THE

SWORD

AND THE

SHIELD

BY CHRISTOPHER ANDREW

THÉOPHILE DELCASSÉ AND THE MAKING OF THE ENTENTE CORDIALE

THE FIRST WORLD WAR: CAUSES AND CONSEQUENCES
(VOLUME 19 OF THE HAMLYN HISTORY OF THE WORLD)

FRANCE OVERSEAS: THE GREAT WAR AND THE CLIMAX OF FRENCH IMPERIAL
EXPANSION (WITH A.S. KANYA-FORSTNER)

THE MISSING DIMENSION: GOVERNMENTS AND INTELLIGENCE COMMUNITIES IN
THE TWENTIETH CENTURY (WITH DAVID DILKS)

HER MAJESTY'S SECRET SERVICE: THE MAKING OF THE
BRITISH INTELLIGENCE COMMUNITY

CODEBREAKING AND SIGNALS INTELLIGENCE

INTELLIGENCE AND INTERNATIONAL RELATIONS, 1900–1945
(WITH JEREMY NOAKES}

KGB: THE INSIDE STORY OF ITS FOREIGN OPERATIONS FROM LENIN TO GORBACHEV
(WITH OLEG GORDIEVSKY)

INSTRUCTIONS FROM THE CENTRE: TOP SECRET FILES ON
KGB FOREIGN OPERATIONS, 1975–1985
(PUBLISHED IN THE USA AS: COMRADE KRYUCHKOV'S INSTRUCTIONS)
(WITH OLEG GORDIEVSKY)

MORE 'INSTRUCTIONS FROM THE CENTRE': TOP SECRET FILES ON KGB
GLOBAL OPERATIONS, 1975–1985
(WITH OLEG GORDIEVSKY)

FOR THE PRESIDENT'S EYES ONLY: SECRET INTELLIGENCE AND THE
AMERICAN PRESIDENCY FROM WASHINGTON TO BUSH

ETERNAL VIGILANCE?
FIFTY YEARS OF THE CIA
(WITH RHODRI JEFFREYS-JONES)

CHRISTOPHER

ANDREW

AND

VASILI

MITROKHIN

BASIC
BOOKS

A MEMBER OF THE

PERSEUS BOOKS GROUP

THE SWORD

AND THE

SHIELD

THE

MITROKHIN

ARCHIVE

AND THE SECRET

HISTORY OF THE

KGB

Published by Basic Books,
A Member of the Perseus Books Group

FIRST EDITION

Designed by Victoria Kuskowski

A CIP catalog record for this book has been applied for from the
Library of Congress.

ISBN 0-465-00310-9

99 00 01 02 / 10 9 8 7 6 5 4 3 2 1

IN MEMORY OF "MA"

CONTENTS

ABBREVIATIONS AND ACRONYMS

AFSA	Armed Forces Security [SIGINT] Agency [USA]
AKEL	Cyprus Communist Party
Amtorg	American-Soviet Trading Corporation, New York
ASA	Army Security [SIGINT] Agency [USA]
AVH	Hungarian security and intelligence agency
AVO	predecessor of AVH
BfV	FRG security service
BND	FRG foreign intelligence agency
CDU	Christian Democratic Union [FRG]
Cheka	All-Russian Extraordinary Commission for Combating Counter-Revolution and Sabotage: predecessor KGB (1917–22)
CIA	Central Intelligence Agency [USA]
COCOM	Coordinating Committee for East-West Trade
Comecon	[Soviet Bloc] Council for Mutual Economic Aid
Comintern	Communist International
CPC	Christian Peace Conference
CPC	Communist Party of Canada
CPCz	Communist Party of Czechoslovakia
CPGB	Communist Party of Great Britain
CPSU	Communist Party of the Soviet Union
CPUSA	Communist Party of the United States of America
CSU	Christian Social Union [FRG: ally of CDU]
DCI	Director of Central Intelligence [USA]
DGS	Portuguese security service
DGSE	French foreign intelligence service
DIA	Defense Intelligence Agency [USA]
DLB	dead letter-box
DRG	Soviet sabotage and intelligence group
DS	Bulgarian security and intelligence service
DST	French security service
F Line	"Special Actions" department in KGB residencies

FAPSI	Russian (post-Soviet) SIGINT agency
FBI	Federal Bureau of Investigation [USA]
FCD	First Chief [Foreign Intelligence] Directorate, KGB
FCO	Foreign and Commonwealth Office [UK]
FRG	Federal Republic of Germany
GCHQ	Government Communications Head-Quarters [British SIGINT Agency]
GDR	German Democratic Republic
GPU	Soviet security and intelligence service (within NKVD, 1922–3)
GRU	Soviet Military Intelligence
GUGB	Soviet security and intelligence service (within NKVD, 1943–43)
Gulag	Labour Camps Directorate
HUMINT	intelligence from human sources (espionage)
HVA	GDR foreign intelligence service
ICBM	intercontinental ballistic missile
IMINT	imagery intelligence
INO	foreign intelligence department of Cheka/GPU/OGPU/ GUGB, 1920–1941; predecessor of INU
INU	foreign intelligence directorate of NKGB/GUGB/MGB, 1941–54; predecessor of FCD
IRA	Irish Republican Army
JIC	Joint Intelligence Committee [UK]
K-231	club of former political prisoners jailed under Article 231 of the Czechoslovak criminal code
KAN	Club of Non-Party Activists [Czechoslovakia]
KGB	Soviet security and intelligence service (1954–1991)
KHAD	Afghan security service
KI	Soviet foreign intelligence agency, initially combining foreign intelligence directorates of MGB and GRU (1947–51)
KKE	Greek Communist Party
KKE-es	breakaway Eurocommunist Greek Communist Party
KOR	Workers Defence Committee [Poland]
KPÖ	Austrian Communist Party
KR Line	Counter-intelligence department in KGB residencies
LLB	live letter box
MGB	Soviet Ministry of State Security (1946–54)

MGIMO	Moscow State Institute for International Relations
MI5	British security service
MI6	alternative designation for SIS [UK]
MOR	Monarchist Association of Central Russia ("The Trust")
N Line	Illegal support department in KGB residencies
NATO	North Atlantic Treaty Organization
NKGB	People's Commisariat for State Security (Soviet security and intelligence service, 1941 and 1943–6)
NKVD	People's Commisariat for Internal Affairs (incorporated state security, 1922–3, 1934–43)
NSA	National Security [SIGINT] Agency [USA]
NSC	National Security Council [USA]
NSZRiS	People's [anti-Bolshevik] Union for Defence of Country and Freedom
NTS	National Labour Alliance (Soviet émigré social-democratic movement)
Okhrana	Tsarist security service, 1881–1917
OMS	Comintern International Liaison Department
OSS	Office of Strategic Services [USA]
OT	Operational Technical Support (FCD)
OUN	Organisation of Ukrainian Nationalists
OZNA	Yugoslav security and intelligence service
PCF	French Communist Party
PCI	Italian Communist Party
PCP	Portuguese Communist Party
PFLP	Popular Front for the Liberation of Palestine
PIDE	Portuguese Liberation Organization
PLO	Palestine Liberation Organization
POUM	Workers Unification Party (Spanish Marxist Trotskyist Party in 1930s)
PR Line	political intelligence department in KGB residences
PSOE	Spanish Socialist Party
PUWP	Polish United Workers [Communist] Party
RCMP	Royal Canadian Mounted Police
ROVS	[White] Russian Combined Services Union
RYAN	*Raketno-Yadernoye Napadenie* (Nuclear Missile Attack)
SALT	Strategic Arms Limitation Talks
SAM	Soviet surface-to-air missile

SB	Polish Security and intelligence service
SCD	Second Chief [Internal Security and Counter-Intelligence] Directorate, KGB
SDECE	French foreign intelligence service; predecessor of DGSE
SDI	Strategic Defense Initiative ('Star Wars')
SED	Socialist Unity [Communist] Party [GDR]
SIGINT	intelligence derived from interception and analysis of signals
SIS	Secret Intelligence Service [UK]
SK Line	Soviet colony department in KGB residencies
SKP	Communist Party of Finland
SOE	Special Operations Executive [UK]
SPD	Social Democratic Party [FRG]
Spetsnaz	Soviet special forces
SR	Socialist Revolutionary
S&T	scientific and technological intelligence
Stapo	Austrian police security service
Stasi	GDR Ministry of State Security
Stavka	Wartime Soviet GHQ/high command
StB	Czechoslovak security and intelligence service
SVR	Russian (post-Soviet) foreign intelligence service
TUC	Trades Union Congress [UK]
UAR	United Arab Republic
UB	Polish security and intelligence service; predecessor of SB
UDBA	Yugoslav security and intelligence service; successor to OZNA
VPK	Soviet Military Industrial Commission
VVR	Supreme Military Council [anti-Bolshevik Ukranian underground]
WCC	World Council of Churches
WPC	World Peace Council
X Line	S&T department in KGB residencies

THE EVOLUTION OF THE KGB, 1917–1991

December 1917	Cheka
	↓
February 1922	Incorporated into NKVD (as GPU)
	↓
July 1923	OGPU
	↓
July 1934	Reincorporated in NKVD (as GUGB)
	↓
February 1941	NKGB
	↓
July 1941	Reincorporated in NKVD (as GUGB)
	↓
April 1943	NKGB
	↓
March 1946	MGB
	↓
October 1947– November 1951	Foreign Intelligence transferred to KI
	↓
March 1953	Combined with MVD to form enlarged MVD
	↓
March 1954	KGB

The term KGB is used both generally to denote the Soviet State Security organisation throughout its history since its foundation as the Cheka in 1917 and, more specifically, to refer to State Security after 1954 when it took its final name.

THE TRANSLITERATION OF
RUSSIAN NAMES

We have followed a simplified version of the method used by the U.S. Board on Geographic Names and BBC Monitering Service. Simplifications include the substitution of "y" for "iy" in surnames (Trotsky rather than Trotskiy) and of "i" for "iy" in first names (Yuri rather than Yuriy). The "y" between the letters "i" and/or "e" is omitted (for example, Andreev and Dmitrievich—not Andreyev and Dmitriyevich), as is the apostrophe used to signify a soft sign.

In cases where a mildly deviant English version of a well-known Russian name has become firmly established, we have retained that version, for example: Beria, Evdokia (Petrova), *Izvestia,* Joseph (Stalin), Khrushchev, Nureyev and the names of Tsars.

FOREWORD

I have written this book in consultation with Vasili Mitrokhin, based on the extensive top secret material (described in Chapter 1) which he has smuggled out from the KGB foreign intelligence archive. For the past quarter of a century, Mitrokhin has passionately wanted this material, which for twelve years he risked his life to assemble, to see the light of day. He wished to reveal "how thin the thread of peace actually was during the Cold War." From that passion this book has been born. I have felt it my duty to ensure that this material, which offers detailed and often unique insights into the workings of the Soviet State and the history of the Soviet Union, achieves the level of public awareness and recognition that it deserves.

Like all archives, those of the KGB require interpretation in the light of previous research and related documents. The end notes and bibliography provide full details of the additional sources used to place Mitrokhin's revelations in historical context. These sources also provide overwhelming corroborative evidence for his genuineness as a source.

Codenames (also known as "worknames" in the case of KGB officers) appear in the text in capitals. Many KGB codenames were used more than once. In such cases, the text and index make clear which individual is referred to. It is also important to note that, although certain individuals were targeted by the KGB, and may have been given codenames, this does not mean that the persons named were conscious or witting agents or sources—or even that they were aware that they were being targeted for recruitment or political influence operations. Similarly, the fact that an individual may have endorsed a position that was favorable to the Soviet Union does not necessarily mean that this person was working as an agent, or agent of influence, for the KGB. The KGB frequently gave prominent policymakers codenames in order to protect the identity of their targets, and to order recruited KGB agents to target such individuals.

For legal reasons, some of the Soviet agents identified in KGB files can be referred to in this book only by their codenames. In a limited number of cases, chiefly because of the risk of prejudicing a possible prosecution, no reference can be made to them at all. These omissions do not, so far as I am aware, significantly affect the main conclusions of any chapter.

Christopher Andrew

O N E

THE MITROKHIN ARCHIVE

This book is based on unprecedented and unrestricted access to one of the world's most secret and closely guarded archives—that of the foreign intelligence arm of the KGB, the First Chief Directorate (FCD). Hitherto the present Russian foreign intelligence service, the SVR (*Sluzhba Vneshnei Razvedki*), has been supremely confident that a book such as this could not be written. When the German magazine *Focus* reported in December 1996 that a former KGB officer had defected to Britain with "the names of hundreds of Russian spies," Tatyana Samolis, spokeswoman for the SVR, instantly ridiculed the whole story as "absolute nonsense." "Hundreds of people! That just doesn't happen!" she declared. "Any defector could get the name of one, two, perhaps three agents—but not hundreds!"[1]

The facts, however, are far more sensational even than the story dismissed as impossible by the SVR. The KGB defector had brought with him to Britain details not of a few hundred but of thousands of Soviet agents and intelligence officers in all parts of the globe, some of them "illegals" living under deep cover abroad, disguised as foreign citizens. No one who spied for the Soviet Union at any period between the October Revolution and the eve of the Gorbachev era can now be confident that his or her secrets are still secure. When the British Secret Intelligence Service (SIS) exfiltrated the defector and his family from Russia in 1992, it also brought out six cases containing the copious notes he had taken almost daily for twelve years, before his retirement in 1984, on top secret KGB files going as far back as 1918. The contents of the cases have since been described by the American FBI as "the most complete and extensive intelligence ever received from any source."

The KGB officer who assembled this extraordinary archive, Vasili Nikitich Mitrokhin, is now a British citizen. Born in central Russia in 1922, he began his career as a Soviet foreign intelligence officer in 1948, at a time when the foreign intelligence arms of the MGB (the future KGB) and the GRU (Soviet military intelligence) were temporarily combined in the Committee of Information.[2] By the time Mitrokhin was sent on his first foreign posting in 1952,[3] the Committee had disintegrated and the MGB had resumed its traditional rivalry with the GRU. His first five years in intelligence were spent in the paranoid atmosphere generated by the final phase of Stalin's dictatorship, when the intelligence agencies were ordered to conduct witch-hunts throughout the Soviet Bloc against mostly imaginary Titoist and Zionist conspiracies.

In January 1953 the MGB was officially accused of "lack of vigilance" in hunting down the conspirators. The Soviet news agency Tass made the sensational announcement that for the past few years world Zionism and Western intelligence agencies had been conspiring with "a terrorist group" of Jewish doctors "to wipe out the leadership of the Soviet Union." During the final two months of Stalin's rule, the MGB struggled to demonstrate its heightened vigilance by pursuing the perpetrators of this non-existent plot. Its anti-Zionist campaign was, in reality, little more than a thinly disguised anti-Semitic pogrom. Shortly before Stalin's sudden death in March 1953, Mitrokhin was ordered to investigate the alleged Zionist connections of the *Pravda* correspondent in Paris, Yuri Zhukov, who had come under suspicion because of his wife's Jewish origins. Mitrokhin had the impression that Stalin's brutal security supremo, Lavrenti Pavlovich Beria, was planning to implicate Zhukov in the supposed Jewish doctors' plot. A few weeks after Stalin's funeral, however, Beria suddenly announced that the plot had never existed, and exonerated the alleged conspirators.

By the summer of 1953 most of Beria's colleagues in the Presidium were united in their fear of another conspiracy—that he might be planning a *coup d'état* to step into Stalin's shoes. While visiting a foreign capital in July, Mitrokhin received a top secret telegram with instructions to decipher it himself, and was astonished to discover that Beria had been charged with "criminal anti-Party and anti-state activities." Only later did Mitrokhin learn that Beria had been arrested at a special meeting of the Presidium on June 26 after a plot organized by his chief rival, Nikita Sergeyevich Khrushchev. From his prison cell, Beria wrote begging letters to his former colleagues, pleading pathetically for them to spare his life and "find the smallest job for me":

> You will see that in two or three years I'll have straightened out fine and will still be useful to you . . . I ask the comrades to forgive me for writing somewhat disjointedly and badly because of my condition, and also because of the poor lighting and not having my pince-nez.

No longer in awe of him, the comrades simply mocked his loss of nerve.

On December 24 it was announced that Beria had been executed after trial by the Supreme Court. Since neither his responsibility for mass murder in the Stalin era nor his own record as a serial rapist of under-age girls could be publicly mentioned for fear of bringing the Communist regime into disrepute, he was declared guilty instead of a surreal plot "to revive capitalism and to restore the rule of the bourgeoisie" in association with British and other Western intelligence services. Beria thus became, following Yagoda and Yezhov in the 1930s, the third Soviet security chief to be shot for crimes which included serving as an (imaginary) British secret agent. In true Stalinist tradition, subscribers to the *Great Soviet Encyclopedia* were advised to use "a small knife or razor blade" to remove the entry on Beria, and then to insert a replacement article on the Bering Sea.[4]

The first official repudiation of Stalinism was Khrushchev's now-celebrated secret speech to a closed session of the Twentieth Congress of the Communist Party of the Soviet Union (CPSU) in February 1956. Stalin's "cult of personality," Khrushchev declared, had been responsible for "a whole series of exceedingly serious and grave perversions of Party principles, of Party democracy, of revolutionary legality." The speech was reported to the KGB Party organization in a secret letter from the Central Committee. The section to which Mitrokhin belonged took two days to debate its contents. He still vividly recalls the conclusion of the section's chairman, Vladimir Vasilyevich Zhenikhov (later KGB resident in Finland): "Stalin was a bandit!" Some Party members were too shocked—or cautious—to say anything. Others agreed with Zhenikhov. None dared ask the question which Mitrokhin was convinced was in all their minds: "Where was Khrushchev while all these crimes were taking place?"

In the aftermath of the secret speech Mitrokhin became too outspoken for his own good. Though his criticisms of the way the KGB had been run were mild by Western standards, late in 1956 Mitrokhin was moved from operations to the FCD archives, where his main job was answering queries from other departments and provincial KGBs.[5] Mitrokhin discovered that Beria's personal archive had been destroyed on Khrushchev's orders so as to leave no trace of the compromising material he had collected on his former colleagues. Ivan Aleksandrovich Serov, chairman of the KGB from 1954 to 1958, dutifully reported to Khrushchev that the files had contained much "provocative and libelous" material.[6]

Mitrokhin was an avid reader of the Russian writers who had fallen out of favor in the final years of Stalinist rule and began to be published again during the mid-1950s. The first great literary event in Moscow after Stalin's death was the publication in 1954, for the first time since 1945, of new poems by Boris Pasternak, the last leading Russian author to have begun his career before the Revolution. Published in a literary magazine under the title "Poems from the Novel *Doctor Zhivago*," they were accompanied by a brief description of the epic but still unfinished work in which they were to appear. However, the completed text of *Doctor Zhivago*, which followed the meandering life of its enigmatic hero from the final phase of Tsarist rule to the early years of the Soviet regime, was judged far too subversive for publication and was officially rejected in 1956. In the novel, when Zhivago hears the news of the Bolshevik Revolution, "He was shaken and overwhelmed by the greatness of the moment, and thought of its significance for the centuries to come." But Pasternak goes on to convey an unmistakable sense of the spiritual emptiness of the regime which emerged from it. Lenin is "vengeance incarnate" and Stalin a "pockmarked Caligula."

Pasternak became the first Soviet author since the 1920s to circumvent the banning of his work in Russia by publishing it abroad. As he handed the typescript of *Doctor Zhivago* to a representative of his Italian publisher, Giangiacomo Feltrinelli, he told him with a melancholy laugh: "You are hereby invited to watch me face the firing squad!" Soon afterwards, acting on official instructions, Pasternak sent a telegram to Feltrinelli insisting that his novel be withdrawn from publication; privately, however, he wrote a letter telling him to go ahead. Published first in Italian in November 1957, *Doctor Zhivago* became a bestseller in twenty-four languages. Some

Western critics hailed it as the greatest Russian novel since Tolstoy's *Resurrection,* published in 1899. Official outrage in Moscow at *Doctor Zhivago's* success was compounded by the award to Pasternak of the 1958 Nobel Prize for Literature. In a cable to the Swedish Academy, Pasternak declared himself "immensely thankful, touched, proud, astonished, abashed." The newspaper of the Soviet Writers' Union, the *Literaturnaya Gazeta,* however, denounced him as "a literary Judas who betrayed his people for thirty pieces of silver—the Nobel Prize." Under immense official pressure, Pasternak cabled Stockholm withdrawing his acceptance of the prize "in view of the significance given to this award in the society to which I belong."[7]

Though Pasternak was not one of his own favorite authors, Mitrokhin saw the official condemnation of *Doctor Zhivago* as typifying Khrushchev's cultural barbarism. "The development of literature and art in a socialist society," Khrushchev boorishly insisted, "proceeds . . . as directed by the Party." Mitrokhin was so outraged by the neo-Stalinist denunciations of Pasternak by Moscow's literary establishment that in October 1958 he sent an anonymous letter of protest to the *Literaturnaya Gazeta.* Though he wrote the letter with his left hand in order to disguise his handwriting, he remained anxious for some time that his identity might be discovered. Mitrokhin knew from KGB files the immense resources which were frequently deployed to track down anonymous letter-writers. He was even worried that, by licking the gum on the back of the envelope before sealing it, he had made it possible for his saliva to be identified by a KGB laboratory. The whole episode strengthened his resentment at Khrushchev's failure to follow his secret speech of 1956 by a thoroughgoing program of de-Stalinization. Khrushchev, he suspected, had personally ordered Pasternak's persecution as a warning to all those inclined to challenge his authority.

As yet, however, Mitrokhin pinned his faith not on the overthrow of the Soviet regime but on the emergence of a new leader less tainted than Khrushchev by his Stalinist past. When, late in 1958, Serov was replaced as KGB chairman by one of his leading critics, Aleksandr Nikolayevich Shelepin, Mitrokhin believed that the new leader had emerged. Aged only forty, Shelepin had made his reputation as a guerrilla commander during the Second World War. As head of the Communist Youth League (Komsomol) from 1952 to 1958, he had mobilized thousands of young people from Khrushchev's "Virgin Lands" campaign to turn vast areas of steppe into arable farmland. Though many of the new collective farms were later ruined by soil erosion, in the short term the campaign seemed a spectacular success. Soviet newsreels showed endless lines of combine-harvesters as they advanced through prairies rippling with grain and stretching as far as the eye could see.

As Mitrokhin had hoped, Shelepin rapidly established himself as a new broom within the KGB, replacing many veteran Stalinists with bright young graduates from Komsomol. Mitrokhin was impressed by the way that when Shelepin gave televised speeches, he looked briefly at his notes, then spoke directly to the viewer—instead of woodenly reading from a prepared text like most Soviet leaders. Shelepin sought to give the KGB a new public image. "Violations of socialist legality," he claimed in 1961, "have been completely eliminated . . . The Chekists [KGB officers] can look the Party and the Soviet people in the eye with a clear conscience." Mitrokhin also remembers Shelepin for an act of personal kindness to a close relative.

Like Beria before him and Andropov after him, Shelepin's ambitions stretched far beyond the chairmanship of the KGB. As a twenty-year-old university student, he was once asked what he wanted to become. According to the Russian historian Roy Medvedev, he instantly replied, "A chief!"[8] Shelepin saw the KGB as a stepping stone in a career which he intended to take him to the post of First Secretary of the CPSU. In December 1961 he left the KGB but continued to oversee its work as chairman of the powerful new Committee of Party and State Control. The new KGB chairman was Shelepin's youthful but less dynamic protégé, thirty-seven-year-old Vladimir Yefimovich Semichastny. On Khrushchev's instructions, Semichastny resumed the work of pruning the archives of material which too vividly recalled the Presidium's Stalinist past, ordering the destruction of nine volumes of files on the liquidation of Central Committee members, senior intelligence officers and foreign Communists living in Moscow during the Stalin era.[9]

Mitrokhin continued to see Shelepin as a future First Secretary, and was not surprised when he became one of the leaders of the coup which toppled Khrushchev in 1964. Memories of Beria, however, were still too fresh in the minds of most of the Presidium for them to be prepared to accept a security chief as Party leader. For most of his colleagues, Leonid Ilich Brezhnev, who had succeeded Khrushchev as First (later General) Secretary, was a far more reassuring figure—affable, lightweight and patient in reconciling opposing factions, though skillful in outmaneuvering his political rivals. By 1967 Brezhnev felt strong enough to sack the unpopular Semichastny and sideline the still-ambitious Shelepin, who was demoted from heading the Committee of Party and State Control to become chairman of the comparatively uninfluential Trade Union Council. On arriving in his spacious new office, Shelepin found that his predecessor, Viktor Grishin, had what Medvedev later euphemistically described as "a specially equipped massage parlor" in an adjoining room. Shelepin took revenge for his demotion by circulating stories about Grishin's sexual exploits around Moscow.[10]

The main beneficiary of the downfall of Semichastny and the sidelining of Shelepin was Yuri Vladimirovich Andropov, who became chairman of the KGB. Andropov had what some of his staff called a "Hungarian complex." As Soviet ambassador in Budapest during the Hungarian Uprising in 1956, he had watched in horror from the windows of his embassy as officers of the hated Hungarian security service were strung up from lampposts. Andropov remained haunted for the rest of his life by the speed with which an apparently all-powerful Communist one-party state had begun to topple. When other Communist regimes later seemed at risk—in Prague in 1968, in Kabul in 1979, in Warsaw in 1981—he was convinced that, as in Budapest in 1956, only armed force could ensure their survival.[11] Since leaving Hungary in 1957 Andropov had been head of the Central Committee Department responsible for relations with Communist parties in the Soviet Bloc. His appointment in 1967 as the first senior Party official brought in to head the KGB was intended by Brezhnev to secure political control of the security and intelligence systems. Andropov went on to become the longest-serving and most politically astute of all KGB chiefs, crowning his fifteen years as chairman by succeeding Brezhnev as General Secretary in 1982.

THE FIRST GREAT crisis of Andropov's years at the KGB was the attempt by the Czechoslovak reformers of the Prague Spring to create what the Kremlin saw as an unacceptably unorthodox "socialism with a human face." Like Khrushchev's Secret Speech, the invasion of Czechoslovakia by the forces of the Warsaw Pact in August 1968 was an important staging post in what Mitrokhin calls his "intellectual odyssey." Stationed in East Germany during the Prague Spring, Mitrokhin was able to listen to reports from Czechoslovakia on the Russian-language services of the BBC World Service, Radio Liberty, Deutsche Welle and the Canadian Broadcasting Company, but had no one with whom he felt able to share his sympathy for the Prague reforms. One episode about a month before Soviet tanks entered Prague left a particular impression on him. An FCD Department V ("special tasks") officer, Colonel Viktor Ryabov, said to Mitrokhin that he was "just off to Sweden for a few days," but made clear by his expression that Sweden was not his real destination. A few days after Ryabov's return, he told Mitrokhin there would be an interesting article in the following day's *Pravda,* implying that it was connected with his mission. When Mitrokhin read the report the next day that an "imperialist arms dump" had been discovered in Czechoslovakia, he realized at once that it had been planted by Ryabov and other Department V officers to discredit the reformers.

Soon after the crushing of the Prague Spring, Mitrokhin heard a speech given by Andropov in the KGB's East German headquarters at Karlshorst in the Berlin suburbs. Like Shelepin, Andropov spoke directly to the audience, rather than—like most Soviet officials—sticking to a prepared platitudinous text. With an ascetic appearance, silver hair swept back over a large forehead, steel-rimmed glasses and an intellectual manner, Andropov seemed far removed from Stalinist thugs such as Beria and Serov. His explanation for the invasion of Czechoslovakia was far more sophisticated than that given to the Soviet public. It had, he insisted, been the only way to preserve Soviet security and the new European order which had emerged from the Great Patriotic War. That objective political necessity, Andropov claimed, was accepted even by such unorthodox figures as the great physicist Pyotr Kapitza, who had initially shown some sympathy for the Prague revisionists. Mitrokhin drew quite different conclusions from the Warsaw Pact invasion. The destruction of Czechoslovak "socialism with a human face" proved, he believed, that the Soviet system was unreformable. He still vividly recalls a curiously mythological image, which henceforth he saw increasingly in his mind's eye, of the Russian people in thrall to "a three-headed hydra": the Communist Party, the privileged *nomenklatura* and the KGB.

After his return to Moscow from East Germany, Mitrokhin continued to listen to Western broadcasts, although, because of Soviet jamming, he had frequently to switch wavelengths in order to find an audible station. Often he ended up with only fragments of news stories. Among the news which made the greatest impression on him were items on the *Chronicle of Current Events,* a samizdat journal first produced by Soviet dissidents in 1968 to circulate news on the struggle against abuses of human rights. The *Chronicle* carried on its masthead the guarantee of freedom of expression in the United Nations Universal Declaration of Human Rights, daily abused in the Soviet Union.

As the struggle against "ideological subversion" intensified, Mitrokhin saw numerous examples of the way in which the KGB manipulated, virtually at will, the Soviet justice system. He later copied down the sycophantic congratulations sent to Andropov by A. F. Gorkhin, chairman of the Soviet Supreme Court, on the fiftieth anniversary of the founding of the Cheka in December 1967:

> The Soviet Courts and the USSR Committee of State Security [KGB] are of the same age. But this is not the main thing which brings us together; the main thing is the identity of our tasks . . .
>
> We are glad to note that the State Security agencies and the Courts solve all their complicated tasks in a spirit of mutual understanding and sound professional relations.[12]

Mitrokhin saw mounting evidence both in the classified in-house journal, *KGB Sbornik,* and in FCD files of Andropov's personal obsession with the destruction of dissent in all its forms and his insistence that the struggle for human rights was part of a wide-ranging imperialist plot to undermine the foundations of the Soviet state. In 1968 Andropov issued KGB Chairman's Order No. 0051, "On the tasks of State security agencies in combating ideological sabotage by the adversary," calling for greater aggression in the struggle against both dissidents at home and their imperialist supporters.[13] One example of this greater aggression which left Mitrokhin, as an ardent admirer of the Kirov Ballet, with a sense of personal outrage was the plan which he discovered in FCD files to maim the ballet's star defector, Rudolf Nureyev.[14]

By the beginning of the 1970s Mitrokhin's political views were deeply influenced by the dissident struggle, which he was able to follow both in KGB records and Western broadcasts. "I was a loner," he recalls, "but I now knew that I was not alone." Though Mitrokhin never had any thought of aligning himself openly with the human rights movement, the example of the *Chronicle of Current Events* and other samizdat productions helped to inspire him with the idea of producing a classified variant of the dissidents' attempts to document the iniquities of the Soviet system. Gradually the project began to form in his mind of compiling his own private record of the foreign operations of the KGB.

Mitrokhin's opportunity came in June 1972 when the First Chief (Foreign Intelligence) Directorate left its overcrowded central Moscow offices in the KGB headquarters at the Lubyanka (once the pre-Revolutionary home of the Rossiya Insurance Company) and moved to a new building south-east of Moscow at Yasenevo, half a mile beyond the outer ringroad. Designed by a Finnish architect, the main Y-shaped seven-story office building was flanked on one side by an assembly hall and library, on the other by a polyclinic, sports complex and swimming pool, with pleasant views over hills covered with birch trees, green pastures, and—in summer—fields of wheat and rye. To the other KGB directorates, most of which worked in cramped conditions in central Moscow, Yasenevo was known—with more envy than condescension—as "The Woods."

For the next ten years, working from private offices both in the Lubyanka and at Yasenevo, Mitrokhin was alone responsible for checking and sealing the approximately 300,000 files[15] in the FCD archive prior to their transfer to the new headquarters. While supervising the checking of files, the compilation of inventories and the writing of index cards, Mitrokhin was able to inspect what files he wished in one or other of his offices. Few KGB officers apart from Mitrokhin have ever spent as much time reading, let alone noting, foreign intelligence files. Outside the FCD archives, only the most senior officers shared his unrestricted access, and none had the time to read more than a fraction of the material noted by him.

Mitrokhin's usual weekly routine was to spend each Monday, Tuesday and Friday in his Yasenevo office. On Wednesdays he went to the Lubyanka to work on the FCD's most secret files, those of Directorate S which ran illegals—KGB officers and agents, most of Soviet nationality, working under deep cover abroad disguised as foreign citizens. Once reviewed by Mitrokhin, each batch of files was placed in sealed containers which were transported to Yasenevo on Thursday mornings, accompanied by Mitrokhin who checked them on arrival.[16] Unlike the other departments, who moved to the new FCD headquarters in 1972, Directorate S remained based in the Lubyanka for a further decade.

Mitrokhin thus found himself spending more time dealing with the files of Directorate S, the most secret in the FCD, than with those of any other section of Soviet foreign intelligence. The illegals retained a curious mystique within the KGB. Before being posted abroad, every illegal officer was required to swear a solemn, if somewhat melodramatic, oath:

> Deeply valuing the trust placed upon me by the Party and the fatherland, and imbued with a sense of intense gratitude for the decision to send me to the sharp edge of the struggle for the interest of my people . . . as a worthy son of the homeland, I would rather perish than betray the secrets entrusted to me or put into the hand of the adversary materials which could cause political harm to the interests of the State. With every heartbeat, with every day that passes, I swear to serve the Party, the homeland, and the Soviet people.[17]

The files showed that before the Second World War the greatest foreign successes had been achieved by a legendary group of intelligence officers, often referred to as the "Great Illegals." After the Second World War, the KGB had tried to recreate its pre-war triumphs by establishing an elaborate network of "illegal residencies" alongside the "legal residencies" which operated under diplomatic or other official cover in foreign capitals.

The records of Directorate S revealed some remarkable individual achievements. KGB illegals successfully established bogus identities as foreign nationals in a great variety of professions ranging from Costa Rican ambassador to piano tuner to the

Governor of New York. Even in the Gorbachev era, KGB propaganda continued to depict the Soviet illegal as the supreme embodiment of the chivalric ideal in the service of secret intelligence. The retired British KGB agent George Blake wrote in 1990:

> Only a man who believes very strongly in an ideal and serves a great cause will agree to embark on such a career, though the word "calling" is perhaps appropriate here. Only an intelligence service which works for a great cause can ask for such a sacrifice from its officers. That is why, as far as I know, at any rate in peacetime, only the Soviet intelligence service has "illegal residents."[18]

The SVR continues the KGB tradition of illegal hagiography. In July 1995, a month after the death of the best-known American-born illegal, Morris Cohen, President Yeltsin conferred on him the posthumous title of Hero of the Russian Federation.

The files of Directorate S noted by Mitrokhin reveal a quite different kind of illegal. Alongside the committed FCD officers who maintained their cover and professional discipline throughout their postings, there were others who could not cope when confronted by the contrast between the Soviet propaganda image of capitalist exploitation and the reality of life in the West. An even darker secret of the Directorate S records was that one of the principal uses of the illegals during the last quarter of a century of the Soviet Union was to search out and compromise dissidents in the other countries of the Warsaw Pact. The squalid struggle against "ideological subversion" was as much a responsibility of Directorate S as of the rest of the FCD.

MITROKHIN WAS UNDERSTANDABLY cautious as he set out in 1972 to compile his forbidden FCD archive. For a few weeks he tried to commit names, codenames and key facts from the files to memory and transcribe them each evening when he returned home. Abandoning that process as too slow and cumbersome, he began to take notes in minuscule handwriting on scraps of paper which he crumpled up and threw into his wastepaper basket. Each evening, he retrieved his notes from the wastepaper and smuggled them out of Yasenevo concealed in his shoes. Gradually Mitrokhin became more confident as he satisfied himself that the Yasenevo security guards confined themselves to occasional inspections of bags and briefcases without attempting body searches. After a few months he started taking notes on ordinary sheets of office paper which he took out of his office in his jacket and trouser pockets.

Not once in the twelve years which Mitrokhin spent noting the FCD archives was he stopped and searched. There were, however, some desperately anxious moments. From time to time he realized that, like other FCD officers, he was being tailed—probably by teams from the Seventh (Surveillance) or Second Chief (Counterintelligence) Directorates. On one occasion while he was being followed, he visited the Dynamo Football Club sports shop and, to his horror, found himself standing next to two English visitors whom his watchers might suspect were spies with whom he had arranged a rendezvous. If he was searched, his notes on top secret files would be instantly discovered. Mitrokhin quickly moved on to other sports shops, hoping to convince his watchers that he was on a genuine shopping expedition. As he approached his apartment block, however, he noticed two men standing near the door to his ninth-floor flat. By the time he arrived, they had disappeared. FCD officers had standing instructions to report suspicious incidents such as this, but Mitrokhin did not do so for fear of prompting an investigation which would draw attention to the fact that he had been seen standing next to English visitors.

Each night when he returned to his Moscow flat, Mitrokhin hid his notes beneath his mattress. On weekends he took them to a family dacha thirty-six kilometers from Moscow and typed up as many as possible, though the notes became so numerous that Mitrokhin was forced to leave some of them in handwritten form. He hid the first batches of typescripts and notes in a milk-churn which he buried below the floor.[19] The dacha was built on raised foundations, leaving just enough room for Mitrokhin to crawl beneath the floorboards and dig a hole with a short-handled spade. He frequently found himself crawling through dog and cat feces and sometimes disturbed rats while he was digging, but he consoled himself with the thought that burglars were unlikely to follow him. When the milk-churn was full, he began concealing his notes and typescripts in a tin clothes-boiler. Eventually his archive also filled two tin trunks and two aluminum cases, all of them buried beneath the dacha.[20]

Mitrokhin's most anxious moment came when he arrived at his weekend dacha to find a stranger hiding in the attic. He was instantly reminded of the incident a few years earlier, in August 1971, when a friend of the writer Aleksandr Solzhenitsyn had called unexpectedly at his dacha while Solzhenitsyn was away and surprised two KGB officers in the attic who were probably searching for subversive manuscripts. Other KGB men had quickly arrived on the scene and Solzhenitsyn's friend had been badly beaten. Andropov cynically ordered Solzhenitsyn to be "informed that the participation of the KGB in this incident is a figment of his imagination."[21] The incident was still fresh in Mitrokhin's mind when he arrived at the dacha because he had recently noted files which recorded minutely detailed plans for the persecution of Solzhenitsyn and the "active measures" by which the KGB hoped to discredit him in the Western press. To his immense relief, however, the intruder in the attic turned out to be a homeless squatter.

During summer holidays Mitrokhin worked on batches of his notes at a second family dacha near Penza, carrying them in an old haversack and dressing in peasant clothes in order not to attract attention. In the summer of 1918 Penza, 630 kilometers southeast of Moscow, had been the site of one of the first peasant risings against Bolshevik rule. Lenin blamed the revolt on the *kulaks* (better-off peasants) and furiously instructed the local Party leaders to hang in public at least one hundred of them so that "for hundreds of kilometers around the people may see and tremble . . ."[22] By the 1970s, however, Penza's counter-revolutionary past was long forgotten, and Lenin's bloodthirsty orders for mass executions were kept from public view in the secret section of the Lenin archive.

One of the most striking characteristics of the best literature produced under the Soviet regime is how much of it was written in secret. "To plunge underground," wrote Solzhenitsyn, "to make it your concern not to win the world's recognition—Heaven forbid!—but on the contrary to shun it: this variant of the writer's lot is peculiarly our own, purely Russian, Russian and Soviet!"[23] Between the wars Mikhail Bulgakov had spent twelve years writing *The Master and Margarita,* one of the greatest novels of the twentieth century, knowing that it could not be published in his lifetime and fearing that it might never appear at all. His widow later recalled how, just before his death in 1940, Bulgakov "made me get out of bed and then, leaning on my arm, he walked through all the rooms, barefoot and in his dressing gown, to make sure that the manuscript of *The Master* was still there" in its hiding place.[24] Though Bulgakov's great work survived, it was not published until a quarter of a century after his death. As late as 1978, it was denounced in a KGB memorandum to Andropov as "a dangerous weapon in the hands of [Western] ideological centers engaged in ideological sabotage against the Soviet Union."[25]

When Solzhenitsyn began writing in the 1950s, he told himself he had "entered into the inheritance of every modern writer intent on the truth":

I must write simply to ensure that it was not forgotten, that posterity might some day come to know of it. Publication in my own lifetime I must shut out of my mind, out of my dreams.

Just as Mitrokhin's first notes were hidden in a milk-churn beneath his dacha, so Solzhenitsyn's earliest writings, in minuscule handwriting, were squeezed into an empty champagne bottle and buried in his garden.[26] After the brief thaw in the early years of "de-Stalinization" which made possible the publication of Solzhenitsyn's story of life in the gulag, *One Day in the Life of Ivan Denisovich,* he waged a time-consuming struggle to try to prevent the KGB from seizing his other manuscripts until he was finally forced into exile in 1974.[27] It did not occur to Mitrokhin to compare himself with such literary giants as Bulgakov and Solzhenitsyn. But, like them, he began assembling his archive "to ensure that the truth was not forgotten, that posterity might some day come to know of it."

THE KGB FILES which had the greatest emotional impact on Mitrokhin were those on the war in Afghanistan. On December 28, 1979 Babrak Karmal, the new Afghan leader chosen by Moscow to request "fraternal assistance" by the Red Army which had already invaded his country, announced over Kabul Radio that his predecessor, Hafizullah Amin, an "agent of American imperialism," had been tried by a "revolutionary tribunal" and sentenced to death. Mitrokhin quickly discovered from the files on the war which flooded into the archives that Amin had in reality been assassinated, together with his family and entourage, in an assault on the Kabul presidential palace by KGB special forces disguised in Afghan uniforms.[28]

The female clerks who filed KGB reports on the war in the archives after they had been circulated to the Politburo and other sections of the Soviet hierarchy had so much material to deal with that they sometimes submitted to Mitrokhin thirty files at a time for his approval. The horrors recorded in the files were carefully concealed from the Soviet people. The Soviet media preserved a conspiracy of silence about the systematic destruction of thousands of Afghan villages, reduced to forlorn groups of uninhabited, roofless mud-brick houses; the flight of four million refugees; and the death of a million Afghans in a war which Gorbachev later described as a "mistake." The coffins of the 15,000 Red Army troops killed in the conflict were unloaded silently at Soviet airfields, with none of the military pomp and solemn music which traditionally awaited fallen heroes returning to the Motherland. Funerals were held in secret, and families told simply that their loved ones had died "fulfilling their internationalist duty." Some were buried in plots near the graves of Mitrokhin's parents in the cemetery at Kuzminsky Monastery. No reference to Afghanistan was allowed on their tombstones. During the Afghan War Mitrokhin heard the first open criticism of Soviet policy by his more outspoken colleagues at Yasenevo. "Doesn't the war make you ashamed to be Russian?" an FCD colonel asked him one day. "Ashamed to be Soviet, you mean!" Mitrokhin blurted out.

When Mitrokhin retired in 1984, he was still preoccupied with the Afghan War. He spent the first year and a half of his retirement sorting through his notes, extracting the material on Afghanistan, and assembling it in a large volume with a linking narrative. Despite Gorbachev's call for *glasnost* after he became Party leader in 1985, Mitrokhin did not believe the Soviet system would ever allow the truth about the war to be told. Increasingly, however, he began to think of ways of transporting his archive to the West and publishing it there.

One novel method suggested itself on May 28, 1987, when a single-engine Cessna piloted by a nineteen-year-old West German, Matthias Rust, crossed the Finnish border into Soviet airspace and flew undetected for 450 miles before landing in Red Square. After an hour of confusion, during which Kremlin security guards wondered whether Rust was an actor in a film, he was taken away to the KGB's Lefortovo Prison. Mitrokhin briefly considered but quickly abandoned the idea of using a microlite from a KGB sports club to fly with his archive in the opposite direction to Finland.

The most practical of the various schemes considered by Mitrokhin before the collapse of the Soviet Union was to get a position on the local Party committee which issued permits for foreign travel, obtain permits for himself and his family, then book reservations on a cruise from Leningrad to Odessa in the Black Sea. At one of the cruise's West European ports of call, Mitrokhin would make contact with the authorities and arrange to leave his archive in a dead letter-box near Moscow for collection by a Western intelligence agency. He eventually abandoned the idea because of the difficulty of separating himself from the Soviet tour group and the ever-watchful group leaders for long enough to tell his story and arrange the hand-over.

As the Berlin Wall came down in November 1989 and the Soviet Bloc began to disintegrate, Mitrokhin told himself to be patient and wait for his opportunity. In the meantime he carried on typing up his handwritten notes in his Moscow flat and at the two family dachas, assembling some of them in volumes covering the FCD's chief target countries—first and foremost the United States, known in KGB jargon as the "Main Adversary." He shared the relief of most Muscovites at the failure of the hardline coup in August 1991 to depose Gorbachev and reestablish the one-party Soviet state. It came as no surprise to Mitrokhin that the chief ringleader in the failed coup was Vladimir Aleksandrovich Kryuchkov, head of the FCD from 1974 to 1988 and chairman of the KGB from 1988 until the coup.

Though Kryuchkov proved better at public relations than most previous KGB chairmen, he had long represented much of what Mitrokhin most detested in the FCD. As a young diplomat at the Soviet embassy in Budapest, Kryuchkov had caught the eye of the ambassador, Yuri Andropov, by his uncompromising opposition to the "counter-revolutionary" Hungarian Uprising of 1956. When Andropov became KGB chairman in 1967, Kryuchkov became head of his personal secretariat and a loyal supporter of his obsessive campaign against "ideological subversion" in all its forms. The files seen by Mitrokhin showed that, as head of the FCD, Kryuchkov collaborated closely with the KGB Fifth (Ideological Subversion) Directorate in the war against dissidents at home and abroad.[29] He had made a senior member of the Fifth Directorate, I. A. Markelov, one of the deputy heads of the FCD with responsibility for coordinating the struggle against ideological subversion.[30] The failed coup of August 1991 marked an appropriately discreditable end to Kryuchkov's KGB career. Instead of shoring up the Soviet Union and the one-party state, it served only to hasten their collapse.

On October 11, 1991, the State Council of the disintegrating Soviet Union abolished the KGB in its existing form. The former FCD was reconstituted as the SVR, the foreign intelligence service of the Russian Federation, independent of the internal security service. Instead of repudiating its Soviet past, however, the SVR saw itself as the heir of the old FCD. Mitrokhin had seen the FCD file on the SVR's newly appointed head, Academician Yevgeni Maksimovich Primakov, previously Director of the Institute of World Economics and International Relations and one of Gorbachev's leading foreign policy advisers. The file identified Primakov as a KGB co-optee, codenamed MAKSIM, who had been sent on frequent intelligence missions to the United States and the Middle East.[31] Primakov went on to become Boris Yeltsin's Foreign Minister in 1996 and Prime Minister in 1998.

IN THE FINAL months of 1991, the breakup of the Soviet Union and the relative weakness of frontier controls at the new borders of the Russian Federation at last opened the way to the West for Mitrokhin and his archive. In March 1992 he boarded an overnight train in Moscow bound for the capital of one of the newly independent Baltic republics.[32] With him he took a case on wheels, containing bread, sausages and drink for his journey on top, clothes underneath, and—at the bottom— samples of his notes. The next day he arrived unannounced at the British embassy in the Baltic capital and asked to speak to "someone in authority." Hitherto Mitrokhin had had an image of the British as rather formal and "a bit of a mystery." But the young female diplomat who received him at the embassy struck him as "young, attractive and sympathetic," as well as fluent in Russian. Mitrokhin told her he had brought with him important material from KGB files. While he rummaged at the bottom of his bag to extract his notes from beneath the sausages and clothes, the diplomat ordered tea. As Mitrokhin drank his first cup of English tea, she read some of his notes, then questioned him about them. Mitrokhin told her they were only part of a large personal archive which included material on KGB operations in Britain. He agreed to return to the embassy a month later to meet representatives from the Secret Intelligence Service.

Emboldened by the ease with which he had crossed the Russian frontier in March, Mitrokhin brought with him on his next trip to the Baltic capital 2,000 typed pages which he had removed from the hiding place beneath his dacha near Moscow. Arriving at the British embassy on the morning of April 9, he identified himself to the SIS officers by producing his passport, Communist Party card and KGB pension certificate, handed over his bulky typescript and spent a day answering questions about himself, his archive and how he had compiled it. Mitrokhin accepted an invitation to return to the embassy about two months later to discuss arrangements for a visit to Britain. Early in May the SIS Moscow station reported to London that Mitrokhin planned to leave Moscow on an overnight train on June 10. On June 11 he arrived in the Baltic capital carrying a rucksack containing more material from his archive. Most of his meeting with SIS officers was spent discussing plans for him to be debriefed in Britain during the following autumn.

On September 7, escorted by SIS, Mitrokhin arrived in England for the first time. After the near chaos of post-Communist Moscow, London made an extraordinary impression on him—"the model of what a capital city should be." At the time, even the heavy traffic, dotted with the black cabs and red doubledecker buses he had seen only in photographs, seemed but proof of the capital's prosperity. While being debriefed at anonymous safe houses in London and the countryside, Mitrokhin took the final decision to leave Russia for Britain, and agreed with SIS on arrangements to exfiltrate himself, his family and his archive. On October 13 he was infiltrated back into Russia to make final arrangements for his departure.

On November 7, 1992, the seventy-fifth anniversary of the Bolshevik Revolution, Mitrokhin arrived with his family in the Baltic capital where he had first made contact with SIS. A few days later they arrived in London to begin a new life in Britain. It was a bittersweet moment. Mitrokhin was safe and secure for the first time since he had begun assembling his secret archive eighteen years previously, but at the same time he felt a sense of bereavement at separation from a homeland he knew he would probably never see again. The bereavement has passed, though his attachment to Russia remains. Mitrokhin is now a British citizen. Using his senior citizen's railcard to travel the length and breadth of the country, he has seen more of Britain than most who were born here. Since 1992 he has spent several days a week working on his archive, typing up the remaining handwritten notes, and responding to questions about his archive from intelligence services from five continents. Late in 1995 he had his first meeting with Christopher Andrew to discuss the preparation of this book. Though *The Sword and the Shield* could not have been written in Russia, Mitrokhin remains as convinced as he was in 1972 that the secret history of the KGB is a central part of the Soviet past which the Russian people have the right to know. He also believes that the KGB's worldwide foreign operations form an essential, though often neglected, part of the history of twentieth-century international relations.

NO WORD LEAKED out in the British media about either Mitrokhin or his archive. Because material from the archive was passed to so many other intelligence and security services, however, there were, unsurprisingly, some partial leaks abroad. The first, slightly garbled reference to Mitrokhin's archive occurred in the United States nine months after his defection. In August 1993 the well-known Washington investigative journalist Ronald Kessler published a bestselling book on the FBI based in part on sources inside the Bureau. Among his revelations was a brief reference to a sensational "probe by the FBI into information from a former KGB employee who had had access to KGB files":

> According to his account, the KGB had had many hundreds of Americans and possibly more than a thousand spying for them in recent years. So specific was the information that the FBI was quickly able to establish the source's credibility . . . By the summer of 1993, the FBI had mobilized agents in most major cities to pursue the cases. A top secret meeting was called at Quantico [the FBI National Academy] to plot strategy.[33]

Kessler did not name any of the "many hundreds of Americans" identified by the defector. An unnamed "US intelligence official" interviewed by the *Washington Post* "confirmed that the FBI had received specific information that has led to a 'significant' ongoing investigation into past KGB activities in the United States," but declined to be drawn in on "how many people are implicated."[34] *Time* reported that "sources familiar with the case" of the KGB defector had identified him as a former employee of the First Chief Directorate, but had described Kessler's figures for the number of "recent" Soviet spies in the United States as "highly exaggerated."[35]

Mitrokhin's notes do indeed contain the names of "many hundreds" of KGB officers, agents and contacts in the United States active at various periods since the 1920s. Kessler, however, wrongly suggested that this number applied to "recent years" rather than to the whole history of Soviet espionage in the United States. Though his figures were publicly disputed, the suggestion that the KGB defector had gone to the United States rather than to Britain went unchallenged.[36] When no further information on the unidentified defector was forthcoming, media interest in the story quickly died away.

There was no further leak from Mitrokhin's archive for over three years. In October 1996, however, reports in the French press alleged that Charles Hernu, Defence Minister from 1981 to 1985, had worked for Soviet Bloc intelligence services from 1953 until at least 1963, and that, when informed by the French security service, the DST, President François Mitterrand had hushed the scandal up.[37] *Le Monde* reported that from 1993 onwards British intelligence had passed on to the DST "a list of about 300 names of diplomats and officials of the Quai d'Orsay alleged to have worked for

Soviet Bloc intelligence."[38] In reality, French diplomats and Foreign Ministry officials made up only a minority of the names in Mitrokhin's notes supplied by the SIS to the DST. Charles Hernu was not among them.[39] None of the media reports on either side of the Channel related the SIS lists of Soviet agents in France to Kessler's earlier story of a defector with extensive access to KGB files.

In December 1996 the German weekly *Focus* reported that, according to "reliable sources," SIS had also provided the BfV, the German security service, with the names of several hundred German politicians, businessmen, lawyers and police officers who had been involved with the KGB. On this occasion the SIS source was identified as a Russian defector who had had extensive access to the KGB archives. A later article in *Focus* reported:

> The Federal Prosecutor has been examining numerous detailed new leads to a hitherto undiscovered agent network of the former Soviet secret service, the KGB, in Germany. The researchers in Karlsruhe are primarily concentrating on Moscow sources who were taken on by the successors to the KGB and have probably been reactivated since the end of the Cold War.
>
> The basis for the research is extensive information on agents which a Russian defector smuggled into London from the Moscow secret service. After intensive analysis, the British secret service passed all information on KGB connections in Germany to the BfV in Cologne in early 1996.[40]

In July 1997 another leak from Mitrokhin's archive occurred in Austria. Press reports quoted a KGB document giving directions for locating a secret arms dump of mines, explosives and detonators, codenamed GROT, hidden in a dead letter-box near Salzburg in 1963, which had been intended for use in sabotage operations:

> Leave the town of Salzburg by the Schallmoser Haupstrasse leading to Highway No. 158. At a distance of 8 km from the town limit, in the direction of Bad Ischl-Graz, there is a large stone bridge across a narrow valley. Before reaching this bridge, leave the federal highway by turning right on to a local road which follows the valley in the direction of Ebenau; then go on 200 meters to the end of the metal parapet, which stands on the left-hand side of the road. On reaching the end of the parapet, turn left at once and follow a village road leading in the opposite direction. The DLB is located about 50 meters (60 paces) from the turn-off point leading from the main road on to the village road . . .[41]

Though the Austrian press did not mention it, the document came from Mitrokhin's archive, which also revealed that in 1964 road repair works had covered the entrance to the DLB, raised the ground level, and changed the layout of the surrounding area. The KGB had decided not to try to recover and relocate the GROT arms dump. Attempts by the Austrian authorities to find the dump in 1997 also failed.[42] Mitrokhin's notes reveal that similar KGB arms and radio caches, some of them booby-trapped, are scattered around much of Europe and North America.[43]

The press leak which came closest to revealing the existence of Mitrokhin's archive was a further article in the German weekly *Focus*, in June 1998. *Focus* reported that a colonel in the FCD registry with access to "all the files on Moscow's agents" had smuggled handwritten copies of them out of KGB headquarters to his dacha near Moscow. In 1992 he had defected to Britain and, according to *Focus*, SIS agents had brought the "explosive" notes hidden in the dacha back to London.[44] Four years later, in an operation codenamed WEEKEND, SIS had allegedly briefed the BfV on the German material in the archive. According to *Focus*, "The defector has presented the BfV with hundreds of leads to Moscow's spy network in the Federal Republic of Germany." A "high-ranking BfV official" was said to have commented, "We were quite shocked at how much [the defector] knew. Moscow clearly possesses tons of blackmail material." The BfV was reported to have received new leads on fifty espionage cases and to have begun twelve new investigations.[45]

The *Focus* article, however, inspired widespread skepticism—partly because the story of a top secret KGB archive exfiltrated from a Russian dacha seemed inherently improbable, partly because the only detailed example given by *Focus* of the intelligence it contained was the sensational allegation that the former Chancellor, Willy Brandt, "the icon of Germany's Social Democrats," had been a Soviet spy during the Second World War. The Brandt story was instantly dismissed as "completely absurd" by Yuri Kobaladze, head of the SVR press bureau. When asked why in this instance the SVR was abandoning its usual practice of not commenting on individuals alleged to be Russian spies, Kobaladze replied:

> It would naturally be very flattering to have such a high-ranking politician on our list of credits, but in the interests of preserving historical truth we felt it necessary to reject this fiction, which could be misused for political purposes.

Kobaladze also dismissed the story of the secret archive in a KGB colonel's dacha as a myth. The source of the Brandt story, he insisted, could only be a former KGB major in the Oslo residency, Mikhail Butkov, who had defected to Britain in 1991.[46]

Though wrong about the secret archive, Kobaladze was right to reject the allegation that Brandt had been a Soviet spy. Mitrokhin's notes reveal that the KGB archives do indeed contain a file on Brandt (codenamed POLYARNIK), which shows that while in Stockholm during the Second World War he passed on information to the NKVD residency. But, as the file makes clear, Brandt was also in touch with British and American intelligence officers—as well as with the Norwegian former secretary of Leon Trotsky, regarded by the NKVD as the greatest traitor in Soviet history.[47] Brandt's overriding motive was to provide any information to all three members of the wartime Grand Alliance which might hasten the defeat of Adolf Hitler. In the case of the Soviet Union, he calculated—accurately—that his best channel of communication with Moscow was via the Stockholm residency. The real embarrassment in the POLYARNIK file concerns the role not of Brandt but of the KGB. In 1962, almost certainly with Khrushchev's personal approval, the KGB embarked on an operation to blackmail Brandt by threatening to use the evidence of his wartime dealings with the Stockholm residency to "cause unpleasantness" unless he agreed to cooperate. The attempted blackmail failed.[48]

LIKE THE BfV and Austrian counter intelligence, a number of other security services and intelligence agencies around the world from Scandinavia to Japan have been pursuing leads from Mitrokhin's archive for several years—usually unnoticed by the media. Most of the leads have been used for counterintelligence purposes—to help resolve unsolved cases and neutralize SVR operations begun in the KGB era—rather than to mount prosecutions. There have, however, been a number of convictions which derive from Mitrokhin's evidence.

On one occasion, Mitrokhin himself was almost called to give evidence in court. The case concerned Robert Lipka, an army clerk assigned in the mid-1960s to the National Security Agency (NSA, the US SIGINT service), whom Mitrokhin had identified as a KGB agent.[49] In May 1993 FBI agent Dmitri Droujinsky contacted Lipka, posing as "Sergei Nikitin," a GRU officer based in Washington. Lipka complained that he was still owed money for his espionage over a quarter of a century earlier, and was given a total of $10,000 by "Nikitin" over the next few months. He appeared confident that he could no longer be prosecuted. "The statute of limitations," he told "Nikitin," "has run out." "Nikitin" corrected him: "In American law the statute of limitations for espionage never runs out." Lipka replied that, whatever the legal position, he "would never admit to anything." After a lengthy FBI investigation, Lipka was arrested in February 1996 at his home in Millersville, Pennsylvania, and charged with handing classified documents to the Soviet Union.[50]

Since Lipka denied all charges against him, Mitrokhin expected to give evidence at his trial in the U.S. District Court, Philadelphia, in May 1997. But, in what the *Philadelphia Inquirer* termed "a surprising turnaround" in the courtroom, Lipka "exploded into tears as he confessed that he had handed over classified information to KGB agents." Lipka had been persuaded by his lawyer, Ronald F. Kidd, to accept a prosecution offer of a plea bargain which would limit his sentence to eighteen years' imprisonment with time off for good behavior, rather than continue to plead not guilty and face the prospect of spending the rest of his life in jail. Though Mitrokhin's name was never mentioned in court, it was the evidence he had obtained from KGB files which seems to have prompted Lipka's change of heart. "We saw how significant the evidence was," his lawyer told reporters. "But the government also realized they couldn't go through a full trial and not have the mystery witness exposed." The "mystery witness" was Mitrokhin. After Lipka's confession, U.S. Assistant Attorney Barbara J. Cohan admitted, "We had a very sensitive witness who, if he had had to testify, would have had to testify behind a screen and under an assumed name, and now we don't have to surface him at all."[51] "I feel like Rip Van Spy," said Lipka when he was sentenced in September 1997. "I thought I had put this to bed many years ago and I never dreamed it would turn out like this." As well as being sentenced to eighteen years' imprisonment and fined 10,000 dollars, Lipka was ordered to repay the further 10,000 dollars from FBI funds given him by "Nikitin."[52]

There are many other "Rip Van Spies" whose memories of Cold War espionage are likely to be reawakened by Mitrokhin's archive. Some will recognize themselves in the pages which follow. About a dozen important cases which are still being actively pursued—including several in leading NATO countries—cannot be referred to for legal reasons until they come to court. Only a small minority of the Soviet agents whose codenames appear in this volume, however, are likely to be prosecuted. But, as the SVR embarks on the biggest and most complex damage assessment in Russian intelligence history, it has to face the unsettling possibility that some of the spies identified by Mitrokhin have since been turned into double agents.

After each of the revelations from Mitrokhin's archive mentioned above, the SVR undoubtedly conducted the usual damage assessment exercise in an attempt to determine the source and seriousness of the leak. Its official statement in 1996 (effectively reaffirmed as recently as June 1998), which dismissed as "absolute nonsense" the suggestion that the names of several hundred Soviet agents could possibly have been given by a defector to any Western intelligence agency, demonstrates that the conclusions of these exercises were very wide of the mark. Not until the publication of this book was announced in 1999 did the SVR seem to begin to grasp the massive hemorrhage of intelligence which had occurred.

SOME OF THE files noted by Mitrokhin give a vivid indication of the ferocity with which the Centre (KGB headquarters) has traditionally responded to intelligence leaks about its past foreign operations. The publication in 1974 of John Barron's *KGB: The Secret Work of Soviet Secret Agents*,[53] based on information from Soviet defectors and Western intelligence agencies, generated no fewer than 370 KGB damage assessments and other reports. The resident in Washington, Mikhail Korneyevich Polonik (codenamed ARDOV), was instructed to obtain all available information on Barron, then a senior editor at *Reader's Digest*, and to suggest ways "to compromise him."[54] Most of the "active measures" used by the KGB in its attempts to discredit Barron made much of his Jewish origins, but its fabricated claims that he was part of a Zionist conspiracy (a favorite theme in Soviet disinformation) appear to have had little resonance outside the Middle East.[55]

The active measures employed against some of the journalists who wrote articles based on Barron's book were more imaginative. Doctored versions of blank "information cards" from the Austrian Stapo (security police) registry previously obtained by KGB agents were used to compromise Austrian journalists judged to have used material from *KGB: The Secret Work of Soviet Secret Agents* to undermine the "peace-loving" policies of the USSR. Fabricated entries on the cards prepared by Service A, the FCD active measures specialists, purported to show that the Stapo believed the journalists concerned to be hand-in-glove with the CIA. Photocopies of the cards were then circulated among the Austrian media. The files noted by Mitrokhin list other KGB countermeasures against Barron's book in countries as far afield as Turkey, Cyprus, Libya, Lebanon, Egypt, Iran, Kuwait, Somalia, Uganda, India, Sri Lanka and Afghanistan.[56]

The other study of the KGB which did the most to arouse the ire of the Centre was the history published in 1990 by Christopher Andrew and Oleg Gordievsky, *KGB: The Inside Story of Its Foreign Operations from Lenin to Gorbachev*, which drew on KGB documents and other information obtained by Gordievsky while working as a British agent inside the KGB from 1974 to 1985.[57] The Centre predictably responded with active measures against both the book and its authors.[58] (Some indication of its continuing hostility to Gordievsky is provided by the fact that, at the time of this writing, he is still under sentence of death in Moscow.) There was, however, one important new element in the reaction of the KGB, and of its chairman Kryuchkov in particular, to the publication of the history by Andrew and Gordievsky. In a top secret "Chairman's Order" of September 1990 emphasizing the importance of influence operations and other active measures ("one of the most important functions of the KGB's foreign intelligence service"), Kryuchkov instructed that "wider use should be made of archive material" to publicize a "positive" image of the KGB and "its more celebrated cases."[59]

The first approach to a Western writer offering material from KGB archives intended to create this "positive" image was to the mercurial John Costello, a freelance British historian who combined flair for research with a penchant for conspiracy theory.[60] In 1991 Costello published a book on the mysterious flight to Britain fifty years previously of Hitler's deputy Führer, Rudolf Hess, which drew on KGB records selected by the SVR as well as Western sources, and argued (implausibly, in the view of most experts on the period) that the key to the whole affair was a plot by British intelligence.[61] Two years later, in collaboration with the SVR consultant (and former FCD officer) Oleg Tsarev, Costello published a somewhat less controversial biography of the inter-war Soviet intelligence officer Aleksandr Orlov which was described on the dustjacket as "The first book from the KGB archives—the KGB secrets the British government doesn't want you to read." The book began with tributes to the disgraced former chairman of the KGB, Vladimir Kryuchkov, and the last head of the FCD, Leonid Vladimirovich Shebarshin, for initiating the project. Costello added a note of "personal gratitude" to the SVR "for the ongoing support that they have given to this project which has established a new precedent for openness and objectivity in the study of intelligence history, not only in Russia, but the rest of the world."[62]

The Costello–Tsarev combination set the pattern for other collaborations between Russian authors selected or approved by the SVR and Western writers (who have included both well-known historians and a senior retired CIA officer): a project initially sponsored, but later abandoned, by Crown Books in the United States. For each volume in the series, which covers topics from the inter-war period to the early Cold War, the SVR has given the authors exclusive access to copies of previously top secret documents selected by it from KGB archives. All the books published so far have contained interesting and sometimes important new material; several are also impressive for the quality of their historical analysis. Their main weakness, for which the authors cannot be blamed, is that the choice of KGB documents on which they are based has been made not by them but by the SVR.[63]

The choice is sometimes highly selective. During the 1990s, for example, the SVR has made available to Russian and Western authors four successive tranches from the bulky file of the KGB's most famous British agent, Kim Philby.[64] In order to preserve both Philby's heroic image and the reputation of Russian foreign intelligence, however, the SVR has been careful not to release the record of Philby's final weeks as head of the SIS station in the United States (the climax of his career as a Soviet spy), when money and instructions intended for Philby were mislaid, and he fell out with his incompetent controller who was subsequently recalled to Moscow in disgrace. Mitrokhin's notes on those parts of the Philby file still considered by the SVR unsuitable for public consumption reveal this farcical episode for the first time.[65]

The SVR has publicly denied even the existence of some of the files which it finds embarrassing. While writing a history of KGB-CIA rivalry in Berlin before the construction of the Wall, based partly on documents selected by the SVR, the Russian and American authors (one of them a former deputy head of the FCD) asked to see the file of the KGB agent Aleksandr Grigoryevich Kopatzky (alias Igor Orlov). The SVR replied that it had no record of any agent of that name. Its only record of "Igor Orlov" was, it claimed, of a visit made by him to the Soviet embassy in Washington in 1965, when he complained of FBI harassment and enquired about asylum in the USSR.[66] Though still officially an unperson in the SVR version of Russian intelligence history, Kopatzky was in reality one of the KGB's most highly rated agents. His supposedly non-existent KGB file, noted by Mitrokhin, reveals that he had no fewer than twenty-three controllers.[67]

As well as initiating an unprecedented series of collaborative histories for publication in the West, the SVR has produced a number of less sophisticated works for the Russian market. In 1995, to mark the seventy-fifth anniversary of the foundation of the Soviet foreign intelligence service, of which it sees itself as the heir, the SVR published a volume on the careers of seventy-five intelligence officers—all, it appears, *sans peur et sans reproche*—which differs little from the uncritical hagiographies of the KGB era.[68] In 1995 the SVR also began the publication of a multi-volume official history of KGB foreign operations which by 1997 had reached the beginning of the Great Patriotic War.[69] Though a mine of mostly reliable factual information, it too presents a selective and sanitized view of Soviet intelligence history. It also preserves, in a mercifully diluted form, some of the traditional conspiracy theories of the KGB. The literary editor of the official history, Lolly Zamoysky, was formerly a senior FCD analyst, well known within the Centre and foreign residencies for his belief in a global Masonic-Zionist plot.[70] In 1989 he published a volume grandly entitled *Behind the Façade of the Masonic Temple*, which blamed the Freemasons for, *inter alia*, the outbreak of the Cold War.[71]

The underlying rationale for the SVR's selection of topics and documents for histories of past operations is to present Soviet foreign intelligence as a dedicated and highly professional service, performing much the same functions as its Western counterparts but, more often than not, winning the contest against them.[72] Even under Stalin, foreign intelligence is presented as the victim rather than the perpetrator of the Terror[73]—despite the fact that during the later 1930s hunting down "enemies of the people" abroad became its main priority.[74] Similarly, the SVR seeks to distance the foreign intelligence operations of the FCD during the Cold War from the abuse of human rights by the domestic KGB. In reality, however, the struggle against "ideological subversion" both at home and abroad was carefully coordinated. The KGB took a central role in the suppression of the Hungarian Uprising in 1956, the crushing of the Prague Spring in 1968, the invasion of Afghanistan in 1979, and the pressure on the Polish regime to destroy Solidarity in 1981. Closely linked to the persecution of dissidents within the Soviet Union were the FCD's PROGRESS operations against dissidents in the rest of the Soviet Bloc and its constant harassment of those who had taken refuge in the West.[75] By the mid-1970s the FCD's war against ideological subversion extended even to operations against Western Communist leaders who were judged to have deviated from Moscow's rigid Party line.[76]

On these and many other operations, Mitrokhin's archive contains much material from KGB files which the SVR is still anxious to keep from public view. Unlike the documents selected for declassification by the SVR, none of which are more recent than the early 1960s, his archive covers almost the whole of the Cold War. Most of it is still highly classified in Moscow. The originals of some of the most important documents noted or transcribed by Mitrokhin may no longer exist. In 1989 most of the huge multi-volume file on the dissident Andrei Sakharov, earlier branded "Public Enemy Number One" by Andropov, was destroyed. Soon afterwards, Kryuchkov announced that all files on other dissidents charged under the infamous Article 70 of the criminal code (anti-Soviet agitation and propaganda) were being shredded.[77] In a number of cases, Mitrokhin's notes on them may now be all that survives.

Vasili Mitrokhin has thus made it possible to extend what John Costello praised in 1993 as the "new precedent for openness and objectivity in the study of intelligence history" set by Kryuchkov and his SVR successors far beyond the limits any of them could have envisaged.

T W O

FROM LENIN'S CHEKA TO STALIN'S OGPU

For most of Mitrokhin's career in the KGB, the history of its domestic operations was something of an embarrassment even to its own historians. During the late 1930s the KGB (then known as the NKVD) had been the chief instrument of Stalin's Great Terror, the greatest peacetime persecution in European history. The KGB officers club in the Lubyanka, its Moscow headquarters, lacked even the usual boardroom photographs of past chairmen; most were more suited to a chamber of horrors than to a hall of fame. Three had been shot after being found guilty of horrific crimes (some real, others imaginary): Genrikh Yagoda in 1938, Nikolai Yezhov in 1940 and Lavrenti Beria in 1953. A fourth—Ivan Serov—blew his brains out in 1963. KGB historians in the post-Stalin era tended to take refuge from the blood-stained reality of their Stalinist past and homicidal former chairmen by returning to an earlier, mostly mythical, Leninist golden age of revolutionary purity.

The KGB traced its origins to the foundation on December 20, 1917, six weeks after the Bolshevik Revolution, of the Cheka, the first Soviet security and intelligence agency. Throughout Mitrokhin's career, KGB officers styled themselves Chekists (Chekisty) and were paid their salaries not on the first but on the twentieth of each month ("Chekists' Day") in honor of the Cheka's birthday. The KGB also adopted the Cheka symbols of the sword and the shield: the shield to defend the revolution, the sword to smite its foes. Outside the Lubyanka, the KGB's Moscow headquarters, stood a huge statue of the Polish-born head of the Cheka, Feliks Dzerzhinsky, venerated in countless official hagiographies as the selfless, incorruptible "Knight of the Revolution" who slew the dragon of counter-revolution which threatened the young Soviet state. He had been a professional revolutionary for over twenty years before the Revolution, spending eleven of those years in Tsarist prisons, penal servitude or exile. KGB training manuals quoted his description of the Chekist as a man with "a warm heart, a cool head and clean hands." Like Lenin, he was an incorruptible workaholic, prepared to sacrifice both himself and others in the defense of the Revolution.[1] In the headquarters of the KGB First Chief (Foreign Intelligence) Directorate at Yasenevo, the main object of veneration was a large bust of Dzerzhinsky on a marble pedestal constantly surrounded by fresh flowers.

The KGB's effusive public tributes to its saintly founding father concealed the degree to which Dzerzhinsky derived his intelligence tradecraft from the Cheka's much smaller Tsarist predecessor, the Okhrana. The Bolsheviks had extensive first-hand experience of the Okhrana's expertise in the use of penetration agents and *agents provocateurs.* In July 1913 Lenin had discussed the difficult problem of Okhrana penetration with two of his chief lieutenants, Lev Kamenev and Grigori Zinovyev, and the leader of the Bolshevik deputies in the Duma, Roman Malinovsky. All were agreed that there must be an unidentified Okhrana agent in close contact with the Bolshevik deputies. The agent was in even closer contact than Lenin realized. It was Roman Malinovsky. After Okhrana files later revealed his identity, he was shot in the Kremlin gardens on the first anniversary of the Bolshevik Revolution.[2]

The Cheka's success in penetrating its opponents derived in large part from its imitation of the techniques employed by Malinovsky and other Tsarist agents. Dmitri Gavrilovich Yevseyev, the author of two of the Cheka's earliest operational manuals, *Basic Tenets of Intelligence* and *Brief Instructions for the Cheka on How to Conduct Intelligence,* based his writings on detailed study of Okhrana tradecraft. Though the Cheka was "an organ for building the dictatorship of the proletariat," Yevseyev insisted—like Dzerzhinsky—that it must not hesitate to learn from the experience of "bourgeois" intelligence agencies.[3]

The Cheka's early priorities were overwhelmingly domestic. Dzerzhinsky described it as "an organ for the revolutionary settlement of accounts with counter-revolutionaries,"[4] a label increasingly applied to all the Bolsheviks' opponents and "class enemies." Within days of its foundation, however, the Cheka had also taken its first tentative steps in foreign intelligence collection. The career of the first agent sent on a mission abroad, Aleksei Frolovich Filippov, was sadly at variance with the heroic image which KGB historians struggled to maintain in their descriptions of the Leninist era. Born in 1870 and trained as a lawyer, Filippov had made a career before the Revolution as a newspaper publisher. At the end of 1917 he was recruited by Dzerzhinsky to go on intelligence assignments to Finland under cover as a journalist and businessman. Before departing on his first mission in January 1918, Filippov gave a written undertaking "on a voluntary basis, without receiving payment, to pass on all the information which I hear in industrial, banking and particularly in conservative [nationalist] circles."[5]

On January 4 Lenin publicly recognized the independence of Finland, formerly part of the Tsarist Empire, then immediately set about trying to subvert it. A putsch at the end of the month by Finnish Communists, supported by the Russian military and naval garrison in Helsinki, seized control of the capital and much of southern Finland. The Communists were quickly challenged by a defense corps of Finnish nationalists led by the former Tsarist officer General Karl Mannerheim.[6] Filippov's main Cheka assignment was to report on Mannerheim, his dealings with the Germans, and the mood of the sailors who had supported the putsch. Early in April 1918, however, German forces intervened in Finland, and by the end of the month both the Communist putsch and Filippov's brief career as the first Soviet foreign agent were at an end.[7]

DURING THE CIVIL war, which began in May 1918 and continued for two and a half years, the Bolshevik regime had to fight for its survival against powerful but divided White Russian armies. Behind all the forces arraigned against them, the Bolshevik leaders saw a vast conspiracy orchestrated by Western capitalism. "What we are facing," declared Lenin in July, "is a systematic, methodical and evidently long-planned military and financial counter-revolutionary campaign against the Soviet Republic, which all the representatives of Anglo-French imperialism have been preparing for months."[8] In reality, though the young Soviet regime had many enemies both at home and abroad, there was no carefully planned, well coordinated imperialist plot to bring it down. The illusion that such a plot existed, however, helped to shape the Cheka's early operations against its imperialist foes.

In the course of the civil war, the Cheka claimed to have uncovered and defeated a series of major conspiracies by Western governments and their intelligence agencies to overthrow the Bolshevik regime. The first such conspiracy in the summer of 1918 was the "envoys' plot," also known as the "Lockhart plot" (after its instigator, Robert Bruce Lockhart, a junior British diplomat). According to a KGB history published in 1979, "One could say without exaggeration that the shattering blow dealt by the Chekists to the conspirators was equivalent to victory in a major military battle."[9] That is what the Cheka had claimed in 1918 and what most of Mitrokhin's colleagues continued to believe over half a century later. In reality, however, the "envoys' plot" was mounted not by a coalition of capitalist governments but by a group of politically naive Western diplomats and adventurous secret agents who were left largely to their own devices during the chaotic early months of the Bolshevik regime and became involved in farcically inept attempts to overthrow it. The best-known of the secret agents was Sidney Reilly of the British Secret Intelligence Service (then known as MI1c), whose exploits oscillated between high adventure and low farce, and whose increasing tendency to fantasy later led to his exclusion from SIS. Reilly announced his arrival in Moscow on May 7, 1918 in bizarre but characteristic fashion by marching up to the Kremlin gates, announcing that he was an emissary from the British prime minister, Lloyd George (who had probably never heard of him), and unsuccessfully demanding to see Lenin.

By far the most sophisticated part of the "envoys' plot" was devised not by the envoys themselves or their secret agents but by the Cheka, possibly at Lenin's suggestion, as a trap for Western conspirators. In August 1918 the Cheka officer Yan Buikis, posing as an anti-Bolshevik conspirator named Shmidkhen, succeeded in persuading Lockhart, Reilly and the French consul-general that Colonel Eduard Berzin, commander of a Latvian regiment in the Kremlin (in reality a Cheka *agent provocateur*), was ready to lead an anti-Bolshevik rising. To finance Berzin's proposed coup, Reilly gave him 1,200,000 roubles which Berzin promptly passed on to the Cheka.[10] Reilly's schemes for the coup varied. At one point he imagined himself leading a detachment of Latvian troops on to the stage of the Bolshoi Theatre during the Congress of Soviets, seizing Lenin, Trotsky and other Bolshevik leaders, and shooting them on the spot.[11] However, Reilly was also attracted by an alternative scheme not to execute Lenin and Trotsky, but instead to remove their trousers, parade them in their underpants through the streets of Moscow, and so "hold them up to ridicule before the world."[12]

Reilly's fantasies however were overtaken by events. On August 30 the head of the Petrograd Cheka, Moisei Solomonovich Uritsky, was assassinated by a former member of the moderate Workers' Popular Socialist Party, Leonid Kannegiser.[13] In an unrelated attack on the same day, Lenin was shot and seriously wounded by the Socialist Revolutionary, Fanya (Dora) Kaplan. "I shot Lenin because I believe him to be a traitor [to Socialism]," Kaplan told her Cheka interrogators.[14] In the aftermath of both shootings, Dzerzhinsky decided to wind up the "envoys' plot," which the Cheka itself had been largely responsible for orchestrating. On September 2 it was announced that the Cheka had "liquidated . . . the conspiracy organized by Anglo-French diplomats . . . to organize the capture of the Council of People's Commissars and the proclamation of military dictatorship in Moscow; this was to be done by bribing Soviet troops." Predictably, the statement made no mention of the fact that the plan to bribe Soviet troops and stage a military coup had been devised by the Cheka itself and that the diplomats had been drawn into the conspiracy by *agents provocateurs* relying on Okhrana tradecraft. On September 5 Dzerzhinsky and Zinovyev, the Petrograd Party boss, issued a further statement declaring that the Anglo-French conspirators had been the "organizers" of the attempt on Lenin's life and the "real murderers" of Uritsky. Dzerzhinsky did not, however, reveal Reilly's plan to remove Lenin's and Trotsky's trousers. Though happy to publicize, or invent, Western involvement in assassination plots against Lenin, the Cheka dared not disclose a plot to hold him up to ridicule.[15]

The attempt on Lenin's life, the killing of Uritsky and the announcement of the "liquidation" of "the envoys' plot" were quickly followed by the declaration of the Red Terror. With the Bolsheviks engaged in a bitter civil war against their White enemies, the Cheka set out to terrorize the regime's opponents. Lenin himself, only three weeks before the attempt on his own life, had written to the Bolsheviks in Penza, and probably elsewhere, urging them to organize public executions to make the people "tremble" "for hundreds of kilometers around." While still recovering from his wounds, he instructed, "It is necessary secretly—and *urgently*—to prepare the terror."[16] On October 15 Uritsky's successor in Petrograd, Gleb Ivanovich Boky, proudly reported to Moscow that 800 alleged counterrevolutionaries had been shot and another 6,229 imprisoned. Among those arrested, and probably executed, in Petrograd was the Cheka's first foreign agent, Alexei Filippov. His liquidation was due, in all probability, not to the failure of his Finnish missions but to his "bourgeois" origins, which marked him down as an enemy of the people in the paranoid atmosphere of the Red Terror.[17] Twenty years later Boky was himself to fall victim to the even greater paranoia of Stalin's Terror.[18]

Berzin and Buikis, the Cheka *agents provocateurs* who had helped orchestrate the "envoys' plot," subsequently became victims of their own deception. Berzin's career initially prospered. He was awarded the Order of the Red Banner for his role as *agent provocateur,* joined the Cheka and later became head of a forced labor camp in the Kolyma goldfields which had one of the highest death rates in Stalin's gulag. In 1937, however, he was arrested and shot as an enemy of the people.[19] The exact charges leveled against Berzin are not known, but it is likely that they included accusations that he had actually collaborated with Western plotters in 1918. In the somewhat paranoid Stalinist interpretation of the "envoys' plot," his collaborator Buikis (alias "Shmidkhen") was portrayed as a covert counter-revolutionary rather than a Cheka officer carrying out his orders. That remained the accepted interpretation even in classified KGB histories during Mitrokhin's early career. Buikis survived the Terror only by concealing his identity. Not until the mid-1960s did research in the KGB archives reestablish "Shmidkhen's" true identity and his real role in 1918.[20]

Throughout Mitrokhin's career, KGB historians continued to interpret all plots and attacks against the young Soviet regime as "manifestations of a unified conspiracy" by its class enemies at home and the "imperialist powers" abroad.[21] The reality was very different. Had there been "a unified conspiracy," the regime would surely have lost the civil war. If two or three divisions of Western troops had landed in the Gulf of Finland in 1919, they could probably have forced their way to Moscow and overthrown the Bolsheviks. But in the aftermath of the First World War not even two or three divisions could be found. Those American, British, French and Japanese troops who intervened against the Red Army served mainly to discredit the White cause and thus actually to assist the Bolsheviks. They were too few to affect the military outcome of the civil war but quite sufficient to allow the Bolsheviks to brand their opponents as the tools of Western imperialism. Most Bolsheviks were, in any case, sincerely convinced that during the civil war they had faced a determined onslaught from the full might of Western capitalism. That illusion continued to color Soviet attitudes to the West throughout, and even beyond, the Stalin era.

THE CHEKA'S INTELLIGENCE operations both at home and abroad were profoundly influenced not merely by the legacy of the Okhrana but also by the Bolsheviks' own pre-Revolutionary experience as a largely illegal clandestine underground. Many of the Bolshevik leadership had become so used to living under false identities before 1917 that they retained their aliases even after the Revolution: among them the Russian nobleman Vladimir Ilyich Ulyanov,[22] who kept the pseudonym Lenin, and the Georgian Joseph Vissarionovich Dzhugashvili, who continued to be known as Stalin. Both Lenin and Stalin retained many of the habits of mind developed during their underground existence. On highly sensitive matters Lenin would insist no copy be made of his instructions and that the original either be returned to him for destruction or destroyed by the recipient. Happily for the historian, his instructions were not always carried out.[23]

Stalin continued to doctor his own pre-Revolutionary record during the 1920s, changing even the day and year of his birth; the correct date (December 6, 1878) was not made public until 1996.[24] During a visit to the secret section of the Moscow Main Archives Directorate (Glavarkhiv), Mitrokhin was once shown an Okhrana file on Dzhugashvili. The file cover and title followed standard Okhrana format, but, on looking inside, Mitrokhin discovered that the contents had been entirely removed. The probability is that the Okhrana had compromising materials on the young Dzhugashvili, and that at the first opportunity Stalin arranged for the file to be gutted. In typical Soviet bureaucratic fashion, however, the cover was preserved since the existence of the file was indelibly recorded in the secret registers. Mitrokhin suspects that whoever emptied the file, presumably on Stalin's instructions, was later eliminated to preserve the dark secret of its missing contents.[25] What Stalin was most anxious to destroy may well have been evidence that he had been an Okhrana informer. Though it falls well short of conclusive proof, a possible trace of that evidence still survives. According to reports from an Okhrana agent discovered in the State Archive of the Russian Federation, Baku Bolsheviks before the First World War "confronted Dzhugashvili-Stalin with the accusation that he was a provocateur and an agent of the Security Police. And that he had embezzled Party funds."[26]

From almost the beginning of the civil war in 1918, in keeping with the Bolshevik tradition of operating under false identities, the Cheka began sending officers and agents under various disguises and pseudonyms behind enemy lines to gather intelligence. By June 1919 the number of these "illegals" was sufficiently large to require the foundation of an illegals operations department (later to become Directorate S of the KGB First Chief Directorate).[27] KGB classified histories note that henceforth "illegal" operations became "an inseparable part of foreign intelligence." On December 20, 1920, the third anniversary of the Cheka's foundation, a new foreign department (Innostranyi Otdel or INO) was set up to direct all operations beyond Soviet borders. During the early years of Soviet Russia, when the Communist regime remained an international pariah, it had few official missions abroad capable of providing official cover for "legal" intelligence stations ("residencies" in Cheka jargon) and thus relied chiefly on illegals. As diplomatic and trade missions were established in foreign capitals, each was given a "legal residency" headed by a "resident" whose identity was officially communicated only to the ambassador or head of the mission. Illegals, sometimes grouped in "illegal residencies," operated without the benefit of diplomatic or official cover and reported directly to INO in Moscow.[28]

During the civil war of 1918–20, foreign intelligence collection was of minor importance by comparison with the Cheka's role in assisting the victory of the Red Army over its White enemies. Like the KGB later, the Cheka liked to quantify its successes. In the autumn of 1919, probably the turning point in the civil war, it proudly claimed that during the first nineteen months of its existence it had discovered and neutralized "412 underground anti-Soviet organizations."[29] The Cheka's most effective method of dealing with opposition was terror. Though its liking of quantification did not extend to calculating the number of its victims, it is clear that the Cheka enormously outstripped the Okhrana in both the scale and the ferocity of its onslaught on political opposition. In 1901, 4,113 Russians were in internal exile for political crimes, of whom only 180 were on hard labor. Executions for political crimes were limited to those involved in actual or attempted assassinations. During the civil war, by contrast, Cheka executions probably numbered as many as 250,000, and may well have exceeded the number of deaths in battle.[30]

At the time of the October Revolution, it had never occurred to Lenin that he and the Bolshevik leadership would be responsible for the rebirth of the Okhrana in a new and far more terrible form. In *The State and Revolution,* which he had almost completed in the summer of 1917, he had claimed that there would be no need for a police force, let alone a political police, after the Revolution. Though it would be necessary to arrange for "the suppression of the minority of exploiters by the majority of wage slaves of yesterday," such suppression would be "comparatively easy." The "proletarian dictatorship" which would preside over the rapid destruction of the bourgeois order would require a minimum of rules, regulation and bureaucracy. Lenin had never foreseen the possibility of mass opposition to a revolution carried out in the name of the people.[31] But, once in power, he used whatever methods were necessary to retain it, claiming always that the Bolsheviks were defending "the people's power" and refusing to accept the reality that he had made himself the infallible leader (*Vozhd*) of the world's first one-party state.

APPROPRIATELY, THE MEMORIAL erected next to the Lubyanka in the closing years of the Soviet era to commemorate "the victims of totalitarian repression" consists of a large block of granite taken not from Stalin's gulag but from a concentration camp established by Lenin on the shores of the White Sea in the autumn of 1918. Many Chekists regarded brutality against their class enemies as a revolutionary virtue. According to a report from the Cheka in Morshansk:

> He who fights for a better future will be merciless towards his enemies. He who seeks to protect poor people will harden his heart against pity and will become cruel.[32]

Even at a time when the Soviet regime was fighting for its survival during the civil war, many of its own supporters were sickened by the scale of the Cheka's brutality. A number of Cheka interrogators, some only in their teens,[33] employed tortures of scarcely believable barbarity. In Kharkhov the skin was peeled off victims' hands to produce "gloves" of human skin; in Voronezh naked prisoners were rolled around in barrels studded with nails; in Poltava priests were impaled; in Odessa, captured White officers were tied to planks and fed slowly into furnaces; in Kiev cages of rats were fixed to prisoners' bodies and heated until the rats gnawed their way into the victims' intestines.[34]

Though Lenin did not approve of such sadism, he was content to leave "excesses" to be corrected by Dzerzhinsky. Brushing aside complaints of Cheka brutality, he paid fulsome tribute to its role in helping to win the civil war. The Cheka, he claimed, had proved a "devastating weapon against countless conspiracies and countless attempts against Soviet power by people who are infinitely stronger than us":

> Gentlemen capitalists of Russia and abroad! We know that it is not possible for you to love this establishment. Indeed, it is not! [The Cheka] has been able to counter your intrigues and your machinations as no one else could have done

when you were smothering us, when you had surrounded us with invaders, and when you were organizing internal conspiracies and would stop at no crime in order to wreck our peaceful work.[35]

Some of the most secret documents in Dzerzhinsky's archive carry a note that only ten copies were to be made: one for Lenin, the rest for Cheka department chiefs.[36] Lenin's absorption in the affairs of the Cheka extended even to operational detail. He sent Dzerzhinsky advice on how to carry out searches and conduct surveillance, and instructed him that arrests were best carried out at night.[37] Lenin also took a somewhat naive interest in the application of new technology to the hunt for counter-revolutionaries, telling Dzerzhinsky to construct a large electromagnet capable of detecting hidden weapons in house-to-house searches. Though the experiment was tried and failed, Dzerzhinsky had some difficulty in persuading Lenin that, "Magnets are not much use in searches."[38]

Far more important than Lenin's sometimes eccentric interest in intelligence techniques and technology was his belief in the central importance of the Cheka to the defense of the Bolshevik one-party state against imperialism and counter-revolution. The extent of Lenin's and Dzerzhinsky's fear of imperialist subversion is well illustrated by their deep suspicion of the aid which they felt forced to accept in August 1921 from the American Relief Association (ARA) to feed millions of starving Soviet citizens. Lenin was convinced that the ARA was a front for United States intelligence, and ordered the closest surveillance of all its members. Once the ARA began work, he was equally convinced that it was using food as an instrument of subversion. He complained to Dzerzhinsky's deputy, Iosif Stanislavovich Unshlikht, that foreign agents were "engaged in massive bribery *of hungry and tattered Chekists* [Lenin's emphasis]. The danger here is extremely great." Lenin insisted that urgent steps be taken to "*feed and clothe* the Chekists" in order to remove them from imperialist temptation.[39]

Though the United States still had no peacetime espionage agency, the Cheka reported that over 200 of the 300 ARA staff, who were devoting all their energies to dealing with one of the most terrible famines in modern European history, were in reality undercover intelligence officers who "could become first-class instructors for a counter-revolutionary uprising." The Cheka also alleged that the ARA was building up a large food supply in Vienna so that "in the event of a coup [it] could provide immediate support to the White government."[40] Lenin was far more exercised by the ARA's non-existent intelligence operations than by the approximately five million Russians and Ukrainians who starved to death. Without the massive aid program of the ARA, which in 1922 was feeding up to eleven million people a day, the famine would have been far worse. Even after the ARA had departed, however, Soviet intelligence remained convinced that it had been, first and foremost, an espionage rather than a humanitarian agency. A quarter of a century later, all surviving Russian employees of ARA were made to sign confessions that they had been American spies.[41]

The priorities of Soviet intelligence under Lenin, and still more under Stalin, continued to be shaped by greatly exaggerated beliefs in an unrelenting conspiracy by Western governments and their intelligence agencies. To understand Soviet intelligence operations between the wars, it is frequently necessary to enter a world of smoke and mirrors where the target is as much the product of Bolshevik delusions as of real counter-revolutionary conspiracy. The Soviet propensity to conspiracy theory derived both from the nature of the one-party state and from its Marxist–Leninist ideology. All authoritarian regimes, since they regard opposition as fundamentally illegitimate, tend to see their opponents as engaged in subversive conspiracy. Bolshevik ideology further dictated that capitalist regimes could not fail to be plotting the overthrow of the world's first and only worker–peasant state. If they were not visibly preparing an armed invasion, then their intelligence agencies must necessarily be secretly conspiring to subvert Soviet Russia from within.

INO'S FIRST TWO heads served between them for a total of barely eighteen months. The first foreign intelligence chief to make his mark was Mikhail Abramovich Trilisser, appointed as head of INO in 1922—undoubtedly with Lenin's personal approval. Trilisser was a Russian Jew who had become a professional revolutionary in 1901 at the age of only eighteen. Like Dzerzhinsky, he had spent much of his early career in exile or in Tsarist prisons. Before the First World War, he had specialized in tracking down police spies among Bolshevik émigrés. While serving with the Cheka in 1918, he was reputed to have been caught by "bandits" and hung from a tree, but to have been cut down just in time by Red forces who successfully revived him. Unlike any of his successors, Trilisser sometimes traveled abroad to meet INO agents.[42] At least until Lenin was incapacitated by his third stroke in March 1923, he continued to take an active, though sometimes ill-informed, interest, in INO reports. He noted, for example, that somewhat inaccurate information received in 1922 from one of the Cheka's few early British sources, the journalist Arthur Ransome (later famous as a children's novelist), was "very important and, probably, fundamentally true."[43]

The early priorities of INO foreign operations, approved by Lenin, were:

the identification, on the territory of each state, of counter-revolutionary groups operating against the Russian Socialist Federal Soviet Republic;
the thorough study of all organizations engaged in espionage against our country;
the elucidation of the political course of each state and its economic situation;
the acquisition of documentary material on all the above requirements.[44]

The "counter-revolutionary groups" which were of most immediate concern to Lenin and the Cheka after the civil war were the remnants of the defeated White armies and the Ukrainian nationalists. After the last White forces left Russian soil late in 1920, they stood no realistic chance of mounting another serious challenge to Bolshevik rule. That, however, was not Lenin's view. "A beaten army," he declared, "learns much." He estimated that there were one and a half to two million anti-Bolshevik Russian émigrés:

We can observe them all working together irrespective of their former political parties ... They are skillfully taking advantage of every opportunity in order, in one way or another, to attack Soviet Russia and smash her to pieces ... These counter-revolutionary émigrés are very well informed, excellently organized and good strategists.[45]

In the early and mid-1920s INO's chief target thus became the émigré White Guards, based mainly in Berlin, Paris and Warsaw, who continued to plot—far less effectively than Lenin supposed—the overthrow of the Bolshevik regime.

The other "counter-revolutionary" threat which most concerned Lenin and the Bolshevik leadership came from Ukrainian nationalists, who had fought both Red and White forces in an attempt to win their independence. In the winter of 1920 and the spring of 1921 the entire Ukrainian countryside was in revolt against Bolshevik rule. Even after the brutal "pacification" of Ukraine by the Red Army and the Cheka, partisan groups who had taken refuge in Poland and Romania continued to make cross-border raids.[46] In the spring of 1922 the Ukrainian GPU received intelligence reports that Simon Petlyura's Ukrainian government-in-exile had established a "partisan headquarters" under General Yurko Tutyunnik which was sending secret emissaries to the Ukraine to establish a nationalist underground.[47]

The GPU was ordered not merely to collect intelligence on the émigré White Guards and Ukrainian nationalists but also to penetrate and destabilize them.[48] Its strategy was the same against both opponents—to establish bogus anti-Bolshevik undergrounds under GPU control which could be used to lure General Tutyunnik and the leading White generals back across the frontier.

The first step in enticing Tutyunnik back to Ukraine (an operation codenamed CASE 39) was the capture of Zayarny, one of his "special duties" officers, who was caught crossing the frontier in 1922. Zayarny was successfully turned back by the GPU and sent to Tutyunnik's headquarters with bogus reports that an underground Supreme Military Council (Vysshaya Voyskovaya Rada or VVR) had been established in Ukraine and was anxious to set up an operational headquarters under Tutyunnik's leadership to wage war against the Bolsheviks. Tutyunnik was too cautious to return immediately but sent several emissaries who attended stage-managed meetings of the VVR, at which GPU officers disguised as Ukrainian nationalists reported the rapid growth of underground opposition to Bolshevik rule and agreed on the urgent need for Tutyunnik's leadership. Like Zayarny, one of the emissaries, Pyotr Stakhov, a close associate of Tutyunnik, was recruited by the GPU and used as a double agent.

Attempts to persuade Tutyunnik himself to return to Ukraine finally succeeded on June 26, 1923.[49] Tutyunnik, with his bodyguard and aides, arrived at a remote hamlet on the Romanian bank of the river Dniester, where Zayarny met him with the news that the VVR and Pyotr Stakhov were waiting on the other side. At 11 p.m. a light from the Ukrainian bank signaled that it was safe for Tutyunnik and his entourage to cross the river. Still cautious, Tutyunnik sent his bodyguard to make sure that no trap had been laid for him. Stakhov returned with the bodyguard to reassure him. According to an OGPU report, Tutyunnik told him, "Pyotr, I know you and you know me. We won't fool each other. The VVR is a fiction, isn't it?" "That is impossible," Stakhov replied. "I know them all, particularly those who are with me [today]. You know you can rely on me . . ." Tutyunnik got into the boat with Stakhov and crossed the Dniester. Once he was in the hands of the OGPU, letters written by Tutyunnik or in his name were sent to prominent Ukrainian nationalists abroad saying that their struggle was hopeless and that he had aligned himself irrevocably with the Soviet cause. He was executed six years later.[50]

OPERATIONS AGAINST THE White Guards resembled those against Ukrainian nationalists. In 1922 the Berlin residency recruited the former Tsarist General Zelenin as a penetration agent within the émigré community. A later OGPU report claimed, possibly with some exaggeration, that Zelenin had engineered "a huge schism within the ranks of the Whites" and had caused a large number of officers to break away from Baron Peter Wrangel, the last of the White generals to be defeated in the civil war. Other OGPU moles praised for their work in disrupting the White Guards included General Zaitsev, former chief of staff to the Cossack Ataman A. I. Dutov, and the ex-Tsarist General Yakhontov, who emigrated to the United States.[51]

The OGPU's greatest successes against the White Guards, however, were two elaborate deception operations, codenamed SINDIKAT ("Syndicate") and TREST ("Trust"), both of which made imaginative use of *agents provocateurs*.[52] SINDIKAT was targeted against the man believed to be the most dangerous of all the White Guards: Boris Savinkov, a former Socialist Revolutionary terrorist who had served as deputy minister of war in the provisional government overthrown in the Bolshevik Revolution. Winston Churchill, among others, was captivated by his anti-Bolshevik fervor. "When all is said and done," Churchill wrote later, "and with all the stains and tarnishes there be, few men tried more, gave more, dared more and suffered more for the Russian people." During the Russo-Polish War of 1920, Savinkov was largely responsible for recruiting the Russian People's Army which fought under Polish command against the Red Army. Early in 1921 he founded a new organization in Warsaw dedicated to the overthrow of the Bolshevik regime: the People's Union for Defence of Country and Freedom (NSZRiS), which ran an agent network inside Soviet Russia to collect intelligence on the Bolsheviks and plan uprisings against the regime.

The first stage of the operation against Savinkov, SINDIKAT-1, successfully neutralized the NSZRiS agent network with the help of a Cheka mole within his organization. Forty-four leading members of the NSZRiS were paraded at a show trial in Moscow in August 1921.[53] SINDIKAT-2 was aimed at luring Savinkov back to Russia to star in a further show trial and complete the demoralization of his émigré supporters. Classified KGB histories give the main credit for the operation to the head of the OGPU counter-intelligence department, Artur Khristyanovich Artuzov (later head of INO), the Russian son of an immigrant Swiss-Italian cheesemaker, assisted by Andrei Pavlovich Fyodorov and Grigori Sergeyevich Syroyezhkin.[54] Though SINDIKAT-2 made skillful use of *agents provocateurs*, however, KGB records fail to acknowledge how much they were assisted by Savinkov's own increasing tendency to fantasize. During a visit to London late in 1921 he claimed improbably that the head of the Russian trade delegation had suggested that he join the Soviet government. Savinkov also alleged that Lloyd George and his family had welcomed him at Chequers by singing "God Save the Tsar"; in reality, the song was a hymn sung in Welsh by a Welsh choir at a pre-Christmas celebration. In July 1923 Fedorov, posing as a member of an anti-Bolshevik underground, visited Savinkov in Paris, where he had installed his headquarters after the collapse of the NSZRiS, and persuaded him to send his aide, Colonel Sergei Pavlovsky, back to Russia with Fedorov for secret talks with the non-existent underground. Once in Moscow, Pavlovsky was turned in by the OGPU and used to lure Savinkov himself to Russia for further talks. On August 15 Savinkov crossed the Russian border with some of his supporters and walked straight into an OGPU trap. Under OGPU interrogation Savinkov's resistance swiftly collapsed. At a show trial on August 27 Savinkov made an abject confession of his counter-revolutionary sins:

> I unconditionally recognize Soviet power and no other. To every Russian who loves his country I, who have traversed the entire road of this bloody, heavy struggle against you, I who refuted you as no one else did, I tell you that if you are a Russian, if you love your people, you will bow down to worker–peasant power and recognize it without any reservations.[55]

The deception of Savinkov continued even after he was sentenced to fifteen years in jail. He failed to realize that his cellmate, V. I. Speransky, was an OGPU officer, later promoted for his success in gaining Savinkov's confidence and surreptitiously debriefing him over a period of eight months.[56] Savinkov did not long survive Speransky's final report on him. KGB files appear to contain no contemporary record of how he met his death. According to the SVR's implausible current version of events, Savinkov fell or jumped from an upper-story window after a congenial "drinking bout with a group of Chekists"—despite a heroic attempt to save him by Grigori Syroyezhkin.[57] It seems more likely that Syroyezhkin pushed him to his death.[58]

Even more successful than SINDIKAT was operation TREST, the cover name given to a fictitious monarchist underground, the Monarchist Association of Central Russia (MOR), first invented by Artuzov in 1921 and used as the basis of a six-year deception.[59] By 1923 the OGPU officer Aleksandr Yakushev, posing as a secret MOR member able to travel abroad in his official capacity as a Soviet foreign trade representative, had won the confidence during visits to Paris of both Grand Duke Nikolai Nikolayevich, cousin of the late Tsar Nicholas II, and General Aleksandr Kutepov of the [White] Russian Combined Services Union (ROVS). The leading victim of the deception, however, was the former SIS agent Sidney Reilly, an even greater fantasist than Savinkov. Reilly had become a tragicomic figure whose hold on reality was increasingly uncertain. According to one of his secretaries, Eleanor Toye, "Reilly used to suffer from severe mental crises amounting to delusion. Once he thought he was Jesus Christ." The OGPU, however, failed to grasp that Reilly was now of little significance, regarding him instead as a British masterspy and one of its most dangerous opponents. On September 26, 1925 it succeeded in luring him, like Savinkov a year before, across the Russian frontier to a meeting with bogus MOR conspirators.[60]

Reilly's resistance after his arrest did not last much longer than Savinkov's. His KGB file contains a letter, probably authentic, to Dzerzhinsky dated October 30, 1925, in which he promised to reveal all he knew about British and American intelligence as well as Russian émigrés in the West. Six days later Reilly was taken for a walk in the woods near Moscow and, without warning, shot from behind. According to an OGPU report, he "let out a deep breath and fell without a cry." Among those who accompanied him on his final walk in the woods was Grigori Syroyezhkin, the probable assassin of Savinkov a year earlier. Reilly's corpse was put on private display in the Lubyanka sickbay to allow OGPU officers to celebrate their triumph.[61] Appropriately for a career in which myth and reality had become inextricably confused, rumors circulated for many years in the West that Reilly had escaped execution and adopted a new identity. The TREST deception was finally exposed in 1927, to the embarrassment of the intelligence services of Britain, France, Poland, Finland and the Baltic states who had all, in varying degrees, been taken in by it.[62]

AS WELL AS engaging in permanent conflict with counter-revolution, both real and imagined, Soviet intelligence between the wars also became increasingly successful in penetrating the main imperialist powers. It had two major operational advantages over Western intelligence agencies. First, while security in Moscow became obsessional, much Western security remained feeble. Secondly, the Communist parties and their "fellow travelers" in the West gave Soviet intelligence a major source of ideological recruits of which it took increasing advantage.

While operation TREST was at its height, INO, the OGPU's foreign intelligence service, succeeded in making its first major penetration of the British foreign service. The penetration agent was an Italian messenger in the British embassy in Rome, Francesco Constantini (codenamed DUNCAN), who was recruited in 1924 by the OGPU residency with the help of an Italian Communist, Alfredo Allegretti, who had worked as a Russian embassy clerk before the Revolution. Despite his lowly status, Constantini had access to a remarkable range of diplomatic secrets.[63] Until the Second World War, the Foreign Office did not possess a single security officer, let alone a security department. Security in many British embassies was remarkably lax. In Rome, according to Sir Andrew Noble, who was stationed at the embassy in the mid-1930s, it was "virtually non-existent." Embassy servants had access to the keys to red boxes and filing cabinets containing classified documents, as well as—probably—the number of the combination lock on the embassy safe. Even when two copies of a diplomatic cipher were missing in 1925, it did not occur to British diplomats that they might have been removed by Constantini—as they almost certainly were.[64]

For more than a decade Francesco Constantini handed over a great variety of diplomatic documents and cipher material. Probably from an early stage he also involved his brother, Secondo, who worked as an embassy servant, in the theft of documents. In addition to despatches on Anglo-Italian relations exchanged between London and the Rome embassy, Constantini was often able to supply the "confidential print" of selected documents from the Foreign Office and major British missions designed to give ambassadors an overview of current foreign policy.[65] By January 1925 he was providing, on average, 150 pages of classified material a week. Constantini made no secret of his motives. The Rome residency reported to the Centre, "He collaborates with us exclusively for money, and does not conceal the fact. He has set himself the goal of becoming a rich man, and that is what he strives for." In 1925 the Centre pronounced Constantini its most valuable agent. Convinced of a vast, nonexistent British plot to destroy the Soviet state, it counted on agent DUNCAN to provide early warning of a British attack, and instructed the Rome residency:

> England is now the organizing force behind a probable attack on the USSR in the near future. A continuous hostile cordon [of states] is being formed against us in the West. In the East, in Persia, Afghanistan and China we observe a similar picture . . . Your task (and consider it a priority) is to provide documentary and agent materials which reveal the details of the English plan.

The Rome residency's pride in running the OGPU's leading agent is reflected in its flattering descriptions of him. Constantini was said to have the face of "an ancient Roman," and to be known to his many female admirers as "the handsome one."[66] By 1928 the OGPU suspected him—accurately—of also supplying documents to Italian intelligence. Despite suspicions about Constantini's honesty, however, there was no mistaking the importance of the material he supplied. Maksim Litvinov, who by the late 1920s was the dominating figure in the People's Commissariat for Foreign Affairs, pronounced it "of great use to me."[67]

THE OGPU'S FIRST successful penetration of the British foreign service was overshadowed in 1927 by an embarrassing series of well-publicized intelligence failures. The security of the rapidly expanding foreign network of OGPU and Fourth Department (Military Intelligence) residencies was threatened by the vulnerability of early Soviet cipher systems to Western cryptanalysts, by the inexperience of some of the first generation of INO officers, and by errors in the selection and training of foreign Communists as agents. The International Liaison Department (OMS) of the Communist International provided a ready pool of enthusiastic volunteers for Soviet intelligence operations. Some, such as the German Richard Sorge, were to be numbered among the greatest spies of the century. Others ignored orthodox tradecraft and neglected standard security procedures.

In the spring of 1927 there were dramatic revelations of Soviet espionage in eight different countries. In March a major OGPU spy ring was uncovered in Poland; a Soviet trade official was arrested for espionage in Turkey; and the Swiss police announced the arrest of two Russian spies. In April a police raid on the Soviet consulate in Beijing uncovered a mass of incriminating intelligence documents; and the French Sûreté, arrested members of a Soviet spy ring in Paris run by Jean Crémet, a leading

French Communist. In May Austrian foreign ministry officials were found passing classified information to the OGPU residency, and the British Home Secretary indignantly announced to the House of Commons the discovery of "one of the most complete and one of the most nefarious spy systems that it has ever been my lot to meet."[68]

Following this last discovery, Britain—still regarded in the Soviet Union as the leading world power and its most dangerous enemy—formally broke off diplomatic relations, and senior ministers read out to the Commons decrypted extracts from intercepted Soviet telegrams. To tighten the security of Soviet diplomatic and OGPU communications after the dramatic revelation of British codebreaking successes, the laborious but virtually unbreakable "one-time pad" cipher system was introduced. As a result, Western cryptanalysts were able to decrypt almost no further high-grade Soviet communications until after the Second World War.[69]

THE MOST WORRYSOME as well as the most plentiful foreign intelligence in 1927 concerned Japan. Since 1925 INO had been able to intercept the secret communications of both Japan's military mission and its consulate-general in the northeast Chinese city of Harbin. Remarkably, instead of using diplomatic bags and their own couriers, Japanese official representatives in Harbin corresponded with Tokyo via the Chinese postal service. The OGPU recruited the Chinese employees who were used to take Japanese official despatches to the Harbin post office, and sent expert teams of letter-openers to examine and photograph the despatches, before sending them on their way in new envelopes with copies of Japanese seals. Professor Matsokin, a Japanese specialist from Moscow,[70] was employed by INO in Harbin to peruse the despatches and send translations of the most important promptly to the Centre. There was ample evidence in the intercepts forwarded to Moscow of designs by the Japanese military on China and the Soviet Far East. But the most troubling document, intercepted in July 1927, was a secret memorandum written by Baron Gi-ishi Tanaka, the Japanese prime minister and foreign minister, which advocated the conquest of Manchuria and Mongolia as a prelude to Japanese domination over the whole of China, and predicted that Japan "would once again have to cross swords with Russia."[71]

A second copy of the memorandum was obtained in Japanese-occupied Korea by the residency at Seoul, headed by Ivan Andreevich Chichayev (later wartime resident in London). A Japanese interpreter, codenamed ANO, recruited by the INO residency, succeeded in extracting the document, along with other secret material, from the safe of the Japanese police chief in Seoul.[72] A copy of the Tanaka memorandum was later leaked by INO to the American press to give the impression that it had been obtained by an agent working for the United States.[73] As recently as 1997 an SVR official history continued to celebrate the simultaneous acquisition of the memorandum in Harbin and Seoul as "an absolutely unique occurrence in intelligence operations."[74] Though somewhat exaggerated, this judgment accurately reflects the enormous importance attached at the time to the discovery of Tanaka's prediction of war with Russia.

The acute anxiety in Moscow caused by the breach of diplomatic relations with Britain and the apparent threat from Japan was clearly reflected in an alarmist article by Stalin, published a few days after he received the Tanaka memorandum:

IT IS HARDLY open to doubt that the chief contemporary question is that of the threat of a new imperialist war. It is not a question of some indefinite and immaterial "danger" of a new war. It is a matter of a real and material threat of a new war in general, and war against the USSR in particular.[75]

The fact that Constantini had failed to provide anything remotely resembling a British version of the Tanaka memorandum did not lead either Stalin or the conspiracy theorists of the Centre to conclude that Britain had no plans to attack the Soviet Union. They believed instead that greater efforts were required to penetrate the secret councils of the Western warmongers. Stalin, who had emerged as the clear victor in the three-year power struggle which followed Lenin's death, demanded more intelligence on the (mostly imaginary) Western plots against the Soviet Union which he was sure existed.

In an effort to make Soviet espionage less detectable and more deniable, the main responsibility for intelligence collection was shifted from "legal" to "illegal" residencies, which operated independently of Soviet diplomatic and trade missions. In later years the establishment of a new illegal residency became an immensely time-consuming operation which involved years of detailed training and the painstaking construction of "legends" to give the illegals false identities. The largely improvised attempt to expand the illegal network rapidly in the late 1920s and early 1930s, without the detailed preparation which later became mandatory, brought into OGPU foreign operations both unconventional talent and a number of confidence tricksters. Among the secret scandals discovered by Mitrokhin in KGB files was that of the illegal residency established in Berlin in 1927 with the Austrian Bertold Karl Ilk as resident and Moritz Weinstein as his deputy. A later investigation concluded that the Centre should have noted the "suspicious speed" with which the Ilk–Weinstein residency claimed to be expanding its agent network. Within two months it was reporting operations in Britain, France and Poland as well as in Germany. Ilk refused to provide more than sketchy information on his agents' identity on security grounds. His failure to supply detailed biographies was reluctantly accepted by the Centre, which was still reeling from the widespread unmasking of OGPU networks in the spring of 1927. It gradually became clear, however, that the core of the Ilk–Weinstein illegal network consisted of their own relatives and that some elements of it were pure invention. Its agent operations in Britain and France were discovered to be "plain bluff," though an effective way of obtaining funds from the Centre for Ilk and Weinstein. The network in Germany and Poland, while not wholly fictitious, was under surveillance by the local police and security services. The Centre closed down the entire residency in 1933, though without attracting the publicity occasioned by the intelligence failures of 1927.[76]

THE MAIN INFLUENCE on the evolution of the OGPU and its successors during the Stalinist era was the change in the nature of the Soviet state. Much of what was later called "Stalinism" was in reality the creation of Lenin: the cult of the infallible leader, the one-party state and a huge security service with a ubiquitous system of surveillance and a network of concentration camps to terrorize the regime's opponents. But while Lenin's one-party state left room for comradely debate within the ruling party, Stalin used the OGPU to stifle that debate, enforce his own narrow orthodoxy and pursue vendettas against opponents both real and imagined. The most vicious and long-lasting of those vendettas was against Leon Trotsky, Lenin's former Commissar for War.

In its early stages at least, the OGPU's campaign against Trotsky and his supporters was characterized by a bizarre combination of brutality and farce. When Trotsky refused to recant and admit his "crimes against the Party," he was sent into internal exile at Alma-Ata, a town in a remote corner of Kazakhstan on the Chinese border. The OGPU detachment which came to his Moscow flat on the morning of January 17, 1928 to take him into exile found Trotsky still in his pajamas. When he refused to come out, the OGPU broke down the door. Trotsky was surprised to recognize the officer leading the detachment as one of his former bodyguards from the civil war. Overcome with emotion at the sight of the ex-Commissar for War, the officer broke down and sobbed, "Shoot me, Comrade Trotsky, shoot me." Trotsky calmed him down, told him it was his duty to obey orders however reprehensible, and adopted a posture of passive resistance while the OGPU removed his pajamas, put on his clothes and carried him to a car waiting to transport him to the Trans-Siberian Express.[77]

Save for a few hunting trips, Trotsky spent most of his time in Alma-Ata at his desk. Between April and October 1928 he sent his supporters about 550 telegrams and 800 "political letters," some of them lengthy polemical tracts. During the same period he received 700 telegrams and 1,000 letters from various parts of the Soviet Union, but believed that at least as many more had been confiscated en route.[78] Every item in Trotsky's intercepted correspondence was carefully noted by the OGPU, and monthly digests of them were sent both to Vyacheslav Rudolfovich Menzhinsky (Dzerzhinsky's successor) and to Stalin.[79] Stalin, who never failed to overreact to opposition, cannot but have been unfavorably impressed by letters which regularly described him and his supporters as "degenerates."

OGPU reports on Trotsky and his followers were written in a tone of self-righteous outrage. No counter-revolutionary group since the October Revolution, it declared, had dared to behave "as insolently, boldly and defiantly" as the Trotskyists. Even when brought in for interrogation, Trotsky's supporters refused to be intimidated by their interrogators. Most declined to reply to questions. Instead they submitted impudent written protests, such as: "I consider the struggle I am engaged in to be a Party matter. I shall explain myself to the Central Control Commission, not to the OGPU." Early in 1928 the OGPU carried out its first mass arrests of Trotskyists, incarcerating several hundred of them in Moscow's Butyrka prison. The Butyrka, however, had not yet descended into the brutal squalor for which it became infamous during the Great Terror a decade later, nor had the spirit of Trotsky's followers been broken. On their first night in prison the Trotskyists staged a riot, kicking down doors, breaking windows and chanting politically incorrect slogans. "Such," reported the OGPU indignantly, "was the behavior of the embittered enemies of the Party and Soviet power."[80]

The liquidation of the Trotskyist heresy and the maintenance of ideological orthodoxy within the Communist one-party state required, in Stalin's view, Trotsky's removal from the Soviet Union. In February 1929 the great heretic was deported to Turkey and given 1,500 dollars by an OGPU escort to enable him to "settle abroad."[81] With Trotsky out of the country, the tone of OGPU reports on the destabilization and liquidation of his rapidly dwindling band of increasingly demoralized followers became more confident. According to one report, "a massive retreat from Trotskyism began in the second half of 1929." Some of those who recanted were turned into OGPU agents to inform on their friends. The same report boasts of the subtlety of the methods used to undermine the credibility of the "counter-revolutionary" hard core. Individual Trotskyists were summoned to OGPU offices from their workplaces, left standing around in the corridors for several hours, then released without explanation. On returning to work they could give no credible account of what had happened. When the process was repeated their workmates became increasingly suspicious and tended to believe rumors planted by the OGPU that they were employed by them as informers. Once the "counter-revolutionaries" were discredited, they were then arrested for their political crimes.[82]

Stalin, however, was far from reassured. He increasingly regretted the decision to send Trotsky abroad rather than keep him in the Soviet Union, where he could have been put under constant surveillance. One episode only six months after Trotsky was sent into exile seems to have made a particular impression on Stalin. In the summer of 1929 Trotsky received a secret visit from a sympathizer within the OGPU, Yakov Blyumkin. As a young and impetuous Socialist Revolutionary in the Cheka in 1918, Blyumkin had assassinated the German ambassador in defiance of orders from Dzerzhinsky. With Trotsky's help, however, he had been rehabilitated and had risen to become chief illegal resident in the Middle East. Blyumkin agreed to transmit a message from Trotsky to Karl Radek, one of his most important former supporters, and to try to set up lines of communication with what Trotsky termed his "co-thinkers" in the Soviet Union.[83] Trilisser, the head of foreign intelligence, was probably alerted to Blyumkin's visit by an OGPU agent in Trotsky's entourage. He did not, however, order Blyumkin's immediate arrest. Instead he arranged an early version of what later became known as a "honey trap." Trilisser instructed an attractive OGPU agent, Yelizaveta Yulyevna Gorskaya (better known as "Lisa," or "Vixen"),[84] to "abandon bourgeois prejudices," seduce Blyumkin, discover the full extent of his collaboration with Trotsky, and ensure his return to the Soviet Union. Once lured back to Moscow, Blyumkin was interrogated, tried in secret and shot. According to the later OGPU defector Aleksandr Mikhailovich Orlov, Blyumkin's last words before his execution were, "Long live Trotsky!" Soon afterwards "Lisa" Gorskaya married the OGPU resident in Berlin (and later in New York), Vasili Mikhailovich Zarubin.[85]

As Stalin became increasingly preoccupied during the early 1930s with the opposition to him within the Communist Party, he began to fear that there were other, undiscovered Blyumkins within INO. But Trotsky himself had not yet been targeted for assassination. The main "enemies of the people" outside the Soviet Union were still considered to be the White Guards. General Kutepov, the head of the ROVS in Paris, was brave, upright, teetotal, politically naive and an easy target for the OGPU. His entourage was skillfully penetrated by Soviet agents, and *agents provocateurs* brought him optimistic news of a nonexistent anti-Bolshevik underground. "Great movements are spreading across Russia!" Kutepov declared in November 1929. "Never have so many people come from 'over there' to see me and ask me to collaborate with their clandestine organizations." Unlike Savinkov and Reilly, however, Kutepov resisted attempts to lure him back to Russia for meetings with the bogus anti-Communist conspirators. With Stalin's approval, the OGPU thus decided to kidnap him instead and bring him back for interrogation and execution in Moscow.[86]

Overall planning of the Kutepov operation was given to Yakov Isaakovich ("Yasha") Serebryansky, head of the euphemistically titled "Administration for Special Tasks."[87] Before the Second World War, the administration functioned as a parallel foreign intelligence service, reporting directly to the Centre with special responsibility for sabotage, abduction and assassination operations on foreign soil.[88] Serebryansky later became a severe embarrassment to official historians anxious to distance Soviet foreign intelligence from the blood-letting of the late 1930s and portray it as a victim rather than a perpetrator of the Great Terror. An SVR-sponsored history published in 1993 claimed that Serebryansky was "not a regular member of State Security," but "only brought in for special jobs."[89] KGB files show that, on the contrary, he was a senior OGPU officer whose Administration for Special Tasks grew into an élite service, more than 200-strong, dedicated to hunting down "enemies of the people" on both sides of the Atlantic.[90]

Detailed preparations for the kidnaping of Kutepov were entrusted by Serebryansky to his illegal Paris resident, V. I. Speransky, who had taken part in the deception of Savinkov six years earlier.[91] On the morning of Sunday, January 26, 1930 Kutepov was bundled into a taxi in the middle of a street in Paris's fashionable seventh *arrondissement.* Standing nearby was a Communist Paris policeman who had been asked to assist by Speransky so that any bystander who saw the kidnaping (one did) would mistake it for a police arrest. Though the Centre commended the kidnaping as "a brilliant operation," the chloroform used to overpower Kutepov proved too much for the general's weak heart. He died aboard a Soviet steamer while being taken back to Russia.[92]

The Kutepov operation was to set an important precedent. In the early and mid-1930s the chief Soviet foreign intelligence priority remained intelligence collection. During the later years of the decade, however, all other operations were to be subordinated to "special tasks."

THREE

THE GREAT ILLEGALS

On January 30, 1930 the Politburo (effectively the ruling body of both the Party and the Soviet Union) met to review INO operations and ordered it to increase intelligence collection in three target areas: Britain, France and Germany (the leading European powers); the Soviet Union's western neighbors, Poland, Romania, Finland and the Baltic states; and Japan, its main Asian rival.[1] The United States, which established diplomatic relations with the Soviet Union only in 1933, was not mentioned. Though the first Soviet illegal had been sent across the Atlantic as early as 1921,[2] the USA's relative isolation from world affairs made American intelligence collection still a secondary priority.[3]

On Politburo instructions, the main expansion of INO operations was achieved through increasing the number of illegal residencies, each with up to seven (in a few cases as many as nine) illegal officers. By contrast, even in Britain and France legal residencies operating under diplomatic cover in Soviet embassies had three officers at most and sometimes only one. Their main function was to provide channels of communications with the Centre and other technical support for the more highly regarded illegals.[4] During the 1920s both legal and illegal residencies had had the right to decide what agents to recruit and how to recruit them. On succeeding Trilisser as head of INO in 1930, however, Artur Artuzov, the hero of the SINDIKAT and TREST operations, complained that the existing agent network contained "undesirable elements." He decreed that future agent recruitment required the authorization of the Centre. Partly because of problems of communication, his instructions were not always carried out.[5]

The early and mid-1930s were to be remembered in the history of Soviet foreign intelligence as the era of the "Great Illegals," a diverse group of remarkably talented individuals who collectively transformed OGPU agent recruitment and intelligence collection. Post-war illegals had to endure long training periods designed to establish their bogus identities, protect their cover and prepare them for operations in the West. Their pre-war predecessors were successful partly because they had greater freedom from bureaucratic routine and more opportunity to use their own initiative. But they also had to contend with far softer targets than their successors. By the standards of the Cold War, most inter-war Western security systems were primitive. The individual flair of the Great Illegals combined with the relative vulnerability of their targets to give some of their operations a much more unorthodox, at times even eccentric, character than those of the Cold War.

Some of the ablest of the Great Illegals were not Russians at all, but cosmopolitan, multilingual Central Europeans who had worked in the Comintern underground before joining the OGPU and shared a visionary faith in the Communist millennium.[6] Arnold Deutsch, the chief recruiter of students and young graduates at Cambridge University (discussed in chapter 4), was an Austrian Jew. The most successful of the Fourth Department (Military Intelligence) illegals was the German Richard Sorge, later described by one of his Comintern admirers as a "startlingly good-looking . . . romantic, idealistic scholar," who exuded charm.[7] While Sorge's main successes were achieved posing as a Nazi journalist in Japan, those of the OGPU/NKVD illegals mostly took place in Europe.

Though the Great Illegals are nowadays best remembered, particularly in Britain, for their recruitment of young, talented, ideological agents, their first major successes were the less glamorous but scarcely less important acquisition of diplomatic ciphers and documents from agents motivated by money and sex rather than ideology. Codebreaking is often supposed to depend on little more than the cryptanalytic genius of brilliant mathematicians, nowadays assisted by huge networks of computers. In reality, most major twentieth-century codebreaking coups on which information is available have been assisted—sometimes crucially—by agent intelligence on code and cipher systems. Tsarist codebreakers had led the world chiefly because of their skill in stealing or purchasing the codes and ciphers of foreign powers. Ten years before the First World War the British ambassador in St. Petersburg, Sir Charles Hardinge, discovered that his head Chancery servant had been offered the then enormous sum of 1,000 pounds to steal the embassy's main cipher. Though the Okhrana failed on this occasion, it succeeded on many others. Hardinge was disconcerted to be told by a Russian statesman that he "did not mind how much I reported in writing what he had told me in conversation, but he begged me on no account to telegraph as all our [ciphered] telegrams are known!" The Okhrana became the first modern intelligence service to make one of its major priorities the theft of foreign ciphers to assist its codebreakers. In so doing it set an important precedent for its Soviet successors.[8]

Research on the making of Stalin's foreign policy has, as yet, barely begun to take account of the large volume of Western diplomatic traffic which the Great Illegals and the codebreakers were instrumental in providing.

THE DOCUMENTS OBTAINED from Francesco Constantini in the British embassy in Rome from 1924 onwards included important cipher material.[9] KGB records, however, give the main credit for the OGPU's early successes in obtaining foreign diplomatic ciphers to the most flamboyant of the Great Illegals, Dmitri Aleksandrovich Bystroletov, codenamed HANS or ANDREI, who operated abroad under a series of aliases, including several bogus titles of nobility. His was one of the portraits of the leading heroes of foreign intelligence later chosen to hang on the walls of the secret "memory room" at the KGB First Chief (Foreign Intelligence) Directorate in Yasenevo (now the headquarters of the SVR). Bystroletov was a strikingly handsome, multilingual extrovert, born in 1901, the illegitimate son of a Kuban Cossack mother and—Bystroletov later persuaded himself—the celebrated novelist Aleksei Tolstoy.[10]

A hagiography of Bystroletov's career published by the SVR in 1995 unsurprisingly fails to mention either his fantasy about the identity of his father or the fact that one of his first claims to fame within the OGPU was the seduction of female staff with access to classified documents in foreign embassies and ministries:[11] a technique later employed on a larger scale by Soviet Bloc intelligence agencies in operations such as the "secretaries offensive" in West Germany. A report noted by Mitrokhin quaintly records that Bystroletov "quickly became on close terms with women and shared their beds." His first major conquest for the OGPU occurred in Prague, where in 1927 he seduced a 29-year-old woman in the French embassy whom the OGPU codenamed LAROCHE.[12] Over the next two years LAROCHE gave Bystroletov copies of both French diplomatic ciphers and classified communications.[13]

Bystroletov's unconventional flamboyance may help to explain why he never achieved officer rank in Soviet intelligence and remained simply an illegal agent,[14] attached in the early 1920s and late 1930s to the illegal Berlin residency of Boris Bazarov (codenamed KIN).[15] Unlike Bystroletov, more conventional OGPU officers missed a number of opportunities to recruit agents with access to diplomatic ciphers. One such opportunity, which later led to a personal rebuke by Stalin to the OGPU personnel responsible, occurred in Paris in August 1928. A stranger, later identified as the Swiss businessman and adventurer Giovanni de Ry (codenamed ROSSI), presented himself at the Soviet embassy and asked to see the military attaché, or the first secretary.[16] According to a later account by Bystroletov based on an embassy report, de Ry was a short man whose red nose contrasted colorfully with his yellow briefcase.[17] He allegedly told the OGPU resident, Vladimir Voynovich:[18]

> This briefcase contains the codes and ciphers of Italy. You, no doubt, have copies of the ciphered telegrams of the local Italian embassy. Take the briefcase and check the authenticity of its contents. Once you have satisfied yourself that they are genuine, photograph them and give me 200,000 French francs.

De Ry also offered to provide future Italian diplomatic ciphers for a similar sum. Voynovich took the ciphers into a back room, where they were photographed by his wife. He then returned the originals to de Ry, denounced them as forgeries, ordered him out of the embassy and threatened to call the police. Though the Centre later changed its mind, at the time it commended Voynovich for his astuteness in obtaining Italian ciphers at no cost to the OGPU.[19]

Exactly a year later, in August 1929, there was another, similar walk-in at the Paris embassy. On this occasion the visitor was a cipher clerk from the Foreign Office Communications Department, Ernest Holloway Oldham, then accompanying a British trade delegation in Paris. Voynovich seems to have tried to repeat the deception practiced on de Ry a year earlier. Oldham, however, was more cautious than de Ry, brought no cipher material with him, tried to prevent his identity being discovered and sought to limit his contact with the OGPU to a single transaction. He identified himself only as "Charlie," misled Voynovich by claiming to work in the Foreign Office printing department, and announced that he could obtain a copy of the British diplomatic cipher. Oldham asked for 50,000 pounds, Voynovich beat him down to 10,000 pounds and they agreed on a meeting in Berlin early the following year.[20]

Before that meeting took place, the work of the Paris embassy and OGPU residency was disrupted by the defection of the Soviet chargé d'affaires, Grigori Besedovsky, in October 1929. Accused of counter-revolutionary "plotting," Besedovsky made a dramatic escape over the embassy wall, pursued by OGPU guards who had orders to return him to Moscow for interrogation and, almost certainly, execution. Besedovsky's memoirs, published in 1930, caused outrage in the Centre. They denounced Stalin as "the embodiment of the most senseless type of oriental despotism," and revealed a number of OGPU secrets: among them the offers of Italian and British ciphers to the Paris residency by unidentified walk-ins.[21]

These revelations led to Bystroletov's urgent recall to Moscow. At the Lubyanka, Abram Aronovich Slutsky (later head of foreign intelligence) showed him a copy of Besedovsky's memoirs. Opposite the reference to the deception of de Ry, the unidentified walk-in who had provided Italian ciphers in 1928, the instruction "Reopen!" had been penciled in the margin by Stalin himself. Slutsky instructed Bystroletov to return to Paris at once, discover the identity of the walk-in swindled two years earlier, renew contact and obtain further ciphers from him. "Where can I find him?" Bystroletov asked. "That's your business," Slutsky replied. "You have six months to track him down."[22]

Bystroletov ran de Ry to ground in a Geneva bar. Believing that, after the fraud practiced on him in Paris two years earlier, de Ry might reject an approach from the OGPU, Bystroletov decided to use what later became known as the "false flag" technique and pretended to be working for the Japanese intelligence service. Though de Ry was not deceived for long by the "false flag," he agreed to sell further Italian ciphers which he claimed to be able to obtain from a corrupt Italian diplomat. Future meetings with de Ry usually took place in Berlin, where the diplomat was allegedly stationed. KGB records, possibly incomplete, show that de Ry was paid at least 200,000 French francs.[23]

Bystroletov was also given the task of tracing the unidentified British walk-in (Ernest Oldham) who had offered to sell Foreign Office ciphers to the Paris residency. In April 1930, at the meeting arranged in the previous year, Oldham (codenamed ARNO by the OGPU) handed over only part of a diplomatic cipher, probably as a precaution against being double-crossed, and demanded a 6,000-dollar down-payment before providing the rest. The OGPU tried to locate him after the meeting but discovered that he had given a false address.[24]

Probably soon after his first meeting with de Ry, Bystroletov succeeded in tracking down Oldham in a Paris bar, struck up a conversation with him, won his confidence and booked into the hotel where he was staying. There Bystroletov revealed himself to Oldham and his wife Lucy as an impoverished Hungarian aristocrat who had fallen, like Oldham, into the clutches of Soviet intelligence. With his wife's approval, Oldham agreed to provide Foreign Office ciphers and other classified documents to Bystroletov to pass on to the OGPU. Oldham was given a first payment of 6,000 dollars, a second of 5,000 dollars, then 1,000 dollars a month. Bystroletov portrayed himself throughout as a sympathetic friend, visiting the Oldhams on several occasions at their London home in Pembroke Gardens, Kensington. Oldham's documents, however, were handed over at meetings in France and Germany.

Having originally tried to hold the OGPU at arm's length, Oldham became increasingly nervous about the risks of working as a Soviet agent. In order to put pressure on him, Bystroletov was accompanied to several of their meetings by the head of the illegal residency in Berlin, Boris Bazarov (codenamed KIN), who posed as a rather menacing Italian Communist named da Vinci. With Bazarov and Bystroletov playing the hard man/soft man routine, Oldham agreed to continue but took increasingly to drink. Bystroletov strengthened his hold over Lucy Oldham (henceforth codenamed MADAM) by putting his relationship with her on what an OGPU report coyly describes as "an intimate footing."[25]

Though Bystroletov successfully deceived the Oldhams, he seems to have been unaware that the Oldhams were also deceiving him. At their first meeting, Oldham explained that he was "a lord, who worked out ciphers for the Foreign Office and was a very influential person," rather than, in reality, a minor functionary. At later meetings Oldham claimed that he traveled abroad on a diplomatic passport illegally provided for him by a Foreign Office friend named Kemp whom he alleged, almost certainly falsely, was in the Secret Intelligence Service. Having helped Bystroletov to acquire a British passport in the name of Robert Grenville, Oldham told him that the passport had been personally issued by the Foreign Secretary, Sir John Simon, who believed it to be for a minor British aristocrat of his acquaintance, Lord Robert Grenville, then resident in Canada. "I didn't know Lord Robert was here in Britain," Simon was alleged to have remarked to Oldham. Mrs. Oldham also specialized in tall stories. She told Bystroletov that she was the sister of an army officer named Montgomery who, she claimed, held the (non-existent) post of head of the intelligence service at the Foreign Office;[26] a later note on the KGB file, probably dating from the 1940s, identified the mysterious and possibly mythical Montgomery as Field Marshal Earl Montgomery of Alamein! Expert though Bystroletov proved as an agent controller, his ignorance of the ways of the Foreign Office and the British establishment made him curiously gullible—though perhaps no more so than the Centre, which was also taken in.[27]

De Ry, meanwhile, was providing Bystroletov at meetings in Berlin with a mixture of genuine diplomatic documents (Italian ciphers probably chief among them) and colorful inventions. According to Bystroletov, when asked whether some of his material was genuine, he replied indignantly, "What kind of question is that? Of course they are . . . Your Japanese are idiots. Write and tell them to start printing American dollars. Instead of paying me 200,000 genuine francs, give me a million forged dollars and we'll be quits." The Centre was taken in by at least some of de Ry's inventions. Possibly to disguise the fact that he was also trying to sell Italian ciphers to the French and other purchasers, he claimed that Mussolini's son-in-law, Count Galeazzo Ciano di Cortellazzo (later Italian foreign minister), had organized "an extensive trade in ciphers" and, when a cipher was missing from the Berlin embassy, had ordered the liquidation of an innocent scapegoat to divert attention from himself. Since the OGPU believed that Western intelligence agencies, like itself, organized secret assassinations, it had surprisingly little difficulty in crediting de Ry's improbable tale.[28] De Ry appears to have tried to deceive the OGPU on two other occasions by putting it in contact with bogus officials who claimed to have German and British diplomatic ciphers for sale.[29]

The Centre attached great importance, however, to an introduction provided by de Ry to his friend the Paris businessman Rodolphe Lemoine, an agent and recruiter of the French foreign intelligence service, the military Deuxième Bureau.[30] Born Rudolf Stallmann, the son of a wealthy Berlin jeweler, Lemoine had begun working for the Deuxième Bureau in 1918 and acquired French citizenship. Intelligence for Lemoine was a passion as well as a second career. According to one of his chiefs in the Deuxième Bureau, "He was as hooked on espionage as a drunk is on alcohol." Lemoine's greatest coup was the recruitment in 1931 of a German cipher and SIGINT clerk, Hans-Thilo Schmidt, whose compulsive womanizing had run him into debt. For the next decade Schmidt (codenamed HE and ASCHE by the French) was the Deuxième Bureau's most important foreign agent.[31] Some of the intelligence he provided laid the foundations for the breaking of the German Enigma machine cipher by British cryptanalysts in the Second World War.[32]

After Bystroletov had made the initial contact with Lemoine (codenamed REX by the Deuxième Bureau and JOSEPH by the OGPU), he was instructed to hand the case over to another, less flamboyant Soviet illegal, Ignace Reiss (alias "Ignace Poretsky," codenamed RAYMOND) so that he could concentrate on running Oldham. At meetings with Lemoine, Reiss posed initially as an American military intelligence officer. Lemoine appeared anxious to set up an exchange of intelligence on Germany and foreign cipher systems, and supplied a curious mixture of good and bad intelligence as evidence of the Deuxième Bureau's willingness to cooperate. An Italian cipher which he provided in May 1931 seems to have been genuine. In February 1932, however, Lemoine reported the sensationally inaccurate news that Hitler (who became German chancellor less than a year later) had made two secret visits to Paris and was in the pay of the Deuxième Bureau. "We French," he claimed, "are doing everything to hasten his rise to power." The Centre dismissed the report as disinformation, but ordered meetings with Lemoine to continue and for him to be paid, probably with the intention of laying a trap which would end in his recruitment.[33]

In November 1933 Lemoine brought with him to meet Reiss the head of the SIGINT section of the Deuxième Bureau, Gustave Bertrand, codenamed OREL ("Eagle") by the Centre. To try to convince Bertrand that he was an American intelligence officer willing to exchange cipher material, Reiss offered him Latin American diplomatic ciphers. Bertrand, predictably, was more interested in European ciphers.[34] Soon after his first meeting with Bertrand, Reiss informed Lemoine that he worked not for American intelligence but for the OGPU. The Centre probably calculated that it had caught Lemoine in a trap, forcing him either to admit to his superiors that he had been both paid and deceived by the OGPU or to conceal that information and risk being blackmailed into working for the Soviet Union. The blackmail failed.[35] Lemoine had probably realized for some time that Reiss, whom he knew as "Walter Scott," worked for Soviet intelligence. Reiss had several further meetings with Lemoine and Bertrand, at which they exchanged intelligence on Italian, Czechoslovak and Hungarian ciphers.[36]

WHILE REISS WAS maintaining contact with Lemoine, Bystroletov was finding Oldham increasingly desperate to extricate himself from the OGPU. By the summer of 1932 Bystroletov feared that Oldham's worsening alcoholism and carelessness at work would attract the attention of MI5. The Centre concluded that Oldham's increasingly erratic behavior also risked exposing Bystroletov to a terrible revenge from the supposedly ruthless British intelligence services. On September 17, in recognition of his bravery in the face of nonexistent British assassination squads, it presented him with a rifle carrying the inscription "For unstinting struggle against Counter-Revolution, from your colleagues in the OGPU."[37]

On September 30, 1932, less than a fortnight after Bystroletov received his rifle, Oldham resigned from the Foreign Office, unable to stand the pressures of his double life.[38] To his despair, the OGPU still refused to leave him in peace. Over the next year Bystroletov extracted from him details of all his former colleagues in the Communications Department, hoping to recruit at least one of them as Oldham's successor. As his drinking got further out of control, Oldham became convinced that his arrest was only a matter of time. His wife told Bystroletov that her husband believed that the permanent under-secretary at the Foreign Office, Sir Robert Vansittart, had personally put him under observation and that British intelligence was also on the trail of Bystroletov.[39] Though there was probably no substance to these fears, the Centre took them seriously. The OGPU trouble-shooter and "flying illegal" Teodor Maly reported to the Centre from London on July 6 that Bystroletov was in great danger:

It is possible that ANDREI [Bystroletov] will be liquidated by the enemy. None the less I have not given an order for his immediate departure. For him to depart now would mean the loss of a source of such importance [Oldham] that it would weaken our defense and increase the power of the enemy. The loss of ANDREI is possible today, as is that of other colleagues tomorrow. The nature of their work makes such risks unavoidable.[40]

The Centre replied on August 10:

Please inform ANDREI that we here are fully aware of the self-denial, discipline, resourcefulness and courage that he has shown in the very difficult and dangerous conditions of recent days while working with ARNO.[41]

Bystroletov continued to receive high praise for his skill in outwitting a British version of the Serebryansky Service which existed only in the conspiratorial imagination of the OGPU.

On September 29, 1933, almost a year to the day after his resignation from the Foreign Office, Oldham was found unconscious in the gas-filled kitchen of his house in Pembroke Gardens, rushed to the hospital and pronounced dead on arrival. An inquest found that he had taken his life by "coal gas suffocation" while of "unsound mind."[42] The Centre had no doubt that Oldham had been murdered. Its report on his death concluded: "In order to avoid a scandal the [British] intelligence service had ARNO physically eliminated, making his death appear to be suicide." It believed, however, that Bystroletov had disguised his identity so successfully that the Foreign Office believed Oldham had been working for French rather than Soviet intelligence.[43]

Oldham's suicide did little if anything to alert the Foreign Office to the chronic problems of its own security and that of British embassies abroad.[44] Still concerned by fears that he was being pursued by a secret British assassination squad, however, Bystroletov failed to grasp how relatively unprotected a target the Foreign Office remained. He concluded that a safer recruiting ground was Geneva, where several of Oldham's former colleagues were working as cipher clerks with the British delegation to the League of Nations. In December 1933 he made contact there with Raymond Oake (codenamed SHELLEY), one of the most promising potential recruits in the communications department identified by Oldham.[45] Oake had good reason to resent his underprivileged status. Since joining the Foreign Office in 1920 he had remained in the lowly rank of "temporary clerk" without pension rights.[46] Bystroletov handed over the cultivation of Oake to the Dutch artist Henri Christian ("Han") Pieck, who operated as an OGPU illegal codenamed COOPER.[47]

Pieck was almost as flamboyant an extrovert as Bystroletov, with a convivial manner which won him a wide circle of friends and acquaintances among British officials and journalists in Geneva. He invited Oake and other cipher clerks to stay at his house in The Hague where he lavished charm and hospitality on them while assessing them as possible recruits. Oake's main service to Soviet intelligence was to provide an introduction to Captain John H. King, who joined the Foreign Office communications department as a "temporary clerk" in 1934[48] and subsequently became a far more important agent than Oake himself. Pieck reported that King had been born in Ireland, considered himself Irish rather than British and, though anti-Soviet, also "hated the English." Estranged from his wife and with an American mistress to support, he found it difficult to live on his modest Foreign Office salary. Pieck cultivated King with patience and skill. On one occasion he and his wife took King and his lover for an expensive touring holiday in Spain, staying at the best hotels. Mrs. Pieck complained that the whole holiday had been "a real ordeal" and that King and his mistress were "incredibly boring."[49] The Piecks' hospitality, however, paid off handsomely. Seven months after his first meeting with Pieck, King (henceforth codenamed MAG) began to hand over large amounts of classified material, including Foreign Office telegrams, ciphers and secret daily and weekly summaries of diplomatic correspondence.[50]

AN ANALYSIS BY the Centre concluded that about 30 percent of King's material was the same as that provided by Francesco Constantini (DUNCAN), the long-serving

OGPU agent in the British embassy at Rome.[51] The overlap was, almost certainly, regarded as useful for checking the authenticity of the documents received from both agents. It was a sign of the importance attached to Constantini's intelligence that Abram Aronovich Slutsky, who succeeded Artuzov as head of INO in 1934, decided to transfer him from the legal residency in Rome to another of the Great Illegals, Moisei Markovich Akselrod (codenamed OST or OSTO), one of the leading Soviet agent controllers. Born into a Jewish family in Smolensk in 1898, Akselrod had been a member of the Russian branch of the Zionist socialist organization Poale Zion, until its dissolution in 1922. He then joined the Bolsheviks and in 1925 began a career in INO.[52] Like most of the Great Illegals, Akselrod was a remarkable linguist—fluent in Arabic, English, French, German and Italian—and, according to a fellow illegal, a man of "extraordinary culture" with "a fine indifference to risk."[53] In 1934 he traveled to Rome on an Austrian passport to establish a new illegal residency and act as Constantini's controller. He had his first meeting with Constantini in January 1935.[54]

Few—if any—Soviet controllers ever met an agent as frequently as Akselrod saw Constantini. At times they had almost daily meetings. On October 27, 1935 the Centre cabled Akselrod: "Between September 24 and October 14 you met [Constantini] 16 times. There must be no more than two or three meetings a week." It is not difficult to understand Akselrod's enthusiasm for agent DUNCAN. Constantini supplied him with a remarkable range of documents and cipher material from embassy red boxes, diplomatic bags, filing cabinets and—probably—the embassy safe. Far from consisting simply of material on British–Italian relations, the documents included Foreign Office reports and British ambassadors' despatches on a great variety of major international issues, which were sent for information to the Rome embassy. A Centre report noted on November 15, 1935 that no fewer than 101 of the British documents obtained from Constantini since the beginning of the year had been judged sufficiently important to be "sent to Comrade Stalin": among them the Foreign Office records of talks between Sir John Simon, the British Foreign Secretary, Anthony Eden, junior Foreign Office minister (who became Foreign Secretary at the end of the year), and Hitler in Berlin; between Eden and Litvinov, the Soviet Commissar for Foreign Affairs, in Moscow; between Eden and Joseph Beck, the Polish foreign minister, in Warsaw; between Eden and Edvard Beneš, the Czechoslovak foreign minister, in Prague; and between Eden and Mussolini in Rome.[55]

A striking omission from the Centre's list of the most important Foreign Office documents supplied to Stalin was Eden's account of his talks with him during his visit to Moscow in March 1935—despite the fact that this document was sent to the Rome embassy and was probably among those obtained by Constantini.[56] Since this was Stalin's first meeting with a minister from a Western government, their talks were of unusual significance. The most likely explanation for the Centre's failure to send the British record of the meeting to the Kremlin is that Slutsky feared to pass on to Stalin some of Eden's comments about him. INO would have been unembarrassed to report the fact that Eden was impressed by Stalin's "remarkable knowledge and understanding of international affairs." But it doubtless lacked the nerve to repeat Eden's conclusion that Stalin was "a man of strong oriental traits of character with unshakeable assurance and control whose courtesy in no way hid from us an implacable ruthlessness." The Centre was probably also nervous about reporting some of the opinions attributed by Eden to Stalin—for example, that he was "perhaps more appreciative of [the] German point of view than Monsieur Litvino[v]."[57] There was no more dangerous activity in Moscow than repeating criticisms of Stalin or attributing heretical opinions to him.

The British ambassador in Moscow, Viscount Chilston, optimistically reported that, as a result of Eden's visit, "the Soviet Government appears to have got rid of the bogey in their minds, that we were encouraging Germany against Soviet plans for Eastern security."[58] Stalin, however, rarely—if ever—abandoned a conspiracy theory and remained deeply suspicious of British policy. In a communiqué at the end of his talks in Moscow, Eden had welcomed the Soviet Union's support for the principle of collective security, following its entry the previous year into the League of Nations (hitherto denounced by Moscow as the "League of Burglars"). But Stalin must have learned from Foreign Office documents that Eden was disinclined to involve the Soviet Union in any collective security arrangements designed to contain Nazi Germany.[59] To Stalin's deeply suspicious mind, this reluctance was further evidence of a British plot to focus German aggression in the east.[60] Though he was content to entrust most day-to-day diplomacy to the efficient and far more pragmatic Litvinov, it was Stalin who determined the strategic thrust of Soviet foreign policy.

The Centre had suspected for some time that its principal source of British diplomatic documents over the last decade, the mercenary agent Francesco Constantini (DUNCAN), had been selling some material to Italian intelligence as well as to the NKVD. It had dramatic confirmation of these suspicions in February 1936, when a British assessment of the Italo-Ethiopian war—purloined by Constantini from the British embassy—was published on the front page of the *Giornale d'Italia*.[61] On being challenged by Akselrod, Constantini was forced to admit that he had supplied some documents to the Italians, but concealed the large scale on which he had done so. Constantini also admitted in 1936 that he had lost his job in the British embassy, though he apparently omitted that he had been sacked for dishonesty. He tried to reassure Akselrod by telling him that he had a former colleague in the embassy who would continue to supply him with classified documents. The colleague was later identified as Constantini's brother Secondo (codenamed DUDLEY), who had worked as a servant in the embassy Chancery for the previous twenty years.[62]

Secondo Constantini, however, took fewer precautions than his brother Francesco. In January he stole a diamond necklace belonging to the ambassador's wife from a locked red box (normally used for diplomatic documents rather than jewelery) which was kept in the ambassador's apartment next to the Chancery. The ambassador, Sir Eric Drummond (soon to become Lord Perth), who had previously dismissed the idea that the British diplomatic documents appearing in the Italian press might have been purloined from his embassy, now began to grasp that embassy security might, after all, require serious attention. Since the Foreign Office had no security officer, it was forced to seek the help of Major Valentine Vivian, the head of

SIS counter-intelligence. Vivian modestly disclaimed significant expertise in embassy security but, in view of the even greater lack of expertise in the Foreign Office, agreed to carry out an investigation.[63] Once in Rome, he quickly discovered an appalling series of basic lapses. The embassy files, safe and red boxes were all insecure and "it would not be impossible or even difficult for unauthorized persons to spend long periods in the Chancery or Registry rooms."

Vivian quickly identified Secondo Constantini as the man probably responsible for the theft both of the diamond necklace and of at least some of the documents supplied to Italian intelligence:

> S. Constantini . . . has been employed in the Chancery for twenty-one years. He might, therefore, have been directly or indirectly responsible for any, or all, of the thefts of papers or valuables which have taken place, or are thought to have taken place, from this Mission. He was, I understand, not quite free of suspicion of being himself concerned in a dishonest transaction for which his brother [Francesco], then also a Chancery servant, was dismissed a short time ago. Moreover, though the Diplomatic Staff at the time did not connect him with the matter, I am clear in my own mind that the circumstances of the loss of two copies of the "R" Code from a locked press [filing cabinet] in the Chancery in 1925 point towards S. Constantini, or his brother, or both, as the culprits.[64]

Though Sir Eric Drummond politely welcomed Vivian's recommendations for improvements in the security of his embassy, he took little action.[65] In particular, neither he nor most of his staff could credit the charges against Secondo Constantini, whom they regarded as "a sort of friend of the family."[66] Instead of being dismissed, agent DUDLEY and his wife were—amazingly—invited to London in May 1937 as the guests of His Majesty's Government at the coronation of King George VI, as a reward for his long and supposedly faithful service.[67]

When Secondo Constantini returned from his expense-paid junket in London, he was able to resume supplying classified British documents to his brother Francesco, who passed them on for copying by both Akselrod's illegal residency and Italian intelligence before returning them to embassy files. The Centre regarded the whole improbable story of Constantini's continued access to embassy files after Vivian's investigation as deeply suspicious. Unable to comprehend the naivety of the British foreign service in matters of embassy security, it suspected instead some deep-laid plot by British and/or Italian intelligence. Regular meetings with Francesco Constantini were suspended in August 1937.[68]

THE CIPHER MATERIAL obtained from the Constantini brothers, Captain King and other agents in Western embassies and foreign ministries was passed to the most secret section of Soviet intelligence, a joint OGPU/Fourth Department SIGINT unit housed not in the Lubyanka but in the Foreign Affairs building on Kuznetsky Bridge. According to Evdokia Kartseva (later Petrova), who joined the unit in 1933, its personnel were forbidden to reveal even the location of their office to their closest relatives.[69] Like most young women in the unit, Kartseva was terrified of its head, Gleb Ivanovich Boky, who had made his reputation first in conducting the "Red Terror" in Petrograd in 1918, then in terrorizing Turkestan later in the civil war.[70] Though in his mid-fifties, Boky still prided himself on his sexual athleticism and arranged group sex weekends at his dacha. Kartseva lived in fear of being invited to the orgies. During the night shift, when she felt most vulnerable, she wore her "plainest and dullest clothes for fear of attracting [Boky's] unwelcome attention."[71]

Despite the personal depravity of its chief, the combined OGPU/Fourth Department unit was the world's largest and best-resourced SIGINT agency. In particular, thanks to Bystroletov and others, it received more assistance from espionage than any similar agency in the West. The records seen by Mitrokhin show that Boky's unit was able to decrypt at least some of the diplomatic traffic of Britain, Austria, Germany and Italy.[72] Other evidence shows that Boky's unit was also able to decrypt some Japanese, Turkish[73] and—almost certainly—American[74] and French[75] cables. No Western SIGINT agency during the 1930s seems to have collected so much political and diplomatic intelligence.

The unavailability of most of the decrypts produced by Boky's unit makes detailed analysis of their influence on Soviet foreign policy impossible. Soviet SIGINT successes, however, included important Japanese decrypts on the negotiation of the Anti-Comintern Pact between Germany and Japan. The published version of the Pact, concluded in November 1936, merely provided for an exchange of information on Comintern activities and cooperation on preventive measures against them. A secret protocol, however, added that if either of the signatories became the victim of "an unprovoked [Soviet] attack or threat of attack," both would immediately consult together on the action to take and do "nothing to ease the situation of the USSR." Moscow, unsurprisingly, read sinister intentions into this tortuous formula, though Japan was, in reality, still anxious not to be drawn into a European war and had no intention of concluding a military alliance. Three days after the signing of the Anti-Comintern Pact, Litvinov publicly announced in a speech to a Congress of Soviets that Moscow knew its secret protocol. His speech also contained a curious veiled allusion to codebreaking:

> It is not surprising that it is assumed by many that the German–Japanese agreement is written in a special code in which anti-Communism means something entirely different from the dictionary definition of this word, and that people decipher this code in different ways.[76]

The success of Boky's unit in decrypting Italian diplomatic traffic probably provided intelligence on Italy's decision to join the Anti-Comintern Pact in the following year.

THANKS TO ITS penetration agents and codebreakers, as well as to primitive Foreign Office security, Soviet intelligence was able to gather vastly more intelligence on the foreign policy of its main Western target, Great Britain, than the much smaller

British intelligence community was able to obtain on Soviet policy. Since 1927 British codebreakers had been unable to decrypt any high-level Soviet communications (though they had some success with the less sophisticated Comintern ciphers). SIS did not even possess a Moscow station. In 1936 the British ambassador, Viscount Chilston, vetoed a proposal to establish one on the grounds that it would be "liable to cause severe embarrassment." But without an SIS presence he despaired of discovering anything of importance about Soviet policy-making.[77]

The Soviet capacity to understand the political and diplomatic intelligence it collected, however, never approached its ability to collect that intelligence in the first place. Its natural tendency to substitute conspiracy theory for pragmatic analysis when assessing the intentions of the encircling imperialist powers was made worse during the 1930s by Stalin's increasing tendency to act as his own intelligence analyst. Stalin, indeed, actively discouraged intelligence analysis by others, which he condemned as "dangerous guesswork." "Don't tell me what you think," he is reported to have said. "Give me the facts and the source!" As a result, INO had no analytical department. Intelligence reports throughout and even beyond the Stalin era characteristically consisted of compilations of relevant information on particular topics with little argument or analysis.[78] Those who compiled them increasingly feared for their life expectancy if they failed to tell Stalin what he expected to hear. Their main priority as they trawled through the Centre's treasure trove of British diplomatic documents and decrypts was to discover the anti-Soviet conspiracies which Comrade Stalin, "Lenin's outstanding pupil, the best son of the Bolshevik Party, the worthy successor and great continuer of Lenin's cause," knew were there. The main function of Soviet foreign intelligence was thus to reinforce rather than to challenge Stalin's misunderstanding of the West.

A characteristic example of the Centre's distorted but politically correct presentation of important intelligence was its treatment of the Foreign Office record of the meeting in March 1935 between Sir John Simon, Anthony Eden and Adolf Hitler in Berlin. Copies of the minutes were supplied both by Captain King in the Foreign Office and by Francesco Constantini in the Rome embassy.[79] Nine days before the meeting, in defiance of the post-First World War Treaty of Versailles, Hitler had announced the introduction of conscription. The fact that the meeting—the first between Hitler and a British foreign secretary—went ahead at all was, in itself, cause for suspicion in Moscow. On the British side the talks were mainly exploratory—to discover what the extent of Hitler's demands for the revision of the Treaty of Versailles really was, and what prospect there was of accommodating them. Moscow, however, saw grounds for deep suspicion. While disclaiming any intention of attacking the Soviet Union, Hitler claimed that there was a distinct danger of Russia starting a war, and declared himself "firmly convinced that one day cooperation and solidarity would be urgently necessary to defend Europe against the . . . Bolshevik menace." Simon and Eden showed not the slightest interest in an anti-Bolshevik agreement, but their fairly conventional exchange of diplomatic pleasantries had sinister overtones in Moscow. According to the Foreign Office record, "The British Ministers were sincerely thankful for the way in which they had been received in

Berlin, and would take away very pleasant memories of the kindness and hospitality shown them."[80]

The British record of the talks ran to over 23,000 words. The Russian translation circulated by the Centre to Stalin and others in the Soviet leadership came to fewer than 4,000. Instead of producing a conventional précis the Centre selected a series of statements by Simon, Eden, Hitler and other participants in the talks, and assembled them into what appeared as a continuous conversation. The significance of some individual statements was thus distorted by removing them from their detailed context. Probably at the time, certainly subsequently, one of Simon's comments was misconstrued as giving Germany *carte blanche* to take over Austria.[81]

Doubtless in line with Stalin's own conspiracy theories, the Centre interpreted the visit by Simon and Eden to Berlin as the first in a series of meetings at which British statesmen not only sought to appease Hitler but gave him encouragement to attack Russia.[82] In reality, though some British diplomats would have been content to see the two dictators come to blows of their own accord, no British foreign secretary and no British government would have contemplated orchestrating such a conflict. The conspiracy theories which were born in Stalin's Moscow in the 1930s, however, have—remarkably—survived the end of the Soviet era. An SVR official history published in 1997 insists that the many volumes of published Foreign Office documents as well as the even more voluminous unpublished files in the Public Record Office cannot be relied upon. The British government, it maintains, is still engaged in a conspiracy to conceal the existence of documents which reveal the terrible truth about British foreign policy before the Second World War:

Some documents from the 1930s having to do with the negotiations of British leaders with the highest leadership of Fascist Germany, including directly with Hitler, have been kept to this day in secret archives of the British Foreign Office. The British do not want the indiscreet peering at the proof of their policy of collusion with Hitler and spurring Germany on to its eastern campaign.[83]

FOUR

THE MAGNIFICENT FIVE

Among the select group of inter-war heroes of foreign intelligence whose portraits hang today on the walls of the SVR's Memory Room at Yasenevo is the Austrian Jew Arnold Deutsch, probably the most talented of all the Great Illegals. According to an SVR official eulogy, the portrait immediately "attracts the visitor's attention" to "its intelligent, penetrating eyes, and strong-willed countenance." Deutsch's role as an illegal was not publicly acknowledged by the KGB until 1990.[1] Even now, some aspects of his career are considered unsuitable for publication in Moscow.

Deutsch's academic career was one of the most brilliant in the history of Soviet intelligence. In July 1928, two months after his twenty-fourth birthday and less than five years after entering Vienna University as an undergraduate, he was awarded the degree of PhD with distinction. Though his thesis had been on chemistry, Deutsch had also become deeply immersed in philosophy and psychology. His description of himself in university documents throughout his student years as an observant Jew (*mosaisch*)[2] was probably intended to conceal his membership of the Communist Party. Deutsch's religious faith had been replaced by an ardent commitment to the Communist International's vision of a new world order which would free the human race from exploitation and alienation. The revolutionary myth image of the world's first worker–peasant state blinded both Deutsch and the ideological agents he later recruited to the increasingly brutal reality of Stalin's Russia. Immediately after leaving Vienna University, Deutsch began secret work as a courier for OMS, Comintern's international liaison department, traveling to Romania, Greece, Palestine and Syria. His Austrian wife, Josefine, whom he married in 1929, was also recruited by OMS.[3]

Deutsch's vision of a new world order included sexual as well as political liberation. At about the time he began covert work for Comintern, he became publicly involved in the "sex-pol" (sexual politics) movement, founded by the German Communist psychologist and sexologist Wilhelm Reich, which opened clinics to bring birth control and sexual enlightenment to Viennese workers.[4] At this stage of his career, Reich was engaged in an ambitious attempt to integrate Freudianism with Marxism and in the early stages of an eccentric research program on human sexual behavior which later earned him an undeserved reputation as "the prophet of the better orgasm."[5] Deutsch enthusiastically embraced Reich's teaching that political and sexual repression were different sides of the same coin and together paved the way for fascism. He ran the Munster Verlag in Vienna which published Reich's work and other "sex-pol" literature.[6] Though the Viennese police were probably unaware of Deutsch's secret work for OMS, its anti-pornography section took a keen interest in his involvement with the "sex-pol" movement.[7]

Remarkably, Deutsch combined, at least for a few years, his role as an open disciple of Reich with secret work as a Soviet agent. In 1932 he was transferred from OMS to the INO, and trained in Moscow as an OGPU illegal with the alias "Stefan Lange" and the codename STEFAN. (Later, he also used the codename OTTO.) His first posting was in France, where he established secret crossing points on the Belgian, Dutch and German borders, and made preparations to install radio equipment on French fishing boats to be used for OGPU communications in times of war.[8] Deutsch owed his posthumous promotion to the ranks of KGB immortals to his second posting in England.

The rules protecting the identities and legends of illegals in the mid-1930s were far less rigid and elaborate than they were to become later. Early in 1934 Deutsch traveled to London under his real name, giving his profession as "university lecturer" and using his academic credentials to mix in university circles. After living in temporary accommodation, he moved to a flat in Lawn Road, Hampstead, the heartland of London's radical intelligentsia. The "Lawn Road Flats," as they were then known, were the first "deck-access" apartments with external walkways to be built in England (a type of construction later imitated in countless blocks of council flats) and, at the time, were probably Hampstead's most avant-garde building. Deutsch moved into number 7, next to a flat owned by the celebrated crime novelist Agatha Christie, then writing *Murder on the Orient Express*. Though it is tempting to imagine Deutsch and Christie discussing the plot of her latest novel, they may never have met. Christie lived elsewhere and probably visited Lawn Road rarely, if at all, in the mid-1930s. Deutsch, in any case, is likely to have kept a low profile. While the front doors of most flats were visible from the street, Deutsch's was concealed by a stairwell which made it possible for him and his visitors to enter and leave unobserved.[9] Deutsch strengthened his academic cover by taking a postgraduate course in psychology at London University and possibly by part-time teaching.[10] In 1935 he was joined by his wife, who had been trained in Moscow as a radio operator.[11]

KGB files credit Deutsch during his British posting with the recruitment of twenty agents and contact with a total of twenty-nine.[12] By far the most celebrated of these agents were a group of five young Cambridge graduates, who by the Second World War were known in the Centre as "The Five": Anthony Blunt, Guy Burgess, John Cairncross, Donald Maclean and Kim Philby. After the release of the enormously popular Western *The Magnificent Seven* in 1960, they were often referred to as the "Magnificent Five." The key to Deutsch's success was his new strategy of recruitment, approved by the Centre, based on the cultivation of young radical highfliers from leading universities before they entered the corridors of power. As Deutsch wrote to the Centre:

Given that the Communist movement in these universities is on a mass scale and that there is a constant turnover of students, it follows that individual Communists whom we pluck out of the Party remain will pass unnoticed, both by the Party itself and by the outside world. People forget about them. And if at some time they do remember that they were once Communists, this will be put down to a passing fancy of youth, especially as those concerned are scions of the bourgeoisie. It is up to us to give the individual [recruit] a new [non-Communist] political personality.[13]

Since the universities of Oxford and Cambridge provided a disproportionate number of Whitehall's highest fliers, it was plainly logical to target Oxbridge rather than the red brick universities elsewhere. The fact that the new recruitment was based chiefly on Cambridge rather than Oxford was due largely to chance: the fact that the first potential recruit to come to Deutsch's attention, Kim Philby, was a graduate of Trinity College, Cambridge. Of the other members of the "Magnificent Five," all recruited as a direct or indirect consequence of Philby's own recruitment, three (Blunt, Burgess and Cairncross) also came from Trinity College and the fourth (Maclean) from the neighboring Trinity Hall.[14]

Deutsch's recruitment strategy was to prove a spectacular success. By the early years of the Second World War all of the Five were to succeed in penetrating either the Foreign Office or the intelligence community. The volume of high-grade intelligence which they supplied was to become so large that Moscow sometimes had difficulty coping with it.

AFTER GRADUATING FROM Cambridge in June 1933 with the conviction that "my life must be devoted to Communism," Philby spent most of the next year in Vienna working for the MOPR (the Russian acronym of the International Workers Relief Organization) and acting as a courier for the underground Austrian Communist Party.[15] While in Vienna he met and married a young Communist divorcee, Litzi Friedman, after a brief but passionate love affair which included his first experience of making love in the snow ("actually quite warm, once you got used to it," he later recalled).[16] The first to identify Philby's potential as a Soviet agent—and probably to draw him to the attention of Arnold Deutsch—was Litzi's friend Edith Suschitsky, who was herself recruited by Deutsch and given the unimaginative codename EDITH.[17]

In May 1934 Kim and Litzi Philby returned to London, arriving some weeks after Deutsch. Several months earlier Edith Suschitsky had also taken up residence in London, marrying another recruit of Deutsch's, an English doctor named Alex Tudor Hart. The newly married couple were given the joint codename STRELA ("Arrow").[18] In June 1934 Edith Tudor Hart took Philby to his first meeting with Deutsch on a bench in Regent's Park, London. According to a later memoir written by Philby for the KGB, Deutsch instructed him, "We need people who could penetrate into the bourgeois institutions. Penetrate them for us!"[19] At this early stage, however, Deutsch did not tell Philby that he was embarking on a career as a Soviet agent. Instead, he gave him the initial impression that he was joining Comintern's underground war against international fascism. Philby's immediate task, Deutsch told him, was to break all visible contact with the Communist Party and to try to win the confidence of British pro-German and pro-fascist circles.[20] As was not uncommon at this period, Philby's first codename, given him immediately after his meeting with Deutsch, had two versions: SÖHNCHEN in German or SYNOK in Russian—both roughly equivalent to "Sonny" in English.[21]

Half a century later, Philby still remembered his first meeting with the man he knew as "Otto" as "amazing":

> He was a marvelous man. Simply marvelous. I felt that immediately. And [the feeling] never left me . . . The first thing you noticed about him were his eyes. He looked at you as if nothing more important in life than you and talking to you existed at that moment . . . And he had a marvelous sense of humor.[22]

It is difficult to imagine any other controller in the entire history of the KGB as ideally suited as Deutsch to the Cambridge Five. Though four of the Five graduated from Cambridge with first-class honors,[23] Deutsch's academic career was even more brilliant than theirs, his understanding of human character more profound and his experience of life much broader. He combined a charismatic personality and deep psychological insight with visionary faith in the future of a human race freed from the exploitation and alienation of the capitalist system. His message of liberation had all the greater appeal to the Cambridge Five because it had a sexual as well as a political dimension. All the Five were rebels against the strict sexual mores as well as the antiquated class system of inter-war Britain. Burgess and Blunt were homosexuals, Maclean a bisexual and Philby a heterosexual athlete. Cairncross, a committed heterosexual, later wrote a history of polygamy which concluded with a quotation from George Bernard Shaw: "Women will always prefer a 10 percent share of a first-rate man to sole ownership of a mediocre man."[24] Cairncross plainly considered himself first-rate rather than mediocre. Graham Greene was charmed by Cairncross's book. "Here at last," he wrote to Cairncross, "is a book which will appeal strongly to all polygamists."[25]

During almost four years as an illegal controlling British agents, Deutsch served under three illegal residents, each of whom operated under a variety of aliases: Ignati Reif, codenamed MARR; Aleksandr Orlov, codenamed SCHWED ("Swede"); and Teodor Maly, successively codenamed PAUL, THEO and MANN. By 1938 all three were to become victims of the Terror. Reif and Maly were shot for imaginary crimes. Orlov defected just in time to North America, securing his survival by threatening to arrange for the revelation of all he knew about Soviet espionage should he be pursued by an NKVD assassination squad.[26] Somewhat misleadingly, a KGB/SVR-sponsored biography of Orlov published in 1993 claimed that he was "the mastermind" responsible for the recruitment of the Cambridge agents.[27] There are probably two reasons for this exaggeration. The first is hierarchical. Within the Soviet *nomenklatura* senior bureaucrats commonly claimed, and were accorded, the credit for their subordinates' successes. The claim that Orlov, the most senior intelligence officer involved in British operations in the 1930s, "recruited" Philby is a characteristic example of this common phenomenon.[28] But there are also more contemporary reasons for the inflation of Orlov's historical importance. It suits the SVR, which sees itself as the inheritor of the finest traditions of the KGB First Chief Directorate, to seek to demonstrate the foolishness of Western intelligence and security services by claiming that they failed for over thirty years to notice that the leading recruiter of the Cambridge Five and other agents was living under their noses in the United States. For several years before his death in 1973, the KGB tried to persuade Orlov to return to a comfortable flat and generous pension in Russia, where he would doubtless have been portrayed for propaganda purposes as a man who, despite being forced to flee from Stalin's Terror, had—like Philby—"kept faith with Lenin's Revolution" and used his superior intelligence training to take in Western intelligence agencies for many years.[29]

In reality, Orlov spent only just over a year in London—ten days in July 1934, followed by the period from September 1934 to October 1935.[30] During that period Deutsch, who was subordinate in rank to Orlov, had to seek his approval for his intelligence operations. On occasion Orlov took the initiative in giving instructions to Deutsch. But the files noted by Mitrokhin make clear that the grand strategy which led to the targeting of Philby and other young Cambridge high-fliers was devised not by Orlov but by Deutsch.[31] And, as Philby himself acknowledged, no other controller equaled Deutsch's tactical skill in implementing that strategy.

Philby's first major service to Soviet intelligence was to direct Deutsch to two other potential Cambridge recruits, Donald Maclean and Guy Burgess.[32] If not already a committed Communist by the time he entered Trinity Hall, Cambridge, in 1931, Donald Maclean became one during his first year. As the handsome, academically gifted son of a former Liberal cabinet minister, Maclean must have seemed to Deutsch an almost ideal candidate to penetrate the corridors of power. On his graduation with first-class honors in modern languages in June 1934, however, Maclean showed no immediate sign of wanting a career in Whitehall. His ambition was either to teach English in the Soviet Union or to stay at Cambridge to work for a PhD. In the course of the summer he changed his mind, telling his mother that he intended to prepare for the Foreign Office entrance examinations in the following year.[33] That change of heart reflected the influence of Deutsch. The first approach to Maclean was made through Philby in August 1934. Deutsch reported that Philby had been instructed to meet Maclean, discuss his job prospects and contacts and ask him to open contact with the Communist Party and begin work for the NKVD. Maclean agreed. For the time being, however, the Centre refused to sanction meetings between Deutsch and Maclean, and contact with him for the next two months was maintained through Philby. Maclean's first codename, like Philby's, had two versions: WAISE in German, SIROTA in Russian—both meaning "Orphan" (an allusion to the death of his father two years earlier).[34]

For some months Guy Burgess, then in his second year as a history research student at Trinity College preparing a thesis he was never to complete, had been enthused by the idea of conducting an underground war against fascism on behalf of the Communist International. Ironically, in view of the fact that he was soon to become one of the Magnificent Five, he seems to have been inspired by the example of the *Fünfergruppen,* the secret "groups of five" being formed by German Communists to organize opposition to Hitler. Maclean was, very probably, among the Communist friends with whom he discussed the (in reality rather unsuccessful) German groups of five.[35] When Maclean admitted, against his instructions, that he had been asked to engage in secret work,[36] Burgess was desperate for an invitation to join him.

In December 1934 Maclean arranged a first meeting between Deutsch and Burgess.[37] Deutsch already knew that Burgess was one of the most flamboyant figures in Cambridge: a brilliant, gregarious conversationalist equally at home with the teetotal intellectual discussions of the Apostles, the socially exclusive and heavy-drinking Pitt Club and the irreverent satirical revues of the Footlights. He made no secret either of his Communist sympathies or of his enjoyment of the then illegal pleasures of homosexual "rough trade" with young working-class men. A more doctrinaire and less imaginative controller than Deutsch might well have concluded that the outrageous Burgess would be a liability rather than an asset. But Deutsch may well have sensed that Burgess's very outrageousness would give him good, if unconventional, cover for his work as a secret agent. No existing stereotype of a Soviet spy remotely resembled Burgess.[38] When invited to join the Comintern's underground struggle against fascism, Burgess told Deutsch that he was "honored and ready to sacrifice everything for the cause." His codename MÄDCHEN[39] ("Little Girl," by contrast with Philby's codename "Sonny") was an obvious reference to his homosexuality.

Deutsch initially told both Maclean and Burgess, like Philby, that their first task was to distance themselves from the left and conform to the ideas of the establishment in order to penetrate it successfully.[40] Maclean successfully persuaded his mother, Lady Maclean, that he had "rather gone off" his undergraduate flirtation with Communism. In August 1935 he passed the Foreign Office exams with flying colors. When asked about his "Communist views" at Cambridge, Maclean decided to "brazen it out":

> "Yes," I said, "I did have such views—and I haven't entirely shaken them off." I think they must have liked my honesty because they nodded, looked at each other and smiled. Then the chairman said: "Thank you, that will be all, Mr. Maclean."[41]

In October 1935, as a new member of His Majesty's Diplomatic Service, Maclean became the first of the Magnificent Five to penetrate the corridors of power.

Burgess went about burying his Communist past with characteristic flamboyance. Late in 1935 he became personal assistant to the young rightwing gay Conservative MP Captain "Jack" Macnamara. Together they went on fact-finding missions to Nazi Germany which, according to Burgess, consisted largely of homosexual escapades with like-minded members of the Hitler Youth. Burgess built up a remarkable range of contacts among the continental "Homintern." Chief among them was

Edouard Pfeiffer, chef de cabinet to Edouard Daladier, French war minister from January 1936 to May 1940 and prime minister from April 1938 to March 1940. Burgess boasted to friends that, "He and Pfeiffer and two members of the French cabinet . . . had spent an evening together at a male brothel in Paris. Singing and dancing, they had danced around a table, lashing a naked boy, who was strapped to it, with leather whips."[42]

In February 1935 there was a security alert at the London illegal residency. Reif, operating under the alias "Max Wolisch," was summoned for an interview at the Home Office and observed a large file in the name of Wolisch on his interviewer's desk. Orlov reported to the Centre that the British authorities appeared to have been "digging around but could not come up with anything and decided to get rid of him." Reif obeyed Home Office instructions to arrange for his prompt departure. Orlov feared that MI5 might also be on the trail of Deutsch and announced that as a precaution he was taking personal control of Philby, Maclean and Burgess, by now sometimes referred to as the "Three Musketeers." Orlov believed that his own cover as an American businessman selling imported refrigerators from an office in Regent Street was still secure. In October, however, there was another security alert when he accidentally encountered a man who, some years earlier, had given him English lessons in Vienna and knew his real identity. Orlov made a hasty exit from London, never to return, leaving Deutsch to resume the running of the Cambridge recruits.[43]

Under Deutsch's control, Philby, Maclean and Burgess rapidly graduated as fully fledged Soviet agents. They may not have been told explicitly that they were working for the NKVD rather than assisting Comintern in its underground struggle against fascism, but they no longer needed formal notification. As Deutsch wrote later in a report for the Centre, "They all know that they are working for the Soviet Union. This was absolutely understood by them. My relations with them were based upon our Party membership." In other words, Deutsch treated them not as subordinate agents but as comrades working under his guidance in a common cause and for the same ideals. Later, less flexible controllers than Deutsch were unhappy that Philby, Burgess and Maclean appeared to consider themselves as officers, rather than agents, of Soviet intelligence.[44] It came as a considerable shock to Philby after his defection to Moscow in 1963 to discover that, like other foreign agents, he did not possess, and would never be allowed to acquire, officer rank—hence his various attempts to mislead Western journalists into believing that he was Colonel, or even General, Philby of the KGB.[45] In his memoirs, published in 1968, Philby repeated the lie that he had "been a Soviet intelligence *officer* for some thirty-odd years."[46]

AFTER THE SECURITY scares of 1935, Deutsch and the illegal residency took increased precautions to evade MI5 and Special Branch surveillance. Before preparing for a meeting with an agent, usually in London, Deutsch would be driven out of town, watching carefully to see if the car was being followed. Once satisfied that he was not being tailed, he returned to London by public transport, changing several times en route. During his travels Deutsch concealed film of secret documents inside hairbrushes, travel requisites and household utensils. Reports to the Centre were usually sent in secret ink to an address in Copenhagen for forwarding to Moscow.[47]

Though the KGB and SVR released interesting material in the early 1990s on the "Three Musketeers," they avoided any reference to Norman John ("James") Klugmann, recruited by Deutsch in 1936.[48] Klugmann and the young Marxist poet John Cornford, "James and John," were the two most prominent Communist Party activists in Cambridge. Though Cornford was killed in the Spanish Civil War in 1937, just after his twenty-first birthday, Klugmann went on to become head of the Party's Propaganda and Education Department, a member of the political committee (in effect its Politburo) and the Party's official historian. He had become a Communist at Gresham's School, Holt, where he had been a friend and contemporary of Donald Maclean. Klugmann won an open scholarship in modern languages to Trinity College, Maclean a slightly less prestigious exhibition to the neighboring Trinity Hall. Both graduated with first-class honors. Like Maclean, Anthony Blunt's conversion to Communism owed something to Klugmann's influence. Blunt found him "an extremely good political theorist" who "ran the administration of the Party with great skill and energy . . . It was primarily he who decided what organizations and societies in Cambridge were worth penetrating [by the Communists]."[49] Klugmann had an unshakable conviction that British capitalism was close to collapse. "We simply *knew*, all of us, that the revolution was at hand," he later recalled. "If anyone had suggested it wouldn't happen in Britain for say thirty years, I'd have laughed myself sick."[50]

Since Klugmann was one of Britain's most active young Communists, there was little prospect that, like the Five, he could convincingly distance himself from the Party and penetrate the "bourgeois apparatus." Deutsch saw another role for Klugmann: as a talent-spotter for the NKVD, capable, when necessary, of persuading Communist students to engage in underground work rather than conventional Party militancy. Before Deutsch recruited Klugmann, the NKVD obtained the approval of the British Party leadership. There was never any likelihood that the British general secretary, Harry Pollitt, would object. Like most Western Communist leaders he believed that the interests of the Communist International required unconditional support for the Soviet Union, whatever the twists of policy in the Kremlin. With Pollitt's consent, Klugmann was recruited by Deutsch as agent MER.[51] The refusal by the SVR until 1998 to admit Klugmann's recruitment was due to the involvement of the British Communist Party.[52] One of the KGB's most closely guarded secrets was the extent to which, as late as the 1980s, it expected the leaders of "fraternal parties" in the West to assist in the recruitment of agents and the fabrication of "legends" for its illegals.[53]

IN THE SPRING of 1936 the Centre appointed another of the Great Illegals, Teodor Maly (codenamed MANN), head of the illegal London residency.[54] Like Deutsch, Maly was later included among the intelligence immortals whose portraits hung on the walls of the First Chief Directorate Memory Room. Hungarian by birth, Maly had entered a Catholic monastic order before the First World War but had volunteered for military service in 1914.[55] He was taken prisoner while serving as second lieutenant in the Austro-Hungarian army on the Russian front in 1916, and spent the rest of the war in a series of POW camps. Maly later told one of his agents:

> I saw all the horrors, young men with frozen limbs dying in the trenches . . . I lost my faith in God and when the Revolution broke out I joined the Bolsheviks. I broke with my past completely . . . I became a Communist and have always remained one.[56]

Maly was originally posted to London in January 1936 to run the Foreign Office with cipher clerk Captain King (previously controlled by Pieck), to whom he introduced himself as an executive of the fictitious Dutch bank which King believed was paying him for classified documents. In April Maly was appointed illegal resident and henceforth shared with Deutsch in the running of the Cambridge agents. Like Deutsch, he impressed them with both his human sympathy and his visionary faith in the Communist millennium.[57]

During the early months of 1937 Deutsch and Maly completed the recruitment of the Magnificent Five. At the beginning of the year, Burgess, by then a producer at the BBC, arranged a first meeting between Deutsch and Anthony Blunt, French linguist, art historian and Fellow of Trinity College, Cambridge.[58] Though the title of "Fourth Man" later accorded Blunt was a media invention rather than a KGB sobriquet, he was both the fourth of the Five to be recruited and, over forty years later, the fourth to be publicly exposed. Until the war Blunt's chief role for the NKVD was that of talent-spotter. His first recruit, by agreement with Deutsch, was a wealthy young American Communist undergraduate at Trinity, Michael Straight (codenamed NIGEL).[59] Shortly after his own first meeting with Deutsch, Blunt invited Straight to his elegant rooms in Trinity. Straight was still shattered by the news a fortnight earlier that his close friend, John Cornford, had died a hero's death in the Spanish Civil War. "Our friends," Blunt told him, had been giving much thought to his future. "They have instructed me to tell you . . . what you must do." "What friends?" Straight asked. "Our friends in the International, the Communist International," Blunt replied. The "friends" had decided that Straight's duty was to break all overt connection with the Party, get a job in Wall Street after his graduation later that year and provide Comintern with inside information. Straight protested. Cornford had given his life for the International. "Remember that," Blunt told him. A few days later, Straight agreed. "In the course of a week," Straight wrote later, "I had moved out of the noisy, crowded world of Cambridge into a world of shadows and echoes." His only meeting with Deutsch, whom he mistook for a Russian, took place in London just after his graduation. Deutsch asked him for some personal documents. Straight gave him a drawing. Deutsch tore it in two, gave him one half back and told him the other half would be returned to him by a man who would contact him in New York.[60]

The last of the Magnificent Five to be recruited, and later the last to be publicly exposed, was the "Fifth Man," John Cairncross, a brilliant Scot who in 1934 had entered Trinity at the age of twenty-one with a scholarship in modern languages, having already studied for two years at Glasgow University and gained a *licence ès lettres* at the Sorbonne.[61] His passionate Marxism led the *Trinity Magazine* to give him the nickname "The Fiery Cross," while his remarkable facility as a linguist led the same magazine to complain, "Cairncross . . . learns a new language every fortnight."[62] Among his college teachers in French literature was Anthony Blunt, though Cairncross later claimed that they never discussed Communism.[63] In 1936, after graduating with first-class honors, Cairncross passed top of the Foreign Office entrance examinations, one hundred marks ahead of the next candidate (though he did less well at the interview).[64]

After Blunt had acted as talent-spotter, the initial approach to Cairncross early in 1937 was entrusted by Deutsch to Burgess[65]—much as Philby had made the first recruitment overture to Maclean in 1934. The actual recruitment of Cairncross shortly afterwards was entrusted to James Klugmann.[66] On April 9 Maly informed the Centre that Cairncross had been formally recruited and given the codename MOLIÈRE.[67] Had Cairncross known his codename, he might well have objected to its transparency but would undoubtedly have found appropriate the choice of his favorite French writer, on whom he later published two scholarly studies in French. For reasons not recorded in KGB files, the codename MOLIÈRE was later replaced by that of LISZT.[68] In May Klugmann arranged Cairncross's first rendezvous with Deutsch. According to Cairncross's admittedly unreliable memoirs, the meeting took place one evening in Regent's Park:

> Suddenly there emerged from behind the trees a short, stocky figure aged around forty, whom Klugmann introduced to me as Otto. Thereupon, Klugmann promptly disappeared . . .[69]

Deutsch reported to Moscow that Cairncross "was very happy that we had established contact with him and was ready to start working for us at once."[70]

Among the pre-Second World War Foreign Office documents available to both Maclean and Cairncross, and thus to the NKVD, were what Cairncross described as "a wealth of valuable information on the progress of the Civil War in Spain."[71] Only in a few cases, however, is it possible to identify individual documents supplied by Maclean and Cairncross which the Centre forwarded to Stalin, probably in the form of edited extracts.[72] One such document, which seems to have made a particular impression on Stalin, is the record of talks with Hitler in November 1937 by Lord Halifax, Lord President of the Council (who, three months later, was to succeed Eden as Foreign Secretary).[73] Halifax's visit to Hitler's mountain lair, the "Eagle's Nest" at Berchtesgaden, got off to a farcical start. As the aristocratic Halifax stepped from his car, he mistook Hitler for a footman and was about to hand him his hat and coat when a German minister hissed in his ear, "*Der Führer! Der Führer!*"[74] The Centre, however, saw the whole meeting as deeply sinister. The extracts from Halifax's record of his talks with Hitler, tailored to fit Stalin's profound distrust of British policy, emphasized that Britain viewed Nazi Germany as "the bastion of the West against Bolshevism" and would take a sympathetic view of German expansion to the east.[75] Though Halifax's assessment of Hitler, whom he regarded as "very sincere," was lamentably naive, his record of his comments on Germany's role in defending the West against Communism were much more qualified than the Centre's version of them. He told Hitler:

> Although there was much in the Nazi system that offended British opinion (treatment of the Church; to a perhaps lesser extent, the treatment of Jews; treatment of Trade Unions), I was not blind to what he had done for Germany and to the achievement from his point of view of keeping Communism out of his country and, as he would feel, of blocking its passage West.

Halifax also said nothing to support German aggression in eastern Europe. His aim—unrealistic though it was—was to turn Hitler into "a good European" by offering him colonial concessions in order to persuade him to limit his European ambitions to those he could achieve peacefully. Halifax made clear, however, that Britain was prepared to contemplate the peaceful revision of Versailles:

> I said that there were no doubt . . . questions arising out of the Versailles settlement which seemed to us capable of causing trouble if they were unwisely handled, e.g. Danzig, Austria, Czechoslovakia. On all these matters we were not necessarily concerned to stand for the status quo as today, but we were concerned to avoid such trouble of them as would be likely to cause trouble. If reasonable settlements could be reached with the free assent and goodwill of those primarily concerned we certainly had no desire to block them.

Such statements were music to Hitler's ears—not because he was interested in the peaceful revision of Versailles, but because he interpreted Halifax's rather feeble attempt at conciliation as evidence that Britain lacked the nerve to fight when the time came for him to begin a war of conquest.[76] Stalin, characteristically, saw a much more sinister purpose behind Halifax's remarks and persuaded himself that Britain had deliberately given the green light to Nazi aggression in the east. The Foreign Office documents supplied by Maclean and Cairncross which recorded British attempts to appease Hitler were used by the Centre to provide the evidence which Stalin demanded of a deep-laid British plot to turn Hitler on the Soviet Union.

THOUGH KIM PHILBY ultimately became the most important of the Magnificent Five, his career took off more slowly than those of the other four. He abandoned an attempt to join the civil service after both his referees (his Trinity director of studies and a family friend) warned him that, while they admired his energy and intelligence, they would feel bound to add that his "sense of political injustice might well unfit him for administrative work." His only minor successes before 1937 were to gain a job on an uninfluential liberal monthly, the *Review of Reviews,* and become a member of the Anglo-German Fellowship, contemptuously described by Churchill as the "Heil Hitler Brigade." As Philby later acknowledged, he would often turn up for meetings with Deutsch "with nothing to offer" and in need of reassurance. The outbreak of the Spanish Civil War gave him his first important intelligence mission. He eventually persuaded a London news agency to give him a letter of accreditation as a freelance war correspondent and arrived in Spain in February 1937. "My immediate assignment," he wrote later in his memoirs, "was to get first-hand information on all aspects of the fascist war effort." As usual, his memoirs fail to tell the whole truth.[77]

A few weeks after Philby's departure, the London illegal residency received instructions, undoubtedly approved by Stalin himself, to order Philby to assassinate General Francisco Franco, leader of the nationalist forces.[78] Maly duly passed on the order but made clear to the Centre that he did not believe Philby capable of fulfilling it.[79] Philby arrived back in London in May without even having set eyes on Franco and, Maly told the Centre, "in a very depressed state." Philby's fortunes improved, however, after he was taken on by *The Times* as one of its two correspondents in nationalist Spain.[80] At the end of the year he became a minor war hero. Three journalists sitting in a car in which he had been traveling were fatally injured by an artillery shell. Philby himself was slightly wounded. He reported modestly to *Times* readers, "Your correspondent . . . was taken to a first aid station where light head injuries were speedily treated." "My wounding in Spain," wrote Philby later, "helped my work—both journalism and intelligence—no end." For the first time he gained access to Franco, who on March 2, 1938 pinned on his breast the Red Cross of Military Merit. Then, as Philby reported, "all sorts of doors opened for me."[81]

The doors, however, opened too late. By the time Philby gained access to Franco, the NKVD assassination plot had been abandoned. Since the spring of 1937 the Centre had been increasingly diverted from the war against Franco by what became known as the civil war within the Civil War. The destruction of Trotskyists became a higher priority than the liquidation of Franco. By the end of 1937 the hunt for "enemies of the people" abroad took precedence over intelligence collection. The remarkable talents of the Magnificent Five had yet to be fully exploited. INO was in turmoil, caught up in the paranoia of the Great Terror, with most of its officers abroad suspected of plotting with the enemy. The age of the Great Illegals was rapidly drawing to a brutal close.

FIVE

TERROR

Though "special tasks" only began to dominate NKVD foreign operations in 1937, the problem of "enemies of the people" abroad had loomed steadily larger in Stalin's mind since the early 1930s as he became increasingly obsessed with the opposition to him inside the Soviet Union. The most daring denunciation of the growing brutality of Stalin's Russia was a letter of protest sent to the Central Committee in the autumn of 1932 by a former Party secretary in Moscow, Mikhail Ryutin, and a small band of supporters. The "Ryutin platform," whose text was made public only in 1989, contained such an uncompromising attack on Stalin and the horrors which had accompanied collectivization and the First Five Year Plan over the previous few years that some Trotskyists who saw the document believed it was an OGPU provocation.[1] It denounced Stalin as "the evil genius of the Russian Revolution, motivated by vindictiveness and lust for power, who has brought the Revolution to the edge of the abyss," and demanded his removal from power: "It is shameful for proletarian revolutionaries to tolerate any longer Stalin's yoke, his arbitrariness, his scorn for the Party and the laboring masses."[2]

At a meeting of the Politburo Stalin called for Ryutin's execution. Only Sergei Mironovich Kirov dared to contradict him. "We mustn't do that!" he insisted. "Ryutin is not a hopeless case, he's merely gone astray." For the time being Stalin backed down and Ryutin was sentenced to ten years in jail.[3] Five years later, during the Great Terror, when Stalin had gained the virtually unchallenged power of life and death over Soviet citizens, Ryutin was shot.

During the early 1930s Stalin lost whatever capacity he had once possessed to distinguish personal opponents from "enemies of the people." By far the most dangerous of these enemies, he believed, were the exiled Leon Trotsky (codenamed STARIK, "Old Man," by the Centre)[4] and his followers. "No normal 'constitutional' paths for the removal of the governing [Stalinist] clique now remain," wrote Trotsky in 1933. "The only way to compel the bureaucracy to hand over power to the proletarian vanguard is by force." Henceforth Stalin used that assertion to argue that the Soviet state was faced with a threat of forcible overthrow, which must itself be forcibly prevented.[5]

Opposition to Stalin resurfaced at the 1934 Party Congress, though in so muted a form that it passed unnoticed by the mass of the population. In the elections to the

Central Committee, Stalin polled several hundred votes fewer than Kirov, who was assassinated, probably on Stalin's orders, at the end of the year. What increasingly obsessed Stalin, however, were less the powerless remnants of real opposition to him than the gigantic, mythical conspiracy by imperialist secret services and their Trotskyist hirelings. Though the paranoid strain in what Khrushchev later called Stalin's "sickly suspicious" personality does much to explain his obsession with conspiracy theory, there was an impeccable Leninist logic at the heart of that obsession. Stalin claimed Lenin's authority for his insistence that it was impossible for the imperialists *not* to attempt to overthrow the world's first and only worker–peasant state:

> We are living not only in a State, but in a system of States, and the existence of the Soviet Republic side by side with imperialist States is in the long run unthinkable. But until that end comes, a series of the most terrible clashes between the Soviet Republic and bourgeois States is unavoidable.

It was equally inevitable, Stalin argued, that the enemies without would conspire with traitors within. Only "blind braggarts or concealed enemies of the people," he declared, would dispute this elementary logic.[6] Those who disagreed thus automatically branded themselves as traitors.

Despite Stalin's increasing obsession during the 1930s with Trotskyist conspiracy, Trotsky never really represented any credible threat to the Stalinist regime. He spent his early years in exile trying vainly to find a European base from which to organize his followers. In 1933 he left Turkey for France, then two years later moved on to Norway, but his political activity in all three countries was severely restricted by the reluctant host governments. In 1937, having finally despaired of finding a European headquarters, Trotsky left for Mexico, where he remained until his assassination three years later. The chief European organizer of the Trotskyist movement for most of the 1930s was not Trotsky himself but his elder son, Lev Sedov, who from 1933 was based in Paris. It was Sedov who, until his death in 1938, organized publication of his father's *Bulletin of the Opposition* and maintained contact with Trotsky's scattered supporters. Sedov's entourage, like his father's, was penetrated by the OGPU and NKVD. From 1934 onwards his closest confidant and collaborator in Paris was an NKVD agent, the Russian-born Polish Communist Mark Zborowski, known to Sedov as êtienne and successively codenamed by the Center MAKS, MAK, TULIP and KANT. Sedov trusted "Étienne" so completely that he gave him the key to his letterbox, allowed him to collect his mail and entrusted him with Trotsky's most confidential files and archives for safekeeping.[7]

AS THE CHIEF headquarters of both the Trotskyist movement and the White Guards, Paris became for several years the main center of operations for the NKVD Administration for Special Tasks, headed by "Yasha" Serebryansky, which specialized in assassination and abduction. Serebryansky's illegal residency in Paris had other targets, too. The most prominent was the mercurial Jacques Doriot, a rabble-rousing orator who during the early 1930s was considered a likely future contender for the leadership of the French Communist Party.[8] In the early months of 1934, he aroused the ire of Moscow by calling on the Party to form an anti-fascist Popular Front with the socialists, still officially condemned in Moscow as "social fascists." Doriot was summoned to Moscow to recant but refused to go. He was expelled from the Party for indiscipline in June 1934, ironically at the very moment when the Communist International, in a rapid volte-face instantly accepted by the French Communist Party, decided in favor of a Popular Front policy.

Doriot responded with a series of increasingly bitter attacks on both Stalin's "oriental" despotism and the French Communist leadership, whom he derided as "Stalin's slaves." The Centre, fearing the effect of Doriot's impassioned and now subversive oratory on the French left, ordered Serebryansky to keep him under continuous surveillance. In 1935, after almost the whole non-Communist press had publicized Doriot's revelation that the French Communist Party received secret instructions and funds from Moscow, the Centre instructed Serebryansky to draw up plans for his liquidation.[9] The order to go ahead with the assassination seems never to have been given, perhaps because of the triumph of the Popular Front in the 1936 elections and Doriot's foundation soon afterwards of the neofascist Parti Populaire Français. Doriot's public vindication of the Communist charge that he was a fascist collaborator provided the Centre with a propaganda victory which his assassination would have spoiled rather than enhanced.[10]

Among other assassinations which Serebryansky was ordered to organize was that of the leading Nazi Hermann Goering, who was reported to be planning a visit to Paris. The Administration for Special Tasks ordered its Paris residency to recruit a sniper and find a way of infiltrating him into the airport, probably Le Bourget, at which Goering was expected to land.[11] Goering, however, failed to visit France and the sniper was stood down. The files seen by Mitrokhin give no indication of the Centre's motive in ordering an assassination which was undoubtedly authorized by Stalin himself. The probability is, however, that the main objective was to damage relations between France and Germany rather than to strike a blow against Nazism. The assassination on French soil in 1932 of the President of the Republic and the King of Yugoslavia by a non-Communist assassin doubtless encouraged the Centre to believe that it could avoid responsibility for the killing of Goering if an opportunity arose.

Despite the numerous other duties of Serebryansky's Paris residency, its main task remained the surveillance and destabilization of French Trotskyists. Until 1937 Lev Sedov, thanks to his misplaced but total confidence in "Étienne" Zborowski, was such an indispensable source on the POLECATS (as the Trotskyists were codenamed by the Centre) that he was not marked down as a target for liquidation.[12] In the autumn of 1936 Zborowski warned the Centre that, because of his financial problems, Trotsky was selling part of his archive (formerly among the papers entrusted by Sedov to Zborowski for safekeeping) to the Paris branch of the International Institute of Social History based in Amsterdam. Serebryansky was ordered to set up a task force to recover it, codenamed the HENRY group. He began by renting the flat immediately above the institute in the rue Michelet in order to keep it under surveillance. On

Serebryansky's instructions, Zborowski, then working as a service engineer at a Paris telephone exchange, was ordered to cause a fault on the Institute's telephone line in order to give him a chance to reconnoitre the exact location of the Trotsky papers and examine the locks. When the Institute reported the fault on its line, however, one of Zborowski's colleagues was sent to mend the fault instead. Zborowski promptly put the Institute's phone out of action once again and on this occasion was called to make the repair himself. As he left the Institute, having mended the fault and closely inspected the locks to the front and back doors, he was given a five franc tip by the director, Boris Nikolayevsky, a prominent Menshevik émigré classed by the NKVD as an "enemy of the people."[13]

Serebryansky fixed the time for the burglary at two o'clock on the morning of November 7, 1936, and ordered it to be completed by 5 a.m. at the latest. Since his agents were unable to find keys to fit the Institute locks, he decided to cut them out with a drill powered by an electric transformer concealed in a box filled with sawdust and cotton wool to deaden the sound.[14] The burglars broke in unobserved and left with Trotsky's papers. Both Sedov and the Paris police immediately suspected the NKVD because of both the professionalism of the burglary and the fact that money and valuables in the Institute had been left untouched. Sedov assured the police that his assistant "Étienne" Zborowski was completely above suspicion, and in any case kept the main archive, which had not been stolen, at his home address. Ironically, Sedov suggested that the NKVD might have learned of the transfer of a part of the archive as the result of an indiscretion by the Institute director, Nikolayevsky.[15]

The extraordinary importance attached by the Centre to the theft of the papers was demonstrated by the award of the Order of the Red Banner to the HENRY group.[16] The operation, however, was as pointless as it was professional. The papers stolen from the Institute (many of them press cuttings) were of no operational significance whatever and of far less historical importance than the Trotsky archive which remained in Zborowski's hands and later ended up at Harvard University.[17] But by the mid-1930s Stalin had lost all sense of proportion in his pursuit of Trotskyism in all its forms, both real and imaginary. Trotsky had become an obsession who dominated many of Stalin's waking hours and probably interfered with his sleep at night. As Trotsky's biographer, Isaac Deutscher, concludes:

The frenzy with which [Stalin] pursued the feud, making it the paramount preoccupation of international communism as well as of the Soviet Union and subordinating to it all political, tactical, intellectual and other interests, beggars description; there is in the whole of history hardly another case in which such immense resources of power and propaganda were employed against a single individual.[18]

The British diplomat R. A. Sykes later wisely described Stalin's world view as "a curious mixture of shrewdness and nonsense."[19] Stalin's shrewdness was apparent in the way that he outmaneuvered his rivals after the death of Lenin, gradually acquired absolute power as General Secretary, and later out-negotiated Churchill and Roosevelt during their wartime conferences. Historians have found it difficult to accept that so shrewd a man also believed in so much nonsense. But it is no more possible to understand Stalin without acknowledging his addiction to conspiracy theories about Trotsky (and others) than it is to comprehend Hitler without grasping the passion with which he pursued his even more terrible and absurd conspiracy theories about the Jews.

GENRIKH GRIGORYEVICH YAGODA, head of the NKVD from 1934 to 1936, was far less obsessed by Trotsky than Stalin was. Stalin's chief grudge against him was probably a growing conviction that he had been deliberately negligent in his hunt for Trotskyist traitors.[20] His nemesis arrived in September 1936 in the form of a telegram from Stalin and his protégé, Andrei Zhdanov, to the Central Committee declaring that Yagoda had "definitely proved himself incapable of unmasking the Trotskyite–Zinovyevite bloc" and demanding his replacement by Nikolai Ivanovich Yezhov.

As head of the NKVD for the next two years, Yezhov carried through the largest scale peacetime political persecution and blood-letting in European history, known to posterity as the Great Terror.[21] One NKVD document from the Yezhov era, which doubtless reflected—and probably slavishly imitated—Stalin's own view, asserted that "the scoundrel Yagoda" had deliberately concentrated the attack on the "lower ranks" of "the right-wing Trotskyite underground" in order to divert attention from its true leaders: Zinovyev, Bukharin, Rykov, Tomsky, Kamenev and Smirnov. Yagoda, it was claimed, had either sacked or sidelined NKVD staff who had tried to indict these former heroes of the Leninist era for their imaginary crimes.[22] All save Tomsky, who committed suicide, were given starring roles in the show trials of 1936 to 1938, gruesome morality plays which proclaimed a grotesque conspiracy theory uniting all opposition at home and abroad by the use of elegantly absurd formulae such as: "Trotskyism is a variety of fascism and Zinovyevism is a variety of Trotskyism." In the last of the great show trials Yagoda, despite a plea for mercy written "on bended knees," was himself unmasked as a leading Trotskyist conspirator. The chief author of the gigantic conspiracy theory, which became undisputed orthodoxy within the NKVD and provided the ideological underpinning of the Great Terror, was Stalin himself.[23] Stalin personally proofread the transcripts of the show trials before their publication, amending the defendants' speeches to ensure that they did not deviate from their well-rehearsed confessions to imaginary conspiracies.[24] NKVD records of the period proclaim with characteristic obsequiousness that, "The practical organization of the work exposing the right-wing Trotskyite underground was supervised personally by Comrade Stalin, and in 1936–8 crippling blows were delivered to the rabble."[25]

"Crippling blows" against both real and imaginary Trotskyist "rabble" were struck outside as well as inside the Soviet Union. The beginning of the Spanish Civil War in July 1936 opened up a major new field of operations for Serebryansky's Administration for Special Tasks and for INO as a whole. The struggle of the Spanish republican government to defend itself against the nationalist rebellion led by General Francisco Franco fired the imagination of the whole of the European left as a crusade against international fascism: 35,000 foreign volunteers, most of them Communist, set out for Spain to join the International Brigades in defense of the republic. In October 1936 Stalin declared in an open letter to Spanish Communists: "Liberation of Spain from the yoke of the Spanish reactionaries is not the private concern of Spaniards alone, but the common cause of all progressive humanity." From the outset, however, the NKVD was engaged in Spain in a war on two fronts: against Trotskyists within the republicans and the International Brigades, as well as against Franco and the nationalist forces. The former illegal resident in London, Aleksandr Orlov, sent to Spain as legal resident after the outbreak of the Civil War, confidently assured the Centre in October, "The Trotskyist organization POUM [Partido Obrero de Unificacion Marxista] can be easily liquidated."[26]

WHILE ORLOV COORDINATED the NKVD's secret two-front war within Spain, Serebryansky conducted operations from abroad. Serebryansky organized training courses in Paris for saboteurs from the International Brigades, run by GIGI, a French Communist mechanic who usually worked without pay, FRANYA, a female Polish student paid 1,500 francs a month, and LEGRAND, on whom no further details are available. The greatest sabotage success reported by Serebryansky was the claim by the ERNST TOLSTY group of illegals, based in the Baltic and Scandinavia, to have sunk seventeen ships carrying arms to Franco.[27] One of the leading saboteurs was a young German Communist, Ernst Wollweber, who twenty years later was to become head of the Stasi in East Germany.[28] An NKVD inquiry after the Civil War concluded, however, that some of the reports of sinkings were fabrications.[29]

The main NKVD training grounds for guerrillas and saboteurs were within Spain itself at training camps supervised by Orlov at Valencia, Barcelona, Bilbao and Argen. Orlov later boasted of how his guerrilla platoons succeeded in blowing up power lines and bridges and in attacking enemy convoys far behind the nationalist lines. As an SVR-sponsored biography of Orlov acknowledges, his larger purpose was "to build up a secret police force under NKVD control to effect a Stalinization of Spain." The chief Soviet military adviser in republican Spain, General Jan Berzin, formerly head of Red Army intelligence, complained that Orlov and the NKVD were treating republican Spain as a colony rather than an ally.[30]

In the spring of 1937 Orlov and Serebryansky were ordered to move from the surveillance and destabilization of Trotskyist groups to the liquidation of their leaders. While Serebryansky began preparing the abduction of Sedov,[31] Orlov supplied the republican government with forged documents designed to discredit POUM as "a German-Francoist spy organization." On June 16 the head of POUM, Andreu Nin, and forty leading members were arrested, its headquarters closed and its militia battalions disbanded. Less than a week later Nin disappeared from prison. An official investigation announced that he had escaped. In reality, he was abducted and murdered by a "mobile squad" of NKVD assassins, supervised by Orlov. Nin was one of many Trotskyists in Spain, both real and imagined, who met such fates. Until Orlov defected to the United States in 1938, fearing that he too had been placed on an NKVD death list, he lived in some luxury while organizing the liquidation of enemies of the people. A young volunteer in the International Brigades summoned to his presence was struck by how strongly he reeked of eau de cologne, and watched enviously as he consumed a large cooked breakfast wheeled in on a trolley by a white-coated servant. Orlov offered none of it to the famished volunteer, who had not eaten for twenty-four hours.[32]

Though unusually forthcoming about Orlov, who, because of his defection, never qualified for the KGB Valhalla, the SVR has been much more reluctant to release material on the Spanish Civil War which might damage the reputation of the traditional heroes of Soviet foreign intelligence: among them Hero of the Soviet Union Stanislav Alekseyevich Vaupshasov, long celebrated for his daring exploits behind enemy lines during the Second World War. With four Orders of Lenin, two Orders of the Great Patriotic War and a chestful of other medals, Vaupshasov was probably the Soviet Union's most profusely decorated intelligence hero. As recently as 1990 he was honored by a commemorative postage stamp. Vaupshasov's murderous pre-war record, however, is still kept from public view by the SVR. In the mid-1920s he led a secret OGPU unit in numerous raids on Polish and Lithuanian border villages, dressed in Polish and Lithuanian army uniforms. In 1929 Vaupshasov was sentenced to death for murdering a colleague, but managed to have the sentence commuted to ten years in the gulag. He was quickly released and resumed his career as one of the NKVD's leading experts in assassination. Among Vaupshasov's duties in Spain was the construction and guarding of a secret crematorium which enabled the NKVD to dispose of its victims without leaving any trace of their remains. Many of those selected for liquidation were lured into the building containing the crematorium and killed on the spot.[33]

The NKVD agent in charge of the crematorium was José Castelo Pacheco (code-named JOSE, PANSO and TEODOR),[34] a Spanish Communist born in Salamanca in 1910, who was recruited by Orlov's deputy resident, Leonid Aleksandrovich Eitingon, in 1936.[35] In 1982, some years after Castelo's death, the KGB received a letter from a female relative appealing for a pension and claiming that he had told her before his death, "If you have any problems and there is no other way out, I mean only in extreme circumstances, then contact my Soviet comrades." Though Castelo's file showed that he had promised never to reveal any details of his work as a Soviet agent, there was an obvious risk that his relative had discovered his work in the NKVD crematorium. The Centre therefore concluded that to refuse her request might have "undesirable consequences." In January 1983 she was summoned to the consular department of the Soviet embassy in Madrid by the resident and told that, though she had no legal right to a pension, it had been decided to make her an *ex gratia* payment of 5,000 convertible roubles, then the equivalent of 6,680 US dollars. No reference was made to Castelo's work for the NKVD.[36]

REMARKABLY, MANY OTHERWISE admirable studies of the Stalin era fail to mention the relentless secret pursuit of "enemies of the people" in western Europe. The result, all too frequently, is a sanitized, curiously bloodless interpretation of Soviet foreign policy on the eve of the Second World War which fails to recognize the priority given to assassination. Outside Spain, the main theater of operations for the NKVD's assassins was France, where their chief targets were Lev Sedov and General Yevgeni Karlovich Miller, Kutepov's successor as head of the White Guard ROVS. In the summer of 1937 Serebryansky devised similar plans to liquidate both. Sedov and Miller were each to be kidnapped in Paris, smuggled on board a boat waiting off the Channel coast, then brought to the Soviet Union for interrogation and retribution. The first stage in the abduction operations was the penetration of their entourages.

Like Sedov's assistant "Étienne" Zborowski, Miller's deputy, General Nikolai Skoblin, was an NKVD agent. Probably unknown to Skoblin, Serebryansky also used an illegal, Mireille Lyudvigovna Abbiate (codenamed AVIATORSHA, "aviator's wife"), to keep Miller under surveillance. Abbiate was the daughter of a French music teacher in St. Petersburg, born and brought up in Russia. When her family returned to France in 1920, she had stayed in Russia and married the aviator Vasili Ivanovich Yermolov (hence her later codename). In 1931, when she traveled to France to visit her parents, she was recruited by the NKVD. During her visit she recruited her brother, Roland Lyudvigovich Abbiate, who also became an illegal with the codename LETCHIK ("pilot"). AVIATORSHA rented a flat next to General Miller, secretly forced an entry, stole some of his papers and installed a hidden microphone which enabled her to bug his apartment.[37] On September 22, 1937, like Kutepov seven years earlier, Miller disappeared in broad daylight on a Paris street. The Sûreté later concluded that Miller had been taken to the Soviet embassy, killed and his body placed in a large trunk which was then taken by a Ford truck to be loaded on a Soviet freighter waiting at Le Havre. Several witnesses reported seeing the trunk being loaded on board. Miller, however, was still alive inside the trunk, heavily drugged. Unlike Kutepov in 1930, he survived the voyage to Moscow, where he was interrogated and shot. Skoblin, who fell under immediate suspicion by Miller's supporters, fled to Spain.[38] Mireille Abbiate, whose role went undetected, was awarded the Order of the Red Star, then reassigned to the operation against Sedov.[39]

Planning for the abduction of Sedov was at an advanced stage by the time Miller disappeared. A fishing boat had been hired at Boulogne to take him on the first stage of his journey to the Soviet Union.[40] The operation, however, was aborted—possibly as a result of the furor aroused in France by the NKVD's suspected involvement in Miller's abduction. A few months later Sedov met a different end. On February 8, 1938 he entered hospital with acute appendicitis. "Étienne" Zborowski helped to persuade him that, to avoid NKVD surveillance, he must have his appendix removed not at a French hospital but at a small private clinic run by Russian émigrés, which was in reality an easier target for Soviet penetration. No sooner had Zborowski ordered the ambulance than, as he later admitted, he alerted the NKVD. But, for alleged security reasons, he refused to reveal the address of the clinic to French Trotskyists. Sedov's operation was successful and for a few days he seemed to be making a normal recovery. Then he had a sudden relapse which baffled his doctors. Despite repeated blood transfusions, he died in great pain on February 16 at the age of only thirty-two. The contemporary files contain no proof that the NKVD was responsible for his death.[41] It had, however, a sophisticated medical section, the Kamera, which experimented with lethal drugs and was capable of poisoning Sedov. It is certain that the NKVD intended to assassinate Sedov, just as it planned to kill Trotsky and his other leading lieutenants. What remains in doubt is whether Sedov was murdered by the NKVD in February 1938 or whether he died of natural causes before he could be assassinated.[42]

Sedov's death enabled the NKVD to take a leading role in the Trotskyist organization. Zborowski became both publisher of the *Bulletin of the Opposition* and Trotsky's most important contact with his European supporters. While unobtrusively encouraging internecine warfare between the rival Trotskyist tendencies, Zborowski impeccably maintained his own cover. On one occasion he wrote to tell Trotsky that the *Bulletin* was about to publish an article entitled "Trotsky's Life in Danger," which would expose the activities of NKVD agents in Mexico. In the summer of 1938 the defector Aleksandr Orlov, then living in the United States, sent Trotsky an anonymous letter warning him that his life was in danger from an NKVD agent in Paris. Orlov did not know the agent's surname but said that his first name was Mark (the real first name of "Étienne" Zborowski), and gave a detailed description of his appearance and background. Trotsky suspected that this letter and others like it were the work of NKVD *agents provocateurs*. Zborowski agreed. When told about one of the accusations against him, he is reported as having given "a hearty laugh."[43]

Following the death of Sedov, the NKVD's next major Trotskyist target in Europe was the German Rudolf Klement, secretary of Trotsky's Fourth International, whose founding conference was due to be held later in the year.[44] On July 13, 1938 the NKVD abducted Klement from his Paris home. A few weeks later his headless corpse was washed ashore on the banks of the Seine. The founding conference of the Fourth International in September was a tragicomic event, attended by only twenty-one delegates claiming to represent mostly minuscule Trotskyist groups in eleven countries. The Russian section, whose authentic members had probably been entirely exterminated, was represented by Zborowski. The American Trotskyist Sylvia Angeloff, one of the conference translators, was accompanied by her Spanish lover, Ramón Mercader, an NKVD illegal posing as a Belgian journalist who was later to achieve fame as Trotsky's assassin in Mexico City.[45]

BY 1938 SEREBRYANSKY's Administration for Special Tasks was the largest section of Soviet foreign intelligence, claiming to have 212 illegal officers operating in sixteen countries: the USA, France, Belgium, Holland, Norway, Denmark, Sweden, Finland, Germany, Latvia, Estonia, Poland, Romania, Bulgaria, Czechoslovakia and China. After Trotskyists, the largest number of "enemies of the people" pursued abroad by the NKVD during the Great Terror came from the ranks of its own foreign intelligence service.[46] When receiving reports from Moscow of show trials and the unmasking of their colleagues as agents of imperialist powers, intelligence officers stationed abroad had to pay careful attention not merely to what they said but also to their facial expressions and body language. Those who failed to respond with sufficiently visible or heartfelt outrage to the non-existent conspiracies being unveiled in Moscow were likely to have adverse reports sent to the Centre—frequently with fatal consequences.

After the trial of Lenin's former lieutenants Zinovyev, Kamenev and other "degenerates" in August 1936, the Centre received an outraged communication from the Paris legal residency regarding the unsatisfactory level of indignation displayed by the military intelligence officer Abram Mironovich Albam (codenamed BELOV):

> BELOV does not appear to feel a deep hatred or a sharply critical attitude towards these political bandits. During discussions of the trial of the Trotskyite–Zinovyevite bandits, he retreats into silence. BELOV was hoping that the sixteen convicted men would be shown mercy, and, when he read about their execution in the newspaper today, he actually sighed.[47]

Albam's subversive sigh helped to convict not merely himself but also a number of his colleagues of imaginary crimes. His file lists thirteen of his acquaintances who were subsequently arrested; at least some, probably most, were shot. Albam's wife, Frida Lvovna, tried to save herself by disowning her arrested husband. "The most horrible realization for an honest Party member," she wrote indignantly to the NKVD, "is the fact that he was an enemy of the people surrounded by other enemies of the people."[48]

Both at home and abroad the Great Terror favored the survival of the most morally unfit. Those who were quickest to denounce their colleagues for imaginary crimes stood the greatest chance of being among the minority of survivors. The fact that Yakov Surits, ambassador in Berlin at the beginning of the Great Terror, was one of the few senior diplomats to survive may well have owed something to his expertise in denunciation. Surits sought to head off denunciation by the head of the legal residency in his embassy, B. M. Gordon, by denouncing Gordon first. At the outset of the Terror, Surits drew to the attention of the Centre that a Soviet diplomat with whom Gordon was on friendly terms was a former Socialist Revolutionary who frequently visited relatives in Prague "where other SR émigrés reside."[49] After the show trial of the "Trotskyite–Zinovyevite Terrorist Center" in January 1937, Surits reported disturbing evidence of Gordon's Trotskyite sympathies:

> On February 2 a Party meeting was held in the Berlin embassy. Gordon, B. M., the resident and Communist Party organizer, delivered a report on the trial of the Trotskyite Center.
>
> Gordon did not say a word about the fact that his rabble of bandits had a specific program of action; he did not say why this scum hid its program from the working class and from all working people; why it led a double life; why it went deeply underground.
>
> He did not dwell on the reasons why after all the enemies managed to cause damage for so many years.
>
> He did not deal with the question why, despite wrecking, sabotage, terrorism and espionage, our industry and transport constantly made progress and continue to make progress.
>
> He did not touch on the international significance of the trial.[50]

Surits, however, was unaware that he was himself being simultaneously denounced for similar failings by one of his secretaries, who wrote virtuously to the Centre:

> To this day the office of Comrade Surits is adorned with a portrait of Bukharin with the following inscription: "To my dear Surits, my old friend and comrade, with love—N. Bukharin." I deliberately do not take it down, not because I greatly enjoy looking at it, but because I want to avoid the cross looks which Comrade Surits gave me when I removed the portrait of Yenukidze.
>
> I am waiting for him to remove it himself, since if Bukharin was indeed once his close friend, he must now be his enemy, as he has become the enemy of our Party and of the whole working class. The portrait should immediately have been thrown into the fire.
>
> That, really, is all that I considered it my Party duty to report to you. After the adoption of the Stalin Constitution [of 1936] which has granted us great rights and put us under great obligations, calling us to exercise discipline, honest work and vigilance, I could not remain silent about these facts.[51]

In 1937–8, following the recall and liquidation of all or most of their officers, many NKVD residencies ceased to function. Though the residencies in London, Berlin, Vienna and Tokyo did not close, they were reduced to one or, at the most, two officers each.[52] Most of the Great Illegals were purged with the rest. Among the first to fall under suspicion was the London head of probably the NKVD's most successful illegal residency, Teodor Maly, whose religious background and revulsion at the use of terror made him an obvious suspect. He accepted the order to return to Moscow in June 1937 with an idealistic fatalism. "I know that as a former priest I haven't got a chance," he told Aleksandr Orlov. "But I have decided to go there so that nobody can say: 'That priest might have been a real spy after all.' "[53] Once in Moscow he was denounced as a German spy, interrogated and shot a few months later. Moisei Akselrod, head of the illegal residency in Italy and controller of DUNCAN, the most productive source of intelligence on Britain during the previous decade, was also recalled to Moscow. After a brief period in limbo, he too was executed as an enemy of the people.[54]

Amid the paranoia of the Great Terror, Arnold Deutsch's Jewish–Austrian origins and unorthodox early career made him automatically suspect in the Centre. After the recall of Maly, Akselrod and other illegals, he must have feared that his own turn would not be long in coming. In an effort to extend his visa he had recently contacted a Jewish relative in Birmingham, Oscar Deutsch, president of a local synagogue and managing director of Odeon Theatres. Arnold sometimes visited his Birmingham relatives for Friday night sabbath dinners, and Oscar promised to provide work to enable him to stay in Britain.[55] These contacts doubtless added to the suspicions of the Centre.

Remarkably, however, Deutsch survived. He may well have owed his survival to the defection in July 1937 of a Paris-based NKVD illegal, Ignace Poretsky (alias Reiss, codenamed RAYMOND). Poretsky was tracked down in Switzerland by a

French illegal in the "Serebryansky Service," Roland Abbiate (alias "Rossi," code-named LETCHIK), whose sister Mireille, also in the "Serebryansky Service," was simultaneously preparing the abduction of General Miller in Paris.[56] To lure Poretsky to his death, Abbiate used one of his friends, Gertrude Schildbach, a German Communist refugee who was persuaded to write to Poretsky to say that she urgently needed his advice. Schildbach refused a request to give Poretsky a box of chocolates laced with strychnine (later recovered by the Swiss police), but enticed him into a side-road near Lausanne where Abbiate was waiting with a machine-gun. At the last moment Poretsky realized that he was being led into a trap and tried to grab hold of Schildbach. His bullet-ridden body was later discovered, clutching in one hand a strand of her greying hair.[57]

The NKVD damage assessment after Poretsky's defection concluded that he had probably betrayed Deutsch, with whom he had been stationed in Paris a few years earlier, to Western intelligence services.[58] Deutsch's classification as a victim of Trotskyite and Western conspiracy helped to protect him from charges of being part of that conspiracy. He was recalled to Moscow in November 1937, not, like Maly, to be shot, but because the Centre believed he had been compromised by Poretsky and other traitors.

The liquidation of Maly and recall of Deutsch did severe and potentially catastrophic damage to the NKVD's British operations. All contact was broken with Captain King (MAG), the cipher clerk in the Foreign Office recruited in 1935, since the NKVD damage assessment absurdly concluded that Maly "had betrayed MAG to the enemy."[59] The files noted by Mitrokhin do not record what the damage assessment concluded about the Cambridge recruits, but, since Maly knew all their names, there were undoubtedly fears that they too had been compromised. Those fears must surely have been heightened by the defection in November of Walter Krivitsky, the illegal resident in the Netherlands. Though Krivitsky seems not to have known the names of any of the Cambridge Five, he knew some details about them, including the fact that one of them was a young journalist who had been sent to Spain with a mission to assassinate Franco.[60]

After Deutsch's recall to Moscow, the three members of the Five who remained in England—Burgess, Blunt and Cairncross—were out of direct contact with the Centre for nine months. They were so highly motivated, however, that they continued to work for the NKVD even as the illegal residency which had controlled them was disintegrating. Burgess, who had been allowed by Deutsch and Maly to consider himself an NKVD officer rather than an agent wholly dependent on instructions from his controller, continued recruiting agents on his own initiative. He saw himself as continuing and developing Deutsch's strategy of recruiting bright students at Oxford as well as Cambridge who could penetrate Whitehall.

Burgess intended his chief talent-spotter at Oxford to be Goronwy Rees, a young Welsh Fellow of All Souls and assistant editor of the *Spectator.* Rees had first met Burgess in 1932 and, though resisting Burgess's attempt to seduce him, had none the less been deeply impressed by him: "It seemed to me that there was something deeply original, something which was, as it were, his very own in everything he had to say."[61]

It was probably a book review by Rees late in 1937 which persuaded Burgess that he was ready for recruitment. The misery of mass unemployment in south Wales, wrote Rees, was

> misery of a special and peculiar kind . . . and to many people it implies a final condemnation of the society which has produced it . . . If you tell men and women, already inclined by temperament and tradition to revolutionary opinions, that their sufferings are caused by an impersonal economic system, you leave them but one choice. Lenin could not do better.

One evening, probably at the beginning of 1938, sitting in Rees's flat with, as usual, a bottle of whiskey between them, Burgess told him that his *Spectator* review showed that he had "the heart of the matter in him." Then, according to Rees, he added with unusual solemnity, "I am a Comintern agent and have been ever since I came down from Cambridge."[62] In later years Rees was to try to give the impression that he did not agree to become an agent. His KGB file makes clear that he was recruited—though it confirms that Burgess asked him not to work for the NKVD but "to help the Party."[63] As an NKVD case officer with whom Burgess made contact later in the year reported to the Centre, he regarded Rees (henceforth codenamed FLEET or GROSS) as a key part of his Oxbridge recruitment strategy:

> The kind of work which he would do with great moral satisfaction and with absolute confidence in its success and effectiveness is the recruitment by us of young people graduating from Oxford and Cambridge Universities and preparing them to enter the civil service. For this kind of work he has such assistants as TONY [Blunt] in Cambridge and GROSS [Rees] in Oxford. MÄDCHEN [Burgess] always returns to this idea at every meeting . . ."[64]

Though unhappy with Burgess's undisciplined recruiting methods, the Centre regarded Rees as potentially an important agent. Three of Britain's leading appeasers—Lord Halifax, the Foreign Secretary; Sir John Simon, then Home Secretary; and Geoffrey Dawson, editor of *The Times*—were nonresident Fellows of All Souls. The Center attached exaggerated importance to the fact that Rees met all three from time to time on high table. It also overestimated the influence of Rees's friend Sir Ernest Swinton, a retired major-general who had been Chichele Professor of Military History since 1925 and was referred to by the Centre as "General Swinton."[65]

WHILE BURGESS WAS pressing ahead enthusiastically with his Oxbridge recruitment strategy, INO was in turmoil. On February 17, 1938 its head, Abram Slutsky, was found dead in his office, allegedly from a heart attack. But at his lying in state in the NKVD officers' club, his senior staff noticed on his face the tell-tale signs of cyanide poisoning.[66] Yagoda, meanwhile, was confessing at his trial to working for the German, Japanese and Polish intelligence services, to poisoning his predecessor, Menzhinsky, and to attempting to poison his successor, Yezhov.[67] By the end of the year, Slutsky's two immediate successors as head of INO, Zelman Pasov and Mikhail Shpigelglas, had also been shot as enemies of the people.[68] INO collapsed into such confusion during 1938 that for 127 consecutive days not a single foreign intelligence report was forwarded to Stalin.[69] In December Yezhov was replaced as head of the NKVD by Lavrenti Pavlovich Beria; a few months later he was accused of treasonable conspiracy with Britain, Germany, Japan and Poland.[70] As NKVD officers went home in the evening, each one must have wondered whether the knock at the door in the early hours would signal that his own doom was nigh.

Most of the INO officers who were interrogated and brutally tortured during the late 1930s in the name of the vast conspiracy theories of Stalin and his NKVD chiefs did not live to tell the tale. One of the few who did was the first of the Great Illegals, Dmitri Bystroletov. In 1937 Bystroletov had been sent on a mission to Berlin to contact a Soviet agent on the Reichswehr general staff. He later claimed that, before he left, he was embraced by Yezhov. "Be proud that we have given you one of our best sources," Yezhov told him. "Stalin and your fatherland will not forget you."[71] Early in 1938, however, Bystroletov was suspended from duty and transferred to the Moscow Chamber of Commerce, where he worked until his arrest in September.[72] During Bystroletov's interrogation by Colonel Solovyev, Yezhov entered the room and asked what he was accused of. When told he was charged with spying for four foreign powers, Yezhov replied "Too few!", turned on his heels and left.[73]

When Bystroletov refused to confess to his imaginary crimes, Solovyev and his assistant, Pushkin, beat him with a ball-bearing on the end of an iron rope, breaking two of his ribs and penetrating a lung. His skull was fractured by one of the other instruments of torture, a hammer wrapped in cotton wool and bandages, and his stomach muscles torn by repeated kicks from his interrogators. Convinced that he would die if the beating continued, Bystroletov signed a confession dictated to him by Solovyev. For most INO officers, torture and confession to imaginary crimes were followed by a short walk to an execution chamber and a bullet in the back of the head. Bystroletov, however, survived to write an account of his interrogation. Though sentenced to twenty years' imprisonment in 1939, he was rehabilitated during the Second World War. By the time he was released, his wife, Shelmatova, sent to the gulag as the spouse of an enemy of the people, had killed herself by cutting her throat with a kitchen knife. His elderly mother poisoned herself.[74]

AFTER THE DISINTEGRATION of the London illegal residency following the liquidation of Maly and the recall of Deutsch, the Centre planned to hand over the running of its main British agents to the legal residency at the Soviet embassy in Kensington. In April 1938 a new resident, Grigori Grafpen (codenamed SAM), arrived to take charge.[75] The massacre of many of the most experienced INO officers had a dramatic effect on the quality of NKVD tradecraft. Deutsch, Orlov and Maly had taken elaborate precautions to avoid surveillance before meeting their agents. But an inexperienced emissary from the Centre who came to inspect Grafpen's residency had so little idea about tradecraft that he assumed it was safe to operate in the immediate environs of the embassy. He reported naively to Moscow, "Next to the Embassy there is a park [Kensington Gardens] which is convenient . . . for holding meetings with agents, as one can simply give the appearance of having gone out for a walk in this park."[76]

Grafpen's first priority was to renew contact with Donald Maclean, then the most productive of the Cambridge Five and able to smuggle large numbers of classified documents out of the Foreign Office. On April 10 a young and apparently inexperienced female NKVD officer, codenamed NORMA, met Maclean in the Empire Cinema in Leicester Square. A few days later Maclean came to NORMA's flat with a large bundle of Foreign Office documents which she photographed, before giving the undeveloped film to Grafpen for shipment to Moscow. Either on that occasion or soon afterwards, the young British agent and his Soviet case officer followed the photography session by going to bed together. In defiance of her instructions, NORMA also told Maclean, probably in bed, that his current codename (which he was not supposed to know) was LYRIC.[77]

In September 1938 Maclean left for his first foreign posting as third secretary in the Paris embassy, preceded by an effusive testimonial from the Foreign Office personnel department:

> Maclean, who is the son of the late Sir Donald Maclean . . . has done extremely well during his first two years here and is one of the mainstays of the Western Department. He is a very nice individual indeed and has plenty of brains and keenness. He is, too, nice-looking and ought, we think, to be a success in Paris from the social as well as the work point of view.[78]

As Maclean was leaving for Paris, the Munich crisis was reaching its humiliating climax with the surrender of the Czech Sudetenland to Nazi Germany. On September 30 the British prime minister, Neville Chamberlain, returned to a hero's welcome in London, brandishing the worthless piece of paper bearing Hitler's signature which, he claimed, meant not only "peace with honor" but "peace for our time." For the Cambridge Five, incapable of imagining that less than a year later Stalin would sign a pact with Hitler, Munich was further confirmation of the justice of their cause.

During the Munich crisis Cairncross had access to Foreign Office files containing what Burgess described as "the very best information imaginable" on British policy, which he passed to the NKVD via Klugmann and Burgess.[79] Cairncross's documents on the attempted appeasement of Germany, which reached its nadir with the Munich agreement, were used by the Centre to provide further evidence for the conspiracy theory that the secret aim of British foreign policy, supported by the French, was "to lure Germany into an attack on Russia." Though the chief advocate of this theory was Stalin, it was also fervently espoused by INO. Throughout the Cold War, the claim that Britain's aim at Munich had been not merely to appease Hitler but also to drive him into a conflict with the Soviet Union remained unchallenged orthodoxy among KGB historians. As late as the mid-1990s, Yuri Modin, the post-war controller of the Five, was still insisting that, "This claim was neither propaganda nor disinformation but the unvarnished truth, proven by the documents obtained for us by Burgess" (chiefly, no doubt, from Cairncross).[80]

After Maclean's posting to Paris during the Munich crisis, Cairncross was intended by the Centre to succeed him as its chief source within the Foreign Office. The London resident, Grafpen, bungled the transition. Cairncross's prickly personality and lack of social graces had not won the same encomiums from his colleagues or the Foreign Office personnel department as Maclean's more patrician manner. In December 1938 he moved to the Treasury.[81] At almost the same moment as Cairncross's departure for the Treasury, though for unconnected reasons, Grafpen was recalled to Moscow. Given the atmosphere of the time, he may actually have been relieved, after being "unmasked" as a Trotskyist on his arrival, to be sentenced to only five years in a labor camp rather than being led to an execution cellar in the Lubyanka basement.[82] En route for Moscow in December 1938, Grafpen accompanied NORMA (renamed ADA since her earlier indiscretion) to Paris where she was due to resume contact with Maclean. ADA reported that Maclean was having an affair with an American student at the Sorbonne, Melinda Marling, whom he was later to marry. She also discovered that Maclean, now drinking heavily, had admitted that while drunk he had told both his mistress and his brother that he was working for Soviet intelligence.[83] ADA remained in Paris, filming the documents provided by Maclean from embassy files, then passing the film to an illegal codenamed FORD for transmission to the Centre.[84]

The news in December 1938 of Maclean's drunken security lapse was balanced by a spectacular success. In the same month Burgess reported, probably via Paris, that he had succeeded in joining the Secret Intelligence Service. He had been taken on by SIS's newest branch, Section D, founded earlier in the year to devise dirty tricks ranging from sabotage to psychological warfare (delicately described as ways of "attacking potential enemies by means other than the operations of military force") for use in a future war.[85] Instead of being elated by the news, however, the Centre appeared almost paralyzed by fear and suspicion.

THE EXPOSURE OF two London illegal residents, Reif and Maly, and the legal resident, Grafpen, as imaginary enemy agents, combined with the defection of Orlov, put the entire future of intelligence operations in Britain in doubt. The illegal residency had been wound up and, with one exception, the staff of the legal residency were recalled to Moscow.[86] The only remaining INO officer in London, Anatoli Veniaminovich Gorsky, was poorly briefed about even the most important British agents. In the summer of 1939, when Philby was due to return to London after the end of the Spanish Civil War, Gorsky told the Centre, "When you give us orders on what to do with SÖHNCHEN, we would appreciate some orientation on him, for he is known to us only in the most general terms."[87]

An assessment in the Centre concluded that intelligence work in Britain "was based on doubtful sources, on an agent network acquired at the time when it was controlled by enemies of the people and was therefore extremely dangerous." It concluded with a recommendation to break contact with all British agents—the Five included.[88] Though contact was not yet broken, the Five seem to have been held at arm's length for most of 1939. Intelligence from them was accepted, often without any visible interest in it, while the Centre continued to debate the possibility that some or all were *agents provocateurs*. ADA reported that Philby "frequently" complained to Maclean about the NKVD's lack of contact with, and interest in, him.[89] Litzi Philby (MARY) and Edith Tudor Hart (EDITH), who were used by Burgess and others as couriers to make contact with the NKVD in Paris in 1938–9, grumbled that their expenses were not being paid. Gorsky reported to the Centre in July 1939:

> MARY announced that, as a result of a four-month hiatus in communications with her, we owe her and MÄDCHEN £65. I promised to check at home [the Centre] and gave him £30 in advance, since she said they were in material need . . . MARY continues to live in [France] and for some reason, she says on our orders, maintains a large flat and so on there.

The Centre replied:

> At one time, when it was necessary, MARY was given orders to keep a flat in Paris. That is no longer necessary. Have her get rid of the flat and live more modestly, since we will not pay. MARY should not be paid £65, since we do not feel that we owe her, *for anything*. We confirm the payment of £30. Tell her that we will pay no more.[90]

To a remarkable degree, however, the ideological commitment of the main British agents survived the turmoil in the Centre. In 1938 Burgess recruited one of his lovers, Eric Kessler, a Swiss journalist turned diplomat on the staff of the Swiss embassy in London. Later codenamed OREND and SHVEYTSARETS ("Swiss"), Kessler proved a valuable source on Swiss–German relations.[91] Probably in 1939, Burgess recruited another foreign lover, the Hungarian Andrew Revoi, later leader of the exiled Free Hungarians in wartime London. Codenamed TAFFY ("Toffee"), he was described in his KGB file as a pederast; the same source also claimed that he had "had homosexual relations with a Foreign Office official." Ironically, in 1942 Burgess was also to recruit Revoi as an MI5 source.[92]

Kim and Litzi Philby, still good comrades according to KGB files though they both now had different partners, made a probably even more important recruitment in 1939: that of the Austrian journalist H. P. Smolka, whom Litzi had known in Vienna. Soon after the Nazi Anschluss, which united Austria with Germany in 1938, Smolka became a naturalized British subject with the name of Peter Smollett. Codenamed ABO by the Centre, Smollett later succeeded in becoming head of the Russian section in the wartime Ministry of Information.[93]

The signature of the Nazi–Soviet Non-Aggression Pact in Moscow on August 23, 1939 was an even bigger blow to the morale of the NKVD's British agents than the turmoil in the Centre. Exchanging toasts with Hitler's foreign minister, Joachim von Ribbentrop, Stalin told him, "I can guarantee, on my word of honor, that the Soviet Union will not betray its partner." The ideological agents recruited during the 1930s had been motivated, at least in part, by the desire to fight fascism. Most, after varying degrees of inner turmoil, overcame their sense of shocked surprise at the conclusion of the Nazi–Soviet Pact. Over the previous few years, they had become sufficiently indoctrinated, often self-indoctrinated, in Stalinist double-think to perform the intellectual somersaults required to sustain their commitment to the vision of the Soviet Union as the world's first worker–peasant state, the hope of progressive mankind.

A minority of the ideological agents in the West, however, were so sickened by the Nazi–Soviet Pact that they ended their connection with the NKVD. The most important of those who broke contact in Britain was FLEET, Goronwy Rees. During a visit to Moscow in 1993, Rees's daughter Jenny was informed, accurately, during a briefing by an SVR representative that Rees had refused to cooperate after the Pact: "We hear no more of him after that." At the end of the briefing, Jenny Rees asked perceptively: "You know something else, do you, about Rees that you are not going to tell me?"[94] The SVR did indeed. The most important of the secrets that the SVR was unwilling to reveal was that Burgess, by now an SIS officer, panicked when Rees decided to break away, sent an urgent message to the Centre warning that Rees might betray both himself and Blunt, and asked for Rees to be assassinated. The Centre refused. Rees's KGB file, however, records that he did not betray Burgess and Blunt because of his "old friendship" with Burgess. In an attempt to make betrayal less likely, Burgess told Rees that he too had been disillusioned by the Nazi–Soviet Pact and had ended illegal work for the Communist Party.[95] Maclean was also deeply worried by Rees's "defection." Years later, as he was beginning to crack under the strain of his double life as British diplomat and Soviet agent, he spat at Rees: "You used to be one of us, but you ratted!"[96]

The doubts about Moscow felt by some of the NKVD's British agents after the Nazi–Soviet Pact were more than matched by the Centre's doubts about its agents. The Center launched an investigation into the possibility that Philby was either a German or a British agent.[97] Since Philby had provided the original leads which led to the recruitment of Burgess and Maclean, and ultimately to all the Cambridge recruits, doubts about him reflected on the whole British agent network. The lowest point in the history of NKVD operations in Britain came at the beginning of 1940 when Gorsky, the last member of the London legal residency, was withdrawn to Moscow, leaving not a single NKVD officer active in Britain. A file in the KGB archives records, "The residency was disbanded on the instruction of Beria [head of the NKVD]."[98] Beria's reasons are not recorded, at least in the files examined by Mitrokhin, but chief among them was undoubtedly the recurrent fear that the British agent network was deeply suspect. In February 1940 the Centre issued orders for all contact with Philby to be broken off.[99] Contact with Burgess was terminated at about the same time.[100]

DURING THE LATER 1930s the hunt for "enemies of the people" replaced intelligence collection as the main priority of NKVD foreign operations. The NKVD's most active foreign intelligence agency was Serebryansky's Administration for Special Tasks, whose persecution of INO officers steadily diminished the flow of foreign intelligence and degraded its analysis at the Center. Even the executioners abroad, however, were not immune from the Terror at home. Serebryansky himself became one of the victims of his own witch-hunt. Though he held the Order of Lenin for his many victories over enemies of the people, he was recalled to Moscow in November 1938 and exposed as "a spy of the British and French intelligence services." An inquiry later concluded that his network contained "a large number of traitors and plain gangster elements." Though the allegations of espionage for Britain and France were absurd, the charge that Serebryansky had inflated both the size of his illegal network and the scale of its accomplishments in reports to the Centre was probably well founded.[101]

Serebryansky's successor was Pavel Anatolyevich Sudoplatov, who a few months earlier had assassinated the émigré Ukrainian nationalist leader Yevkhen Konovalets with an ingeniously booby-trapped box of chocolates. In March 1939 Sudoplatov became deputy head of foreign intelligence, thus bringing "special tasks" and INO into closer association than ever before.[102] He was personally instructed by Stalin that his chief task was to send a task force to Mexico to assassinate Leon Trotsky. The killing of Trotsky, codenamed operation UTKA ("Duck"), had become the chief objective of Stalin's foreign policy. Even after the outbreak of the Second World War in September 1939, discovering the intentions of Adolf Hitler remained a lower priority than arranging the liquidation of the great heretic. Sudoplatov's task force was composed of Spanish and Mexican NKVD agents recruited during the Civil War, supervised by his deputy, Leonid Eitingon, whose long experience of "special actions" included the liquidation of "enemies of the people" in Spain.[103]

The task force consisted of three groups. The first was an illegal network headed by the Spanish Communist Caridad Mercader del Rio (codenamed MOTHER), who was both recruited and seduced by Eitingon, one of the NKVD's most celebrated womanizers.[104] The most important agent in Caridad Mercader's group was her son Ramón (codenamed RAYMOND),[105] who traveled on a doctored Canadian passport in the name of Frank Jacson (an eccentric NKVD spelling of Jackson). Like Eitingon, Ramón Mercader employed seduction as an operational technique, using his affair with the American Trotskyist Sylvia Ageloff to penetrate Trotsky's villa near Mexico City. His opportunity came when Ageloff began work as one of Trotsky's secretaries early in 1940. Each day Mercader drove her to Trotsky's villa in the morning and returned to collect her after work. Gradually he became a well-known figure with the guards and some of Trotsky's entourage, who, in March 1940, allowed him into the villa for the first time. Mercader's role at this stage was still that of penetration agent rather than assassin, with the task of reporting on the villa's defenses, occupants and guards.[106]

The attack on the villa was to be led by a second group of agents drawn from veterans of the Spanish Civil War, headed by the celebrated Mexican Communist painter David Alfaro Siqueiros (codenamed KONE),[107] who was animated by an exuberant ideological mix of art, revolution, Stalinism and exhibitionism. Both Mercader and Siqueiros were later to become well known for their involvement in operation UTKA. KGB files, however, also reveal the involvement of a shadowy third group of assassins headed by one of the most remarkable of all Soviet illegals, Iosif Romualdovich Grigulevich (then codenamed MAKS and FELIPE), who had taken a leading role in liquidating Trotskyists during the Spanish Civil War, as well as training saboteurs and arsonists to operate behind Franco's lines.[108] It is a measure of Grigulevich's skill in assuming false identities that, though born a Lithuanian Jew,[109] he was to succeed, a decade later, in passing himself off as a Costa Rican diplomat.[110] Early in 1940 he recruited Siqueiros's former pupil, the painter Antonio Pujol (codenamed JOSE), whom he later described as lacking in initiative but "very loyal, exceptionally reliable and quite bold," to act as Siqueiros's second-in-command in the assault on Trotsky's villa.[111] Grigulevich's other recruits included his future wife and assistant, the Mexican Communist Laura Araujo Aguilar (codenamed LUISA).[112]

A key part of the assault plan was the infiltration in April 1940 of a young American agent, Robert Sheldon Harte (codenamed AMUR), posing as a New York Trotskyist, as a volunteer guard in Trotsky's villa. Harte's role was to open the main gate when the assault group staged its surprise attack in the middle of the night.[113] Though enthusiastic, he was also naive. Grigulevich decided not to brief him on what would happen after he opened the villa gate.

KGB records identify Grigulevich as the real leader of the assault on Trotsky's villa.[114] Grigulevich's role in the attack was two-fold: to ensure that Siqueiros's assault group gained entrance to the villa compound, and to try to inject some element of discipline into the attack. Left to his own devices, Siqueiros would have led the assault with all guns blazing but probably have made few attempts to cover his tracks. On the evening of May 23, 1940 Siqueiros and a group of about twenty followers put on a mixture of army and police uniforms and armed themselves with pistols and revolvers. As they did so, according to one of their number, they "laughed and joked as if it were a feast day."[115] Then, with Pujol carrying the only machine-gun, Grigulevich and the assault group set off to assassinate Trotsky.[116]

On arriving at the villa in the early hours of May 24, Grigulevich spoke to the American volunteer guard, Harte, who opened the gate.[117] The assault group raked the bedrooms with gun fire to such effect that the Mexican police later counted seventy-three bullet holes in Trotsky's bedroom wall. Remarkably, however, Trotsky and his wife survived by throwing themselves beneath their bed. Though an incendiary bomb was thrown into the bedroom of their small grandson, he too escaped by hiding under his bed.[118] Harte was shocked by the attack—particularly, perhaps, by the attempt to kill Trotsky's grandchild. He angrily told the assault group that, had he known how they would behave, he would never have let them in. To prevent Harte revealing what had happened, he was taken away and shot.[119] A few months later, Siqueiros was tracked down and arrested.[120] Grigulevich, however, managed to smuggle himself, Pujol and Laura Araujo Aguilar out of the country without his identity being discovered by the Mexican police. From 1942 to 1944 he ran an illegal residency in Argentina which, according to KGB files, planted more than 150 mines in cargoes and ships bound for Germany.[121]

The failure of the attack on Trotsky's villa, followed by the dispersal of Siqueiros's gunmen, led to the promotion of Ramón Mercader from penetration agent to assassin. Mercader succeeded partly because he was patient. Five days after the raid he met Trotsky for the first time. Amiable as ever, he gave Trotsky's grandson a toy glider and taught him how to fly it. Over the next three months he paid ten visits to the villa, sometimes bringing small presents with him and always taking care not to overstay his welcome. Finally, on August 20, he brought an article he had written and asked for Trotsky's advice. As Trotsky sat reading it at his study desk, Mercader took an icepick from his pocket and brought it down with all the force he could muster on the back of Trotsky's skull.[122]

Mercader had expected Trotsky to die instantly and silently, thus allowing him to make his escape to a car nearby where his mother and her lover, Eitingon, were waiting. But Trotsky, though mortally wounded, let out "a terrible piercing cry." ("I shall hear that cry all my life," said Mercader afterwards.) Mercader was arrested and later sentenced to twenty years in jail.[123] Eitingon persuaded his mother to flee with him to Russia, promising to marry her if she did so. In Moscow Señora Mercader was welcomed by Beria, received by Stalin in the Kremlin and decorated with the Order of Lenin. But within a few years, abandoned by Eitingon and denied permission to leave Russia, she was consumed with guilt at having turned her son into an assassin and then leaving him to languish in a Mexican jail.[124]

Ramón Mercader kept the Stalinist faith throughout his twenty years in prison. History, he claimed, would see him as a soldier who had served the cause of the working-class revolution by ridding it of a traitor. KGB files reveal (contrary to most published accounts) that when Mercader was finally released and traveled to Moscow in 1960, he was awarded the title Hero of the Soviet Union, along with a general's pension and a three-room apartment, and was personally congratulated by Khrushchev. Twenty years after the assassination of Trotsky, the liquidation of enemies of the people abroad still remained, on a reduced scale, a significant part of KGB foreign operations.[125]

S I X

WAR

During the later months of 1940, with Trotsky dead and the worst of the blood-letting inside INO at an end, the Centre sought to rebuild its foreign intelligence network. Until the Great Terror, all new recruits to INO had been trained individually at secret apartments in Moscow and kept strictly apart from other trainees. By 1938, however, so many INO officers had been unmasked as (imaginary) enemies of the people that the Centre decided group training was required to increase the flow of new recruits. NKVD order no. 00648 of October 3 set up the Soviet Union's first foreign intelligence training school, hidden from public view in the middle of a wood at Balashikha, fifteen miles east of the Moscow ringroad. Given the official title Shkola Osobogo Naznacheniya (Special Purpose School), but better known by the acronym SHON, it drew its recruits either from Party and Komsomol members with higher education or from new university graduates in Moscow, Leningrad, Kiev and elsewhere.[1]

Since most of the new recruits had experienced only the cramped, squalid living conditions of crowded city apartment blocks, collective farms and army barracks, an attempt was made to introduce them to gracious living so that they would feel at ease in Western "high society." Their rooms were furnished with what an official history solemnly describes as "rugs, comfortable and beautiful furniture, and tastefully chosen pictures on the walls, with excellent bed linens and expensive bedspreads."[2] With no experience of personal privacy, the trainees would have been disoriented by being accommodated separately even if space had allowed, and so were housed two to a room. The curriculum included four hours' teaching a day on foreign languages, two hours on intelligence tradecraft, and lectures on the CPSU, history, diplomacy, philosophy, religion and painting—an eclectic mix designed both to reinforce their ideological orthodoxy and to acquaint them with Western bourgeois culture.[3] There were also regular musical evenings. Instructors with experience living in the West gave the trainees crash courses in bourgeois manners, diplomatic etiquette, fashionable dressing and "good taste."[4] During its first three years, SHON taught annual intakes totalling about 120 trainees—all but four of them male.[5]

The most successful of SHON's first intake of students was Pavel Mikhailovich Fitin, whose early career had been spent in an agricultural publishing house. In February 1938 he had been recruited by the NKVD's internal training school to fill one of the many vacancies caused by the liquidation of "enemies of the people" within its ranks. In October he was transferred to SHON, where, according to an official hagiography, his "high intellect and outstanding organizational ability" made an immediate impression. After only a few months, with his training still incomplete, he was drafted into foreign intelligence. In May 1939 he was appointed head of INO. At age thirty-one, Fitin was both the youngest and most inexperienced foreign intelligence chief in Soviet history. At the time of his sudden promotion his prospects must have seemed poor. During the chaotic previous fifteen months three of his predecessors had been liquidated and a fourth transferred.[6] Fitin, however, proved remarkably tenacious. He remained head of INO for seven years, the longest period anyone had held that office since the 1920s, before losing favor and returning to provincial obscurity.[7]

Towards the end of 1940, four INO officers were despatched to London on Fitin's orders to reopen the legal residency. The new resident was Anatoli Veniaminovich Gorsky (codenamed VADIM), the last intelligence officer to be withdrawn from London before the residency had closed that February.[8] Gorsky was a grimly efficient, humorless, orthodox Stalinist, a far cry from the Great Illegals of the mid-1930s. Blunt found him "flat-footed" and unsympathetic.[9] Another of his wartime agents described him as "a short, fattish man in his mid-thirties, with blond hair pushed straight back and glasses that failed to mask a pair of shrewd, cold eyes."[10] Like Fitin, Gorsky owed his rapid promotion to the recent liquidation of most of his colleagues.

Gorsky returned to London, however, far better briefed than during his previous tour of duty, when he had been forced to ask the Centre for background material on Kim Philby.[11] On Christmas Eve 1940 he reported that he had renewed contact with SÖHNCHEN. The Centre appeared jubilant at Gorsky's report. In the summer of 1940 Burgess had succeeded in recruiting Philby to Section D of SIS, which soon afterwards was merged into a new organization, the Special Operations Executive (SOE), instructed by Churchill to "set Europe ablaze" through subversive warfare behind enemy lines. Following the six-week defeat of France and the Low Countries, the Prime Minister's orders proved wildly optimistic. The Centre, however, warmly welcomed Gorsky's report that Philby "was working as a political instructor at the training center of the British Intelligence Service preparing sabotage agents to be sent to Europe." There was, however, one major surprise in Philby's early reports. "According to SÖHNCHEN's date," Gorsky informed the Centre, "[SOE] has not sent its agents to the USSR yet and is not even training them yet. The USSR is tenth on the list of countries to which agents are to be sent." Wrongly convinced that the Soviet Union remained a priority target, a skeptical desk officer in the Centre underlined this passage and placed two large red question marks in the margin.[12]

Early in 1941, the London residency renewed contact with the other members of the Five. Maclean continued to provide large numbers of Foreign Office documents. Unlike Philby, Burgess had failed to secure a transfer from Section D to SIS to SOE and had returned to the BBC. Blunt, however, had succeeded in entering the Security Service, MI5, in the summer of 1940. As well as providing large amounts of material from MI5 files, Blunt also ran as a sub-agent one of his former Cambridge pupils, Leo Long (codenamed ELLI), who worked in military intelligence.[13] Among the early intelligence provided by Blunt from MI5 files was evidence that during the two years before the outbreak of the Second World War the NKVD had abandoned one of its best-placed British agents. In the summer of 1937, at the height of the paranoia generated by the Great Terror, the Centre had jumped to the absurd conclusion that Captain King, the Foreign Office cipher clerk recruited three years earlier, had been betrayed to British intelligence by Teodor Maly, the illegal resident in London. Blunt revealed that King had gone undetected until his identification by a Soviet defector at the outbreak of war.[14]

Cairncross too had succeeded in occupying what the Centre considered a prime position in Whitehall. In September 1940 he left the Treasury to become private secretary to one of Churchill's ministers, Lord Hankey, Chancellor of the Duchy of Lancaster. Though not a member of the War Cabinet (initially composed of only five senior ministers), Hankey received all cabinet papers, chaired many secret committees and was responsible for overseeing the work of the intelligence services.[15] By the end of the year Cairncross was providing so many classified documents—among them War Cabinet minutes, SIS reports, Foreign Office telegrams and General Staff assessments—that Gorsky complained there was far too much to transmit in cipher.[16]

During 1941 London was easily the NKVD's most productive legal residency. According to the Centre's secret statistics, the residency forwarded to Moscow 7,867 classified political and diplomatic documents, 715 on military matters, 127 on economic affairs and 51 on British intelligence.[17] In addition it provided many other reports based on verbal information from the Five and other agents. It is difficult to avoid the conclusion that, until the Soviet Union entered the war, most of this treasure trove of high-grade intelligence was simply wasted. Stalin's understanding of British policy was so distorted by conspiracy theory that no amount of good intelligence was likely to enlighten him. Despite the fact that Britain and Germany were at war, he continued to believe—as he had done since the mid-1930s—that the British were plotting to embroil him with Hitler. His belief in a non-existent British conspiracy helped to blind him to the existence of a real German plot to invade the Soviet Union.

THE LEGAL RESIDENCY in the Berlin embassy resumed work in 1940 at about the same time as that in London. The NKVD had lost touch with its most important German agent, Arvid Harnack (codenamed CORSICAN), an official in the Economics Ministry, in June 1938. Early on the morning of September 17, 1940 contact was resumed by the newly arrived deputy Berlin resident, Aleksandr Mikhailovich Korotkov (alias "Erdberg," codenamed SASHA and DLINNY). The fact that Korotkov simply knocked on Harnack's door and arranged their next meeting in the Soviet embassy is evidence both of the decline in tradecraft caused by the liquidation of most experienced INO officers and of the fact that the Gestapo was at this stage of the war far less omnipresent than was widely supposed.

A fellow member of the German Communist underground, Reinhold Schönbrunn, later recalled:

Harnack . . . had little sense of humor, and we, his colleagues, did not feel at ease in his presence. There was something of the puritan in the man, something narrow and doctrinaire. But he was extremely devoted.

Like Burgess and Philby, Harnack was so highly motivated that he had carried on recruiting intelligence sources even during the two and a quarter years that he was out of contact with the Centre. Korotkov reported that Harnack was in touch with a loose network of about sixty people, although he could not "personally vouch for every person":

> CORSICAN's description of the way that they camouflage their operations is that, while not all of the members of the circle know one another, something of a chain exists. CORSICAN himself tries to remain in the background although he is at the heart of the organization.[18]

The most important of the sources cultivated by Harnack was a lieutenant in the Luftwaffe intelligence service, Harro Schulze-Boysen, codenamed STARSHINA ("Senior"), whose dynamic personality provided a striking contrast with that of the dour Harnack. Leopold Trepper, who knew them both, found Schulze-Boysen "as passionate and hot-headed as Arvid Harnack was calm and reflective." His tall, athletic frame, fair hair, blue eyes and Aryan features were far removed from the Gestapo stereotype of the Communist subversive. On March 15, 1941 the Centre ordered Korotkov to make direct contact with Schulze-Boysen and persuade him to form his own network of informants independent of Harnack. Schulze-Boysen needed little persuasion.[19]

Even a more experienced intelligence officer than Korotkov would have found Harnack, Schulze-Boysen and their groups of agents difficult to run. Both networks put themselves at increased risk by combining covert opposition to the Nazi regime with espionage for the Soviet Union. Schulze-Boysen and his glamorous wife, Libertas, held evening discussion groups for members of, and potential recruits to, an anti-Hitler underground. Libertas's many lovers added to the danger of discovery. As young resisters pasted anti-Nazi posters on Berlin walls, Schulze-Boysen stood guard over them dressed in his Luftwaffe uniform, with his pistol at the ready and the safety catch off.[20]

The most important intelligence provided by the Harnack and Schulze-Boysen networks in the first half of 1941 concerned Hitler's preparations for operation BARBAROSSA, the invasion of Russia. On June 16 Korotkov cabled the Centre that intelligence from the two networks indicated that "[a]ll of the military training by Germany in preparation for its attack on the Soviet Union is complete, and the strike may be expected at any time."[21] Similar intelligence arrived from NKVD sources as far afield as China and Japan. Later KGB historians counted "over a hundred" intelligence warnings of preparations for the German attack forwarded to Stalin by Fitin between January 1 and June 21.[22] Others came from military intelligence. All were wasted. Stalin was as resistant to good intelligence from Germany as he was to good intelligence from Britain.

The Great Terror had institutionalized the paranoid strain in Soviet intelligence assessment. Many NKVD officers shared, if usually to a less grotesque degree, Stalin's addiction to conspiracy theory. None the less, the main blame for the catastrophic failure to foresee the surprise attack on June 22 belongs to Stalin himself, who continued to act as his own chief intelligence analyst. Stalin did not merely ignore a series of wholly accurate warnings. He denounced many of those who provided them. His response to an NKVD report from Schulze-Boysen on June 16 was the obscene minute: "You can send your 'source' from the German air force to his whore of a mother! This is not a 'source' but a disinformer. J. Stalin."[23] Stalin also heaped abuse on the great GRU illegal Richard Sorge, who sent similar warnings from Tokyo, where he had penetrated the German embassy and seduced the ambassador's wife. Sorge's warnings of operation BARBAROSSA were dismissed by Stalin as disinformation from a lying "shit who has set himself up with some small factories and brothels in Japan."[24]

Stalin was much less suspicious of Adolf Hitler than of Winston Churchill, the evil genius who had preached an anti-Bolshevik crusade in the civil war twenty years earlier and had been plotting against the Soviet Union ever since. Behind many of the reports of impending German attack Stalin claimed to detect a disinformation campaign by Churchill designed to continue the long-standing British plot to embroil him with Hitler. Churchill's personal warnings to Stalin of preparations for BARBAROSSA only heightened his suspicions. From the intelligence reports sent by the London residency, Stalin almost certainly knew that until June 1941 the Joint Intelligence Committee (JIC), the body responsible for the main British intelligence assessments, did not believe that Hitler was preparing an invasion. It reported to Churchill as late as May 23 that "the advantages . . . to Germany of concluding an agreement with the USSR are overwhelming."[25] The JIC assessments were probably regarded by Stalin as further proof that Churchill's warnings were intended to deceive him. Stalin's deep suspicions of Churchill and of British policy in general were cleverly exploited by the Germans. As part of the deception operation which preceded BARBAROSSA, the Abwehr, German military intelligence, spread reports that rumors of an impending German attack were part of a British disinformation campaign.

By early June, reports of German troop movements toward the Soviet frontier were too numerous to be explained, even by Stalin, simply as British disinformation. At a private lunch in the German embassy in Moscow, the ambassador, Count von der Schulenberg, revealed that Hitler had definitely decided on invasion. "You will ask me why I am doing this," he said to the astonished Soviet ambassador to Germany, Vladimir Georgyevich Dekanozov. "I was raised in the spirit of Bismarck, who was always an opponent of war with Russia." Stalin's response was to tell the Politburo, "Disinformation has now reached ambassadorial level!"[26] On June 9, or soon afterwards, however, Stalin received a report that the German embassy had been sent orders by telegram to prepare for evacuation within a week and had begun burning documents in the basement.[27]

Though Stalin remained preoccupied by a non-existent British conspiracy, he increasingly began to suspect a German plot as well—though not one which aimed at surprise attack. As it became ever more difficult to conceal German troop movements, the Abwehr spread rumors that Hitler was preparing to issue an ultimatum, backed by some display of military might, demanding new concessions from the Soviet Union. It was this illusory threat of an ultimatum, rather than the real threat of German invasion, which increasingly worried Stalin during the few weeks and days before BARBAROSSA. He was not alone. A succession of foreign statesmen and journalists were also taken in by the planted rumors of a German ultimatum.[28]

Beria sought to protect his position as head of the NKVD by expressing mounting indignation at those inside and outside the NKVD who dared to send reports of preparations for a German invasion. On June 21, 1941 he ordered four NKVD officers who persisted in sending such reports to be "ground into labor camp dust." He wrote to Stalin on the same day with his characteristic mix of brutality and sycophancy:

> I again insist on recalling and punishing our ambassador to Berlin, Dekanozov, who keeps bombarding me with "reports" on Hitler's alleged preparations to attack the USSR. He has reported that this attack will start tomorrow . . . But I and my people, Iosif Vissarionovich, have firmly embedded in our memory your wise conclusion: Hitler is not going to attack us in 1941.[29]

Also in jeopardy for providing intelligence on the forthcoming German invasion was the senior INO officer Vasili Mikhailovich Zarubin, later chief resident in the United States.[30] Early in 1941 Zarubin was sent to China to meet Walter Stennes, German adviser to the Chinese nationalist leader Chiang Kai-shek. Stennes had once been deputy head of Hitler's stormtroopers, the Sturmabteilung, but developed a grudge against him after being sacked in 1931. In 1939 Stennes was approached by the NKVD Chungking residency and agreed to supply intelligence on Hitler. In February 1941 Zarubin reported to the Centre that a visitor from Berlin had secretly assured Stennes that "an attack against the USSR by the Germans . . . was being planned for the end of May this year" (the original date set by Hitler but later postponed).[31] Zarubin cabled on June 20: "The FRIEND [Stennes] repeats and confirms categorically—based on absolutely reliable information—that Hitler has completed preparations for war against the USSR."[32] Fitin outraged Beria by taking these and similar warnings seriously. An SVR official history concludes, probably correctly, "Only the outbreak of war saved P. M. Fitin from the firing squad."[33]

The devastating surprise achieved by the German invasion in the early hours of June 22 was made possible both by the nature of the Soviet intelligence system at the time and by the personal failings of the dictator who presided over it. In Whitehall the patient, if uninspired, examination of intelligence reports through the committee system eventually turned the belief that Germany saw the "overwhelming" advantages of a negotiated settlement with Russia into recognition that Hitler had decided to attack. In Moscow the whole system of intelligence assessment was dominated by the fearful sycophancy encapsulated in the formula "sniff out, suck up, survive," and by a culture of conspiracy theory.

Stalin had institutionalized both a paranoid strain and a servile political correctness which continued to distort in greater or lesser degree all intelligence assessment even after the outbreak of the Great Patriotic War in 1941. From 1942 to 1944 the Cambridge Five, probably the ablest group of Soviet wartime agents, were to be seriously suspected by the Centre of being double agents controlled by British intelligence simply because their voluminous and highly classified intelligence sometimes failed to conform to Stalin's conspiracy theories.[34] The responsibility, however, did not rest with Stalin alone. Some degree of distortion in intelligence assessment remained inherent in the autocratic nature of the Soviet system throughout the Cold War. The Centre always shrank from telling the Kremlin what it did not want to hear. The last head of KGB foreign intelligence, Leonid Shebarshin, confessed in 1992 that until Gorbachev introduced a measure of *glasnost,* the KGB "had to present its reports in a falsely positive light" which pandered to the predilections of the political leadership.[35]

IN THE EARLY months of the Great Patriotic War, while the German forces advancing into Russia were sweeping all before them, Stalin faced the even more terrifying prospect of a two-front war. Ribbentrop instructed the German embassy in Japan, "Do everything to rouse the Japanese to begin war against Russia . . . Our goal remains to shake hands with the Japanese on the Trans-Siberian Railway before the beginning of winter." Opinion in Tokyo was initially divided between those who favored the "northern solution" (war with the Soviet Union) and the supporters of the "southern solution" (war with Britain and the United States). Sorge, deeply distrusted by Stalin, sought to provide reassurance from Tokyo that the advocates of the "southern solution" were gaining the upper hand. But on October 18 Sorge was arrested and his spy ring rapidly rounded up.

SIGINT was more influential than Sorge in persuading Stalin that there would be no Japanese attack. Late in 1938 the combined NKVD/Fourth Department SIGINT unit had been broken up. The NKVD section moved into the former Hotel Select on Dzerzhinsky Street, where it concentrated on diplomatic traffic; most, but not all, military communications were the responsibility of the cryptanalysts of the GRU (successor to the Fourth Department). In February 1941 the NKVD cryptanalysts had been integrated into a new and enlarged Fifth (Cipher) Directorate, with, at its heart, a research section responsible for the attack on foreign codes and ciphers. The chief Japanese specialist in the section, Sergei Tolstoy, went on to become the most decorated Soviet cryptanalyst of the war, winning two Orders of Lenin. In the autumn of 1941, a group led by him replicated the success of American codebreakers a year earlier in breaking the main Japanese diplomatic cipher, codenamed by the Americans and since known to Western historians as PURPLE. The teetotal American codebreakers had celebrated their success by sending out for a case of Coca-Cola. Tolstoy is unlikely to have had time to celebrate at all. The Japanese diplomatic decrypts which he provided, however, were of enormous importance. Japan, they made clear, would not attack the Soviet Union.[36]

The reassurance about Japanese intentions provided by SIGINT enabled Stalin to shift to the west half the divisional strength of the Far Eastern Command. During

October and November 1941, between eight and ten rifle divisions, together with about a thousand tanks and a thousand aircraft, were flung into the fight against Germany. These forces, together with other Red Army divisions which had been held in reserve, may well have saved the Soviet Union from defeat. As Professor Richard Overy concludes in his study of the eastern front, "It was not the tough winter conditions that halted the German army [in December 1941] but the remarkable revival of Soviet military manpower after the terrible maulings of the summer and autumn."[37]

As well as providing reassurance that Japan did not propose to attack the Soviet Union, SIGINT also gave indications of its move towards war with Britain and the United States, though the diplomatic decrypts contained no mention of plans for a surprise attack on Pearl Harbor. A decrypted telegram from Tokyo to its Berlin embassy (probably copied to the Moscow embassy) on November 27, 1941, ten days before Pearl Harbor, instructed the ambassador:

> See Hitler and Ribbentrop, and explain to them in secret our relations with the United States . . . Explain to Hitler that the main Japanese efforts will be concentrated in the south and that we propose to refrain from deliberate operations in the north [against the Soviet Union].[38]

Soviet cryptanalysts, however, were unable to match the success of the British wartime SIGINT agency at Bletchley Park in breaking the main high-grade ciphers used by the German armed forces. They failed to do so partly for technological reasons. Soviet intelligence was unable to construct the powerful electronic "bombs," first constructed at Bletchley Park in 1940 to break the daily settings of the German Enigma machine cipher. It was even further from being able to replicate COLOSSUS, the world's first electronic computer used by Bletchley from 1943 to decrypt the *Geheimschreiber* messages (radio signals based on teleprinter impulses enciphered and deciphered automatically) which for the last two years of the war yielded more operational intelligence than the Enigma traffic. But there was a human as well as a technological explanation for the inferiority of Soviet to British SIGINT. The Soviet system would never have tolerated the remarkable infusion of unconventional youthful talent on which much of Bletchley's success was built. Alan Turing—the brilliant eccentric who buried his life savings (converted into silver ingots) in the Bletchley Woods, forgot where he had hidden them, but went on to be chiefly responsible for the invention of COLOSSUS—was one of many British cryptanalysts who would surely have been incapable of conforming to the political correctness demanded by the Stalinist system.[39] Some British ULTRA—the SIGINT derived from decrypting high-grade enemy traffic—was, however, passed officially to Moscow in a disguised form, and in an undisguised form by several Soviet agents.[40]

JUST AS THE KGB later sought to take refuge from the horrors of its Stalinist past by constructing a Leninist golden age of revolutionary purity, so it also sought to reinvent its record during the Great Patriotic War of 1941–5 as one of selfless heroism—best exemplified by its role in special operations and partisan warfare behind enemy lines. According to Pavel Anatolyevich Sudoplatov, head of the wartime NKVD Directorate for Special Tasks and Guerrilla Warfare, "This chapter in NKVD history is the only one that was not officially rewritten, since its accomplishments stood on their own merit and did not contain Stalinist crimes that had to be covered up."[41] In reality, the NKVD's wartime record, like the rest of its history, was extensively doctored.

Among the best-publicized examples of the NKVD's bravery behind enemy lines were the heroic deeds of its detachment in the Ukrainian Black Sea port of Odessa during the 907-day occupation by German and Romanian forces. The detachment based itself in the catacombs there, a maze of underground tunnels used to excavate sandstone for the construction of the elegant nineteenth-century buildings which still line many of Odessa's streets and boulevards. With over a thousand kilometers of unmapped tunnels as well as numerous entrances and exits, the catacombs made an almost ideal base for partisan warfare. In 1969, on the twenty-fifth anniversary of VE Day, a section of the catacombs on the outskirts of Odessa was opened as the Museum of Partisan Glory, which throughout the remainder of the Soviet era received over a million visitors a year.[42]

After the Second World War, however, the sometimes heroic story of the struggle to liberate Odessa from enemy occupation was hijacked by the KGB to refurbish its dubious wartime record. Pride of place in the Museum of Partisan Glory is given to the exploits of the NKVD detachment headed by Captain Vladimir Aleksandrovich Molodtsov, who was posthumously made a Hero of the Soviet Union and suffered the indignity of having his whole life transformed into that of a Stalinist plaster saint. The origins of Molodtsov's heroism were officially traced back to selfless devotion in overfulfilling his norms as a miner during the first Five Year Plan. "What a wonderful thing it is," he was said to have declared in 1930, "not to notice or watch the time during the working day, not to wait for the end of the shift but to seek to prolong it, to run behind the [coal] trolley, to be bathed in sweat and at the end of the shift to emerge victorious in fulfilling the plan!"[43]

The Museum of Partisan Glory contains a "reconstruction" of the NKVD detachment's underground headquarters, complete with dormitories, ammunition depot, workshops, fuel store, kitchen and meeting room with—inevitably—a portrait of Lenin (but not of Stalin) on the wall.[44] Nearby is a vertical shaft 17 meters long linking the headquarters to the surface, through which it received messages and food from its agents in Odessa. During the Soviet era numerous films, books, magazine and newspaper articles, many promoted by the KGB, celebrated the heroic feats of the NKVD detachment in holding at bay thousands of German and Romanian troops in Odessa before giving their lives in defense of the fatherland.

Mitrokhin owed his discovery of the true story of the catacombs to a colleague in the FCD Illegals Directorate S, who borrowed the multi-volume Odessa file and, when he returned it, told Mitrokhin he might find it interesting. The file began by recording the despatch of Molodtsov's detachment of six NKVD officers to Odessa shortly before it fell to the Germans in October 1941, with orders to establish an underground residency which would organize reconnaissance, sabotage and special operations behind the German lines. In Odessa they were joined by thirteen members of the local NKVD Special Department, commanded by Lieutenant V. A. Kuznetsov. According to the official version of events, the two groups held a Party/Komsomol meeting on the evening of October 15 immediately before going down into the catacombs to set up their base. What actually took place, according to the KGB file, was a raucous dinner party and heavy drinking which ended in a fight between the Moscow and Odessa NKVD detachments. The next day the two groups entered the catacombs still at daggers drawn, with Molodtsov and Kuznetsov each claiming overall command. Over the next nine months Muscovites and Odessans combined operations against the Germans and Romanians with internecine warfare among themselves.[45]

Molodtsov's end may well have been genuinely heroic. According to the official Soviet version, he was captured by the enemy in July 1942 but refused to beg for his life, courageously telling his captors, "We are in our own country and will not ask the enemy for mercy."[46] The rest of the history of the Odessa catacombs, however, was an NKVD horror story. After Molodtsov's execution, Kuznetsov disarmed his detachment and put them under guard inside the catacombs. All but one, N. F. Abramov, were executed on Kuznetsov's orders on charges of plotting against him. As conditions in the catacombs deteriorated, the Odessans then proceeded to fall out among themselves. The dwindling food supply became moldy; and, with their kerosene almost exhausted, the detachment was forced to live in semidarkness. On August 28 Kuznetsov shot one of his men, Molochny, for the theft of a piece of bread. On September 27 two others, Polschikov and Kovalchuk, were executed for stealing food and "lack of sexual discipline." Fearing that he might be shot next, Abramov killed Kuznetsov a month later. In his notebook, later discovered in the catacombs and preserved in the KGB Odessa file, Abramov wrote:

> The former head of the Third Special Department of the Odessa district of the NKVD, State Security Lieutenant V. A. Kuznetsov, was shot by me with two bullets in the temple in the underground "Mirror Factory" [the base in the catacombs] on October 21, 1942.

By this time, following several other deaths at the hands of the enemy, only three NKVD officers remained alive in the catacombs: Abramov, Glushchenko and Litvinov. Abramov and Glushchenko together killed Litvinov, then began to eye each other suspiciously in the semi-darkness.

Glushchenko wrote in his diary that Abramov wanted to surrender: "We are beaten. There is no victory to wait for. He told me not to be frightened of committing treason or being shot as he has friends in German intelligence." On February 18, 1943, apparently suffering from hallucinations, Glushchenko wrote, "[Abramov] was bending over, attending to his papers. I took my pistol from my belt and shot him in the back of the head." Over the next few months Glushchenko spent much of his time outside the catacombs in his wife's Odessa flat, finally abandoning the underground base on November 10, 1943. After the liberation of Odessa by the Red Army

in April 1945 Glushchenko returned with members of the Ukrainian NKVD to collect equipment and compromising papers from the catacombs, but was fatally
wounded when a grenade he picked up exploded in his hands.[47]

For almost twenty years, the Centre believed that no survivor of the Odessa catacombs remained to cast doubt on the heroic myth it had constructed. In 1963, however, the KGB was disconcerted to discover that Abramov had not been killed by
Glushchenko after all, but had escaped and was living in France. His father, who may
also have known the true story of the Odessa catacombs, was reported to have emigrated to the United States. Abramov's supposed widow, Nina Abramova, who had
been working in the KGB First Chief Directorate, was quietly transferred to another
job. The myth of the NKVD heroes of the Odessa catacombs was left undisturbed.[48]

According to statistics in KGB files, the NKVD ran a total of 2,222 "operational
combat groups" behind enemy lines during the Great Patriotic War.[49] Mitrokhin
found no realistic appraisal, however, of the effectiveness of partisan warfare. Contrary to the claims of post-war Soviet hagiographers, the combat groups seem only
rarely to have tied down German forces larger than themselves.[50] Because about half
of all partisans were NKVD personnel or Party officials, they were frequently
regarded with acute suspicion by the peasant population on whom they depended for
local support. The virtual collapse of partisan warfare in the western Ukraine, for
example, was due largely to the hostility of the inhabitants to the Party and the
NKVD. Though partisan warfare became more effective after Stalingrad, there were
important areas—notably Crimea and the steppes—where it never became a significant factor in the fighting on the eastern front.[51]

OUTSIDE EUROPE, THE NKVD's most successful attacks on German targets were
mounted by an illegal residency in Argentina,[52] headed by Iosif Romualdovich
Grigulevich (codenamed ARTUR), a veteran both of sabotage operations in the
Spanish Civil War and of the first attempt to assassinate Trotsky in Mexico City.[53] In
September 1941 an official Argentinian inquiry reached the hysterical conclusion,
endorsed by the Chamber of Deputies but rejected by the government, that the German ambassador was the head of over half a million Nazi stormtroopers operating
under cover in Latin America.[54] During the months after Pearl Harbor, Argentina
and Chile were the only Latin American states not to break off diplomatic relations
with Germany and Japan. The rumors of Nazi plots among Argentina's quarter of a
million German speakers, pro-German sympathies in its officer corps, and the presence of an Argentinian military purchasing mission in Berlin until 1944, helped to
persuade the Centre that Argentina was a major Nazi base. Though this belief was
greatly exaggerated, it was shared by OSS, the US wartime foreign intelligence
agency, which reported that Dr. Ramón Castillo, president of Argentina from 1941
to 1943, was in the pay of Hitler.[55] Such reports, passed on to the Centre by its agents
in OSS and the State Department,[56] doubtless reinforced Moscow's suspicions of
Nazi plots in Argentina.

After the outbreak of war the German merchant navy was unable to run the gauntlet of the Royal Navy and enter Argentinian ports. Grigulevich's residency, however,

reported in 1941 that copper, saltpetre, cotton and other strategic raw materials were being exported from Argentina in neutral vessels to Spain, whence they were being secretly transported overland through France to Germany. To disrupt this export trade, Grigulevich recruited a sabotage team of eight Communist dockyard workers and seamen, headed by a Polish immigrant, Feliks Klementyevich Verzhbitsky (code-named BESSER), who in December 1941 obtained a job as a blacksmith in the port of Buenos Aires. The first major exploit of Verzhbitsky's group was to burn down the German bookshop in Buenos Aires, which Grigulevich regarded as the main center of Nazi propaganda. Thereafter it concentrated on planting delayed-action incendiary devices on ships and in warehouses containing goods bound for Germany.[57] Grigulevich also ran smaller sabotage and intelligence networks in Chile and Uruguay. The approximately seventy agents in his far-flung illegal residency were to remain the basis of Soviet intelligence operations in Argentina, Uruguay and—to a lesser extent—Chile during the early years of the Cold War as well as the Second World War.[58]

Between the beginning of 1942 and the summer of 1944, according to statistics in KGB files, over 150 successful incendiary attacks were mounted by Grigulevich's agents against German cargoes, and an unspecified number of Spanish, Portuguese and Swedish vessels sunk. One, probably exaggerated, assessment by the Centre claims that the attacks succeeded early in 1944 in halting German exports from Buenos Aires.[59] A more serious problem for Germany than Soviet sabotage, however, was the change of government in Argentina. A military coup in the summer of 1943, followed by the uncovering of a Nazi espionage network, led Argentina to sever diplomatic relations with Germany in January 1944.[60]

For most of the war communications between Grigulevich's residency and the Centre were slow and spasmodic, depending on occasional couriers between Buenos Aires and the New York residency.[61] In the summer of 1944, shortly after the NKGB had established a legal residency in Uruguay, Grigulevich was summoned to Monte-video to give a detailed report on his intelligence operations, finances and agent net-works since the beginning of the Great Patriotic War. The Centre had become alarmed at the scale of his incendiary attacks on neutral shipping and feared that his cover might be blown. In September it ordered him to suspend sabotage operations and limit himself to intelligence collection in Argentina, Brazil and Chile.[62] Once instructed to stop work by Grigulevich, Verzhbitsky began making grenades for the underground Argentinian Communist Party but was seriously injured in October by an explosion in his workshop which cost him his left arm and the sight in one eye. Grigulevich reported that he behaved with great bravery during police investigation, sticking to a prepared cover story that a personal enemy had planted explosives on him, hidden in a packet of dried milk. In 1945 Verzhbitsky was smuggled out of prison and exfiltrated by the Argentinian Communist Party across the border into Uruguay, where he lived on a Party pension.[63]

Remarkable though they were, the sabotage operations run from Buenos Aires had no perceptible influence on the course of the Great Patriotic War. Once the alarmism of the summer of 1944 had died down, however, they greatly enhanced Grigulevich's reputation in the Centre as saboteur and assassin. His successes in wartime Argentina help to explain his later selection for the most important assassination mission of the Cold War.[64] By contrast, Grigulevich's chief saboteur, Verzhbitsky, was regarded as an embarrassment because of his disablement. His request to emigrate to the Soviet Union in 1946 was brusquely turned down. In 1955, however, when Verzhbitsky, by then completely blind, applied again, his application was accepted—possibly for fear that he might otherwise reveal his wartime role.[65] On arrival in the Soviet Union, Verzhbitsky was awarded an invalidity pension of 100 roubles a month, but his application for membership of the Soviet Communist Party was turned down.[66]

DESPITE INDIVIDUAL ACTS of heroism, the NKVD and NKGB (as its security and intelligence components were renamed in 1943) deserve to be remembered less for their bravery during the Second World War than for their brutality. After the forcible incorporation into the Soviet Union of eastern Poland in September 1939, followed by the Baltic states and Moldavia in the summer of 1940, the NKVD quickly moved in to liquidate "class enemies" and cow the populations into submission.[67] On June 25, 1941, three days after the beginning of Hitler's invasion, the NKVD was ordered to secure the rear of the Red Army by arresting deserters and enemy agents, protecting communications and liquidating isolated pockets of German troops. In August 1941 Soviet parachutists disguised as Germans landed among the villages of the Volga German Autonomous Region and asked to be hidden until the arrival of the Wehrmacht. When they were given shelter, the whole village was exterminated by the NKVD. All other Volga Germans, however loyal, were deported by the NKVD to Siberia and northern Kazakhstan, with enormous loss of life.[68]

When the Red Army took the offensive in 1943, the NKVD followed in its wake to mop up resistance and subversion. Beria reported proudly to Stalin at the end of the year:

> In 1943, the troops of the NKVD, who are responsible for security in the rear of the Active Red Army, in the process of cleaning up the territory liberated from the enemy, arrested 931,549 people for investigation. Of these, 582,515 were servicemen and 394,034 were civilians.

Of those arrested, 80,296 were "unmasked," in many cases wrongly, as spies, traitors, deserters, bandits and "criminal elements."

Stalin used the NKVD to punish and deport entire nations within the Soviet Union whom he accused of treachery: among them Chechens, Ingushi, Balkars, Karachai, Crimean Tartars, Kalmyks and Meskhetian Turks. In response to Stalin's instructions to reward "those who have carried out the deportation order in an exemplary manner," Beria replied:

> In accordance with your instructions, I submit a draft decree of the Presidium of the Supreme Soviet of the USSR on decorations and medals for the most outstanding participants in the operation involving the deportation of the

Chechens and Ingushes. 19,000 members of the NKVD, NKGB and Smersh took part, plus up to 100,000 officers of the NKVD forces . . .

As on this occasion, many of the NKVD and NKGB personnel decorated during the war received their medals not for valor against the enemy but for crimes against humanity.[69]

THE WARTIME RECORD of Soviet intelligence on the eastern front was patchy. Up to the end of 1942 the main espionage system providing intelligence from Nazi Germany and occupied Europe was a loosely coordinated GRU illegal network linked to the NKVD Harnack and Schulze-Boysen groups, codenamed the *Rote Kappelle* ("Red Orchestra") by the Abwehr. The "musicians" were the radio operators who sent coded messages to Moscow; the "conductor" was the Polish Jew Leopold Trepper, alias Jean Gilbert, known within the network as *le grand chef.* The *Rote Kappelle* had 117 agents: 48 in Germany, 35 in France, 17 in Belgium and 17 in Switzerland.[70] The network was gradually wound up during the later months of 1942 as German radio direction-finding tracked down the "musicians." Trepper himself was captured as he sat in a dentist's chair in occupied Paris on December 5. According to the Abwehr officer who arrested him, "For a second he was disturbed; then he said in perfect German, 'You did a fine job.'" Only Rado's GRU illegal residency in Switzerland, known as the Rote Drei after its three main radio transmitters, which was out of reach of German intelligence, continued work for another year until it was shut down by the Swiss.[71]

Though both Trepper and Rado were sentenced to ten years' imprisonment in Moscow after the war, it was later alleged by Soviet historians that intelligence from the *Rote Kappelle* had been of enormous assistance to the Red Army. In reality, intelligence did not begin to have a significant influence on Soviet military operations until after Trepper was arrested and most of his network wound up. Military intelligence failed to detect the sudden German turn south which captured Kiev in September 1941, and was taken aback by the intensity of the October assault on Moscow. The loss of Kharkov in May 1942 was due partly to the fact that the Stavka (a wartime combination of GHQ and high command) was expecting another attack on the capital. The Wehrmacht's move south in the summer again took the Stavka by surprise. Throughout the German advance to Stalingrad and the Caucasus, Soviet forces were constantly confused about where the next blow would fall. When the Red Army encircled Axis forces at Stalingrad in November 1942, it believed it had trapped 85,000 to 90,000 troops; in reality it had surrounded three times as many.[72]

The NKVD's main role at Stalingrad was less in providing good intelligence than in enforcing a ferocious discipline within the Red Army. About 13,500 Soviet soldiers were executed for "defeatism" and other breaches of military discipline in the course of the battle, usually by a squad from the NKVD Special Detachment. Before execution, most were ordered to strip so that their uniform and boots could be reused. The NKVD postal censorship seized on any unorthodox or politically incorrect comment in soldiers' letters to their families as evidence of treachery. A lieutenant who wrote "German aircraft are very good . . . Our anti-aircraft people shoot down only very few of them" was, inevitably, condemned as a traitor. In the 62nd Army alone, in the first half of October 1942, the NKVD claimed that "military secrets were divulged in 12,747 letters."[73] The great victory at Stalingrad, sealed by the surrender of the German Field Marshal Friedrich Paulus, twenty-two generals and 91,000 troops early in 1943, was achieved in spite of, rather than because of, the contribution of the NKVD.

Stalingrad was followed by a major improvement in the quality of Soviet military intelligence on the eastern front, made possible in part by massive supplies of radio equipment from the Americans and the British.[74] At the end of 1942 the Stavka established special-purpose radio battalions, each equipped with eighteen to twenty radio-intercept receivers and four direction-finding sets. The result, according to a Soviet historian given access to the battalions' records, was "a qualitative jump in the development of radio-electronic combat in the Soviet army." Though Soviet crypt-analysts lacked the state-of-the-art technology which enabled Bletchley Park to decrypt high-grade Enigma and Geheimschreiber messages, they made major advances during 1943—reluctantly assisted by German cipher personnel captured at Stalingrad—in direction-finding, traffic analysis and the breaking of lower-grade hand ciphers. In 1942–3 they also had the benefit of Luftwaffe Enigma decrypts supplied by an agent inside Bletchley Park.

All these improvements were evident during the battle of Kursk in the summer of 1943 when the Red Army defeated the last great German offensive on the eastern front. Intelligence reports captured by the Wehrmacht from the Red Army during the battle revealed that Soviet SIGINT had located the positions and headquarters of the 6th, 7th and 11th Panzer Divisions, II and XIII Panzer Corps, and Second Army HQ. Aerial reconnaissance before and during Kursk was also on a larger scale and more successful than ever before.[75]

Victory at Kursk opened the way to an almost continuous advance by the Red Army on the eastern front which was to end with Marshal Zhukov accepting the surrender of Berlin in May 1945. With a four-to-one superiority in men over the Wehrmacht, large amounts of military equipment from its Western allies and growing dominance in the air, the Red Army, though suffering enormous losses, proved unstoppable. In the course of its advance, the Red Army sometimes captured lists of the daily settings for periods of up to a month of the Wehrmacht's Enigma machines, as well as some of the machines and their operators. During the final stages of the war these captures sometimes enabled Soviet cryptanalysts to decrypt spasmodically a still unknown number of Enigma messages.[76]

Despite the improvements after Stalingrad, however, the quality of Soviet intelligence on the eastern front—in particular the SIGINT—never compared with the intelligence on Germany available to their Western allies. The ULTRA intelligence provided to British and American commanders was, quite simply, the best in the history of warfare. The Soviet Union's most striking intelligence successes during the Great Patriotic War, by contrast, were achieved not against its enemies but against its allies in the wartime Grand Alliance: Britain and the United States.

SEVEN

THE GRAND ALLIANCE

For most of the inter-war years the United States had ranked some way behind Britain as a target for INO operations. Even in the mid-1930s the main Soviet espionage networks in the United States were run by the Fourth Department (Military Intelligence, later renamed the GRU) rather than by the NKVD. Fourth Department agents included a series of young, idealistic high-flyers within the federal government, among them: Alger Hiss and Julian Wadleigh, both of whom entered the State Department in 1936; Harry Dexter White of the Treasury Department; and George Silverman, a government statistician who probably recruited White.[1] Like the Cambridge Five, the Washington moles saw themselves as secret warriors in the struggle against fascism. Wadleigh wrote later:

> When the Communist International represented the only world force effectively resisting Nazi Germany, I had offered my services to the Soviet underground in Washington as one small contribution to help stem the fascist tide.[2]

The main NKVD operations in the United States during the mid-1930s were run by an illegal residency established in 1934 under the former Berlin resident, Boris Bazarov (codenamed NORD), with Iskhak Abdulovich Akhmerov (YUNG), a Soviet Tartar, as his deputy.[3] Bazarov was remembered with affection by Hede Massing, an Austrian agent in his residency, as the warmest personality she had encountered in the NKVD. On the anniversary of the October Revolution in 1935 he sent her fifty long-stemmed red roses with a note which read:

> Our lives are unnatural, but we must endure it for [the sake of] humanity. Though we cannot always express it, our little group is bound by love and consideration for one another. I think of you with great warmth.

Though Akhmerov, by contrast, struck Massing as a "Muscovite automaton," he was less robotic than he appeared.[4] Unknown to Massing, Akhmerov was engaged in a passionate love affair with his assistant, Helen Lowry, the cousin of the American Communist Party leader, Earl Browder, and—unusually—gained permission from the Centre to marry her.[5]

Bazarov's and Akhmerov's recruits included three agents in the State Department: ERIKH, KIY and "19."[6] Probably the most important, as well as the only one of the three who can be clearly identified, was agent "19," Laurence Duggan, who later became chief of the Latin American Division.[7] To Hede Massing, Duggan seemed "an extremely tense, high-strung, intellectual young man." His recruitment took some time, not least because Alger Hiss was simultaneously attempting to recruit him for the Fourth Department. In April 1936 Bazarov complained to the Centre that the "persistent Hiss" showed no sign of abandoning the attempt.[8] A year later, in the midst of the Moscow show trials, Duggan told Akhmerov that he was afraid that, if he "collaborated" with Soviet intelligence, he might be exposed by a Trotskyite traitor. By the beginning of 1938, however, Duggan was supplying Akhmerov with State Department documents which were photographed in the illegal residency and then returned. In March Duggan reported that his close friend Sumner Welles, undersecretary at the State Department from 1938 to 1945, had told him he was becoming too attracted to Marxism and had given him a friendly warning about his left-wing acquaintances.[9] Duggan's future in the State Department, however, seemed as bright as that of Donald Maclean in the Foreign Office.

The Centre also saw a bright future for Michael Straight (codenamed NOMAD and NIGEL), the wealthy young American recruited shortly before his graduation from Cambridge University in 1937.[10] Its optimism sprang far more from Straight's family connections than from any evidence of his enthusiasm for a career as a secret agent. Straight's job hunt after his return to the United States began at the top—over tea at the White House with Franklin and Eleanor Roosevelt. With some assistance from Mrs. Roosevelt, he obtained a temporary, unpaid assignment in the State Department early in 1938. Soon afterwards, he received a phone call from Akhmerov, who passed on "greetings from your friends at Cambridge University" and invited him to dinner at a local restaurant. Akhmerov introduced himself as "Michael Green," then ordered a large meal. Straight watched as he ate:

> He was dark and stocky, with broad lips and a ready smile. His English was good; his manner was affable and easy. He seemed to be enjoying his life in America.

Ahkmerov seemed to accept that it would be some time before Straight had access to important documents, but was evidently prepared to wait. Before paying the bill, he delivered a brief lecture on international relations. Straight was "too stunned to think clearly." Though Straight claims that he was "unwilling to become a Soviet agent in the Department of State," he plainly did not say so to Akhmerov. The two men "parted as friends" and Straight agreed to continue their meetings.[11]

With the approach of war in Europe, the Centre's interest in the United States steadily increased. In 1938 the NKVD used the defection of the main Fourth Department courier, Whittaker Chambers, as a pretext for taking over most of the military intelligence agent network, with the notable exception of Alger Hiss.[12] In the United States, as elsewhere, however, the expansion of NKVD operations was disrupted by the hunt for imaginary "enemies of the people." Ivan Andreyevich Morozov (codenamed YUZ and KIR), who was stationed in the New York legal residency in 1938–9, sought to prove his zeal to the Centre by denouncing the Resident, Pyotr Davidovich Gutzeit (codenamed NIKOLAI), and most of his colleagues as secret Trotskyists.[13] In 1938 both Gutzeit and Bazarov, the legal and illegal residents, were recalled and shot.[14] Morozov's denunciation of the next legal resident, Gayk Badalovich Ovakimyan (codenamed GENNADI), was less successful and may have prompted Morozov's own recall in 1939.[15]

Bazarov was succeeded as illegal resident by his former deputy, Iskhak Akhmerov, who henceforth controlled most political intelligence operations in the United States.[16] Mitrokhin noted the codenames of eight rather diverse individuals in whom the Centre seemed to place particularly high hopes on the eve of the Second World War:[17] Laurence Duggan (agent "19," later FRANK) in the State Department;[18] Michael Straight (NIGEL), also in the State Department; Martha Dodd Stern (LIZA), daughter of the former US ambassador to Germany, William E. Dodd, and wife of the millionaire Alfred Kaufman Stern (also a Soviet agent); Martha's brother, William E. Doss, Jr. (PRESIDENT), who had run unsuccessfully for Congress as a Democrat and still had political ambitions; Harry Dexter White in the Treasury Department (KASSIR, later JURIST); an agent codenamed MORIS (probably John Abt) in the Justice Department";[19] Boris Morros (FROST), the Hollywood producer of Laurel and Hardy's *Flying Deuces* and other box-office hits;[20] Mary Wolf Price (codenamed KID and DIR), an undeclared Communist who was secretary to the well-known columnist Walter Lippmann; and Henry Buchman (KHOSYAIN, "Employer"), owner of a women's fashion salon in Baltimore.[21]

In August 1939, however, political intelligence operations in the United States, as in Britain, were partially disrupted by the signing of the Nazi–Soviet Pact. Laurence Duggan broke off contact with Akhmerov in protest.[22] Others who had serious doubts included Michael Straight. At a meeting in October in a restaurant below Washington's Union Station, Akhmerov tried to reassure him. "Great days are approaching!" he declared. With the beginning of the Second World War, revolution would spread like wildfire across Germany and France.[23] Straight was unimpressed and failed to attend the next meeting.[24] Duggan and Straight are unlikely to have been the only agents to break contact, at least temporarily, with the NKVD.

Further disruption to NKVD operations in the United States followed Akhmerov's recall, soon after his last meeting with Straight, to Moscow where he was accused by Beria of treasonable dealings with enemies of the people.[25] Though, for unknown reasons, the charges were dropped, Akhmerov was placed in the NKVD reserve and remained under suspicion for the next two years while his record was thoroughly checked. For the first time, the center of NKVD operations in the United States was moved, after Akhmerov's recall, to the legal residency headed by Gayk Ovakimyan, later known to the FBI as the "wily Armenian." Ovakimyan found himself terribly overworked, all the more so since he was also expected to take an active part in the complex preparations for Trotsky's assassination in Mexico City. He would sometimes return home exhausted after meeting as many as ten agents in a single day.[26]

Ovakimyan's main successes were in scientific and technological (S&T), rather than political, intelligence. He was unusual among INO officers in holding a science doctorate from the MVTU (Moscow Higher Technical School) and, since 1933, had operated under cover as an engineer at Amtorg (American–Soviet Trading Corporation) in New York. In 1940 he enrolled as a graduate student at a New York chemical institute to assist him in identifying potential agents.[27] Ovakimyan was the first to demonstrate the enormous potential for S&T in the United States. In 1939 alone NKVD operations in the United States obtained 18,000 pages of technical documents, 487 sets of designs and 54 samples of new technology.[28]

Ovakimyan was probably also the first to suggest using an INO officer, under cover as an exchange student, to penetrate the Massachusetts Institute of Technology. The first such "student," Semyon Markovich Semyonov (codenamed TVEN), entered MIT in 1938. The scientific contacts which he made over the next two years, before changing his cover in 1940 to that of an Amtorg engineer, helped to lay the basis for the remarkable wartime expansion of S&T collection in the United States. One of his colleagues in the New York residency was struck by Semyonov's "large eyes which, while he was talking to somebody, [revolved] like parabolic antennae."[29] By April 1941 the total NKVD agent network in the United States numbered 221, of whom forty-nine were listed in NKVD statistics as "engineers" (probably a category which included a rather broad range of scientists).[30] In the same month the Centre for the first time established separate departments in its major residencies to specialize in scientific and technological intelligence operations (later known as Line X), a certain sign of their increasing priority.[31]

According to an SVR official history, the sheer number of agents with whom Ovakimyan was in contact "blunted his vigilance." In May 1941 he was caught by the FBI in the act of receiving documents from agent OCTANE, briefly imprisoned, freed on bail and allowed to leave the country in July.[32] But for the remarkably lax security of the Roosevelt administration, the damage to NKVD operations might have been very much worse than the arrest of Ovakimyan. On September 2, 1939, the day after the outbreak of war in Europe, Whittaker Chambers had told much of what he knew about Soviet espionage in the United States to Adolf Berle, Assistant Secretary of State and President Roosevelt's adviser on internal security. Immediately afterwards, Berle drew up a memorandum for the President which listed Alger Hiss, Harry Dexter White and the other leading Soviet agents for whom Chambers had acted as courier. One of those on the list was a leading presidential aide, Lauchlin Currie (mistranscribed by Berle as Lockwood Curry). Roosevelt, however, was not interested. He seems to have dismissed the whole idea of espionage rings within his administration as absurd. Equally remarkable, Berle simply pigeon-holed his own report. He did not even send a copy to the FBI until the Bureau requested it in 1943.[33]

IMMEDIATELY AFTER THE Japanese attack on Pearl Harbor and Hitler's declaration of war on the United States in December 1941, Vassili Zarubin (alias Zubilin, codenamed MAKSIM) was appointed legal resident in New York. Already deeply suspicious of British commitment to the defeat of Nazi Germany, Stalin also had doubts about American resolve. He summoned Zarubin before his departure and told him that his main assignment in the United States was to watch out for attempts by Roosevelt and "US ruling circles" to negotiate with Hitler and sign a separate peace. As resident in New York, based in the Soviet consulate, Zarubin was also responsible for subresidencies in Washington, San Francisco, and Latin America.[34] Though fragmentary, the evidence suggests that Stalin continued to take a direct personal interest in overseeing intelligence operations against his allies.

A brief official SVR biography portrays Zarubin's wartime record in New York (and later in Washington) as one of unblemished brilliance.[35] In reality, his abrasive personality and foul-mouthed behavior caused immediate uproar. Zarubin's preference for the operations officers whom he brought with him (among them his wife, Yelizaveta Yulyevna Zarubina)[36] and his unconcealed contempt for existing residency staff led to open rebellion. Two of the operations officers whom he insulted, Vasili Dmitryevich Mironov and Vasili Georgyevich Dorogov, went to the remarkable lengths of reporting "his crudeness, general lack of manners, use of street language and obscenities, carelessness in his work, and repugnant secretiveness" to the Centre, and asking for his recall along with his almost equally unpopular wife. Feuding within the residency continued throughout the Second World War.[37]

Zarubin's recruitment strategy was simple and straightforward. He demanded that the leaders of the Communist Party of the United States (CPUSA) identify supporters and sympathizers in government establishments suitable for work as agents.[38] When Zarubin arrived in New York, the CPUSA leader Earl Browder (codenamed RULEVOY—"Helmsman") was serving a prison sentence for using a false passport during his frequent secret journeys to the Soviet Union. His first contact was therefore with Eugene Dennis (born Francis X. Waldron, codenamed RYAN), a Moscow-trained Comintern agent who later succeeded Browder as CPUSA general secretary. Dennis reported that a number of Communists (mostly secret Party members) were joining the first professional American foreign intelligence agency, the Office of the Coordinator of Information, reorganized in June 1942 as the Office of Strategic Services (OSS). Shortly before the foundation of OSS, Browder left prison to resume the Party leadership. He was, Dennis told Moscow, "in a splendid mood."[39]

Among the first Soviet agents to penetrate OSS was Duncan Chaplin Lee (codenamed KOCH), who became personal assistant to its head, General "Wild Bill" Donovan. Donovan had a relaxed attitude to the recruitment of Communists. "I'd put Stalin on the OSS payroll," he once said, "if I thought it would help us defeat Hitler." Throughout the Second World War the NKVD knew vastly more about OSS than OSS knew about the NKVD.[40]

Browder's recruitment leads also included foreign Communists and fellow travelers who had taken refuge in the United States. Among the most important was the French radical politician Pierre Cot, six times Minister of Air and twice Minister of Commerce in the short-lived governments of the prewar Third Republic. Cot had probably been recruited by the NKVD in the mid-1930s, but seems to have drifted out of touch during the chaotic period which followed the purge of much of Soviet foreign intelligence and had condemned the signing of the Nazi–Soviet Pact. Rebuffed by General Charles de Gaulle, the leader of the Free French after the fall of France in 1940, Cot spent the next few years in the United States.[41] In November Browder reported to Moscow: "Cot wants the leaders of the Soviet Union to know of his willingness to perform whatever mission we might choose, for which purpose he is even prepared to break faith with his own position."[42] Probably a month or so after his arrival in New York, Zarubin approached Cot and, with his habitual brusqueness, pressed Cot to begin active work as a Soviet agent forthwith. Cot's KGB file records that he was taken aback by the peremptory nature of Zarubin's summons and insisted that one of the leaders of the French Communist Party exiled in Moscow give his approval.[43] On July 1 Zarubin reported to the Centre "the signing on of Pierre Cot" as agent DAEDALUS.[44] In 1944 Cot was to be sent on a three-month mission to Moscow on behalf of de Gaulle's provisional government. He concluded the report on his mission: "Liberty declines unceasingly under capitalism and rises unceasingly under socialism."[45]

Though the Centre was plainly impressed by the quality of Communist recruits talent-spotted by Browder, it cautioned Zarubin against over-reliance on them:

> We permit the use of the Communist [Party members'] illegal intelligence capabilities . . . as a supplement to the Residency's operations, but it would be a mistake to turn these capabilities into the main basis of operations.[46]

At almost the same moment in December 1941 when Zarubin arrived in New York as legal resident, Iskhak Akhmerov (successively codenamed YUNG and ALBERT) returned to reestablish the illegal residency, also based in New York, which he had been ordered to abandon two years earlier. Though he had previously used Turkish and Canadian identity documents, on this occasion he carried a doctored US passport which he had acquired in 1938.[47] Unlike Zarubin, Akhmerov avoided all contact with Browder—despite the fact that his wife and assistant, Helen Lowry (codenamed MADLEN and ADA), was Browder's niece.[48] In March 1942 the Akhmerovs moved from New York to Baltimore, a more convenient location from which to run agents based in Washington. There Akhmerov, whose stepfather had been a furrier, opened a fur and clothes business in partnership with a local Soviet agent, KHOSYAIN, to give himself a cover occupation.[49]

Michael Straight (NIGEL), in whom Akhmerov had placed such high hopes before the Second World War, refused to resume work as a Soviet agent. Straight had one last meeting with Akhmerov in Washington early in 1942, declined any further meeting, shook hands and said goodbye.[50] Most other pre-war agents, however, were successfully reactivated, among them Laurence Duggan (FRANK)[51] and Harry Dexter White (JURIST).[52] Henry Wallace, vice-president during Roosevelt's third term of office (1941 to 1945), said later that if the ailing Roosevelt had died during that period and he had become president, it had been his intention to make Duggan his Secretary of State and White his Secretary of the Treasury.[53] The fact that Roosevelt survived three months into an unprecedented fourth term in the White House, and replaced Wallace with Harry Truman as vice-president in January 1945, deprived Soviet intelligence of what would have been its most spectacular success in penetrating a major Western government. The NKVD succeeded none the less in penetrating all the most sensitive sections of the Roosevelt administration.

Akhmerov's most productive Washington network was a group of Communists and fellow travelers with government jobs run by Nathan Gregory Silvermaster (successively codenamed PAL and ROBERT), a statistician in the Farm Security Administration, later seconded to the Board of Economic Warfare.[54] "Greg" Silvermaster retained the untarnished idealism of the revolutionary dream. A chronic sufferer from bronchial asthma, which often left him gasping for breath, he believed that, "My time is strictly limited, and when I die I want to feel that at least I have had some part in building a decent life for those who come after me."[55]

Akhmerov believed, probably correctly, that, despite the security risks involved in Silvermaster's unorthodox tradecraft, he was able to obtain far more intelligence from his increasing number of sources than if each of them was run individually by a Soviet controller. Silvermaster himself disdained the NKVD's bureaucratic "orthodox methods." Though most of his sources must have been aware of the ultimate destination of their intelligence, the network was run under what Akhmerov termed "the Communist Party flag." Informants regarded themselves as helping the CPUSA, which would in turn assist its Soviet comrades.[56]

To limit the security risks, Akhmerov placed two cut-outs between himself and the Silvermaster group. The first was a courier, Elizabeth Bentley (codenamed MIRNA, then, more condescendingly, UMNITSA—"Good Girl"), a Vassar graduate who in 1938, at the age of thirty, had been persuaded to break her visible links with the CPUSA in order to work for the NKVD. Every fortnight Bentley collected classified documents microfilmed by Silvermaster and his wife in her knitting bag. She reported not to Akhmerov himself but to another Soviet illegal in his residency, Jacob Golos (ZVUK—"Sound"), whom she knew as "Timmy." Golos broke NKVD rules by seducing Bentley during a New York snowstorm. According to Bentley's enthusiastic description of the seduction, she felt herself "float away into an ecstasy that seemed to have no beginning and no end." Encouraged by Golos's unprofessional example, Bentley mixed friendship and espionage in a way which would have horrified the Centre. Each Christmas she used NKVD funds to buy carefully chosen presents, ranging from whiskey to lingerie, for the agents in Silvermaster's group. These, she said later, were "the good old days—the days when we worked together as good comrades."[57]

Like Zarubin's, Akhmerov's illegal residency recruited non-American as well as American agents. Among the most important was the British journalist and wartime intelligence officer Cedric Belfrage (codenamed CHARLIE), who joined British Security Coordination (BSC) in New York shortly after the United States entered the war.[58] Directed by the SIS head of station, Sir William Stephenson, for much of the war, BSC handled intelligence liaison with the Americans on behalf of MI5 and SOE as well as SIS.[59] Belfrage volunteered his services to Soviet intelligence. Like a number of other American agents in the United States, he made his initial approach to Earl Browder, who passed him on to Golos.[60] Given the unprecedented number of wartime secrets exchanged by the British and American intelligence communities, Belfrage had access to an unusually wide range of intelligence.

The rolls of microfilm forwarded by Akhmerov's illegal residency to the Centre via the legal residency in New York increased almost four-fold in the space of a year, from fifty-nine in 1942 to 211 in 1943. Zarubin none the less regarded Akhmerov's refusal to have direct dealings with the CPUSA leadership and his roundabout methods of controlling the Silvermaster group as feeble and long-winded. Akhmerov himself, Zarubin complained, had a "dry and distrustful" manner—which may well have been true as far as his relations with Zarubin were concerned. Zarubin had a much higher opinion of Akhmerov's wife, Helen Lowry, whom he regarded as more quick-witted, more business-like in manner, and—because of her American upbringing—better able to make direct contact with US agents.[61]

THERE WAS THUS a breathtaking gulf between the intelligence supplied to Stalin on the United States and that available to Roosevelt on the Soviet Union.[62] Whereas the Centre had penetrated every major branch of Roosevelt's administration, OSS—like SIS—had not a single agent in Moscow. At the Tehran Conference of the Big Three in November 1943—the first time Stalin and Roosevelt had met—vastly superior intelligence gave Stalin a considerable negotiating advantage. Though there is no precise indication of what intelligence reports and documents were shown to Stalin before the summit, there can be no doubt that he was remarkably well briefed. He was almost certainly informed that Roosevelt had come to Tehran determined to do his utmost to reach agreement with Stalin—even at the cost of offending Churchill. FDR gave proof of his intentions as soon as he arrived. He declined Churchill's proposal that they should meet privately before the conference began, but accepted Stalin's pressing invitation that—allegedly on security grounds—he should stay at a building in the Soviet embassy compound rather than at the US legation. It seems not to have occurred to Roosevelt that the building was, inevitably, bugged, and that every word uttered by himself and his delegation would be recorded, transcribed and regularly reported to Stalin.[63]

Stalin must also have welcomed the fact that Roosevelt was bringing to Tehran his closest wartime adviser, Harry Hopkins, but leaving behind his Secretary of State, Cordell Hull. Hopkins had established a remarkable reputation in Moscow for taking the Russians into his confidence. Earlier in the year he had privately warned the Soviet embassy in Washington that the FBI had bugged a secret meeting at which Zarubin (apparently identified by Hopkins only as a member of the embassy) had passed money to Steve Nelson, a leading member of the US Communist underground.[64] Information sent to Moscow by the New York residency on the talks between Roosevelt and Churchill in May 1943 had also probably come from Hopkins.[65] There is plausible but controversial evidence that, in addition to passing confidences to the Soviet ambassador, Hopkins sometimes used Akhmerov as a back channel to Moscow, much as the Kennedys later used the GRU officer Georgi Bolshakov. Hopkins's confidential information so impressed the Centre that, years later, some KGB officers boasted that he had been a Soviet agent.[66] These boasts were far from the truth. Hopkins was an American patriot with little sympathy for the Soviet system. But he was deeply impressed by the Soviet war effort and convinced that,

"Since Russia is the decisive factor in the war she must be given every assistance and every effort must be made to obtain her friendship."[67] "Chip" Bohlen, who acted as American interpreter, later described Hopkins's influence on the President at the Tehran summit as "paramount."[68]

It was at Tehran, Churchill later claimed, that he realized for the first time how small the British nation was:

> There I sat with the great Russian bear on one side of me, with paws out-stretched, and on the other side the great American buffalo, and between the two sat the poor little English donkey . . .[69]

Despite the closeness of the British-American wartime "special relationship" and Roosevelt's friendship with Churchill, his priority at Tehran was to reach agreement with Stalin. He told his old friend, Frances Perkins, the Secretary of Labor, how

> Winston got red and scowled, and the more he did so, the more Stalin smiled. Finally, Stalin broke out into a deep, hearty guffaw, and for the first time in three days I saw light. I kept it up until Stalin was laughing with me, and it was then that I called him "Uncle Joe." He would have thought me fresh the day before, but that day he laughed and came over and shook my hand.
>
> From that time on our relations were personal . . . We talked like men and brothers.[70]

In the course of the Tehran Conference, Hopkins sought out Churchill privately at the British embassy, and told him that Stalin and Roosevelt were adamant that Operation OVERLORD, the British-American cross-Channel invasion of occupied France, must take place the following spring, and that British opposition must cease. Churchill duly gave way. The most important political concession to Stalin was British-American agreement to give the post-war Soviet Union its 1941 frontier, thus allowing Stalin to recover his territorial gains ill-gotten under the Nazi–Soviet Pact: eastern Poland, the Baltic states and Moldova. The Polish government-in-exile in London was not consulted.

Stalin returned to Moscow in high spirits. The United States and Britain seemed to have recognized, as a Russian diplomat put it privately, Russia's "right to establish friendly governments in the neighboring countries."[71] Roosevelt's willingness to go so far to meet Stalin's wishes at Tehran had derived chiefly from his deep sense of the West's military debt to the Soviet Union at a time when the Red Army was bearing the overwhelming brunt of the war with Germany. But there is equally no doubt that Stalin's negotiating success was greatly assisted by his knowledge of the cards in Roosevelt's hand.[72]

Despite the considerable success of the legal and illegal American residencies in penetrating the Roosevelt administration, however, they had failed totally in one important respect. Part of Zarubin's original brief from the Centre had been to recruit agents from among the large German-American community who could be used against Germany. In the end he recruited not a single one. When asked to explain this omission, he told the Centre that most German-Americans were Jews and therefore unsuitable.[73] The Centre, like Zarubin, had become so engrossed in the intelligence offensive against its allies that it appears to have judged leniently his failure against the enemy.

WARTIME INTELLIGENCE GATHERING continued to expand in Britain as well as the United States. At the beginning of 1942 a second legal residency began to operate in London under Ivan Andreyevich Chichayev (JOHN) alongside that of Anatoli Gorsky (successively HENRY and VADIM). Unlike Gorsky, who remained in charge of the agent network, Chichayev announced his presence in London to the authorities and was responsible for intelligence liaison with both the British and allied governments-in-exile.[74] Chichayev also ran an agent network of émigré officials from central and eastern Europe who kept him informed of British negotiations with the Polish government-in-exile, the Czechoslovak president, Edvard Bene˘s, King Peter of Yugoslavia and his prime minister, Ivan Subăs.[75]

The Cambridge Five, meanwhile, continued to generate a phenomenal amount of intelligence. For 1942 alone Maclean's documents filled more than forty-five volumes in the Centre archives.[76] Philby too was providing large quantities of highly classified files. Since September 1941 he had been working in Section V (Counter-intelligence) of SIS. Though Section V was then located in St. Albans, rather than in SIS London headquarters at Broadway Buildings, it had the advantage of being next door to the registry which housed SIS archives. Philby spent some time cultivating the archivist, Bill Woodfield, with whom he shared a common appreciation of pink gin. As Philby later recalled, "This friendly connection paid off."[77] Over a period of months, Philby borrowed the operational files of British agents working abroad and handed them to Gorsky in batches to be photographed.[78] Early in April 1942 the Centre completed a lengthy analysis of the SIS records removed by Philby up to the end of the previous year. Though praising SÖHNCHEN for "systematically sending a lot of interesting material," it was puzzled that this material appeared to show that SIS had no agent network in Russia and was conducting only "extremely insignificant" operations against the Soviet Union. Centre analysts had two reasons for disputing these entirely accurate conclusions. First, though at least partly aware that the evidence used to convict some of their liquidated predecessors of working for British intelligence was fraudulent, they remained convinced that SIS had been conducting major operations against the Soviet Union, using "their most highly skilled agents," throughout the 1930s. The reality—that SIS had not even possessed a Moscow station—was, so far as the Centre was concerned, literally unbelievable. The Centre refused to believe that the Soviet Union was a smaller priority for British intelligence (which was, in truth, almost wholly geared to the war effort) than Britain was for Soviet intelligence:

If the HOTEL [SIS] has recruited a hundred agents in Europe over the past few years, mainly from countries occupied by the Germans, there can be no doubt that our country gets no less attention.[79]

Such reports merely echoed Stalin's own acute suspicions of his British allies.

The intelligence from the London residency during the first year of the Great Patriotic War which ultimately had the greatest impact on both Stalin and the Centre came from Cairncross. On September 25, 1941 Gorsky telegraphed Moscow:

> I am informing you very briefly about the contents of a most secret report of the Government Committee on the development of uranium atomic energy to produce explosive material which was submitted on September 24, 1941 to the War Cabinet.[80]

The secret committee which produced the report was the Scientific Advisory Committee, chaired by Lord Hankey, whose codename BOSS reflects the fact he was Cairncross's employer.[81] The report which Cairncross gave Gorsky was the first to alert the Centre to British plans to build the atomic bomb.[82]

Vitally important though that report, and others on the atomic bomb despatched from London over the next few months, proved to be, they had a delayed impact in Moscow. When Cairncross's first report arrived, Stalin and the Stavka were preoccupied by the German advance which in October 1941 forced them to evacuate the capital. It was not until March 1942 that Beria sent Stalin a full assessment of British atomic research. The British high command, he reported, was now satisfied that the theoretical problems of constructing an atomic bomb had been "fundamentally solved," and Britain's best scientists and major companies were collaborating on the project.[83] At Beria's suggestion, detailed consultations with Soviet scientists followed over the next few months.[84]

In June 1942 President Roosevelt ordered an all-out effort, codenamed the MANHATTAN project, to build an American atomic bomb. Though it was another year before British participation in the project was formally agreed, the NKVD discovered that Roosevelt and Churchill had discussed cooperation on the building of the bomb during talks in Washington on June 20.[85] On October 6, following extensive consultations with Soviet scientists, the Centre submitted the first detailed report on Anglo-American plans to construct an atomic bomb to the Central Committee and the State Defence Committee, both chaired by Stalin.[86] By the end of the year, Stalin had decided to begin work on the construction of a Soviet atomic bomb.[87] In taking that momentous decision in the middle of the battle of Stalingrad, the main turning point in the war on the eastern front, Stalin was not thinking of the needs of the Great Patriotic War, since it was clear that the bomb could not be ready in time to assist in the defeat of Germany. Instead, he was already looking forward to a post-war world in which, since the United States and Britain would have nuclear weapons, the Soviet Union must have them too.[88]

For most of the Great Patriotic War Moscow collected more atomic intelligence from Britain than from the United States. In December 1942 the London residency received a detailed report on atomic research in Britain and the United States from a Communist scientist codenamed "K." Vladimir Barkovsky, head of scientific and technological intelligence (S&T) at the residency, later reported that "K" "works for us with enthusiasm, but . . . turns down the slightest hint of financial reward." With the help of a duplicate key personally manufactured by Barkovsky from a wax impression provided by "K," he was able to remove numerous classified documents from colleagues' safes as well as his own. The most valuable, in the Centre's view, were those on "the construction of uranium piles." At least two other scientists, codenamed MOOR and KELLY, also provided intelligence on various aspects of TUBE ALLOYS, the British atomic project.[89]

The most important of the British atom spies, the Communist physicist Klaus Fuchs, a naturalized refugee from Nazi Germany, was initially a GRU rather than an NKVD/NKGB agent. Fuchs was a committed Stalinist who was later to take part in the construction of the first atomic bomb. Before the war he had been an enthusiastic participant in dramatized readings of the transcripts of the show trials organized by the Society for Cultural Relations with the Soviet Union, and impressed his research supervisor, the future Nobel Laureate Sir Neville Mott, with the passion with which he played the part of the prosecutor Vyshinsky, "accusing the defendants with a cold venom that I would never have suspected from so quiet and retiring a young man." Late in 1941, Fuchs asked the leader of the German Communist Party (KPD) underground in Britain, Jürgen Kuczynski, for help in passing to the Russians what he had learned while working on the TUBE ALLOYS project at Birmingham University. Kuczynski put him in touch with Simon Davidovich Kremer, an officer at the GRU London residency, who irritated Fuchs by his insistence on taking long rides in London taxis, regularly doubling back in order to throw off anyone trying to tail them.[90]

In the summer of 1942 Fuchs was moved on to another and more congenial GRU controller, SONYA (referred to in KGB files under the alternative codename FIR),[91] who he almost certainly never realized was the sister of Jürgen Kuczynski. They usually met near Banbury, midway between Birmingham and Oxford, where SONYA lived as Mrs. Brewer, a Jewish refugee from Nazi Germany. SONYA remembered the material she collected from Fuchs as "just strings of hieroglyphics and formula written in such tiny writing that they just looked like squiggles:"

> Klaus and I never spent more than half an hour together when we met. Two minutes would have been enough but, apart from the pleasure of the meeting, it would arouse less suspicion if we took a little walk together rather than parting immediately. Nobody who did not live in such isolation can guess how precious these meetings with another German comrade were.[92]

SONYA later became the only woman ever to be made an honorary colonel of the Red Army, in recognition of her remarkable achievements in the GRU[93] But though it has been publicly acknowledged that she ran other agents besides Fuchs during her time in Britain, both the SVR and the GRU have gone to some pains to conceal the existence of the most important of them: Melita Stedman Norwood, née Sernis (codenamed HOLA). Norwood's file in the Centre shows her to have been, in all probability, both the most important British female agent in KGB history and the longest-serving of all Soviet spies in Britain.[94]

HOLA was born in 1912 to a Latvian father and British mother, joined the Communist Party of Great Britain (CPGB), married another Party member employed as a mathematics teacher in a secondary school, and from the age of twenty onwards worked as a secretary in the research department of the British Non-Ferrous Metals Association. Talent-spotted in 1935 by one of the CPGB's founders, Andrew Rothstein, she was recommended to the NKVD by the Party leadership and recruited two years later. Like the Magnificent Five, Norwood was a committed ideological agent inspired by a myth-image of the Soviet Union which bore little relationship to the brutal reality of Stalinist rule. Her forty-year career as a Soviet agent, however, nearly ended almost as soon as it began. She was involved with a spy ring operating inside the Woolwich Arsenal, whose three leading members were arrested in January 1938, tried and imprisoned three months later. MI5 failed, however, to detect clues to her identity contained in a notebook taken from the ringleader, Percy Glading (codenamed GOT), and after a few months "on ice" she was reactivated in May 1938. It is a sign of the Centre's high opinion of Norwood that contact with her was maintained at a time when it was broken with many other agents, including some of the Five, because of the recall or liquidation of most foreign intelligence officers.[95]

Contact with Norwood was suspended, however, after the temporary closure of the London residency early in 1940. When reactivated in 1941, she was for unexplained reasons handed over to SONYA of the GRU rather than to an NKVD controller. Her job at the Non-Ferrous Metals Association gave her access to extensive S&T documents which she passed on to SONYA and subsequent controllers. By the final months of the war Norwood was providing intelligence on the TUBE ALLOYS project. According to Mitrokhin's notes on her file, she was assessed throughout her career as a "committed, reliable and disciplined agent, striving to be of the utmost assistance."[96]

By the beginning of 1943, aware of American plans to build the first atomic bomb, the Centre was even more anxious to collect atomic intelligence in the United States than in Britain. One certain indication of the importance attached by the Centre to monitoring the MANHATTAN project was the dispatch of its head of scientific and technological intelligence, Leonid Romanovich Kvasnikov (ANTON), to New York where he became deputy resident for S&T in January 1943.[97] Igor Vasiliyevich Kurchatov, the newly appointed scientific head of the Soviet atomic project, wrote to Beria on March 7:

My examination of the [intelligence] material has shown that their receipt is of enormous and invaluable significance to our nation and our science. On the one hand, the material has demonstrated the seriousness and intensity of the scientific research being conducted on uranium in Britain, and on the other hand, it has made it possible to obtain important guidelines for our own scientific research, by-passing many extremely difficult phases in the development of this problem, learning new scientific and technical routes for its development, establishing three new areas for Soviet physics, and learning about the possibilities for using not only uranium-235 but also uranium-238.[98]

While Beria was reading the report, a new top-secret laboratory was starting work at Los Alamos in New Mexico to build the first atomic bomb. Los Alamos contained probably the most remarkable collection of youthful talent ever assembled in a single laboratory. A majority of the scientists who worked on the bomb were still in their twenties; the oldest, Robert Oppenheimer, the head of the laboratory, was thirty-nine. Los Alamos eventually included twelve Nobel Laureates.

In April 1943, a month after the opening of Los Alamos, the New York residency reported an important source on the MANHATTAN project. An unknown woman had turned up at the Soviet consulate-general and delivered a letter containing classified information on the atomic weapons program. A month later the same woman, who again declined to give her name, brought another letter with details of research on the plutonium route to the atomic bomb. Investigations by the New York residency revealed that the woman was an Italian nurse, whose first name was Lucia, the daughter of an anti-fascist Italian union leader, "D." At a meeting arranged by the residency through the leaders of the Friends of the USSR Society, Lucia said that she was acting only as an intermediary. The letters came from her brother-in-law, an American scientist working on plutonium research for the Du Pont company in Newport while completing a degree course in New York, who had asked his wife Regina to pass his correspondence to the Soviet consulate via her sister Lucia. The scientist—apparently the first of the American atom spies—was recruited under the codename MAR; Regina became MONA and Lucia OLIVIA.[99]

In June the New York residency forwarded intelligence on uranium isotope separation through gaseous diffusion from an unidentified agent codenamed KVANT ("Quantum") working for the MANHATTAN project. KVANT demanded payment and was given 300 dollars.[100] On July 3, after examining the latest atomic intelligence from the United States, Kurchatov wrote to the NKVD (probably to Beria in person):

> I have examined the attached list of American projects on uranium. Almost every one of them is of great interest to us . . . These materials are of enormous interest and great value . . . The receipt of further information of this type is extremely desirable.[101]

As yet, however, atomic intelligence from the United States was less detailed than that obtained from Britain in 1941–2.[102] Among those who supplied some of the further intelligence requested by Kurchatov was MAR, who in October 1943 was transferred to the Du Pont plant in Hanford, Washington State, which produced plutonium for the MANHATTAN project. He told his controller that his aim was to defeat the "criminal" attempt of the US military to conceal the construction of an atomic bomb from the USSR.[103] Other sources of atomic intelligence included a "progressive professor" in the radiation laboratory at Berkeley, California,[104] and— probably—a scientist in the MANHATTAN project's metallurgical laboratory at Chicago University.[105] The mercenary KVANT seems to have faded away, but by early 1944 another agent, a Communist construction engineer codenamed FOGEL (later PERS), was providing intelligence on the plant and equipment being used in the MANHATTAN project.[106] There is, however, no reliable evidence that Soviet intelligence yet had an agent inside Los Alamos.[107]

The penetration of the MANHATTAN project was only the most spectacular part of a vast wartime expansion of Soviet scientific and technological espionage. S&T from the United States and Britain made a major contribution to the development of Soviet radar, radio technology, submarines, jet engines, aircraft and synthetic rubber, as well as nuclear weapons.[108] Atomic intelligence was codenamed ENORMOZ ("Enormous"), jet propulsion VOZDUKH ("Air"), radar RADUGA ("Rainbow").[109] A. S. Yakovlev, the aircraft designer and Deputy Commissar of the Aviation Industry, paid handsome, though private, tribute to the contribution of S&T to the Soviet aircraft which bore his name.[110] Political and military intelligence from inside all the main branches of the Roosevelt administration also continued to expand, thanks chiefly to the increasing activity of Akhmerov's Washington networks. The rolls of film of classified documents sent by his illegal residency to Moscow via New York increased from 211 in 1943 to 600 in 1944.[111]

THE QUALITY OF political intelligence from Britain probably exceeded even that from the United States, partly as a result of the greater coordination of British government and intelligence assessment through the War Cabinet and the Joint Intelligence Committee (of which there were no real equivalents in the United States, despite the existence of bodies with similar names). The wartime files of the London residency contain what Mitrokhin's summary describes as "many secrets of the British War Cabinet," correspondence between Churchill and Roosevelt, telegrams exchanged between the Foreign Office, the embassies in Moscow, Washington, Stockholm, Ankara and Tehran, and the minister-resident in Cairo, and intelligence reports.[113] From the summer of 1942 to the summer of 1943, the intelligence reports included ULTRA decrypts direct from Bletchley Park, the main wartime home of the British SIGINT agency, where John Cairncross spent a year as a Soviet agent. His controller, Anatoli Gorsky, whom, like the rest of the Five, he knew as "Henry," gave him the money to buy a second-hand car to bring ULTRA to London on his days off.[113] Because of the unprecedented wartime collaboration of the Anglo-American intelligence communities, the London residency was also able to provide American as well as British intelligence.[114]

The problem for the professionally suspicious minds in the Centre was that it all seemed too good to be true. Taking their cue from the master conspiracy theorist in the Kremlin, they eventually concluded that what appeared to be the best intelligence ever obtained from Britain by any intelligence service was at root a British plot. The Five, later acknowledged as the ablest group of agents in KGB history, were discredited in the eyes of the Centre leadership by their failure to provide evidence of a massive, non-existent British conspiracy against the Soviet Union. Of the reality of that conspiracy, Stalin, and therefore his chief intelligence advisers, had no doubt. In October 1942 Stalin wrote to the Soviet ambassador in Britain, Ivan Maisky:

All of us in Moscow have gained the impression that Churchill is aiming at the defeat of the USSR, in order then to come to terms with the Germany of Hitler or Brüning at the expense of our country.[115]

Always in Stalin's mind when he brooded on Churchill's supposed wartime conspiracies against him was the figure of Hitler's deputy Führer, Rudolf Hess, whom, he told Maisky, Churchill was keeping "in reserve." In May 1941 Hess had made a bizarre flight to Scotland, in the deluded belief that he could arrange peace between Britain and Germany. Both London and Berlin correctly concluded that Hess was somewhat deranged. Stalin, inevitably, believed instead that Hess's flight was part of a deeply laid British plot. His suspicions deepened after the German invasion in June. For at least the next two years he suspected that Hess was part of a British conspiracy to abandon its alliance with the Soviet Union and sign a separate peace with Germany.[116] At dinner with Churchill in the Kremlin in October 1944 Stalin proposed a toast to "the British intelligence service which had inveigled Hess into coming to England:" "He could not have landed without being given signals. The intelligence service must have been behind it all."[117] Stalin's mood at dinner was jovial, but his conspiracy theory was deadly earnest. If his misunderstanding of Hess's flight to Britain did not derive from Centre intelligence assessments, it was certainly reinforced by them. As late as the early 1990s the same conspiracy theory was still being publicly propounded by a KGB spokesman who claimed that in 1941 Hess "brought the Führer's peace proposals with him and a plan for the invasion of the Soviet Union." That myth is still, apparently, believed by some of their SVR successors.[118]

On October 25, 1943 the Centre informed the London residency that it was now clear, after long analysis of the voluminous intelligence from the Five, that they were double agents, working on the instructions of SIS and MI5. As far back as their years at Cambridge, Philby, Maclean and Burgess had probably been acting on instructions from British intelligence to infiltrate the student left before making contact with the NKVD. Only thus, the Centre reasoned, was it possible to explain why both SIS and MI5 were currently employing in highly sensitive jobs Cambridge graduates with a Communist background. The lack of any reference to British recruitment of Soviet agents in the intelligence supplied either by SÖHNCHEN (Philby) from SIS or by TONY (Blunt) from MI5 was seen as further evidence that both were being used to feed disinformation to the NKGB:

> During the entire period that S[ÖHNCHEN] and T[ONY] worked for the British special services, they did not help expose a single valuable ISLANDERS [British] agent either in the USSR or in the Soviet embassy in the ISLAND [Britain].

There was, of course, no such "valuable agent" for Philby or Blunt to expose, but that simple possibility did not occur to the conspiracy theorists in the Centre. Philby's accurate report that "at the present time the HOTEL [SIS] is not engaged in active work against the Soviet Union" was also, in the Centre's view, obvious disinformation.[119]

Since the Five were double agents, it followed that those they had recruited to the NKVD were also plants. One example which particularly exercised the Centre was the case of Peter Smollett (ABO), who in 1941 had achieved the remarkable feat of becoming head of the Russian department in the wartime Ministry of Information. By 1943 Smollett was using his position to organize pro-Soviet propaganda on a prodigious scale. A vast meeting at the Albert Hall in February to celebrate the twenty-fifth anniversary of the Red Army included songs of praise by a massed choir, readings by John Gielgud and Laurence Olivier, and was attended by leading politicians from all parties. The film *USSR at War* was shown to factory audiences of one and a quarter million. In September 1943 alone, the Ministry of Information organized meetings on the Soviet Union for 34 public venues, 35 factories, 100 voluntary societies, 28 civil defense groups, 9 schools and a prison; the BBC in the same month broadcast thirty programs with a substantial Soviet content.[120] Yet, because Smollett had been recruited by Philby, he was, in the eyes of the Centre, necessarily a plant. His apparently spectacular success in organizing pro-Soviet propaganda on an unprecedented scale was thus perversely interpreted as a cunning plot by British intelligence to hoodwink the NKVD.[121]

Even the hardened conspiracy theorists of the Centre, however, had some difficulty in explaining why the Five were providing, along with disinformation, such large amounts of accurate high-grade intelligence. In its missive to the London residency of October 25, the Centre suggested a number of possible answers to this baffling problem. The sheer quantity of Foreign Office documents supplied by Maclean *might* indicate, it believed, that, unlike the other four, he was not *consciously* deceiving the NKVD, but was merely being manipulated by the others to the best of their ability. The Centre also argued that the Five were instructed to pass on important intelligence about Germany which did not harm British interests in order to make their disinformation about British policy more credible.[122]

The most valuable "documentary material about the work of the Germans" in 1943 was the German decrypts supplied by Cairncross from Bletchley Park. A brief official biography of Fitin published by the SVR singles out for special mention the ULTRA intelligence obtained from Britain on German preparations for the battle of Kursk when the Red Army halted Hitler's last major offensive on the eastern front.[123] The Luftwaffe decrypts provided by Cairncross were of crucial importance in enabling the Red Air Force to launch massive pre-emptive strikes against German airfields which destroyed over 500 enemy aircraft.[124]

The Centre's addiction to conspiracy theory ran so deep, however, that it was capable of regarding the agent who supplied intelligence of critical importance before Kursk as part of an elaborate network of deception. It therefore ordered the London residency to create a new independent agent network uncontaminated by the Five. But, though the Five were "undoubtedly double agents," the residency was ordered to maintain contact with them. The Centre gave three reasons for this apparently contradictory decision. First, if British intelligence realized that their grand deception involving the Five had been discovered, they might well intensify their search for the new network intended to replace them. Secondly, the Centre acknowledged that, despite the Five's "unquestionable attempts to disinform us," they were none the less providing "valuable material about the Germans and other matters." Finally, "Not all the questions about this group of agents have been completely cleared up." The Centre was, in other words, seriously confused about what exactly the Five were up to.[125]

To try to discover the exact nature of the British intelligence conspiracy, the Centre sent, for the first time ever, a special eight-man surveillance team to the London residency to trail the Five and other supposedly bogus Soviet agents in the hope of discovering their contacts with their non-existent British controllers. The same team also investigated visitors to the Soviet embassy, some of whom were suspected of being MI5 *agents provocateurs*. The new surveillance system was hilariously unsuccessful. None of the eight-man team spoke English; all wore conspicuously Russian clothes, were visibly ill at ease in English surroundings and must frequently have disconcerted those they followed.[126]

The absurdity of trailing the Five highlights the central weakness in the Soviet intelligence system. The Centre's ability to collect intelligence from the West always comfortably exceeded its capacity to interpret what it collected. Moscow's view of its British allies was invariably clouded by variable amounts of conspiracy theory. The Soviet leadership was to find it easier to replicate the first atomic bomb than to understand policy-making in London.

EIGHT

VICTORY

Given the closeness of the British-American "special relationship," the Centre inevitably suspected that some of the President's advisers sympathized with Churchill's supposed anti-Soviet plots.[1] Suspicions of Roosevelt himself, however, were never as intense as those of Churchill. Nor did the Centre form conspiracy theories about its American agents as preposterous as those about the Cambridge Five. Perhaps because the NKVD had penetrated the OSS from the moment of its foundation, it was less inclined to believe that United States intelligence was running a system of deception which compared with the supposed use of the Five by the British. The CPUSA's assistance in the operation to assassinate Trotsky, combined with the enthusiasm with which it "exposed and weeded out spies and traitors,"[2] appeared to make its underground section a reliable recruiting ground. Vasili Zarubin's regular contacts with the CPUSA leader, Earl Browder, plainly convinced him of the reliability of those covert Party members who agreed to provide secret intelligence.

By the spring of 1943, however, the Centre was worried about the security of its large and expanding American agent network. Zarubin became increasingly incautious both in his meetings with Party leaders and in arranging for the payment to them of secret subsidies from Moscow. One of the files noted by Mitrokhin records censoriously, "Without the approval of the Central Committee, Zarubin crudely violated the rules of clandestinity." On one occasion Browder asked Zarubin to deliver Soviet money personally to the Communist underground organization in Chicago; the implication in the KGB file is that he agreed. On another occasion, in April 1943, Zarubin traveled to California for a secret meeting with Steve Nelson, who ran a secret control commission to seek out informants and spies in the Californian branch of the Communist Party, but failed to find Nelson's home. Only on a second visit did he succeed in delivering the money. On this occasion, however, the meeting was bugged by the FBI which had placed listening devices in Nelson's home.[3] The Soviet ambassador in Washington was told confidentially by none other than Roosevelt's adviser, Harry Hopkins, that a member of his embassy had been detected passing money to a Communist in California.[4]

Though Zarubin became somewhat more discreet after this "friendly warning," his cover had been blown. Worse was yet to come. Four months later Zarubin was secretly denounced to the FBI by Vasili Mironov, a senior officer in the New York residency who had earlier appealed unsuccessfully to the Centre for Zarubin's recall.[5] In an extraordinary anonymous letter to Hoover on August 7, 1943, Mironov identified Zarubin and ten other leading members of residencies operating under diplomatic cover in the United States, himself included, as Soviet intelligence officers. He also revealed that Browder was closely involved with Soviet espionage and identified the Hollywood producer Boris Morros (FROST) as a Soviet agent. Mironov's motives derived partly from personal loathing for Zarubin himself. He told Hoover, speaking of himself in the third person, that Zarubin and Mironov "both hate each other." Mironov also appears to have been tortured by a sense of guilt for his part in the NKVD's massacre of the Polish officer corps in 1940. Zarubin, he told Hoover, "interrogated and shot Poles in Kozelsk, Mironov in Starobelsk." (In reality, though Zarubin did interrogate some of the Polish officers, he does not appear to have been directly involved in their execution.) But there are also clear signs in Mironov's letter, if not of mental illness, at least of the paranoid mindset generated by the Terror. He accused Zarubin of being a Japanese agent and his wife of working for Germany, and concluded bizarrely: "If you prove to Mironov that Z is working for the Germans and Japanese, he will immediately shoot him without a trial, as he too holds a very high post in the NKVD."[6]

By the time Mironov's extraordinary denunciation reached the FBI, Zarubin had moved from New York to Washington—a move probably prompted by the steady growth in intelligence of all kinds from within the Roosevelt administration. As the senior NKVD officer in the United States, Zarubin retained overall control in Washington of the New York and San Francisco residencies; responsibility for liaison with the head of the CPUSA, Browder, and with the head of the illegal residency, Akhmerov; and direct control of some of his favorite agents, among them the French politician Pierre Cot and the British intelligence officer Cedric Belfrage, whom he took over from Golos.[7]

With his cover blown, however, Zarubin found life in Washington difficult. One of his most humiliating moments came at a dinner for members of the Soviet embassy given early in 1944 by the governor of Louisiana, Sam Houston Jones.[8] After dinner, as guests wandered round the governor's house in small groups, a lady who appeared to know that Zarubin was a senior NKGB officer, turned to him and said, "Have a seat, General!" Zarubin, whose fuse and sense of humor were both somewhat short, took the seat but replied stiffly, "I am not a general!" Another guest, who identified himself as an officer in military intelligence, complimented the lady on her inside knowledge. He then caused Zarubin further embarrassment by asking for his views on the massacre of 16,000 Polish officers, some of whose bodies had been exhumed in the Katyn woods. Zarubin replied that German allegations that the officers had been shot by the NKVD (as indeed they had) were a provocation intended to sow dissension within the Grand Alliance which would deceive only the naive.[9]

Zarubin subsequently sought to persuade the Centre that his humiliating loss of cover was due not to his own indiscretion but to the fact that the Americans had somehow discovered that he had interrogated imprisoned Polish officers in Kozelsk. The Centre was unimpressed. In a letter to the Central Committee, the NKGB Personnel Directorate reported that his period as resident in the United States had been marked by a series of blunders.[10] Mironov not long before had informed on Zarubin to Hoover, now appears to have written to Stalin, accusing Zarubin of being in contact with the FBI.[11] In the summer of 1944, both Zarubin and Mironov were recalled to Moscow. Anatoli Gorsky, who until a few months earlier had been resident in London, succeeded Zarubin in Washington.[12]

Once back in Moscow, Zarubin quickly succeeded in reestablishing his position at the expense of Mironov and was appointed deputy chief of foreign intelligence. By the time he retired three years later, allegedly on grounds of ill health, he had succeeded in taking much of the credit for the remarkable wartime intelligence obtained from the United States, and was awarded two Orders of Lenin, two Orders of the Red Banner, one Order of the Red Star, and numerous medals.[13] Mironov, by contrast, was sentenced soon after his return to Moscow to five years in a labor camp, probably for making false accusations against Zarubin. In 1945 he tried to smuggle out of prison to the US embassy in Moscow information about the NKVD massacre of Polish officers similar to that which, unknown to the Centre, he had sent to the FBI two years earlier. On this occasion Mironov was caught in the act, given a second trial and shot.[14]

Even after the recall of Zarubin and Mironov, feuding and denunciations continued within the American residencies. As with Mironov's bizarre accusations, some of the feuds had an almost surreal quality about them. In August 1944 the newly appointed resident in San Francisco, Grigori Pavlovich Kasparov, telegraphed to the Centre a bitter denunciation of the resident in Mexico City, Lev Tarasov, who, he claimed, had bungled attempts to liberate Trotsky's assassin, Ramón Mercader, and had adopted a "grand lifestyle." As well as renting a house with grounds and employing two servants in addition to the staff allocated to him, Tarasov was alleged to be spending too much time breeding parrots, poultry and other birds.[15] The fate of Tarasov's denounced parrots is not recorded.

There was dissension too in New York, where the inexperienced 28-year-old Stepan Apresyan (MAY) had been appointed resident early in 1944, despite the fact that he had never previously been outside the Soviet Union. His appointment was bitterly resented by his much more experienced deputy, Roland Abbiate (alias "Vladimir Pravdin," codenamed SERGEI), whose previous assignments had included the liquidation of the defector Ignace Poretsky. Operating under cover as the Tass bureau chief in New York, Abbiate had a grasp of American conditions which greatly exceeded Apresyan's, but his career continued to be held back by the fact that, although he had been born in St. Petersburg in 1902, his parents were French and had returned to France in 1920. Abbiate had returned with them, living in France until his recruitment by the OGPU as an illegal in 1932.[16]

As a stop-gap measure to compensate for Apresyan's now visible incompetence, the Centre gave Abbiate virtually equal status with Apresyan in the autumn of 1944 in running the residency. Abbiate responded by telegraphing to Moscow a scathing attack on Apresyan, whom he condemned as "incapable of dealing with the tasks which are set him" or of gaining the respect of his staff:

MAY [Apresyan] is utterly without the knack of dealing with people, frequently showing himself excessively abrupt and inclined to nag, and too rarely
finding time to chat with them. Sometimes our operational workers . . . cannot
get an answer to an urgent question from him for several days at a time . . . A
worker who has no experience of work abroad cannot cope on his own with the
work of directing the TYRE OFFICE [New York residency].

The real responsibility, Abbiate clearly implied, rested with the Centre for appointing such an obviously unsuitable and unqualified resident.[17] The civil war between
the resident and his deputy continued for just over a year before ending in victory for
Abbiate. In March 1945 Apresyan was transferred to San Francisco, leaving Abbiate
as resident in New York.[18]

WHILE THE WASHINGTON and New York residencies were both in some turmoil in
the summer of 1944, sanity was returning to London. The Magnificent Five were
officially absolved of all suspicion of being double agents controlled by the British.
On June 29 the Centre informed the London residency, then headed by Konstantin
Mikhailovich Kukin (codenamed IGOR),[19] that recent important SIS documents
provided by Philby had been largely corroborated by material from "other sources"
(some probably in the American OSS, with whom SIS exchanged many highly classified reports):[20] "This is a serious confirmation of S[ÖHNCHEN]'s honesty in his
work with us, which obliges us to review our attitude toward him and the entire
group." It was now clear, the Centre acknowledged, that intelligence from the Five
was "of great value," and contact with them must be maintained at all costs:

> On our behalf express much gratitude to S[ÖHNCHEN] for his work . . . If
> you find it convenient and possible, offer S[ÖHNCHEN] in the most tactful
> way a bonus of 100 pounds or give him a gift of equal value.

After six years in which his phenomenal work as a penetration agent had been frequently undervalued, ignored or suspected by the Centre, Philby was almost pathetically grateful for the long overdue recognition of his achievements. "During this
decade of work," he told Moscow, "I have never been so deeply touched as now with
your gift and no less deeply excited by your communication [of thanks]."[21]
    High among the intelligence which restored the Centre's faith in Philby were his
reports, beginning early in 1944, on the founding by SIS of a new Section IX "to study
past records of Soviet and Communist activity." Urged on by his new controller, Boris
Krötenschield (alias Krotov, codenamed KRECHIN), Philby succeeded at the end of
the year in becoming head of an expanded Section IX, with a remit for "the collection
and interpretation of information concerning Soviet and Communist espionage and
subversion in all parts of the world outside British territory." As one of his SIS colleagues, Robert Cecil, wrote later, "Philby at one stroke had . . . ensured that the
whole post-war effort to counter Communist espionage would become known in the
Kremlin. The history of espionage records few, if any, comparable masterstrokes."[22]

At about the same time that Philby was given his present, Cairncross was belatedly rewarded for his contribution to the epic Soviet victory at Kursk. Krötenschield informed him that he had been awarded one of the highest Soviet decorations, the Order of the Red Banner. He opened a velvet-lined box, took out the decoration and placed it in Cairncross's hands. Krötenschield reported to the Centre that Cairncross was visibly elated by the award, though he was told to hand it back for safekeeping in Moscow.[23] The award came too late, however, to achieve its full effect. In the summer of 1943, exhausted by the strain of his regular car journeys to London to deliver ULTRA decrypts to Gorsky, and probably discouraged by Gorsky's lack of appreciation, Cairncross had left Bletchley Park. Though he succeeded in obtaining a job in SIS, first in Section V (Counterintelligence), then in Section I (Political Intelligence), his importance in the Centre's eyes now ranked clearly below that of Philby.[24] Unlike Philby, Cairncross did not get on well with his SIS colleagues. The head of Section I, David Footman, found him "an odd person, with a chip on his shoulder."[25]

Encouraged by the Centre's new appreciation of their talents, the other members of the Five—Maclean, Burgess and Blunt—became even more productive than before. In the spring of 1944 Maclean was posted to the Washington embassy, where he was soon promoted to first secretary. His zeal was quickly apparent. According to one of his colleagues, "No task was too hard for him; no hours were too long. He gained the reputation of one who would always take over a tangled skein from a colleague who was sick, or going on leave, or simply less zealous." The most sensitive, and in the NKGB's view probably the most important, area of policy in which Maclean succeeded in becoming involved by early 1945 was Anglo-American collaboration in the building of the atomic bomb.[26]

Burgess increased his usefulness to the NKGB by gaining a job in the Foreign Office press department soon after Maclean was posted to Washington. Claiming no doubt that he required access to a wide range of material to be adequately informed for press briefings, Burgess regularly filled a large holdall with Foreign Office documents, some of them highly classified, and took them to be photographed by the NKGB. The holdall, however, was almost his undoing. At a meeting with Krötenschield, Burgess was approached by a police patrol, who suspected that the bag contained stolen goods. Once reassured that the two men had no housebreaking equipment and that the holdall contained only papers, the patrol apologized and proceeded on its way. Though Burgess may subsequently have used a bag which less resembled that of a housebreaker, his productivity was unaffected. According to one of the files examined by Mitrokhin, of the Foreign Office documents provided by Burgess in the first six months of 1945, 389 were classified "top secret."[27]

Blunt's productivity was prodigious too. In addition to providing intelligence from MI5, he continued to run Leo Long in military intelligence, and in the crucial months before D-Day gained access to Supreme Headquarters Allied Expeditionary Force (SHAEF), not far from MI5 headquarters.[28] Part of Blunt's contribution to NKGB operations in London was to keep the residency informed of the nature and extent of MI5 surveillance. Intelligence which he provided in 1945 revealed that MI5 had discovered that his Cambridge contemporary, James Klugmann, was a Communist spy. In 1942 Klugmann had joined the Yugoslav section of SOE Cairo, where his intellect, charm and fluent Serbo-Croat gave him an influence entirely disproportionate to his relatively junior rank (which eventually rose to major). As well as briefing Allied officers about to be dropped into Yugoslavia, he also briefed the NKGB on British policy and secret operations. In both sets of briefings he sought to advance the interests of Tito's Communist partisans over those of Mihailovich's royalist Chetniks. For four months in 1945 he served in Yugoslavia with the British military mission to Tito's forces. Blunt was able to warn Krötenschield that MI5 listening devices in the British Communist Party headquarters in King Street, London, had recorded a conversation in which Klugmann boasted of secretly passing classified information to the Yugoslav Communists.[29]

WITH THE EXCEPTION of the Five, potentially the most important Soviet spy in Britain was the nuclear physicist Klaus Fuchs, recruited by the GRU late in 1941.[30] When Fuchs left for the United States late in 1943 as part of the British team chosen to take part in the MANHATTAN project, he was—though he did not realize it—transferred from GRU to NKGB control and given the codename REST (later changed to CHARLES).[31] Earlier in 1943, the Centre had instructed its residencies in Britain and the United States that "[t]he brain centers [scientific research establishments] must come within our jurisdiction." Not for the first time, the GRU was forced to give way to the demands of its more powerful "neighbor."[32] In 1944 Melita Norwood, the long-serving Soviet agent in the British Non-Ferrous Metals Association, ceased contact with SONYA of the GRU and was given an NKGB controller.[33] In March 1945, after her employer won a contract from the TUBE ALLOYS project, Norwood gained access to documents of atomic intelligence[34] which the Centre described as "of great interest and a valuable contribution to the development of work in this field." She was instructed to say nothing about her espionage work to her husband, and in particular to give no hint of her involvement in atomic intelligence.[35] Atomic intelligence from London and the American residencies was complementary as well as overlapping. According to Vladimir Barkovsky, head of S&T at the London residency, "In the USA we obtained information on how the bomb was made and in Britain of what it was made, so that together [intelligence from the two countries] covered the whole problem."[36]

On February 5, 1944 Fuchs had his first meeting in New York's East Side with his NKGB controller, Harry Gold (codenamed successively GOOSE and ARNO), an industrial chemist born in Switzerland of Russian parents.[37] Fuchs was told to identify himself by carrying a tennis ball in his hand and to look for a man wearing one pair of gloves and carrying another.[38] Gold, who introduced himself as "Raymond," reported to Leonid Kvasnikov, head of S&T at the New York residency (later known as Line X), that Fuchs had "greeted him pleasantly but was rather cautious at first."[39] Fuchs later claimed, after his arrest in 1949, that during their meetings "the attitude of 'Raymond' was at all times that of an inferior." Gold admitted, after his own arrest by the FBI, that he was overawed by the extraordinary intelligence which Fuchs provided and had found the idea of an atomic bomb "so frightening that the only thing I could do was shove it away as far back in my mind as I could and simply not think on the matter at all."[40]

On July 25, 1944 the New York residency telegraphed the Centre: "Almost half a year of contact established with REST [Fuchs] has demonstrated the value of his work for us." It asked permission to pay him a "reward" of 500 dollars. The Centre agreed, but, before the money could be handed over, Fuchs had disappeared.[41] It was over three months before Gold discovered that Fuchs had been posted to Los Alamos, and he did not renew contact with him until Fuchs returned to the east coast on leave in February 1945.[42]

During 1944 Kvasnikov's responsibilities were extended: he was given the new post of S&T resident for the whole of the United States—a certain indication of the increasing priority of atomic espionage.[43] Late in 1944 Kvasnikov was able to inform the Centre that, in addition to Fuchs, there were now two more prospective spies at Los Alamos.

The first, David Greenglass, was recruited through a group of S&T agents run by Julius Rosenberg (codenamed successively ANTENNA and LIBERAL), a 26-year-old New York Communist with a degree in electrical engineering. Like Fuchs, the members of the Rosenberg ring, who included his wife Ethel, had been rewarded with cash bonuses in the summer. The ring was producing so many classified documents to be photographed in Kvasnikov's apartment that the New York residency was running dangerously short of film. The residency reported that Rosenberg was receiving so much intelligence from his agents that he was finding it difficult to cope: "We are afraid of putting LIBERAL out of action with overwork."[44]

In November 1944 Kvasnikov informed the Centre that Ethel Rosenberg's sister, Ruth Greenglass (codenamed WASP), had agreed to approach her husband, who worked as a machinist at Los Alamos.[45] "I was young, stupid and immature," said David Greenglass (codenamed BUMBLEBEE and CALIBRE) later, "but I was a good Communist." Stalin and the Soviet leadership, he believed, were "really geniuses, every one of them." "More power to the Soviet Union and abundant life for their peoples!" "My darling," Greenglass wrote to his wife, "I most certainly will be glad to be part of the community project [espionage] that Julius and his friends [the Russians] have in mind."[46]

The New York residency also reported in November 1944 that the precociously brilliant nineteen-year-old Harvard physicist Theodore Alvin ("Ted") Hall, then working at Los Alamos, had indicated his willingness to collaborate. As well as being inspired by the myth-image of the Soviet worker–peasant state, which was an article of faith for most ideological Soviet agents, Hall convinced himself that an American nuclear monopoly would threaten the peace of the post-war world. Passing the secrets of the MANHATTAN project to Moscow was thus a way "to help the world," as well as the Soviet Union. As the youngest of the atom spies, Hall was given the appropriate, if transparent, codename MLAD ("Young"). Though only one year older, the fellow Harvard student who first brought Hall into contact with the

NKGB, Saville Savoy Sax, was codenamed STAR ("Old").[47] Hall himself went on to become probably the youngest major spy of the twentieth century.

THE PENETRATION OF Los Alamos was part of a more general surge in Soviet intelligence collection in the United States during the last two years of the war, as the NKGB's agents, buoyed up by the remorseless advance of the Red Army towards Berlin and the opening of a second front, looked forward to a glorious victory over fascism. The number of rolls of microfilm sent by Akhmerov's illegal residency to Moscow via New York grew from 211 in 1943 to 600 in 1944 and 1,896 in 1945.[48] The Centre, however, found it difficult to believe that espionage in the United States could really be as straightforward as it seemed. During 1944–5 the NKGB grew increasingly concerned about the security of its American operations and sought to bring them under more direct control.[49] Among its chief anxieties was Elizabeth Bentley's habit of socializing with the agents for whom she acted as courier. When Bentley's controller and lover, Jacob Golos, died from a sudden heart attack on Thanksgiving Day 1943, Akhmerov decided to dispense with a cut-out and act as her new controller. Bentley's first impressions were of a smartly dressed "jaunty-looking man in his mid-thirties" with an expansive manner. (Akhmerov was actually forty-two). She soon realized, however, that "despite the superficial appearance of a boulevardier, he was a tough character."[50] For the next six months, though Bentley continued to act as courier for the Silvermaster group in Washington, she felt herself under increasing pressure.

In March 1944 Earl Browder passed on to her another group of Washington bureaucrats who had been sending him intelligence which he had previously passed on to Golos.[51] Bentley regarded Victor Perlo (RAIDER), a government statistician who provided intelligence on aircraft production, as the leader of the group—probably because he acted as spokesman during her first meeting with them.[52] Akhmerov, however, believed that the real organizer was Charles Kramer (LOT), a government economist, and was furious that the Perlo/Kramer network had been handed over by Browder not to him but to Bentley. For over a year, he told the Centre, Zarubin and he had wanted to make direct contact with the group, but Browder had failed to arrange it. "If we work with this group," Akhmerov added, "it will be necessary to remove [Bentley]."[53]

Bentley appealed to Browder for support as she struggled to remain the courier for the Washington networks. "Night after night, after battling with [Akhmerov]," wrote Bentley later, "I would crawl home to bed, sometimes too weary to undress." Eventually, Bentley agreed to arrange a meeting between Akhmerov and Silvermaster (PAL). Soon afterwards, according to Bentley, Akhmerov told her, "almost drooling with arrogance:" "Earl [Browder] has agreed to turn Greg [Silvermaster] over to me . . . Go and ask him." "Don't be naive," Browder told Bentley the next day. "You know that when the cards are down, I have to take my orders from them."[54] Akhmerov reported to the Centre that Bentley had taken her removal from the Silvermaster group "very much to heart . . . evidently supposing that we do not trust her. She is offended at RULEVOY [Browder] for having consented to our liaison with PAL."[55]

Bentley was also removed from contact with the Perlo/Kramer group. Gorsky tried to placate her by inviting her to dinner at a waterfront restaurant in Washington. He made a bad start. "I hope the food is good," he said. "Americans are such stupid people that even when it comes to a simple matter like cooking a meal, they do it very badly." "Ah, yes," he added, seeing Bentley's expression change. "I had forgotten for the moment that you, too, are an American." Gorsky went on to tell her that she had been awarded the Order of the Red Star ("one of the highest—reserved for all our best fighters") and showed her a facsimile: "We all think you've done splendidly and have a great future before you." GOOD GIRL was not to be placated.[56] A year later she secretly began telling her story to the FBI.

The Centre was also worried by increased FBI surveillance of the New York Soviet consulate, which housed the legal residency, and by a warning from Duncan Lee (KOCH) in September 1944 that the OSS Security Division was compiling a list of Communists and Communist sympathizers in OSS.[57] The Centre's nervousness was shared by some of its best agents. Bentley found Lee himself "on the verge of cracking up . . . so hypercautious that he had taken to crawling around the floor of his apartment on hands and knees examining the telephone wires to see if they had been tampered with."[58] Another highly placed Soviet agent, the senior Treasury official Harry Dexter White (JURIST), told his controller that, though he was unconcerned for his own personal security and his wife had prepared herself "for any self-sacrifice," he would have to be very cautious because of the damage to the "new course" (the Soviet cause) which would occur if he were exposed as a spy. He therefore proposed that in the future they have relatively infrequent meetings, each lasting about half an hour, while driving around in his car.[59]

There was a further alarm in November which, according to Bentley, followed an urgent warning from an agent in the White House, Roosevelt's administrative assistant Lauchlin Currie. Currie reported that "the Americans were on the verge of breaking the Soviet code."[60] The alarm appears to have subsided when it was discovered that Currie had wrongly concluded that a fire-damaged NKGB codebook obtained by OSS from the Finns would enable Soviet communications (which went through a further, theoretically impenetrable, encipherment by "one-time pad") to be decrypted.[61] (Given the phenomenal success of Anglo-American codebreakers in breaking the highest grade German and Japanese ciphers, Currie's mistake is understandable.) At Roosevelt's insistence, Donovan returned the NKGB codebook to the Soviet embassy. A doubtless bemused Fitin sent Donovan his "sincere thanks."[62]

DESPITE ALL THE Centre's anxiety that Soviet espionage was about to be exposed, and despite all the confusion in the residencies, the NKGB's eager American and British agents continued to provide intelligence remarkable for both its quantity and quality. The NKGB proudly calculated after the war that the grand total of its wartime agents and informers ("confidential contacts") around the world had been 1,240, who had provided 41,718 items of intelligence. Approximately 3,000 foreign intelligence reports and documents had been judged important enough to be sent to the State Defense Committee and the Central Committee. Eighty-seven foreign intelligence officers were decorated for their wartime work.[63]

Moscow made far better use of S&T than of its political intelligence, which was always likely to be ignored or regarded with suspicion when it disagreed with Stalin's conspiracy theories—or with those of the Centre, which were closely modeled on his. S&T from the West, by contrast, was welcomed with open and unsuspicious arms by Soviet scientists and technologists. A. F. Ioffe, the director of the USSR Academy of Sciences Leningrad Physics and Technological Institute, wrote of wartime S&T:

> The information always turns out to be accurate and for the most part very complete . . . I have not encountered a single false finding. Verification of all the formulae and experiments invariably confirms the data contained in the materials.[64]

The most valuable S&T concerned the atomic program. Kurchatov reported to Beria on September 29, 1944 that intelligence revealed the creation for the MAN-HATTAN project of "a concentration of scientific and engineering-technical power on a scale never before seen in the history of world science, which has already achieved the most priceless results."[65] According to NKGB calculations, up to November 1944 it had acquired 1,167 documents on nuclear research, of which 88 from the United States and 79 from Britain were judged of particular importance.[66] The most important, however, were yet to come.

On February 28, 1945 the NKGB submitted to Beria its first comprehensive report on atomic intelligence for two years—also the first to be based on reports from inside Los Alamos. Five months before the successful test of the first atomic bomb at Alamogordo in southern New Mexico, the Centre was informed of all the main elements in its construction. The information which Fuchs had passed to Gold on the east coast in mid-February arrived too late to be included in the Centre's assessment. The report passed to Beria was, almost certainly, based chiefly on intelligence from the nineteen-year-old Theodore Hall and technical sergeant David Greenglass. There can be little doubt that Hall's intelligence, delivered to the New York residency by his friend, Saville Sax, was the more important. It was probably Hall who first revealed the implosion method of detonating the bomb, though a more detailed report on implosion by Fuchs reached Kurchatov on April 6.[67]

In the spring of 1945 Sax was replaced as courier between Hall and the New York residency by Leontina ("Lona") Cohen, codenamed LESLIE. "Lona" had been recruited in 1941 by her husband Morris (codenamed LUIS), who had become a Soviet agent during the Spanish Civil War while serving in the International Brigades. The couple, later to figure among the heroes of Soviet intelligence, were collectively codenamed the DACHNIKI ("Vacationers"), but their careers as agents were interrupted by Morris's conscription in 1942. "Lona" was reactivated early in 1945 to act as a courier to both Los Alamos and the Anglo-Canadian atomic research center at Chalk River, near Ottawa, which was also penetrated by Soviet agents. While she made contact with Hall, Gold acted as courier for Fuchs and Greenglass. Each of the three Soviet agents was completely ignorant of the espionage conducted by the other two.[68]

It is probable that both Fuchs and Hall independently furnished the plans of the first atomic bomb, each of which the Centre was able to crosscheck against the other.[69] Fuchs and Hall also independently reported that the test of the first atomic bomb had been fixed for July 10, 1945,[70] though in the end weather conditions caused it to be postponed for six days. A month later the Pacific War was at an end. Following the bombing of Hiroshima and Nagasaki on August 6 and 9, Japan surrendered.

Lona Cohen spent the final dramatic weeks of the Pacific War in New Mexico, waiting for Hall to deliver the results of the Alamogordo test. After missing rendezvous in Albuquerque on three consecutive Sundays, Hall finally handed a set of highly classified papers to his courier, probably soon after the Japanese surrender.[71] On catching the train back to New York, Lona Cohen was horrified to see military police on board searching passengers' luggage. With remarkable presence of mind she thrust Hall's documents inside a newspaper and gave it to a policeman to hold while she opened her purse and suitcase for inspection. The policeman handed the newspaper back, inspected her purse and suitcase, and Mrs. Cohen returned safely to New York.[72]

Thanks chiefly to Hall and Fuchs, the first Soviet atomic bomb, successfully tested just over four years later, was to be an exact copy of the Alamogordo bomb. At the time, however, the Centre found it difficult to believe that the theft of two copies of perhaps the most important secret plans in American history could possibly escape detection. The sheer scale of its success made the NKGB fear that the penetration of the MANHATTAN project would soon be uncovered by the Americans.

The NKGB officer in charge of intelligence collected from Los Alamos in 1945 was Anatoli Antonovich Yatskov (alias "Yakovlev," codenamed ALEKSEI), an engineer recruited by the NKVD in 1939 who succeeded Kvasnikov as S&T resident in the United States.[73] He is nowadays remembered as one of the heroes of Russian foreign intelligence.[74] At the time, however, the Centre was bitterly critical of him. In July 1945 it concluded that his carelessness had probably compromised MLAD, and denounced his "completely unsatisfactory work with the agents on ENORMOZ [the MANHATTAN project]."[75] At the very moment of Soviet intelligence's greatest ever triumph in the United States, the acquisition of the plans of the first atomic bomb, the Centre wrongly feared that the whole ENORMOZ operation was in jeopardy.

The GRU, as well as the NKGB, had some striking successes in the wartime United States. Though Soviet military intelligence had been forced to surrender both Fuchs and the majority of its more important pre-war American agents to the more powerful NKGB, it had succeeded in retaining at least one of whom the Centre was envious in 1945. Gorsky reported to the Centre a conversation between Akhmerov and ALES (Alger Hiss), who had been working for the GRU for the past ten years.[76] Though Hiss was a senior diplomat, Akhmerov said that the GRU had generally appeared little interested in State Department documents, and had asked Hiss and a small group of agents, "for the most part consisting of his relations," to concentrate on military intelligence.[77] Late in 1944, however, Hiss's role as a Soviet agent took on a new significance when he became actively engaged in preparations for the final meeting of the wartime Big Three at Yalta in the Crimea in February 1945.

Yalta was to prove an even bigger success for Soviet intelligence than Tehran. This time both the British and the American delegations, housed respectively in the ornate Vorontsov and Livadia Palaces, were successfully bugged. The mostly female personnel used to record and transcribe their private conversations were selected and transported to the Crimea in great secrecy. Not till they arrived at Yalta did they discover the jobs that had been assigned to them.[78] The NKGB sought, with some success, to distract both delegations from its surveillance of them by lavish and attentive hospitality, personally supervised by a massive NKGB general, Sergei Nikiforovich Kruglov. When Churchill's daughter, Sarah, casually mentioned that lemon went well with caviar, a lemon tree appeared, as if by magic, in the Vorontsov orangery. At the next Allied conference, in Potsdam, General Kruglov was rewarded with a KBE, thus becoming the only Soviet intelligence officer to receive an honorary knighthood.

Stalin was even better informed about his allies at Yalta than he had been at Tehran. All of the Cambridge Five, no longer suspected of being double agents, provided a regular flow of classified intelligence or Foreign Office documents in the run-up to the conference, though it is not possible to identify which of these documents were communicated to Stalin personally. Alger Hiss actually succeeded in becoming a member of the American delegation. The problem which occupied most of the time at Yalta was the future of Poland. Having already conceded Soviet dominance of Poland at Tehran, Roosevelt and Churchill made a belated attempt to secure the restoration of Polish parliamentary democracy and a guarantee of free elections. Both were outnegotiated by Stalin, assisted once again by a detailed knowledge of the cards in their hands. He knew, for example, what importance his allies attached to allowing some "democratic" politicians into the puppet Polish provisional government already established by the Russians. On this point, after initial resistance, Stalin graciously conceded, knowing that the "democrats" could subsequently be excluded. After first playing for time, Stalin gave way on other secondary issues, having first underlined their importance, in order to preserve his allies' consent to the reality of a Soviet-dominated Poland. Watching Stalin in action at Yalta, the permanent undersecretary at the Foreign Office, Sir Alexander Cadogan, thought him in a different league as a negotiator to Churchill and Roosevelt: "He is a great man, and shows up very impressively against the background of the other two aging statesmen." Roosevelt, in rapidly failing health and with only two months to live, struck Cadogan, by contrast, as "very woolly and wobbly."[79]

Roosevelt and Churchill left Yalta with no sense that they had been deceived about Stalin's true intentions. Even Churchill, hitherto more skeptical than Roosevelt, wrote confidently, "Poor Neville Chamberlain believed he could trust Hitler. He was wrong. But I don't think I'm wrong about Stalin."[80] Some sense of how

Moscow felt that good intelligence had contributed to Stalin's success at Yalta is conveyed by Moscow's congratulations to Hiss. Gorsky reported to the Centre in March 1945, after a meeting between Akhmerov and Hiss:

> Recently ALES [Hiss] and his whole group were awarded Soviet decorations. After the Yalta conference, when he had gone on to Moscow, a Soviet personage in a very responsible position (ALES gave to understand that it was Comrade Vyshinsky [Deputy Foreign Minister]) allegedly got in touch with ALES and at the behest of the military NEIGHBOURS [GRU] passed on to him their gratitude and so on.[81]

The NKGB's regret at failing to wrest Hiss from the NEIGHBOURS must surely have intensified in April when he was appointed acting Secretary-General of the United Nations "organizing conference" at San Francisco.[82]

BEHIND THE VICTORIOUS Red Army as it swept into central Europe during the final months of the war came detachments of Smersh (short for *Smert Shpionam*, "Death to Spies!"), a military counter-intelligence agency detached from the NKVD in 1943 and placed directly under the control of Stalin as Chairman of the State Defense Committee and Defense Commissar.[83] Smersh's main mission was to hunt for traitors and Soviet citizens who had collaborated with the enemy. On Stalin's instructions, it cast its net remarkably wide, screening well over five million people. The million or more Soviet POWs who had survived the horrors of German prison camps were treated as presumed deserters and transported to the gulag, where many died.

In their anxiety to honor obligations to their ally, both the British and American governments collaborated in a sometimes barbarous repatriation. So far as Britain was concerned, the most controversial part of the forced repatriation was the handover of Cossacks and "dissident" Yugoslavs from south Austria to the Red Army and Tito's forces respectively in May and June 1945. Most had collaborated with the enemy, though sometimes only to a nominal degree. On June 1 battle-hardened soldiers of the 8th Argylls, some of them in tears, were ordered to break up a Cossack religious service and drive several thousands of unarmed men, women and children into cattle trucks with rifle butts and pick handles. There were similar horrors on succeeding days. Some of the Cossacks killed themselves and their families to save them from torture, execution or the gulag. Most of the 45,000 repatriated Cossacks were Soviet citizens, whom Churchill and Roosevelt had agreed at Yalta to return to the Soviet Union. But a minority, variously estimated at between 3,000 and 10,000 were so-called "old émigrés" who had left Russia after the civil war, had never been citizens of the Soviet Union, and were not covered by the Yalta agreement. They too were repatriated against their will.[84]

Among the "old émigrés" were a group of White generals—chief among them Pyotr Krasnov, Andrei Shkuro and Sultan Kelech Ghirey[85]—whom the NKGB and its predecessors had been pursuing for a quarter of a century. A Smersh detachment was sent to Austria with orders to track them down. Its initial inquiries to the British about their whereabouts met with no response other than the claim that no information was available. After heavy drinking at a dinner for Anglo-Russian troops, however, a British soldier blurted out that, until recently, the generals had been at a camp in the village of Gleisdorf.[86] A group of Smersh officers drove immediately to Gleisdorf where they discovered that, though the generals had left, Shkuro's mistress Yelena (surname unknown) was still there. Yelena was lured out of the camp on the pretense that she had a visitor. As she approached the Smersh car, she suddenly saw the Russian officers inside and froze with fear. She was quickly bundled into the car and revealed, under no doubt brutal interrogation, that the White generals had appealed for the Supreme Allied Commander, Field Marshal Alexander, for protection. Yelena also disclosed that the generals had with them fourteen kilograms of gold.[87] What happened next is of such importance that Mitrokhin's note on it deserves to be quoted as fully as possible:

> The Chekists [Smersh officers] raised the matter of the generals again at a meeting with . . . [a British] lieutenant-colonel. They mentioned where the generals were. The Chekists proposed that they should approach the question of the generals' fate in a business-like way. "What do you mean by that?" asked the Englishman. They explained to him. If the British would hand them over quietly at the same time as the Cossacks were repatriated, they could keep the generals' gold. "If the old men remain with you, you and your colleagues will get no benefit at all. If you accept our alternative, you will get the gold." The lieutenant-colonel thought a while and then agreed. He talked with two of his colleagues about the details of the operation. On the pretext that they were being taken to Alexander's headquarters for talks, the generals were put into cars without any of their belongings and driven to Odenburg [Judenburg] where they were handed over to the Chekists. From the hands of Smersh they were transferred to Moscow, to the Calvary of the Lubyanka.[88]

No corroboration is available from any other source for the claim in a KGB file that a British army officer (and perhaps two of his colleagues) had been bribed into handing over the White generals. Given the failure on the ground to distinguish the minority of non-Soviet Cossacks from the rest, they might well have been surrendered to Smersh in any case. The generals would probably have survived, however, if their petitions had reached Field Marshal Alexander, who might well have granted them. But the petitions mysteriously disappeared en route.[89]

The speed and injustice of the "repatriation" derived chiefly from the desire of military commanders on the spot to be rid of an unwelcome problem as soon as possible, combined with the belief that individual screening to determine which Cossacks were not of Soviet nationality would be a complex, long drawn out, and in some cases impossible task. On May 21 Brigadier Toby Low of 5 Corps, which was in charge of the "repatriation," issued an order defining who were to be regarded as Soviet citizens. The one White Russian group which could be collectively identified as non-

Soviet, the Schutzkorps, commanded by Colonel Anatol Rogozhin, was, he instructed, not to be repatriated. But those to be "treated as Soviet Nationals" included the "Ataman Group" (of which General Krasnov was a leading member) and the "Units of Lt.-Gen. Shkuro." Low added that "[i]ndividual cases [appeals] will NOT be considered unless particularly pressed," and that "[i]n all cases of doubt, the individual will be treated as a Soviet National."[90]

When all allowance is made for the difficulties of combining loyalty to allies with respect for the human rights of the Cossacks, the brutality with which the repatriation was conducted remains perhaps the most ignominious episode in twentieth-century British military history. "I reproach myself for just one thing," the 76-year-old White general Krasnov later told the NKGB. "Why did I trust the British?" On May 27, just before 3 A.M., a time of day much favored by Soviet Security, General Shkuro was awakened by an unidentified British officer, who told him he was under arrest and took him to be held under close guard well away from the Cossack camp. Another, or perhaps the same, British officer later delivered an "urgent," though bogus, invitation to General Krasnov to a conference with Field Marshal Alexander, his former comrade-in-arms during the Russian civil war. Smersh photographers were waiting to record the historic moment when the NKGB's oldest enemies were turned over to it.[91] For the British army it was a shameful moment. For Stalin, Smersh and the NKGB, it was a famous victory.

ΠIΠΕ

FROM WAR TO COLD WAR

At the end of the Second World War, the Centre faced what it feared was impending disaster in intelligence operations against its wartime allies. The first major alarm occurred in Ottawa, where relations among NKGB and GRU personnel working under "legal" cover in the Soviet embassy were as fraught as in New York. The situation was worst in the GRU residency.[1] On the evening of September 5, 1945 Igor Gouzenko, a GRU cipher clerk at the Soviet embassy in Ottawa, secretly stuffed more than a hundred classified documents under his shirt and attempted to defect. He tried hard to hold his stomach in as he walked out of the embassy. "Otherwise," his wife said later, "he would have looked pregnant."

Defection turned out to be more difficult than Gouzenko had imagined. When he sought help at the offices of the Ministry of Justice and the *Ottawa Journal*, he was told to come back the next day. But on September 6 both the Ministry of Justice and the *Ottawa Journal*, which failed to realize it was being offered the spy story of the decade, showed no more interest than on the previous evening. By the night of September 6 the Soviet embassy realized that both Gouzenko and classified documents were missing. While Gouzenko hid with his wife and child in a neighbor's flat, NKGB men broke down his door and searched his apartment. It was almost midnight before the local police came to his rescue and the Gouzenko family at last found sanctuary.[2]

As well as identifying a major GRU spy ring, Gouzenko also provided fragmentary intelligence on NKGB operations. Some months later Lavrenti Beria, the Soviet security supremo, circulated to residencies a stinging indictment of the incompetence of the GRU and, he implied, the NKGB in Ottawa:

> The most elementary principles of security were ignored, complacency and self-satisfaction went unchecked. All this was the result of a decline in political vigilance and sense of responsibility for work entrusted by the Party and the government. G[ouzenko]'s defection has caused great damage to our country and has, in particular, very greatly complicated our work in the American countries.[3]

The fear of being accused of further breaches of security made the Ottawa residency unwilling to take any initiative in recruiting new agents. According to a later damage assessment, Gouzenko's defection "paralyzed intelligence work [in Canada] for several years and continued to have a most negative effect on the work of the residency right up to 1960." In the summer of 1949 the acting resident in Ottawa, Vladimir Trofimovich Burdin (also known as Borodin), newly arrived from Moscow, wrote to the Centre to complain about his colleagues' inertia:

> The residency not merely lost all its previous contacts in Canadian circles but did not even try to acquire new ones . . . The Soviet colony closed in on itself and shut itself off from the outside world, becoming wholly preoccupied with its own internal affairs.

The Centre agreed. The residency, it concluded, had "got stuck in a rut."[4]

For the rest of Gouzenko's life the KGB tried intermittently and unsuccessfully to track him down. In 1975, after a Progressive Conservative MP, Thomas Cossit, requested a review of Gouzenko's pension, the Ottawa residency deduced that Gouzenko lived in his constituency. The residency also reported that Cossit and Gouzenko had been seen together at an ice hockey match during a visit to Canada by the Soviet national team. A KGB officer stationed in Ottawa, Mikhail Nikolayevich Khvatov, sought to cultivate Cossit in the hope of discovering Gouzenko's whereabouts. He had no success and the residency subsequently reported that parliamentary questions by Cossit were "clearly anti-Soviet in tone." Some years later the KGB began to search for compromising material on Cossit's private life and prepare active measures to discredit him. He died in 1982 before the campaign against him had begun.[5]

Gouzenko's defection in September 1945 also caused alarm at NKGB residencies in Britain and the United States. As head of SIS Section IX (Soviet Counterintelligence) Philby was kept well informed of the debriefing of Gouzenko and reported "an intensification of counter-measures" against Soviet espionage in London. The Centre responded with instructions for tight security procedures to ensure that "the valuable agent network is protected from compromise." Boris Krötenschield (aka "Krotov"), the controller of the residency's most important agents, was told to hand over all but Philby to other case officers and to reduce the frequency of meetings to once a month: "Warn all our comrades to make a thorough check when going out to a meeting and, if surveillance is observed, not to attempt under any circumstances to evade the surveillance and meet the agent . . ." If necessary, contact with British agents was to be temporarily broken off.[6]

Even greater alarm was caused by the attempted defection of an NKGB officer in Turkey, Konstantin Dmitryevich Volkov. On August 27, 1945 Volkov wrote to the British vice-consul in Istanbul, C. H. Page, requesting an urgent appointment. When Page failed to reply, Volkov turned up in person on September 4 and asked for political asylum for himself and his wife. In return for asylum and the sum of 50,000 pounds (about a million pounds at today's values), he offered important files and information obtained while working on the British desk in the Centre. Among the most highly rated Soviet agents, he revealed, were two in the Foreign Office (doubtless Burgess and Maclean) and seven "inside the British intelligence system," including one "fulfilling the function of head of a section of British counter-espionage in London" (almost certainly Philby).[7]

On September 19 Philby was startled to receive a report of Volkov's meeting with Page by diplomatic bag from the Istanbul consulate.[8] He quickly warned Krötenschield.[9] On September 21 the Turkish consulate in Moscow issued visas for two NKGB hatchet men posing as diplomatic couriers. The next day Philby succeeded in gaining authorization from the chief of SIS, Sir Stewart Menzies, to fly to Turkey to deal personally with the Volkov case. Due to various travel delays he did not arrive in Istanbul until September 26. Two days earlier Volkov and his wife, both on stretchers and heavily sedated, had been carried on board a Soviet aircraft bound for Moscow.[10] During the flight back to London Philby drafted a cynical report to Menzies on the possible reasons for Volkov's detection by the NKGB. As he wrote later,

> Doubtless both his office and his living quarters were bugged. Both he and his wife were reported to be nervous. Perhaps his manner had given him away; perhaps he had got drunk and talked too much; perhaps even he had changed his mind and confessed to his colleagues. Of course, I admitted, this was all speculation; the truth might never be known. Another theory—that the Russians had been tipped off about Volkov's approach to the British—had no solid evidence to support it. It was not worth including in my report.[11]

Under interrogation in Moscow before his execution, Volkov admitted that he had asked the British for political asylum and 50,000 pounds, and confessed that he had planned to reveal the names of no fewer than 314 Soviet agents.[12] Philby had had the narrowest of escapes. With slightly less luck in Ottawa a few weeks earlier, Gouzenko would not have been able to defect. With slightly more luck in Istanbul, Volkov would have succeeded in unmasking Philby and disrupting the MGB's British operations.

The Gouzenko and Volkov alarms occurred at a remarkably busy period for the London residency, headed until 1947 by Konstantin Kukin (codenamed IGOR). From September 11 to October 2, 1945 the Council of Foreign Ministers of the five permanent members of the UN Security Council (the United States, Soviet Union, Britain, France and China) held its first meeting in London to discuss peace treaties with defeated enemy states and other post-war problems. The residency's penetration of the Foreign Office gave it an unusually important role. Throughout the meeting, according to KGB files, the Soviet ambassador, Ivan Maisky, placed greater reliance on residency staff than on his own diplomats, forcing them to extend each working day into the early hours of the following morning.[13] The Security Council meeting, however, was a failure, publicly exposing for the first time the deep East–West divisions which by 1947 were to engender the Cold War.

At this and subsequent meetings of the Security Council, Stalin's foreign minister, Vyacheslav Mikhailovich Molotov, depended heavily on the intelligence supplied by the MGB's Western agents. Indeed, he tended to take it for granted. "Why," he roared on one occasion, "are there no documents?" At the London conference which opened in November 1947, he appears to have received some Foreign Office documents even before they reached the British delegation.[14]

The MGB's most important sources during the meetings of the Council of Foreign Ministers from 1945 to 1949 were British. Thanks to the kidnapping of Volkov, four of the wartime Magnificent Five were able to carry on work as full-time Soviet agents after the war. The exception was Anthony Blunt, who was under such visible strain that the Centre did not object to his decision to leave MI5. Shortly before he returned to the art world in November 1945 as Surveyor of the King's Pictures, Blunt made one extraordinary outburst which at the time was not taken seriously. "Well," he told his MI5 colleague Colonel "Tar" Robertson, "it's given me great pleasure to pass on the names of every MI5 officer to the Russians!" The Centre may well have hoped that Leo Long (codenamed ELLI), whom Blunt had run as a sub-agent in military intelligence during the war, would succeed him in the Security Service. Blunt recommended Long for a senior post in MI5 but the selection board passed him over, allegedly by a narrow margin, in favor of another candidate. Long moved instead to the British Control Commission in Germany, where he eventually became Deputy Director of Intelligence. There he resisted attempts to put him in regular contact with a case officer—a recalcitrance which the Centre attributed in part to the fact that Blunt had ceased to be his controller. Among the occasional services which Blunt continued to perform for the Centre were two or three visits to Germany to seek intelligence from Long.[15]

Unlike Blunt, three of the Magnificent Five—Philby, Burgess and Maclean— were all at their peak as Soviet agents, and Cairncross still close to his, when the Cold War began. Philby remained head of SIS Section IX until 1947, when he was appointed head of station in Turkey, a position which enabled him to betray agents who crossed the Russian border as well as their families and contacts inside the Soviet Union. Maclean established a reputation as a high-flying young diplomat in the Washington embassy, where he remained until 1947. In 1946 Burgess, who had joined the Foreign Office in 1944, became personal assistant to Hector McNeil, Minister of State to Ernest Bevin in the post-war Labor government.[16] After the war John Cairncross returned to the Treasury, where the London residency renewed contact with him in 1948.[17] Cairncross's main job at the Treasury over the next few years was to authorize expenditure on defense research. According to his Treasury colleague G. A. Robinson:

> [Cairncross] thus knew not just about atomic weapons developments but also plans for guided missiles, microbiological, chemical, underwater and all other types of weapons. He also needed to know, *inter alia*, about projected spending on aeronautical and radar research and anti-submarine detection, research by the Post Office and other bodies into signals intelligence, eavesdropping techniques, etc. He . . . could legitimately ask for any further details thought necessary to give Treasury approval to the spending of money.[18]

Cairncross's controller, Yuri Modin, was, unsurprisingly, "overjoyed by the quality of [his] information."[19]

The new security procedures introduced in the wake of the Gouzenko and Volkov alarms made controlling the London residency's agents far more laborious and time-consuming than during or before the war. On average, before every meeting with an agent, each case officer spent five hours moving on foot or by public transport (especially the London Underground) between locations he had studied previously in order to engage in repeated checks that he was not under surveillance. Once at the meeting place, both the case officer and the agent were required to establish visual contact and to satisfy themselves that the other was not being watched before they approached each other. If either had any doubts, they would fall back on one of three previously agreed alternative rendezvous. The system pioneered in London was later introduced into other residencies.[20]

The London residency also pioneered the use of radio intercept units to identify and monitor surveillance of its operations by the police and MI5. In addition to the main interception unit in the residency, mobile units were established in embassy cars to check the areas in which meetings took place with agents.[21] However, the Centre's experiment with the eight-man surveillance team sent to London during the Second World War to carry out checks on agents and visitors to the Soviet embassy, as well as to discover the surveillance methods used by British intelligence, was discontinued. A report in KGB archives records that, handicapped by its lack of fluency in English, the team had "no major successes."[22] The experiment was probably a total failure.

The London residency's attempts to enforce the strictest standards of secrecy and security had only a limited effect on Guy Burgess. On one occasion, while coming out of a pub where he had established visual contact with his case officer, he dropped his briefcase and scattered secret Foreign Office papers over the floor. There were frequent complaints that he turned up for meetings the worse for drink and with his clothing in disarray.[23] When George Carey-Foster, head of the embryonic security branch in the Foreign Office, first encountered Burgess in 1947, he was struck by his "disheveled and unshaven appearance. He also smelt so strongly of drink that I enquired who he was and what his job was." Yet Burgess could still display fragments of the charm and brilliance of his Cambridge years. Late in 1947, probably to get rid of him, Hector McNeil recommended Burgess to the parliamentary under-secretary at the Foreign Office, Christopher Mayhew, who was then organizing the Information Research Department (IRD) to counter Soviet "psychological warfare." Mayhew made what he later described as "an extraordinary mistake:" "I interviewed Burgess. He certainly showed a dazzling insight into Communist methods of subversion and I readily took him on." Burgess went the rounds of British embassies selling IRD's wares while simultaneously compromising the new department by reporting all its plans to Yuri Ivanovich Modin, who became his case officer in 1947 and acquired a reputation as one of the ablest agent controllers in Soviet intelligence. The chorus of protests at Burgess's undiplomatic behavior led to his removal from the IRD and transfer to the Foreign Office Far Eastern Department in the autumn of 1948.[24] Though it disturbed the Centre, Burgess's frequently outrageous conduct paradoxically strengthened his cover. Even to most of those whom he outraged he seemed as unlike a Soviet spy as it was possible to imagine.

Modin was also concerned about Nikolai Borisovich Rodin (alias "Korovin"), who succeeded Kukin as London resident in 1947. Rodin considered himself above the tight security regulations on which he insisted for the other members of the residency. According to Modin, who loathed him personally, Rodin was "known to go to clandestine meetings in one of the embassy cars, and sometimes was foolhardy enough to place direct calls to agents in their offices." But, in the rigidly hierarchical world of Soviet intelligence, Modin felt that "there was nothing I could do about it. It was hardly my place to denounce my superior in the service." As head of Faculty Number One (Political Intelligence) in the FCD Andropov Institute in the early 1980s, Modin was less inhibited. He dismissed Rodin as an arrogant, pretentious nonentity.[25]

THOUGH THE MGB's most important British agents were still undetected at the end of the 1940s, many of their American counterparts had been compromised. The Centre had complained as early as March 1945 that the membership of the Silvermaster spy ring was an open secret among "many" Washington Communists and that Harry Dexter White's Soviet "connection" had also become known. It denounced "not only the falling off in the [New York] Residency's work of controlling and educating probationers [agents], but also the lack of understanding by our operational workers of the most elementary rules in our work."[26]

The defections later in 1945 of Igor Gouzenko and Elizabeth Bentley confirmed the Centre's worst fears. In September J. Edgar Hoover reported to the White House and the State Department that Gouzenko had provided information on the activities of a number of Soviet spies in the United States, one of whom was "an assistant to the Secretary of State" (almost certainly Alger Hiss). On November 7 Bentley, who had first contacted the FBI six weeks earlier, began revealing what she knew of Soviet espionage to its New York field office. Next day Hoover sent President Truman's military aide a first list of fourteen of those identified by Bentley as supplying information to "the Soviet espionage system:" among them Assistant Secretary of the Treasury Harry Dexter White, OSS executive assistant Duncan C. Lee and Roosevelt's former aide Lauchlin Currie.[27] Bentley's defection, in turn, revived FBI interest in Whittaker Chambers' earlier evidence of pre-war Soviet espionage by Hiss, White and others.[28]

On November 20 Gorsky, the Washington resident whom Bentley knew as "A1," met her for the last time in front of Bickford's cafeteria on 23rd Street and Sixth Avenue in New York. Unaware that they were under surveillance by the FBI, Gorsky arranged their next meeting for January 20. According to Bentley, he told her that she might soon be needed "back in undercover work." By the time the date for their next rendezvous had arrived, however, Gorsky was back in Moscow.[29] His hasty departure was probably due to the discovery of Bentley's defection.[30] A few months later the resident in New York, Roland Abbiate (alias "Pravdin"), whose wife was known to Bentley, was also withdrawn.[31] A damage assessment in the Centre concluded that Bentley did not know the real name, address or telephone number of her previous controller, Iskhak Akhmerov, the illegal resident in the United States. As a precaution, however, he and his wife were recalled to Moscow.[32]

The almost simultaneous recall of Gorsky, Abbiate and Akhmerov left the MGB without experienced leadership in the United States. There were few senior officers at the Centre with first-hand knowledge of North America capable of succeeding them. In any case, as Yuri Modin later acknowledged, "We were leery of sending people out of the Soviet Union for fear of defections. Most of our officers worked in Moscow, with the result that the few men posted in foreign countries had a workload so crushing that many of them cracked under the pressure."[33] Akhmerov was not replaced as illegal resident until 1948.[34] Gorsky's two successors as chief legal resident in the United States both became bywords for incompetence in the Centre. Grigori Grigoryevich Dolbin, who arrived to replace Gorsky in 1946, had to be replaced in 1948 after showing signs of insanity (due, it was rumored in Moscow, to the onset of hereditary syphilis). His successor, Georgi Aleksandrovich Sokolov, was reprimanded by the Centre before being recalled in 1949.[35]

The most effective damage limitation measure taken by the MGB after Bentley's defection was to break off contact with most of the wartime American agents whose identities were known to her. As a result, Bentley's many leads resulted in not a single prosecution. The FBI began its investigations too late to catch any of the spies named by Bentley in the act of passing on classified information, and it was unable to use evidence from wiretaps in court. The Centre, however, failed to grasp the extent of the legal obstacles which confronted the FBI and continued to fear for several years that it would succeed in mounting a major spy trial.

The Centre's fears were strengthened by a major American codebreaking success, later codenamed VENONA. For its high-grade diplomatic and intelligence communications the Soviet Union had used since 1927 a virtually unbreakable cipher system known in the West as the "one-time pad."[36] During and immediately after the Second World War, however, some of the one-time pads were reissued, thus becoming vulnerable—though it took several years for American and British codebreakers to exploit the difficult opportunity offered to them by Soviet cryptographic carelessness. Late in 1946 Meredith Gardner, a brilliant cryptanalyst in the US Army Security [SIGINT] Agency, began decrypting some of the wartime messages exchanged between the Centre and its American residencies. By the summer of 1947 he had accumulated evidence from the decrypts of massive Soviet espionage in the wartime United States. In 1948 ASA called in the FBI. From October special agent Robert Lamphere began full-time work on VENONA, seeking to identify the agents (some still active) whose codenames appeared in the VENONA decrypts.[37] Remarkably, however, the Central Intelligence Agency was not informed of VENONA until late in 1952.[38] Even more remarkably, President Truman appears not to have been told of the decrypts, perhaps for fear that he might mention them to the Director of Central Intelligence, head of the CIA, at one of his weekly meetings with him. VENONA showed in graphic detail how OSS, the CIA's wartime predecessor, had been heavily penetrated by Soviet agents. Both Hoover and the Chairman of the Joint Chiefs of Staff, General Omar N. Bradley, seem to have suspected—wrongly—that the same was true of the Agency.[39]

The Centre learned the VENONA secret in 1947—five years earlier than the CIA—from an agent in ASA, William Weisband (codenamed ZHORA).[40] The son of Russian immigrants to the United States, Weisband was employed as a Russian linguist and roamed around ASA on the pretext of looking for projects where his linguistic skills could be of assistance. Meredith Gardner recalls Weisband looking over his shoulder at a critical moment in the project late in 1946, just as he was producing one of the first important decrypts—an NKGB telegram of December 2, 1944 which revealed Soviet penetration of Los Alamos.[41]

For the Centre, VENONA represented a series of unpredictable timebombs which threatened to explode over the next few years. It had no means of knowing precisely what NKGB telegrams would be decrypted in whole or part, or which Soviet agents would be compromised by them. Moscow's anxieties were heightened by the public controversy which broke out in the United States in the summer of 1948 over Soviet espionage. In July 1948 Elizabeth Bentley gave evidence in public for the first time to the House Committee on Un-American Activities and achieved instant media celebrity as the "Red Spy Queen." In evidence to the committee in early August, Whittaker Chambers identified Hiss, White and others as members of a secret pre-war Communist underground. The Centre wrongly feared that the committee hearings would be the prelude to a series of show trials which would expose its wartime espionage network.

DURING THE LATE 1940s Soviet foreign intelligence operations were further confused by a major reorganization in Moscow, prompted by the American National Security Act of July 1947 which established a Central Intelligence Agency "for the purpose of coordinating the intelligence activities of the several government departments and agencies in the interest of national security." Though that coordination was never fully achieved, Molotov argued that the unified foreign intelligence apparatus envisaged by the National Security Act would give the United States a clear advantage over the fragmented Soviet system. The solution, he argued, was to combine the foreign intelligence directorates of both the MGB and the GRU under a single roof. Molotov's proposal had the further advantage, from Stalin's viewpoint, of weakening the power of Beria, whose protégé, Viktor Semyonovich Abakumov, headed the MGB.[42] In July 1947 the foreign intelligence directorates of the MGB and GRU were combined to form a new unified foreign intelligence agency, the Committee of Information (Komitet Informatsii or KI).[43] Under the new, highly centralized system, even the operational plans for arranging meetings with, and investigating the reliability of, important agents required the prior approval of the KI.[44]

The appointment of Molotov as first chairman of the Committee of Information gave the Foreign Ministry greater influence on foreign intelligence operations than ever before. The first deputy chairman, responsible to Molotov for day-to-day operations, was the relatively pliant Pyotr Vasilyevich Fedotov, who had become the MGB foreign intelligence chief in the previous year.[45] Like most of the Centre management, Fedotov had almost no experience of the West. Roland Abbiate, the former resident in New York and probably the senior intelligence officer best acquainted with the West, was sacked on the formation of the KI. His file records that he was given no explanation for his dismissal and that "it was a terrible blow for him." Though the reason for the sacking is not recorded, it may well have been related to his foreign Jewish ancestry, which is duly noted in his file. Abbiate was briefly reinstated after Stalin's death, then sacked again and later committed suicide.[46]

Molotov sought to strengthen Foreign Ministry control of KI operations by appointing Soviet ambassadors in major capitals as "chief legal residents" with authority over both civilian (ex-MGB) and military (ex-GRU) residents. In the jaundiced view of the later KGB defector Ilya Dzhirkvelov:

This resulted in incredible confusion. The residents, the professional intelligence officers, resorted to incredible subterfuges to avoid informing their ambassadors about their work, since the diplomats had only amateurish knowledge of intelligence work and its methods . . .[47]

Some diplomats, however, became directly involved in intelligence operations. After the troubles in the Washington residency which led to the recall of two successive residents in 1948–9, the Soviet ambassador, Aleksandr Semyonovich Panyushkin, took personal charge for a year. He acquired such a taste for intelligence that he later became head of the KGB First (foreign intelligence) Chief Directorate.[48]

In 1949 Molotov, now out of favor with Stalin, was succeeded as both Foreign Minister and chairman of the KI by his former deputy, Andrei Vyshinsky, who had made his reputation as the brutal prosecutor in the prewar show trials. Vyshinsky retained a sycophantic devotion to Beria which showed itself even on the telephone. According to one of his successors, Andrei Gromyko, "As soon as he heard Beria's voice Vyshinsky leapt respectfully out of his chair. The conversation itself also presented an unusual picture: Vyshinsky cringed like a servant before his master."[49] Unlike Molotov, Vyshinsky had little interest in KI affairs, handing over the chairmanship after a few months to Deputy Foreign Minister Valerian Zorin. Fedotov was succeeded as first deputy chairman in charge of day-to-day operations by the more brutal and decisive Sergei Romanovich Savchenko, like Vyshinsky a protégé of Beria. Savchenko seems to have answered to Beria rather than the Foreign Ministry.[50]

By the time Vyshinsky succeeded Molotov, much of the Committee of Information had unraveled. In the summer of 1948, after a prolonged dispute with Molotov, Marshal Nikolai Aleksandrovich Bulganin, Minister for the Armed Forces, began withdrawing military intelligence personnel from KI control and returning them to the GRU. Probably with the support of Beria, Abakumov then embarked on a long drawn out struggle to recover control of the remnants of the KI. At the end of 1948 all residency officers in the EM (Russian émigré) and SK (Soviet colonies abroad) Lines returned to the MGB. The KI was finally wound up and the rest of its foreign intelligence responsibilities returned to the MGB late in 1951.[51]

THE MAIN LEGACY of the KI period to the subsequent development of Soviet intelligence was a renewed emphasis on illegals who, it was believed, would eventually establish a more secure and better-concealed foundation for foreign intelligence operations than the legal residencies, particularly in the United States. The Fourth (Illegals) Directorate of the KI, formed by combining the illegals sections of the MGB and the GRU, had a total staff of eighty-seven, headed by Aleksandr Mikhailovich Korotkov, who had made his reputation during pre-war missions to assassinate "enemies of the people" on foreign soil. In 1949, by which time military personnel in the directorate had returned to the GRU, forty-nine illegals were in training.[52] Korotkov set up departments specializing in the selection of illegals, their training and the fabrication of documentation to support their legends. By 1952 the documentation department had forged or doctored 364 foreign identity documents, including seventy-eight passports. Illegal support (Line N) officers were sent by the Centre to all major legal residencies.[53]

The first priority of the Fourth Directorate was the creation of a new illegal residency in New York to rebuild its American intelligence operations. The man selected as illegal resident, the first since Akhmerov's departure from the United States at the beginning of 1946, was Vilyam ("Willie") Genrikhovich Fisher, codenamed MARK, probably the only English-born Soviet intelligence officer.[54] Fisher's parents were Russian revolutionaries of the Tsarist era who had emigrated in 1901 to Newcastle-on-Tyne, where Vilyam had been born in 1903.[55] In 1921 the family returned to Moscow, where Fisher became a Comintern translator. During military service in 1925–6, he was trained as a radio operator and, after a brief period in the Fourth Department (Military Intelligence), was recruited by INO (OGPU foreign intelligence) in 1927. He served as a radio operator in residencies in Norway, Turkey, Britain and France until 1936, when he was appointed head of a training school for radio operators in illegal residencies.[56]

Fisher was fortunate not to be shot during the Great Terror. His file records that, as well as being automatically suspect because of his English background, he had been "referred to in positive terms" by a series of "enemies of the people," and his wife's brother was accused of being a Trotskyite. Though dismissed by the NKVD at the end of 1938, he survived to be reemployed during the Great Patriotic War in a unit training radio operators for guerrilla and intelligence operations behind German lines.[57]

Fisher's training as an illegal began in 1946 under the personal supervision of Korotkov, the head of the MGB Illegals Department. His legend was unusually complicated. Fisher assumed one identity during his journey to the United States in

1948 and another shortly after his arrival. The first identity was that of Andrei Yurgesovich Kayotis, a Lithuanian born in 1895 who had emigrated to the United States and become an American citizen. In November 1947 Kayotis crossed the Atlantic to visit relatives in Europe. While he was in Denmark, the Soviet embassy issued a travel document enabling him to visit Russia and retained his passport for use by Fisher. In October 1948 Fisher traveled to Warsaw on a Soviet passport, then traveled on Kayotis's passport via Czechoslovakia and Switzerland to Paris, where he purchased a transatlantic ticket on the SS *Scythia*. On November 6 he set sail from Le Havre to Quebec, traveled on to Montreal and—still using Kayotis's passport—crossed into the United States on November 17.[58]

On November 26 Fisher had a secret meeting in New York with the celebrated Soviet illegal I. R. Grigulevich (codenamed MAKS), who had taken part in the first attempt to assassinate Trotsky in Mexico City and had led a Latin American sabotage group during the war attacking ships and cargoes bound for Germany.[59] Grigulevich gave Fisher 1,000 dollars and three documents in the name of Emil Robert Goldfus: a genuine birth certificate, a draft card forged by the Centre and a tax certificate (also forged). Fisher handed back Kayotis's documents and became Goldfus. The real Goldfus, born in New York on August 2, 1902, had died at the age of only fourteen months. Fisher's file records that his birth certificate had been obtained by the NKVD in Spain at the end of the Spanish Civil War, at a time when it was collecting identity documents from members of the International Brigades for use in illegal operations, but gives no other details of its provenance. According to the legend constructed by the Centre, Goldfus was the son of a German house painter in New York, had spent his childhood at 120 East 87th Street, left school in 1916 and worked in Detroit until 1926. After further periods in Grand Rapids, Detroit and Chicago, the legendary Goldfus had returned to New York in 1947. The legend, however, was far from perfect. The Centre instructed Fisher not to seek employment for fear that his employer would make inquiries which would blow his cover. Instead, he was told to open an artist's studio and claim to be self-employed.[60] As Fisher mingled with other New York artists, his technique gradually improved and he became a competent, if rather conventional, painter. He surprised friends in the artistic community with his admiration for the late nineteenth-century Russian painter Levitan, of whom they had never heard, but made no mention of Stalinist "socialist realism," with which he was probably also in sympathy. Fisher made no secret of his dislike for abstract painting. "You know," he told another artist, "I think most contemporary art is headed down a blind alley."[61]

In 1949, as the basis of his illegal residency, Fisher was given control of a group of agents headed by Morris Cohen (codenamed LUIS and VOLUNTEER), which included his wife Lona (LESLE).[62] Following Elizabeth Bentley's defection, the Centre had temporarily broken contact with the Cohens early in 1946, but renewed contact with them in Paris a year later and reactivated them in the United States in 1948.[63] The most important agent in the VOLUNTEER network was the physicist Ted Hall (MLAD), for whom Lona Cohen had acted as courier in 1945 when he was passing atomic intelligence from Los Alamos.[64] Early in 1948, Hall, then working for his PhD at Chicago University, had joined the Communist Party together with his wife Joan, apparently with the intention of abandoning work as a Soviet agent and working for the campaign of the Progressive candidate, the naively pro-Soviet Henry Wallace, in the presidential election.[65] Morris Cohen, however, persuaded Hall to return to espionage. On August 2, 1948 the Washington residency telegraphed the Centre:

> LUIS has met MLAD. He has persuaded him to break contact with the Progressive organization and concentrate on science. Important information obtained on MLAD's two new contacts. They have declared their wish to transmit data on ENORMOZ [the nuclear program], subject to two conditions: MLAD must be their only contact and their names must not be known to officers of ARTEMIS [Soviet intelligence].[66]

The VOLUNTEER network expanded to include, in addition to MLAD, three other agents: ADEN, SERB and SILVER.[67] Two of these were undoubtedly the two nuclear physicists contacted by Hall. Though their identities remain unknown, the Centre clearly regarded their intelligence as of the first importance. According to an SVR history, "the Volunteer group . . . were able to guarantee the transmittal to the Centre of supersecret information concerning the development of the American atomic bomb."[68]

In recognition of the VOLUNTEER group's success, Fisher was awarded the Order of Red Banner in August 1949.[69] A year later, however, his illegal residency was disrupted by the arrest of Julius and Ethel Rosenberg, for whom Lona Cohen had acted as courier. Both the Cohens were quickly withdrawn to Mexico, where they were sheltered for several months by the Soviet agents OREL ("Eagle") and FISH—both members of the Spanish Communist Party in exile[70]—before moving on to Moscow. The Cohens were to resurface a few years later, under the names Peter and Helen Kroger, as members of a new illegal residency in Britain.[71] Hall's career as a Soviet spy was also interrupted. In March 1951 he was questioned by an FBI team which was convinced that he was guilty of espionage but lacked the evidence for a prosecution.[72]

Under his later alias "Rudolf Abel," Fisher was to become one of the best-known of all Soviet illegals, whose career was publicized by the KGB as a prime example of the success and sophistication of its operations in the West during the Cold War. In reality, Fisher never came close to rivaling the achievements of his wartime predecessor, Iskhak Akhmerov. During eight years as illegal resident, he appears never to have identified, let alone recruited, a single promising potential agent to replace the VOLUNTEER network.[73] Unlike Akhmerov, however, he did not have the active and enthusiastic assistance of a well-organized American Communist Party (CPUSA) to act as talent-spotters and assistants. Part of the reason for Fisher's lack of success was the post-war decline and persecution of the CPUSA.[74]

THE MOST IMPORTANT American agent recruited during the early Cold War, Aleksandr ("Sasha") Grigoryevich Kopatzky, was a walk-in. Kopatzky had been born in the city of Surozh in Bryansk Oblast in 1923,[75] and had served as a lieutenant in Soviet intelligence from August 1941 until he was wounded and captured by the Germans in December 1943. While in a German hospital he agreed to work for German intelligence. During the last two months of the war he served as an intelligence officer in General Andrei Vlasov's anti-Soviet Russian Army of Liberation which fought the Red Army in alliance with the Wehrmacht. At the end of the war, Kopatzky was briefly imprisoned by the American authorities in the former concentration camp at Dachau.[76]

Despite his service in the NKVD, Kopatzky's anti-Soviet credentials seemed so well established that he was invited to join the American-supervised German intelligence service established in 1946 at Pullach, near Munich, by General Reinhard Gehlen, the former Wehrmacht intelligence chief on the eastern front.[77] In 1948 Kopatzky further distanced himself from his Soviet past by marrying the daughter of a former SS officer, Eleonore Stirner, who had been briefly imprisoned for her activities in the Hitler Youth. Eleonore later recalled that her husband "drank a lot of vodka. He kissed ladies' hands . . . He was very punctual, shined his shoes, did his gymnastics in the morning, had a neat haircut, short hair all his life. And he was a very good shot. Sasha liked to hunt and talked of hunting tigers in Siberia with his father." Many years later, after Sasha's death, it suddenly occurred to Eleonore, while watching a televised adaptation of a John Le Carré novel, that her husband might have married her to improve his cover. That realization, she says, "came like a mountain of bricks on me."[78] By their wedding day Kopatzky was probably already planning to renew contact with Soviet intelligence.

The SVR still regards the Kopatzky case as extremely sensitive. It insisted as recently as 1997 that no file exists which suggests that Kopatzky, under any of his aliases, ever engaged in "collaboration . . . with Soviet intelligence."[79] Mitrokhin, however, was able to take detailed notes from the bulky file which the SVR claims does not exist. The file reveals that in 1949 Kopatzky visited the Soviet military mission in Baden-Baden, and was secretly transported to East Berlin where he agreed to become a Soviet agent.[80] Soon afterwards, he infiltrated the anti-Soviet émigré organization Union of the Struggle for Liberation of the Peoples of Russia (SBONR), based in Munich, which had close links with the CIA. In 1951, doubtless to his Soviet controllers' delight, he was recruited by the CIA station in West Berlin as "principal agent."[81] Successively codenamed ERWIN, HERBERT and RICHARD by the Centre, Kopatzky received a monthly salary of 500 marks in addition to his income from the CIA. Among his earliest successes was, on November 5, 1951, to get one of his fellow CIA agents, the Estonian Vladimir Kivi (wrongly described in Kopatzky's file as an "American intelligence chief"), drunk, transport him to East Berlin and hand him over to Soviet intelligence.[82] Though Kopatzky was not a CIA staff officer and never worked at Agency headquarters, he did enormous damage to Agency operations in Germany for more than a decade.[83] According to his file, no fewer than twenty-three KGB legal operational officers and one illegal "met and worked with him"—a certain indication of how highly the Centre rated him.[84]

THROUGHOUT THE COLD WAR, Soviet intelligence regarded the United States as its "main adversary." In second place at the beginning of the Cold War was the United States's closest ally, the United Kingdom. In third position came France.[85] Before the Second World War, France had been a major base for NKVD foreign operations. Her crushing defeat in June 1940, however, followed by the German occupation of northern France, the establishment of the collaborationist Vichy regime in the south (later also occupied by the Germans) and Hitler's invasion of the Soviet Union in June 1941 drastically reduced the scope for Soviet penetration. The NKGB did, however, establish a strong presence within Communist sections of the French Resistance.

There were two main groups of Soviet agents in wartime France: one in Paris of about fifty Communists and fellow travelers headed by LEMOINE (transliterated into the Cyrillic alphabet as LEMONYE), and another of over twenty-five headed by HENRI, based on Toulouse, with, from 1941, a subgroup in Paris. According to KGB records, the LEMOINE group, most of whom believed they were working for the Communist Party rather than the NKGB, "was disbanded because of treachery." Though six members of the HENRI group (KLOD, LUCIEN, MORIS, ROBERT and ZHANETTA) were caught and shot by the Germans, the core of the group survived.[86]

At the end of the war Soviet intelligence had much greater freedom of action in France than in either the United States or Britain. The *Parti Communiste Français* (PCF) publicly congratulated itself on its undeniably heroic role in the wartime Resistance, proudly termed itself *le parti des fusillés* ("the party of the shot"), and greatly inflated the numbers of its fallen heroes. From August 1944, when General de Gaulle invited the PCF to join the Provisional Government, there were Communist ministers for the first time in French history. According to an opinion poll in May 1945, 57 percent of the population thought that the defeat of Germany was due principally to the Soviet Union (20 percent gave the most credit to the United States, 12 percent to Britain). In the elections of October 1945 the PCF, with 26 percent of the vote, emerged as the largest party in France. By the end of the year it had almost 800,000 members. Though support for the PCF had almost peaked, there were many who hoped—or feared, particularly after de Gaulle's resignation early in 1946—that France was on the road to becoming a Communist-controlled "people's democracy." One socialist minister privately complained, "How many senior civil servants, even at the very top, are backing Communism to win!"[87]

The Centre's first instructions to the newly re-established Paris residency after the Liberation, dated November 18, 1944, instructed it to profit from the "current favorable situation" to renew contact with the pre-war agent network and recruit new agents in the foreign and interior ministries, intelligence agencies and political parties and organizations. Inspired by the success of scientific and technological intelligence-gathering in Britain and the United States, the Centre sent further instructions on February 20, 1945, ordering the residency to extend its recruitment to the Pasteur and

Curie Institutes and other leading research bodies.[88] The appointment of the ardent Communist and Nobel Laureate Frédéric Joliot-Curie as the French government's Director of Scientific Research doubtless delighted the Centre. Joliot-Curie assured Moscow that "French scientists . . . will always be at your disposal without asking for any information in return."[89]

During 1945 the Paris residency sent 1,123 reports to Moscow, based on intelligence from seventy sources. Its operational problems derived not from any lack of agents but from a shortage of controllers. Up to February 1945 the residency had only three operational officers.[90] In May MARCEL of the wartime HENRI group was instructed to set up a new group to assist in the penetration of the post-war foreign and domestic intelligence agencies, the foreign ministry and the political parties, and in re-establishing control over agents in the provinces.[91] By November the number of operational officers in the Paris residency had increased to seven, supported by six technical staff, but there was to be no further increase for several years. In addition to recruiting new agents, the residency was ordered to check individually every agent recruited before the war. Unsurprisingly, its 1945 reports were criticized for lack of depth and insufficient attention to the most valuable agents.[92]

The next available statistics on the intelligence supplied by the Paris residency cover the period from July 1, 1946 to June 30, 1947, when it supplied 2,627 reports and documents, well over double the total for 1945. It also had some major recruiting successes. In 1944 WEST, recruited by HENRI from the Resistance in the previous year, joined the newly founded foreign intelligence agency the DGER (from January 1946 the Service de Documentation Extérieure et de Contre Espionnage (SDECE)), working first on the British, then the Italian, desk. His file records that he provided "valuable information on the French, Italian and British intelligence services." Though WEST (later renamed RANOL) was dismissed in 1945 and moved to a career in publishing, he retained contact with some of his former colleagues. RATYEN, the first of his recruits to be identified in the files noted by Mitrokhin, was dismissed from SDECE in 1946. In 1947 WEST recruited two, more important SDECE officers, codenamed CHOUAN (or TORMA) and NOR (or NORMAN).[93]

Soviet penetration was assisted by the chronic infighting within SDECE. In May 1946 André Dewavrin (alias "Passy"), de Gaulle's wartime intelligence chief and the first head of SDECE, was arrested on a charge of embezzlement of which he was later found innocent.[94] For the next few years Dewavrin's successor, Henri Ribière, and his deputy, Pierre Fourcaud, were engaged in such bitter feuding that Fourcaud was forced to deny accusations that he had sabotaged the brakes of Ribière's car and caused a near fatal accident. On one occasion, during the fractious daily meeting of SDECE division heads, Ribière drove his deputy out of the room with his walking stick. As one SDECE officer complained, "[D]ivision heads, finding themselves with conflicting orders from their director and his deputy, did not know what to do."[95]

In the year up to June 30, 1947, the Paris residency forwarded to the Centre 1,147 documents on the French intelligence services, 92 on French intelligence operations against the Soviet Union and 50 on other intelligence agencies.[96] The files noted by

Mitrokhin record that both CHOUAN and NOR worked on political intelligence (SDECE Section d'études politiques). CHOUAN was employed for a time in the American department of SDECE, but by 1949 was working on Soviet Bloc affairs. NOR specialized in intelligence on Italy.[97] WEST was paid 30,000 francs a month by the Paris residency, and in 1957 was given 360,000 francs to buy a flat.[98] Ivan Ivanovich Agayants, the Paris resident from 1946 to 1948, was fond of boasting of his success in penetrating SDECE. In a lecture at the Centre in 1952 he sneeringly described French intelligence as "that prostitute I put in my pocket."[99]

Penetration of the Foreign Ministry at the Quai d'Orsay proved more difficult. During a visit to Moscow in June 1946, the Communist trade union leader Benoît Frachon reported pessimistically:

> The officials of the Foreign Ministry represent a very closed caste . . . well known for their reactionary views. Our situation at the ministry is very precarious. We have only one Party member. This is the private secretary of [Georges] Bidault [the Foreign Minister], who knows that she is Communist—so we do not have total confidence in her. Among the diplomats in foreign postings, only the embassy secretary in Prague is Communist.

The Communist embassy secretary was almost certainly Étienne Manac'h, who went on to become French ambassador in Beijing (1969–75).[100] Manac'h, codenamed TAKSIM, had first made contact with Soviet intelligence while stationed in Turkey in 1942. His KGB file describes him as a confidential contact rather than an agent, who provided information from time to time "on an ideological-political basis" until 1971. His information was clearly valued by the Centre. During his twenty-nine years' contact with the KGB he had six case officers, the last of whom—M. S. Tsimbal—was head of the FCD Fifth Department, whose responsibilities included operations in France.[101]

The KGB's most important Cold War agents in the Foreign Ministry were cipher personnel rather than diplomats. Ultimately the most valuable and longest-serving agent recruited by the Paris embassy at the end of the war was probably a 23-year-old cipher officer in the Quai d'Orsay codenamed JOUR (transliterated into the Cyrillic alphabet as ZHUR). The large amount of Foreign Ministry documents and cipher materials provided by JOUR were despatched from Paris to Moscow in what his file describes as "a special container," and enabled much of the cipher traffic between the Quai d'Orsay and French embassies abroad to be decrypted. In 1957 he was secretly awarded the Order of the Red Star. JOUR was still active a quarter of a century later, and in 1982 was awarded the Order of the Friendship of Peoples for his "long and fruitful co-operation."[102]

The dismissal of Communist ministers from the French government in May 1947 made further Soviet penetration of the official bureaucracy more difficult. The Centre complained in April 1948 that: the residency had no agents close to the leadership of the Gaullist *Rassemblement du Peuple Français,* the Christian

Democrat MRP and other "reactionary" political parties; it had failed to penetrate the Soviet section of SDECE; intelligence on the British and American embassies was poor; and inadequate progress had been made in penetrating the Commissariat on Atomic Energy and other major targets for scientific and technological intelligence.[103]

A plan was drawn up to remedy these failings and to promote active measures "to compromise people hostile to the USSR and the French Communist Party." Once again, Moscow was not fully satisfied with the results achieved. In the five-month period from September 1 to February 1, 1949, the Paris residency submitted 923 reports, of which 20 percent were judged sufficiently important to pass on to the Central Committee. The Centre noted, however, that "the requirement set by the leadership with regard to political intelligence had still not been adequately met." During the eleven months from February 1 to December 31 the residency supplied 1,567 reports. Though 21 percent were passed to the Central Committee, the reports were criticized for failing to "reveal the innermost aspects of events" and for "not making it possible to identify the plans of ruling circles in their struggle with democratic [pro-Soviet] forces."[104]

The decline in the number of reports to the Centre during 1949—about forty a month fewer than during the latter months of 1948—was due chiefly to what the files describe as a "deterioration in the operational situation" at the beginning of the year, caused by heightened surveillance by the internal security service, the Direction de la Surveillance du Territoire (DST), and the Sûreté. On March 12, 1949 the Centre warned the Paris residency of the danger of continuing to meet agents on the street or in cafés and restaurants and advised it to make much greater use of dead letter-boxes, messages in invisible ink and radio communication. The residency was also instructed to train its agents to recognize and evade surveillance, and to instruct them on how to behave if questioned or arrested. A month later the residency reported to the Centre that, though it was impracticable to abandon completely street meetings with agents, security had been much improved. Case officers were now forbidden to go directly from the embassy or any other Soviet premises to meet an agent. Before each meeting the officer was picked up by a residency driver at a prearranged location and driven to the area of the rendezvous, after elaborate security checks designed to detect surveillance. Following the meeting the case officer would pass on any materials supplied by the agent to another residency officer in a "brush contact" as they walked past each other. Both times and places of meetings with agents were regularly changed, and more rendezvous were arranged in churches, theaters, exhibitions and locations outside Paris.[105]

As a further security precaution, the frequency of meetings with agents was also reduced. The six most valuable were seen twice a month, ten other agents were met once a month and another seven once every two months. Less important agents were either put on ice or contacted by pre-arranged signals only as the need arose. After a year operating the new security procedures, the Paris residency reported that operating conditions had improved. On April 22, 1950 it informed the Centre that it was in contact with almost fifty agents—twice as many as a year before.[106] For most of the next decade the residency was to provide better intelligence than its counterparts in Britain and the United States.[107]

THE ORGANIZATIONAL CONFUSION of Soviet foreign intelligence in the late 1940s was reflected in the running of its three most productive British agents. Remarkably, even Kim Philby had no regular controller during his term as head of station in Turkey from 1947 to 1949. Except during visits to London, he communicated with Soviet intelligence via Guy Burgess. Burgess's behavior, however, was becoming increasingly erratic. To his controller, Yuri Modin, it seemed "that his nerve was going, and that he could no longer take the strain of his double life."[108] A trip by Burgess to Gibraltar and Tangier in the autumn of 1949 turned into what Goronwy Rees called a "wild odyssey of indiscretions": among them failing to pay his hotel bills, publicly identifying British intelligence officers and drunkenly singing in local bars, "Little boys are cheap today, cheaper than yesterday." Burgess was surprised not to be sacked on his return to London.[109] Once back in the Foreign Office, however, he resumed his career as a dedicated Soviet agent, supplying large quantities of classified papers. On December 7, 1949, for example, he handed Modin 168 documents, totaling 660 pages. KGB files also credit Burgess with using Anglo-American policy differences over the People's Republic of China, established in October 1949, to cause friction in the "Special Relationship."[110]

Donald Maclean was under even greater strain than Burgess. His posting to Cairo in October 1948 as counselor and head of chancery at the age of only thirty-five seemed to set him on a path which would lead him to the top of the diplomatic service, or a position close to it. But Maclean became deeply depressed at his insensitive handling by the Cairo residency. The documents he supplied were accepted without comment and no indication was given by the Centre of what was expected of him. In December 1949 Maclean attached to a bundle of classified diplomatic documents a note asking to be allowed to give up his work for Soviet intelligence. The Cairo residency gave so little thought to running Maclean that it forwarded his note unread to Moscow. Incredibly, the Centre also ignored it. Not till Maclean sent another appeal in April 1950, asking to be released from the intolerable strain of his double life, did he attract the Centre's attention. It then read for the first time the letter he had sent four months earlier.[111]

While the Centre was deliberating, Maclean went berserk. One evening in May, while in a drunken rage, he and his drinking companion Philip Toynbee broke into the flat of two female members of the US embassy, ransacked their bedroom, ripped apart their underclothes, then moved on to destroy the bathroom. There, Toynbee later recalled, "Donald raises a large mirror above his head and crashes it into the bath, when to my amazement and delight, alas, the bath breaks in two while the mirror remains intact." A few days later Maclean was sent back to London where the Foreign Office gave him the summer off and paid for treatment by a psychiatrist who diagnosed overwork, marital problems and repressed homosexuality. In the autumn, apparently back in control of himself, at least in office hours, he was made head of the American desk in the Foreign Office.[112]

The impact of Burgess's and Maclean's intelligence in Moscow was heightened by the outbreak of the Korean War in June 1950. Maclean's deputy on the American desk, Robert Cecil, later concluded that the Kremlin must have found the documents provided by Maclean "of inestimable value in advising the Chinese and the North Koreans on strategy and negotiating positions."[113] In addition to supplying classified documents, Maclean and Burgess also put their own anti-American gloss on them and thus strengthened Soviet fears that the United States might escalate the Korean conflict into world war. For perhaps the first time in his diplomatic career, Maclean showed open sympathy in a Foreign Office minute with the crude Stalinist analysis of the inherently aggressive designs of American finance capital. There was, he said, "some point" to the argument that the American economy was now so geared to the military machine that all-out war might seem preferable to a recession produced by demobilization.[114]

The Centre's most prized British agent, however, remained Kim Philby, who, it was hoped, would one day rise to become Chief of the Secret Service. In the autumn of 1949 he was appointed SIS station commander in Washington. Philby was exultant. His new posting, he later wrote, brought him "right back into the middle of intelligence policy-making" and gave him "a close-up view of the American intelligence organizations."[115]

Before his departure for the United States, Philby was "indoctrinated" into the VENONA secret. Though aware of the possibility that one of the decrypts might identify him as a Soviet agent, he was doubtless reassured to discover that VENONA provided comparatively little information on NKGB activities in Britain.[116] The bulk of the Soviet intelligence decrypts concerned operations in the United States. In late September 1949, immediately after the successful test of the first Soviet atomic bomb, Philby discovered during his VENONA briefing that the atom spy CHARLES in Los Alamos had been identified as Klaus Fuchs. The Centre promptly warned those of its American agents who had been in contact with Fuchs that they might have to escape through Mexico.[117] It did not, however, succeed in warning Fuchs, who in April 1950 was sentenced to fourteen years' imprisonment.[118]

On his arrival in Washington in October 1949, Philby quickly succeeded in gaining regular access to VENONA decrypts. That access became particularly important after the arrest and imprisonment in the following year of William Weisband, the American agent who had first revealed the VENONA secret to the Centre.[119] Philby's liaison duties with the CIA allowed him to warn the Centre of American as well as British operations against the Soviet Bloc, even enabling him to provide the geographical coordinates of parachute drops by British and American agents.[120] When writing his memoirs later, Philby was sometimes unable to resist gloating over the fate of the hundreds of agents he betrayed. Referring to those who parachuted into the arms of the MGB, he wrote with macabre irony, "I do not know what happened to the parties concerned. But I can make an informed guess."[121]

Philby's success in Washington was achieved despite, rather than because of, the assistance given him by the KI/MGB in Washington. The chaotic state of the Washington residency, which led to the recall of two successive residents in 1948–9,[122] made Philby refuse to have any contact with any legal Soviet intelligence officers in the United States.[123] For almost a year Philby's sole contact with the Centre was via messages sent to Burgess in London.[124]

In the summer of 1950 Philby received an unexpected letter from Burgess. "I have a shock for you," Burgess began. "I have just been posted to Washington." Philby later claimed in his memoirs that he had agreed to put Burgess up in his large neo-classical house at 4100 Nebraska Avenue during his tour of duty at the Washington embassy to try to keep him out of the spectacular "scrapes" for which he was now notorious.[125] The "scrapes," however, continued. In January 1951 Burgess burst in on a dinner party given by the Philbys and drew an insulting (and allegedly obscene) caricature of Libby Harvey, wife of a CIA officer. The Harveys stormed out, Aileen Philby retired to the kitchen and Kim sat with his head in his hands, repeatedly asking Burgess, "How could you? How could you?"[126]

Despite Burgess's scrapes in the United States, he fulfilled an important role as courier between Philby and his newly appointed case officer, a Russian illegal code-named HARRY (GARRI in Cyrillic transliteration), who had arrived in New York a few months before Burgess began his posting at the Washington embassy. HARRY had been born Valeri Mikhaylovich Makayev in 1918. In May 1947 he had been sent to Warsaw to establish his legend as a US citizen who had lived for some years in Poland. As evidence of his bogus identity the Centre gave him an out-of-date US passport issued in 1930 to Ivan ("John") Mikhailovich Kovalik, born in Chicago to Ukrainian parents in 1917.[127] The real Kovalik, whose identity Makayev assumed, had been taken to Poland as a child by his parents in 1930, later settling in the Soviet Union; he died in 1957 in Chelyabinskaya Oblast.

After two years in Warsaw, Makayev was able to obtain a new US passport in the name of Kovalik with the help of a female clerk at the American embassy. The MGB discovered that in November 1948, without informing the embassy, the clerk had married a Polish citizen with whom she planned to return to the United States after her tour of duty. Anxious to keep her marriage secret, she was pressured by the MGB into swearing under oath that she was personally acquainted with Kovalik and his parents and could vouch for his good character. According to Makayev's file, his application for a new US passport was "processed in an expeditious manner and with significant deviations from the rules." The corrupt embassy clerk received a reward of 750 dollars.[128]

On March 5, 1950 Makayev left Gdynia for the United States on board the ship Batory.[129] The Centre concluded that his cover, like Fisher's, could best be preserved within New York's cosmopolitan artistic community. Soon after his arrival, he began an affair with a Polish-born ballerina, codenamed ALICE, who owned a ballet studio in Manhattan. Makayev's gifts as a musician probably exceeded Fisher's as a painter. After a brief period working as a furrier, he succeeded in obtaining a job teaching musical composition at New York University.[130]

The Centre had high hopes of Makayev. He was given 25,000 dollars to establish a new illegal American residency to run parallel with Fisher's. Two other Soviet illegals were selected to work under him: Reino Hayhanen (codenamed VIK), who had assumed a bogus Finnish identity, and Vitali Ivanovich Lyampin (DIM or DIMA), who had an Austrian legend. Two dedicated communications channels were prepared for the new residency: a postal route between agents MAY in New York and GERY in London, and a courier route using ASKO, a Finnish seaman on a ship which traveled between Finland and New York. Makayev impressed the Centre by getting to know the family of the Republican senator for Vermont, Ralph E. Flanders. His main mission, however, was to act as controller of Moscow's most important British agent, Kim Philby.[131]

Burgess's first journey as a courier between Philby in Washington and Makayev in New York took place in November 1950.[132] The main pretext for his journeys to New York was to visit his friend Alan Maclean (younger brother of Donald), private secretary to the British representative at the United Nations, Gladwyn Jebb.[133] Once the liaison established by Burgess was working smoothly, Philby agreed to meet Makayev himself. Burgess, however, continued to act as the usual method of communication between Philby and his case officer.[134] His visits to Alan Maclean became so frequent that Jebb formed the mistaken impression that the two men "shared a flat." Conversations with Alan doubtless also helped Burgess keep track of Donald Maclean's unstable mental state.[135]

Some of the most important intelligence which Philby supplied to Makayev directly concerned Maclean. The VENONA decrypts to which he had access contained a number of references to an agent codenamed HOMER operating in Washington at the end of the war, but initially only vague clues to his identity. Philby quickly realized that HOMER was Maclean, but was informed by the Centre that "Maclean should stay in his post as long as possible" and that plans would be made to rescue him "before the net closed in."[136] The net did not begin to close until the winter of 1950–1. By the end of 1950 the list of suspects had narrowed to thirty-five. By the beginning of April 1951 it had shrunk to nine.[137] A few days later a telegram decrypted by Meredith Gardner finally identified HOMER as Maclean. It revealed that in June 1944 HOMER's wife was expecting a baby and living with her mother in New York[138]—information which fitted Melinda Maclean but not the wife of any other suspect.

There still remained a breathing space of at least a few weeks in which to arrange Maclean's escape. The search for the evidence necessary to convict him of espionage, complicated by the decision not to use VENONA in any prosecution, made necessary a period of surveillance by MI5 before any arrest. The plan to warn Maclean that he had been identified as a Soviet agent was worked out not by the Centre but by Philby and Burgess.[139] In April 1951 Burgess was ordered home in disgrace after a series of escapades had aroused the collective wrath of the Virginia State Police, the State Department and the British ambassador. On the eve of Burgess's departure from New York aboard the *Queen Mary,* he and Philby dined together in a Chinese restaurant where the piped music inhibited eavesdropping and agreed that Burgess would convey a warning to both Maclean and the London residency as soon as he reached Britain.[140]

Philby was even more concerned with his own survival than with Maclean's. If Maclean cracked under interrogation, as seemed possible in view of his overwrought condition, Philby and the rest of the Five would also be at risk. Mitrokhin's notes on the KGB file record: "STANLEY [Philby] demanded HOMER's immediate exfiltration to the USSR, so that he himself would not be compromised."[141] He also extracted an assurance from Burgess that he would not accompany Maclean to Moscow, for that too would compromise him. Immediately after his return to England on May 7, Burgess called on Blunt and asked him to deliver a message to Modin, whom Blunt knew as "Peter." According to Modin, Blunt's anxious appearance, even before he spoke, indicated that something was desperately wrong. "Peter," he said, "there's serious trouble. Guy Burgess has just arrived back in London. HOMER's about to be arrested . . . Donald's now in such a state that I'm convinced he'll break down the moment they question him." Two days later the Centre agreed to Maclean's exfiltration.[142]

Meanwhile Burgess had seen Maclean and was worried that, despite (or because of) his nervous exhaustion, he might refuse to defect. He reported to Modin and the London resident, Nikolai Rodin, that Maclean could not bring himself to leave his wife Melinda, who was expecting their third child in a few weeks' time. When Rodin reported Maclean's hesitations to Moscow, the Centre telegraphed, "HOMER *must* agree to defect." Melinda Maclean, who had been aware that her husband was a Soviet spy ever since he had asked her to marry him, agreed that, for his own safety, he should leave for Moscow without delay.[143] It was clear, however, that Maclean would need an escort. On May 17 the Centre instructed the London residency that Burgess was to accompany him to Moscow. Burgess initially refused to go, recalling his promise to Philby not to defect, and seemed to Modin "close to hysteria." Rodin, however, seems to have persuaded Burgess to go by giving the impression that he would not need to accompany Maclean all the way, and would in any case be free to return to London. In reality, the Centre believed that Burgess had become a liability and was determined to get him to Moscow—by deception, if necessary—and keep him there. "As long as he agreed to go with Maclean," wrote Modin later, "the rest mattered precious little. Cynically enough, the Centre had . . . concluded that we had not one but two burnt-out agents on our hands."[144]

Though the Foreign Secretary, Herbert Morrison, had secretly authorized the interrogation of Maclean, no date had been decided for it to begin.[145] The London residency, however, mistakenly believed that Maclean was to be arrested on Monday, May 28, and made plans for his exfiltration with Burgess during the previous weekend. It reported to the Centre that surveillance of Maclean by MI5 and Special Branch ceased at 8 p.m. each day and at weekends. (It may not have realized that there was no surveillance at all of Maclean at his home at Tatsfield on the Kent–Surrey border.) The residency also discovered that the pleasure boat *Falaise* made weekend round-trip cruises from Southampton, calling in at French ports, which did not require passports. Burgess was instructed to buy tickets for himself and Maclean under assumed names for the cruise leaving at midnight on Friday, May 25. That evening Burgess arrived at Tatsfield in a hired car, had dinner with the Macleans, then drove off with Donald to Southampton where they were just in time to board the *Falaise* before it set sail. The next morning they left the boat at St. Malo, made their way to Rennes and caught the train to Paris. From Paris they took another train to Switzerland, where they were issued false passports by the Soviet embassy in Berne. In Zurich they bought air tickets to Stockholm via Prague, but left the plane at Prague, where they were met by Soviet intelligence officers.[146] By the time Melinda Maclean had reported that her husband had not returned home after the weekend, Burgess and Maclean were behind the Iron Curtain.[147]

Once in the Soviet Union, Burgess was told that he would not be allowed back to Britain but would receive an annual pension of 2,000 roubles.[148] Modin later complained that his talents were wasted by the Centre: "He read a lot, walked and occasionally picked up another man for sex . . . He might have been very useful to [the KGB]; but instead he did nothing because nothing was asked of him, and it was not in his nature to solicit work."[149] Maclean was rather better treated than Burgess. He settled in Kuibyshev, took Soviet citizenship under the name Mark Petrovich Fraser, was awarded an annual pension twice that of Burgess and taught for the next two years at the Kuibyshev Pedagogical Institute. In September 1953, in an operation codenamed SIRA, his wife and three children were exfiltrated from Britain to join him in Kuibyshev.[150]

THE CENTRE CONGRATULATED itself that the successful exfiltration of Burgess and Maclean had "raised the authority of the Soviet intelligence service in the eyes of Soviet agents."[151] That, however, was not Philby's view. At a meeting on May 24, Makayev had found him "alarmed and concerned for his own security" and insistent that he would be put "in jeopardy" if Burgess as well as Maclean fled to Moscow.[152] The first that Philby learned of Burgess's defection with Maclean was during a briefing about five days later by the MI5 liaison officer in Washington. "My consternation [at the news]," wrote Philby later, "was no pretense." Later that day he drove into the Virginia countryside and buried the photographic equipment with which he had copied documents for Soviet intelligence in a forest—an action he had mentally rehearsed many times since arriving in Washington two years earlier.[153] Just when Philby most needed his controller's assistance, however, Makayev let him down. The New York legal residency left a message and 2,000 dollars in a dead letter-box for HARRY to deliver to Philby. Makayev failed to find them and Philby never received them.[154]

An inquiry by the Centre into Makayev's conduct in New York, prompted by his failure to help Philby, was highly critical. It found him guilty of "lack of discipline," "violations of the Centre's orders" and "crude manners"—a defect blamed on his neglected childhood. Plans for Makayev to found a new illegal residency in the United States were canceled and he was transferred to Fisher's residency so that he could receive expert supervision. His performance, however, failed to improve. While returning to New York from leave in Moscow, he lost a hollow imitation Swiss coin which contained secret operational instructions on microfilm. After a further inquiry at the

Centre, Makayev was recalled and his career as an illegal terminated. Attempts to recover 9,000 dollars allotted to him in New York (2,000 dollars in bank accounts and 7,000 dollars in stocks) were unsuccessful and the whole sum had to be written off.[155]

The Centre calculated that since their recruitment in 1934–5, Philby, Burgess and Maclean had supplied more than 20,000 pages of "valuable" classified documents and agent reports.[156] As Philby had feared, however, the defection of Burgess and Maclean did severe, though not quite terminal, damage to the careers in Soviet intelligence of the other members of the Magnificent Five. Immediately after the defection, Blunt went through Burgess's flat, searching for and destroying incriminating documents. He failed, however, to notice a series of unsigned notes describing confidential discussions in Whitehall in 1939. In the course of a lengthy MI5 investigation, Sir John Colville, one of those mentioned in the notes, was able to identify the author as Cairncross. MI5 began surveillance of Cairncross and followed him to a hurriedly arranged meeting with his controller, Modin. Just in time, Modin noticed the surveillance and returned home without meeting Cairncross. At a subsequent interrogation by MI5, Cairncross admitted passing information to the Russians but denied being a spy. Shortly afterwards he received "a large sum of money" at a farewell meeting with Modin, resigned from the Treasury and went to live abroad.[157]

Immediately after the defection of Burgess and Maclean, the Centre instructed Modin to press Blunt to follow them to Moscow. Unwilling to exchange the prestigious, congenial surroundings of the Courtauld Institute for the bleak socialist realism of Stalin's Russia, Blunt refused. "I know perfectly well how your people live," Blunt told his controller, "and I can assure you it would be very hard, almost unbearable, for me to do likewise." Modin, by his own account, was left speechless. Blunt was rightly confident that MI5 would have no hard evidence against him. Soviet intelligence had few further dealings with him.[158]

As Philby had feared, the defection of his friend and former lodger, Burgess, placed him under immediate suspicion. The Director of Central Intelligence, General Walter Bedell Smith, promptly informed SIS that he was no longer acceptable as its liaison officer in Washington. On his return to London, Philby was officially retired from SIS. In December 1951 he was summoned to a "judicial inquiry" at MI5 headquarters—in effect an informal trial, of which he later gave a misleading account in his memoirs. According to one of those present, "There was not a single officer who sat through the proceedings who came away not totally convinced of Philby's guilt." Contrary to the impression Philby sought to create in Moscow after his defection twelve years later, many of his own former colleagues in SIS shared the opinion of MI5. But the "judicial inquiry" concluded that it would probably never be possible to find the evidence for a successful prosecution. Within SIS Philby retained the support of a loyal group of friends to whom he cleverly presented himself as the innocent victim of a McCarthyite witch-hunt. Soviet intelligence had no further contact with him until 1954.[159]

Philby seems never to have realized that Burgess's sudden defection was the result not of his own loss of nerve but of a cynical deception by the Centre, and never forgave Burgess for putting him in jeopardy. By the time Philby himself finally defected to Moscow in 1963, Burgess was on his death bed. He asked his old friend to visit him at the KGB hospital in Pekhotnaya Street. Philby refused to go.[160] His sense of grievance was increased by his own reception in Moscow. Philby had long believed that he was an officer in the Soviet foreign intelligence service and was shocked to discover that, as a foreign agent, he would never be awarded officer rank. Worse still, he was not fully trusted by the leadership either of the KGB or its First Chief (Foreign Intelligence) Directorate. Not until the sixtieth anniversary celebrations of the October Revolution, fourteen years after his arrival in Moscow, was the KGB's most celebrated Western agent at last allowed to enter its headquarters.[161]

TEN

THE MAIN ADVERSARY

Part 1: North American Illegals in the 1950s

One of the most remarkable public appearances ever made by a Soviet illegal took place on November 6, 1951, when "Teodoro B. Castro" attended the opening in Paris of the Sixth Session of the United Nations General Assembly as an adviser to the Costa Rican delegation. Castro was, in reality, Iosif Romualdovich Grigulevich (variously codenamed MAKS, ARTUR and DAKS),[1] a Lithuanian Jew whose main previous expertise had been in sabotage and assassination. He had trained saboteurs during the Spanish Civil War, taken a leading role in the operations to kill Trotsky in Mexico and had run a wartime illegal residency in Argentina which specialized in the sabotage of ships and cargoes bound for Germany.[2] While in Argentina, Grigulevich had begun to develop an elaborate Latin American legend for use after the war.[3]

Late in 1949, Grigulevich and his wife, Laura Araujo Aguilar (a Mexican illegal agent codenamed LUIZA), set up an illegal residency in Rome. Posing as Teodoro Castro, the illegitimate son of a dead (and childless) Costa Rican notable, Grigulevich established a small import–export business to provide cover for his intelligence work. In the autumn of 1950 he made the acquaintance of a visiting delegation from Costa Rica which included the leading Costa Rican politician of his generation, José Figueres Ferrer, head of the founding junta of the Second Republic which had restored constitutional government and later President of the Republic in 1953–5 and 1970–4. Grigulevich's success in winning Figueres's confidence must have exceeded his wildest expectations. Hoodwinked by Grigulevich's fraudulent account of his illegitimate birth, Figueres told him they were distant relatives. Thereafter, according to Grigulevich's file, he became the friend and confidant of the future president, using the Centre's money to invest with him in an Italian firm importing Costa Rican coffee.[4]

In October 1951, under his cover name Teodoro Castro, Grigulevich was appointed Costa Rica's chargé d'affaires in Rome. A month later he was chosen as an adviser to the Costa Rican delegation to the Sixth Session of the UN General Assembly at its meeting in Paris. During the assembly he was introduced to the US Secretary of State, Dean Acheson, and the British Foreign Secretary, Anthony Eden—but not, apparently, to the Soviet Foreign Minister, Andrei Vyshinsky.[5] Vyshinsky's usual oratorical style at international gatherings was tedious and long-winded. On this occasion, however, he arrived with a caged dove, intended to represent the innocent victims of imperialist aggression, then proceeded to speak with the brutal sarcasm for which he had been infamous as prosecutor during the show trials of the Great Terror. Referring to a speech by President Truman on arms limitation, Vyshinsky declared in the course of a lengthy diatribe, "I could hardly sleep all night last night having read that speech. I could not sleep because I kept laughing."[6]

Among the other targets for Vyshinsky's sarcasm was the Costa Rican delegation. One of the motions debated by the General Assembly was the call by the Greek delegation for the return to Greece of the children evacuated to the Soviet Bloc during the Greek civil war. At Acheson's request, the Costa Rican delegation agreed to support the motion. Doubtless to his extreme embarrassment, Grigulevich was chosen to draft a speech in favor of it to be delivered by Jorge Martínez Moreno. He did his best to limit the offense to the Soviet delegation by somewhat vacuous rhetoric which emphasized "the anxiety and the interest with which [the Costa Rican] delegation had always considered any threat liable to endanger the peace of the world," and congratulated the UN Special Committee on the Balkans "for its work of observation and conciliation, thanks to which . . . although the Balkans remained a danger, at least world peace had been safeguarded." The Soviet delegation was unimpressed. Probably unaware of Castro's real identity, Vyshinsky condemned the speech as the ramblings of a diplomatic clown.[7]

Vyshinsky's denunciation, however, did nothing to damage Grigulevich's diplomatic career. On May 14, 1952 he presented his letters of credence as Envoy Extraordinary and Minister Plenipotentiary of Costa Rica in Rome to the Italian president, Luigi Einaudi. According to his file, Grigulevich was on good terms with the American ambassador, Ellsworth Bunker, and his successor, Claire Boothe Luce, and successfully cultivated the Costa Rican nuncio to the Vatican, Prince Giulio Pacelli, a nephew of Pope Pius XII. Grigulevich had a total of fifteen audiences with the Pope. He also made friends with one of Italy's leading post-war politicians, the Christian Democrat Alcide de Gasperi (Prime Minister, 1945–53), who gave him a camera inscribed "In token of our friendship."[8]

Grigulevich's astonishing transformation from Soviet saboteur and assassin into a popular and successful Latin American diplomat, combined with the initial success of "Willie" Fisher's illegal residency in providing "supersecret" nuclear intelligence from the United States,[9] seemed to vindicate the Centre's early Cold War strategy of attempting to recreate the age of the Great Illegals. The role of the post-war illegals was considered to be potentially even more important than that of their illustrious predecessors. If the Cold War turned into hot war, as the Centre thought quite possible, Soviet embassies and the legal residencies they contained would have to be withdrawn from NATO countries, leaving the illegals to run wartime intelligence operations.

DESPITE THE EARLY Cold War success of Grigulevich and Fisher, the mood in the Centre at the beginning of the 1950s was anything but triumphalist. As a result of the identification of Soviet spies in the VENONA decrypts, following the earlier revelations by Bentley, Chambers and Gouzenko, the Centre had to set about rebuilding almost its entire American agent network while operating under far closer FBI surveillance than ever before.[10] It could no longer count on significant help from the Communist Party of the United States (CPUSA), which during the Second World War had assisted Soviet penetration of the Roosevelt administration, the intelligence community and the MANHATTAN project.[11] In 1949 Gene Dennis, the CPUSA general secretary, and ten other party leaders were tried on charges of advocating the forcible overthrow of the federal government. Dennis and nine of the defendants were sentenced to five years in jail, the eleventh was jailed for three years, and all the defense attorneys were found in contempt of court. After the Supreme Court upheld the sentences in 1951, more than a hundred other leading Communists were convicted on similar charges. For most of the decade the Party was forced into a largely underground existence.[12]

The Centre was also greatly exercised by the unprecedented publicity given to Soviet intelligence operations in the United States. On January 24, 1950 Klaus Fuchs began confessing his wartime espionage at Los Alamos to his British interrogators. The next day, in New York, Alger Hiss was sentenced to five years' imprisonment for perjury in denying espionage charges before a Grand Jury. On February 2 Fuchs was formally charged in London, and the menace of Soviet atomic espionage burst on to the front pages of the American press. A week later the previously little-known Wisconsin senator, Joseph R. McCarthy, falsely claimed to have the names of 205 State Department Communists who were "shaping" American foreign policy. Despite his outrageous inventions and exaggerations, McCarthy rapidly won a mass following. He did so because he succeeded in striking a popular chord. To many Americans the idea of an "enemy within," given plausibility by the convictions of Hiss and Fuchs (followed a year later by those of the Rosenbergs), helped to explain why the United States, despite its immense power, seemed unable to prevent the onward march of world Communism and the emergence of the Soviet Union as a nuclear superpower. As late as January 1954 opinion polls found 50 percent of Americans with a favorable opinion of McCarthy and only 29 percent opposed to him.

President Truman's claim in 1951 that "the greatest asset that the Kremlin has is Senator McCarthy" was, in the long run, to be proved right. McCarthy ultimately did more for the Soviet cause than any agent of influence the KGB ever had. His preposterous self-serving crusade against the "Red Menace" made liberal opinion around the world skeptical of the reality of Moscow's secret intelligence offensive against the Main Adversary. Even Julius and Ethel Rosenberg, executed one after the other in the same electric chair at New York's Sing Sing Prison in 1953, were widely believed to have been framed. It took some years, however, for the Centre to grasp the enormous propaganda advantages of McCarthyism. At the time the Centre was chiefly concerned by the increased difficulties created by "spy mania" in the United States for its attempts to recruit and run new American agents.

McCarthyism reinforced the Centre's belief in the importance of expanding its illegal presence on the territory of the Main Adversary. While legal residencies based in official Soviet missions were inevitably subject to increasingly sophisticated FBI surveillance, illegal residencies could operate freely so long as they remained unidentified. Since his arrival in the United States in 1947 "Willie" Fisher (MARK) had attracted no suspicion whatsoever—despite the fact that his agent, Theodore Hall, was interrogated by the FBI in 1951 after his identity was disclosed by the VENONA decrypts.[13] The Centre also took seriously the possibility that illegal residencies might have to take over all intelligence operations if war or other crises led to the expulsion of Soviet missions and legal residencies. The preparations for a major expansion of the illegal residencies were enormously detailed. In 1954 the Illegals Directorate drew up plans for a network of 130 "documentation agents" whose sole responsibility was to obtain birth certificates, passports and other documents to support the illegals' legends.[14] Operations officers specializing in illegal documentation were posted in twenty-two Western and Third World residencies, as well as in China and all Soviet Bloc KGB liaison missions.[15]

There were, however, more serious obstacles than the Centre was willing to acknowledge than the expansion of its illegal networks. The age of the Great Illegals—brilliant cosmopolitans such as Deutsch and Maly, able to inspire others with their own visionary faith in the future of the Soviet system—had gone, never to return. Turning Soviet citizens brought up in the authoritarian, intellectually blinkered command economy of Stalin's Russia into people who could pass as Westerners and cope successfully with life in the United States was to prove a daunting, as well as time-consuming, business. Recruiting high-flying ideologically committed American agents was also vastly more difficult during the Cold War than during the 1930s or the Second World War. The Soviet Union had lost much of its appeal even to young radical intellectuals alienated by the materialism and injustices of American society. It was deeply ironic that when McCarthy's self-serving campaign against the Red Menace was at its height, Soviet penetration of the American government was at its lowest ebb for almost thirty years.

The Centre was further hampered by its own cumbersome bureaucracy, complicated during the final years of the Stalinist era by the rise and fall of the Committee of Information (KI) as the overseer of Soviet foreign intelligence.[16] In the course of the Cold War, the organization of the Illegals Directorate changed eight times, and the role assigned to it was modified on fourteen different occasions.[17] Aleksandr Korotkov, the head of the directorate during the first decade of the Cold War, had no experience of life in the West and little understanding of the problems faced by illegals in the United States. Few of his grandiose plans for illegal operations against the Main Adversary were ever realized.

Throughout the 1950s, the Centre struggled to establish even one more illegal residency in the United States to add to that of Fisher. The first attempt to found a second residency collapsed in ignominious failure, the recall in 1951 of Makayev (HARRY), the intended resident, and the disappearance of 9,000 dollars of KI funds. The next attempt was more cautious. Using a strategy which it was later to repeat, the Centre decided to send a potential illegal resident to Canada, wait until he was well established, and only then move him on to the more difficult terrain of the Main Adversary. The first Soviet illegal to use Canada as a staging post for the United States was the 30-year-old Yevgeni Vladimirovich Brik (codenamed HART), who landed in Halifax, Nova Scotia, in November 1951 with instructions to take up residence in Montreal.

Brik had the great advantage of a bilingual education. From 1932 to 1937 he had been a pupil at the Anglo-American School in Moscow,[18] subsequently spending several years in New York, where his father worked for Amtorg, the Soviet trade mission in the United States,[19] before returning to serve in the Red Army during the Great Patriotic War. In 1948 Brik was instructed to cultivate Western pupils at his old school in order to test his suitability for intelligence work in North America. Having succeeded in that exercise to the Centre's satisfaction, he began a two-year training course in 1949, covering ciphers, secret writing, use of short-wave radio, selection and use of dead letter-boxes, anti-surveillance precautions and methods of intelligence collection. Brik was also taught the trade of a watchmaker in order to enable him to start a small business in Canada.[20]

For his journey to Canada, Brik adopted the identity of a Canadian "live double," Ivan Vasilyevich Gladysh (codenamed FRED), recruited in July 1951 specifically to provide cover for him. On instructions from the Centre, Gladysh crossed the Atlantic to Britain, then traveled through France and West Germany to Vienna, where he met Brik. In Vienna Gladysh briefed Brik on the details of his life in Canada and his journey to Europe, then gave him his Canadian passport. Brik pasted his own photograph in the passport in place of Gladysh's and set off across the Atlantic.[21] After landing at Halifax, Brik took a train to Montreal and went to the station lavatories. On one of the cubicle doors he saw the chalk mark he had been told to expect. He went inside, removed the top of the cistern and found taped to the underside the birth certificate and other documents belonging to another "live double," David Semyonovich Soboloff.[22] Soboloff (codenamed SOKOL) had been born in Toronto in 1919 but at the age of sixteen had emigrated with his family to the Soviet Union. In 1951 he was working as a teacher at the Magnitogorsk Mining and Metallurgical Institute. For the remainder of his time in Canada Brik became David Soboloff. In July he obtained a passport in his name.[23]

Brik succeeded in persuading the Centre that there was no realistic possibility of establishing himself as a watchmaker in Montreal, and that he should open a one-man photographic studio instead. While in Montreal, he was instructed to begin making plans for emigration to the United States.[24] Brik, however, proved an even more disastrous choice than Makayev as the potential head of an illegal American residency. Without telling the Centre, in October 1953 he began a passionate affair with the wife of a Canadian soldier living in Kingston, Ontario.[25] In order not to break contact with her, Brik persuaded the Centre that it would be premature for him to move to the United States. Before long he admitted to his lover that he was a Russian spy living under a false identity and tried to persuade her to leave her husband. She refused but begged him to go to the RCMP (Royal Canadian Mounted Police) and make a voluntary confession.[26]

In November 1953 Brik gave in to his lover's pleas and telephoned the RCMP headquarters in Ottawa. Terry Guernsey, the head of the diminutive B (Counter-intelligence) Branch of the RCMP Security Service, decided to run Brik (codenamed

GIDEON by B Branch) as a double agent in order to uncover as much as possible about Soviet intelligence operations in Canada. GIDEON proved unusually difficult to run, particularly when his lover broke off their affair, and his drinking ran periodically out of control. On one occasion, after consuming more than a bottle of Old Tom gin, he rang the Montreal *Gazette* and, to the horror of the RCMP officer monitoring his telephone calls, said in a drunken slur, "I'm a Russian spy. Do you want a story?" Like the *Ottawa Journal* which had turned away Gouzenko in September 1945, the *Gazette* failed to realize it was being offered the spy story exclusive of the decade and dismissed the caller as a drunk.[27]

Until the summer of 1955 it did not occur to the KGB that the illegal HART (Brik) might now be a double agent. Once it was satisfied that he had successfully established his bogus identity and cover profession in Montreal, the Centre proceeded to the next stage in his development as an illegal resident whose main role would be as an agent controller. Between 1951 and 1953 the Ottawa legal residency, spurred on by Moscow's criticism of its inertia since the defection of Gouzenko, recruited eleven agents (all apparently fairly low-level) with the assistance of the Canadian Communist Party. Five were Communists and most supplied scientific and technological intelligence.[28] By transferring some of the agents to an illegal controller, the Centre hoped to overcome the problems created by the RCMP security service's surveillance of the Ottawa embassy.

By the time the KGB realized that Brik was under RCMP control, it had put him in touch with five agents. Three were male: LISTER, a Toronto Communist of Ukrainian origin born in 1919; LIND, an Irish-Canadian Communist employee of the A. V. Roe aircraft company, also resident in Toronto; and POMOSHCHNIK, the Communist owner of a radio and television sales and service business in Ottawa.[29] The intelligence supplied by LIND included plans for the CF-105 Avro Arrow, then among the most advanced jet fighter aircraft in the world.[30] Brik also knew the identities of EMMA and MARA, two female agents used as "live letterboxes" (LLBs) for communications with the Centre. EMMA, who had been recruited while studying at the Sorbonne in 1951, took the Canadian External Affairs Ministry entrance examination, but was unsuccessful. In 1954 she opened an arts and crafts shop in Quebec. MARA was a French fashion designer, born in 1939, the co-owner of a furniture shop in Paris who was used as an LLB for KGB communications from Canada.[31]

The Centre later concluded that Brik had betrayed all five of the agents with whom he had been put in contact. He was unaware, however, of the identity of Hugh Hambleton, ultimately the most important of the agents recruited by the Ottawa legal residency in the early 1950s. Hambleton had been born in Ottawa in 1922 and had spent some of his childhood in France, where his father was a Canadian press correspondent. During the Second World War he served as an intelligence officer with the Free French in Algiers and, after the Liberation, in Paris, before becoming French liaison officer with the US army's 103rd Division in Europe. In 1945 he transferred to the Canadian army and spent a year based in Strasbourg analyzing intelligence on occupied Germany, and interrogating prisoners-of-war. Unsurprisingly, the post-war years seemed dull by comparison. "To be important, to have people pay attention to you," he once said, "that is what counts in life."[32] The KGB gave him the recognition which he craved.

Hambleton's KGB file reveals for the first time that he emerged from the war as a committed Communist and was talent-spotted by the Centre's "Canadian friends." Harry Baker, one of the Canadian Communist leaders, picked him out at Party meetings and later vouched for his ideological reliability. Another Party member, codenamed SVYASHCHENIK ("Priest"), carried out background checks on him. In 1952 Hambleton was recruited as a Soviet agent by the Ottawa resident, Vladimir Trofimovich Burdin, and given the codename RIMEN (later changed to RADOV). Two years later Hambleton moved to Paris where he began postgraduate research in economics at the Sorbonne. In 1956 he gained a job in the economics directorate of NATO, whose headquarters were then on the outskirts of Paris. Over the next five years Hambleton handed over what his KGB file describes as "a huge quantity of documents," most of which were assessed by the Centre as "valuable or extremely valuable in content."[33] Though Brik was unaware of his existence, Hambleton was eventually betrayed twenty years later by another Soviet illegal.[34]

Early in 1955, probably as part of its preparations to transfer Brik to the United States, the Centre made plans to move another illegal resident, codenamed ZHANGO, to Canada. ZHANGO was a 49-year-old Russian, Mikhail Ivanovich Filonenko, who had been given the genuine birth certificate, and had assumed the identity, of Joseph Ivanovich Kulda. Born on July 7, 1914 in Alliance, Ohio, Kulda had emigrated to Czechoslovakia with his parents in 1922. Filonenko's wife, Anna Fyodorovna (codenamed successively MARTA and YELENA), took the identity of Mariya Navotnaya, a Czech born on October 10, 1920 in Manchuria. Anna was Czech on her father's side; before marrying Filonenko she had spent two years in Czechoslovakia perfecting her grasp of the language and improving her legend. Posing as Czechoslovak refugees, the Filonenkos were initially unsuccessful in their applications for Canadian visas, but with the help of the UN Refugees Commission (later the UNHCR) gained entry to Brazil in 1954.[35] In 1955 the Centre made plans to move Filonenko on to join Brik in Canada, where he was to have the new codename HECTOR. Brik duly informed the RCMP of HECTOR's planned arrival.[36]

The KGB was saved in the nick of time from a major intelligence disaster, which, it believed, would have included the arrest and show trial of Filonenko, by a walk-in to the Ottawa residency. On July 21, 1955 a heavily indebted 39-year-old RCMP corporal, James Morrison, who for some years had taken part in surveillance of the Ottawa embassy, got in touch with Burdin's successor as resident, Nikolai Pavlovich Ostrovsky (codenamed GOLUBEV), and reported that Brik had been "turned" eighteen months earlier. He was acting, he claimed, out of sympathy for the USSR and a desire to prevent a repetition of the Gouzenko affair which had done so much damage to Soviet–Canadian relations ten years earlier. Morrison's request for 5,000 dollars, however, provides a better indication of his motives.[37] Unknown to Ostrovsky, he had already been caught embezzling RCMP funds with which he hoped to pay off the debts caused by his taste for high living. Remarkably, instead of being sacked, Morrison was allowed to refund the money he had stolen. Ironically, he was to use money from the KGB to repay the RCMP.[38]

The Centre initially suspected that the intelligence from Morrison (later codenamed FRIEND) was an elaborate "provocation" by the RCMP, but decided to interrogate Brik in Moscow. Fortunately for the KGB, it had already been decided in June that Brik would travel to the Soviet Union for a holiday and reunite with his wife later in the summer.[39] Though understandably nervous at the thought of returning to Moscow, he appears to have been confident of his ability to continue to outwit the KGB.[40] Before leaving Canada, Brik was briefed by Charles Sweeny of the RCMP and Leslie Mitchell, the SIS liaison officer in Washington, and asked to find out what he could about the fate of Burgess and Maclean, as well as to identify as many KGB officers as possible during his visit. They told him that if he needed assistance in Moscow it would be provided by the British SIS, since Canada had no foreign intelligence service. He was given details of one rendezvous point with an SIS officer, the location of two dead letter-boxes and signal sites to indicate when a DLB had been filled. If it became necessary to arrange an escape, SIS would leave in a DLB a short-wave radio, money, a pistol with silencer, false Soviet passports for himself and his wife, the internal travel documents needed to go to the town of Pechenga near the Soviet–Norwegian border and a map showing where to cross the frontier.[41]

The Centre took great care not to arouse Brik's suspicions before his departure. His first stop, arranged in June, was in Brazil, where he was due to meet Filonenko (HECTOR) on August 7. Filonenko was warned not to attend the meeting, but the prearranged rendezvous was kept under KGB observation. When Brik arrived on August 7, the KGB watchers reported that he had two companions, thus providing strong circumstantial evidence that he was now a double agent. Apparently undeterred by Filonenko's failure to meet him, Brik continued to Moscow via Paris and Helsinki. The residents in both capitals were ordered to give him a friendly welcome and discuss with him the travel arrangements for his return to Canada. A KGB strong-arm man was, however, sent to Finland in case Brik had any last-minute doubts about going to Moscow. If necessary, a Soviet agent in the Finnish police agreed to arrange for his expulsion to the Soviet Union.[42]

On August 19, 1955 Brik arrived at Moscow airport and was immediately arrested. He at first denied that he was a double agent, but his file records that he subsequently broke under "pressure" and "told all."[43] His confession confirmed everything reported to the Ottawa residency by James Morrison (FRIEND), who was then paid the 5,000 dollars he had asked for. Morrison volunteered for further payment what the Centre considered "valuable" information about the organization, personnel and operations of the RCMP and, in particular, its security service.[44]

On September 4, 1956, at a closed session of the Military Collegium of the Supreme Court, Brik was sentenced to fifteen years in prison. The fact that he escaped the death penalty was presumably due to his cooperation in what his file describes as "an operational game." Brik was not allowed to meet any member of the SIS station in the Moscow embassy, probably for fear that he would blurt out what had happened to him, but instructed to arrange a rendezvous which he did not keep.

By keeping the rendezvous site under surveillance, the KGB was able to identify Daphne (later Baroness) Park, the member of the British embassy who turned up there, as an SIS officer. During the "operational game" Brik was allowed to live at home with his family in order to try to give SIS the impression that he was still at liberty. The KGB discovered, probably by bugging his apartment, that he tried unsuccessfully to persuade his wife to flee abroad.[45]

Morrison continued for three years to work as a Soviet agent. Including the 5,000 dollars he received for betraying Brik, he was paid a total of 14,000 dollars by the KGB. The Centre, however, became increasingly dissatisfied with the quality of the information he supplied. In September 1955 Morrison was posted to Winnipeg as part of a unit investigating drug smuggling from the United States, and lost much of his previous access to RCMP intelligence. His last meeting with a Soviet controller took place on December 7, 1957. Morrison asked for help in paying off a debt of 4,800 dollars. The deputy resident in Ottawa, Rem Sergeevich Krasilnikov (ARTUR), however, paid him only 150 dollars and told him that he would need to arrange a transfer to Ottawa and get better access to RCMP intelligence if he wished to earn more money. Morrison failed to turn up to his next pre-arranged meeting with Krasilnikov and broke off further contact with the KGB. In 1958 the Ottawa residency discovered from press reports that Morrison had been dismissed from the RCMP and given a two-year suspended sentence for fraud.[46]

Though Morrison's warning in 1955 had helped to contain the damage done to KGB operations by Brik's twenty-one months as a double agent, that damage was none the less considerable. The Centre was forced to abandon its plan for a second illegal residency in the United States based on Brik and Filonenko. In addition to betraying five KGB agents, Brik had also identified to the RCMP a number of KGB officers in the Ottawa legal residency, all of whom were withdrawn from Canada.[47]

ANOTHER PLAN BY the Centre to establish a further illegal residency in the United States also collapsed in the mid-1950s. The intended illegal resident was Vladimir Vasilyevich Grinchenko (codenamed RON and KLOD), who had taken the identity of Jan Bechko, the son of a Slovak father and a Ukrainian mother. Since 1948 Grinchenko and his wife, Simona Isaakovna Krimker (codenamed MIRA), had been based in Buenos Aires, where in 1951 they had gained Argentinian citizenship. In 1954 the Centre planned to transfer them to the United States. At the last moment, however, it was discovered that the FBI had obtained Grinchenko's fingerprints while he was working as an agent on a Soviet ship visiting North America. Grinchenko was hurriedly redeployed to France, where, a few months later, his career as an illegal was ended by what his file describes as "a gross breach of security." In August 1955 his Argentinian passport, French residence permit, student card and expense account were all stolen from his hotel room in Paris. So was the photograph of, and a letter in Russian from, another KGB illegal codenamed BORIS. Both Grinchenko and BORIS were hurriedly recalled to Moscow.[48]

Though the Centre did not yet realize it, its one established American residency was by now also in trouble. Unlike Makayev (HARRY), Brik (HART) and

Grinchenko (KLOD), "Willie" Fisher (MARK), the illegal resident in New York, was a paragon of both self-discipline and ideological dedication.[49] His chief assistant, Reino Hayhanen, however, was to prove even less reliable than Brik.

Hayhanen had taken the identity of a "live double," Eugene Nikolai Maki, who had been born in the United States in 1919 to a Finnish-American father and a New York mother, and at the age of eight had emigrated with his parents to the Finnish-speaking Soviet Republic of Karelia. In 1938 Maki had been arrested on suspicion of espionage but had been released, given the codename DAVID and employed by the Interior Ministry to inform on the families of other Karelian victims of the Terror. In 1949 Maki surrendered his birth certificate to Hayhanen, who spent most of the next three years in Finland taking over Maki's identity with the help of a Finnish Communist, Olavi Åhman, who had been recruited as a Soviet agent in 1939.[50]

On October 20, 1952 Hayhanen, now codenamed VIK, arrived in New York on board the *Queen Mary*, and spent most of the next two years establishing his new identity, collecting his salary from dead letter-boxes in the Bronx and Manhattan and periodically drawing attention to himself by heavy drinking and violent quarrels with his Finnish wife Hannah.[51] The Centre, doubtless unaware of Hayhanen's disorderly behavior, sent him congratulations on his "safe arrival" in a microfilm message hidden inside a hollowed-out nickel. Like Makayev a year or so earlier, Hayhanen mislaid the nickel, which in the summer of 1953 was used, possibly by Hayhanen himself, to buy a newspaper from a Brooklyn newsboy. The newsboy accidentally dropped the nickel in a stairway and was amazed to see it break in two and a minute microfilm drop out. He handed both the coin and the microfilm to the New York police, who passed them on to the FBI. Though it was some years before the number groups in the microfilm message could be decrypted, the fact that they had been typed on a Cyrillic typewriter helped to alert the Bureau to the presence in New York of a Soviet illegal.[52] It is highly unlikely that VIK informed the Centre that the coin and microfilm were missing.

In the summer of 1954 Hayhanen at last began work as Fisher's assistant. One of his first tasks was to deliver a report from a Soviet agent in the United Nations secretariat in New York, a French economist codenamed ORIZO, to a dead letter-box for collection by the New York legal residency. ORIZO's report probably concerned two American nuclear physicists whom he had been instructed to cultivate.[53] The report, however, never arrived.[54] Doubtless alarmed at this breach of security, ORIZO asked to stop working for the KGB, but was ultimately persuaded to carry on.[55]

Though disturbed by the weakness of Hayhanen's tradecraft, Fisher failed to grasp that he was an alcoholic fraudster who posed a serious threat to the future of his residency. During a visit to Bear Mountain Park in the spring of 1955, Fisher and Hayhanen buried 5,000 dollars which Hayhanen was later supposed to deliver to the wife of Morton Sobell, a convicted Soviet spy and member of the Rosenberg spy ring, who had been sentenced to thirty years in jail. Hayhanen later reported, "I located Helen Sobell and gave her the money and told her to spend it carefully." In fact, he kept the 5,000 dollars for himself.[56]

Early in 1956 the police were called to the home of the "Makis" home at Peekskill in Hudson Valley, where they found both Hayhanen and his wife drunk; Hayhanen had a deep knife wound in his leg, which he claimed was the result of an accident. Later that year he was found guilty of drunken driving and had his license suspended. In January 1957 Hayhanen was due to return to Moscow on leave. Initially, he could not bring himself to go, fabricating a series of stories to justify his delay. He first told Fisher that he was being tailed by three men, then claimed that the FBI had taken him off the *Queen Mary*, on which he had booked a passage. The unsuspecting Fisher told Hayhanen to leave the country as soon as possible to escape FBI surveillance and gave him 200 dollars for his travel expenses. On April 24 Hayhanen set sail aboard *La Liberté* for France. Arriving in Paris on May Day, he made contact with the KGB residency and was given another 200 dollars to complete his journey to Moscow. Four days later, instead of returning to Russia, he entered the American embassy in Paris, announced that he was a KGB officer and began to tell his story.[57]

Though the KGB did not discover the defection until August, it warned Fisher, probably in late May or early June, that Hayhanen had failed to arrive in Moscow, and instructed him as a precaution to leave the United States, using a new set of identity documents. Fisher disobeyed his orders and stayed.[58] He was arrested early on the morning of June 21 while staying in a New York hotel on East 28th Street and flown to the Alien Detention Facility in McAllen, Texas, for questioning.[59] After a few days spent stonewalling his questioners Fisher finally admitted that he was a Russian who had been living under false identities in the United States, and gave as his real name that of a deceased friend and KGB colleague, Rudolf Ivanovich Abel. The Centre, Fisher knew, would realize what had happened as soon as it saw the name Abel on the front pages of the American newspapers.[60]

FISHER'S ARREST MARKED a major strategic defeat for KGB operations against the Main Adversary. The Centre's early Cold War strategy in the United States had been based on the creation of an illegal network which would run major agents such as Hall and Philby, and eventually penetrate the administration to approximately the level achieved during the Great Patriotic War. Fisher's failure, however, appears to have left the KGB without a single illegal residency in the United States. Instead of adopting a more realistic strategy with far more limited aims, the Centre persisted with its plan to revive the era of the Great Illegals and blamed its initial failure on a series of operational errors.

The Centre's investigations of the cases of Makayev (HARRY), Brik (HART) and Hayhanen (VIK) all revealed flaws in the selection of the first generation of Cold War illegals. Hayhanen's file in the KGB archives contains many warning signs which should have been evident well before he was despatched to the United States in 1952. In both the Soviet Union and Finland he had a record for getting into debt and borrowing money, as well as for unusually complicated sexual liaisons. Though already married in the Soviet Union, Hayhanen entered into a bigamous marriage in Finland—without informing the Centre beforehand—with Hannah Kurikka, with whom he later lived in the United States. The report on Hayhanen prepared for the leadership of the KI in 1949, however, glossed over his character weaknesses and insisted that his operational failings would be rectified during training. Mitrokhin noted after reading Hayhanen's file in the KGB archives:

> It was obvious that the KGB wanted to keep VIK in intelligence work no matter what, regardless of signs that he was in trouble, because they did not want to expose any of their operations, because the training of a replacement would be difficult and time-consuming, and because they regretted wasting so much time and money on VIK.[61]

Hayhanen's Russian wife was informed of his defection, divorced him and went back to her maiden name, Moiseyeva. In 1957 the chairman of the KGB received a letter from a woman named M. M. Gridina asking for news of Hayhanen, who, she said, was the father of her 12-year-old son. The KGB was less frank with Gridina than with Moiseyeva. She was told that the KGB had never employed Hayhanen and did not know his whereabouts, but had heard rumors that he had committed a serious crime against the Soviet state and was wanted by the police. Gridina replied that she would tell her son that his father had been killed fighting the Germans during the Great Patriotic War.[62] In fact, Hayhanen died in the United States in 1961. At the time it was alleged that he had been killed in a car accident on the Pennsylvania turnpike; in reality he seems to have died from cirrhosis of the liver.[63]

On November 15, 1957 the 55-year-old "Rudolf Abel" was sentenced to thirty years in jail. His American lawyer, James Donovan, was struck by "Abel's" "uncanny calm" as he listened to what was, in effect, a life sentence: "This cool professional's self-control was just too much for me."[64] "Abel's" wife, Ilya, who had last seen her husband when he returned on leave to Moscow in the summer of 1955, made less attempt to disguise her feelings. She wrote bitterly to the Centre that it was not simply a question of waiting for twenty-five or thirty years but "I do not know if my husband will ever return." For the past seven years she had worked as a harpist in a circus orchestra; however, when she criticized the KGB after her husband was jailed, she was made redundant on the pretext that the orchestra no longer needed a harpist. The Centre rejected Ilya "Abel's" pleas for help in finding another job, but granted her a pension of 51 roubles a month.[65]

At Atlanta Penitentiary, in Georgia, where "Rudolf Abel" had been sent to serve his sentence, he became friends with two other convicted Soviet spies. He played chess with Morton Sobell, whose wife had failed to receive the 5,000 dollars embezzled by Hayhanen.[66] "Abel" also received a number of small favors from Kurt Ponger, an Austrian-born American in the penitentiary's dental section who had been sentenced in 1953 to a term of five to fifteen years' imprisonment for conspiracy to commit espionage while serving in the US army in Austria. Ponger's file in the KGB archives reveals that he had been a Soviet agent since 1936, but that after his arrest the Centre had wrongly concluded that he was a double agent whose arrest had been deliberately staged by the Americans in order to discredit the Soviet Union in Austrian public opinion. "Abel" had no doubt that Ponger was a genuine Soviet agent and later tried to persuade the KGB to give Ponger financial assistance after he was freed in September 1962.[67]

"Abel" served only just over four years of his sentence. On February 10, 1962 he was exchanged on the Glienicker Bridge, which linked West Berlin with Potsdam, for the shot-down American U-2 pilot Gary Powers.[68] The exchange was treated by the KGB as a major operation, codenamed LYUTENTSIA, coordinated by Vladimir Trofimovich Burdin, the former resident in Ottawa. An undercover KGB group was stationed in West Berlin to watch for signs of American military activity in the area of the bridge. On the bridge itself, hidden in the offices of the East German Customs Service, was a KGB armed operational group. Close at hand, but also out of view from the Western side of the bridge, was another armed group which had accompanied Powers from Potsdam for the exchange. At the Soviet checkpoint, a specially trained officer from the 105th Regiment was put in command of a detail of submachine gunners. The East Germans provided a reserve unit of twenty men armed with submachine guns and grenades.[69]

The Centre congratulated itself on the fact that its absurdly large, concealed military presence had gone almost unobserved.[70] "Abel's" lawyer was more impressed by the fact that the American guard who accompanied his client on to the bridge was "one of the largest men I have ever seen. He must have been six feet seven inches tall and weighed perhaps three hundred pounds."[71] After the exchange of "Abel" for Powers, the Glienicker Bridge became famous during the Cold War as the "Bridge of Spies." The KGB file on operation LYUTENTSIA records that its total non-military cost (food, train tickets, hotel bills, various items for "Abel" and his wife and daughter, and a celebration dinner) came to 5,388 marks 90 pfennigs. Walter Ulbricht, the East German leader, did not share the Centre's satisfaction at the success of the operation. He complained to the Soviet ambassador, Pervukhin, on February 15 that his government had not been adequately informed and that the failure to include East German police among Powers's escort showed lack of respect for the sovereignty of the German Democratic Republic. Ulbricht followed his verbal protest with a diplomatic note citing other Soviet slights.[72]

In the United States, "Abel's" paintings and prints became collectors' items. The Attorney-General, Robert Kennedy, asked the Soviet embassy to find out whether "Abel" would be willing to give the US government a portrait of his brother, President Kennedy, which he had painted in Atlanta Penitentiary, and allow it to be hung in the White House. The Centre suspected a plot. The proposal to display "Abel's" portrait in the White House was, it believed, a provocation, though it was not certain what exactly it was intended to provoke. Robert Kennedy's request was turned down.[73]

"Abel" received an unpublicized hero's welcome on his return to Moscow, being received in turn by Vladimir Yefimovich Semichastny, chairman of the KGB, Aleksandr Mikhailovich Sakharovsky, head of the KGB First Chief (Foreign Intelligence) Directorate, and General Pyotr Ivashutin, head of the GRU.[74] At Semichastny's prompting, "Abel" wrote to Khrushchev to thank him personally for the supposed part he had taken in securing his release: ". . . I am especially touched by the fact that, amidst the great variety of your Party and governmental concerns, you found the time to think about me as well."

Though it suited the Centre, for the sake of its own reputation in the Party hierarchy, to portray "Abel's" mission to the United States as an operational triumph by a dedicated Chekist, brought to a premature conclusion only by an act of treachery for which he bore no responsibility, it was well aware that in reality he had achieved nothing of real significance. He had been arrested in 1957 only because he had disobeyed instructions to leave the country after Hayhanen had failed to return to Moscow.[75]

The Centre took advantage of the fact that "Abel" was portrayed in the American media as a master spy of heroic stature. That impression was strengthened by the sympathetic portrayal of him in *Strangers on a Bridge,* an account by his lawyer of his trial, imprisonment and exchange for Powers published in 1964. Donovan made clear that he "admired Rudolf as an individual," and quoted Allen Dulles, Director of Central Intelligence from 1953 to 1961, as telling him, "I wish we had three or four just like him in Moscow right now . . ." He ended his book by printing a letter "Abel" had sent him from Moscow, enclosing two rare, sixteenth-century, vellum-bound Latin editions of *Commentaries on the Justinian Code.* "Please accept them," "Abel" wrote, "as a mark of my gratitude for all that you have done for me."[76]

All this was music to the Centre's ears.[77] The myth of the master spy Rudolf Abel replaced the pedestrian reality of Fisher's illegal residency. The inconvenient lack of heroic exploits to celebrate was glossed over by the assurance that, though there were many of them, they remained too secret to celebrate in public.[78] The real "Willie" Fisher, however, became increasingly disillusioned. After his return to Moscow, he was given a chair in a corner of the FCD Illegals Directorate but was denied even a desk of his own. When a friend asked him what he did, he replied disconsolately, "I'm a museum exhibit."[79]

ELEVEN

THE MAIN ADVERSARY

Part 2: Walk-ins and Legal Residencies in the Early Cold War

The KGB's chief successes against the Main Adversary during the presidencies of Dwight D. Eisenhower (1953–61) and John F. Kennedy (1961–3) derived not from its grand strategy for new illegal residencies, which collapsed for several years after FISHER's arrest, but from a series of walk-ins. The most important was probably a CIA "principal agent" in West Berlin and Germany, Alexsandr ("Sasha") Grigorye-vich Kopatzky, alias "Koischwitz" (successively codenamed ERWIN, HERBERT and RICHARD), who had offered himself for recruitment by Soviet intelligence in 1949.[1] Trained by the KGB in secret writing and microphotography, he was paid a total of 40,000 West German and 2,117 East German marks during the 1950s, as well as being rewarded for his success with several gold watches.[2]

Kopatzky was employed at one of the focal points of American intelligence oper-ations. The CIA's West Berlin station was situated only a few miles from the greatest concentration of Soviet forces anywhere in the world. One of Kopatzky's chief tasks was to find East German women willing to have sex with Soviet soldiers and act as CIA agents. By taking an active part in the station's attempt to recruit Soviet per-sonnel and encourage defections, he was able to find numerous opportunities to sab-otage its operations. Among the wealth of intelligence which Kopatzky provided were the identities of more than a hundred American intelligence officers and agents in East Germany; some were arrested while others were turned into double agents. He also assisted a number of KGB operations to "dangle" bogus agents intended to deceive the CIA station. In 1952 he helped to organize the bogus defection of Soviet agent VIKTOR, who was later employed by the Voice of America radio station and supplied what Kopatzky's file terms "valuable information."[3]

After Kopatzky was briefly imprisoned for drunken driving in 1954, his name was changed by the CIA to "Igor Orlov," so that his criminal record would not appear on his application for US citizenship.[4] In 1957, with his cover as a CIA (but not Soviet) agent largely blown in Berlin, Orlov was taken to Washington with his family and given further operational training by the Agency. He then returned to Europe to take part in various CIA operations in Germany and Austria.[5] In 1960 the CIA at last began to suspect that "Orlov" was working for the KGB. A later damage assessment at the Centre concluded that the extraordinary number of KGB officers who had been in direct contact with him—over twenty during the last decade—might have helped to place him under suspicion.[6] In order to prevent Orlov defecting before the case against him had been established, the CIA promised him a new job with the Agency in Washington, sacked him on his arrival in January 1961 and began an intensive investigation.[7] Orlov made contact with his new Soviet controller, I. P. Sevastyanov, an operations officer at the Washington residency, got a job as a truck driver and heard nothing for several years from either the CIA or the FBI. In 1964 he bought a picture-framing gallery in Alexandria, Virginia, paid for in part, no doubt, by his earnings from the KGB.[8]

By the time he opened his gallery, Orlov may well have felt confident that the case against him could never be proved. His confidence evaporated in the spring of 1965 when the FBI arrived on his doorstep, spent several days searching his home, questioned his wife Eleonore and summoned him to take a polygraph test. Orlov seems to have panicked. Under surveillance and unable to make covert contact with the KGB, he went into the Soviet embassy on 16th Street through a rear door, vainly hoping to enter unobserved.[9] The Washington residency arranged with him an exfiltration plan which was agreed to by Moscow. Encouraged by "Abel's" star rating as a master spy and his American lawyer's affectionate memoir of him, the Centre intended to turn the exfiltration into a publicity stunt. It planned a press conference in Moscow at which Orlov would be presented as a Soviet illegal who had performed heroic deeds behind the German lines on the eastern front during the Second World War and later penetrated the CIA. Orlov would then publish his life story, which would be used as an "active measure" to glamorize the KGB and denigrate its Main Adversary.[10]

The plan, however, had to be called off. Orlov's wife flatly refused to go to Moscow with their two young sons, so he decided to tough it out in Washington.[11] Though the FBI kept the "Orlov" file open, they were never able to prove a case against him. Their investigation, like that of the CIA, however, was based on one false assumption. After his defection in December 1961, KGB Major Anatoli Golitsyn had provided some clues which helped to confirm suspicions about Orlov. Golitsyn correctly said that a Soviet spy whose real surname began with a K had been active in Berlin and West Germany, but wrongly said that his codename, rather than his real name, was SASHA. The CIA and FBI both wrongly concluded that Aleksandr ("Sasha") Kopatzky, alias "Igor Orlov," was agent SASHA.[12] Orlov's KGB file shows that he was at various stages of his career successively ERWIN, HERBERT and RICHARD, but never SASHA, and that he remained a Soviet agent until a few years before his death in 1982. After a press article in 1978 claimed that Orlov was a Soviet spy, the KGB broke off contact with RICHARD.[13] In 1992, ten years after Orlov's death, the Gallery Orlov, run by his widow, was still described by a Washington guide as "a hangout for espionage writers."[14]

West Berlin and West Germany, where Kopatzky (aka Orlov) had first offered his services to the KGB in 1949, were the KGB's most successful recruiting grounds for disgruntled US military personnel. The most important was probably Robert Lee Johnson, codenamed GEORGE, a disaffected army sergeant and part-time pimp in West Berlin.[15] In 1953 Johnson and his prostitute fiancée, Hedy, crossed into East

Berlin and asked for political asylum. The KGB, however, persuaded Johnson to stay in the West, earn a second salary by spying for the Soviet Union and pay off his old scores against the US army. Despite his involvement in prostitution, alcohol abuse and gambling (not to mention espionage), Johnson succeeded in gaining employment as a guard from 1957 to 1959 at missile sites in California and Texas, where he purloined documents, photographs and, on one occasion, a sample of rocket fuel for the KGB.[16]

Johnson's most productive period as a Soviet agent began in 1961 when he was stationed as a guard in the US Armed Forces Courier Centre at Orly Airport, near Paris, one of the main nerve centers in the classified military communications system. Over the next two years he handed over 1,600 pages of top secret documents to his controller. Among them were ciphers and daily key-tables for the Adonis, KW-9 and HW-18 cipher machines; the operational plans of the US armed forces command in Europe; documents on the production of American nuclear weapons; lists and locations of targets in the Soviet Bloc; US intelligence reports on Soviet scientific research, aviation and missile development; and SIGINT evidence on the state of readiness of the East German Air Force. Collectively the documents provided an extraordinary and highly classified insight both into American forces in Europe and into what they knew about the forces of the Warsaw Pact.[17] Johnson was finally arrested in 1964 after a tip-off from the KGB defector Yuri Nosenko.[18]

IN THE UNITED STATES itself the most remarkable KGB walk-ins during the Eisenhower presidency were two employees of the National Security [SIGINT] Agency, 31-year-old Bernon F. Mitchell and 29-year-old William H. Martin. On September 6, 1960, in Moscow's House of Journalists, Mitchell and Martin gave perhaps the most embarrassing press conference in the history of the American intelligence community. The greatest embarrassment was the public revelation that NSA had been decrypting the communications of some of the United States' allies. Among them, said Martin, were "Italy, Turkey, France, Yugoslavia, the United Arab Republic [Egypt and Syria], Indonesia, Uruguay—that's enough to give a general picture, I guess."[19]

Though the defection of the two NSA employees was a spectacular publicity coup, Mitchell's KGB file reveals that it fell some way short of the Centre's expectations.[20] Somewhat surprisingly, Mitchell had been recruited by NSA in 1957 despite admitting to six years of "sexual experimentations" up to the age of nineteen with dogs and chickens. His gifts as a mathematician were presumably thought more important than his farmyard experiences. During Martin's positive vetting, acquaintances variously described him as irresponsible and an insufferable egotist but—like his friend Mitchell—a gifted mathematician. Politically naive and socially inadequate, Mitchell and Martin were seduced by the Soviet propaganda image of the USSR as a state committed to the cause of peace whose progressive social system could offer them the personal fulfillment they had failed to find in the United States.[21]

In December 1959, Mitchell flew from Washington to Mexico City, in defiance of NSA regulations, entered the Soviet embassy and asked for political asylum in the USSR, giving ideological reasons as the motive for his action.[22] The KGB residency made strenuous attempts to persuade him to stay on inside NSA as a defector-in-place, but without success. Mitchell agreed to a secret meeting with another KGB officer in Washington but maintained his insistence on emigrating to the Soviet Union with Martin. Once there, however, he promised to reveal all he knew about NSA.

On June 25, 1960, at the beginning of three weeks' summer leave, Mitchell and Martin boarded Eastern Airlines flight 307 at Washington National Airport, bound for New Orleans. There, after a brief stopover, they took another flight for Mexico City, stayed the night at the Hotel Virreyes, then caught a Cubana Airlines plane to Havana.[23] In July they were exfiltrated from Cuba to the Soviet Union. KGB code-breakers were disappointed in the amount of detailed knowledge of NSA crypt-analysis possessed by Mitchell and Martin. Their most important intelligence, in the Centre's view, was the reassurance they were able to provide on NSA's lack of success in breaking current high-grade Soviet ciphers.[24] However, the KGB similarly remained unable to decrypt high-grade US cipher systems.[25]

Security was so lax at NSA's Fort Meade headquarters that no attempt was made to track Mitchell and Martin down until eight days after they had been due to return from their three-week vacation. Inside Mitchell's house NSA security officers found the key to a safe deposit box, which Mitchell had deliberately left for them to find. Inside the box in a nearby bank they found a sealed envelope bearing a request, signed by both Mitchell and Martin, that its contents be made public. The envelope contained a lengthy denunciation of the US government and the evils of capitalism and a bizarre eulogy of life in the Soviet Union, including the claim that its emancipated women were "more desirable as mates."[26]

By decision no. 295 of the Communist Party of the Soviet Union, dated August 11, 1960, Mitchell and Martin were given political asylum and monthly allowances of 500 roubles each—about the same as their NSA salaries and well above Soviet salary scales.[27] In the autumn Mitchell was given a job in the Institute of Mathematics at Leningrad University; Martin began doctoral research at the same institute. Both defectors quickly put their beliefs about the desirability of Soviet mates to the test. Mitchell married Galina Vladimirovna Yakovleva, a 30-year-old assistant professor in the piano music department of the Leningrad Conservatory. Martin, who changed his name to Sokolovsky, married a Russian woman whom he met on holiday on the Black Sea.[28]

Within a few years the Centre found both Mitchell and Martin considerably more trouble than they were worth. Predictably, both defectors rapidly became disillusioned with life in the Soviet Union. Martin, whom the Centre regarded as the more impressionable of the two, was gullible enough to believe a tale concocted by the KGB that they had both been sentenced *in absentia* to twenty years' hard labor by a closed session of the US Supreme Court. He was eventually shown a bogus copy of the judgment in order to persuade him to put all thought of returning home out of his mind. Mitchell was more skeptical and by the 1970s appeared determined to leave. As chairman of the KGB, Yuri Andropov gave personal instructions that under no circumstances was either Mitchell or Martin to be allowed to go, for fear of deterring other potential defectors from the West. In a further attempt to deter Martin he was shown an article by Yuri Semyonov in *Izvestia* claiming that American agents had been found in possession of poison ampoules, and was led to believe that these were intended for Mitchell and himself. Mitchell correctly suspected that the story had been fabricated by the KGB. Galina Mitchell was also anxious to leave, but the KGB put pressure on her mother to persuade Galina to change her mind. After their applications for visas had been rebuffed by Australia, New Zealand, Sweden and Switzerland, as well as the United States, the Mitchells told the Soviet authorities on March 29, 1980 that they had given up their attempts to emigrate.[29] But there were persistent reports afterwards that Mitchell was still trying to leave.[30]

FOR MOST OF the Cold War, the Washington and New York legal residencies had little success in providing the intelligence from inside the federal government which had been so plentiful during the Second World War. Their limitations were clearly exposed during the two years before the most dangerous moment of the Cold War, the Cuban missile crisis of 1962.

The vacuum left by the lack of KGB high-grade political intelligence from the United States was partly filled by dangerous nonsense from elsewhere, some of which reflected the paranoid strain in Soviet analysis. On June 29, 1960 the KGB chairman, Aleksandr Nikolayevich Shelepin, personally delivered to Khrushchev an alarmist assessment of American policy, based on a misinformed report from an unidentified NATO liaison officer with the CIA:

> In the CIA it is known that the leadership of the Pentagon is convinced of the need to initiate a war with the Soviet Union "as soon as possible" . . . Right now the USA has the capability to wipe out Soviet missile bases and other military targets with its bomber forces. But over the next little while the defense forces of the Soviet Union will grow . . . and the opportunity will disappear . . . As a result of these assumptions, the chiefs at the Pentagon are hoping to launch a preventive war against the Soviet Union.

Khrushchev took the warning seriously. Less than a fortnight later he issued a public warning to the Pentagon "not to forget that, as shown at the latest tests, we have rockets which can land in a pre-set square target 13,000 kilometers away."[31]

Moscow followed the presidential elections of 1960 with close attention. Khrushchev regarded the Republican candidate, Richard Nixon, as a McCarthyite friend of the Pentagon hawks, and was anxious that Kennedy should win. The Washington resident, Aleksandr Semyonovich Feklisov (alias "Fomin"), was ordered to "propose diplomatic or propaganda initiatives, or any other measures, to facilitate Kennedy's victory." The residency tried to make contact with Robert Kennedy but was politely rebuffed.[32]

Khrushchev's view of Kennedy changed after the CIA's abortive and absurdly inept attempt to topple Fidel Castro by landing an American-backed "Cuban brigade" at the Bay of Pigs in April 1961. In the immediate aftermath of the Cuban débâcle, Kennedy despairingly asked his special counsel, Theodore Sorensen, "How could I have been so stupid?"[33] The young president, Khrushchev concluded, was unable to control the "dark forces" of American capitalism's military–industrial complex.[34] At a summit meeting with Kennedy at Vienna in June, Khrushchev belligerently demanded an end to the three-power status of Berlin and a German peace treaty by the end of the year. The two superpowers seemed set on a collision course. Kennedy said afterwards to the journalist James Reston:

> I think [Khrushchev] did it because of the Bay of Pigs. I think he thought anyone who was so young and inexperienced as to get in that mess could be taken, and anyone who got into it and didn't see it through had no guts. So he just beat the hell out of me.[35]

On July 29, 1961 Shelepin sent Khrushchev the outline of a new and aggressive global grand strategy against the Main Adversary designed to "create circumstances in different areas of the world which would assist in diverting the attention and forces of the United States and its allies, and would tie them down during the settlement of the question of a German peace treaty and West Berlin's proposal." The first part of the plan was to use national liberation movements around the world to secure an advantage in the East–West struggle and to "activate by the means available to the KGB armed uprisings against pro-Western reactionary governments." At the top of the list for demolition Shelepin placed "reactionary" regimes in the Main Adversary's own backyard in Central America, beginning in Nicaragua where he proposed coordinating a "revolutionary front" in collaboration with the Cubans and the Sandinistas. Shelepin also proposed destabilizing NATO bases in western Europe and a disinformation campaign designed to demoralize the West by persuading it of the growing superiority of Soviet forces. On August 1, with only minor amendments, Shelepin's masterplan was approved as a Central Committee directive.[36] Elements of it, especially the use of national liberation movements in the struggle with the Main Adversary, continued to reappear in Soviet strategy for the next quarter of a century.

During the Kennedy administration, however, the role of the KGB in Washington was less important than that of the GRU. In May 1961 GRU Colonel Georgi Bolshakov, operating under cover as head of the Washington bureau of the Tass news agency, began fortnightly meetings with the Attorney-General, Robert Kennedy. Bolshakov succeeded in persuading Robert Kennedy that, between them, they could short-circuit the ponderous protocol of official diplomacy, "speak straightly and frankly without resorting to the politickers' stock-in-trade propaganda stunts" and set up a direct channel of communication between President Kennedy and First Secretary Khrushchev. Forgetting that he was dealing with an experienced intelligence professional who had been instructed to cultivate him, the President's brother became convinced that "an authentic friendship grew" between him and Bolshakov:

> Any time that he had some message to give to the President (or Khrushchev had) or when the President had some message to give to Khrushchev, we went through Georgi Bolshakov . . . I met with him about all kinds of things.[37]

Despite Bolshakov's success, GRU intelligence assessment of American policy was abysmal. In March 1962 it produced two dangerously misinformed reports which served to reinforce the KGB's earlier warning that the Pentagon was planning a nuclear first strike. The GRU claimed that in the previous June the United States had made the decision to launch a surprise nuclear attack on the Soviet Union in September 1961, but had been deterred at the last moment by Soviet nuclear tests which showed that the USSR's nuclear arsenal was more powerful than the Pentagon had realized. The woefully inaccurate Soviet intelligence reports of Washington's plans for thermonuclear warfare coincided with a series of real but farcically inept American attempts to topple or assassinate Moscow's Cuban ally, Fidel Castro—actions ideally calculated to exacerbate the paranoid strain in Soviet foreign policy.

In March 1962 Castro urged the KGB to set up an operations base in Havana to export revolution across Latin America.[38] Then, in May, Khrushchev decided to construct nuclear missile bases in Cuba—the most dangerous gamble of the Cold War. He was partly motivated by his desire to impress Washington with Soviet nuclear might and so deter it from further (non-existent) plans for a first strike. At the same time he intended to make a dramatic gesture of support for the Cuban revolution.[39]

The Soviet gamble was taken in the belief that Washington would not detect the presence of the Cuban missile sites until it was too late to do anything about them. That belief was mistaken for two reasons. First, high-altitude U-2 spy planes were able to photograph the construction of the missile bases. Secondly, American intelligence analysts were able to make sense of the confusing U-2 photographs because they possessed plans of missile site construction and other important intelligence secretly supplied by Colonel Oleg Vladimirovich Penkovsky, a spy in the GRU run jointly by the British SIS and the CIA. All the main American intelligence reports on the Cuban bases during the missile crisis were later stamped IRONBARK, a codeword indicating that they had made use of Penkovsky's documents.[40]

As the construction of nuclear missile bases in Cuba began, Bolshakov continued to provide reassurance, probably as part of a deliberate deception strategy, that Khrushchev would never countenance such an aggressive policy. When U-2 spy planes revealed the existence of the bases in mid-October, while they were still in the course of construction, thus beginning the Cuban missile crisis, Robert Kennedy turned on Bolshakov. "I bet you know for certain that you have your missiles in Cuba," he remonstrated. Bolshakov denied it. According to Sorensen, "President Kennedy had come to rely on the Bolshakov channel for direct private information from Khrushchev, and he felt personally deceived. He *was* personally deceived."[41]

At the moment in the Cold War when the Kremlin most urgently needed good intelligence from Washington, the KGB residency was unable to provide it. During the Second World War Soviet agents had penetrated every major branch of the Roosevelt administration. The Centre had been better informed on some important aspects of American policy (notably the MANHATTAN project) than Roosevelt's vice-presidents or most members of his cabinets.[42] During the Cuban missile crisis, by contrast, the Washington residency's sources were limited to agents and contacts in the press corps and foreign embassies (especially those of Argentina and Nicaragua).

Some of the intelligence which Feklisov, the resident, sent to Moscow was simply gossip. He had no source capable of penetrating the secret deliberations of EXCOMM, Kennedy's closest advisers who assembled in the cabinet room on October 16 and met in daily session for the next thirteen days until the crisis was resolved. Aleksandr Sakharovsky, the head of the FCD, wrote dismissively on several of Feklisov's telegrams at the height of the missile crisis, "This report does not contain any secret information."[43]

The relative lack of influence of the KGB on Khrushchev's policy during the crisis also reflected the limitations of its chairman. In December 1961 the influential Aleksandr Shelepin had been succeeded as chairman by his less able protégé, Vladimir Semichastny, who knew so little about intelligence and was so unattracted by the post offered to him that he accepted it only under pressure from Khrushchev. Khrushchev made clear that his main reason for appointing Semichastny was to ensure the political loyalty of the KGB rather than to benefit from his advice on foreign policy. There is no sign in any of the files noted by Mitrokhin that Semichastny ever followed Shelepin's example of submitting to Khrushchev ambitious grand strategies for combating the Main Adversary. During the missile crisis Semichastny had not a single meeting with Khrushchev and was never invited to attend meetings of the Presidium (an enlarged Politburo which for the previous decade had been the main policy-making body).

Nor did Khrushchev ever ask for, or receive from, the KGB any assessment of the likely American response to the placing of nuclear missile bases in Cuba.[44] As foreign intelligence chief, Sakharovsky seems to have had little insight into American policy-making. Though apparently a competent bureaucrat in the Soviet mold, his first-hand experience of the outside world was limited to Romania and other parts of eastern Europe. His melancholy expression was probably, as one of his subordinates has written, "due to the enormous pressures of the job."[45] Among the pressures was the need to conform to the highest standards of political correctness. The FCD rarely submitted assessments save at the specific request of the Foreign Ministry, the International Department of the Central Committee or the Presidium. Most of what it termed its "analyses" were, in reality, little more than digests of information on particular topics which generally avoided arriving at conclusions for fear that these might conflict with the opinions of higher authority. The supreme authority during the missile crisis was Khrushchev himself rather than the Presidium. To a remarkable degree he both determined Soviet policy and, like Stalin before him, acted as his own chief intelligence analyst.[46]

Intelligence did, however, have some influence on Khrushchev's policy during the final stages of the crisis. On October 25 he indicated to the Presidium that, in order to resolve the crisis, it might ultimately be necessary to dismantle the missile bases in return for a US guarantee not to invade Cuba. Khrushchev, however, was not yet ready to make such a proposal. He changed his mind during the night of October 25–6 after a GRU report that US Strategic Air Command had been placed on nuclear alert. Hitherto he had hoped to save face by obtaining the removal of US missile bases in Turkey in return for stopping the construction of Soviet missile sites in Cuba. On the morning of October 26, however, wrongly fearing that an American invasion of Cuba might be imminent, he dictated a rambling and emotional plea for peace to Kennedy which asked for a US guarantee of Cuban territorial integrity but made no mention of the Turkish missile bases. Within twenty-four hours, Khrushchev had changed his mind. On October 27, having concluded that an American invasion was not imminent after all, he sent another letter insisting that the Turkish bases must be part of the deal.[47]

Shortly after Khrushchev had sent his second letter, Soviet air defense in Cuba, apparently as a result of a failure in the chain of command, shot down an American U-2 spy plane over Cuba, killing the pilot. Khrushchev panicked. Reports that Kennedy was to make a speech on national television at noon on October 28 wrongly persuaded him that the President might be about to announce an invasion of Cuba. Khrushchev gave in and accepted Kennedy's terms: a unilateral withdrawal of "all Soviet offensive arms" from Cuba. To make sure his message reached Kennedy in time, he ordered it to be broadcast over Radio Moscow.[48]

THE HUMILIATION OF the Soviet climbdown at the end of the missile crisis, which led two years later to Khrushchev's overthrow in a Kremlin palace coup, was strengthened in the Centre by the discovery of a series of penetrations by, and defections to, the CIA. In December 1961 a KGB officer, Major Anatoli Mikhailovich Golitsyn, walked into the American embassy in Helsinki and was exfiltrated to the United States. In September 1962 the KGB arrested GRU Colonel Oleg Penkovsky, who for the past eighteen months had been providing high-grade intelligence to the British and Americans.[49]

The damage report on Golitsyn produced the usual stereotyped denunciation of his motives. Since it was impossible to criticize either the KGB or the Soviet system, it followed that the basic cause of all defections was the moral failings of the defectors themselves—in particular, "the virus of careerism" unscrupulously exploited by Western intelligence services:

> The treason of Golitsyn, an ambitious and vain man, provides a typical example of a person representing the tribe of careerists. In the mid-1950s he reacted painfully to a demotion in his position: he could not tolerate having his mistakes and blunders pointed out and commented on. Emphasizing his exceptional qualities, he said that only bad luck had prevented him from becoming a highly successful senior officer during the Stalin period. [Late in 1961] Golitsyn made persistent attempts to learn the contents of the evaluation written on him for Moscow, which was negative. The [Helsinki] Residency believes that he succeeded in learning its essence and, knowing from the experience of others that he could expect a serious talk in the personnel department and a demotion in rank, he defected to the United States.[50]

Like all defectors, Golitsyn was given an insulting codename—in his case, GOR-BATY ("Hunchback").[51] Measures taken to discredit him included the arrest of a

Soviet smuggler (codenamed MUSTAFA), who was persuaded to implicate Golitsyn in contraband operations across the Finnish border. An article in the newspaper *Sovetskaya Rossiya* on September 27, 1962 condemned Golitsyn's (fictitious) involvement with smugglers.[52]

Despite the Centre's attempt to belittle Golitsyn, the damage assessment after his defection concluded that he had been able to betray a wide range of intelligence to the CIA on the operations of most of the "Lines" (departments) at the Helsinki and other residencies, as well as KGB methods of recruiting and running agents.[53] Between January 4 and February 16, 1962 the Centre sent instructions to fifty-four residents on the action required to limit the damage to current operations. For the time being, all meetings with important agents were to be suspended and contact limited to "impersonal means" such as dead letter-boxes.[54]

As well as providing important intelligence on KGB methods and leads to a number of Soviet agents, however, Golitsyn also confused the CIA with a series of increasingly extravagant conspiracy theories. He persuaded the head of the CIA counter-intelligence staff, James Angleton, that the KGB was engaged in a gigantic global deception, and that even the Sino-Soviet split was a charade to deceive the West. Golitsyn was later to maintain that the Prague Spring in Czechoslovakia was also a KGB description.[55] It did not occur to the Centre that Golitsyn's defection, by infecting a small but troublesome minority of CIA officers with his own paranoid tendencies, would ultimately do the Agency more harm than good.

In November 1963 Aleksandr Nikolayevich Cherepanov of the KGB Second Chief Directorate (internal security and counter-intelligence), sent the American embassy in Moscow a packet of highly classified papers dealing with the surveillance and entrapment of diplomats and other foreigners in Russia, together with a note offering his services to the CIA. In the ambassador's absence, the deputy head of mission feared that the documents were part of a KGB provocation. Though the head of the CIA station was allowed to photograph the documents, the originals, despite his protests, were returned to the Russians. Cherepanov fled from Moscow but was arrested by KGB border guards on the frontier with Turkestan on December 17, 1963. He admitted during interrogation that the operational secrets he had revealed to the Americans included the use of "spy dust" (*metka*), special chemicals applied to suspects' shoes to facilitate tracking. Cherepanov was sentenced to death at a secret trial in April 1964. The Centre's damage assessment of the case concluded:

> It is not possible to determine why the Americans betrayed Cherepanov. Either they suspected that his action was a KGB provocation or they wanted to burden the KGB with a lengthy search for the person who had sent the package to the embassy.[56]

Though the CIA was not responsible for Cherepanov's betrayal, it was shortly to make another, even more serious error. In February 1964 Yuri Ivanovich Nosenko, a KGB officer serving on the Soviet disarmament delegation in Geneva, who had begun working for the Agency in June 1962, defected to the United States. Nosenko's CIA debriefers, however, wrongly concluded that he was a KGB plant.[57]

Unaware of the CIA's horrendous misjudgement, the Centre regarded Nosenko's defection as a serious setback. Its damage assessment began with the usual character assassination, claiming that Nosenko (henceforth codenamed IDOL), had been infected—like Golitsyn—with the "virus of careerism:"

> Nosenko, who lusted for power, did not hide his ambitions and obtained a high position. The leadership of Department 1 at Headquarters will not forget Nosenko's hysterical reaction when he was informed of their plans to promote him from deputy chief to chief of section [otdeleniye]. "The chief of the directorate has promised that I will replace the head of the department [otdel]," he shouted shamelessly. The characteristics of careerism were evident in many curious facets of his life. When he became the deputy chief of another department, Nosenko was ashamed of his rank [KGB captain], which was below that normally associated with his position. He would return unsigned any documents with "Captain" on them, and would only sign documents on which his perceptive subordinates had not indicated his rank.[58]

Throughout the Cold War, the KGB had much greater success in collecting scientific and technological intelligence (S&T) on the Main Adversary than penetrating the federal government. In 1963 the S&T department of the FCD was given enhanced status as Directorate T.[59] Most of its tasking came from the Military—Industrial Commission (VPK), which was responsible for overseeing weapons production,[60] and was obsessed with American armaments and advanced technology—almost to the exclusion of the rest of the world. In the early 1960s over 90 percent of VPK requirements concerned the Main Adversary.[61] Among the American S&T obtained by the KGB during these years was intelligence on aircraft and rocket technology, turbojet engines (from a source in General Electric), the Phantom jet fighter, nuclear research, computers, transistors, radio electronics, chemical engineering and metallurgy.[62] S&T agents in the United States identified in Mitrokin's notes (though with few details of their accomplishments) include: STARIK and BOR (or BORG), who worked as research scientists for the US air force; URBAN, identified by Mitrokhin as a department head at Kellogg (probably the M. W. Kellogg Technology Company in Houston), who had served as an agent since 1940;[63] BERG, a senior engineer probably employed by Sperry-Rand (UNIVAC);[64] VIL, who worked for the chemical manufacturers Union Carbide; FELKE, an agent in Du Pont de Nemours, the chemical, biomedical and petroleum conglomerate; USACH, of the Brookhaven National Laboratory at Upton, New York, which carried out government research on nuclear energy, high-energy physics and electronics; and NORTON of RCA, which manufactured electronic, telecommunications and defense equipment.[65]

During the Cold War, unlike the Second World War, the dwindling band of American Communists and fellow travelers rarely had access to the S&T sought by the KGB. Most S&T agents recruited in the United States seem to have spied for money. Two such mercenary spies were caught by the FBI during the mid-1960s: John Butenko, who worked for an ITT subsidiary which did classified work for Strategic Air Command, and Colonel William Whalen, who provided intelligence on missiles and atomic weapons.[66] In 1963 the New York residency supplied 114 classified S&T documents, totaling 7,967 pages, and 30,131 unclassified documents, totaling 181,454 pages, as well as 71 "samples" of state-of-the-art technology and other items. Washington sent the Centre 37 classified documents (3,944 pages) and 1,408 unclassified documents (34,506 pages).[67]

Some of the best American S&T, however, came from residencies outside the United States. Possibly the most important was in the field of computer technology, where the Soviet Union had fallen far behind the West. The experimental Soviet BESM-1, produced in 1953, was judged by a Western expert to be "a respectable computer" for its time, with a capability superior to that of the UNIVAC-1 introduced in 1951. The BESM-2, however, which went into production in 1959, was only a third as fast as the IBM-7094, introduced in 1955, and one-sixteenth as fast as the IBM-7090 of 1959. Because of the embargo on the export of advanced technology to the Soviet Union maintained by COCOM (the embargo coordinating committee of NATO members and Japan), the computers legally imported from the West were barely more powerful than their Soviet counterparts.[68] During the 1960s the attempt to catch up with Western computer technology was based largely on espionage.

The KGB's main source of computer S&T was, almost certainly, IBM, which manufactured over half the computers in use around the world in the mid-1960s. Within IBM, the most important KGB agent identified in Mitrokhin's notes was ALVAR, a naturalized French citizen born in Tsarist Russia, whose motives—unlike most Americans in the S&T network—may well have been ideological. Probably the KGB's longest-serving Line X agent, ALVAR had been recruited by the NKVD in 1935. By the 1950s he held a senior post at IBM's European headquarters in Paris, and in 1958 was awarded the Order of the Red Banner for his work as a Soviet agent. ALVAR carried on working for the KGB until his retirement in the late 1970s, when he was awarded a Soviet pension of 300 dollars a month in addition to his company pension—a certain sign of the Centre's appreciation of him.[69]

In the early 1960s the Paris residency supplied intelligence on American transistor manufacture which, according to KGB files, both improved the quality of Soviet transistors and brought forward the start of mass production by one and a half years. It also provided S&T on computer networking systems which were later imitated by the Soviet defense ministry.[70] The most likely source of the intelligence on both transistor production and computer networks was ALVAR. From 1964, however, the Paris residency also had an agent, codenamed KLOD, in Texas Instruments.[71]

Among other agents who provided technology and S&T from IBM was a Nordic national, codenamed KHONG. From 1960 to 1966 KHONG worked for a European affiliate of IBM, and purchased embargoed materials and samples worth 124,000 dollars, which he passed on to the KGB. In both 1961 and 1962 he was questioned by the local US embassy on the reasons for his purchases, but appears to have satisfied the embassy on both occasions. KHONG's motives, unlike ALVAR's, seem to have been mainly financial. He was initially paid 10 percent commission, subsequently raised to 15 percent, on his purchases from IBM. KHONG later worked for the United Nations in a number of countries. The fact that he had a total of twelve controllers during his career as a Soviet agent is evidence that the Centre considered him an important source. By the time contact with him ceased in 1982, a year after his retirement, the KGB had held about 150 meetings with him.[72]

The Soviet Union often found it more difficult to use than to collect the remarkable S&T which it collected from American businesses, most of them defense contractors. In 1965 the Politburo criticized the fact that there was a time lag of two to three years before Soviet industry began exploiting S&T.[73] Even the computer technology stolen by the KGB did no more than, at best, stabilize the striking gap between East and West.[74] The gap was not to be explained by any lack of expertise among Soviet scientists and mathematicians. As one Canadian expert wrote in 1968, "Westerners who know Soviet computer scientists can testify to their competence and their thorough knowledge of the field."[75] The continued backwardness of the Soviet computer industry, despite the expertise of Soviet scientists and the remarkable S&T obtained by the KGB, reflected the cumbersome inefficiency of the Soviet command economy, in which technological innovation had to run the gauntlet of a complex and unresponsive state bureaucracy.

Rather than accept any share of responsibility for the failure to make efficient use of much of the S&T acquired from the West, the VPK chairman, L. V. Smirnov, blamed the KGB for not obtaining enough of it. In a letter to the KGB chairman, Semichastny, in April 1965, Smirnov complained that over 50 percent of the top priority S&T tasks assigned to the KGB between two and four years earlier had still not been fulfilled. Semichastny replied that steps had been taken to improve the KGB's ability to meet its assignments, but criticized the VPK for underestimating the current difficulty of collecting S&T from American targets. Since some of the same scientific and technological developments were taking place in Britain, France, Japan and West Germany, the VPK should pay greater attention to targets in these countries.[76] In the following year groups of Line X officers operating against American targets were stationed in residencies in Argentina, Australia, Brazil, Denmark, Finland, India, Israel, Lebanon, Mexico, Morocco, Norway, Switzerland, Turkey, the United Arab Republic and a number of other Third World countries.[77]

Despite Smirnov's criticisms, the KGB's performance in S&T collection was, on balance, a success story. As Smirnov himself acknowledged, the FCD fulfilled almost half of the VPK's demanding tasks against the Main Adversary with a few years at most. Measured against the spectacular successes of twenty years earlier, however, when the Centre had received the plans of the atomic bomb—the world's greatest scientific secret—from two different agents and important nuclear intelligence from several more, even the successes of the early 1960s were bound to seem somewhat disappointing. The decline was irreversible. Most of the Soviet spies who penetrated every major branch of the Roosevelt administration had been ideological agents, seduced by the myth-image of Stalin's Russia as the world's first worker–peasant state, pointing the way to a new Socialist society. During the early Cold War, even among American radicals, the vision faded. Most of the successors to the wartime ideological moles were mercenary walk-ins and corrupt employees of defense contractors willing to sell their companies' secrets.

Though the KGB could not bring itself to accept it, the golden age of the high-flying American ideological agent had gone, never to return.

APPENDIX

SOME FAVORITE KGB *YAVKAS* (MEETING PLACES) IN THE 1960'S

Baltimore: by the Clayton men's clothing store on North Avenue.

Boston: the music hall; by the State Hilton Hotel.

Chicago: the Chicago Institute of Fine Arts buildings; by the movie theater on State Street; by the Lake State movie theater; and by the men's tie store on Randolph Street.

Cleveland: by the Khipp movie theater.

Indianapolis: by the notice board on Market Street.

Los Angeles: by the newspaper stand "Out of Town Papers" on Las Palmas Avenue; by the entrance to the movie theaters Viltern and Star Theater; by the display windows on Hollywood Boulevard, the furniture store MacMahon Brasses; near the entrance to the Hotel Roosevelt.

Newark: by the Newark train station, on the bench by the monument to Sergeant Donan A. Bazilone.

New Haven: by the Taft Hotel; by the Sherman movie theater.

New York (Bronx): by the David Marcus movie theater; by the restaurant Savarin; by the display windows of the store Wilma's Party Center; under the awning of the Middletown Inn Restaurant at 3188 Middletown Road.

Philadelphia: by the Randolph and Stanton movie theaters; by the Silvanna Hotel.

Portland: by the parking lot on the main street; by the Parker movie theater.

Rochester: by the Randolph movie theater.

Sacramento: by the Tower movie theater, and near the advertisements at the café Camilia Lodge.

St. Paul: by the display windows of the St. Paul Hotel; by the Strand movie theater.

San Francisco: by the Metro movie theater on Union Street; by Fosters Restaurant, Simms Café, and Comptons Café (in the downtown area); the Canterbury Hotel.

Seattle: by the movie theater Orpheum Cinema on Fifth Avenue; by the City Motel on Queen Anne Avenue.

Syracuse: by the Cates movie theater.

Union City, New Jersey: by the A&P supermarket.

Washington area: the telephone booth by the entrance to the Hot Shoppes Restaurant in the center of Hyattsville, a Washington suburb; by the entrance to the grocery store in the Aspen Hill Shopping Center on Georgia Avenue in Maryland, six miles north of Washington.

TWELVE

THE MAIN ADVERSARY

Part 3: Illegals after "Abel"

In 1966 the lack of high-grade political intelligence from the United States led the KGB Collegium, a senior advisory body headed by the Chairman, to call for a major improvement in intelligence operations against the Main Adversary. The chief method by which it proposed to achieve this improvement, however, was one which had already been attempted unsuccessfully during the 1950s: the creation over the next few years of a network of illegal residencies which would take over the main burden of intelligence operations from the legal residencies in New York, Washington and San Francisco.[1]

Not until six years after the arrest of "Rudolf Abel" in 1957 did the KGB succeed in establishing another illegal residency on the territory of the Main Adversary. Though there were brief missions to or through the United States by a number of illegals, the first to have taken up residence who is recorded in the files noted by Mitrokhin was KONOV, a Muscovite of Greek origin born in 1912, who took the identity of Gerhard Max Kohler, a Sudeten German born in Reichenberg (now part of the Czech Republic) in 1917. KONOV was a war veteran and radio specialist who worked as head of a laboratory in Leningrad until his recruitment by the KGB in April 1955. He spent the next four years in East Germany, working as an engineer, establishing his German cover identity and studying both his next destination, West Germany, and his ultimate target, the United States. The KGB, which specialized in arranged marriages for its illegals, found him a German wife and assistant previously employed by the Stasi, codenamed EMMA, who took the identity of Erna Helga Maria Decker, born on September 2, 1928 near Breslau (now in Poland).[2]

In October 1959, posing as East German refugees, KONOV and EMMA crossed to the FRG, where KONOV found work as a radio engineer. In 1962 he began corresponding with American radio and electronics companies and obtained several job offers. After visiting the United States as a tourist, he accepted employment in a company which in 1963 enabled EMMA and himself to obtain immigrant visas. KONOV seems to have been the first post-war illegal sent to the United States to concentrate on scientific and technological intelligence (S&T). Specializing in electronic measuring devices, he took part in a number of international exhibitions and—according to his file—made several inventions. KONOV's S&T was so highly rated by the Centre that it won him two KGB awards. On June 20, 1970, after living for seven years in the United States as Gerhard and Erna Kohler, KONOV and EMMA became American citizens, swearing their oaths of allegiance in Newark Courthouse.[3]

By the time KONOV entered the United States in 1963, two other KGB illegals were already established in Canada, both intended by the Centre for subsequent transfer to the Main Adversary. Nikolai Nikolayevich Bitnov (codenamed ALBERT) had arrived in Canada in 1961. The basis of the legend painstakingly constructed for Bitnov was a fabricated version of the life history of Leopold Lambert Delbrouck, who had been born in Belgium in 1899, emigrated to Russia with his family at the age of eight and died there in 1946. In the fictitious version of Delbrouck's career constructed by the Centre, however, Delbrouck had married a Romanian woman, set up home in Gleiwitz in Germany (now Gliwice in Poland) and then moved to Romania, where he died in 1931. While in Gleiwitz, the couple had supposedly had a son, Jean Leopold Delbrouck, whose identity Bitnov assumed. Bitnov's wife, Nina (codenamed GERA), took over the identity of a "dead double," Yanina Batarovskaya, who had been born in France in 1928 and died in Lithuania in 1956.[4]

Early in 1956, now age thirty, Bitnov moved with his wife to Romania to establish his legend with the help of the Romanian intelligence service, the DGSP. In April 1957, using identity documents forged by the Centre, they succeeded in obtaining passports from the Belgian diplomatic mission in Bucharest.[5] Six months later, they moved to Geneva so that Bitnov could enroll in a business school and learn how to operate as a businessman in the West. From late 1958 to the summer of 1961 the couple lived in Liège, establishing Belgian identities and obtaining new passports which, unlike those issued in Bucharest, made no reference to their residence in Romania and were thus less likely to arouse suspicion in North America. In July 1960, the Bitnovs emigrated to Canada.[6]

The Centre probably intended that Bitnov should move on after a few years to the territory of the Main Adversary. Initially, however, he was ordered, like Brik (HART) a decade earlier, to establish himself under business cover in Canada. Despite his course in Geneva, however, Bitnov proved a hopeless businessman. First, he invested 2,000 dollars of KGB funds in a business which bought up land with mineral rights and sold them to mining companies. After two years the company went bankrupt. Then Bitnov spent 2,000 dollars purchasing a directorship in a car dealership which went into liquidation only two months later. Unwilling to pour good money after bad into any more of his investment schemes, the Centre ordered him to look for paid employment. After a period on unemployment benefits, Bitnov found a poorly paid job as a bookkeeper which, he complained, left him little or no time for intelligence work. Having achieved nothing of any significance as an illegal, he was recalled to Moscow in 1969.[7] The following year, he was given a pension and sent into early retirement at the age of only forty-five.[8] The fact that the Centre persevered with Bitnov for so long was further evidence of the strength of its determination to establish a network of illegal residencies in North America.

Bitnov was unaware that in February 1962, only seven months after his own arrival in Canada, another illegal, codenamed DOUGLAS, had landed with his wife and four-year-old son at Montreal airport. DOUGLAS was Dalibar Valoushek, a 33-year-old Czech border guard recruited by the KGB with the assistance of its Czechoslovak counterpart, the StB.[9] He took the identity of a Sudeten German, Rudolf Albert Herrmann, who had died in the Soviet Union during the Second World War. According to Valoushek's legend, Herrmann had survived the war and made his home in East Germany, then taken refuge in the West to escape the Communist regime. His wife, Inga (codenamed GERDA), a Sudeten German whose family had moved to the GDR, took the identity of Ingalore Noerke, a "dead double" who had been killed during the wartime bombing of Stettin. At the end of 1957 the Valousheks fled to the West, loudly proclaiming their hatred of the East German regime. They spent the next four years strengthening their legends as anti-Communist refugees while Valoushek learned how to run a small business.[10]

Once in Canada, Valoushek proved a much better businessman than Bitnov—though not quite as successful as published accounts of his career (which do not give his real identity) have suggested. Soon after his arrival in Canada he bought Harold's Famous Delicatessen in downtown Toronto, which he and Inga, as "Rudi" and "Inga Herrmann" made a popular rendezvous for staff from the nearby studios of the Canadian Broadcasting Company. After two years Valoushek sold the delicatessen, got a job as a CBC sound engineer and took courses in film-making. His first major assignment was on a film advertising campaign for the Liberal Party. By the mid-1960s he had a reputation as a popular and successful film-maker. At the 1967 Liberal convention, which elected Pierre Trudeau as party leader, Trudeau leaned off the stage and playfully popped grapes into "Rudi Herrmann's" mouth.[11] Though Valoushek's business appeared prosperous, however, his KGB file reveals that the Centre had to provide 10,000 dollars to cover trading losses.[12]

In 1967 Valoushek became the controller of the KGB's most important Canadian agent, Hugh Hambleton (RADOV).[13] After losing his job at NATO on security grounds in 1961 (though without any charges being brought against him), Hambleton had spent the next three years taking a PhD at the London School of Economics, returning to Canada in 1967 to become a professor in the economics department at Laval University in Quebec. Once back in Quebec, Hambleton's contact with the KGB dwindled. He met an officer from the legal residency three times in Ottawa, on each occasion talking to him in a car parked near the main post office. Hambleton, however, disliked his new controller, who tried unsuccessfully to persuade him to apply for a job in External Affairs. After an interval during which Hambleton failed to turn up for meetings in Ottawa, Valoushek was sent to Quebec to renew contact with him. During a congenial dinner at the Château Frontenac overlooking the Saint Lawrence river, the two men established a mutual rapport and Hambleton agreed to resume his career as a Soviet agent.[14] Over the next few years, he traveled to a great variety of destinations, combining research on academic projects with work for the KGB. He remained in touch with Valoushek until 1975, meeting him in Trinidad and Haiti, as well as Canada and the United States. But Hambleton's travels were so far flung that it required a considerable number of KGB officers to maintain contact with him.[15]

In 1968, a year after becoming Canadian citizens, Valoushek and his family were transferred to the United States to found a new illegal residency in the New York area. His first KGB contact was IVANOVA, a young Russian woman who, having formerly worked as an agent of the KGB Second Chief Directorate inside the Soviet Union, had been allowed (perhaps even encouraged) to marry an American visitor and had moved to the United States. IVANOVA gave Valoushek 15,000 dollars to establish himself and had several further secret meetings with him to pass on instructions from the Centre and letters from his Czech relatives.[16] With the funds provided by IVANOVA, Valoushek made a 12,000 dollar downpayment on a secluded house fifteen miles north of New York, in Hartsdale,[17] joined the New York Press Club and began work as a freelance cameraman and commercial photographer. His first major assignment from the KGB was to penetrate the Hudson Institute, a leading New York think tank. The Centre had been excited by a report from Hambleton giving information on the Institute's members and believed it to be a major potential source of intelligence on American global strategy and defense policy.[18]

IN MAY 1962, three months after Valoushek's arrival, BOGUN, another Soviet illegal, had landed in Canada. The Centre intended that, after establishing himself in Canada, BOGUN, like DOUGLAS, should transfer to the territory of the Main Adversary. BOGUN was Gennadi Petrovich Blyablin, a 38-year-old Muscovite who had taken the identity of Peter Carl Fisher, born in Sofia in 1929 of a German father and Bulgarian mother. Like Valoushek, he perfected his German legend by living in East Germany, then moved to the West in 1959, posing as a refugee. The Centre allowed him three years to settle, legalize his status and find work in West Germany before sending him to Canada. On March 9, 1961 Blyablin married his KGB-approved partner, LENA, in Hanover. In December they obtained their West German passports before setting off for Canada five months later.[19]

While Valoushek found cover as a film-maker, Blyablin established himself as a freelance press photographer—a profession which provided numerous opportunities and pretexts for traveling around Canada and further afield. In February 1965, following the Centre's instructions, Blyablin and his wife moved to the United States on immigrant visas. His main task over the next three years was photographing and providing intelligence on major military, scientific and industrial targets around the United States.[20]

In 1968, however, Blyablin attracted the attention of the FBI during his investigation of major targets in the United States and had to be hurriedly recalled, together with his wife, to Moscow.[21] It was later discovered that some of his correspondence with the Centre, routed via agent SKIF, had been intercepted. SKIF was Karo Huseinjyan, an ethnic Armenian born in Cyprus in 1919 was Karo Huseinjyan, an ethnic Armenian born in Cyprus in 1919 who owned a jewelry shop in Beirut and provided a forwarding service for a number of illegals. A Centre investigation disclosed that letters from Blyablin, dated April 7 and July 27, 1968, sent via Huseinjyan, had been steamed open.[22]

A year before Blyablin's sudden recall, RYBAKOV, another Soviet illegal, had arrived in the United States. RYBAKOV was Anatoli Ivanovich Rudenko, whose early career was strikingly similar to Blyablin's. Like Blyablin, Rudenko was a Muscovite born in 1924 who had assumed a bogus German identity, spent several years in East Germany working on his legend and then moved to the West. Rudenko was given the identity documents of Heinz Walter August Feder, born in Kalisch on November 6, 1927.[23] While in East Germany he had trained as a piano tuner and repairer. After crossing to West Germany in April 1961, posing as a refugee from Communism, he found a job with the world-famous piano manufacturers Steinway in Hamburg. Though Rudenko was told that his ultimate destination was the United States, in 1964 he was sent to work with a musical instrument company in London, probably in order to accustom him to an English-speaking environment.[24]

Rudenko's period in London almost ended in disaster. Once, while returning from Brussels, where he had received his maintenance allowance from a KGB operations officer, he was stopped at Heathrow and 500 pounds were found on him which he had failed to declare. Rudenko was fortunate to find a sympathetic customs officer. The money, he pleaded, was his life savings, the product of many sacrifices over the years. He was allowed to keep the 500 pounds and no action was taken against him.

In 1966 he went to New York on a tourist visa and visited the Manhattan showrooms of Steinway & Sons on West 57th Street, who offered Rudenko a job with a salary of 80 dollars a week. With Steinway's assistance, he gained a work permit and traveled to the United States on his German passport in July 1967. In New York Rudenko became piano tuner to a series of celebrities—among them Nelson Rockefeller, Governor of New York, unsuccessful candidate for the Republican nomination in 1964 and future vice-president of the United States.[25] Rockefeller was regarded in Moscow as the "patron" of Henry Kissinger, who in January 1969 became President Nixon's National Security Adviser (and later Secretary of State).[26] While professor at Harvard during the 1960s, Kissinger had served as Nelson's paid part-time adviser and speechwriter, receiving a severance pay gift of 50,000 dollars when he joined the Nixon administration. "He has a second-rate mind but a first-rate intuition about people," Kissinger once said of Rockefeller. "I have a first-rate mind but a third-rate intuition about people."[27]

To the Centre it must have seemed that Rudenko had penetrated one of the innermost sanctums of the capitalist system, which the Rockefeller family had seemed to epitomize for three generations. Nelson's second wife, "Happy," said of him in the mid-1960s, "He believed he could have it all. He always had." The six square miles of Nelson's Westchester estate were one of the world's most valuable properties and contained some of the most spectacular art treasures in any private collection. Theodore White once offered to exchange his Manhattan townhouse on East 64th Street for a single Tong Dynasty horse from the Westchester collection.[28] Though Rudenko's occasional visits to Westchester impressed the Centre, however, they achieved nothing of significance.

Penetrating the houses of the great and good appears to have become almost an end in itself for Rudenko, even though his access to some of new York's most distinguished pianos failed to give him any intelligence access. Among the well-known musicians whose pianos he tuned was the world's most famous pianist, the Russian-born Vladimir Horowitz, who for the past twenty years had lived on East 94th Street near Central Park. In 1965, after a twelve-year hiatus caused by a mixture of psychiatric problems and colitis attacks, Horowitz had returned to the concert platform at the age of sixty-two, becoming, with Luciano Pavarotti, one of the two most highly paid classical musicians in the world. The recital instrument which he chose for his comeback was the Steinway concert grand numbered CD 186, which had to be tuned to an exact 440-A with a key pressure of 45 grams instead of the usual 48 to 52.[29]

Overimpressed by Rudenko's access to the pianos of new York's celebrities, the Centre made detailed plans for him to become head of a new illegal residency whose chief targets would be the US mission to the United Nations and a New York think tank, concentrating on relatively junior employees with access to classified information—in particular, single women whose loneliness made them sexually vulnerable and poorly paid employees with large families who were open to financial inducements.[30]

Just as the new residency was about to be established in New York, however, the Centre noticed what Rudenko's file refers to as "irregularities" and "suspicious behavior" and lured him back to Moscow in April 1970 for what he was probably told were final instructions before beginning work. Exactly what the Centre suspected is not known, but, since Rudenko was interrogated under torture, it may well have feared he was working as a double agent for the FBI. What he revealed was much less serious, but bad enough to end his career as an illegal. Soon after arriving in Hamburg in 1961, Rudenko had met BERTA, a 32-year-old ladies' hairdresser, whom he had suggested recruiting as a Soviet agent. The Centre refused and ordered him to break off all relations with her. During his interrogation in 1970, Rudenko admitted that he had secretly defied his instructions, married BERTA and taken her with him to New York. Worse still, he had taken down radio messages from the Centre and decoded them in her presence. Her parents had discovered that he was a spy, but believed he was working for East Germany. Rudenko also admitted that he was having an affair with a female accountant (codenamed MIRA) in Pennsylvania.[31]

As part of the Centre's damage limitation exercise it instructed Rudenko to write to both BERTA and MIRA letters designed to convince both of them and, if necessary, the FBI that he had left the United States because of the breakdown of his marriage. He told BERTA that he had found it impossible to live with her any longer and urged her not to waste time trying to track him down since she would never find him. In the letter to MIRA, Rudenko was allowed to express his love for her and pain at their separation within what his file quaintly describes as "permissible bounds" and his pain at the separation from her. But, he explained somewhat unconvincingly, his sudden departure from the United States had been the only way to escape from his wife. Both letters were posted by the KGB in Austria, giving no other indication of where Rudenko was living.[32]

THE SUCCESSIVE FAILURES of Makayev (HARRY), Brik (HART), Hayhanen (VIK), Grinchenko (KLOD), Bitnov (ALBERT), Blyablin (BOGUN) and

Rudenko (RYBAKOV) underscored the Centre's difficulty in finding illegals capable of fulfilling its expectations in North America. Fisher/"Abel" (MARK) was, in many ways, the exception who proved the rule. He was able to survive, if not actually succeed, as an illegal resident in the United States because of a long experience of the West which went back to his Tyneside childhood, an ideological commitment which probably predated even the Bolshevik Revolution and a thirty-year career as a foreign intelligence officer, most of it under Stalin, from which he had emerged scarred but battle-hardened. Other Cold War illegals in the United States were psychologically less well prepared for the stress of their double lives. All had to come to terms with a society which was strikingly different from the propaganda image of the Main Adversary with which they had been indoctrinated in Moscow. Unlike KGB officers stationed in legal residencies, illegals did not work in a Soviet embassy, where they were constantly subject to the ideological discipline imposed by the official hierarchy. They also had to cope with a much greater degree of personal isolation, which they could diminish only by friendships and sexual liaisons which were liable to undermine their professional discipline. No wonder that some illegals, like Rudenko, had affairs which they tried to conceal from the Centre; that others, like Hayhanen, took to drink and embezzlement; and that others, like Bitnov, found it difficult to survive in an alien market economy.

Illegals had also to face unreasonable, and ultimately impossible, expectations from the Centre. Until almost the end of the Cold War, no post-war Soviet leader, KGB chairman or foreign intelligence chief had either any personal experience of living in the West or any realistic understanding of it. Accustomed to strong central direction and a command economy, the Centre found it difficult to fathom how the United States could achieve such high levels of economic production and technological innovation with so little apparent regulation. The gap in its understanding of what made the United States tick tended to be filled by conspiracy theory. The diplomat, and later defector, Arkadi Shevchenko noted of his Soviet colleague:

> Many are inclined to the fantastic notion that there must be a secret control center somewhere in the United States. They themselves, after all, are used to a system ruled by a small group working in secrecy in one place. Moreover, the Soviets continue to chew on Lenin's dogma that bourgeois governments are just the "servants" of monopoly capital. "Is not that the secret command center?" they reason.[33]

However much the Centre learned about the West, it never truly understood it. Worse still, it thought it did.

THE CENTRE'S FAITH in the future of illegal operations in the United States was remarkably unaffected by the many failures and disappointments of the 1950s and 1960s. At the beginning of the 1970s the Centre still had high hopes of KONOV and DOUGLAS. It also had remarkably ambitious projects for the next decade. A plan drawn up in the late 1960s envisaged establishing and putting into operation between 1969 and 1975 ten illegal residencies in the United States, two in Canada, two in Mexico, and one each in Argentina, Brazil, Chile, Uruguay and Venezuela. For use in wartime and other major crises it was also planned to create five "strategic communications residencies" to maintain contact with the Centre if legal residencies were unable to operate: two in the United States, one in Canada and two in Latin America.[34]

This visionary program was to prove hopelessly optimistic. The 1970s produced another crop of serious setbacks in illegal operations in the United States—among them the collapse of the illegal residencies of KONOV and DOUGLAS. When KONOV and EMMA swore their oaths of allegiance as American citizens in 1970, their neighbors apparently regarded them as a model married couple. In reality, the increasing friction between them had begun to affect their operational effectiveness. In 1971 they flew to Haiti to be divorced, but informed only the Centre and their New York lawyer. On their return they still contrived to keep up appearances as a married couple by living together in their New Jersey apartment. EMMA, however, asked the Centre to find her a new partner. In October 1972 KONOV was recalled to Moscow, where he died three years later. EMMA was dismissed from the KGB.[35]

Valoushek's career as the illegal DOUGLAS was to end a few years later in even greater ignominy. His first assignment in the United States, to penetrate the Hudson Institute, was wholly unrealistic. As Valoushek later complained, had he been able to use his real identity and mention his postgraduate degrees from Charles University, Prague, and Heidelberg, he might have made contact with senior members of the Institute. But posing as photographer and cameraman without higher education he had no worthwhile opportunity to do so.[36] In 1970, unreasonably dissatisfied with Valoushek's progress, the Centre took him off the Hudson Institute assignment.[37]

The Vaklousheks' elder son, Peter Herrmann, born in 1957, had a brilliant school academic record and was expected to have opportunities to recruit within American universities that his parents did not. In 1972 Valoushek revealed his true identity to Peter, told the Centre he had done so and said that his son was ready to join the KGB. Moscow accepted the offer and agreed to pay Peter's university fees. In the summer of 1975, shortly before entering McGill University in Montreal, Peter began training in Moscow and started his career as an illegal with the German codename ERBE ("Inheritor"). In 1976 he moved from McGill to Georgetown University, where he was instructed to report on students whose fathers had government jobs (especially if they had character flaws which could be exploited), as well as on "progressive" students and professors opposed to the imperialist policies of the United States. He was also told to try to find a part-time job in the Georgetown Center for Strategic and International Studies, make friends with Chinese students and discover as much as possible about them.[38]

By the end of the academic year, Peter Herrmann's brief career as a teenage illegal was over. Early in May 1977 Valoushek was arrested by the FBI and given the choice of being charged with espionage, together with his wife and son, or of working as a double agent. He later told the espionage writer John Barron that after his arrest he worked as a double agent under FBI control for over two years until the Bureau discontinued the operation. "Rudi [Valoushek] gave us his word and he kept it," the FBI told Barron. "We must keep our word to him." On September 23, 1979 an unmarked furniture van removed all the contents of the "Herrmann" household in Andover Road, Hartsdale. The Valoushek family left to start new lives elsewhere under new identities.[39]

Valoushek's KGB file, however, gives a very different account of his relations with the FBI. For well over a year after his arrest, he included deliberate errors and warning signs in his messages to the Centre as an indication that he was working under instructions from the FBI. The KGB failed to notice that anything was wrong until it was warned by an agent early in October 1978 that Valoushek had been turned. Soon afterwards the Centre summoned him to a meeting in Mexico City with the Washington deputy resident, Yuri Konstantinovich Linkov (codenamed BUROV). The FBI told him to keep the rendezvous in order to continue the double agent deception. Valoushek began his meeting with Linkov by admitting that he and his family had been under Bureau control since the spring of the previous year. He suspected that he had been betrayed by LUTZEN, who had defected in West Germany in 1969.[40] He complained that he had done his best to warn the Centre, but that no one had paid attention to his warnings. A subsequent investigation by the counter-intelligence department of the FCD Illegals Directorate uncovered an extraordinary tale of incompetence. A series of warnings and deliberate errors in Valoushek's communications since May 1977 had been overlooked and messages he had posted to the residencies in Vienna and Mexico City had simply been ignored.[41]

Immediately after Valoushek's warning to the KGB in Mexico City in October 1978, the KGB warned Hambleton that contact with his controller would be temporarily broken for security reasons. Instead of being told that Valoushek had defected, however, he was simply given a vague warning that "progressive" people and organizations were under increased surveillance. He was instructed to destroy all compromising materials and to deny everything if he was questioned. In case of emergency, he was advised to escape to East Germany. Hambleton, however, remained confident that he had covered sufficient of his tracks to prevent a case from being brought against him. In June 1979 he sent a confident message to the KGB in secret writing, saying that there was no cause for alarm.[42]

At 7:15 a.m. on November 4, 1979 RCMP officers arrived at Hambleton's Quebec City apartment with a search warrant. For the next two and a half years there was extensive press speculation and numerous questions about Hambleton in the Canadian parliament, but no Canadian prosecution. On March 3, 1980, the first day of the new Trudeau administration, the FBI made an apparent attempt to force its hand by producing Valoushek (under a pseudonym) for a press conference at Bureau headquarters, where he publicly identified Hambleton as one of his agents. Hambleton shrugged off the charges. Though appearing to revel in detailed descriptions of his secret contacts with Moscow by short-wave radio and other hocus pocus, he insisted that he was not a spy: "A spy is someone who regularly gets secret material, passes it on, takes orders, and gets paid for it. I have never been paid."[43] According to Hambleton's KGB file, however, between September 1975 and December 1978 alone he was paid 18,000 dollars.[44] In May 1980 the Canadian Ministry of Justice, apparently convinced that there was still insufficient evidence, announced that Hambleton would not be prosecuted. Thereafter media interest in the case gradually died down. Two years later, however, Hambleton was arrested during a visit to London, tried under the Official Secrets Act and sentenced to ten years in jail.[45]

Valoushek's intended successor as illegal resident in the United States was probably Klementi Alekseyevich Korsakov, codenamed KIM, born in 1948 in Moscow to a Russian father and a German mother. Korsakov's mother, who died in 1971, had herself been a KGB illegal, codenamed EVA. Korsakov seems to have been selected as a potential illegal while still a child and, like his mother, was given bogus identity documents by the East Germans. According to his legend, Korsakov was Klemens Oskar Kuitan, an illegitimate child born in Dalleghof in 1948. Like many other Soviet illegals, he and his mother posed as East German refugees, entering West Berlin in 1953 and moving to the FRG a year later. In 1967, at the age of eighteen, Korsakov obtained a West German passport. After his mother's death, he spent several years in Vienna, first at an art school, then taking an advertising course, while simultaneously training secretly for illegal intelligence work. In 1978, after two transatlantic trips to familiarize himself with life in the United States, he moved to New York.

Once he had begun work as a KGB illegal, however, Korsakov quickly became disillusioned. In January 1980, while undergoing further training in Moscow, he secretly entered the United States embassy, identified himself as an illegal, gave the identities of a number of other KGB officers (among them Artur Viktorovich Pyatin, head of Line N (illegals support) in Washington) and was debriefed by the CIA station. Since Korsakov was nominally a West German citizen, it was decided to transfer him secretly to the embassy of the FRG to arrange for his exfiltration. Mitrokhin's notes do not record whether the KGB had observed him entering the American embassy, but they were waiting for him when he arrived at Moscow airport to return to the West. After lengthy interrogation, Korsakov was sent to the Kazanskaya psychiatric hospital, where, like a number of prominent Soviet dissidents, he was falsely diagnosed as schizophrenic.[46]

THIRTY YEARS AFTER the beginning of the Cold War, the Centre's grand strategy for a powerful chain of illegal residencies running American agent networks as important as those during the Second World War had little to show for an enormous expenditure of time and effort. At the end of the 1970s, following a string of previous failures, Valoushek's illegal residency was under the (albeit imperfect) control of the FBI and Korsakov was preparing to defect.

Particularly galling for the Centre was the fact that probably the most remarkable penetration of the Main Adversary by an illegal during the Cold War was achieved not by the KGB but by its junior partner, the Czechoslovak StB. In 1965 two StB illegals, Karl and Hana Koecher, arrived in New York, claiming to be refugees from persecution in Czechoslovakia. Fluent in Russian, English and French as well as Czech, Karl Koecher found a job as a consultant with Radio Free Europe while studying first for a master's degree at Indiana University, then for a doctorate at Columbia. Among his professors at Columbia was Zbigniew Brzezinski, who later became President Carter's National Security Adviser. All the time, he posed as a virulent anti-Communist, even objecting to the purchase of an apartment in his East Side building in New York by the tennis star Ivan Lendl—simply because of Lendl's Czech origins. In 1969, a year before gaining his PhD, Karl Koecher was appointed lecturer in philosophy at Wagner College, Staten Island. Hana, meanwhile, worked for a diamond business which gave her regular opportunities to travel to Europe and act as courier for the StB. The Koechers may also have been the most sexually active illegals in the history of Soviet Bloc intelligence, graduating from "wife-swapping" parties to group orgies at New York's Plato's Retreat and Hell Fire sex clubs which flourished in the sexually permissive pre-AIDS era of the late 1960s and 1970s.

With the blessing of the StB, the Koechers later revealed some of their colorful careers to the Washington investigative journalist Ronald Kessler.[47] Karl Koecher's KGB file, however, reveals that he withheld important details. In 1970 he was summoned back to Prague to take part in an StB active measure designed to unmask alleged CIA operations using Czech emigrés. Koecher, however, was too attached to his swinging lifestyle to leave New York, refused to return and for the next four years broke off contact with the StB.[48] In 1971 he succeeded in becoming a naturalized US citizen; his wife was granted citizenship a year later.

Karl Koecher seems to have devised a plan to mend his fences with the StB by penetrating the CIA. In 1973 he moved to Washington and obtained a job as translator in the Agency's Soviet division, with a top secret security clearance. His chutzpah was such that only three weeks later he demanded a better job:

My present position is by no means one which would require a PhD. I am interested in intelligence work, and I want to stay with the agency and do a good piece of work. But I also think that it would only be fair to let me do it in a position intellectually far more demanding than the one I have now . . .

Probably as a result of his complaints, Koecher was later asked to write intelligence assessments based on some of the Russian and Czech material which he translated and transcribed from tape recordings.

Sex in Washington struck Koecher as even more exciting than in New York. In the mid-1970s, he later claimed nostalgically, Washington was "the sex capital of the world." The Koechers joined the "Capitol Couples," who met for dinner at The Exchange restaurant on Saturday evenings before moving on for group sex in a hotel or private house, as well as becoming members of a private club of Washington swingers at Virginia's In Place, about ten of whose members worked for the CIA. Hana, blonde, attractive and ten years younger than her husband, later boasted that she had had sex with numerous CIA personnel, Pentagon officials, reporters from major newspapers and a US Senator. The organizer of "Capitol Couples" remembered her as "strikingly beautiful; warm, sweet, ingratiating; incredibly orgasmic."

Karl, however, "was a bit strange . . . The women he was with said he was a terrible lover, very insensitive. His wife was everything he wasn't."[49]

In 1974, having penetrated the CIA, Karl Koecher renewed contact with the StB, which consulted the KGB about whether to reactivate him. Henceforth he became a KGB agent with the codename RINO, as well as being an StB illegal. The Koechers' adventures in Washington sex clubs are unlikely to have provided the StB and KGB with more than compromising information and gossip about Washington officials, most of it of no operational significance. Far more important was the classified Soviet and Czech material translated by Karl Koecher for the CIA which he forwarded to the KGB. Andropov personally praised his intelligence as "important and valuable."[50] In 1975 Koecher left full-time Agency employment, but continued on contract work, based in New York. Among the subjects of his assessments was the decision-making process in the Soviet leadership.[51]

In 1975 Koecher supplied the KGB's New York residency with highly rated intelligence on CIA operations against the Soviet Union in the Third World. As well as arranging meetings in New York, his KGB case officers also met him in Austria and France.[52] Among his most important counter-intelligence leads was evidence that the CIA had recruited a Soviet diplomat. Following an apparently lengthy investigation, the KGB identified the diplomat as Aleksandr Dmitryevich Ogorodnik, then working in the American department at the Foreign Ministry. Soon after his arrest in 1977, Ogorodnik agreed to write a full confession but complained that the pen given him by his interrogator was too clumsy for him to use. As soon as he was given his own pen back, he removed a concealed poison capsule, swallowed it before the guard could stop him and died in the interrogation room.[53]

In the early 1980s the Koechers were themselves betrayed by a CIA agent in the StB. Arrested in 1984, they returned to Czechoslovakia less than two years later as part of a deal which allowed the imprisoned Russian dissident Anatoli Shcharansky to emigrate to Israel. According to a newspaper report, as they crossed the Glienicker Bridge from West Berlin to East Germany:

> With his moustache and fur-lined coat, Karl F. Koecher looked like nothing so much as a fox. His wife, Hana, wore a mink coat and high white mink hat. Blonde and sexy, with incredibly large blue eyes, she looked like a movie star.

"The KGB thinks highly of me," Karl Koecher later boasted to Ronald Kessler.[54] There was a curious sequel to the Koechers' espionage careers in the West. In 1992 Hana succeeded in obtaining a job in the commercial section at the British embassy in Prague. She was sacked two years later after a Czech journalist revealed her background.[55]

AT THE BEGINNING of the 1980s, despite all the setbacks of the previous thirty years, the Centre's plans for the expansion of illegal networks on the territory of the Main Adversary still remained remarkably ambitious—though not to quite the same degree as a decade earlier. Instead of the ten illegal residencies which it had intended to establish within the United States by 1975, the Centre planned to have six by 1982. Between them, the six residencies were supposed to have three to four sources in each of a series of major penetration targets: the White House, the State Department, the Pentagon and what were described as "related institutions"—among them the Hudson Institute, the Rand Corporation, Columbia University's School of International Relations, Georgetown University's Center for Strategic Studies and the West German affiliates of Stanford University's Center for Strategy and Research. The Centre also planned the "active recruitment" of students at Columbia, New York and Georgetown Universities.[56]

It is clear that the KGB had some success in deploying illegals against the Main Adversary in the 1980s. For example, Mitrokhin's notes record that in 1983 the illegal couple GORT and LUIZA were operating in the United States, but give no details of their achievements.[57] However, even the KGB's downgraded plan for six illegal residencies, each with agents at the heart of the Reagan administration, was hopelessly unrealistic. The scale of the Centre's ambitious projects for illegal operations against the Main Adversary in the later years of the Cold War reflected not the reality of the 1980s but the spell still cast by the triumphs of the Great Illegals half a century before.

THIRTEEN

THE MAIN ADVERSARY

Part 4: Walk-ins and Legal Residencies in the Later Cold War

Ｙuri Andropov became KGB chairman in 1967 with extravagant expectations of the potential contribution of political intelligence to Soviet foreign policy, particularly towards the United States. In a report to KGB Party activists soon after his appointment, he declared that the KGB must be in a position to influence the outcome of international crises in a way that it had failed to do during the Cuban missile crisis five years earlier. He ordered the preparation within three to four months of a First Chief (Foreign Intelligence) Directorate report to the Central Committee on the current and future policy of the Main Adversary and its allies. The principal weakness of current operations in the United States, Andropov complained, was the lack of American agents of the caliber of the Britons Kim Philby, George Blake and John Vassall, or the West German Heinz Felfe. Only by recruiting such agents, he insisted, could the FCD gain access to really high-grade intelligence.[1]

Almost from the moment he became a candidate (non-voting) member of the Politburo in 1967, Andropov established himself as a powerful voice in Soviet foreign policy. In 1968 he emerged as the chief spokesman of those calling for "extreme measures" to crush the Prague Spring.[2] During the 1970s he became co-sponsor, with the foreign minister, Andrei Gromyko, of the main foreign policy proposals brought before the Politburo (of which both were full, voting members from 1973). Dmitri Ustinov, who became Defense Minister in 1977, sometimes added his signature to the proposals worked out with Gromyko. According to the long-serving Soviet ambassador in Washington, Anatoli Dobrynin:

> Andropov had the advantage of familiarity with both foreign policy and military issues from the KGB's broad sources of information . . . Gromyko and Ustinov were authorities in their respective domains but laid no special claim to each other's fields in the way that Andropov felt comfortable in both.[3]

Under Andropov, the FCD, which had traditionally been wary of taking the initiative in issuing intelligence assessments, for fear that they might contradict the opinions of higher authority, reformed and expanded its analytical branch.[4] On a number of occasions Andropov circulated slanted assessments to the Politburo in an attempt to influence its policy.[5]

Andropov became one of Brezhnev's most trusted advisers. In January 1976, for example, he sent the General Secretary a strictly personal eighteen-page letter, which began sycophantically:

> This document, which I wrote myself, is intended for you alone. If you find something in it of value to the cause, I shall be very glad, and if not, then I ask you to consider it as never having happened.[6]

Though careful not to criticize Brezhnev even in private discussions with senior KGB officers,[7] Andropov was well aware of both his intellectual limitations and declining health, and set out to establish himself as heir-apparent. The General Secretary paid little attention to the details of foreign policy. Dobrynin quickly discovered that what most interested Brezhnev about foreign affairs were the pomp and circumstance of ceremonial occasions:

> . . . the guards of honor, the grand receptions for foreign leaders in the Kremlin, the fulsome publicity, and all the rest. He wanted his photo taken for his albums, which he loved to show. He much preferred a fine ceremony signing final documents rather than working on them.

During one meeting with Dobrynin, Brezhnev disappeared upstairs and reemerged in field marshal's uniform, his chest clanking with medals. "How do I look?" he asked. "Magnificent!" Dobrynin dutifully replied.[8] From 1974 onwards a series of mild strokes caused by arteriosclerosis of the brain left Brezhnev a semi-invalid. At the rear of the cavalcade of black Zil limousines which accompanied Brezhnev wherever he went was a resuscitation vehicle. By the mid-1970s one of his closest companions was a KGB nurse, who fed him a steady stream of pills without consulting his doctors.[9]

THOUGH ANDROPOV STRENGTHENED both his own influence and that of the KGB in the making of Soviet foreign policy, his ambitious plans for dramatically improved political intelligence on the Main Adversary were never realized. Line PR (political intelligence) in the American residencies failed to live up to his high expectations. In 1968, a scandal arose over the New York resident, Nikolai Panteleymonovich Kulebyakin, a former head of the FCD First (North American) Department. After the Centre had received a complaint against him, probably from within his residency, an enquiry revealed that he had entered the KGB with a bogus curriculum vitae. Contrary to the claims in his CV, he had never completed his school education and had evaded military service. Fearing that Kulebyakin might defect if he were confronted with his crimes in Washington, he was told he had been promoted to deputy director of the FCD and summoned home to take up his new office. On arriving in Moscow, however, he was summarily dismissed from the KGB and expelled from the Communist Party.[10]

Thanks chiefly to two walk-ins, Line PR in Washington performed rather better than New York during the mid- and late 1960s. In September 1965 Robert Lipka, a twenty-year-old army clerk in NSA, caused great excitement in the Washington residency by presenting himself at the Soviet embassy on Sixteenth Street, a few blocks from the White House, and announcing that he was responsible for shredding highly classified documents. Lipka (code-named DAN) was probably the youngest Soviet agent recruited in the United States with access to high-grade intelligence since the nineteen-year-old Ted Hall had offered his services to the New York residency while working on the MANHATTAN project at Los Alamos in 1944. Lipka's file notes that he quickly mastered the intelligence tradecraft taught him by Line PR. Over the next two years he made contact with the residency about fifty times via dead letter-boxes, brush contacts and meetings with a case officer.[11]

The youthful head of Line PR, Oleg Danilovich Kalugin, spent "countless hours" in his cramped office in the Washington residency sifting through the mass of material provided by Lipka and choosing the most important documents for cabling to Moscow.[12] Lipka's motives were purely mercenary. During the two years after he walked into the Washington embassy, he received a total of about 27,000 dollars, but regularly complained that he was not paid enough and threatened to break contact unless his remuneration was increased. Lipka eventually did break contact in August 1967, when he left NSA at the end of his military service to study at Millersville College in Pennsylvania and probably concluded that his loss of intelligence access made it no longer worth his while maintaining contact with the Washington residency. To discourage the KGB from trying to renew contact, Lipka sent a final message claiming that he had been a double agent controlled by US intelligence. In view of the importance of the classified documents he had provided, however, the KGB had no doubt that he was lying. Attempts by both the residency and illegals to renew contact with Lipka continued intermittently, without success, for at least another eleven years.[13]

Only a few months after Lipka ceased working as a Soviet agent, the Washington residency recruited another walk-in with access to SIGINT. The most important Cold War agent recruited in Washington before Aldrich Ames walked in in 1985 was probably Chief Warrant Officer John Anthony Walker, a communications watch officer on the staff of the Commander of Submarine Forces in the Atlantic (COM-SUBLANT) in Norfolk, Virginia. Late in 1967 he entered the Soviet embassy and announced, "I'm a naval officer. I'd like to make some money and I'll give you some genuine stuff in return." Despite his junior rank, Walker had access to very high-level intelligence—including the key settings of US naval ciphers. The sample batch of his material, which he brought with him to the embassy, was examined with amazement by Kalugin and the Washington resident, Boris Aleksandrovich Solomatin. According to Kalugin, Solomatin's "eyes widened as he leafed through the Walker papers. 'I want this!' he cried." Walker, they later agreed, was the kind of spy who turns up "once in a lifetime." Enabling Soviet codebreakers to crack US navy codes, claims Kalugin, gave the Soviet Union "an enormous intelligence advantage" by allowing it to monitor American fleet movements.[14]

Walker, described in a fitness report from his commanding officer in 1972 as "intensely loyal" with "a fine sense of personal honor and integrity," found photographing top secret documents and cipher material with a Minox camera in the COMSUBLANT communications center so easy that he was later to claim, "K Mart has better security than the Navy." He went on to form a spy-ring by recruiting a naval friend, Jerry Whitworth, and his own son and elder brother.[15] For Kalugin the greatest surprise of both the Lipka and Walker cases was their revelation of "how incredibly lax security still was at some of the United States' top secret installations."[16]

After the foundation in 1968 of the ultra-secret Sixteenth Department to handle SIGINT material collected by the FCD, Walker was transferred to its control and thus no longer figured on the Washington residency's agent list.[17] Solomatin, however, was careful to ensure that he retained personal oversight of the running of what became the Walker family spying throughout the extraordinary eighteen years of its existence.[18] The reflected glory of the Lipka and Walker cases was to win Solomatin the Order of the Red Banner and, later, promotion to deputy head of the FCD. Kalugin's career also benefited; in 1974 he became the FCD's youngest general.[19]

Most walk-ins were less straightforward than Lipka and Walker. During the 1970s KGB residencies, especially that in Mexico City, had to deal with a growing number of "dangles"—double agents controlled by the US intelligence community who offered their services as Soviet agents. One of the most successful dangles was MAREK, a master sergeant of Czech descent at the Fort Bliss army base in Texas, who visited the Soviet embassy in Mexico in December 1966 and offered information on electronic equipment used by the US army. Recruited in June 1968, he had numerous meetings over the next eight years with a grand total of twenty-six case officers in Mexico, West Germany, Switzerland, Japan and Austria. In May 1976, however, the KGB learned from the former CIA officer Philip Agee (PONT) that MAREK was a US dangle, run in a joint CIA/Defense Intelligence Agency operation of which he had personal knowledge.[20]

By the late 1970s a special Pentagon panel was selecting classified documents which were given to American dangles, mostly non-commissioned officers selected by the DIA to strengthen their credibility as Soviet spies. As well as providing a potential channel for disinformation in a conflict or crisis, large amounts of KGB time and energy were wasted in distinguishing dangles from genuine walk-ins. The most successful of the real Soviet recruits, Aldrich Ames, said later that the refusal of the Red Army to release classified documents made it impossible for Soviet dangles to compete with those of the United States:

> Even if a document were of no real value, no one in the Soviet military was willing to sign off on releasing it, knowing that it was going to be passed to the West. They were afraid that a few months later, they would be called before some Stalin-like tribunal and be shot for treason.[21]

Throughout the Cold War the main weakness of the Washington residency was its inability to recruit agents able to provide high-level political intelligence from within the federal government. At the end of the 1960s, however, it had one non-agent source to which it attached great importance. A line PR officer, Boris Sedov, operating under cover as a Novosti journalist, had succeeded in making contact with Henry Kissinger while he was still a professor at Harvard University. According to Kalugin, "We never had any illusions about trying to recruit Kissinger: he was simply a source of political intelligence." When Kissinger became an adviser to Nixon during the 1968 election campaign, he began to use Sedov to pass messages to Moscow that Nixon's public image as an unreconstructed Cold War warrior was false and that he wanted better relations with the Soviet Union. After Nixon's election victory, Brezhnev sent personal congratulations to him via Sedov together with a note expressing the hope that together they would establish better US—Soviet relations. While the presidential campaign had been underway, the long-serving Soviet ambassador, Anatoli Dobrynin, had tolerated Sedov's secret contacts with Kissinger. Once Nixon entered the White House and Kissinger became his National Security Adviser, however, he insisted on taking over the back channel to the Kremlin himself.[22]

When Kissinger took over as Secretary of State in 1973, Dobrynin became the only ambassador in Washington who was allowed to enter the State Department unobserved via the underground garage.[23] The Washington residency complained to the Centre that Kissinger had forbidden his officials to meet members of the Soviet embassy outside office hours, thus making it impossible for residency officers to develop contacts of their own within the State Department and "check Kissinger's true intentions when negotiating with Ambassador Dobrynin."[24] During his twenty-three years in Washington from 1963 to 1986, Dobrynin's access to a series of major policy-makers from Dean Rusk under Kennedy to George Shultz under Reagan was never equaled by the Washington residency.[25]

Line PR at the New York residency had no success in recruiting "valuable agents" within the US administration either. The United Nations, however, was a much softer target. Of the more than 300 Soviet nationals employed in the UN Secretariat, many were KGB and GRU officers, agents and co-optees. KGB officers operating under diplomatic cover became the trusted personal assistants to successive UN secretaries-general: Viktor Mechislavovich Lesiovsky to U Thant, Lesiovsky and Valeri Viktorovich Krepkogorsky to Kurt Waldheim and Gennadi Mikhaylovich Yevstafeyev to Javier Pérez de Cuéllar.[26] The KGB made strenuous attempts to cultivate Waldheim in particular, arranging for the publication of flattering articles about him in the Soviet press and selecting a painting of Samarkand by a Soviet artist which was personally presented to him by Lesiovsky and Krepkogorsky when he visited the USSR.[27]

According to Arkadi Nikolayevich Shevchenko, the Russian under secretary-general at the UN who defected in 1978, Lesiovsky and Krepkogorsky were given largely routine responsibilities by Waldheim, checking the order of speakers at the General Assembly or representing him at innumerable diplomatic receptions, but were frozen out of sensitive UN business by what they claimed was Waldheim's "Austrian mafia." The UN Secretariat in New York none the less became a much more successful recruiting ground than the federal government in Washington. Shevchenko frequently saw Lesiovsky in the delegates' lounge, "buying drinks for an ambassador, telling amusing stories, procuring hard-to-get theater or opera tickets, name dropping, ingratiating himself."[28] The Secretary-General's KGB personal assistants spent much of their time cultivating and trying to recruit members of foreign missions and the UN Secretariat from around the world.[29]

The Centre, however, frequently expressed disappointment with political intelligence operations by the New York residency outside the United Nations. The residency's work was seriously disrupted in 1973 when it discovered that the FBI had detailed information on the activities of some of its operations officers, as well as of three "developmental" agents (codenamed GREK, BREST and BRIZ).[30] A report at the end of 1974 concluded that Line PR's performance had been unsatisfactory for some time past:

> For a number of years the Residency has not been able to create an agent network capable of fulfilling the complex requirements of our intelligence work, especially against the US We have not succeeded in achieving this goal in 1974, either, although there has been some progress in this line. There have been several recruitments (SUAREZ, DIF, HERMES) and confidential contacts have been acquired. But these results still do not move us any closer to fulfilling our basic task.[31]

None of the three new agents was of major significance. SUAREZ was a Colombian journalist recruited by Anatoli Mikhailovich Manakov, a KGB officer operating under cover as *Komsomolskaya Pravda* correspondent in New York. A few years later SUAREZ succeeded in gaining US citizenship.[32] DIF was a US businessman who provided political and economic assessments.[33] HERMES, potentially the most important of the three new recruits, was Ozdemir Ahmet Ozgur, a Cypriot born in 1929. In 1977, the New York residency was able to arrange through Arkadi Shevchenko for Ozgur to gain a post at the UN Secretariat. When Shevchenko defected in 1978, however, the KGB was forced to break off all contact with HERMES.[34]

DIF, the US businessman, was also included in the Washington residency's list of its Line PR agents in 1974. Line PR had nine other agents: GRIG, MAGYAR, MORTON, NIK, RAMZES, REM, ROMELLA, SHEF and STOIC.[35] GRIG remains unidentified but is reported as operating in Canada.[36] MAGYAR was a leading peace activist.[37] MORTON was a prominent lawyer recruited in 1970 but taken off the agent list in 1975 because of his advancing years. On his retirement he put the Washington residency in touch with his son, who was also a partner in a well-known law firm.[38] NIK was a Colombian who worked on US—Colombian cultural exchange programs.[39] RAMZES was an American professor with contacts in Congress, academe, the press and Latin America.[40] REM was an Italian employee of the UN Secretariat.[41] ROMELLA was a Latin American diplomat in the UN Secretariat, who made contact with the KGB to seek its help in renewing her contract at the UN before it expired in 1975; she supplied both classified documents and recruitment leads.[42] SHEF was a professor at McMaster University, recruited during a visit to Lithuania in 1974.[43] STOIC was a Latin American diplomat in the UN Secretariat.[44] As in New York, none of the Washington Line PR agents had high-level access to any branch of the federal government.

Though the New York residency had some successes in electronic eavesdropping, in active measures and in scientific and technological intelligence, its Line PR network mostly consisted of agents at the UN and in émigré communities, only a minority of whom had US citizenship.[45] The largest concentration of agents was within the Soviet colony itself, most of whom inhabited the residential complex in Riverdale. According to KGB statistics, in 1975 the colony numbered 1,366 Soviet employees and dependents. Of the 533 employees, seventy-six were officially classed as agents and sixteen as "trusted contacts."[46] Most, however, were chiefly concerned with informing on their colleagues to Line SK (Soviet Colony) in the residency. The Centre's assessment in 1974 stressed the limitations of Line PR's New York agents:

> Not one of these agents has access to secret American information. The basic thrust of operations with this network therefore consists of using it for the collection of information from UN diplomatic sources, and from several American [non-agent] sources.[47]

Lacking any high-level agents in the federal government, Line PR officers in New York and Washington, usually operating under cover as diplomats or journalists, devoted much of their time to collecting insider gossip from well-placed non-agent sources in Congress and the press corps.[48] As head of Line PR in Washington from 1965 to 1970, Kalugin got to know the columnists Walter Lippmann, Joseph Kraft and Drew Pearson; Chalmers Roberts and Murray Marder of the *Washington Post;* Joseph Harsch of the *Christian Science Monitor;* Carl Rowan, former director of the US Information Agency; and Henry Brandon of the London *Times.* Kalugin's role when he called at their offices or lunched with them in Washington restaurants was not that of agent controller or recruiter. Instead, he "would act like a good reporter," carefully noting their assessments of the current political situation: "Rarely did I come up with a scoop for the Politburo, but the reporting of our [PR] section enabled Soviet leaders to have a better sense of American political realities . . ." During the 1968 presidential election campaign some of Kalugin's sources provided corroboration for Sedov's reports, based on conversations with Kissinger, that, if elected, Nixon would prove much less anti-Soviet than Moscow feared. One of Kalugin's most important contacts was Senator Robert Kennedy who, but for his assassination just after he had won the California presidential primary, might have won the 1968 Democratic nomination. Before his death Kennedy presented Kalugin with a tie-pin showing the PT-109 torpedo boat which his brother had captained during the war. Line PR officers in Washington also had regular meetings with such leading senators as Mike Mansfield, William Fulbright, Mark Hatfield, Charles Percy, Eugene McCarthy, George McGovern and Jacob Javits. The Centre liked to boast to the

Politburo that its assessments of American policy were based on access to the Congressional élite.[49]

Most of the political reporting of the Washington residency was thus based on non-secret sources—to the considerable annoyance of some of the Soviet diplomats whose far smaller foreign currency allowances gave them less freedom to entertain their contacts in Washington restaurants. Despite his insistence on keeping the back channel to himself, Dobrynin took a more benign view of the residency's work, and seemed genuinely interested in what it discovered from both its contacts and agents.[50] "In too many Soviet embassies," Dobrynin complained, "normal personal relations between the ambassador and the KGB resident were the exception rather than the rule." Ambassador and resident frequently became locked in bitter rivalry as each sought "to show who really was the boss in the embassy" and to demonstrate to Moscow the superiority of his own sources of information.[51]

As resident in Washington from 1965 to 1968 Solomatin had got on well with Dobrynin. When he became resident in New York in 1971, however, he quickly began to feud with Yakov Malik, the Soviet representative at the United Nations. Malik strongly objected to Solomatin's attempts to develop contacts whom he wished to cultivate himself—among them David Rockefeller, brother of Nelson and chairman of Chase Manhattan Bank.[52] Malik was fascinated by Rockefeller's 30,000-name card file of his contacts around the world, cross-indexed by country, city and business. On a visit to the chairman's sprawling seventeenth-floor office at the sixty-story Chase Manhattan building, Malik asked to see a sample from the file. Rockefeller picked out the card for Khrushchev.[53] Malik also vigorously opposed Solomatin's contacts with the veteran diplomat Averell Harriman, regarded in Moscow as one of the most influential American advocates of better relations with the Soviet Union.[54] In co-operation with Dobrynin, Harriman later returned from retirement to act as unofficial channel of communication between Brezhnev and Jimmy Carter during the transition period after Carter's 1976 election victory.[55] Solomatin complained to the Centre that Malik's objections to his attempts to cultivate Rockefeller and Harriman were "characteristic" of his general obstructionism.[56] He failed, however, to tell the Centre that there was not the slightest prospect of recruiting either Rockefeller or Harriman.

In an attempt to improve the quality of agent recruitment in the United States, the director of the Institute of Psychology in the Academy of Sciences, Boris Fyodorovich Lomov, a "trusted contact" of the KGB, was sent in 1975 to advise the New York residency on techniques of cultivation.[57] In 1976 the Centre devised an elaborate incentive scheme to reward successful recruiters, with inducements ranging from medals and letters of appreciation to accelerated promotion, new apartments and cash bonuses in hard currency (which would make possible the purchase of Western consumer goods that could be shipped back to Moscow at the end of the officer's tour of duty).[58]

As chairman of the KGB, Andropov seemed unable to grasp the difficulties of penetrating the US administration. During the mid-1970s he initiated a series of hopelessly impracticable recruitment schemes. Following Nixon's resignation in

August 1974 after the Watergate scandal, Andropov instructed the Washington residency to establish contact with five members of the former administration: Pat Buchanan and William Safire, former advisers and speechwriters to Nixon; Richard Allen, Deputy National Security Adviser during the first year of Nixon's administration; C. Fred Bergsten, an economist on the National Security Council (NSC); and S. Everett Gleason, an NSC veteran who died three months after Nixon's resignation.[59] All were wildly improbable recruits. In 1975 Andropov personally approved a series of equally improbable operations designed to penetrate the "inner circles" of a series of well-known public figures: among them George Ball, Ramsey Clark, Kenneth Galbraith, Averell Harriman, Teddy Kennedy and Theodore Sorensen.[60] Somewhat humiliatingly for the FCD, the KGB's most productive agent during the 1976 election campaign was a Democratic activist with access to the Carter camp who had been recruited during a visit to Russia by the Second Chief Directorate.[61]

The KGB's most successful strategy for cultivating American policy-makers was to use the prestigious academic cover of the Moscow Institute of the United States and Canada. The secret 1968 statute of the institute kept at the Centre authorized the KGB to task it to research aspects of the Main Adversary which were of interest to it, to provide KGB officers with cover positions, to invite prominent American policy-makers and academics to Moscow and to undertake intelligence-related missions to the United States. Among the KGB's cover positions at the institute was that of deputy director, occupied by Colonel Radimir Bogdanov (codenamed VLADIMIROV), sometimes described behind his back as "the scholar in epaulets."[62] The KGB's most important agent at the institute was its director, Georgi Arbatov, codenamed VASILI, who built up a large circle of high-level contacts in the United States and was regularly required to cultivate them.[63] According to Kissinger:

> [Arbatov] was especially subtle in playing to the inexhaustible masochism of American intellectuals who took it as an article of faith that every difficulty in US—Soviet relations had to be caused by American stupidity or intransigence. He was endlessly ingenious in demonstrating how American rebuffs were frustrating the peaceful, sensitive leaders in the Kremlin, who were being driven reluctantly by our inflexibility into conflicts that offended their inherently gentle natures.[64]

Though Arbatov's access to US policy-makers raised KGB hopes of a major penetration of the federal government, Mitrokhin found no evidence in the files of any significant recruitment which resulted from it. In the Centre's view, Arbatov's most important contact during the 1970s was former Under-Secretary of Defense Cyrus Vance, codenamed VIZIR ("Vizier"). During a visit to Moscow in the spring of 1973, Vance unsurprisingly agreed with Arbatov on the need to "increase the level of mutual trust" in US—Soviet relations. Arbatov reported that he had told Vance—doubtless to no effect—that the majority of the American press corps in Moscow were propagating "a negative propagandistic" image of the USSR at the behest of the Zionist lobby in the United States. In 1976 Arbatov was sent on another mission to the United States. While there he claimed an addition 200 dollars for "operational expenses" from the New York residency for entertaining Vance and others. From such inconsequential meetings the Centre briefly formed absurdly optimistic hopes of penetrating the new American administration after Jimmy Carter's victory in the presidential election of November 1976 and his appointment of Vance as Secretary of State. On December 19 Andropov personally approved operations against Vance which were probably intended to make him at least a "trusted contact" of the KGB. The operations were, of course, doomed to failure. Vance's file records that, once he entered the Carter administration, any possibility of unofficial access to both him and his family dried up.[65] Doubtless to the frustration of the Centre, Ambassador Dobrynin continued to have a private entrée to the State Department via its underground garage, just as he had done during Kissinger's term as Secretary of State, and prided himself on maintaining through Vance the "confidential channel" between White House and Kremlin which the Centre had briefly deluded itself into believing it could take over.[66]

The Centre's early expectations of the Carter administration were so unrealistic that it even devised schemes to cultivate his hardline National Security Adviser, Zbigniew Brzezinski. The FCD drew up a plan to send Arbatov's deputy, Bogdanov, whom Brzezinski had met previously, to Washington "to strengthen their relationship and to convey to him some advantageous information." On January 3, 1977 Andropov also approved an operation to collect "compromising information" on Brzezinski as a means of putting pressure on him. Unsurprisingly, as in the case of Vance, the Centre's early hopes of cultivating Brzezinski quickly evaporated, and the Centre concentrated instead on devising "active measures" to discredit him.[67]

KGB Decree No. 0017 of May 26, 1977 declared that there was an urgent need for better intelligence on the Carter administration. The Centre's evaluations of the work of the Washington and New York residencies in both 1977 and 1978 make clear that this requirement was not met. Line PR's agent network in the United States was once again declared incapable of meeting the objectives assigned to it. Not a single agent had direct access to major penetration targets.[68]

Lacking reliable, high-level sources within the administration, the Centre, as frequently happened, fell back on conspiracy theories. Early in 1977 Vladimir Aleksandrovich Kryuchkov, head of the FCD and a protégé of Andropov, submitted to him a report entitled "On CIA Plans to Recruit Agents Among Soviet Citizens," revealing a non-existent CIA masterplan to sabotage Soviet administration, economic development and scientific research:

> ... Today American intelligence is planning to recruit agents among Soviet citizens, train them and then advance them into administrative positions within Soviet politics, the economy and science. The CIA has drafted a program to subject agents to individual instruction in espionage techniques and also intensive political and ideological brainwashing ... The CIA intends that individual agents working in isolation to carry out policies of sabotage and distortion of superiors' instructions will be coordinated from a single center

within the US intelligence system. The CIA believes that such deliberate action by agents will create internal political difficulties for the Soviet Union, retard development of its economy and channel its scientific research into dead ends.

Andropov considered this improbable top secret conspiracy theory so important that on January 24, 1977 he forwarded it under his signature to the other members of the Politburo and Central Committee.[69]

THE CENTRE HARBORED far fewer illusions about the incoming Reagan administration in January 1981 than it had done about Carter four years earlier. Any hope that Reagan's anti-Soviet speeches during the election had been mere campaign rhetoric quickly faded after his inauguration. In April 1981, after a trip to the United States at the Centre's request, Arbatov sent a report on the new administration to Andropov and Kryuchkov. At a dinner in the White House he had been able to observe Reagan for one and a half hours from a distance of only fifteen meters. Though Reagan seemed to be acting the role of president, he played the part with genuine emotion. Tears came to his eyes when the flags of the four armed services were brought into the room and when he stood up and placed his hand on his heart as the national anthem was played. Nancy Reagan's eyes never left her husband. Her adoring expression reminded Arbatov of a teenage girl suddenly placed next to her favorite pop star. Though Reagan's speech to the assembled journalists was "exceptionally shallow," the President played to perfection the role of "father of the nation," a great leader who had kept his humanity, a sense of humor and the common touch.[70]

Both the Centre and the Kremlin took a less benign view of Reagan. In a secret speech to a major KGB conference in May 1981 a visibly ailing Brezhnev denounced Reagan's policies as a serious threat to world peace. He was followed by Andropov, who was to succeed him as general secretary eighteen months later. To the astonishment of most of the audience, the KGB chairman announced that, by decision of the Politburo, the KGB and GRU were for the first time to collaborate in a global intelligence operation, codenamed RYAN—a newly devised acronym for *Raketno-Yadernoye Napadenie* ("Nuclear Missile Attack"). RYAN's purpose was to collect intelligence on the presumed, but non-existent, plans of the Reagan administration to launch a nuclear first strike against the Soviet Union—a delusion which reflected both the KGB's continuing failure to penetrate the policy-making of the Main Adversary and its recurrent tendency towards conspiracy theory.[71] "Not since the end of the Second World War," Andropov informed foreign residencies, "has the international situation been as explosive as it is now."[72] As Brezhnev's successor in November 1982, Andropov retained full control over the KGB; his most frequent visitors were senior KGB officers.[73] Throughout his term as general secretary, RYAN remained the FCD's first priority.

For several years Moscow succumbed to what its ambassador in Washington, Anatoli Dobrynin, fairly described as a "paranoid interpretation" of Reagan's policy.[74] Most residencies in Western capitals were less alarmist than Andropov and the KGB leadership. When Oleg Antonovich Gordievsky joined the London residency in June 1982 he found all his colleagues in Line PR skeptical about operation RYAN. None, however, were willing to risk their careers by challenging the Centre's assessment. RYAN thus created a vicious circle of intelligence collection and assessment. Residencies were, in effect, ordered to search out alarming information. The Centre was duly alarmed by what they supplied and demanded more.[75] The Washington resident, Stanislav Andreyevich Androsov, a protégé of Kryuchkov, was at pains to provide it.[76]

The Centre interpreted the announcement of the SDI ("Star Wars") program in March 1983 as part of the psychological preparation of the American people for nuclear war. On September 28, 1983 the terminally ill Andropov issued from his sickbed a denunciation of American policy couched in apocalyptic language unparalleled since the depths of the Cold War. "Outrageous military psychosis" had taken over the United States. "The Reagan administration, in its imperial ambitions, goes so far that one begins to doubt whether Washington has any brakes at all preventing it from crossing the point at which any sober-minded person must stop." Alarm within the Centre reached a climax during the NATO exercise "Able Archer 83," held in November 1983 to practice nuclear release procedures. For a time the KGB leadership was haunted by the fear that the exercise might be intended as cover for a nuclear first strike. Some FCD officers stationed in the West were by now more concerned by the alarmism in the Centre than by the threat of a Western surprise attack.[77]

Operation RYAN wound down (though it did not end) during 1984, helped by the death of its two main proponents, Andropov and defense minister Ustinov, and by reassuring signals from London and Washington, both worried by intelligence on Soviet paranoia.[78] The alarmist RYAN reports obediently provided by KGB residencies were merely an extreme example of Line PR's habitual tendency to tell Moscow what it wanted to hear. One political intelligence officer later admitted:

> In order to please our superiors, we sent in falsified and biased information, acting on the principle "Blame everything on the Americans, and everything will be OK." That's not intelligence, it's self-deception![79]

During the first Reagan administration, as at other periods, the Centre would have gained a far more accurate insight into American policy by reading the *New York Times* or *Washington Post* than by relying on the reports of its own residencies. One of the most striking signs of Gorbachev's "new thinking" on foreign policy after he became general secretary in 1985 was his early dissatisfaction with the FCD's political reporting. In December 1985 Viktor Mikhailovich Chebrikov, KGB chairman since 1982, summoned a meeting of the KGB leadership to discuss a stern memorandum from Gorbachev "on the impermissibility of distortions of the factual state of affairs in messages and informational reports sent to the Central Committee of the CPSU and other ruling bodies." The meeting sycophantically agreed on the need to avoid sycophantic reporting and declared the duty of all Chekists both at home and abroad to fulfill "the Leninist requirement that we need only the whole truth."[80]

Gorbachev was far more impressed initially by the performance of FCD's Directorate T. Throughout the Cold War the KGB had greater success in collecting scientific and technological intelligence (S&T) than in its political intelligence operations against the Main Adversary. Infiltrating US defense contractors and research institutes proved far easier than penetrating the heart of the federal government. S&T also rarely suffered from the political correctness which distorted the reporting of Line PR in residencies and political intelligence assessments at the Centre. What remained at least partially taboo, however, was the difficulty experienced by Soviet state-run industry in making full use of the extraordinary S&T which it received. In 1971, for example, the defense and electronics industry ministries began a joint project to duplicate Westinghouse cathode-ray tubes. Two years later, because of production problems at the State Optical Institute, little progress had been made.[81] It was ideologically impossible to learn the lessons of failures such as this, for to do so would have involved a recognition of the inferiority of the Soviet command economy to the market economies of the West. FCD reports thus concentrated on the structural contradictions of Western capitalism while glossing over the far more serious economic problems of the Soviet Bloc.[82]

In 1970 the New York and Washington residencies each ran nine Line X agents and five "trusted contacts."[83] In 1973 the new position of head S&T resident for the United States was established in New York, with responsibility for coordinating Line X operations by the three American residencies, as well as attempts to evade the embargo on the export of advanced technology to the Soviet Union. By 1975 Directorate T had seventy-seven agents and forty-two trusted contacts working against American targets inside and outside the United States.[84]

Mitrokhin's notes identify thirty-two of the S&T agents and trusted contacts active in the United States during the 1970s, mostly recruited in the same decade. A further eight whose espionage is not dated in the notes were also probably active in the 1970s.[85] The companies for which they worked included some of the leading American defense contractors: among them IBM, McDonnell Douglas and TRW.[86] The S&T agent network also contained scientists with access to important defense-related projects at some of the United States' best-known research institutes: among them MIKE at the Massachusetts Institute of Technology,[87] and TROP in the Argonne National Laboratory at the University of Chicago.[88] In addition to the civilian S&T agent network, there were also KGB agents in the armed forces who provided intelligence on the latest military technology: among them JOE, an army electronics engineer who provided "valuable information" on military communications systems,[89] and NERPA, who in 1977 was engaged in weapons research at the US army's Material Development and Readiness Command (DARCOM).[90]

Though Mitrokhin's information on the extent and targets of the S&T network on the territory of the Main Adversary is far more extensive than any previously available account, it is not comprehensive.[91] There is, for example, no mention in

Mitrokhin's notes of the Californian drug dealer Andrew Daulton Lee, who in 1975–6 provided the KGB residency in Mexico City with the operating manual for the Rhyolite surveillance satellite and technical data on other satellite systems. Lee's source was his friend Christopher Boyce, an employee of Rhyolite's manufacturer, TRW Corporations in Redondo Beach. Among the TRW secrets passed on to the KGB was detailed information on how American spy satellites monitored Soviet missile tests. In 1977 Lee and Boyce were arrested, tried and sentenced to, respectively, life and forty years' imprisonment. Both achieved celebrity status as the subjects of the bestselling book and film *The Falcon and the Snowman*.[92] One of the KGB files noted by Mitrokhin reveals that only a year after the arrest of Lee and Boyce the KGB recruited another, possibly even more important, spy in TRW with the codename ZENIT. While Boyce had been only a clerk (though with access to classified documents), ZENIT was a scientist.[93]

Directorate T was proud of its achievements, particularly against the Main Adversary, and anxious to bring them to the attention of the Soviet leadership. Brezhnev was informed in 1972 that S&T had produced a saving during the past year of over a hundred million convertible roubles.[94] Among the successes singled out for Brezhnev's attention was intelligence on the construction of the American space shuttle and preparations for unmanned flights to Mars. This, he was told, would solve a number of current problems in the development of Soviet space technology. S&T intelligence on the pelletization of seeds, he was further assured (doubtless unrealistically), would increase the Soviet grain harvest by 20 to 30 per cent and shorten growing time.[95] In 1973 Directorate T reported that it had acquired over 26,000 documents and 3,700 "samples." Though only a minority of this material was classified, it included top secret information on the Saturn rocket, the Apollo space missions, the Poseidon, Honest John, Redeye, Roland, Hydra and Viper missiles, the Boeing 747 jumbo jet and computer technology subsequently plagiarized in the construction of the Minsk-32 computer.[96]

The triumphs of S&T collection figured prominently in the Chekist Hall of Fame opened by the FCD at Yasenevo in 1977 to mark the sixtieth anniversary of the October Revolution. Directorate T's exhibit claimed that during the previous five-year period it had obtained over 140,000 S&T documents and more than 20,000 "samples." These were alleged to have produced an economic benefit of over one billion roubles for the Soviet economy and to have advanced research work in a number of branches of science and technology by periods of from two to six years.[97]

Leonid Sergeyevich Zaitsev, the dynamic and ambitious head of Directorate T appointed in 1975, argued that it should be allowed to leave the FCD and become an independent directorate within the KGB. It would, he claimed, need a budget of only 1 percent per annum of the value of the S&T which it supplied to Soviet industry and agriculture.[98] The head of the FCD, Kryuchkov, however, was determined not to allow such a prestigious part of his intelligence empire to escape from his control. Despite failing to win its freedom, Directorate T increasingly operated independently from the rest of the FCD. Its new recruits mostly came from scientific or engineering backgrounds, had their own curriculum in the Andropov Institute (the FCD academy) and trained separately from those in other departments. In foreign residencies Line X officers mixed relatively little with their colleagues in other lines.[99]

The Military—Industrial Commission (VPK), which was mainly responsible for overseeing Directorate T, showed greater interest in non-American targets than during the early Cold War.[100] The United States none the less remained a more important S&T target than the rest of the world combined. In 1980 61.5 percent of the VPK's information came from American sources (some outside the USA), 10.5 percent from West Germany, 8 percent from France, 7.5 percent from Britain and 3 percent from Japan.[101] In 1980 the VPK gave instructions for 3,617 "acquisition tasks," of which 1,085 were completed within a year, benefiting 3,396 Soviet research and development projects.[102] Directorate T was its chief collection agency.

Directorate T owed much of its success in meeting so many of the VPK's requirements to its numerous collaborators in the Soviet scientific community, who numbered approximately 90 agent-recruiters, 900 agents and 350 trusted contacts during the mid-1970s.[103] Among these collaborators—probably the largest network of talent-spotters in the history of S&T—were some of the Soviet Union's leading scientists. All Western scientists—particularly in the United States—in fields related to Directorate T's "acquisition tasks" were potential targets for the KGB. The first approach to a targeted scientist usually came from a Soviet colleague in a similar field, who would try to establish cooperation at a personal or institutional level. Directorate T would then seek to recruit the more naive or corrupt of the Western scientists approached in this way as agents or trusted contacts.[104] Among the Directorate's agent-recruiters was the director of the Physics and Energy Institute of the Latvian Academy of Sciences (codenamed VITOS), who in 1973 recruited MIKE, a senior physicist at MIT.[105] SATURN, a department head at McDonnell Douglas, was recruited in 1978 with similar assistance from the Lithuanian Academy of Sciences.[106]

The KGB also took an active part in the selection of Soviet students for academic exchange programs with the United States and trained many of them as talent-spotters. Students were told to seek places at universities and research institutes within easy reach of the residencies at New York (Brooklyn Polytechnic, MIT, Rensselaer Polytechnic and the universities of Columbia, Cornell, Harvard, New York and Princeton), Washington (American, Catholic, Georgetown, George Washington and Maryland Universities) and San Francisco (the University of California at Berkeley and San Francisco, California Institute of Technology, University of Southern California and Stanford).[107]

Directorate T's success in penetrating American targets was greatly assisted by poor security in some of its target companies and research institutes. Appearing in 1985 before a Senate committee investigating security among defense contractors, Christopher Boyce testified that he and colleagues at TRW "regularly partied and boozed it up during working hours with the 'black vault'" housing the Rhyolite satellite project. Bacardi rum, he claimed, was kept behind the cipher machines and a cipher-destruction device used as a blender to mix banana daiquiris and Mai-Tais.[108] Security failures in most other companies probably took less exotic and alcoholic forms.

Since most major American companies operated abroad, they were vulnerable to penetration outside as well as inside the United States. In the mid-1970s seventeen major US companies and research institutes were targeted by KGB residencies in western Europe: among them IBM by the London, Paris, Geneva, Vienna and Bonn residencies; Texas Instruments by Paris; Monsanto by London and Brussels; Westinghouse Electric by Brussels; Honeywell by Rome; ITT by Stockholm; and the National Institutes of Health by Copenhagen.[109] European residencies were assisted by a number of walk-ins. In 1974, for example, a Canadian resident of Los Angeles (later given the codename SPRINTER) entered the Soviet embassy in Helsinki, announced that he worked for an electro-optical company which was developing laser anti-missile systems and infra-red sights for firearms, tanks, ships and aircraft, and offered to sell its secrets.[110] Like SPRINTER, most of the KGB's S&T network in the United States appear to have been mercenary spies.

SIGINT added substantially to the S&T provided by agents. The SIGINT stations within the Washington, New York and San Francisco residencies (whose operations are discussed in chapter 21) succeeded in intercepting the telephone and fax communications of the Brookhaven National Laboratory and a series of major companies. Mitrokhin's notes, however, do not make it possible to assess the proportion of S&T provided by SIGINT rather than HUMINT.

Since before the Second World War S&T had been regarded as an essential means of preventing Soviet military technology and weapons systems from falling behind the West's. According to one report noted by Mitrokhin, over half the projects of the Soviet defense industry in 1979 were based on S&T from the West.[111] Andropov claimed in 1981 that all the tasks in military S&T set for the KGB had been successfully completed.[112] According to an official US report, based largely on documents supplied during the early 1980s by Vladimir Vetrov (codenamed FAREWELL), a French agent in FCD Directorate T:

> The Soviets estimate that by using documentation on the US F-18 fighter their aviation and radar industries saved some five years of development time and 35 million roubles (the 1980 dollar cost of equivalent research activity would be $55 million) in project manpower and other developmental costs. The manpower portion of these savings probably represents over a thousand man-years of scientific research effort and one of the most successful individual exploitations ever of Western technology.
>
> The documentation of the F-18 fire-control radar served as the technical basis for new lookdown/shootdown engagement radars for the latest generation of Soviet fighters. US methods of component design, fast-Fourier-transform algorithms, terrain mapping functions, and real-time resolution-enhancement techniques were cited as key elements incorporated into the Soviet counterpart.[113]

Other successful military projects made possible by S&T were the construction of a Soviet clone of the AWACS airborne radar system and the construction of the Blackjack Bomber modeled on the American B1-B.[114]

From the late 1970s onwards increasing emphasis was also put on the contribution of S&T to the Soviet economy. Directorate T calculated that the main branches of civilian industry were ten years behind their Western counterparts.[115] In January 1980 Andropov instructed Directorate T to draw up S&T collection plans designed to resolve current problems in Soviet agriculture, metallurgy, power-generation, engineering and advanced technology.[116] Of the 5,456 "samples" (machinery, components, microcircuits, etc.) acquired by Directorate T during 1980, 44 percent went to defense industries, 28 percent to civilian industry via the State Committee for Science and Technology (GKNT) and 28 percent to the KGB and other government agencies. In the same, possibly exceptional year, just over half the intelligence obtained by Directorate T came from allied intelligence services, chief among them the East German HVA and the Czechoslovak StB.[117]

Among the HVA's greatest S&T successes was its penetration of IBM. According to the head of the HVA, Markus Wolf, the East German microelectronics company Robotron "became so heavily dependent on surreptitiously acquiring IBM's technological advances that it was, in effect, a sort of illegal subsidiary of that company."[118] Though well behind the West, Robotron was rather better than its Soviet equivalents in exploiting IBM computer technology. The KGB's name-trace system SOUD ("System for Operational and Institutional Data") used East German computers.[119]

S&T collection continued to expand during the 1980s. At a meeting of senior FCD staff early in 1984 Kryuchkov reported that, "In the last two years the quantity of material and samples handed over to civilian branches of industry has increased by half as much again." This, he claimed, had been used "to real economic effect," particularly in energy and food production. Kryuchkov characteristically failed to mention that the sclerotic nature of Soviet economic management made it far harder to exploit S&T in the civilian economy than in the imitation of Western armaments. His obsession with operation RYAN also left him dissatisfied with Directorate T's intelligence on the weapons systems at the heart of Reagan's non-existent plans for a nuclear first strike. "As previously," Kryuchkov complained, "we are experiencing an acute shortage of secret information about new types of weapon and their means of delivery." The FCD "work plan" for 1984 laid down as Directorate T's main intelligence priorities:

> military technology measures taken by the Main Adversary to build up first-strike weapons: the quantitative increase in nuclear munitions and means of delivery (MX missile complexes, Trident, Pershing-2, cruise missiles, strategic bombers); replacement of one generation of nuclear missiles by another (Minuteman, Trident-2), the development of qualitatively new types of weapons (space devices for multiple use for military purposes, laser and pencil beam weapons, non-acoustic anti-submarine defense weapons, electronic warfare weapons, etc.).

The second priority was "information and specimens of significant interest for civilian branches of the USSR's economy."[120]

Like other Soviet leaders, Gorbachev doubtless took it for granted that Soviet military technology required S&T from the West. He was probably more interested, however, in the use of S&T to invigorate the civilian economy. In an address to embassy staff in London on December 15, 1984, three months before he became general secretary, he singled out for praise the achievements of Directorate T and its Line X officers in foreign residencies.[121] It was already clear that Gorbachev regarded the covert acquisition of Western technology and scientific research as an important part of economic *perestroika.*

The dramatic improvement in East—West relations during the later 1980s offered new opportunities for Directorate T, which produced 25–40,000 S&T "information reports" and 12–13,000 "samples" a year. In 1986 it estimated their value at 550 million roubles; in 1988 and 1989 it put the figure at one billion roubles a year.[122] In the later 1980s about 150 Soviet weapons systems were believed by Western experts to be based on technology system stolen from the West.[123]

AS WELL AS being impressed by the achievements of Directorate T, Gorbachev also seems to have revised his initially critical opinion of the political intelligence provided by the FCD. During the early 1980s Kryuchkov had repeatedly berated his subordinates for their lack of success in recruiting important American agents, and demanded "a radical improvement." As late as February 1985 he denounced "the low standard" of operations against the Main Adversary and "the lack of appreciable results" by KGB residencies in recruiting US citizens.[124]

A walk-in to the Washington embassy two months later came as the answer to Kryuchkov's prayers. By the time Aldrich Ames offered his services to the KGB in April 1985 he had been working for the CIA for eighteen years. Within two months he had betrayed twenty Western (mostly American) agents: among them Dmitri Polyakov, a GRU general who had worked for the FBI and CIA for over twenty years; Oleg Gordievsky, a British agent in the KGB who had just been appointed resident in London; Adolf Tolkachev, an electronics expert who had provided high-grade intelligence on the Soviet avionics system; and at least eleven other KGB and GRU officers stationed in various parts of the world. A majority were shot, though Gordievsky made an epic escape from Russia, with SIS assistance, while under KGB surveillance. Collectively, they had represented probably the most successful Western agent penetration of the Soviet Union since the Bolshevik Revolution. Ames's main motive for betraying them was probably greed. By the time of his arrest nine years later, the KGB and its successor agency had paid him almost three million dollars (probably more than any other agent in Russian history) and had promised him another two.[125] As Gorbachev embarked on a new course in policy towards the United States, he was doubtless impressed by the fact that the KGB had, for the first time, recruited a major agent within the CIA. The FCD also appears to have responded to Gorbachev's demand for less crudely biased reporting on the Main Adversary and its allies. According to Leonid Vladimirovich Shebarshin, then one of Kryuchkov's deputies, "the FCD no longer had to present its reports in a falsely positive light,"[126] though many of its officers must surely have found it difficult to throw off the habits of a lifetime.

In December 1987 Gorbachev took Kryuchkov with him on his historic visit to Washington to sign with President Reagan the first arms control treaty to reduce the nuclear arsenals of the superpowers. Never before had a head of the FCD accompanied a Soviet leader on a visit to the West. Gorbachev's confidence in Kryuchkov—which he would later bitterly regret—doubtless reflected his high opinion of the FCD's success both in gathering an unprecedented volume of S&T and in penetrating the CIA. During the visit to Washington Kryuchkov had dinner at the Maison Blanche restaurant, unnoticed by other diners, with the Deputy Director of Central Intelligence, Robert Gates (later DCI). Gates wrote later:

> Looking back, it is embarrassing to realize that, at this first high-level CIA—KGB meeting, Kryuchkov smugly knew that he had a spy—Aldrich Ames—at the heart of CIA, that he knew quite well what we were telling the President and others about the Soviet Union, and that he was aware of many of our human and technical collection efforts in the USSR.[127]

In October 1988 Kryuchkov achieved his ambition of becoming the first foreign intelligence chief to become chairman of the KGB. His valedictory address on leaving the FCD was a remarkable mixture of the old and new thinking. "Democratization and *glasnost* are the motive force of *perestroika*," he declared, "and we shall not win through without them:"

> Unless we have an objective view of the world, seeing it unadorned and free of clichés and stereotyped ideas, all claims about the effectiveness of our foreign policy operations will be nothing but empty words.

The old suspicions and conspiracy theories about the United States, however, still lurked not far below the surface of Kryuchkov's address. Without mentioning operation RYAN by name, he sought to justify the principles on which it was based:

> Many of [the FCD's] former responsibilities have not been removed from the agenda. The principal one of these is not to overlook the immediate danger of nuclear conflict being unleashed.

And he added a warning about what he alleged was the continuing brutality of "provocation operations" by Western intelligence services; he claimed that there had been over 900 such operations during the first half of 1988 alone.[128] Kryuchkov began 1989 with a dramatic demonstration of the new climate of East—West relations, becoming the first chairman in KGB history to receive the United States ambassador in his office. Thereafter he embarked on an unprecedented public relations campaign designed to win over Western as well as Soviet opinion. "The KGB," he declared, "should have an image not only in our country but worldwide which is consistent with the noble goals I believe we are pursuing in our work."[129]

After a brief power struggle, Kryuchkov was succeeded as head of the FCD by the 53-year-old Leonid Shebarshin, the first man with experience of working in countries outside the Soviet Bloc to run foreign intelligence since the Second World War.[130] One of Shebarshin's main jobs at the beginning of the Gorbachev era had been to prepare intelligence reports for the Party leadership. The fact that he leapfrogged several more senior candidates for his new post is a certain indication that his briefing had impressed Gorbachev.[131] Foreign intelligence officers interviewed by *zvestia* after Shebarshin's resignation in September 1991 described him as "the first really competent head of the FCD in decades."[132] According to Shebarshin, his main initial brief from Gorbachev was "to ensure the West did not cheat on arms control."[133]

The tactical victories of the FCD against the Main Adversary which impressed Gorbachev failed to avert strategic defeat. Directorate T's very success in stealing Western secrets merely underlined the structural problems of the Soviet economy. Despite S&T worth a billion roubles a year and the Soviet Union's large numbers of scientists and engineers, Soviet technology fell steadily further and further behind the West. Gorbachev's reforms served only to weaken further the command economy, without establishing a market economy in its stead. There was a bread shortage even after the good harvest of 1990.[134] No amount of either economic or political intelligence could stave off the disintegration of the failing Soviet system.

As the Soviet Union's economic problems multiplied during 1990 and separatist movements strengthened, the Centre's traditional suspicions of the Main Adversary revived. Kryuchkov did not place all the blame for Russia's ills on imperialist plots. "The main sources of our trouble, in the KGB's view," he declared, "are to be found inside the country." But he accused the CIA and other Western intelligence services of promoting "anti-socialist" and separatist forces as part of a "secret war against the Soviet state."[135] According to Shebarshin, Gorbachev failed to heed the FCD's warnings. "He and his friends lived in a world of self-delusion . . . We were hitching our wagon to the Western train."[136] With Gorbachev, in the Centre's view, unwilling to offend the Americans, Kryuchkov began to publicize some of the KGB's neglected conspiracy theories. In December 1990 he denounced a (non-existent) Western plot, "akin to economic sabotage," to "deliver impure and sometimes infected grain, as well as products with an above-average level of radioactivity or containing harmful substances."[137] In February 1991 first Kryuchkov's deputy, Viktor Fyodorovich Grushko, and then the new prime minister, Valentin Pavlov, denounced an equally imaginary plot by Western banks to undermine the rouble. The fullest public version of the Centre's theory of a vast American-led conspiracy to subvert the Soviet Union was set out in April 1991 in a speech by the head of KGB assessments, Nikolai Sergeyevich Leonov, formerly deputy head of the FCD, responsible for operations in North and South America. The goal of US policy, he declared, was "to eliminate the Soviet Union as a united state." Gorbachev, he implied, was refusing to listen:

The KGB has been informing the leadership of the country about this in time and detail. We would not want a repetition of the tragic situation before the Great Patriotic War against Germany, when Soviet intelligence warned about the imminent attack of Nazi Germany but Stalin rejected this information as wrong and even provocative. You know what this mistake cost us.

Further dramatic evidence of the resurgence of the KGB leadership's traditional conspiracy theories about the Main Adversary came in a speech by Kryuchkov to a closed session of the Supreme Soviet on June 17. Kryuchkov read out a hitherto top secret FCD report to the Politburo of January 1977, "On CIA Plans to Recruit Agents Among Soviet Citizens," which denounced an imaginary CIA masterplan to sabotage the Soviet administration, economy and scientific research. This plan, Kryuchkov claimed, remained actively in force.[138] The CIA's most important agent, he solemnly informed Gorbachev, was his own closest adviser, Aleksandr Yakovlev, allegedly recruited while an exchange student at Columbia University over thirty years earlier.[139]

As Kryuchkov later complained, Gorbachev did not take such nonsense seriously. Nor, no doubt, did many FCD officers with the first-hand experience of the West which the KGB Chairman lacked. Kryuchkov was now Gorbachev's most dangerous opponent, convinced that, having tamely accepted the collapse of the Soviet Bloc in 1989, Gorbachev was now presiding over the disintegration of the Soviet Union. In August 1991 he became the chief organizer of the coup which attempted to topple Gorbachev and preserve the Union.

FOURTEEN

POLITICAL WARFARE

Active Measures and the Main Adversary

T he philosophers," wrote Marx, "have only *interpreted* the world in various ways; the point, however, is to *change* it."[1] In addition to collecting intelligence and producing politically correct assessments of it, the KGB also sought to influence the course of world events by a variety of "active measures" (*aktivinyye meropriatia*) ranging from media manipulation to "special actions" involving various degrees of violence. Inspired by exaggerated accounts of its heroic defeat of counter-revolutionary conspiracies between the wars and a desire to impress the political leadership, it frequently overestimated its own effectiveness.

Throughout the Cold War the United States was the main target for KGB active measures as well as for intelligence collection. Most were at the non-violent end of the active measures spectrum—"influence operations" designed to discredit the Main Adversary. A conference of senior FCD officers in January 1984 reaffirmed a priority which had remained unchanged since the end of the Second World War: "Our chief task is to help to frustrate the aggressive intentions of American imperialism . . . We must work unweariedly at exposing the adversary's weak and vulnerable points."[2] Much of what was euphemistically described as "exposure" was in reality disinformation fabricated by Service A, the active measures branch of the FCD, and spread by Line PR officers in foreign residencies. Line PR officers were supposed to spend about 25 percent of their time on active measures, though in practice some failed to do so.

The wide variation in the sophistication of the disinformation generated by Service A reflected the uneven quality of its personnel. About 50 per cent of its officers were specialists in active measures. Some of the remaining 50 per cent were rejects from other departments. Few of the ablest and most ambitious FCD recruits wanted jobs in Service A; it rarely offered the opportunity of overseas postings and was widely regarded as a career dead end.[3] There were, of course, exceptions. Yuri Modin, the last controller of the Magnificent Five, became an active measures specialist, was appointed deputy head of Service A and subsequently had a successful Line PR posting spreading disinformation in India before becoming head of political intelligence at the Andropov Institute.[4] Many Service A officers, however, had little, if any, experience of living in the West and relied on crude conspiracy theories about the capitalist and Zionist plotters who supposedly operated a secret "command center" in the

United States.[5] Successive chairmen of the KGB and heads of the FCD, none of whom until the late 1980s had worked in foreign residencies, were influenced by the same theories.

IT WOULD HAVE been wholly out of character had the Centre failed to interpret President Kennedy's assassination by Lee Harvey Oswald in Dallas on November 22, 1963 as anything less than conspiracy. The deputy chairman of the KGB reported to the Central Committee in December:

> A reliable source of the Polish friends [the Polish intelligence service], an American entrepreneur and owner of a number of firms closely connected to the petroleum circles of the South, reported in late November that the real instigators of this criminal deed were three leading oil magnates from the South of the USA—Richardson, Murchison and Hunt, all owners of major petroleum reserves in the southern states who have long been connected to pro-fascist and racist organizations in the South.[6]

It was not difficult to find circumstantial "evidence" for this simplistic conspiracy theory, particularly as regards the oil magnate and anti-Communist buffoon H. L. Hunt. "The Communists need not invade the United States," Hunt once preposterously declared. "Pro-Bolshevik sentiment in the US is already greater than when the Bolsheviks overthrew the Kerensky government and took over Russia."[7]

Hunt's son, Bunker, was one of a group of right-wing mavericks who had paid for a full-page advertisement in the Dallas *Morning News* on the day of Kennedy's visit, accusing the President of being a Communist stooge—a charge which prompted Kennedy to say he was "heading into nut country."[8] The Dallas strip-club owner Jack Ruby, who shot and fatally wounded Oswald on November 24, had visited the Hunt offices shortly before Kennedy's assassination.[9]

The KGB reported that a journalist from the *Baltimore Sun* "said in a private conversation in early December that on assignment from a group of Texas financiers and industrialists headed by millionaire Hunt, Jack Ruby, who is now under arrest, proposed a large sum of money to Oswald for the murder of Kennedy." Oswald had subsequently been shot by Ruby to prevent him revealing the plot.[10] Khrushchev seems to have been convinced by the KGB view that the aim of the right-wing conspirators behind Kennedy's assassination was to intensify the Cold War and "strengthen the reactionary and aggressive elements of American foreign policy."[11]

The choice of Oswald as Kennedy's assassin, the KGB believed, was intended to divert public attention from the racist oil magnates and make the assassination appear to be a Communist plot.[12] The Centre had strong reasons of its own to wish to deflect responsibility for the assassination from Oswald. It was deeply embarrassed by the fact that in 1959 Oswald had defected to Russia, professing disgust with the American way of life and admiration for the Soviet system. Initially the KGB had suspected that he might have been sent on a secret mission by the CIA, but eventually concluded that he was an unstable nuisance and were glad to see the back of him when he returned to Texas with his Russian wife in 1962. After Oswald's return the FBI at first similarly suspected that he might be a Soviet agent but then seems to have made the same jaundiced assessment of him as the Centre.[13] KGB suspicions of Oswald revived, however, when he wrote to the CPUSA in August 1963 asking whether it might be better for him to continue the fight against "anti-progressive forces" as a member of the "underground" rather than as an open supporter of "Communist ideals." Jack Childs (codenamed MARAT), an undeclared member of the CPUSA who acted as one of its main points of contact with the KGB, warned Moscow that Oswald's letter "was viewed as an FBI provocation." The fact that, unknown to the KGB, Childs was himself an FBI agent renders his warning unusually ironic.[14]

The Warren Commission, appointed by President Lyndon B. Johnson to investigate Kennedy's assassination, reported in September 1964 that it had found "very persuasive" evidence that Oswald had acted alone and none of a conspiracy. Though the report was flawed, its main conclusions are probably accurate.[15] Service A, which may well have been genuinely persuaded that Kennedy was the victim of a right-wing conspiracy, succeeded in sponsoring its first counterblast even before the Warren Report appeared. The publisher was Carl Aldo Marzani (codenamed NORD), an Italian-born American Communist and Soviet agent, probably recruited before the Second World War, who was extensively used by the KGB for active measures.[16] Early in 1960 the New York residency recommended to the Centre that Marzani be given 6–7,000 dollars to enable his Liberty Book Club to continue publishing pro-Soviet material:

> NORD is an extremely energetic person and is quite devoted to his task. Despite his financial difficulties, he is struggling to keep SEVER [North, the Liberty Book Club publishing company] afloat. SEVER, together with its commercial bookselling network, the Prometheus Book Club, has been in existence for fourteen years. During this time it has published and distributed more than 200 titles of a progressive nature, by both American and foreign authors. The catalogue of the SEVER publishing firm lists around fifty titles, and the Prometheus Book Club has 7,000 members. Books are also sent to 8,000 addresses on an individual basis.

The international department of the Central Committee was plainly impressed. In May 1960 it approved a secret grant of 15,000 dollars, more than twice the sum suggested by the New York residency.[17]

Marzani's productions during 1960 included his own translation of a rapturous endorsement of the Soviet system by an Italian Communist:

> It is the duty of every Socialist, of every democrat, of every modern man, to deepen his understanding of the USSR . . . We are today capable of continuing to transform the world, thanks to the successes of the USSR, thanks to the successes in a series of other countries, thanks to the struggles which we all wage

in our own lands. We can, and we will, extend the civilization that was born in October 1917.[18]

In September 1961 the CPSU Central Committee allocated another 55,000 dollars for the next two years to allow Marzani to expand his publications. He was given a further 10,000 dollars a year to cover advertising costs.[19] When the young KGB officer Oleg Kalugin, stationed in New York in the early 1960s under cover as a Radio Moscow reporter, paid his first visit to one of Marzani's receptions, he found his apartment "filled with a motley assortment of Communists, liberals, and KGB spooks—all of them watched, undoubtedly, by FBI informers in attendance."[20]

Among the books published by Marzani in 1964 was the first volume on the Kennedy assassination to appear in the United States, *Oswald: Assassin or Fall-Guy?* by the German writer Joachim Joesten. At the beginning of the book Joesten expresses his "heartfelt thanks . . . to Carl Marzani, a shrewd and hard-hitting publisher in the finest American tradition, who put his whole heart and soul in this book;" Marzani succeeded in publishing it within five weeks of receiving the manuscript.[21] Joesten supported Moscow's line in pinning the blame for the assassination on a conspiracy by right-wing racists, chief among them "oil magnate H. L. Hunt:"

> They all feared that Mr. Kennedy, with his test-ban treaty, his neutralization of Laos, his dislike of Latin-American militarists, and his quiet feelers towards Castro, intended to put an end to the Cold War, cut back the arms budget and bring under control the Warfare State—that "military-industrial complex" which President Eisenhower had excoriated, and warned the nation about, in his farewell address.[22]

According to Joesten, Oswald was "an FBI *agent provocateur* with a CIA background" who had been judged expendable, used as a fall guy and murdered to prevent him giving evidence.[23] *Oswald: Assassin or Fall-Guy?* thus established two themes which were to recur in Soviet and Russian active measures for the next thirty years: a plot by Hunt and other right-wing fanatics; and the involvement of the CIA. At the time, however, Joesten's book was overshadowed by the publication of the Warren report and further undermined by the publicity given to Joesten's Communist background.[24]

The KGB correctly identified the New York lawyer Mark Lane as the most talented of the first wave of conspiracy theorists researching the JFK assassination. According to one report made on him, probably by the New York residency:

> Mark Lane is well known as a person with close ties to Democratic Party circles in the US. He holds liberal views on a number of current American political problems and has undertaken to conduct his own private investigation of the circumstances surrounding the murder of J. Kennedy.[25]

Joesten praised Lane as "brilliant and courageous" and dedicated his own book to him: "Neither the 'police state tactics' of the FBI—to use [Lane's] own words—nor the conspiracy of silence of the press magnates, could sway him from doggedly pursuing the truth."[26] Together with student assistants and other volunteers, Lane founded the Citizens' Committee of Inquiry in a small office on lower Fifth Avenue and rented a small theater at which, each evening for several months, he gave what became known as "The Speech," updating the development of his conspiracy theory. "This alternative method of dissent was required," writes Lane, "because not a single network radio or television program permitted the broadcast of a word of divergence from the official view."[27] Though it dared not take the risk of contacting Lane directly, the New York residency sent him 1,500 dollars to help finance his research through the intermediary of a close friend whom Lane's KGB file identifies only as a trusted contact. While Lane was not told the source of the money, the residency suspected that he might have guessed where it came from; it was also concerned that the secret subsidy might be discovered by the FBI.[28]

The same intermediary provided 500 dollars to pay for a trip by Lane to Europe in 1964. While there, Lane asked to visit Moscow in order to discuss some of the material he had found. The Centre regretfully concluded that inviting him to Russia would reveal its hand in too blatant a way and his proposed trip was "tactfully postponed." Trusted contacts were, however, selected from among Soviet journalists to encourage him in his research. Among them was the KGB agent Genrikh Borovik, who later maintained regular contact with Lane. Lane's *Rush to Judgment,* published in 1966, alleged complicity at the highest levels of government in the Kennedy assassination.[29] It was top of that year's hardback bestseller list and went on to become the bestselling paperback of 1967, as well as enjoying what Lane modestly describes as "enormous success around the world" and causing "a dramatic change in public perception" of the assassination.[30]

During the late 1960s and early 1970s, Lane's success was less enormous. The most popular books on the assassination were now those that exposed some of the excesses of the conspiracy theorists.[31] CPUSA leaders who visited Moscow in 1971, though describing *Rush to Judgment* as "advantageous to the Communists," claimed that Lane's main motive was his own self-aggrandizement.[32] In the mid-1970s, however, the dramatic revelations of real conspiracy in the Nixon White House and of CIA assassination plots against several foreign statesmen gave the conspiracy theorists a new lease on life.[33] The KGB, predictably, was anxious to lose no opportunity to promote active measures which supported the increasingly popular theory that the CIA was behind Kennedy's assassination. Its chief target was the former CIA officer turned Watergate conspirator E. Howard Hunt (sometimes confused with the Texan oil millionaire H. L. Hunt), who had been wrongly accused of being in Dallas on the day of the assassination.

The centerpiece of the active measure against Howard Hunt, codenamed ARLINGTON, was a forged letter to him from Oswald, allegedly written a fortnight before the assassination. The letter used phrases and expressions taken from actual letters written by Oswald during his two years in the Soviet Union, was fabricated in a clever imitation of his handwriting.

Dear Mr. Hunt,

I would like information concerning my position.

I am only asking for information. I am suggesting that we discuss the matter fully before any steps are taken by me or anyone else.

Thank-you.

Lee Harvey Oswald[34]

The implication, clearly, was that Oswald wanted to meet Hunt before going ahead with the assassination.

Before being used, the forgery was twice checked for "authenticity" by the Third Department of the KGB's OTU (operational technical) Directorate. In 1975 photocopies of it were sent to three of the most active conspiracy buffs, together with covering letters from an anonymous wellwisher who claimed that he had given the original to the Director of the FBI, Clarence Kelly, who appeared to be suppressing it. The Centre was doubtless disappointed that for almost two years its forgery received no publicity. In 1977, however, the letter was published by Penn Jones, the retired owner of a small Texas newspaper and self-published author of four books about the assassination. The *New York Times* reported that three handwriting experts had authenticated the letter. Oswald's widow also identified her husband's handwriting.[35] Experts summoned by the House Select Committee on Assassinations in 1978 concluded more prudently that they were unable to reach a "firm conclusion" because of the absence of the original document.[36]

The Centre was somewhat put out, however, by the fact that initial press reaction to its forgery centered chiefly on the likelihood of the letter being addressed to the late Texan oil millionaire H. L. Hunt (the central character in its own original conspiracy theory), rather than the KGB's current intended target, the Watergate conspirator Howard Hunt. Service A believed there had been a CIA plot to disrupt its own plot. The KGB reported that an "orchestrated" American press campaign was seeking to divert public attention from Oswald's connections with the American intelligence community by concentrating on H. L. Hunt instead. In April 1977, soon after the publication of the forged letter, the KGB informed the Central Committee that it was launching additional active measures to expose the supposed role of the "American special services" in the Kennedy assassination.[37] By 1980 Howard Hunt was complaining that, "It's become an article of faith that I had some role in the Kennedy assassination."[38]

By the late 1970s the KGB could fairly claim that far more Americans believed some version of its own conspiracy theory of the Kennedy assassination, involving a right-wing plot and the US intelligence community, than still accepted the main findings of the Warren Commission. Soviet active measures, however, had done less to influence American opinion than the Centre believed. By their initial cover-ups the CIA and the FBI had unwittingly probably done more than the KGB to encourage the sometimes obsessional conspiracy theorists who swarmed around the complex and confusing evidence on the assassination. Allen Dulles, the recently retired DCI on the Warren Commission, had deliberately not informed the commission that the CIA had plotted the assassination of Castro. On the very day of Kennedy's assassination, the Agency had supplied an agent with a murder weapon for use against Castro. J. Edgar Hoover too had held back important information. He discovered, to his horror, that Oswald had not been included on the FBI's security index of potentially disloyal citizens, despite having written a threatening letter to the Bureau after his return from Russia and subsequently making an appointment to see a KGB officer in Mexico City. After reading a report on "investigative deficiencies in the Oswald case," Hoover concluded that, if it became public, the report would destroy the FBI's reputation.[39]

The information withheld by Dulles and Hoover would have been most unlikely to undermine the Warren Commission's conclusion that Oswald had been a lone assassin. But, when it became public in the mid-1970s, it inevitably encouraged the belief that there had been other cover-ups which pointed to the involvement of the intelligence community. The Watergate scandal, and the revelations of intelligence abuses which followed, created a perfect breeding ground for the spread of conspiracy theories.[40] Though most of the major abuses had been ordered or authorized by successive presidents, the belief grew that, in the words of Senator Frank Church, chairman of the Senate Select Committee to Study Governmental Operations with Respect to Intelligence Activities, the CIA had been "behaving like a rogue elephant on the rampage."[41]

SERVICE A SEIZED eagerly on Church's ill-chosen metaphor. The KGB's most valuable asset in its active measures to discredit the Agency was an embittered former CIA operations officer in Latin America, Philip Agee (codenamed PONT),[42] who had been forced to resign in 1968 after complaints at his heavy drinking, poor financial management and attempts to proposition wives of American diplomats.[43] Though he remained in the West, Agee became, in effect, the CIA's first defector. In 1973 he approached the KGB residency in Mexico City and offered what the head of the FCD's Counter-intelligence Directorate, Oleg Kalugin, called "reams of information about CIA operations." The suspicious KGB resident, however, found Agee's offer too good to be true, concluded that he was part of a CIA plot and turned him away. According to Kalugin:

> Agee then went to the Cubans, who welcomed him with open arms . . . The Cubans shared Agee's information with us. But as I sat in my office in Moscow reading reports about the growing list of revelations coming from Agee, I cursed our officers for turning away such a prize.[44]

In January 1975 Agee published an uncompromisingly hostile memoir of his career in the CIA entitled *Inside the Company: CIA Diary*, which identified approximately 250 Agency officers and agents and claimed that "millions of people all over the world had been killed or had their lives destroyed by the CIA and the institutions it supports."[45] The self-congratulatory KGB file on the book claims, doubtless with some exaggeration, that it was "prepared by Service A, together with the Cubans."[46]

Mitrokhin's notes do not indicate exactly what the KGB and its Cuban ally, the DGI, contributed to Agee's text. As Agee himself acknowledged, however: "Representatives of the Communist Party of Cuba [the DGI] . . . gave important encouragement at a time when I doubted that I would be able to find the additional information I needed."[47] While Agee was writing his book in Britain, the KGB maintained contact with him through its co-optee, Edgar Anatolyevich Cheporov, London correspondent of the Novosti news agency and the *Literaturnaya Gazeta*.[48] At Service A's insistence, Agee removed all references to CIA penetration of Latin American Communist parties from his typescript before publication.[49]

Because of legal problems in the United States, *Inside the Company* was first published in Britain, where it was an instant bestseller. The London *Evening News* called it "a frightening picture of corruption, pressure, assassination and conspiracy." The *Economist* commended it as "inescapable reading." Probably most valuable of all, from Service A's viewpoint, was a review in the *Spectator* by Miles Copeland, a former CIA station chief in Cairo, who described *Inside the Company* as "as complete an account of spy work as is likely to be published anywhere." With enthusiastic support from a number of journalists, Agee then set about unmasking the members of the CIA London station, some of whom were surprised emerging from their homes by press photographers. An American theater director staged a production satirizing the Agency in front of a number of CIA officers' houses. "For a while," claimed Agee, "the CIA in Britain was a laughing stock." The left-wing Labor MP Stan Newens promoted a Commons bill, signed by thirty-two of his colleagues, calling for the CIA station to be expelled. Encouraged by Agee's success in Britain, there was a rush by the media in other parts of Europe to expose the CIA stations in their own capitals.[50]

The six-month delay between the publication of the British and American editions of *Inside the Company*, and the associated legal difficulties, merely served to increase media interest in the United States and ensure its place high on the bestseller list. A review of *Inside the Company* in the CIA's classified in-house journal, *Studies in Intelligence*, acknowledged that it was "a severe body blow" to the Agency: "A considerable number of CIA personnel must be diverted from their normal duties to undertake the meticulous and time-consuming task of repairing the damage done to its Latin-American program . . ."[51]

On November 16, 1976 a deportation order served on Agee requiring him to leave England turned his case, much to the delight of the Centre, into a *cause célèbre*. According to one of the files noted by Mitrokhin:

> The KGB employed firm and purposeful measures to force the Home Office
> to cancel their decision . . . The London residency was used to direct action by
> a number of members of the Labor Party Executive, union leaders, leading parliamentarians, leaders of the National Union of Journalists to take a stand
> against the Home Office decision.[52]

On November 30 the first in a series of well-publicized meetings to protest against the deportation order was held in London, with speakers including Judith Hart, former Labor Minister of Overseas Development, the leading Labor left-winger Ian Mikardo, Alan Sapper of the film and TV technicians union and the distinguished historian E. P. Thompson. An active defense committee[53] based at the National Council of Civil Liberties organized petitions, rallies and pickets of the Home Office. In the Commons Stan Newens sponsored a protest supported by over fifty MPs and led a delegation to see the Home Secretary, Merlyn Rees. Agee addressed sympathetic meetings in Birmingham, Blackpool, Brighton, Bristol, Cambridge, Cardiff, Coventry, London, Manchester and Newcastle. At his appeal against deportation in January and February 1977, Agee's character witnesses included Stan Newens, Judith Hart, former Home Office minister Alex Lyon, former US Attorney-General Ramsey Clark, Kissinger's former aide Morton Halperin and Sean MacBride, Nobel Peace Prize winner and UN High Commissioner for Namibia. Hart and another ex-Labor minister, Barbara Castle, sponsored a motion, supported by 150 MPs, to reform the appeals procedure. According to Agee's KGB file, "Campaigns of support for PONT were initiated in France, Spain, Portugal, Italy, Holland, Finland, Norway, Mexico and Venezuela." After Agee's appeals had failed, the final act in the long drawn-out protest campaign was a Commons debate on May 3. The *Guardian*, which supported Agee's appeal, commented:

> When Merlyn Rees . . . decided that Philip Agee and [American journalist] Mark Hosenball must go, he must equally have known there would be a fuss. But did he realize the endlessly stretching, deeply embarrassing nature of that fuss—the evidence at a length to rival *War and Peace*, the press conferences, the parade of fervent witnesses?[54]

Though Agee was eventually forced to leave England for Holland on June 3, 1977, the KGB was jubilant at the "deeply embarrassing nature of [the] fuss" his deportation had caused. The London residency's claim that it had been able to "direct" the campaign by prominent Labor politicians and others in support of Agee was, however, greatly exaggerated.[55] It doubtless did not occur to the vast majority of Agee's supporters to suspect the involvement of the KGB and the DGI.[56]

After Agee's well-publicized expulsion from Britain, the KGB continued to use him and some of his supporters in active measures against the CIA.[57] Among the documents received by Agee from what he described as "an anonymous sender" was an authentic copy of a classified State Department circular, signed by Kissinger, which contained the CIA's "key intelligence questions" for fiscal year 1975 on economic, financial and commercial reporting.[58] KGB files identify the source of the document as Service A.[59] In the summer of 1977 the circular was published in a pamphlet entitled "What Uncle Sam Wants to Know about You," with an introduction by Agee. While acknowledging that it was "not the most gripping document in the world," Agee claimed that it demonstrated the unfair assistance secretly given to US companies abroad by the American intelligence community.[60]

In 1978 Agee and a small group of supporters began publishing the *Covert Action Information Bulletin* in order to promote what Agee called "a worldwide campaign to destabilize the CIA through exposure of its operations and personnel."[61] Files noted by Mitrokhin claim that the *Bulletin* was founded "on the initiative of the KGB" and that the group running it (collectively codenamed RUPOR), which held its first meeting in Jamaica early in 1978, was "put together" by FCD Directorate K (counterintelligence).[62] The *Bulletin* was edited in Washington by Bill Schaap, a radical lawyer codenamed RUBY by the KGB, his wife, the journalist Ellen Ray, and another journalist, Louis Wolf, codenamed ARSENIO. Agee and two other disaffected former members of the CIA, Jim and Elsie Wilcott (previously employed by the Agency as, respectively, finance officer and secretary), contributed articles and information.[63] There is no evidence in Mitrokhin's notes that any member of the RUPOR group, apart from Agee, was conscious of the role of the DGI or KGB.

The first issue of the *Covert Action Information Bulletin* was launched by Agee and the RUPOR group at a Cuban press conference on the eve of the Eleventh World Festival of Youth and Students, held to coincide with the Havana carnival in the summer of 1978. Agee also produced advance copies of another book, *Dirty Work: The CIA in Western Europe*, coauthored by himself and Wolf, which contained the names and biographical details of 700 CIA personnel who were, or had been, stationed in western Europe. "Press reaction," wrote Agee, "was not disappointing. In the next few days we learned by telephone from friends in the States and elsewhere that most of the major publications carried stories about the *Bulletin* and *Dirty Work*. Perfect."[64]

The Centre assembled a task force of personnel from Service A and Directorate K, headed by V. N. Kosterin, assistant to the chief of Service A, to keep the *Covert Action Information Bulletin* supplied with material designed to compromise the CIA. Among the material which the task force supplied for publication in 1979 was an eighteen-page CIA document entitled "Director of Central Intelligence: Perspectives for Intelligence, 1976–1981." The document had originally been delivered anonymously to the apartment of the Washington resident, Dmitri Ivanovich Yakushkin, and at the time had been wrongly assessed by both the residency and the Centre as a "dangle" by US intelligence.[65] Agee's commentary on the document highlighted the complaint by DCI William Colby that recent revelations of its operations were among the most serious problems the CIA had to face.[66] Kosterin's task force, however, became increasingly concerned about the difficulty of finding enough secret material for the *Bulletin*, and recommended that it look harder for open-source material, ranging from readers' letters to crises around the world which could be blamed on the CIA—among them the Jonestown massacre in Guyana, when 900 members of the American religious cult the "People's Temple" had been persuaded to commit mass suicide or had been murdered.[67]

Following what Service A believed was the success of *Dirty Work: The CIA in Western Europe*, Agee began work with Wolf on a sequel, *Dirty Work II: The CIA in Africa*. Early in 1979 Oleg Maksimovich Nechiporenko of Directorate K and A. N. Itskov of Service A met Agee in Cuba and gave him a list of CIA officers working on the African continent.[68] Shortly before *Dirty Work II* was finished, Agee decided not to be publicly identified as one of the authors for fear that he might lose his residence permit in Germany, where he now lived. He also changed his official role on the *Covert Action Information Bulletin* from editor to "editorial adviser." "How that would save my residence in Germany," Agee later acknowledged, "was a little obscure . . . but such was my fear that I was barely rational—at least on this point."[69] Nechiporenko and Itskov agreed with Pedro Pupo Perez, the head of the DGI, that publication of *Dirty Work II* should be timed to coincide with the conference of ninety-two heads of non-aligned nations to be held in Havana, presided over by Fidel Castro, in September 1979.[70]

By Agee's own count, *Dirty Work II* brought the total number of CIA officials exposed by him and the RUPOR team to about 2,000. For the KGB it had been a remarkably effective active measure. The Senate Intelligence Committee reported in 1980:

> In recent years members of the House and Senate Intelligence Committees . . . have become increasingly concerned about the systematic effort by a small group of Americans . . . to disclose the names of covert intelligence agents . . . Foremost among them has been Philip Agee . . . The destructive effect of these disclosures has been varied and wide-ranging . . .
>
> The professional effectiveness of officers who have been compromised is substantially and sometimes irreparably damaged. They must reduce or break contact with sensitive covert sources and continued contact must be coupled with increased defensive measures that are inevitably more costly and time-consuming. Some officers must be removed from their assignments and returned from overseas at substantial cost, and years of irreplaceable area experience and language skills are lost.
>
> Since the ability to reassign the compromised officer is impaired, the pool of experienced CIA officers who can serve abroad is being reduced. Replacement of officers thus compromised is difficult and, in some cases, impossible. Such disclosures also sensitize hostile security services to CIA presence and influence foreign populations, making operations more difficult.

All thirteen members of the House Intelligence Committee sponsored the Intelligence Identities Protection Bill, popularly known as the "Anti-Agee Bill," which eventually became law in June 1982. Agee himself had been deprived of his American passport in 1981 and traveled over the next few years on passports issued by, successively, Maurice Bishop's Marxist-Leninist regime in Grenada and the Sandinista government in Nicaragua. His influence, by now, was in sharp decline. As he complained, "My 1983 call for a continent-wide action front against the CIA's people in Latin America went nowhere. People had other preoccupations and priorities."[71]

LIKE THE CIA, the FBI was inevitably a major target of KGB active measures. Until the death of J. Edgar Hoover in 1972, many of these measures were personally directed against the Bureau's long-serving, aging and irascible director. Service A employed three simple and sometimes crude techniques. The first was to portray

Hoover as in league with extremists such as the ultra right-wing John Birch Society, whose founder regarded even the former Republican president Dwight D. Eisenhower as "a dedicated conscious agent of the Communist conspiracy." Service A had acquired both some of the society's stationery and samples of its leaders' signatures from its California headquarters to assist it in its forgeries. In November 1965 it fabricated a letter of good wishes from Hoover to the leader of the John Birch Society, reminding him that the FBI funds put at his disposal would enable the society to open several more branches.[72]

A second, more sophisticated form of active measures concerned alleged FBI abuses of civil rights. Operation SPIRT was designed to demonstrate that the head of the Passport Office in the State Department, Frances Knight, was a secret FBI agent whose loyalty was to Hoover rather than to the Secretary of State. In 1967 Service A forged a letter from Ms. Knight to Hoover and arranged for it to be sent to the celebrated columnist Drew Pearson, who published it in the *Washington Post* on August 4.[73] The fabricated letter reported that a situation of "extreme urgency" had arisen as a result of press enquiries about an alleged FBI request to her for information on Professor H. Stuart Hughes, a Harvard critic of American policy in Vietnam:

> I am seriously afraid that this may indicate preparations for a sustained press campaign against us. We have already discussed the attitude of the Secretary of State towards the long-established practice of the department making inquiries at the request of the FBI . . .
>
> Forgive me if I sound alarmist, but I am quite certain from what I have heard that a principle of vital importance is at stake which affects the whole conduct of the government and, in particular, the effectiveness of the Bureau.

Ms. Knight told Hoover she was unwilling to commit too much to paper and suggested an urgent meeting with him.[74] Knight and Hoover both dismissed the letter as a forgery, but the fact that neither denied the FBI's contacts with the Passport Office persuaded the KGB that at least some of its mud had stuck.[75]

A third line of attack deployed by Service A against Hoover was to accuse him of being a homosexual.[76] The truth about Hoover's probably severely repressed sexuality is unlikely ever to be known. Later, much-publicized claims that he was a gay cross-dresser whose wardrobe included a red dress and boa, which made him look like "an old flapper," and a black dress, "very fluffy, with flounces, and lace stockings," which he wore with a black curly wig, rest on little more than the discredited testimony of a convicted perjurer, Susan Rosenstiel, who claimed to have seen Hoover so attired. Nor is there any reliable evidence that Hoover and his deputy, Clyde Tolson, who shared his house, ever had a homosexual relationship. But attempts to portray him as a heterosexual are also less than convincing. Hoover had no known female liaisons. As his staunchly loyal number three, "Deke" DeLoach, acknowledges, probably the only person he had ever loved was his mother: "Hoover's capacity to feel deeply for other human beings [was] interred with her in the Old Congressional Cemetery near Seward Square."[77]

The later commercial success, admittedly in a more prurient period, of fanciful stories of Hoover at gay transvestite parties suggests that in fabricating stories of his homosexual affairs in the late 1960s Service A had hit upon a potentially promising active measures theme. DeLoach was later depressed to discover how readily such stories were accepted as "undeniable truth:"

"Tell us about Hoover and Tolson," people would say.
"Was it obvious?"
"Did everyone know what was going on?"[78]

As sometimes happened, however, Service A spoiled a plausible falsehood by surrounding it with improbable amounts of conspiracy theory. It sent anonymous letters, intended to appear to come from the Ku Klux Klan, to the editors of leading newspapers, accusing Hoover of personally selecting for promotion in the FBI homosexuals from whom he expected sexual favors. Not content with turning the FBI into "a den of faggots," Hoover had also allegedly been engaged for several decades in a larger gay conspiracy to staff the CIA and the State Department with homosexuals. The national security of the United States, claimed the letters, was now seriously at risk.[79] Service A's belief that major newspapers would take seriously nonsense of this kind, especially emanating from the Ku Klux Klan, was graphic evidence of the limitations in its understanding of American society. The letters had, predictably, no observable effect.

THE MOST CELEBRATED victim of the FBI's own active measures was the great civil rights leader Martin Luther King. Hoover's obsessive belief that King was "a tom cat with degenerate sexual urges" and his simmering resentment at King's criticism of the FBI led him to make the preposterous allegation to a group of journalists in 1964 that "King is the most notorious liar in the country." When his staff urged him to insist that his outburst was off the record, Hoover refused. "Feel free," he told the journalists, "to print my remarks as given." The active measures against King were organized, apparently without Hoover's knowledge, by FBI Assistant Director William C. Sullivan. In December 1964 Sullivan sent King a tape recording of some of his adulterous sexual liaisons which the Bureau had obtained by bugging his room in Washington's Willard Hotel. With the tape was an anonymous letter which purported to come from a disillusioned former supporter:

King, look into your heart. You know you are a complete fraud and a great liability to all of us Negroes . . . You could have been our greatest leader. You, even at an early age, have turned out to be a dissolute, abnormal moral imbecile . . . You are finished. You will find on the record for all time . . . your hideous abnormalities . . . What incredible evilness. It is all there on the record.[80]

King was probably the only prominent American to be the target of active measures by both the FBI *and* the KGB. By the mid-1960s the claims by the CPUSA leadership that secret Party members within King's entourage would be able to "guide" his policies had proved to be hollow.[81] To the Centre's dismay, King repeatedly linked the aims of the civil rights movement not to the alleged worldwide struggle against American imperialism but to the fulfillment of the American dream and "the magnificent words of the Constitution and the Declaration of Independence." He wrote in his inspirational "Letter from Birmingham Jail" in 1963:

> I have no despair about the future . . . We will reach the goal of freedom in Birmingham [Alabama] and all over the nation, because the goal of America is freedom . . . We will win our freedom because the sacred heritage of our nation and the eternal will of God are embodied in our echoing demands.[82]

Having given up hope of influencing King, the Centre aimed instead at replacing him with a more radical and malleable leader. In August 1967 the Centre approved an operational plan by the deputy head of Service A, Yuri Modin, former controller of the Magnificent Five, to discredit King and his chief lieutenants by placing articles in the African press, which could then be reprinted in American newspapers, portraying King as an "Uncle Tom" who was secretly receiving government subsidies to tame the civil rights movement and prevent it threatening the Johnson administration. While leading freedom marches under the admiring glare of worldwide television, King was allegedly in close touch with the President.[83]

The same operational plan also contained a series of active measures designed to discredit US policy "on the Negro issue." The Centre authorized Modin:

- To organize, through the use of KGB residency resources in the US, the publication and distribution of brochures, pamphlets, leaflets and appeals denouncing the policy of the Johnson administration on the Negro question and exposing the brutal terrorist methods being used by the government to suppress the Negro rights movement.

- To arrange, via available agent resources, for leading figures in the legal profession to make public statements discrediting the policy of the Johnson administration on the Negro question.

- To forge and distribute through illegal channels a document showing that the John Birch Society, in conjunction with the Minuteman organization, is developing a plan for the physical elimination of leading figures in the Negro movement in the US.[84]

Service A sought to exploit the violent images of the long, hot summers which began in August 1965 with race riots in Watts, the black Los Angeles ghetto, which resulted in thirty-six deaths, left 1,032 injured and caused damage estimated at over 40 million dollars. The Centre seems to have hoped that as violence intensified King would be swept aside by black radicals such as Stokeley Carmichael, who told a meeting of Third World revolutionaries in Cuba in the summer of 1967, "We have a common enemy. Our struggle is to overthrow this system . . . We are moving into open guerrilla warfare in the United States." Traveling on to North Vietnam, Carmichael declared in Hanoi, "We are not reformists . . . We are revolutionaries. We want to change the American system."[85]

King's assassination on April 4, 1968 was quickly followed by the violence and rioting which the KGB had earlier blamed King for trying to prevent. Within a week riots had erupted in over a hundred cities, forty-six people had been killed, 3,500 injured and 20,000 arrested. To "Deke" DeLoach, it seemed that, "The nation was teetering on the brink of anarchy."[86] Henceforth, instead of dismissing King as an Uncle Tom, Service A portrayed him as a martyr of the black liberation movement and spread conspiracy theories alleging that his murder had been planned by white racists with the connivance of the authorities.[87]

Simultaneously the Centre implemented a series of active measures designed to weaken the internal cohesion of the United States and undermine its international reputation by inciting race hatred. In 1971 Andropov personally approved the fabrication of pamphlets full of racist insults purporting to come from the extremist Jewish Defense League, headed by Meir Kahane, calling for a campaign against the "black mongrels" who, it was claimed, were attacking Jews and looting Jewish shops. Thirty pamphlets were mailed to a series of militant black groups in the hope of producing "mass disorders in New York." At the same time forged letters were sent to sixty black organizations giving fictitious details of atrocities committed by the League against blacks and calling for vengeance against Kahane and his chief lieutenants. Probably to the Centre's disappointment, Kahane was assassinated some years later, not by a black militant but by an Arab.

On at least one occasion, the Centre ordered the use of explosives to exacerbate racial tensions in New York. On July 25, 1971 the head of the FCD First (North American) Department, Anatoli Tikhonovich Kireyev, instructed the New York residency to proceed with operation PANDORA: the planting of a delayed-action explosive package in "the Negro section of New York." Kireyev's preferred target was "one of the Negro colleges." After the explosion the residency was ordered to make anonymous telephone calls to two or three black organizations, claiming that the explosion was the work of the Jewish Defense League.[88]

The attempt to stir up racial tensions in the United States remained part of Service A's stock-in-trade for the remainder of the Cold War. Before the Los Angeles Olympics in 1984, for example, Line PR officers in the Washington residency mailed bogus communications from the Ku Klux Klan to the Olympic committees of African and Asian countries.[89] Among the racial taunts devised by Service A for inclusion in the mailings was the following:

THE OLYMPICS—FOR THE WHITES ONLY!
African monkeys!
A grand reception awaits you in Los Angeles!
We are preparing for the Olympic games by shooting at black moving targets.
In Los Angeles our own Olympic flames are ready to incinerate you. The high-

est award for a true American patriot would be the lynching of an African monkey.
Blacks, Welcome to the Olympic games in Los Angeles!
We'll give you a reception you'll never forget!

This and other active measures on the same theme made front-page news in many countries. When Attorney-General William French Smith denounced the letters as KGB forgeries, Moscow predictably feigned righteous indignation at Washington's anti-Soviet slanders.[90]

THE CENTRE'S ASSESSMENT of "anti-Sovietism" in the United States changed radically at the beginning of the 1970s. In 1968 the Kremlin had been so anxious to prevent the election of the veteran anti-Communist Richard Nixon that it had secretly offered to subsidize the campaign of his Democratic opponent, Hubert Humphrey.[91] Once in office, however, Nixon rapidly emerged as the architect of détente. More Soviet–American agreements were signed in 1972–3 than in the entire forty years since the establishment of diplomatic relations between Moscow and Washington. Nixon's resignation in August 1974, under threat of impeachment for his involvement in the Watergate scandal, caused both dismay and deep suspicion in Moscow. Seen from the Kremlin, Nixon's attempts to conceal the use of dirty tricks against his opponents were, as Dobrynin later acknowledged, "a fairly natural thing to do. Who cared if it was a breach of the Constitution?" The conspiracy theorists in the Centre convinced themselves that Nixon's dramatic fall from power was due far less to public indignation over Watergate than to conspiracy by the enemies of détente—in particular the "Jewish lobby," who were campaigning for unrestricted emigration by Soviet Jews to Israel, and the military–industrial complex, which was anxious to prevent lower arms expenditure.[92]

The key figure in holding together the anti-Soviet coalition, in the Centre's view, was the liberal Democrat, Senator Henry "Scoop" Jackson. Kissinger too regarded Jackson as "the indispensable link between the liberals, preoccupied with human rights [in the Soviet Union], and the conservatives, who became anxious about any negotiations with the Soviets." "Jackson," one commentator has written, "was not the type of leader who needed an impassioned aide to tell him what to think, but he had one anyway: Richard Perle, an intense, razor-sharp scourge of the Soviets who, despite his cherubic smile, earned the sobriquet Prince of Darkness from the legions he had engaged in bureaucratic battle." Perle was the leader of what the KGB saw as a particularly dangerous part of the Jewish lobby: an informal group on Capitol Hill which included both paid Israeli lobbyists and congressional staffers.[93]

Jackson was propelled into battle in August 1972 by the Soviet announcement of an exit tax on emigrants, theoretically designed to repay the costs of their state-funded education but whose main practical effect would have been to reduce Jewish emigration to a trickle. In October Jackson introduced an amendment to the Nixon Trade Reform Bill barring the Soviet Union from receiving most-favored nation status and trade credits until it had lifted restrictions on emigration. Though Moscow quickly dropped the exit tax, Jackson maintained his amendment. For the next two years Kissinger conducted a shuttle diplomacy between Moscow and Jackson, trying vainly to obtain enough Soviet concessions on Jewish emigration to persuade Jackson to back down. "For a long time," said Kissinger later, "I did not realize that Jackson could not be placated."[94]

Dobrynin reported to Moscow that Jackson "kept escalating his demands" in order to win the backing of the Jewish lobby for his attempt to win the Democratic nomination at the 1976 election.[95] The New York resident, Boris Solomatin, informed the Centre that Jackson appeared to be in a strong position for the presidential primaries:

Jackson's strong point is the fact that, during his nearly thirty-five years in Congress, he has never been involved in any sort of political or personal scandal. In the post-Watergate period the personal integrity of a presidential candidate has had exceptionally great significance. It is necessary to find some stains on the Senator's biography and use them to carry out an active measure which will compromise him. We must discuss with the American friends [the CPUSA] the most effective ways and means of opposing Jackson's plans to become president of the USA.

Others in the Centre cynically concluded that Jackson's reticence about his private life "probably points to the existence of compromising information which could be used to discredit him and his family." The KGB's search for "compromising information" was extraordinarily wide-ranging. Despite the fact that Jackson's parents had left Norway as long ago as 1885, the Oslo residency was ordered in 1974 to make a detailed investigation of his Norwegian relatives. As the American residencies examined Jackson's long political career with a fine toothcomb, the most promising area which seemed to emerge was his sexuality. Jackson's file in the Centre records that his marriage at the age of forty-nine "amazed many of his colleagues, who had considered him a confirmed bachelor." Intensive KGB research, however, found no more incriminating evidence of homosexuality than the fact that for many years Jackson had shared an apartment in Washington with a male childhood friend.[96]

Lacking any proof that Jackson had ever been a practicing homosexual, the Centre decided to fabricate it in an active measure codenamed operation POROK. In 1976 Service A forged an FBI memorandum, dated June 20, 1940, in which Hoover reported to the Assistant Secretary of Justice that Jackson was a homosexual. Photocopies of the forgery were sent to the *Chicago Tribune,* the *Los Angeles Times,* the *Topeka Capital* and Jimmy Carter's campaign headquarters. Service A also sought to exploit a number of incidents during the 1976 primary campaign. After an argument with a gay rights activist at a press conference in March, Jackson told him that he did not want his vote. During a television appearance in April, Jackson declared that "homosexuality leads to the destruction of the family." The KGB sent these statements, together with bogus documents purporting to show that Jackson and Perle were members of a gay sex club, to, among others: Senator Edward Kennedy, who was thought "personally hostile to Jackson;" the columnist Jack Anderson; and the magazines *Playboy* and *Penthouse*.

Because of Jackson's continuing influence on the ratification of Soviet–American arms limitation agreements, operation POROK continued long after he had failed to gain the Democratic nomination. One of the aims of the operation during 1977 was to incite the gay press into attacking Jackson as a closet gay who hypocritically attacked homosexuality in public for his own political advantage. Early in May a Service A officer in New York posted a forged FBI document to the California-based magazine *Gay Times* reporting that Jackson had been an active homosexual while working as a state prosecutor in the early 1940s. Handwritten on the forgery was the heading "Our Gay in the US Senate." Like the rest of operation POROK, the forgery had no discernible effect on Jackson's career.

THE CENTRE'S MAIN target within the Carter administration, which took office in 1977, was the Polish-born National Security Adviser, Zbigniew Brzezinski, previously an ill-chosen KGB target for cultivation.[97] As Brzezinski later acknowledged, he and Secretary of State Cyrus Vance engaged in a "prolonged and intense" debate over policy to the Soviet Union. The result, according to Vance, was an unstable balance between the "visceral anti-Sovietism" of Brzezinski and his own "attempt to regulate dangerous competition" between the superpowers.[98] "When Carter spoke on foreign affairs," complained Dobrynin, the Soviet ambassador, "we tended to hear echoes of the anti-Sovietism of Brzezinski."[99] The aim of Service A was to diminish Brzezinski's influence relative to Vance's and, if possible, to engineer his dismissal.

The Centre ordered its American residencies to begin a trawl for potentially damaging information on Brzezinski as wide-ranging as that which preceded operation POROK. Was Brzezinski concealing Jewish origins? Was he having an affair with the actress Candice Bergen? Was there any compromising material on his relations with, among others, his deputy David Aaron, his special assistant Karl Inderfurth, Ambassador Richard Gardner and the Polish émigré community?[100]

Though muckraking in the United States appears to have proved unproductive, the Centre was supplied with what it believed was sensational evidence of Brzezinski's secret career in the CIA by the Bulgarian intelligence service. Probably under pressure from his interrogators, Henrich Natan Shpeter, a Bulgarian economist who had confessed to working for both American and Israeli intelligence, produced a bizarre account of a visit to Bulgaria in 1963 by Brzezinski, then a professor at Columbia University, as a guest of the Academy of Sciences. Shpeter allegedly claimed that Brzezinski was a CIA officer who contacted him by using a password, received intelligence from him and gave him further instructions for intelligence operations. In addition, even in 1963, according to Shpeter, Brzezinski had a major role in framing US policy towards the Soviet Bloc.

Shpeter's story, in short, was strikingly similar to those expected of defendants in Stalinist show trials. The Centre, however, was easily seduced by attractive conspiracy theories and used Shpeter's bizarre tale as the basis of an active measure codenamed operation MUREN. Service A drafted a bogus report on Brzezinski by an

Israeli Zionist organization which included allegedly authentic details of his involvement in Shpeter's espionage. The report went on to denounce Brzezinski as "a secret anti-Semite" and declared that the Zionists had compromising information on his private life which would seriously discredit him.

The Centre decided to deliver this bizarre document to the US embassy in Israel, convinced that its contents were so sensational that they would be brought to carter's as well as Vance's attention. On August 20, 1978 the report was inserted through the half-open window of a car parked by an American diplomat on a street in East Jerusalem.[101] In all probability, the US embassy dismissed the document as the work of a mildly deranged conspiracy theorist. Service A, however, persuaded itself that it had succeeded in putting Brzezinski's career in jeopardy. It seized on press articles during and after the negotiation of the Camp David agreement between Egypt and Israel in September 1978—which appeared to show that Vance had established himself as Carter's main foreign policy adviser—as proof that Brzezinski had been demoted. In November 1978 the deputy head of Service A, L. F. Sotskov, proudly reported to Andropov that operation MUREN had been successfully completed. Though the MUREN file fails to mention it, that judgment was doubtless revised the following year. The hardening of Carter's policy to the Soviet Union was evident even before the Soviet invasion of Afghanistan at the end of 1979.[103]

PROBABLY NO AMERICAN policymaker at any time during the Cold War inspired quite as much fear and loathing in Moscow as Ronald Reagan during his first term as president. Active measures against Reagan had begun during his unsuccessful bid for the Republican nomination in 1976. The Centre had no doubt that Reagan was far more anti-Soviet than either the incumbent president, Gerald Ford, or the Democratic contender, Jimmy Carter. As in the cases of Jackson and Brzezinski, Service A was ordered to embark on a remarkably wide-ranging quest for compromising material. The Centre ordered, *inter alia,* an investigation of reports that Reagan's health had been affected by his father's alcoholism.[104] During his childhood Christmases, Reagan later recalled, "there was always a threat hanging over our family. We knew holidays were the most likely time for Jack [Reagan senior] to jump off the wagon."[105] But such painful childhood memories were not the stuff of which successful active measures were made. Apart from confirming Reagan's reputation as a Cold War warrior, Service A seems to have discovered nothing more damaging than alleged evidence of his "weak intellectual capabilities." Service A successfully planted anti-Reagan articles in Denmark, France and India,[106] where they found more fertile soil than in the United States, but it is barely conceivable that KGB active measures had any influence on Reagan's failure to win the Republican nomination in 1976.

The Centre was less involved in trying to influence the 1980 presidential election than it had been four years earlier. Moscow saw little to choose between what it now saw as a Carter administration dominated by Brzezinski's hard line policies and Reagan's long-standing anti-Sovietism. "Fed up with Carter and uneasy about Reagan," wrote Dobrynin, "it decided to stay on the fence." After Reagan's election, Moscow quickly regretted its fence-sitting, convinced that the new administration represented "the most conservative, chauvinist, and bellicose part of American politics . . . pressing for the restoration of American world leadership after the defeat in Vietnam." To Dobrynin's dismay, the Kremlin succumbed to a "paranoid interpretation" of Reagan's policy, fearful—particularly during 1983—that he was planning a nuclear first strike. Dobrynin discovered from the Washington resident, Stanislav Andreyevich Androsov, the instructions for the vast KGB–GRU operation RYAN designed to detect Reagan's non-existent preparations for the surprise attack. But RYAN remained so secret that most Soviet ambassadors were kept in ignorance of it.[107]

It was probably the extreme priority attached by the Centre to discrediting the policies of the Reagan administration which led Andropov to decree formally on April 12, 1982, as one of the last acts of his fifteen-year term as chairman of the KGB, that it was the duty of all foreign intelligence officers, whatever their "line" or department, to participate in active measures.[108] Ensuring that Reagan did not serve a second term thus became Service A's most important objective. On February 25, 1983 the Centre instructed its three American residencies to begin planning active measures to ensure Reagan's defeat in the presidential election of November 1984. They were ordered to acquire contacts on the staffs of all possible presidential candidates and in both party headquarters. Residencies outside the United States were told to report on the possibility of sending agents to take part in this operation. The Centre made clear that *any* candidate, of either party, would be preferable to Reagan. Residencies around the world were ordered to popularize the slogan "Reagan Means War!" The Centre announced five active measures "theses" to be used to discredit Reagan's foreign policy: his militarist adventurism; his personal responsibility for accelerating the arms race; his support for repressive regimes around the world; his administration's attempts to crush national liberation movements; and his responsibility for tension with his NATO allies. Active measures "theses" in domestic policy included Reagan's alleged discrimination against ethnic minorities; corruption in his administration; and Reagan's subservience to the military–industrial complex.[109]

Reagan's landslide victory in the 1984 election was striking evidence of the limitations of Soviet active measures within the United States. Even on university and college campuses Reagan was surprised by the (admittedly less than unanimous) "outpouring of affection and support:" "These students in the eighties seemed so different from those that I'd dealt with as governor a decade earlier."[110] Though Service A was never willing to admit it, there was little it could do to undermine a popular president. Its attacks on Reagan fell on much more fertile ground in Europe and the Third World, however, where his populist appeal to the American way was frequently ridiculed.

ACTIVE MEASURES AGAINST the Main Adversary were usually more effective outside than inside the United States. One of Service A's most successful tactics was its use of forgeries of US documents shown in confidence to Third World leaders to alert them to supposedly hostile operations against them by the CIA and other American agencies. Since most of these forgeries were never made public, the United States was not usually able to challenge their authenticity. One characteristic example in the files noted by Mitrokhin was operation KULBIT in the Republic of Guinea in 1975. The operation was based on three French language leaflets attacking the government of President Sekou Touré, allegedly produced by the CIA station in the Guinean capital, Conakry, but in reality fabricated by Service A in Moscow. To heighten the dramatic impact of the forgeries, the Soviet ambassador in Conakry telephoned the Minister of Security, Mussa Diakite, at 6 p.m. on October 16, 1975 to tell him that a special emissary had arrived from Moscow with top secret information for the President of great importance. At 9 p.m. the ambassador and O. A. Seliskov, deputy head of FCD Directorate K, were ushered by Diakite into the presence of Sekou Touré. Seliskov handed the President the three fabricated CIA leaflets, the first of which began with an attack on the high level of Guinean unemployment. According to the KGB file on operation KULBIT, on seeing the reference to unemployment, Sekou Touré turned to Diakite, waved the pamphlet in his face and angrily exclaimed, "The filthy imperialists!" Seliskov then described various alleged plots by the CIA station to overthrow the President, making the plots appear all the more convincing by incorporating into them various pieces of information which he knew were already known to the Guinean security service. Sekou Touré, by now "in an emotional state," pounded the table and declared, "We will take decisive action against the US intelligence officers you have identified. They will be expelled within twenty-four hours!" When he calmed down, the President observed, as Service A had intended, that some of Seliskov's information coincided with intelligence already in the possession of his security service.[111]

Sekou Touré was profuse in his thanks for the KGB disinformation: "We highly appreciate the concern shown by our Soviet comrades. This is not Chile, and we are not going to allow the same events [the overthrow of the President] to happen in our country." He asked Seliskov how his top secret information on the machinations of the CIA, supposedly obtained from "important and reliable sources in the United States," should be handled. "At your own discretion," replied Seliskov graciously. Sekou Touré asked him to convey his "deepest gratitude" to the appropriate Soviet authorities and asked to be kept informed about future imperialist threats to the security of the Guinean Republic.[112]

The fabrication of compromising US documents and imaginary CIA plots continued into the Gorbachev era. In addition to the "silent forgeries" shown privately to Sekou Touré and other gullible political leaders around the world, forgeries were used to promote media campaigns: among them, in 1987, a forged letter from the DCI, William Casey, on plans to overthrow the Indian prime minister, Rajiv Gandhi; in 1988, bogus instructions from Reagan to destabilize Panama; and in 1989, a fabricated letter from the South African foreign minister, "Pik" Botha, referring to a sinister but non-existent secret agreement with the United States.[113]

Probably the most successful anti-American active measure of the Gorbachev era, promoted by a mixture of overt propaganda and covert action by Service A, was the story that the AIDS virus had been "manufactured" by American biological warfare specialists at Fort Detrick in Maryland. An East German, Russian-born physicist, Professor Jacob Segal, claimed on the basis of "circumstantial evidence" (later wholly discredited) that AIDS had been artificially synthesized at Fort Detrick from two natural viruses, VISNA and HTLV-1. Thus fortified by spurious scientific jargon, the AIDS fabrication not merely swept through the Third World, but took in some of the Western media as well. In October 1986 the conservative British *Sunday Express* made it its main front-page story. During the first six months of 1987 alone, the story received major news coverage in over forty Third World countries.

At the very height of its success, however, the AIDS fabrication was compromised by a combination of Western protests and "new thinking" in Soviet foreign policy. "We tell the truth and nothing but the truth," Gorbachev proudly proclaimed at a Moscow press conference in July 1987. Faced with official American protests and the repudiation of the AIDS story by the international scientific community, the Kremlin for the first time showed signs of embarrassment at a successful active measures campaign. In August 1987 US officials in Moscow were informed that the story was officially disowned and Soviet media coverage of it came to an abrupt halt.

The AIDS fabrication, however, was swiftly followed by other, equally scurrilous anti-American active measures in the Third World, some of which also seduced sections of the Western media. Among the most successful was the "baby parts" story, alleging that rich Americans were butchering Third World children in order to use their bodies for organ transplants in the United States. In September 1988 a motion in the European Parliament condemning the alleged trafficking in "baby parts," proposed by a French Communist MEP, passed on a show of hands in a poorly attended session.[114]

Even the end of the Cold War did little to diminish the enthusiasm for active measures of both Kryuchkov, who became chairman of the KGB in 1988, and Leonid Shebarshin, who succeeded him as head of the FCD. Shebarshin, who had made his reputation as resident in India from 1975 to 1977 in part by the success of his active measures operations, was wont to speak "nostalgically about the old days, about disinformation—forging documents, creating sensations for the press."[115]

Not all KGB personnel, however, shared their chiefs' continuing enthusiasm for active measures. Kryuchkov complained in September 1990 that some FCD officers in both Moscow and foreign residencies "underestimate the importance and the role of measures designed to promote influence." He issued a formal "Order of the Chairman of the KGB" requiring "refinement of the work of the foreign intelligence service in the field of active measures" and insisting that "their importance in intelligence work is continuing to grow:"

> In effect the joint political and operational scenario and the interests of the Soviet state and its society require the KGB foreign intelligence service to introduce active measures with greater ingenuity, inventiveness and secrecy which will enhance the level of their effectiveness . . . Work on active measures is to be considered one of the most important functions of the KGB's foreign intelligence service.

The FCD training school, the Andropov Institute, was instructed to prepare new "specialist courses in active measures." Among the most important "themes" for active measures was to frighten off support by the West—in particular the United States—for nationalist movements in the Baltic republics and other parts of the Soviet Union:

> In Western government and political circles and in influential émigré groups, it is important . . . to strengthen the conviction that an adventurist gamble on the disintegration of the Soviet Federation and statehood would lead to a disruption of contemporary international relations with the attendant unpredictable consequences.[116]

Amid the active measures promoted by the SVR in the mid-1990s there remained some echoes of its KGB past. Yeltsin's memoir, *The View from the Kremlin*, published in the West in 1994, ends with an appendix which contains two specially selected examples of KGB documents in the secret archives of the Russian president. One concerns the assassination of John F. Kennedy. The KGB documents on this topic, probably drawn to Yeltsin's attention by the SVR (then headed by Yevgeni Primakov), support the theory formerly propagated by Service A that Oswald had been selected as the assassin by "a group of Texas financiers and industrialists headed by millionaire Hunt:"

> Oswald was the most suitable figure for executing a terrorist act against Kennedy because his past allowed for the organization of a widespread propaganda campaign accusing the Soviet Union, Cuba, and the US Communist party of involvement in the assassination. But . . . Ruby and the real instigators of Kennedy's murder did not take into account the fact that Oswald suffered from psychiatric illness. When Ruby realized that after a prolonged interrogation Oswald was capable of confessing everything, Ruby immediately liquidated Oswald.[117]

No conspiracy theory of the Cold War era seems to have greater staying power than that generated by the death of President John F. Kennedy.

FIFTEEN

PROGRESS OPERATIONS

Part 1: Crushing the Prague Spring

The KGB and its predecessors had played a crucial part in the creation of the Soviet Bloc after the Second World War. Throughout eastern Europe, Communist-controlled security services, set up in the image of the KGB and overseen—except in Yugoslavia and Albania—by Soviet "advisers," supervised the transition to so-called "people's democracies." Political development in most east European states followed the same basic pattern. Coalition governments with significant numbers of non-Communist ministers, but with the newly founded security services and the other main levers of power in Communist hands, were established immediately after German forces had been driven out. Following intervals ranging from a few months to three years, these governments were replaced by bogus, Communist-run coalitions which paved the way for Stalinist one-party states taking their lead from Moscow.[1]

The German Communist leader Walter Ulbricht announced to his inner circle on his return to Berlin from exile in Moscow on April 30, 1945: "It's got to look democratic, but we must have everything under our control."[2] Because a democratic façade had to be preserved throughout eastern Europe, the open use of force to exclude non-Communist Parties from power had, so far as possible, to be avoided. Instead, the new security services took the lead in intimidation behind the scenes, using what became known in Hungary as "salami tactics"—slicing off one layer of opposition after another. Finally, the one-party people's democracies, purged of all visible dissent, were legitimized by huge and fraudulent Communist majorities in elections rigged by the security services.[3]

During the early years of the Soviet Bloc, Soviet advisers kept the new security services on a tight rein. The witch-hunts and show trials designed to eliminate mostly imaginary supporters of Tito and Zionism from the leadership of the ruling Communist Parties of eastern Europe were orchestrated from Moscow. One of the alleged accomplices of the Hungarian Minister of the Interior, László Rajk, in the non-existent Titoist plot for which Rajk was executed in 1949, noted how, during his interrogation, officers of the Hungarian security service "smiled a flattering, servile smile when the Russians spoke to them" and "reacted to the most witless jokes of the [MGB] officers with obsequious trumpetings of immoderate laughter."[4]

Even after Stalin's death, any Soviet Bloc intelligence officer of whom the KGB disapproved became a marked man. Among them was Ernst Wollweber, head of the

East German Stasi from 1953 to 1957, whose long connection with Soviet intelligence went back to his years as an NKVD agent in the 1930s, specializing in marine sabotage. Wollweber, however, had come to dislike Moscow's habit of issuing peremptory orders and resented the fact that the KGB kept him ill-informed on its operations in West Germany. The KGB also distrusted Wollweber's current mistress, Clara Vater, a German Communist who, like many of her comrades, had been unjustly imprisoned during Stalin's Terror.[5] Remarkably, it placed both her and her daughter, whom Wollweber had adopted, under surveillance inside East Germany. Wollweber was succeeded in 1956 by the sycophantically pro-Soviet Erich Mielke, who remained in office with Moscow's blessing until 1989, becoming one of the world's longest serving intelligence chiefs.[6]

ON EACH OF the three occasions when the Red Army intervened to restore pro-Soviet orthodoxy in a wayward Communist state—Hungary in 1956, Czechoslovakia in 1968, Afghanistan in 1979—the KGB played a prominent part in what was euphemistically termed the process of "normalization." When the Hungarian uprising began in October 1956 with mass demonstrations calling for free elections and the withdrawal of Soviet troops, the KGB chairman, General Ivan Aleksandrovich Serov, flew to Budapest to take personal charge of KGB operations. At an emergency meeting of security and police officers in the interior ministry, Serov denounced their reluctance to fire on the demonstrators: "The fascists and imperialists are bringing out their shock troops into the streets of Budapest, and yet there are still comrades in your country's armed forces who hesitate to use arms!" Sandor Kopácsi, the Budapest chief of police, who was soon to side with the freedom fighters, replied scornfully:

> Evidently the comrade adviser from Moscow has not yet had time to inform himself of the situation in our country. We need to tell him that these are not "fascists" or other "imperialists" who are organizing the demonstration; they come from the universities, the handpicked sons and daughters of peasants and workers, the fine flower of our country's intelligentsia which is demanding its rights . . .[7]

A quarter of a century later Kopácsi still vividly recalled the long, withering glare in his direction from Serov's steel-blue eyes. Shortly before Kopácsi escaped to the West, Serov told him, "I'm going to have you hanged from the highest tree in Budapest!" On the evening of November 3, 1956 a Hungarian delegation headed by Pál Maléter, the minister of defense, was invited to Soviet military headquarters at Tokol to discuss final details of the Red Army's withdrawal from Hungarian soil. At midnight, while toasts were being drunk, Serov, brandishing a Mauser pistol, burst into the room at the head of a group of KGB officers and arrested Maléter and his colleagues. A series of mock executions over the next few hours convinced each member of the Hungarian delegation that all his colleagues had been shot.[8] At 4 a.m. on November 4 the Red Army began the suppression of the Hungarian uprising. Serov and his deputy, KGB General K. Grebennik, who became military commandant of Budapest, stayed on to supervise the "normalization."[9]

Though it was not until after the Prague Spring of 1968 that the Red Army intervened again to enforce Soviet ideological orthodoxy, Moscow showed growing anxiety during the 1960s at increasing Western influence within the Soviet Bloc. The KGB reported that the West was engaged in wide-ranging "subversive activity in the political and ideological sphere against the socialist countries . . . seeking to persuade the population of the superiority of the Western way of life." The "subversion" took many forms: broadcasting, propagandist publications, information distributed by Western embassies, East–West cultural and scientific exchanges, tourism and letter-writing. In the Centre's view, Western radio stations such as the BBC World Service and Radio Liberty threatened to cause "immense harm" by broadcasting propaganda designed to weaken the fraternal ties between the Soviet Union and the socialist states of eastern Europe.[10] What most worried the KGB was that "the broadcasts were popular with the intelligentsia and young people." According to statistics probably obtained from its Hungarian ally, the AVH, over 20 per cent of young people in Hungary listened to Western radio stations.[11] During 1964 approximately fifty million postal items were exchanged between Hungarian citizens and the West, eight million more than in 1963. The KGB was also exercised by the growth in east European visitors to the West, who were in danger of returning with subversive ideas. In 1964 168,000 Hungarians and 150,000 Czechoslovaks visited Western countries. Worse still, in the Centre's view, many were unsupervised during their visits. The KGB complained that its Polish ally, the SB, had no officers in its foreign residencies who were responsible for monitoring the behavior of Polish tourists and Poles studying abroad. In 1964 34,500 Poles traveled to the West as individuals rather than as members of groups.[12]

The KGB kept somewhat bizarre statistics of "harmful attitudes" and "hostile acts" in the Soviet Bloc, which it tended to lump together: such disparate phenomena as enthusiasm for Western pop music with cases of ideological deviation. In both 1965 and 1966 Hungarian young people were said to have been guilty of approximately 87,000 "harmful attitudes" and "hostile acts." According to classified official statistics, the figure fell reassuringly, if somewhat surprisingly, to 68,000 in 1968 and remained at about that level for the next decade. Disturbingly, however, about 30 per cent of the cases recorded concerned members of the Communist youth organization, Komsomol.[13]

"The West's subversive activities," complained one KGB report, were "harming the cause of Socialist construction" throughout the Soviet Bloc, encouraging nationalist tendencies in the states of eastern Europe and damaging their ties with the Soviet Union. The greatest harm was being done among the intelligentsia and young people. The KGB noted "an unhealthy tendency" among writers towards "ideological co-existence" with the West and a growing belief that literature was no business of the Party. Students showed a worrying tendency to set up independent non-Party organizations for "free discussion on the model of English clubs." One undated KGB report picked out two subversive texts currently attracting "growing interest:" *The*

New Class by the heretical Yugoslav Communist Milovan Djilas, and the works of the late nineteenth-century German philosopher Friedrich Nietzsche.[14]

It is easy to see why Djilas's devastating exposé of the Soviet system as a co-optive oligarchy run by a privileged Party *nomenklatura* should have been seen as so subversive. In 1963 the twenty-year-old Russian dissident Vladimir Bukovsky was sent to psychiatric hospital for possessing a copy of it. Even for KGB officers *The New Class* was seen as a potentially dangerous text. When General Oleg Kalugin finally read the book in the KGB library in 1981, twenty-four years after its publication in the West, he found himself secretly agreeing with it.[15] Why Nietzsche should have been mentioned in the same breath as Djilas is more puzzling. His call for a "revaluation of all values" so that the life force of the strongest should not be hampered by the weak, though bearing some relation to the actual practice of Stalinism, was ideological anathema. But the works of Nietzsche, unlike those of Djilas, were scarcely likely to subvert the youth of the Soviet Bloc. The author of the KGB report probably knew no more about the great German philosopher than that he was a well-known enemy of Marxism.

The first stirrings of reform in Czechoslovakia in the mid-1960s, however, caused relatively little concern in the Centre. The chief target of the reformers, the aging and truculent Czechoslovak Communist Party (CPCz) leader, Antonín Novotný, was increasingly regarded in Moscow as a neo-Stalinist nuisance rather than as a bulwark against revisionism. In December 1967 Brezhnev made an unscheduled one-day visit to Prague at the request of Novotný, who was under pressure to relinquish the post of First Secretary, which he had hitherto combined with that of president. Brezhnev refused to intervene, telling Novotný bluntly to deal with the problem himself.[16] Deprived of Soviet support, Novotný gave way to the reformers.

The election of the 46-year-old Alexander Dubček as the new First Secretary on January 5, 1968 initially aroused no disquiet in either the Kremlin or the Centre. Dubček had spent most of his childhood in the Soviet Union, graduating with honors from the Moscow Higher Party School in 1958, and was condescendingly known within the KGB as "Our Sasha." When the Czechoslovak attempt to create "Socialism with a human face" began, the FCD Eleventh (East European) Department at first concluded that "Our Sasha" was being cleverly manipulated by "bourgeois elements" in the CPCz. Once it became clear that Dubček was himself one of the moving forces behind the reforms, the Centre felt a sense of personal betrayal.[17]

Dubček believed, in retrospect, that Moscow took a secret decision to use the Red Army to crush the Prague Spring little more than two months after he succeeded Novotný:

Under Novotný and his predecessors, the Soviets had been permitted to control the Czechoslovak armed forces and secret police in various ways, which included an implicit "right" to approve key appointments. It was apparently not until mid-March that they realized that their proxies might be fired and replaced without their consent and decided to step in.[18]

In reality Brezhnev remained unsure about the wisdom of military intervention until almost the eve of the August invasion. The Soviet prime minister, Alexei Kosygin, shared some of Brezhnev's doubts.[19] Both, however, gradually gave way to the hard-liners in the Politburo.

The case for military intervention was first put at the Politburo meeting on March 21 by the Ukrainian Party secretary, Petr Yefimovich Shelest, who declared that the fate of the whole "socialist camp" was at stake in the Prague Spring. Though it was "essential to seek out the healthy [pro-Soviet] forces in Czechoslovakia more actively," he argued that "military measures" would also be necessary. Shelest was vigorously supported by the KGB chairman, Yuri Andropov, who called for "concrete measures" to prepare for armed intervention.[20] Though as yet only a candidate (non-voting) member of the Politburo, Andropov became an increasingly influential voice during the Czechoslovak crisis, willing to challenge Kosygin and other more senior figures who appeared reluctant to use force.[21]

As Soviet ambassador in Budapest in 1956, Andropov had played a key role in suppressing the Hungarian Revolution. His insistence that the threat of counter-revolution had reached a critical stage helped to persuade an initially reluctant Khrushchev to agree to military intervention.[22] An admiring junior diplomat in the Soviet embassy later recalled how Andropov had been the first to "see through" the reformist prime minister, Imre Nagy, and had seemed completely in control of events even as Soviet tanks entered Budapest: "He was so calm—even when bullets were flying, when everyone else at the embassy felt like we were in a besieged fortress."[23] As well as being an uncompromising advocate of force, Andropov had demonstrated his mastery of deception, successfully persuading Nagy that the Red Army was being withdrawn while simultaneously plotting his overthrow. When the Hungarian commander-in-chief phoned the Prime Minister's office early on November 4 to report the Soviet attack, Nagy told him, "Ambassador Andropov is with me and assures me there's been some mistake and the Soviet government did not order an attack on Hungary. The Ambassador and I are trying to call Moscow."[24]

In Czechoslovakia in 1968, as in Hungary in 1956, Andropov's strategy was based on a mixture of deception and military might. Among the main instruments of deception during the Prague Spring were KGB illegals, all disguised as Westerners. Their deployment in Czechoslovakia in the first of what were henceforth termed PROGRESS operations marked a major innovation in the KGB's use of illegals. Hitherto illegals had been sent overwhelmingly to the West rather than the East. Most of those deployed within the Soviet Bloc had been sent on missions (codenamed BAYKAL) either to cultivate Western tourists or to monitor contacts between Soviet citizens and Westerners. In 1966 and 1967, for example, a number of illegals were sent to Bulgarian Black Sea resorts to mingle with the growing number of Western holidaymakers and look for possible recruits.[25] The illegal Stanislav Federovich Malotenko visited tourist areas of Ukraine, Bulgaria, Romania and Czechoslovakia posing as a Western visitor in order to investigate, *inter alia*, "how willingly women agents agreed to have intimate relations with foreigners without permission" from the KGB.[26]

During the Prague Spring illegals, posing as Western tourists, journalists, business people and students, were for the first time used in significant numbers in a country of the Soviet Bloc for both intelligence collection and active measures. Czechoslovak counter-revolutionaries, the Centre believed, would be much franker in revealing their subversive designs to those they believed Western sympathizers than to their neighbors in eastern Europe. Even within the FCD the PROGRESS operation in Czechoslovakia was known only to a small circle of senior officers. Initially the PROGRESS file was kept in the office of the head of Directorate S (Illegals), General Anatoli Ivanovich Lazarev, though, as operations in Czechoslovakia expanded, the group within the directorate who were privy to the secret also widened.[27]

Of the first twenty illegals selected by the Centre for PROGRESS operations in Czechoslovakia during 1968,[28] at least five (GROMOV, SADKO, SEVIDOV, VLADIMIR and VLAS)[29] and probably another two (GURYEV and YEVDOKI-MOV)[30] posed as West Germans. There were also three bogus Austrians (ARTYO-MOVA, DIM and VIKTOR)[31] and three bogus Britons (BELYAKOV, USKOV and VALYA),[32] two fictitious Swiss (ALLA[33] and SEP[34]), one Lebanese (YEFRAT[35]) and one Mexican (ROY[36]).[37] Probably in March, Andropov ordered that by May 12 at least fifteen of the illegals should be deployed in Czechoslovakia—more than had ever been despatched to any Western country in so short a period of time. Each was given a monthly allowance of 300 dollars as well as travel expenses and enough money to rent an apartment.[38]

Andropov also expanded the KGB legal representation in Prague. In addition to the KGB liaison office, headed by M. G. Kotov, which had been operating in the headquarters of the StB (its Czechoslovak equivalent) for the past twenty years, Andropov secretly established an undeclared KGB residency, headed by V. V. Surzhaninov, which began work in the Soviet embassy on April 26.[39] The deputy head of FCD Directorate S, G. F. Borzov, and another senior Line N officer, V. K. Umnov, were sent to the residency to co-ordinate the work of the illegals.[40] The main task both of the residency's Line PR and of the KGB liaison with the StB was to identify reliable, pro-Soviet members of the CPCz to form a quisling government after a Soviet invasion. At the top of their list the KGB put four hardline members of the CPCz Presidium—Alois Indra, Jozef Lenárt, Drahomir Kolder and Vasil Bil'ak—and a former minister of the interior, Rudolf Barák, who had been dismissed and imprisoned in 1962, officially for embezzlement of Party funds but in reality for using the StB to collect an incriminating dossier on Novotný.[41]

KGB officers in Prague had little difficulty in arranging meetings with Indra, Lenárt, Kolder and Bil'ak, who were regular visitors to the Soviet embassy. It was considered too risky, however, to approach Barák directly after his release from prison early in May. Instead, the KGB residency used a female illegal, Galina Leonidovna Linitskaya (codenamed ALLA), operating with a Swiss passport in the name of Maria Werner, to make the first approach to Barák. For some years the vivacious ALLA had specialized in making contact with Western visitors to the Soviet Union who were of interest to the KGB. Her KGB file primly complains that she was "too sexually stimulated" and, despite having a daughter, "not a family person" (not a criticism which appears in the files of male illegals). ALLA had first met Barák in 1961, when he was minister of the interior, and succeeded in renewing contact with him soon after his release from prison. At ALLA's request, Barák agreed to a meeting with B. S. Ivanov of the KGB residency.[42]

Indra, Lenárt, Kolder and Bil'ak were all to prove stalwarts of the neo-Stalinist regime which later presided over the destruction of "Socialism with a human face." Barák, however, proved far less useful than the Prague residency had hoped, partly because of resentment—even by some pro-Soviet members of the CPCz leadership—at his brutality as minister of the interior when he had been in charge of the StB. He was not fully rehabilitated until 1975, seven years after his release from prison.[43]

THE KGB ILLEGALS deployed in Czechoslovakia had two main tasks: to penetrate the allegedly counter-revolutionary groups springing up during the Prague Spring in order to report on their subversive intentions; and to implement a series of active measures designed to discredit them. The main task of penetration was entrusted to YEFRAT, GURYEV, YEVDOKIMOV, GROMOV and SADKO.[44] Their chief targets were what the Centre saw as the main sources of subversive ideas:

- the Union of Writers (in particular its chairman, Eduard Goldst Åcker, and vice-chairman, Jan Procházka, and the celebrated authors Pavel Kohout and Milan Kundera);
- radical journals which had escaped Communist control such as the Union of Writers' *Literární Listy* and the Socialist Party's *Svobodne slovo,* as well as the increasingly unorthodox Communist Party newspaper, *Rudé právo;*
- leading reformists in television and radio (in particular Jiří Pelikán, the director-general of Czechoslovak television);
- Charles University, especially its philosophy department, which took the lead in pressing for a new law protecting academic freedom, and leading student activists such as Lubomír Holeček and Jiří Måller;
- K-231, a club of former political prisoners who had been jailed under the notorious Article 231 of the Czechoslovak criminal code;
- KAN, the club of non-Party activists, formed in early April to give those who were not Party members the opportunity to participate in public life and share in the building of "a new political system—hitherto never realized in history—democratic socialism;"
- and the Socialist and People's Parties, struggling to recover the independent existence they had lost after the Communist coup in 1948.[45]

One of the defining moments of the Prague Spring, which epitomized the new climate of political freedom and the near-collapse of official censorship, was the May Day procession through the capital, seen on television throughout the country. Instead of the usual tedious display of sycophantic admiration for the Party leadership and platitudinous slogans celebrating friendship with the Soviet Union, there was a spontaneous celebration of popular support for the reform movement combined with irreverent messages for Moscow such as the banners proclaiming "With the Soviet Union for ever—but not a day longer!" and "Long live the USSR—but at its own expense!" Dubček remembered the day "with deep emotion," "truly touched" by the support for him from the former political prisoners of K-231 and the non-Party activists of KAN. For Moscow, however, the day was an outrageous counter-revolutionary provocation which demonstrated that the Czechoslovak one-party state was in mortal danger.[46]

The danger was all the greater because, in the Centre's view, the StB was becoming increasingly unreliable. Probably Moscow's leading *bête noire* in Oldřich Černík's government, which took power in April, was the interior minister, Josef Pavel, who was responsible for the StB. Ironically, the KGB placed much of the blame for Pavel's appointment on Lubomír Štrougal, who later turned against the reformists and played a prominent part in the return to pro-Soviet orthodoxy. According to a report in the KGB files, Štrougal came into Černík's office soon after his appointment as prime minister and, fearing that the office was bugged, asked him to come for a stroll by the river Vltava, which runs through the center of Prague. During their walk Štrougal urged Černík to give Pavel the interior ministry. Because Pavel had spent some years in prison during the early 1950s, Štrougal argued that he could be relied upon to ensure that the police and the StB did not abuse their powers. Černík allegedly agreed with his arguments.[47] In late April, soon after becoming Interior Minister, Pavel announced that both the ministry and the StB were henceforth to be under government—not Party—control, and that a series of senior officials were to be sacked. Among them was the pro-Soviet head of the StB, Josef Houska, who was dismissed in June. Some weeks before he left, he handed the KGB photocopies of a series of StB personnel files.[48]

On May 10 Aleksei Kosygin, the Soviet prime minister, sent Černík, his Czech counterpart, an outraged letter complaining, among other things, that "agents and saboteurs" disguised as Western tourists had been able to penetrate Czechoslovakia because of poor border security.[49] What Kosygin predictably failed to mention, however, was that the most active agents and all the saboteurs with Western passports were KGB illegals. On the very day he sent his letter, GROMOV (Vasili Antonovich Gordievsky) and GURYEV (Valentin Aleksandrovich Gutin), both posing as West Germans, were attempting to kidnap two of the most eloquent tribunes of the Prague Spring.[50] GROMOV had recent experience in kidnapping. Only a month earlier he had been decorated for an assignment in Sweden, which involved exfiltrating another illegal, FAUST, who was considered by the Centre to have developed a persecution syndrome. Once back in the Soviet Union, FAUST had been sent to a psychiatric hospital for a year, then released and sacked from the KGB.[51]

The targets selected for exfiltration by GROMOV and GURYEV in May 1968 were Professor Václav Černý and Jan Prochízka.[52] Václav Černý (codenamed TEMNY),[53] one of Czechoslovakia's leading authorities on Romance literature, had been expelled from his chair at Charles University after the Communist coup in 1948 but re-emerged during the Prague Spring as a founder member of KAN and an eloquent advocate of academic freedom. At the June 1967 Congress of the Writers Union, Jan Prochízka had been one of those who took the lead in denouncing official censorship and demanding "freedom of creativity."[54] Claiming to be concerned for his safety, GURYEV tried to persuade Černý that he was in serious personal danger (presumably from the hardline opponents of reform) and offered to find him a temporary hiding place. GROMOV delivered a similar message to Prochízka. Once persuaded of the need to hide, both Černý and Prochízka were to be handed over to thugs from Service V (the FCD "special actions" department), who would drive them in a car with CD plates which could cross unchecked into East Germany.[55] If they resisted, Černý and Prochízka were to be subdued with what the operational file euphemistically describes as "special substances."

The operation, however, was a miserable failure. After the persecution Černý had suffered during the previous twenty years, GURYEV could not persuade him that he was in any greater danger than usual. GROMOV discovered to his dismay that Prochízka had been supplied with a bodyguard by Pavel. The Centre had also overlooked the language problems involved in the operation. Though Černý was a good linguist, Prochízka spoke only Czech. Posing as a non-Czech-speaking West German, GROMOV found it difficult to communicate with him. Though he could probably have made himself understood in Russian, he would have risked revealing his real identity.[56] After a few weeks GURYEV and GROMOV abandoned their kidnap attempts.

In addition to their other missions during the Prague Spring, the illegals were tasked with a series of active measures collectively codenamed KHODOKI ("go-betweens"), which were intended to justify a Soviet invasion by fabricating evidence of a counter-revolutionary conspiracy by Czechoslovak "rightists" and Western intelligence services.[57] Posing as sympathetic Westerners, the illegals tried to persuade editors and journalists to publish attacks on the Soviet Union and other provocative articles. They also attempted to interest Černý and K-231 in accepting aid from a fictitious underground organization allegedly supplied with arms by the West. Josef Houska, the StB chief sacked by Pavel in June, was secretly informed of operation KHODOKI and agreed to co-operate with it.[58]

By mid-July, as part of KHODOKI, the illegals had succeeded in planting fabricated evidence of preparations for an armed coup. On July 19 *Pravda* reported the discovery of a "secret cache" of American weapons near the West German border, some conveniently contained in packages marked "Made in USA," which had allegedly been smuggled into Czechoslovakia by "revenge seekers and champions of the old order." The Soviet authorities, it claimed, had also obtained a copy of an American "secret plan" to overthrow the Prague regime. The press throughout the Soviet Bloc followed up *Pravda*'s story with reports that hidden Western weapons were being discovered all over Czechoslovakia. Simultaneously bogus intelligence was fed to the StB implicating K-231 and KAN in a counter-revolutionary conspiracy with Western intelligence services.[59]

The Soviet Politburo met to consider its next step in the crisis on the same day that *Pravda* produced its first report on the fictitious counter-revolutionary arms caches. Brezhnev began the meeting by proposing a final meeting with the Czechoslovak leadership to try to reach a negotiated settlement. Only if that failed should they take "extreme measures." Andropov emerged as the chief spokesman of those who wanted extreme measures immediately. Bilateral talks, he argued, would achieve little, while any delay would increase the threat from "the rightists:" "They are fighting for survival now, and they're fighting frenziedly . . . Both we and they are making preparations, and theirs are very thorough. They are preparing the working class, the workers' militia [for a conflict]." It was a bad-tempered meeting. Andropov became involved in a furious argument with Kosygin, whom he accused of "attacking" him, presumably because of his call for immediate military intervention. "I am not attacking you," retorted Kosygin. "On the contrary, it is you who are attacking me!" The only full member of the Politburo who supported Andropov's opposition to a final meeting with the CPCz leadership was K. T. Mazurov. However, the foreign minister, Andrei Gromyko, like Andropov a non-voting member of the Politburo and later his close ally, probably summed up the majority view when he declared that meeting Dubček and his colleagues was no more than a necessary preliminary to invasion: "Clearly they will not accept our proposals. But then we can move to a decision about taking extreme measures . . ."[60]

As Gromyko had predicted, the meeting between the CPCz Presidium and the Soviet Politburo at the border town of Čierní nad Tisou from July 29 to August 1 ended without agreement. After an StB investigation, Pavel reported to the CPCz Presidium that the alleged counter-revolutionary arms caches were a "provocation." Though the weapons themselves were American, of Second World War vintage, some of them were in Soviet-made packaging. Other intelligence linking K-231 and KAN with Western secret services was also discovered to be fabricated.[61] The KGB illegals behind operation KHODOKI, however, went undetected. Mitrokhin's notes on KGB files lend some, though not conclusive, support to the claim by an StB defector that the KGB planned to murder the Soviet wives of a number of Czechoslovak citizens in August and blame their deaths on counter-revolutionaries. The plan was apparently discovered by the StB and aborted.[62]

At a meeting of the CPCz Party committee of the StB early in August, the head of StB foreign intelligence, Shuoj Frouz (codenamed FARKAC), argued that the KGB advisers in the StB were violating the principles of Czechoslovak–Soviet intelligence liaison and should be recalled to Moscow. A report of the meeting, at which other StB officers supported Frouz, was quickly relayed to the KGB.[63] After the Soviet invasion, those who had demanded the recall of the KGB advisers were arrested—with the significant exception of Frouz, who may well have made the demand on KGB instructions in order to identify the main anti-Soviet elements in the StB in advance of the invasion.[64]

As well as producing fabricated evidence of a Western plot for public consumption, Andropov supplied the Politburo throughout the crisis with slanted intelligence designed to strengthen its resolve to intervene. Probably the most important accurate intelligence on American policy to reach the Centre during the Prague Spring came from the Washington residency, where the dynamic 34-year-old head of Line PR,

Oleg Kalugin, gained access to what he reported were "absolutely reliable documents" proving that neither the CIA nor any other agency was manipulating the Czechoslovak reform movement. These documents, however, failed to conform to Andropov's conspiracy theory of an imperialist plot and were thus kept from the Politburo. On returning to Moscow, Kalugin was amazed to discover that the Centre had ordered that "my messages should not be shown to anyone, and destroyed." Instead, on Andropov's orders, "The KGB whipped up the fear that Czechoslovakia could fall victim to NATO aggression or to a coup."[65]

At a meeting in Moscow on August 18, the leaders of the Soviet Union and the other four "reliable" members of the Warsaw Pact—Bulgaria, East Germany, Hungary and Poland—formally agreed on the invasion of Czechoslovakia, the biggest armed action in Europe since the end of the Second World War.[66] At 4 p.m. on August 20 a meeting of "reliable" members of the StB was briefed by Pavel's pro-Soviet deputy, Viliam Šalgovič, on plans for the invasion which was to begin that night and assigned tasks to assist the Warsaw Pact forces. Josef Houska, dismissed by Pavel two months earlier, returned to take charge of the StB.

At about 9 a.m. on the morning of August 21, with Soviet forces already in key positions in Prague, the StB veteran Lieutenant Colonel Bohumil Molnír, who had been given a specially engraved automatic pistol by the former KGB chairman, Ivan Serov, for his assistance in crushing the Hungarian Revolution in 1956, briefed the group of StB officers selected by the KGB to arrest Dubček and the reformist majority on the CPCz Presidium.[67] Escorted by KGB officers, the arrest group proceeded to Dubček's office in the Central Committee building, where one of them announced in what seemed to Dubček the "mechanical voice" of a second-rate amateur actor: "I am placing you in custody in the name of the Workers' and Peasants' Government led by Comrade Indra." He added, after a pause in which he seemed to be remembering his lines, that Dubček and his colleagues would shortly be brought before a revolutionary tribunal, also headed by Alois Indra.[68]

Indra and the other leading members of the quisling government-in-waiting selected by Moscow were already in the Soviet embassy ready to take power.[69] But at this point the invasion plan had to be modified. Indra and his co-conspirators had mistakenly assured Moscow that the invasion would be supported by a majority of the CPCz leadership.[70] The fact that Dubček retained a majority on the Presidium as well as overwhelming popular support forced Moscow to abandon its plan for a puppet regime and bring Dubček and his colleagues to the Kremlin, under KGB escort, to be browbeaten into a degree of submission. Brezhnev stuck to the fabricated KGB story that "anti-socialist" forces had been preparing a coup:

> Underground command posts and arms caches have now come to light. We don't want to make charges against you personally, that you're guilty. You might not even have been aware of it . . .

As the discussion proceeded over the next few days, however, the Soviet Politburo passed from attempts to justify the invasion and the pretense of comradely solidarity to intimidation and coercion. Dubček felt he had no option but to concede the main Soviet demands: "It could not have been otherwise. We were managing the affairs of an occupied country where the barrel of a Soviet gun was trained on our every move." On August 26 the Czechoslovak delegation signed a secret protocol accepting a "temporary" occupation by forces of the Warsaw Pact. The decisions of the Extraordinary Fourteenth Congress of the CPCz hurriedly convened on August 22, which had condemned the invasion, were annulled. Some of the leading reformists in the Party, government, radio and television who had most outraged Moscow were dismissed.[71]

The Kremlin intended the Moscow protocol only as the beginning of a process of "normalization" which would rapidly turn the Prague Spring into winter. As a later official history of the CPCz complained:

> The Right . . . still held the decisive positions in the Party, the state apparatus and the mass media . . . The Marxist-Leninist forces in the Party and society led a difficult and complicated struggle from August 1968 to April 1969, characterized by the gradual suppression of the Right.[72]

Of particular concern to Andropov was the continued strength of the "Right" in the StB, despite Houska's arrest of some leading reformists. According to KGB reports from Prague, the situation was most serious in foreign intelligence:

> In the [StB] First [foreign intelligence] Directorate nationalist passions were inflamed and there were acts of an anti-Soviet nature: removal of the Soviet flag, [hostile] slogans, attacks on Soviet military units sent to protect the old premises of the First Directorate, intelligence officers going underground, handing in their official passes, and stopping work in protest at the arrival of Soviet troops.

The Centre was outraged by a series of resolutions passed by the plenary committee of the StB First Directorate Communist Party:

1. Communists of the First Directorate Communist Party Organization welcome the return of the Czechoslovak delegation from Moscow and express their joy that comrades Dubček, Smrkovský, Černík, Kriegel, Svoboda and others will have the possibility of resuming their constitutional and Party duties. [In fact, on Soviet insistence, Kriegel was sacked.]

   In expressing their confidence in them, the Communists of the First Directorate Party Organization will continue to give these comrades their full support in implementing the [reformist] action program of the Czechoslovak Communist Party.
2. The First Directorate Communist Party Organization expresses concern about the contents of the final communiqué on the talks in Moscow, which

reflects the fact that the talks were held in conditions of inequality, under pressure and with occupation forces present in the Czechoslovak Socialist Republic.

3. The Communists again express their full support for the lawfully elected leadership of the Czechoslovak Intelligence Service and welcome its return to carry out its duties. The Communists demand an urgent investigation into all incidents in which the orders of this leadership, and also the orders of the Minister of Internal Affairs Pavel [sacked at Moscow's insistence], were contravened. In this connection, it is also essential to determine what role was played by officers of the USSR KGB.

The Party Organization recognizes the decisions of the Fourteenth Congress [annulled by the Moscow protocol] as lawful and places responsibility for the crisis on the Soviet troops.[73]

The KGB discovered that the StB resident in New York, codenamed PATERA, was trying vainly to persuade the Czechoslovak foreign minister, Jiří Hájek, to address the United Nations Security Council on the Soviet invasion, in defiance of the Moscow protocol. "If we did not raise the Czechoslovak question in the Security Council," PATERA insisted, "the nation would declare us to be traitors."[74] The StB resident in Washington, his eyes brimming with tears, told Oleg Kalugin, "My children will hate you for what you've done to my country. They will never forgive you for what happened."[75] It took several years for "healthy forces," as the KGB referred to the Soviet loyalists in the StB, to eradicate all trace of revisionism.

After the Soviet invasion KGB illegals remained central to Andropov's strategy for penetrating and destabilizing "rightist" forces.[76] PROGRESS operations in Czechoslovakia were augmented by other Soviet Bloc intelligence services. On August 25 Mielke, who had deployed East German illegals in Czechoslovakia during the Prague Spring, informed the Centre that he was sending a further contingent to Prague, together with Stasi officers to direct their operations and liaise with the KGB residency.[77] In September Andropov and Sakharovsky, the head of the FCD, traveled to Warsaw and agreed a plan for the SB (the Polish KGB) to use both agents and illegals to penetrate the Czechoslovak "counter-revolutionary underground," émigré groups and hostile intelligence services.[78]

The most valuable unwitting KGB source among the ranks of Czechoslovak "counter-revolutionaries" identified in the files seen by Mitrokhin was Leo Lappi (codenamed FREDDI), a former political prisoner and founder member of K-231. The fact that, though a Czechoslovak citizen, Lappi was an ethnic German made him far easier to cultivate than the majority of Czechoslovak citizens who were not fluent in Western languages. The first contact with Lappi was made by ALLA, posing as a German-speaking Swiss, in October 1968.[79] After about two months his cultivation was handed over to another female illegal, ARTYOMOVA, who had assumed the identity of an Austrian businesswoman.[80] From February 1969 onwards, Lappi's case officer was FYODOROV, who, using a West German passport in the name of Walter Brade, for the next decade became the leading illegal specializing in Czechoslovak operations. Since ALLA and ARTYOMOVA had reported that Lappi let rooms to foreigners, FYODOROV made initial contact with him on the pretext that he was a businessman looking for accommodation in Prague.[81]

Lappi had no idea that ALLA, ARTYOMOVA and FYODOROV were KGB illegals sent on missions to assist in the destruction of the last remnants of "socialism with a human face." Instead, they successfully persuaded him that they were Western supporters of the Prague Spring, anxious to do what they could to assist in its restoration. Given the almost universal revulsion in the West at the Soviet occupation, Lappi's misplaced trust in his new Swiss, Austrian and German friends was an understandable mistake, cynically exploited by FYODOROV. Lappi's confidence in FYODOROV was so complete that he left him in charge of his flat when he went on holiday to Romania. He introduced FYODOROV both to K-231 activists and to leaders of the Christian Democrat, People's and Socialist Parties, which had tried to re-establish themselves during the Prague Spring. Lappi regularly acted as translator at FYODOROV's meetings with them. Some of FYODOROV's reports on his meetings with the counter-revolutionaries were rated so highly by the Centre that they were forwarded to the Politburo.[82]

What the KGB files do not, of course, report are the feelings of the illegals as they betrayed the sometimes heroic survivors of the Prague Spring. Unlike the leaders of the Soviet Union and the Soviet public, who had no first-hand experience of the world outside the Soviet Bloc, the illegals knew the West and the reality of life in Czechoslovakia too well to have deluded themselves into believing that they were engaged in a moral crusade to defend socialist values against Western imperialism. There were recurrent complaints in FCD Directorate S that after postings abroad illegals sometimes returned with an "incorrect" attitude towards life in the Soviet Union.[83] Occasionally their attitudes were so incorrect that their careers were cut short. In 1966 the KGB liaison office in Budapest virtuously reported to the Centre a series of politically incorrect observations made by the female illegal ERNA while returning from leave in Moscow to her posting in Canada. Among the comments said to have "shocked" her fellow KGB officers were the following:

> In Moscow I was afraid to express my views frankly on certain subjects. After all, I could see that they thought that I had become more than a bit bourgeois.
>
> Why did the Party allow a second cult of personality to develop in respect of Khrushchev? I cannot understand how Khrushchev could take decisions on important Party and state matters all on his own. And what were the other members of the Central Committee doing? Were the consequences of the cult of Stalin not still fresh in their minds?
>
> What is the point now of launching so many Sputniks? Would it not be better to attend to more important things on earth? Twenty years have gone by since the end of the war, but people do not have the material goods which they need and deserve, and which the humblest inhabitants of the West have long enjoyed![84]

Very few illegals dared to voice such seditious comments openly. But the fact that some undoubtedly thought such thoughts cannot fail to have bred in them an increasing cynicism, heightened in some cases by their experiences in Czechoslovakia.

Some insight into the attitude of GROMOV, one of the first five illegals assigned to the penetration of "rightist" groups during the Prague Spring, is provided by the recollections of his younger brother, Oleg Antonovich Gordievsky, who worked from 1963 to 1972 in the FCD Illegals Directorate and Line N in the Copenhagen residency. GROMOV had been born in 1933 and, in Oleg's view, "had grown up among boys brutalized by war," becoming a cynical, materialistic adult who much preferred life in the West to the relative privations of Czechoslovakia. When Oleg was informed during his training that he had to choose between learning Czech and Swedish, his brother told him he would be an idiot not to choose Swedish: "If you take Czech, you'll spend the rest of your life sitting in the pathetic consular departments in Prague and Bratislava . . . [But] Sweden's a nice country . . . From there you can go anywhere in Europe."[85] There are signs of a less blatant cynicism towards the Czechs in FYODOROV's reports to the Centre. He wrote of the role of the Red Army in Czechoslovakia: "The Soviet forces play the role of a policeman standing at a crossroads where there is heavy traffic; everyone notices him and this disciplines the traffic." The Czechoslovak population, in other words, was being cowed into submission.[86]

In the case of a minority of illegals, their Czechoslovak experiences probably had more serious consequences than simply an increased level of cynicism. A few years later ALLA attempted to commit suicide. Though her KGB file attributes the episode solely to the fact that her partner had left her,[87] it is difficult to believe that the betrayal of the Czechoslovaks ALLA had befriended did not add to her emotional scars. A more common reaction by the illegals to their experiences in Czechoslovakia was probably to turn to alcohol. Unable to stop drinking even after he contracted hepatitis B during a mission in south-east Asia, GROMOV died in 1972 at the age of only thirty-nine.[88] Both BOGUN and his wife also became alcoholics. In 1976 he was admitted for "a full course of anti-alcohol therapy" at the Burdenko military hospital, while his wife was treated for alcoholism in the psycho-neurological department of the Central KGB Polyclinic. The previous few years, during which BOGUN had worked extensively on PROGRESS operations in Czechoslovakia and elsewhere in eastern Europe, seem to have taken a much heavier psychological toll than his earlier period as an illegal in the United States.[89]

In the case of one member of the Illegals Directorate there is no doubt about the shattering impact of the Soviet invasion of Czechoslovakia. For GROMOV's brother, Oleg Gordievsky, then serving in Copenhagen, "It was that dreadful event, that awful day, which determined the course of my own life." The crushing of the Prague Spring convinced him that the Soviet one-party state was, by its very nature, destructive of human liberties. He spent much of the next few years secretly pondering how to work for its overthrow before taking the decision to become a British penetration agent within the KGB.[90]

SIXTEEN

PROGRESS OPERATIONS

Part 2: Spying on the Soviet Bloc

Dubček later described the eight months after the Soviet invasion as "an organized retreat, in which no inch of territory was given up without calculated resistance."[1] It was a retreat, however, which was doomed to end in defeat. Dubček's position and that of the other leading reformers was steadily undermined by a combination of Soviet pressure, the old guard within the CPCz and former allies who decided to throw in their lot with the invaders to save their own careers.

The immediate pretext for Dubček's removal was the World Ice Hockey Championship in Stockholm in March 1969. On March 21, Dubček later recalled, "The whole country watched [on TV] as Czechoslovakia played the Soviets; it was much more than ice hockey, of course. It was a replay of a lost war . . ." The national rejoicings after the Czechoslovak victory led the KGB to prepare, with assistance from its stooges in the StB, an anti-Soviet riot to follow the next match between Czechoslovakia and the USSR on March 28. Shortly before the match a team of police agents disguised as city workers unloaded a pile of paving stones in front of the offices of the Soviet airline, Aeroflot, in Wenceslas Square. Prague police documents show that the whole operation was directly supervised by a Soviet agent in the Czech ministry of the interior.[2] Immediately after the Czechoslovak team had defeated the Soviets for the second time in a week, StB plain clothes personnel mingling with the celebrating crowd began to throw the conveniently placed stones at the Aeroflot office. The office furniture was dragged out on to the pavement and set alight.

Moscow now had the fabricated evidence it required to demand that, "The counter-revolution must be beheaded." Dubček believed he had no option but to resign. "Otherwise the Soviets would set up another provocation that could lead to further public turmoil and even a bloodbath."[3] On April 17 he was succeeded as First Secretary of the Czechoslovak Party by the Slovak first secretary, Gustáv Husák. As Dubček broadcast the news of his replacement, he broke down and wept.

PROGRESS operations in Czechoslovakia continued. A senior officer from FCD Directorate S, Dmitri Kirillovich Vetrov, arrived in Prague to supervise and coordinate the work of the illegals as they penetrated the ranks of the unrepentant reformists.[4] Posing as a Swiss sympathizer with the Prague Spring, Galina Vinogradova (ALLA) was instructed to cultivate Ladislav Lebovič (codenamed KHAN), one of the trainers of the victorious Czechoslovak ice hockey team which was viewed with deep suspicion in the Centre.[5] The illegal Yuri Linov (KRAVCHENKO), who pretended to be Austrian, succeeded in gaining the confidence of the international chess grand master and sports columnist Luděk Pachman, one of the organizers of the illegal broadcasts transmitted in the aftermath of the Soviet invasion. As soon as Linov had identified those of Pachman's friends and associates who were ready to continue "the struggle against the Soviet occupiers," Pachman himself was arrested and imprisoned.[6]

Though delighted by Dubček's departure, the KGB liaison office in Prague remained unenthusiastic about his successor, Gustáv Husák, who had been imprisoned in 1952 on trumped-up charges as an alleged Trotskyist and "bourgeois nationalist." "Spending nine years in prison," it reported, "has left its mark on Husák's psychology, in that he shows unwarranted indulgence towards clear adversaries of the Czechoslovak Communist Party line." The KGB liaison office complained to the Centre that there was "no genuine internal unity" within the CPCz leadership, which was divided between "internationalists" such as Bil'ak and Indra, who had supported Soviet intervention in August 1968, and "realists" led by Štrougal, who had opposed intervention but now accepted it as a fact of life. The two sides were engaged in a power struggle, seeking to gain key positions and place their supporters within the Party apparatus.[7] Over the next year both realists and internationalists had some successes. In January 1970 Štrougal replaced Černík as prime minister. Simultaneously, however, Bil'ak was put in charge of an operation to purge the CPCz of all reformists during the introduction of new Party cards.[8] A fellow hardliner, Miloš Jakeš, head of the Central Committee's Control and Auditing Committee, became his right-hand man and regularly reported on the progress of the purge to the KGB liaison office.[9] Seventeen years later Jakeš was to succeed Husák as general secretary of the CPCz.

The Centre's assessment of the work of the KGB liaison office and residency in Prague during 1970 concluded:

> The bloc of revisionist and anti-socialist forces in the Czechoslovak Socialist Republic has suffered a political defeat; the legal ideological centers of the right-wing have been eliminated; the main ideologists of Czechoslovak renewal have been removed from the political arena and expelled from the Party; and measures have been taken to purge the state apparatus of the most active carriers of the right-wing danger. However, it would not be right to suppose that with the exchange of Party cards the Czechoslovak Communist Party has totally purged its ranks of hostile and alien elements.[10]

Indra, whom Moscow had originally intended to take power after the invasion at the head of a "Workers' and Peasants' Government," was reported by the liaison office to be "biding his time," waiting for an opportunity to press his claims as general secretary.[11] His wait was to prove in vain.

KGB agents and Soviet sycophants within the CPCz continued to protest that Štrougal and other former reformists retained far too much influence at the expense of the Soviet Union's true friends. One informant in the Ministry of the Interior,

Jaroslav Zeman, complained that Štrougal was discriminating against the internationalists: "And what sort of person is Štrougal? In 1968 he was preparing to emigrate to the West and had currency and documents ready for his escape." While turncoats prospered under Štrougal's patronage, "Officials who cooperate with the USSR are looked down on in the Czechoslovak Socialist Republic; they are kept in the dark, and are not promoted or rewarded."[12]

By January 1971 310 foreign intelligence officers had been dismissed and 170 expelled from the Party. The whole of the senior staff of the internal StB had been replaced along with many more junior officers.[13] The Centre, however, was not satisfied. The KGB liaison office was instructed during 1971 to press the interior ministry and the StB "in a tactful manner" to carry out a thorough reorganization of Czechoslovak intelligence "in view of the fact that the central apparatus was tainted and the possibility that committed agents of the adversary were present in it." The Centre wished for active assistance from a reformed StB in the collection of scientific and technological intelligence, the deployment of illegals and other FCD operations.[14]

Despite continuing doubts about the reliability of some StB personnel, the KGB liaison office reported that the minister of the interior, Radko Kaska, displayed a satisfactory level of subservient cooperation:

> We have not noticed any unjustified or non-objective information from Kaska. Up to the present he has informed us frankly and in detail about internal political processes in Czechoslovakia and about the situation within the Ministry of Internal Affairs.[15]

The KGB was provided with copies of StB operational orders and reports, and proposed staff changes were submitted for its approval.[16] At Husák's instructions, Kaska began secretly collecting material on "leading right-wing personalities" in order to determine how many could be held to have broken state laws.[17] The KGB was, however, embarrassed to be asked by Kaska in March 1971 whether it had any "adverse information" on past contacts with the West by the chairman of the National Assembly, Dalibor Hanes. The Centre was concerned that, if it replied to Kaska's enquiry, it would give the (perfectly accurate) impression that "the KGB is engaged in collecting information on officials of fraternal Parties in friendly countries." The head of the KGB liaison office in Prague, Ye. G. Sinitsyn, was instructed to reply that it had "no reports of links between Hanes and foreign intelligence," but that, since it followed the principle of not spying on its allies, it would be unable to respond to such requests in future. Sinitsyn was privately informed by the Centre that Bil'ak had complained to the Soviet ambassador that Hanes had "taken up incorrect positions" during the Prague Spring and that his father had been responsible for "crushing workers' demonstrations in Slovakia" between the wars.[18] Soon afterwards Hanes was replaced as chairman of the National Assembly by the impeccably orthodox Indra.[19]

On May 4, 1971 Kaska met Semyon Konstantinovich Tsvigun, KGB deputy chairman, to report on the progress of "normalization."[20] Tsvigun owed his job almost solely to the fact that he was one of Brezhnev's oldest drinking partners. Kalugin found him "downright stupid but relatively harmless."[21] Tsvigun cannot have been wholly reassured by Kaska's briefing. Over the past two years, Kaska told him, about 450,000 CPCz members had left or been expelled, "making contact between the Party and the population more difficult."[22] With one exception, the heads of all directorates in the interior ministry had been replaced. In all, about 3,000 of its employees in the StB and other agencies had been dismissed. There was, however, still widespread evidence of anti-Soviet feeling. Soviet films and plays were systematically boycotted. At the Czechoslovak premiäre of the film *The Kremlin Chimes* there were only five people in the audience; at the second showing there were only ten. There were numerous anonymous threats, malicious rumors and acts of sabotage on the railways. But there were also successes to report. The StB had succeeded in setting up a bogus organization dedicated to "socialism with a human face," in order to smoke out secret supporters of the Prague Spring. Finally, Kaska assured Tsvigun that he and his ministry were in close touch with the KGB liaison office and its head, General Sinitsyn.[23]

In the spring of 1972 Andropov had a private meeting with Kaska. His manner was more assertive than that of Tsvigun a year earlier. He insisted that opposition forces were still strong, despite the "stabilization" in Czechoslovakia and the strengthening of the Communist Party's authority, and that they were being infiltrated by Western intelligence services. Agent penetration of the opposition therefore remained essential.[24] The opposition source to which Andropov attached most importance probably remained Leo Lappi (FREDDI). Still posing as a committed West German supporter of the Prague Spring, the illegal FYODOROV had regular meetings with Lappi in Prague and East Berlin. On January 25, 1972 Fyodor Konstantinovich Mortin, who had succeeded Sakharovsky as head of the FCD, sought Andropov's permission to trick Lappi into becoming a Soviet agent by a "false flag" deception which concealed the role of the KGB. Andropov gave his approval on January 29 and FYODOROV went ahead with the recruitment, claiming to be working for the West German BND. An additional reason for the Centre's interest in Lappi was that his brother Karl was a West German citizen who, according to KGB files, was "close" to two prominent FRG politicians.[25]

Despite Kaska's personal sycophancy towards his KGB advisers and the extensive purge which he had overseen, the Centre remained dissatisfied with the ideological purity of the StB. In August 1972 Andropov reported to the CPSU Central Committee that "internal adversaries" in the StB were striving to prevent the completion of "normalization."[26] A further KGB report to the Central Committee in November cited complaints from its agents and informers within the Czechoslovak Ministry of Internal Affairs that leading posts in the ministry continued to be occupied by "people who do not inspire political confidence."[27] The KGB also received numerous protests from its informants that the disgraced leaders of the Prague Spring and their families were being insufficiently persecuted. Viliam Šalgovič, who had assisted the Soviet invasion in 1968 and had been promoted to the CPCz Central Committee in 1970, complained that the children of "right-wing leaders" were being allowed to enter the universities. Worse still, the children of three disgraced former members of the Presidium—Dubček, Štefan Sádovský and Julius Turček—had been given "excellent marks" in their entrance examinations.[28]

Šalgovič's complaint reflected the self-righteous vengefulness of the Soviet sycophants rather than any failure to purge the universities. In 1969–70 900 out of 3,500 university professors were dismissed. All Czech literary and cultural journals were closed down. Unemployed academics and writers were forced to seek new careers as lavatory cleaners, building laborers and boiler-room stokers. Soon after winning the Nobel Prize for Literature in 1972, Heinrich Böll described Czechoslovakia as "a veritable cultural cemetery."[29]

MANY OF THE reports received by the Centre throughout the period of "normalization" concerned continued covert feuding within the CPCz leadership. In December 1972 Jakeš complained to the KGB liaison office that Husák had ordered the telephones of all Presidium members to be tapped. The working atmosphere within the Central Committee was now, he claimed, so poisonous that the Novotný era appeared, by comparison, a golden age.[30] In February 1973 Jakeš and three other leading Soviet loyalists—Presidium members Karel Hoffmann and Antonín Kapek and party secretary Miloslav Hruškovič—again protested to the KGB about what they claimed were "attempts to squeeze out internationalist Communists from important posts."[31] Among other intrigues within the Party leadership reported by the KGB to Moscow during 1973 was the claim that the realist Prime Minister Štrougal was seeking to ingratiate himself with Husák's internationalist deputy Bil'ak by methods which included giving Bil'ak's daughter a present costing 10,000 crowns, debited to the budget of the Czechoslovak television service.[32]

On February 28, 1973 Kaska was killed in an aircrash while visiting his Polish opposite number and was succeeded as Minister of Internal Affairs by Jaromír Obzina, who promptly gave a sycophantic display of his internationalist credentials. "For the CPSU and for Comrade Brezhnev," he told the KGB liaison, he was "ready to carry out any assignment."[33] Obzina, however, quickly became caught up in Husák's attempts to increase his personal prestige by combining, like Novotný before the Prague Spring, the post of President of the Republic with that of General Secretary of the CPCz. At the end of 1973, probably at Husák's request, Obzina began trying to win over internationalists opposed to his ambitions for the presidency. According to KGB reports from Prague, a group of Soviet loyalists headed by Hoffmann, Indra, Jakeš and Kapek (all in close touch with both the KGB and the Soviet embassy) continued to resist any attempt to combine the two posts.[34] The growing senility of Ludvík Svoboda, who had succeeded Novotný as president in 1968, however, played into Husák's hands. In May 1975 he replaced the by now demented Svoboda as head of state. Rudé právo celebrated the occasion by publishing five large photographs of Husák, each showing him in the company of one of the leaders of the five Warsaw Pact countries who had invaded Czechoslovakia in August 1968.[35]

At the time of Husák's apotheosis, Dubček was working as a mechanic with the Slovak Forestry Commission under constant surveillance and frequent harassment by the StB.[36] On October 2, 1975 the Centre reported to Brezhnev that Dubček had sent compromising material on Husák to the Western media. Based on information supplied by Dubček, the West German and Austrian press had reported that during the war Husak had accompanied a group of Nazi journalists to the Katyn Wood near Smolensk, where the Germans had exhumed the bodies of several thousand Polish officers shot by the NKVD (an atrocity blamed by Moscow on the Germans). Dubček was twice summoned for questioning by the StB at the Slovakian interior ministry. The KGB was deeply dissatisfied by the outcome. "At the interrogation," it informed Brezhnev, "Dubček conducted himself provocatively, categorically refusing to answer questions and declaring that in future he would protest against being subjected to pressure." Dubček refused to sign either a denial that he had provided the information on Husák or a protest at the use of his name by the Western press, and threatened to react "decisively" if "repressive measures" were taken against him. Husák meanwhile wrote to Obzina to protest his innocence of the charges against him.[37]

Despite Husák's success in capturing the presidency, his power was more circumscribed than Novotný's a decade earlier. His second-in-command, the internationalist Bil'ak, enjoyed greater authority and influence than any other deputy in eastern Europe. Having rejected the idea of a regime wholly dominated by notorious hardliners, the Kremlin, with some misgivings, regarded the Husák–Bil'ak combination as the best available. A KGB report from Prague at the end of the decade reported in thinly disguised language that, despite growing friction between Husák and Bil'ak, neither was attempting to topple the other because they knew that Moscow would not allow it:

> Business-like relations between the leaders of Czechoslovakia are being maintained largely because of the fact that Husák Bil'ak and other members of the Presidium of the Czechoslovak Communist Party know that the top leadership of the CPSU gave their full, firm and uncompromising support to Husák and Bil'ak. For both, this is a serious restraining factor for maintaining normal working relations between the two of them, and the situation in the Presidium of the Czechoslovak Communist Party largely depends on their mutual relations.[38]

Despite its jaundiced view of the political leadership, the KGB liaison office in Prague was fully satisfied with the willingness of Obzina and the StB to do its bidding. Obzina, it reported, kept it "objectively informed" both about what took place in the CPCz Presidium and about the activities of each of its members, Husák included.[39] Sinitsyn reported in 1977 that there were "operational contacts" between KGB and StB residencies in twenty-six countries.[40] In 1975 the StB had agreed to a Soviet request to open a residency in Albania, a country which the KGB found hard to penetrate.[41] In 1976, when the StB discovered that Jozef Grohman, editor-in-chief of the state technical literature publishing house and the Czechoslovak representative at UNESCO, was working for West German intelligence, Obzina invited the Centre to send KGB officers to Prague to help in the investigation of the Grohman case at what he deferentially termed "a higher professional level."[42] Sinitsyn concluded his annual report from Prague in 1977:

Our friends hand over to us all their cipher traffic with the residencies, whether it is of an information nature or operational; they also hand over telegrams from ambassadors. Our friends keep practically no secrets from us.[43]

The crushing of the Prague Spring and the "normalization" which followed marked a turning point in the KGB's policy towards eastern Europe. The PROGRESS operations by illegals pioneered in Czechoslovakia were extended to the rest of eastern Europe to monitor the state of public opinion, penetrate subversive groups and watch for signs of "ideological sabotage" by Western intelligence agencies. From 1969 onwards the KGB was also allowed to recruit agents and confidential contacts throughout the Soviet Bloc. In addition to the KGB liaison offices in the countries of the Warsaw Pact, the Centre now established, as in Czechoslovakia, secret residencies operating under diplomatic cover in Soviet embassies.[44]

In March 1968, partly as a result of the Prague Spring, there had been several weeks of confrontation between Warsaw students and the police, during which the aging Polish leader Władisław Gomułka had seemed in danger of losing control. Gomułka survived in the short term only because of his steadfast backing for intervention in Czechoslovakia and the Kremlin's desire to avoid simultaneous upheavals in another part of the Soviet Bloc. His position, however, was already under threat from his eventual successor, Eduard Gierek. According to reports from the KGB liaison office in Warsaw, the hardline, anti-Semitic minister of the interior, Mieczysław Moczar, who was responsible for the SB (the Polish KGB), feared that his own position would also be threatened under Gierek and began plotting to prevent his succession. Compromising material on Gierek was passed, on Moczar's instructions, to Radio Free Europe via an SB agent. Moczar also ordered the bugging of a series of leading figures in the PUWP, the Polish Communist Party.[45]

Late in 1970 Gomulka's position was fatally undermined by a new round of public protest. On December 14 workers at the Baltic shipyards of Gdańsk, Gdynia and Szczecin struck in protest at a sudden rise in food prices. Clashes next day with security forces left 300 strikers and demonstrators dead.[46] According to KGB reports from Warsaw, the order to open fire on the shipyard workers was given by Zenon Kliszko, Gomułka's closest supporter on the Politburo, and General Grzegorz Korczyński, deputy defense minister and a supporter of Gierek.[47] The KGB also forwarded to Moscow the minutes of the Polish Politburo meeting held to discuss the crisis on December 19. With Gomułka in a Party clinic suffering from nervous exhaustion, the meeting was chaired by the prime minister, Józef Cyrankiewicz, who asked the Minister of Defense, General Wojciech Jaruzelski, to report on the situation.

Jaruzelski's assessment sealed Gomułka's fate. He reported that 350 tanks and 600 troop carriers had been deployed in Gdańsk and Gdynia alone. If unrest on a similar scale occurred in Warsaw, he could not guarantee the security of the capital, though special measures would be taken to protect Party and government buildings. Army morale was seriously affected. On the Baltic coast it was being met with shouts of "Gestapo!" and "Murderers!" Jaruzelski was followed by Moczar, who summarized SB and other reports reaching the interior ministry. The Party, he said, has never found itself so helpless in the face of a crisis. Hitherto, even when times were hardest, Party members had felt they were fighting for "a righteous cause"—but no longer. In Party meetings, when the Politburo letter justifying the price increases was read out, some Communists were reduced to tears and left the room. The rise in family allowances from 15 to 25 zlotys caused derision among rank and file members, stunned by the leadership's incomprehension of ordinary living conditions. After an agitated debate it was agreed that Gomułka should be replaced as first secretary by Gierek. There was then an acrimonious discussion about who should tell Gomułka to submit his resignation, before it was finally decided to send Cyrankiewicz and the hitherto faithful Kliszko.[48]

Gomułka's downfall marked the first occasion anywhere in Europe since the Second World War when spontaneous working-class protest had brought about a change of political leadership.[49] The Centre was predictably alarmed at the extent and success of the popular revolt and immediately embarked on a PROGRESS operation to assess how far it had been contained. A group of illegals, posing once again as Western visitors, were instructed to investigate the role of the Catholic Church in organizing protest, its attitude towards the Gierek regime and the general mood of the population.[50] Among the illegals was the experienced Gennadi Blyablin (BOGUN), disguised as a West German press photographer, who was given a list of five individuals to cultivate and told to persuade two or three of them to "co-operate under false flag," in the belief that they were supplying information not to the KGB but to West German wellwishers. Probably the most important name on the list was that of Father Andrzej Bardecki, personal assistant to Cardinal Archbishop Karol Wojtyła of Kraków, whom the Centre considered the leading ideological influence on the Polish Church. The KGB doubtless did not foresee that less than eight years later Wojtyła would become the first Polish pope, but it showed some foresight in identifying him as a potential threat to the Communist regime.[51]

DURING 1971, IN addition to the illegals sent on PROGRESS operations to Czechoslovakia and Poland, thirteen were deployed in Romania, nine in Yugoslavia, seven in East Germany, four in Hungary and three in Bulgaria.[52] Though all had broadly similar objectives, there were also specific causes of KGB concern in each country.[53] The priority given to Romania in 1971 reflected growing Soviet displeasure at the foreign policy of its leader, Nicolae Ceauşescu, who combined a nepotistic version of neo-Stalinism at home with increasing independence from the Warsaw Pact abroad. After condemning the invasion of Czechoslovakia, Ceauşescu was rewarded in the following year by a state visit from Richard Nixon, the first by an American president to Communist eastern Europe. In 1970 Ceauşescu paid the first of three visits to the United States. Moscow showed its displeasure at his visit to Beijing in 1971 by staging Warsaw Pact maneuvers on the Romanian borders.[54]

KGB reports on Romania were written in a tone which combined indignation with deep suspicion:

Exploiting the anti-Soviet line of the Chinese Communist Party and of the Chinese government, the Romanian leadership has set out on the path of so-called autonomy and independence from the Soviet Union . . . Nationalism is flourishing in Romania. Its authors and advocates are the very same Party and government leaders.

The Romanian Communist Party leadership does not openly reveal its territorial claims; but it does everything to demonstrate that historically, ethnically and in other ways Moldavia and the Chernovitsy Oblast belong to Romania. The statement made by Mao in conversation with Japanese socialists about the USSR's illegal acquisition of Bessarabia [Moldavia] has been developed in Romania.

The French newspaper *Le Monde* has twice published articles casting doubt on the legality of Bessarabia's inclusion in the [Soviet] Union. It is not impossible that the initiative for publishing the articles came from Romania.[55]

The illegals sent to Romania under Western disguise in 1971 were ordered to collect intelligence on Romanian relations with the United States and China; Romanian claims on Soviet territory in Bessarabia and north Bukovina; the political and economic basis of opposition to the Soviet Union; the position of German and Hungarian minorities; the Ceauşescu cult; and the state of the Romanian Communist Party.[56] The illegals' main sources included staff of the Party newspaper *Scintea* and the German language *Volk und Kultur*.[57]

PROGRESS OPERATIONS IN Yugoslavia during 1971 were prompted chiefly by the most serious internal crisis since Tito's break with Moscow in 1948. The dramatic resurgence of nationalist tensions during the Croat Spring of 1971 culminated at the end of the year with Tito's arrest of the Croat Communist leaders and 400 Croat nationalists and in his resumption of direct control over the Croat secret police. The claim that Yugoslav socialism was resolving ethnic rivalries was exposed as an illusion.[58] The illegals were given a long list of institutions in which they were instructed to "strike up acquaintances:" the Academy of Sciences, the Public Opinion Institute in Belgrade, the editorial offices of *Kommunist*, *Politika* and *Borba*, the Tanjug Agency, the Institute for International Politics and Economics at Belgrade University, Zagreb University, Yugoslav businesses and the Union of Journalists (in particular, the writer Dobrica Ćosić, who was believed to be close to Tito). Some of the reports sent back to the Centre by illegal courier, radio and the post were judged sufficiently important to be forwarded to Brezhnev.[59]

BY FAR THE largest KGB presence in eastern Europe was in East Germany. Ever since the Second World War there had been a large KGB enclave within the headquarters of the Soviet military administration in the Berlin suburb of Karlshorst. During the period which preceded the establishment of the GDR it had closely monitored political parties, churches, trade unions and public opinion within the Soviet zone of Germany. Though the KGB claimed after the foundation of the GDR that the role of its Karlshorst base was to mount operations against the FRG and other Western countries, as well as to provide liaison with the Stasi, it also continued to monitor developments within East Germany.[60] In 1971 the intelligence personnel stationed at Karlshorst, not including liaison officers, totaled 404, of whom forty-eight were operations officers working under cover. Another forty-seven KGB operations officers were stationed elsewhere in the GDR.[61]

The advent of Willy Brandt's socialist–liberal coalition in West Germany in 1969 offered opportunities for détente which Moscow was more anxious to pursue than Walter Ulbricht, the aging and inflexible neo-Stalinist leader of East Germany. KGB reports from Karlshorst complained that, after the invasion of Czechoslovakia, Ulbricht was posing as the wisest and most far-sighted statesman of the Soviet Bloc, implying (probably correctly) that he had been quicker than Brezhnev to identify the subversive nature of the Dubček regime.[62] Ulbricht's refusal to abandon his commitment to a united "socialist" Germany made him unwilling to consider an agreement with Brandt involving, for the first time, mutual recognition by the FRG and the GDR.[63]

By 1969, if not before, both Willi Stoph, the East German prime minister, and Erich Honecker, who had overseen the building of the Berlin Wall, were fueling Moscow's growing irritation with Ulbricht at meetings with the KGB and the Soviet ambassador, Pyotr Andreyevich Abrasimov. Ulbricht, they reported, had described Soviet cut-price imports of East German uranium as "the plundering of the GDR's natural resources." When Abrasimov suggested that allowance needed to be made for Ulbricht's age (he was seventy-six in 1969), Stoph and Honecker retorted that he should have resigned when he was seventy.[64] In 1971 Ulbricht was kicked upstairs to the newly created post of Party chairman, and succeeded as Party leader by Honecker. In the following year the GDR and FRG formally recognized each other's existence as separate states.

Though bickering continued within the Party leadership, the KGB's main concern was "the impact of the adversary's ideology on citizens of the GDR" through Western broadcasts and visits by West Germans. The Centre calculated in the mid-1970s that "500,000 citizens are hostile to the existing system and the [Western] adversary will for a long time retain a base of support in the GDR."[65] A long-running KGB operation, codenamed LUCH, monitored opinion within the East German population and Party, contacts between East and West Germans and alleged "attempts by the USA and the FRG to harm the building of socialism" in the GDR. In 1974 the section of the Karlshorst KGB responsible for LUCH was raised in status to a directorate.[66]

The majority of the Centre's intelligence on East Germany, however, came from the Stasi, whose network of internal informers was vastly greater than the KGB's. The GDR had seven times as many informers per head of population as Nazi Germany.[67] In 1975 65 percent of all reports from Soviet Bloc security services received by the Centre came from the Stasi.[68] Some of the reports were, in effect, classified East German opinion polls. In an opinion survey of factory workers in 1974, for example, 20.6 percent of those questioned "considered that friendship with the

USSR restricted the GDR's autonomy and brought more benefit to the Soviet Union than to the GDR." A majority, when asked to explain the phrase "achieving working-class power," claimed not to know what it meant. Some of the comments on the phrase, however, were described in the report forwarded to the Centre as "bitter, wounding and vicious." Among them were "Working-class power is all right [in theory], but what is it like in practice?"; "This is just a slogan!"; and "Justice for every worker, not just for a newly created privileged group!" Given the inevitable caution of those questioned in expressing politically incorrect views, the real level of dissatisfaction was probably considerably higher. Both the size of the KGB's Karlshorst base and the volume of intelligence from the Stasi made the Centre less dependent on PROGRESS operations by illegals for intelligence from East Germany than from the rest of eastern Europe.[69]

THE KGB'S MAIN concern in Hungary was the extent of Jewish influence within the Party and the AVH (the Hungarian KGB). Always prone to Zionist and anti-Semitic conspiracy theories, the Centre was deeply disturbed by Hungarian reluctance to agree in 1969 to its suggestion for holding "an anti-Zionist conference in Budapest of progressive Jews opposed to the policy of Israel" or for assisting the KGB in making an anti-Zionist film alleging cooperation between Hitler and Hungarian Zionists. "The Hungarian security agencies," the Centre concluded, "were forced to look over their shoulder when working on the [anti-]Zionist line, as Jewish nationalists within the leadership of the highest Party organs were morbidly cautious with regard to this sector of work." The KGB also looked askance at the number of Jews within the Hungarian interior ministry, among them—it reported—two deputy ministers, the heads of the AVH First and Third Directorates (responsible, respectively, for foreign intelligence and the surveillance of domestic political opposition), the head of the police directorate and the head of military counter-intelligence. The situation was worst of all in foreign intelligence, where, according to KGB calculations, thirteen of the seventeen department chiefs were Jewish.[70]

The illegals sent to Hungary on PROGRESS operations in 1971 posing as Western visitors were sent primarily to investigate the extent of Zionist influence. They were instructed to report on attitudes to Israel and its trade and economic relations with Hungary, "the links of Hungarian organizations and individuals with Zionist circles" and the situation in the Writers' Union and other "creative unions" (where Jewish influence was also believed to be strong). The illegals were also told to "identify anti-Semitic attitudes," presumably in the hope that they would discover popular opposition to the number of Hungarian Jews in high places. According to an alarmist Centre assessment, "Pro-Zionist domination was entrenched in Party, state and public organizations."[71]

DURING 1972 PROGRESS operations were extended to areas of nationalist unrest within the Soviet Union. On October 4, 1972 KGB Directive No. 150/3-10807 instructed the FCD Illegals Directorate to investigate the mood of the population and the activities of Western tourists in the Baltic republics. The Centre's analysis of the reports received from ARTYOM, FYODOROV, SEVIDOV and VLAS was uniformly depressing. Posing as Western visitors, all four illegals noted inefficient administration; an apathetic workforce "just sitting out the appointed [working] hours, with no pride in their profession;" intolerance between ethnic groups; and widespread drunkenness. The population of the Baltic republics were, however, "well informed about events in the West and in the Soviet Union." Letters were taken to the West by foreign tourists, frequently written by people anxious to enter into marriages of convenience with Westerners to provide pretexts for emigration: "Many people of either sex marry ethnic Jews, although they themselves are not Jews; their only aim is to leave the USSR." As frequently occurred with analyses of internal dissidence, the main scapegoats were the Jews. Because they were "conscious of the moral support of Israel and the USA and other Western countries," they were alleged to be even more idle than the rest of the population—admitting to the illegals that "We work just enough to avoid being sacked."[72]

ALL OVER EASTERN Europe the illegals appear to have given franker, and therefore more depressing, assessments of public attitudes than the KGB liaison offices and residencies, who were under pressure to produce flattering accounts of local reaction to dreary set-piece speeches by Soviet leaders. Even in Bulgaria most of the population had lost their traditional sense of Slav kinship with Soviet Russia. According to one report:

> Anti-Sovietism flourishes on Bulgarian television. Though not openly expressed . . . it finds a fertile breeding ground. The so-called "spots," featuring Soviet films about the Soviet Union and Soviet life, cause the population to switch off their television sets.[73]

When the illegal TANOV was sent on a two-month PROGRESS mission to Bulgaria in 1974, posing as a Western journalist preparing travel brochures, he was advised by the Centre to win the confidence of the Bulgarians he talked to by giving them presents. Everywhere he went he found resentment at the low standard of living and the well-founded conviction that Bulgaria was being pressurized by the Soviet Union to squander resources on Cuba and other profligate foreign friends, as well as on a huge police and state security system. From the Centre's viewpoint, the only silver lining in TANOV's bleak report was that Bulgarians were too afraid of the DS, their security service, to grumble publicly.[74]

PROBABLY THE MOST depressing intelligence on the Soviet Bloc to reach the Centre during the 1970s came from Czechoslovakia. An illegal reported after a PROGRESS mission in 1976:

> The population of the country hates the Russians. The Czechs cannot even make an objective judgment of the skills of Soviet artists performing on tour in Czechoslovakia. The following is a typical comment: "It may be that the artists

are performing well professionally, but because they are Russians I can't bear to watch them."[75]

Lines in plays which were capable of being interpreted as "negative allusions" to the Soviet Union, such as "Love for the enemy is not love" in Gorin's *Till Eulenspiegel*, were liable to provoke storms of applause from the audience.[76]

In view of the popular rejoicings after the Czechoslovak defeat of the Russian team in the 1969 World Ice Hockey Championships in Stockholm, there was considerable anxiety before the 1979 world championships which were held in Prague. A special commission headed by one of the leading internationalists on the CPCz Presidium, Antonín Kapek, tried to ensure good crowd behavior by introducing a variety of security measures, arranging for ticket allocations to Party organizations and conducting what was called "educational work" among both players and spectators. Most of its efforts proved in vain.

Throughout the championships, which opened at the end of April, Brezhnev received regular reports from both the KGB and the Soviet embassy in Prague. They made dismal reading. Irrespective of who the Russian team was playing, the Czechoslovak spectators cheered the other side and shouted anti-Soviet insults. The United States, Canadian and West German teams, by contrast, all received a warm reception. The KGB reported that the Soviet defeat of the Czechoslovak team was "greeted coldly" even by Štrougal and other ministers in the government box. After the match senior CPCz officials avoided members of the Soviet embassy.

The KGB did, however, succeed in preventing one potentially acute embarrassment. After the Soviet match against East Germany, a Russian player who had taken proscribed stimulants was summoned to a drug test. Had he failed the test, as no doubt he would have done, the Soviet victory might have been annulled. The KGB reported proudly to Brezhnev that, "as a result of measures taken by the [Prague] residency," the player concerned was let off the drug test.[77]

KGB reports from Prague complained that, after the Soviet team won the world championship, the medal ceremony was conducted in English and German with no Russian translation. At the gala reception which followed, the Russians were coldshouldered. The Soviet flag was ripped from the team. Even the CPCz newspaper *Rudé právo* paid more attention to the Canadian, Swedish and Finnish teams than to the Soviet world champions.[78]

The KGB was also outraged at the sometimes visible lack of enthusiasm displayed by Czechoslovak representatives at tedious official celebrations in the Soviet Union. The Centre wrote a damning report on the behavior of Miroslav Vasek, head of a delegation from the Czechoslovak ministry of culture at the Ninth Conference of Ministers of Culture of the Socialist Countries, held in Moscow in July 1978. At the end of this doubtless mind-numbing occasion, Vasek had had the impertinence to leave behind in his room at the Hotel Mir both the souvenir conference folder and a series of probably unreadable volumes solemnly presented to him by the Soviet ministry of culture: *Lenin: Revolution and Art*, *Brezhnev: A Brief Biography*, *Sixty Jubilee Years: Facts and Figures about the Achievements of Culture and Art in the Soviet Union* and

Protection of Historical and Cultural Monuments in the USSR. The KGB report insisted that these valuable items had been deliberately "abandoned, not simply forgotten." The Centre was not prepared for this outrage to be passed over. A full report on it was sent both to Andropov and to the KGB liaison office in Prague.[79]

For all the KGB's dissatisfaction with the state of Czechoslovak public opinion and the fractious leadership of the CPCz, the Communist one-party state in Czechoslovakia was under no visible threat at the end of the 1970s. At the beginning of 1977 a series of small dissident groups came together in "Charter 77," which described itself as "a free, informal, open community of people of different convictions, different faiths and different professions, united by the will to strive, individually and collectively, for the respect of civil and human rights." Within six months, over 750 courageous individuals had signed the Charter. All endured public vilification and persecution, ranging from attacks on the street to prison sentences and incarceration in psychiatric hospitals. One of the founders, the philosopher Jan Patocka, died after a brutal interrogation by the StB. The power of the StB, the sense of powerlessness induced in the mass of the population by the process of "normalization" and the presence of Soviet troops robbed Charter 77 of any chance of recapturing the mass enthusiasm generated by the promise nine years earlier of "socialism with a human face."[80]

Throughout the Soviet Bloc the KGB's east European clones, urged on by the Centre, were among the moving forces during the decade which followed the Prague Spring in the creation of an intellectually monotone and moribund society. Václav Havel, one of the founders of Charter 77 (and later the first president of the post-Communist Czech Republic), wrote later of this period:

> I remember the first half of the 1970s in Czechoslovakia as the time when "history stopped" . . . History has been replaced by pseudo-history, with its calendar of regularly returning official anniversaries, Party congresses, festivities and mass sport meetings . . . Totalitarian power has brought "order" in the organic "disorder" of history, thereby numbing it as history. The government, as it were, nationalized time. Hence, time meets with the sad fate of so many other nationalized things: it has begun to wither away.[81]

The clock which had stopped in eastern Europe with the suppression of the Prague Spring in 1968 was to start again ten years later with the election of a Polish pope.

SEVENTEEN

THE KGB AND WESTERN
COMMUNIST PARTIES

The KGB and Western Communist Parties Throughout the Cold War, Communist parties around the world dismissed claims that they were involved in Soviet espionage as crude McCarthyite slander. KGB files, however, give the lie to most of their denials. From the 1920s onwards Western Communists were regularly asked for help in intelligence operations, which they usually considered their fraternal duty to provide. Most leaders of even the largest Western parties equally considered it the fraternal duty of the Communist Party of the Soviet Union (CPSU) to provide, via the KGB, annual subsidies whose existence they indignantly denied. Knowledge of the KGB connection in the fields of both espionage and finance was the preserve of small and secretive inner circles within each Party leadership.

In the immediate aftermath of the Second World War, the most active assistance in Soviet agent recruitment came from four Communist Parties which were briefly included in coalition governments: the French Parti Communiste Français (PCF), the Italian Partito Comunista Italiano (PCI), the Austrian Kommunistische Partei Österreichs (KPÖ) and the Finnish Suomen Kommunistinen Puolue (SKP).

AS SHOWN IN chapter 9, the PCF assisted after the Liberation in a major penetration of the French intelligence community which continued for at least a quarter of a century. From July 1, 1946 to June 30, 1947 the Paris residency forwarded to the Centre a total of 1,289 French intelligence documents.[1] By the early 1950s the KGB's chief collaborator inside the PCF was Gaston Plissonnier (codenamed LANG), a life-long Soviet loyalist who had established himself by 1970 as second-in-command to the Party leader.[2] Though little known to the French public and a poor public speaker with a thick regional accent, Plissonnier was a master in the arcane procedures of "democratic centralism" by which the Party leadership imposed its policies on its members.[3] As well as providing inside information on the PCF, he assisted the KGB in identifying potential agents and other intelligence operations.[4] During the later 1970s Plissonnier also passed on reports from an agent in the entourage of President Boumedienne of Algeria.[5]

IN ITALY, AS in France, Communist ministers sat in post-war coalition governments until the spring of 1947. At the end of 1945 the PCI had 1,760,000 members—twice as many as the PCF. All over Italy, photographs of Stalin, affectionately known as *Baffone* ("Walrus moustache"), were pasted on factory walls and stuck to machinery. "We were all under the impression," one of the Communist ministers, Fausto Gallo, later acknowledged, "that the wind was blowing our way."[6] Washington feared that Gallo and his colleagues might be right. The National Security Council concluded in November 1947, "The Italian Government, ideologically inclined towards Western democracy, is weak and is being subjected to continuous attack by a strong Communist Party." The very first CIA covert action was an operation to aid the Christian Democrats against the Communists in the 1948 general election by laundering over 10 million dollars from captured Axis funds for use in the campaign.[7]

As in France, the post-war popularity of the Communist Party and the brief period of Communist participation in government created the best opportunities Soviet intelligence was ever to enjoy in Italy for agent penetration. Like JOUR, probably the most important of the post-war French recruits, DARIO, the longest-serving and probably the most valuable Italian agent, was a foreign ministry employee. Born in 1908, and trained as a lawyer, DARIO worked as a journalist and state official in agriculture during the early years of fascist Italy. In 1932 he was recruited as a Soviet agent on an "ideological basis" but, on instructions from his controller, pretended to be a supporter of Mussolini and in 1937 succeeded in enrolling in the Fascist Party. Before the outbreak of war he obtained a job in the foreign ministry, ironically dealing with Soviet and Comintern affairs and succeeded in recruiting three foreign ministry typists (codenamed DARYA, ANNA and MARTA) who regularly supplied him with what the Centre considered "valuable" classified documents. For almost forty years DARIO was instrumental in obtaining a phenomenal amount of classified foreign ministry material.[8] His remarkable career as a Soviet agent, however, was temporarily interrupted during the war. In 1942, following the discovery by the Italian police of an illegal GRU residency with which DARIO was in contact, he was arrested and imprisoned, surviving a period at the end of the war in a German concentration camp from which he was liberated by the Red Army.[9]

Once back in Italy, DARIO reestablished contact with DARYA and MARTA, both of whom agreed once again to give him foreign ministry documents. Probably on Soviet instructions, instead of joining the PCI he became a member of the Italian Socialist Party led by Pietro Nenni, but was expelled in 1946 after he was denounced as a former fascist and threatened with prosecution. At the request of the Rome residency, the Communist leader, Palmiro Togliatti, secretly interceded with Nenni and DARIO was given back his Socialist Party membership. Togliatti's intervention, however, leaked out and DARIO was publicly identified as having links with the Soviet embassy. He succeeded, none the less, in recruiting two more foreign ministry typists: TOPO (later renamed LEDA), who for fifteen years provided what the Centre considered "valuable documents," and NIKOL (later INGA), who also supplied "consistently valuable" information. Probably soon after her recruitment under a false flag (not identified in Mitrokhin's notes), TOPO and DARIO were married.[10] In March 1975, forty-three years after DARIO's recruitment, he and his wife were awarded the Order of the Red Star. He finally retired in May 1979 after one of the longest careers as a Soviet agent in the history of the FCD.[11]

In the immediate aftermath of the Second World War the Rome residency also achieved a highly successful penetration of the interior ministry, thanks chiefly to a Communist civil servant, codenamed DEMID, who acted as agent-recruiter. On instructions from the residency, DEMID left the Communist Party immediately after his recruitment in 1944. His first major cultivation inside the ministry was QUESTOR, whom he helped to obtain a job in the cipher department. By 1955 the penetration of the Italian interior ministry, begun by DEMID, was considered so important that control of it was handed over to a newly established illegal residency in Rome, headed by Ashot Abgarovch Akopyan, a 40-year-old Armenian from Baku codenamed YEFRAT.[12]

THE THIRD STATE in which Soviet agent penetration was assisted by Communist participation in post-war coalition governments was Austria. Though placed under joint occupation until 1955 by the Soviet Union, United States, Britain and France (a cumbersome arrangement likened by Karl Renner, the first post-war chancellor, to "four elephants in a rowing boat"), Austria—unlike Germany—was allowed to govern itself. In Renner's provisional government, formed in April 1945, the Communists were given three ministries, including the key post of Minister of the Interior taken by Franz Honner. In the November 1945 elections, however, the Austrian Communist Party (KPÖ), which had expected to do as well as the French PCF, picked up a mere 5 percent of the vote and was given only the comparatively unimportant ministry of electrification in the new coalition. The KPÖ left government altogether two years later, and its two half-hearted attempts to stage a *coup d'état* in 1947 and 1950 failed to gain serious Soviet support.[13]

Franz Honner used his seven months in 1945 to pack the Austrian federal police force (Bundespolizei) with Communist Party members. Though many were purged or sidelined by Honner's socialist successor, Oskar Helmer,[14] Soviet penetration of the Austrian police, especially its security service (Staatspolizei or Stapo), continued until the 1980s. In an attempt to evade Helmer's purge, Communists in the police force were instructed to disavow or conceal their Party membership.[15] The files noted by Mitrokhin record the recruitment of a series of major KGB police agents: EDUARD in 1945,[16] VENTSEYEV in 1946,[17] PETER in 1952,[18] two further recruits in 1955, ZAK in 1974[19] and NADEZHDIN in 1978.[20] There may well have been others; Mitrokhin's list is probably not exhaustive. At least some of them took part in operations (one of them codenamed EDELWEISS) to remove and copy top secret documents held in the safe of the head of the Stapo. In 1973 Andropov personally authorized the payment to one of its Stapo agents of a reward of 30,000 Austrian schillings.[21]

IN THREE OF the four countries of Scandinavia—Denmark, Norway and Finland—Communist ministers also served in post-war coalitions. By far the most influential of the Scandinavian Communist parties was the Finnish SKP.[22] Alone among Germany's eastern allies, Finland was not forced to become part of the Soviet Bloc. At the end of the Second World War, however, Stalin still kept his options open. In 1945, at Soviet insistence, the SKP was given several key positions within the Finnish government, secretly instructed via a "special channel" on their relations with "bourgeois parties," and held in readiness for a possible *coup d'état*. That Finland was not in the end forced to become a people's democracy was probably due chiefly to memories of the Winter War in 1939–40, when the greatly outnumbered Finns had inflicted heavy casualties on the Soviet invaders. Stalin was well aware that the price of Finnish incorporation in the Soviet Bloc might be another blood bath.[23] Finland was, however, deprived of 12 percent of its territory, forced to pay enormous reparations (five times those of Italy) and required to sign a non-aggression pact in 1948.

In Finland, as in Austria, the Communists succeeded in 1945 in claiming the key post of minister of the interior. But whereas the Austrian Communist Franz Honner left office after only seven months, his Finnish counterpart, Yrjî Leino, continued in power for three years. Leino's aim, like Honner's, was "to deprive the bourgeoisie of one of its most important weapons in supporting reactionary policies, the police force." By the end of 1945 the security police had been purged and reconstituted as a new force, usually known as Valpo. As Leino later acknowledged, "the new recruits were naturally, as far as possible, Communists."[24] The rapidity of the purges and the inexperience of the new recruits, however, led to a good deal of confusion. According to Leino, "Valpo in SKP hands never became the kind of weapon that had been hoped for . . . They did not have the skill to use it to advantage in the right way." Leino himself found it increasingly difficult to cope. By 1947 he was drinking heavily and sometimes absent from his office for days on end. At the end of the year he was summoned to Moscow, given a severe dressing down by two senior members of the Politburo, instructed to resign from the Finnish government and told to go for a health cure in the Soviet Union. Though Leino refused to tender his resignation, he was dismissed by President Paasikivi in April 1948 on the grounds that he no longer enjoyed the confidence of Parliament. His dismissal brought to an end Communist participation in the Finnish government.[25] Leino's memoirs, completed ten years later, caused such embarrassment in Moscow that, at the insistence of the Soviet ambassador in Helsinki, the whole edition was destroyed on the eve of publication, leaving only a few copies in private circulation.[26]

THE REMOVAL FROM power by 1948 of all those Western Communist parties which had taken part in post-war coalitions reduced, but did not end, their ability to assist Soviet intelligence penetration of government bureaucracies. By far the biggest disappointment experienced by the Centre at the beginning of the Cold War in its relations with fraternal parties in the West, however, was the dramatic decline in the assistance offered by the Communist Party of the United States (CPUSA). From the mid-1930s to the onset of the Cold War, Communism had been a major force in the American labor movement, a significant influence on the liberal wing of the Democratic Party and a rite of passage for several hundred thousand young radicals. During the Second World War the Party had played an important part in assisting Soviet penetration of the Roosevelt administration, the MANHATTAN project and the intelligence community.[27] The onset of the Cold War, however, dealt the CPUSA a blow from which it never fully recovered.

In 1949 Gene Dennis, the general secretary, and ten other Party leaders were put on trial for advocating the forcible overthrow of the federal government. Dennis and nine of the defendants were sentenced to five years in jail, the eleventh was jailed for three years and all the defense attorneys were found in contempt of court. After the Supreme Court upheld the sentences in 1951, more than a hundred other leading Communists were convicted on similar charges. For most of the 1950s the Party was forced into a largely underground existence. It was deeply ironic that when McCarthyism was at its height the CPUSA was among those Western parties which were least able to give assistance to Soviet espionage. Not till the Supreme Court backed away from its earlier decision in 1957 was the CPUSA able to regroup. By the time the Party had drawn up a new membership list in 1958, there were only 3,000 open members and a much smaller number of undeclared members left.[28]

What the CPUSA might have achieved during the 1950s had it been less perse-cuted was well illustrated by the neighboring Canadian Party, which in 1951–3 assisted the Ottawa residency in the recruitment of Hugh Hambleton, probably the most important Canadian agent of the Cold War, and ten other agents.[29] Like most other Western parties, the Canadian Communist Party also provided help in docu-menting illegals—among them Konon Trofimovich Molody (codenamed BEN), the most celebrated of the Cold War illegal residents in Britain.[30] In 1957, with the help of the Canadian Communist Party, the Ottawa residency succeeded in obtaining a new passport for the illegal resident in the United States, "Willie" Fisher (better known as "Rudolf Abel") in the name of Robert Callan, born on March 10, 1903 in Fort William, Ontario. "Abel," however, was arrested before he could adopt his new identity. The Ottawa residency was subsequently fearful that the clerk who issued the passport might recognize the photograph of "Abel" published in the press after his arrest in June 1957 as that of "Robert Callan." Unsurprisingly, the clerk, who doubt-less saw—and paid little attention to—many photographs a day, seems not to have noticed.[31]

One of the rare cases in which the assistance given by Western Communists in fabricating the legend of a Soviet illegal became public was that of Reino Hayhanen (codenamed VIK), who was helped to adopt the identity of the Finn Eugene Maki by the Finnish Communist Olavi Åhman (codenamed VIRTANEN). When Hay-hanen defected to the FBI in 1957, Åhman and his wife were secretly taken into hid-ing in the Soviet Union. For almost twenty years Åhman pleaded to go back to Finland, but the Finnish Communist Party insisted that he stay in Russia for fear that his return would expose it to "anti-Communist propaganda." In 1975 the Party leader, Ville Pessi (codenamed BARANOV), finally relented. Åhman was allowed back home and awarded a KGB pension of 200 roubles a month.[32]

A number of Western Communist parties were also asked to provide various kinds of assistance to KGB illegals. In 1957 a group of undeclared members of the French Communist Party, recommended by the PCF leadership, began training as radio operators for illegal residencies. Initially the new recruits found difficulty in transcribing the coded number groups broadcast in test transmissions from the Centre. By the end of the year, however, some had successfully completed their training course.[33]

The files seen by Mitrokhin give no sense that the Centre's demands on the fraternal assistance of Western Communist parties declined in the course of the Cold War. On the contrary, the KGB's solicitations of its "friends" appear to have been greater during the 1970s than in the previous decade. The increased deployment of experienced illegals in eastern Europe after the Prague Spring and the difficulty experienced by the FCD in finding enough suitably qualified and well-motivated Soviet replacements led it to seek renewed inspiration from the era of the Great Illegals, some of the greatest of whom—the Austrian Arnold Deutsch and the German Richard Sorge chief among them—had been Communists from other European countries. Deutsch's career, however, still remained top secret, not least because two of his most important recruits, Anthony Blunt and John Cairncross, were still at liberty in the West. Sorge, by contrast, was the best-publicized member of the Soviet intelligence pantheon. he had been posthumously declared Hero of the Soviet Union in 1964 and further honored by the first postage stamps ever issued to commemorate a spy. Sorge's reputation as a romantic heart-throb added to his popular appeal. His was the example chosen by the Centre to inspire a new generation of non-Soviet KGB illegals.[34]

The recruitment campaign began on the eve of the Twenty-fourth Congress of the Soviet Communist Party (CPSU) in April 1971. The FCD took advantage of the presence in Moscow of a large number of leaders of fraternal parties in the West to ask some of them to search out a new generation of Sorges. The files noted by Mitrokhin record meetings between senior FCD officers and six different Western Communist leaders to discuss the recruitment of illegals. There may well have been many more such approaches.

Shortly before the Party congress opened, the former resident in Copenhagen, Leonid Sergeyevich Zaitsev, met Knud Jespersen, the chairman of the Danish Communist Party, at the Sovetskaya Hotel, and asked him to find "two or three" totally reliable, dedicated Communists, loyal to the Soviet Union, who could be trained to become "Danish Richard Sorges." They should be male, between twenty and forty years of age, and preferably undeclared rather than open Party members. If married, their wives would have to meet the same conditions. Potential Danish Sorges would also need to be well educated and in a suitable occupation—such as journalist, businessman or foreign language student. According to Zaitsev, Jespersen responded enthusiastically, saying that he fully understood both the importance and the secrecy of the request, and already had one candidate in mind, whose details he would send to the current resident in Copenhagen, Anatoli Aleksandrovich Danilov.[35]

Meanwhile at the Ukraina Hotel, I. P. Kisliak, a former operations officer at the Athens residency, was asking Kostas Koliannis, first secretary of the Greek Communist Party, to find "one or two" Greek Richard Sorges. Like Zaitsev, Kisliak emphasized that candidates must be "totally reliable ideologically," but added that they also needed "charm."[36] At a subsequent meeting with Ezekias Papaioannou, general secretary of AKEL (the Cyprus Communist Party), Kisliak was slightly less demanding. Though Cypriot candidates would require high moral, political and professional qualities, they need not necessarily be "the equals of Richard Sorge."[37]

While Zaitsev and Kisliak were approaching the heads of the Danish, Greek and Cypriot Parties, Anatoli Ivanovich Lazarev, head of the FCD Illegals Directorate, was engaged in talks with Gaston Plissonnier, the second-in-command of the French Communist Party. Plissonier agreed to select two or three undeclared members of the PCF with the potential to become French Sorges and later suggested two possible candidates. He was also asked to supply the KGB with the names of poorly paid (and, by implication, corruptible) staff in the French foreign ministry whose work included photocopying classified documents.[38]

One of the FCD's approaches to a leading member of a fraternal delegation to the Twenty-fourth Party Congress took place in hospital. Geinrich Fritz of the Austrian Communist Party (KPô) Central Committee suffered an acute attack of sciatica shortly before the congress opened and was taken for treatment to the CPSU Central Committee Polyclinic at Kuntsevo. While undergoing treatment in Ward 103, he was visited by Ivan Alekseyevich Yerofeyev, deputy head of the Fourth (German and Austrian) Department, who raised the question of finding "one or two" Austrian Sorges. Fritz said that the KPô chairman, Franz Muhri, refused to become involved in intelligence matters because of his precarious position within the Party. However, Fritz agreed to find suitable candidates himself and to keep N. V. Kirilenko, head of Line PR at the Vienna residency, informed of his progress.[39]

The most cautious of the Party leaders whose responses to the 1971 illegal recruiting drive were noted by Mitrokhin was the general secretary of the Communist Party of Canada (CPC), William Kashtan. Though a rigidly orthodox pro-Soviet loyalist, Kashtan "made much of the practical difficulties." The CPC had to be particularly careful to avoid any suspicion of involvement with the KGB, he explained, because of memories of the Gouzenko affair in 1945, when the Party's only MP, Fred Rose, and its national organizer, Sam Carr, had both been exposed as Soviet agents. Kashtan was assured that he was expected only to select reliable candidates, provide character references and suggest ways of making contact with them. The KGB would do the rest and ensure that, even in the event of "complications," he would not become involved. Kashtan is said to have replied that this arrangement "suited him completely."[40]

During the Twenty-fourth Party Congress senior FCD officers also held discussions with at least eight leaders of Latin American Communist parties. The aim was not as yet to solicit a new generation of Latin American Sorges, but rather to identify potential agents in registry offices who could supply the documents required to support illegals' legends.[41] Within a year or so, however, the Centre was actively seeking Latin illegals to operate in North America.[42] In 1975 Kryuchkov personally approached the general secretary of the Argentinian Communist Party, Alvarez Arnedo, to "seek help from our Argentinian friends in building up the illegal agent apparatus of Soviet intelligence." According to the KGB record of the conversation, Arnedo was "wholly sympathetic."[43] During 1975 Andropov also gave personal instructions for approaches to Communist Party leaders in Syria, Iraq and Lebanon as part of a quest for Arab illegals.[44]

OVER A QUARTER of a century after the collapse of the post-war coalitions which had given Communists a brief experience of office in France, Italy, Austria and Scandinavia, Communist ministers once again entered a Western government. They did so as a result of the Portuguese Revolution of April 1974, when the so-called Armed Forces Movement of young, radical officers ended over forty years of civilian dictatorship and promised both to restore democracy and to end Portugal's colonial wars in Africa. Within days the Communist and Socialist leaders, Álvaro Cunhal and Mário Soares, had returned from exile, standing together in front of their delirious supporters jointly clutching the same red carnation. Soares paid tribute to Cunhal, his former teacher, as "a remarkable man, with a luminous, penetrating glance that bespoke great inner strength."[45] But Cunhal was also a hardline Soviet loyalist who in 1968 had been the first Western Communist leader to support the crushing of the Prague Spring. Though the differences between himself and Soares gradually widened, they were to serve together in a series of coalition governments until the summer of 1975.

In June 1974 Portugal and the Soviet Union established diplomatic relations for the first time since the October Revolution. Six months later Cunhal had his first meeting with the KGB resident in Lisbon, Svyatoslav Fyodorovich Kuznetsov (codenamed LEONID), who operated under diplomatic cover in the recently established Soviet embassy. Though the meeting took place in a Portuguese Communist Party (PCP) safe house, both men were so fearful their conversation might be bugged that they conducted an entirely silent dialogue with pencil and paper. It was agreed that the KGB would train two reliable Party members to detect eavesdropping equipment so that their future discussions could be by word of mouth. Cunhal also undertook to hand over material on the Portuguese security service, NATO (of which Portugal had been a founder member) and other "matters of interest to the KGB."[46]

Shortly after the revolution of April 1974, a commission of enquiry was given access to the files of the brutal security service of the deposed regime (known successively as the PIDE and DGS), whose vast network of informers had almost rivaled those of the Soviet Bloc. Since the PCP, whose 22-member Central Committee had between them spent 308 years in jail, had been the chief target of the PIDE/DGS, it was, unsurprisingly, well represented on the commission.[47] As well as passing on large numbers of PIDE/DGS documents (some of which concerned collaboration with Western intelligence services), the PCP also provided the Lisbon residency with files from Portuguese military intelligence and the new security service established after the revolution. According to one of the files noted by Mitrokhin, the total weight of the classified material provided by the PCP to the Lisbon residency in the mid-1970s came to 474 kilograms. In January 1976 a special section was created within the FCD Fifth Department to work on the Portuguese documents which in their microfilm version filled 68,138 frames. Mitrokhin's summary of the Centre's report on the material concludes:

Extremely important information was obtained about the structure, methods of work and agent networks of the Special [intelligence] Services of the USA, France, the FRG and Spain on the territory of Portugal; on their cooperation with and the agent networks of PIDE/DGS in Portugal and its former colonies; on the armed forces of Portugal and of a number of other countries; on the methods of work of the Portuguese Special Services against the Soviet Union and other socialist countries; on the agent operational situation in the country and at target establishments of interest to the KGB; [and] on individuals of operational interest to the KGB.[48]

Service A made use of the documents, in both authentic and doctored form, as the basis of active measures designed to discredit the CIA, French and West German intelligence services.[49]

In April 1975, at Portugal's first free post-war elections, the Communists gained only 12.5 percent of the vote—one third of the support won by the socialists under Soares. Cunhal, however, shrugged off the setback, confident that real power would remain with the Armed Forces Movement, which had made the revolution a year before. "The elections," he told an interviewer, "have nothing or very little to do with the dynamics of revolution . . . I promise you there will be no parliament in Portugal." Cunhal's prediction proved hopelessly mistaken. His support within the Armed Forces Movement crumbled after the failure of a left-wing coup in November, and new elections in April 1976 gave the Communists only 14.5 percent of the vote, as compared with the socialists' 35 percent. Soares became prime minister and Cunhal led the PCP into opposition.[50]

The PCP leadership continued in opposition to talent-spot for the KGB.[51] During talks in Moscow in July 1977 the FCD asked PATRICK, a member of the PCP Politburo, to identify PCP members suitable for training as illegal agents to operate against NATO. PATRICK saw no difficulty in using experienced Party members for particular intelligence assignments, but was less happy with using them as long-term illegals since this would require them to give up their work for the PCP. Once back in Lisbon, however, PATRICK suggested the names of five possible candidates "without heavy Party responsibilities" and provided blank Portuguese passports and other identity documents to assist in the fabrication of their legends.[52]

While the FCD was holding discussions with PATRICK in July 1977, an almost identical approach was being made to the veteran chairman of the Finnish Communist Party (SKP), Ville Pessi (codenamed BARANOV), then on holiday in the Soviet Union. Pessi agreed to suggest the names of four or five undeclared members of the SKP or trusted fellow travellers to train as illegal agents who could be used against American and NATO targets in the United States, Norway, Denmark or the Low Countries. He was also asked to find another one or two potential agents in registry offices or other locations able to provide the documentation required for the fabrication of illegals' legends.[53] At about the same time that PATRICK and BARANOV were engaged in discussions in Moscow, Andropov authorized an approach in

Dublin by the resident, Mikhail Konstantinovich Shadrin (codenamed KAVERIN), to a leading Irish Communist (codenamed GRUM), who cannot be identified for legal reasons. GRUM agreed that two undeclared members of the Party should be selected for training as the first Irish illegals.[54]

The approaches to Communist Parties outside the Soviet Bloc coincided with a series of exhortations from Kryuchkov, the head of the FCD, to residencies to improve their Line N (Illegal support) performance. Increasingly close surveillance of legal residencies by Western counterintelligence agencies made the expansion of the illegal network of increasing importance. Kryuchkov was not satisfied, however, with the efforts made by residencies to follow up recruiting leads for illegal agents provided by Western Communist Parties and other sources. He complained in a circular of April 1978:

In a number of residencies Line N work has been only half-heartedly pursued on the part of residents; the deep study of those who could be utilized for illegal espionage, especially as special [illegal] agents, has not been conducted sufficiently purposefully . . .[55]

By the mid-1970s most Western, Latin American and some Middle Eastern, North African and Asian Communist Parties had been drawn into the quest for a new generation of illegals.[56] There is, however, no evidence that the almost global recruiting program conducted by the KGB and fraternal parties turned up another Arnold Deutsch or Richard Sorge.[57] So far as the recruiting leads produced by Western Communist leaders are concerned, Mitrokhin's notes reveal no major successes and a number of failures.

The failures included Maria, a Portuguese Communist language teacher recommended as a potential illegal agent by PATRICK of the PCP Central Committee. The Centre planned to recruit Maria as the assistant and wife of an illegal KGB officer, Aleksandr Nikolayevich Kunosenko (codenamed YEFREMOV), who was being trained for work in Brazil. A meeting arranged between YEFREMOV and his proposed bride in East Germany, however, ended in disaster. Maria found Kunosenko physically unattractive and refused to sleep with him; her recruitment was discontinued. Without Maria's assistance, Kunosenko failed to become sufficiently fluent in Portuguese. In 1981 plans for his posting to Brazil were cancelled and he was redeployed in Directorate S headquarters.[58]

Among the more promising illegal agents discovered as a result of leads from Western Communist Parties were a French couple, LIMB and his wife DANA, who were recruited in 1973. LIMB was recommended by the PCF as a man "devoted to Communist ideals" but not to be used against French targets. After two years' training, however, LIMB's first recorded success was talent-spotting a French recruit. MARCEL, LIMB's recruitment lead, worked in the *mairie* of a Paris suburb and was recruited as a KGB agent in 1975, probably to provide documentation for KGB illegals. In December 1975 LIMB (then aged thirty-six) and DANA were deployed to

Belgium, where they set up a small business printing invitation and visiting cards near the headquarters of SACEUR (Supreme Allied Commander Europe). But their attempts over the next year to cultivate NATO personnel met with little or no success. By the end of 1976 they had returned to France, settled in the Bordeaux region and abandoned their brief careers as KGB illegal agents.[59]

Thirty or forty years before, the recruiting drive for illegal agents would doubtless have met with much greater success. Its apparent failure in the 1970s reflected the inability of the Soviet Union under Brezhnev's geriatric leadership to recapture the idealism of an earlier generation of ideological agents inspired by the utopian vision of the world's first worker—peasant state. By the mid-1970s most of the leading Western Communist Parties were tainted by what Moscow considered the "Eurocommunist" heresy, which advocated a parliamentary road to socialism within a multi-party system rather than slavish imitation of the Soviet model.[60] Within the new generation of young Western Marxists, unconditional pro-Soviet loyalists were a dwindling breed—if not yet an endangered species.

JUST AS THE Centre expected fraternal assistance from the leaders of Western Communist parties, so the parties themselves depended in varying degrees on subsidies from Moscow secretly delivered by the KGB. The subsidies, like involvement in intelligence operations, were closely guarded secrets within each Party leadership. When stories of "Moscow gold" occasionally leaked out during the Cold War, they were dismissed as McCarthyite disinformation. The Centre, however, was well aware that some details of its secret subsidies were known to Western intelligence agencies. During the late 1970s, for example, the Soviet ambassador in Ottawa, Aleksandr Nikolayevich Yakovlev (later one of Gorbachev's leading advisers), protested to Andropov, Gromyko and Boris Ponomarev, head of the Central Committee's International Department, against the practice of Canadian Communist Party representatives—in particular the Party leader, William Kashtan—of calling at the embassy to collect funds (codenamed "US wheat") from the resident, Vladimir Ivanovich Mechulayev. The residency had already warned Kashtan that he was taking a considerable risk. By 1980 the Centre was convinced that the Canadian authorities were aware that subsidies to the CPC were being funded by the Soviet-owned Ukrainskaya Kniga [Ukrainian Book] Company, based in Toronto. The FCD informed Ponomarev on October 20:

> The Canadian Special [intelligence] Services are carrying out a study of the financial situation of the Communist Party of Canada which it is proposed to complete within 15–18 months. A preliminary report prepared by the federal government quotes data based on the results of an analysis of the channels and size of the financial receipts in the CPC treasury in 1970. The Special Services have only fragmentary information about subsequent years, but these give grounds to suppose that the methods of financing the activities of the CPC remain as before. According to the data of the Special Services, the CPC bud-

get in 1970 amounted to 158,850 dollars (according to unconfirmed reports, in 1979 it was more than 200,000 dollars). This sum is made up of Party membership dues from CPC members (13,500 dollars or 8.5 percent), receipts from legacies from "deceased loyal members of the Party" (the amount cannot be estimated), voluntary payments and also direct transfers of cash by Soviet representatives and contributions to CPC funds from the income of the Ukrainskaya Kniga Company. It is noted that the first three sources of income provide approximately 30–35 percent of the Party's total budget. The remaining part [65–70 percent] comes from the USSR and from Ukrainskaya Kniga. The Special Services report concentrates on an analysis of the mechanism for supplying funds along the last two channels. [Canadian] Counter-intelligence concludes that the USSR finances the CPC by means of "physical transfer of cash" by officials of the Soviet embassy in Ottawa, to be put at the disposal of Party functionaries under pretext of covering the expenses of Party activists on the occasion of their journeys to Socialist countries.[61]

The seizure by Boris Yeltsin's government of the archives of the Soviet Communist Party (CPSU) after the failed coup of August 1991 led to the publication for the first time of documentary evidence showing that during the 1980s alone, at a time when the Soviet Union was chronically short of hard currency, the CPSU had distributed over 200 million dollars to fraternal parties outside the Soviet Bloc. The Central Committee's International Department had tried to destroy the records of the payments shortly before the confiscation of its archive, but the metal paper clips which held the documents together jammed the shredding machines and saved some of them from destruction.[62]

THOUGH THE LARGEST subsidies for most of the Cold War seem to have gone to the French PCF and Italian PCI, the two leading Western Parties, the biggest per capita donations probably went to the Communist Party of the United States. The disproportionate share of Soviet funds channelled to the CPUSA reflected Moscow's desire to encourage the revival of Communism on the territory of the Main Adversary after the near disintegration of the Party in the mid-1950s. The CPUSA repaid Soviet generosity with an impeccable ideological orthodoxy which became particularly valued in Moscow when the heresy of Eurocommunism later took hold of the major west European Communist Parties.

In April 1958 a veteran member of the CPUSA leadership, Morris Childs (whose aliases included "Morris Summers," "Ramsey Kemp Martin" and "D. Douglas Mozart") was invited to Moscow to discuss financial help for his ailing party. Boris Ponomarev, the head of the Central Committee international department, offered 75,000 dollars for the current year and 200,000 dollars for 1959, initially channelled via the Canadian Communist Party.[63] From 1961 to 1980 the conduits for Soviet subsidies were Childs (codenamed KHAB) and his brother Jack (alias "D. Brooks," codenamed MARAT), an undeclared Communist who had worked for Comintern in the 1930s. Until the late 1970s Morris Childs usually visited Moscow at least once a year to submit the CPUSA budget and request for funds, receive instructions from the International Department and the KGB and take part in discussions on American affairs. Jack acted as the main point of contact for the handover of money in the United States. The normal procedure was for the Centre to send a coded message to a CPUSA radio operator in New York containing details of the next transmission of funds. The message would then be passed to Jack Childs, who would decode it and inform his brother, Gus Hall (leader of the CPUSA from 1959 and codenamed PALM), or Hall's wife Elizabeth that the next delivery was imminent.[64]

From 1968 the CPUSA radio operator who passed messages from the Centre on to Jack Childs was another undeclared party member of Russian descent, Albert Friedman, codenamed FORD, who worked as a salesman in a Manhattan radio store on East 49th Street. Using the alias Weber, Friedman had worked between the wars at Comintern's radio school in Moscow, training other underground radio operators. In January 1969 he travelled to Moscow for further training,[65] but performed so well that his instructor told him, "You know more than I do" and invited him to lunch.[66] Though Friedman paid Party dues, his membership of the CPUSA was known only to the KGB and a small group within the Party leadership.[67] What neither the KGB nor CPUSA leaders knew, however, was that since the end of the Second World War Friedman had been an FBI agent in the Party, codenamed CLIP. He passed every word of the Centre's communications on to the Bureau.[68]

By the late 1960s Soviet subsidies to the CPUSA amounted to well over a million dollars a year; a decade later they were more than two million. Jack Childs (MARAT) usually took delivery of Soviet subsidies from KGB operations officers during "brush passes" at pre-arranged locations in New York, all at precisely 3:05 p.m. During 1974, for example, money-transfer operations (then codenamed VAL-DAY) took place at four locations in Lower Manhattan: 10 Pine Street, 10th floor (codenamed DINO); 11 Broadway, 9th floor (FRED); 120 Wall Street, 7th floor (POST); and 81 New Street, 2nd floor (ROLAND). All four addresses were chosen by the New York residency because they had several entrances and exits. MARAT and the KGB operations officer chosen to hand the money over to him entered and left the building selected for their brush contact through different doors. In order to lessen the increasing bulk of the packages of money handed over in brush contacts, the denomination of the bills contained in them was raised in 1974 from 20 dollars to 50 dollars and 100 dollars.[69] On the grounds that it was too dangerous to pass the money to Hall, who was under close surveillance by the FBI, the New York police and the Internal Revenue Service, Jack Childs gave much of it to his brother Morris for safekeeping.[70]

As well as acting as a conduit for Soviet subsidies, Jack Childs also regularly exchanged written messages with the New York residency either through brush contacts or "dead drops." Like brush contact sites, dead drops were all given codenames; those in use in 1974 were MANDI, LYUSI, OPEY, RIBA and OVERA. Messages were normally sent on undeveloped film from a Minox camera placed in a magnetic container. One of the files noted by Mitrokhin records that between July 1975 and August 1976 MARAT took part in five VALDAY operations and nine to exchange secret messages (five by brush contact, four by dead drop). In an emergency the residency could arrange an urgent meeting with MARAT by ringing a designated telephone number at precisely five minutes past noon and asking for Dr. Albert. On being told, "There is no Dr. Albert here" the residency officer would reply, "Sorry, must have the wrong number." He would then meet MARAT at 3:05 p.m. the same day at a Brooklyn location codenamed ELLIOT, at the entrance to the Silver Road pharmacy on the corner of Avenue J and East 16th Street, next to the subway station. MARAT identified himself by carrying a copy of *Time* magazine and placing a Bandaid on his left hand. The operations officer asked him, "Do you have the time?" When MARAT replied, "It's 3:05 sharp," he produced a business card from one of MARAT's former employers with a note by KHAB, his brother Morris, on the back.[71]

The elaborate security employed by the KGB in contacts with both MARAT and KHAB suffered, however, from one fatal flaw. Since the early 1950s both had been FBI agents.[72] By 1974 the Centre had become suspicious, particularly about KHAB (Morris Childs). He had not been imprisoned during the anti-Communist witchhunts of the 1950s, nor had he been arrested for travelling abroad on false passports (a fact of which the FBI was believed to be aware). A 1967 report by the Senate Judiciary Committee had referred to him under the names Morris Chilovsky (his name at birth) and Morris Summers (one of his aliases) and mentioned his pre-war links with Soviet intelligence. The Centre also found suspicious KHAB's determination to accompany Gus Hall on all his trips to Russia and his "nervousness" when Moscow bypassed him and his brother and communicated directly with Hall. In March 1974 Vladimir Mikhailovich Kazakov, head of the FCD First (North American) Department, reported to Andropov and the Central Committee:

> Although [Morris] Childs enjoys the trust of Comrade Gus Hall, his direct involvement in the financial affairs of the US Communist Party constitutes a real threat to this special channel [for the transmission of Soviet funds]. In addition, certain doubtful and suspicious elements in M. Childs's behavior lead one to believe that he is possibly being used by US intelligence.

Kazakov also urged that Hall be persuaded to find a substitute for MARAT (Jack Childs), whom he described as absent-minded and in poor health.

At a meeting with Hall in Moscow on May 8, another senior FCD officer, B. S. Ivanov, tried to persuade him that the time had come to retire both the Childs brothers, whose long involvement in secret work placed them under increasing danger of FBI surveillance. Ivanov suggested a number of alternative methods of transferring Soviet funds to the CPUSA, among them opening a Swiss bank account or using a cover business in the United States. But, though Hall said he had found a "reliable comrade" to replace Jack Childs, he took no action and the International Department, which evidently did not take Kazakov's warning very seriously, did not insist.[73]

In 1975 Morris and Jack Childs were awarded the Order of the Red Banner; Morris received his in person from Brezhnev during a Moscow banquet. Back in the United States both brothers lived in some style, embezzling about 5 percent of the Soviet funds sent to the CPUSA as well as receiving a salary from the FBI. Morris posed as a wealthy businessman with a penthouse in Chicago, expensively furnished with antiques, paintings and oriental carpets, as well as apartments in Moscow and New York. Gus Hall, who naively believed both brothers to be independently wealthy, sometimes asked them to buy clothes for his family.[74]

Among the intelligence which the Childs brothers reported to the FBI for more than twenty years were the claims of the CPUSA leadership to influence on the black civil rights movement. In 1958 Jack Childs had reported a boast by James Jackson, Party secretary in charge of "Negro and Southern Affairs," that "most secret and guarded people" were "guiding" the civil rights leader Martin Luther King.[75] According to one KGB file, Dobrynin, the Soviet ambassador, later asked Hall to stop bringing Jackson, whom he described as "poorly trained politically," to meetings with him; he also requested the Soviet mission to the UN (by which he probably meant the KGB New York residency) to break off contact with Jackson.[76]

There was, however, some substance to the claim that the CPUSA had penetrated King's entourage. The Childs brothers reported that one of King's advisers, Stanley D. Levison, a New York lawyer and entrepreneur, was a secret Party member.[77] Levison drafted sections of King's 1958 book, *Stride Toward Freedom*, and helped prepare his defense against trumped-up charges of perjury on his Alabama tax returns in 1960.[78] Levison also introduced into King's entourage a secret black member of the CPUSA, Hunter Pitts "Jack" O'Dell.[79] The FBI, who put Levison under surveillance, reported that he was meeting Viktor Lesiovsky, a KGB officer working as special assistant to the UN Secretary-General, U Thant.[80] It was Levison's alleged influence on King which in 1963 led Attorney-General Robert Kennedy to authorize the bugging of King's hotel rooms. Though the bugs produced recordings of a number of King's sexual liaisons, in which President Lyndon B. Johnson took a prurient interest, they provided no evidence of Communist influence on him.[81]

At the beginning of the Carter administration in 1977, the CPUSA leadership made exaggerated claims of its influence over King's former executive secretary, Andrew Young (codenamed LUTHER), newly appointed as US representative at the United Nations. According to Hall, "Young himself did not know that several of his close friends in Atlanta were covert Communists, and he listened to them. The Party, while observing the required clandestinity, would cautiously exert an influence on Young in the necessary areas."[82] Lesiovsky's cover as assistant to U Thant gave him a number of opportunities for discussions with Young. Though he claimed to have obtained "important information" from the discussions, he reported—less optimistically than Hall—that, while Young hoped for better US–Soviet relations, his attitude to the Soviet Union was fundamentally "negative."[83]

Though Hall tended to overstate the influence of undeclared members of the CPUSA within the Democratic Party, there was at least one to whom the Centre attached real importance during the 1970s: a Democratic activist in California recruited as a KGB agent during a visit to Russia. The agent, who is not identified by name in the reports noted by Mitrokhin, had a wide circle of influential contacts in the Democratic Party: among them Governor Jerry Brown of California, Senator Alan Cranston, Senator Eugene McCarthy, Senator Edward Kennedy, Senator Abraham Ribicoff, Senator J. William Fulbright and Congressman John Conyers, Jr. During the 1976 presidential election the agent was able to provide inside information from within the Carter camp and a profile of Carter himself, which were particularly highly valued by the Centre since it had so few high-level American sources. On one occasion he spent three hours discussing the progress of the campaign at a meeting with Carter, Brown and Cranston in Carter's room at the Pacific Hotel. His report was forwarded to the Politburo. During the final stages of the campaign the agent had what the KGB claimed were "direct and prolonged conversations" with Carter, Governor Brown and Senators Cranston, Kennedy, Ribicoff and Jacob Javits. Andropov attached such importance to the report on these conversations that he forwarded it under his signature to the Politburo immediately after Carter's election.[84]

IN NOVEMBER 1977 the Centre sent a memorandum to the Central Committee complaining that, despite several requests to Hall to replace the Childs brothers, they were still running the American end of the "covert channel of communication with the US Communist Party." During Jack's illness in August and September, Morris had replaced him as the CPUSA's representative at a meeting with a KGB officer in New York:

> His use in the special channel operation is very risky, since [Morris] Childs is known to the intelligence service—as is evidenced by the US Senate Judiciary Committee's report for 1967, where he is referred to as a person who uses several names and has contact with the KGB. Because of this, one cannot exclude the possibility that the FBI has him under covert surveillance.

On November 10 Kazakov and Ivanov raised the question of replacing the Childs brothers at another meeting with Hall in Moscow. Hall said that he had three candidates in mind as a replacement for Jack Childs—John Vogo and the Applekhoums [? Appleholmes] brothers.[85] He would make his final choice in the near future and announce his decision by a coded telegram to Moscow reporting the completion of a draft article on colonialism. The number of the draft indicated in the telegram (first, second or third) would indicate which candidate he had selected. Jack Child's successor would then apply for a visa at the Soviet consulate in Vienna so that he could receive one and a half to two months of "special training" in Moscow. Hall also suggested that the KGB use the wife of his personal chauffeur and bodyguard as an additional channel of communication in New York. The residency could telephone her at work, identifying itself by using the *parole*, "This is Mr. Budnik calling about the old furniture. My friend from Hoboken suggested contacting you."[86]

Once again, however, Hall delayed taking action. The Childs brothers continued to take part in the "special channel operation" for the remainder of the decade. One of the files noted by Mitrokhin records that during the eight months up to April 1978 Jack Childs conducted nineteen operations: three VALDAY money transfers, two meetings with KGB officers, five dead drops, six brush contacts and three operations to signal contacts.[87] By the spring of 1980, however, the FBI had concluded that the Childs were in imminent danger of being compromised. On May 28, as a pretext for withdrawing from the "special channel," Morris Childs told Hall that unidentified men had been calling on his neighbors making enquiries about him and he feared he might have to go into hiding to avoid arrest. He handed Hall 225,437 dollars in cash, which, he claimed, was all the money from Moscow in his possession. Jack Childs, who had been in failing health for some time, died in a New York hospital on August 12. Morris and Eva Childs retired to a luxurious condominium north of Miami with spectacular views over the Atlantic. In 1987, at a special ceremony at FBI headquarters, Morris was presented by President Reagan with the Presidential Medal of Freedom. He and his brother Jack, who was awarded the same medal posthumously, thus became the only spies ever to be decorated by both the Soviet Union and the United States.[88]

Throughout the decades when the Childs brothers operated the secret channel to Moscow, the CPUSA had been wholly marginal to American politics. In four presidential elections between 1972 and 1984 Gus Hall never received more than 59,000 votes; after falling to 35,000 in 1984, he decided to support the Democrats in 1988. After dropping well below 10,000 members in the mid-1970s, the Party staged a modest revival but in the later 1980s was only about 15,000 strong.[89] Hall, however, continued to inhabit a fantasy world in which the CPUSA had a major influence on American politics. He wrote to Boris Ponomarev, the head of the International Department, in the autumn of 1981:

> More than at any moment in recent history, I am convinced that our Party can be an important factor in slowing down, stopping and reversing the present reactionary policies of the Reagan administration. Tens of millions have become disillusioned. They are moving towards mass actions, and millions are in ideological flux. Our Party can be an important and even a decisive factor in influencing and moving these masses.

As on this occasion, Hall's fantasy assessments of the CPUSA's growing influence were accompanied by appeals for Soviet subsidies, which for most of the 1980s ran at 2 million dollars a year. In 1987 Hall asked for a large increase:

> I can only argue that because our party works in the decaying heart of imperialism whatever we do in influencing events in the United States has an impact on world developments. And, because of the crisis of the Reagan presidency, which is deep and chronic now, our Party's work has had and continues to have a growing impact on the politics of our country.

Therefore, in the context of the struggle against US imperialism and the policies of the Reagan administration, our party must be seen as an important, and even indispensable, factor.

The CPUSA's subsidy for the following year was put up to three million dollars.[90]

Morris Childs believed that the remarkable generosity of Soviet donations to the CPUSA (200 dollars a member in 1987) was due partly to the fact that the Kremlin took Gus Hall's claims at least semi-seriously and "ludicrously overestimated the influence of the American party."[91] The generosity was also due, however, to the ideological servility of Hall and the CPUSA leadership. According to Dorothy Ray Healey, a prominent party militant for forty-five years:

Under Gus's leadership the American CP had picked up the dubious distinction of being the chief ideological sheepdog in the international Communist movement, barking on command when any of the other lambs threatened to stray from the fold. The Soviet leaders would contact Gus and tell him what they wanted him to say, he would say it, and then *Pravda* could run a story saying that embattled American Communists speaking from the heartland of world imperialism had thus-and-such to say about whatever issue was of particular concern to the Soviets at the moment.[92]

EIGHTEEN

EUROCOMMUNISM

A conference of eighty-five Communist parties held in Moscow in 1960 unanimously reaffirmed loyalty to the Soviet Union as an unshakeable article of faith for Communists in both East and West:

> The Communist Party of the Soviet Union has been, and remains, the universally recognized vanguard of the world Communist movement, being the most experienced and steeled contingent of the international Communist movement.

By the end of the decade, however, the CPSU leadership was outraged to find its infallibility being called into question by the emergence of what was later termed "Eurocommunism." The Eurocommunist heresy made its first public appearance after the suppression of the Prague Spring in 1968, when a number of Western parties ventured some, mostly timid, criticisms of the Soviet invasion. The leadership of the PCI (Partito Comunista Italiano), later the dominant force in Eurocommunism, reaffirmed "the profound, fraternal and genuine ties that unite the Italian Communist Party to the Soviet Union and the CPSU," but denied the right of the Soviet Union to intervene militarily "in the internal life of another Communist Party or another country."[1]

"The profound, fraternal and genuine ties" which bound the PCI to the Soviet Union even after Soviet tanks had entered Prague had a secret dimension of which very few Italian Communists outside the Direzione were aware. After the Colonels' coup in Athens in April 1967, the PCI general secretary, Luigi Longo, and other party leaders had become alarmed by the possibility of an Italian military putsch on the Greek model. In the summer of 1967, Giorgio Amendola, on behalf of the PCI Direzione, formally requested Soviet assistance in preparing the Party for survival after a coup as an illegal underground movement. Politburo decision no. P50/P of August 15 authorized the FCD to draw up a program which was intended to give the PCI its own intelligence unit with fully trained staff and a clandestine radio communications system. Details of the program were agreed in talks in Moscow between ANDREA, the head of the PCI's illegal apparatus, and senior Central Committee officials and KGB officers. Between October 1967 and May 1968 three Italian radio operators completed a four-month KGB training course. Other Party members took courses in producing bogus identity documents, following a syllabus which devoted ninety-six hours to the production of rubber stamps and document seals, six to the art of embossing with synthetic resins, six to changing photographs on identity documents, six to making handwritten entries on documents and twelve to "theoretical discussions." These and other secret training programs continued at least until the end of the 1970s. The PCI leadership also asked the KGB to check its headquarters for listening devices.[2]

After the immediate PCI protest at the suppression of the Prague Spring in 1968, open criticism quickly subsided. Before the PCI Twelfth Congress in February 1969, both Boris Ponomarev, head of the Central Committee's International Department, and senior KGB officers put heavy pressure on Luigi Longo and other Party leaders to tone down their comments on Cezchoslovakia in speeches to the conference. In reports to the CPSU Central Committee, Ponomarev and the KGB claimed the credit for the fact that, despite the retention of some "ambiguous phrases," all references to "intervention" and "occupation" by the Soviet Union and its allies in the Warsaw Pact were removed. Nor was there any call by the PCI for the withdrawal of Warsaw Pact forces from Czechoslovakia.[3] In a private discussion in 1970 with Nikita Ryzhov, the Soviet ambassador, Longo "particularly emphasized that for the Italian Communists friendship with the CPSU and the Soviet Union was not a formality but a real necessity for their existence."[4]

Longo also depended heavily on Soviet subsidies. He was at his most importunate when a general election was called one year ahead of schedule in May 1972. The original CPSU Politburo allocation for the election year was 5,200,000 dollars—2 million more than in 1971. After a further appeal from Longo, it provided another 500,000 dollars. Longo then wrote another begging letter, to which Brezhnev sent a personal reply, delivered by the Rome resident, Gennadi Fyodorovich Borzov (alias "Bystrov"), on April 4:

Dear Comrade Longo,

We have received your letter requesting additional assistance to meet expenses relating to the Italian Communist Party's participation in the electoral campaign.

We well understand the difficult nature of the situation in which this campaign is taking place, and the need for the intense activity which your Party must exert in this connection in order to win the elections and resist the forces of reaction.

As you, Comrade Longo, know, we have already allocated an additional US $500,000 for the Italian Communist Party to take part in the electoral campaign, thus bringing the total [contribution] this year to US $5,700,000.

In the light of your request, we once again carefully studied all the possibilities open to us, and decided to give the Italian Communist Party further assistance to the amount of US $500,000. Unfortunately, at the present time, there is no more that we can do.

> With Communist greetings,
> [Signed] L. Brezhnev
> General Secretary of the CPSU Central Committee[5]

After handing the letter to Longo, Borzov reported to the Centre:

The Ambassador [Nikita Ryzhov] declared that as we had gone behind his back he intended to telegraph Comrade Brezhnev about this. Bearing in mind Ryzhov's difficult character, and his extremely sensitive reaction to things of this kind, this particular incident has greatly exacerbated the Ambassador's attitude towards us.

The Centre ordered Borzov to do his best to pacify the Ambassador:

Tell Ryzhov that you assumed he would be made aware in Moscow of the decision taken by the Instantsiya [CPSU leadership]. On your own behalf, ask Comrade Ryzhov to treat all this with proper understanding and not to attach exaggerated importance to what has happened; tell him that our relations with him will continue to be businesslike and that the Ambassador will be fully informed about all our contacts with our friends [the PCI].[6]

In October 1972, Borzov reported that the "friends" had handed back three 100-dollar notes which had, embarrassingly, turned out to be forgeries.[7]

Until 1976 the transfer of funds to the Communist Party was a far more straightforward business in Rome than in the United States or many other parts of the world. Since leading Italian Communists regularly called at the Soviet embassy, it was thought unnecessary to resort to the clandestine rigmarole of brush contacts and dead-drops. The most dependable Soviet loyalist on the PCI Direzione, who was in regular contact with the KGB, simply selected a series of emissaries who drove to the embassy and collected the money, having first checked that their cars were not being followed. The KGB residency's KOMETA radio-listening post simultaneously monitored the wavelengths used by Italian police and security forces in order to detect any signs of surveillance. As an additional precaution, the emissary was followed to and from the embassy by a PCI car.[8] Moscow provided further financial assistance through lucrative contracts with PCI-controlled companies in business ventures ranging from Soviet oil imports to hotel construction in the Soviet Union.[9]

The PCI's fears of a right-wing military coup were revived by the overthrow of President Salvador Allende's Unidad Popular government in Chile by the armed forces in September 1973. In December the PCI took secret delivery from the KGB of three SELENGA radio stations in order to enable Party headquarters to maintain contact with local branches if the PCI was forced underground. Party radio technicians were trained in Russia to operate the new system. In the aftermath of a coup the

SELENGA radios would transmit messages to Moscow which would then be retransmitted to local PCI underground groups by powerful Soviet transmitters.[10]

The renewed fear of an Italian putsch, however, also drove the PCI in directions which caused concern in Moscow that the West's largest Communist Party was succumbing to ideological heresy. In a series of articles entitled "Reflections on Italy after the Events in Chile," Enrico Berlinguer (who had succeeded Longo as general secretary in 1972) proposed, in a phrase which became famous, a *compromesso storico* ("historic compromise") with the Socialists and the ruling Christian Democrats.[11] Berlinguer was unlike any previous major Communist leader with whom the Kremlin had had to deal. His wife Letizia was a devout Catholic and he had agreed to their children being brought up in the Catholic faith. Longo had done his best to persuade Moscow that, despite his Catholic family, Berlinguer was the best available candidate and that his three main rivals, Giorgio Amendola, Gian Carlo Pajetta and Pietro Ingrao, were unsuitable for the post of general secretary. Amendola, according to Longo, "had a great deal of the bourgeois democrat about him and had too often committed revisionist errors;" Pajetta, "whose authority was dwindling, was too short-tempered and would not promote [Party] unity;" Ingrao was "superficial and given to unrealistic theoretical speculation." Berlinguer, however, represented the new generation of Party leaders who had emerged since the Second World War.[12] Moscow was far from reassured.

Berlinguer's original proposal for a "historic compromise" was conceived chiefly as a defense against the prospect of a right-wing coup, justified by Lenin's dictum that revolutionaries must know when to retreat. Gradually, however, the proposal evolved into a more ambitious—and, in Moscow's view, heretical—strategy, in which Catholic traditions of solidarity would combine with Communist collective action to produce a new political and social order. During 1975 Berlinguer emerged as the chief spokesman of what became known as Eurocommunism. The PCI joined with the Spanish PCE and French PCF in issuing what was, in effect, a Eurocommunist manifesto, distancing themselves from the Soviet model of socialism and committing themselves to free elections, a free press and a parliamentary road to socialism within a multi-party system.[13]

At a secret meeting with Ryzhov on December 12, 1975, a KGB informant on the Direzione accused Berlinguer and the Party leadership of "a cowardly rejection of Leninism" and growing hostility to the Soviet Union. He appealed to the CPSU to issue a public criticism of the PCI line: "This will almost split the party, but it is the only way to save the situation." The informant also claimed that the PCI leadership was planning to disrupt the conference of European Communist Parties, due to be held in East Berlin in the summer of 1976, by using it as a platform for its revisionist views.[14]

During the preparations for the East Berlin conference the Kremlin issued a series of thinly veiled public warnings to the Eurocommunists not to misbehave. Berlinguer, however, was not to be intimidated. During the Italian election campaign in June, he made what Moscow considered his most outrageous statement yet. Italian membership of NATO, Berlinguer declared, was on balance an advantage: "This guarantees us the kind of socialism that we want—to be precise, socialism in liberty, socialism of a pluralist kind." The Kremlin responded with a scathing, though secret, letter of protest. Of far more significance so far as most of the PCI Direzione was concerned, however, was the fact that the Party received a record 34.5 percent of the vote (up 7.3 percent since 1972). At the East Berlin conference on June 29–30 the clash between the CPSU and the Eurocommunists was thinly papered over by a bland communiqué calling for "internationalist solidarity." The speeches of Berlinguer and other leading heretics, which drew attention to flaws in "existing socialism" (in other words, the Soviet model), were published in *Pravda* only in a censored version.[15]

In December 1976 the Bulgarian leader, Todor Zhivkov, always a faithful mouthpiece for the Kremlin, denounced Eurocommunism as one of the bourgeois propagandists' "main lines of ideological subversion against proletarian internationalism."[16] The Kremlin's scope for a direct, frontal assault on Berlinguer, however, was limited by his immense popularity. Instead, Andropov instructed Kryuchkov, the head of the FCD, to prepare active measures to discredit him and other tribunes of Eurocommunism.[17] A report prepared by the FCD for the Central Committee claimed that Berlinguer owned a plot of land in Sardinia, and had been involved in dubious building contracts worth tens of billions of lira.[18]

Remarkably, while hoping to destabilize Berlinguer by leaking evidence of his alleged corruption, Moscow continued to subsidize the PCI. The total subsidy for 1976 was 6.5 million dollars.[19] According to KGB files, however, the "operational situation" for the transfer of money in Rome had become more difficult. The newly appointed resident, Boris Solomatin (previously stationed in New York), concluded in 1976 that handing over money at the embassy was insufficiently clandestine. He agreed with Guido Cappelloni (codenamed ALBERTO), head of the PCI Central Committee administration department, that it would be safest for the money transfers to take place early on Sunday mornings at pre-arranged locations in the Rome suburbs which had been carefully checked beforehand by both the residency and the PCI. The route of the car used by the "friend" who received the money was kept under careful surveillance by PCI members; he then transferred the money to another car which delivered it to a secret Party office.[20]

Despite its hostility to Berlinguer and Eurocommunism, the Soviet Politburo also continued to authorize KGB training in underground operations of specially selected Italian Communists. In 1979, for example, the PCI sent three Party members to Moscow for instruction by the FCD "Illegals" Directorate S. One was trained to act as radio and cipher instructor, another as a disguise specialist and the third in the fabrication of false documents.[21]

Not all the conflicts between the PCI Direzione and the Communist parties of the Soviet Bloc became public. The most serious secret dispute in the late 1970s concerned the covert assistance given by a number of east European intelligence services to terrorist groups in the West. East Germany became, in the words of its last, non-Communist, minister of the interior, Peter-Michael Diestel, "an Eldorado for terrorists."[22] What most concerned the leaders of the PCI, however, was support by the

Czechoslovak StB for the Italian Brigate Rosse (Red Brigades).[23] Their anxieties reached a peak on March 16, 1978, when the Red Brigades ambushed a car carrying the president of the Christian Democrats, Aldo Moro, in the center of Rome. Moro's chauffeur and his police escort were gunned down and Moro himself was bundled into a waiting car. For the next fifty-four days, while Moro was held prisoner in a secret hiding place, the nation agonized over whether or not to negotiate with the Red Brigades to save his life.[24]

Though the PCI Direzione publicly maintained that there could be no deals with terrorists, it was privately tormented by the fear that news of the support given to the Red Brigades by the StB would leak out. Speaking for the Direzione, Arturo Colombi complained to the Czechoslovak ambassador in Rome, Vladimir Koucky, that a PCI delegation to Prague had been fobbed off when it had tried to raise the issue of help to the Red Brigades, some of whom, it believed, had been invited to Czechoslovakia. On May 4, 1978 Amendola warned Koucky that, if Moro's kidnappers were caught and put on trial, the assistance given them by the StB "could all come out." On this occasion, Rhyzov, the Soviet ambassador, sided with the PCI, telling Koucky "he had warned Czechoslovak representatives about contacts with the Red Brigades, but they would not listen to him." Rhyzov was convinced that the StB residency in Rome was still secretly in touch with the Red Brigades. "You got a pennyworth of benefit [from the Red Brigades]," he told Koucky, "but did a hundred times more damage."[25]

The Italian authorities failed to discover Moro's hiding place in time. On May 9, 1978 he was murdered by his kidnappers and his body left in the boot of a car in the center of Rome, midway between the headquarters of the PCI and those of the Christian Democrats. In the outpouring of grief and soul-searching which followed Moro's assassination there was—to the relief of the Direzione—no mention of the involvement of the StB with the Red Brigades. During the police hunt for terrorist radio stations over the next few years, however, the PCI leadership became increasingly anxious that their own might be discovered. In June 1981 the PCI leadership informed the Rome residency that, for security reasons, the three radio stations installed by the KGB for clandestine Party use eight years earlier had been destroyed.[26]

The Soviet invasion of Afghanistan at the end of 1979 and the imposition of martial law in Poland two years later destroyed any semblance of a reconciliation between Moscow and the PCI. At a meeting of the PCI Central Committee in January 1982, only the KGB's main contact voted against a motion condemning Soviet interference in Polish affairs. Berlinguer declared that the October Revolution had "exhausted its propulsive force," implying in effect that the CPSU had lost its revolutionary credentials. The Direzione called on the west European left to work for the "democratic renewal" of the countries of the Soviet Bloc. *Pravda* denounced the PCI's declarations as "truly blasphemous." There followed what the Italians called *lo strappo*—a brief but highly polemical breach of relations between the PCI and CPSU.

Within the Italian Party leadership, the hardliner Armando Cossutta was a lone voice in taking Moscow's side in the quarrel.[27] A decade later, as the Soviet Union was disintegrating, evidence leaked out that Soviet subsidies to the PCI had continued on a reduced scale in the 1980s. But, according to one commentator, "It soon became clear that if Soviet funds had been channelled into Italy, they went through the hands . . . of Cossutta, either to shore up a failing newspaper with pro-Soviet sympathies (*Paese Sera*) or to help finance his own activities against the PCI's leaders."[28] The final recorded payments—700,000 dollars in 1985, 600,000 dollars in 1986 and 630,000 dollars in 1987—were used solely to provide "material support" to what the CPSU International Department and the KGB (but probably not Gorbachev) considered "the healthy forces in the PCI," chief among them Cossutta and *Paese Sera*.[29]

BERLINGUER APART, THE Eurocommunist of whom Moscow was most suspicious was Santiago Carrillo, leader of the PCE (Partido Comunista de España). Even as a teenage militant, Carrillo had shown precocious leadership qualities. In 1936, at the age of only nineteen, mocked by his opponents as "the chrysalis in spectacles," he engineered a fusion between the socialist and communist youth movements and became chairman of the combined organization. During the Spanish Civil War, Carrillo became a close friend of the celebrated NKVD illegal, saboteur and assassin Iosif Grigulevich, whom he subsequently chose as his son's secular "godfather."[30] Taking refuge in Moscow in 1939 after Franco's victory in Spain, Carrillo proved his Stalinist orthodoxy by denouncing his own father, to whom he wrote with self-righteous fanaticism, "Between a Communist and a traitor there can be no relations of any kind." He later claimed, implausibly, "If there was any fear of Stalin in the Soviet Union, I did not see it. For many years only a minority knew about the trials and the purges."[31]

After becoming general secretary of the exiled PCE in 1959, however, Carrillo gradually evolved towards Eurocommunism. In 1968 the PCE executive committee condemned Soviet intervention in Czechoslovakia; its leading Soviet loyalists, Agustín Gómez, Eduardo García and General Enrique Líster, were expelled in 1969–70.[32] In July 1975 the PCI and PCE jointly issued a "solemn declaration that their conception of the march towards socialism in peace and freedom expresses not a tactical attitude but a strategic conviction." After Franco's death in November, Carrillo began to plan the PCE's reemergence as a legal party. Late in 1976, without informing Moscow, he returned secretly to Spain from his French headquarters. On December 6 the Centre sent an urgent telegram to the Madrid residency, telling it to investigate rumors that Carrillo was in Spain and, if so, to find out whether he had returned on his own initiative or after a secret agreement with the Christian Democrat prime minister, Adolfo Suárez.[33]

In fact Carrillo had returned in order to try to force Suárez's hand. On December 10 he gave a public news conference, thus compelling the Prime Minister to decide whether to risk the wrath of the army and the right by legalizing the PCE or to risk alienating the main democratic parties by refusing to do so. Though Carrillo was arrested on December 22, he was set at liberty a few days later and met secretly with Suárez. The formal legalization of the PCE followed in April 1977.[34]

Just as in Italy, the KGB's principal point of contact with the PCI was with a Soviet loyalist, so the Madrid residency's main source within the PCE was the most pro-Soviet member of its executive committee, Ignacio Gallego, codenamed KOBO. Until March 1976 Soviet subsidies to the PCE had been forwarded via the French Communist Party, the PCF. By Politburo decision no. P-1/84 of March 16, however, the KGB was instructed to make payments directly to Gallego. At least some of these payments were intended for Gallego himself, rather than the PCE executive as a whole, so that he could "work on his contacts." On December 6, 1976 the Politburo approved a payment to Gallego of 20,000 dollars (decision no. P37/39-OP) for the purchase of a flat in Madrid. Though his public criticism of Carrillo was muted, the Madrid residency reported that in private Gallego was bitterly critical, denouncing him as "a danger to the Spanish Communist Party and the international Communist movement."[35]

Early in 1977, through his wife LORA, Gallego passed on to the Madrid residency Carrillo's draft of a joint declaration to be issued at a summit meeting of the leaders of the PCE, PCI and PCF, as well as the proofs of Carrillo's forthcoming book, *"Eurocomunismo" y Estado* (*"Eurocommunism" and the State*).[36] The Centre was scandalized by the criticisms in both documents of the Soviet Union—though, in the event, Berlinguer and Georges Marchais, general secretary of the PCF, rejected the most trenchant passages of the draft communiqué.[37] Gallego informed the KGB that the left-wing daily *Pueblo* planned to send a correspondent to Moscow to interview Soviet dissidents. Thus forewarned, the Madrid embassy refused the correspondent a visa.[38]

With the restoration of parliamentary democracy for the first time since the Spanish Civil War, the PCE was widely expected—not least by Carrillo—to achieve as dominant a position on the left in Spain as the PCI had in Italy. Its socialist rival, the PSOE, had adapted itself less well both to underground opposition to the autocratic Franco regime and to maintaining party organization during almost forty years of exile. In the 35-year-old Felipe González, however, the socialists had a dynamic, telegenic leader whose youthful appeal to voters was far more effective than Carrillo's. During the campaign for the parliamentary elections of June 1977 the PCE also found it more difficult than the PSOE to free itself of an extremist image. To Moscow's satisfaction, Carrillo's Eurocommunist campaign was at least mildly disrupted by the return from the Soviet Union in May of the 83-year-old president of the PCE, Dolores Ibárruri, whom Carrillo had succeeded as general secretary almost twenty years earlier. Known as *La Pasionaria* ("passion flower"), Ibárruri had been the most charismatic orator of the Civil War, famous around the world for her cries of defiance in the face of fascism: "Better to die on your feet than live on your knees!"; "Better to be the widow of a hero than the wife of a coward!" Franco's supporters spread rumors that she had once cut a priest's throat with her own teeth.[39] Though Ibárruri's appearances during the 1977 election campaign were limited by her age and weak heart, she lost no opportunity to praise the achievements of the Soviet Bloc—"countries where socialism is being built." Carrillo tried to dilute the impact of her speeches by implying that she was out of touch and bound to the Soviet Union by the death of her only son while fighting for the Red Army at Stalingrad.

At the parliamentary elections of June 1977, the first free elections in Spain for forty-one years, the electorate rejected the extremes of both left and right. The PCE won only 9 percent of the vote, as compared with the 34 percent of Suárez's Union of the Democratic Centre and the 28 percent of the socialists. Among the new Communist deputies was Gallego, who became deputy chairman of the PCE parliamentary group. Believing Carrillo's position to be much weaker than Berlinguer's, the Kremlin tried to rally opposition to him in the PCE. Shortly after the election, the Moscow *New Times* published a vituperative review of Carrillo's *"Eurocommunism" and the State.* Carrillo, it declared, might appear to be talking simply about differences in tactics and strategy between different Communist Parties, but his real views were "exactly those of the imperialist adversaries of Communism."[40] The CPSU International Department drafted an attack on Carrillo's revisionism, then arranged for its publication under the signatures of three members of the PCE. A letter containing a similar attack, signed by 200 Spanish Communists, was circulated as a leaflet.[41]

During 1978 the public controversy between the PCE and CPSU died down. In private, however, Carrillo was more critical than ever. According to a report from Gallego forwarded by the Madrid residency, he condemned the Soviet Union in one off-the-record outburst as "a semi-feudal state, dominated by a privileged bureaucracy which is cut off from the people," with a far less democratic way of life than the United States.[42] After the Soviet invasion of Afghanistan at the end of 1979, Carrillo made some of his criticisms public. In January 1980 he wrote to the CPSU Central Committee attacking the invasion as political adventurism and blaming Soviet as well as American policy for the intensification of the Cold War.[43] Though some local Party organizations supported Soviet intervention, Carrillo was backed by a majority of the PCE executive. Gallego, meanwhile, continued to receive about 30,000 dollars a year from the KGB.[44] The Madrid resident, Viktor Mikhailovich Filippov, reported that though Gallego stuck "as far as possible" to the political line recommended by the residency, there was little he could do to galvanize open opposition without isolating himself on the executive. In Filippov's view, Carrillo remained in firm control of his party.[45] In reality, torn between Eurocommunists and hardliners, and with the Catalan Communists losing faith in Carrillo's leadership, the PCE had begun to disintegrate.[46]

There were also divisions within the socialists as Felipe González tried to turn the PSOE into a social democratic party. After a party congress in May 1979 reaffirmed the Marxist nature of the PSOE, González resigned, only to return in triumph four months later when an extraordinary party congress recognized the non-Marxist as well as Marxist "contributions which have helped to make socialism the great alternative for emancipation of our time." In the 1982 parliamentary elections the PSOE won a sweeping victory. With González as prime minister, the socialists dominated Spanish politics for the next decade. Support for the PCE, meanwhile, was dwindling away. In 1982 it gained only 3.8 percent of the vote—down from 10.5 percent in 1979. Carrillo was forced to resign as general secretary, to be succeeded by Gerardo Iglesias. According to González, "Carrillo managed to accomplish in record time what Franco could not do in forty years of the dictatorship. He has dismembered the Communist Party in Spain."

The KGB also placed much of the blame for the collapse of PCE support on Carrillo personally, though its analysis differed from that of González. A book by an officer at the Madrid residency, Anatoli Krasikov, operating under cover as a Tass journalist, claimed that Carrillo's Eurocommunism and rejection of Marxism—Leninism had led the Party into "sharp internal strife" and electoral disaster: "Large numbers of activists, including very prominent ones who had struggled against Francoism and fought for the democratization of the country, were driven out of the Party."[47] Boris Ponomarev, the head of the international department, declared in a secret report early in 1983 that there was no prospect of a PCE revival so long as Carrillo or his protégés retained influence in it.[48]

In January 1984 Moscow supported, and probably financed, the foundation by Gallego of a breakaway Partido Comunista de los Pueblos de España. *Pravda* welcomed Gallego's denunciation of Eurocommunism and his announcement that the new party would be an "integral part" of the international Communist movement.[49] The PCPE, however, never became more than a splinter party. In 1986 the rump of the PCE merged with two smaller left-wing parties to form the Izquierda Unida (United Left).

THE THIRD OF the main Eurocommunist parties in the mid-1970s was the PCF (Parti Communiste Français), led by Georges Marchais, who had previously made a reputation as an uncompromising Stalinist. In 1957 he shouted angrily at a Party militant who dared to express doubts about Stalin's purges and the Soviet suppression of the Hungarian Uprising: "Yes, [the Soviets] arrested people, they imprisoned people! Well, I tell you they didn't arrest enough! They didn't imprison enough! If they had been tougher and more vigilant they wouldn't have got into the situation they find themselves in now!" François Mitterrand once complained, "Insult is [Marchais's] way of saying hello."[50]

As Marchais consolidated his power in the PCF as deputy general secretary in 1970 and general secretary two years later, the Centre grew increasingly suspicious of him. Despite his early Soviet loyalism, the KGB reported to the Central Committee in March 1976 that, according to its informants in "circles close to Marchais," he had been gradually moving away from "the principles of proletarian internationalism" for some time. The KGB's chief informant on Eurocommunist tendencies inside the PCF was Marchais's second-in-command, Gaston Plissonier, who had assisted Soviet intelligence operations since at least the early 1950s.[51] Like his fellow Soviet loyalists in Italy and in Spain, Plissonier was also the main conduit for Moscow's secret subsidies to the PCF.[52]

In June 1972 the PCF formed an electoral alliance and agreed a "common program of government" with the socialists and left-wing radicals. A few months later, according to the KGB, Marchais told his closest associates (doubtless including Plissonnier) that he condemned both the invasion of Czechoslovakia in 1968 and the continuing persecution of dissidents within the Soviet Union. Marchais was also deeply irritated by the Kremlin's apparent benevolence towards France's Gaullist governments, which, he claimed, "hampered the French Communist Party's revolutionary struggle." Since President de Gaulle had withdrawn France from the integrated NATO command in 1966, Moscow had seen Gaullism as potentially a more disruptive force in western Europe than a left-wing French government, even one which included Communists. Marchais tried to persuade the Kremlin that its assessment was mistaken. In 1972, doubtless intending his warning to be passed on to Moscow, he secretly threatened the East German leader, Erich Honecker:

> If the Socialist countries [the Soviet Bloc] do not take account of the French Communist Party's warning that the French government is shifting towards Atlantic [pro-American] positions, and if they do not give the Party the proper assistance in the struggle to overthrow the regime, they would be faced with a refusal by the French Communist Party to support their policy, as happened at the time of the Czechoslovak events [in 1968].

Publicly, the Kremlin appeared to pay little heed. Before the second round of the 1974 French presidential elections, the Soviet ambassador called on the neo-Gaullist candidate, Valéry Giscard d'Estaing, apparently implying that Moscow favored his election rather than that of Mitterrand, who had PCF support.[53] Behind the scenes, however, the KGB was engaged in active measures aimed—unsuccessfully—at securing Giscard's defeat.[54]

At the beginning of 1976 Marchais privately rebuked the PCF newspaper, *L'Humanité,* for failing to send a correspondent to meet the exiled Russian dissident, Leonid Plyushch, on his arrival in Paris after being freed from incarceration in a Soviet mental hospital. The Centre interpreted Marchais's gradual move towards Eurocommunism less in terms of ideological evolution than personal ambition. Even Berlinguer was reported by the KGB as criticizing Marchais for his narrow nationalism and comparing him to the Romanian autocrat Nicola Ceauşescu. The Centre concluded that Marchais would stop at nothing to satisfy his personal vanity.[55]

The KGB reported to the Central Committee that it was not until the Twenty-second Congress of the PCF in February 1976 that Marchais felt sufficiently confident of support for his increasingly heretical views within the Party hierarchy to dare to express them openly, despite the opposition of Plissonnier.[56] The congress adopted an ambitious Eurocommunist agenda. Marchais took the lead in rejecting the traditional aim of a "dictatorship of the proletariat," in criticizing the "limitations on democracy" in the Soviet Bloc and in committing the PCF to "a democratic road to socialism" which would "foster the free expression of many trends of thought." To scandalized Soviet loyalists within the PCF, the new Eurocommunist platform seemed to "legalize counter-revolution."[57] Over the next eighteen months the CPSU Central Committee sent three angry letters to the PCF complaining about its policies.[58] Behind the scenes the KGB accompanied such irate correspondence with active measures. Among them was operation YEVROPA, begun in 1977 and based on forged CIA documents which purported to reveal an American plot to destroy the unity of the PCF. The Centre hoped that YEVROPA would set some of the Central Committee against Marchais, presumably by implying that he was playing into the hands of the CIA.[59]

The KGB, however, had misjudged the strength of Marchais's ideological deviations. The PCF's Eurocommunist flirtation had been part of the price it had paid for the alliance with the socialists. The flirtation ended in the summer of 1977 after it became clear that, instead of confirming the Communists as the largest party on the French left, it had led to them being overtaken by the socialists. In September 1977 the left-wing alliance collapsed amid mutual recriminations. Thereafter Marchais and the PCF Central Committee gradually returned to an increasingly uncritical Soviet loyalism.[60] In October 1978 the Centre cancelled an active measure devised by the Paris residency to drive a wedge between the PCF and PCI, probably because it was no longer considered necessary.[61]

The KGB report on Marchais submitted to the Central Committee in March 1976 reported that he had hanging over him the exposure of his war record.[62] Marchais had claimed in 1970 that he had been "requisitioned" in December 1942 to work in a German factory at Lipheim building Messerschmitt fighter aircraft, but had escaped in January 1943 and returned to France.[63] The Centre, however, claimed to know "from reliable sources" that the French authorities had documents showing that, far from being forced to work in Germany, he had signed a voluntary contract for a job at Lipheim. The KGB report on Marchais was so hostile that in 1976 it may well have contemplated using his war record to discredit him, just as it hoped to use Berlinguer's allegedly shady building contracts to destroy his reputation.[64] It is unclear, however, whether the KGB did anything to bring to light a document, which was published in 1977 by Auguste Lecoeur, a former member of the PCF Politburo, and the right-wing weekly *Minute,* showing that Marchais had voluntarily accepted work in the Messerschmitt factory. Marchais claimed that the document was forged and brought a libel suit against both Lecoeur and *Minute.* At the opening of the trial in September 1977 he burst into tears. He lost both that case and another libel suit in the following year. In March 1980 *L'Express* published a wartime German document which appeared to show not merely that Marchais had gone voluntarily to work in Germany but that he had stayed there until 1944. On this occasion Marchais did not sue but maintained his innocence, declaring that he was the victim of an improbable plot by his rivals in the 1981 presidential elections: "That is why, at the origin of this calumny, there have been successively discovered close collaborators of Giscard d'Estaing, of Chirac, and of François Mitterrand."[65]

The PCF entered the 1980s in a mood of unswerving loyalty to Moscow. No other leader of a major Western Communist Party matched the zeal with which Marchais defended the Soviet invasion of Afghanistan in December 1979. Two years later the PCF sycophantically greeted the outlawing of Solidarity and the declaration of a state of emergency in Poland as a "triumph" for the Polish Communist Party. At the same time, however, the PCF was in steep electoral decline. In the 1981 presidential election Marchais gained only 15 percent of the vote—easily the Party's worst result since the Second World War. In 1986 the PCF vote fell even more precipitously, to 6.8 percent, in the parliamentary elections.[66]

THE GORBACHEV ERA brought a sea change in the CPSU's relations with foreign Communist Parties. The PCF and Moscow's other most faithful Western followers were increasingly outraged to discover that their loyalism was no longer appreciated. Gorbachev himself appeared far more interested in imaginative heresy than in intellectually sclerotic orthodoxy. Eurocommunism seemed to have conquered the Kremlin. As head of the CPSU delegation to Berlinguer's funeral in June 1984, Gorbachev was deeply impressed by the spontaneous outpouring of grief by a million and a half mourners crowded into Rome's Piazza San Giovanni.[67] One of the first signs of his "new thinking" when he became CPSU general secretary in March 1985 was the fact that the only European Communist leader included in his meetings with world statesmen after Chernenko's funeral was Berlinguer's successor, Alessandro Natta. Ponomarev was visibly shocked. How could it be, he asked his colleagues in the international department, that despite the presence of so many leaders of "good" Communist Parties in Moscow, Gorbachev had bestowed his favor instead on the general secretary of the "bad" PCI?[68]

Over the next five years Gorbachev repeatedly conferred with PCI leaders, praised their policies and used them as sounding boards for his "new thinking" on social democracy and East–West relations.[69] In Spain Gorbachev showed far less interest in the tattered remnants of the PCE[70] than in the ruling Socialist Party. Gorbachev's press secretary, Andrei Grachev, once asked him which foreign politician he felt closest to. Gorbachev's reply was unhesitating: Felipe González. According to Grachev, Gorbachev "did not just appreciate 'Felipe,' he loved him."[71]

Dependence on secret Soviet subsidies, however, persuaded some of the affronted hardline foreign Communist leaders to swallow their pride. In June 1987, Marchais sent a groveling message to Gorbachev conveying his "deepest gratitude" for meeting him in May and asking for "emergency financial aid" of 10 million francs (1.65 million dollars) to prepare for the 1988 presidential elections.[72] Noting that the PCF had already received 2 million dollars during 1987, the Politburo none the less agreed to supply another million via the KGB.[73]

For Gus Hall, the hardline leader of the ever-faithful CPUSA, Gorbachev's "new thinking" proved too much in the end. Goaded for the first time in his career into open disagreement with Moscow, he launched a public attack on Gorbachev's reforms in 1989, only for his secret Soviet subsidies to be abruptly cut off. The impact on the CPUSA was devastating. Plunged into an immediate financial crisis, it was forced in 1990 first to cut the publication of the Party newspaper, the *People's Daily World*, from five to two days a week, then to turn it into a weekly.[74] Armando Cossutta spoke for many traditional Moscow loyalists in Western Communist Parties when he declared his disgust after the failure of the August 1991 Moscow coup that "the term 'Communism' is now a dirty word even in the land of Lenin."[75]

ΠΙΠΕΤΕΕΠ

IDEOLOGICAL SUBVERSION

Part 1: The War Against the Dissidents

Soviet "dissidents" made their first public appearance on Constitution Day (December 5) 1965, when a group of about two hundred organized a demonstration in Pushkin Square, Moscow, in support of the authors Andrei Sinyavsky and Yuli Daniel, who were shortly to go on trial accused of attempting to subvert the Soviet system through their writings. Some of the demonstrators briefly succeeded in unfurling banners reading "Respect the Constitution!" and "We Demand an Open Trial for Sinyavsky and Daniel!", before being frogmarched to the police station by plain clothes members of the KGB. Henceforth the term used to describe democratic and human rights activists in the Soviet Union was the English word "dissidents" rather than its Russian equivalent *inakomysliashchii*—probably as part of an official attempt to portray such people as stooges of the West rather than as the authentic voice of Russian protest.[1]

The KGB had been unusually slow to track the two writers down. Sinyavsky, using the pseudonym "Abram Tertz," had begun publishing his work in the West, initially in Paris, in 1959. His friend Daniel, employing the alias "Nikolai Arzhak," had followed suit in 1961. After extensive analysis of the publications of "Tertz" and "Arzhak" by Soviet writers and literary critics who were KGB agents and co-optees, opinion in the Centre was divided on their real identity. One school of thought claimed that the intimate knowledge of Moscow life displayed by both authors showed that they were living in the Soviet Union and had smuggled their work abroad for publication. This view was supported by the Paris residency, which forwarded a report that the manuscript for "Tertz's" book, *The Trial Begins* (*Sud Idyot*), had reached France from Moscow. Others within the Centre sided with literary analysts who argued that "inaccuracies" in the authors' depiction of Moscow life showed that they were living in the West, and cited other (mistaken) KGB reports that both "Tertz" and "Arzhak" were living in western Europe.[2] The KGB was further confused by the fact that Sinyavsky used a Jewish pseudonym, thus giving rise to the mistaken belief that he was Jewish himself. The official Soviet press later denounced the choice of pseudonym as "a squalid provocation." According to a writer in *Izvestia*:

> By publishing anti-Soviet tales under the name of Abram Tertz in foreign publications, Sinyavsky was attempting to create the impression that anti-

Semitism exists in our country and that a writer with a name such as Abram Tertz has to seek publishers in the West if he wants to write "frankly" about Soviet life.[3]

After several years' fruitless surveillance of the wrong writers, a KGB agent in the Moscow literary world, codenamed YEFIMOV, reported early in 1964 that an author named Yuli Daniel was in possession of "anti-Soviet material." Simultaneously the KGB in Yalta sent a report from another agent who claimed that Daniel had the manuscript of "a story for which he could be given fifteen years' imprisonment." The surveillance of Daniel quickly led the KGB to Sinyavsky. In May 1964 the Centre began operation EPIGONI to obtain proof that Sinyavsky and Daniel were the authors of the "anti-Soviet" volumes published in the West, to discover where they kept their manuscripts and find out how they smuggled them out of the Soviet Union. The KGB arranged for Sinyavsky's employer, the Gorky Institute of World Literature, to send him on a business trip away from Moscow. During his absence it conducted a detailed search of his flat and installed bugging devices. Searching and bugging Daniel's apartment proved to be more difficult. His two-room flat with shared kitchen at 85 Leninsky Prospekt was reported to be "constantly occupied by his family, a friend and a dog." Eventually, a KGB officer, posing as the relative of a neighbor, succeeded in staying in the flat, taking wax impressions of the keys and creating an opportunity for a detailed search.[4]

It took over a year for operation EPIGONI to achieve significant results. Though the KGB lacked proof, it correctly concluded that Sinyavsky's first attempts to smuggle his work to the West had been assisted by Héläne Zamoyska, the daughter of a former French naval attaché, whom he had met while she was studying at Moscow University.[5] In the summer of 1965 the KGB intercepted a letter to Sinyavsky, signed "Alfreda" but giving no return address, inviting him to meet her at the Hotel Bucharest in Moscow. Having discovered that "Alfreda" was Alfreda Aucouturier, a friend of Hécläne Zamoyska, the KGB hoped to catch Sinyavsky in the act of handing over a manuscript to her. Sinyavsky and Daniel were both placed under 24-hour surveillance and a "special operational group" was formed to catch Madame Aucouturier red-handed. Despite bugging a visit made by Madame Aucouturier to Sinyavsky's flat and filming a later meeting between them near the Rechnoy Vokzal metro station, the group failed to detect any manuscript being handed over. It was disappointed again when it searched Madame Aucouturier's luggage at the Russo-Polish frontier on September 8.[6] A long interrogation also failed to produce results. The KGB's unsuccessful attempts to persuade Aucouturier to admit that "Tertz's" real name was Sinyavsky merely made her realize how thin their evidence was against him.[7]

Shortly after Madame Aucouturier was allowed to leave Russia, Sinyavsky and Daniel were arrested and taken to Lefortovo prison in Moscow. Under interrogation both confessed that they had published works under pseudonyms in the West, but denied that they were anti-Soviet. They also refused to admit that Madame Zamoyska had smuggled their manuscripts out of Russia. According to surveillance reports before their arrest, Sinyavsky and Daniel had been suspicious of all new acquaintances, sensibly fearing that they might be KGB agents. In Lefortovo prison, however, Sinyavsky fell for one of the oldest deceptions in the KGB's repertoire. A stoolpigeon codenamed MIKHAILOV (probably the illegal Geli Fyodorovich Vasilyev)[8] was introduced into his cell and succeeded in gaining his confidence. Before MIKHAILOV's "release" in November, Sinyavsky asked him to pass on a series of signs and passwords to his wife to enable her to communicate secretly with him during prison visits. MIKHAILOV's information and surveillance of Sinyavskaya's meetings with her husband provided what the EPIGONI file describes as "invaluable material relating to Sinyavsky's contacts." The most important of these contacts was Andrei Remizov, head librarian at the Moscow Library of Foreign Literature.[9]

Remizov confessed during interrogation that, under the pseudonym "Ivanov," he had published in the West the play *Is There life on Mars?* and the essay "American Pangs of the Russian Conscience," which had appeared in *Encounter* magazine in 1964.[10] He also admitted that, during a visit to France, he had delivered one of Sinyavsky's manuscripts to Hélène Zamoyska.[11] The KGB seems to have planned originally to put Remizov on trial with Sinyavsky and Daniel. When Remizov became suicidal, however, the plan changed. It was decided instead to use Remizov primarily as a prosecution witness against Sinyavsky and Daniel. His own case was treated separately and he was placed under 24-hour suicide watch. To prevent further contact with the wives of Sinyavsky and Daniel, who were trying to persuade him not to give evidence, Remizov was sent on official business by the Ministry of Culture to Kursk and Tula, where he remained on suicide watch until the trial. Surveillance of Daniel's wife showed that she was collecting a dossier of material for publication in the West before the trial. The KGB successfully planted on her an illegal posing as a sympathetic Western businessman who delivered the dossier not to the West but to the KGB.[12]

Though many Soviet writers had been persecuted for unorthodox opinions without due legal process, Sinyavsky and Daniel were the first to be put on trial simply for what they had written. The trial in February 1966 was officially a public one, with both defendants being granted their "full rights." As the *New York Herald Tribune* observed, "These rights included the right to be laughed at by a hand-picked audience of 70 persons . . . [and] the right to have only the prosecution side of the case reported in some detail to those who cannot claim access to the "open" trial because they have no passes."[13] The stage-managed proceedings were, however, spoiled by the failure of the defendants to play the roles allotted to them. Against all the traditions of Soviet show trials, Sinyavsky and Daniel refused either to admit guilt or to show contrition.

Despite the sycophantic audience, the prosecution was visibly disconcerted by the courageous and articulate defendants. Sinyavsky exposed the elementary confusion in a prosecution case which identified the opinions of fictional characters with those of their authors. He was also able to refer to the bugging of his flat before he was interrupted in mid-sentence.[14] The state prosecutor, undeterred either by his own mental confusion or by his uncertain grasp of the law,[15] concluded with an absurdly melo-dramatic denunciation of the two authors' work: "They pour mud on whatever is most holy, most pure—love, friendship, motherhood. Their women are either monsters or bitches. Their men are debauched." But the most serious crime committed by Sinyavsky and Daniel was that of ideological subversion:

> The social danger of their work, of what they have done, is particularly acute at this time, when ideological warfare is being stepped up, when the entire propaganda machine of international reaction, connected as it is with the intelligence services, is being brought into play to contaminate our youth with the poison of nihilism, to get its tentacles into our intellectual circles by hook or by crook . . .[16]

Sinyavsky was sentenced to seven years in a labor camp, Daniel to five.

The promised official transcript of the trial never appeared—a sure sign of the weakness of the prosecution case. An unofficial transcript, however, assembled by supporters of the defendants, was published in the West. To penetrate the dissidents who had come together in support of Sinyavsky and Daniel, the Centre selected two illegals in their late twenties, Anatoli Andreyevich Tonkonog (codenamed TANOV) and his wife Yelena Timofeyevna Fyodorova (TANOVA). Tonkonog reported that the sale of the transcripts of the trial of Sinyavsky and Daniel in the West had been organized by an entrepreneurial KGB agent, Nikolai Vasilyevich Dyakonov (codenamed GOGOL), who had worked for the Novosti Press Agency in the United States and other Western countries. According to one of Tonkonog's informants, Dyakonov was "a real wheeler-dealer" who dealt in foreign currency and sold Russian abstract paintings and unpublished literary works to Western buyers.[17]

Though the KGB evidently considered that the prosecution of Dyakonov would be too embarrassing, after a long investigation it put on trial in January 1968 four young dissidents who had compiled the transcript and other documents concerning the trial of Sinyavsky and Daniel: Aleksandr Ginzburg, Yuri Galanskov, Alexei Dobrovolsky and Vera Lashkova. Ginzburg and Galanskov had for some years taken leading roles in the production of samizdat journals. Their trial proceeded in much the same manner as that of Sinyavsky and Daniel. The courtroom audience was, once again, picked by the KGB and the defense was prevented from calling most of its witnesses. The two principal defendants, Ginzburg and Galanskov, again refused to contribute to the success of their own show trial and were sentenced to five and seven years in labor camp respectively. Emboldened by the courage of the defendants and the interest of the Western media, Daniel's wife, Larisa Bogoraz, and a fellow dissident, Pavel Litvinov, issued an impassioned denunciation of the conduct of the trial to foreign correspondents, with a request "that it be published and broadcast by radio as soon as possible."[18] Tonkonog later reported that the small demonstration in Red Square in August 1968 against Soviet military intervention in Czechoslovakia was also organized by Larisa Bogoraz. On this occasion Litvinov and other dissidents tried to dissuade her, but ten of them joined her when she insisted on going ahead. The KGB inevitably broke up the demonstration and arrested the demonstrators.[19]

THUS FAR THE writer who most concerned the Soviet authorities, Aleksandr Solzhenitsyn, codenamed PAUK ("Spider") by the KGB,[20] had escaped arrest. Solzhenitsyn had been saved in part by his celebrity. The labor camp novel *One Day in the Life of Ivan Denisovich*, which changed him almost overnight from an obscure provincial teacher of mathematics and physics into a world-renowned author, had been published in 1962 with the personal blessing of Khrushchev. During a sweep of Moscow dissidents shortly after the arrest of Sinyavsky and Daniel in September 1965, the KGB had discovered and confiscated manuscripts which Solzhenitsyn had left for safekeeping at the home of a friend. The KGB reported to the Central Committee that the manuscripts provided proof that "Solzhenitsyn indulges in politically damaging statements and disseminates slanderous fabrications." Both the KGB chairman, Vladimir Semichastny, and the Public Prosecutor, Roman Rudenko, were, however, uncertain how to proceed against such a celebrated writer, and simply referred Solzhenitsyn's manuscripts to the Writers' Union, which did not supply the denunciation expected of it for another eighteen months. By the time the Central Committee considered the matter in March 1967, Solzhenitsyn had sent his latest novel, *Cancer Ward*, to the West and had almost finished *The Gulag Archipelago*, his epic study of the labor camps. Within the Central Committee, the initiative in calling for "decisive measures" to deal with Solzhenitsyn's "anti-Soviet activities" came from Andropov, who succeeded Semichastny as KGB chairman in the summer of 1967.[21]

For the remaining seventeen years of his life, Andropov remained the dissidents' most determined opponent within the Soviet leadership. First-hand involvement in crushing the Hungarian uprising, reinforced by second-hand experience of the Prague Spring during his first year as KGB chairman, convinced him that one of the chief threats to the Soviet Bloc was Western-sponsored ideological subversion:

> The enemy gives direct and indirect support to counter-revolutionary elements, engages in ideological sabotage, establishes all sorts of anti-Socialist, anti-Soviet and other hostile organizations and seeks to fan the flames of nationalism. Graphic confirmation of this is provided by the events in Czechoslovakia . . . [22]

In the wake of the Prague Spring, Andropov set up a new KGB Fifth Directorate to monitor and crack down on dissent in all its forms. Specialized departments within the directorate were responsible for the surveillance of intellectuals, students, nationalists from ethnic minorities, religious believers and Jews.[23]

Solzhenitsyn increasingly became one of Andropov's personal obsessions. The announcement in October 1970 that the great subversive had won the Nobel Prize for Literature prompted the KGB chairman to submit to the Politburo a memorandum, also signed by Rudenko, enclosing a draft decree to deprive Solzhenitsyn of his citizenship and expel him from the Soviet Union:

When analyzing the materials on Solzhenitsyn and his works, one cannot fail to arrive at the conclusion that we are dealing with a political opponent of the Soviet state and social system . . . If Solzhenitsyn continues to reside in the country after receiving the Nobel Prize, it will strengthen his position, and allow him to propagandize his views more actively.[24]

Andropov, however, did not persuade a majority of the Politburo. Brezhnev showed more sympathy for the contrary views of his crony, Nikolai Shchelokov, the interior minister, who argued in the autumn of 1971 that Solzhenitsyn needed to be won over, not persecuted: "One of the higher-ups needs to sit down and talk with him, to remove the bitter taste that persecution has, no doubt, left in his mouth." Brezhnev underlined—apparently approvingly—a series of comments in a memorandum by Shchelokov which must have been anathema to Andropov:

In resolving the Solzhenitsyn question we must analyze past mistakes made in dealing with people in the arts . . . The "Solzhenitsyn Problem" was created by literary administrators who should have known better . . . In this case what needs to be done is not to execute our enemies publicly but smother them with embraces.[25]

Henceforth Shchelokov, so far as Andropov was concerned, was a marked man. After Brezhnev's death he was charged by Andropov with corruption but committed suicide before going on trial.[26]

In the autumn of 1971, however, Andropov knew better than to attack openly opinions approved by Brezhnev. But he was not prepared to give up. In March 1972 Andropov made a further attempt to persuade the Politburo to expel Solzhenitsyn from the Soviet Union, providing further "indisputable" evidence that "he was deliberately and irrevocably embarked on the path of struggle with the Soviet government and will wage this struggle regardless of everything." Though agreeing that Solzhenitsyn was "a true degenerate," the Politburo—doubtless to Andropov's extreme displeasure—was still not willing to send him into exile.[27]

THE OTHER DISSIDENT who most obsessed Andropov from the early 1970s onwards was the nuclear physicist and Academician Andrei Sakharov, codenamed ASKET ("Ascetic") by the KGB, "father" of the Soviet H-bomb and three times Hero of Socialist Labor. Though out of favor with the scientific establishment, he retained an official dacha in Zhukovka as well as his flat in Moscow. Late in 1970, Sakharov and two fellow physicists, Valeri Chalidze and Andrei Tverdokhlebov, founded the Committee for Human Rights and persuaded Solzhenitsyn to become a corresponding (though not very active) member.[28] Like Solzhenitsyn, Sakharov's international stature made it difficult for the KGB to persecute him as freely as less well-known dissidents. His KGB file makes the absurd claim that Sakharov "used his authority to influence the decisions of the judiciary and create a hullabaloo around the trials of anti-social elements" such as Vladimir Bukovsky, put on trial in January

1972 for compiling evidence about the committal of himself and other dissidents to mental hospitals.[29] The real burden of the KGB complaint was that Sakharov and his committee had some modest success in limiting, though not in preventing, the abuse of the legal process.

In October 1972 the 37-year-old illegal Georgi Ivanovich Kotlyar, codenamed BERTRAND, succeeded in winning Sakharov's confidence and establishing what the Centre considered a "trusted relationship" with him and his wife Elena Bonner. Kotlyar had been born in France and succeeded in passing himself off as one "Alain Boucaut," a French archaeologist who had been working in Mexico for the past decade. His success in maintaining his cover and providing intelligence on Sakharov and Bonner won him high praise from both Filipp Denisovich Bobkov, head of the Fifth Directorate, and his deputy, Nikashin.[30] Attempts were also made to plant agents on Solzhenitsyn, among them the pianist Miroka Kokornaya (transparently codenamed MIROKA), who regularly went on concert tours abroad. A KGB operation in 1973 to persuade Solzhenitsyn to use MIROKA as a courier to the West failed.[31]

In the summer of 1973 the KGB at last succeeded in staging what it considered a successful show trial, during which the defendants incriminated themselves in the best Stalinist tradition, and other dissidents were duly demoralized. The victims of this traditional travesty of Soviet justice were Pyotr Yakir and Viktor Krasin, leading members of the group which produced the samizdat *Chronicle of Current Events*. Yakir was the son of an army commander shot during the Great Terror, and had spent much of his life in prison. At the time of his arrest in June 1972, he was known by other dissidents to be close to breaking point and drinking heavily. After the trial of Bukovsky, the KGB had overheard him saying, "I can't take it any more. I couldn't face another sentence myself—I haven't the strength." Before his arrest, Yakir circulated a statement saying that any confession extracted from him in jail should be disregarded.[32] Though exhausted by many years of persecution, Yakir somehow found the strength to resist during the early stages of his interrogation before finally breaking under prolonged pressure. In the brutally triumphant words of his chief interrogator, "He began to assess his actions and the contents of the anti-Soviet literature which he had distributed fairly objectively and politically correctly." Yakir was finally persuaded to put his signature to a formulaic KGB-dictated confession:

> In the course of the investigation, I have come to understand that I committed a whole series of criminal acts: I have signed letters with a defamatory content which asserted that in our country people are sentenced for their beliefs; I have given a number of interviews to foreign correspondents which contained slanderous assertions; I kept, duplicated and distributed documents of similar content; and I frequently passed tendentious information to foreign correspondents who used this for propaganda purposes.
>
> Having grasped the seriousness of what I have done, I sincerely repent. Not only will I not do this again in the future, but I shall do my utmost to influence people who are close to me and to demonstrate the error of their positions.[33]

The breaking of Krasin under interrogation caused much greater surprise in dissident circles than that of Yakir. According to his KGB file, "[Krasin] stood out because of the particularly hostile attitude to the Soviet system which he had adopted in his youth, his stubbornness and consistency in his work, and his readiness to see things through to the end, regardless of the obstacles." He was co-author of the samizdat *Legal Instructions,* which advised all those summoned for interrogation by the KGB to refuse to answer questions. On seven occasions between 1968 and 1972 when he himself had been questioned by the KGB, Krasin had faithfully followed his own advice. After prolonged surveillance, however, the Fifth Directorate concluded that a "polite and calm" interrogation with "absolutely no sneering," combined with a sympathetic stoolpigeon in his cell, would eventually wear down his resistance. Krasin was known to be willing to disagree with other dissidents, and during 1971–2 had become increasingly despondent about their prospects. There were, he said, "few defenders at the final barricades."[34]

As expected, Krasin began his lengthy interrogation in defiant mood. When his interrogator, Lieutenant-Colonel Pavel Aleksandrovsky, asked, "Why do you refuse to say what you have been doing if you do not consider it criminal?" Krasin replied, "I do not consider it criminal, but you do. Therefore, if I were to tell you, I would be giving you incriminating material which I do not want to do." The first breach in Krasin's defenses was made by the KGB agent in his cell, who pretended that he had been arrested for dealing in foreign currency and appealed for Krasin's advice on how to face the charges against him. Instead of simply telling him not to answer questions, Krasin showed him how to frame the best defense during his interrogation. Full of praise for Krasin's knowledge of the criminal code, the stoolpigeon then urged him to follow his own advice and challenge the charges against him:

> You are very clever. Fancy knowing the law so well! You can stand up to any interrogator. It would be impossible to trick you or frighten you! If you can prove that what you did was not criminal, then you will be helping your friends who are still free!

Krasin's KGB cellmate claimed to have been converted from his previous political skepticism to Krasin's dissident opinions, and gradually persuaded him that by standing up for those views during his interrogation he would be continuing his fight for Russian democracy. According to the absurdly stilted language of the interrogation report, "The agent also introduced the beauty of nature and the significance of art and literature into their conversations. This rekindled Krasin's love of life and made him forget his bitter disenchantment." Rumors fed to him that Yakir was now talking to his interrogator seem finally to have persuaded Krasin to take his cellmate's advice. "The idea that Yakir was giving full, true and detailed evidence," declared his interrogator Aleksandrovsky dramatically, "hung over him like the sword of Damocles."[35]

Krasin's early replies to Aleksandrovsky's questions were extremely cautious. Initially he limited himself to refuting alleged evidence that he had attempted to subvert or weaken Soviet power, refusing to answer anything he considered a leading question. He prepared written answers to those questions he accepted, sometimes preparing and correcting several drafts before handing one of them to his interrogator. This laborious procedure continued for two months, during which Krasin provided what the KGB considered "only worthless information." Like all good interrogators, however, Aleksandrovsky was patient. "The importance of these first interrogations," he believed, "was that they enabled psychological contact to be established."

The first sign of a breakthrough came on September 27, 1972. As usual Krasin insisted that, "The accusation against me is monstrous. I cannot do what is against my conscience. I cannot admit that I am guilty of something that I have not done or repent of crimes which have not been committed." But, for the first time, he seemed to accept that his career as a dissident was at an end. "I will not," he announced, "carry on with my work." Krasin added that he did not believe Aleksandrovsky's main aim was to sentence him to another term in a labor camp. Henceforth the scope of the interrogation was broadened. Each day Aleksandrovsky allowed Krasin to choose the subject for discussion but tried, when the opportunity arose, to develop their conversation in ways which showed the hopelessness of his position and of the dissident cause. While discussing the fight against counter-revolution in the Dzerzhinsky era, Aleksandrovsky mentioned the case of the arch anti-Bolshevik Boris Savinkov, who had been lured back to Russia in August 1924. Krasin's KGB cellmate was primed to raise the question of how long Savinkov's interrogation had lasted. The answer, which Krasin doubtless discovered from a book lent him by his interrogator, was that after only nine days Savinkov publicly renounced his "bloody struggle" against the Bolshevik regime and declared that he unconditionally recognized the Soviet state.[36] When Krasin asked him why Savinkov had recanted, Aleksandrovsky replied that he had seen the hopelessness of his situation, realized that his struggle against Soviet power was doomed to failure and understood that his actions were against the interests of the Russian people.

Whenever Krasin expressed interest in a subject during interrogation, Aleksandrovsky would try to find him relevant books and articles which would have a "positive influence" on him. He was thought to be particularly impressed by the stirring account by the British journalist Alexander Werth in his book *Russia at War* of the endurance and triumph of the Soviet people during the Great Patriotic War. On one occasion Krasin was even given copies of the banned periodical *Posev,* published by the émigré NTS (social democrat organization), which contained articles by himself and Yakir. Krasin was seen to rub his hands with anticipation as he opened the pages of the periodical. After a time, he put the copies of *Posev* down in disgust, declaring that it was "White Guard drivel" and that he had never read "anything so primitive and bereft of ideas." From his reading of the file, Mitrokhin suspected that Krasin had been given fabricated copies of the periodical specially designed to arouse his indignation.

Krasin's separation from his wife, Yemelkina, who was banished into internal exile at Yesineysk, was also used to increase the emotional pressure on him. Alexandrovsky noted cynically, "Krasin loved his wife greatly and was ready to do anything for her sake." On visiting Yemelkina at Yesineysk, he found that she too was desperate to be reunited with her husband. Probably as a condition of being allowed to visit Krasin, Yemelkina agreed to reveal where she had hidden "anti-Soviet literature." After an emotional reunion with his wife in January 1973, Krasin gave Aleksandrovsky the locations of four hiding places containing sixty allegedly subversive foreign publications and 140 microfilms (totaling 5,000 frames) of other "anti-Soviet texts."[37] Further pressure on Krasin was exerted during visits from his mother and other relatives and friends, all of whom had been expertly intimidated by the KGB.[38]

Even after Krasin had agreed to plead guilty to the charges against him, however, he refused for almost two months to incriminate his friends. Step by step Aleksandrovsky overcame his resistance. First, Krasin agreed to talk about dissidents who had already confessed, then about foreign correspondents who had left Moscow and Soviet émigrés in the USA and Israel who were, as he put it, "beyond the reach of the KGB." Next he identified people who, he said, had not committed any criminal offense but had merely read "anti-Soviet literature" and had been present when foreign correspondents were given the *Chronicle of Current Events*. Then, almost overnight, what remained of Krasin's resistance to informing on his fellow dissidents collapsed. He spent ten days writing by hand a document of over a hundred pages setting out the evidence against dissidents, identifying sixty of them and giving details of numerous incidents previously unknown to the Fifth Directorate—among them the origins of the *Chronicle of Current Events*. To a triumphant Aleksandrovsky it seemed as though Krasin was "unburdening himself of a great weight."

At Aleksandrovsky's prompting, Krasin then spent two months composing an appeal to his fellow dissidents which was read aloud at a meeting in Yakir's flat in April 1973 and, according to a KGB report, "made a strong impact." "We started by demanding that the laws should be observed," declared Krasin, "but ended up breaking them. We forgot the basic truth that we are citizens of the USSR and are bound to respect and keep the laws of our state." Fifty-seven dissidents named by Krasin and Yakir were summoned for interrogation by the Moscow KGB. Some were subjected to emotional confrontations with Krasin and Yakir, who appealed to them to end the dissident campaign. According to KGB records, forty-two capitulated. Another eight "vacillated in evaluating their activities" but "gave assurances that they would not commit any anti-social acts in future." Only seven remained completely unrepentant; all were given official cautions and put under "operational surveillance." During 1973 a total of 154 people associated with the dissident movement were cautioned by the Moscow KGB, eighty of them "for possessing, writing and distributing ideologically harmful material and for anti-social and politically harmful conduct."

The trial of Yakir and Krasin opened in Moscow on August 27, 1973. Solzhenitsyn dismissed it in advance as "a dismal repetition of the clumsy Stalin–Vyshinsky farces:"

> In the 1930s . . . these farces, despite the primitive stagecraft, the smeared grease-paint, the loudness of the prompter, were still a great success with "thinking people" among Western intellectuals . . . But if no [foreign] correspondents are to be admitted to the trial, it means that it has been pitched two grades lower still.

Western correspondents were, however, invited to a KGB press conference at which Yakir and Krasin paraded their guilt and remorse in front of television cameras.[39] The transformation of Krasin seemed so remarkable that some dissidents wrongly suspected he had been a KGB agent all along.[40]

In the Centre, the show trial was regarded as a triumph. Basking in the approval of their superiors, the case officers of Yakir and Krasin wrote a self-congratulatory article in the classified in-house quarterly, *KGB Sbornik*, explaining how "the detailed tactics worked out for the interrogation of the accused" and the "deeply thought-out cultivation within the [prison] cell" by well-trained stoolpigeons had combined to "determine the positive results which were obtained at the hearing of the case."[41]

SAKHAROV AND SOLZHENITSYN, however, still remained beyond the punitive arm of the KGB. While the trial of Yakir and Krasin was in progress they raised the stakes in their campaign by publicly criticizing the concessions made by the United States to the Soviet Union in the name of East–West détente. On September 17 Sakharov addressed a public appeal to the US Congress, asking it to support the Jackson–Vanik amendment opposing most-favored nation status for the USSR until it ended restrictions on emigration:

> The amendment does not represent interference in the internal affairs of socialist countries, but simply a defense of international law, without which there can be no mutual trust.[42]

Sakharov's letter, printed in capital letters in the *Washington Post*, was credited with persuading Congress to pass the amendment, despite the opposition of the Nixon administration.

The Politburo reacted with predictable fury. Brezhnev absurdly denounced Sakharov's letter as "not just an anti-State and anti-Soviet deed, but a Trotskyist deed." They had, he declared, tolerated the behavior of Solzhenitsyn and Sakharov for far too long: "We should have stopped them right away." Andropov, now a full (voting) member of the Politburo, sought to maintain the collective outrage of his colleagues by a series of slanted intelligence reports. Solzhenitsyn and Sakharov, he declared, had "stepped up the peddling of their services to reactionary imperialist, and particularly Zionist, circles," and were being manipulated by, or actually colluding with, Western intelligence agencies. On February 7, 1974 Andropov submitted to the Politburo a further draft decree to deprive Solzhenitsyn of his citizenship and expel him from the Soviet Union. Simultaneously, he sent an alarmist personal letter to Brezhnev, implying that there would be serious discontent among senior Party and Military figures unless the decree was approved:

> . . . I think it impossible, despite our desire not to harm international relations, to delay the solution of the Solzhenitsyn problem any longer, because it could have extremely unpleasant consequences for us inside the country.

This time the KGB pressure on Brezhnev and his colleagues was successful. On February 11 the Politburo formally approved "the proposals of Comrade Andropov."[43] Three days later, Solzhenitsyn was forcibly put on board an Aeroflot flight to Frankfurt by KGB officers. As the plane took off, he crossed himself and bowed to the homeland he might never see again.[44]

From Frankfurt Solzhenitsyn moved on to Zurich, where he rented a house in the city center. Paradoxically it was easier for the KGB to penetrate his entourage in Switzerland than in Russia. Abroad, among strangers, Solzhenitsyn found it far more difficult than at home to distinguish friend from foe. The KGB was quick to take advantage of his sympathy for the survivors of the Prague Spring by using StB agents in the Czech émigré community to win his confidence. The first to do so was the Russian-born StB officer Valentina Holubová.[45] Though the files noted by Mitrokhin do not record her first meeting with Solzhenitsyn, she seems to have arrived on his doorstep on his first day in Zurich, claiming to be from Ryazan (where he had been a schoolteacher) and bearing a bouquet of roses and lilac. She gave him a note containing an old Ryazan proverb and said the lilac was to remind him of the lilac that bloomed in Ryazan each spring.[46] Within a few weeks, at most, Holubová and her husband, Dr. František Holub (also an StB agent), had succeeded in ensconcing themselves as Solzhenitsyn's unofficial advisers in Zurich, with Valentina also acting as his part-time secretary and spokeswoman.[47]

In March 1974 the Holubs took Solzhenitsyn to see an exhibition of paintings by the artist Lucia Radova at a gallery in the village of Pfúffikon, not far from Zurich, owned by the Czech émigré Oskar Krause. When Krause told him that he too had been a political prisoner, imprisoned in Czech jails, Solzhenitsyn embraced him and burst into tears. The Holubs then introduced him to the young Czech writer Tomáš Řezáč (codenamed REPO), like themselves an StB officer who had penetrated the émigré community posing as a dissident. Solzhenitsyn later agreed that Dr. Holub should edit the work of the seven translators producing a Czech edition of *The Gulag Archipelago*, while Řezáč would translate the long narrative poem, *Prussian Nights*, which Solzhenitsyn had written in prison in 1949.[48]

Solzhenitsyn thus became the latest in a long line of leading Soviet émigrées, stretching back to the inter-war White Guard and Trotskyist leaders, who unwittingly included Soviet agents among their most trusted advisers.[49] The thought of Holub and Řezáč translating the works of the great heretic was bound to give the Centre some pause for thought. But

> It was deemed to be operationally justified for REPO to translate all Solzhenitsyn's materials, without declining to translate various anti-Soviet texts or attempting to tone them down, since he might otherwise lose Solzhenitsyn's confidence and the texts would in any case be translated by someone else.

Because of the importance of the PAUK (Solzhenitsyn) case, REPO's instructions were personally drawn up, doubtless in consultation with the KGB, by the head of StB foreign intelligence, Hladik, and his deputy, Dovin.[50]

Intelligence from the Holubs and Řezáč allowed the KGB to monitor Solzhenitsyn's contacts with supporters inside the Soviet Union as well as his activities in the West. Andropov reported to the Politburo on May 2:

[Solzhenitsyn] is hatching plans to conduct subversive activity against the USSR. Residing in Zurich, he has established, in particular, contacts with representatives of the Czechoslovak émigrés in Switzerland, with the assistance of whom he intends to arrange the illegal delivery of his writings and other material of an anti-Soviet nature to the Soviet Union. Solzhenitsyn stated in a discussion with the Czechoslovak émigrés that his future activities would be subordinate primarily to the interests of the "opposition inside the USSR."

Following usual practice, Andropov did not identify his sources by name; in particular he did not reveal to the Politburo that the main émigrés with whom Solzhenitsyn had had these conversations were StB agents. On July 24 he reported that Solzhenitsyn had set up a "Russian Social Fund," using royalties from his books, to "assist the families of political prisoners detained in Soviet camps." As on other occasions, Andropov also gave a woefully distorted assessment of Solzhenitsyn's influence in exile. "Available information," he informed the Politburo, ". . . indicates that after Solzhenitsyn's deportation abroad, interest in him in the West is steadily on the decline." At that very moment, volume I of *The Gulag Archipelago* was a runaway bestseller, with a print run of 2 million paperbacks in the USA alone.[51] KGB assessments on Solzhenitsyn, as on some other subjects, were distorted at two levels. First, residencies in varying degrees told the Centre what it wanted to hear. Secondly, Andropov told the Politburo what *he* wanted it to hear—which in the summer of 1974 emphasized the correctness of the decision to send Solzhenitsyn into exile but did not include the phenomenal Western sales figures of his books.

On September 19, 1974 Andropov approved a large-scale, "multifaceted plan" (no. 5/9-16091) to discredit and destabilize Solzhenitsyn and his family and cut his links with dissidents in the Soviet Union. A Fifth Department officer with experience of the PAUK case was sent to Switzerland on long-term assignment to direct a series of operations against Solzhenitsyn.[52] The KGB sponsored a series of hostile books and articles, among them a memoir published under the name of his first wife, Natalia Reshetovskaya, but probably mainly composed by Service A. In 1975 Řezáč suddenly disappeared from Zurich, taking the manuscript of *Prussian Nights* with him, and made his way to Moscow to begin work on a biography intended to destroy Solzhenitsyn's reputation. Shortly afterwards, Solzhenitsyn realized that he had also been betrayed by the Holubs, on whom he had relied ever since he had arrived in Zurich, and broke all contact with them.[53] Andropov gave orders to maintain "an atmosphere of distrust and suspicion between PAUK and the people around him" by feeding Solzhenitsyn constant rumors that others in his circle were KGB agents or deceiving him in a variety of ways.

The plan to destabilize Solzhenitsyn also sought "to create a state of nervousness within his family" through a constant stream of threats against his children and the sending of suspicious packages which looked as if they might contain explosives.[54] The Sakharovs were subjected to similar treatment. Shortly before Elena Bonner was due to have eye surgery, they were sent photographs of eyes gouged out of their sockets and other horrifying eye injuries. At Christmas 1974 they received dozens of envelopes containing photographs of car accidents, brain surgery and monkeys with electrodes implanted in their brains.[55] All such threats, Solzhenitsyn told *Time* magazine, "come from one and the same organization"—the KGB.[56]

What is most striking about the KGB's campaign against Solzhenitsyn during his Swiss exile is the enormous priority and resources devoted to it. The "plan of agent operational measures" to be implemented during 1975 against Solzhenitsyn and the émigrée journal, *Kontinent,* with which he was associated, was jointly agreed late in the previous year by Kryuchkov, Grigorenko and Bobkov (heads of the First Chief, Second Chief and Fifth Directorates). It had nineteen sections, of which the first three alone provided for twenty different hostile operations.[57] The residencies in Berne, Geneva, Karlshorst, London, Paris, Rome and Stockholm were all involved in implementing the "agent operational measures" and a series of joint operations were planned with other Soviet Bloc intelligence agencies.[58] In July 1976 plans for yet more active measures, jointly proposed once again by Kryuchkov, Grigorenko and Bobkov, were approved by Andropov.[59]

The destabilization campaign had some success. Swiss newspapers reported that Solzhenitsyn asked for, but did not receive, police protection. KGB harassment in Zurich was probably at least partly responsible for his decision to move to the United States in 1976.[60] Since his expulsion from Russia two years earlier, Solzhenitsyn had lost some of the immense moral authority he had formerly possessed as a persecuted dissident. Dismayed by what he saw as Western indifference to the Soviet menace, he took to denouncing, sometimes in apocalyptic tones, the moral failings of a West he did not fully understand. After settling in Vermont, he became a virtual recluse on his fifty-acre estate behind an eight-foot-high chainlink fence topped with barbed wire, as he devoted himself to writing a series of historical novels on Russia in the years leading up to the October Revolution.

Solzhenitsyn's life as a recluse (with occasional excursions to deliver the 1978 Harvard Commencement Address and other solemn pronouncements on East and West) may well have spared him further KGB penetration of his entourage of the kind that had taken place in Zurich. Previously, on August 23, 1975, Andropov had approved a draft directive (no. 150/S-9195), jointly proposed by the heads of the First Chief and Fifth Directorates, Kryuchkov and Bobkov, establishing as the main priority in operations against émigrés the infiltration of at least one illegal into Solzhenitsyn's inner circle. When Solzhenitsyn moved to the United States, L. G. Bolbotenko, a Line KR officer in the New York residency, was put in charge of operations against him. Though there were numerous active measures designed to discredit Solzhenitsyn and embroil him with other émigrés, there is no evidence that any illegal succeeded in gaining his confidence.[61]

Despite failing to penetrate Solzhenitsyn's Vermont fastness, the KGB seems to have been broadly satisfied by the later 1970s that the great writer's reputation in the

West had declined dramatically. In the summer of 1978, the FCD and Fifth Directorate jointly arranged the screening of a video of Solzhenitsyn's Harvard Address to a meeting of leading KGB and Party figures. It was an extraordinary moment in Soviet history. Never before, almost certainly, had such an audience gathered together to hear a lecture by a leading opponent of the Soviet system.[62] The Moscow notables watched, probably intently, as Solzhenitsyn gave his Commencement audience in Harvard Yard, while drizzle moistened their academic gowns, an uncompromising "measure of bitter truth." He denounced those in the West whose silence and inertia had made them "accomplices" in the suffering imposed on those who lived under Communist rule. Corrupted by materialism and selfish individualism, the West had become morally impoverished: "Two hundred or even fifty years ago, it would have seemed quite impossible, in America, that an individual be granted boundless freedom with no purpose, simply for the satisfaction of his whims . . ." Though many in Harvard Yard were skeptical, and some were probably seething, they dutifully followed tradition and cheered Solzhenitsyn's address.[63]

The KGB screening of the address was followed by commentaries from FCD and Fifth Directorate officers. Though Mitrokhin's brief notes report only their conclusions, they probably cited the hostile reception accorded to Solzhenitsyn's "bitter truth" by *The New York Times* and the *Washington Post*. The *Times* leader writer found "Mr. Solzhenitsyn's world view . . . far more dangerous than the easy-going spirit which he finds so exasperating," while the *Post* denounced his "gross misunderstanding of western society." The KGB commentators were agreed that Solzhenitsyn had alienated his American listeners by his "reactionary views and intransigent criticism of the US way of life—a fact which could not fail to have a negative effect on his authority in the eyes of the West and his continued use in anti-Soviet propaganda." The meeting of KGB and Party notables agreed that no active measures were required to counter the Harvard Address.[64] Solzhenitsyn, they evidently believed, had discredited himself.

TWENTY

IDEOLOGICAL SUBVERSION

Part 2: The Victory of the Dissidents

On August 1, 1975 the Soviet leadership committed what turned out to be a strategic blunder in its war against the dissidents. As part of the Helsinki Accords on Security and Co-operation in Europe, the United States, Canada and all European states save Albania and Andorra agreed to protect a series of basic human rights. Though Andropov warned against the consequences, a majority of the Politburo shared Gromyko's confident view that "We are masters in our house"—that the Soviet Union would be free to interpret the human rights provisions of the Helsinki Accord as it saw fit. In fact, as Zbigniew Brzezinski predicted, the accord "put the Soviet Union on the ideological defensive."[1] Henceforth its human rights critics both at home and abroad could justly claim that it was in breach of an international agreement it had freely entered into.

The most influential of those critics was, increasingly, Andrei Sakharov. From the KGB's viewpoint, both the importance and the difficulty of discrediting Sakharov before world opinion were heightened by his being awarded the Nobel Peace Prize in October 1975. The Oslo residency had been instructed to do all in its power to prevent the award, but was forced to confess that it was powerless to influence the Nobel Peace Prize committee which, it claimed, was wholly composed of "reactionaries"—chief amongst them its chairwoman, the Labor Party deputy Aase Lionaes.[2] Sakharov pronounced the Peace Prize "a great honor not just for me but also for the whole human rights movement":

> I feel I share this honor with our prisoners of conscience—they have sacrificed their most precious possession, their liberty, in defending others by open and non-violent means.[3]

Just over a week after he received news of the award, the first of the "Sakharov Hearings," held in response to an appeal launched by Sakharov and other dissidents a year earlier, opened in Copenhagen to hear evidence of Soviet human rights abuses—almost all of them in breach of the Helsinki Accords.

On November 22 Andropov approved a document entitled "Complex Operational Measures to Expose the Political Background to the Award of the Nobel Peace Prize to Sakharov." The sheer range and ambitiousness of the active measures proposed indicated Sakharov's increasing prominence as a KGB target. In collaboration, where necessary, with other KGB directorates, the FCD was instructed:

- to inspire articles and speeches by public and political personalities in Norway, Finland, Sweden, Denmark, Britain and the FRG, to develop the theme that the award of the Nobel Peace Prize to Sakharov was an attempt by certain political circles to slow down the process of détente . . .
- to organize articles and speeches by representatives of public and political circles through KGB assets in Finland, France, Italy and Britain, to demonstrate the absurdity of attempting to link the award of the Peace Prize to Sakharov to a decision relating to the all-European [Helsinki] Conference . . .
- to organize the mailing of letters and declarations protesting about the award of the Peace Prize to Sakharov to the Nobel Committee of the Norwegian Storting [parliament] and to influential press organs in various Western countries . . .
- to pass material compromising Sakharov to the Danish, Swedish and Finnish press, hinting at his links with reactionary organizations financed by the CIA and other Western special services;
- to take steps designed to persuade S. Haffner, the leading political observer of the West German *Stern* magazine to make negative comments on the award of the Nobel Peace Prize to Sakharov. Haffner had already made sharp criticisms in the FRG press when Sakharov was put forward for the Peace Prize in 1973;
- to pass information to the "dissident" emigration in western Europe designed to exacerbate relations between Sakharov and Solzhenitsyn . . .
- with the help of agents of influence among prominent Chilean émigrés (in Algeria and Mexico), to disseminate the text of a [bogus] telegram of congratulations supposedly sent by General Pinochet [who had led the coup against President Allende] to Sakharov on the occasion of the award of the Nobel Peace Prize;
- to inspire pronouncements by leading Chilean émigrés in Italy, the FRG and France, expressing the outrage of all Chilean patriots at the award of the Nobel Peace Prize to Sakharov, who in 1973 had welcomed the overthrow of the Allende government and in return for this had been awarded the title of "Honorary Citizen" by Pinochet;
- to inspire public statements by public personalities in the Arab countries, condemning the Nobel Committee's decision on Sakharov, presenting this as a deal between Sakharov and the Zionists, in return for Sakharov's pronouncements on the question of Jewish emigration from the Soviet Union, as the Zionists had a decisive influence on the Nobel Committee when it awarded the Nobel Peace Prize for 1975. It should be noted that the "Sakharov Hearings" in Copenhagen were also a form of payment to Sakharov by the Zionists in return for his pro-Israel activity;

- to make available through Novosti for publication abroad a series entitled "Who Defends Sakharov?," dealing with [alleged pro-Sakharov] criminals sentenced in the Soviet Union for bribery (Shtern), theft (Leviyev), instigation of terrorism (Bukovsky, Moroz).[4]

The main fabrications intended to discredit Sakharov personally—his links with Western intelligence agencies, his support for the Pinochet regime and his plots with the Zionists—were all further developed in active measures over the next few years.[5] The files examined by Mitrokhin, however, record few immediate successes for the operations approved by Andropov in November 1975. The best the Oslo residency could do to provoke Norwegian opposition to Sakharov's award was to claim the credit for an article in *Dagbladet* ridiculing his wife Elena Bonner, who in December 1975 collected the award in place of Sakharov after he was denied an exit visa. The author of the article claimed that Bonner, a heavy smoker, was constantly providing "free publicity for the tobacco industry" and should have received a cigarette lighter rather than the Nobel Prize.[6]

In Oslo to see Bonner collect the award on behalf of Sakharov was the Soviet émigré Vladimir Maximov, editor-in-chief of the journal *Kontinent*, which published news of dissidents throughout eastern Europe in Russian, English, French, German and Italian editions. The first issue in September 1974 had opened with a ringing declaration by Solzhenitsyn:

> The intelligentsia of eastern Europe speaks with the united voice of suffering and knowledge. All honor to *Kontinent* if it is able to make his voice heard. Woe (which will not be long in coming) to western Europe if its ears fail to hear.[7]

Kontinent rapidly established Maksimov as second only to Solzhenitsyn in the KGB's list of émigrées enemies. Among the most ingenious of the many active measures used to discredit him in 1976 was one which followed the discovery that a car used by Eduard Mihailovich Serdinov (codenamed TKACHEV), an operations officer in the New York residency, had been bugged by the FBI. It was decided to stage a conversation in the car between Serdinov and a KGB agent from the Soviet community which, it was hoped, would deceive the FBI:

SERDINOV: By the way, Solzhenitsyn's chum Maksimov is also becoming more and more insolent. He is turning into an open enemy.
AGENT: Which Maksimov do you mean?
SERDINOV: That Parisian one—from the *Kontinent.*
AGENT: Oh, don't pay any attention to him! I have heard here from "certain people" . . . well, from "them" [i.e. the KGB] . . . that he is their agent and that he even underwent special training with them before he left the Soviet Union.

Other active measures were devised to reinforce the impression that Maksimov was a KGB agent.[8] Whether any of them actually succeeded in deceiving the FBI or any other Western intelligence agency remains in doubt.

Doubtless to the intense irritation of the Centre, *Kontinent* was able to publicize the formation during 1976 and 1977 of "Helsinki Watch Groups" in Moscow, Ukraine, Lithuania, Georgia and Armenia to monitor Soviet compliance with the terms of the Helsinki Accords.

At a meeting of the KGB Collegium in 1976, Andropov branded Sakharov "Public Enemy Number One,"[9] a title he retained for the next nine years. The active measures campaign against him continued to expand for several years, with attacks on his wife Elena (codenamed LISA—"Vixen"—by the KGB) forming an increasingly large part of it. A list of current and impending active measures compiled in February 1977 included thirteen "operations to compromise ASKET[Sakharov]"; seven "measures to cut off ASKET and LISA from their close contacts engaged in antisocial activity and to cause dissension in their circle;" eight "measures to hinder the hostile activity of ASKET and LISA;" and four "measures to distract ASKET and LISA from their hostile activity." Such was the pedantic precision of active measures terminology that "hindrance" operations were carefully distinguished from those whose purpose was merely to "distract." The main responsibility for directing and coordinating these thirty-two operations fell upon V. N. Shadrin, head of the Ninth Department of the Fifth Directorate.[10] It was a measure of the courage and character of Sakharov and Bonner that their sanity and determination survived the KGB's best efforts to destroy them.

The thirteen compromise operations were remarkably diverse. As usual, they involved a number of forgeries: among them a bogus State Department evaluation which dismissed Sakharov as a worn-out political dilettante and a fabricated letter from Radio Liberty's Russian staff denouncing his links with the Zionists. Somewhat more bizarrely, attempts were made to link Sakharov with the gay liberation movement. Letters bearing the forged signatures of Sakharov and a Belorussian "group of homosexuals" were sent to gay rights organizations in Britain and Scandinavia, with the aim of prompting them to send letters in reply.

The Western "bourgeois press" and its Moscow correspondents were fed stories—apparently without much success—claiming that Sakharov's family suffered from hereditary mental illness, which affected both his children and his brother, and that he himself had degenerated into "a tired, weak-willed man," "unable to take independent decisions" because of his domineering wife. Instructions were given for suitably gullible foreign correspondents to be invited to meet the Deputy Procurator-General, S. I. Gusev, who would provide "objective information about the nature of the official warning given to ASKET about his provocative actions."[11]

The most vicious of the active measures were directed against Elena Bonner both because Sakharov's worldwide reputation for integrity made him a less vulnerable target than his less well-known wife, and because attacks on Bonner wounded Sakharov more deeply than those on himself. During Sakharov's fifteen years of persecution, his only resort to physical violence was to slap the face of Nikolai Yakovlev, one of the writers used by the KGB to libel Bonner.[12] The character assassination of Bonner began in earnest with an article entitled "Madame Bonner—Sakharov's Evil Genius?" planted in the New York Russian-language newspaper *Russkiy Golos* (*Russian Voice*) by an agent codenamed YAK, in July 1976.[13] Simultaneously, Bonner began to receive letters prepared by Service A but purporting to come from one "Semyon Zlotnik," who claimed to know the secrets of her "dark past" and demanded money with menaces.[14]

The "dark past" fabricated by the KGB over the next few years was an explosive mixture of sex and violence. "In her dissolute youth," it was claimed, "[Bonner] had developed an almost professional knack for seducing and subsequently sponging off older men of considerable stature." During the war she had allegedly seduced the poet Vsevelod Bagritsky, then hounded his wife to her grave by bombarding her with obscene telephone calls. Her next victim, according to the KGB libel, was a well-known engineer, "Moisei Zlotnik" ("uncle" of the fictitious Semyon Zlotnik), who was jailed for murdering his wife on instructions from Bonner. To escape justice, Bonner was said to have become a nurse on a wartime hospital train—only to be sacked when her seduction of the elderly doctor in charge was discovered by the doctor's daughter. Among Bonner's fictitious post-war conquests was her equally elderly, married French uncle, Leon Kleiman; the affair was said to have continued even after she "ensnared" Sakharov.[15] The KGB went to enormous pains to fabricate this account of Bonner's supposedly homicidal sexual appetites, even sending an illegal to France in 1977 to recover some of the papers of Leon Kleiman (who had died five years earlier) to assist in the production of Service A's forgeries.[16]

Unsurprisingly, the KGB found considerable difficulty for several years in placing this libellous fiction in the Western "bourgeois press." It eventually appeared as a "world exclusive" in the Sicilian newspaper *Sette Giorni*, whose staff—according to the Rome residency—included a "confidential contact" codenamed KIRILL.[17] On April 12, 1980 *Sette Giorni* printed a sensational story headlined "WHO IS ELENA BONNER? The Wife of Academician Sakharov Perpetrator of Several Murders." An unnamed member of the editorial staff was reported to have met the elusive "Semyon Zlotnik" while on holiday in Paris, and to have learned the story from him. *Sette Giorni* cited at some length a series of Service A forgeries, among them a letter from "Moisei Zlotnik" to Bonner reproaching her for persuading him to murder his wife: "You acted precisely, cold-bloodedly and rationally . . . And your demand 'to bump her off' seemed as natural as remembering that I should give you your favorite chocolates on your birthday." The article also cited an equally fraudulent diary supposedly written by Leon Kleiman describing his seduction by Bonner and denouncing her obsession with "subjugating others" to her will.[18] The Rome residency proudly sent fifty copies of the *Sette Giorni* article to the Centre, together with subsequent readers' letters denouncing Bonner, most of which had been written or prompted by the residency itself.[19] When reporting on the operation to the Central Committee, the KGB is unlikely to have mentioned that *Sette Giorni* was a little-known provincial newspaper with a print run of only 20,000.[20]

To increase the pressure on Bonner, and through her on Sakharov, attempts were made to deprive her of the support of family and friends. The first of the active measures devised by the KGB early in 1977 "to cut off ASKET and LISA from their close contacts engaged in anti-social activity and to cause dissension in their circle" listed seven different methods of harassing her daughter from her first marriage, Tanya, and son-in-law, Efrem Yankelevich, in order to force them to emigrate. The harassment succeeded. On September 5, 1977 Bonner said goodbye to Tanya and Efrem at Sheremetyevo airport.

The Centre showed equal ingenuity in attempting to alienate the Sakharovs' friends. Agents in the dissident movement were instructed to "cause dissension between ASKET and LISA on the one hand and their contacts involved in anti-social activity" by circulating disparaging comments about other dissidents supposedly made by Sakharov and Bonner.[21]

The two sets of KGB active measures designed to "hinder the hostile activity of ASKET and LISA" also had the unstated aim of making daily life impossible for both of them. The "hindrance" operations were designed to "create abnormal [living] conditions" in as many ways as possible. Though the KGB did not yet dare to withdraw Sakharov's driving license, no other member of his or Bonner's families was allowed to obtain—or retain—a license. An agent codenamed MORVIKOV was instructed to stir up trouble between the couple and Andrei Sakharov's children. The "distraction" operations included flooding the Sakharovs with bogus requests for help from people who had fallen foul of the Soviet legal system or who simply sought their advice on non-existent problems.[22] The cumulative effect of the KGB's active measures took an inevitable toll—particularly on the health of Bonner, who was suffering from a heart condition. There were times, she wrote later, "when it was difficult for me to walk even a hundred yards, when even sitting at the typewriter made me break out in a cold sweat." Simply thinking about the allegations about her private life made her feel sick—or even that she was about to have a heart attack.[23]

THE EXTENT OF the Sakharovs' covert persecution was due partly to the fact that the KGB did not yet dare imprison them. The president of the Soviet Academy of Sciences solemnly assured his American opposite number that "not one hair of Dr. Sakharov's head" would be harmed—though, as Bonner wryly remarked, the promise meant little since Sakharov was almost bald.[24] During 1977, however, there was a wave of arrests of other well-known dissidents, among them the two most prominent members of the "Helsinki Watch Groups": the veteran civil rights campaigner Aleksandr Ginzburg, victim of the botched 1968 show trial, and the physicist Yuri Orlov, founder of the Moscow group. Andropov's characteristically slanted intelligence reports to the Politburo sought to implicate both in the ideological subversion campaigns allegedly run by Western intelligence agencies:

The enemy's special services and ideological centers are applying serious efforts to invigorate and extend the hostile activity of anti-Soviet elements on the territory of the Soviet Union. Especially notable is the effort of Western special services to organize an association of persons opposing the existing state and social order in our country . . . The need has thus emerged to terminate the actions of Orlov, Ginzburg and others once and for all, on the basis of existing law . . .[25]

Orlov and Ginzburg were arrested in February 1977. A month later it was the turn of the leading Jewish human rights activist and "refusenik" Anatoli Shcharansky. For the next year all three withstood the best efforts of teams of KGB interrogators to cajole and bully them into cooperating in their own show trials. On December 29, 1977 Orlov's chief investigator, Captain Yakovlev, made what amounted to a formal admission of failure. After Yakovlev showed him the official charge sheet, Orlov took notes of it but "refused to sign it, saying that he wholly rejected the charge." The record of the interrogation on that day (reproduced as an appendix to this chapter) shows Orlov, ten months after his arrest, obviously getting the better of his interrogator. When asked whether he understood the charge against him, Orlov replied that it was not clear to him, and that he had been shown no "evidence that my actions had the intention of undermining or weakening the Soviet regime." He put in writing a complaint that "[i]t has never been explained to me precisely and unambiguously what is meant by the words 'undermining,' 'weakening,' and even 'Soviet regime.' " Interrogator Yakovlev offered no explanation. Orlov went on to complain against the manner of Yakovlev's interrogation: "You first make an assertion of your own, and then ask whether this is a fact. This is the typical way of putting a leading question." Orlov claimed that the documents he had circulated on behalf of the Helsinki Watch Group had had a beneficial effect. They had been studied by "progressive forces in the West," such as the French and Italian Communist parties, "whose criticism has clearly improved certain aspects of human rights in the USSR." Fewer people were being sent to prison camps or being mistreated in psychiatric hospitals, and fewer children from unregistered Christian sects were being taken away from their parents. Yakovlev, as usual, had no answer. Orlov made a written protest that his previous request for Yakovlev to be taken off his case had been turned down.[26]

The most striking feature of Orlov's trial in May 1978, apart from his own courageous defiance, was the pathetic spectacle of fifteen prosecution witnesses insisting that Soviet citizens enjoyed all the freedoms guaranteed by the Helsinki Accords. For campaigning for those very freedoms, Orlov was sentenced to seven years' imprisonment, followed by five in exile.

Ginzburg, who was tried two months later, knew that, as a re-offender, he was liable to a ten-year sentence. But, to his surprise:

> They played a little game with me. The prosecution told the court that he was only asking for eight years, because I had helped the police in the Shcharansky case. It was a lie, but it was a good piece of character assassination for them to use in their propaganda and to make life hard for me in the camps.[27]

Shcharansky's trial, held at the same time as Ginzburg's, had moments of farce as well as brutality. At one point a witness named Platonov was asked, "What can you tell us about the case of Shcharansky?" "Nothing," he replied. "I'm not familiar with the case." But Ginzburg, he declared, had behaved very badly. It quickly became clear that Platonov had turned up in the wrong court. The trial ended, however, in a great moral victory for Shcharansky. He declared in his closing address:

> I am proud that I came to know and work with such people as Andrei Sakharov, Yuri Orlov and Aleksandr Ginzburg, who are carrying on the best traditions of the Russian intelligentsia. But most of all, I feel part of a marvelous historical process—the process of the national revival of Soviet Jewry and its return to the homeland, to Israel.
>
> For two thousand years the Jewish people, my people, have been dispersed all over the world and seemingly deprived of any hope of returning. But still, each year Jews have stubbornly, and apparently without reason, said to each other, "Next year in Jerusalem!" And today, when I am further than ever from my dream, from my people and from my Avital [Shcharansky's wife], and when many difficult years of prisons and camps lie ahead of me, I say to my wife and to my people, "Next year in Jerusalem!"
>
> And to the court, which has only to read a sentence that was prepared long ago—to you I have nothing to say.[28]

The KGB's main fear in the aftermath of the show trials of Orlov, Ginzburg and Shcharansky was that Orlov, like Sakharov three years earlier, would be awarded the Nobel Peace Prize. The KGB residency in Norway was ordered to give the highest priority to an active measures campaign, personally overseen by Andropov himself, designed to discredit Orlov and ensure that his candidacy failed.[29] On October 27, 1978 the Oslo resident, Leonid Alekseyevich Makarov (codenamed SEDOV), rang Suslov, the Politburo's leading ideologist, in the middle of the night to pass on the good news that the prize had gone instead to the Egyptian and Israeli leaders Anwar Sadat and Menachem Begin. Makarov succeeded in claiming more of the credit than he deserved for what was regarded by the KGB as a famous victory. In a notably immodest telegram to the Centre, he reported that the residency had successfully "carried out complex active measures through reliable assets in order to disrupt the anti-Soviet operation" to award the prize to Orlov. It claimed to have brought pressure to bear during conversations with a series of Norwegian political leaders, chief among them Knut Frydenlund, the foreign minister, Reiulf Steen, chairman of the Norwegian Labor Party and of the Parliamentary Foreign Policy Committee, Tor Halvorsen, chairman of the Central Federation of Trade Unions and of the Board of the Norway—USSR Friendship Society, and Trygve Bratteli, a former prime minister and chairman of the Parliamentary Labor Party Group:

> In the course of these conversations, the provocative nature and anti-Soviet bias of the agitation around Yuri Orlov was emphasized . . . It was pointed out that the political leadership of Norway needed to show proper responsibility for the state and development of bilateral relations between our countries. The

conversations produced the desired response in influential circles of the Norwegian Labor Party. The work that we did exerted useful influence on the foreign policy leadership of Norway and, in our opinion, made it possible for the residency's task to be carried out—to prevent the award of the Nobel Peace Prize to Yuri Orlov and his Committee.[30]

The Centre gave Makarov as much credit as he gave himself. Viktor Fedorovich Grushko, head of the FCD Third Department (whose responsibilities included Scandinavia), telegraphed congratulations on "the determination and operational effectiveness which the residency has shown while carrying out this work."[31]

ANDROPOV REMAINED AS obsessed with ideological subversion during his final years as KGB chairman as he had been at the outset. The war against subversion extended even to abstract painting. A joint report in 1979 by the KGB Moscow Directorate and the Moscow department of the Fifth Directorate proudly reported that, over the past two years, "it proved possible to use agents to prevent seven attempts by avant-garde artists to make provocative arrangements to show their pictures." Four "leaders of the avant-garde artists" had been recruited as agents. Surveillance of the "creative intelligentsia" was an important part of "the task of the [KGB] agencies to protect the intelligentsia from the influence of bourgeois ideology":

> Creative workers produce individualistic works; they are cut off from the positive influence of the collective for forming and training their personality; they develop an egocentric attitude towards reality, one that is based on strictly personal perceptions, personal interest, arrogance, ambition and over-estimation of their importance.[32]

Andropov told a Fifth Directorate conference in March 1979 that the KGB could not afford to ignore the activities of a single dissident, however obscure:

> Our enemies—and even certain comrades from Communist Parties in Western countries—often bring up this question: "If, as you say, you have constructed a developed socialist society, then do various anti-social phenomena or the negative activities of an insignificant handful of people really represent a threat to it? Are they really capable of shaking the foundations of socialism?"
> Of course not, we reply, if one takes each act or politically harmful trick individually. But if one takes them all together, combining their content with their purpose as regards ideological sabotage, then every such act represents a danger. And we cannot ignore it. We simply do not have the right to permit even the smallest miscalculation here, for in the political sphere any kind of ideological sabotage is directly or indirectly intended to create an opposition which is hostile to our system—to create an underground, to encourage a transition to terrorism and other extreme forms of struggle, and, in the final analysis, to create the conditions for the overthrow of socialism.

The experience of Hungary in 1956 and Czechoslovakia in 1968 showed that behind the Soviet dissidents were "the main organizers of ideological sabotage—the intelligence services and subversive centers of the imperialist nations. The struggle against them must be decisive, uncompromising, and merciless." Within the Soviet Union the "twelve-year ideological struggle" of the Fifth Directorate showed that repression worked:

> The Check lists have learned to quash undesirable and hostile phenomena in their initial stages. This is confirmed by the facts. Of the 15,580 people who were suppressed last year, only 107 showed themselves to be hostile a second time.[33]

In 1980 even Sakharov ceased to be untouchable. While being driven to the Academy of Sciences on January 22 he was arrested, taken to the prosecutor's office and told that he and his wife were to be exiled to Gorky, a city closed to Westerners: "You are forbidden to go beyond the city limits of Gorky. You'll be kept under surveillance, and you are forbidden to meet with or contact foreigners or criminal elements [dissidents].[34] The KGB Fifth Directorate organized a series of workplace meetings in Gorky as well as broadcasts on local radio and television in an attempt to ensure that Sakharov and Bonner were reduced to pariah status throughout their exile. To the KGB's embarrassment, however, Sakharov's banishment to Gorky was quickly followed by an unconnected period of social unrest which it feared would become known in the West. In May there was a strike at the car factory there. In September and October, after a series of four murders in Gorky, rumors spread rapidly round the city that murders were in fact occurring daily but were being officially concealed. In the ensuing panic schools suspended some of their classes and factories canceled night shifts. There were numerous letters to the authorities pleading for the murderers to be caught. To the Centre's relief, however, the mayhem in Gorky passed unnoticed in the West.[35]

During the early 1980s the dissident movement seemed at its lowest ebb since its emergence in the 1960s. Most leading dissidents were in labor camps or exile. Those who remained at liberty were under constant KGB surveillance. Samizdat literature was reduced to a trickle. During the second half of the 1980s, however, the dissidents found themselves, to their great surprise, rapidly transformed from "anti-social elements" into the prophets of *perestroika*. The chief agent of this transformation was Mikhail Gorbachev.

"When I became General Secretary," writes Gorbachev in his *Memoirs*, "I considered it an important task to rescue Academician Sakharov from exile."[36] The record of his statements in both public and private during his first year as Soviet leader, however, tells a more complicated story. At a Politburo meeting on August 29, 1985, Gorbachev announced that he had received "a letter from a certain Mr. Sakharov, whose name will not be unknown to you. He asks us to allow his wife Bonner to go abroad for medical treatment and visit relatives." The KGB chairman, Viktor Chebrikov, reported that Sakharov was in poor health: "He has largely lost his position as a political figure and recently we have heard nothing new from him. So perhaps Bonner ought to be allowed abroad for three months." Chebrikov appeared to believe the propaganda image of Bonner sedulously cultivated by the KGB over the previous decade: "We must not forget that [Sakharov] acts very much under Bonner's influence . . . She has one hundred per cent influence over him." "That's what Zionism does for you!" joked Gorbachev. Chebrikov added that, with Bonner away, Sakharov might even be willing to reach some sort of accommodation.[37] Though he did not tell the Politburo, Chebrikov was doubtless aware from KGB surveillance reports that Sakharov had welcomed Gorbachev's election as general secretary with the comment: "It looks as if our country's lucky. We've got an intelligent leader!"[38]

Aleksandr Yakovlev, the most influential reformer among Gorbachev's advisers, secretly asked two officials of the Central Committee's international information department, Andrei Grachev and Nikolai Shishlin, to prepare a case which would persuade the Politburo to end Sakharov's exile. According to Grachev, both Yakovlev and Gorbachev realized that neither democratic reform nor the normalization of East—West relations could proceed so long as Sakharov's banishment continued. But "the delicacy of the problem was indicated by Yakovlev's conspiratorial tone" as he emphasized the need to avoid attracting the attention of the KGB. Grachev and Shishlin had to conduct an elaborate covert operation even to obtain copies of Sakharov's works without Chebrikov realizing what they were up to. On December 1, 1986 Gorbachev finally considered the time to be ripe to raise the Sakharov question at the Politburo, and gained its approval to end his exile.[39] On December 15 two electricians, escorted by a KGB officer, arrived at Sakharov's Gorky flat and installed a telephone. At 10 a.m. the next day he received a call from Gorbachev. "You [and Bonner] can return to Moscow together," Gorbachev told him. "You have an apartment there . . . Go back to your patriotic work!"[40]

Though Gorbachev probably had in mind Sakharov's work at the Academy of Sciences, by far his greatest impact was on the transition to a democratic political system—in changing the Soviet Union from what the Marquis de Custine, a French visitor to Tsarist Russia over a century and a half earlier, had described as a "nation of mutes." Custine had famously prophesied:

Nations are mute only for a time—sooner or later the day of discussion arises . . . As soon as speech is restored to this silenced people, one will hear so much dispute that an astonished world will think it has returned to the confusion of Babel.[41]

"The day of discussion" arrived in Russia on May 25, 1989, with the opening of the first session of the Congress of People's Soviets, the product of the first contested elections since 1917. Gorbachev later acknowledged that, of all the deputies elected to the congress, Sakharov was "unquestionably the most outstanding personality."[42] At the time, however, Gorbachev viewed Sakharov with a mixture of irritation and admiration. Sakharov wanted the congress to abolish the one-party state, curb the power of the KGB and establish a directly elected office of president. "If only we had listened more carefully to Andrei Dmitriyevich [Sakharov]," Gorbachev said later, "we might have learned something." But Gorbachev was not ready to end the Communist Party's monopoly of power. He could not decide, Sakharov complained, whether he was "the leader of the *nomenklatura* or the leader of *perestroika*," When the popular weekly *Argumenti i Fakti* published a poll showing that Sakharov was by far the most popular politician in the country, Gorbachev was so enraged that he threatened to sack the editor. Tension between Sakharov and Gorbachev renewed at the next session of the congress in December 1989. Gorbachev brushed aside an attempt by Sakharov to present him with tens of thousands of telegrams calling for an end to the one-party state. A few days later, Sakharov died suddenly of a heart attack. At his lying in state, Gorbachev and the Politburo stood bare-headed for several minutes in front of the open coffin of the man once described by Andropov as "Public Enemy Number One."[43]

Sakharov's premature death was in all likelihood partly due to the strain of his and Bonner's earlier persecution, and to the lack of proper medical treatment during their Gorky exile. "The totalitarian system probably killed him," said the democratic journalist Vitali Korotich. "I'm only glad that before he died Sakharov dealt the system a mortal blow."[44] In 1990 the text of a long letter (previously available only in samizdat) calling for democratic political change addressed by Sakharov and two other dissidents to the Soviet leadership twenty years earlier was exhumed from the CPSU archives and published for the first time. Since Gorbachev had become general secretary, almost every issue raised in the "subversive" appeal of 1970 had been placed on the political agenda and acted upon.[45] Simultaneously, Solzhenitsyn's works, banned from bookshops and library shelves since 1974, had become bestsellers.

The dissidents were not the main agent for change in Gorbachev's Soviet Union. As at other celebrated turning points in modern Russian history—among them the turn to the West in the early eighteenth century, the end of feudalism in 1861, collectivization and crash industrialization after 1929—change came chiefly from the top. The Soviet system was transformed, and ultimately destroyed, by Gorbachev's courageous but misguided attempt to reform the unreformable. The dissidents, however, played a major role in changing the political consciousness of the Soviet élite. One KGB report of the mid-1970s quotes Solzhenitsyn as saying that the main task of the dissident movement was "a moral and ideological preparation of the Russian intelligentsia to oppose the Soviet regime."[46] Against all the odds, the dissidents largely succeeded in fulfilling that mission. A small and persecuted minority, powerless save for the strength and courage of its convictions, only feebly supported by the West, defeated a determined campaign to silence them by the world's largest and most powerful security and intelligence service. Nowhere in the world during the final third of the twentieth century did a radical intelligentsia make a greater contribution to the destruction of an anti-democratic political system.

APPENDIX

THE INTERROGATION OF YURI ORLOV ON DECEMBER 29, 1977

The Interrogation of Yuri Orlov on December 29, 1977 According to official announcements in Moscow, Fifth Directorate interrogation records of the interrogation of dissidents have been destroyed. Mitrokhin's copy may therefore be the only surviving transcript of Orlov's interrogation. A copy was sent by the Fifth Directorate to the FCD to form part of the dossier being used to prepare active measures to discredit Orlov in the West and prevent him receiving the Nobel Peace Prize. Mitrokhin's growing sympathy for the dissidents is reflected in the fact that he copied the whole of this and some other documents dealing with their persecution, rather than following his usual practice of copying extracts, making notes or writing précis.

The interrogation was conducted by Captain Yakovlev, senior investigator for especially important cases with the investigation department of the KGB Directorate for Moscow and Moscow Oblast under the USSR Council of Ministers, assisted by Assistant Procurator Chistyakov of Moscow City:

QUESTION: You have been shown the resolution dated December 29, 1977 summoning you as the accused in criminal case No. 474, charged with committing a crime specified in Section 1 of Article 70 of the RSFSR Criminal Code.

Do you understand the nature of the charge?

ORLOV: No, it is not clear to me. I have not been shown evidence that my actions had the intention of undermining or weakening the Soviet regime, or any other evidence; instead of which, as I see it, the charge presented to me contains emotional phrases which obscure the nature of the case.

QUESTION: Do you admit you are guilty of the charge?

ORLOV: No, I do not. I do not see any proof of my guilt; I do not feel guilty, in my own conscience.

QUESTION: Do you admit the facts of preparing, duplicating and disseminating the documents specified in the charge against you?

ORLOV: Since these documents are qualified as deliberately slanderous fabrications, uttered with the intention of undermining or weakening the Soviet regime, I refuse to answer your question.

QUESTION: The investigation has established that you were a direct participant in the preparation, duplication and dissemination of the documents cited in the charge, and in a number of cases you were their author. The contents of these documents, as the materials of the case show, are of a slanderous nature, defaming the Soviet State and social order. What can you say about that?

ORLOV: In answer to that question, I should like to say the same thing as I have said in answer to the previous question, namely that I do not see any evidence, and do not feel guilty in my own conscience.

QUESTION: It has also been established that you acted deliberately to undermine and weaken the Soviet regime. What do you have to say about that?

ORLOV: I do not believe that this has been established. I rely on my own inner conviction, on my experience and on my thoughts.

QUESTION: Do you believe that the imperialist States and their agencies, to which you addressed the majority of the documents which incriminate you, are not interested in weakening and undermining the Soviet regime but in strengthening it? Is that how we must interpret you?

ORLOV: I protest against such a manner of putting questions, when you first make an assertion of your own, and then ask whether this is a fact. This is the typical way of putting a leading question. The very problem set out in your positive assertion derives from the interpretation of general aspects of détente, or, on the contrary, of the Cold War, the mutual interest of the peoples in making common progress and, in particular, progress in the field of human rights or, on the other hand, their mutual interest in internal troubles arising because of the lack of such progress. The problem also derives from the interpretation of what international organizations one may turn to, and to which ones one may not (or, perhaps, one must not approach any international organizations?). It derives from the interpretation of whether international obligations on human rights may be verified at an international level; whether they can be criticized by the international public; when such criticism is permissible, and when it becomes interference in internal affairs; does in general criticism of breaches of human rights in a particular society undermine its structure or improve it; which human rights are organically linked with the regime, and which are not; and the same applies to breaches of the rights. Besides, as is well known, my documents have been used in the West by those progressive forces whose criticism has clearly improved certain aspects of human rights in the USSR. I have in mind statements by Communists in France, Italy and probably others, and also criticism from various left-wingers, their meetings and so forth, and also statements by representatives of Workers' Parties, Socialists and Social Democrats. One must bear in mind that criticism from hostile forces can be useful for the regime; for example, criticism of capitalism by the USSR has undoubtedly strengthened that system and prolonged its existence. However, I did not appeal to hostile forces, but either to the international pubic as a whole, or to left-wingers, including Communists, or to members of governments irrespective of regime, if it was a question of formal international obligations. All criticism, both internal and external, has led to the following shifts in the field of human rights in the USSR: as the result of the 1977 reforms, the number of people imprisoned in the camps is actually falling; a clause has been introduced in the constitution concerning the unacceptability of persecution for criticism, the very persecution which was one of the reasons why Soviet citizens appealed to Western public opinion; the number of psychiatric repressions has been reduced; there has been a clear reduction, and possibly a total stop, to instances of children being virtually taken away from members of certain religious communities following decisions by the judicial authorities, and so forth. For these reasons, I can consider that your question has no direct relevance to the case.

QUESTION: How do you explain your reluctance to give objective testimony on the substance of the charge?

ORLOV: I ask you to explain the term "objective testimony." In my view, I have spoken about the very substance of the case.

QUESTION: Do you have anything to add?

ORLOV: I wish to write additional comments in my own hand.

[Written comments by Orlov]

In the first place, I want to add that I did not sign the charge sheet, although I read it, in part because I requested that the investigator who has just put the charge to me be taken off the case, and I do not accept the Procuracy's rejection of my request.

Secondly, I want to explain further why I do not understand the substance of the charge. The accusation is based on an interpretation of Article 70 of the RSFSR criminal code which is not clear to me: it has never been explained to me precisely and unambiguously what is meant by the words "undermining," "weakening" and even "Soviet regime," how the presence or absence of "purpose" is to be interpreted, what is considered as "defamatory" and what is not, and so on.

I have read through the record; my answers have been written verbatim, and I do not have any corrections or observations.

[Signed] Yu. Orlov.[47]

TWENTY-ONE

SIGINT IN THE COLD WAR

One of the largest gaps in histories of Cold War intelligence operations and international relations in both East and West concerns the role of signals intelligence (SIGINT). The role of the ULTRA intelligence generated by British and American codebreakers in hastening victory over Germany and Japan during the Second World War is now well known. Research on post-war SIGINT, by contrast, has barely begun. With the exception of the VENONA decrypts of mostly wartime Soviet communications, British and American SIGINT records for the Cold War remain completely closed. Other declassified files, however, show that SIGINT sometimes had an important influence on British and American policy. An in-house CIA history concludes that during the Korean War SIGINT became "a critically important source of information." During the 1956 Suez Crisis, the British Foreign Secretary, Selwyn Lloyd, wrote to congratulate the director-general of the British SIGINT agency, GCHQ, on the "volume" and "excellence" of the Middle Eastern decrypts it had produced and to say "how valuable" the decrypts had proved to be.[1] In 1992, after the end of the Cold War, President George Bush described SIGINT as "a prime factor" in his foreign policy.[2]

In both Britain and the United States Cold War SIGINT operations were controlled by a single agency. Soviet SIGINT was more fragmented. The GRU had responsibility for intercepting and decrypting military communications, the KGB for diplomatic and other civilian traffic. An attempt early in the Cold War to combine the SIGINT operations of the two agencies was short-lived. Until the late 1960s KGB SIGINT, ciphers and communications were the primary responsibility of the Eighth Chief Directorate.[3] The volume of SIGINT supplied to the Soviet leadership was very large. The KGB annual report sent to Khrushchev early in 1961 reveals that during 1960 the Eighth Chief Directorate decrypted 209,000 diplomatic cables sent by representatives of fifty-one states. No fewer than 133,200 of these intercepts were forwarded to the Central Committee (chiefly, no doubt, to its international department).[4] By 1967 the KGB was able to decrypt 152 cipher systems employed by a total of 72 states.[5] Though the text of all these decrypts remains inaccessible in the archives of the Eighth and Sixteenth directorates, FCD files and other sources contain important information on KGB SIGINT operations and some of the results achieved by them. Both FCD residencies abroad and the Second Chief Directorate (SCD) within the Soviet Union made impressive contributions to these operations.

David Kahn, the leading Western historian of SIGINT, plausibly concludes that, on present evidence, bugs and agent penetration contributed more than cryptanalysis to Soviet SIGINT successes during the Cold War.[6] The SCD had a long tradition of bugging Moscow embassies. For over thirty years after the establishment of Soviet—American diplomatic relations in 1933, the United States embassy was one of its most successful targets. A navy electrician who conducted the first electronic sweep of the embassy in 1944 discovered 120 hidden microphones. For a time, according to a member of the embassy staff, more "kept turning up, in the legs of any new tables and chairs that were delivered, in the plaster of the walls, any and everywhere."[7] The embassy seems to have been lulled into a false sense of security by its failure to find more bugs during the early years of the Cold War. In reality, it remained highly vulnerable to increasingly sophisticated Soviet electronic eavesdropping until at least the mid-1960s.

In 1952 the new American ambassador, George Kennan, ordered a thorough search of both the embassy and his own residence. The security experts sent from Washington asked him to dictate the text of an old diplomatic despatch in his study in order to help them discover any voice-activated listening device. As he continued his dictating, one of the experts suddenly began hacking away at the wall behind a wooden replica of the Great Seal of the United States. Finding nothing in the wall, he then attacked the seal itself with a mason's hammer and triumphantly extracted from it a pencil-shaped bug which had been relaying Kennan's every word (and no doubt those of previous ambassadors) to Soviet eavesdroppers. Next morning Kennan noted a "new grimness" among the Soviet guards and embassy staff: "So dense was the atmosphere of anger and hostility that one could have cut it with a knife."[8]

In 1953 work began on a new US embassy in Tchaikovsky Street. During its construction American security personnel stood guard each day to prevent the installation of listening devices, particularly on the two top floors which were to contain the CIA station, the ambassador's office and the cipher rooms. The day-long security vigil, however, served little purpose since the guards were withdrawn at night, thus allowing KGB personnel ample opportunity to bug the embassy. Charles "Chip" Bohlen, who had succeeded Kennan as ambassador, later blamed the extraordinary decision to leave the new embassy unguarded overnight on "carelessness" (presumably his own) and the desire "to save money."[9] "Carelessness" in matters of security was by now an embassy tradition.

During a heated discussion with US ambassador Foy Kohler in 1962, Khrushchev made clear—to the dismay of the KGB—that he knew the ambassador had personally opposed the supply of steel tubing manufactured in the West for the construction of natural gas pipelines in the Soviet Union.[10] Though Kohler probably deduced that Khrushchev knew the contents of some of his cables to Washington, he seems not to have realized that the information came from the bugging of his own embassy. In 1964, however, acting on intelligence from the KGB defector Yuri Nosenko, the embassy discovered over forty bugs concealed in bamboo tubes built into the walls behind the radiators in order to shield them from metal detectors.[11] Remarkably, most studies of US—Soviet relations take no account whatever of the almost continuous hemorrhage of diplomatic secrets from the United States Moscow embassy for more than thirty years.

FROM THE 1960s onwards the KGB also had a series of successes in bugging American and British embassies in the Third World, as well as the intelligence stations for which they provided diplomatic cover. The planting of listening devices on targets outside the Soviet Union was the responsibility of the FCD OT (Operational Technical Support) Directorate (also known as the Fourteenth Department), whose officers in residencies had a wide range of duties which included providing the equipment for clandestine photography of classified documents, short-range radio communication and the construction of apparently innocent objects (such as hairbrushes and cans of shaving cream) which could be used to conceal film and other espionage paraphernalia. Each of the OT eavesdropping devices, often remote-controlled, was individually constructed in order to assist concealment in the target area, which was always carefully reconnoitered beforehand. The devices were fixed in place either by FCD operations officers or by local agents employed as cleaners, electricians, plumbers, furniture makers and telephone company technicians.[12]

One of the FCD's most successful eavesdropping operations against a British target was directed at the chief SIS station in the Middle East, which was located in the British embassy building in Beirut (codenamed OVRAG, "Ravine").[13] During the early 1960s a Lebanese maid in the embassy, Elizabeth Aghasapet Ghazarian, was talent-spotted by a bishop in the Armenian Orthodox church, codenamed OLAF, who had been recruited as a Soviet agent in 1947.[14] In 1964 Ghazarian was herself recruited as agent ZOLUSHKA ("Cinderella").[15] By January 1966 she had successfully planted a radio microphone (STEREO-1) in the office of the ambassador, Sir Derek Riches. On February 4 ZOLUSHKA succeeded in concealing another radio microphone (STEREO-2), about the size of a matchbox, behind the desk of the Old Etonian SIS head of station, Peter Lunn (codenamed PHOENIX), who worked under diplomatic cover as the embassy first secretary.[16]

The Centre was briefed on Lunn's background and career by his former colleague Kim Philby, who had worked in Beirut as a journalist and SIS agent from 1956 until his defection to Moscow in 1963, soon after SIS obtained proof of his treachery.[17] Lunn was one of Britain's leading skiers; he had been captain of the British team at the 1936 Winter Olympics and was the author of a series of well-known skiing manuals.[18] He and Philby joined SIS at almost the same moment in 1941.[19] After his defection Philby informed the KGB that Lunn had been awarded the CMG (the highest decoration then given to any SIS officer save the Chief) for his success in the planning and operation of a 500-meter tunnel under East Berlin which in 1955–6 tapped Soviet and East German telephone lines. The Centre rather admired Lunn's professionalism and calm, self-assured manner. According to a report on operation RUBIN in 1967:

> Peter Lunn has many agents, who collect information on intelligence services of socialist countries and their representatives in the Middle East, on the activ-

ities of the intelligence service of the United Arab Republic [the short-lived union of Egypt and Syria], on oil policy (via a fluctuating agent network), on relations between Arab countries and the USSR and carry out the cultivation of Egyptian intelligence officers. In his agent work Lunn shows caution, experience, puts a high priority on security with agent contacts. With those agents who do not know that Lunn works under embassy cover he used the assumed name Joseph and met either at a clandestine rendezvous or at the flat of his secretary . . . For meetings with agents who are personally known to Lunn, he used his flat or business premises in the city. Lunn is demanding, strives to give his agents set tasks and to ensure they are carried out clearly. He is very economical when paying rewards to his agents, he adheres strictly to the rule that, firstly, it is only necessary to pay for information when it is unobtainable without paying and, secondly, that payment is only for that information which can be used actively.

Lunn's only major weakness, in the Centre's view, was his relaxed attitude to station security. The KGB eavesdroppers overheard one of his staff suggest extra security measures. They must have been relieved to hear Lunn reply that no further measures were necessary. The bugging of the office of the Beirut head of station, codenamed operation RUBIN, continued for three and a half years after Lunn was recalled to a post at SIS headquarters in November 1967.[20]

The deputy head of the FCD, Mikhail Stepanovich Tsymbal, reported to Andropov in 1967 that RUBIN had identified over fifty British agents in the Middle East and Europe: "Of the greatest interest is the identification of an SIS agent group consisting of a courier and two agents in the highest government circles of Iraq." SIS was also alleged to have "an important agent" in Egypt "with access to President Nasser," and "sub-sources" who included the foreign minister of one Middle Eastern country and the army chief-of-staff of another.[21]

Operation RUBIN also revealed that SIS had penetrated the Lebanese Communist Party. Its most important penetration agent was a lawyer who was a member of the Party's Politburo and a personal friend of its general secretary, Nicolas Chaoui. On September 27, 1967 the Centre informed the Soviet Politburo that, in addition to keeping SIS well informed on the affairs of the Lebanese Communist Party, the lawyer had provided intelligence on contacts between the Party leadership and the retiring Soviet ambassador, and on Soviet involvement in the affairs of the Lebanese and Syrian peace movements and of the Cairo Peace Conference. The Centre, however, was reluctant to warn Chaoui that one of his closest associates was an SIS agent, probably for fear that he would confront the agent, who in turn would alert SIS to the penetration of its operations.

In 1971, a year after SIS had discovered the bugging of its Beirut station, the Soviet Politburo gave permission for Chaoui to be briefed during a visit to Moscow. At a meeting in the international department of the CPSU on December 25, Pavel Yefimovich Nedosekin, a senior FCD officer, informed Chaoui that the lawyer was regarded by SIS as "one of its very valuable agents" and had given it secret information about the Lebanese Communist Party and two of the most important Soviet front organizations, the World Peace Council and the Afro-Asian Solidarity Committee. Though doubtless somewhat shocked, Chaoui admitted that, as early as 1949, he had received a report of a confidential meeting between the lawyer and a British consul; he added that since 1968 the lawyer had twice been to London, ostensibly for treatment to a cataract. Chaoui acknowledged that he had no intelligence department capable of protecting Party security, and promised to take immediate action to set one up.[22]

Among other unwelcome revelations of operation RUBIN was the discovery that SIS had succeeded in planting six agents in the KGB, the GRU and the Czechoslovak StB. The most important appears to have been SHAUN, the owner of an advertising bureau in Damascus, who was discovered to be a double agent run by Lunn's deputy, BARITONE. A Centre damage assessment concluded that SHAUN had compromised a series of KGB operations in which he had taken part, among them the recruitment of the Spanish cipher clerk GOMEZ (arrested after his return to Spain); the attempted recruitment of an unidentified member of the West German embassy in Damascus; and contacts between the Soviet military attaché and the chief of the Syrian general staff. SHAUN had also reported to SIS on an affair between the KGB resident in Damascus and the wife of a Soviet doctor. Andropov was tersely informed that "measures have been taken to neutralize the consequences of SHAUN's treachery."[23]

In January 1967 ZOLUSHKA also succeeded in placing a bug in BARITONE's office in the SIS Beirut station. In addition to running SHAUN, he was discovered to have sixteen agents inside the Lebanese Communist Party and other left-wing organizations. A detailed study of the SIS officers in Lebanon, Jordan, Syria and elsewhere identified through the bugging of the Beirut station led the Centre to draw a number of general conclusions which, surprisingly, it does not seem to have fully grasped before. The report on operation RUBIN concluded, correctly, that the cover posts occupied by SIS officers in British embassies were rarely as high as counselor and never higher; most were first, second or third secretaries, and seldom headed any of the main embassy departments such as trade and information. SIS personnel did not keep to the daily diplomatic routine, spent more time outside the embassy, lived in worse accommodation, drove older cars and gave fewer large receptions at their homes than British diplomats, but had higher expense allowances and arranged more meetings in restaurants and other public places. Philby had doubtless made such points before, but KGB debriefers still tended to seek only detailed classified information from agents and defectors and failed to use them to add to their general understanding of the West. By the late 1960s Philby was, unsurprisingly, deeply depressed and drinking heavily, convinced that the KGB had "no idea" of how to profit from his vast experience.[24]

In 1967 ZOLUSHKA was rewarded for her work as a KGB agent with the secret granting of Soviet citizenship. For the next four years she continued to provide classified documents and other intelligence from the British embassy and the SIS station in Beirut. In 1971, after she had been questioned about the discovery of the radio microphones, she was hurriedly exfiltrated to the Soviet Union, settled in Armenia and given a modest pension of 120 roubles. In 1978, after the Armenian KGB reported to the Centre that the pension was insufficient, Andropov approved an increase to 180 roubles.

BECAUSE OF THE closeness of Anglo-American intelligence cooperation, eavesdropping on the SIS Beirut station also produced intelligence on the CIA. The KGB discovered plans for, and was able to forestall, a joint CIA/SIS operation to bug the Beirut bureau of Novosti.[25] In 1969 the KGB residency began an operation which, it was hoped, would penetrate the CIA station (codenamed OMUT ("Whirlpool"))[26] as successfully as ZOLUSHKA had penetrated that of SIS. On KGB instructions, one of its Lebanese agents, a hotel owner codenamed MARAT, founded an employment agency designed to attract maids and domestic servants who could be used in operations against the Main Adversary. The most promising applicant to the agency was Mary Matrosian (codenamed VERA), a Lebanese maid from an Armenian family living in Syria. Until 1967 she had worked in the American ambassador's residence in Beirut, but had taken refuge with her family in Syria after the outbreak of the Arab—Israeli Six Day War. On her return to Beirut in 1969, MARAT's agency found her domestic work with a series of American diplomatic families. VERA was recruited by MARAT under a false flag to provide information on her employers and remove papers from their homes. MARAT told her the information was needed by Armenian community and church leaders in order to keep them informed of potential threats to the security of the Armenian people. In 1971 MARAT handed her over to a controller from the Beirut residency, who posed as a fellow Armenian. With VERA's (possibly unwitting) help, the KGB succeeded in bugging the apartment of the CIA officer for whom she worked.[27]

KGB files record a number of other KGB attempts to bug CIA stations, though none seems to have been as successful as operation RUBIN. Among the most vulnerable US embassies was that in Conakry, the capital of Guinea. One of the files noted by Mitrokhin contains a brief reference to the successful bugging of an American diplomat's apartment in Conakry in 1965.[28] Much fuller details are available on the bugging of the Conakry embassy during the 1970s, when sub-Saharan Africa became for the first time a priority area for both Soviet foreign policy and KGB operations.[29] In December 1972 a Guinean employee of the embassy recruited by the KGB (codenamed successively RUM and SANCHO) succeeded in installing a radio-operated eavesdropping device in the office of the ambassador, Terence Todman (succeeded in May 1975 by William Harrop). RUM/SANCHO was instructed that, if detected, he was to tell his interrogators that he had been paid to place the bug by a Chinese diplomat whose visiting card he was given. The bug (replaced by an improved version in January 1974) was so well concealed, however, that it went undetected during three annual checks on embassy security. The KGB monitoring post which recorded Todman's dictation and conversations with embassy and CIA staff (operation REBUS) was situated in an apartment only thirty meters from the ambassador's office.

The voice-activated bug was sometimes activated by Todman's engaging habit of bursting into song or whistling cheerfully to himself. In general, however, operation

REBUS provided what the Centre considered information "of great operational value" on US policy to African liberation movements as well as on State Department assessments of Soviet–American relations and Soviet policy in Africa. The volume of intelligence was so large that two English-speaking operations officers, Anatoli Mikhaylovich Zheleznoy and Yuri Yefimovich Tatuzov, were seconded from the KGB residency in Addis Ababa to process it. In July 1975 bugged conversations in the ambassador's office revealed that the embassy was aware there had been a leak in its communications with Washington and had asked the State Department for help in reviewing embassy security. Though strongly tempted to remove the bug, the Conakry residency decided not to do so for fear of compromising RUM/SANCHO. According to a KGB damage assessment, when the bug in the ambassador's office was discovered in September, "suspicion fell entirely on the Guinean Special [Intelligence] Services." RUM/SANCHO went undetected and remained on the embassy staff.[30]

The KGB's most ambitious bugging operation against a US diplomatic mission during the later Cold War was the bugging of a new eight-storey Soviet-built embassy building in Moscow on which construction began in 1979. The CIA was warned in 1980 by a defector from the Eighth Chief Directorate, Viktor Sheymov, that "the KGB was going to make the building itself a giant system of sensors that could pick up virtually anything." Officials in Washington, however, rashly concluded that any sensor installed by the KGB could be detected and removed before it was used. Five years later they discovered they had made an expensive mistake. Further investigation revealed a series of highly sophisticated bugs built into the fabric of the building which made it, according to a member of the House Foreign Affairs Committee, "an eight-storey microphone plugged into the Politburo." Steel-reinforcing rods set into the concrete were designed to serve as antennae. A power source, codenamed BATWING by the CIA, which was discovered embedded in a concrete wall, was estimated to be able to last for a century. One US official, interviewed by the *Washington Post*, commented, "Our technical people were astounded at the level of sophistication. One man from the CIA said, 'These are the kind of things that are only on the drawing boards here.'" For the KGB as well as the State Department, however, the operation ended in expensive failure. The new embassy building was never occupied.[31]

MOST EAVESDROPPING OPERATIONS using bugs planted in foreign embassies or overseas targets were short-term, unlikely to last more than a few years. By the late 1960s the FCD's most important and long-term SIGINT operations were run by specialized posts within its residencies in foreign capitals which intercepted local telephone and radio communications. The earliest such intercept post appears to have been that set up in the Mexico City residency in 1963. Codenamed RADAR, it was given the task of intercepting the communications of the US embassy and CIA station, but had only limited success.[32] The most successful of the residency posts created to intercept the communications of the Main Adversary were those set up in the United States itself. The first, codenamed POCHIN ("Start" or "Initiative"), started life in 1966 on the top floor of the Soviet embassy on Sixteenth Street in Washington, a few blocks from the White House. In 1967 a similar post, codenamed PROBA

("Test" or "Trial"), was established by the New York residency. There were eventually five POCHIN intercept posts in various Soviet establishments in and around Washington and four PROBA posts in the New York region.[33]

By 1970 POCHIN-1 (at the embassy) and POCHIN-2 (in the embassy residential complex) had transformed intelligence collection by the Washington residency.[34] According to Oleg Kalugin, head of Line PR:

> We were able to overhear the communications of the Pentagon, the FBI, the State Department, the White House, the local police, and a host of other agencies. These communications all were broadcast on open, non-secure channels, but nevertheless a surprising amount of useful material was relayed over the airways.[35]

Among the intelligence which most impressed the Centre was secret data on the vetting of ninety candidates for posts in the first Nixon administration. In 1969–70 twenty-three POCHIN intercepts were considered sufficiently important to be shown to leading members of the Politburo.

During the same period PROBA-1 (in the Soviet mission to the UN) and PROBA-2 (in the large embassy "dacha" at Glen Cove on Long Island) intercepted diplomatic traffic sent and received by the UN missions of Argentina, Brazil, Canada, France, Portugal, Spain and Venezuela, as well as some US military cables and the communications of Radio Liberty and Radio Free Europe. According to the PROBA files, the intelligence from these intercepts was given "a high evaluation" by both Foreign Minister Gromyko and the Soviet UN representative, Yakov Malik.[36]

THE KGB'S SIGINT operations against the Main Adversary were greatly assisted by a series of agents and defectors—all of them walk-ins—with access to highly classified intelligence on American cryptanalysis and/or cipher systems. In 1960 two NSA employees, Bernon F. Mitchell and William H. Martin, who had made contact with the KGB a year earlier in Mexico City, were exfiltrated by the FCD to Moscow, where they continued being debriefed for several years.[37] In 1963 Staff Sergeant Jack E. Dunlap committed suicide after several years spent smuggling top secret documents out of NSA headquarters at Fort Meade for the GRU. Shortly before Dunlap's suicide, another NSA defector, Victor Norris Hamilton, arrived in Moscow. In 1965 Robert Lipka, a young army clerk at NSA responsible for the shredding of highly classified documents, began handing many of them over to the KGB. Lipka is the last KGB agent inside the NSA identified in the files seen by Mitrokhin. (A retired NSA employee, Ronald Pelton, was, however, to provide valuable intelligence to the Washington residency in the early 1980s.) Shortly after Lipka left NSA in 1967, Chief Warrant Officer John Walker, a communications watch officer on the staff of the commander of submarine forces in the Atlantic (COMSUBLANT), began an eighteen-year career as a KGB agent, supplying detailed information on US naval ciphers.[38]

During the late 1960s both the New York and Washington residencies had a series of other striking SIGINT successes. Late in 1969 operation PRESSING, run by the New York residency, succeeded in concealing remote-controlled radio transmitters in UN offices used by the chairman of the Security Council. The devices, hidden in wooden boards, were fixed beneath bookcases and constructed from Western materials to conceal their Soviet origin. Simultaneously, operation KRAB, which almost certainly had to be approved by the Politburo, succeeded in bugging the secretariat of the UN secretary-general, U Thant (codenamed BROD). A radio-controlled eavesdropping device was also concealed in the offices of the Ghanaian mission to the UN.[39]

In 1969 the Washington residency succeeded in concealing a remote-control radio-operated bugging device in the meeting room of the Senate Foreign Relations Committee. The device, once again constructed from Western materials, continued to function for at least four years. In February 1973 information (which may have been inaccurate) reached the residency from press sources that a bug had been found attached to the underside of the press table in the Foreign Relations Committee room. The KGB was puzzled by the report since its own listening device was fixed beneath the seat of a chair rather than under the table and still appeared to be functioning normally. Expecting its bug to be discovered, Service A prepared a story claiming that it had been placed by the DGSE, the French foreign intelligence service. To the KGB's surprise, however, the media lost interest in the episode and no report of the bug beneath the chair appeared in the press.[40]

EARLY IN 1968 the KGB achieved its most important penetration of British SIGINT operations since John Cairncross had entered Bletchley Park in 1942. Corporal Geoffrey Arthur Prime, then working in the RAF SIGINT station at Gatow in West Berlin, handed a message to a Russian officer at a Soviet checkpoint asking Soviet intelligence to make contact with him. Prime's note was passed not to the FCD but to the comparatively lowly KGB Third Directorate, whose main responsibility was the surveillance and security of Soviet armed forces but which sometimes succeeded in making (usually low-level) recruits among Western troops stationed in Germany. Anxious to steal a march over the more prestigious FCD by gaining the credit for Prime's recruitment, a Third Directorate officer left him a message, inviting him to a rendezvous in East Berlin, in a small magnetic cylinder attached to his car door. At the meeting which followed and at subsequent rendezvous, Prime agreed to work as a KGB agent but explained that his service with the RAF was due to end in August 1968. In agreement with his Third Department case officers he applied, successfully, for a job processing Russian intercepts at GCHQ, the British SIGINT agency.

Prime was a sexual and social misfit who blamed many of his problems on the capitalist system and, as he later acknowledged, developed "a misplaced idealistic view of Russian Communism." He was, however, skillfully handled by his controllers. In September 1968, before taking up his job in GCHQ, Prime spent a week in the KGB compound at Karlshorst in the East Berlin suburbs being trained in radio transmission, cipher communications, microdots, photography of documents with a Minox camera and the use of dead letter-boxes. Before flying to Britain, he was given a briefcase containing a set of one-time cipher pads, secret writing materials and 400 pounds in banknotes. He continued working as a Soviet agent in GCHQ for almost nine years, spending most of his time transcribing and translating intercepts. Among the intelligence supplied by Prime during his final year working for GCHQ in 1976–7 were details of British successes and failures in decrypting Soviet traffic. Though his GCHQ colleagues were struck by his morose appearance, they put it down to his unhappy marriage and failure to be promoted.[41]

The expansion of KGB SIGINT operations during the late 1960s led to a reorganization at the Centre. Hitherto the KGB Eighth Directorate had handled SIGINT as well as ciphers and communications. Probably in 1968 Andropov established a new Sixteenth Directorate,[42] headed by Nikolai Nikolayevich Andreev, to specialize exclusively in SIGINT. Its operations were among the most highly classified in the whole of the KGB. The Sixteenth Directorate worked closely with the Sixteenth Department of the FCD, founded at about the same time, which was given responsibility for residency intercept posts, operations to acquire foreign codes and ciphers and attempts to penetrate other SIGINT agencies.[43] On May 15, 1970 Andropov approved a plan for radio-intercept posts (some were already functioning) in fifteen residencies: Washington, New York, Montreal, Mexico, Tokyo, Peking, Teheran, Athens, Rome, Paris, Bonn, Salzburg, London, Reykjavik and Belgrade. During 1971 these fifteen posts intercepted a total of 62,000 diplomatic and military enciphered cables from 60 countries, as well as more than 25,000 plain text messages.[44]

The most important intercept posts, operated by the Sixteenth Department with the assistance of OT personnel, remained the Washington area POCHIN and New York PROBA stations. The most striking achievement of the POCHIN stations during the 1970s was the interception of many of the messages exchanged between Washington, via Andrews Air Force Base, and the aircraft taking the President, Secretary of State and other senior members of the administration on overseas trips. ANTON, one of the POCHIN operational officers, was awarded the Order of the Red Star for his success in intercepting US communications during Kissinger's visit to London in July 1974 for talks with the British Foreign Secretary (and future prime minister), James Callaghan.[45] The Centre's particular interest in these intercepts doubtless derived from the fact that the main purpose of Kissinger's visit was to brief Callaghan on Nixon's recent visit to Moscow—his last foreign trip before his resignation at the height of the Watergate scandal.[46] Soon afterwards the PROBA stations succeeded in intercepting Kissinger's telephone conversations with Callaghan and the Turkish foreign minister, Professor Turan Gânes, during the crisis caused by the Turkish invasion of northern Cyprus on July 21.[47] The KGB was thus able to monitor the dramatic way in which, as Kissinger later recalled:

> During the night of July 21–22, we forced a cease-fire by threatening Turkey that we would move [US] nuclear weapons from forward positions—especially where they might be involved in a war with Greece.[48]

Not all the intercepts of Kissinger's conversations concerned affairs of state. On one occasion he was heard talking to his fiancée, Nancy Maginnes, shortly before their marriage in 1974. According to Kalugin's somewhat censorious recollection:

He apparently had just given a speech and, in his egotistical way, was asking her what she thought of it. He was saying, in effect, "How did I look? You really thought I sounded well?" The transcript showed Kissinger to be a vain and boastful man.

Word came back from Moscow that Andropov "loved the intercepted conversation." He enjoyed boasting to some of his Politburo colleagues that the KGB was able to eavesdrop on the intimate conversations of the US National Security Adviser.[49]

THE COMPLEX ANTENNAE sprouting on the roofs of Soviet missions gradually alerted Western SIGINT agencies to the presence of the intercept stations within.[50] Though probably unaware the KGB had successfully gained access to his own communications, Kissinger protested to Ambassador Dobrynin on August 15, 1975 at the interception of radio and telephone conversations by the Soviet embassy. The Centre drafted a robust reply:

> It is advisable that, when there is a meeting with Kissinger, if he again raises that issue, the Soviet ambassador should state that the antennae set up on the Soviet embassy's roof are being used on the basis of the principle of [diplomatic] reciprocity to ensure communications with Moscow, as well as to receive general radio and television transmissions. These antennae are in no way a contradiction of the embassy's status. It should be brought to the attention of the Secretary of State that the US government should prevent the installation of equipment, including that on buildings close to the embassy, which would impede the normal operation of the USSR embassy's radio station.[51]

Kissinger was inhibited in pursuing his protest by the knowledge that NSA also ran SIGINT operations from the US embassy in Moscow. In 1971 columnist Jack Anderson had revealed in the *Washington Post* that the embassy had succeeded in intercepting the microwave radio and telephone communications exchanged between the large black ZIL limousines of Politburo members as they sped around Moscow.[52] Kissinger seems, however, to have been genuinely alarmed by the electronic countermeasures taken to frustrate SIGINT operations run from the Moscow embassy. In November 1975 he told Dobrynin that it was believed that the American ambassador, Walter Stoessel, had developed leukemia as a result of prolonged exposure to electromagnetic radiation directed against the embassy. On instructions from Moscow, Dobrynin replied that the electromagnetic field around the embassy did not exceed Soviet health standards. Dobrynin claims that he was privately informed by the State Department during the Carter administration that a study had concluded that there was, in fact, no evidence of damage to the health of embassy personnel.[53]

Kissinger's protests failed to halt the continued expansion of POCHIN and PROBA operations. Summaries and transcripts of POCHIN intercepts grew from 2,600 pages in 1975 to 7,000 in 1976. During these two years 800 reports based on the intercepts were cabled to the Centre from the Washington residency. Among the communications to and from Andrews Airforce Base intercepted during 1976 were important messages dealing with Secretary of Defense Donald Rumsfeld's visits to the NATO Nuclear Planning Group in January and June, and to US armed forces headquarters in Europe in February; and on Kissinger's meetings with British, French, West German and South African leaders.[54] In 1977 POCHIN summaries and transcripts increased again to over 10,500 pages,[55] covering foreign visits by, among others, Vice-President Walter Mondale and Secretary of State Cyrus Vance.[56] For much of the Carter administration the POCHIN posts also intercepted a substantial amount of State Department material; the KGB kept a card file on all the officials mentioned in it.[57]

Given the KGB's lack of high-level penetration agents in Washington during the 1970s, it seems likely that POCHIN and other SIGINT operations were the Centre's most important source of intelligence on the foreign and defense policies of the Ford and Carter administrations. The general effect of this intelligence was probably benign—to limit the natural predisposition of the Centre to conspiracy theories about American policy. During the 1979 crisis caused by American protests at the presence of a Soviet "combat brigade" in Cuba, for example, POCHIN intercepts of Pentagon telephone discussions and other communications enabled the Washington residency to reassure Moscow that the United States had no plans for military intervention.[58]

The most important intelligence provided by the POCHIN stations during the 1970s and early 1980s, however, was probably military. The intercepts provided highly classified information on the Trident, MX, Pershing-2, Cruise and surface-to-air missile systems; the F-15, F-16, F-18, B-52 and B-1 aircraft; and the AWACS early warning system. From 1973 onwards the main priority of the New York PROBA stations was also scientific and technical intelligence, particularly in the military field. Its most striking success during the remainder of the decade was the interception of fax communications from the Brookhaven National Laboratory on Long Island and a series of major companies, among them Boeing, Fairchild, General Dynamics, Grumman, Hughes, IBM, Lockheed and Sperry Rand. Fax intercepts on military projects included important material on the design and development of the A-10, B-1, EF-111A and F-14 aircraft; the anti-missile defense program; and the anti-submarine defense system. By 1976 an intercept post, codenamed VESNA ("Spring"), was operating in the San Francisco residency, successfully intercepting fax and telephone communications of defense contractors and other high-tech companies on the West Coast.[59]

The KGB residencies in New York, Washington and San Francisco also had radio-intercept posts (codenamed, respectively, RAKETA, ZEFIR and RUBIN) which monitored FBI (codenamed FIRMA) communications in order to keep track of surveillance of its operations. In New York during the 1970s the RAKETA post monitored continuously six FBI shortwave radio communications channels.[60] Its eavesdroppers quickly became used to Bureau jargon. According to a report in KGB files:

FBI look-out posts and surveillance teams communicate using simple codes, slang expressions and pre-arranged phrases which are easily deciphered by the RAKETA operator. Conversations between the look-out posts and a surveillance team consist of short dialogues in which the post informs the team of the target's number and the direction he is moving in up to an intersection and beyond.

Daily radio intercept of the operation of the FBI dispatch center provides a picture of the operational environment and the FBI's conduct of operations in the city. Whenever the [KGB] residency is conducting an operation in the city, the RAKETA operator monitors the operation of the FBI's radio center; if necessary, an operations officer can be given a danger signal prior to his going out to the site where an operation is to be conducted, [or told] to back off from an operation if he has been detected by surveillance. The RAKETA post makes note of local citizens who have come to the attention of the FBI, and they are put on file in the KONTAKT system [the FCD's computerized name-trace system].

For several years the New York residency deluded itself into believing that it was able to detect every instance of street surveillance of KGB personnel by the FBI.[61] In 1973, however, it realized that it had been taken in. Having discovered that the FBI was aware of the activities of some of its operations officers, as well as of three "developmental" agents, it finally grasped that the apparent simplicity of FBI surveillance techniques was actually a means of diverting the residency's attention from far more sophisticated methods which it had failed to detect. The residency's operations were temporarily disrupted as it tried to come to terms with methods of surveillance it did not fully understand.[62]

THE RUNNING COSTS for the main intercept posts in KGB residencies around the world in 1979 show that the Washington and New York operations were by far the most expensive.[63] The SIGINT post in the Havana residency, the third most expensive, was also focused chiefly on the United States. All other intercept posts were also instructed to give priority, when possible, to the communications of the Main Adversary. The most important of the KGB's foreign intercept posts targeted on the United States from outside, however, was located not in a residency but in the large SIGINT base set up by the GRU at Lourdes in Cuba in the mid-1960s to monitor US navy communications and other high-frequency transmissions.[64] On April 25, 1975 a secret Soviet government decree (no. 342—115) authorized the establishment of a new KGB SIGINT station (codenamed TERMIT-P) within the Lourdes base, which began operations in December 1976. Run by the Sixteenth Directorate, TERMIT-P had a fixed 12-meter dish antenna and a mobile 7-meter dish antenna mounted on a covered lorry, which enabled it to intercept microwave communications "downlinked" from US satellites or transmitted between microwave towers.[65] Other large GRU/Sixteenth Directorate SIGINT stations established in the late 1970s included those in South Yemen and at Cam Ranh Bay in Vietnam. The biggest, however, remained the Lourdes complex, which continued to grow steadily over the next decade. President Reagan declared in 1983:

> The Soviet intelligence collection facility less than 100 miles from our coast is the largest of its kind in the world. The acres and acres of antennae fields and intelligence monitors are targeted on key US military installations and sensitive activities. The installation, in Lourdes, Cuba, is manned by 1,500 Soviet technicians, and the satellite ground station allows instant communication with Moscow. This 28-square-mile facility has grown by more than 60 percent in size during the past decade.

A joint report by the Departments of State and Defense in 1985 estimated that the total personnel at the Lourdes SIGINT base had increased further to 2,100.[66]

By the early 1980s all KGB residencies possessed an intercept post.[67] Each post was required to submit an annual report to the Centre in November, giving details of encrypted and plain text material intercepted over the past year; the proportion of operationally significant intercepts; newly discovered communications channels of intelligence value; characteristics of the "radio-intelligence environment" in the country concerned; the handling and fulfillment by the intercept post of its SIGINT assignments; measures taken to protect the security and secrecy of its operations; conclusions about past performance and proposals for the future.[68]

In 1980 the Washington area POCHIN posts reported that, as a result of new security precautions, it had become much more difficult to intercept the communications of the federal government.[69] The residency there, however, reported one major new SIGINT success. In September 1980, after two years' planning, in an operation codenamed FLAMINGO, the residency succeeded in bugging the conference room of System Planning Corporation (SPC), a private company in Arlington, Virginia, which did research for the Pentagon. Viktor Vasilyevich Lozenko (codenamed MARVIN), a Line X (scientific and technological intelligence) officer under diplomatic cover at the Washington residency, had noticed that the SPC conference room was also used for meetings of the Society for Operational Research, of which he was a member. The day before he left Washington at the end of his tour of duty, he succeeded in fixing the listening device—a battery-powered rod a quarter of a meter long—underneath a table in the room. The signal from the bug was monitored from a command post in a car with diplomatic number plates, fitted with a T-shaped antenna built into the front windshield, which took up position at one of nine locations situated at distances of 300–500 meters from the SPC offices.

For the next ten and a half months operation FLAMINGO provided what the Centre considered "highly important" intelligence on the current and future deployment of US nuclear weapons in Europe, on American chemical weapons, on the US navy's chances of survival in a nuclear conflict, and on the US position on the SALT-2 talks. On January 27, 1981 a senior Pentagon official presented a classified report at a meeting entitled "Current Status and Trends in the Advancement of the US Nuclear Forces in the Central European Theater of War." Among the issues discussed at the meeting were: American mobilization capabilities; the effectiveness of laser guidance systems; plans for the destruction of 730 tons of chemical weapons which were now unusable; and the extent of US intelligence on, and requirements concerning, Soviet chemical weapons. Other meetings in the bugged conference room, also attended by senior Pentagon officials, discussed the current status and proposed reforms of the US armed forces. The operation came to an end not because the listening device was discovered but because its power supply gradually ran out.[70]

Four of the KGB officers involved in operation FLAMINGO received the Order of the Red Star: Lozenko, who selected the location and placed the bug; V. I. Shokin, who supervised the operation; the head of the POCHIN station Yuri Nikolayevich Marakhovsky, who played a leading role in collecting and processing the intelligence collected from the SPC conference room; and Yuri Vasilyevich Gratsiansky, head of the residency's Operational—Technical Support section, who was responsible for the technical side of the operation. Three other residency officers received lesser awards.[71]

SOVIET SIGINT OPERATIONS, like those of the United States, were assisted by allied agencies. The UKUSA Security Agreement concluded in 1948 between the United States, the United Kingdom, Canada, Australia and New Zealand provided for the division of collection tasks and the sharing of the product between their SIGINT services.[72] The KGB, however, was determined to give its allies only limited access to its cryptanalytic secrets. In January 1975 Andropov approved "Regulations on the Principles and Directions of Co-operation with the Security Agencies of the Socialist Countries in Decryption Operations," drafted by the Sixteenth Directorate. Its two guiding principles were, first, that joint operations with the "friends" (allied agencies) were to be under KGB control; second, that cryptographic information supplied to allied agencies "should not disclose the level of the latest [Soviet] achievements in the field of cryptanalysis:"

> Bearing in mind that at the present time the related services of our friends have acquired a certain experience of working on and exploiting [SIGINT] targets by the methods of electronic [computer-based] cryptanalysis, there is some possibility that in future our friends may try to apply these methods independently against other targets as well. In these conditions, it is essential to strengthen further the co-operation between the Sixteenth Directorate and the related services of our friends with a view to exclude uncontrolled operations which could cause irreparable harm to the Sixteenth Directorate with regard to the application of the methods of electronic cryptanalysis.

On no account were the "friends" to learn of the existence of the top secret training school for KGB cryptanalysts; they were to be given the impression that all training took place at the Centre. Though, on occasion, allied agencies could be given cipher communications from shortwave transmissions intercepted by the Sixteenth Directorate, they were never allowed access to SIGINT from residency intercept posts, satellite communications or telegraph lines within the Soviet Union.[73]

Despite the Sixteenth Directorate's reluctance to share most SIGINT secrets with its intelligence allies, it depended on their assistance. With the growing complexity of computer-generated cipher systems, Soviet cryptanalysts were increasingly dependent on the penetration of foreign embassies to steal cipher materials and, when possible, bug cipher machines and teleprinters. During 1974 alone joint operations by the FCD Sixteenth Department and its Soviet Bloc allies succeeded in abstracting cipher material from at least seven embassies in Prague, five in Sofia, two in Budapest and two in Warsaw.[74] Soviet Bloc intelligence services also shared some of their agents in Western embassies and foreign ministries with the KGB. Among those who were particularly highly rated by the KGB Sixteenth Directorate was a Bulgarian agent codenamed EPIR, a security official in the Greek foreign ministry recruited by Bulgarian intelligence in 1966. Over the next ten years he assisted in the removal of over 12,000 classified pages of documents from the ministry.[75]

A conference of the KGB leadership in May 1981 included in its main priorities the recruitment of agents from the cipher personnel of the United States, Britain, France, West Germany and China. Andropov reaffirmed that priority in a special directive issued after he succeeded Brezhnev as general secretary in 1982.[76] He also approved the secret award of the Order of the Friendship of Peoples to the KGB's longest-serving cipher officer agent, JOUR in the French foreign ministry, in recognition of his "long and fruitful co-operation" over the previous thirty-seven years.[77] The FCD Sixteenth Department, headed by A. V. Krasavin, had plans to create another forty or fifty intercept posts in Soviet establishments around the world by the end of the decade. It calculated optimistically that the volume of intercepted communications would increase by five to eight times its present level if the current rate of expansion were maintained.[78]

According to Viktor Makarov, who served in the Sixteenth Directorate from 1980 to 1986, the European states whose diplomatic traffic was decrypted with varying frequency during these years included Denmark, Finland, France, Greece, Italy, Sweden, Switzerland and West Germany. There was, he believes, no penetration of high-grade British cipher systems during that period.[79] An inner circle within the Politburo—consisting, in 1980, of Brezhnev, Andropov, Gromyko, Kirilenko, Suslov and Ustinov—were sent a daily selection of the most important intercepts. A larger selection was forwarded each day to the heads of the First and Second Chief Directorates.[80] Though neither selection is yet available for research, both will one day be sources of major importance for historians of Soviet foreign policy.

In addition to obviously important items such as Kissinger's and Vance's meetings with foreign leaders, the intercepts selected for the inner circle of the Politburo undoubtedly also included, whenever possible, Western responses to their public pronouncements. Vyacheslav Ivanovich Gurgenev (alias "Artemov"), deputy head of the FCD, complained publicly in 1991:

Our service has had enough trouble in the past trying to collect responses to every "brilliant" initiative by our leaders. This kind of work tended to corrupt people who started out with the illusion of doing something useful.[81]

Residencies around the world were expected to provide prompt reports of favorable responses to every major speech by the Soviet leadership. When no such responses occurred, they were commonly invented to avoid the risk of offending the Politburo.[82] Since the Sixteenth Directorate was able, by the later 1960s, to decrypt at least some of the diplomatic traffic of over seventy states,[83] its chances of finding some suitable response among the thousands of decrypts produced each week were much greater than those of even the most active residency.

In the pre-*glasnost* era controversial references to Soviet leaders were routinely edited out of translations of diplomatic decrypts. Makarov recalls seeing an intercepted cable from the Swedish ambassador in Moscow in August 1984 discussing the likely power struggle which would follow the demise of the ailing Konstantin Chernenko. Among the passages removed or doctored in the Russian translation was a disparaging reference to Gorbachev's wife, Raisa Maximovna. On another occasion Makarov was ordered to remove from a diplomatic telegram he had decrypted the sentence, "Gorbachev is like Andropov." Such excisions were known within the Sixteenth Directorate as "minding the words."[84]

DURING THE 1980s SIGINT agencies in both East and West began to face two formidable new technological challenges: the use of fiber optics in global telecommunications and the greatly increased availability of highly sophisticated encryption systems. Neither the KGB nor any other SIGINT agency seems to have devised a system of intercepting messages which passed along fiber-optic lines as streams of light. In the late 1980s Britain installed a highly secure fiber-optic trunk system, codenamed BOXER, which linked 200 military installations. Simultaneously, the development of Public Key Cryptography by mathematicians at the Massachusetts Institute of Technology and the Weizmann Institute in Israel, and subsequent refinements such as Phil Zimmermann's PGP (Pretty Good Privacy) system, made ciphers which were difficult, if not impossible, for SIGINT agencies to crack, available to anyone with a powerful desktop computer and modem.[85]

The SIGINT-related files seen by Mitrokhin, which end in 1982, do not explain how the KGB sought to respond to these new challenges. It is clear from other evidence, however, that Soviet SIGINT operations continued to expand, at least in volume, during the Gorbachev era. Those of the GRU, targeted chiefly on the armed forces of the United States, NATO and China, were on an even larger scale than the KGB's. By the end of the 1980s the Red Army had 40 SIGINT regiments, 170 SIGINT battalions and over 700 SIGINT companies. Since the launch of *Kosmos 189* in 1967, the GRU Space Intelligence Directorate had put over 130 SIGINT satellites into orbit. More than 60 Soviet surface ships and over 20 different types of aircraft were used for SIGINT collection. The GRU and KGB had between them over 500 SIGINT ground stations in the Soviet Union and around the world. In all, the GRU and KGB SIGINT network probably employed about 350,000 intercept operators, processors, cryptanalysts and other technical specialists, a majority of them military personnel—about five times as many as the NSA and US Service Cryptological Authorities, which together had an estimated 60,000 to 70,000 personnel.[86] According to Vladimir Rubakov, a senior KGB officer interviewed shortly before the reorganization of Soviet intelligence in 1991, SIGINT operations consumed a quarter of the KGB budget.[87]

In December 1991 the former Eighth and Sixteenth Directorates of the KGB were reconstituted as an independent service, the Federal Agency for Government Communications and Information (FAPSI in its Russian acronym), responsible for communications security, ciphers and SIGINT. Russian SIGINT operations today are on a significantly smaller scale than those of the former Soviet Union. One of the least noticed consequences of the disintegration of the Soviet Bloc was the dismantling of the great majority of the 150 ground stations in former Warsaw Pact countries.[88] Some of the most important stations outside the Russian Federation, however, still survive—among them the large SIGINT complexes near Tallinn in Estonia and at Lourdes in Cuba (though the Lourdes personnel was reduced by over half to a total of about 1,000 in 1993).[89] The residencies of the SVR, the Russian foreign intelligence service, continue to contain active intercept posts. Though FAPSI operates with somewhat reduced resources, faces harder targets and probably finds it increasingly difficult to match NSA's state of the art technology, Russian SIGINT still has a global reach.

T W E N T Y - T W O

SPECIAL TASKS

Part 1: From Marshal Tito to Rudolf Nureyev

Assassination had been an integral part of Stalin's foreign policy. During the late 1930s he had been obsessed with NKVD operations to liquidate Trotsky and his leading foreign supporters. The final act of his foreign policy before he died in 1953 was a plan to assassinate Josip Tito, who had succeeded Trotsky as the leading heretic of the Soviet Bloc.

At the height of the Terror, Tito (born Josip Broz) had, ironically, been one of the few leading Yugoslav Communists (most then living in exile in Moscow) who were trusted by the NKVD. On becoming secretary general of the purged Yugoslav Party in 1937, he had dutifully denounced his persecuted and liquidated comrades, in impeccable Stalinist invective, as Trotskyists, traitors, factionalists, spies and anti-Party elements. He apologized personally to Stalin for his own lack of vigilance in choosing as his first wife a woman who had since been unmasked as an (imaginary) Gestapo agent. When Tito became wartime leader of the Communist partisans, an NKVD agent, Josip Kopinić, codenamed VAZHDUH ("Air"), acted as his radio link with Moscow.[1] At the end of the war, the NKGB resident, Saveli Vladimirovich Burtakov (codenamed LIST), presented the head of Tito's Bureau of People's Protection, Alexander-Leka Ranković, with a portrait of Stalin. Apparently deeply moved, Ranković (codenamed MARKO by the Centre) replied that it was the most precious gift he could possibly have received.[2] There was no sign yet of the violent confrontation between Tito and Stalin which was to erupt only three years later. Despite his own subsequent loathing for Stalinism, the leading Yugoslav communist Milovan Djilas later acknowledged:

> The fact is that not a single Party leader was anti-Soviet—not before the war, not during, not after . . . Stalin and the Soviet Union were our corner-stone and point of spiritual origin . . . [3]

There were already signs by the end of the war, however, that Tito (codenamed OREL ("Eagle") by the Centre) would be less sycophantic to Moscow than most other leaders of the emerging Soviet Bloc. Unlike other Bloc members, the Yugoslav partisans had defeated the Germans and Italians chiefly through their own efforts rather than the sacrifices of the Red Army. Tito declared ominously soon after VE Day, "We will not be dependent on anyone ever again." Burtakov reported to the Centre:

> Side by side with his positive qualities—popularity, good looks, an expressive face, spirit and willpower—OREL also has the following negative traits: lust for power, lack of modesty, arrogance and insincerity. He considers himself to be the absolute authority, prefers unquestioning obedience, dislikes an exchange of views and criticism of his orders; he is irritable, hot-tempered and curt; he loves to strike poses.

Burtakov also believed Tito was less than frank about his dealings with Britain, "although outwardly he makes a show of his supposed hostility towards the Allies, especially the British."[4]

Tito and Ranković, in turn, took a dim view of Burtakov, who became notorious for his habit of looting jewelry, crystal, china and rugs from Yugoslav mansions (a practice he was to repeat when posted to Romania and Czechoslovakia).[5] At the end of 1945 Burtakov was replaced as chief adviser to the Bureau of People's Protection (OZNA) by Arseni Vasilyevich Tishkov, known to the Yugoslavs as Timofeyev.[6]

The post-war MGB had residencies in Belgrade, Zagreb, Ljubljana and Skopje, as well as four sub-residencies elsewhere in Yugoslavia,[7] whose imperious behavior caused increasing resentment at Soviet intrusion into Yugoslav affairs. An inspection by the Centre reported that MGB advisers "interfered roughshod in the internal affairs of the Bureau of People's Protection, and applied pressure in order to obtain information." Information refused by OZNA's leaders was surreptitiously obtained from its junior officers.[8] What caused most resentment in Belgrade, however, was MGB recruitment of Yugoslav agents. Tito was unaware that two of his own ministers—Andriya Hebrang, minister of industry, and Streten Žujović, finance minister—were among them. He was, however, outraged at a Soviet attempt in 1945 to seduce and recruit Dusica Petrović, the female officer in charge of Yugoslav ciphers. When informed of the case by Ranković, Tito exploded: "A spy network is something we will not tolerate! We've got to let them know right away."[9] Tishkov, however, continued to demand from Tito and Ranković offices for himself and the Soviet "advisers" inside OZNA headquarters, with the right to be informed of all agent files and operations.[10]

Of all Tito's early signs of independence, the one which caused most alarm in Moscow was probably his plan for a Balkan federation—interpreted by Stalin as a potential challenge to Soviet hegemony. In March 1948 the Soviet Union recalled its advisers and angrily denounced the Yugoslav Party as riddled with both ideological heresy and British spies. On June 28 Cominform (the post-war successor to Comintern) expelled the Yugoslavs and appealed to "healthy elements" in the Party to overthrow the leadership. Tito's flattering secret codename OREL ("Eagle") was hurriedly downgraded to STERVYATNIK ("Carrion Crow").[11] Stalin, however, initially overestimated the ease with which "Carrion Crow" could be overthrown. "I shall shake my little finger," he boasted to Khrushchev, "and there will be no more Tito." When that failed, "he shook everything else he could shake;" but without success. Tito's hold over the Party, army and state machinery remained secure.

In the summer of 1948 the MGB and UDBA (OZNA's successor) began a vicious intelligence war. Hebrang and Žujović, the two Soviet moles in Tito's cabinet, were arrested. Other Soviet agents were discovered in Tito's bodyguard, of whom the most senior was Major-General Momo Jurović (codenamed VAL). According to Djilas, the UDBA discovered an MGB plot to wipe out the Yugoslav Politburo with automatic rifles while they were relaxing in the billiards room at Tito's villa. The UDBA's use of terror against Cominforn "traitors" rivaled in horror, if not in scale, that of the NKVD against Soviet "enemies of the people" a decade before. Djilas mournfully told Ranković, "Now we are treating Stalin's followers just as he treated his enemies!"[12] The MGB and its allied intelligence services simultaneously engaged in a purge of mostly imaginary Titoist conspirators throughout the Soviet Bloc. Their most celebrated victims were the Hungarian interior minister, László Rajk, and seven alleged accomplices who confessed at a carefully rehearsed show trial in Budapest to taking part in a vast non-existent plot hatched by Tito and the CIA.[13]

The final, and most ingenious, of the MGB plans to assassinate Tito involved one of the most remarkable of all Soviet illegals, Iosif Grigulevich (at this time codenamed MAKS or DAKS), who had taken a leading part in the first, narrowly unsuccessful, attempt on Trotsky's life in Mexico City in May 1940, had run a Latin American sabotage network during the Second World War, and in 1951—posing as Teodoro Castro—had become Costa Rican chargé d'affaires (later Minister Plenipotentiary) in Rome.[14] Since Costa Rica had no diplomatic mission in Belgrade, Grigulevich was also able to obtain the post of non-resident envoy to Yugoslavia. The MGB reported to Stalin in February 1953:

> While fulfilling his diplomatic duties in the second half of the year 1952, [MAKS] twice visited Yugoslavia, where he was well received. He had access to the social group close to Tito's staff and was given the promise of a personal audience with Tito. The post held by MAKS at the present time makes it possible to use his capabilities for active measures against Tito.[15]

Grigulevich volunteered for the role of assassin. At a secret meeting with senior MGB officers in Vienna early in February 1953 he suggested four possible ways to eliminate "Carrion Crow:"

1. To administer a lethal dose of pneumonic plague from a silent spray concealed in his clothing during a personal audience with Tito. (Grigulevich would be inoculated with an antidote beforehand.)
2. To obtain an invitation to the reception for Tito to be given during his forthcoming visit to London by the Yugoslav ambassador, with whom Grigulevich was on friendly terms. Grigulevich would shoot Tito with a

silenced pistol, then spray tear gas at the reception to cause panic and assist his escape.

3. To use the previous method at a diplomatic reception in Belgrade.

4 To present Tito with jewelry in a booby-trapped box which would release a lethal poison gas as soon as it was opened.

Grigulevich was asked to submit more detailed proposals to the Centre, Meanwhile, the MGB assured Stalin that there was no doubt that "MAKS, because of his personal qualities and experience in intelligence work, is capable of accomplishing a mission of this kind."[16]

The use of an accredited Central American diplomat as Tito's assassin was intended to conceal as effectively as possible the hand of the MGB. Using his Costa Rican alias, Grigulevich composed a farewell letter addressed to his Mexican wife to be made public and used to reinforce his Latin American cover if he were captured or killed during the assassination attempt.[17] On March 1, 1953 the MGB reported to Stalin that MAK's attempt to "rub out" Tito had, unfortunately, not yet taken place. This disappointing report, which Stalin read at about midnight, may well have been the last document he saw before he suffered a fatal stroke in the early hours of March 2.[18]

After Stalin's death three days later, plans for the assassination were suspended. That May Grigulevich was hurriedly withdrawn to Moscow when the pre-war Soviet defector Aleksandr Orlov began publishing reminiscences of Stalin and the NKVD in *Life* magazine. The Centre feared that Orlov, who knew of Grigulevich's sabotage missions before and during the Spanish Civil War, might blow his cover—though, in the event, he did not do so.[19] So far as the puzzled Costa Rican foreign ministry and Rome diplomatic corps were concerned, Grigulevich and his wife simply disappeared into thin air. A note on his KGB file in 1980 records that Western intelligence services had, apparently, never identified the missing Teodoro Castro as the Soviet illegal Iosif Grigulevich. Back in Moscow, Grigulevich had successfully completed a doctoral dissertation, become a senior scientific researcher at the Ethnographic Institute of the Soviet Academy of Sciences in 1958, and thereafter made a new life for himself as a leading writer and academic authority on Latin America, ethnography and religion, becoming vice-president of the Soviet—Cuban and Soviet—Venezuelan Friendship Societies.[20]

UNDER KHRUSHCHEV, PLOTS to assassinate Tito were replaced by attempted conciliation with Belgrade. The public Soviet—Yugoslav conflict was formally concluded during a state visit by Khrushchev to Belgrade in May 1955. Assassination was far less central to Khrushchev's foreign policy than it had been to Stalin's. It remained, however, as it had done throughout the Stalin era, a basic part of Soviet policy for dealing with the leaders of anti-Soviet émigré groups: in particular, the Organization of Ukrainian Nationalists (OUN) and the rival Social-Democratic National Labor Union (NTS). As Party secretary in the Ukraine, Khrushchev had ordered the secret poisoning by the MGB of, among others, the nationalist Oleksander Shumsky and of Archbishop Romzha of the Uniate (Catholic) church.[21]

The first major foreign assassination target of the post-Stalin era was Georgi Sergeyevich Okolovich, one of the leaders of the NTS organization in West Germany. The training of Okolovich's intended assassin, Nikolai Khokhlov, was personally overseen by the MGB head of foreign intelligence, Aleksandr Semyonovich Panyushkin. Khokhlov's instructors included Mikhail Rubak, a Soviet judo champion, and Lieutenant-Colonel Godlevsky, winner of five national pistol tournaments. The execution weapon was an electrically operated gun, fitted with a silencer and concealed inside a cigarette packet, which fired cyanide bullets developed in the Centre's secret arms laboratory at Khozyaistvo Zheleznovo. Khokhlov, however, proved to be more squeamish than the assassins of the Stalin era and was at least half-persuaded by some of the NTS publications which he read while plotting Okolovich's assassination. On February 18, 1954 Khokhlov called at Okolovich's flat in Frankfurt. His introduction was somewhat disconcerting. "Georgi Sergeyevich," he told him, "I've come to you from Moscow. The Central Committee of the Communist Party of the Soviet Union has ordered your assassination." He then informed the startled Okolovich that he had decided not to murder him. Instead, Khokhlov defected to an initially skeptical CIA. On April 20 he gave a sensational press conference at which he revealed the assassination plan and displayed his exotic murder weapon to the world's media.[22]

In April 1955, following a prolonged post-mortem at the Centre in the wake of Khokhlov's well-publicized defection, "special actions" were made the responsibility of the reorganized FCD Thirteenth Department, which was represented in residencies by a newly created Line F. Its duties were to prepare and conduct sabotage in collaboration with the GRU; to carry out other "special actions" involving the use of force, ranging from kidnapping to assassination; and to steal Western military technology (a responsibility later handed over to FCD Directorate T on its foundation in 1963).[23]

SABOTAGE OPERATIONS REPLACED assassination as the most important "special actions" of the Thirteenth Department during and beyond the Khrushchev era. The main priority of these operations consisted of the identification of targets in the West and preparations for their destruction by Soviet sabotage and intelligence groups (*diversionnye razvedyvatelnye gruppy* or DRGs) and the local Communist "resistance" in the event of an East—West conflict. One of Line F's earliest tasks followed the conclusion of the four-power Austrian State Treaty, signed in Vienna in May 1955, which ended the post-war occupation by the wartime allies. Before the withdrawal of the Red Army, the KGB was instructed to select and fill a series of secret arms caches. Among the many sites recorded in the files examined by Mitrokhin were the villages of Mayerling, Mollram, Weinersdorf, Heiligenkreuz and Semmering; the Stift Gîttweig monastery; and two ruined castles, Schloss Starhemberg and Schloss Merkenstein. KGB archives contain detailed plans and written descriptions of these and other locations. The plan of the ruins of Schloss Starhemberg, for example, shows a 7.65 caliber Walter pistol, with a cartridge clip and 21 rounds of ammunition, concealed in a crack in the outer wall at ground level 1.5 meters to the left of an old pine tree; and a 6.35 caliber Walter pistol, with a cartridge clip and 21 live rounds, hidden in the castle courtyard 1.5 meters from an old pear tree. At Schloss Merkenstein a 7.65 caliber Mauser pistol, with cartridge clip and 21 rounds of ammunition, was concealed in a niche underneath a large stone to the left of the gateway arch; a Walter pistol, also with cartridge clip and 25 rounds, was hidden in a crevice in the wall.[24]

In May 1964, the KGB residency in Vienna made a sample check of the second Schloss Merkenstein cache, and was disturbed to discover that the cover in which the arms had been wrapped had rotted away. Four of the twenty-one rounds of ammunition had disappeared and were assumed to have fallen deeper into the crevice; the other seventeen rounds had deteriorated and were no longer safe to use. The Walter pistol, once rust had been removed, as found to be still serviceable. The Centre prudently decided to leave the other caches undisturbed.[25]

Potential sabotage targets and landing sites for Soviet sabotage and intelligence groups (DRGs) are recorded in KGB·files with the same meticulous detail as the location of the secret arms caches.[26] By 1959, if not earlier, the most vulnerable points of power-transmission lines, oil pipelines, communications systems and major industrial complexes in most, if not all, NATO countries were being systematically reconnoitered and marked on the Thirteenth Department's maps. In the summer of 1959 a KGB agent obtained a temporary job at an electricity substation near Worms in order to assist the preparation of plans to sabotage electric power lines crossing the Rhine.[27] From October 2 to 30, 1959 a Soviet delegation of energy experts, headed by the deputy minister for the construction of power plants and including a KGB officer, used a visit to the United States to reconnoiter sabotage targets in power stations and electricity lines.

Files on suitable landing sites and bases for the DRGs which would attack these and other targets included detailed information on the terrain, landmarks, climate in different seasons, prevailing winds, populated areas and local customs. Where the DRGs were to land by sea rather than by air, there were further details on the coastline, tides and operating conditions for submarines and motor boats.[28] Much of the information was collected by local agents and by Soviet citizens who were allowed to travel to the West for family reunions. An attempt was also made to recruit illegal agents in the main NATO countries and Japan to assist the DRGs. According to a Thirteenth Department file:

> People who are suitable as special [illegal] agents for Line F operations are 20 to 45 years old. Persons from aristocratic and bourgeois-conservative circles are of no interest. Preference is given to the following professions: electricians, mechanics, toolmakers, chemists, qualified engineers, technicians and highly skilled workers—primarily citizens of the United States, France, Canada, Britain, West Germany, Italy and Japan. People who adhere strictly to church dogma and rules are not suitable, nor are people with a tendency towards alcoholism, drug addiction and sexual deviations. In order to provide explanations for the characteristics and routines involved in the operations being carried out, it is desirable to select people who travel frequently around their own country

as well as to other countries—people who own houses, second homes, country dachas, farmsteads and plots of land.[29]

The Thirteenth Department's preparations for wartime sabotage operations inevitably overlapped with those of the GRU. The resulting duplication of effort was made worse by the traditional rivalry and distrust between the two agencies. On April 7, 1960 the CPSU Central Committee issued Decision No. P-274-XIVI, calling for closer co-ordination between the KGB and GRU. This and other exhortations, however, had little practical effect. In September 1963 the Centre complained that the leadership of the GRU was making no serious attempt to co-ordinate its operations with those of the KGB.[30]

The KGB found it easier to collaborate with the intelligence agencies of other Soviet Bloc countries, who were usually willing to accept a subordinate role, and sought their help in a number of Line F operations. According to Markus Wolf, head of the HVA (Stasi foreign intelligence) from 1952 to 1986, the Centre offered its allies lethal nerve toxins and poisons which were fatal on contact with the skin for use during "special actions." Wolf claims that he refused all but a small supply of "truth drugs," which he had analyzed by an HVA doctor:

> He came back shaking his head in horror. "Use those without constant medical supervision and there is every chance that the fellow from whom you want the truth will be dead as a dodo in seconds," he said.

In his memoirs Wolf seeks to distance himself from KGB assassination attempts. He claims, for example, that the KGB assassinated Aleksandr Trushnovich, the NTS leader in West Berlin, "while attempting to kidnap him."[31] KGB files tell a rather different story. In April 1954 Heinz Gleske, a Stasi officer operating undercover in West Germany, lured Trushnovich to his home, where he was kidnapped and handed over to the KGB at Karlshorst. Gleske then issued a statement, claiming that Trushnovich had become disillusioned with the West and had "voluntarily" defected to East Germany. The Centre awarded Gleske the Order of the Red Star.[32]

Even with some assistance from its allies, the KGB's "special actions" against NTS and OUN leaders during the Khrushchev era had a mixed record of success—not least because of the doubts of its assassins. In an attempt to disguise its involvement in an attempt to murder the NTS president, Vladimir Poremsky, the Thirteenth Department hired the services of a German contract killer, Wolfgang Wildprett. Like Khokhlov, however, Wildprett had second thoughts, decided not to go ahead with the "special action" and in December 1955 informed the West German police. In September 1957 a Thirteenth Department attempt to poison Khokhlov himself with radioactive thallium (chosen in the belief that it would degrade and leave no trace at autopsy) also failed.

These failures, however, were followed by the successful assassination of two leading Ukrainian émigrés: the main NTS ideologist, Lev Rebet, in October 1957 and the OUN leader, Stephen Bandera, in October 1959.[33] The Thirteenth Department assassin in both cases, only twenty-five years of age when he killed Rebet, was Bodgan Stashinsky, who operated out of the KGB compound at Karlshorst. His murder weapon, specially constructed by the KGB weapons laboratory, was a spray gun which fired a jet of poison gas from a crushed cyanide ampule and caused death by cardiac arrest. The Centre calculated, correctly, that an unsuspecting pathologist was likely to diagnose the cause of death as heart failure. Stashinsky tested his weapon by taking a dog into a wood near Karlshorst, tying it to a tree and firing at it. The dog had immediate convulsions and died in a few moments. Confident of the deadliness of his spray gun, Stashinsky killed both Rebet and Bandera by lying in wait for them in darkened stairways. In December 1959, he was summoned to Moscow. At a ceremony in the Centre, Aleksandr Nikolayevich Shelepin, chairman of the KGB, read aloud a citation praising Stashinsky "for carrying out an extremely important government assignment" and presented him with the Order of the Red Banner. Stashinsky was told he would be sent on a course to perfect his English before being sent on a three- to five-year assignment in the West to carry out further "special actions."[34]

Like Khokhlov and Wildprett, however, Stashinsky had second thoughts about his career as an assassin, encouraged by his East German girlfriend, Inge Pohl, whom he married in 1960. In August 1961, the day before the Berlin Wall sealed off the escape route from the East, the couple defected to the West. Stashinsky confessed to the murders of Rebet and Bandera, was tried at Karlsruhe in October 1962 and sentenced to eight years' imprisonment. The judge declared that the main culprit was the Soviet government which had institutionalized political murder. Heads were quick to roll within the KGB. According to Anatoli Golitsyn, who defected four months after Stashinsky, at least seventeen KGB officers were sacked or demoted.[35] More importantly, the Khokhlov and Stashinsky defections led both the KGB leadership and the Politburo to reassess the risks of "wet affairs" (assassination attempts). Fearful of attracting more of the worldwide publicity generated by Khokhlov's press conference and Stashinsky's trial, the Politburo abandoned assassination as a normal treatment of policy outside the Soviet Bloc, resorting to it only on rare occasions such as in the elimination of President Hafizullah Amin of Afghanistan in December 1979.[36]

Among the chief beneficiaries of the KGB's declining enthusiasm for assassination plots was probably Nikita Khrushchev. Vladimir Semichastny, then the KGB chairman, claims that he was approached in 1964 by Leonid Brezhnev, the ringleader of the plot to oust Khrushchev, and asked to arrange his "physical elimination." Semichastny refused.[37] He did, however, agree to bug Khruschchev's private telephone lines. With the KGB's assistance, the plotters achieved a substantial element of surprise. When Khrushchev left for a holiday on the Black Sea in the autumn of 1964, he was seen off by smiling colleagues. When he returned on October 13, summoned to attend an urgent meeting of the Presidium, he was met at the airport only by Semichastny and a senior security officer from the KGB. "They've all gathered in the Kremlin and are waiting for you," Semichastny told him. Khrushchev surrendered to the inevitable without a struggle, agreeing to resign on the grounds of "advanced age and poor health." Thereafter, he was relegated almost to the status of unperson, not mentioned again in the press until *Pravda* published a brief note in 1970 recording his death.[38]

THOUGH ITS ASSASSINATION operations declined, the Centre showed increasing interest during the 1960s and 1970s in collaboration with "anti-imperialist" guerrilla and terrorist groups in the Third World. In January 1961 Khrushchev publicly pledged Soviet assistance for "movements of national liberation." The abortive, CIA-backed invasion of Cuba at the Bay of Pigs three months later strengthened his determination to do so. On August 3 he told a private meeting of Warsaw Pact leaders in Moscow, "I wish we could give imperialism a bloody nose!"[39] The Centre believed it had devised a way to do so which would conceal the role of the KGB.

The aggressive global grand strategy against the Main Adversary, devised in the summer of 1961 by Shelepin and approved by Khrushchev and the Central Committee, envisaged the use of national liberation movements both in operations against the United States and its allies and in promoting "armed uprisings against reactionary pro-Western governments." At the top of the list of national liberation movements cultivated by the KGB was the newly founded Sandinista National Liberation Front (FSLN) in Nicaragua, which was dedicated to following the example of the Cuban revolution and overthrowing the brutal pro-American dictatorship of the Somoza dynasty.[40] The FSLN leader, Carlos Fonseca Amador, codenamed GIDROLOG ("Hydrologist"), was described by the Centre as "a trusted agent."[41] Sandinista guerrillas formed the basis for a KGB sabotage and intelligence group established in 1966 on the Mexican US border with support bases in the area of Ciudad Juarez, Tijuana and Ensenada. Its leader, Manuel Ramón de Jesus Andara y Ubeda (codenamed PRIM), traveled to Moscow for training in Line F operations. Among the chief sabotage targets across the US border were military bases, missile sites, radar installations and the oil pipeline (codenamed START) which ran from El Paso in Texas to Costa Mesa, California. Three sites on the American coast were selected for DRG landings, together with large-capacity dead-drops in which to store mines, explosive, detonators and other sabotage materials. A support group codenamed SATURN was given the task of using the movements of migrant workers (*braceros*) to conceal the transfer of agents and munitions across the border. SATURN's headquarters was a hotel belonging to a Russian-born agent, codenamed VLADELETS ("Proprietor"), in Ensenada fifty miles from the US border in the Baja California. VLADELET's two sons, both born in Mexico but assessed by the KGB as "Russian patriots," owned a gas station which was selected as a hiding place for DRGs and their equipment as well as a base from which to conduct sabotage in the United States.[42]

Canada in the north, like Mexico in the south, was intended by the Thirteenth Department (reorganized in 1965 as Department V) as a base for cross-border operations by DRGs against the Main Adversary. In 1967 a number of frontier crossings were reconnoitred: among them areas near the Lake of the Woods and International Falls in Minnesota, and in the region of the Glacier National Park in Montana. The KGB believed that one of its targets in Montana, the Flathead dam, generated "the largest power supply system in the world." Department V identified a point (codenamed DORIS) on the South Fork river about three kilometers below the dam, where it could bring down a series of pylons on a steep mountain slope which would take a lengthy period to repair. It also planned a probably simultaneous operation in which DRG commandos would descend on the Hungry Horse dam at night, take control of it for a few hours and sabotage its sluices.

The state with the largest number of targets, however, was almost certainly New York, where DRG's based along the Delaware river, in the Big Spring Park near Harrisburg, Pennsylvania, and at other locations planned to disrupt the power supply of the entire state before taking refuge in the Appalachian mountains. In examining the target files of the Thirteenth Department and Department V, Mitrokhin was invariably struck by the thoroughness with which each target had been reconnoitred. The file on the port of New York (target GRANIT), for example, included details of ships' berths, warehouses, communications systems, port personnel and security procedures. As always, the port's most vulnerable points were carefully marked.[43]

As well as being a base of KGB "special tasks" against the United States, Canada was also an important target in its own right. Operation KEDR ("Cedar"), begun by the Ottawa residency in 1959, took twelve years to complete an immensely detailed reconnaissance of oil refineries and oil and gas pipelines across Canada from British Columbia to Montreal. Each target was photographed from several angles and its vulnerable points identified. The most suitable approach roads for sabotage operations, together with the best getaway routes, were carefully plotted on small-scale maps.[44]

Line F operations in north America were part of a much larger strategy. In the event of war with NATO, Moscow planned a massive campaign of sabotage and disruption behind enemy lines. But sabotage on a more modest scale was also envisaged in crises (not precisely defined in files seen by Mitrokhin) which stopped short of war. Within Europe, residencies in NATO countries and some neutral states (notably Austria, Sweden and Switzerland) were all expected to make detailed plans for the sabotage of four to six major targets a year.[45] In 1964–6, for example, Line F in West Germany planned "special actions" against the Wilhelmshaven–Wesseling oil pipeline; fuel and lubricant depots in Wilhelmshaven and Unterpfaffenhoven; the main electrical substations in Brauweiler and Rommerskirchen and in the hamlet of Feinau; the NATO military transit base in the harbor of Bremerhaven; the FRG government war bunker; the Howaldswerft shipbuilding docks at Kiel and the Weser A G in Bremen; and the main US army arms depot at Misau. On instructions from the Centre, the Bonn residency purchased uniforms and work clothes, used by Bundeswehr soldiers, railway personnel, forestry workers, gamekeepers and roadworkers, to be worn as disguise by DRG saboteurs, for whom landing sites were selected in the Black Forest and Bavaria. Arms and radio equipment for use in the sabotage missions were hidden in dead-drops near the targets.[46] The standard DRG arms package, packed in a container designed for long-term storage, consisted of: equipment for blowing up railway track; one "Cherepakha" (tortoise) mine with 3 additional explosive charges; 4 "Ugolok" devices (purpose not specified in Mitrokhin's notes); explosives designed to destroy the main supports of high-voltage power transmission pylons; 3 6-meter-long detonator fuses; and 2 Karandash ("pencil") detonators with a two-hour delay.[47]

Each arms cache might include more than one container. Radio transmitters and receivers were usually concealed in separate caches, sometimes with local currency for use by the DRGs. In August 1965, for example, 10,000 deutschmarks were placed in the TREZUBETS cache near Bonn; several attempts to locate it a decade later all failed and the money was written off.[48]

Italy was divided by the Centre into four main zones of operations, each with two landing sites and bases for DRGs: the foothills of the Alps (with sites near Venice and in the Milan–Turin region), the remainder of the north (with sites in the Arno valley and the Livorno–Pisa–Florence area), the center and the south. Each site for parachute landings by DRGs had to be a level area without buildings of approximately 1 by 1.5–2 kilometers. In each zone, a large arms cache was hidden in land or property belonging to an experienced agent; radio equipment and money were hidden in dead-drops. The Rome residency was instructed to buy samples of the uniforms worn by the armed services, police, *carabinieri*, railway and forestry workers, as well as typical clothing of the local inhabitants near the landing sites. For the use of DRGs in the most northerly region, the residency was asked to acquire badges from Alpine units of the armed services. Line F prepared files on power-transmission lines, oil pipelines, bridges, tunnels and military installations within a 120-kilometer radius of each landing site. A four-volume file was prepared on former members of the Italian wartime resistance who, it was hoped, would assist in sabotage missions.[49]

Similar sabotage plans were made for all Department V's target countries. Each DRG landing site was known as a DOROZHKA ("runway"), each of its bases as a ULEY ("beehive").[50] Among the most sinister remnants of the Cold War, still scattered around north America, most of western and central Europe, Israel, Turkey, Japan and some other parts of the world, are the caches of KGB arms and radio equipment intended for use by the DRGs. Mitrokhin's notes include precise details of their locations in a number of countries. Some are booby-trapped with MOLNIYA ("lightning") explosive devices designed to destroy their contents if the caches are opened, and are highly dangerous.[51] Indeed, one or more of the caches may already have caused explosions mistakenly attributed to other causes.

LATE IN 1998, the Swiss authorities began removing a radio cache in woods near Berne identified by Mitrokhin,[52] which exploded when fired on by a water-cannon. A spokesman for the Federal Prosecutor's office issued a warning that if any further caches were discovered, they should not be touched: "Anyone who tried to move the [KGB] container would have been killed."[53] In Belgium, radio sets were safely removed from three other KGB caches (codenamed ALPHA-1, ALPHA-2 and ALPHA-5).[54] Given the dangerous condition of an unpredictable number of the KGB's Cold War radio and arms caches, the SVR now has no excuse for failing to reveal their exact locations to the governments of all the countries in which they have been hidden.

In addition to using Line F officers in KGB residencies to run or supervise its operations, the Thirteenth Department and its successor also had a small group of illegals, trained in sabotage techniques and other "special actions," who moved around the world from one sabotage target or "wet job" to another.[55] The most active was Igor Vitalyevich Voytetsky (codenamed PAUL), who began training as an illegal in 1956 at the age of twenty-three. Voytetsky's father, Gleb Pavlovich Shlyandin, had committed suicide at the height of the Great Terror in 1937. His mother, Sofya Davidovna Rudnitskaya, who worked as a music teacher, had remarried Vitali Panteleymonovich Voytetsky, a film director in the Gorky Film Studio. According to his legend, Voytetesky was "Emil Evraert," the son of a Belgian father, Ernst Evraert, and a German mother, Hedwig Marta Althammer. Ernst Evraert had lived in Russia since 1933; "Hedwig Althammer" did not exist. However, a KGB agent, codenamed RAG, who worked for the commune of Bellecour in the Belgian province of Hainault, made a bogus entry in the commune records which purported to show that PAUL and his fictitious mother had lived there from October 15, 1943 to December 14, 1944. On the strength of this entry and forged identity documents provided by the FCD Illegals Directorate S, PAUL obtained a Belgian passport in the name of Emil Evraert on November 8, 1962, then crossed the Channel to England.

On January 30, 1963, in Dover Register Office, Voytetsky married another KGB illegal, Yulia Ivanovna Gorankova (codenamed VIRGINIA), who was then able to apply for genuine Belgian identity documents to replace her forged West German passport. Assisted by Gorankova, Voytetsky embarked on a full-time career as an illegal working for the Thirteenth Department.[56] His first assignment was in Northern Ireland, where he selected sites for airborne and maritime landings by DRGs. He then reconnoitred landing sites in Scotland, where he also identified suitable bases for wartime "resistance movements" by Scottish Communists, prepared large deaddrops for sabotage equipment, identified vulnerable sections of oil pipelines and other targets and selected agents for carrying out sabotage operations. Over the next decade, before becoming an illegal trainer in 1975, Voytetsky carried out similar assignments in Austria, Belgium, Canada, France, Greece, Hong Kong, Israel, Italy, Spain, Turkey and the United States—probably the first ever saboteur's world tour.[57]

THOUGH THE FCD greatly expanded its sabotage capability during the 1960s, it became increasingly confused about the traditional speciality of its "special actions" department—the liquidation of "enemies of the people" abroad. The targets of most of the assassination plots during the 1960s and 1970s recorded in the KGB files seen by Mitrokhin concerned the KGB's own defectors, all of whom were sentenced to death for treason during secret trials held *in absentia*. Despite the risks of further bad publicity in the West if they were hunted down, the Centre was determined not to allow the belief to spread within KGB ranks that traitors could escape their just deserts:

> The KGB must intensify the spirit of hatred towards the enemy and traitors. Significant harm is done by the comforting theory that losses are inevitable in wars between intelligence services. At meetings and in reports, betrayals are sometimes called compromises. Compromises, by which is meant operational failures, are usually provoked by skillful dangles by the enemy. Equating these

two concepts usually leads to the moral justification of traitors, and creates an image of them as victims of the intelligence skills of the enemy. Defectors do not go unpunished. Their punishment is described in such proverbs as: "The traitor Judas is hated everywhere." "A mercenary dog deserves a stake through the heart" and "A traitor is his own murderer."[58]

Deep concern in the Centre at the damage done by Anatoli Golitsyn's defection from the Helsinki residency in December 1961 strengthened its determination to deter future defectors. Unaware of the confusion caused inside the CIA by Golitsyn's increasingly extravagant conspiracy theories, the KGB regarded his defection as a serious setback.[59] His case prompted a major review by the Centre of its procedures for liquidating traitors outside the Soviet Union. In November 1962 Semichastny, who had succeeded Shelepin as KGB chairman, a year earlier, approved a plan for "special actions" against a group of "particularly dangerous traitors," jointly drawn up by the heads of the First and Second Chief Directorates, Aleksandr Mikhailovich Sakharovsky and Oleg Mikhailovich Gribanov:

> As these traitors, who have given important state secrets to the opponent and caused great political damage to the USSR, have been sentenced to death in their absence, this sentence will be carried out abroad.

The oldest name on the death list was that of the former GRU cipher clerk Igor Gouzenko, who had defected in 1945. The remainder were more recent KGB defectors: Anatoli Golitsyn, Pyotr Deryabin, Yuri Rastvorov, Vladimir and Evdokia Petrov, Reino Hayhanen, Nikolai Khokhlov and Bogdan Stashinsky.[60] The plan approved by Semichastny instructed the Thirteenth Department to train assassins to carry out the death sentences on the traitors. The FCD Counter-Intelligence Department (later Directorate K) was to track them down in their foreign refuges, in collaboration with the Second Chief Directorate, which would maintain surveillance of the traitors' relatives inside the Soviet Union, monitor their correspondence and carry out periodic searches of their homes.[61] In Golitsyn's case it was hoped that he would emerge from hiding to give evidence to a Congressional committee and provide an opportunity for a KGB assassin.[62]

In 1964 reports appeared in the American press that the former illegal Reino Hayhanen, who had betrayed "Willie" Fisher (alias "Rudolf Abel"), had been killed in a road accident. FCD personnel were informed that the "accident" had been arranged by the Thirteenth Department. Though KGB had, in reality, no hand in Hayhanen's death, most foreign intelligence officers were taken in by their chief's disinformation.[63] The truth, which the Centre could not bring itself to admit even to its own officers, was that it rarely succeeded in tracking down any of those on the list of "particularly dangerous traitors" and that, even when it did so, it could not devise methods of assassinating them which did not carry unacceptable risks.

During the 1960s, the names of several further defectors were added to the list of "particularly dangerous traitors" to be liquidated abroad. The first was Yuri Nosenko, a KGB officer who had made secret contact with the CIA in June 1962 while serving on the Soviet disarmament delegation in Geneva and who defected to the United States in January 1964.[64] Unlike any of the other defectors on the 1962 list of "particularly dangerous traitors," Nosenko was imprisoned, though not executed. By a terrible irony, however, his jailers were not the KGB but the CIA. Golitsyn had claimed that the KGB would send a series of bogus defectors in an attempt to discredit him. Nosenko, he insisted, was one of them. Tragically, Nosenko's debriefers, like Angleton, the chief of the counterintelligence staff, believed Golitsyn. They paid too much attention to some of the apparent gaps and discrepancies in Nosenko's story—notably the confusion over his rank. They also wrongly concluded that some of his information was too good to be true—particularly his accurate report in the wake of Kennedy's assassination that Oswald's file in the Centre showed that the KGB considered him mentally unstable and had declined to use him as an agent, despite his period in the Soviet Union. And they foolishly regarded as suspicious rather than rational Nosenko's lack of support for Golitsyn's conspiracy theories. Pete Bagley, chief of the counterintelligence branch of the CIA's Soviet Division, complained, "[Nosenko] made everything sound less sinister than Golitsyn. To me, Golitsyn's version was simply superior." For four years and eight months Nosenko was imprisoned by the CIA in miserable conditions, without reading material or human contact, while his interrogators insisted he admit that he was a KGB plant. Few cases in American intelligence history have been so appallingly mishandled.[65]

The KGB knew nothing of the CIA's ill-founded suspicions. Ironically, while Nosenko was languishing in solitary confinement in a prison cell, the Centre was working on a plan for both him and Golitsyn to be assassinated by the illegal PAUL, if they visited the 1967 Montreal World Fair (which, for rather different reasons, neither did).[66]

The Centre's continuing inability to track down its traitors was well illustrated by the case of the illegal Yevgeni Runge (codenamed MAKS), who defected with his wife Valentina Rush (ZINA) to the CIA in Germany in October 1967. Following the KGB's traditional practice of using insulting codenames for defectors, MAKS was renamed GNIDA ("Nit"). Like his predecessors, he was secretly condemned to death in absentia. Enormous efforts involving several other Soviet Bloc services were devoted to operation TREZOR, the long and unsuccessful attempt to track down and liquidate Runge. More than fifty of the Runges' friends and relatives in the Soviet Union, East and West Germany were placed under surveillance; every item of their correspondence which passed through the Soviet Bloc was opened and examined; their homes were bugged and secretly searched. The Stasi mounted a support operation, codenamed COBRA, which set out to cultivate Valentina Rush's sister, Renata Ludwig, and one of her relatives, Ernst Buchholz, who lived in West Berlin. After fifteen years of failure, operation COBRA was finally abandoned.

The KGB also sought the assistance of other Soviet Bloc intelligence services in finding an assassin capable of liquidating Runge in north America, where it was assumed he had taken refuge. The Centre's preferred candidate was a Hungarian-born West German criminal, codenamed JAGUAR, who had been recruited by the

AVH for "special actions" against anti-Communist Hungarian émigrés. On July 1, 1968 JAGUAR blew up the Danube printing house in Munich, which produced émigré publications. He also set fire to the editorial offices of two Hungarian émigré newspapers, putting one of them out of business. For these operations JAGUAR received 40,000 Hungarian forints and 1,000 West German marks from the AVH. Impressed by his "special actions" in Munich, the KGB decided to employ him for operation TREZOR. JAGUAR was shown photographs of Runge and his wife and agreed to hunt them down. Once he had left for the United States, however, he disappeared without trace—together, presumably, with the operational funds allocated to him by the KGB. Following JAGUAR's disappearance, the Centre asked the East German Stasi and the Bulgarian DS whether they had contacts among American gangsters or mafiosi who would take out a contract on Runge. Neither was able to suggest a suitable assassin.[67]

AS WELL AS attempting to liquidate major traitors, the Thirteenth Department and Department V were also responsible for administering lesser punishments to other defectors whose crimes were not considered to merit the death penalty. The November 1962 plan for dealing with defectors also specified "special action" against the world-famous ballet dancer Rudolf Nureyev, who had defected at Le Bourget airport in Paris during a tour by the Kirov Ballet in 1961.[68] The KGB had begun a campaign of intimidation immediately after Nureyev's defection. On the night of his first major performance with a Western company, when he was due to dance the part of the Blue Bird in a Paris production of *Sleeping Beauty*, he received emotional letters from both his parents and his former ballet teacher, appealing to him not to betray the fatherland. Having steeled himself to go ahead, Nureyev then found his performance interrupted:

> I had barely come on to the stage . . . when shouting and whistling broke out, almost drowning Tchaikovsky's music. I went on dancing the Blue Bird, but beyond the haze of the footlights . . . I was perfectly aware that some communists were trying to sabotage the performance. I could hardly hear the music and I saw pieces of what looked like glass thrown on to the stage at me but I kept on dancing.[69]

The KGB's early attempts at intimidation failed. On February 21, 1962, amid a blaze of publicity, Nureyev made his Covent Garden debut, dancing with Margot Fonteyn in *Giselle*. To those who saw that unforgettable performance and the twenty-three curtain calls which followed, it was already clear that one of the greatest partnerships in the history of dance had been born.[70] The Centre was outraged not merely by the public adulation of a notorious defector but also by Nureyev's publication a few months later of memoirs describing his "leap to freedom" in the West. Though the November 1962 plan of campaign against leading defectors did not specify the nature of the "special action" to be employed against him, it was clear from the context that it would henceforth involve a good deal more than sprinkling broken glass on the stage.[71] Subsequent FCD directives discussed schemes (which were never successfully implemented) to break one or both of Nureyev's legs.[72]

In the summer of 1970 one of Nureyev's best-known near-contemporaries, Natalia Makarova, defected from the Kirov Ballet during a London season at the Royal Festival Hall. The KGB report on the defection predictably condemned her as a "politically immature individual, with low moral qualities."[73] In reality, the main motive for her defection, like Nureyev's, had been the quest for greater artistic freedom.[74] A joint memorandum by the heads of the First and Second Chief Directorates proposed that, if a way could be found to injure Nureyev without the hand of the KGB being obvious, a similar "special action" should be undertaken against Makarova. As usual, the reference in their memorandum to physical injury was expressed in euphemistic bureaucratic prose:

> Depending on the results of special actions taken with respect to Nureyev, aimed at lessening his professional skills, [the KGB] should consider carrying out a similar action with respect to Makarova, in order to localize the negative effect of her forthcoming performances in Britain and the United States. If the British propaganda organs are activated and information provided by her is used to slander Soviet life, additional measures will be devised.[75]

An approach was made by the Centre to the Bulgarian intelligence service to seek the possible assistance of one of their agents in a company where Makarova was due to dance. On one occasion Makarova was slightly hurt in an accident behind the stage caused by a beam falling from the set. The files seen by Mitrokhin, however, do not make clear whether this was the first nearly successful "special action" by the KGB against a defecting ballerina or merely an act of clumsiness by a stagehand.[76]

Since the defection of the reluctant assassin, Bogdan Stashinshky, in 1960, KGB operations against traitors living in the West had been totally unsuccessful. Though enormous amounts of time and resources had been devoted to tracking down defectors and preparing to kill and maim them, the only successful liquidation claimed by the Centre, the assassination of Hayhanen, was entirely fraudulent. It is just possible that the KGB was responsible for the minor injury to Natalia Makarova. But the probability is that its pursuit of traitors during the decade up to 1970 ended in complete failure.

APPENDIX 1

INSTRUCTIONS FOR DISARMING THE MOLNIYA ["LIGHTNING") EXPLOSIVE DEVICE

Instructions for Disarming the MOLNIYA Explosive DeviceFCD Directorate S guidance to residencies on the correct procedure for removing radio transmitters from booby-trapped caches

1. When digging out the container from the earth, take care not to strike the handle by chance. Dig until the upper surface of the container with the handle comes to light; remove the board and the plywood which cover the container.

2. The handle must only be turned and the container tilted and taken out of the hole after the explosive device has been disarmed.

3. In order to disarm the device, one must have a pocket torch battery of not less than 3.5 volts. Attach two wires of 30–50 cm length to the battery, with sharp probes at the end (a nail or a needle).

4. Without taking the container out of the cache, place one of the battery contacts on the body of the container, and the other on the left lock fitting, assuming that the lid of the container faces the operator. The contact points must be applied after scratching the paintwork on the body of the container and on the lock fitting.

5. When contact is made with the battery, a "click" should be heard inside the container; this indicates that the explosive device has been disarmed. If there is no "click," check the contact points again and repeat the operation to disarm the device.

6. If when the operation is repeated there is still no "click," it is forbidden to take the container out of the cache and the cache must be filled in. To open the container and remove the electric detonators from the two-way radio:

   – remove the padlocks and lift the lid of the container with the key which is inside the container. Unscrew the four screws and remove the metal casing under which the two-way radio is located in the ALIOT packaging;

   – cut each of the wires which connect the container with the ALIOT packaging and remove the package from the container.[77]

APPENDIX 2

EXAMPLE OF BOOBY-TRAPPED RADIO CACHE PUT IN PLACE BY THE BERNE RESIDENCY

On May 15, 1966, the KGB residency in Berne, Switzerland carried out an operation to deposit a booby-trapped BR-3U agent radio transmitter no. 624471/2329 in a hiding place codenamed CACHE no. 3. In July 1972, the residency was ordered to check the area where the transmitter had been buried and to devise an operation to remove it. Directorate S sent Berne the following description of the route to the cache and of its location:

Cache No. 3

Leaving Friburg by the Avenches road. Six kilometers from Friburg, the road goes through the township of Belfaux. There is a farm standing on its own on the right-hand side of the road as you leave Belfaux. About 100 meters beyond this farm, a track on the right-hand side goes up to a wood on a hillock. The entrance to this track is immediately opposite a railway crossing. Go up this track to the edge of the wood, where there is a large covered chapel with the image of a saint and benches for sitting.

A path passes by the chapel on the edge of the wood. Take 55 steps along the path from the left-hand side of the chapel (as you face it). At that point, on the right-hand side, there is a stone pillar inscribed with the letters F C, and next to it on the left there is a large pine tree (the only one in the sector between the chapel and the little pillar). Start counting steps again from the edge of the path. Proceed at right angles to the path, passing between the pine tree and the little pillar. After taking 36 steps, you will be at the point between two large leafy trees, the only ones in the sector. The distance between the trees is three paces. The area between the trees has been used for the cache.

If no motor car is available, one can reach the cache by rail from Friburg, alighting at Belfaux and proceeding on foot. The distance from the Belfaux railway station up to the cache is about 1,500 m.

There are three containers in the cache: a case, a waterproof package and a stone.

The case container has an explosive device which was made live by means of the MOLNIYA ["Lightning"] system when it was put into the cache.

A board has been put on top of the case container in order to protect the handle when the cache is opened.

Close to the center of the cache, a glass jar has been buried 30 cm below the surface, and above the suitcase a 15 cm length of metal piping has been stuck vertically into the earth, the upper end being 5–7 cm below the surface. These items were placed there for the special purpose of indicating whether the cache had been opened by third parties. At the same time, they can act as markers during the excavation. The overall depth of the cache is 1 m. The case contains a BR-3U radio transmitter.

After inspecting the area, the Berne residency reported to the Centre that, because of the lack of leaf cover at the site, it would be difficult to conceal signs of excavation. It would also be difficult to devise a cover story for the presence of operational officers in the area of the cache for one or two hours, which might well attract attention. Directorate S eventually proposed to the leadership of the FCD that the cache be written off, partly because of the difficulties of excavation, and partly because the fact that the shelf life of the MOLNIYA device had expired might make removal of the transmitter hazardous. The proposal was approved.[78]

The cache was eventually emptied in December 1998 by Swiss Federal police using the finding instructions from Mitrokhin's archive reproduced above. The MOLNIYA device was, as Directorate S had anticipated, dangerously unstable and exploded when fired on by a water cannon.[79] (See illustrations.)

APPENDIX 3

EXAMPLES OF RADIO CACHES PUT IN PLACE BY THE ROME RESIDENCY

Examples of Radio Caches Put in Place by the Rome Residency(a) Description of the Route to the MEZHOZERNY ("Inter-lake") cache and location of the cache

On April 15, 1962, a BR-3U radio transmitter no. 609072/9126 was placed in a waterproof package in the MEZHOZERNY cache.

The MEZHOZERNY cache is located 30 km from Rome in a wooded area between Lakes Albano and Nemi, 50 m from the Via dei Laghi, on the right-hand side of the road when traveling from Rome to Velletri.

Leave Rome by the Appia Antica, and 17 km later (the lower end of Champino airfield) turn left into the Via dei Laghi, leading to Velletri. Proceed for 13 km along the Via dei Laghi up to the 13 km milestone and continue in the same direction for 120 m beyond the 13 km milestone and at that point a broad path goes off to the right into a wood.

Go along this path for 90 m up to a fork where there are two paths, continue along the path to the right which begins 10 m from four large stones on the main path.

These two paths go round either side of a hillock. After following the right-hand path for 15 m from the point where it branches off, turn left and go up the hill for 7–8 m. On the hill and on its slopes there are holes, apparently left after trees had been uprooted. Among all these holes there is a group of four which are side by side.

The cache in which the load was secreted is a square hole which is next to another large hole of irregular shape like the figure eight.

At the bottom of the hole a chamber has been dug in the direction of the fork in the paths and it is in this that the trunk with the two-way radio has been placed. It is covered with earth and stones to a depth of 55–60 cm. After the case had been covered with 25 cm of earth a first marker was placed: two lengths of green wire were put across the spot diagonally and the case was then covered with another 50 cm of earth, when a yellow wire was also placed diagonally across the spot; this was then covered with a 55–60 cm layer of earth. On the opposite side of the hole there is a large stone.

The distance from the Via dei Laghi and Ariccia–Rocca di Papa crossroads up to the broad footpath when traveling away from Rome is about 1,450 m.[80]

(THE CACHE WAS emptied by the Rome residency on February 6, 1970, apparently because of concern that the condition of its contents might be deteriorating and becoming unsafe.)[81]

(b) Description of the Route to the MARINO Cache and Its Location

On September 20, 1962, two containers were placed on the MARINO cache: a notebook with instructions on the removal and packing of the two-way radio, and a capsule containing instructions for operating the two-way radio together with schedules for two-way and one-way communication; all the materials were on soft film in English.

The MARINO cache consisted of a cleft at the foot of an ancient tree which had been expanded into the root system of the tree.

The cache was located at a point 6 km along the Via dei Laghi after leaving Rome. Proceed along the Rome–Albano road, turn left into the Via dei Laghi, and continue for 6.3 km. From the 6 km milestone, the road begins to turn sharply just in face of the Marino hamlet. In the middle of the bend, two unmetaled village tracks go off to the left and the right of the road. Between the track to the right of the road and the road itself there is a sector overgrown with tall bushes. Among these bushes there is one ancient tree 25 m from the road. The MARINO cache is at the foot of this tree in the root system on the side opposite to the road, at a depth of 25 cm from the surface.

Two containers are wrapped in cellophane and placed in a metal sweet tin measuring $18 \times 10 \times 4$ cm, the edges of which have been stuck down with insulating tape. The objects have been covered with earth and a stone placed on top.[82]

(The cache was emptied by the Rome residency on February 7, 1970.)[83]

FOR REASONS OF public safety it is impossible to publish the locations of any of the KGB radio and arms caches which have not been cleared, since an unknown number are booby-trapped or in otherwise dangerous condition.

TWENTY-THREE

SPECIAL TASKS

Part 2: The Andropov Era and Beyond

On becoming chairman of the KGB in 1967, Andropov immediately announced his intention to revive KGB "special actions" as an essential tool of Soviet policy during the Cold War. The FCD, he declared, "must take the offensive in order to paralyze the actions of our enemies and to get them involved in a struggle in conditions which are unfavorable to them."[1] Two years earlier dissatisfaction with the recent record of the Thirteenth Department, which was responsible for FCD special actions, had led to its reorganization as Department V.[2] Following Andropov's call for a new "offensive to paralyze the actions of our enemies," the main priority of Department V became "special actions of a political nature"—the peacetime use of sabotage and other forms of violence in the furtherance of Soviet policy.[3] Line F officers in residencies were instructed to show greater ingenuity in devising special actions in which the hand of the KGB would be undetectable. All of the newly devised sabotage proposals employed the same standardized coded jargon. Each act of sabotage was termed a "Lily" (*Liliya*), the explosive device a "Bouquet" (*Buket*), the detonator a "Little Flower" (*Tsvetok*), the explosion of the device a "Splash" (*Zaplyv*) and the saboteur the "Gardener" (*Sadovnik*).[4]

The most important special action being planned at the beginning of the Andropov era was in Greece, where a group of army colonels seized power in April 1967, suspended parliamentary government and declared martial law. The Greek Communist Party (KKE) was driven underground and its leaders temporarily lost touch with Moscow. In July 1967 the KGB was formally instructed by the CPSU Central Committee to renew contact with the underground Party (a task it had doubtless already begun) and to give it "political and material assistance."[5] The "material assistance" included both financial subsidies, usually handed over to Party representatives in Budapest,[6] and help in preparing for guerrilla warfare. The Centre decreed that Department V's main priority for 1968 should be to set up sabotage and intelligence groups (DRGs) on Greek territory to prepare for an uprising against the military regime.[7] Department V also made preparations for possible guerrilla operations in Italy. The leaders of the PCI were seriously afraid of an Italian military putsch on the Greek model and had requested Soviet assistance in preparing the Party for the possibility that, like the KKE, it would have to transform itself into an illegal underground movement.[8]

In 1968, all KGB residencies were sent operational letters headed "Recommendations for Creating the Necessary Conditions on the Territory of a Potential Adversary for Special Group [DRG] Operations in an Emergency." The letter to the resident in Athens, Ivan Petrovich Kislyak (codenamed MAYSKY), added: "It is not possible that the course of events will in practice require us to assist local progressive forces in the near future, and we must therefore make preparations for this in advance."[9] The Centre issued instructions that all locally recruited DRGs operating in Greece were to be headed by KGB agents, but that this was to be concealed from other members of the groups.[10] In 1968 the illegal PAUL was sent to Greece with orders to select "runways" (*doroshki*) for the landing of airborne Soviet DRGs and bases—"beehives" (*ulya*)—from which to operate, as well as to check the suitability of those sites identified earlier. "Runway ALFA," reconnoitered by PAUL, was located in the southern part of the Thessalia plain, about forty kilometers north-west of the town of Lamia. "Runway BETA" was on the north-west of the Thessalia plain, four or five kilometers south of the Kalambaka settlement. The wooded hilly districts of Belasitsa, Piri and Sengal were chosen as areas suitable for smuggling agents and equipment across the Bugarian—Greek border.[11]

In August 1968 the Bulgarian DS confidently informed the Centre that it was capable of overthrowing the Greek junta with the assistance of one of its agents, whom it identified as the former head of a Greek intelligence agency. The Bulgarian Central Committee had approved the proposed *coup d'état* in Athens and instructed the leadership of its intelligence service to coordinate plans for it with the KGB and the CPSU Central Committee.[12] The KGB files seen by Mitrokhin do not explain why the Bulgarian proposal was turned down. There were, however, at least three probable reasons. The Centre may well have assessed the risks of failure more highly than the Bulgarians. The Politburo, which at almost the moment the Bulgarian proposal reached it was deciding on the invasion of Czechoslovakia, was doubtless disinclined to give its simultaneous approval to a risky coup attempt in Greece. Further complications were caused by the split in the Greek Communist Party which, after the suppression of the Prague Spring, divided into the pro-Soviet KKE and the Eurocommunist KKE-es. Brillakis (codenamed SEMYON), who had hitherto been one of the KGB's chief contacts in the underground Greek Party, refused further meetings with the Athens residency in protest at the Warsaw Pact invasion of Czechoslovakia.[13]

Though the KGB continued to channel large amounts of money into the KKE,[14] it seems to have made little progress in setting up DRGs on Greek soil. The main material successfully smuggled across the Greek—Bulgarian border was not sabotage equipment into Greece but the archives of the KKE which were taken in the opposite direction. Weighing 14 tons, filling 1,598 packages and four crates, guarded by thirty Greek Communists, they were transported from Bulgaria to Romania and thence to the Soviet Union, where they were deposited for safekeeping in the town of Ivanovo.[15]

AMONG DEPARTMENT V'S most ambitious proposals for special actions during 1968 was an operation to distract Western opinion from the suppression of the

Prague Spring by sabotaging a major oil pipeline, codenamed ZVENO ("Link"), near the Austrian end of Bodensee Lake, which was believed by the Centre to carry 10 million tons of oil a year between Italy and West Germany. By breaching the pipeline at the point where it crossed the Rhine canal, Department V calculated that it could pollute the Bodensee, and thus contaminate the main source of drinking water on the West German—Austrian frontier. To carry the explosive, the Vienna residency purchased four Western-manufactured 1-liter thermos flasks, as well as ten ballpoint pens—presumably to conceal the detonators. The scapegoats for the environmental disaster caused by the explosion were to be Italian extremists allegedly retaliating for acts of sabotage carried out by South Tyrol terrorists.

ZVENO set the pattern for most Department V peacetime special actions: immensely laborious and detailed preparations, followed by a reluctant decision not to go ahead because of the political risks involved—in particular, the possibility that, despite all the precautions taken, the hand of the KGB might somehow be discovered. The operation was postponed several times, kept under review for a number of years and finally abandoned.[16]

Many, perhaps most, of the proposed special actions in Europe were intended to cause dissension within NATO. A characteristic example (reproduced at the end of this chapter) was the proposal by the Athens residency in April 1969 for a bomb attack on the Turkish consulate-general in Thessaloniki, which would be blamed on a Greek extremist. Though complimenting the Athens residency on its initiative, the Centre once again dared not take the risk of giving the go-ahead. Instead, on May 12, 1969, it sent a temporizing reply:

> We approve the work carried out by the residency to collect material with the aim of preparing a Lily [sabotage operation] against the YAYTSO [Turkish consulate-general] target. We have put this target on file and if the need arises we shall return to the question of carrying out a Lily against it.
>
> We ask you to keep the YAYTSO target under observation as far as possible, in order to collect additional data and to take account of possible changes.[17]

Probably the first Department V plan approved by Sakharovsky, the head of the FCD, for a major special action in Britain was operation EDDING, a scheme to disrupt preparations for the investiture of the 20-year-old Prince Charles as Prince of Wales on July 1, 1969. Security at the ceremony itself in Caernavon Castle, when the Queen presented Prince Charles with the coronet, rod, ring, sword and mantle of his office in front of 4,000 invited guests and a worldwide television audience of 500 million, was expected to be too tight for a special action. Instead, about a month beforehand, Department V proposed to blow up a small bridge on the road from Porthmadog to Caernavon, near the junction of the A487 and the A498, using British-manufactured gelignite. On the eve of the explosion a letter was to be sent to the Welsh Nationalist MP Gwynfor Evans, at the House of Commons, warning him that MI5 and Scotland Yard were planning a "provocation" in order to discredit the Welsh Nationalists and provide a pretext for a major security clampdown in Wales.

When the explosion took place Evans and his colleagues were then expected to unmask the conspiracy by the "British organs of power" against Welsh liberties. Though backed by the FCD, however, operation EDDING was postponed by higher authority—either Andropov or the Politburo (the file does not specify which)—doubtless because of the fear, once again, that KGB involvement might come to light.[18]

A CENTRE REPORT in 1969 subjected the past record of both the Thirteenth Department and Department V to scathing criticism. Only the training of sabotage and intelligence groups (DRGs) was judged reasonably satisfactory. Some special tasks had proved beyond the capacity of both the Thirteenth Department and its successor to implement; others had become redundant. The report argued that there was little point in making elaborate preparations for DRGs to sabotage American and NATO military installations which were also targeted by the considerably more numerous GRU *spetsnaz,* and in many cases by the Soviet nuclear missile strike force. It was noted that, during the previous three years, there had been only one successful "special action of a political nature"—operation PEPEL ("Ashes") in Istanbul (although what this was exactly remains unclear).[19] The report, however, predictably failed to mention that the lack of special actions involving the peacetime use of sabotage and other forms of violence was due chiefly to Andropov's refusal to sanction the proposals put to him.

Andropov's reluctance to accept the risks of the peacetime special actions for which he had called on becoming chairman forced him to rethink his strategy. Having reassessed the scope for direct involvement by the KGB, he increasingly turned to using terrorist proxies. Among the first opportunities for their use was a new wave of troubles in Northern Ireland. On November 6, 1969 the general secretary of the Irish Communist Party, Michael O'Riordan, a veteran of the International Brigades,[20] forwarded a request for Soviet arms from the Marxist IRA leaders Cathal Goulding and Seamus Costello. According to O'Riordan:

> There has always existed more or less good relations between the IRA and the Irish Communists. We not only conduct a number of public and anti-imperialist activities together, but for more than a year a secret mechanism for consultations between the leadership of the IRA and the Joint Council of the Irish Workers' Party and the Communist Party of Northern Ireland has existed and is operating. They unfailingly accept our advice with regard to tactical methods used in the joint struggle for civil rights and national independence for Ireland.[21]

The IRA had been widely criticized by its supporters for failing to defend the Catholic community during the Belfast troubles of August 1969, when seven people had been killed, about 750 injured and 1,505 Catholic families had been forced out of their homes—almost five times the number of dispossessed Protestant households. One Catholic priest reported that his parishioners were contemptuously calling the IRA, "I

Ran Away."[22] In his message to Moscow, O'Riordan said that during the "August crackdown" the IRA had failed to act as "armed defender" of the nationalist community because "its combat potential was weakened by the fact that it had previously concentrated its efforts on social protests and educational activity." He claimed that there was now a real possibility of civil war in Northern Ireland between the two communities, and of serious clashes between British troops and the Catholics. Hence the IRA's appeal for arms. In a report to the Central Committee, Andropov insisted that, before going ahead with an arms shipment, it was essential to verify O'Riordan's ability "to guarantee the necessary conspiracy in shipping the weapons and preserve the secret of their source of supply."[23] It was more than two and half years before Andropov was sufficiently satisfied on both these points to go ahead with the arms shipment.

While talks were continuing with O'Riordan, the illegal PAUL was instructed to explore the possibility of using extremist Quebec separatists in special actions against the United States.[24] Given the violence of the terrorist methods employed by the FLQ (*Front de Libération du Québec*) and its apparent interest in Cuban and Soviet Bloc assistance, the hopes placed in it by the Centre were by no means fanciful. In 1969 the FLQ bombed both the home of the Montreal mayor and the National Defense Headquarters in Ottawa. During 1970 it failed in its attempts to kidnap the American and Israeli consuls-general in Montreal, but succeeded in kidnapping British trade official James Cross and Quebec labor minister Pierre Laporte. Cross was eventually released in return for a promise of safe conduct to Cuba for his kidnappers, but Laporte was murdered—strangled by the chain of the crucifix he wore around his neck.[25]

Though PAUL probably succeeded in making at least indirect contact with the FLQ, the Centre almost certainly decided that the risks of establishing a direct KGB—FLQ connection were too great. The KGB did, however, seek to cover its own tracks by circulating forged documents indicating that the CIA was involved with the FLQ. On September 24, 1971 the *Montreal Star* published a photocopy of a bogus CIA memorandum dated October 20, 1970:

> Subject Quebec. Sources advise that urgent action be taken to temporarily break contact with the FLQ militants since the Canadian government's measures may have undesirable consequences.

Questions followed in the Canadian parliament. Prime Minister Pierre Trudeau declared that if the CIA was operating in Canada, it was "without the knowledge or consent of the government."[26] Twenty years later the forged memorandum was still being quoted in Canadian publications, even by some academic authorities.[27] Further forgeries suggesting CIA involvement with Quebec extremists were circulated on the eve of the visit to Canada by President Nixon in 1972.[28]

ANDROPOV'S FRUSTRATION AT the difficulty of mounting peacetime special tasks which would leave no trace of the KGB's involvement was heightened by his mistaken conviction that the CIA was pursuing its own series of special tasks against KGB officers and other Soviet citizens living abroad. In a letter to Brezhnev of May

21, 1970, headed "of special importance," Andropov gave three instances of actual or attempted "abductions" by the CIA: the unsuccessful attempt to abduct the KGB officer Georgi Petrovich Pokrovsky in Tokyo on March 17, 1966; similarly, Yuri Sergeevich Pivovarov of the GRU in Buenos Aires on March 29, 1970; and the disappearance without trace of a Novosti correspondent in Delhi, Yuri Aleksandrovich Bezmenov, on March 9, 1970.[29]

Andropov's allegations derived not from any real CIA program of covert action but from his own addiction to conspiracy theory. Pivovarov had been the victim of an attempted kidnap and assassination by the right-wing Argentinian terrorist group Mano ("Hand"), which claimed to be avenging the kidnapping of a Paraguayan diplomat by left-wing terrorists.[30] Most other cases of alleged CIA special actions against KGB officers were in reality cases of actual or attempted defection. Some FCD officers realized—as Andropov did not—that "abductions" were convenient fictions used by residencies to conceal the shameful reality of defection. Such was the case, for example, in the disappearance of Bezmenov. Anxious to save face, the Delhi residency had reported that he had been abducted, and his son (the closest surviving relative) was given financial compensation.[31] In reality, as Bezmenov later admitted:

> I decided to stay in India to become a kind of hippie and get to now the country. Unfortunately, I started reading local newspaper and found out the Indian police were looking for me. I panicked. I tried to make a deal with smugglers to take me out of the country, but they either wanted too much money or didn't trust me.

Eventually Bezmenov approached the CIA, who exfiltrated him first to Greece, where he was debriefed, then resettled him in Canada.[32] The KGB abandoned the myth of Bezmenov's abduction after he was seen visiting an exhibition in Montreal in 1974, and ordered his bewildered son to return all the money they had paid to him.[33]

The conspiracy theorists in the Centre, however, remained convinced that the CIA was out to abduct KGB officers, as well as to induce them "to commit treason" (in other words, to defect). That belief survived until the end of the Cold War. When Kryuchkov became the first head of the FCD to visit Washington in 1987, Robert Gates, then deputy DCI, found it impossible to persuade him that a Soviet scientist, Vladimir Valentinovich Aleksandrov, who had gone missing in Spain, had not been physically abducted by the CIA.[34]

In his letter to Brezhnev of May 21, 1970, Andropov insisted that the CIA dared to engage in "brazen" provocations towards the KGB only because of "the lack of appropriate measures on our part." It was, he argued, high time to retaliate in kind and abduct a CIA officer to teach the Americans a lesson. To avoid the risk that a KGB special action might go wrong and become publicly known, Andropov asked Brezhnev's permission to use a proxy.

The precedent set by the previous use of Sandinista guerrillas against American targets in central and north America.[35] encouraged both Andropov and Department V to consider the use of Palestinian terrorists as proxies in the Middle East and

Europe. The man chiefly responsible for exporting Palestinian terrorism to Europe was Dr Wadi Haddad, deputy leader of the Marxist-Leninist Popular Front for the Liberation of Palestine (PFLP), headed by Dr George Habash. In 1968–9 Haddad had attracted favorable attention in the Centre with a spate of aircraft hijackings and attacks on Israeli offices and Jewish businesses in European capitals. In 1970 he was recruited by the KGB as agent NATSIONALIST. Andropov reported to Brezhnev:

> The nature of our relations with W. Haddad enables us to control the external operations of the PFLP to a certain degree, to exert influence in a manner favorable to the Soviet Union and also to carry out active measures in support of our interests through the organization's assets while observing the necessary conspiratorial secrecy.[36]

Andropov sought Brezhnev's approval to use Haddad for a special action against the CIA:

> It appears expedient to carry out an operation to abduct the deputy CIA resident in Lebanon . . . and to have him taken to the Soviet Union both as a retaliatory measure and with the aim of possibly obtaining reliable information [from him] about the plans and specific operations of the USA in the Middle East. It is planned to carry out the operation through a reliable agent of the Beirut residency, NATSIONALIST [Haddad], who directs the sabotage operations of the Popular Front for the Liberation of Palestine and is experienced in carrying out aggressive measures.
>
> The essence of the operational plan is that [the CIA officer] would be abducted by NATSIONALIST's reliable fighters in Beirut or its surroundings and would be delivered illicitly to a place which we selected in the Damascus region, where he would be handed over to our operational officers. From Damascus, he would be taken illegally to the USSR on one of our special aircraft or on board ship.
>
> Bearing in mind that the Palestinian guerrilla organizations have recently stepped up their activities in Lebanon against American intelligence and its agents, the Lebanese authorities and the Americans would suspect Palestinian guerrillas of carrying out the above operation. The ultimate purpose of the operation would be known only to NATSIONALIST, on the foreign side, and to the KGB officers directly involved in planning the operation and carrying it out, on the Soviet side.
>
> I request your authority to prepare and carry out the above operation.

Brezhnev gave his consent on May 25, 1970. The Beirut residency then passed on to Haddad a detailed dossier on the CIA officer (codenamed VIR), his home address (a fourth-floor apartment), car (a light blue Ford Comet with diplomatic number-plates), route to and from work at the US embassy and personal habits. It was noted, for example, that VIR regularly went for walks accompanied by his black poodle.

Haddad agreed to select three of the "most experienced and reliable" gunmen to kidnap VIR. As soon as he had been seized, his captors would press over his mouth and nose a mask impregnated with a general anaesthetic supplied by Department V. While VIR was unconscious, he would be given an injection (also provided by the KGB) which would leave him disoriented and unable to resist when he recovered consciousness. The PFLP would then drive VIR, dressed in fedayeen clothes, into Syria along a route carefully reconnoitered by the KGB and hand him over to Line F officers from the Damascus residency in a hamlet near Zabadani. From there he was to be exfiltrated by the KGB to the Soviet Union.[37]

One of Haddad's probable reasons for agreeing to work as a Soviet agent was to obtain arms for the PFLP. In July 1970 Brezhnev agreed to an initial request from Andropov that Haddad be supplied from the KGB arsenal with five RPG-7 hand-held anti-tank grenade launchers for terrorist operations. The head of Department V, Nikolai Pavlovich Gusev, and his assistant, Aleksei Nikolayevich Savin, then met Haddad to discuss the handover of further arms supplies which it was agreed to deliver under cover to darkness in an inflatable rubber boat at a pre-arranged spot near Aden. Control of the operation, codenamed VOSTOK ("East"), was entrusted to the deputy head (later head) of Department V, Aleksandr Ivanovich Lazarenko. On the orders of the defense minister, Marshal Ustinov, the arms for Haddad were loaded on an intelligence-gathering vessel of the Pacific Fleet, the *Kursograf,* at Vladivostok. With S. M. Grankin from Department V on board to supervise the handover, the *Kursograf* then set sail for the gulf of Aden to rendezvous with Haddad's motor launch at a point 12°34′ north and 45°12′ east, at 2100 hours local time. As arranged, Haddad signaled his presence with a 360-degree red signal light. The *Kursograf* extinguished its lights, locked on to the launch's radio beacon and signaled its presence with two brief flashes, repeated after a short interval. On receiving the answering signal (four brief flashes) from Haddad, the *Kursograf* launched the rubber boat containing the arms supplies and gave the agreed signal "Load launched" (three brief flashes) twice. Haddad's launch gave the same signal in reply, then made a "dot-dash" signal twice as soon as it had picked up the arms.

The arms supplied to Haddad consisted of 50 West German pistols (10 with silencers) and 5,000 rounds of ammunition; 50 captured MG-ZI machine guns with 10,000 rounds of ammunition; 5 British-made Sterling automatics with silencers and 36,000 rounds of ammunition; 50 American AR-16 automatics with 30,000 rounds of ammunition; 15 booby-trap mines manufactured from foreign materials; and 5 radio-controlled SNOP mines, also assembled from foreign materials. The two varieties of mine were considered some of the most sophisticated small weapons in the Soviet arsenal, and, like some of the silencers given to Haddad, had never previously been supplied even to other members of the Warsaw Pact. The SNOP mines could be detonated by radio signal at distances of up to two kilometers in cities and fifteen to twenty kilometers in the countryside.

The successful completion of operation VOSTOK was greeted in the Centre as a major triumph. On the recommendation of the FCD, and with the approval of Rear Admiral Radchenko, head of the KGB Special Department in the Pacific Fleet,

VOSTOK souvenirs (each valued at 600 roubles) and cash bonuses of 600 roubles were awarded to seven of the naval commanders who had taken part: Captain V. P. Lebedev, commander of the *Kursograf;* Captains (First Rank) A. G. Shtyrov and E. P. Lopatin; Captains (Second Rank) G. S. Babkov and V. I. Avramenko; and Lieutenant Commanders A. V. Garnitsky and A. S. Klimchuk. The Centre also sent a formal letter of thanks to the Chief of Naval Staff, Admiral of the Fleet N. D. Sergeyev.

The Centre was to make what it considered successful use of Haddad and the PFLP in a number of special actions in the Middle East, particularly against Israel (which will be covered in the next volume of this book). But operation VINT, the attempt by the PFLP to abduct the deputy head of the CIA station in Beirut, ended in failure. VIR varied his daily routine and Haddad's gunmen found it impossible to implement the original plan for his abduction. During 1971 Department V devised a number of alternative plans to kidnap VIR. One simply proposed that Haddad arrange VIR's assassination. All failed. So did operation INTIKAM, an attempt to use PFLP terrorists to kill two Soviet defectors, P. S. Branzinkas and his son (codenamed PIRATY, "Pirates"), who in 1970 hijacked an Aeroflot aircraft and escaped to Turkey. The operational file records that NATSIONALIST did not realize how difficult the assignment would be, and overestimated his capabilities."[38]

Plans to make larger use of the PFLP to hunt down Soviet defectors were largely abandoned. Andropov's decision to use Haddad for special actions, and Brezhnev's approval for it, none the less marked a turning point in the history of KGB operations. Henceforth, other Soviet Bloc intelligence services were to follow the Soviet lead in using, or conniving in the use of, terrorist groups.[39]

LIKE THE OPERATIONS of the Thirteenth Department during the Khrushchev era, those of Department V were seriously compromised by defections. The most important defector was the Line F officer in the London residency, Oleg Adolfovich Lyalin, an expert in hand-to-hand combat as well as a highly proficient marksman and parachutist who had been recruited by MI5 as a defector-in-place in the spring of 1971. During the six months before he defected in September, Lyalin provided details of KGB sabotage plans in London, Washington, Paris, Bonn, Rome and other Western capitals. In addition to compromising preparations for a number of peacetime special actions, he revealed Department V's hair-raising contingency plans for operations during periods of international crisis or conflict which would be carried out by illegals, local agents and sabotage and intelligence groups (DRGs) who would infiltrate each target country.[40]

In Washington, according to Oleg Kalugin, head of Line PR and deputy resident, Line F "did everything from plotting ways to poison the capital's water systems to drawing up assassination plans for US leaders."[41] Projected sabotage in Britain included plans to flood the London Underground, blow up the early-warning station at Fylingdale, North Yorkshire, and destroy V-bombers on the ground. Some of Department V's schemes were as bizarre as any of those devised by the CIA in its unsuccessful attempts to kill Castro a decade earlier. One plan revealed by Lyalin was for KGB agents posing as messengers and delivery men to scatter colorless poison capsules along Whitehall corridors of power which would kill all those who crushed them underfoot. Though the British government released few details about Lyalin after his defection, the Attorney General told the Commons that he was charged with "the organization of sabotage within the United Kingdom" and "the elimination of individuals judged to be enemies of the USSR."

The Centre was caught completely off-guard by Lyalin's defection and the almost simultaneous action against the London residency taken by the British government. On September 24, 1971 the Permanent Under-Secretary at the Foreign and Commonwealth Office, Sir Denis Greenhill, summoned the Soviet chargé d'affairs, Ivan Ivanovich Ippolitov (a KGB agent), and informed him that 90 KGB and GRU officers stationed in Britain under official cover were to be expelled and another fifteen, then on leave in the Soviet Union, would not be allowed to return, making a grand total of 105 expulsions.[42] Many of the Soviet intelligence officers concerned had been known to MI5 and SIS for some time, but over the past six months Lyalin had confirmed a number of probable identifications and added new names to the list.[43] Preparations for operation FOOT, as the mass expulsion was codenamed in Whitehall, had been under secret discussion throughout that time. In a joint memo to the Prime Minister, Edward Heath, on July 30, the Foreign and Home Secretaries, Sir Alec Douglas Home and Reginald Maudling, argued that the sheer numbers of KGB and GRU officers in London were "more than the Security Service can be expected to contain."[44] The horrendous nature of some of the Department V sabotage plans revealed by Lyalin added weight to the arguments for expulsion.

Almost immediately after Ippolitov's return from the FCO on Friday September 24, the MI5 surveillance team near the Soviet embassy in Kensington Palace Gardens reported that a KGB officer had been seen sprinting across the road from the residency opposite, no doubt summoned by telephone for an urgent briefing on the mass expulsion.[45] In the short term Lyalin's defection probably caused even greater concern than operation FOOT. Over the weekend the Centre informed the Soviet leadership that Lyalin was likely to compromise Department V operations in other countries. On Monday September 27 Brezhnev cut short a tour of eastern Europe for an emergency meeting of the Politburo in the VIP lounge at Moscow airport. Shortly afterwards most Line F officers were recalled from Western capitals, leaving Department V effectively crippled and unable to fulfill its task of coordinating sabotage operations abroad in time of crisis.[46] The Centre investigation into the London débâcle, which, as was traditional, emphasized the alleged personal depravity of the defector, claimed that Lyalin had seduced the wives of a number of his Soviet colleagues in London, and heavily criticized the former resident, Yuri Nikolayevich Voronin, for covering up Lyalin's misdeeds to avoid a scandal.[47] The head of the FCD Third Department, whose responsibilities included operations in Britain, was among those senior KGB officers who were demoted or sacked as a result.[48]

JUST AS STASHINSKY's defection in 1961 had made the Centre much more cautious in ordering assassinations, so Lyalin's defection a decade later dealt a further blow to its plans for peacetime sabotage. Department V found itself in limbo pending a reorganization which took three and a half years to complete. The files seen by Mitrokhin record no new schemes for KGB "special political actions" during the few years immediately after Lyalin's "treachery." (It is, of course, possible that some special actions are recorded in files not seen by Mitrokhin.) One example of the Centre's declining enthusiasm for such operations which made a particular impression on Mitrokhin was its response to the defection of another star of the Kirov Ballet, Mikhail Baryshnikov, while on a tour of Canada in June 1974. Baryshnikov's flawless classical style and apparently effortless grace had made him one of Mitrokhin's personal favorites. Among the intercepted messages sent to Baryshnikov after his defection which found their way into his KGB file, Mitrokhin noted one from a female balletomane in Leningrad which told him that he "was, is and forever will be my dear little brother . . . one of the brightest, most beautiful and most notable people I have ever met." Unsurprisingly, the KGB kept Baryshnikov under close observation after his defection. Its agents included another ballet dancer, codenamed MORIS, who also reported on Nureyev and Makarova. What struck Mitrokhin, however, was the apparent lack of plans to maim Baryshnikov similar to those which had been devised, though not apparently implemented, against Nureyev and Makarova a few years earlier.[49]

Despite the KGB's increased reluctance to take the risks involved in implementing directly special actions in the West, it continued to use—or connive at the use of—terrorist groups as proxies in the struggle against the United States and its allies. The Centre's mood, however, remained distinctly cautious. It was almost three years before the arms requested by the IRA in November 1969 through the intermediary of the Irish Communist leader, Michael O'Riordan, were finally delivered by the KGB. Shortly after the request had been made, the IRA had split into two: the Officials under Cathal Goulding and the Provisionals led by Sean MacStioftin.[50] The sympathies of the KGB were wholly with the Marxist Officials rather than the more nationalist Provisionals. Though Goulding's long-term aim was to create a non-sectarian, non-military, all-Ireland revolutionary movement, the Officials were responsible for some of the bloodiest episodes in the Troubles of the early 1970s. The only answer to the "forces of imperialism and exploitation," Goulding declared in 1971, lay "in the language that brings these vultures to their senses most effectively, the language of the bomb and the bullet." The Official IRA's bloodthirsty attempts to upstage the Provisionals ended by alienating some of its own supporters. In February 1972 a bomb planted at the Aldershot headquarters of the Parachute Regiment killed seven people, including a Catholic priest and five women canteen workers. Nationalist anger at the killing of an off-duty British soldier on home leave in Derry on May 21 led the Officials' army council to announce a ceasefire eight days later. Since the Officials reserved the right to take what they described as "defensive action," however, the ceasefire had little immediate effect. Though Goulding gradually succeeded in scaling down "military operations," local militants continued terrorist attacks during the remainder of 1972 and 1973.[51]

On July 3, 1972 the Irish Communist leader, Michael O'Riordan, wrote to remind the CPSU Central Committee that the arms he had first requested on behalf of the IRA in November 1969 had still not been received. Since then, on behalf of the Official IRA, he had held numerous discussions on the means of shipment with the KGB's "technical specialists:" "The fact that there has not been the slightest leak of information for two and a half years proves, in my opinion, a high level of responsibility with regard to keeping the secret, so to speak." Andropov agreed. On August 21 he presented to the Central Committee a "Plan for the Operation of a Shipment of Weapons to the Irish Friends," codenamed SPLASH. SPLASH was a variant of operation VOSTOK, which had delivered arms to Haddad and the PFLP two years earlier. Once again, the weapons and munitions—2 machine-guns, 70 automatic rifles, 10 Walther pistols, 41,600 cartridges, all of non-Soviet origin to disguise the involvement of the KGB—were transported by a Soviet intelligence-gathering vessel, on this occasion the *Reduktor.* On this occasion, the arms, in waterproof wrapping, were submerged to a depth of about 40 meters on the Stanton sandbank, 90 kilometers from the coast of Northern Ireland, and attached to a marker buoy of the kind used to indicate the presence of fishing nets below the surface. KGB laboratories carefully examined the arms shipment before it left to ensure that there was no trace of Soviet involvement. The Walther pistols were lubricated with West German oil, the packaging was purchased abroad by KGB residencies and it was specified that the marker buoy should be Finnish or Japanese. A few hours after the arms had been deposited on the sandbank, they were retrieved by a fishing vessel belonging to the "Irish friends," whose crew were unaware of their contents.[52] Operation SPLASH was supervised on board the *Reduktor* by an officer from the 8th Department of Directorate S (the successor to Department V). Several further Soviet arms shipments to the Official IRA were delivered by similar methods.[53]

The KGB can have had few illusions about the likely use of the arms it supplied, since the man in charge of their collection from the sandbank was the Officials' most hard-line terrorist, Seamus Costello.[54] Late in 1974, after a dispute with Goulding, Costello was expelled from the Officials and founded a new Trotskyite movement, the Irish Republican Socialist Party (IRSP). The Officials set up four assassination squads to liquidate the dissidents, but came off worse in a series of shoot-outs in the spring of 1975. They had, however, rather the better of a feud later in the year with the Provisionals. The Official IRA eventually succeeded in murdering Costello in 1977.[55] The probability is that some of the arms smuggled into Ireland by the KGB were used in the internecine warfare between republican paramilitaries.

As well as shipping arms to the Official IRA, the KGB also continued to use some Third World terrorists and guerrillas—notably the PFLP and the Sandinistas—as proxies. In Latin America, the KGB found itself—somewhat to its irritation—being upstaged by its Cuban ally, the DGI. By 1970, in the Centre's view, the DGI had effectively "expropriated" the Sandinista ISKRA guerrilla group. In 1969 the DGI financed the guerrilla operation to free the FSLN (Sandinista) leader, Carlos Fonseca Amador (GIDROLOG), from a Costa Rican jail, where he had been imprisoned for bank robbery.[56] Fonseca was recaptured shortly after his jailbreak, but freed again and flown to Cuba after the Sandinista hijack of a plane carrying American executives of the United Fruit Company, who were released in exchange.[57] The DGI also organized guerrilla training for the Sandinistas in Cuba, and gave them 100,000 dollars to purchase weapons. The head of the DGI, Manuel Piñeiro Losado, whose nickname "Redbeard" reflected his fiery temperament, told the deputy head of the FCD, Boris Semenovich Ivanov,

> Of all the countries in Latin America, the most active work being carried out by us is in Nicaragua. Aid is being given to partisan groups headed by C[arlos] Fonseca. This movement has influence and could go far.

At a meeting with Fonseca in February 1971, Piñeiro restated the conviction of the Cuban leadership that for most Latin American countries armed conflict was the only path to liberation. Though Cuba remained willing to offer the Sandinistas "any kind of support and assistance," they would need to make major changes in their organization if they were to avoid the defeats and heavy losses they had suffered during the past decade. The Centre concluded that future attempts to use the Sandinistas for special actions against United States targets would have to be made in collaboration with the DGI.[58]

The KGB did, however, retain a number of agents within the Sandinistas, among them GRIN (not identified by Mitrokhin's notes), who was used to identify possible operations in which the KGB could make use of the FSLN. In May 1974 a Sandinista delegation visited the Soviet embassy in Havana and delivered a letter to the CPSU Central Committee asking for assistance. The most dramatic Sandinista attack on a United States target was the attempt, assisted by the DGI with the personal blessing of Fidel Castro, to kidnap Turner B. Shelton, the American ambassador in Managua and a close friend of the Somoza family.[59] Remarkably, Shelton and President Anastasio Somoza Debayle appeared together on the 1974 twenty cordoba note, the ambassador's head inclined deferentially towards the president; the note quickly became known as the *sapo* ("toady").[60] The original plan of attack appears to have been for a guerrilla group to force an entry into the US embassy during a diplomatic reception.[61] On December 27, 1974, however, an unexpected opportunity arose during a party in honor of Shelton given by the former minister of agriculture, José Maria (Chema) Castillo. A Sandinista working undercover as a waiter at the reception telephoned the guerrilla group to report that Castillo's house was poorly guarded, providing an excellent opportunity to kidnap the ambassador.[62]

Shelton escaped kidnap by the skin of his teeth. He left the reception minutes before a well-drilled assault group of Sandinistas (ten male, three female) stormed Castillo's mansion at 10:50 p.m. Finding the ambassador gone, they killed his host, held the rest of the guests hostage and demanded that the Archbishop of Managua act as mediator. After several days of tense negotiations, President Somoza released eighteen imprisoned FSLN members, paid a million-dollar ransom for the release of the hostages, agreed to publish a 12,000-word denunciation of himself and US imperialism and provided a plane to fly the Sandinistas to Cuba.[63] On the Sandinistas' arrival at Havana, the Cubans took possession of the million dollars.[64]

Though the FSLN had won an enormous propaganda victory, the period of brutal martial law which followed in Nicaragua led to the death of many of its guerrillas and internal conflict among the Sandinistas over how to wage a victorious guerrilla war.[65] Still in awe of the Russian revolutionary tradition,[66] Fonseca turned to Moscow for advice. On February 14, 1975 he asked the Soviet embassy in Havana to arrange a trip to Moscow for himself and other Sandinistas so that they could study and learn from both Bolshevik experience before the October Revolution and methods of partisan warfare during the Great Patriotic War. He also requested further financial assistance.[67] Late in 1975, probably soon after his return from Moscow,[68] Fonseca traveled secretly to Nicaragua to try to resolve the factional conflict within the FLSN. On November 8, 1976 he was killed in a shoot-out with a National Guard patrol. After the Sandinista victory in 1979, Fonseca was reburied as a Hero of the Revolution.[69]

IN FEBRUARY 1976 the Politburo approved increase staffing and funding for the FCD Illegals Directorate S. As part of the reorganization of the enlarged Directorate by KGB order no. 0046 of April 12, 1976, the former Department V was formally incorporated into it as Department 8 with, by 1980, 23 operational officers at headquarters out of the total for the directorate of 400.[70] The head of Department 8, Vladimir Grigoryevich Krasovsky, mournfully reflected on the decline of KGB special actions in recent years. His self-image as a man of action was symbolized by the cigarette lighter mounted on a fragmentation hand grenade which he kept on his desk. But, he complained, "We move paper from place to place. That's all we do!.[71] Department 8's most basic task—the liquidation of traitors who had fled abroad— was by now an almost hopeless one. But the Centre could not bring itself either to give up the ritual of passing death sentences on KGB defectors or to abandon the pretence that the sentences would one day be carried out.

According to Oleg Kalugin, head of FCD Directorate K (counterintelligence) from 1973 to 1979, the KGB succeeded in tracking down only two post-war defectors, one in Australia (probably Vladimir Petrov) and the other in the United States (probably Pyotr Deryabin)—both of whom had defected in the 1950s. "The hell with them—they're old men now!" Andropov told Kalugin. ". . . Find Oleg Lyalin or Yuri Nosenko, and I will sanction the execution of those two!"[72] Probably in 1974, Nikolai Fyodorovich Artamonov (codenamed LARK), a former Soviet naval officer working as an analyst in the US Office of Naval Intelligence under the alias "Nicholas Shadrin," told his KGB controller that he could discover the whereabouts of Nosenko who, he claimed, was living near Washington.[73] In 1975 a KGB agent among the Russian Orthodox clergy in the United States found a gangster willing to take out a contract on Nosenko for 100,000 dollars. But before he could do so, the gangster was arrested for other crimes.[74] Almost simultaneously, Artamonov was discovered to be a double agent working for the FBI. In December 1975, after being lured to Austria, ostensibly to meet a new controller, he was bundled into a car by operations officers from the Vienna residency who intended to exfiltrate him to Moscow for questioning. The sedative injected into Artamonov to stop him struggling in the back seat was so powerful that it killed him. Kryuchkov, however, was delighted that at last a traitor had received his just deserts. "Which medal do you want?" he asked

Kalugin. "The October Revolution or the Combat Red Banner?" Kalugin chose the Red Banner.[75]

From 1976 to 1981 the Line KR (counterintelligence) officer E. R. Ponomarev (codenamed KEDROV) was stationed at the Washington residency with the sole task of tracking down defectors and was given the cover post of deputy head of the Consular Department in order to give him a pretext for making enquiries in the Departments of Immigration and Naturalization, as well as in lawyers' offices. Ponomarev also gained access to the file of purchasers at a Russian-language bookshop and cultivated academics thought likely to come into contact with defectors.[76] His five years in Washington appear to have been an expensive waste of time and effort.

Some of the KGB's Soviet Bloc allies, in particular the Bulgarian Durzhavna Sigurnost (DS), were much less cautious than the Centre in their pursuit of defectors. The zeal with which the DS hunted down traitors who had fled abroad owed much to the personal outrage with which the Bulgarian dictator, Todor Zhivkov, the most colorful and grotesque of the rulers of eastern Europe, responded to émigré criticism and mockery. The best known of the émigré writers, Georgi Markov, broadcast regular commentaries on the corruption and excesses of the Zhivkov regime in the Bulgarian-language services of the BBC World Service and Radio Free Europe, ridiculing Zhivkov himself as a man with a "a distastefully mediocre sense of humor," the bullying manner of "a village policeman," a penchant for "pompous phrases" and the deluded conviction that he was a great huntsman.

In 1974 Boris Arsov, another of the defectors who had dared to attack the excesses of the Zhivkov regime, suddenly disappeared from his flat in Aarhus, Denmark, where he had been publishing the Bulgarian émigré newspaper *Levski*. Two months later he resurfaced in Sofia and was sentenced to fifteen years' imprisonment. An official statement during Arsov's trial virtually admitted that he had been kidnapped by the DS:

> Arsov was playing with fire. The timely activity of the State Security stopped his dangerous activity. This only shows that the hand of justice is longer than the legs of the traitor.

In 1975 Arsov was officially declared to have been found dead in his prison cell. At about the same time three Bulgarian exiles who had been helping others to defect— Ivan Kolev, Peter Nezamov and Vesselina Stoyova—were shot in Vienna. The assassin, quickly identified by the Austrian police, was a DS agent who had penetrated the émigré group and escaped to Sofia after the murders.[77]

The KGB eventually became embroiled in DS special political actions. Early in 1978 General Dimitar Stoyanov, Bulgarian interior minister and head of the DS, appealed to the Centre for help in liquidating Georgi Markov, then living in London and accused of "slandering Comrade Zhivkov" in his many radio broadcasts. The request was considered at a meeting chaired by Andropov and attended by Kryuchkov, Vice Admiral Mikhail Usatov (Kryuchkov's deputy) and Oleg Kalugin, head of FCD counterintelligence. Though reluctant to take the risks involved in helping the Bulgarians, Andropov eventually accepted Kryuchkov's argument that to refuse would be an unacceptable slight to Zhivkov. "But," he insisted, "there is to be no direct participation on our part. Give the Bulgarians whatever they need, show them how to use it and send someone to Sofia to train their people. But that's all."

The Centre made available to the DS the resources of its top secret poisons laboratory, the successor to the Kamera of the Stalinist era, attached to the OTU (Operational Technical) Directorate and under the direct control of the KGB chairman. Sergei Mikhailovich Golubev, head of FCD security and a poisons specialist, was put in charge of liaison with the Bulgarians. The murder weapon eventually chosen was concealed in an American umbrella, one of a number purchased at Golubev's request by the Washington residency in order to disguise the KGB connection if the weapon was ever discovered. The tip was converted by OTU technicians into a silenced gun capable of firing a tiny pellet containing a lethal dose of ricin, a highly toxic poison made from castor-oil seeds. On September 7, 1978, while Markov was waiting at a bus stop on Waterloo Bridge, he felt a sudden sting in his right thigh. Turning instinctively, he saw a man behind him who had dropped his umbrella. The stranger apologized, picked up his umbrella and got into a taxi waiting nearby. Though Markov felt no immediate ill effects, he became seriously ill next day and died in hospital on September 11. During the autopsy a tiny pellet was recovered from Markov's thigh, but the ricin, as Golubev had calculated, had decomposed. Markov's assassination alerted another Bulgarian émigré, Vladimir Kostov, to the significance of an earlier, unexplained attack he had been subject to in Paris on August 26. Nearly a month later, on September 25, a steel pellet of the kind that had killed Markov was removed, still intact, from Kostov's back. During a visit to Sofia soon afterwards, Kalugin was presented by General Stoyanov with an expensive Browning hunting rifle in gratitude for KGB assistance in the murder of Markov.[78]

THE CHIEF ADDITION to Soviet special tasks capability during the later Cold War was the creation of KGB special forces (*spetsnaz*) with the foundation of the Alpha group in 1974, on Andropov's personal instructions.[79] Intended for foreign operations and initially kept secret from all but a minority of FCD officers, the special forces grew steadily in numbers during the late 1970s. Their first major operation, by far the most important special action of the Andropov era, was the murder of President Hafizullah Amin of Afghanistan, who seized power in a blood-thirsty palace coup in September 1979.[80] Cautious though Andropov had become in ordering assassinations, he convinced himself that in this case he had no option. Amin, he believed, was contemplating ending the Communist regime in Afghanistan and turning to the West. There were even reports, which Andropov appears to have taken seriously, that Amin was plotting with the CIA.[81] As during the Czechoslovak crisis in 1968,[82] Andropov took the lead in insisting on the enforcement of the "Brezhnev doctrine" which asserted Moscow's right to prevent the defection of any member of the Soviet Bloc.

For the first time since its foundation, Department 8 of FCD Directorate S (Illegals) moved into the front line of KGB operations. Its plot to assassinate Amin, operation AGAT ("Agate"), formed part of a larger invasion plan.[83] By late November, after Amin had demanded the replacement of A. M. Puzanov, the Soviet ambassador, Andropov and defence minister Ustinov, the two leading hawks in the Politburo, were agreed on the need for Soviet military intervention as well as the elimination of Amin.[84] Early in December, Andropov sent Brezhnev a handwritten letter, reporting "alarming information [intelligence] about Amin's secret activities, forewarning of a possible shift to the West," bringing with it both the end of Communist rule and a catastrophic loss of Soviet influence.[85] On December 8 Andropov and Ustinov jointly obtained Brezhnev's approval for a draft invasion plan.[86]

While Marshal Akhromeyev and the General Staff operations group in charge of the invasion established their headquarters near the Afghan border in Uzbekistan, the head of Directorate S, Vadim Vasilyevich Kirpichenko, and the head of Department 8, Vladimir Krasovsky, flew secretly into Kabul to supervise the overthrow of Amin. Day-to-day control of operation AGAT was entrusted to Krasovsky's deputy, A. I. Lazarenko. A team from the KGB Seventh (Surveillance) Directorate flew in to monitor Amin's movements. Meanwhile, elaborate attempts were made to avoid arousing Amin's suspicions. His requests for military supplies were granted and two radio stations were constructed for him. On December 23, however, the KGB residency in Kabul reported that Amin's suspicions had been aroused both by Western radio reports of Soviet troop movements and the frequent flights into the Soviet airbase at Bagram, outside Kabul. The main invasion began at 3 p.m. (local time) on December 25.[87]

According to some accounts of the Soviet invasion, Amin was successfully duped into believing that the Red Army was arriving to provide him with "fraternal assistance" against anti-Communist rebels.[88] The Kabul residency thought otherwise. On December 26 it reported to the Centre the publication of an article in the English-language *Kabul Times* entitled "The Will of the People will be the Deciding Factor." Though the article made no direct reference to the massive arrival of Soviet troops, it ended with the slogan "Down with the interventionists!" The residency concluded:

> As the Afghan press is subject to strict censorship, the article could not have been published without the sanction of Amin. The time chosen to print the article was not a coincidence. It was printed in an English language newspaper, a language which few Afghans understand. It was clearly intended to turn the pro-Western sections of the population against the Soviet troops and to enable the mass media in the West to make an immediate fuss about the Soviet intervention in Afghanistan. In general the article reflects the ambiguous and cautious attitude of Amin and his entourage towards the increased Soviet military presence in Afghanistan.[89]

The assault on the presidential palace on December 27 was led by 700 members of the KGB Alpha and Zenith special forces, dressed in Afghan uniforms and traveling in military vehicles with Afghan markings. The signal for the attack to begin was the detonation of an explosive device concealed some days earlier beneath a tree in the central square of the capital. The palace guards, however, put up much stiffer resistance than had been expected, and over a hundred of the KGB troops were killed before the palace was taken and Amin gunned down. Among the casualties was the leader of the assault group, Colonel Grigori Boyarinov, commandant of the Department 8 special operations training school at Balashikha.[90]

It was normal KGB procedure for the portraits of officers who fell in combat to be displayed in black frames at the Centre as a sign of mourning. On this occasion, since the fallen heroes of operation AGAT were so numerous, Andropov decided not to put their hundred portraits on display. Some of the survivors, however, were honored for their part in the operation. Kirpichenko was promoted from major-general to lieutenant-general, and soon afterwards made First Deputy Head of the FCD. Lazarenko was promoted from colonel to major-general. Leonid Aleksandrovich Kozlov of Department 8 was made a Hero of the Soviet Union.[91] The head of Line N (Illegals Support) at the Kabul residency, Ismail Murtuza Ogly Aliev, was awarded the Order of the Red Star, as were an unknown number of the members of the assault group who had stormed the presidential palace.[92]

Immediately after the storming of the palace, the exiled Afghan Communist and veteran KGB agent Babrak Karmal, who had been chosen by Moscow to succeed Amin, asked senior KGB officers in Kabul to assure Comrade Andropov that, as president, he would unswervingly follow his advice. He also called for the "severest punishment" of Amin's former associates and all those who had opposed Soviet troops. Karmal was fulsome in his praise for the heroism shown by the KGB and other special forces who had stormed the presidential palace:

> As soon as we have decorations of our own, we would like to bestow them on all the Soviet troops and Chekists [KGB officers] who took part in the fighting. We hope that the government of the USSR will award orders to these comrades.[93]

The long-drawn-out Afghan War (which will be covered in volume 2 of this book) rescued Department 8 from the doldrums into which it had lapsed for most of the 1970s. In 1982 its special operations training school at Balashikha set up a "Training Centre for Afghanistan," headed by V. I. Kikot, previously a Line F officer in Havana, who was well-informed on the Cuban experience of irregular warfare.[94] Department 8 also made an intensive study of the methods used both by the Palestinians against the Israelis and by the Israelis against Palestinian camps in Lebanon.[95] Balashikha made a significant, though unquantifiable, contribution to the increasing use of special forces and methods of terrorizing the population—among them incendiary bombs, napalm, poison gas, tiny mines scattered from the air, even booby-trapped toys which maimed children and so demoralized their parents. But though Soviet forces and the terror campaign drove a quarter of the Afghan population into refugee camps in Pakistan, they failed to win the war.

WITH THE INTENSIFICATION of the Cold War in the early years of the Reagan presidency and fears in the Centre that the new president was planning a nuclear first strike, Andropov became increasingly willing, both as KGB chairman and as Brezhnev's successor from 1982 to 1984, to use, or connive in the use of, terrorism against United States and NATO targets. With Andropov's knowledge (and doubtless his blessing), East Germany became what its last, non-Communist, interior minister, Peter-Michael Diestel, later called "an Eldorado for terrorists." Among East Germany's favorite terrorist groups was the West German Red Army Faction (RAF). Contemptuous of working-class reluctance to make a revolution and inspired by slogans such as "Don't argue—destroy!," the well-educated members of the RAF saw themselves as the militant vanguard of the deplorably inert proletariat, committed to the destruction of the "bourgeois power structures" of both the FRG and NATO. After a series of successful terrorist attacks in the mid-1970s, however, a grand offensive planned by the RAF in 1977 failed, and four of its leaders committed suicide in prison.

Thanks to the sanctuary offered by East Germany to its main surviving activists from 1977 onwards, the RAF was able to regroup. With training, weapons, funds and false identity documents provided by the Stasi, the Red Army Faction launched a new offensive during the early 1980s. In August 1981 a car bomb attack on the European headquarters of the US airforce at Ramstein in West Germany injured seventeen people; a month later RAF terrorists made an unsuccessful rocket attack in Heidelberg on the car of General Frederick Kroesen. During another terrorist offensive in 1984–5, the RAF attempted to blow up the NATO school at Oberammergau, bombed the US airbase at Frankfurt/Main, and attacked American soldiers at Wiesbaden. The Stasi also connived in the bombing of the La Belle discothèque in West Berlin, helping to transport the explosives which killed an American sergeant and a Turkish woman and wounded 230 people, including fifty US servicemen. Other Stasi contacts included the Provisional IRA, the Basque ETA and Carlos the Jackal.[96]

In 1983, at the height of operation RYAN (the combined KGB/GRU attempt to find (nonexistent) evidence of US and NATO plans for a surprise nuclear attack), Andropov ordered preparations by Department 8 for terrorist attacks on British, American and NATO targets in Europe. Plans were made for a campaign of letter bombs to be sent to Mrs. Thatcher's office at 10 Downing Street and to a series of prominent US and NATO representatives.[97] At about the same time the KGB organized a series of dead drops in bars and restaurants near American bases in West Germany, intended to conceal explosives which could be detonated in a manner that would give the impression of terrorist attacks. The dead drop sites included behind a vending machine, in a ventilation cavity under a sink, on a wooden beam over a lavatory and underneath a paper-towel dispenser. By the time the sites were discovered by the CIA in 1985, however, operation RYAN was winding down and plans for a KGB terrorist campaign against NATO targets had been shelved.[98]

In August 1983, while RYAN was still in full swing, the Centre instructed the main residencies in European NATO countries to step up their search for NATO preparations for

the secret infiltration of sabotage teams with nuclear, bacteriological and chemical weapons into the countries of the Warsaw Pact; [and] the expansion of the network of sabotage-training intelligence schools and increase in the recruitment of émigrés from the socialist countries and persons who know the language of these countries, and the creation of émigré military formations and sabotage and intelligence teams.[99]

Though, as with most of the requirements for operation RYAN, there was no such intelligence to collect, the Centre's instructions give an important insight into Moscow's contingency plans for the role of Department 8 and its DRGs in an attack on NATO.

THE DECLINE AND fall of the Cold War brought a further decline in KGB special actions. The last major special action of the Soviet era was directed not against the traditional Main Adversary and its NATO allies, but against the reformers within the Soviet Union. On December 8, 1990 Kryuchkov, who had become KGB chairman two years earlier, summoned to his office in the Lubyanka his former chief-of-staff, Vyacheslav Zhizhin, now deputy chief of the FCD, and Alexei Yegorov of Counter-intelligence. There he instructed them to prepare a report on the measures needed to "stabilize" the country following the declaration of a state of emergency—in other words, the "special" and other actions required to preserve one-party rule and a centralized Soviet state.

Over the next eight months Kryuchkov repeatedly tried and failed to persuade Gorbachev to agree to the declaration of a state of emergency and the "stabilization" of the Soviet Union. The point of no return for himself and his co-conspirators was the agreement on July 23, 1991 of the text of a new Union Treaty which would have transferred many of the powers of central government to the republics. On August 4 Gorbachev, whom Kryuchkov had placed under close surveillance some months earlier as SUBJECT 110, left for his summer holidays in a luxurious dacha at Foros on the Crimean coast, intending to return to Moscow for the signing of the Union Treaty on August 20. The day after Gorbachev's departure, Kryuchkov and his fellow plotters—chief among them the defence and interior ministers, Dmitri Yazov and Boris Pugo (former head of the Latvian KGB)—met at OBJECT ABC, a KGB sanatorium equipped with swimming pool, saunas, masseuses and cinema. There they secretly constituted themselves as the State Committee for the State of Emergency, and met over the next fortnight to make preparations for a coup which would forestall the signing of the Union Treaty. The committee ordered the printing of 300,000 arrest forms and the supply by a factory in Pskov of 250,000 pairs of hand-cuffs. Kryuchkov called all KGB personnel back from holiday, placed them on alert and doubled their pay. Two floors of cells in the Lefortovo prison were emptied to received important prisoners and a secret bunker prepared for the committee in the Lubyanka in case the going got rough.

On August 18 the plotters made a final attempt to intimidate Gorbachev into declaring a state of emergency. Having failed, they kept him incommunicado under house arrest in Foros and announced next day that the president was prevented by "ill health" from performing his duties, and that Vice-President Gennadi Yanayev had become acting president (in fact a mere figurehead) at the head of an eight-man State

Committee for the State of Emergency. The plotters quickly discovered, however, that the old autocratic machinery of the one-party state was in too serious a state of disrepair for them to be able to turn back the clock. The Alpha group *spetsnaz* was supposed to storm the Moscow White House, the seat of government of the Russian Federation, and arrest its president, Boris Yeltsin, but failed to do either. Not one of the 7,000 reformers on the plotters' detention list was arrested. The coup crumbled farcically and ignominiously in only four days. Pugo committed suicide. "Forgive me," he wrote in a note to his children and grandchildren. "It was all a mistake. I lived honestly, all my life." As Yazov was being led to a prison van, he said to those who arrested him, "Everything is clear now. I am such an old idiot. I've really fucked up." Kryuchkov lacked sufficient self-knowledge to reach a similar conclusion.[100]

The result of the final special action organized by the KGB was thus the precise opposite of what Kryuchkov and his fellow plotters had intended, accelerating both the collapse of the Communist one-party state and the disintegration of the Soviet Union. The coup also ended in unprecedented humiliation for the KGB. On the evening of August 21 a heavy crane arrived in front of the Lubyanka and, before a cheering crowd, hoisted the giant statue of Felix Dzerzhinsky by a noose around his neck, toppled him from his pedestal and dragged him away to a field near the Tretyakov gallery, which became a graveyard for statues of the Soviet regime.

APPENDIX

"SPECIAL POLITICAL ACTION" PROPOSED BY THE ATHENS RESIDENCY TO THE CENTRE IN APRIL 1969

Our operational letter no. 24/[Line]F of April 14, 1969 sets out a draft plan for carrying out a Lily [sabotage operation] against the target codenamed VAZA ["Vase"].

The operation is codenamed YAYTSO ["Egg"].

The aim and purpose of the operation is to cause moral and political damage to the south-east wing of NATO.

Constant disagreements between Greece and Turkey cause great concern to the leadership of the USA and NATO and are a weak link in American policy in the area of southeast Europe.

Carrying out a Lily on the VAZA could exacerbate relations between Greece and Turkey.

The operation would be carried out in the name of a Greek who had come from Turkey and was dissatisfied with the situation of the Greek minority there (there can also be another variant [pretext] for carrying out the sabotage).

VAZA is a two-storey house in Thessaloniki. The house and its annex belong to the Turkish consulate-general . . . There is no furniture, only a table, iron troughs and a cooking stove.

On the upper floor of the house there are displays with Atat;Anrk [the Turkish national hero]'s clothes and a photographic portrait of him. Apart from a desk there is no furniture.

Next to the VAZA, about 15–20 m away, there is the two-storey building of the Turkish consulate-general. This house is also used as living accommodation for consulate officials.

The VAZA and the consulate have a common courtyard. (A detailed description of the layout of the houses and the courtyard is attached.)

The most suitable place for planting a Bouquet [explosive device] is in the bushes growing about one meter from the VAZA.

The VAZA is not open to the general public. It can be visited with the permission of the Turkish consulate; a special official is assigned to watch over the VAZA and to accompany visitors to the VAZA.

The VAZA and the consulate are guarded round the clock by two gendarmes. The guard posts are mobile and the approaches to VAZA are restricted. The most convenient time to approach the target is at nightfall.

Specifications of the Bouquet:

The size and weight of the Bouquet must be related to the results which are desired from the attack on the VAZA. Evidently, there is no point in causing serious damage to the VAZA; it is better to achieve a moral and political effect. When calculating the force of the Bouquet, one must bear in mind that the distance from the Splash [explosion] to the consulate living quarters is 15–20 m.

. . . In order to increase the impact and achieve the desired results, the Bouquet must be wrapped in a newspaper published in Turkey for Greek citizens.

The temperature in Thessaloniki ranges in winter from below zero to 14°C, while in summer it ranges from 24°C upwards. Occasionally there are thick fogs.

The Gardener [saboteur] must be sent to the country as a foreign tourist at the height of the tourist season. The greatest influx of tourists occurs from June to August. According to his identity documents, the Gardener's identity documents must show him to be a citizen of a country friendly to Greece or a neutral state (the USA, Britain, West Germany, Austria, France, Italy, Canada, Libya), excluding the Scandinavian countries, Denmark, Holland and Belgium.

On arriving in Athens the Gardener can hire a motor car, visit historical sites in the south of the country and some of the islands. Simultaneously, the Gardener is acclimatizing himself and becoming fully accustomed to the situation in the country.

After collecting the Bouquet from the residency via a DLB [dead letterbox], the Gardener travels to Thessaloniki by rail.

The estimated time span for carrying out the Lily and for the Gardener's activities is as follows:

AFTER ARRIVING IN Athens, the Gardener can hire a motor car the next day, spend one or two days in Athens and its suburbs, then travel the following route by car: Athens–Pátrais–Spártia–Návplion–Epidhauros–Kóinthos–Athens. This route will take the Gardener four or five days. On arriving in Athens, the Gardener books into a hotel. The next day he places a signal indicating he is ready to carry out the DLB operation to receive the Bouquet. The DLB operation takes place next day.

After collecting the Bouquet, the Gardener leaves by the next train to Thessaloniki, having previously booked out from the hotel. A train leaves Athens at 11:42, and arrives at Thessaloniki at 19:29; he travels in a first-class compartment.

At Thessaloniki he does not stay at a hotel. In order to acquaint himself with the situation around the VAZA he walks past the VAZA after checking for surveillance.

As darkness falls, the Gardener goes off on a route of his own choice, but at the final stage goes into the old fort, where he inserts the little flower [detonator] into the Bouquet. From the northern gates of the fort, the Gardener goes down Isail Street which leads to the VAZA and comes out on St. Paul Street. This takes 15–20 minutes.

On coming out on to Isail Street, the Gardener goes from the garage towards St. Paul Street. While moving along the [VAZA] fence, the Gardener causes the Splash [explosion]. The Gardener can throw the Bouquet into the bushes which are close to the VAZA fence or he can drop the Bouquet on the ground inside the VAZA fence. (A diagram of the route and of the location of the installations is attached.)

After completing the Splash, the Gardener goes out on Áyios Dhimitrios Street and moves in the direction of the stadium (20–25 minutes walk). In the stadium area there is some waste ground where the Gardener can bury the TWA or BOAC airline bag used for keeping and transporting the Bouquet. From Thessaloniki, the Gardener can go to Athens by train or air (buying the air ticket 5–10 minutes before takeoff, using any surname).

If the situation does not permit the Gardener to put the Bouquet together, then he can get rid of it . . . in the area of the stadium where there is some waste ground. If he attracts the attention of the VAZA security guard, he must say that he is a foreign tourist going from the fort to the Delta Hotel, where he intends to spend the night, but that this is his first visit to the town and he is not sure of the way to the hotel.[101]

Vasili Mitrokhin fishing in East Germany; a photograph presented to him by the Stasi.

Mitrokhin during his KGB career: (left) on a hunting expedition; (right) returning from fishing.

Mitrokhin working on papers from his archive.

Уважаемый
Василий Никитич!

Коллектив сотрудников отдела сердечно поздравляет Вас с 60-летием со дня рождения.

40 лет жизни Вы отдали службе в органах государственной безопасности. 35 лет Вы состоите в нашей славной Коммунистической партии.

В славных рядах советских чекистов на протяжении всей своей деятельности Вы отдавали все свои силы, знания и энергию делу служения нашей Социалистической Родине.

За образцовое выполнение обязанностей Вы отмечались правительственными наградами, поощрялись руководством Главка и Комитета государственной безопасности.

Сегодня, в день Вашего юбилея, примите, уважаемый Василий Никитич, наши сердечные пожелания здоровья, счастья, а также успехов в Вашей дальнейшей деятельности на благо нашей Родины.

Dear Vasili Nikitich,

The collective's employees wish you a very happy 60th birthday.

You devoted 40 years of your life to the state security service and for 35 years you were a member of our glorious Communist Party.

In the glorious ranks of the Soviet Chekists and in advancing its work, you devoted all of your strength, knowledge and energy to serving our Socialist Motherland.

In the discharge of your responsibilities you received Government decorations and were an inspiration to the head of and the Committee for State Security.

Dear Vasili Nikitich, today, on the day of your jubilee, please accept our heartfelt good wishes of health, happiness and also of success in your work in the future for the sake of our motherland.

KGB certificate given to Mitrokhin on his 60th birthday.

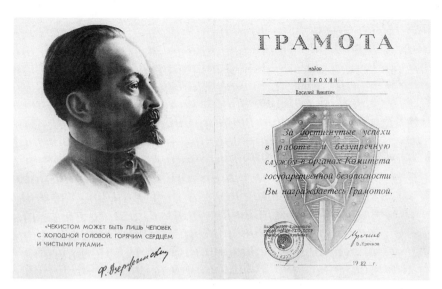

Certificate signed by Vladimir Kryuchkov (below sword and shield emblem on the right), head of foreign intelligence, commending Mitrokhin for his work. In 1988 Kryuchkov (below) became chairman of the KGB; three years later he led the unsuccessful coup against Gorbachev.

© Camera Press

Mitrokhin's KGB pension book, recording his retirement in 1984.

Checkmate

How the FBI Broke Spy Case That Baffled Agency for 30 Years

A Tip and a Risky Gamble On Meaning of 'Roeck' Cracked KGB Scheme

'You Mean to Kill Him?'

Robert Lipka (codenamed DAN); a leading Cold War Soviet agent in the United States arrested after Mitrokhin supplied the FBI with extracts from his KGB file. On being sentenced to 18 years' imprisonment in 1997, almost 30 years after his work as an agent ended, Lipka ruefully commented, 'I feel like Rip Van Spy'.

Lipka's arrest, as reported by the *Wall Street Journal*, 21/11/96, republished by permission (above right).

        "Дан"—Роберт Стефен Липка,16.6.1945 г.р.,уроженец Шагара Фоллс,
Нью-Йорк,в сентябре 1965 года посетил посольство в Вашингтоне и предложил
продавать документы НСА,сказал,что в 1963 году окончил разведывательную
школу,работает в бюро В форте Халабад,обязанности его распределять документы и уничтожать их.Был завербован,получено от него более 200 важных
документов НСА,ЦРУ,госдепартамента и других ведомств,подлинность их не
вызывала сомнений,высоко оценено,проведено около 50 операций по связи.
"Дан" хорошо освоил технику тайниковых и моментальных операций,постоянные
условия связи и вызов на экстренную встречу.За время сотрудничества ему
уплочено около 27 тысяч долларов,но был недоволен,требовал более высокой
оплаты,угрожал.В июле 1967 года порвал отношения с резидентурой,известил
через тайник,что якобы работал под контролем спецслужб США.Но анализ
сотрудничества показал,что сигнал этот нельзя принимать за чистую монету,
так как никогда не был близок идеологически,работал исключительно на
материальной основе,материалы наносили ущерб национальным интересам США
и безусловно спецслужбы в случае выхода на "Дана" стремились бы поймать
оперативника с поличным.Вероятно,"Дан" убедился,что советская разведка
даром денег не даёт,платит только за действительно ценные материалы,а
возможная помощь в период учёбы будет настолько мала,что не оправдывает
риска контакта.
В апреле и ноябре 1968 года проводилась установка "Дана" по адресам при
помощи нелегалов.Оперработник письмом вызывал на встречу "Дана",в 1969-
73 годах резидентура и нелегальная служба вели поиск его.
   Жена "Дана"—Патрисия Липка,работала в госпитале:403 Ланкастер авеню
г.Ланкастер.

Extract from Mitrokhin's notes on Lipka's KGB file.

Moisei Akselrod (right), who operated in Italy in the mid-1930s, posing as an Austrian businessman.

The classified British diplomatic documents which he obtained from a source inside the British embassy in Rome were so highly rated by the Centre that in 1935 over 100 of them were passed on to Stalin. Two years later, however, Akselrod became an innocent victim of the Stalinist Great Terror, was denounced as a traitor and executed.

Dr. Arnold Deutsch (main photo below), the principal recruiter and early controller of the Magnificent Five, five young Cambridge graduates (clockwise from top: Kim Philby, Donald Maclean, Guy Burgess, Anthony Blunt and John Cairncross) recruited in the mid-1930s. As well as having an even more brilliant academic record than any of the Five, Deutsch was also a collaborator of the leading sexologist Wilhelm Reich.

Iosif Grigulevich (portrayed in 1974, at the age of 61). Grigulevich was a master of impersonation. After the Second World War, he passed himself off as the Costa Rican Teodoro Castro, became a friend of the president and was appointed Costa Rican envoy to Rome. As well as specializing in sabotage and assassination, Grigulevich also made a career as an academic authority and writer on Latin America.

Morris and Lona Cohen, the KGB's leading American illegal agents. In 1954 Paddy Costello, a Soviet agent in the New Zealand legation in Paris, supplied them with New Zealand passports (above) in the names of Peter and Helen Kroger, which they used to move to London to join the illegal residency of Konon Molody. In 1995 Morris Cohen was posthumously made Hero of the Russian Federation by President Yeltsin.

Konon Molody (BEN), KGB illegal resident in Britain from 1955 to 1961, with one of his many girlfriends in London. He did not, however, hit it off with the KGB's most important and long-serving female British agent, HOLA. After only two months HOLA was moved to another controller.

Gentlemen's lavatory at the Classics Cinema, Baker Street, London, used by Molody as a dead letter-box. Notes and radio spare parts were hidden in a condom inside the cistern.

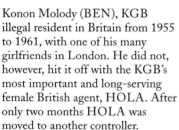

Vasili Gordievsky. In 1968, with a false West German passport, Gordievsky was one of a number of illegals posing as Western supporters of the Prague Spring who were sent to Czechoslovakia to cultivate and compromise the reformers. This was the first of numerous PROGRESS operations in which illegals were used to monitor dissidence and disaffection in the Soviet Bloc.

Vasili's brother, Oleg Gordievsky (above), disgusted by the suppression of the Prague Spring, later became an SIS agent inside the KGB.

The Czechoslovak illegals Karl and Hana Koecher who worked for the KGB as well as for the StB in the 1970s and early 1980s. Karl Koecher seems to have been the first illegal to find employment with the CIA. The KGB chairman and future Soviet leader, Yuri Andropov, personally praised his intelligence as "important and valuable." The Koechers were *habitués* of Washington and New York sex clubs where they had sex with personnel from the CIA, Pentagon and other parts of the federal government. The photograph was taken after their return to Prague in 1986.

6   NEWS   DIARY   THE TIMES SATURDAY NOVEMBER 29 1969

'I'm in a little firm in a firm . . . anywhere in London I can get on the phone to someone I know I can trust, that talks the same as me . . .'
—Detective-sergeant John Symonds, of Camberwell CID

Meetings observed by The Times.—Left: Detective-inspector Robson, of Scotland Yard, gesticulating, and Detective-sergeant Harris with Michael Smith beside Mr. Smith's Wolseley car, on November 5. Above: Sergeant Harris and Inspector Robson walking off. Below: Detective-sergeant Symonds meeting Mr. Smith in the same Wolseley on November 21. The white Vauxhall in which he arrived is parked some yards behind.

In 1969 a front-page story in *The Times* (London) charged Detective Sergeant John Symonds and other corrupt Met officers with being in the pay of the London underworld. In 1972, while awaiting trial, Symonds fled abroad and spent the next eight years working as a KGB agent in four continents under false Australian, British and Canadian identities. In 1980 he broke contact with the KGB, returned to Britain and was sentenced to two years in jail for corruption. Interviewed in *The Times* (London) in 1994 (headline below), he said that he had roamed the world living off his wits but concealed his KGB connection.

Confessions of a bent copper

3 | KGB RADIO AND ARMS CACHES

Mitrokhin succeeded in copying files giving the exact locations and other details of some of the caches located in almost every Western country, most intended for use by illegals. Some, probably many, were booby-trapped.

Mitrokhin's copy of the instructions for defusing the Molniya ("lightning") explosive devices (above) attached to many of the caches (see chapter 22, appendix 1).

i

ii

Directions (i) to a booby-trapped radio cache, located near the Swiss town of Befaux (see chapter 22, appendix 2). The first major landmark referred to in the directions is a chapel (ii) on the edge of a wood. The next marker, 50 paces along the path to the left of the chapel is a stone block (iii), marked FC [Fôret Cantonale]. The site in which the cache was buried in 1966 is another 36 paces away, between two large trees (iv), one reduced to a stump since the instructions were drawn up. The Swiss federal police excavated the cache in December 1998, using Mitrokhin's notes, and discovered a metal container and waterproof packet (v) buried one metre deep beneath a large stone.

Inside the booby-trapped container (bottom), were a radio transmitter, radio receiver and cipher machine (top); the waterproof packet contained a radio antenna and other accessories (bottom right of top picture). The Molniya device attached to the container was discovered to be in a dangerous condition, and was exploded after Swiss police examination. Though not revealing the location of the cache, the police issued a warning that attempting to remove or open any similar caches was likely to cause death or serious injury. Most of the booby-trapped caches hidden in unknown quantities throughout the West must now also be in a dangerous condition.

© Camera Press

The trial in 1966 of the dissident writers, Andrei Sinyavsky (bearded) and Yuli Daniel, accused of publishing allegedly anti-Soviet works in the West. Though many Soviet writers had been imprisoned or executed in the Stalin era, Sinyavsky and Daniel were the first to be subjected to a show trial. Jeered by a courtroom audience chosen by the KGB, they were accused of "pouring mud on whatever is most holy."

© Scanpix

Elena Bonner receives the 1975 Nobel Peace Prize on behalf of her husband, Andrei Sakharov, watched by the president of the Peace Prize Committee, Aase Lionaes. One of the priorities of KGB foreign operations was to prevent other dissidents receiving Nobel Peace Prizes.

Mitrokhin's copy of the KGB record of the interrogation of the dissident Yuri Orlov (inset) in December 1977. (See translation in the appendix to chapter 20.) It is claimed in Moscow that the originals of this and similar documents concerning those charged with "anti-Soviet" agitation and propaganda have been destroyed. Orlov's failure to win the Nobel Peace Prize was celebrated by the KGB as a major victory.

© Corbis

Aleksandr Solzhenitsyn, delivering his celebrated Commencement address at Harvard University in 1978, four years after he was expelled from Russia. The Centre arranged a secret viewing of a video of the speech by a Moscow audience of KGB and Party notables.

KGB envelope in which Mitrokhin kept his notes and copies of documents from Andrei Sakharov's file, now officially said to have been destroyed.

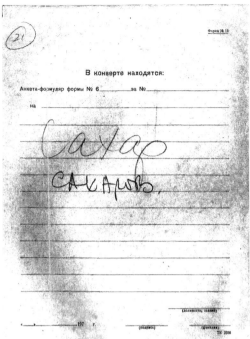

Sakharov, denounced by Andropov as "Public Enemy Number One," with Bonner in internal exile at Gorky in the early 1980s. Both were objects of an extraordinary number of KGB "active measures" (some involving forged documents), designed to demoralize them and destroy their reputations in the West. The KGB's campaigns of libels against Bonner were particularly vicious—partly because they wounded Sakharov more deeply than those against himself.

TШЕПTY-FOUR

COLD WAR OPERATIONS AGAINST BRITAIN

Part 1: After the Magnificent Five

Soviet intelligence operations in Britain from the 1930s onward fall into three distinct phases. First, there was a golden age, begun by the Great Illegals, during which the KGB collected better intelligence (even if it did not always understand it) than any other hostile intelligence agency in British history. Next came a silver age during the 1950s and 1960s, which included fewer—though still substantial—intelligence successes. The third phase, in the 1970s and 1980s, qualifies, at best, as a bronze age, with few major successes and some spectacular failures.

The golden age of Soviet intelligence operations in Britain came to an end in 1951 with the flight of Burgess and Maclean to Moscow and the recall of Philby from Washington.[1] The files noted by Mitrokhin, however, reveal for the first time that one major ideological agent recruited in the mid-1930s, Melita Norwood (HOLA), continued to operate after the demise of the Magnificent Five.[2] From March 1945 onward, while working in the research department of the British Non-Ferrous Metals Association, she had been able to provide intelligence on the TUBE ALLOYS project to build Britain's first atomic bomb.

After the Second World War there was a recurrence of the wartime rivalry between NKGB and GRU for control of Norwood. Her first post-war controller was an NKGB/MGB officer at the London residency, Nikolai Pavlovich Ostrovsky. During the Committee of Information (KI) period in the early Cold War, however, when the MGB and GRU combined their foreign intelligence services, Norwood had two GRU controllers: Galina Konstantinovna Tursevich and Yevgeni Aleksandrovich Oleynik. In April 1950, following the conviction of the atom spy Klaus Fuchs and the MI5 interrogation of SONYA, the wartime GRU controller of both Norwood and Fuchs, Norwood was temporarily put "on ice" for fear that she might have been compromised. Contact, however, was resumed in 1951. Within about a year, following the demise of the Committee of Information, control of Norwood was reclaimed by the Centre from the GRU.[3]

In October 1952, a few months after Norwood returned to the MGB, the first British atomic bomb was successfully tested on the Monte Bello islands off the north-west coast of Australia, hitherto known chiefly for their pearl divers and shipwrecks. Stalin had been far better briefed on the construction of the bomb than most British ministers. Attlee never allowed discussion of the TUBE ALLOYS project by his whole cabinet, later claiming censoriously that "some of them were not fit to be trusted with secrets of this kind." Churchill was amazed, after winning the 1951 election, to discover that Attlee had concealed the 100-million-pound cost of the atomic bomb from both Parliament and most of his ministers.[4]

Over the next twenty years Norwood had seven different controllers: six officers of the KGB London residency (Yevgeni Aleksandrovich Belov, Georgi Leonidovich Trusevich, Nikolai Nikolayevich Asimov, Vitali Yevgenovich Tseyrov, Gennadi Borosovich Myakinkov and Lev Nikolayevich Sherstnev) and one illegal (BEN). For security reasons Norwood actually met her controllers only four or five times a year, usually in the suburbs of south-east London to hand over the documents she had been collecting.[5]

The rivalry between the Centre and the GRU for control of Norwood during the Second World War and the early Cold War—decided in both cases in the Centre's favor—gives a clear indication of her importance as an agent. According to her file, some of the S&T which she supplied "found practical application in Soviet industry." (Mitrokhin's notes, alas, give no further details.) In 1958 HOLA was awarded the Order of the Red Banner. Two years later she was rewarded with a life pension of 20 pounds a month, payable with immediate effect, despite the fact that she was twelve years off from retirement at the Non-Ferrous Metals Association. Norwood, however, was an ideological agent who did not work for money. After her retirement she refused further payment, saying she had enough to live on and did not need it.[6]

Norwood also acted as agent-recruiter. The only recruit identified in Mitrokhin's notes, however, is the civil servant HUNT, whose cultivation Norwood began in 1965. In the fourteen years after HUNT's recruitment in 1967, he provided S&T and intelligence on British arms sales (on which no further details are available). In the late 1970s the London residency gave him 9,000 pounds to found a small business, probably in the hope that he could use it to supply embargoed technology.[7]

SO FAR AS is known, no Soviet agent recruited after the Second World War ever penetrated the British intelligence community quite as successfully as Philby, Blunt and Cairncross. Within a few months of Philby's dismissal from SIS in June 1951, however, the MGB began the recruitment of another SIS officer, the 29-year-old George Blake, né Behar. Blake had been born in Rotterdam of a naturalized British father (by origin a Sephardic Jew from Constantinople) and a Dutch mother who called their son George in honor of King George V. During the Second World War Blake served successively in the Dutch Resistance and in the Royal Navy, before joining SIS in 1944. There was much that SIS had failed to discover about its new recruit, notably the influence on him of his older cousin, Henri Curiel, co-founder of the Egyptian Communist Party, a man—according to Blake—with "immense charm and a dazzling smile [which] made him very attractive, not only to women, but to all who met him." In 1949 Blake was posted by SIS to South Korea, working under diplomatic cover as vice-consul in Seoul. A year later, shortly after the outbreak of the Korean War, he was interned by the invading North Koreans.[8]

In the autumn of 1951 Blake handed his captors a note, written in Russian and addressed to the Soviet embassy, saying that he had important information to communicate. At a meeting with Vasili Alekseyevich Dozhdalev of the KGB, he identified himself as an SIS officer and volunteered to work as a Soviet agent. Following a favorable assessment by Dozhdalev, the London resident, Nikolai Borisovich Rodin (alias "Korovin"), traveled to Korea to complete Blake's recruitment as agent DIOMID, and arranged to meet him in the Netherlands after the end of the Korean War. According to Sergei Aleksandrovich Kondrashev, who became Blake's controller in Britain in October 1953, the Centre considered him so important that no other member of the London residency was permitted to know either DIOMID's identity or the fact that he worked for SIS.[9]

KGB files give Blake the credit for two major successes during the 1950s. First, his intelligence—together with previous information from Philby and that supplied by Heinz Felfe,[10] a Soviet agent in the West German BND—is said to have made possible the "elimination of the adversary's agent network in the GDR in 1953–5."[11] In his memoirs, published in 1990, Blake claimed that he had betrayed almost 400 Western agents in the Soviet Bloc, but insisted that none had come to any harm—an improbable assertion swiftly denied by, among others, Oleg Kalugin. According to Blake, some of those he betrayed "are today taking an active part in the democratic movements of their respective countries in eastern Europe." Many more, however, were executed in the 1950s.[12]

Blake's second major achievement as a Soviet agent was to alert the Centre to one of the most remarkable Western intelligence operations of the Cold War—the secret construction of a 500-meter underground tunnel from West to East Berlin built to intercept landlines running from the Soviet military and intelligence headquarters in Karlshorst. At a meeting with his controller on the top deck of a London bus in January 1954, Blake handed over a carbon copy of the minutes of an SIS—CIA conference on the tunnel project, codenamed operation GOLD. Blake was posted to the SIS Berlin station in April 1955, one month before the tunnel became operational. The Centre, however, dared not interfere either with the tunnel's construction or with its early operations for fear of compromising Blake, who had established himself as by far its most important British agent.

By the time the KGB staged an "accidental" discovery of the tunnel in April 1956, operation GOLD had yielded over 50,000 reels of magnetic tape recording intercepted Soviet and East German communications. The intelligence yield was so considerable that it took over two years after the end of the operation to process all the intercepts. Though the FCD was able to protect its own communications, it was curiously indifferent to the interception of those of the rival GRU and of Soviet armed forces. There is no evidence to support past claims that the intelligence generated by operation GOLD was muddied by significant amounts of KGB disinformation. CIA and SIS intelligence reports on the operation contained important new information on the improved nuclear capability of the Soviet air force in East Germany; its new fleet of bombers and twin-jet radar-equipped interceptors; the doubling of Soviet bomber strength and the creation of a new fighter division in Poland; over one hundred air force installations in the USSR, GDR and Poland; the organization, bases and personnel of the Soviet Baltic Fleet; and installations and personnel of the Soviet atomic energy program. In the era before spy planes and spy satellites (the first U-2 overflight of the Soviet Union did not occur until July 1956), this intelligence was of particular value to a West still ignorant about much of the capability of the Soviet armed forces.[13]

One of the messages intercepted in the Berlin tunnel revealed the existence of a Soviet agent working for British intelligence in Berlin, but it was not until 1961 that evidence from the Polish SB defector Michał Goleniewski identified the agent as Blake.[14] Blake was sentenced to forty-two years in jail but served only five before escaping from Wormwood Scrubs with the help of three former inmates who had befriended him, the Irish bomber Sean Bourke and the peace protesters Michael Randle and Pat Pottle. On October 22, 1966 Blake knocked a loosened iron bar out of his cell window, slid down the roof outside and dropped to the ground, then climbed over the outer wall with a nylon rope ladder thrown to him by Bourke. Hidden in the Randle family dormobile, Blake was driven to East Berlin, where a fortnight later he was joined by Bourke. Once in Moscow, Blake and Bourke rapidly fell out. Blake writes in his memoirs that, "Arrangements were made for [Bourke] to return to Ireland."[15] He does not mention, and may not have known, that on the instructions of Sakharovsky, the head of the FCD, Bourke was given before his departure a drug designed to cause brain damage and thus limit his potential usefulness if he fell into the hands of British intelligence. Bourke's premature death in his early forties probably owed as much to KGB drugs as to his own heavy drinking.[16]

WHILE RUNNING BLAKE as an agent inside SIS during the 1950s, the KGB also had ambitious plans to recruit leading British politicians. Among the targets recorded in the files noted by Mitrokhin was Tom Driberg, Labor MP, journalist, member of Labor's National Executive from 1949 to 1974 and party chairman in 1957–8.[17] In 1956, shortly after Burgess and Maclean gave the first press conference since their flight to Moscow, claiming to have come to Moscow "to work for the aim of better understanding between the Soviet Union and the West," Driberg provided the opportunity for his own recruitment by requesting an interview with Burgess.[18] The two men had become friends during the War—brought together by common interests which included, according to Driberg's biographer, "contempt for the bourgeoisie" and "healthy appetites for alcohol and young men."[19] With the approval of the KGB, Burgess agreed to the interview, doubtless informing the Centre that Driberg was one of the most promiscuous homosexuals in British public life.

Whenever it saw an opportunity, the Second Chief Directorate (SCD) went to great pains to compromise foreign diplomats and Western politicians visiting Moscow by using female or male "swallows" to seduce them, photographing their sexual liaisons and then blackmailing them into "cooperation." A year before Driberg visited Moscow, for example, John Vassall, a homosexual clerk in the office of the

British naval attaché at the British embassy, had been lured to a party organized by the SCD. Soon afterward, Vassall recalled:

> I was shown a box of photographs of myself at the party . . . After about three photographs I could not stomach any more. They made one feel ill. There I was, caught by the camera, enjoying every sexual activity . . . having oral, anal or a complicated array of sexual activities with a number of different men.

For the next seven years, while working at the Moscow embassy and at the Admiralty in London, Vassall handed over thousands of highly classified documents on British and NATO weapons development and naval policy.[20]

As a compulsive "cottager" in public lavatories, Driberg proved even easier to recruit than Vassall. Instead of being compromised by an elaborate SCD sexual entrapment, Driberg obligingly compromised himself. During his visit to Moscow he discovered, to his delight, "a large underground urinal just behind the Metropole Hotel, open all night, frequented by hundreds of questing Slav homosexuals—standing there in rigid exhibitionist rows, motionless save for the hasty grope and the anxious or beckoning glance over the shoulder—and tended only by an old woman cleaner who never seemed to notice what was going on."[21] If the cleaner failed to notice the distinguished British visitor to the urinal, the KGB undoubtedly did not. Among Driberg's sexual partners on that or subsequent evenings in Moscow was an agent of the Second Chief Directorate. Soon afterward, Driberg was confronted with "compromising material" on his sexual encounters (probably photographs similar to those shown to Vassall) and recruited as agent LEPAGE.[22] Somewhat absurdly, in view of the use of blackmail, Driberg's file alleges that "ideological affinity," going back to his teenage membership of the Communist Party, played a subsidiary part in his recruitment.

For the next twelve years, Driberg was used both as a source of inside information from the Labor National Executive and to promote active measures.[23] The importance of his role within the Labor Party may well have been exaggerated by the Centre, especially after he became party chairman in 1957. "Even before he held this post, whose nature often misleads foreign observers," writes the political commentator Alan Watkins, "Driberg was assumed by several Russian politicians to be leader of the Labor Party. This was on account partly of his great episcopal manner, and partly of his ability to get on well with Russians."[24] Driberg was, none the less, wonderfully placed to report to his controller on both the evolution of Labor policy and the rivalries within the Party leadership. His mixture of political information and gossip was so highly rated by the KGB that it was passed on to the Politburo.[25]

Driberg's first active measure as agent LEPAGE was the publication in 1956 of a disingenuous study of Guy Burgess which concluded that he had never been a Soviet agent. At the time Driberg was temporarily out of the Commons, working as a freelance journalist, seriously short of money and being hounded by his bank manager. The book on Burgess brought him more money than anything else in his writing career, including the then-astounding sum of 5,000 pounds for its serialization in the *Daily Mail*.[26] After his initial meeting with Burgess in Moscow, Driberg went back to London, drafted in about a month a short biography entitled *Guy Burgess: A Portrait with Background*, then returned to Moscow to go through the proofs. "Presumably," he wrote later, "Guy had shown each chapter to his colleagues or superiors."[27] The proofs, in other words, had been carefully vetted by the KGB.

Driberg later described how, during their evenings together in Moscow, he had seen Burgess "getting a bit sozzled on vodka." The KGB, however, would tolerate no reference to Burgess's alcoholism. Driberg's biography thus quotes Burgess as saying that, despite his previous heavy drinking in the West, he no longer drank vodka in Moscow except—improbably—as "the best cure for an upset stomach:" "You know, Tom, living in a Socialist country *does* have a therapeutic effect on one." Driberg praised the "passionate sincerity" of Burgess's convictions and "his courage in doing what he thought right" to work for "better understanding between the Soviet Union and the West." Burgess and Maclean, claimed Driberg, had been the victims of British media attacks as outrageous as "the extreme excesses of the McCarthy witch hunt" in the United States:

> That does not mean that I personally agree with the decision that Burgess and Maclean took. As a Socialist, I take the view that, on the whole, one should go on working for Socialism by such means as are available in one's own country—in Britain, specifically, through the Labor Party. But this is a matter on which opinions differ . . .

While it was "silly for Western Socialists to defend every action of the Soviet Government," the achievements of Soviet industrial democracy deserved to be better known in the West. Driberg extolled the example of a Party meeting he had attended in a Moscow machine-tool factory:

> At this meeting a large percentage of those available to attend were present voluntarily to take an active, proud and responsible part in the running of their factory; and they seemed to feel that it was indeed theirs, as the workers at a factory in Dagenham or Coventry or Detroit can never, as things are, feel that the factories in which they work are theirs.[28]

The propaganda impact of Driberg's book was somewhat spoiled by the fact that, just as it was published in November 1956, Soviet tanks entered Budapest to crush the Hungarian Uprising. His KGB file records, however, that he continued to be used for KGB active measures.[29] Though Mitrokhin's summary of the file gives few details, the Centre probably considered Driberg's main use as an agent of influence to support the campaign within the Labor Party for unilateral nuclear disarmament. At the Scarborough party conference in October 1960, the left proved strong enough to pass two unilateralist motions, despite the impassioned opposition of Hugh Gaitskell, party leader, who implored his supporters to "fight and fight and fight again to save the party we love." Doubtless to the Centre's delight, Driberg was made a member of the "Committee of Twelve," appointed by the NEC to draft a new defense policy. Though Gaitskell complained that Driberg was behaving on the committee "like a tired snake," his supporters pushed through a pro-NATO and anti-unilateralist policy later adopted by the 1961 party conference, which reversed the vote at Scarborough a year earlier.[30]

It is unlikely that, after the publication of his biography of Guy Burgess, the KGB had any major subsequent influence on Driberg's speeches and articles—though it doubtless tried to claim some of the credit for his denunciation of the British nuclear deterrent and America's role in Vietnam. Driberg's campaigns on these and other left-wing causes sprang from conviction rather than KGB dictation. His main usefulness to the Centre probably lay in enabling it to boast to the Politburo that it had an agent at the heart of the Labor leadership who would probably figure in the next Labor government.

The Centre was doubtless deeply disappointed when there was no place for Driberg in the government formed by Gaitskell's successor, Harold Wilson, after the Labor election victory of 1964. Wilson distrusted him too much to think of making him a minister.[31] Together with Ian Mikardo, Driberg formed the left-wing Tribune Group, which opposed many of Wilson's policies from the back benches. After Wilson won an increased majority in 1966, however, the Tribune Group's protests became less effective. The *Daily Express* compared the impact of a protest organized by Driberg and Mikardo against a proposed wage freeze to that of "a piece of wet cod dropping in a snowdrift."[32] Driberg began to try to distance himself from the KGB, end secret contacts and limit himself to official meetings with Soviet diplomats and intelligence officers under diplomatic cover. When the KGB tried to increase pressure on him, he broke off contact altogether in 1968.[33]

Agent LEPAGE's decision—in KGB jargon—to "refuse to cooperate" may have been related to his worsening health. In January 1968, while on a tour of Cyprus as chairman of the Parliamentary Labor Party, he had a minor heart attack. Though warned that the attack might have been triggered by "overdoing it" sexually, Driberg insisted on inviting Cypriot youths into his hospital bed. Later in the year, after his return to London, he spent several further months in hospital with a detached retina, becoming blind in one eye. At the end of 1970, he decided to retire at the following election.[34]

It is uncertain whether Wilson ever learned from MI5 that Driberg was a Soviet agent. He was, however, informed in the late 1960s that a defector from the Czechoslovak StB, Josif Frolik, had reported that Driberg had been in the pay of the StB.[35] Frolik claimed that the StB had been warned off by the KGB on the grounds that Driberg was "their man."[36] Mitrokhin's brief summary of Driberg's file contains no reference to a Czech connection. But his notes on the file of another agent in the Labor Party, the journalist Raymond Fletcher, who served as MP for Ilkeston from 1964 to 1983, record that he was involved with the StB as well as the KGB.

When Fletcher (codenamed PETER) was recruited by the London residency in 1962,[37] he was preparing a scathing attack on Conservative defense policy, published in the following year under the title *£60 a Second on Defense,* which called for major defense cuts and the abandonment of the British nuclear deterrent. Fletcher ridiculed most of the security measures designed to prevent British defense secrets reaching the Soviet Union. "Classification," he declared, "is more a device for concealing incompetence than for concealing information from a potential enemy:"

> If the object of the deterrent exercise is to convince the Soviet Union that . . . "unacceptable damage" can be inflicted if aggression is embarked upon, why conceal the methods by which it is to be inflicted? We do not, of course. Such is the dismal state of our security procedures that it is a safe bet that more is known about British security procedures in the Kremlin than in the House of Commons.[38]

Shortly before his election as Labor MP in 1964, the Centre learned that Fletcher was also "cooperating" with the StB. On this occasion, instead of warning off the Czechs—as allegedly happened in the case of Driberg—the KGB seems to have broken off contact with Fletcher. The Centre was also disturbed by a report from the Polish SB that a letter in the possession of the British Communist Party appeared to show (almost certainly wrongly) that Fletcher had been "cooperating" since 1957 with the CIA.[39]

A few months before his death in 1991, Fletcher admitted that during the 1960s he had contacts at the Czechoslovak embassy in London whom "it was later claimed were intelligence personnel," but that he had thought "I was safe because I reported all my contacts to Goronwy Roberts at the Foreign Office." MI5, he implied, thought differently. They were, he declared, "a complete bunch of bastards" who "tried to break my nerve and nearly broke my spirit."[40] If, as Fletcher believed, MI5 did have him under surveillance, his KGB file suggests that they had some reason to do so.

The most important British politician identified in the files noted by Mitrokhin as a target for KGB recruitment was Harold Wilson. Given the extent of his contacts with the Soviet Union, unusual for a Western politician in the early years of the Cold War, Wilson was an almost inevitable target. As President of the Board of Trade and the youngest member of the Attlee cabinet from 1947 to 1951, Wilson had been actively involved in promoting East—West trade. He increased that involvement during Labor's thirteen years in opposition after 1951. His *Tribune* pamphlet *In Place of Dollars,* published in 1952, urged the government to relax controls on "strategic" exports to the Soviet Bloc and ignore the inevitable American protests which would follow. In May 1953, two months after the death of Stalin, he became the first major British politician to visit Moscow since the Berlin crisis five years earlier. There he renewed his acquaintance with Anastas Mikoyan, with whom he had established friendly relations during visits in 1947, and held wide-ranging talks with the Soviet foreign minister, Vyacheslav Molotov. On his return to London, Wilson addressed a special meeting of the Parliamentary Labor Party (PLP) and was congratulated by Attlee on a "magnificent inside report" on post-Stalin Russia.[41] Wilson's information on British politics seems to have been rated equally highly by the Russians. According to his KGB file, it was passed on to the Politburo.[42] There is, however, no indication that any of Wilson's conversations with Soviet officials (some, inevitably, undercover KGB officers) was any more confidential than his talk to the PLP.

During his years in opposition Wilson accepted a series of consultancies with firms trading with the Soviet Union, which paid him, on average, about 5,000 pounds a year.[43] According to his KGB file, one of the firms with which Wilson was involved breached the COCOM embargo on "strategic" exports.[44] Wilson's official biographer, Philip Ziegler, accepts that this was probably the case: "The export of many items was forbidden; inevitably a grey area grew up in which trading might or might not be illegal. Some of Wilson's associates strayed into that area or even beyond it."[45] The high value placed by the KGB on Wilson's political gossip, together with the dubious nature of some of his business contacts, probably explain the Centre's decision in 1956 to give him the codename OLDING and open an "agent development file" in the hope of recruiting him. The file records, however, that, "The development did not come to fruition."[46]

Allegations that Wilson was ever a KGB agent derive not from credible evidence but from unfounded conspiracy theories, some of them elaborated by the KGB officer Anatoli Golitsyn, who may have known of the existence of the "agent development file" and claimed after his defection in December 1961 that Wilson was a Soviet mole. When Gaitskell died suddenly in 1963, Golitsyn developed the bizarrely improbable theory that he had been poisoned by the KGB to enable Wilson to succeed him as Labor leader. Sadly, a minority of British and American intelligence officers with a penchant for conspiracy theory—among them James Angleton of the CIA and Peter Wright of MI5—were seduced by Golitsyn's fantasies.[47] Wright went on to devise several conspiracy theories of his own, among them the claim that thirty MI5 officers later conspired against Harold Wilson.[48]

Far from using Wilson as an agent or confidential contact after he became prime minister in 1964, the London residency commissioned articles attacking various of his policies by an agent codenamed DAN, recruited in 1959, who contributed to the left-wing weekly *Tribune.* DAN's file records that he published material given him by the KGB and wrote articles on "theses" devised by Service A, the active measures section at the Centre. Though Mitrokhin's brief notes on the file do not record whether DAN received regular payment, they do mention that in February 1967 he was given a "reward" of 200 pounds.[49]

The most prominent British journalist targeted by the Centre during the early years of the Cold War to be identified in the KGB files noted by Mitrokhin was Edward Crankshaw. From the start of the Cold War until some years after his retirement in 1968, Crankshaw was Britain's most authoritative commentator on Soviet affairs. During the Second World War he had served for two years with the British Military Mission in Russia. In 1947 he was "half-flattered, half-bullied" by the editor of the *Observer,* David Astor, into returning to Moscow as the paper's Russian and East European correspondent. For the next generation, he kept up what he called "a continual running commentary on what I thought the Russians were up to" in the *Observer,* its globally syndicated Foreign News Service, the *New York Times Sunday*

Magazine and "lectures and broadcasts all over the place."[50] Crankshaw's voluminous "running commentary," diffused around the world, was a source of continuous annoyance to both the Kremlin and the Centre. "There is only one group of people in the world today," he wrote in 1951, "which is actively and deliberately . . . committed to the downfall of our society: the group of Russians who form the government of the Soviet Union."[51]

The KGB tried various methods of bringing pressure on Crankshaw to modify his views—all without success. Some of the methods used were attempts to exploit his sexual liaisons in Moscow. Though "slight and gentlemanly in appearance," according to his entry in the *Dictionary of National Biography,* "Crankshaw controlled a wild and independent nature."[52] While serving with the wartime military mission, he had lived with the artist T. S. Andreyevskaya and her friend E. S. Rosinevich. In 1948 both were arrested, forced to confess to being British spies and sent to labor camp.[53] Crankshaw was not intimidated, but the fate of the two women may well have inspired a moving description by him in 1948 of others who suffered similar fates:

> Another thing you become aware of in the north, and which dominated your ideas, is forced labor in its many different forms. As you sit at breakfast in your hotel you hear the dreadful sound of a woman wailing, half hysterically, in the street outside. And looking out you see thirty or forty women and girls being marched along the frozen street by guards with fixed bayonets, each woman with a small bundle. You do not know where they are going; but you know that they are being marched away against their will, that the call came suddenly and roughly, and that behind them they are leaving homes which are, as it were, still warm, while they trudge through the snow with nothing but their bundles.[54]

In 1959 photographs were taken of Crankshaw while engaged in what Mitrokhin's notes describe as "sexual frolics."[55] If the photographs were shown to Crankshaw, as was usual in such cases, he was, once again, not intimidated— although the episode may have helped to inspire his reminder in the *Observer* that past atrocities committed by the KGB remained "part of the present:"

> Still no voice in the Soviet Union can be heard to say that the collectivization, the mass arrests, the deportations and killings were appalling crimes, past now, but never to be forgotten, and this means in effect that for all the remarkable changes since Stalin, the Khrushchev Government is still condoning those crimes.[56]

Soon after Andropov became KGB chairman in 1967, he gave his approval for an operation designed either to blackmail Crankshaw by using the photographs taken in 1959, and perhaps on other occasions, or to discredit him by sending them to the *Observer.* The operation, however, was abandoned at the urging of the London residency, which no doubt calculated correctly that Crankshaw would not give way to blackmail and that his editor would stand by him.[57]

Though the photographs of Crankshaw's "sexual frolics" were never published, similar pictures were used in an active measure codenamed operation PROBA designed to discredit the Conservative MP Commander Anthony Courtney, who had aroused the ire of the Centre by campaigning against the growing size of the London residency.[58] In 1965 the KGB produced a leaflet containing photographs of Courtney having sex with an unidentified woman, and circulated copies to his wife, other MPs and newspaper editors. Though intended to give the impression that Courtney was having an adulterous affair, the photographs had in fact been taken by the SCD four years earlier during a trip by Courtney, then a widower, to a Moscow trade fair. While in Moscow Courtney had been seduced by an Intourist guide who visited him in a hotel room fitted with a concealed KGB camera. The ensuing scandal, which began with a story in *Private Eye,* was largely responsible for Courtney's failure to hold his seat at the 1965 general election.[59] The KGB file on operation PROBA also claimed the credit for the breakdown of Courtney's marriage and the failure of his business career.[60]

The KGB's main targets for sexual compromise operations throughout the Cold War were foreign embassies in Moscow. The files noted by Mitrokhin suggest that few, if any, embassies escaped some degree of penetration by KGB swallows. The most successful seduction within the British embassy during the Brezhnev era, though it achieved far less than the entrapment of John Vassall, was probably that of a 30-year-old married male diplomat codenamed KAREV, who was seduced by his family's Russian maid, codenamed CH. On KGB instructions, using a stratagem successfully deployed against a number of foreign diplomats, CH pretended to be pregnant and sought KAREV's help in arranging an abortion, for which she claimed to have received help from an embassy protection officer. KAREV was persuaded to show his gratitude by giving some biographical information on embassy personnel, including the identities of SIS officers working under diplomatic cover. To compromise KAREV further, CH then pretended that she was pregnant again and needed help in arranging another abortion. Soon afterward CH was arrested on KGB instructions for being found in possession of Western currency given her by KAREV. On this occasion KAREV sought the help of a Soviet official, whom he probably realized was a KGB officer, both to arrange the second fictitious abortion and to have charges against CH dropped. Since KAREV's tour of duty in Moscow was about to end, he was persuaded to agree to a meeting with a KGB officer during his next posting. Once out of Moscow, however, KAREV succeeded in holding the KGB at arm's length. On being shown his file, Philby advised against attempting to compromise KAREV publicly, as in the case of Commander Courtney, probably because the hand of the KGB would have been too obvious.[61]

IN BRITAIN, AS in the United States,[62] the Centre's strategy during much of the Cold War was based on the attempt to establish a network of illegal residencies which would prove more difficult for MI5 to monitor than the legal residency at the Soviet embassy, and which could continue to operate if the Cold War turned into hot war. Its first post-war choice of illegal resident was Konon Trofimovich Molody (codenamed BEN), the son of two Soviet scientists, who seems to have been selected in childhood as a potential foreign intelligence officer. In 1932, at only ten years of age, he was sent, with official approval, to live with an aunt in California and attend secondary school in San Francisco, where he became fluent in English before returning to Moscow in 1938. During the Great Patriotic War he joined the NKVD and, according to a stilted official hagiography, "made frequent sorties into the enemy's rear . . . brilliantly displaying such qualities as boldness and valor." After the war Molody took a degree in Chinese and worked as a Chinese language instructor before beginning training as an illegal in 1951.[63]

Like some of the illegals chosen for postings in the United States, Molody began by establishing his cover in Canada, where he arrived in 1954 using the identity of a Canadian Communist "live double." MICK, a member of the Central Committee of the Canadian Communist Party, had persuaded the Party member to give him his passport in the previous year when he discovered that it had never been used for foreign travel. Though the live double was told that his passport would be for Party use, MICK passed it to Vladimir Pavlovich Burdin of the Ottawa residency via a senior member of the Canadian—Soviet Friendship Society codenamed SVYASHCHENNIK ("Clergyman").[64] The Centre replaced the photograph on the passport with that of Molody and gave it to him for his journey to Canada. Once in Canada, Molody obtained a new passport in the name of a "dead double," Gordon Arnold Lonsdale (codenamed KIZH), who had been born in Cobalt, Ontario, in 1924, emigrated as a child to the Soviet Union with his Finnish mother and died in 1943.[65] A Canadian Royal Commission later concluded:

> Canada has acquired a dubious international reputation with regard to her passports, and there is evidence that hostile intelligence services have concentrated on the acquisition of Canadian documentation because of this relative ease of procurement.[66]

In March 1955, Molody traveled to London using his new identity as "Gordon Lonsdale" and enrolled as a student on a Chinese course at the School of Oriental and African Studies (SOAS). The Centre selected SOAS for two main reasons. First, since the course taken by Molody did not lead to a degree, he was not asked to provide the documentation on his previous education normally required of British university students. Secondly, as a qualified lecturer in Chinese and the author of a Russian—Chinese textbook, Molody found little difficulty in coping with the course requirements while spending most of his time establishing the KGB's first post-war illegal residency in Britain. His main problem at SOAS was the need to conceal from his tutors the fact that they had little, if anything, to teach him.[67] Molody's contact in the legal London residency was the Line N (Illegal Support) officer, V. A. Dmitriyev, who provided him with money and instructions from the Centre, as well as microdot letters from his family in Moscow, delivered via dead letter-boxes and at face-to-face meetings.[68] "When is Daddy coming, and why has he gone away?" asked Molody's small son Trofim in one letter. ". . . What a *stupid* job Daddy has got."[69]

While at SOAS, Molody began, with the Centre's approval, to establish a cover profession as a London businessman. Using KGB funds, he set himself up as the director of several companies operating juke boxes, vending machines and one-armed bandits. According to a KGB file, the vending machines included chewing-gum dispensers at no fewer than two hundred different sites, thus offering Molody frequent pretexts for journeys in the Greater London area to meet Dmitriyev, the two other members of his residency and his agents. An electronic locking device produced by one of the firms in which Molody was a partner won a gold medal at the 1960 International Inventors Exhibition in Brussels.[70] In retirement, Molody made the wildly exaggerated claim that he had been the KGB's first multimillionaire illegal resident. He boasted to a Soviet interviewer:

> Let me remind you that all the working capital and profits from my four companies (millions of pounds sterling) which were increasing year by year without any help from me, were "socialist property." Strange but true![71]

The radio operators and technical support team in Molody's illegal residency were the veteran American agents Morris and Lona Cohen (LUIS and LESLEY, collectively known as the DACHNIKI), who had been hastily recalled to Moscow after the arrest of the Rosenbergs.[72] In May 1954 the Cohens were issued with passports in the name of Peter and Helen Kroger by a Soviet agent at the New Zealand consulate in Paris, Paddy Costello (codenamed LONG), who later became professor of Russian at Manchester University.[73] "Peter Kroger's" cover profession in London was that of antiquarian bookseller. Like BEN, LUIS and LESLEY were extroverts with an active social life. One of their friends in the London book trade later recalled many convivial evenings at their house in Ruislip:

> Here you received good food, good wine, and the most wonderful hospitality . . . Peter cultivated the acquaintance of everyone he could, and he and his wife were liked by all. He attended the Bibliomites' darts matches and drank pint for pint. He played for the Guv'nors versus the Bibs, in their annual cricket match, wielding his willow like a baseball bat, and trying to knock home runs, to everybody's amusement.[74]

George Blake, who was to meet Konon Molody while both were imprisoned in Wormwood Scrubs, later eulogized him as "a perfect example of what an 'illegal resident' should be . . . a man who believes very strongly in an ideal and serves a great cause."[75] During his years in London, however, Molody became cynical about the prospects of recruiting a new generation of ideological spies like Blake, inspired by working for a great cause. He later told a Soviet interviewer:

> The average Englishman is apolitical and indifferent. He really couldn't care less who is governing him, where the country is going or whether the Common

Market is a good or bad thing. All that interests him is his own wage packet, his job and keeping the wife happy.

Molody also took a jaundiced view of the kind of Cold War recruits on whom he believed the KGB should concentrate in Britain:

A good agent is one whose vital statistics are the following: he works, for example, in a military department and holds a middle-ranking but key position giving him access to information; he doesn't aspire to a higher office, has a chip on his shoulder about being a failure (let's say that ill-health prevented him finishing studies at the general staff college); he drinks (an expensive habit); he has a weakness for the fair sex (which is also not cheap); he is critical of his own government and loyal to the resident's government.[76]

The accounts of Molody's career released by the KGB and SVR carefully conceal the fact that late in 1958 he was given control of the KGB's longest-serving British agent, Melita Norwood (HOLA), whose ideological commitment seems never to have wavered over more than forty years. Molody met Norwood for the first time on December 23 and received from her the usual batch of documents from the safes of the Non-Ferrous Metals Association. For reasons not recorded in Mitrokhin's notes, however, Norwood was returned only two months later to the control of the legal London residency.[77] Perhaps Norwood was repelled by the signs of Molody's high-living, womanizing lifestyle. Or perhaps Molody simply lacked the ability to control an ideological agent.

The files on the Molody residency seen by Mitrokhin suggest that it successfully ran only two agents: Harry Houghton and his mistress Ethel Gee (codenamed SHAH and ASYA).[78] Houghton, a former NCO in the Royal Navy, closely resembled Molody's jaundiced stereotype of the British agent. He worked as a civilian clerk in the Underwater Weapons Establishment at Portland, where, helped by Gee, who was employed as a filing clerk, he had easy access to top secret information on anti-submarine warfare and nuclear submarines. Houghton's later memoirs provide striking evidence of how successfully his controller concealed his low opinion of him. Though Molody, as his Moscow interviews make clear, regarded agents such as Houghton as mildly contemptible moral inadequates, Houghton was pathetically convinced that, from their first meeting, "[t]here was a real camaraderie between us." Molody deceived Houghton so successfully that he even persuaded him that he regarded going to bed with any of his many girlfriends as "absolutely out."[79]

Like Blake, Houghton was identified by MI5 as a result of information from the defector Michał Goleniewski. Surveillance of Houghton led to the discovery of "Lonsdale," who was then followed on a visit to the "Krogers" in Ruislip. A search of the "Krogers' " house uncovered a powerful high-speed radio transmitter used for communications with the Centre and a short-wave radio used for receiving messages from Moscow on high-frequency bands, both hidden in a cavity beneath the kitchen floor; one-time cipher pads hidden in flashlights and a cigarette lighter; a microdot reader concealed in a box of face powder; equipment for microdot construction; a cookery jar containing magnetic iron oxide used for printing high-speed morse messages on to tape; thousands of pounds, dollars and travelers checks; and seven passports.[80] At their trial in 1961 Molody was sentenced to twenty-five years in prison, the Cohens to twenty, Houghton and Gee to fifteen.

Molody was freed in a spy exchange in 1964. His misleading memoirs, published a year later under his alias "Gordon Lonsdale," with the approval of the CPSU Central Committee, contained a variety of disinformation—including the pretense that the "Krogers" were entirely innocent. The London residency reported a "negative reaction" to the memoirs by the British Communist Party leadership, on the grounds that they amounted to a formal admission that the Soviet Union engaged in espionage against the West.[81] In 1969 the Cohens were exchanged for the imprisoned British lecturer Gerald Brooke. At a dinner in their honor at a KGB dacha on November 25, 1969, Andropov personally presented them with the Order of the Red Star. Other top brass from the Centre present at the dinner included Sakharovsky, the FCD chief, and Lazarev, the head of the illegals directorate. 5,000 roubles were spent furnishing a Moscow apartment for the Cohens on Malaya Bronnaya, where the same KGB top brass attended a flat-warming party in April 1970.[82]

The Centre remained anxious, however, to keep the Cohens away from other Western defectors in Moscow—partly because it clung to the fiction that they were Polish and had gone to live in Poland. On June 7, 1971, while returning to his flat from a shopping expedition, Morris Cohen accidentally bumped into George Blake, whom he had first met several years earlier when they were both imprisoned in Wormwood Scrubs. The KGB file on the meeting notes that both expressed "genuine joy" at their reunion, exchanged telephone numbers and agreed to arrange another meeting. The Centre, however, separately instructed both Blake and the Cohens to devise pretexts to cancel their arrangement. According to the KGB record of a bugged telephone conversation, Cohen rang Blake to tell him that he was about to go on holiday and would, after all, not be able to meet him in the near future. Blake replied that he quite understood and would himself be leaving for his dacha in a few days' time. The two men never met again.[83] The Cohens, however, retained an honored place in the KGB pantheon. Lona died in 1993 at the age of eighty, Morris two years later at the age of ninety. By order of President Yeltsin, Morris Cohen was posthumously awarded the title of Hero of the Russian Federation.[84]

Molody's career ended less happily. Once back in Moscow, his experience of life in the West made him, like a number of other former illegals, increasingly disillusioned with the Soviet system. According to Blake:

> He was particularly critical of the inefficient and often incompetent way Soviet industrial enterprises were run and international trade was conducted. Being an outspoken man who had the good of his country at heart, he made his views known. Criticism of any kind was not appreciated in those days and he soon fell from favor and found himself relegated to a position of relatively minor importance.[85]

Molody also took to drink. One Saturday in October 1970 he went on a mushroom-collecting expedition near the town of Medyi with his wife and two friends from the air force. Immediately after his second glass of vodka, he suffered a stroke, lost the power of speech and died a few days later in hospital at the age of only forty-eight.[86] He lay in state on a funeral bier in the KGB officers' club while colleagues displayed his large collection of medals on velvet cushions and Andropov and other top brass came to pay their respects.[87] Shortly before his death, a team of writers commissioned by the Centre had completed, with Molody's assistance, a new biography of him entitled *Special Mission,* some extracts of which were published in the Soviet press. In 1972, however, it was decided, with Andropov's approval, not to publish the book abroad and to suspend publication in the Soviet Union for fear that it would "fan the flames of spymania" in the West.[88]

After Molody's death, his long-suffering wife, Galina Ivanovna, who had seen very little of him during his career as an illegal, also took to drink. Over the next few years she was treated several times for alcoholism. In 1976 a monument to Molody costing 2,000 roubles was erected on his grave in Moscow's Donskoy Monastery, next to that of another well known illegal of the 1950s, William Fisher (alias "Abel"). In the same year, the CPSU Central Committee awarded his widow a pension of 120 roubles.[89]

Mitrokhin saw frequent references in KGB files to visits to Britain made by other Soviet illegals during the twenty years after Molody's arrest but found no evidence that any fully functioning illegal KGB residency to replace BEN's was established during that period—though it is possible that such evidence exists in files he did not see. One of the principal candidates chosen to succeed BEN in London appears to have been the comparatively youthful Eduard Ivanovich Koslov (codenamed YEVDOKIMOV), born in 1934. With the help of the agent RAG, an official in a Belgian commune,[90] Koslov obtained identity documents in the name of the non-existent Jean-Louis de Mol, which he used to obtain a Belgian passport in 1961. Over the next few years, he went through an elaborate acclimatization period to strengthen his cover, studying at a Swiss foreign language school, working as an electronic machine operator in Zurich, then in a Stuttgart insurance company. In 1966 he returned to Belgium, took up residence in Dinant and obtained a new passport valid until 1970. Before he could move on to Britain or the United States, however, Koslov aroused the suspicions of the Belgian security service and was hurriedly recalled to Moscow. At the time of his recall, his account in the Banque de Bruxelles (no. A-04-18295) contained 39,000 Belgian francs; the Centre considered it too dangerous to withdraw the money and wrote it off. Unable henceforth to travel in the West, Koslov worked instead on PROGRESS operations in Bulgaria, Czechoslovakia, Hungary and the Soviet Union, posing as a British, American or Belgian tourist.[91]

DESPITE THE APPARENT failure of its attempts to establish a new illegal residency after the arrest of Molody and the Cohens, the KGB's British operations achieved a series of significant successes during the following decade. The Centre discovered a simple but effective method of making life easier for the London legal residency. Under four successive residents—Nikolai Grigoryevich Bagrichev (1962–4),[92]

Mikhail Timofeyevich Chizhov (1964–6), Mikhail Ivanovich Lopatin (acting resident, 1966–7)[93] and Yuri Nikolayevich Voronin (1967–71)—the size of the residency steadily increased. Between 1960 and 1970, KGB and GRU personnel in London grew from about fifty to over 120—more than in Washington or any other Western capital. The intelligence services of other Soviet Bloc countries also rapidly expanded their British operations. The aim, which was partially successful, was to swamp the overstretched MI5 with more intelligence officers than they could hope to keep under effective surveillance.[94]

When the Czechoslovak StB officer Josef Frolik was posted to London in 1964, he was told that "the British service was so short of funds and men that it would be relatively easy to throw off their tails."[95] MI5's job became even harder at the beginning of Voronin's term as resident, in 1967, when one of his operations officers, Aleksei Nikolayevich Savin (codenamed RUSLAN),[96] recruited a clerk in the Greater London Council (GLC) motor licensing department, Sirioj Husein Abdoolcader, who had access to the registration numbers of all Security Service and Special Branch vehicles. A series of sophisticated MI5 mobile surveillance operations was compromised by the ability of the London residency to identify the vehicles used.[97]

The London residency's greatest successes during the Brezhnev era were in scientific and technological intelligence (S&T), particularly in the defense field. In 1967 Lopatin, the residency's main S&T expert in the mid-1960s, became one of the founders of a new FCD Directorate T, specializing in this field and serviced by Line X (S&T) officers in residencies abroad. The head of Line X in London from the beginning of 1968 until his expulsion in the summer of 1971 was Lev Nikolayevich Sherstnev, a tough but amiable engineer who spoke almost flawless English with a Canadian accent and had a passion for Western hi-fi.[98]

In addition to the veteran Norwood, Mitrokhin's notes identify at least ten other Line X agents active in the late 1960s: MERCURY, a chemist recruited in 1958;[99] SAKS, an employee of a British aircraft company, recruited in Germany, probably in 1964, "for material reward;"[100] YUNG, an aeronautical and computer engineer recruited in 1965;[101] NAGIN, a chemical engineer recruited in 1966;[102] ACE, an aeronautical engineer recruited in 1967, who supplied voluminous documentation on aero engines and flight simulators;[103] HUNT, the civil servant recruited by Norwood in 1967;[104] AKHURYAN, a nuclear physicist recruited in 1968;[105] STARIK, an aeronautical design engineer recruited in 1968;[106] DAN, an engineer in the British subsidiary of an American company, recruited in 1969 "for material reward;"[107] and STEP, a laboratory assistant recruited in 1969 for a monthly salary of 150 dollars.[108] Mitrokhin's notes also identify four further Line X agents operating in the 1970s who may well have been recruited in the 1960s: a virologist, a research scientist in a pharmaceutical laboratory,[109] an engineer at a nuclear reactor,[110] and COOPER, who worked in the new products department of a pharmaceutical company.[111]

MI5 was hampered in its response to the upsurge of KGB and GRU S&T operations not merely by its own overstretched resources but also by the difficulty (which it was, understandably, not anxious to advertise) of bringing successful prosecutions. Unless it could obtain confessions or catch agents in the act of handing over material, it was usually impossible to secure convictions. Its difficulties were exemplified by the trial in 1963 of Dr. Giuseppe Martelli, a 39-year-old Italian physicist employed for the previous year at the Culham Laboratories of the Atomic Energy Authority. Arrested as a result of a lead from a KGB defector, Martelli was found in possession of a record of meetings with Nikolai Karpekov and other KGB officers, a set of partly used one-time pads for cipher communications hidden inside an ingeniously constructed cigarette case, and instructions for photographing documents. But possession of espionage paraphernalia (unlike housebreaking equipment) is not in itself a crime and Martelli had no official access to classified information, though he was in contact with people who had. Martelli admitted meeting Karpekov, but claimed he was engaged in an ingenious scheme to turn the tables on a blackmail attempt by the KGB. He was acquitted.[112]

During the mid- and late 1960s there were only two successful British prosecutions of Soviet spies in Britain. In 1965 Frank Bossard, a 52-year-old projects officer at the Ministry of Aviation was sentenced to twenty-one years in jail for passing top secret details of British guided weapon development to the GRU. An investigation after Bossard's arrest revealed a criminal record which had never been properly investigated. Twenty years earlier he had served six months' hard labor for fraud. In 1968 Douglas Britten, an RAF chief technician, was also sentenced to twenty-one years in jail for giving the KGB highly classified information from RAF signals units in Cyprus and Lincolnshire. A Security Commission inquiry after Britten's conviction disclosed Britten's history of financial problems and his record as an "accomplished liar."[113]

The work of Line X in the London residency was supplemented by KGB officers sent to Britain under cover either as members of trade and scientific delegations or as postgraduate students. Among the KGB postgraduates was A. V. Sharov of Directorate T, who began work for a PhD in engineering at London University in November 1966 and was awarded his doctorate on October 22, 1969. On KGB instructions, Sharov returned to London to take his degree in person in January 1971 and embark on a lecture tour arranged by the Academy of Sciences which was intended by the Centre to enable him to identify possible recruits in the scientific community.[114]

Probably the most important Line PR postgraduate at a British university in the mid-1960s was Gennadi Fedorovich Titov (codenamed SILIN), who studied at University College, London. Titov went on to become resident in Norway in 1971 at the relatively youthful age of thirty-nine;[115] in 1984 he was promoted to the rank of KGB general, and by the time of the 1991 coup ranked third in the KGB hierarchy. KGB officers and agents disguised as students were also used to uncover links between Western church groups and religious minorities in the Soviet Union. In September 1970 ABRAMOV (not identified in Mitrokhin's notes) enrolled at a Baptist college in England, where he made contacts who revealed plans in Sweden and West Germany to smuggle religious literature into Russia by car, hidden in specially constructed secret compartments.[116]

Since the demise of the Magnificent Five and the arrest of George Blake, the Centre had seen as the main weakness of its British operations its failure to recruit a new generation of young, ideologically committed high-flyers. The simple truth, which the Centre could not bring itself to accept, was that the Soviet Union had lost most of its former ideological appeal. The aging apparatchiks who ruled Brezhnev's Soviet Union lacked the luster of both the interwar myth—image of the world's first worker—peasant state and the far more accurate wartime image of the state which had been chiefly responsible for the defeat of Nazism. Most young Western radicals of the late 1960s were attracted not to ideologically servile Communist Parties but to the libertarian movements of the New Left. Moscow, however, refused to accept that this was more than a passing phase. The Centre sought to use the exploits of Kim Philby to inspire a new generation of radical idealists to follow his example.

On his defection to Moscow in 1963, Philby had been dismayed to discover that he held only agent status in the KGB, did not hold officer rank and was not even to be allowed to set foot inside the Lubyanka. For the first five years of his Moscow exile, however, he was kept occupied by long debriefing sessions, helping to ghost-write the memoirs of Konon Molody (published under his alias "Gordon Lonsdale") and writing a sprightly but tendentious memoir of his own career as a Soviet agent inside SIS, published in 1968 under the title of *My Silent War*.[117] Philby made no mention of the disappointments of life in Moscow. Instead, he claimed that, "As I look over Moscow from my study window, I can see the solid foundations of the future I glimpsed at Cambridge." Philby concluded his preface with words which were intended to inspire others:

> It is a sobering thought that, but for the power of the Soviet Union and the Communist idea, the Old World, if not the whole world, would now be ruled by Hitler and Hirohito. It is a matter of great pride to me that I was invited, at so early an age, to play my infinitesimal part in building up that power . . . When the proposition [to join Soviet intelligence] was made to me, I did not hesitate. One does not look twice at an offer of enrollment in an élite force.[118]

Scarcely had *My Silent War* been published than an American high school student, inspired by Philby's example, arrived in Moscow on a tourist visa and offered his services to the KGB. Though aged only sixteen (the youngest Western recruit recorded in the files seen by Mitrokhin), he was signed up in July 1968, with Andropov's personal approval, as agent SYNOK ("Sonny")[119]—the same codename as that which had been given to Philby on his recruitment in 1934.[120] SYNOK's file notes that he came from a well-to-do family, had an idealistic commitment to the Soviet Union and was imbued with a romantic notion of intelligence work. After a second meeting with SYNOK in Mexico on October 19, it was decided to train him as an illegal agent. Over the next few months, however, either SYNOK or his parents had second thoughts and he failed to show up at the next pre-arranged rendezvous in London.

It may be a sign of how few other bright, ideologically committed young Westerners were inspired to follow Philby's example (no others are recorded in Mitrokhin's notes) that the KGB continued intermittently to try to renew contact with SYNOK for more than a decade. In 1978 a KGB officer discovered from SYNOK's father that he was in Mexico, but failed to track him down. Two years later, his mother was tricked into revealing that he was in San Francisco and giving his address. In December 1980 the operations officer who had met him in Mexico twelve years earlier wrote to SYNOK in San Francisco, inviting him to another meeting in Mexico and giving an East German cover address to which to reply. When no reply was received, the KGB seems, at long last, to have given up.[121]

Though a new generation of Philbys failed to materialize, memories of the Magnificent Five continued to enhance the prestige of the London residency. Even in the Gorbachev era, operations in Britain during the Second World War and the quarter century afterward were still held up as a model for young intelligence officers at the FCD training school, the Andropov Institute. The three main faculty heads in the institute had all made their reputations in the London residency. Yuri Modin, who was in charge of political intelligence training, was a former controller of the Magnificent Five. Ivan Shishkin, head of counter-intelligence, had run Line KR in London from 1966 to 1970. Vladimir Barkovsky, who ran S&T espionage training, had specialized in that field in London from 1941 to 1946.[122]

If the golden age of KGB operations in London had ended with the demise of the Magnificent Five in 1951, the silver age came to an even more abrupt conclusion twenty years later with the defection of Oleg Lyalin and the mass expulsion of 105 KGB and GRU officers.[123] Henceforth MI5 surveillance was no longer swamped by the sheer numbers of Soviet intelligence personnel. Oleg Gordievsky remembers the British operation FOOT as "a bombshell, an earthquake of an expulsion, without precedent, an event that shocked the Centre profoundly."[124] According to Oleg Kalugin, "our intelligence gathering activities in England suffered a blow from which they never recovered."[125] For the remainder of the Cold War the KGB probably found it more difficult to collect high-grade intelligence in London than in almost any other Western capital.

TWENTY-FIVE

COLD WAR OPERATIONS AGAINST BRITAIN

Part 2: After Operation FOOT

Despite Moscow's public expressions of righteous indignation after the expulsion of 105 KGB and GRU officers from London in September 1971, the Centre knew that it had suffered a public relations disaster. The centerpiece of its active measures campaign to turn the tables on British intelligence and discredit the British expulsions was the former rising star of SIS, Kim Philby. Philby, however, was in no fit state to be seen in public. Since the publication of his memoirs in 1968, the KGB seemed to have no further use for him and Philby roamed round Russia on a series of almost suicidal drinking bouts which sometimes left him oblivious of where he was, uncertain whether it was night or day. During the early 1970s he was slowly pulled back from alcoholic oblivion by Rufa, "the woman I had been waiting for all my life."[1]

Though the Centre judged, no doubt correctly, after operation FOOT that Philby was still in no condition to give a press conference, it used a lengthy interview with him in *Izvestia* on October 1, 1971 to denounce the "slanderous allegations" in the "right-wing bourgeois British press" that the Soviet officials expelled from London had been engaged in espionage. In striking contrast with the far more sophisticated tone of Philby's memoirs published three years earlier, the interview regurgitates a series of stereotypical denunciations of British "ruling circles:"

> It should be said that spy mania, the fabrication of slanderous inventions in regard to the Soviet Union, is nothing new in the activities of the ruling circles in England. Definite, concrete political aims are always behind such activities.
>
> This time also, the intensive anti-Soviet provocation and the large scale of the false accusations in regard to Soviet officials in London, as well as the timing of this action, reveal the premeditated character of the activities of the Conservatives who now hold power.
>
> These activities are directed at putting the brakes on the process of lessening tension in Europe.
>
> It is no accident that, as was reflected in the English bourgeois press, government circles showed evident displeasure at, and I should say fear of, the foreign policy of the Soviet Union, which is directed towards normalization of the international situation.

Philby can scarcely have composed these turgid platitudes himself. The probability is that they were simply submitted to him by the KGB for signature. Philby added to them some personal memories of the anti-Soviet "psychological warfare" conducted by British intelligence—though there was a certain irony to his claim that "SIS did not interrupt their subversive operations against the Soviet Union even at the time of the war against Hitler's Germany."[2] In reality, the lack of evidence of anti-Soviet subversion in the wartime SIS reports provided by Philby had led the Centre to suspect him of disinformation.[3] The fact that Philby identified SIS officers, real and alleged, who had been stationed in the Middle East since he had defected from Beirut in 1963 is further evidence that much, if not all, of his interview was scripted for him by the Centre.[4] Among the British intelligence officers in Beirut identified in his interview was the young David Spedding who, a quarter of a century later, became chief of SIS.[5]

So, far from limiting the damage done by the London expulsions, Philby's interview turned into another public relations fiasco. Tass was promptly sued for libel by four prominent Lebanese citizens named in the interview as British agents: Robert Abella, editor-publisher of the Beirut weekly *Al Zaman;* Dori Chamoun, son of former President Camille Chamoun; Emir Farid Chehab, former Lebanese security chief; and Ahmed Isbir, a deputy in the Lebanese parliament.[6] The Soviet ambassador in Beirut sought to distance his government from the law suit by declaring that the whole affair was "purely journalistic" and that "the Soviet Union as a state had no connection with it." He quickly backtracked, however, when the head of the Tass bureau in Beirut, Nikolai Borisovich Filatov, was included in the law suit, claiming that Tass was "a government news agency" and that Filatov was covered by diplomatic immunity.[7] To make matters worse, the Communist lawyer chosen by the embassy to act for Tass was believed by the Centre to be an SIS agent.[8] Before the case came to trial the Beirut residency withdrew Filatov and his family to Moscow.[9] In May 1972 the Tass Lebanese bureau chief, Raymond Saadeh, who was unable to claim diplomatic immunity, was sentenced to two months' imprisonment and ordered to pay damages of 40,000 Lebanese pounds to each of the plaintiffs—a sentence later reduced on appeal to a fine of 1,000 and damages of 10,000 Lebanese pounds each (a total of about 6,000 pounds sterling). Tass was further humiliated by being ordered to report the judgment against it. The story appeared in *The Times* under the headline, "Tass ordered to pay for libel by Mr. Kim Philby."[10]

The miserable sequel to Philby's *Izvestia* interview did little either to persuade Philby that the KGB any longer had a serious use for his talents or to assist in his rehabilitation. When Oleg Kalugin met him for the first time at the beginning of 1972, a month after Philby's marriage to Rufa, he found "a wreck of a man:"

The bent figure caromed off the walls as he walked. Reeking of vodka, he mumbled something unintelligible to me in atrocious, slurred Russian.

Over the next few years Kalugin and other Young Turks within the FCD gradually succeeded in rehabilitating Philby, using him to devise active measures and run seminars for young officers about to be posted to Britain, Ireland, Australasia and Scandinavia. Kryuchkov and the FCD old guard, however, remained suspicious of Philby and refused to allow him into Yasenevo.[11] Philby's lack of status continued to rankle with him. He liked to give Western journalists the impression that he was Colonel—or even General—Philby of the KGB. In reality, he remained agent TOM.

IN THE IMMEDIATE aftermath of the mass expulsions of September 1971, most of the London residency's agents were put on ice. The Centre calculated that the residency would be unlikely to resume normal operations, even on a reduced scale, until mid-1974 at the earliest.[12]

The much reduced number of KGB and GRU officers in London found themselves under considerably tighter surveillance. On September 17, 1971, Abdoolcader, the KGB agent in the GLC motor licensing department, was arrested after a tip-off from Lyalin, who had been his case officer for the previous two years. In his wallet was a postcard addressed to Lyalin, giving the latest registration numbers of MI5 surveillance vehicles. Abdoolcader was jailed for three years.[13]

With the previous resident, Voronin, declared *persona non grata* and known intelligence officers refused British visas, a junior Line KR officer, Yevgeni Ivanovich Lazebny, who had the cover position of security officer at the Soviet trade delegation and had somehow escaped expulsion, was made acting resident. During his fourteen months in charge, Lazebny tried to preserve his cover by keeping his office at the trade delegation and visiting the embassy each day to supervise the work of the residency.[14]

Though out of his depth when it came to running intelligence operations, Lazebny insisted on elaborate and time-consuming security precautions which further complicated the life of the residency. No one was allowed to enter the residency wearing an overcoat for fear that it might be used to conceal material being smuggled in or out. Briefcases, bags and packages were also forbidden, and the shoes of operations officers were X-rayed for bugs or any hidden compartments. All mail and furniture bought or repaired locally were also X-rayed. The embassy administrative officer, M. V. Loshkarov, was disciplined for placing a bulk order at a London store for electric lamps which Lazebny feared might be bugged. Oil cans, batteries, even knots in woodwork, were regularly inspected to make sure they contained no bugs or secret compartments.[15]

At the end of 1972 Lazebny was succeeded as resident by the Latvian Yakov Konstantinovich Lukasevics (alias "Bukashev"),[16] who continued to insist on elaborate security procedures. In 1971–2 the residency received agent reports that MI5 had a source either among the officials of the Soviet trade delegation or among the inspectors of industrial equipment. Though a time-consuming hunt for the traitor continued until 1976, it yielded no result. It was eventually concluded that the agent reports might have been planted by MI5 to distract the residency from its operational priorities. The residency's fears of British penetration had, however, some foundation. An extensive network of bugging devices was discovered at the trade delegation, which contained outposts of both the KGB and GRU residencies.[17]

Following the 1971 expulsions, Cuban and east European intelligence services were asked by the Centre to help plug the intelligence gap in London.[18] The KGB also sought to compensate in some degree for its diminished residency by expanding its agent network among the diplomats and staff of the London embassy. By 1973 nineteen members of the embassy were listed in Centre files as KGB agents, among them the ambassador's deputy, Ivan Ippolitov.[19] Some of the KGB officers who were expelled from, or denied entry to, Britain, were redeployed to Commonwealth capitals with substantial British expatriate communities—notably Delhi, Colombo, Dar-es-Salaam, Lagos and Lusaka.[20] The files seen by Mitrokhin record few major recruitments of British agents by the redeployed officers. In 1974, however, three operations officers in an east African residency—S. S. Sarmanov, G. M. Yermolev and N. T. Krestnikov—were given awards for recruiting a British journalist, TOM, and his wife IRENE. TOM and IRENE, however, proved of limited usefulness. Early in 1976 TOM moved to Asia and was briefly used to report on other Western residents. He failed, however, to gain access to any classified information and in April 1976 Kryuchkov decided to break operational contact with him.[21]

THE FIRST SECTION of the London residency to resume something like normal operations after the 1971 expulsions, albeit slowly and on a reduced scale, was Line X (S&T). During 1972 plans were made to renew contact with six of its most highly rated agents: the veteran Melita Norwood (HOLA) in the British Non-Ferrous Metals Association, first recruited in 1937; ACE, an aeronautical engineer; HUNT, a civil servant recruited by Norwood; YUNG, an aeronautics and computer engineer; NAGIN, a chemical engineer; and STEP, a laboratory assistant.[22] Though Mitrokhin's notes give only an incomplete account of how the six agents were reactivated, it is clear that it was a lengthy business, probably preceded by prolonged and painstaking surveillance to ensure that none was under MI5 observation. Contact with HUNT was not re-established until 1975, and even then it was thought safer to use a French agent, MAIRE, rather than an operations officer from the London residency, as his controller.[23]

When contact was renewed with Melita Norwood in London in 1974, it was discovered that she had retired two years earlier. Since she no longer had access to classified material, regular contact was discontinued. HOLA, however, retained a high reputation in the Centre as probably its longest-serving British agent with a highly productive record which included intelligence on the British nuclear program. She seems to have remained throughout her career a true believer in the Soviet Union. During a visit to Moscow with her husband in 1979, forty-two years after her original recruitment, she was offered a further financial reward but declined, saying she had all she needed to live on.[24]

By 1974 Line X at the London residency had nine operations officers (seven fewer than before operation FOOT), headed by the deputy resident, Oleg Aleksandrovich Yakimov, and had successfully resumed contact with most of the Line X agents put on ice in September 1971.[25] The most productive of the reactivated agents was, almost certainly, the aeronautical engineer ACE, recruited in the late 1960s.[26] By the time he died in the early 1980s, ACE's product file consisted of about 300 volumes, each of about 300 pages. Most of these 90,000 pages consisted of technical documentation on new aircraft (among them Concorde, the Super VC-10 and Lockheed L-1011), aero-engines (including Rolls-Royce, Olympus-593, RB-211 and SNEY-505) and flight simulators. ACE's material on the flight simulators for the Lockheed L-1011 and Boeing 747 were the foundation for a new generation of Soviet equivalents. ACE also recruited under false flag (probably that of a rival company) an aeroengine specialist codenamed SWEDE. Remarkably, ACE was paid a monthly salary of only 225 pounds, raised to 350 pounds in 1980.[27]

Despite the exclusion from Britain of known KGB and GRU officers, the KGB was still able to send Line X agents and "trusted contacts" from Soviet universities to Britain on scientific exchanges and for postgraduate or postdoctoral research in engineering and the natural sciences. Most went either to universities and polytechnics in the London area or to Oxford and Cambridge.[28] "Targets of operational interest," where it was hoped that KGB agents and trusted contacts could identify potential recruits, included Churchill College, King's College, St. Catharine's College and Trinity Hall at Cambridge University; Magdalen, Queen's and Trinity Colleges at Oxford; King's College, University College, the London School of Economics, the School of Oriental and African Studies and the School of Slavonic Studies at London University.[29]

Some of the Soviet scientists who came to conduct research in Britain were KGB officers. In May 1975, for example, Dr. Hugh Huxley of the British Medical Research Council's molecular biology laboratory at Cambridge invited Academician Frank, director of the USSR Academy of Sciences Biophysics Institute, to send a member of his institute to carry out research at the laboratory. Unknown to Huxley, the invitation was misappropriated by the KGB. The scientist sent to Cambridge was Valeri Vasilyevich Lednev of Directorate T.[30] At about the time Lednev embarked on his British assignment, the head of Directorate T, Mikhail Lopatin, who had been in charge of S&T collection in Britain in the mid-1960s, arrived in London to advise the residency on the expansion of Line X operations.[31]

Though not comprehensive, Mitrokhin's notes suggest that there were fewer new British Line X recruits during the 1970s than in the decade before operation FOOT. The earliest post-FOOT recruit definitely identified by Mitrokhin is CHRISTINA, who was recruited in 1973—probably in the Soviet Union.[32] It is unclear from Mitrokhin's notes whether four other Line X agents operating in Britain in the early 1970s were recruited before or after the mass expulsion of KGB and GRU officers.[33] Because of the difficult operating conditions in London, at least six (probably more) Line X agents either met their case officers outside Britain or were controlled by other European residencies.[34]

The most important British S&T agent recruited during the decade after operation FOOT was, almost certainly, Michael John Smith (codenamed BORG), a Communist electronics engineer.[35] The secretary of the Surrey Communist Party in the early 1970s, Richard Geldart, recalls Smith as an "out-and-out Tankie"—a hardline supporter of the crushing of the Prague Spring by Soviet tanks: "Not to put too fine a point on it, he was the total nerd. There was socializing going on, but he was not part of it."[36] A Line X officer at the London residency, Viktor Alekseevich Oshchenko (codenamed OZEROV), made initial contact with Smith in a pub near Smith's flat at Kingston-on-Thames after a trade union meeting held in May 1975 before the referendum on British membership of the EEC. On instructions from Oshchenko, Smith left the Communist Party, ceased trade union activity, became a regular reader of the *Daily Telegraph,* joined a local tennis club and—as his operational file quaintly puts it—"endeavored to display his loyalty to the authorities."

In July 1976, helped by bureaucratic confusion in MI5, caused by the remarkable coincidence that the Surrey Communist Party contained another Michael John Smith, he gained a job as a test engineer in the quality assurance department of Thorn—EMI Defense Electronics at Feltham, Middlesex. Within a year he was working on the top secret project XN-715, developing and testing radar fuses for Britain's freefall nuclear bomb.[37] The KGB passed the documents on project XN-715 provided by Smith to N. V. Serebrov and other nuclear weapons specialists at a secret Soviet military research institute codenamed Enterprise G-4598, who succeeded in building a replica of the British radar fuse. Smith's intelligence, however, seemed too good to be true. Serebrov and his colleagues were puzzled as to how Smith had been able to obtain the radio frequency on which the detonator was to operate. This information, they believed, was so sensitive that it should not have appeared even in the top secret documents on the design and operation of the detonator to which Smith had access. Armed with a knowledge of the radio frequency, Soviet forces would be able to create radio interference which could prevent the detonator from operating. One possibility which occurred to the specialists was that the frequency supplied by Smith *might* be merely a test frequency which would not be used in actual military operations. But they remained suspicious of the extent of the detailed highly classified information which Smith had been able to supply.[38]

The Centre also seems to have been suspicious of the ease and speed with which a well-known pro-Soviet Communist had been able to gain access to one of Britain's most highly classified nuclear secrets so soon after going through the motions of leaving the Party and switching from the *Morning Star* to the *Daily Telegraph.* Its suspicions that Smith's intelligence on the radar fuse might have been a sophisticated deception seem to have strengthened when he told his controller in 1978 that he had lost his security clearance and, for the time being, could no longer provide classified information. (Though Smith did not realize it at the time, MI5 had discovered its earlier error and secretly informed Thorn—EMI of Smith's Communist past.)[39]

To try to resolve its doubts the Centre devised a series of tests to check Smith's reliability. The first test, which Smith seems to have passed, was to remove two packets of secret material from a dead letter-box in Spain. The second, more elaborate check on Smith, personally approved by Andropov and termed in KGB jargon "a psycho-physiological test using a non-contact polygraph," was conducted in Vienna in August 1979 by Boris Konstantinovich Stalnov and two OT (operational—technical support) officers. Stalnov began with a brief prepared speech, duly entered in Smith's file:

I am personally satisfied with the way things are going and with our mutual relations and I am therefore extremely glad to congratulate you. From today you are a full member of our organization. This means that the organization will take care of you. Believe me, you will have gained friends who are ready to come to your help in any circumstances. Your participation and help to the organization will be duly recognized. The organization is based on two principles: voluntary participation and sincerity.

The first means that, having joined the organization of your own free will, you may leave it at any time if you think it necessary, without any [adverse] consequences for yourself, provided you give prior notice.

As for the second principle, sincerity, you must inform us of all details which directly or indirectly affect the interests of our organization. This is understandable as the security of both sides depends on it. Joining the organization is also in a certain sense a formal act. In connection with this I am required to put a number of questions to you. I regard this as a pure formality. You should do the same.

It will simplify the task and save time if you simply answer "yes" or "no."

Smith was then asked over 120 questions and his replies secretly recorded. Subsequent analysis of the recording and Smith's response to each question persuaded the Centre—doubtless to its immense relief—that he was not, as it had thought possible, engaged in a grand deception orchestrated by British intelligence. Though Smith had been led to suppose that the "psycho-physiological test" was a routine formality, it had never been used before by the KGB outside the Soviet Union. The Centre was so pleased with its success that it decided to use the same method to check other agents. It none the less decided to give Smith a third (and apparently final) test of his "sincerity" by instructing him to remove a container holding two rolls of film from a DLB in the Paris suburbs and to deliver it to a KGB officer in Lisbon.[40] The KGB would doubtless have been able to detect any attempt by Smith or another intelligence agency to open the container.

From 1979 onward Smith was paid a 300-pound monthly retainer by the KGB. His file also records additional payments for documents supplied by him of 1,600 pounds, 750 pounds, 400 pounds and 2,000 pounds. Though Mitrokhin's notes do not record the dates of these payments, they probably relate chiefly to Smith's two years in Thorn—EMI Defense Electronics.[41] The excitement of working for the KGB, copying highly classified documents, emptying DLBs and going to secret assignations with his case officers in foreign capitals seems to have rescued Smith from his earlier existence as a "total nerd." A hint of the exotic began to enliven a previously drab lifestyle. In 1979 he got married, took up flamenco dancing, began experimenting with Spanish and Mexican cuisine, and gave dinner parties at which guests were served his homemade wine.[42]

Smith was so taken with his life as a secret agent that he made strenuous efforts to recover the security clearance he had lost in 1978, even drafting a personal appeal two years later to Margaret Thatcher to intercede on his behalf. "There is a cloud over me which I cannot dispel," he complained to the Prime Minister. "I have been wrongly suspected and have lost my position most unjustly." Though Smith seems never to have posted his letter to Mrs. Thatcher, in June 1980 he succeeded in putting his case to an MI5 officer. Smith began by denying that he had ever been a Communist, was confronted with evidence that he had, then apologized for lying and said he had joined the Party only to find a girlfriend.[43] Amazingly, Smith's campaign to recover his security clearance survived even this setback. More amazingly still, a few years later it succeeded.[44]

In 1980 7.5 percent of all Soviet scientific and technological intelligence came from British sources.[45] As well as providing what it claimed was enormous assistance to Soviet research and development, especially in the military field, Directorate T also prided itself on obtaining commercial secrets which drove down the cost of contracts with Western companies. One British example of which it was particularly proud during the later 1970s was the negotiation of the contract for two large methane production plants with the companies Davy Power Gas and Klickner INA Industrial Plants.[46] The original price quoted by the British consortium was 248 million convertible roubles, as compared with the 206 million allocated for the project by the Soviet Council of Ministers. An operation conducted in the Peking Hotel, Moscow, on March 23, 1977 by Directorate T with the assistance of the Moscow KGB, probably based on a combination of eavesdropping and the secret photocopying of company documents, obtained commercial intelligence which—according to a report by the Ministry of Foreign Trade—made it possible to negotiate a reduction of 50.6 million roubles on the price of the contract. On October 24, 1977 Andropov formally commended fifteen KGB officers for their part in the operation. Ironically, the British prime minister, James Callaghan, subsequently wrote to his Soviet opposite number, Alexei Kosygin, to thank the Soviet government for awarding the contract to a British firm.[47]

THE PR AND KR Lines at the London residency appear to have had less success during the 1970s than Line X. The only known Soviet agent within the British intelligence community, Geoffrey Prime of GCHQ, was run not by the residency but by Third Directorate controllers who met him outside Britain.[48] The most highly placed Line PR agent active during the decade after operation FOOT identified in Mitrokhin's notes was WILLIAM, a trade union official and former Communist. WILLIAM was recruited during a visit to the Soviet Union by Boris Vasilyevich Denisov, a KGB officer working under cover as a Soviet trade union (AUCCTU) official, and agreed to provide inside information on the TUC and the Labor Party. After a meeting with WILLIAM in London in December 1975, however, his case officer reported that he had become anxious about his role as a Soviet agent. Though reaffirming his desire to help his Soviet comrades, WILLIAM said that he was distrusted by less progressive trade union officials because of his Marxist views and worried that word of his Soviet connection would leak out and damage his chances of becoming leader of his union.[49] Lacking any really important British agents, Line PR tended to exaggerate the significance of second-rate agents such as WILLIAM and its other sources of inside information on British politics and government policy.

The political contact of which Line PR was proudest was Harold Wilson (code-named OLDING), who became honorary president of the Great Britain—USSR Association after his resignation as prime minister in 1976. The first secretary at the Soviet embassy responsible for liaison with the association, Andrei Sergeyevich Parastayev, periodically called on Wilson, nominally to discuss its affairs with him. The fact that Parastayev was a KGB agent allowed the residency to claim that it had secured access to the former prime minister. Though not claiming that Wilson was a "confidential contact" (let alone an agent), the residency reported that he freely provided political information.[50] Mitrokhin's notes give no examples of what the information comprised, but if Wilson's observations to Parastayev resembled his private comments to some of his British friends and acquaintances, they would certainly have attracted the attention of the Centre and probably have been passed to the Politburo. Roy Jenkins noted in 1978, for example, that Wilson "did not think there was much future for the [Callaghan] Government, or indeed the Labor Party."[51]

The Centre claimed that disinformation from Service A had been passed to Wilson, probably via Parastayev, with the intention that it should reach the Labor government.[52] It is highly unlikely, however, that the disinformation had any significant influence on Wilson, let alone on the Callaghan government. In retirement, though remaining firmly anchored in the Labor Party, Wilson moved steadily to the right. According to his official biographer, Philip Ziegler, by 1977 his dislike of the far left equaled that of "the most conservative of capitalists."[53] Nor did Wilson show great sympathy for Soviet foreign policy. His KGB file reports that, after the invasion of Afghanistan, he canceled a visit to the USSR and refused to hold any further meetings of the Great Britain—USSR Association.[54]

By the 1970s Line PR in London, as in other residencies, was supposed to spend 25 percent of its time on active measures[55] and send annual statistics to the Centre on the number of its influence operations. These totaled 160 in 1976 and 190 in 1977.[56] During 1977 Line PR officers reported that they had initiated 99 discussions which allegedly "influenced" politicians, journalists and other opinion-formers, and claimed to have successfully prompted 26 public announcements, 20 publications, the sending of more than 20 letters and telegrams, 9 questions in Parliament, 5 press conferences, 4 meetings and demonstrations and 3 television and radio broadcasts. In addition, it had distributed three brochures and one forged document produced by Service A, which was responsible for active measures at the Centre.[57]

In order to gain credit from the Centre, residencies invariably tried to exaggerate the success of their active measures. While working at the Centre, Oleg Gordievsky was told that in 1977 or 1978 the London resident, Yakov Lukasevics, had been asked by Andropov whether his residency possessed the means to influence British policy. "Why yes, we can exert influence," Lukasevics replied. "We have such channels." "I do not think you can," Andropov told him. "I think you are too hasty in answering that question."[58] The files noted by Mitrokhin confirm Andropov's skepticism.

The KGB's attempts to recruit agents of influence in the British media to use for active measures seems to have met with limited success by comparison with France and some other European countries. The journalist DAN, probably the London residency's most reliable agent of influence during the 1960s,[59] broke contact during the 1970s—probably after he was put on ice in the aftermath of operation FOOT. Several attempts by the residency to reactivate DAN failed and he was eventually written off some time in the early 1980s.[60]

Probably the most ambitious scheme devised by the London residency during the 1970s for the recruitment of a prominent agent of influence was targeted on Dr. Mervyn Stockwood, the socialist Bishop of Southwark.[61] In October 1975 Stockwood delivered a public protest against a "Call to the Nation," jointly issued by Archbishop Donald Coggan of Canterbury and Archbishop Stuart Blanch of York, claiming that it put too much emphasis on the need for individual responsibility and too little on the social injustices which caused so much human misery. The most remarkable feature of Stockwood's protest, however, was that he chose to make it in the pages of the Communist *Morning Star*, and that he included in it an extraordinary tribute to the Soviet Bloc:

> Those of us who have visited Socialist counties in Europe know that if a Communist government were to be established in Britain the West End would be cleared up overnight, and the ugly features of our permissive society would be changed within a matter of days. And heaven help the porn merchants and all engaged in the making of fortunes through the commercial exploitation of sex.[62]

Sixteen Labor MPs signed a motion "marveling at the innocence" of Stockwood's understanding of Communist regimes. Another fifty backbenchers supported a motion supporting the archbishops against his criticisms. One told the *Guardian*, "The Marxists seem now to have penetrated the higher echelons of the established Church."[63] The Soviet embassy, possibly on the initiative of the residency, established what a KGB file describes as "close contact" with Stockwood.

Hopes in the residency of the bishop's potential for active measures reached their peak when he arranged a dinner party with Gordon McLennan, general secretary of the British Communist Party, as guest of honor, to which, apparently, at least one Soviet official (who, unknown to Stockwood, was a KGB officer) was also invited.[64] Though Mitrokhin's note on the dinner is tantalizingly brief, it seems to have been a boisterous evening. Stockwood frequently drank heavily at dinner parties to the extent that his friend Princess Margaret sometimes feared for the furniture at Kensington Palace.[65] Over dinner Stockwood asked McLennan what the Communist Party thought about the Church of England. McLennan replied that the Church was a "moral force in society," but regretted that, "Unlike before and during the War, we do not see members of the clergy at progressive meetings and demonstrations." Stockwood retorted, "We also don't see you at demonstrations at the Soviet embassy!"[66] The residency seems to have concluded reluctantly that the Bishop's tendency to launch into criticisms of the Soviet Union rendered him unsuitable for active measures.

THE EXAMPLES OF active measures noted by Mitrokhin suggest that the residency, in its reports to the Centre, sought to inflate a series of mostly modest successes. A characteristic example was its attempt to claim the credit for an article in the *Guardian* by Richard Gott (codenamed RON) attacking the role of the CIA in the overthrow and death of the Marxist president of Chile, Salvador Allende, in 1973, and denouncing the military junta of General Augusto Pinochet which had seized power.[67] Gott later denied reports that he had been a KGB agent, but acknowledged that after the Chilean coup he had been contacted by Yuri Mikhailovich Solonitsyn (who he later realized was a KGB officer) and had "quite a sort of interesting session" with him on Chile, as well as a series of subsequent meetings with both Solonitsyn and Gennadi Federovich Titov, later number Three in the KGB hierarchy.[68] While the details of Gott's articles may sometimes have been influenced by "interesting sessions" with Solonitsyn and Titov, his support for revolutionary movements in Latin America and loathing for American "imperialism" were so well established that he would have required little encouragement from the KGB to denounce either Pinochet or the CIA.[69]

The London residency was equally prone to exaggerate its influence in the House of Commons. It tried to take the credit, for example, for the following parliamentary question put by the Labor MP James Lamond to Fred Mulley, Secretary of State for Defense in the Callaghan government, on February 21, 1978:

> Does my right honorable friend agree that to deploy the neutron bomb in western Europe must lower the threshold of nuclear war? Does he accept that President Brezhnev was in earnest when he said in the Kremlin [*Conservative shouts of* "Were you there?"] that the Soviet Union would develop similar weapons at enormous cost, if the neutron bomb were placed in western Europe? That would be a cost that neither the Warsaw Pact nor NATO could afford and would serve only unnecessarily to increase the enormous arms expenditure of the world.[70]

There is absolutely no evidence that James Lamond had any conscious link with the KGB. He was, however, vice-president of the World Peace Council (WPC) and appears not to have realized that this was the leading Soviet front organization, devoted to pinning all the blame for the nuclear arms race on Western warmongering.[71] Lamond's parliamentary question, which received a noncommittal reply, derived from a much larger WPC campaign against the neutron bomb rather than from a brilliant initiative by the London residency.

The Centre usually responded relatively uncritically to exaggerated claims by residencies of the success of their active measures. It suited the Centre as much as the London residency to be able to inform the Politburo that it was able to inspire questions in the House of Commons and articles in the *Guardian*.

Despite Line PR's attempts to inflate the importance of its active measures, it also had some undoubted successes. The *Observer* and the *New Statesman* were among a number of British print media taken in during the early 1980s by forged anti-American and anti-South African documents fabricated by Service A.[72] The *Observer* printed a bogus memorandum from the Zaire security council under the headline, "US and S. Africa in Angola Plot."[73] The *New Statesman* published a forged letter from South African military intelligence to Jeane Kirkpatrick, US ambassador to the UN, conveying its "gratitude" and referring to a birthday present sent to her "as a token of appreciation."[74] As late as 1986, the conservative *Sunday Express* based its main front page story on reports (also concocted by Service A) that the AIDS virus had originally been developed as part of an American biological warfare program.[75] Claims that KGB active measures had succeeded in producing significant shifts in British opinion, however, were based on little more than wishful thinking.

The KGB's shortage of major agents in the British media helps to explain why it chose a Danish rather than a British journalist, Arne Herløv Petersen (codenamed KHARLEV and PALLE) for its first major active measure against Margaret Thatcher after she became prime minister in 1979. Originally a confidential contact of the Copenhagen residency, Petersen had been invited to Moscow in the mid-1970s to "deepen the relationship."[76] Thereafter he was regularly used as an agent of influence not merely to write articles along lines suggested by his case officers but to publish, also under his own name, articles and pamphlets written in English by Service A. The first of the KGB/Petersen co-productions attacking Thatcher was a 1979 pamphlet, entitled *Cold Warriors*, which gave her pride of place as Europe's leading anti-Soviet crusader. The next Petersen pamphlet ghostwritten by Service A, *True Blues*, published in 1980, was solely devoted to an onslaught on Thatcher. It made the mistake of attempting satire—a weak area of the KGB's usually heavy-handed active measures—and carried the feeble subtitle "The Thatcher that Couldn't Mend her own Roof." The Service A author had an even feebler grasp of English geography, believing Mrs. Thatcher's birthplace of Grantham in Lincolnshire to be "in the suburbs of London." Though the Centre appears to have been curiously proud of them, both pamphlets (probably intended chiefly for mailing to British "opinion-formers") had negligible influence.[77]

THOUGH MITROKHIN HAD unrestricted access to FCD files, their sheer volume meant that his notes on them are bound to contain significant gaps. The possibility thus remains that the KGB had important Cold War British sources not identified by him. It is unlikely, however, that there were many of them. Oleg Gordievsky has confirmed that during his posting to the London residency from 1982 to 1985, which included two years as head of Line PR and a few months as resident-designate, Line PR and, probably, Line KR were running no British agents of major importance.[78] There remains the possibility of British agents recruited and run by residencies and illegals outside the United Kingdom[79]—a list by Mitrokhin of KGB agents, contacts and "developmentals" (targets under cultivation) includes a tantalizing one-line reference to a British agent run from Karlshorst whose operational file in 1981 ran to fifteen volumes.[80]

The most remarkable British agent identified by Mitrokhin outside the field of S&T to have been recruited after operation FOOT was also run by Line KR outside the United Kingdom. Given the codename SCOT, he was a bent London copper: Detective Sergeant John Symonds of the Metropolitan Police, who became probably the most peripatetic of all the KGB's British agents.[81] The London residency, however, was able to claim no credit for his recruitment.

On November 29, 1969, the day that *The Times* published photographs of the footprints on the moon of Apollo 12 astronauts, it also carried a front page story headlined "London Policeman in Bribe Allegations. Tapes Reveal Planted Evidence." Conversations secretly recorded by two undercover *Times* reporters were said to prove that Symonds and at least two other detectives were "taking large sums of money in exchange for dropping charges, for being lenient with evidence in court, and for allowing a criminal to work unhindered." Symonds, then aged thirty-three, admitted to the reporters that he was a member of what he called "a little firm in a firm"—corrupt detectives in the pay of criminals such as south London gang boss Charlie Richardson.[82]

While awaiting trial at the Old Bailey in 1972, Symonds went into hiding for several months, then fled abroad. His KGB file reveals that he used a passport obtained in the name of his girlfriend's mentally handicapped brother, John Frederick Freeman, and had his passport photograph authenticated as that of Freeman by the mistress of a member of the Richardson gang. In his absence, the two other corrupt policemen identified by *The Times* were sentenced to six and seven years' imprisonment. In August 1972 Symonds entered the Soviet embassy in Rabat, told his story, said that his money was running out and offered his services to the KGB.[83] To be certain that his story attracted the Centre's attention, he gave the name of a Special Branch officer guarding the defector Oleg Lyalin, and alleged that he was probably corruptible. Symonds also made the dramatic claim that Denis Healey, the Secretary of State for Defense, regularly bribed Chief Superintendent Bill Moody of the Met "to smooth over certain unpleasantness."[84] Though Moody was later convicted of accepting huge bribes from the underworld and sentenced to twelve years' imprisonment, the allegation that Healey was involved in the bribery was wholly fraudulent. The Centre, however, took Symonds's tall story at its improbable face value.[85]

Symonds spent the next eight years as a KGB agent. Noting that he was "of attractive appearance," the Centre decided to use him as its first British "Romeo spy," using seduction and romance, rather than the traditional cruder KGB techniques of sexual compromise and blackmail, to recruit or obtain classified information from a series of female officials. In 1973 Symonds was posted to Bulgaria in order to cultivate suitable targets at Black Sea resorts popular with Western tourists. Symonds's most important sexual conquest was the wife of an official in an FRG government ministry. Over the next few years he paid a number of visits to Bonn to continue the affair. Intelligence from Symonds's German girlfriend in 1975 was considered so important by the Centre that it was made the subject of a personal report to Andropov.[86]

Symonds was used by the KGB to attempt the seduction of female officials, mostly Western embassy staff, on four continents. His next assignment, after beginning his affair with the woman from Bonn, was to target women at American and

British missions in Africa during the latter part of 1973. At the end of the year, however, he fell ill in Tanzania with what his KGB file describes as "tropical fever," and had to travel to Moscow for medical treatment. As soon as he had recovered, Symonds was ordered to cultivate a member of the British embassy staff in Moscow, codenamed VERA, who had been observed going for long solitary walks in her spare time. Posing as Jean-Jacques Baudouin, a Canadian businessman attending the 1974 International Polymer Exhibition in Moscow, Symonds succeeded in staging an apparently chance encounter with VERA and striking up a friendship with her. Though Symonds's file claims that VERA became "attached" to him and gave him details of her next posting as well as her home address in Britain, there is no indication that she passed on to him any more than unimportant personal gossip about some of her colleagues and superiors in Moscow and London. The Centre, however, considered her a potentially valuable source for identifying other, more vulnerable female targets in the British embassy.[87]

In 1976, on KGB instructions, Symonds set out on a long journey which took him from Bulgaria through Africa and India to south-east Asia. In India he cultivated an English woman (codenamed JILL), an Israeli and at least five American women. In 1977, however, while in Singapore pursuing a secretary at a Western diplomatic mission who had been identified as a target for cultivation by the local KGB residency, Symonds believed that he had come under surveillance, took a flight to Athens and returned to Bulgaria. An assessment by Directorate K of Symonds's work over the previous five years concluded that he had shown no sign of dishonesty in his dealings with the KGB, had obtained material "of significant operational interest" and—but for the fact that his existing travel documents had aroused the suspicion of Western security services—still had considerable potential as a KGB agent. At the request of Kalugin, the head of Directorate K, Kryuchkov instructed the Illegals Directorate to give Symonds a new identity.[88]

The identity chosen for Symonds was that of a "dead double," Raymond Francis Everett (codenamed FORST), an Australian who had died in childhood during the Second World War.[89] On July 23, 1978 Symonds flew from Moscow to Tokyo *en route* to Australasia, carrying a forged British passport in the name of Everett, a genuine birth certificate in the same name and 8,000 US dollars. Once in Australia Symonds was to abandon the British passport and use the birth certificate to obtain an Australian passport in the name of the dead double. Symonds began by spending several months in New Zealand developing his legend so that, once in Australia, he could pose as an Australian who had spent some years in New Zealand.[90]

In November 1978 SCOT traveled to Australia with a group of rugby supporters and began to cultivate Margaret, the manageress of a small travel agency, in the hope that she would provide the necessary reference for his passport application. Symonds's cynical report on Margaret was probably typical of the way he had sized up the previous women he had been instructed to seduce. Margaret, he claimed, was tall, thin, plain, round-shouldered, had hair on her upper lip and was bound to be flattered by his attentions. Symonds pursued her with flowers, chocolates, presents and invitations to dinner. Unfortunately for Symonds, Margaret was honest as well as unattractive. When he asked her to act as a referee, she refused on the grounds that the law required her to have known him for at least a year. By now Symonds's money had almost run out. Arrangements for him to receive more money via the Canberra residency broke down and his landlord locked him out when he failed to pay the rent. A female schoolteacher whom he persuaded to put him up also threw him out after a fortnight. At one point Symonds was reduced to spending several nights in a Salvation Army hostel. Eventually, with the help of a French bank in Sydney, he was able to withdraw 5,000 US dollars from a bank account he had opened in the name of Freeman (his first alias) in Senegal.[91]

Early in 1979, using a reference he had forged himself, Symonds at last succeeded in obtaining an Australian passport in the name of his dead double, Raymond Everett. Soon afterward, he caught a flight to Rome, from where he traveled to Vienna by train to meet his KGB controller. By now, however, Symonds had become seriously confused by the complications of acquiring a new Australian identity. Unwilling to risk using his new Australian passport, he strapped it to his leg beneath his sock and traveled instead on the bogus British passport he had come to Australia to replace. Once in Vienna, he handed over the new passport to his controller, then returned to Moscow via Belgrade.[92]

After his return to Moscow, Andropov, Kryuchkov and Grigori Fyodorovich Grigorenko (head of the Second Chief Directorate) jointly approved a plan for Symonds to cultivate a secretary at the British embassy, posing once again as a Canadian businessman. His target on this occasion was ERICA, a friend of his earlier target VERA, whom he had first met five years earlier. The operation failed—partly, perhaps, because of Symonds's increasingly run-down appearance. Symonds's file records that "his physical characteristics did not appeal to ERICA."[93]

The failed cultivation of ERICA appears to have been Symonds's last operation as a Romeo agent. His file notes that, since his return from Australia, he had become more and more difficult to handle and resentful of what he claimed was the KGB's lack of trust and interest in him. A medical report on Symonds prepared without his knowledge concluded that he was emotionally unstable, suffering from a psychological disorder and had become hypersensitive and inconsistent in his judgments. In 1980 Symonds left Moscow for Sofia, intending to marry his current girlfriend, "Nellie," an agent of the Bulgarian intelligence service. The couple, however, soon fell out and Symonds requested permission to leave for western Europe. Before the Centre had replied to his request, Symonds succeeded in making his own way to Vienna and thence to Britain.[94] In April 1980, accompanied by his solicitor, he surrendered himself to the Central Criminal Court, which had issued a warrant for his arrest for corruption eight years earlier.[95]

The Centre's main fear after Symonds's return was that he might reveal his career as a KGB agent. Should he do so, it was decided to dismiss his revelations as fantasy. The Bulgarian medical authorities were asked to prepare a certificate stating that he was mentally deranged.[96] The certificate, however, was not needed. At his trial, in which he conducted his own defense, former Detective Sergeant Symonds made no reference to his Soviet connection, which remained completely unknown to the prosecution. Instead, he claimed that he had spent eight years on the run from crooked senior detectives who had threatened to kill him if he gave evidence in court. Symonds was sentenced to two years' imprisonment on three charges of corruptly obtaining a total of 150 pounds from a London criminal. The prosecution offered no evidence on five further counts of corruption. Symonds was indignant at the verdict. "I decided to return, hoping to have a fair trial," he told the court. "I have not had a fair trial and that is all I have to say."[97]

AT ALMOST THE moment that Symonds returned to England in 1980 to face trial, Lukasevics left for Moscow at the end of his eight-year term as London resident. The Centre, unimpressed by his performance, concluded that he had made inadequate progress in rebuilding the residency's agent network after the 1971 expulsions and banished him to his native Latvia.[98] Lukasevics's successor, the heavy-drinking Arkadi Vasilyevich Guk (codenamed YERMAKOV), is remembered by Oleg Gordievsky, who served under him, as "a huge, bloated lump of a man, with a mediocre brain but a large reserve of low cunning." He owed his overpromotion to London resident largely to the British policy of refusing visas to known, and more able, Soviet intelligence officers. Guk's naturally suspicious mind gave rise to a number of conspiracy theories: among them the conviction that many of the advertisement hoardings on the London Underground concealed secret look-out posts from which MI5 kept watch for KGB officers and other suspicious travelers.[99]

During Guk's first year as resident, a series of operations officers were sent home in disgrace. In 1980 Yuri Sergeyevich Myakov (codenamed MOROZOV), who had been posted to London three years earlier, was recalled for an allegedly serious breach of security: showing KGB material to the GRU residency without first gaining Guk's approval.[100] In 1981 Guk also insisted on the recall of Aleksandr Vladimirovich Lopukhin, an operations officer working in London under cover as correspondent for *Komsomolskaya Pravda* since 1979, whom he denounced for unsatisfactory performance, keeping himself apart from Soviet colleagues and preferring a Western lifestyle.[101] Also in 1981 the head of Line N (Illegals Support), Anatoli Alekseyevich Zamuruyev (codenamed ZIMIN), who had occupied a cover position in the secretariat of the Cocoa Organization since 1977, was declared to be mentally ill and sent back to Moscow.[102]

When Oleg Gordievsky arrived in London as a Line PR officer in the summer of 1982, he found the residency a "hotbed of intrigue." For the previous eight years he had been SIS's most important penetration agent inside the KGB. His presence in London eventually compromised almost all residency operations. In 1983 Gordievsky was promoted to head of Line PR and deputy resident. On being appointed resident-designate in January 1985, he was able to fill in most of the remaining gaps in his knowledge of the KGB's British operations.

Among the intelligence passed by Gordievsky to MI5 was information on the attempt by one of its own officers, Michael Bettaney, a disaffected alcoholic in the counter-espionage directorate, to volunteer as a Soviet agent. On Easter Sunday 1983 Bettaney put through Guk's letter-box in Holland Park an envelope containing the case put by MI5 for expelling three Soviet intelligence officers in the previous month, together with details of how all three had been detected. Bettaney offered to provide further information and gave instructions on how to contact him. Guk thus found himself presented with the first opportunity for a quarter of a century to recruit an MI5 or SIS officer. His addiction to conspiracy theory, however, persuaded him to look the gift horse in the mouth. The whole affair, he suspected, was a British provocation. The head of Line KR, Leonid Yefremovich Nikitenko, who was reluctant to disagree with the irascible Guk, concurred. Gordievsky said little but informed SIS.

In June and July, Bettaney stuffed two further packets of classified information from Security Service files through Guk's door, unwittingly providing what Guk believed was clinching evidence of an MI5 provocation. Understandably despairing of Guk, Bettaney decided to try his luck with the KGB in Vienna instead. He was arrested on September 16, a few days before he planned to fly out. Guk's reputation never recovered. Shortly after Bettaney was sentenced to twenty-three years' imprisonment the following spring, Guk himself was declared *persona non grata* by the British authorities.[103]

Guk's four, somewhat incompetent years as London resident included the most dangerous phase of operation RYAN. The whole of Line PR in London were skeptical about the Centre's fear that NATO was making plans for a nuclear first strike against the Soviet Union. None, however, were willing to risk their careers by challenging the alarmist assumptions on which RYAN was based. As a result, the residency's chief priority from 1981 until at least the early months of 1984 was the preparation of fortnightly reports on its search for non-existent evidence of NATO preparations for nuclear aggression. The Centre's alarmism reached its peak in November 1983 during the NATO exercise ABLE ARCHER, which it feared might be used to begin the countdown to a first strike. In his annual review of the work of the London residency at the end of 1983, Guk was forced to admit "shortcomings" in obtaining intelligence on "specific American and NATO plans for the preparation of surprise nuclear missile attack against the USSR." During the early months of 1984, helped by reassuring signals from London and Washington, the mood in Moscow gradually lightened. In March Nikolai Vladimirovich Shishlin, a senior foreign affairs specialist in the Central Committee (and later an adviser to Gorbachev), addressed the staff of the London embassy and KGB residency on current international problems. He made no mention of the threat of surprise nuclear attack. The bureaucratic momentum of operation RYAN, however, took some time to wind down. When the London residency grew lax in the early summer of 1984 about sending its pointless fortnightly reports, it received a reprimand from the Centre telling it to adhere "strictly" to the original RYAN directive.[104]

Like his predecessor, Lukasevics, Guk tried to compensate for his residency's failings by exaggerating the success of its active measures. In particular, he sought to take some of the credit for the resurgence of the British peace movement caused by the intensification of the Cold War in the early 1980s. Twenty years earlier, the KGB had been suspicious of the British peace movement, fearing that it might detract from the authority of the World Peace Council.[105] During Guk's years as resident, however, most sections of the peace movement spent more time campaigning against American than against Soviet nuclear weapons. In July 1982 Guk briefed the newly arrived embassy counselor, Lev Parshin, about a mass demonstration in London against the deployment of US cruise missiles. Although a few KGB agents and contacts joined the march, the demonstration had been wholly organized by the Campaign for Nuclear Disarmament (CND) without any assistance from the residency. Guk, however, assured Parshin, "It was us, the KGB residency, who brought a quarter of a million people out on to the streets!"[106]

The main authentic successes of the London residency during Guk's four years in London were, as during the previous two decades, in scientific and technological intelligence gathering. Between 1980 and 1983 Gennadi Fyodorovich Kotov (code-named DEYEV), a Line X officer working under cover in the Soviet trade delegation, ran twelve agents and obtained 600 items of S&T information and samples.[107] Another Line X officer, Anatoli Alekseyevich Chernyayev (codenamed GRIN), who operated under diplomatic cover from 1979 to 1983, obtained 800 items of classified information. He was expelled in 1983 during a round of tit-for-tat expulsions. A Centre report concluded that, despite his expulsion, Chernyayev might not have been definitely identified by MI5 as a KGB officer.[108] Its author, however, was unaware that Gordievsky had identified the entire KGB residency.

Following Guk's expulsion in the spring of 1984, Nikitenko, the head of Line KR, was made acting resident. In January 1985 the Centre decided that he was to return to Moscow in the spring and that the post of resident should go to Gordievsky. And so, when Mikhail Gorbachev succeeded Konstantin Chernenko as general secretary in March 1985, the London residency was at its operational nadir, with an SIS agent about to assume command of it.

Only a month later, however, the Washington main residency achieved one of its greatest post-war triumphs. On April 16 Aldrich Ames, a senior officer in the CIA's Soviet division, walked into the lobby of the Soviet embassy on Sixteenth Street and handed a guard a letter addressed to the resident, Stanislav Andreyevich Androsov. Ames claims that his original aim was a one-time scam to extract 50,000 dollars from the KGB by revealing the names of three apparent CIA spies in the Soviet Union whom he knew were really double agents controlled by the Centre. Only later, he insists, did he identify Gordievsky and over twenty other genuine Western agents, a majority of whom were shot. According to Viktor Cherkashin, head of Line KR (counter-intelligence) in Washington, however, Ames's letter of April 16, 1985 included, in addition to the names of the double agents, the identities of two *real* American agents—one of them a colleague of his in the Washington residency. Both were executed. Though Ames insists that he did not betray Gordievsky until June 13, it is quite possible that he did so earlier.[109]

By mid-May 1985 the Centre had reached the alarming conclusion that its resident-designate in London was a British agent—although it remains unclear whether it based that conclusion on intelligence from Ames. On May 17 Gordievsky received a summons to return to the Centre for consultations before formally taking up the post of resident. In Moscow he was drugged and interrogated, but no admission of guilt extracted from him. On May 30 Gordievsky was given a period of leave during which the Centre placed him under constant surveillance, doubtless in the hope that he would be caught making contact with SIS or provide other compromising evidence. He was well aware that, whether or not further evidence was obtained against him, it had already been decided to execute him as a British agent. On July 20, however, Gordievsky was successfully exfiltrated across the Finnish border in the boot of an SIS car—the only escape in Soviet history by a Western agent under KGB surveillance. In October thirty-one Soviet intelligence personnel identified by Gordievsky were expelled from London. Owing to the lack of any more senior candidate, the inexperienced Aleksandr Smagin, formerly KGB security officer at the Soviet embassy, was appointed as the new London resident.[110]

The greatest known success of KGB operations in Britain during the Gorbachev era was the reactivation of Michael Smith, probably the most important British Line X agent since the retirement of Norwood. When Mitrokhin last saw Smith's file in 1984, he had been trying for six years without success to recover the security clearance which had made him such a valuable agent in the Thorn—EMI Weapons Division in 1976–8. By now, the Centre was close to writing him off. The last contact with Smith noted on his file was in March 1983. In 1984 it was decided to put him "on ice" for the next three years.[111] In December 1985, however, Smith was taken on as a quality assurance engineer by the GEC Hirst Research Centre at Wembley, in north-west London, where seven months later he was given limited security clearance for defense contracts on a need-to-know basis.[112]

In 1990 Line X at the London residency renewed contact with Smith, arranging meetings either in the graveyard of the church of St. Mary at Harrow on the Hill or in the nearby Roxeth recreation park at South Harrow. Security procedures were devised at each site to warn Smith if it was under surveillance. At St. Mary's church he was told to look for a white chalk line on the vicarage wall near a fire hydrant. If the line was uncrossed, it was safe for him to enter the graveyard. He was also told to look at the church noticeboard. A small green dot, usually on a drawing pin, indicated that the meeting with his case officer was still on; a red dot was a warning to leave immediately. Though Smith had originally been an ideological agent, his motives had become increasingly mercenary. At meetings between 1990 and 1992 he was given a total of over 20,000 pounds for material from GEC defense projects, some of which he spent on an expensive flamenco guitar, a musical keyboard and computer equipment. Smith became increasingly confident and careless. When he was arrested in August 1992, the police found documents on the Rapier ground-to-air missile system and Surface Acoustic Wave military radar technology in a Sainsbury's carrier bag in the boot of his Datsun.[113]

IN THE COURSE of the Cold War, there had been a remarkable transformation in the balance of intelligence power between Britain and the Soviet Union. When the Cold War began, at a time when Britain possessed no major intelligence assets in Moscow, the KGB was still running the Magnificent Five (Blunt, admittedly, on a part-time basis) and had other major agents inside the British nuclear project. So far as is known at present, there were no comparable British agents during the closing years of the Cold War, though it is impossible to exclude the possibility (not, however, a probability) that there may have been a British Ames who has so far gone undetected. SIS, by contrast, attracted a series of KGB officers either as penetration agents or as defectors—among them Oleg Gordievsky, Vladimir Kuzichkin, Viktor Makarov, Mikhail Butkov and Vasili Mitrokhin.[114] Other defectors exfiltrated by SIS included the leading Russian scientist Vladimir Pasechnik, who provided extraordinary intelligence on the vast Soviet biological warfare program.[115] There may well have been other agents and defectors whose names have yet to be revealed. On present evidence, during the final phase of the Cold War SIS had clearly the better of its intelligence duel with the KGB.

TWENTY-SIX

THE FEDERAL REPUBLIC OF GERMANY

The Soviet intelligence offensive against West Germany during the Cold War had three distinguishing characteristics. First, the division of Germany made the Federal Republic (FRG) easier to penetrate than any other major Western state. So many refugees fled to the West from the misnamed German Democratic Republic (GDR)—about three million before the building of the Berlin Wall in 1961—that it was not difficult to hide hundreds, even thousands, of East German and Soviet agents among them. Among the bogus refugees were a series of illegals. Some were KGB officers of Soviet nationality who had spent several years establishing false German identities in the secure environment of the GDR, many of whom moved on to operate against north American and other targets.[1] Others were East German illegal agents recruited and trained by the KGB, most of whom were deployed against targets in the Federal Republic.[2]

Secondly, the FRG was the only Western state on which Moscow received even more high-grade intelligence from an allied agency—the Stasi's foreign section, the Hauptverwaltung Aufklúrung (HVA)[3]—than it did from the KGB. From 1952 to 1986 the HVA was headed by Markus Johannes "Mischa" Wolf, probably the ablest of the Soviet Bloc intelligence chiefs. Wolf was the son of a well-known German Communist doctor and writer who had been forced to flee to Moscow after Hitler's rise to power. He owed his appointment as head of East German foreign intelligence shortly before his thirtieth birthday to his devoted Stalinism and hence the confidence he inspired in the KGB (then the MGB), as well as to his own ability. In 1947 he told his friend Wolfgang Leonhard that East German Communists would have to give up the idea of the "separate German way to socialism" mentioned in their Party program. When Leonhard, who worked in the Party central secretariat, told him he was wrong, Wolf replied, "There are higher authorities than your central secretariat!" Shortly afterward, the "higher authorities" in Moscow did indeed put an end to talk about the "separate German way."[4] Wolf has never suffered from false modesty. "As even my bitter foes would acknowledge," he boasts in retirement, "[the HVA] was probably the most efficient and effective such service on the European continent."[5]

The third distinguishing characteristic of Soviet intelligence operations in West Germany was that, in addition to receiving HVA reports, the KGB's own penetration of the FRG was powerfully assisted by its East German allies. As well as establishing legal residencies in Bonn, Cologne and Hamburg,[6] the KGB was also able to run West German operations from its base at Karlshorst in the Berlin suburbs. This was the largest Soviet intelligence station outside the USSR, using East German illegals and other agents supplied by the Stasi and HVA. Though the KGB was, in principle, responsible for funding its Karlshorst station, in the mid-1970s the GDR was contributing 1.3 million marks a year to its running costs.[7]

The first major recruitments by the Karlshorst KGB in the FRG which are recorded in the files noted by Mitrokhin occurred in 1950. SERGEYEV (also codenamed NIKA), a young West German Communist recruited in that year, was instructed to distance himself from the Communist Party in order to allow him to provide intelligence on the Trotskyists in the FRG, with whom—despite their political insignificance—the Centre remained obsessed for ideological reasons. His file records that early in his career as an agent he provided the intelligence which made possible the abduction of Weiland, a leading Trotskyist, from West Berlin by a special actions snatch squad.[8] SERGEYEV became one of the KGB's longest serving West German agents and by 1963 was receiving a salary of 400 deutschmarks a month. A Centre report on his work claims that, "With his help, in 1951–74, Trotskyist organizations in the FRG and western Europe were cultivated and compromised." Simultaneously, SERGEYEV served for some years as a respected north German *Bürgermeister*. Fearing that he was under surveillance, the KGB broke contact with him in 1981, giving him a final payment of 3,000 deutschmarks.[9]

Karlshorst's main achievement in the early years of the Federal Republic was the penetration of the semi-official West German foreign intelligence agency, the Gehlen Org, which from 1956 was officially attached to the Federal Chancellery as the Bundesnachrichtendienst (BND). In March 1950 Karlshorst recruited "for material reward" an unemployed former SS captain, Hans Clemens (codenamed KHANNI), who in the following year gained a job in the Gehlen Org. Over the next decade he supplied what his file describes as "valuable information" on the FRG intelligence community: "This made it possible to prevent the exposure of valuable agents, and to disrupt operations directed against Soviet missions in the FRG."[10] Clemens's greatest success, however, was to recruit a former SS comrade, Heinz Felfe (codenamed KURT), whom he successfully recommended for a job in the Gehlen Org.[11] With the active assistance of Karlshorst, Felfe rapidly established himself as one of the most successful agents of the Cold War. According to a KGB report, his intelligence, when combined with that from the British spies George Blake and Kim Philby, made possible "the elimination of the adversary's agent network in the GDR" during the period 1953 to 1955.[12]

In 1953 Felfe astounded his colleagues in the Gehlen Org by announcing that he had set up an agent network in Moscow headed by a Red Army colonel. Much of the intelligence from the non-existent network—a blend of fact and fiction fabricated by the Centre—was passed on to the West German chancellor, Konrad Adenauer, in Bonn. Simultaneously, Felfe was providing Karlshorst with large numbers of FRG intelligence reports. Urgent reports went by radio; the remainder were despatched in the false bottoms of suitcases, on film concealed in tins of babyfood, via dead letter-boxes, or through a Gehlen Org courier, Erwin Tiebel, who was also working for Karlshorst. By 1958 Felfe had established himself as the German Philby, becoming—like Philby in SIS fourteen years earlier—head of Soviet counter-intelligence in the BND. Unlike Philby, however, his motives had more to do with vanity than with ideology. He was, he told himself, the supreme intelligence professional, recognized as the rising star of the BND yet outwitting it at the same time. Karlshorst was careful to boost his ego, encouraging him to believe that his achievements were eclipsing even those of Richard Sorge. "I wanted," Felfe said later, "to rank as top class with the Russians." A CIA officer who served in Germany during the 1950s concluded after Felfe's arrest in 1961:

> The BND damage report must have run into tens of thousands of pages. Not only were agents and addresses compromised, but ten years of secret agent reports had to be re-evaluated: those fabricated by the other side, those subtly slanted, those from purely mythical sources.[13]

Soon after Andropov became KGB chairman in 1967, he singled out Felfe—along with Philby, Blake and Vassall—as the kind of past agent whose recruitment was, once again, urgently needed in order to keep the Soviet leadership abreast of the development of Western policy.[14]

THE FRG WAS a major target for KGB active measures as well as intelligence collection. The chief priority of both KGB and HVA influence operations during the 1950s and 1960s was to discredit as many West German politicians as possible as neo-Nazis and "revenge-seekers." Disinformation almost always works most effectively when it includes a basis of fact. In the early years of the FRG, there was no shortage of real ex-Nazis in positions of power and influence to denounce in active measures campaigns. Among the most effective denouncers was the Reuters correspondent in Berlin, John Peet, who had been recruited as an NKVD agent during the Spanish Civil War. In 1950 Peet defected to East Berlin, somewhat disconcerted by the excessively clandestine preparations made for the defection by his East German case officer. All Peet expected was a phone call inviting him to coffee from an East Berlin professor who frequently visited his West Berlin flat. Instead, the professor rang him and, in what struck Peet as a curiously high-pitched voice, declared, "PRIMROSE has a message for DAFFODIL. 1600 hours on Monday. I repeat, 1600 hours on Monday." Once in East Berlin, Peet announced at a press conference:

> I simply cannot consent to take part any longer in the warmongering which threatens not only the Soviet Union and the People's Democracies, but which is also well on the way to converting my motherland, Britain, into a powerless American colony.[15]

From 1952 to 1975 Peet edited the fortnightly *Democratic German Report,* which spent much of its time denouncing the past records (often supplied by Wolf) of West

German politicians, diplomats, industrialists, lawyers, generals and police chiefs. Peet regarded as his "prize exhibit" Adenauer's most important aide, Hans Globke, who had drafted the infamous official commentary on Hitler's 1935 race laws.[16]

Peet's propaganda was powerfully reinforced by the KGB-arranged defection in July 1954 of Otto John, first head of the FRG security service, the Bundesamt für Verfassungsschutz (BfV). Like Peet four years earlier, John gave a press conference at which he denounced the alleged revival of Nazism in West Germany. In December 1955 John reappeared in the West, claiming that he had been drugged by Wolfgang Wohlgemuth, a doctor working for the KGB. The West German supreme court was skeptical. According to other evidence, John was a heavy drinker who had been observed crossing to the East in a "cheerful" rather than comatose condition, after Wohlgemuth had plied him with whisky and played on his fears of a Nazi revival. In December 1959 he was sentenced to four years in jail, but served only eighteen months. Considerable mystery still surrounds the John case. The head of the KGB Karlshorst apparat, Yevgeni Petrovich Pitovranov, reported to the Centre in July 1954 that John had come for discussions in East Berlin because he "wished to maintain contact with us to discuss political problems and joint action against the Nazis of East Germany." John's decision to remain in the East, however, was made under KGB pressure. According to one of the KGB officers involved in the John case:

> We wanted to recruit him, but he turned us down. Because it was necessary that John remain in East Berlin, we put a sleeping pill in his coffee . . . After sleeping for about thirty hours, he was worked over by specialists from the KGB with psychological pressure. He finally said that he would cooperate with us.

Among the deceptions used to persuade John to remain in the East was a fake Western news broadcast announcing that he had already defected to the GDR.[17]

The HVA and KGB had at their disposal an archive in East Berlin which held Wehrmacht, SS and Nazi records seized by the Red Army. In two large volumes of material on real and alleged war criminals and neo-Nazis, the HVA's active measures department, Abteilung X, combined authentic archival documents and fabricated evidence to form a damning indictment of the West German political, business and military élite.[18] Abteilung X also concocted an additional, highly discreditable chapter to the memoirs of Reinhard Gehlen, first head of the BND, in an imitation of his handwriting.[19]

The most celebrated West German target of the KGB and the HVA was Willy Brandt, codenamed POLYARNIK ("Polar").[20] From the moment Brandt became *Bürgermeister* of Berlin in October 1957, he was the victim of a series of active measures operations designed first to discredit and then to blackmail him. Given Brandt's heroic record of resistance to Hitler, it was plainly unrealistic to include him in the KGB's list of neo-Nazi conspirators. Instead, by distorting his early career and war record, KGB and HVA active measures sought, at various times, to portray him as a Gestapo informer, an anti-German émigré, a collaborator with SIS and the CIA and even as a former Soviet agent.

In 1931, shortly before his eighteenth birthday, Willy Brandt (born Herbert Frahm) had become leader of the youth section of the Sozialistische Arbeiterpartei (SAP), a left-wing breakaway party from the socialist SDP. After Hitler's rise to power in 1933, Brandt went into exile, traveling to Norway carrying only a briefcase containing the first volume of Marx's *Das Kapital,* a few shirts and 100 marks. Once in Oslo he established himself as the SAP representative and began a career as a journalist. In February 1937 he traveled to Spain, ostensibly as a journalist covering the Civil War but also to act as liaison between SAP members of the International Brigades and the neo-Trotskyist POUM militia. Brandt quickly denounced the "blind terror" waged by the Communists, on Soviet instructions, against POUM and other left-wing heretics:

> The truth of the matter is: the Comintern is determined to destroy all forces that refuse to obey its orders. It is for this reason that the whole international labor movement must rise against it.

Brandt in turn was, absurdly, denounced by the Communists as "an agent of Franco" and "a spy of the Gestapo."[21]

The earliest reference to Brandt in his KGB file is a description of him in 1936 as a member of the Danzig Trotskyists. The other reports on Brandt during the late 1930s, all of them hostile, accurately reflect the paranoia of the Great Terror. There are fabricated claims that POLYARNIK had been tasked by the Paris Sñreté to infiltrate POUM, that he had betrayed many members of the SDP to the Gestapo and that he was involved in the murder in Spain of Mark Rein, son of a prominent Russian Menshevik, who had in reality been killed by the NKVD.[22]

After Hitler's invasion of the Soviet Union in June 1941, Brandt's attitude to Moscow changed. The NKVD residency in Stockholm, whither Brandt had moved after the German occupation of Norway, reported that there had been a split in the ranks of "Norwegian Trotskyists." Some, including Brandt, were now willing to cooperate with the Soviet Union to secure the defeat of Hitler. In the autumn of 1941 M. S. Okhunev (codenamed OLEG), an operations officer at the Stockholm residency, called on Brandt but found him out and left his card. The following evening Brandt visited the Soviet embassy and spent three hours talking to Okhunev and the NKVD resident, Mikhail Sergeyevich Vetrov. Brandt said that he ran a news agency whose clients included the American press, was ready to do anything to hasten the destruction of Nazism and would be happy to send stories from "Soviet comrades" to the United States (which had not yet entered the war)—if necessary, disguising their source. Vetrov and Okhunev replied that the most important contribution he could make to the war effort would be to gather intelligence from his Norwegian friends on German forces and operations in Norway. Brandt agreed, and for the next nine months had clandestine meetings once a fortnight with officers from the Stockholm residency. On one occasion he was handed 500 kroner, probably to meet his expenses, and gave a receipt.

Among the intelligence supplied by Brandt from his Norwegian sources was information on the German battleship *Tirpitz,* which left the Norwegian port of

Trondheim in March 1942 to attack Arctic convoys. Brandt informed the NKVD that he had passed the same information to the British, who tried and failed to sink it.[23] He also supplied the Stockholm residency with information on German pressure on Sweden to join the Anti-Comintern Pact and on plans (never implemented) to ban the Swedish Communist Party. In the summer of 1942, after the arrest by the Swedish police of two Czech agents of the residency, TERENTY and VANYA,[24] Brandt refused further secret rendezvous with NKVD officers, despite pressure from the residency to continue them. He did, however, agree to come openly to the Soviet embassy, sometimes to meet intelligence officers operating under diplomatic cover.[25]

None of this makes POLYARNIK a Soviet agent. The Stockholm residency reported in 1943 that Brandt had also been in touch with British and American intelligence officers in Sweden, as well as with Trotsky's Norwegian former secretary, who remained deeply suspect as far as the Centre was concerned.[26] Brandt's overriding motive was to provide any information to all three members of the Grand Alliance which might contribute to the defeat of Hitler. In the case of the Soviet Union, he calculated accurately that his best channel of communication with Moscow was via the Stockholm residency.

The first attempt to discredit Brandt after his election as Berlin *Bürgermeister* in 1957 was a lengthy operation carried out jointly by the KGB and HVA in 1958–9 to use tendentious versions of his wartime record and other fabrications to show him as an agent of British and American intelligence. But, as the file on the operation acknowledges, "This did not produce the desired result, and Brandt's position as a politician was not undermined."[27] Wolf next proposed reviving the old slander that Brandt had been a Gestapo agent during his Norwegian exile, but the East German leadership ordered the plan to be aborted due to lack of credible evidence.[28]

In the 1961 West German elections Brandt stood as the SDP candidate for the chancellorship. The campaign was the dirtiest in the history of the FRG. Brandt was assailed by what he denounced as "a right-wing barrage of mud." The fact that he had spent the Nazi years in exile led to accusations that he was unpatriotic, while his background as a left-wing socialist gave rise to insinuations that he was a crypto-Communist. Brandt was deeply depressed by the "political pornography" used to discredit him. "My opponents," he later admitted, "were sometimes successful to the extent that they kept me from my work for days on end." Sensing his vulnerability, the Stasi gave secret but, in Brandt's view, "vigorous encouragement" to some of the charges fabricated against him.[29]

Though the SDP succeeded in cutting the Christian Democrat majority (thanks largely to the building of the Berlin Wall during the campaign), the Centre decided to threaten Brandt with far more damaging evidence than had surfaced during the elections. On November 16, 1962 Semichastny, the KGB chairman, formally approved a blackmail operation proposed by Sakharovsky, the head of the FCD. Though there is no mention of it in the file seen by Mitrokhin, the operation was also, almost certainly, approved by Khrushchev, still smarting from the humiliating outcome of the Cuban missile crisis in the previous month.[30] The operational plan was for Brandt to be approached by the *Izvestia* correspondent, Polyanov, to whom he had given an interview earlier in the year. On this occasion, Polyanov would be accompanied by an undercover KGB operations officer who would tell Brandt, "We would like to resume our confidential relations with you in order to develop together sensible solutions to the West Berlin question." If Brandt refused, he was to be told, "We have sufficient means to cause you unpleasantness, and therefore assume that you will reconsider your position." The threat was in fact largely bluff. Sakharovsky had been annoyed to discover that the original documents in Brandt's wartime operational file had been destroyed in 1959 (an inconceivable action had he actually been an agent), among them such apparently compromising items as his receipt for 500 kroner for the Stockholm residency. Brandt, however, would be unaware of this. The operational plan approved by Semichastny confidently asserts that Brandt must believe that "there are materials in our possession which could compromise him."[31]

Mitrokhin did not see the report on the meeting with Brandt.[32] It is clear, however, that—if it went ahead—Brandt brushed the attempted KGB blackmail aside. Semichastny and Sakharovsky had almost certainly intended, with Khrushchev's approval, to soften up Brandt before a meeting with the Soviet leader. In January 1963, while on a visit to East Berlin, Khrushchev duly invited Brandt to a meeting. Already convinced of the need to reach a *modus vivendi* between the FRG and GDR as well as to settle the Berlin question, Brandt was willing to accept. Opposition to the proposed meeting from the Christian Democrats in the ruling West Berlin coalition, however, persuaded him to refuse. According to Brandt:

> Khrushchev must have taken my refusal as an affront. Ambassador [Pyotr Andreyevich] Abrasimov later gave me a vivid description of the total dismay that overcame his erstwhile master when the news was communicated to him. Khrushchev, caught in the act of changing, almost dropped his trousers with surprise . . .[33]

Brandt's four and a half years as West Germany's first SDP chancellor, from October 21, 1969 to May 6, 1974, marked the high water mark of the HVA and KGB intelligence offensive in the FRG. Wolf's greatest success was the penetration of the Chancellor's office by Günter Guillaume (codenamed HANSEN). In 1956 Guillaume and his wife Christel, both HVA officers, had staged a carefully orchestrated "escape" from East Germany, set up small businesses in Frankfurt to act as cover for their intelligence work and become active, apparently staunchly anti-Communist, members of the SDP. By 1968 Guillaume had become chairman of the Frankfurt SDP and an elected member of the Frankfurt city council, thus becoming the only HVA officer (as opposed to agent) ever to hold public office in the FRG. In November 1969, three weeks after Brandt became chancellor, Guillaume gained a job in his office, initially as an assistant dealing with trade unions and political organizations. Hardworking and efficient, with a jovial down-to-earth manner, he was promoted in 1972 to become the Chancellor's aide for relations with the SDP, as well as being put in charge of Brandt's travel arrangements. His reports were so highly rated in the Centre that they were personally forwarded by Andropov to foreign minister Gromyko.[34]

The key intelligence requirement placed on Guillaume concerned Brandt's *Ostpolitik*, which he defined as having "a threefold aim: improved relations with the Soviet Union, normal relations with the east European states, and a *modus vivendi* between the two parts of Germany." In his "Report on the State of the Nation" to the Bundestag at the beginning of 1970, Brandt called for "cooperative togetherness" between the FRG and GDR. In the course of the year he became the first chancellor to visit East Germany, and signed treaties with the Soviet Union and Poland.[35] "Through Guillaume's judgments," writes Wolf in his memoirs, "we were able to conclude sooner rather than later that Brandt's new *Ostpolitik*, while still riven with contradictions, marked a genuine change of course in West German foreign policy."[36] Moscow reached the same conclusion. After Brandt's visit to East Germany, however, Karlshorst reported "a noticeable rise in his popularity,"[37] which caused some concern to the GDR leadership. During his visit, as the crowds chanted, "Willy, Willy!," Brandt mischievously asked the East German prime minister, Willi Stoph, whether the name being chanted was spelled with a "y" or an "i." Stoph remained stony-faced.[38]

With the Christian Democrats in open opposition to Brandt's *Ostpolitik*, the Centre was now concerned not to compromise Brandt but to keep him in power. By the spring of 1972 a series of defections from the SDP and its Free Democrat allies had reduced Brandt's majority to four. With more defections in the offing, the fate of *Ostpolitik* hung in the balance. In April 1972, confident of success, the CDU (Christian Democrat) leader, Rainer Barzel, tabled a motion of no confidence.[39] With the blessing of the Centre, Wolf made a possibly critical secret intervention in the Bundestag with the aim of keeping Brandt in power.

Shortly before the crucial vote of confidence, the HVA had recruited a corrupt CDU deputy, Julius Steiner, as an agent with the codename SIMSON.[40] Wolf paid Steiner 50,000 marks to vote for Brandt.[41] Barzel's no confidence motion failed by two votes. At a general election in November, Brandt won a more secure parliamentary majority, with the SDP for the first time beating the Christian Democrats in the popular vote.[42] The HVA continued to run SIMSON as an agent in the new Bundestag. In February 1973 Steiner agreed to a contract with the HVA (euphemistically described as the "Structural Working Group of the GDR Council of Ministers"), under which he was paid a retainer of 3,000 marks a month. Soon afterward (the date is not recorded by Mitrokhin), Wolf reported to the Centre that Steiner was in contact with the BfV, the West German counter-intelligence agency, and thus useless as an agent.[43] In June the Munich weekly *Quick* published a photograph of a bank deposit slip showing that 50,000 marks had been paid into Steiner's account the day after the April 1972 vote of confidence, thus provoking a public scandal which was quickly dubbed "Bonn's Watergate" or "Rhinegate." Steiner acknowledged being recruited as an HVA agent but claimed that he had worked as a double agent with the approval of the BfV, and said that the 50,000 marks had come from the SDP chief whip, Karl Wienand[44]—a charge denied by Wienand (who, it later transpired, was also an HVA agent).[45] A parliamentary inquiry decided that there was no conclusive evidence of bribery.[46]

By the time of Brandt's victory in the November 1972 elections, Guillaume was at the peak of his career as a penetration agent, attending all meetings of the SDP party and parliamentary leadership. On May 29, 1973, however, Günter Nollau, head of the BfV, informed Hans-Dietrich Genscher, the interior minister, that Guillaume was under suspicion of espionage and had been placed under surveillance. (Their recollections later differed over how serious the suspicions reported by Nollau were.)[47] Shortly afterward, alerted—according to Wolf's not wholly reliable account—by the BfV's clumsy surveillance of Guillaume's wife, the HVA ordered both Günter and Christel Guillaume to suspend their intelligence work.[48] At 6:30 a.m. on April 24, 1974 the Guillaumes were arrested at their Bonn apartment. In a curious breach of espionage tradecraft, Guillaume virtually admitted his guilt. Dressed only in a bathrobe, he declared defiantly, "I am an officer of the [East German] National People's Army!" According to Genscher, "It was basically only Guillaume's own declaration which convicted him."[49]

Wolf now argues that his success in penetrating Brandt's entourage was "equivalent to kicking a football into our own goal." The political scandal caused by Guillaume's arrest was the immediate cause of Brandt's resignation on May 6, 1974. The HVA, Wolf concludes, "unwittingly helped to destroy the career of the most far-sighted of modern German statesmen."[50]

THE HVA OPERATIONS in West Germany which had had the greatest influence on the KGB's own methods were probably those of its "Romeo spies (a phrase invented by the Western media but later taken over by Wolf himself).[51] The KGB had specialized in the sexual entrapment of Western diplomats and visitors to Moscow since the 1930s. The entrapment followed a straightforward sequence: the use of attractive female or male swallows as sexual bait, the seduction of the target, the secret photography of the sexual encounter (and, on occasion, the interruption of the encounter by a supposedly outraged "spouse" or "relative"), followed by blackmail.[52] Wolf's tactics were both more subtle and more effective. Love, or a plausible semblance of it, was capable of generating more intelligence over a longer period than brief sexual encounters.[53] The main targets of the Romeo spies were lonely female secretaries, most in their thirties or forties, employed in West German ministries and intelligence agencies.

Beginning in the late 1950s, the KGB base in Karlshorst began imitating the HVA's "secretaries offensive." Indeed, the KGB files seen by Mitrokhin show that some of the "secretary spies" later thought to be HVA agents were in fact working for the KGB. Karlshorst's initial targets were female employees in the Bonn Foreign Ministry identified by a KGB agent in the ministry's personnel department, Gisela Herzog (codenamed MARLENE), recruited in 1954—without, apparently, the use of a Romeo spy. Herzog herself married an official from the French defense ministry in 1958 and moved to Paris. The first victim of the KGB's secretaries offensive was Herzog's friend Leonore Heinz (codenamed LOLA), secretary to a foreign ministry department head. Her seducer was Heinz Sütterlin (codenamed WALTER), a West German from Freiburg recruited by the KGB in 1957, whose first name, confusingly, was identical to Leonore's surname. When Herzog heard in 1958 that the 30-year-old Leonore Heinz had succumbed to Sütterlin's advances, she became conscience-stricken. Probably foreseeing Heinz's devastation when she discovered that she had been deceived, Herzog wrote to the Centre, "I should like to say that you should not involve LOLA in co-operation with us through Sütterlin. She would be very disillusioned." "I do ask you," she wrote on another occasion, "to please leave LOLA in peace."[54] The Centre, predictably, paid no attention.

In December 1960 Heinz Sütterlin and Leonore Heinz were married. Over the next year Sütterlin frequently discussed with his wife the danger that the Cold War might turn into hot war. At a time when the West German leadership were building themselves nuclear shelters, he argued that they had to be concerned for their own safety. Leonore agreed to confide in him everything she knew about East—West relations. In 1961, at first unwittingly, she was included in the KGB agent network. Two years later, Sütterlin reported to the Centre that, without mentioning the KGB, he had told his wife he was passing on her information to an organization dedicated to preventing nuclear war:

> I told LOLA that there is one great organization in the world which regards the preservation of peace as its task. This organization requests one great favor from her. She must continue to work in the foreign ministry and report to me everything that she finds out . . . The organization thinks well of her work . . . She has agreed to cooperate in every way she can, and declared that she regards it as the duty of every decent person to seek to tie the hands of warmongers. She declined to receive money for her help. I believe that in LOLA we have an assistant on whom one may rely totally.

Though his wife refused payment, Sütterlin received 1,000 marks a month.

From 1964 onward, Sütterlin handed film of documents LOLA had smuggled out of the ministry to the East German illegal Eugen Runge (codenamed MAKS), who was working for the Karlshorst KGB. Runge, in turn, left the film in a dead letter-box which was emptied by the Bonn residency. After Leonore at last realized that she was working for the Soviet Bloc, Runge had a personal meeting with her. He found her unperturbed by her discovery. Leonore said that she trusted her husband absolutely, and that her work in the cause of peace was a job that had to be done. Sütterlin told Runge that Leonore was also motivated by "hatred for the caste of haughty foreign ministry officials" and "derived satisfaction from causing as much damage as she could."[55] His comment supplies a missing element in traditional explanations of the success of the HVA and KGB secretaries offensive. Though most of the secretaries began spying for love, their espionage was probably sustained, at least in part, by the arrogance of some of their better-educated and better-paid male superiors.

In 1967 Runge defected to the CIA, betraying both Leonore and Heinz Sütterlin. Runge told his debriefers, "We received [FRG diplomatic] documents before they moved across Leonore's desk and on to the code room, and we read the reports brought by diplomatic couriers from abroad, mostly even before German Foreign Minister [Gerhard] Schrîder got them." As her friend Gisela Herzog had feared nine years earlier, Leonore was distraught at the discovery that she had been targeted by a Romeo spy. During her police interrogation, she was confronted with a confession by her husband that he had married her not for love but on orders from the KGB. Soon afterward Leonore hanged herself in her cell.[56]

TWO OF THE other most successful seductions in the KGB's secretaries offensive recorded in files seen by Mitrokhin—those of DORIS and ROSIE—also involved a false flag recruitment and the use of East German illegals. The false flag, however, differed from that which had deceived LOLA. DORIS and ROSIE believed they were working not for an underground peace movement but for a secret neo-Nazi group.

DORIS was Margret Hîke, a secretary in the office of the West German president, where she worked successively in the mobilization and security departments. Her Romeo spy was the East German illegal Hans-Jurgen Henze (codenamed HAGEN), who assumed the identity of Franz Becker, a West German living in the GDR.[57] Henze discovered the 33-year-old Hîke by chance. One day in 1968, while looking out of the window of his Bonn apartment, he saw a woman who struck him as a possible civil servant going for a walk alone. Henze stood waiting in a telephone kiosk along her route and, as Hîke passed by, asked if she had change for a phone call. Somehow he also managed to strike up a conversation and, on discovering where she worked, arranged another meeting with her. Gradually, according to Hîke's operational file, "She fell seriously in love and was greatly attached to him." Henze explained that he was a postgraduate student writing a dissertation on the work of the president, but needed additional source material before he could complete it. Hîke supplied documents from work to help finish the fictional thesis. Though less infatuated than Hîke, Henze also became emotionally involved in their relationship and for several years "found it difficult to switch to a business footing." Finally in 1971 or 1972 (the date is unclear from the file), hoping to appeal to Hîke's somewhat extreme right-wing views, he told her he belonged to an organization of "German patriots," based in Brazil, who were committed to the cause of national revival and needed inside information on the Bonn government to continue their work.[58]

Hîke said she had guessed something of the sort and agreed to assist the "German patriots." Henze then persuaded her to sign a contract, allegedly drawn up by his "boss," under which she agreed to provide information from the President's office in return for her expenses and 500 marks a month. Among the intelligence she supplied were the mobilization plans of the Chancellor's office and the major Bonn ministries; details on the government war bunker (which were reported to Brezhnev); despatched from FRG ambassadors in Moscow, Washington and elsewhere; the secret weekly reports to the President from the foreign ministry; a dossier on Brezhnev's visit to the FRG; and accounts of the President's meetings with foreign diplomats. Hîke gradually became dependent on the 500 marks she received each month. In order to leave no trace of it in her own financial records, she gave it to her mother to invest on her behalf, telling her that she found it difficult to save herself.[59] With the help of her mother's investments, Hîke was able to buy a new apartment (Apartment 85, House 16, am Baitzaplen 37, Oberkassel).[60]

After Hîke signed her agent contract, she ceased to take the risks of smuggling classified material back to her flat. Instead, Henze taught her how to photograph documents in the President's office with a miniature camera concealed in a tube of lipstick. On one occasion Hîke's boss entered the room just as she was about to use the camera, but—to her immense relief—failed to notice what she was doing.[61] She usually handed over the film either in Cologne or Zürich. The *yavka* (secret rendezvous) in Cologne was at 8:30 p.m. on the first Tuesday of each month in Kîln-Bayenthal, at the end of Bayenthalgürtel, about fifty meters from the Bismarck column, by a telephone kiosk next to an advertising pillar. Hîke was told to have a copy of *Der Spiegel* in her hand if she was ready to go ahead with the meeting; if she needed to give a danger signal, she was to carry a plastic bag instead. The meetings in Zürich took place at 5 o'clock on Saturday afternoons at Rennweg 35, by the window of a china shop.[62]

Henze was twice awarded the Order of the Red Star for his success in running Hîke as an agent. In 1976 he returned to East Germany but continued to meet her regularly in Cologne and Zürich.[63] Hîke was temporarily put on ice in 1979 during a security scare caused by the investigation of another secretary suspected of spying for the East, but was reactivated a year later with the new codename VERA. By 1980 the "product file" of the documents she had provided filled ten volumes.[64] Though Hîke remained in touch with Henze, she also passed on intelligence through RENATA, a female East German illegal working for the KGB.[65] Among the intelligence she supplied during the early 1980s were details of talks in October 1982 between Foreign Minister Hans-Dietrich Genscher and US Secretary of State George Schultz over the stationing of Pershing II missiles in the FRG. She also took part in two major NATO WINTEX exercises, during which she had been able to provide intelligence on the FRG wartime command and control system, and was able to report on her experience of working inside the secret wartime government bunker in the Eiffel hills near Bonn.

Hîke was arrested in 1985, and quickly confessed. In 1987 she was sentenced to eight years in jail and fined 33,000 marks, the total sum she was believed to have received from the KGB (probably an underestimate). The judge told her that, in passing a relatively lenient sentence, he was taking into account that she had fallen "hopelessly in love" with her recruiter. The British press was curiously divided in its opinion of Hîke. Though the *Daily Telegraph* described her as a "dowdy secretary," she impressed the *Observer* as a "Glamour Spy."[66]

The methods used to recruit Hîke were similar to those employed against Heidrun Hofer (codenamed ROSIE), a secretary in her early thirties in the FRG foreign intelligence service, the Bundesnachrichtendienst (BND).[67] While serving at the BND Paris station during the early 1970s Hofer was seduced by ROLAND, an East German illegal with a military bearing who, like Henze, claimed to be working for a neo-Nazi group of "German patriots."[68] Hofer's deception was taken one stage further than that of Hîke. On February 26, 1973 at Innsbruch in Austria, ROLAND introduced her to VLADIMIR, telling her that he was one of the leaders of the neo-Nazi underground. Next day VLADIMIR met Hofer alone, telling her that he had known Admiral Canaris, wartime head of the Abwehr (German military intelligence), in which her father had served, and discussed the intelligence which he wanted her to supply. Unknown to Hofer, VLADIMIR was, in reality, a senior KGB illegal, Ivan Dmitryevich Unrau, an ethnic German born in Russia in 1914.[69]

In 1974 Hofer was transferred to BND headquarters at Pullach in Bavaria, where she worked successively for the west European and NATO liaison departments, and became engaged to a BND major.[70] Following the end of her affair with ROLAND, the KGB used two further East German illegals, MAZON (who pretended to be ROLAND's father) and FRANK, to maintain contact with her. Both pretended to be members of the neo-Nazi underground.[71] Hofer appears eventually to have realized that she had been recruited under false flag but to have carried on working as a paid KGB agent. On December 21, 1977, possibly as the result of a tip-off to the BND from the French SDECE, she was arrested while driving across the Austrian border to meet her controller. Next day she confessed to being a KGB agent. Hofer showed little emotion until told that her BND fiancé had broken off their engagement. After bursting into tears, she asked for the window to be opened to give her some air, then suddenly leaped to her feet and threw herself from the sixth floor. Though her fall was partially broken by some bushes, she was critically injured.[72]

Apart from Hîke and Hofer, the most successful KGB recruitment made by an East German Romeo spy during the 1970s appears to have been that of Elke Falk (codenamed LENA). After Falk had advertised in a lonely hearts column, she was contacted by the illegal Kurt Simon (codenamed GEORG), who introduced himself as Gerhard Thieme. It is unclear from Mitrokhin's notes what, if any, false flag Simon employed to recruit her. However, with his encouragement, Falk gained a job in 1974 as a secretary in the Chancellor's office,[73] taking with her to work a miniature camera disguised as a cigarette lighter and a bogus can of hairspray in which to store her films.[74] Like Hîke, Falk was a member of the crisis management team during the WINTEX exercises. In 1977 the Centre awarded Simon the Order of the Red Star. Later Falk was moved to the control of two other illegals, one who used the alias "Peter Muller" and a second who was codenamed ADAM.[75] Falk moved from the Chancellor's office to the transport ministry in 1977, then in 1979 to the economic aid ministry two years later.[76] By 1980, when Mitrokhin saw her operational file, it filled seven volumes.[77] Falk was arrested in 1989 but wrongly described at her trial as an HVA rather than a KGB agent. Though sentenced to six and a half years' imprisonment, she served only a few months before being released as part of an East—West spy exchange. Falk was alleged to have received a total of 20,000 marks for her espionage.[78]

NOT ALL THE Romeo spies, however, achieved results. Among the failures was one of the KGB's East German illegals, Wilhelm Kahle (codenamed WERNER), who assumed the identity of a West German living in the GDR. Kahle's cover occupations included working as a laboratory technician in Cologne and Bonn universities and as a German language teacher in Paris. During the early 1970s he set out to cultivate four FRG foreign ministry and embassy secretaries, a female clerk at an American embassy in Europe, an American student at a German university who invited him to her parents' home in the United States and a British secretary at NATO. Kahle's ten-volume file, however, contains no indication that he obtained significant intelligence from any of them. His main West German cultivation was BELLA, who worked at the FRG embassies in Tehran and, from 1975, in London. According to WERNER's file, his attempts to recruit BELLA during her tour of duty in London showed "insufficient determination" and were hampered by a number of operational errors, such as attracting the attention of the embassy security officer. Kahle became more interested in MONA, a French technical translator for a firm of Swedish paper manufacturers in Paris, where he was based from 1975 onward. His file records that he had "intimate relations" with MONA and wished to marry her. The Centre, however, became understandably skeptical both of MONA's intelligence potential and of Kahle's motives in pursuing her. The KGB also discovered, through tapping the telephone and intercepting the correspondence of Kahle's mother in East Germany, that he was fearful of being recalled to Moscow and anxious about the fate of his crystal and porcelain collections in Paris, of which the Centre was previously unaware.[79]

In 1978 Kahle was duly summoned back to Moscow and given a lie-detector test—on the pretext that it would be valuable experience if he were subjected to a polygraph during his next posting. As a further method of discovering what WERNER had really been up to, an impeccably ideologically orthodox female agent, ANITA, was planted on him—the only known example of a Romeo agent being targeted by a "Juliet." ANITA's report confirmed the Centre's suspicions. When she asked why he thought he had been recalled, Kahle replied with a grin that he had become "too comfortable" in Paris, had made many friends and acquaintances and had acquired a well-appointed, attractively furnished apartment which he was reluctant to leave. He had also broken KGB regulations by leaving some of his possessions with MONA and by borrowing 3,000 francs from her. ANITA claimed to be shocked by Kahle's "ideological crisis:"

> It would do him no harm to refresh his knowledge of Marxism-Leninism, and especially the course on the political economy of socialism. He was not imbued with a class instinct, as he had been brought up in a petty bourgeois environment. Life in the West had left its mark on him; as the saying goes, "dripping water wears away stone." His beliefs could be those of the French Communist Party. The dictatorship of the proletariat was like a red rag to a bull for him; he was not convinced of its necessity and he had little faith in the advantages of the socialist planned economy. WERNER had only encountered the chocolate icing side of the West. He had been in contact with people who were contented, rich and successful. He had not seen unemployment and poverty.[80]

As a result of ANITA's report, Kahle appears to have been sidelined. He was formally removed from illegal work in 1982.[81]

APART FROM THE secretary spies, the KGB's most productive penetrations of the West Germany bureaucracy during the 1970s were probably two recruits in the intelligence community. One was awarded the Order of the KGB Badge of Honor (*Znak Pochota*) for his "fruitful collaboration."[82] The other, whose recruitment was personally approved by Andropov himself, was ranked by the KGB's Karlshorst base as among its most valuable agents.[83] By the early 1980s, however, both sources seem to have dried up.

HVA penetrations of FRG intelligence agencies were at least as impressive as those by the KGB. In 1973 Gabriele Gast, who had been recruited by an HVA Romeo three years earlier, joined the BND as an analyst and rose to become deputy head of the Soviet Bloc division in 1987, the most highly placed woman in the male-dominated West German foreign intelligence agency. Gast's motivation was complex. As well as her emotional involvement with her recruiter, she was suspicious of the FRG political system and deeply fascinated by Markus Wolf. According to Wolf, "She needed to feel wanted by me and I gave her my personal attention . . . Sometimes her messages carried the wounded tone of a lover who feels taken for granted." Wolf met her personally seven times. His attentions were richly rewarded. "Gaby's work for us," he recalls, "was flawless. She gave us an accurate picture of the West's knowledge of and its judgments regarding the entire Eastern Bloc. This proved vitally important to us in handling the rise of Solidarity in Poland in the early 1980s." Some of the intelligence assessments by Gast which so impressed Wolf also landed on the desk of Chancellor Kohl and, almost certainly, on those of Andropov, Chernenko and Gorbachev as well.[84]

In 1981 Klaus Kuron of the BfV offered his services by letter to the HVA residency in Bonn. A senior counter-intelligence officer who specialized in running "turned" HVA agents, Kuron was bitter at having been passed over for the top jobs and now found himself in increasing financial difficulty. He struck Wolf as "unembarrassed about his treachery . . . His was a paradigm of unfulfilled ambitions of a type that fester throughout any civil service." The HVA skilfully pandered to his wounded self-esteem as well as paying him a total of almost 700,000 marks in the last eight years of its existence.[85]

In 1985 Hans-Joachim Tiedge, the BfV's counter-intelligence chief, caused even greater surprise than Kuron with his letter four years earlier by arriving drunk and unkempt at the East German border and demanding to defect. Tiedge was a heavy gambler as well as an alcoholic, who had come close to being charged with manslaughter after the death of his wife in a drunken household brawl. "If a case like mine had been presented to me for analysis," he told the HVA, "I would have recommended that I be fired without delay." The first prostitute summoned by Wolf to entertain Tiedge after his defection took one look at him and ran away. But, claims Wolf, "Tiedge had a memory like a computer for names and connections, and filled in a lot of the blanks for us—though not as many as he thought, since he was unaware that his colleague Kuron was in our pay."[86]

PERHAPS THE MOST complex aspect of HVA operations in the FRG concerned its contacts either directly or through intermediaries with politicians. The great majority of meetings between West German politicians and representatives of the GDR were part of a genuine attempt to establish a dialogue, often necessarily out of public view, between East and West. The fact that the Stasi inevitably took a close interest in these encounters is not sufficient to brand those politicians from the FRG who took part in them as collaborators with the HVA. In a small minority of cases, however, such contacts acted as a cover for espionage or something close to it.

The most notorious case of a West German politician acting as an HVA agent is that of Karl Wienand, an SDP parliamentary whip during the Brandt government and one of the closest colleagues of Herbert Wehner, leader of the parliamentary party. After the collapse of East Germany, evidence emerged from Stasi files that Wienand had been an HVA agent from 1970 until the Berlin Wall came down in 1989. In 1996 he was sentenced to two and a half years' imprisonment and fined a million marks—the total of the payments he had received from the HVA.[87] According to Foreign Minister Hans-Dietrich Genscher, Wienand was the only person to enjoy the trust of all three members of the triumvirate which ran the SDP after Brandt's resignation: Helmut Schmidt, the new chancellor, Brandt, who remained party chairman, and Wehner.[88] Wolf claims that Wienand, whose motivation was "extraordinarily materialistic," gave him "an enviable insight" into the policies of, and tensions between, the triumvirate at the top of the SDP. That insight also seems to have impressed the Centre. According to Wolf, the KGB itself made an attempt to "do business" with Wienand, but he "succeeded in dissuading our Soviet colleagues" from doing so.[89]

The most controversial case of a senior West German politician in close contact with the East concerns Herbert Wehner. References to Wehner which have been discovered in Soviet and GDR documents since the fall of the Berlin Wall have led to much speculation as to whether, like his colleague Wienand, he was an agent for the HVA or KGB.[90] The Centre's file on Wehner (codenamed KORNELIS) shows that he was a "confidential contact" of both the KGB and the HVA, but not a fully recruited agent.[91] Wehner's contacts with Soviet intelligence went back to his years as a member of the KPD (German Communist Party) leadership-in-exile in Moscow after Hitler's rise to power. During the Great Terror he had denounced a number of his comrades as traitors,[92] and was considered for recruitment as an NKVD agent. Wehner's KGB file, however, reveals that he himself narrowly escaped execution. One KPD official in exile who denounced Wehner, Heinrich Mayer (codenamed MOST), was executed; another, Erich Birkenhauer (BELFORT), was sentenced to twelve years in the gulag. A third denunciation, by MIRRA, a female NKVD agent among the German Communists, almost led to Wehner's downfall. She reported that Wehner's behavior appeared to indicate that he was "in contact with the Gestapo." On December 15, 1937, Wehner (then known as Herbert Funk) was summoned to NKVD headquarters for questioning. A subsequent note on his file records that he was to be given the impression that he was being recruited as an NKVD agent but that the real purpose was to gather evidence against him in preparation for his arrest. In 1938, the former secretary of the Berlin-Brandenburg KPD district committee, Theodor Beutming, confessed to being a member, with Wehner, of a (nonexistent) "underground German Trotskyist center" in Moscow. On July 22 Yezhov, the NKVD chief, wrote on Beutming's confession, "Where is the memorandum on the arrest of Funk?" A memorandum sent to Yezhov shortly afterwards listed a series of German Communists who had identified Wehner, under NKVD interrogation, as a Gestapo agent.[93]

Wehner seems to have been saved from execution only by the winding down of the Terror and the disgrace, a few months later, of Yezhov. Early in 1940 Comintern sent him to carry out "illegal work" in Sweden, using identity documents in the name of H. M. Kornelis. In June 1941, shortly before Hitler's attack on the Soviet Union, the Centre once again considered Wehner as possible NKVD agent material. It was decided not to recruit him, however, when it was discovered that he had included in a report of the previous October an accurate but politically incorrect warning that an attack by Nazi Germany on the Soviet Union was, sooner or later, inevitable.[94] Wehner was later arrested by the Swedish police and—according to later claims by Markus Wolf—revealed the names of members of the Communist underground in both Sweden and Germany.[95] On emerging from prison Wehner broke away from the Communists and made common cause with the SDP.

Wolf found the post-war Wehner "a person of irreconcilable contradictions." Though playing a major role in turning the SDP from a Marxist into a social democratic party, Wehner remained nostalgic for his Communist roots. In 1973 he had an "intensely emotional" reunion with Ulbricht's successor, Erich Honecker, with whom he had worked as a young Communist in the Saarland almost half a century earlier. Honecker went to enormous pains to arrange the details of the reunion, trying to ensure that a cake prepared for tea at a hunting lodge tasted exactly like one baked for Wehner many years before by Honecker's mother.[96] After Wehner's death in 1990, Honecker claimed that, although he had rejected Communism, "his goal was still the union of the labor movement and the building of a socialist German republic."[97]

According to Wolf, secret contacts with Wehner began in the mid-1950s but were initially regarded with great suspicion by Ulbricht, who absurdly suspected him of being "a British spy." Contact became easier when Wehner became Minister for All-German Affairs in 1966 and began regular meetings with the East German lawyer Wolfgang Vogel, who negotiated on "humanitarian questions" with West German officials. Vogel took his instructions directly from Erich Mielke, the GDR Minister of State Security, and reported to him after each meeting with Wehner. According to Wolf:

> Mielke alone edited the reports on conversations with Wehner for passing on to Honecker. Since drafting was not his strong point, he often locked himself in his room for a whole day to put the Wehner reports into the proper form. Hardly anything in the GDR was more secret than these reports. Apart from the three copies for Honecker, Mielke and myself, there was also a re-edited and censored version of the reports which was sent to our Soviet colleagues.

Mielke boasted to the Centre that Wehner's regular briefings gave the Stasi a direct line to the heart of the West German power structure.[98] Mitrokhin's notes contain none of these briefings. They do include, however, one example from KGB files of the trust placed in Wehner as a "confidential contact." He was informed in 1973—apparently before the news became public—that the editor of the weekly magazine *Quick,* Heinz Van Nouhuys (codenamed NANT), who had been recruited as an HVA agent, was in fact a double agent working for the BfV.[99]

Brandt later concluded that Wehner had been negotiating with the GDR behind his back.[100] It is unlikely, however, that Wehner ever consciously betrayed what he saw as the interests of the FRG. "From his youth onwards," Wolf argued, "he regarded conspiracy as an instrument of power politics and sometimes physical survival. From his first contacts with us . . . he no doubt felt that he was always the stronger party in the political game."[101]

Though the KGB appears to have left the running of Wienand entirely to the HVA and never regarded Wehner as more than a "confidential contact," during the 1970s it had a hitherto unknown agent, codenamed CARDINAL, an SDP official who had been talent-spotted by another KGB agent, MAVR, a West German film-maker. The intelligence provided by CARDINAL included reports on FRG politicians and industrialists, the issues to be raised by Brandt during his visit to Moscow in 1973, Brandt's resignation in 1974, the subsequent state of the SDP leadership and FRG relations with China, Israel and Portugal. As well as being rewarded with an icon and other gifts, CARDINAL was paid 5,000 dollars in 1974, the same sum in 1976 and 11,635 deutschmarks in 1977. Then the doubts began. A detailed study of his "intelligence" by the Centre revealed nothing of significance which had not also appeared in the West German press—apart from some items which the KGB suspected were disinformation. It was concluded that CARDINAL and MAVR had been seeking to ingratiate themselves with the KGB in the hope of gaining its assistance in winning valuable contracts in the Soviet Union. Contact with both was abruptly broken off.[102]

Mitrokhin's notes on KGB attempts to penetrate the Christian Democrats (CDU) are thinner than those on the SDP. He does, however, identify two agents within the CDU, both recruited in 1972; SHTOLPEN, a party adviser,[103] and RADIST, a member of the West Berlin city assembly.[104] No details are available on the intelligence which they provided. Mitrokhin also identifies a leading member of the Free Democrats (FDP), codenamed MARK, who had been recruited as a Soviet agent in East Germany in 1946 on the basis of what were alleged to be "compromising circumstances" arising from his wartime service in the Wehrmacht. A few years later MARK succeeded in fleeing to the West, where he rapidly embarked on a new career as a politician. In 1956 the KGB resumed contact with him and remained in touch for the next twenty-four years. However, there is no evidence that during that time MARK supplied any significant intelligence. A later Centre assessment concluded that he had passed on information slanted in favor of the political interests of the FDP and had tried to use his contacts with the East to further his own career. In about 1975 one of MARK's parliamentary colleagues told Aleksandr Demyanovich Zakharov, a KGB officer stationed in Karlshorst, that MARK's earlier association with Soviet intelligence had been "a youthful error." In 1980 the Centre finally decided that there was no point in remaining in contact with him.[105]

Both the recycled newspaper stories provided by CARDINAL and the quarter century wasted in trying to extract intelligence from MARK provide further evidence of the limitations of the KGB's political intelligence analysis. Mitrokhin records one occasion on which Andropov issued what amounted to an official rebuke for the poor quality of FCD assessments on the FRG. In October 1977, as part of the preparations for Brezhnev's state visit to West Germany in the following year, Kryuchkov submitted an alarmist report on the likely security problems, claiming that no fewer than 250 terrorist and extremist groups in the FRG were capable of attempting the assassination of the Soviet leader. Andropov replied acerbically:

> Comrade [V. I.] Kevorkov [of the Second Chief Directorate], who has just returned from the FRG, gives a different account of the situation. You should synchronize your watches, as for us this is not a trivial matter.[106]

In the event, Kevorkov's less alarmist assessment proved correct and Brezhnev's visit in May 1978 passed off without incident.[107]

MITROKHIN'S INFORMATION ON the KGB's West German agents, though extensive, is not comprehensive. There is, for example, intriguing evidence in the files seen by Mitrokhin of a KGB agent in the entourage of Egon Bahr, one of Helmut Schmidt's most trusted advisers and a leading architect of *Ostpolitik*. (There is no suggestion that the agent was Bahr himself.) On February 5, 1981 Andropov sent Brezhnev and the CPSU Central Committee an intelligence report (no. 259-A/OV), marked "of special importance," which recounted a telephone conversation on January 27 between Schmidt and Ronald Reagan, whose inauguration as president of the United States had taken place a week earlier, and gave details of Schmidt's subsequent discussions with Bahr and other advisers. To Schmidt's irritation, Reagan asked for a month's delay to the chancellor's visit to Washington, previously arranged for March 3, on the grounds that the President was not yet ready "for a serious discussion of foreign policy problems." Schmidt told his advisers that this was a deliberate delaying tactic by the new Reagan administration "designed to enable Washington to gain time to build up its armaments with the aim of overtaking the USSR in the military field."

The KGB source also reported complaints by Schmidt to Bahr and others that Bonn was flooded with specialists sent by Washington with the aim of halting the growth of commercial contacts between West Germany and the Soviet Union. Schmidt rightly believed that the Reagan administration was out to torpedo the negotiations between Bonn and Moscow on the construction of pipelines to bring natural gas from Siberia to the FRG, which Washington feared would make West Germany dangerously dependent on Soviet energy supplies. Moscow was doubtless delighted by Schmidt's intention to press ahead with the negotiations as quickly as possible in order to present Reagan with a *fait accompli*.[108]

The reliability of the KGB's German source was authenticated in the report sent to Brezhnev and the Central Committee both by Andropov and by Lieutenant-

General Kevorkov, then head of the Seventh Department of the KGB Second Chief Directorate (SCD).[109] Kevorkov's involvement indicates that the source was recruited and controlled not by the FCD but by the SCD, perhaps after being compromised during a visit or posting to Moscow (a characteristic form of SCD blackmail).[110]

Despite some lack of enthusiasm for Schmidt, both the Soviet and East German leadership were anxious to prevent a return to power by the Christian Democrats. According to a KGB file, Honecker secretly made known to the Schmidt government in 1978 that East Germany was willing to take action designed to improve the SDP's apparently declining electoral prospects—for example, by easing travel restrictions between the GDR and FRG.[111] There is no evidence of any response from the SDP.

Moscow's particular *bête noire* was the charismatic, right-wing Bavarian CSU leader, Franz-Josef Strauss, who was chosen as the candidate of the CDU and its CSU allies for the chancellorship in the 1980 elections. According to the minutes of a meeting in Moscow in July 1979 between Andropov and Mielke, the GDR interior minister and head of the Stasi, "It was acknowledged that Strauss was a serious opponent to Schmidt at the Bundestag elections in 1980. It was therefore essential to compromise Strauss and his supporters."[112] Among the KGB active measures agreed by Andropov and Mielke was operation COBRA-2, which used information gathered by an HVA agent, Inge Goliath, former secretary to the head of the main CDU foreign affairs think tank, to fabricate sinister links between the CDU/CSU leadership and right-wing elements in the intelligence agencies. A total of 1,587 copies of a booklet alleging that BND officers had conspired with the opposition against the Schmidt government were circulated to politicians, trade union leaders and other opinion-formers in the FRG. According to the KGB file on COBRA-2, some of the disinformation in the booklet reappeared in the West German press and caused Schmidt to order a judicial enquiry.[113]

The KGB, which had a recurrent tendency to exaggerate the success of its active measures in reports to the Politburo, claimed that COBRA-2 had caused great alarm in the CDU/CSU leadership and had "a positive influence" in ensuring an SDP victory at the 1980 Bundestag elections.[114] Though, in reality, Strauss's election defeat probably owed little—if anything—to Soviet and East German active measures, it undoubtedly came as a considerable relief to the Centre. When the SDP finally fell from power in 1983, the new government was headed not by Strauss but by the less flamboyant Helmut Kohl.

The main aim of KGB active measures during the early 1980s was the attempt to exploit the opposition of the large and militant West German peace movement to the deployment of US medium-range missiles in the FRG. Among the most eloquent opponents of the deployment was the *Bürgermeister* of Saarbrucken, Oskar Lafontaine, later an unsuccessful SDP candidate for the chancellorship (and in 1998 briefly a controversial finance minister in the government of Gerhard Schrîder). It would have been wholly out of character had the Centre, which only a few years earlier had formed absurdly unrealistic plans to recruit Harold Wilson and Cyrus Vance, not also targeted Lafontaine. In 1981 the operations officer, L. S. Bratus, was sent to cultivate him and—predictably—failed in the attempt.[115] The KGB seems, none the less, to have tried to take a largely undeserved share of the credit for the decision by an SDP congress eight months after its 1983 election defeat to oppose the stationing of US medium-range missiles on German soil. A CPSU Central Committee document in 1984 claimed complacently, "Many arguments that had previously been presented by us to the representatives of the SDP have now been taken over by them."[116]

As in other NATO countries, the chief priority of intelligence collection in the FRG during the early 1980s was operation RYAN—the fruitless attempt to discover non-existent Western preparations for a nuclear first strike against the Soviet Union. Markus Wolf and, no doubt, some KGB officers in Karlshorst and West German residencies regarded the whole operation as utterly misconceived. None, however, dared to challenge the paranoid mindset of the Centre. Wolf found his Soviet contacts "obsessed" with RYAN and the threat of a NATO nuclear first strike:

> The HVA was ordered to uncover any Western plans for such a surprise attack, and we formed a special staff and situation center, as well as emergency command centers, to do this. The personnel had to undergo military training and participate in alarm drills. Like most intelligence people, I found these war games a burdensome waste of time, but these orders were no more open to discussion than other orders from above.[117]

Because S&T collection was less distorted by misconceptions of the West than political intelligence, its quality was probably higher. Kryuchkov wrote in a directive to residencies in July 1977:

> Work against West Germany is assuming an increasingly greater importance at the present time in connection with the growth of the economic potential of the FRG and the increase in its influence in the solution of important international issues.
>
> The Federal Republic of Germany is both economically and militarily the leading West European capitalist country. It is the main strategic bridgehead of NATO, where a significant concentration of the adversary's military strength can be observed: the total numerical strength of the forces of the Western allies (including the Bundeswehr) reaches almost a million in the country. This situation distinguishes the FRG from the other European capitalist states and makes it the most important component of the military bloc. Within the FRG, military scientific research studies in the fields of atomic energy, aviation, rocket construction, electronics, chemistry and biology are being intensively pursued.[118]

As Kryuchkov's directive indicates, West Germany, though ranked far behind the United States, had become the chief European target for Line X (S&T) operations. In 1980, 61.5 percent of the S&T received by the Military Industrial Commission (VPK) came from American sources (not all in the United States), 10.5 percent from the FRG, 8 percent from France, 7.5 percent from Britain and 3 percent from Japan. Just over half the intelligence acquired by FCD Directorate T in 1980 (possibly an exceptional year) came from allied intelligence services, the HVA and Czechoslovak StB chief among them.[119]

Among Directorate T's chief targets in the FRG was Germany's largest electronics company, Siemens, whose scientists and engineers included the KGB illegal RICHARD,[120] recruited in East Germany, and at least two other Soviet agents: HELMUT[121] and KARL.[122] HELMUT was unaware that he was a KGB agent and believed that he was working for the HVA.[123]

As in the case of other Western companies, it proved easier to collect S&T from Siemens than to exploit it in the Soviet Union, particularly in the civilian economy. The Centre's paranoid tendencies made it increasingly fearful that the Siemens computers it purloined had been bugged or otherwise tampered with. The FCD's Fifteenth Department (Registry and Archives) planned to use a Siemens computer to store the information on its card files on three million people. Because of the Centre's fear that the computer contained some hidden bug which Soviet experts had failed to detect, however, it remained unused in a storeroom for five years.[124] Less advanced East German computers were eventually used instead.[125]

As well as benefiting from the HVA's extensive S&T operations in the FRG, the KGB's own Line X agents spanned almost the whole of West German high technology. In addition to those in Siemens, Mitrokhin's notes identify twenty-nine other agents of varying importance, some of them working for such major firms as Bayer, Dynamit Nobel, Messerschmitt and Thyssen.[126]

The great majority of these espionage cases never came to court. One of the few which did was that of Manfred Rotsch (EMIL), who was betrayed by a French agent in Directorate T.[127] As head of the planning department in the FRG's largest arms manufacturer, Messerschmitt—Bölkow—Blohm (MBB), Rotsch betrayed many of the secrets of NATO's new fighter bomber, the Tornado (built by MMB jointly with British and Italian manufacturers), the Milan anti-tank missile and the Hot and Roland surface-to-air missiles.[128] Rotsch was a highly professional well-trained spy, communicating with his controllers by microdot messages.[129] His cover too was impeccable. While living an apparently conventional family life of almost tedious tranquility in a Munich suburb, he joined the conservative Christian Social Union and stood as a CSU candidate in Bavarian local elections.[130] Mitrokhin's brief note on EMIL indicates that he had already been recruited by the KGB before he left East Germany, ostensibly as a refugee, in 1954.[131] Rotsch thus may well have been the longest-serving KGB agent planted in the FRG with East German assistance. Arrested in 1984, he was sentenced in 1986 to eight and a half years' imprisonment but exchanged a year later for an East Berlin doctor serving a long prison term of solitary confinement. Though housed with his wife in a luxury East German lakeside villa, Rotsch had grown attached to his life in the West. Within a few months, both returned to their house near Munich and a frosty welcome from their scandalized neighbors.[132]

STASI AND HVA offices were full of busts of Lenin and Dzerzhinsky, commemorative plaques embellished with the sword and shield of the Cheka and other trinkets presented at convivial gatherings of GDR and Soviet intelligence officers at which operational successes against the FRG such as the East German Manfred Rotsch's thirty years as a KGB agent were celebrated and toasts were drunk to the future. After the fall of the Berlin Wall in November 1989, however, the near 40-year collaboration between HVA and KGB, the most successful (though characteristically rather one-sided) intelligence alliance in the Soviet Bloc, ended in East German charges of betrayal by Moscow. Most appeals for help to the Centre after the collapse of the GDR by former HVA officers and agents who feared prosecution in the West were met by an embarrassed silence from the KGB. On October 22, 1990 Wolf wrote to Gorbachev:

> We were your friends. We wear a lot of your decorations on our breasts. We were said to have made a great contribution to your security. Now, in our hour of need, I assume that you will not deny us your help.

Gorbachev, however, did precisely that. Wolf appealed to him to insist on an amnesty for the Stasi and its foreign intelligence service before agreeing to German reunification. Gorbachev refused. "It was," says Wolf bitterly, "the Soviets' ultimate betrayal of their East German friends, whose work for over four decades had strengthened Soviet influence in Europe."[133]

TWENTY-SEVEN

FRANCE AND ITALY DURING
THE COLD WAR

Agent Penetration and Active Measures

For much, probably most, of the Cold War, the Paris residency ran more agents—usually about fifty plus—than any other KGB station in western Europe. Its most remarkable achievement during the Fourth Republic (1946–58) was the penetration of the French intelligence community, especially SDECE, the foreign intelligence agency. An incomplete list in KGB files of the residency's particularly "valuable agents" in 1953 included four officials in the SDECE (codenamed NOSENKO, SHIROKOV, KORABLEV and DUBRAVIN) and one each in the domestic security service DST (GORYACHEV), the Renseignements Généraux (GIZ), the foreign ministry (IZVEKOV), the defense ministry (LAVROV), the naval ministry (PIZHO), the New Zealand embassy (LONG) and the press (ZHIGALOV).[1] In 1954 30 per cent of all reports to the Centre from the Paris residency were based on information from its agents in the French intelligence community.[2]

The basis for Soviet penetration of France during the Cold War had been laid at the end of the Second World War. Thanks both to the leading role played by the Communist Party in the French Resistance and the presence of Communist ministers in government until 1947, the few years after the Liberation had been a golden age for agent recruitment.[3] Though the British and American intelligence communities were probably unaware of the identities of most Soviet agents in France, they were acutely conscious of the weakness of post-war French security and—for that reason—cautious about exchanging classified information with the SDECE and the DST. A 1948 assessment by the British Joint Intelligence Committee (JIC), infused by a somewhat absurd sense of ethnic superiority, blamed the success of Soviet penetration on "inherent defects in the French character" as well as "the wide appeal of Communism in France." Soviet intelligence, the JIC concluded, was able to exploit:

(a)   A natural garrulous tendency in the French character which makes the temptation to pass on "hot" information, albeit in strictest confidence," almost irresistible.

(b)   A lack of "security consciousness" which leads to carelessness and insufficient precautions to guard classified documents.

(c)   A certain decline in moral standards in France, which, together with extremely low rates of pay, must contribute to the temptation to "sell" information . . .[4]

The JIC's supreme confidence in the inherent superiority of British over Gallic security was, presumably, at least slightly deflated three years later by the defection of Burgess and Maclean, Philby's recall from Washington and the suspicion which fell on Blunt and Cairncross.

After the compromise of the British Magnificent Five in 1951, France became for the remainder of the decade the KGB's most productive source of intelligence on Western policy to the Soviet Bloc.[5] The KGB defectors Vladimir and Evdokia Petrov reported in 1954 that the Centre "found intelligence work particularly easy in France . . . The French operational section was littered with what looked like photostat copies of original French documents."[6] The Paris residency obtained important intelligence on Western negotiating positions before both the Berlin Conference early in 1954, the first between Soviet, American, British and French foreign ministers since 1949, and the Geneva four-power summit in July 1955, the first meeting of heads of government since the meeting of the Big Three at Potsdam ten years before.[7] Thanks to the diplomatic ciphers provided by JOUR, a cipher clerk in the Quai d'Orsay recruited in 1945, the Centre also seems to have had access to plentiful French SIGINT. In 1957 JOUR was awarded the Order of the Red Star.[8] It was probably largely thanks to JOUR that during the Cuban missile crisis, the KGB was able to supply the Kremlin with verbatim copies of diplomatic traffic between the Quai d'Orsay and its embassies in Moscow and Washington.[9]

During the early Cold War, the Paris residency also appears to have been the most successful promoter of active measures designed to influence Western opinion and opinion-formers. Between 1947 and 1955 the residency sponsored a series of bogus memoirs and other propagandist works, among them: *J'ai choisi la potence* (*I Chose the Gallows*) by General Andrei Vlasov, who had fought with the Germans on the eastern front; the equally fraudulent *Ma carriäre Ö l'état-major soviétique* (*My Career in the Soviet High Command*) by "Ivan Krylov;" and bogus correspondence between Stalin and Tito, published in the weekly magazine *Carrefour*, in which Tito confessed to being a Trotskyist. The main author of the forgeries was Grigori Besedovsky, a former Soviet diplomat who had settled in Paris. Some of Besedovsky's fabrications, which also included two books about Stalin by a non-existent nephew, were sophisticated enough to deceive even such a celebrated Soviet scholar as E. H. Carr, who in 1955 contributed a foreword to *Notes for a Journal*, fraudulently attributed to the former foreign commissar Maksim Litvinov. The resident in Paris from 1946 to 1948, Ivan Ivanovich Agayants, who had launched the Besedovsky frauds, was later appointed head of the FCD's first specialized disinformation section, Department D (subsequently Service A), founded in 1959.[10]

The post-war Paris residency also had what was, in effect, its own weekly newspaper, focusing on international relations: *La Tribune des Nations* (codenamed ÉCOLE). Founded in 1946 by André Ulmann with the help of Soviet subsidies,[11] the

Tribune's subscribers included both French government departments and foreign embassies. Publicly, Ulmann disclaimed any connection with the French Communist Party (PCF). According to his friend Pierre Daix:

> There was nothing Stalinist about him. He did not even seem like a Communist. He was a progressive intellectual, but without any of the utopian or idealistic nonsense associated with this expression. His feet were firmly on the ground.[12]

Ulmann's KGB file, however, reveals that he was a secret member of the PCF. Recommended by the Party leadership to the Paris residency, he had been recruited as agent DURANT in 1946. From 1948 onwards Ulmann also worked as an agent of the Polish intelligence service, which gave him the codename YULI and provided monthly subsidies of 200,000 francs to help finance the publication of *La Tribune des Nations*.[13] Between 1946 and his death in 1970, Ulmann received a total of 3,552,100 francs from the Paris residency, as well as an (unidentified) Soviet decoration for his work for the KGB.[14] To at least some Paris journalists, however, Ulmann's cover was somewhat transparent. The historian of the PCF, Annie Kriegel, herself a former *militante*, recalls hearing Ulmann being described by one of her friends as "a secret agent disguised as a secret agent."[15]

Despite the Paris residency's successes during the 1950s, the Centre was dissatisfied with the number of its new recruits. It took Moscow some years to accept that, following the end of Communist participation in government in 1947, the pace of subsequent agent recruitment was bound to be slower. In a despatch to the Paris residency on February 3, 1954, the Centre insisted that it step up its campaign to acquire new agents in the foreign ministry, the cabinet secretariat, the SDECE, the DST, the general staff's Deuxiäme Bureau, the armed forces and NATO. "The residency," it complained, "is living on its old capital and is not taking energetic measures to acquire new, valuable sources of information."[16]

In 1955 the Paris residency recruited a major new agent inside NATO, codenamed GERMAIN, who was controlled by an (unidentified) illegal despatched from the Centre. GERMAIN, like JOUR, was later awarded the Order of the Red Star. His wife NINA trained as a KGB radio operator and was given the medal "For combat services."[17] In 1956 a residency agent, DROZDOV, reported that one of his wife's friends, ROZA, who worked at SDECE headquarters, had become pregnant after a one-night stand with "a chance acquaintance." On instructions from the residency, DROZDOV gave ROZA financial help after the birth of her daughter in the following year in the hope of laying the basis for an eventual recruitment. ROZA's cultivation, however, proceeded slowly. By 1961 the residency had concluded that she would rebuff any direct attempt to turn her into a KGB agent, and decided instead on a false flag recruitment. DROZDOV successfully persuaded her to provide regular intelligence reports to assist a fictitious "progressive organization" of which he claimed to be a member.[18] Other French recruits during the early years of the Fifth Republic, established in January 1959 under the presidency of General Charles de

Gaulle, included two cipher clerks (LARIONOV[19] and SIDOROV[20]), two Paris police officers (FRENE[21] and DACHNIK[22]) and two young scientists (ADAM[23] and SASHA[24]). In 1964, like his fellow cipher clerk JOUR seven years earlier, SIDOROV was awarded the Order of the Red Star[25]—a further indication of the success of KGB SIGINT operations in decrypting French diplomatic traffic.

The French embassy in Moscow was also a major KGB target. During the early 1960s both the ambassador, Maurice Dejean, and the air attaché, Colonel Louis Guibaud, were seduced by KGB swallows after elaborate "honeytrap" operations directed by the head of the Second Chief Directorate, Oleg Mikhailovich Gribanov, with the personal approval of Khrushchev. Dejean was beaten up by a KGB officer posing as the enraged husband of the swallow, a Moscow ballerina who had seduced him. Guibaud was confronted with the usual compromising photographs of his sexual liaison. Both seductions, however, failed as intelligence operations. In 1962 Guibaud shot himself with his service revolver. The following year, a defector revealed Gribanov's plan to compromise Dejean, who was recalled to Paris before serious KGB blackmail had begun. De Gaulle welcomed the ambassador home with the now celebrated reproof, "Alors, Dejean, on couche!"[26] The KGB files noted by Mitrokhin reveal for the first time that a third French diplomat in Moscow was successfully targeted by Gribanov. A female member of the embassy staff, codenamed LOUISA, was seduced by a male swallow, confronted with photographs of her seduction and persuaded to work as a Soviet agent. Once back in Paris in the early 1960s, however, she broke off contact with the KGB.[27]

The most successful French recruitment in Moscow recorded in the files seen by Mitrokhin was that of the businessman Franáois Saar-Demichel (codenamed NN) in the 1960s.[28] After fighting in the Resistance, Saar-Demichel had served briefly in the DGER and its successor, the SDECE, before leaving in 1947 to begin a business career. In 1954 he won an exclusive, and lucrative, contract to import Soviet wood pulp for French paper manufacture. A year later, during a visit to Moscow, he was recruited by the SCD as a KGB agent. Acting on instructions from the Centre, Saar-Demichel used his Resistance connections to make contact with some of de Gaulle's leading supporters and contributed almost 15 million francs to the Gaullist cause during the final years of the Fourth Republic.[29]

After the change of regime and de Gaulle's election as President of the Republic, Saar-Demichel succeeded in gaining an entrée to the êlysée and supplied regular reports on his meetings with Soviet leaders during business trips to Moscow. According to Constantin Melnik, security adviser to the first prime minister of the Fifth Republic, Michel Debré, "More than any other political movement, Gaullism was swarming with agents of influence of the obliging KGB, whom we never succeeded in keeping away from de Gaulle." The most important of them may well have been Saar-Demichel. His reports were designed by the Centre to reinforce de Gaulle's belief that Soviet leaders were guided not by Communist ideology but by traditional Russian interests, and to persuade him that they were genuinely anxious for an understanding with France:

My Soviet interlocutors [nowadays] make much less use of Marxist-Leninist phraseology . . . They are very open to dialogue and make a clear distinction between propaganda statements and discussions based on precise facts . . . The dead weight of ideology is fading away, particularly among the new generation. Faced with this transformation of public opinion, the leadership is making no attempt to put a stop to it.[30]

During his visits to Moscow, Saar-Demichel also provided the Centre with regular reports on de Gaulle's foreign policy. He claimed that after the signature of the coopperation treaty between France and West Germany in January 1963, which had been badly received in Moscow, de Gaulle had said privately, "We extended our hand to the Germans so that we could at least be sure they were not holding a knife in theirs."[31]

AS WELL AS collecting intelligence, the Paris residency continued to be energetically engaged in active measures. In its annual report for 1961, the residency proudly reported that it had been responsible for inspiring 230 articles in the press, 11 books and pamphlets, 32 parliamentary questions and statements, 9 public meetings and the circulation of 14,000 copies of 10 posters and flysheets.[32] In addition to André Ulmann (DURANT), editor of *La Tribune des Nations*,[33] the residency's agents of influence included at least two socialist politicians, GILBERT and DROM.[34] GILBERT (later GILES), who was reported to be "close" to the future president, Franáois Mitterrand, was recruited by the Czechoslovak StB in 1955 under the code-name ROTER. KGB contacts with GILBERT began a year later.[35] DROM was first cultivated by the KGB in 1959, recruited as an agent in 1961 and paid a monthly retainer of 1,500 francs for the next twelve years.[36]

The Paris residency's most ambitious active measure during de Gaulle's decade as President of the Fifth Republic was to fund a new news agency, the Centre d'Information Scientifique, Économique et Politique, founded in 1961 by Pierre-Charles Pathé, a newly recruited KGB agent codenamed PECHERIN (later MASON). The journalist son of the millionaire film magnate who had founded Pathé newsreels, he had first come to the residency's attention two years earlier after publishing a naively pro-Soviet *Essai sur le phénomäne soviétique:*

The cruelties of Stalinism were only childhood illnesses. The victory of the Soviet Union is that of a correct vision of the march of history. The USSR, this laboratory of new ideas for the most advanced development of society, will overtake the gigantism of the United States.

From 1961 to 1967 the KGB paid Pathé 6,000 francs a month to publish a weekly newsletter (codenamed OBZOR) from his center, which was sold by subscription but sent free of charge to opinion-formers in politics, business, journalism and diplomacy.[37]

The main purpose of the active measures implemented by Pathé and the Paris residency's other agents of influence during the early Fifth Republic was to damage

Franco-American relations, encourage a Franco-Soviet *rapprochement* and distance France from NATO.[38] Saar-Demichel reported progress on all three fronts. His finest hour as a KGB agent came during a visit to Moscow to negotiate the sale of the French SECAM color system to Soviet television in March 1965, when he told his controller that de Gaulle wished to visit the Soviet Union in the following year. De Gaulle, he claimed, attached no importance to Franco-Soviet ideological differences and had told him:

> Russia was, is, and would continue to be a great power in Europe. The outstanding qualities of the Russian people remained the same whatever the ideology of the Communist government, but at the present time Communist ideology acted as a bond which held together this vast multinational federation. However, it was not ideology but reasons of state which played the main role.

As for the reunification of Germany, to which the Soviet Union was resolutely opposed, de Gaulle wished to postpone it as long as possible: "The later, the better." A doubtless exultant Centre passed on Saar-Demichel's message to the Central Committee.[39]

It remains unclear whether, as the KGB believed, the êlysée had asked Saar-Demichel to sound out Moscow on the question of a state visit—or whether, knowing de Gaulle's wishes, he took the initiative himself. The Centre, however, claimed much of the credit for de Gaulle's decision to distance France from NATO and improve relations with the Soviet Union.[40] In March 1966 France withdrew from the integrated NATO command. Three months later de Gaulle made a triumphal state visit to the Soviet Union. The KGB had, in reality, little influence on either decision. Ever since the United States and Britain had rejected his proposal early in the Fifth Republic to join with France in a three-power directorate at the head of NATO, de Gaulle had been increasingly inclined to distance himself from it. His attempt to use the Soviet Union as a counterweight to American influence in Europe went back to his wartime years as leader of the Free French, when Roosevelt and Churchill had failed to treat him as an equal. "Ah, Monsieur le Secrétaire Général," he told Brezhnev during his visit to Moscow, "how happy we are to have you to help us resist American pressure—just as we are pleased to have the United States to help us resist pressure from the Soviet Union!" But if—contrary to the private boasts of the Centre—KGB active measures did not determine de Gaulle's foreign policy, they played at least a minor role in reinforcing his conviction that the Soviet Union was a traditional great power with an increasingly thin Communist veneer. His report to the French cabinet on his state visit to Russia concurred with the views expressed by Saar-Demichel. The Soviet Union, de Gaulle declared, was "evolving from ideology to technocracy:

> I did not talk to anyone who told me, "I am a Communist militant or a party leader" . . . If one leaves aside their propaganda statements, they are conducting a peaceful [foreign] policy.[41]

KGB active measures may have had a somewhat greater, though doubtless not decisive, influence on the evolution of French public opinion. According to opinion polls after de Gaulle's state visit, 35 percent of French people held a favorable opinion of the Soviet Union (as compared with 25 percent two years earlier) while only 13 percent were hostile. Those with favorable opinions of the United States fell, partly as a consequence of the Vietnam War, from 52 percent in 1964 to only 22 percent at the beginning of 1967.[42]

After the apparent successes of the previous few years, the Paris residency saw little purpose in continuing to fund Pathé's Centre d'Information Scientifique, Économique et Politique, on which it had spent 436,000 francs since 1961. The center closed and its newsletter ceased publication. Pathé continued, however, to work as an agent of influence, writing regular articles in national newspapers under the pseudonym "Charles Morand." From January 1967 to June 1979, he received a total of 218,400 francs in salary, plus 68,423 francs for expenses and bonuses.[43] In 1969 Pathé was one of the organizers of the Gaullist-dominated Mouvement pour l'Indépendance de l'Europe, which the Centre regarded as a potentially valuable means of destabilizing NATO.[44]

KGB PENETRATION OF the French intelligence community continued during the 1960s. Mitrokhin's notes record that at least four French intelligence officers and one former head of department in the Sñreté Générale were active KGB agents during the period 1963–6, but give few details.[45] In the years after de Gaulle's resignation in 1969, the quality, though not the quantity, of the KGB's French recruits seems to have declined. The total number of agents run by the Paris residency rose from 48 in 1971 to 55 in 1974; in 1974 the residency also had 17 confidential contacts.[46] However, the files seen by Mitrokhin contain no indication that the 1974 agents included any senior civil servants or intelligence officers. The KGB had also lost the services of DROM, one of its two leading agents within the Socialist Party. In 1973 he was given "substantial funds" to pay off his debts. Shortly afterwards, however, DROM was reported to be in contact with the DST.[47]

The best indication of the main strengths of the KGB's French agent network in the mid-1970s is a list of thirteen "valuable agents" of the Paris residency who, with Andropov's personal approval, were given substantial New Year gifts in 1973, 1974 and 1975. In each of these three years JOUR was given a bonus of 4,000 francs; ANDRÉ, BROK and FYODOR received 3,000 francs; ARGUS, DRAGUN, DZHELIB and LAURENT 2,000 francs; NANT and REM 1,500 francs; BUKINIST, MARS and TUR 1,000 francs.[48] Two reservations need to be registered about this list. First, it does not include the residency's most important S&T agent, ALAN, who was paid on a different bonus system.[49] (The same may apply to some other Line X agents.) Secondly, three of the agents who received the New Year bonuses were foreign officials stationed in Paris who provided intelligence chiefly on non-French matters. DZHELIB was a staff member of an Asian embassy, who provided ciphers and other classified documents;[50] REM was a Canadian in the Paris headquarters of UNESCO, who acted as an agent-recruiter;[51] BUKINIST worked in a Middle Eastern embassy.[52] The eleven French recruits selected for New Year gifts in 1973–5 do, however, give an important insight into the Centre's and Paris residency's perception of their main French assets.

The most highly rated French agent in the mid-1970s was also the longest-serving: JOUR, the cipher clerk in the Foreign Ministry (codenamed ELITA) recruited thirty years earlier, who was singled out for the largest bonus. During the period 1968–73 he provided intelligence on the cipher machines in the French embassy in Moscow and at NATO headquarters which enabled the Sixteenth (SIGINT) Directorate to decrypt a probably substantial amount of diplomatic traffic. In 1973 JOUR was posted to a French embassy abroad, where contact with him was maintained through dead letter-boxes.[53] Intelligence provided by JOUR probably assisted the bugging of the new teleprinters installed in the Moscow embassy between October 1976 and February 1977. All, remarkably, were left unguarded for forty-eight hours during their journey by rail to Moscow. The bugs secretly fitted to the teleprinters during this period transmitted to the KGB the unenciphered text of all incoming and outgoing embassy telegrams for over six years.[54] The head of the bugging operation, Igor Vasilovich Maslow, was awarded the Order of Lenin and later promoted to head the Sixteenth (SIGINT) Directorate.[55]

Until 1983, thanks to JOUR and Maslov, the Centre had far better information on French policy to the Soviet Union than that of any of France's NATO allies. JOUR simultaneously continued to talent-spot other Foreign Ministry cipher and secretarial personnel. In 1978–9 he cultivated "L" (identified only as a member of the ministry "support staff"), obtained his private address, carried out a background check on his home and facilitated his recruitment by a residency operations officer.[56] During the period 1978–82 no less than six cipher personnel at the Quai d'Orsay were under active KGB cultivation.[57]

A majority of the most highly rated French agents in the mid-1970s (six of the ten who received New Year bonuses in 1973–5: ANDRÉ,[58] BROK,[59] ARGUS,[60] NANT,[61] MARS[62] and TUR[63]) were journalists or involved with the press: a clear indication that, whatever the real effectiveness of KGB disinformation campaigns against French targets, the Centre regarded active measures as one of the main strengths of the Paris residency. Of the three other most valuable French agents, FYODOR held a major position in a foreign policy institute and provided documents on the USA, NATO and China;[64] LAURENT was a scientist in a NATO aeronautical research institute;[65] and DRAGUN was a businessman and agent-recruiter.[66] LAURENT and DRAGUN were probably Line X (S&T) agents. Pathé (MASON), one of the leading agents of influence in the 1960s, had declined in importance and did not figure on the list of most valuable agents in 1973–5. His career, however, was to revive during the second half of the decade.

The Centre's probably exaggerated confidence in the agents of influence run by the PR Line of the Paris residency led it to undertake an ambitious series of active measures throughout the 1970s. According to KGB files, ANDRÉ, a senior journalist, "had access to President Georges Pompidou," who had succeeded de Gaulle in 1969, and to some of his senior ministers, including Pierre Messmer, who became prime minister in 1972, and Foreign Minister Maurice Schumann.[67] Reports from the Paris residency claimed that ANDRÉ was used to pass to Pompidou's office "slanted information" calculated to increase the President's suspicion of the United States.[68] In this, as in most influence operations, it is difficult to estimate the level of success. Given ANDRÉ's access to the highest levels of the Pompidou administration, it is difficult to believe that he was simply ignored. It is equally difficult to credit, however, that he had more than—at best—a marginal influence on French foreign policy. The Centre's reports to the Central Committee tended to claim more credit than it probably deserved for provoking, or worsening, tension within the Atlantic Alliance.

The limitations of KGB active measures in influencing French policy were clearly illustrated by the failure of the LA MANCHE ("English Channel") operation, designed to sow distrust between Pompidou and the British prime minister, Edward Heath, to persuade the President to maintain de Gaulle's veto on British entry into the European Community.[69]

Though the journalist ARGUS appears to have had no direct access to Pompidou, he was in even closer contact than ANDRÉ with Messmer. According to reports from the Paris residency he had regular discussions with the Prime Minister during the campaign for the March 1973 general election and continued to advise him afterwards. The main aim of the KGB disinformation channeled through ARGUS was to damage the electoral prospects of the Gaullist-led ruling coalition by sowing distrust between the Gaullists and their allies. ARGUS falsely alleged to Messmer that Michel Poniatowski, general secretary of the Independent Republicans, and the Reformist Jean-Jacques Servan-Schreiber had secretly agreed to cooperate in undermining the position of Gaullist candidates. On KGB instructions, ARGUS also planted similar disinformation in the press. Other active measures devised by Service A to damage "Atlanticist" (pro-American) candidates included planting false reports that the campaigns of Servan-Schreiber and the Christian Democrat leader, Jean Lecanuet, were being financed by American money. In Servan-Schreiber's constituency of Meurthe-et-Moselle, letters were posted to local notables purporting to come from a neo-Nazi group in the FRG which called on all those "with German blood flowing in their veins" to vote for Servan-Schreiber.[70] While such operations may well have impressed the Centre, it is difficult to believe that they had a significant influence on French voters. Though the vote of the left increased at the general election, the Gaullist-led coalition retained a comfortable majority of seats.

Having greatly exaggerated its success in 1973, the Centre was also confident of its ability to influence the outcome of the May 1974 presidential election. It informed the Central Committee that the Socialist leader, Franáois Mitterrand, standing as the candidate of all the main left-wing parties, had a real chance of victory,[71] and mounted a major active measures campaign against his chief right-wing opponent, Valéry Giscard d'Estaing (codenamed KROT—"Mole"). In one week during the campaign, ten officers of the Paris residency Line PR carried out fifty-six allegedly "significant operational measures."[72]

A leading part in the active measures against Giscard was taken by one of the residency's most highly rated and longest-serving agents, BROK, then a well-connected journalist. Originally recruited as an ideological agent in 1946, BROK had begun working for money within a few years to supplement his income as a journalist and to purchase a Paris apartment. In the mid-1970s he was paid over 100,000 francs a year.[73] As well as having a total of at least ten case officers,[74] BROK was so highly regarded that he had meetings with five heads of the FCD Fifth Department, whose responsibilities included operations in France.[75] During the 1974 presidential election campaign, BROK was provided, on Andropov's personal instructions, with a fabricated copy of supposedly secret campaign advice given to Giscard d'Estaing by the Americans on ways to defeat Mitterrand and Jacques Chaban-Delmas, Giscard's unsuccessful Gaullist rival for the right-wing vote during the first round of the election. The forged document was then shown to Chaban-Delmas and others, doubtless to try to make collaboration between him and Giscard more difficult at the second round, when Giscard was the sole candidate of the right.[76]

The only other operation to discredit Giscard d'Estaing during the 1974 presidential election which is described in detail in Mitrokhin's notes was a somewhat bizarre active measure which reflected the obsession of the KGB's many conspiracy theorists with Zionist intrigues. In France, as in the United States and elsewhere, the Centre believed that a powerful Jewish lobby was at work behind the scenes, manipulating much of the political process.[77] The KGB decided to exploit the murder of a female relative of Giscard d'Estaing in October 1973 to mount an extraordinary operation designed to embroil him with the Jewish lobby. Service A concocted a forged document supposedly distributed by a (non-existent) French pro-Israeli group, claiming that she had been killed by Zionists in revenge for Giscard's part in the prosecution of Jewish financiers while serving as finance minister some years earlier. The Centre was unaccountably proud of the whole absurd operation.[78] In the second round of the presidential election, Giscard defeated Mitterrand by less than 2 percent of the vote. There is no evidence that KGB active measures had the slightest influence on the result.

IN THE MID-1970S *Le Monde* (codenamed VESTNIK—"Messenger"—by the KGB)[79] became embroiled in a controversy over its alleged left-wing, anti-American bias. The most distinguished of its leading conservative critics, Raymond Aron, contrasted *Le Monde*'s readiness to mention US bombing raids on North Vietnam in the same breath as Nazi wartime atrocities with its reluctance to engage in serious, detailed criticism of Soviet abuses of human rights.[80] Solzhenitsyn, whose *Gulag Archipelago* provided the best-documented evidence of those abuses, received particularly unfair treatment. In July 1975 *Le Monde* used a distorted account of a speech by Solzhenitsyn in the United States to smear him as a Nazi sympathizer:

> Alexander Solzhenitsyn regrets that the West joined forces with the USSR against Nazi Germany during the last world war.
>
> He is not alone. Westerners of a previous generation like [the leading French collaborator] Pierre Laval had the same ideas, and people like [the French fascists] Doriot and Déat welcomed the Nazis as liberators.[81]

Two months later, Le Monde reported—also inaccurately—that Solzhenitsyn had accepted an invitation to visit Chile from the brutal military dictatorship of General Pinochet.[82] There is no proof that either of these smears was planted by the KGB. Both, however, were entirely in line with disinformation which the KGB was seeking to plant on the Western press.[83] In 1976 a former member of Le Monde's editorial staff, Michel Legris, published a detailed analysis of what he claimed was its equally biased reporting in favor of the Portuguese Communists, the Cambodian Khmer Rouge and the Palestinian PLO.[84]

The extent of bias in Le Monde reporting during the 1970s still remains controversial, as do claims that it was far readier to condemn American than Soviet policy.[85] KGB files, however, provide some support for the charges of pro-Soviet bias made by Le Monde's critics. Mitrokhin's brief notes on KGB contacts with Le Monde identify two senior journalists and several contributors who were used, in most cases doubtless unwittingly, to disseminate KGB disinformation.[86] During the 1970s and early 1980s the Paris residency claimed to have influenced Le Monde articles on, inter alia, US policy in Iran, Latin America, the US bicentennial, the dangers of American influence in Europe, the threat of a supranational Europe, US plans for the neutron bomb, causes of East–West tension and the war in Afghanistan.[87] In July 1981 Andropov received a message from the leadership of the French Communist Party, urging him to arrange for an invitation to visit Afghanistan to be sent to a named journalist on Le Monde, whose reporting, it claimed, would be "sympathetic."[88] Some years earlier the same journalist had been generous in his praise of Colonel Muhammar Qaddafi. Le Monde's susceptibility to KGB disinformation probably derived chiefly from naivety about Soviet intelligence operations. In the aftermath of Watergate and the revelations of abuses by the US intelligence community, Le Monde showed itself—like some other sections of the media—acutely aware of the sins, real and imagined, of the CIA but curiously blind to the extensive active measures program of the KGB.[89]

Unlike Le Monde, the main news agency, Agence France-Presse, attracted little public controversy. It was, however, successfully penetrated both in Paris and abroad. Mitrokhin's notes identify six agents[90] and two confidential contacts[91] in the agency recruited between 1956 and 1980. The most senior, LAN, was recruited under false flag by the businessman DRAGUN in 1969 and paid 1,500 francs a month, which he was told came from the Italian company Olivetti, supposedly anxious to have inside information on French government policy.[92]

Perhaps the most ambitious active measure begun by the KGB during the presidency of Giscard d'Estaing was the launching of the fortnightly newsletter Synthesis (codenamed CACTUS) by its agent of influence Pierre-Charles Pathé (MASON). The first issue of Synthesis, ostensibly left-wing Gaullist in tone, appeared in June 1976 and was sent free of charge to 500 opinion-formers,[93] among them 70 percent of the Chamber of Deputies, 47 percent of the Senate and 41 journalists.[94] The seventy issues published over the next three years, at a cost to the KGB of 252,000 francs,[95] covered a series of well-worn Service A themes. France was portrayed as the victim of an "underhanded" American economic war in which the US balance of payments deficit allowed Washington to act as a parasite on the wealth of other states.

Giscard d'Estaing was portrayed as an "Atlanticist" who was failing to protect French interests against American exploitation. The United States was a sinister "police democracy" which employed systematic violence against its black minority and all others who stood in its way. The assassination of President Kennedy was "an essential aspect of American democracy." By contrast, Pol Pot's massacres were either played down or explained away and the Vietnamese boat people dismissed as middle-class emigrants.[96]

Pathé's downfall began in 1978 when the DST started tailing his case officer at the Paris residency, Igor Aleksandrovich Sakharovsky (alias "Kuznetsov"), son of a former head of the FCD. After Sakharovsky reported his suspicions that he was being followed to his superiors, his meetings with Pathé were temporarily suspended. When they resumed two months later, Sakharovsky inadvertently led his watchers to Pathé. On July 5, 1979 the radio-intercept post in the Paris residency, while listening into a frequency used by a DST surveillance team, heard its leader announce, "The actors are in place. Let's start the show!" Immediately afterwards Pathé was arrested in the act of receiving money and documents from Sakharovsky.[97] In May 1980 Pathé became the only Soviet agent of influence ever convicted in a Western court. He was sentenced to five years' imprisonment but was released in 1981. During his trial Pathé admitted to having received small sums of money for articles written on Moscow's behalf. His KGB file reveals that, in reality, by the time of his arrest he had received a total of 974,823 francs in salary and expenses.[98]

At almost the same time as the *Synthesis* active measure came to an ignominious end, the Paris residency took the decision to cease funding *La Tribune des Nations*, founded by its agent André Ulmann (DURANT) in 1946. Since Ulmann's death in 1970, further KGB subsidies to the *Tribune*, totaling 1,527,500 francs by 1978, had been channeled through agent NANT, a former associate of Ulmann. In the mid-1970s NANT was considered one of the residency's dozen most valuable agents, providing intelligence obtained from his contacts in official circles as well as carrying out active measures. According to his file, from 1970 to 1978 he supplied 119 intelligence reports, published 78 articles on topics devised by Service A and helped to cultivate 12 potential agents. In the late 1970s, however, the KGB began to suspect him of "dishonesty" and of being in contact with the DST. Contact with NANT was broken off in 1980. Thus ended the longest and most expensive active measures operation ever run by the Paris residency. The KGB files on DURANT, NANT and three agents closely associated with them—VERONIQUE, JACQUELINE and NANCY—fill 26 volumes, totaling over 8,000 pages.[99]

Each year the Paris residency, like other KGB stations abroad, sent the Centre somewhat crude statistics on its active measures. Those for 1979 totaled 188 articles in the press (despite the demise of *Synthesis*), 67 "influence conversations;" 19 operations to convey disinformation by word of mouth; 7 operations involving forged documents; the organization of 2 public meetings; 4 speeches at public gatherings; 2 books; and 4 leaflets.[100] In 1980, largely as a result of the breach with NANT, the number of press articles for which the Paris residency claimed the credit fell to 99. "Influence conversations," however, increased to 79 and operations to convey disinformation verbally to 59. The residency also reported two active measures involving forged documents, and claimed the credit for organizing two public meetings, inspiring sixteen conference speeches and arranging one leaflet distribution.[101]

If Paris residency reports are to be taken literally, the "influence conversations" achieved some striking successes. Several leading French politicians from across the political spectrum as well as a few well-known academics, whom it would be unfair to name, are said to have adopted views on the threat posed by American defense policy, the future of East–West relations and the menace to French national sovereignty from a "supranational Europe." Some of these individuals may well have been imprudent in their contacts with individuals from the Soviet embassy whom they might reasonably have suspected were KGB officers. It seems probable, however, that in many instances the Paris residency merely claimed the credit for policy statements which were relatively favorable to Soviet positions but which it had, in reality, done little to influence. Among the residency's more absurd claims was the boast that KGB active measures "compelled" two of de Gaulle's former prime ministers, Michel Debré and Maurice Couve de Murville, the latter the current head of the Foreign Affairs Commission in the National Assembly, to "defend France's independence from the United States"—a policy to which both were already committed. Though the KGB also claimed to have brought influence to bear on close advisers of the President, Giscard d'Estaing, the Prime Minister, Raymond Barre, the Foreign Minister, Jean Franáois-Poncet, and the Socialist leader, Franáois Mitterrand, this supposed "influence" had no discernible effect on their policies.[102]

KGB policy during the 1981 presidential election campaign was less clear-cut than during the election seven years earlier. At the end of the 1970s the left-wing alliance including both Socialists and Communists, which had supported Mitterrand in 1974, had broken down, and on the first round of the election he had to face opposition from the PCF leader, Georges Marchais, as well as from candidates of the right. Though KGB active measures in 1981 reflected greater hostility to Giscard d'Estaing and the candidates of the right than to Mitterrand, they were no longer, as in 1974, guided by the simple strategy of securing a Mitterrand victory. (It was clear from the outset that Marchais, who won only 15 percent of the vote, had no chance of winning the election.) The individual active measures recorded in the files noted by Mitrokhin suggest that bringing pressure on all the leading candidates was considered a more important objective than ensuring the victory of any one of them. As in 1974, however, the Centre seriously exaggerated its ability to influence the course of events.

In May 1980, Giscard d'Estaing had become the first Western leader to hold talks with Brezhnev since the Soviet invasion of Afghanistan, thus helping to rescue the Soviet Union from its pariah status in the West. In preparing for the meeting, Brezhnev's advisers must have been greatly assisted in their continuing access to all the diplomatic traffic exchanged between Paris and the French embassy in Moscow. On Giscard's return to Paris, he announced, perhaps somewhat naively, that the Soviet Union had agreed to withdraw one of its divisions from Afghanistan.[103] Though Giscard's attitude to the Soviet Union subsequently appeared to harden, the Paris residency embarked on active measures designed to persuade him that he would increase his chances of reelection by presenting himself as "the advocate of dialogue with [eastern Europe] against American domination." Disinformation was sent to a member of Giscard's staff which it was hoped would convince him that the most damaging scandal of his presidency, that of the diamonds given him by "Emperor" Jean Bédel Bokassa of the Central African Republic, had been engineered by the CIA.[104] The residency also claimed the credit for "inciting" attacks by the unofficial Gaullist candidate, Michel Debré, on alleged "departures from Gaullist principles" and pro-American tendencies on the part of the official Gaullist candidate, Jacques Chirac. Other active measures included schemes "to expose pro-Atlantic and pro-Israeli elements" in the policies of Mitterrand and one of his future prime ministers, Michel Rocard.[105]

According to an opinion poll during the campaign, 53 percent of Jewish electors intended to vote for Mitterrand as compared with only 23 percent for Giscard d'Estaing.[106] The KGB was predictably suspicious of Mitterrand's popularity with Jewish voters. As in 1974 the active measures devised by Service A reflected the KGB's anti-Zionist conspiracy theories, in particular its belief in the power of the French Jewish lobby. The most absurd of the residency's operations during the election was probably its attempt to "compromise the Zionists" by passing bogus information to the French authorities purporting to show that they were planning "extremist measures" to disrupt the campaigns of Giscard d'Estaing and Debré.[107] It is highly unlikely that this or any other active measure had any significant influence either on the main candidates or on the outcome of the presidential election.

Mitterrand's success in May 1981 was followed by a landslide Socialist victory in the legislative elections a month later. Though the career of the veteran Socialist Party agent GILES, recruited a quarter of a century earlier, was by then almost over, he remained in touch with his case officer, Valentin Antonovich Sidak (codenamed RYZHOV), who was stationed in Paris from 1978 to 1983 under diplomatic cover as second secretary at the Soviet embassy. He continued to provide Sidak with what the Centre considered inside information from "the close entourage of F[rançois] Mitterrand."[108]

The arrest of Pathé in 1979 and the decision to break off contact with NANT in 1980 caused a major change of strategy in KGB active measures to influence the French press after Mitterrand's election as president in May 1981. An unusually frank enquiry by the FCD Fifth Department concluded—probably correctly—that *Synthesis, La Tribune des Nations* and other periodicals funded by the KGB had had "practically no influence on public opinion." In future the Paris residency was instructed to concentrate on the cheaper and more productive task of acquiring agents in established newspapers and magazines.[109] The value of some of its existing media agents, however, was called into question—among them BROK, probably the KGB's longest-serving journalist recruit. During the 1970s BROK had been one of the best-paid and most highly regarded French agents. A subsequent review of his work concluded, however, that he was "insincere, untruthful in his contacts with operational officers, exaggerating his information and operational possibilities, inflating the value of his information, and developing mercenary tendencies, lack of discipline and failure to carry out assignments." In 1981 BROK's 35-year service as a Soviet agent was abruptly terminated.[110] The Centre continued to seek new agents among French journalists, but concluded that, in a television age, the Western press lacked the influence on public opinion which it had possessed twenty years earlier.[111]

AT THE BEGINNING of the 1980s, partly as a result of the KGB's declining confidence in its Paris agents of influence, the Centre probably regarded S&T as the most successful part of its French operations. By the mid-1970s (if not sooner), the Paris residency had twice as many Line X officers and agents (over twenty of each) as any other residency in the European Community.[112] Line X operations continued to expand during the late 1970s and—probably—the early 1980s. S&T documents sent to the Centre (835 in 1973, 829 in 1974, 675 in 1975) rose to a record 1,021 in the first half of 1977.[113] A total of 36 Line X officers served in Paris for all or part of the period 1974 to 1979, far more once again than in any other EC country.[114] By 1980, if not before, France had become the KGB's third most productive source of S&T, providing 8 percent of all S&T received by the Soviet Military Industrial Commission (VPK).[115]

The most important and best-paid French S&T agent during the 1970s identified in the files noted by Mitrokhin was ALAN (also codenamed FLINT and TELON), an employee of a defense contractor (codenamed AVANTGARDE). ALAN was a walk-in. In 1972 he went to the Paris embassy, explained that he was earning 7,000 francs a month, needed extra money to buy a house (possibly a second home) in the 150,000–200,000 francs price range and was willing to sell his firm's secrets. Over the next six years he provided technical documentation and parts of missile guidance systems, laser weapons, detection systems for high-speed low-flying targets and infrared night-vision equipment for tanks, helicopters and other uses. ALAN's file records that his S&T "fully met the requirements of the highest authorities [Politburo]."[116] In December 1974 his controller, Boris Federovich Kesarev, a Line X officer at the Paris residency, was recommended for the Order of the Red Star in a citation signed personally by Andropov.[117] ALAN was paid over 200,000 francs a year,[118] but was dismissed by his firm in 1978 on suspicion of passing its secrets to a Western intelligence service. The KGB appears to have escaped suspicion.[119]

Apart from ALAN's intelligence, the French S&T most highly rated by the Centre probably concerned France's Ariane rocket and its fuel, *Cryogäne*.[120] From 1974 to 1979 a French engineer, Pierre Bourdiol, recruited by the KGB in 1970, was employed on the Ariane project by SNIAS, the predecessor of the state-owned aerospace group Aerospatiale.[121] Probably in 1979 or 1980, agent KARL, a specialist in electromagnetism, succeeded in obtaining further intelligence on Ariane from an unidentified subsource. KARL was paid a salary of about 150,000 francs a year and received bonuses of over 30,000 francs in 1979 and 1980.[122] In 1982 KARL recruited NIKE, another highly rated Line X agent, who worked in one of the laboratories of the Centre National de Recherches Scientifiques. NIKE was enlisted under false flag, believing he was in the pay of a foreign firm. His file records that his information "satisfied priority requirements" of Directorate T.[123]

Just as Line X operations in France reached their apogee in the early 1980s, they were compromised by a French agent inside Directorate T, Vladimir Ippolitovich Vetrov (codenamed FAREWELL), who had been stationed at the Paris residency from 1965 to 1970. Vetrov was an ardent Francophile, deeply disillusioned with the Soviet system, and resentful at his treatment by Directorate T which had transferred him from operations to analysis. In the spring of 1981 he sent a message, via a French businessman returning from Moscow, to the DST headquarters in Paris, offering his services as a spy. Over the next year Vetrov supplied over 4,000 documents on Soviet S&T collection and analysis. The FAREWELL operation came to an abrupt end after a brutally bizarre episode in a Moscow park in February 1982 whose explanation still remains unclear. While drinking—and probably quarreling—with a KGB secretary with whom he was having an affair, Vetrov was approached by a KGB colleague. Startled, and perhaps fearing that his double life had been discovered, he stabbed his colleague to death. When his lover tried to run away, Vetrov stabbed her too, probably to prevent her revealing what had happened, but she survived to give evidence against him. Though Vetrov began a twelve-year sentence for murder at Irkurksk prison in the autumn of 1981, it was several months before the KGB began to suspect that he was also guilty of espionage. Vetrov wrote his own death sentence with a confession which concluded, "My only regret is that I was not able to cause more damage to the Soviet Union and render more service to France."[124]

Vetrov's documents added enormously to Western intelligence services' knowledge of Soviet S&T operations.[125] In July 1981, two months after he became president, Franáois Mitterrand personally informed Ronald Reagan of the documents being received from FAREWELL. Soon afterwards, Marcel Chalet, the head of the DST, visited Washington to brief Vice-President George Bush, a former Director of Central Intelligence, in greater detail. The first public disclosure of Vetrov's material followed the discovery early in 1983 that bugs in the teleprinters of the French embassy in Moscow had been relaying incoming and outgoing telegrams to the KGB for the previous seven years. Mitterrand responded by ordering the expulsion from France on April 5, 1983 of forty-seven Soviet intelligence officers—the largest such exodus since operation FOOT in Britain twelve years earlier. Many of those expelled, in particular the Line X officers, had been identified by Vetrov. When the Soviet ambassador, Yuli Vorontsev, arrived at the Quai d'Orsay to deliver an official protest, Foreign Minister Claude Cheysson reduced him to silence by producing one of the KGB documents on S&T operations supplied by Vetrov.[126]

THOUGH THE KGB residency in Rome ran less than half as many agents as its counterpart in Paris (just over twenty in the mid-1970s as compared to about fifty in France),[127] the pattern of agent recruitment in the two countries was broadly similar. Immediately after the Second World War Soviet intelligence succeeded, with the assistance of the Communist Party leadership, in penetrating a number of major ministries in both Italy and France. By the 1970s, however, a majority of the best-paid Line PR agents run by the Rome and Paris residencies were journalists rather than civil servants.

As in France, the post-war popularity of the Communist Party and the brief period of Communist participation in government created the best opportunities Soviet intelligence was ever to enjoy in Italy for agent penetration.[128] Like JOUR, probably the most important of the post-war French recruits, DARIO, the longest-serving and probably the most valuable Italian agent, worked in the foreign ministry, where he had recruited his first three female agents before the Second World War. On his return to the ministry after the war, he recruited two more female typists: TOPO (later renamed LEDA), whom he married, and NIKOL (later INGA).[129]

For most of the next three decades DARIO was instrumental in obtaining a phenomenal amount of classified foreign ministry material.[130] During the mid-1950s he succeeded in recruiting three further female agents: VENETSIANKA, who was on the staff of the Italian embassy in Paris; OVOD, on whom Mitrokhin's notes provide no further information; and SUZA, who worked for the diplomatic adviser to President Giovanni Gronchi and gained access to a wide variety of ambassadors' reports and other classified foreign ministry documents.[131] During the early 1960s DARIO's wife LEDA met her case officer from the Rome residency once a week in cinemas and other locations in the city. As she shook hands with him, she passed over a microfilm of the classified foreign ministry documents she had photographed during the previous week.[132]

In 1968 the Centre decided to put DARIO "on ice," and awarded him a pension for life of 180 hard currency roubles a month. Four years later, however, it reactivated him in order to cultivate a female cipher officer in a foreign embassy and another typist at the Italian foreign ministry, who appears to have been given the codename MARA.[133] In March 1975, forty-three years after DARIO's recruitment, he and his wife were awarded the Order of the Red Star. He subsequently collected his pension at regular intervals by traveling abroad either to the Soviet Union or to some other country.[134]

After the Second World War the Rome residency also successfully penetrated the interior ministry, thanks chiefly to DEMID, a ministry official recruited in 1945 who acted as agent-recruiter.[135] DEMID's first major cultivation inside the ministry was a cipher clerk codenamed QUESTOR, who agreed to supply information on the contents of the classified telegrams which he enciphered and deciphered. QUESTOR, however, believed for several years that his information was being passed by DEMID not to Soviet intelligence but to the PCI, and refused to hand over the ciphers themselves. Late in 1953 the Rome residency decided to force the pace and instructed DEMID to offer QUESTOR 100,000 lire for the loan "for a few hours" of the code and cipher books used by the ministry. QUESTOR accepted. On March 3, 1954 DEMID finally told him that he was working not for the PCI but for the KGB, and obtained a receipt from him for the 100,000 lire. Soon afterwards QUESTOR was handed over to the control of STEPAN, an operations officer at the Rome residency, to whom he supplied a phenomenal range of official ciphers to which he succeeded in gaining access. Among them were those of the prefectures, the finance ministry, central and regional headquarters of the *carabinieri,* Italian diplomatic missions abroad, the Italian general staff and the military-run foreign intelligence service,

SIFAR (Servizio Informazioni Forze Armate). QUESTOR also obtained interior ministry lists of Italian Communists, foreign nationals and others who were under surveillance by the Police security service (*Pubblica Sicurezza*).[136]

The Centre considered its penetration of the Italian interior ministry to be so important that in 1955 it handed over control of it to a newly established illegal residency in Rome, headed by YEFRAT ("Euphrates"). YEFRAT was Ashot Abgarovich Akopyan, a 40-year-old Armenian from Baku who had assumed the identity of a live double, Oganes Saradzhyan, a Lebanese Armenian living in the Soviet Union. Like many illegals, he was a gifted linguist, fluent—according to his file—in Arabic, Armenian, Bulgarian, French, Italian, Romanian and Turkish. His wife, Kira Viktorovna Chertenko, an ethnic Russian from Baku, was also an illegal, codenamed TANYA. YEFRAT and TANYA began their careers as illegals in Romania in 1948, obtained Italian visas by bribery and moved to Rome where they acquired passports in the name of Saradzhyan from the Lebanese embassy. YEFRAT's original mission was to prepare the establishment of a new illegal residency in Iran, but in 1952 he and his wife were directed to Egypt instead. In 1954 they were recalled to Rome where YEFRAT was given 19,500 dollars to purchase a business to provide cover for an illegal residency. He was not, however, a successful businessman; an Italian firm with which he was involved went bankrupt.[137]

YEFRAT's residency was given control of DEMID, QUESTOR and a third agent in the interior ministry, CENSOR, who had probably been recruited by DEMID. CENSOR's greatest coup was to abstract top secret documents from the safe of the director general of the security service in the ministry.[138] YEFRAT also succeeded in renewing contact with a former agent, OMAR, who had been sacked from the interior ministry cipher department in 1948 and had obtained a job in what Mitrokhin's notes describe as "a service attached to the American embassy." For unexplained reasons, however, the quantity of high-grade intelligence produced by the agents in the interior ministry declined during the later 1950s. When exhortations by the Centre and a personal meeting between YEFRAT and Lazarev, the head of the Illegals Directorate S, failed to produce results, YEFRAT was recalled and his illegal residency closed. Control of his agents was handed back to the legal Rome residency.[139]

THE ITALIAN EMBASSY in Moscow, like that of France, was a major KGB target. Whereas Second Chief Directorate operations against French diplomats culminated in an embarrassing public scandal, those against the Italian embassy achieved spectacular, unpublicized success. The weapons used against Italian diplomats were the normal stock-in-trade of the SCD: a combination of sexual compromise and blackmail. The SCD's first victim was IKAR ("Icarus"), one of the service attachés in the Italian embassy who was seduced in the late 1950s by a KGB swallow, who then claimed to be pregnant and pretended to have an abortion. IKAR was confronted by an SCD officer, posing as the swallow's enraged husband and signed a document agreeing to become a KGB agent in return for the supposed scandal being hushed up. In addition to providing classified information, IKAR also gave his SCD controller the combination number of his safe and a copy of the cipher he used to communicate with Rome.

IKAR, however, became increasingly anxious at the KGB's hold over him—finally handing his controller a rather pathetic letter, promising to continue work as a Soviet agent but appealing for the undertaking he had signed to be destroyed:

Beneath your cloak, you are holding a dagger at the ready. The day that you trapped me by using methods which I regard as unworthy of your highly respected nation, I tried to convey to you that my attitude to you was friendly. Ignoring these feelings of mine, you have subjected me to various tests. Despite that, you still doubt my loyalty and my good intentions. You continue to hold a gun to my head, while uttering words of friendship and appreciation towards me. If these feelings of yours correspond with reality and are not a mere fiction, then give me some proof—that is to say, the question of destroying the document concerning the circumstances in which I was caught must be resolved between us. If you do not do this, I shall no longer be able to regard you as worthy of my friendship and of my friendly esteem.

I beg you to understand that I need your respect. Therefore, if you think that I am acting under the threat of the materials relating to the circumstances in which I was caught, you judge me wrongly. Find some means of testing my loyalty without threats. I believe that I shall not be found wanting. If you continue to doubt my sincerity, I shall not be able to work while I remain anxious, or continue to respect you.

IKAR was given a copy of his signed undertaking, carefully fabricated to look like the original, and destroyed it with evident relief in the presence of his controller. The original, however, remained in IKAR's file, together with a Russian translation which was later transcribed by Mitrokhin.[140]

Another member of the Italian embassy staff, codenamed PLATON, was also successfully blackmailed into becoming a KGB agent after falling victim to the same SCD honeytrap. The swallow (codenamed R) planted on him by the SCD moved into his Moscow flat, then pretended that she was pregnant. PLATON paid for her to have a (fictitious) abortion (a criminal act under Italian law), was threatened with exposure and agreed to become a KGB agent. By the time Mitrokhin saw PLATON's file in 1976, he had left Moscow and a plan had been drawn up for Georgi Pavlovich Antonov, an Italian-speaking FCD officer formerly stationed in Rome, to renew contact with him in Belgium.[141] Whether PLATON continued as a KGB agent after 1976 remains unknown.

One senior married Italian diplomat in Moscow was the victim of two honeytraps. When first targeted, ENERO (also codenamed INSPECTOR) was having an affair with a secretary at the French embassy. The SCD concluded that he had an insatiable "appetite for women," selected a swallow, agent SUKHOVA, as his maid and secretly photographed them making love. During a visit to Tashkent, ENERO was seduced by another KGB swallow, Diana Georgiyevna Kazachenko, and further photographs were taken of their lovemaking. A Russian friend of ENERO (who, unknown to ENERO, was a KGB officer) then told him that the KGB had come into possession of photographs of him in bed with SUKHOVA, taken by a criminal gang who were about to stand trial, charged with taking compromising photographs which they intended to use for blackmail and extortion. Almost simultaneously, ENERO was informed that Kazachenko's relatives had lodged an official complaint, accusing him of rape and claiming that he had made Kazachenko pregnant. Kazachenko, it was claimed, was now an invalid as a result of medical complications arising from the abortion.

An SCD operations officer, I. I. Kuznetsov, told ENERO that the Soviet authorities were prepared to hush both matters up if he agreed to "help" them. Though ENERO protested that Kuznetsov's proposal was straightforward blackmail, he quickly gave way to it. According to his file, the intelligence he provided included information that the embassy was illegally smuggling into Moscow by diplomatic bag roubles purchased abroad at a fraction of the official exchange rate. Before leaving Moscow in the early 1970s, ENERO agreed to continue work as a KGB agent on his return to Italy and was given an initial payment of 500 US dollars. Soon afterwards Kusnetsov visited him in Rome to introduce his new case officer from the local residency. A year later, however, the residency reported that ENERO was avoiding meetings with his controller and had changed his private address. In 1979 a residency officer resumed contact but, since ENERO was now retired and in poor health, he was removed from the agent network.[142]

The SCD's greatest triumph in its operations against the Italian embassy in Moscow was the recruitment of a senior diplomat, successively codenamed ARTUR and ARLEKINO ("Harlequin"). ARTUR was first recruited by the Czechoslovak StB in the 1960s, which threatened to expose both his affair with a prostitute and his currency speculation unless he agreed to cooperate. When he was posted to Moscow some years later, control of him was transferred by the Czechs to the SCD. ARTUR's file records that he was rewarded with "valuable presents" and all-expenses-paid hunting expeditions in the Moscow area. After his return to Italy, ARTUR continued to work for the KGB until 1983, several years after his retirement, when his much-reduced access to classified information led to his removal from the agent network.[143]

A number of other Italian embassies around the world also contained KGB agents: among them DENIS, a cipher clerk stationed in the Middle East and recruited in 1961;[144] VITTORIO, a former member of the PCI recruited in Latin America in 1970;[145] and PLEMYANNIK ("Nephew"), a cipher clerk in the Middle East recruited with the help of Bulgarian intelligence in 1977.[146] As well as providing large numbers of documents, the KGB's agents inside the Italian foreign ministry and embassies abroad must also have made a major contribution to the success of the Sixteenth Directorate in decrypting Italian diplomatic telegrams, which continued at least until the mid-1980s.[147] Mitrokhin's notes provide very few details on the content of the remarkable number of diplomatic documents which reached the Centre and nothing on the content of the decrypts. The implications of the KGB files on Italy and France to which he had access are, none the less, very great. So great was the Centre's access to classified French and Italian diplomatic traffic that, at numerous points during the Cold War, both France and Italy were conducting, so far as the Soviet Union was concerned, something akin to open diplomacy.

THOUGH LINE X operations in Italy were on about half the scale of those in France, they included some striking successes. In 1970 the co-owners of a small high-tech company, METIL ("Methyl") and BUTIL ("Butyl"), jointly supplied the KGB with full technical documentation on the production of butyl rubber, which was used in the construction of the Soviet Sumgait rubber factory and led to the redesign of production lines at the Nizhnekama Combine and the Kuybyshev Synthetic Rubber Works. Directorate T calculated that their S&T had produced a saving of 16 million roubles. METIL and BUTIL were paid 50,000 dollars. In the mid-1970s BUTIL provided other highly rated intelligence, some from American sources, on chemical and petrochemical processes.[148]

In 1970 the Rome residency had nine Line X officers who ran about ten agents,[149] composed chiefly of businessmen but including an important minority of academics.[150] There was some expansion of S&T operations during the later 1970s both in Rome[151] and in Milan, where a senior Line X officer, Anatoli Vasilyevich Kuznetsov (codenamed KOLIN), was posted in 1978 under consular cover.[152] Probably the most important Line X agent at the end of the 1970s and beginning of the 1980s was UCHITEL ("Teacher"), who taught at a major university and was controlled by Kuznetsov.[153] Using his wide range of academic and business contacts, UCHITEL provided S&T from a total of eight major companies and research institutes in Italy, West Germany, France and Belgium, and carried out other KGB assignments in the USA and FRG. UCHITEL's most valuable intelligence seems to have concerned military aircraft, helicopters, aero-engine construction and airborne guidance systems. Among the intelligence he supplied was information on NATO's newest combat aircraft, the Tornado, jointly developed by Britain, the FRG and Italy.[154] Doubtless unknown to UCHITEL, at least one of his university colleagues, a nuclear physicist codenamed MARIO, was also a KGB agent.[155] Another academic, KARS, who operated as a Line X agent in both Italy and the United States, also appears to have been based at the same university.[156]

Though Soviet scientists working as KGB agents or co-optees used a variety of methods to lure their Western colleagues into secret collaboration, they commonly promised both money and privileged access to Soviet research in their fields. A probably typical example was the agreement, dated September 12, 1976, concluded by Professor Georgi Nikolayevich Aleksandrov (agent AYUN) of the Lenin Polytechnic Institute Imeni Kalinin (LPI) with KULON, a senior member of an Italian research institute:

> In view of the importance of the exchange of scientific and technical information and the timeliness of obtaining information on research in other countries, LPI on the one hand, in the person of its pro-rector for scientific contacts with foreign countries, V. A. Serebryannikov, and [the Italian research institute] on the other hand, in the person of the scientific adviser to its director, Professor [KULON], have agreed as follows:

(1) Professor [KULON] agrees to use his own and LPI's facilities to assist LPI in obtaining scientific and technical information on basic problems of electronics of an applied nature. This scientific and technical information should be in the form of reports and articles which have not been published in journals, or of materials put out by firms on the results of studies by firms and scientific institute laboratories in the United States, the FRG, France, the UK and Japan [Directorate T's five main targets]. If the information is of a confidential nature, it will be transmitted to LPI's pro-rector or his representative at personal meetings, which may be held in one of three countries as agreed. The pro-rector's request will be made in the form of a separate list. LPI will pay in any currency for acquisitions . . .

(2) For its part LPI undertakes to assist Professor [KULON] to publish in closed specialized Soviet journals and to arrange for invitations for him to the USSR in order to learn about other institutions in the USSR and to carry out joint studies, and for familiarization with major hydroelectric stations and power transmission lines.

Most meetings between KULON and his KGB contacts took place in Switzerland.[157] Though KULON seems to have remained a confidential contact, similar approaches to other Western scientists sometimes led to their recruitment as agents.

S&T operations in Italy suffered a serious setback on August 5, 1981 with the unpublicized expulsion of probably the most senior Line X officer, Anatoli Kuznetsov, which caused inevitable KGB anxiety as to whether UCHITEL and his other agents had been detected by Italian counterintelligence. An investigation at the Centre arrived at three possible explanations for the expulsion: that some of Kuznetsov's Line X operations dating from his period at the Paris residency from 1970 to 1975 had come to light; or that his work as security officer for the Soviet colony in northern Italy, which he combined with his Line X work, had blown his cover as consul in Milan; or that his frequent trips from Milan to Turin had aroused suspicion.[158] It does not seem to have occurred to the Centre until its investigation of the FAREWELL case in 1982 that the leak which led to Kuznetsov's downfall might have come from within Directorate T.

BY THE 1970S a majority of the most highly rated Line PR agents run by both the Rome and Paris residencies were journalists. One of the files noted by Mitrokhin contains a list of the thirteen most highly paid political intelligence agents run by the Rome residency at the beginning of 1977.[159] Of the six best-paid, each of whom received 240 hard currency roubles a month, at least three were journalists: FRANK, recruited in 1966, who held a senior position on a major newspaper;[160] POD-VIZHNY ("Agile"), also a well-known journalist;[161] and STAZHER ("Trainee"), who had been recruited in 1969 and worked in the Rome bureau of a news agency.[162] The other three agents paid 240 roubles a month by the Rome residency were DARIO, the veteran agent-recruiter in the Foreign Ministry; NEMETS ("German"), a well-known left-wing politician; and ORLANDO, who cannot be clearly identified from Mitrokhin's notes.[163]

The next best-paid agents of the Rome residency at the beginning of 1977 were six who received 170 roubles a month. No information is available on the occupation of one of the six, ACERO; Mitrokhin's notes reveal his identity and indicate that he was probably recruited not later than 1969, but give no further details.[164] Of the five whose occupations are identified, three—FIDELIO, RENATO and MAVR—were journalists. RENATO, recruited in 1974, was editor of a periodical.[165] FIDELIO, who became an agent in 1975, was director of a press agency.[166] MAVR, a left-wing journalist on a leading Rome daily recruited some years earlier than RENATO or FIDELIO, also acted as agent-recruiter. Among his recruits was ARALDO, a civil servant who, according to MAVR, regarded the whole Italian political establishment as a "den of thieves" and was happy to earn a share of the spoils by selling classified documents.[167]

The other two agents paid 170 roubles a month by the Rome residency were LORETO, a (probably disillusioned) Maoist militant who provided information on China's contacts with its supporters in the European left,[168] and METSENAT ("Patronage"), a corrupt civil servant whose motives were assessed as purely mercenary.[169] The final codename on the January 1977 list of the Rome residency's most valuable agents is that of TURIST, a newspaper publisher who was paid 150 roubles a month.[170] In all, at least seven of the residency's thirteen best-paid recruits, who each received between 150 and 240 roubles a month, were journalists. As in Paris, where a majority of the KGB's most highly rated Line PR agents were also journalists, the Centre's probably exaggerated confidence in their potential as agents of influence led it to undertake an ambitious series of active measures throughout the 1970s.

A Centre report on the Rome residency in August 1977 concluded that it had "an effective and reliable agent network" with sources in the foreign ministry, cabinet office, defense ministry and the main political parties. Each month the residency obtained between 40 and 50 intelligence reports from its agents. It was, however, criticized for its comparative lack of success against American, NATO and European Community targets. The Centre's greatest praise was reserved for the residency's influence operations: "[Its] agents coped successfully with active measures, including those on a large scale." During 1977 operation CRESCENDO, which used forged documents to discredit the human rights policy of the Carter administration, and operation BONZA, targeted against the Chinese, were singled out for particular praise.[171]

The Rome residency's annual statistics for its active measures in 1977 were as follows:

articles published in the bourgeois press: 43
materials distributed: 1
letters drafted: 2
oral information disseminated: 1
conversations of influence: 13

interviews secured: 1
television appearances: 2
exhibitions mounted: 1
parliamentary questions inspired: 2
appeals inspired: 2[172]

Such statistics, of course, mean relatively little unless it can be demonstrated that the active measures to which they refer had a significant influence on Italian opinion. Nowhere in the files examined by Mitrokhin, however, is there any sign of a serious, critical assessment of what active measures in Italy (or in most other countries) had actually achieved. Instead, any sign that Western opinion was hostile to any aspect of American policy or sympathetic to the Soviet Union was liable to be seized on uncritically as evidence of a successful KGB operation. Just as it suited the residencies to exaggerate the success of their active measures, so it also suited the Centre to report these successes to the Politburo.

AT LEAST HALF the Rome residency's best-paid Line PR Italian agents in January 1977 were either taken off the KGB payroll or retired over the next five years.[173] The first to go was TURIST. Apparently disillusioned by the evidence of Soviet abuses of human rights, TURIST made various pretexts for declining to co-operate during 1977 and by the end of the year had broken contact. According to his case officer, he "did not correctly understand and interpret the situation of believers and of the Church itself in the USSR, or that of dissidents." In other words, TURIST had been alienated by the persecution of Soviet religious and political dissidents. An examination of TURIST's file led Mitrokhin to doubt whether he had ever been a fully committed KGB agent.[174]

In 1978 FIDELIO was also removed from the agent network after it was discovered that he was in regular touch with—and doubtless receiving money from—Hungarian intelligence, and had also made contact with the Czechoslovak and Polish services.[175] In 1979 DARIO retired, followed by METSENAT in the following year.[176] Simultaneously, RENATO and FRANK—like TURIST—were becoming disillusioned. RENATO was put on ice in 1980, initially for a four-year period;[177] there is no evidence as to whether contact with him was subsequently resumed. FRANK's case officer complained that he was too easily "influenced by anti-Soviet propaganda" following the Soviet invasion of Afghanistan in December 1979 and the suppression of Solidarity in Poland two years later. FRANK was also reported to be associated with one of those arrested for involvement with the Red Brigades. He was removed from the agent network in 1982.[178]

The disillusion of FRANK, who a few years earlier had been one of the KGB's most highly paid Italian agents, epitomized the problems faced by Service A as it tried to devise new influence operations in the early 1980s. Though no KGB report dared say so, active measures could not possibly repair the damage done to the image of the Soviet Union by the invasion of Afghanistan and the suppression of Solidarity.

THE MOST EFFECTIVE of the KGB's active measures during the early and mid-1980s in Italy and France, as in western Europe as a whole, were those which exploited popular currents of anti-Americanism and the fear of nuclear war. Though the first step in the renewed nuclear arms race had been the Soviet decision in 1978 to begin the deployment of SS20s (a new generation of intermediate-range ballistic missiles), Western peace movements were far more critical of the subsequent decision by NATO to station Pershing II and cruise missiles in Europe from 1983. As Mitterrand once drily observed, "The missiles are in the East, but the peace protests are in the West." It is reasonable to assume, but difficult to prove, that the constant stream of Soviet peace propaganda, reinforced by KGB active measures, encouraged—even if it did not cause—the overconcentration by most Western peace activists on the nuclear menace posed by Reagan and his NATO allies rather than on that from the Soviet Union. In February 1984, Kryuchkov reported to a conference of senior FCD officers, when reviewing active measures over the previous two years:

> Considerable work has been done to provide support for unofficial organizations [such as peace movements] in a number of countries abroad in their struggle against implementation of the American administration's militarist plans.[179]

The Centre's confidence that it now possessed a nerve-hold on Western public opinion was reflected in the first three priorities which it laid down for active measures in 1984, the year before Gorbachev became Soviet leader:

- counteracting attempts by the USA and NATO to destroy the existing military strategic equilibrium and to acquire military superiority over the USSR; compromising the aggressive efforts of imperialist groups and their plans for preparing a nuclear missile war . . .
- deepening disagreements inside NATO . . .
- exposing before the international community the plans made by the USA to launch a war, its refusal to negotiate in good faith with the USSR on limiting armaments; stimulating further development of the anti-war and anti-missile movements in the West, involving in them influential political and public figures and broad strata of the population, and encouraging these movements to take more decisive and coordinated action.[180]

KGB active measures in western Europe were much less successful during the Gorbachev era as a result both of East–West détente and of *glasnost* within the Soviet Union. By 1987 Gorbachev and his advisers were visibly concerned that Western exposure of KGB disinformation might take the gloss off the new Soviet image in the West. The claim that the AIDS virus had been "manufactured" by American biological warfare specialists—one of the most successful active measures of the mid-1980s—was officially disowned by Moscow, though it continued to circulate for several years in the Third World and the more gullible sections of the Western media.

During the later 1980s Soviet front organizations were increasingly exposed as frauds. The most important of them, the World Peace Council, lost most of its remaining credibility in 1989 when it admitted that 90 percent of its income came from the Soviet Union.[181]

In September 1990 Kryuchkov acknowledged in an "Order of the Chairman of the KGB" that there had been a serious decline in the effectiveness of active measures—and in the FCD's faith in them:

> There are very limited opportunities for residencies' access to the mass media in the countries of the West, the progress of acquiring new operational sites is progressing slowly, and there is an absence of the necessary cooperation with the other sections of the Soviet KGB and other Soviet ministries and agencies.

Like other members of the KGB old guard, Kryuchkov refused to accept that the end of the Cold War implied any decline in the importance of active measures either in western Europe or elsewhere.[182] That view still appears to be well-represented in the senior ranks of the SVR today.

TWENTY-EIGHT

THE PENETRATION AND PERSECUTION
OF THE SOVIET CHURCHES

Though paying lip-service to freedom of religion, the Soviet state was the first to attempt to eradicate the concept of God. Marx had famously denounced religion as "the opium of the people," but also spoke with some compassion of its role as "the sigh of the oppressed creature, the heart of a heartless world." Lenin's denunciation of religion, however, was uncompromisingly venomous:

> Every religious idea, every idea of God, every flirting with the idea of God, is unutterable vileness, . . . vileness of the most dangerous kind, "contagion" of the most abominable kind. Millions of filthy deeds, acts of violence and physical contagions are far less dangerous than the subtle, spiritual idea of a God decked out in the smartest "ideological" costumes.[1]

During the 1930s most priests were condemned to a gulag from which few returned. Most churches, with their religious symbols removed or defaced but their onion domes usually left more or less intact, were turned into barns, cinemas and garages, or given over to other secular purposes. After two decades of brutal persecution which had left only a few hundred churches open for worship, the Russian Orthodox Church was unexpectedly revived as a public institution by Stalin's need for its support during the Great Patriotic War. In 1943, after a gap of seventeen years, the Moscow Patriarchate, the Church's administrative center, was formally reestablished.[2] During the remainder of the decade, Orthodox Christians reclaimed and lovingly restored several thousand of their churches.[3]

The Church, however, paid a heavy price for its restoration. The Council for the Affairs of the Russian Orthodox Church (later the Council for Religious Affairs) worked in close cooperation with the NKVD and its successors to ensure the subservience of Church to State.[4] Both Patriarch Aleksi I and Metropolitan Nikolai of Krutitsky and Kolomna, second in the Orthodox hierarchy, joined the World Peace Council, the Soviet front organization founded in 1949, and were highly valued by the KGB as agents of influence.[5] Aleksi declared in 1955:

> The Russian Orthodox Church supports the totally peaceful foreign policy of our government, not because the Church allegedly lacks freedom, but because

Soviet policy is just and corresponds to the Christian ideals which the Church preaches.[6]

The Orthodox Church also took a prominent part in the founding of another front organization, the Christian Peace Conference (CPC), established in 1958 with its headquarters in Prague, in a further attempt to mobilize worldwide Christian support for the "peace policies" of the Soviet Union. At the second conference of the CPC in 1960 delegates from the rest of the world, mostly innocent of its orchestration by Moscow, outnumbered those from the Soviet Bloc.[7]

In 1961, with the KGB's blessing, the Orthodox Church joined the World Council of Churches (WCC). At that very moment Khrushchev was in the midst of a ferocious anti-religious campaign which closed down many of the reopened churches, monasteries and seminaries and disbanded half the Orthodox parishes. The KGB was simultaneously seeking to strengthen its grip on the churches which remained. According to a secret KGB directive of 1961:

> Up to 600 individuals are studying in the two ecclesiastical academies of the Moscow Patriarchate and the five ecclesiastical seminaries. These must be exploited in the interests of the KGB. We must infiltrate our people among the students of these ecclesiastical training establishments so that they will subsequently influence the state of affairs within the Russian Orthodox Church and exert influence on the believers.[8]

The head of the Second Chief Directorate, General Oleg Mikhailovich Gribanov, reported in 1962 that over the previous two years the KGB had infiltrated "reliable agents" into the leading positions of the Moscow Patriarchate, the Catholic dioceses, the Armenian Gregorian Church and other religious groups. These, he predicted, would make it possible to remove remaining "reactionary Church and sectarian authorities" from their posts.[9]

Since the Russian Orthodox delegates to the WCC were carefully selected by the KGB and the Council for Religious Affairs, it is scarcely surprising that they denied—often indignantly—all reports of the persecution of their Church by the Soviet state. According to a KGB report of August 1969:

> Agents ALTAR, SVYATOSLAV, ADAMANT, MAGISTER, ROSHCHIN and ZEMNOGORSKY went to England to take part in the work of the WCC central committee. Agents managed to avert hostile activities [public criticism of Soviet religious persecution] . . .[10]

The most important of the agents at the WCC central committee meeting in Canterbury was the leader of the Russian Orthodox delegation, Metropolitan Nikodim (agent ADAMANT),[11] whose meteoric rise through the Church hierarchy was in itself unmistakable evidence of KGB approval. In 1960, at the age of only thirty-one, Nikodim had become the youngest bishop in Christendom. A year later he was put in charge of the Moscow Patriarchate's foreign relations department, and in 1964 was appointed Metropolitan of Leningrad. Nikodim took the lead in ensuring that there was no reference in the WCC central committee's message to member churches either to the invasion of Czechoslovakia or to religious persecution in the Soviet Bloc. According to a report in the *Church Times:*

> Agreement on the text of the message was not without drama . . . The main critic on the Thursday [August 21] when the fifth draft came up for discussion was the Metropolitan of Leningrad, Archbishop Ni[k]odim.
>
> . . . The Russian leader then dropped a bombshell[:] ". . . If certain amendments are not taken into account which are essential to us, we shall have to reject this letter in holy synod and not send it to our Churches. I am sorry to speak in such sharp terms."
>
> . . . On Friday morning [after redrafting] there was more sweetness and light, and with the Russian leader obviously mollified, the final draft went through rapidly.

The main initiative agreed by the WCC central committee was a call to member churches to become "as fully engaged as possible in the struggle to eradicate racism in whatever form it appears."[12] While welcoming the campaign against racism, the *Church Times* deplored the failure of the WCC to address "grave breaches of human rights" or to offer help to the oppressed: "Czechoslovakia springs to mind as an obvious instance."[13]

The KGB reported that, at the Canterbury conference, its agents had also succeeded "in placing agent KUZNETSOV in a high WCC post." Agent KUZNETSOV was Alexei Sergeyevich Buyevsky, lay secretary of the Moscow Patriarchate's foreign relations department headed by Nikodim. Since joining the department in 1946, Buyevsky had accompanied all the major Russian Orthodox delegations abroad and had met the most important visitors from foreign churches to Moscow. Throughout the 1970s and 1980s he played an active role in the work of the WCC central committee, helping to draft policy statements on international affairs.[14]

In 1973 the Bishop of Bristol told the *Church Times* that, of the 130 members of the WCC central committee, 42 percent were Westerners, 28 percent Eastern Orthodox (mainly Russian), and 30 percent from the Third World (mainly Africa). The Russian Orthodox and Third World majority saw Westerners "primarily as the representatives of 'colonialism' with all the emotional overtones which that contains."[15] KGB agents on the WCC were remarkably successful in dissuading it from paying serious attention to religious persecution in the Soviet Bloc and in persuading it to concentrate instead on the sins of the imperialist West. The Reverend Richard Holloway of the Scottish Episcopal Church told the Nairobi Assembly of the WCC in 1975:

> I have observed there is an unwritten rule operating that says that the USSR must never be castigated in public. Nevertheless it is well known that the

USSR is in the forefront of human rights violations. To mention this fact appears to be unsporting. I think this tradition should end. The USSR should take its place in the public confessional along with the rest of us from white neo-imperialism.[16]

As late as 1989, the Centre claimed that, following the secret implementation of "a plan approved by the KGB leadership," "the WCC executive and central committee adopted public statements (eight) and messages (three) which corresponded to the political direction of Socialist [Communist] countries."[17]

Members of the Orthodox hierarchy sent on missions to foreign church leaders, doubtless with KGB approval, invariably insisted that believers in the Soviet Union enjoyed freedom of religion. In January 1975 Metropolitan Yuvenali of Krutitsky and Kolomna, who had succeeded his cousin Metropolitan Nikodim as the globetrotting chairman of the Patriarchate's foreign relations department,[18] traveled to Britain for the enthronement of the new Archbishop of Canterbury, Dr. Donald Coggan. In an interview on the BBC World Service, Yuvenali condemned the tendency of "certain circles" in Britain, including some in the Church of England, to give a biased and one-sided view of the Orthodox Church in Russia. In a private meeting with Dr. Coggan, he attacked the *Church Times* for its "offensive" stories on religious persecution in Russia and denounced Keston College, the world's leading research center on religion in Communist countries, directed by the Anglican priest Michael Bourdeaux, as "anti-Soviet." Though courteous, Dr. Coggan was more robust than most of the Western council members of the WCC. Yuvenali appeared incredulous as the Archbishop patiently defended the independence of the *Church Times* and the fair-mindedness of Keston College. During a visit to the Soviet Union two years later Dr. Coggan annoyed his hosts by departing from the prepared itinerary to visit Moscow synagogues and the congregation of the imprisoned Baptist minister, Georgi Vins, in Kiev, where he led the singing of the hymn "He Who Would Valiant Be."[19]

Among KGB agents in the Patriarchate's foreign relations department who were regularly used as agents of influence in meetings with Western churches was the monk Iosif Pustoutov, who was recruited in 1970, aged twenty-six, with the code-name YESAULENKO. Over the next few years YESAULENKO was sent on missions to the Netherlands, West Germany, Italy and France. In 1976 he was appointed representative of the Moscow Patriarchate of the Russian Orthodox Church at the Prague headquarters of the Christian Peace Conference. In order to raise his standing in the religious community, his case officer at the Prague residency, Yevgeni Vasilyevich Medvedev, arranged for him to be regularly invited to embassy receptions given by the Soviet ambassador.[20]

It would be both simplistic and unjust to see all the KGB's agents and co-optees in the Orthodox Church and the WCC simply as cynical careerists with no real religious faith—though that may have been true of a minority. Most Russian Orthodox priests probably believed they had no option but to accept some of the demands of state security. One of the best-known dissident priests of the 1970s, Father Dmitri Dudko, later declared:

One hundred percent of the clergy were forced to cooperate to some extent with the KGB and pass on some sort of information—otherwise they would have been deprived of the possibility to work in a parish.

A minority, however, did successfully resist all the pressure placed on them by the KGB. In December 1991, shortly before the dissolution of the Soviet Union, the last deputy chairman of the KGB, Anatoli Oleinikov, told an interviewer that, of the Russian Orthodox priests approached by the KGB, 15 to 20 percent had refused to work for it.[21] The courageous minority who resisted all KGB pressure were inevitably denied advancement. The section of the Orthodox Church most compromised by its association with the KGB was its hierarchy.

It would be wrong, however, to interpret the deference shown by the hierarchy to the KGB simply in terms of the moral inadequacy of individual bishops. The Church was strongly influenced by a centuries-old tradition of Orthodox spirituality which emphasized submission to both God and Caesar. Before the Revolution, obedience to the Tsar had been regarded almost as a religious obligation. The Orthodox Church had traditionally functioned as a department of state as well as a guide to salvation. Metropolitan Nikodim of Leningrad, who headed the Russian Orthodox delegation to the WCC until his sudden death during a visit to the Vatican in 1978, impressed many Western Christians by his deep devotion to the Orthodox liturgy and the apparent intensity of his prayer during church services.[22] Nikodim's admirers included Pope John Paul I, who was with him when Nikodim died of a heart attack and said afterwards that he had pronounced during their meeting "the most beautiful words about the Church that I ever heard."[23] Yet Nikodim was not merely supine in his submission to the Soviet powers-that-be but also a KGB agent.[24] So was his private secretary and confidant, Nikolai Lvovich Tserpitsky, who was recruited in 1971 with the codename VLADIMIR.[25]

A report by the Council for Religious Affairs in 1974 distinguished three categories of Orthodox bishop. The first category

affirm both in words and deed not only loyalty but also patriotism towards the socialist society; strictly observe the laws on cults, and educate the parish clergy and believers in the same spirit; realistically understand that our state is not interested in proclaiming the role of religion and the church in society; and, realizing this, do not display any particular activeness in extending the influence of Orthodoxy among the population.

Among the bishops in this category were Patriarch Pimen, who had succeeded Aleksi I in 1971, and Metropolitan Aleksi of Tallinn and Estonia, who in 1990 was to succeed Pimen as Patriarch Aleksi II.[26] Both were fulsome in their public praise of Soviet leaders. Pimen even claimed to detect "lofty spiritual qualities" in Andropov, the chief persecutor of religious dissent during his patriarchate. On Andropov's death Pimen declared that he would always "remember with heartfelt gratitude" his "benevolent understanding of the needs of our Church."[27]

Like Patriarch Aleksi I, Pimen was used by the KGB to front Soviet "peace" propaganda, paying gushing and sycophantic tribute to Brezhnev's "titanic work in the cause of international peace."[28] In February 1976 he, Metropolitan Aleksi and the other metropolitans on the Holy Synod received special awards from the Soviet Peace Fund "for manifold and fruitful activities of the Russian Orthodox Church in the struggle for peace, security and friendship."[29] A month later the Patriarch was given a similar award by the World Peace Council to mark its twenty-fifth anniversary.[30] In June 1977, Pimen hosted a conference at Zagorsk, organized behind the scenes by the KGB, entitled "Religious Workers for Lasting Peace, Disarmament and Just Relations among Nations," which attracted 663 delegates from 107 countries, representing all the major world religions.[31] The conference approved a call by Pimen to declare the years up to 2,000 "a period of struggle for peace"—thus, in the KGB's view, preempting the danger that the Vatican might take the lead in a similar appeal.[32] A month later Pimen was awarded the Order of the Red Banner "for his great patriotic activities in defense of peace."[33]

The second category of bishops identified by the Council of Religious Affairs in 1974 consisted of those who, though loyal to the state and "correct" in their observance of the laws on religious observance, wished to "heighten the role of the Church in personal, family and public life . . . and select for priestly office young people who are zealous adherents of Orthodox piety." Despite his use as an agent of influence in the World Council of Churches and elsewhere, Metropolitan Nikodim was included in this second category rather than the first—probably because of what was considered his excessive zeal in encouraging religious devotion. The third category of bishops (just under a third of the total) consisted of those "who at different times have made attempts to evade the laws on cults," though without the conspicuous defiance which would have required their removal from office.[34]

The first sign of dissidence within the Orthodox Church to gain worldwide publicity during the Brezhnev era was an appeal to the Fifth Assembly of the World Council of Churches at Nairobi in November 1975 by the banned priest Father Gleb Yakunin and the layman Lev Regelson, who appealed for support for the victims of religious persecution in the Soviet Union—a hitherto taboo subject at WCC meetings.[35] A Swiss delegate was applauded when he proposed that a resolution on "Disarmament, the Helsinki Agreement and Religious Liberty" include the statement:

> The WCC is concerned about restrictions to religious liberty, particularly in the USSR. The Assembly respectfully requests the government of the USSR to implement effectively principle no. 7 [religious and other freedoms] of the Helsinki Agreement.

Metropolitan Yuvenali complained that this proposal offended Christian charity. A KGB agent on the drafting committee, Alexei Buyevsky (KUZNETSOV), working "in the spirit of brotherly love, mutual understanding and the spirit of fellowship," helped produce a formula which avoided any specific reference to the Soviet Union but "recognize[d] that churches in different parts of Europe are living and working under very different conditions and traditions." The WCC's general secretary, the West Indian Methodist Dr. Philip Potter, was asked to prepare a report on religious liberty in all countries which had signed the Helsinki Accords. *The Times* interpreted the WCC resolution as "a sidestep by churches on Soviet curbs."[36]

There were no such prevarications in the denunciation of Western racism and imperialism. One of the keynote speakers at the assembly, Dr. Robert McAffie Brown of the Union Theological Seminary, New York, confessed that, as a white, male middle-class American, he embodied the sins of "racism, sexism, classism and imperialism." In an attempt to avoid "linguistic imperialism," he then began speaking in Spanish, thus forcing most of his audience to reach for their headsets so that they could hear his address translated back into imperialist English. The WCC's refusal to consider non-white racism, such as the expulsion of Ugandan Asians in 1972, led to protests and a walk-out by some British delegates—prompting the comment by Dr. Potter that, "Wherever the British have gone in the world they have established a racist system."[37] At the end of the conference, lobbying by the Soviet-front Christian Peace Conference helped to ensure the election of Metropolitan Nikodim (agent ADAMANT) as one of the WCC's six presidents.[38]

Had Andropov and the KGB leadership kept any sense of proportion about the threat of "ideological subversion" posed by the few brave dissidents within a generally subservient Orthodox Church, they would have been quite satisfied by the outcome of the Nairobi Assembly. In fact, mild though the WCC response to the appeal from Yakunin and Regelson was, it caused outrage at the Centre.[39] Despite complaints by Dr. Potter's critics in the West that he was "openly anti-Western and anti-capitalist,"[40] the KGB claimed that, in reality, he had "anti-Soviet leanings" and was "known for his provocative statements about the absence of freedom of conscience in the USSR."[41] Though he had been given a carefully staged-managed tour of Soviet religious institutions two months before the Nairobi Assembly, Potter had failed to defend them against Yakunin's and Regelson's outrageously accurate criticisms. Metropolitan Filaret of Kiev and Gallich told a Novosti correspondent after the assembly:

> We deplore the prejudiced conviction held by the WCC leadership about our state and the Russian Orthodox Church. WCC general secretary Mr. Potter, by the way, was my guest last September and saw for himself that churches and monasteries were open. While here he attended divine services and said that he was always filled with joy when visiting this peace-loving country, in the midst of such prayerful and happy surroundings. It seemed strange and surprising to us that at the assembly he said nothing about his visit to the Soviet Union, including the Ukraine.[42]

The Centre organized a flood of letters to the ungrateful Dr. Potter from Russian Orthodox clergy, Baptists and other Soviet Christians, protesting at his alleged hostility towards them. It also sought to orchestrate public criticism of Potter by "prominent religious figures" in Britain, Syria and Lebanon, as well as in the Soviet Union.

Further KGB active measures included the publication in Moscow of an English-language book, *Religion Under Socialism,* and the production of a TV documentary, *Freedom of Religion in the USSR,* both involving a probably English-speaking agent codenamed "K" (not identified in Mitrokhin's notes). Attempts were also made to "compromise" Potter personally in various ways and—probably through KGB agents in the WCC—to suggest his replacement as general secretary. Archbishop Kiprian (agent SIMONOV) from the Moscow Church of the Consolation of All Who Sorrow, gave an interview denouncing "fabrications concerning the so-called persecution of believers in the USSR."[43]

The absurdity of the KGB's overreaction to the temporary embarrassment of the Nairobi Assembly and Dr. Potter's handling of it was well illustrated by his report to the WCC central committee in August 1976 on progress to religious liberty in those countries which had signed the Helsinki Accords. His lengthy address said nothing about religious persecution in the Soviet Bloc, despite extensive, well-documented evidence of it submitted by Keston College and others. Dr. Potter did, however, insist that "it is essential for churches in Europe and north America to be aware of the problems created and maintained by European and American domination of other regions of the world."[44]

The most serious act of public defiance within the Orthodox Church during the Brezhnev era was, in the Centre's view, the foundation in December 1976 of the Christian Committee for the Defence of Believers' Rights in the USSR by Father Gleb Yakunin, Hierodeacon Varsonofy (Khaibulin) and a layman, Viktor Kapitanchuk. The declared aim of the committee, which worked in consultation with the Helsinki Monitoring Group, was to help believers of all denominations "exercise their rights in accordance with their convictions."[45] "Yakunin and his associates," reported the Centre, "are in practice engaging in a struggle with the existing order in the USSR . . . proclaiming a national religious revival in Russia as an alternative to Marxist–Leninist ideology":

> The committee has an extensive network of correspondents among religious fanatics; they are the main suppliers of information about the situation of believers in the USSR to places abroad.
>
> In order to cause a schism in the Russian Orthodox Church and to set up a new Church organization taking up anti-Soviet positions, the Christian Committee has launched a campaign to compromise clergy loyal to the Soviet state as unfit to defend the interests of the believers.[46]

By 1980—to the consternation of the KGB—eleven volumes of documents totaling 1,189 pages of Russian text, obtained by the Christian Committee, had been published in the West.[47]

The KGB eventually demolished the Christian Committee by its traditional techniques of destabilization, agent penetration and persecution. The Fifth Directorate concluded that the most vulnerable of the committee's founders was Hierodeacon Varsonofy. With the assistance of GALKIN (an unidentified agent in the Orthodox

Church), Varsanofy was assigned early in 1978 to a church in Vladimir region whose incumbent, VOLZHSKY, was a long-standing KGB agent. Finding it difficult to stay in touch with Yakunin and Kapitanchuk, Varsanofy resigned from the Christian Committee. According to Varsanofy's file, VOLZHSKY introduced him to a sympathetic psychiatrist (also a KGB agent, codenamed BULKIN), who persuaded him that he was suffering from a nervous illness and should give up membership of the Christian Committee in order to reduce the stress he was under and prevent his illness from getting worse. The KGB claimed the credit for inducing Varsonofy "to abandon political activity and concentrate on research work in the field of theology, using materials from the Oblast archives." While he was working in the archives, another KGB agent, codenamed SPIRANSKY, succeeded in winning his confidence and allegedly "deflected Varsanofy from his obsession of becoming the spokesman of believers in the Soviet Union":

> Finally he was persuaded to send a letter to Patriarch Pimen of All Russia and to senior personalities in the Russian Orthodox Church apologizing for the hurt that he had caused.[48]

On September 28, 1978 the Centre secretly promulgated KGB order no. 00122 on "Measures to Strengthen Agent Operational Work in the Struggle with the Subversive Activity of Foreign Clerical Centres and Hostile Elements among Church People and Sectarians": a lengthy document which reflected both the KGB's addiction to conspiracy theory and its obsession with "ideological subversion" of all kinds. It also paid unwitting, if irritated, tribute to the courage of the persecuted believers and the vitality of their faith. Mitrokhin's notes on order no. 00122 include the following:

> Under the pretense of concern for the freedom of belief and the rights of believers in the USSR, imperialist intelligence services and foreign anti-Soviet centers were organizing ideological sabotage, aimed at undermining the moral and political unity of Soviet society and undermining the basis of the Socialist system; they sought to discredit the Soviet state and social order, incite religious organizations towards confrontations with the state and stimulate the emergence of an anti-Soviet underground among sectarians. With encouragement from abroad, hostile elements had launched active organizational and provocational activity aimed at forming illegal groups and organizations within the sectarian milieu, setting up printing presses and establishing contacts with foreign clerical centers.

Following the directives of the May 1975 conference of leading officials of KGB agencies [dealing with religious affairs], it had been possible to carry out measures to strengthen operational positions in international religious organizations, to expose and compromise their leaders, officials and emissaries of clerical centers. Experienced and reliable agents had been infiltrated into the leading circles of some sectarian formations and measures to identify, prevent and terminate the subversive activity of hostile elements among the clerical anti-Soviet underground had become more effective, the further strengthening of the positions of progressive religious figures had been ensured, as well as their active participation in the struggle for peace and other political measures.

Operational work, however, still did not meet present requirements of the present time. The operational situation in a number of sectors of KGB agency work remained tense. The work of disrupting and detaching believers, especially among young people, from the influence of hostile elements was being carried out feebly. Agent positions in the leading ranks of the dissident Baptists, the Catholic and Uniate priesthood, the Pentecostalists, the Adventists and the Jehovah's Witnesses, and among the irregular Moslem clerics, were weak.

The USSR KGB Collegium decided as follows:

1. To raise the level of agent operational work designed to struggle against the subversive activity conducted under the cover of religion by imperialist intelligence services, clerical centers abroad and hostile elements within the country. The basic task was to identify in good time, prevent and put an end to the subversive designs of the adversary to stimulate anti-Soviet activity in the sectarian environment, creating religious formations hostile to the Socialist system and drawing believers into their sphere of influence.
2. The FCD, the SCD and the Fifth Directorate of the KGB were to identify the foreign anti-Soviet clerical organizations which, evidence showed, were being used by the adversary's special services and were to submit proposals for identifying and cutting off subversive channels, identifying and intercepting communication channels with hostile elements in the sectarian milieu . . .
3. The Fifth Directorate and the local KGB agencies were to take steps to put an end to hostile activity designed to undermine loyalty to the Soviet state and the social order by the largest religious organization in the USSR, namely the Orthodox Church; they were to prevent the penetration of individuals with hostile attitudes in the leading ranks of the Church; in 1978–80, they were to take steps to strengthen the operational positions [i.e. the number and quality of agents] within the structure of the Orthodox Church (in Metropolitan provinces, Eparchies, parishes, monasteries and educational establishments), and to compromise and remove reactionary and anti-Soviet elements . . .[49]

The Christian Committee for the Defence of Believers' Rights sought to protect itself against KGB penetration in part by remaining small, never having more than four members at any one time.[50] In May 1979, however, it was joined by Father Vasili Fonchenkov, unaware that nine years earlier he had been recruited by the Fifth Directorate as agent DRUG ("Friend"). According to his file, "He was involved in the cultivation of specific individuals [in the Orthodox Church], carried out his assignments conscientiously and showed initiative." Since 1972 Fonchenkov had been a lecturer at the Zagorsk theological academy as well as holding a position in the foreign relations department of the Moscow Patriarchate. In 1976–7 he had been the incumbent of the church of St. Sergi in East Berlin and editor of *Stimme der Orthodoxie* (*Voice of Orthodoxy*), the journal of the Patriarchate's central European exarchate.[51] His contacts with foreign churches may well have helped to recommend agent DRUG to his unwitting colleagues on the Christian Committee.

The KGB campaign against public dissent in the Orthodox Church reached its peak in 1979–80, with a wave of arrests of leading dissidents—chief among them Father Gleb Yakunin—who were later imprisoned or persuaded to recant. Probably to protect his cover, Fonchenkov was summoned for interrogation by the KGB and issued a statement saying that he was threatened with arrest, but was never charged.[52] During a visit to West Germany in March 1980 Archbishop Pitirim of Volokolamsk (agent ABBAT)[53] bizarrely declared that there had been "no wave of arrests."[54] The first major success of the KGB campaign was to persuade the charismatic Moscow priest Father Dmitri Dudko, whose offenses included calling for the canonization of Orthodox martyrs of the Soviet era, to make a public recantation on Soviet television in June 1980. Dudko's resistance had been broken by a particularly skillful KGB interrogator, Vladimir Sergeyevich Sorokin, whom he had come to regard as "my own brother." He said later that he had hoped that parts of his confession, such as his condemnation of "the sabre-rattling of the Carter administration," would be recognized as words placed in his mouth by the KGB. His reputation, however, never fully recovered.[55]

There was no prospect of a recantation by Yakunin. Only his wife was allowed to attend his trial. The rest of his family and friends, along with the Western press, were refused admittance, while what one correspondent described as "burly young men in ill-fitting suits," selected by the KGB, filed into the courtroom. Probably to protect his cover, Fonchenkov was among those who were turned away.[56] Those called to give evidence against Yakunin included several KGB agents inside the Orthodox Church, among them Iosif Pustoutov (YESAULENKO), former representative of the Moscow Patriarchate at the Prague headquarters of the Christian Peace Conference, who testified to the harmful international consequences of the Christian Committee's work. Yakunin accepted his sentence of five years' imprisonment, followed by five years' internal exile, with the words, "I thank God for this test He has sent me. I consider it a great honor, and, as a Christian, accept it gladly." The British Council of Churches sent an appeal to Brezhnev, urging the court to reconsider its opinion. Attempts to gain the support of the World Council of Churches for a similar appeal met with no response.[57]

A change in WCC rules before its Vancouver Assembly in 1983 ensured that the KGB suffered no repetition of the embarrassment caused by the discussion of the Yakunin and Regelson letter at the previous assembly seven and a half years earlier. Under the new regulations, probably prompted by the KGB agents on the WCC council:

Appeals from groups or individuals for World Council of Churches intervention cannot be acted on by the assembly without the support of delegates or member churches, but will be followed up by the WCC general secretary.

An open letter from Vladimir Rusak, a Russian Orthodox deacon who had been dismissed for writing an unauthorized history of the Church after the October Revolution, appealed to delegates at Vancouver to "stop treating the propagandistic claims of Soviet delegates as the only source of information" on religion in the Soviet Union. He also urged the assembly to hold a frank debate on religious freedom. The mere discussion of the Yakunin–Regelson letter at Nairobi had "yielded some definite results" by embarrassing the authorities into the "hurried publication" of some copies of the Bible. The assembly also received another letter on behalf of thirty-five imprisoned Soviet Christians and 20,000 persecuted Pentecostalists who wished to emigrate to the West. Unsurprisingly, neither letter received support from Soviet delegates and neither was discussed at the assembly.

The embarrassment of the Afghan War was also successfully contained. Despite the desire of a minority of delegates for "a condemnation of Soviet aggression and the unconditional withdrawal of Soviet troops," the final compromise resolution called for a Soviet withdrawal only "in the context of an overall political settlement between Afghanistan and the USSR" (conveniently ignoring the fact that the Kabul regime had been installed by the Soviet invaders) and "an end to the supply of arms to the opposition groups from outside" (in other words, the denial of arms to those resisting the Soviet invasion). These were precisely the conditions which the Soviet Union itself laid down for the withdrawal of its troops. Unsurprisingly, the Russian Orthodox delegation praised the final resolution as "balanced and realistic." The Vancouver Assembly had no such inhibitions in condemning the West. Western capitalism was duly denounced as the main source of injustice in the world, responsible for the evils of sexism, racism, "cultural captivity, colonialism, and neo-colonialism."[58]

The success, in Moscow's view, of the Vancouver Assembly, probably helps to explain why the Centre established as one of the priorities for KGB active measures for 1984:

Exerting influence in our favor on the activity of . . . clerical organizations on the questions of war and peace, and other key contemporary problems.[59]

Looking back on his career in the KGB, Oleg Kalugin concludes that, like "the stranglehold over the Church inside the Soviet Union," the penetration and exploitation of the Russian Orthodox Church abroad was "one of the most sordid and little known chapters in the history of our organization."[60] Mitrokhin came to the same conclusion, commenting at one point in his notes that the files contained "a whirlpool of filth."[61] The KGB used its agents among Russian Orthodox clergy in the West not merely to spy on émigré communities but also to identify possible agent recruits.[62] Though the Russian Orthodox Church in north America was split, the faction which remained loyal to the Moscow Patriarchate was, according to Kalugin, "riddled with KGB agents."[63] Among the agents identified in the files noted by Mitrokhin was a cleric codenamed PETROV, who was sent to north America in the 1970s. His case officers in north America contacted him by using the passwords "Pyotr Mikhailovich," the first name and patronymic of his Fifth Directorate controller in Moscow.[64]

The file on Arkadi Rodyonovich Tyshchuk (VORONOV), a priest who was posted to the Nikolsky Russian Orthodox cathedral in New York from 1977 to 1982, contains evidence of a hostility to the United States which may also have helped to motivate other Orthodox priests in the KGB's north American network. The United States, VORONOV told his KGB case officer, suffered from the sin of pride—"and pride comes before a fall:"

> When a country declares itself to be the most powerful and the richest, and that its government is the smartest and possesses the best weapons—that is not maturity, it is bragging, and is the reason for the downfall of all the powerful nations of the past.

VORONOV usually met his controller from the New York residency either at the Soviet mission to the United Nations, where he went to collect his correspondence from Russia, or on board the ship *Mikhail Lermontov,* which regularly came into port at New York. More difficult to explain than his hostility to the United States was his apparent admiration for the KGB which, according to his file, he bizarrely described as a "good shepherd" and a "true Russian spiritual guardian and shepherd."[65]

Russian Orthodox priests in the West were also used by FCD Directorate S to collect material for use in devising the well-documented legends of KGB illegals. In the early 1970s, for example, two KGB agents in the Moscow Patriarchate were sent to carry out detailed research on parish registers in Canada. Ivan Grigoryevich Borcha (codenamed FYODOR), who worked as a priest in prairie parishes of Ukrainian and Romanian communities, studied registers in Alberta and Saskatchewan. Viktor Sergeyevich Petlyuchenko (PATRIOT), who was assigned to Orthodox parishes in Edmonton, carried out further research in Alberta.[66]

The Russian Orthodox Church, both at home and abroad, took a prominent part in the Rodina ("Motherland") Society founded as a front organization by the KGB in December 1975 to promote "cultural relations with compatriots abroad," and thus provide new opportunities for agent recruitment among émigré communities. Its vice-president, P. I. Vasilyev, was a senior member of the FCD's Nineteenth (Soviet émigré) Department and headed a secret Rodina intelligence section.[67] Metropolitan Aleksi of Tallinn and Estonia (agent DROZDOV),[68] the future Patriarch Aleksi II, who was made a Rodina council member, told its opening conference, "We are all united by our love for our Socialist motherland." Through its exarchates, dioceses and parishes in Europe, America, Asia and Africa, the Orthodox Church "continued to maintain spiritual ties with our compatriots" and was "doing its best to keep these contacts alive and active."[69] Metropolitan Aleksi is unlikely to have been unaware that these contacts were exploited by the KGB. According to a KGB document of 1988, "An order was drafted by the USSR KGB chairman to award an honorary citation to agent DROZDOV" for unspecified services to state security.[70]

THOUGH NEVER FULLY satisfied by the extent of its stranglehold over the Orthodox Church, the KGB was far more concerned by the "subversive" activities of those Christians over whom it had no direct control. The largest of the underground churches was the Greek Catholic (or Uniate) Church of Ukraine (nowadays the Ukrainian Catholic Church), whose liturgy and structure followed the "Eastern Rite" but which accepted the authority of Rome. Fearful at the end of the Second World War that the Uniate Church would provide a focus for Ukrainian nationalism, Stalin set out to terrorize it into submission to Moscow. In 1946 a mock synod in Lviv cathedral, staged by the MGB with the assistance of a small number of Uniate stooges and the blessing of the Orthodox hierarchy, announced the "reunion" of the Greek Catholics with the Russian Orthodox Church. Greek Catholic Archbishop (later Cardinal) Josyf Slipyj wrote later:

> Our priests were given the choice of either joining the "church of the Regime" and thereby renouncing Catholic unity, or enduring for at least ten years the harsh fate of deportation and all the penalties associated with it. The overwhelming majority of priests chose the way of the Soviet Union's prisons and concentration camps.

Almost overnight, the four million Uniate Christians became the world's largest illegal church. All but two of its ten bishops, along with many thousands of priests and believers, died for their faith in the Siberian gulag.[71]

In 1963 Slipyj was expelled to Rome, leaving Bishop (later Archbishop) Vasyl Velychkovsky as effective leader of the underground church. The KGB immediately deployed five agents—TIKHOV, SIDORENKO, ROMANENKO, SOVA and PODOLENIN (none identified in Mitrokhin's notes)—in a series of attempts to discredit Velychkovsky among the persecuted Uniate faithful. TIKHOV, evidently a member of the underground church, periodically sent to Slipyj in the Vatican letters containing disinformation about Velychkovsky fabricated by the Centre. According to KGB files, Slipyj sent his own emissaries to the Ukraine to check the truth of the allegations against his successor, but agents who were planted on them confirmed TIKHOV's fabrications.[72] KGB reports, however, probably overstated the success of their active measures. There is no convincing evidence of a breach between Slipyj and Velychkovsky.

In July 1967 a conference of senior officials of Soviet Bloc intelligence agencies met in Budapest to discuss "work against the Vatican; measures to discredit the Vatican and its backers; and measures to exacerbate differences within the Vatican and between the Vatican and capitalist countries."[73] Two senior KGB officers, Agayants and Khamazyuk, addressed the conference on "The Hostile Activity of the Vatican and of the Catholic and Uniate Clergy on the Territory of the USSR and the Experience of the [KGB] Agencies in Countering this Activity." A third, Kulikov, spoke on "Some aspects of agent operational work against Vatican institutions." On the proposal of the KGB delegation, all but the Romanian representatives agreed on the need to intensify "work against the Vatican in close relation with the work against the Main Adversary." Andropov, who regarded the Uniates as the spearhead of the Vatican's ideological sabotage offensive in the Soviet Union, wrote to the Central Committee, emphasizing the importance of the conference's conclusions.[74]

Andropov's obsession with ideological subversion by the Holy See was doubtless reinforced by the claim in a 1968 intelligence report that the Vatican's Secretariat of State had devised a masterplan to shatter the unity of the Soviet Union and had given the Deputy Secretary of State, Cardinal Giovanni Benelli, the task of implementing it.[75] A Centre assessment of 1969 repeated the claim that the Vatican was out "to shatter the Soviet Union from within with the help of ideological sabotage":

> Church people were disseminating Church propaganda literature, praising the Western way of life, whipping up nationalist feelings among the population of Soviet Republics and sowing distrust among Soviet people towards Soviet and Party agencies.[76]

A professional *antireligioznik* from the Ukraine, speaking at an official conference in 1969, paid unwitting tribute to the continued vitality of the persecuted Uniates:

> Nurturing hopes for the restoration of the Uniate Church, its apologists are work-ing on the clergy who reunited with Orthodoxy, trying to persuade them to repu-diate the "Muscovites" and to adopt openly or secretly a Uniate, pro-Vatican line. In some regions of the Ukraine, illegal schools were organized to train new Uni-ate priests. In a series of localities, the Uniates have willfully opened previously closed churches and have been conducting [unauthorized] religious services . . .[77]

On April 4, 1969 Andropov approved further "measures to intensify the struggle against subversive activity by the Vatican and the Uniates on the territory of the USSR in 1969–70," to be implemented jointly by the FCD, the Fifth (Dissidents and Ideological Subversion) Directorate and local KGBs. The FCD was instructed, somewhat ambitiously, to attempt the agent penetration of all major sections of the Vatican bureaucracy, the Jesuit order, the Russicum and other pontifical colleges training priests for Eastern churches, as well as to make operational contact with three Roman clerics—codenamed APOSTOL, RASS and SLUGA—who had been born in the Soviet Union.[78] Among the few successes in this ambitious program by the end of 1969 which Mitrokhin found in Centre files was the penetration of pon-tifical colleges by KGB agents from the legally established Catholic Church in the Soviet Union, particularly the Baltic republics. PETROV and ROGULIN, both agents of the Fifth Directorate, had arrived in Rome in January 1968 to begin three years' study at the Russicum; in 1969 they went on an intelligence-gathering mission to "Catholic centers" in France and Belgium.[79] During 1969, two KGB agents from

Lithuania, ANTANAS and VIDMANTAS, were studying at the Gregorian University.[80] Two other Lithuanian agents, DAKTARAS (a bishop) and ZHIBUTE, took part in the working commission for the reform of the Canon Law Codex, held at the Vatican from May 21 to June 11, 1969. DAKTARAS told his case officer that, at a papal audience on June 7, Paul VI had told him, "I remember you in my prayers and hope that God will help the clergy and believers [in Lithuania]."[81]

With the assistance of the Hungarian AVH, the KGB also succeeded in cultivating a member of the Vatican's Congregation for the Eastern Church, Uniate Bishop Dudás, who was resident in Hungary. A Fifth Directorate female agent, POTOCHINA, who had probably infiltrated the underground church in Ukraine, traveled regularly to Hungary on the pretext of visiting a relative and—according to her file—succeeded in winning Dudás's confidence.[82] Dudás doubtless never suspected that she was a KGB agent, sent to obtain intelligence on the Vatican's secret contacts with the Ukrainian Uniates.

The operations against the Vatican approved by Andropov in April 1969 also included a series of active measures. The KGB was instructed to find ways of creating distrust between émigré clerics in Rome and Uniates and other Catholics in the Soviet Union. The leading KGB agents in the Russian Orthodox Church who were in contact with the Vatican—DROZDOV (Metropolitan Aleksi), ADAMANT (Metropolitan Nikodim), SVYATOSLAV and NESTEROV (both unidentified)—were instructed "to cause dissension between Vatican organizations such as the Congregation for the Eastern Church, the Secretariat for Christian Unity and the Commission for Justice and Peace." In order to put pressure on the Vatican "to cease its subversive activity," ADAMANT was also instructed to tell his contacts in the Roman Curia that the Soviet government was contemplating establishing autonomous Catholic churches in the Baltic republics and elsewhere in the Soviet Union which would be independent of Rome. The Lithuanian bishop DAKTARAS passed on the same message when he attended a bishop's conference in Rome in October 1969.[83] There is no evidence that any of the active measures had a discernible effect on Vatican policy.

As well as giving higher priority to operations against the Vatican, Andropov also stepped up the persecution of the Ukrainian Uniates. In 1969 the head of the underground church, Bishop Velychkovsky, was arrested and sentenced to three years' imprisonment. The KGB reported that his arrest "greatly helped to achieve a psychological breakthrough in the mind of SERAFIM," another leading figure in the Uniate underground, who was recruited as a KGB agent. According to Mitrokhin's notes on his file:

SERAFIM explained in detail by whom, when and in what circumstances he was tasked to direct monks illegally; he reported incidents of criminal organizational activity by Bishop Velychkovsky and his close contacts; he reported on the situation among underground orders of monks . . . and he drew up a list of Uniate priests operating illegally. SERAFIM's answers were recorded covertly on tape.

Though SERAFIM agreed to "cooperate secretly" with the KGB, he refused to sign the written undertaking required of most informers. His controller did not insist, on the grounds that it would represent too great "a psychological trial for a man of religion" and leave him in fear of "divine punishment in the next world." Another agent, terrified of "being cast into Hell," had once begged the controller, on bended knee, to return his signed undertaking.[84]

In 1971 the KGB also succeeded in recruiting in Lviv one of the leading members of an underground order of Uniate monks, codenamed IRENEY, who served as one of the main points of contact with the Catholic Church in Poland. The Fifth Department regarded IRENEY as a tough nut to crack. If confronted directly with his "illegal activity," he would probably be strong enough to withstand the usual uncompromising interrogation. If given too many details of his activities, he would be able to identify members of the underground church who had informed on him. The KGB decided to begin by mounting a major surveillance operation on IRENEY's sister and "conspiratorial" collaborator, MARIYA. After MARIYA's sudden death, with IRENEY in deep depression, his case officer judged that the time was ripe for "a complex recruitment operation." IRENEY was brought in for interrogation and given extensive details of his ministry in the underground church, carefully designed to give the misleading impression that MARIYA had been informing on him for many years. Mitrokhin's notes give the following summary of the interrogator's self-congratulatory report:

> The monk lost the power of speech; he was totally stunned by this astonishing thought. His wild eyes, trembling hands, and the perspiration which covered his face betrayed his strong spiritual turmoil . . . Judging that denials were useless, [IRENEY] described the membership of the illegal leadership of the monastic order in Ukraine; he named Uniate authorities and monks who had come to Lvov [Lviv] through the tourist channel; and he spoke of his own journey to Poland in 1971 and of the meetings that he had held there. A month later, [IRENEY] was recruited . . . but refused to give a signed undertaking.

IRENEY remained so convinced that his sister had been a KGB agent that, when passing information to his controller, he frequently added the comment, "No doubt my sister told you this." According to his KGB file, he never ceased to marvel at the way in which sister had succeeded in keeping her KGB connection a secret from him.[85]

In 1972, like Slipyj nine years earlier, Bishop Velychkovsky was deported to the Vatican. A year later the KGB managed to gain access to Slipyj. Cardinal Felici invited to the Vatican a leading Uniate cleric from Czechoslovakia, unaware that he was a KGB agent codenamed PROFESSOR. Originally recruited by the Czechoslovak StB, PROFESSOR had been used by the KGB in 1971 to go on a supposedly "pastoral" visitation of the Redemptorist Order in Ukraine in order to provide intelligence on the activities of the underground church and its links with Rome. In September 1973 he met Slipyj in the Vatican. Plans were made for PROFESSOR to meet the Uniate leadership in Lviv, but Mitrokhin's notes do not record whether this meeting went ahead.[86]

In February 1975 a conference of Soviet Bloc intelligence services considered the coordination of operations against, and agent penetration in, the Vatican.[87] The Polish SB, Czechoslovak StB and Hungarian AVH all reported that they had "significant agent positions in the Vatican." Mitrokhin's notes record no such claim by the KGB. As at the similar conference in 1967, however, a hugely ambitious and unrealistic program for agent penetration was drawn up, which included plans to cultivate the Uniate leadership and no fewer than seven cardinals (Casaroli, Willebrands, Kînig, Samorä, Benelli, Poggi and Pignedoli), as well as an elaborate series of active measures to influence and discredit the Catholic Church.[88]

Among the individual targets for character assassination was Velychkovsky's successor as head of the underground Uniate Church, Bishop (later Metropolitan Archbishop) Volodymyr Sternyuk. Agent NATASHA spread disinformation about Sternyuk's alleged sexual immorality and the same stories were passed by other agents to the Vatican. As a result, according to KGB reports, "he lost the support of a significant part of the Uniates."[89] In reality, despite a new and vicious round of religious persecution in the early 1980s, the KGB lost its war against the Uniates. In 1987 Sternyuk emerged from the underground at the age of eighty-one with the status of a national hero, openly acknowledged by Rome as head of the Catholic Church in Ukraine—to the dismay of both the KGB and most of the Orthodox hierarchy. Metropolitan Filaret of Kiev and Galich insisted as late as October 1989, "The Uniates will never be legalized in our country." They were legalized by the end of the year.[90]

AFTER THE UNIATES and other Catholics, the KGB was most concerned during its war against religious "ideological subversion" in the Soviet Union by the activities of the unregistered Protestant churches and sects, which—like the Uniates—were outside direct state control. In the late 1950s the KGB estimated the membership of what it termed "illegal sectarian formations"—chief among them the Reform Baptists, Pentecostalists, Jehovah's Witnesses and Reformed Adventists—at about 100,000.[91]

The fact that throughout the Brezhnev era the KGB continued, on Andropov's instructions, to spend so much time and effort on groups who represented no conceivable threat to the Soviet system is further evidence of its obsession with even the most harmless forms of dissent. Andropov made the keynote of his address to an all-union KGB conference in 1975 the claim that anti-Soviet elements were conspiring against the state "under cover of religion." The first essential in unmasking and defeating the conspiracies was agent penetration:

> This is difficult, since false perceptions of the attitude of the state towards religion which still prevail in their milieu have left a definite mark on the psychology of the believers. Among sectarians there is a prejudice that any assistance to the authorities, including the KGB, is a great sin—treason. There is no trust in the humanism of the Cheka.

Andropov's complaint that believers failed to trust the "humanism" of the KGB provides further evidence of his limited sense of the absurd. To illustrate the difficulties of agent penetration among the ungrateful sectarians, he gave the example of "one candidate for recruitment, who had almost freed himself from errors with regard to the Cheka, and carried out particular assignments from an operational officer:"

> ... One day, however, he declared that meetings with his operational officer were sinful. He explained that the Lord God had appeared to him in a dream, had handcuffed him and asked: "Whose servant art thou?" Greatly shaken by this dream, the potential recruit interpreted it as a warning from God and stopped meeting the Chekist.[92]

Mitrokhin cannot have been the only KGB officer who, as he listened to such speeches or read articles on operations against believers in the classified in-house journal *KGB Sbornik,* secretly admired their courage and their faith. No hint of that admiration, however, appeared in KGB reports.

By the 1960s the KGB leadership had reluctantly concluded that no amount of persecution would wipe out the sectarians altogether. A conference in March 1959 of senior KGB officers leading "the struggle against Jehovists [Jehovah's Witnesses]" concluded that the correct strategy was "to continue measures of repression with measures of disruption."[93] The KGB set out to divide, demoralize and discredit the sectarians, as well as to arrest their most influential leaders on trumped-up charges.

In 1966 Pastors Georgi Vins and Gennadi Kryuchkov, the leaders of the Reform Baptists, probably the largest sectarian group, were jailed for three years. After their release, both went underground to continue their ministry. In 1974 Vins was caught and rearrested. Despite a major international campaign on his behalf, he was sentenced to a further ten years' imprisonment, but was released in a "spy exchange" in 1979 and expelled to the United States. Pastor Kryuchkov remained at liberty until 1989, when he dramatically reappeared in public at an emotional Reform Baptist congress. His success in continuing a secret ministry for almost twenty years without being caught by the KGB remains one of the most astonishing achievements in the history of the Soviet religious underground.[94]

Remarkably, however, the KGB was even more concerned by Jehovah's Witnesses, viewed with indifference or suspicion by most governments around the world, than by the Reform Baptists, whose heroic endurance of persecution attracted international sympathy. The head of the Second Chief Directorate, General Oleg Mikhailovich Gribanov, reported in 1962, "The most hostile of the sectarians are the Jehovists."[95] Since their emergence in the United States in the 1870s, no other Christian sect has spent so much of its energies on prophesying the end of the world. Though many of its detailed prophecies have been discredited and the Apocalypse has been repeatedly postponed, the basic millennarian message of Jehovah's Witnesses has never varied: "The end is near. Christ will reveal himself shortly to bring destruction upon the nations and all who oppose is messianic kingdom."[96]

In the course of the twentieth century Jehovah's Witnesses have been persecuted by many authoritarian regimes. Thousands suffered martyrdom in the death camps of the Nazi Third Reich. No major intelligence agency, however, has been quite as concerned as the KGB by the "Jehovist conspiracy." The Jehovist obsession of senior KGB officers was, perhaps, the supreme example of their lack of any sense of proportion when dealing with even the most insignificant forms of dissent.

Until the Second World War there had been no Jehovah's Witnesses in the Soviet Union. The incorporation of eastern Poland, Lithuania and Moldavia in 1939–40, however, turned thousands of Witnesses into unwilling Soviet citizens.[97] Many were deported to Siberia, accused of being "an American sect."[98] In 1968 the KGB put the total number of Jehovah's Witnesses at about 20,000.[99] The fact that the Witnesses had originated in the United States and still had their world headquarters in Brooklyn was regarded as deeply suspicious by the Centre's many conspiracy theorists.[100] The almost surreal outrage of KGB analysts, as they denounced the Witnesses for describing the Soviet state (like states in general) as the work of the Devil, would not be out of place in Bulgakov's *The Master and Margarita*:

> The sect of the Jehovah's Witnesses or Students of the Bible is a foreign invention. It is dangerous because it is actively engaged in drawing new members into the sect . . . The sectarians call Communists and the Komsomols "sons of the Devil."
>
> They demonstrate that the Soviet state is founded by Satan. Therefore one must not implement Soviet laws, or take part in elections, and they urge people to refuse to serve in the Soviet army. Jehovists extend assistance of all kind to their co-religionists who are in the [labor] camps or in internal exile, supplying them with money, food and clothing.[101]

The Soviet press, meanwhile, accused the Witnesses' Brooklyn headquarters of organizing an aggressive crusade against the countries of the Soviet Bloc.[102]

The Centre was disturbed by reports that, even in labor camps, "the Jehovah leaders and authorities did not reject their hostile beliefs and in camp conditions continued to carry out their Jehovah work." A conference of KGB officers working on operations against Jehovah's Witnesses met at Kishinev in November 1967 to discuss new measures "to prevent the sectarians' hostile work" and "ideological subversion:"

> The agencies were to strengthen in every way their agent positions among Jehovah's Witnesses within the country; they were to collect and build up information about young members of the sect and about the Jehovah authorities for operational purposes, recruitment, compromise and for open countermeasures . . . The conference recognized that it was essential to select and promote to leading positions in the sect, with the help of agents, people who were barely literate, who lacked initiative and were unlikely to stimulate the activity of subordinate units.[103]

The seriousness with which the conference discussed the Jehovist menace was, once again, almost surreal. The allegedly dangerous conspiracy which the Centre devoted so many resources to combating amounted to little more than the attempt by small groups to worship together in private, mostly in each others' homes, and their refusal to perform military service. Yet the conspiracy was judged so dangerous that the conference agreed on the need for agent penetration of the Brooklyn headquarters and its west European branches.[104] It was also feared that Brooklyn might correctly identify some Jehovah's Witnesses who had gone long periods without arrest as KGB agents. The conference therefore agreed on the need to "create a reliable reserved of understudy agents" for use if the existing agents were unmasked.[105]

As well as grossly exaggerating the menace of the Jehovah's Witnesses and other sectarians, the *KGB Shornik* also contained self-congratulatory accounts of the active measures used to destabilize them. One such case study in the mid-1970s concerned the leader of the Jehovah's Witnesses in Khmelnitskaya Oblast, codenamed PAVEL, whose "criminal activities consisted of drawing new members into the sect, conducting illegal gatherings, inducing young believers to refuse to serve in the army, holding and disseminating religious literature." The KGB concocted "well-documented defamatory materials" which were used in a press campaign against him. Even PAVEL's children from his first marriage were persuaded to sign a newspaper article about him. Finally an evening meeting was arranged by the KGB in Shepetovka, attended by local Jehovah's Witnesses, as well as representatives of the Party, provincial administration, collective farms and newspapers, at which PAVEL was subjected to a series of doubtless well-rehearsed denunciations of his alleged indolence, cruelty, egoism and dissolute behavior. The KGB report on the meeting noted with satisfaction that the evening ended in PAVEL's utter humiliation and the "unrestrained sobbing" of his second wife.[106]

Like the other sectarians, Jehovah's Witnesses showed an astonishing capacity to survive persecution. During the Gorbachev era, the KGB's campaign against them gradually disintegrated. In October 1989, doubtless to the outrage of many KGB officers, the head of the European department of the Brooklyn Centre, Willi Pohl, arrived in Moscow as the guest of the Council of Religious Affairs to visit Soviet Witness communities and discuss their future.[107]

DURING THE LATER 1980s the Moscow Patriarchate seemed to be trying neither to fall behind nor to overtake the speed at which the official programs of *glasnost* and *perestroika* were developing. In 1991, a year after succeeding Pimen as Patriarch, Aleksi II, finally dissociated himself and the Russian Orthodox Church from the "declaration of loyalty" to the Soviet system issued by Metropolitan Sergi in 1927. When an interviewer reminded him that, a quarter of a century earlier, the Council for Religious Affairs had classed him as one of those bishops most loyal to the state, the Patriarch asked for forgiveness and understanding of his attitude at the time. As the Soviet Union began to disintegrate in the final months of 1991, Aleksi II declared that "Russia has suffered a severe illness in the form of Communism."[108]

The Russian Orthodox Church, however, continued to be haunted by its past history of KGB penetration. After the failure of the August coup in 1991, the Russian government's Committee on Freedom of Conscience, which included Father Gleb Yakunin, was given access to a section of the KGB archives which showed that some members of the Orthodox hierarchy had been KGB agents. After Yakunin published a selection of the documents, the archives were closed once more; he was accused of having betrayed state secrets to the United States and threatened with a private prosecution.[109] Father Gleb remained defiant. He wrote to the Patriarch in January 1994:

> If the Church is not cleansed of the taint of the spy and informer, it cannot be reborn. Unfortunately, only one archbishop—Archbishop Khrizostom of Lithuania—has had the courage publicly to acknowledge that in the past he worked as an agent, and has revealed his codename: RESTAVRATOR. No other Church hierarch has followed his example, however.
>
> The most prominent agents of the past include DROZDOV—the only one of the churchmen to be officially honored with an award by the KGB of the USSR, in 1988, for oustanding intelligence services—ADAMANT, OSTROVSKY, MIKHAILOV, TOPAZ and ABBAT. It is obvious that none of these or the less exalted agents are preparing to repent. On the contrary, they deliver themselves of pastoral maxims on the allegedly neutral character of informing on the Church, and articles have appeared in the Church press justifying the role of the informer as essential for the survival of the Church in an antireligious state.
>
> The codenames I discovered in the archives of the KGB belong to the top hierarchs of the Moscow Patriarchate.[110]

The letter to Aleksi II was unprecedented in the history of the Russian Orthodox Church—for, as the Patriarch must surely have been aware, DROZDOV, the most important of the KGB agents discovered by Father Gleb in the KGB archives, was in fact himself.

T W E N T Y - N I N E

THE POLISH POPE AND THE RISE
OF SOLIDARITY

For forty years all challenges to the Communist one-party states established in eastern Europe in the wake of the Second World War were successfully contained. Opponents of the regimes usually felt too powerless to organize any visible opposition to them. On the rare occasions when the survival of the one-party state seemed in question—in Hungary in 1956 and Czechoslovakia in 1968—it was swiftly and brutally shored up with an overwhelming show of force. The Polish challenge to the Soviet system, however, eventually succeeded where the Hungarian Uprising and the Prague Spring failed. Though contained for a decade, it was never mastered and eventually began the disintegration of the Soviet Bloc.

The Polish crisis began in a wholly novel and unforeseen way—not, as in Hungary and Czechoslovakia, with the emergence of revisionist governments, but with the election of October 16, 1978 of Cardinal Karol Wojtyła, Archbishop of Kraków, as Pope John Paul II. No Soviet leader was tempted any longer to repeat Stalin's scornful question at the end of the Second World War, "How many divisions has the Pope?" The undermining of the empire built by Stalin after Yalta was begun not by the military might of the West but by the moral authority of the first Polish Pope, which rapidly eclipsed that of the PUWP (the Polish Communist Party).

Boris Aristov, the Soviet ambassador in Warsaw, reported to the Politburo that the Polish authorities regarded the new Pope as "a virulent anti-Communist."[1] The Centre agreed. Since 1971 Wojtyła had been the target of PROGRESS operations designed to monitor his allegedly subversive role in undermining the authority of the Polish one-party state.[2] The day after Wojtyła's election, the head of the KGB mission in Warsaw, Vadim Pavlov, sent Moscow an assessment of him by the SB, the KGB's Polish equivalent:

> Wojtyła holds extreme anti-Communist views. Without openly opposing the Socialist system, he has criticized the way in which the state agencies of the Polish People's Republic have functioned, making the following accusations:
> – that the basic human rights of Polish citizens are restricted;
> – that there is unacceptable exploitation of the workers, whom "the Catholic Church must protect against the workers' government";

– that the activities of the Catholic Church are restricted and Catholics treated as second-class citizens;
– that an extensive campaign is being conducted to convert society to atheism and impose an alien ideology on the people;
– that the Catholic Church is denied its proper cultural role, thereby depriving Polish culture of its national treasures.

In Wojtyła's view, the concept of the one-party state "meant depriving the people of its sovereignty." "Collectivization," he believed, "led to the destruction of the individual and of his personality." The fact that he dared to say what most Polish Catholics thought seemed to both the KGB and the SB evidence of his commitment to ideological subversion.

The SB report forwarded to the Centre reveals that as early as 1973–4 the Polish Procurator-general had considered prosecuting Wojtyła for his sermons. Three of his homilies—in Warsaw on May 5, 1973, in the Kraków steelmaking suburb of Nowa Huta on May 12, 1973 and in Kraków on November 24, 1974—were judged in breach of article 194 of the Criminal Code, which provided for terms of imprisonment of from one to ten years for seditious statements during religious services. According to an SB informant, Wojtyła had declared during one of his sermons, "The Church has the right to criticize all manifestations and aspects of the activity of the authorities if they are unacceptable to the people."[3] Wojtyła, however, was protected by his eminence. Though the UB (predecessor of the SB) had interned the Polish primate, Cardinal Stefan Wyszyński, for three years in the 1950s, by the 1970s the Gierek regime no longer dared to arrest a cardinal. The SB thus lapsed into a tone of largely impotent outrage as it denounced Wojtyła's "moral support to the initiatives of anti-socialist elements."

In June 1976 Gierek repeated the mistake which had led to Gomułka's downfall six years earlier and ordered a sudden increase in food prices. After a wave of protest strikes and riots, the price rises were withdrawn. On September 30 Wojtyła set up a fund to assist the families of those in the Kraków archdiocese who had been imprisoned for taking part in the protests or injured in clashes with the riot police.[4] He also took an active interest in the formation after the strike wave of KOR, the Workers Defence Committee, which sought to create an alliance of workers and dissident intellectuals. According to SB surveillance reports, during the autumn of 1976 Wojtyła had a series of meetings with KOR's founders in the apartment of the writer Bohdan Cywiński, later a prominent Solidarity activist.[5] The SB also reported that he met individually KOR militants from a great variety of backgrounds: among them the dissident Communist Jacek Kuroń, the wartime resistance fighter Jan Józef Lipski, the ex-Maoist Antoni Macierewicz and the writer Jerzy Andrzejewski.[6]

Wojtyła rarely read newspapers, listened to the news on the radio or watched it on television. Every fortnight, however, Father Andrzej Bardecki, the Church's liaison officer with the Catholic weekly *Tygodnik Powszechny* (to which Wojtyła was a regular contributor), came to his study in the archbishop's palace at Kraków and gave him a news briefing.[7] Bardecki had been a target of PROGRESS operations by KGB illegals ever since BOGUN, posing as a West German press photographer, had first made contact with him in 1971.[8] In 1977 another illegal, Ivan Ivanovich Bunyk, codenamed FILOSOV ("Philosopher"), who had been instructed by the Centre to develop sources inside the Polish Church, had a series of meetings with Bardecki. Bunyk had been born in France but had emigrated as a teenager with his Ukrainian family to the Soviet Union in 1947. In 1970 he had returned to France as a KGB illegal, trained as a journalist and set himself up as a freelance writer and poet. On his first meeting with Bardecki in 1977, FILOSOV probably presented him with one or more of the books he had published in France with the aid of KGB subsidies. Though the files noted by Mitrokhin do not include FILOSOV's reports from Poland, there is little doubt that his main priority in cultivating Bardecki was to seek out information on Wojtyła.[9]

SB surveillance reports during 1977 showed Wojtyła aligning himself with a variety of protest movements. On March 23 he received the student organizers of a petition of protest to the authorities and gave them his support.[10] Increasingly he invoked the example of St. Stanisław, the martyred bishop of ancient Kraków whose silver sarcophagus formed part of the high altar in the cathedral, as a symbol of resistance to an unjust state:

> St. Stanisław has become the patron saint of moral and social order in the country . . . He dared to tell the King himself that he was bound to respect the law of God . . . He was also the defender of the freedom that is the inalienable right of every man, so that the violation of that freedom by the state is at the same time a violation of the moral and social order.[11]

It is easy to imagine the rage in the Centre as Wojtyła continued with impunity to defend the rights of the individual against violation by the Polish state.

Among the greatest triumphs of Wojtyła's years at Kraków was the consecration on May 15, 1977 of the great new church at Nowa Huta, constructed after many years of opposition from a regime which had sought to exclude a visible Catholic presence from what it intended as a model "Socialist city."[12] In his sermon to a congregation of over 20,000, Wojtyła gave his blessing to those protesting against the death of a KOR activist, Stanisław Pyjas, who was widely believed—despite official denials—to have been murdered by the SB.[13] That evening a long procession of mourners wound its way through the streets of Kraków to Wawel Castle, where a Committee of Student Solidarity was formed. Similar committees followed in other cities, all independent of the officially sponsored Socialist Union of Polish Students.[14]

As church bells rang out across Poland on October 16, 1978 and the streets filled with excited crowds to celebrate Wojtyła's election as pope, the PUWP Politburo reacted with private shock and alarm. Publicly, the Politburo reluctantly felt compelled to associate itself with the mood of popular rejoicing and sent a lengthy telegram of congratulations to the Vatican, expressing hypocritical joy that for the first time "a son of the Polish nation . . . sits on the papal throne." What particularly disturbed the KGB, however, was the evidence that among many PUWP members, even some senior officials, the joy was genuine.[15] As well as sending official reports on Polish popular rejoicing, KGB officers in Warsaw also unofficially relayed to their colleagues at the Centre some of the political jokes circulating immediately after John Paul II's election. The white smoke from the Vatican chimney, traditionally used to signal the election of a pope, was said to have been followed on this occasion by red smoke; Wojtyła had burned his Party card. According to another satirical account, the new pope had secretly visited the Polish interior minister, who was responsible for the SB, and announced after the election, "Comrade minister! Your important instructions have been carried out!"[16]

Two days after the election, Aristov, the Soviet ambassador, reported to Moscow in more serious vein:

> The leadership of the Polish People's Republic considers that the danger of Wojtyła's move to the Vatican is that it will now clearly be more difficult to use the Vatican as a moderating influence on the Polish episcopate in its relations with the state. The Catholic Church will now make even greater efforts to consolidate its position and increase its role in the social and political life of the country.
>
> At the same time, our friends consider that Wojtyła's departure from the country also has its positive side, since the reactionary part of the episcopate has been deprived of its leader—one who had an excellent chance of becoming Primate of the Polish Catholic Church.

Aristov criticized the Polish Politburo for compromising its ability to resist the Church's future demands by its past weakness in permitting the construction of new churches, the ordination of more priests and larger print-runs for Catholic publications.[17]

At the time of Wojtyła's election, Poland was probably the world's most Catholic country. The KGB estimated that 90 percent of the population were Catholic.[18] With 569 ordinations in 1978, Poland had the highest ratio of priestly vocations to population anywhere on earth. In total, there were 19,193 Polish priests and 5,325 students in seminaries.[19] Somewhat alarmist KGB assessments put the figures higher still.[20] A steady rise in religious practice continued over the next few years. According to a secret study circulated to the PUWP central committee, "This phenomenon emerged particularly acutely among the intelligentsia, especially among persons with higher education." In 1978 25 percent of those with higher education were reported to engage in private prayer at home; by 1983 the figure had risen to over 50 percent. The central committee study plausibly attributed the increase to the "social-political crisis" and the influence of the Polish Pope.[21] Even many Polish Party officials felt in awe of Wojtyła's intense, mystical spirituality. They reported to Moscow that he often spent six to eight hours a day in prayer. On entering his private chapel, aides would sometimes find him lying motionless on the marble floor, his arms outstretched in the shape of a cross.[22]

The KGB privately denounced some of John Paul II's first acts in the Vatican as "anti-Soviet gestures." Among them was his order on the day after his election that the red *zuchetto*—cardinal's skullcap—which he had worn at the papal conclave should be taken to Lithuania by two priests from the Kraków archdiocese and placed on the altar of the church of the Virgin of Mercy in Vilnius.[23] What most concerned the Centre during the early weeks of the new pontificate, however, was the Pope's evident determination to give the Vatican a major voice in world affairs. Though John Paul II's concerns ranged widely over the problems of peacekeeping and human rights around the globe, his first priority was the situation in Poland and eastern Europe.[24] The Centre was particularly suspicious of the Pope's appointment of the Lithuanian-born Andris Backis as one of his chief advisers on the Vatican's relations with the Soviet Bloc. Backis's father had served as pre-war ambassador of independent Lithuania in Paris, and Backis himself was believed to follow in the same "bourgeois" tradition. His appointment was, in the Centre's view, another "anti-Soviet gesture."[25] On November 5 the Pope made his first official visit outside the Vatican to Assisi, the city of St. Francis, patron saint of Italy. A voice from the crowd urged him to remember eastern Europe: "Don't forget the Church of Silence!" "It's not a Church of Silence any more," replied John Paul II, "because it speaks with my voice."[26]

Among the illegals sent on PROGRESS operations to Poland after Wojtyła's election was Oleg Petrovich Buryen (codenamed DEREVLYOV), who posed as the representative of a firm of Canadian publishers. DEREVLYOV claimed to be collecting material about Polish missionaries in the Far East and used this as a pretext for contacting a number of prominent Church figures, most of whom recommended him to others. If arrested by the police or SB, he was told to stick firmly to his cover story and insist that he was a Canadian citizen. In case of real emergency, however, he was instructed to ask to see Colonel Jan Slovikowski of the SB, who appears to have acted as a point of contact for KGB agents who found themselves in difficulty with the Polish authorities. Among DEREVLYOV's most prized contacts was one of the Pope's closest friends, Father Józef Tischner, a fellow philosopher who had helped him found the Papal Theological Academy in Kraków.[27] Tischner was a frequent visitor to Rome and one of those chosen by John Paul II to revive his spirits when he felt trapped in the Vatican.[28]

One of John Paul II's chief ambitions during the first year of his pontificate was to return to Poland. Early in 1979, horrified that the PUWP Politburo was prepared to contemplate a papal visit, Brezhnev rang Gierek to try to dissuade him. "How could I not receive a Polish pope," Gierek replied, "when the majority of my countrymen are Catholics?" Absurdly, Brezhnev urged him to persuade the Pope to have a diplomatic illness: "Tell the Pope—he is a wise man—that he could announce publicly that he cannot come because he has been taken ill." When Gierek failed to see the merit of this odd suggestion, Brezhnev told him angrily, "Gomułka was a better Communist [than you] because he wouldn't receive [Pope] Paul VI in Poland, and nothing awful happened!" The conversation ended with Brezhnev saying, "Well, do what you want, so long as you and your Party don't regret it later"—at which point Brezhnev put the phone down.[29]

On June 2, 1979 more than a million Poles converged on the airport road, on Warsaw's Victory Square and in the Old City, rebuilt from the rubble after the Second World War, to welcome John Paul II on his emotional return to his homeland. Over the next nine days at least ten million people came to see and hear him; most of the remaining twenty-five million witnessed his triumphal progress through Poland on television. At the end of his visit, as the Pope bade farewell to his home city of Kraków, where, he said, "every stone and brick is dear to me," men and women wept uncontrollably in the streets. The contrast between the political bankruptcy of the Communist regime and the moral authority of the Catholic Church was plain for all to see.

The papal visit, the Centre reported to the Politburo, had lived up to its worst expectations.[30] Many Polish Party members, faced with the Pope's "ideological subversion" of the Communist regime, felt that the ideological battle had been lost. During the visit the KGB mission in Warsaw had even thought it possible that KOR militants and anti-Communist workers in Kraków might try to seize power from the Party. Emergency preparations were also made to evacuate the Soviet trade mission in Katowice, which was headed by a KGB officer, to Czechoslovakia.[31] The Centre believed that John Paul II had set out to challenge the foundations of the whole Soviet Bloc. One KGB report emphasized that he had repeatedly called himself not just the "Polish Pope" but, even more frequently, the "Slav Pope."[32] In his homilies he had recalled one by one the baptism of the peoples of eastern Europe: Poles, Croats, Slovenes, Bulgarians, Moravians, Slovaks, Czechs, Serbs, Russians and Lithuanians:

> Pope John Paul II, a Slav, a son of the Polish nation, feels how deeply rooted he is in the soil of history . . . He comes here to speak before the whole Church, before Europe and the world, about those oft-forgotten nations and peoples.[33]

A Politburo document concluded that the Vatican had embarked on an "ideological struggle against Socialist countries." Since the election of John Paul II, papal policy towards Catholic regions of the Soviet Union—especially in Ukraine, Lithuania, Latvia and Byelorussia—had become "more aggressive," aiding and abetting "disloyal priests." On November 13 the Central Committee secretariat approved a six-point "Decision to Work Against the Policies of the Vatican in Relation with Socialist States," prepared by a subcommittee which included Andropov and the deputy chairman of the KGB, Viktor Chebrikov. The KGB was instructed to organize propaganda campaigns in the Soviet Bloc "to show that Vatican policies go against the life of the Catholic Church" and to embark on active measures in the West "to demonstrate that the leadership of the new Pope, John Paul II, is dangerous to the Catholic Church."[34]

One of the chief priorities of SB foreign operations was to build up an agent network among the Poles in Rome and the Vatican. On June 16, 1980 the KGB mission in Warsaw reported to the Centre:

> Our friends [the SB] have serious operational positions [i.e. agents] at their disposal in the Vatican, and these enable them to have direct access to the Pope and to the Roman congregation. Apart from experienced agents, towards

whom John Paul II is personally well disposed and who can obtain an audience with him at any time, our friends have agent assets among the leaders of Catholic students who are in constant contact with Vatican circles and have possibilities in Radio Vatican and the Pope's secretariat.

The Centre responded by proposing a series of KGB/SB "joint long-term operations" with the following aims:

- To influence the Pope towards active support for the idea of international détente [as defined by Moscow], peaceful co-existence and cooperation between states, and to exert a favorable influence on Vatican policy on particular international problems;
- To intensify disagreements between the Vatican and the USA, Israel and other countries;
- To intensify internal disagreements within the Vatican;
- To study, devise and carry out operations to disrupt the Vatican's plans to strengthen the Churches and religious teaching in Socialist countries;
- To exploit KGB assets in the Russian Orthodox Church, the Georgian and the Armenian-Gregorian Churches; to devise and carry out active measures to counteract the expansion of contacts between these Churches and the Vatican;
- To identify the channels through which the Polish Church increases its influence and invigorates the work of the Church in the Soviet Union.

Because of the Polish Politburo's anxiety to avoid confrontation with the Catholic Church, however, the Centre had low expectations of what joint KGB/SB operations were likely to achieve:

In our view, so long as our friends [the SB] remain fearful of damaging the development of relations between the Polish People's Republic and the Vatican and between state and Church, they will not display great initiative in implementing the measures which we propose. Officers in our Centre and in the [Warsaw KGB] mission will need to display some tact and flexibility in order to find ways of solving the task before them.[35]

Moscow's fears that the Polish Politburo lacked the nerve to confront the challenge to its authority were heightened by its apparent capitulation to working-class discontent. Sudden rises in food prices in the summer of 1980 sparked off a strike wave which gave birth to the Solidarity trade union movement under the charismatic leadership of a hitherto unknown 37-year-old electrician from Gdańsk, Lech Wałęsa. The interior ministry informed the KGB mission in Warsaw that it had established an operations center, headed by Stachura, the deputy minister, to direct police and SB operations against the strikers, monitor the situation and produce daily reports. To judge from a report forwarded to Moscow, the Center was remarkably pleased with its own performance: "The operational staff displayed a high degree of conscientiousness and discipline, and an understanding of their duties; combat-readiness was introduced; leave was canceled; and round-the-clock work was introduced." While not claiming "complete success," the operations center claimed to have limited the scale of the strike movement by "eliminating" their printing presses and breaking links between protesters in different parts of the country. In addition, "Attempts by anti-Socialist forces to establish contacts with the artistic, scientific and cultural intelligentsia, in order to enlist their support for the demands of the strikers, were cut short."[36]

The reality, however, was somewhat different. The strikers succeeded in creating inter-factory strike committees to coordinate the protest and dissident intellectuals played an important part in advising them. The final judgment of the KGB mission in Warsaw was in stark contrast to the efforts by the Interior Ministry to defend its performance. The SB, it reported, "did not recognize the extent of the danger in time or the hidden discontent of the working class." And when the strike movement began, both the SB and the police were unable to control it:

> The blame lay chiefly with the leadership of the Interior Ministry, and in particular with Minister Kowalczyk and his deputy Stachura . . . When the strikes intensified in the coastal region, Kowalczyk simply lost his head . . . In the opinion of the KGB mission, it is time to replace Kowalczyk and Stachura with other officers.[37]

On August 24 Aristov sent Moscow the alarming news that the deputy prime minister, Mieczysław Jagielski, was negotiating with Wałęsa and the strike leaders.[38] Next day, the Soviet Politburo set up a commission headed by Suslov, its chief ideologist, to monitor the Polish crisis and propose remedies.[39] On August 27, at the Pope's instigation, the Polish bishops approved a document that explicitly claimed "the right to independence both of organizations representing the workers and of organizations of self-government." Confident of the Pope's backing, Wałęsa was now convinced that the government had little choice but to give in.[40]

The Polish government privately agreed. On August 27 the leading members of the Polish Politburo met Aristov to try to persuade him that the partial disintegration of the PUWP and the hostility to it of much of the Polish people had created "a new situation:"

> We must take a step back in order not to fall into the abyss, and agree on the creation of self-governing trade unions. We have no other political means of normalizing the situation, and it is impossible to use force. By staging a [tactical] retreat, we can regroup Party forces and prepare for offensive action.

The Poles went through the motions of seeking "the opinion of Comrade Brezhnev," recognizing that trade unions free from Party control were "not simply a Polish issue but an issue which affects the interests of the entire Socialist community."[41] In reality, however, all alternatives to the legalization of Solidarity had already been ruled out. The Gdańsk Agreement of August 31, which accepted "the formation of free trade unions as a genuine representation of the working class," made a series of unprecedented political concessions, ranging from the right to strike to an agreement to broadcast Mass every Sunday over the state radio. Wałęsa signed the agreement in front of the television cameras with an outsize, garishly colored pen, which he drew with a flourish from his top pocket. Produced as a souvenir of the papal visit, it had on it a portrait of John Paul II.[42]

THIRTY

THE POLISH CRISIS AND THE CRUMBLING
OF THE SOVIET BLOC

In the view of both the KGB and the Soviet Politburo, the Gdańsk Agreement represented the greatest potential threat to the "Socialist Commonwealth" (the official designation of the Soviet Bloc) since the Prague Spring of 1968. On September 3, 1980 the Politburo agreed a series of "theses for discussion with representatives of the Polish leadership"—a euphemism for demands that the Poles recover the ground lost to Solidarity:

> The [Gdańsk] agreement, in essence, signifies the legalization of the anti-Socialist opposition . . . The problem now is how to prepare a counter-attack and reclaim the positions that have been lost among the working class and the people . . . It is necessary to give overriding significance to the consolidation of the leading role of the Party in society.[1]

The principal scapegoat for the success of Solidarity was Edward Gierek, the Polish first secretary, bitterly criticized by the Soviet ambassador, Aristov, among others, for the loss of Party control.[2] The strikers at the Lenin shipyard had greeted Gierek's television appearances with derisive catcalls. Ordinary Poles summed up their feelings in one of the political jokes with which they privately mocked their Communist leaders:

> QUESTION: What is the difference between Gierek and Gomułka [who had been forced to resign as first secretary in 1970]?
> ANSWER: None, only Gierek doesn't realize it yet![3]

On September 5 Gierek was succeeded by Stanisław Kania, the tough, heavily built and heavy-drinking Party secretary responsible for national security. The KGB in Warsaw reported a satirical comment on the changeover doing the rounds in Poland—"Better Kania than Vanya!" (better, in other words, to put up with an unpopular Polish Communist than have to face a Soviet invasion).[4] It also reported that on September 6 Admiral L. Janczyszyn, the commander-in-chief of the Polish navy, had warned two Soviet admirals that military intervention would end not in "normalization," as in Prague in 1968, but in catastrophe. "If outside troops are brought into Poland," he told them, "there would be a river of blood. You must understand that you're dealing with Poles—not Czechs!"[5]

On September 18 Pavlov, the head of the KGB mission in Warsaw, complained to the Centre that the Kania regime was already repeating the mistakes of its predecessors—looking for compromise with the opposition rather than taking a firm stand against them. The Party rank and file remained demoralized.[6] "The counterrevolution in Poland is in full flood!" Brezhnev dramatically announced to the Politburo on October 29:

> Wałęsa is traveling from one end of the country to another, to town after town, and they honor him with tributes everywhere. Polish leaders keep their mouths shut and so does the press. Not even television is standing up to these anti-Socialist elements . . . Perhaps it really is necessary to introduce martial law.

Brezhnev's assessment was, predictably, strongly supported by Andropov. It was also backed by Mikhail Gorbachev, who had joined the Politburo in the previous year. "We should speak openly and firmly with our Polish friends," he declared. "Up to now they haven't taken the necessary steps. They're in a sort of defensive position, and they can't hold it for long—they might end up being overthrown themselves."[7]

The Politburo was concerned not merely by the situation in Poland itself but also by the contagious effect of Solidarity's success in some parts of the Soviet Union. The PROGRESS operation reports submitted to Andropov in October included one from the illegal SOBOLEV, who has been sent on a mission to Rubtsovsk in the Altay Kray region of Russia, far from the Polish border. His report made depressing reading:

> The situation in the town of Rubtsovsk is unstable. The population has many grounds to be dissatisfied with the situation in the town, antisocial elements are visibly engaged in provocative action, and there could be uncontrolled disorders . . . Believers [practicing Christians] are also ready to speak up, and the population approves the strikes in Poland.
>
> . . . The basic cause of dissatisfaction is food supplies, especially the lack of meat in the shops, poor living conditions and disgraceful public services. The top people are supplied through special channels, and for this there are special stores of foodstuffs and consumer goods. Theft is rampant, and the biggest thieves are officials of the Party city committee and the Soviet executive committee. There is drunkenness everywhere, and many people suffer from alcoholism.
>
> The Polish events have a negative influence and effect on the local population, suggesting that it is possible to improve living and economic conditions on the Polish model.[8]

Among the most successful illegals selected for PROGRESS operations in Poland itself was FILOSOV, still posing as a French writer and poet. According to his KGB file, he made "numerous contacts within Solidarity." Perhaps his most important contact was Tadeusz Mazowiecki, editor-in-chief of the Solidarity weekly, *Tygodnik Solidarność,* to whom he was introduced in November by Father Andrzej Bardecki.[9] Nine years later Mazowiecki was to become prime minister of the first Solidarity-led government.

Early in November, Andropov summoned the new, hardline Polish interior minister, General Mirosław Milewski, for talks in Moscow. Milewski reported that lists had been prepared of more than 1,200 of the "most counter-revolutionary individuals," who would be arrested immediately if martial law were declared. Andropov then launched into an alarmist monologue designed to persuade Milewski that martial law could not be avoided:

> Even if you left Wyszyński [the Polish primate] and Wałęsa in peace, Wyszyński and Wałęsa would not leave you in peace until either they had achieved their aim, or they had been actively crushed by the Party and the responsible part of the workers. If you wait passively . . . the situation slips out of your control. I saw how this happened in Hungary [in 1956]. There, the old leadership waited for everything to normalize itself, and when, at last, it was decided to act, it turned out that no one could be relied upon. There is every reason to fear that the same may happen in Poland also, if the most active and decisive measures are not now taken.
>
> This is a struggle for power. If Wałęsa and his fascist confederates came to power, they would start to put Communists in prison, to shoot them and subject them to every kind of persecution. In such an event, Party activists, Chekists [the SB] and military leaders would be most under threat.
>
> You say that some of your comrades cannot take on the responsibility of taking any aggressive measures against the counter-revolutionaries. But why are they not afraid of doing nothing, since this could lead to the victory of reaction? One must show the Communists, and in the first place the Party activists, the Chekists [the SB] and the military comrades that it is not just a question of defending socialist achievements in Poland, but a question of protecting their own lives, that of their families, who would be subjected to terror by the reaction, if, God forbid, this came to pass.
>
> Sometimes our Polish comrade say that they cannot rely on the Party. I cannot believe this. Out of three million Party members, one can find 100,000 who would be ready to sacrifice themselves. Wyszyński and Wałęsa have roped in the free trade unions and are securing more and more new positions in various spheres in Poland. There are already the first signs that the counter-revolutionary infection is affecting the army.
>
> Comrade Brezhnev says that we must be ready for struggle both by peaceful means and by non-peaceful means.

When Andropov had finished his tirade, Milewski asked him, "You have convinced me, but how am I to convince our comrades back in Warsaw?" Andropov's reply is not recorded.[10]

On December 5 an extraordinary meeting of Warsaw Pact leaders assembled in Moscow to discuss the Polish crisis. Kania heard one speaker after another castigate the weakness of his policies and demand an immediate crackdown on Solidarity and the Church. Otherwise, he was told, Warsaw Pact forces would intervene. Eighteen divisions were already on the Polish borders and Kania was shown plans for the occupation of Polish cities and towns. The meeting was followed by a private discussion between Kania and Brezhnev. Military intervention, Kania insisted, would be a disaster for the Soviet Union as well as for Poland. "OK, we don't march into Poland now," Brezhnev replied, "but if the situation gets any worse we will come."[11]

Brezhnev's threat was probably a bluff. With Soviet forces already at war in Afghanistan and the probability that military intervention in Poland would result in a bloodbath, Western economic sanctions and a global public relations disaster, the Kremlin's strategy was to pressure the Poles into using martial law to end Solidarity's challenge to the Communist one-party state. Ultimately the most effective way of exercising pressure was to threaten invasion by the Red Army. Memories of Hungary in 1956, Czechoslovakia in 1968 and Afghanistan in 1979 meant that very few in either Poland or the West failed to take the threat seriously in 1980.

It took over a year of almost continuous pressure, however, before the Polish Politburo, after a series of personnel changes, finally agreed to declare martial law. The KGB mission in Warsaw reported in December 1980 that, although Milewski was ready to go ahead with the "repression of hostile people," most of the Politburo was not:

> Our friends consider Kania an honest Communist loyal to the Soviet Union and CPSU, but none the less one cannot exclude the possibility of a substantial difference between his point of view and ours, especially on the question of taking decisive measures . . . Lately Comrade Kania has tended not to adopt immediately recommendations by Soviet representatives, displaying doubts and not sharing all of our assessments of the situation in the People's Republic of Poland.[12]

The KGB was also deeply concerned at what it believed was the growing Western intelligence presence in Poland. According to data supplied by the SB, of the 1,300 foreign journalists in Poland at the beginning of 1981 about 150 were members or agents of intelligence agencies. NATO intelligence agencies, it was claimed, "were acquiring firm agent positions within Solidarity."[13]

For much of 1981 the PUWP continued to lose ground to Solidarity. On January 15 Wałęsa was received by John Paul II in the Vatican. "The son," he announced reverently to the world's television cameras, "has come to see the father." Increasingly, the Pope and Wałęsa now appeared as the real leaders of the Polish nation.[14] In his conversations with the KGB, Milewski seemed to despair of defeating the challenge from Solidarity without Soviet military intervention. As the news came in of Wałęsa's meeting with the Pope, Milewski told Aristov, "I am beginning to think that order will come only when Poland has a reliable security guarantee in the form of allied troops . . ."[15] Kania admitted to the Soviet ambassador that the PUWP had lost touch with the Polish people: "This is not a Solidarity slogan but a statement of fact, of the bitter truth." The only forces on which he could rely were the army and the SB.[16]

With martial law as the only solution favored by the Kremlin to deal with the Solidarity crisis, the role of the Polish army became of crucial importance. On February 9, probably as a result of Soviet pressure, the minister of defense, General Wojciech Jaruzelski became Polish prime minister. Slim, erect, habitually wearing dark glasses and an inscrutable expression, Jaruzelski was an enigmatic figure for most Poles. But he had a relatively favorable public image due both to the fact that he had refused to use troops against the workers in 1970 and to the reputation of the armed forces as the most trusted state institution. In KGB reports to Brezhnev, however, Jaruzelski had long been described as "a sincere friend of the Soviet Union."[17] On his instructions, the chief of military intelligence, General Czesław Kiszczak (later interior minister in charge of the SB), had for some time been meeting the KGB mission in Warsaw every two or three days to provide the latest intelligence reports on the crisis from military sources.[18] As Prime Minister, Jaruzelski retained the defense portfolio.

The period up to December 1981 was to be characterized by recurrent Soviet complaints of Polish inaction and Polish attempts to placate the Soviet leadership. During that period the Kremlin was assailed by recurrent doubts as to whether Jaruzelski really possessed the resolve required to enforce martial law. In the end it concluded that no better candidate was available. Soviet doubts about Kania, however, were to prove much more serious.

On March 4 Kania and Jaruzelski were summoned to the Kremlin to be dressed down by Brezhnev and other members of the Politburo. When, the Soviet leaders demanded, would the Polish comrades impose martial law? And how was it that, alone among the Socialist countries, Poland found it so difficult to control the Church?[19] The dressing-down had little effect. A member of the Polish Politburo, Mieczysław Moczar, informed the KGB that Kania had told him, shortly after his return to Warsaw, "In spite of the pressure from Moscow, I don't want to use force against the opposition. I don't want to go down in history as the butcher of the Polish people." According to another of the KGB's Polish informants, Kania said that neither the Party nor the government was ready for a confrontation with Solidarity—"and I'll never ask the Russians for military assistance."[20]

"We have huge worries about the outcome of events in Poland," Brezhnev told the Politburo on April 2. "Worst of all is that our friends listen and agree with our recommendations, but in practice they don't do anything. And a counter-revolution is taking the offensive on all fronts!" Ustinov, the defense minister, declared that if Socialism was to survive in Poland, "bloodshed is unavoidable." "Solidarity," reported Andropov, "is now starting to grab one position after the other." The only solution was renewed pressure on the Poles to declare martial law:

> We have to tell them that martial law means a curfew, limited movement in the
> city streets, strengthening state security [the SB] in Party institutions, factories,
> etc. The pressure from the leaders of Solidarity has left Jaruzelski in terribly

bad shape, while lately Kania has begun to drink more and more. This is a very sad phenomenon. I want to point out that Polish events are having an influence on the western areas of our country too . . . Here, too, we'll have to take tough internal measures.

Next day Kania and Jaruzelski were summoned to meet Andropov and Ustinov in the Soviet equivalent of a Pullman railway coach at the border city of Brest-Litovsk. After caviar and a sumptuous buffet, they were seated at a green-baize-covered table and subjected to six hours of recriminations, demands for the declaration of martial law and threats of Soviet military intervention. Kania and Jaruzelski responded by pleading for more time.[21] On April 7, four days after the meeting at Brest-Litovsk, Mieczysław Moczar had another conversation with Kania which he reported to the KGB. Kania clearly believed that the threat of military intervention was in deadly earnest. "There would be a tragedy on a huge scale if Soviet forces intervene," he told Moczar. "It would take two generations of Poles to remedy the consequences."[22]

The Soviet Politburo believed that such a threat of military intervention was the main restraining influence on Polish "anti-Socialist forces." On April 23 it approved a report on Poland which concluded:

> Solidarity has been transformed into an organized political force, which has the capacity to paralyze the activity of the Party and state organs and take *de facto* power into its own hands. If the opposition has not yet done this, that is primarily because of its fear that Soviet troops would be introduced and because of its hopes that it can achieve its aims without bloodshed and by means of a creeping counter-revolution.

The Politburo agreed, "as a deterrent to counter-revolution," to "exploit to the utmost the fears of internal reactionaries and international imperialism that the Soviet Union might send its troops into Poland." It also decided to maintain "support for Comrades Kania and Jaruzelski, who, despite their well-known waffling, are in favor of defending Socialism." They must, however, be put under "constant pressure to pursue more significant and decisive actions to overcome the crisis and preserve Poland as a Socialist country friendly to the Soviet Union."[23]

On May 13 John Paul II gave his usual Wednesday general audience in St. Peter's Square. As he was waving to the crowds from his open-topped "Popemobile," he was shot from a distance of twenty feet by a Turkish would-be assassin, Mehmet Ali Agca. The bullet passed a few millimeters from the Pope's central aorta; had it hit his aorta, the Pope would have died instantly. John Paul II believed that his life had been saved by a miracle performed by the Virgin of Fatima in Portugal, whose feast day it was. On the first anniversary of the assassination attempt, he made a pilgrimage to Fatima to place Agca's bullet on her altar.[24] If the Pope had died, the KGB would doubtless have been overjoyed. But there is no evidence in any of the files examined by Mitrokhin that it was involved in the attempt on his life.[25]

In the weeks after the assassination attempt, the strongest pressure on Kania and Jaruzelski to declare martial law came from Marshal Viktor Kulikov, the short-tempered commander-in-chief of Warsaw Pact forces. Kulikov accused Jaruzelski of cowardice. "You yourself, Comrade Jaruzelski," he told him, "are afraid of taking decisive action." Though insisting that the time was not ripe for martial law, Jaruzelski accepted Kulikov's insults—according to a KGB report to the Politburo—with remarkable meekness and even offered to resign as prime minister.[26] Kulikov remained deeply suspicious of the motives of both Kania and Jaruzelski, reporting to the Politburo, "It looks as though the leadership of the PUWP and the government is conducting a dishonest political game and is facilitating the accession to power of those backing Solidarity."[27]

The Centre informed the Warsaw KGB mission that the time had come to find both a new first secretary and a new prime minister:

> Kania and Jaruzelski are no longer capable of leading Party and government effectively. They cannot organize the defeat of the opposition, and have been compromised by cooperating for many years with Gierek. There is no doubt that they do not even have the fighting qualities which are essential for political leaders capable of taking decisive measures.

The Centre's preferred candidates on the Polish Politburo to succeed Kania and Jaruzelski were the hardliners Tadeusz Grabski and Stefan Olszowski. Both, it reported, "are imbued with a firm Marxist-Leninist outlook, and are prepared to act decisively and consistently in defense of Socialist interests and of friendship with the Soviet Union."[28] On May 30 Aristov and Pavlov sent a joint telegram to Brezhnev and the Politburo, accusing Kania and Jaruzelski of consistent capitulation to "revisionist elements":

> The present situation requires urgent consideration of the necessity of dismissing [Kania] from his post as first secretary of the central committee and replacing him with a comrade capable of ensuring the survival of the Party's Marxist-Leninist nature and of the Socialist character of the Polish state . . . An analysis of the mood of Party activists shows that the most suitable candidate for post of first secretary of the PUWP central committee is Comrade T. Grabski.[29]

Having discovered that the KGB was plotting against him, Kania lapsed into a tone of almost whimpering self-pity. When Pavlov phoned him on June 7 to ask if he proposed to ring Comrade Brezhnev to reply to another letter from Moscow demanding tough action against Solidarity, Kania replied, "There is probably now no point in my telephoning as everything has already been decided without me [being consulted]." Later that night Kania rang Pavlov back at home in order to appeal for sympathy:

> At this very moment your people [the KGB] are saying that it is necessary to speak up at the Plenum [of the PUWP central committee] against Kania and

Jaruzelski . . . You do not have, and you never have had, more trustworthy friends than me and Jaruzelski . . . I am amazed at the method you have chosen for dealing with me. I do not deserve this . . . There is no need to mobilize the members of the Central Committee against me. It is clear that I shall be on the side of the CPSU . . . It is very bitter sensation for me to realize that I have lost your trust. I feel hurt that you have chosen such a roundabout way to mobilize opinion for an attack on me at the Plenum. I therefore find it difficult to speak to Comrade Brezhnev. What can I say to him?[30]

When Kulikov asked Jaruzelski for his reaction to the latest philippic from Moscow, he replied, "They are hammering me into the ground. I'm a fool for accepting this post [of prime minister]."[31]

During June a group of nine Polish generals approached the KGB with a plan to remove Jaruzelski because of his unwillingness to order martial law and replace him with a new defense minister (presumably one of the plotters), who would arrest the rest of the government, take control of strategic points and seize up to 3,000 counter-revolutionaries who would be deported to elsewhere in the Soviet Bloc. An action group led by the defense minister, containing no members of either the previous government or the Politburo, would then appeal to the rest of the Soviet Bloc for "military assistance to protect Socialism in the Polish People's Republic."[32] Moscow's response to the plan for a military coup is not recorded in the files noted by Mitrokhin. Given its desire to avoid "military assistance" and preserve a semblance of legality, however, it cannot have been attracted by it.

Jaruzelski's main concern seems to have been less his own personal position than to prevent the disaster of Soviet military intervention. On June 22 he held a meeting with the minister of the interior, General Milewski, whom he knew was trusted by the Kremlin. How, asked Jaruzelski, could he "regain the trust of our Soviet comrades?" Milewski replied that, though Soviet confidence in the Polish leadership had been severely damaged, it had not been entirely destroyed: "If there had been none at all, they would have stopped talking to us." Jaruzelski complained that, so far as he was concerned, they had indeed stopped talking. Previously, Kulikov had phoned him almost every day and had frequently come to see him. Recently he had broken all contact. Soviet representatives in Warsaw were instructed to tell Jaruzelski that their confidence in him had indeed been shaken and that it would disappear altogether unless he mended his ways.[33]

Centre files record that in the weeks before the opening of the Ninth PUWP Congress on July 14, the Soviet embassy, the KGB mission and Soviet military representatives "worked among the delegates to identify Party members who followed the Marxist-Leninist line, to establish personal contact with them, and through them to influence the course of the Congress."[34] The Suslov Commission, set up by the Politburo a year earlier to monitor the Polish crisis, gave instructions that the threat of military intervention by the other members of the Warsaw Pact must be "a constant factor in the minds of all Polish political forces."[35] On the eve of the congress, the Centre instructed Pavlov, the head of the KGB mission in Warsaw, to have "a straightforward conversation with S. Kania and Jaruzelski on their weak Party and government work, and remind them of their earlier statements of readiness to cede their Party and government jobs if necessary in the interest of saving the Socialist system in Poland and the unity of Socialist cooperation in Europe." The choice of Kania's successor, in the Centre's view, lay among three leading hardliners: Tadeusz Grabski, Stefan Olszowski and Andrzej Zabínski. All other representatives of "healthy forces" in the PUWP lacked the necessary authority to become first secretary. The KGB also drew up a list of those suitable for election to the Politburo and a hit list of moderates to be removed from the government and Party posts. Top of the hit list was the deputy prime minister, Mieczysław Rakowski, who had threatened to inform the leaders of the Italian and French Communist Parties about Soviet interference in the internal affairs of the PUWP. The Centre concluded that, in view of Jaruzelski's continuing "authority in the country and especially in the army," it would be unwise simply to dismiss him. Rather, it was hoped to kick him upstairs to the less powerful post of president and harness his personal prestige in support of a hardline government.[36]

So far as Moscow was concerned, however, the Ninth PUWP Congress failed to go according to plan. Faced with a blatant Soviet attempt to unseat Kania, the congress rallied round him. But, taking seriously the threat of Soviet invasion, the congress also retained among the leadership some of the chief supporters of the Soviet campaign of intimidation. And though it gave loud applause to Rakowski's speech, it dared not antagonize the Kremlin by electing him to the Politburo. The main consequence of the contradictory outcome of the congress was a near paralysis of government. Women and children marched through Polish cities banging empty pans to protest against food shortages. Encouraged by Solidarity, industrial workers elected factory councils which claimed the right to choose their managers.[37]

The worsening crisis of central government seems to have convinced Jaruzelski that martial law would soon become inevitable. Detailed plans were agreed with Kulikov early in August. At a meeting with Jaruzelski and senior Polish generals on August 12, Kulikov demanded "firmness and still more firmness."[38] On August 21 the new hardline interior minister, General Czesław Kiszczak, formerly head of military intelligence, visited Moscow to report personally to Andropov on secret preparations by the SB and police for the introduction of martial law. Hitherto, he acknowledged, "The Polish leadership has handled Solidarity as if it were an egg which it was afraid to break. We must put a stop to this."[39]

Kiszczak and the SB no longer saw Wałęsa as the main problem. During the previous six months Wałęsa's leadership had become somewhat lackluster as he struggled to recover a clear sense of direction. Solidarity ultimately had to choose between two strategic options: either it had to become a truly revolutionary body capable of overthrowing the Communist one-party state, or it had to accommodate itself to the system and be content with winning a few concessions. Wałęsa found himself unable to opt clearly for either option. He had backed away from a general strike in March when most other leading figures in Solidarity believed the time had come for a showdown. Zbigniew Bujak, chairman of Solidarity in the Warsaw region, concluded that Wałęsa had made a fatal mistake:

General strikes are like swords—once you take them out of the scabbard and fail to use them, they are no more use than useless hunks of iron. Wałęsa in effect demobilized the union . . . It deprived us of our basic weapon and thus became the source of our subsequent defeat. The authorities counted on this when they prepared the martial law operation of December 13.[40]

Kiszczak told Andropov that, though Wałęsa might use aggressive language to appeal to Solidarity "extremists," his thinking was relatively moderate. The main danger now came from Bujak, who was both "anti-Socialist and anti-Soviet:" "He is cleverer than Wałęsa and is closely linked with [the KOR leaders] Kurón and Michnik. The task of the [SB] agencies is to discredit him."

"AT THE PRESENT time," Kiszczak told Andropov, "the Roman Catholic Church does not represent a threat to the PUWP." Milewski had devoted "immense efforts" to the agent penetration of the Church, and the SB was now well-informed about its mood and intentions: "Out of seventy bishops, good contacts are maintained with fifty. This makes it possible to bring influence to bear on the Catholic Church and to prevent undesirable moves."[41] The recent death of the 80-year-old Primate, Cardinal Wyszyński, a friend of Solidarity and for over a generation a courageous defender of religious freedom, had come as an immense relief to the SB (and doubtless to the KGB):

> The new Primate, [Cardinal Józef] Glemp, is not as anti-Soviet as his predecessor. Wyszyński enjoyed immense authority; his word was law. He was the object of a personality cult and his cult exceeded anything imaginable. Glemp is a different kind of man and there are undoubtedly possibilities of exerting influence on him.

Two problems, however, remained in Church–state relations. The first was the Pope, who—according to Kiszczak—was cleverly exploiting the situation in Poland to advance his anti-Communist policies in eastern Europe. The second problem was the moral authority of the Polish Church. The people looked on the Church, not the Party, as the "standard-bearer of morality." "In the immediate future," Kiszczak admitted, "the Party will not be able to change the attitude towards the Catholic Church."

Andropov seems to have hectored Kiszczak rather less than most other Polish leaders he had met over the previous few years. But he ended their meeting in somber mood:

> The class enemy has repeatedly tried to challenge the people's power in the Socialist countries . . . But the Polish crisis is the most long drawn out, and perhaps the most dangerous. The adversary's creeping counter-revolution has long been preparing for the struggle with Socialism.[42]

Solidarity's first national congress (held in two sessions from September 5 to 10 and from September 26 to October 7) provided further evidence of "creeping counter-revolution." Its appeal on September 8 "to the working people of eastern Europe . . . who have entered the difficult road to struggle for a free trade union movement" was denounced by the SB as "a brazen attempt to interfere in the internal affairs of Socialist countries."[43]

Pavlov now seemed satisfied that Jaruzelski was prepared for "decisive measures" to end "the threat from Solidarity." On September 29 he reported to the Centre that he had "advised" Jaruzelski on the line to follow at the plenary meeting of the Central Committee on October 18.[44] The first priority was to get rid of Kania, who, Pavlov reported, continued to pursue "a policy of conciliation" towards Solidarity. Having failed to secure Kania's dismissal at the July Party congress, Moscow was determined to succeed at the October Central Committee plenum. The Centre must have been particularly outraged by Pavlov's account of a secret briefing on Kania's policy given by his supporter, Deputy Prime Minister Kazimierz Barcikowski, on October 2, 1981. According to Barcikowski, Kania was "disenchanted with the Soviet model of Socialism":

> The Soviet system of Socialism had failed the test. The fact that the USSR was systematically buying grain in the West was an indication of serious errors in the management of agriculture . . . The power of the Soviet regime was maintained only through the army and other agencies of coercion. However, in the last two or three years, the situation had begun to change to the Soviet Union's disadvantage. China was significantly strengthening its military power; its military and economic contacts with the USA were a serious threat to the USSR, and pinned down a large number of troops on the far eastern borders. In the last few months, the situation in Afghanistan had sharply deteriorated. It was now clear that it would be impossible to win this conflict politically without the use of mass repressive measures similar to those used by the Americans in Vietnam. If at the present time the USSR still had some strategic advantage over the USA, within three or four years it would lose it, as the Soviet economy would no longer be able to meet the additional expense of developing and producing new types of armaments.

The imposition of the Soviet model of socialism had, Kania believed, "bureaucratized the PUWP" and distorted Leninist principles:

> He regarded it as his main task to do everything to protect the positive processes taking place in Poland, including the Solidarity movement, in order to create a basis for genuine Socialism which, with certain variations, could also find a place in other Socialist countries.[45]

Even Dubček during the Prague Spring had never made such a devastating indictment of the Soviet system.

Pavlov's detailed reports on Kania indicate either that his home had been bugged or that there was an informer in his immediate family. He informed the Centre that on October 5, "Kania came home in a very agitated state and told a narrow circle of his family that the Russian comrades are again plotting to remove him from the post of First Secretary." Kania claimed not to understand why his Soviet "friends" did not tell him frankly that he must resign. If they did so, he would go "without causing a fuss." According to the KGB, Kania's wife was deeply disturbed by his state of mind and anxious for him to resign so that he could recover his health and cease to be "a persecuted politician." But Pavlov did not believe that Kania really intended to go quietly. He reported on October 7 that Kania had instructed Kiszczak to take action against a number of Party members who, he believed (no doubt correctly), were plotting against him.[46] Kiszczak, however, sided with Jaruzelski and the plotters.

Kania's fate was sealed at a stormy confrontation with Jaruzelski, Kiszczak, Milewski (now secretary of the PUWP central committee) and two other Polish generals. Jaruzelski told him that, unless he agreed to preparations for martial law, they would go ahead behind his back—and "decisive" (but unspecified) action would be taken against him personally.[47] On the morning of October 18, just before the opening of the plenary meeting of the central committee, Aristov informed Kania that it was the "unanimous view" in Moscow that he should be replaced as first secretary by Jaruzelski.[48] The central committee duly did Moscow's bidding, and Kania gave way without a struggle. According to KGB reports, Kania said after his dismissal that he was still haunted by memories of the shooting of strikers in 1970. If he had remained first secretary, he would never have been able to give the order to open fire again.[49]

Next day, October 19, Brezhnev telephoned Jaruzelski to congratulate him on his appointment as first secretary, while keeping his existing posts as prime minister and defense minister. "Hello, Wojciech," Brezhnev began. "Hello, my dear, deeply esteemed Leonid Ilyich!" Jaruzelski replied. He maintained the same sycophantic tone throughout the conversation:

> Thank you very much, dear Leonid Ilyich, for the greeting and above all for the confidence you have in me. I want to tell you frankly that I had some inner misgivings about accepting this post and agreed to do so only because I knew that you support me and that you were in favor of this decision. If this had not been so, I would never have agreed to it.

Jaruzelski added that, later in the day, he would be meeting Aristov to discuss the situation in detail and would "be asking for your suggestions on some questions which he, no doubt, will convey to you." Lying effortlessly, Brezhnev told Jaruzelski that the CPSU Politburo had realized long ago that he was the right man for the job.[50] Predictably, he made no mention of the fact that in the course of the summer the KGB had recommended sacking Jaruzelski as well as Kania. In the end, however, the Politburo had reluctantly concluded that only Jaruzelski possessed the authority to declare martial law.[51]

Soviet doubts about Jaruzelski, however, continued. On November 4 Jaruzelski began talks with Wałęsa and Archbishop Glemp at which he proposed their participation in a Front of National Accord which, while it would have no decision-making powers, would keep open dialogue between the state, Church and unions.[52] Though Pavlov and Aristov were in favor of tactics designed to damp down any suspicion by Wałęsa and Glemp that martial law was imminent, they feared that Jaruzelski would end by making real concessions. On November 13 they sent a joint telegram to the Politburo condemning Jaruzelski's indecisiveness and his attempt to conciliate Wałęsa, and urging that he be pressed yet again to declare martial law without further delay.[53] On november 21 the Politburo approved the text of a personal message from Brezhnev to Jaruzelski, berating him for his inaction:

> The anti-Socialist forces are not only gaining sway in many large industrial enterprises, but are also continuing to spread their influence among ever wider segments of the population. Worse still, the leaders of Solidarity and the counter-revolutionaries are still appearing before various audiences and making openly inflammatory speeches aimed at stirring up nationalist passions and directed against the PUWP and against Socialism. The direct consequence of this is the dangerous growth of anti-Sovietism in Poland.
>
> . . . The leaders of the anti-Socialist forces . . . are placing great store by the fact that a new group of recruits will be entering the army who have been worked on by Solidarity. Doesn't this suggest to you that a failure to take harsh measures against the counter-revolutionaries right away will cost you valuable time?[54]

Jaruzelski seems finally to have given way to Soviet pressure at the beginning of December. He told a meeting of the PUWP Politburo on December 5 that, after thirty-six years of the "people's power" in Poland, there sadly seemed no alternative to using "police methods" against the working class. The Politburo unanimously accepted the need to declare martial law.[55] The main details of its implementation were worked out under the supervision of Kiszczak,[56] who briefed Pavlov on December 7. One hundred and fifty-seven SB and other interior ministry personnel had been sent around the provinces in groups of up to five to ensure that preparations had been made to isolate and arrest Solidarity leaders and other "extremists." Pavlov reported to the Centre that the SB had agents "at all levels of Solidarity," and intended that, where possible, these agents should step into the shoes of the arrested activists. Their main task after the declaration of martial law would be to prevent workers from going on strike or taking to the streets.[57] Suspect members of the government and Party leadership were placed under close SB surveillance. Kania's former supporter, Barcikowski, told his friends that the SB followed him wherever he went and recorded all his telephone calls.[58]

On the night of December 8–9 Jaruzelski briefed Marshal Kulikov on the timetable for martial law. Approximately 80,000 personnel had been selected to arrest 6,000 Solidarity activists on the night of either December 11–12 or 12–13.

Troops would begin moving from their barracks at 6 a.m. on the morning after the arrests. Though the plans appeared resolute, however, Jaruzelski did not. "During our discussions," Kulikov reported, "W. Jaruzelski's indecisiveness and wavering and his apprehension about the successful implementation of the plan to impose martial law were palpable." The PUWP, Jaruzelski complained, had little authority left. Six to seven hundred thousand of its members were associated with Solidarity, and it was compromised by numerous instances of theft, bribery and other abuses of the people's trust. For martial law to succeed, it might be necessary for him to appeal for assistance from Warsaw Pact forces—though he asked for East German troops not to be used. "I can assure you that you have no need for concern on that score," Kulikov told him. "The question of assisting you in the event that your own resources become exhausted is being addressed at General Staff level."[59]

On December 9 Milewski brought Pavlov further evidence of Jaruzelski's anxious state of mind. Jaruzelski had still not set a date for the introduction of martial law. If the Church opposed martial law, Jaruzelski had told him, Glemp would turn into "a second Khomeini."[60] Next day the CPSU Politburo met in emergency session to discuss the Polish crisis. It began by hearing a report from Nikolai Baibakov of Gosplan, just returned from a visit to Warsaw to discuss Poland's appeal for economic assistance. Jaruzelski, Baibakov reported, had become an "extremely neurotic" wreck, terrified that Glemp would declare a holy war. Though all the Politburo members who spoke after Baibakov made scathing criticisms of Jaruzelski, none suggested trying to replace him. It was plainly too late for that. There was general agreement, too, that Soviet forces must not intervene. Andropov declared bluntly:

> If Comrade Kulikov actually did speak about the introduction of troops, then I believe he did this incorrectly. We can't risk such a step. We don't intend to introduce troops into Poland. That is the proper position, and we must adhere to it until the end. I don't know how things will turn out in Poland, but even if Poland falls under the control of Solidarity, that's the way it will be.[61]

Jaruzelski complained to Milewski and others that, by refusing to allow Warsaw Pact military intervention if Polish security forces proved unable to cope, the Soviet Politburo had let him down:

> They pressed us to take firm and decisive action, and the Soviet leaders promised to provide all the assistance and support needed. But now, when we have made a firm decision to take action and we would like to discuss it with the Soviet leaders, we cannot get a concrete answer from the Soviet comrades.

Jaruzelski was gloomy about the prospects for martial law without Soviet military support. "We're about to go on the offensive," he told Milewski, "but I'm afraid that later on we'll be branded as conspirators and hanged." Milewski rang Andropov to report what Jaruzelski had said.[62]

Until the very last moment Moscow continued to fear that Jaruzelski's nerve would crack. On December 11 Aristov, Kulikov and Pavlov jointly reported to the Politburo that all the preparations for "operation X" (the enforcement of martial law) had been completed. But:

> In view of W. Jaruzelski's inclination toward vacillation and doubt, we can't exclude the possibility that, under pressure from the episcopate and other forces, he may refuse to take the final decision and will pursue the line of making concessions and agreements. In the light of the current situation, such a step could prove fatal for the PUWP and for the future of Socialism in Poland.[63]

On Saturday December 12 Jaruzelski telephoned Brezhnev and Suslov, asked for and received their approval for operation X to begin that evening.[64] The KGB mission in Warsaw, however, was still not convinced that Jaruzelski would go ahead. He continued to agonize over whether the loss of life which might be necessary to prevent Solidarity turning Poland into "a bourgeois state" could possibly be justified. And if martial law failed, he was convinced that all those responsible for declaring it would be "physically eliminated." "If we fail," said Jaruzelski, "there will be nothing left for me to do but to put a bullet in my head."[65] Pavlov also reported that if Jaruzelski's nerve failed, Olszowski was prepared to stage a coup—provided he had the backing of Moscow. Olszowski's plan of action included the immediate arrest of Solidarity leaders; the prohibition of strikes and protests; the confiscation of food supplies in the countryside; close "economic cooperation" with the Soviet Union; the enforcement of martial law throughout the country; and the sealing of Polish borders.[66]

To Pavlov's relief, Kiszczak, who was in charge of implementing operation X, appeared much more resolute than Jaruzelski. In the course of Saturday December 12 he provided the KGB with the detailed timetable of the operation. At 11:30 p.m., telephone communications throughout the country would be shut down; all embassies would lose their landline connections; communications abroad would cease; and the borders would be closed. Foreign reporters without permanent accreditation would be expelled. The arrests would begin at midnight. Four thousand two hundred would be detained overnight and another 4,500 placed in "protective custody" on Sunday December 13. Wałęsa would be asked to enter talks with the government and arrested if he refused. In a broadcast at 6 a.m. Jaruzelski would declare martial law and announce the creation of a "Military Council for National Salvation." In order to keep people at home and off the streets on Sunday, church services would—unusually—be televised. If necessary, Monday December 14 would be declared a public holiday. The security forces had orders to open fire if they encountered serious resistance. But, Kiszczak warned, there was no guarantee of success:

> If the operation that we have undertaken fails, if we have to pay with our lives, then the Soviet Union will have to be ready to face a hostile state on its west-

ern border, whose leaders will promote nationalism and anti-Sovietism. From the outset they will receive energetic assistance from the imperialist states to an extent sufficient for them to sever all ties with Socialist countries. Poland's Socialist development would be put into reverse for a long period.[67]

In the event, the enforcement of martial law went more smoothly than Jaruzelski had dared to hope. Kryuchkov, who had arrived from Moscow to observe operation X at first hand, must also have been pleasantly surprised. Solidarity was caught off-guard, with most of its leading activists asleep in bed when the security forces arrived to arrest them. Zbigniew Bujak, the most senior Solidarity leader to escape arrest and go underground, said later, "The authorities were clearly planning a sizeable operation against the union. But we never thought it would be as serious as this." There had been so much talk about the growing powerlessness of the Polish government that Solidarity had begun to believe its own rhetoric. Poles awoke on Sunday morning to find an army checkpoint at every crossroads and declarations of martial law posted to every street corner. Jaruzelski's 6 a.m. broadcast was repeated throughout the day, interspersed with Chopin polonaises and patriotic music. Television viewers saw Jaruzelski, dressed in army uniform, sitting at a desk in front of a large Polish flag. "Citizens and lady citizens of the Polish People's Republic!" he began. "I speak to you as a soldier and head of government! Our motherland is on the verge of an abyss!"[68] Many interpreted his speech as a warning that only martial law could save Poland from a Soviet invasion.

In the early hours of the morning Wałęsa had been taken by military escort, accompanied by the minister of labor, Stanisław Ciosek, to a villa on the outskirts of Warsaw. Wałęsa later recalled that he was addressed as "Mr. Chairman," there were apologies for the inconvenience to which he was being put and the razor was removed from the villa's marble bathroom in case he was tempted to commit suicide.[69] Later in the day Ciosek reported to the PUWP Politburo that Wałęsa was in a state of shock, had said that his role as chairman of Solidarity was at an end and that the union would have to be reorganized. He was also alleged to be willing to cooperate with the government. Kiszczak passed on the good news to the KGB mission.[70] Milewski exultantly told Pavlov and Kryuchkov, "Wałęsa cannot hide his terror!"[71] In reality, though stunned by the suddenness of the declaration of martial law, Wałęsa is unlikely to have panicked. He had been arrested over a dozen times before and his wife Danuta was accustomed to the routine of packing a holdall for him to take to prison.[72]

While Wałęsa was being installed in the government villa, Glemp was being visited by Kazimierz Barcikowski, secretary of the Polish Central Committee and president of the Joint Commission for the State and the Episcopate, and Jerzy Kuberski, Minister of Religious Affairs, to be informed of the impending declaration of martial law. Since no telephones were operating, they had arrived unannounced at 3 a.m. at the archbishop's palace, where a patrolman rang the doorbell repeatedly until at last a light went on inside, Glemp was woken and a nun came to let them in. "The whole thing," said Barcikowski, "was a bit theatrical."[73] Contrary to Jaruzelski's alarmist forecasts, Glemp showed no inclination to declare a holy war and no desire to become "a Polish Khomeini." Milewski informed Kryuchkov and Pavlov that Glemp had reacted calmly, with "a certain degree of understanding." Though the declaration of martial law did not surprise him, he had not expected it to occur until after the Christmas holidays.[74]

The immediate concern of the authorities had been the homily that Glemp was due to give on Sunday afternoon at the Jesuit church of Mary Mother of God in Warsaw's Old City.[75] They need not have worried. The keynote of Glemp's sermon was caution. "Opposition to the decisions of the authorities under martial law," he warned, "could cause violent reprisals, including bloodshed, because the authorities have the armed forces at their disposal . . . There is nothing of greater value than human life." "The Primate's words," writes historian Timothy Garton Ash, "were bitterly resented by many Christian Poles who were, at that moment, preparing to risk their own lives for what they considered greater values." Jaruzelski, by contrast, felt an enormous sense of relief. Glemp's homily was broadcast repeatedly on television, printed in the Party newspaper and put up on the walls of army barracks.[76]

On the first day of martial law, Brezhnev rang Jaruzelski to congratulate him on the beginning of operation X.[77] Kryuchkov, Pavlov and Kulikov jointly telegraphed from Warsaw that the first stages of the operation had been successfully completed. "But the most dangerous days," they believed, "will be Monday, Tuesday, and Wednesday of the coming week [December 14–16] when Solidarity activists who are still at large will try to spread disorder among workers and students."[78] "During the next two weeks," Jaruzelski told Kryuchkov, "a great deal will depend on the market situation." The best antidote to Solidarity would be well-stocked shelves in Polish shops for Christmas. He appealed to Moscow to send shoes, children's toys and other consumer goods as quickly as possible: "Any material aid now will cost much less than the expenditure required by the Polish situation if the unthinkable began to happen here."[79]

The worst violence after the declaration of martial law took place at a coal mine near Katowice, where more than 2,000 miners began a sit-in. On Tuesday December 15 helicopters dropped tear gas into the mines, while ZOMO paramilitary police from the ministry of the interior, supported by forty tanks, began firing rubber bullets at the miners. The security forces then attacked the doctors and ambulance drivers who came to tend the wounded.[80] Seven miners were killed and thirty-nine injured; forty-one ZOMO policemen were also injured, though none were killed. Overall, however, casualties were much lower than the SB and KGB had expected. The mere threat of Soviet intervention had proved as effective in crushing opposition as the actual Soviet intervention in Czechoslovakia thirteen years earlier. By the year's end organized opposition to martial law had virtually disappeared. Graffiti on the walls of Polish cities proclaimed optimistically, "Winter Is Yours. Spring Will be Ours!" But Spring did not truly return until 1989 with the formation of a Solidarity-led government and the disintegration of the Communist one-party state.

Jaruzelski gave the main credit for the success of operation X to the SB, ZOMO and other interior ministry personnel. At a meeting in the ministry on December 31 he praised the SB's dedication to Socialism and the high moral and political qualities of its operational officers. "You were the defenders of Socialism in Poland," Jaruzelski told them. "The Polish army contributed to the success, but the main work was done by the Interior Ministry." The SB's principal role now was deep penetration of the opposition movement to provide the intelligence necessary "to neutralize the adversary by the swiftest possible means." In answer to a question about the "mild-ness" of the sentences passed on the strike organizers at Katowice and elsewhere, Jaruzelski said that, though he was personally in favor of more severe punishment, public opinion had to be taken into account: "If we were to impose excessively severe sentences, say ten to twelve years' imprisonment, people would say that we were tak-ing our revenge on Solidarity. So we have to be content with moderate sentences." As usual, an account of the meeting was forwarded to the Centre by the KGB mission in Warsaw.[81]

According to self-congratulatory SB statistics supplied to the KGB, during the year after the declaration of martial law, 701 underground opposition groups were identified, 430 of them associated with the now-illegal Solidarity; 10,131 individuals were interned; over 400 demonstrations dispersed; 370 illegal printing presses and 1,200 items of printing equipment confiscated; the distribution of over 1.2 million leaflets prevented; and 12 underground Solidarity radio stations closed down. A total of 250,000 members of the security forces were allegedly deployed on these opera-tions, among them 90,000 members of police reserve units, over 30,000 soldiers and 10,000 members of the volunteer police reserve.[82] The figures for the deployment of security forces, however, are suspiciously high and may well have been substantially inflated in order to impress Moscow. Jaruzelski commended all those who had taken part in the enforcement of martial law as intrepid defenders of Polish Socialism.

The SB's biggest problem was Wałęsa, whose worldwide celebrity made it impos-sible either to subject him to a show trial or to treat him with the casual brutality meted out to less well-known Solidarity activists. (Even Wałęsa's wife Danuta and their small daughters were subjected to humiliating strip searches.) As the initial shock of internment wore off, however, Wałęsa's old combative spirit returned and he refused to negotiate with the authorities. The SB's first tactic was to try to persuade Wałęsa to follow the more accommodating policy of Cardinal Glemp by giving the Primate's spokesman, Father Alojsy Orszulik, regular access to him.[83] Orszulik was initially accompanied by an interior ministry official later identified as Colonel Adam Pietruszka, deputy head of the SB church department, who three years later was to be implicated in the murder of the Solidarity priest Father Jerzy Popiełuszko. Wałęsa did not take to Orszulik. When urged to give up his resistance to negotiating with the Military Council for National Salvation, Wałęsa shouted, "They'll come to me on their knees!" Polish Catholics did not normally shout at their priests and Orszulik seems to have been shocked. According to Wałęsa, he "disapproved of my lack of Christian humility, and it too us some time to get used to each other."[84]

Wałęsa's clashes with Orszulik had the advantage, so far as the SB was concerned, of alienating Glemp. In January 1982 Kiszczak reported to the KGB, with evident sat-isfaction and possibly some exaggeration, that Glemp was "completely disenchanted with Wałęsa," and believed that the leaders of Solidarity "have learned nothing from events and refuse to budge from their previous positions."[85] The SB also informed the

KGB that Orszulik's visits eventually had a "favorable effect" on Wałęsa.[86] As Wałęsa later acknowledged, he dropped one by one all his conditions for negotiating with the authorities, "finally aligning himself with the church's position."[87]

The SB also tried less subtle methods of influencing and discrediting Wałęsa. While working as a shipyard electrician in the early 1970s, Wałęsa had been in contact with the SB. Among the SB files discovered in the early 1990s after the collapse of the Communist regime was one codenamed BOLEK, whose full contents have yet to be revealed and whose authenticity remains to be established, but which is known to contain alleged details of Wałęsa's role as an SB informer. According to some reports, after seeing a copy of the file in 1992, Wałęsa, by then President of the Polish Republic, began to draft a public statement in which he acknowledged that he had put his signature to "three or four" SB interrogation protocols, but asked for understanding of the difficult position of those pressured by the SB to act as informers in the 1970s. In the end, it is claimed, Wałęsa had second thoughts and scrapped the statement.[88]

The KGB files noted by Mitrokhin do not disclose the exact extent of Wałęsa's cooperation with the SB in the 1970s. But they do reveal that the SB sought to intimidate Wałęsa after his internment by "reminding him that they had paid him money and received information from him." If Wałęsa did indeed act at one stage of his career as a paid informant of the SB, it is easy to imagine the pressure exerted on him to do so, as on the millions of other informers to Soviet Bloc security services. Kiszczak told the KGB that Wałęsa had been confronted by one of his alleged former SB case officers and a conversation between them tape-recorded.[89]

Since the SB did not wish to advertise its vast network of willing and unwilling informers, it made only limited use of Wałęsa's past contact with it in active measures intended to discredit him. Instead, it resorted to a series of fabrications designed to portray Wałęsa as a greedy, foul-mouthed embezzler.[90] To add authentic detail to its forgeries, it stole a tape-recording made by his brother Stanisław during Wałęsa's birthday celebrations on September 29.[91] On November 11, the anniversary of Polish independence, Wałęsa was freed from internment. Moscow was outraged that the news was broadcast in Poland at the same time as the announcement of Brezhnev's death the previous day.[92] Kiszczak sought to reassure Pavlov that, despite Wałęsa's release, active measures were still in hand to compromise Wałęsa.[93] Jaruzelski told Aristov that the material being assembled to discredit Wałęsa included pornographic photographs (presumably of Wałęsa with a mistress) and would expose him as "a scheming, grubby individual with gigantic ambitions." Wałęsa, Jaruzelski claimed, had already lost half the popular authority he had possessed before his internment. Though he remained a potential threat, he no longer had his Solidarity base and would be unable to rebuild his previous alliance with the church.[94]

Moscow was far from reassured. Since the unexpectedly successful introduction of martial law, many of its previous doubts about Jaruzelski had resurfaced. A KGB agent in Jaruzelski's entourage described him as "the offspring of rich Polish landowners" with little sympathy for working people: "His tendency is pro-Western and he surrounds himself with generals who are descendants of Polish landowners and are anti-Soviet in inclination." The agent (presumably something of an anti-

Semite) also reported that Jaruzelski was in contact with "a representative of Polish Zionism": "One should examine whether he himself is not a Zionist." By contrast, Jaruzelski "virtually ignored" the advice of the Soviet ambassador.[95]

The reports of both the KGB mission and the Soviet embassy during 1982 repeatedly condemned Jaruzelski's tolerance of men with revisionist tendencies in the Polish leadership, chief among them Mieczysław Rakowski, whose allegedly defeatist attitude to anti-Socialist forces aroused deep suspicion in Moscow. Rakowski was reported to have told the Council of Ministers in June, "The PUWP is sick. Martial law made it possible to overcome the peak of the opposition, but there is no noticeable change for the better in the attitude of broad layers of the population." The strength of the Catholic Church meant that a policy of confrontation would be mere "adventurism."[96] A report by Rakowski on June 22 concluded that there were "100,000 hostile teachers" in Polish schools, but that it was impossible to sack them all.[97] Jaruzelski was alleged to have told Milewski, "I know that Rakowski is a swine, but I still need him." In a telegram to Brezhnev on June 29, however, Aristov argued that keeping Rakowski and other like-minded individuals in the Polish leadership was "not simply a tactical move, but a strategic line for Jaruzelski, who shares their position on a number of problems": "It is therefore very important at the present stage to continue to exert influence on Comrade W. Jaruzelski."[98]

Pavlov and Aristov continued to press for more arrests and trials of counter-revolutionaries. At a meeting with Kiszczak on July 7, Pavlov denounced the policy of the interior ministry and the SB as "weak and indecisive." Kiszczak replied that there were 40,000 Solidarity activists, and it was impossible to prosecute them all.[99] Four days later Aristov brought Jaruzelski a personal message from Brezhnev and repeated the Soviet demand for more prosecutions. Jaruzelski argued that to try Wałęsa would be impossible because of the international as well as Polish outcry it would produce, and that a trial of leading opposition figures which excluded Wałęsa would lack credibility.[100] The Polish decision in December to suspend (though not yet formally end) martial law caused predictable dismay in Moscow. When pressed by Aristov to keep it in force, however, Jaruzelski delivered something of a lecture, which was duly reported to Moscow:

> We cannot continue martial law as if we were living in a bunker; we want to pursue a dialogue with the people . . . Glemp's latest statements are such that they could even be printed in *Trybuna Ludu* [the Party newspaper]. He appeals for calm, restraint and realism . . . We are, of course, playing a game with the Catholic Church; our aim is to neutralize its harmful influence on the population. The aims of the Church and my aims are still different. However, at this stage we must exploit our common interest in stabilizing the situation in order to strengthen Socialism and the positions of the Party.[101]

Jaruzelski's attitude to Moscow had become visibly less deferential since operation X a year earlier. The KGB mission reported that he had declared on one occasion, "The Soviet comrades are mistaken if they think that the Polish section of the CPSU

Central Committee will make Polish policy as in the days of Gierek. This will not happen. [Those] days are over."[102] Jaruzelski was, initially, favorably impressed by the signs of a new, less hectoring style in the Soviet leadership after Brezhnev's death. He told Kiszczak after a meeting in Moscow with Andropov, Brezhnev's successor, in December 1982:

> This was a genuine conversation on an equal footing between the leaders of the two Parties and countries, not a monologue as was the case earlier with Brezhnev. In a conversation lasting three hours, Andropov said that all Socialist countries must take account of the specific conditions of Poland. The Polish problems were not the concern of one country alone; it was a world problem.

Andropov did, however, express concern about the continued presence of Rakowski and his fellow moderate, Barcikowski, in the Polish leadership. Jaruzelski asked Andropov to trust his judgment on how long to keep them in office. The fact that Andropov appeared so well informed about the Polish situation, Jaruzelski believed, was due chiefly to reports from the KGB mission in Warsaw.[103]

The KGB mission remained deeply suspicious of revisionist tendencies in the Polish leadership. It telegraphed the Centre at the end of 1982:

> Rakowski continues to influence Jaruzelski. They meet constantly to exchange views, not only at work, but also at home, and Rakowski was the first person Jaruzelski met immediately after his return from Moscow.[104]

KGB distrust of Jaruzelski continued to grow during 1983. The Warsaw mission reported that he had given a dangerously defeatist address to the PUWP central committee on January 12:

> Gierek's slogans about the moral and ideological unity of the Poles, the development of Socialism—all this is a fantasy and dreamworld. We have a multi-party system. There is an uneven rate of development of capitalism, but there is also such a thing as the uneven rate of development of Socialism . . . In [the current] situation tactics must prevail over strategy.

Even Lenin, at various moments of his career, had engaged in tactical retreats. Poland, Jaruzelski claimed, must do the same.[105] Pavlov believed that Jaruzelski intended to retreat much too far. The danger that he would do so was greatly increased by the Polish regime's capitulation to Church pressure for a second visit by John Paul II in June. According to Pavlov:

> The episcopate, and right-wing forces within the PUWP and the country at large, seek to influence Jaruzelski and intimidate him with the might of the Church. There are many signs that the right wing and the Church are succeeding in this.[106]

Among other worrying signs of Jaruzelski's susceptibility to right-wing pressure was his willingness to allow family farms and the private ownership of land to be enshrined in the Polish constitution.[107] The Soviet embassy condemned a report presented to the PUWP Politburo on February 1 on "The Causes and Consequences of Social Crises in the History of the Polish People's Republic" as the product of "bourgeois methodology":

[The report] reduces the essence of the class struggle in the Polish People's Republic to conflicts between the authorities and society, thereby deliberately excluding the possibility of analyzing the actions of anti-Socialist forces, and their connections with the West's ideological sabotage centers. There is not a word about the USSR's help in restoring and developing Poland's economy.

After extensive lobbying by the Soviet embassy, which had received an advance copy, the report was rejected and it was agreed that a revised version should be prepared, emphasizing Poland's supposed achievements in Socialist construction under the leadership of the PUWP.[108] Aristov continued, however, to complain that "ideological work remains a most neglected sector of the PUWP's activity," and that the PUWP leadership was failing to master "the revisionist right-wing opportunist bias in the Party." The press was deeply tainted by revisionism and Eurocommunism, while Polish translations of Soviet textbooks were openly disparaged:

Currency has been given to the idea that the Soviet model is unsuitable for Poland; the PUWP is incapable of solving contradictions in the interests of the whole of society, and a "third path" needs to be worked out. There is increasing criticism of real Socialism.[109]

As the time for John Paul II's return to Poland approached, the official mood in both Warsaw and Moscow became increasingly nervous. On April 5, 1983 Pavlov forwarded to Viktor Chebrikov, the KGB chairman, a request from Kiszczak for "material and technical assistance in connection with the Pope's visit": 150 rifles of the kind used for firing rubber bullets, 20 armed personnel carriers, 300 cars for transporting plain clothes personnel and surveillance equipment, 200 army tents and various medical supplies.[110] According to Pavlov, Kiszczak was close to panic, declaring that he could no longer "rely on anyone." SB sources in the Vatican reported that, though statements drafted for John Paul II were usually moderate, he tended to depart from prepared texts, improvise and get carried away. Kiszczak feared that he would do the same in Poland.

The SB's only ground for optimism was the decline in the Pope's health since the assassination attempt in the previous year. "At the present time," said Kiszczak, "we can only dream of the possibility that God will recall him to his bosom as soon as possible." Kiszczak seized eagerly on any evidence which suggested that the Pope's days were numbered. According to one improbable SB report, which he passed on to the KGB, John Paul II was suffering from leukemia but used cosmetics to conceal his condition.[111] Two years earlier the KGB had received an equally inaccurate report from the Hungarian AVH which claimed that the Pope was suffering from cancer of the spinal column.[112] About a fortnight after Kiszczak's appeal for help from the KGB, Aristov reported further evidence that the Polish authorities were wilting under papal pressure. Having at first refused to allow large open-air masses at Kraków and Katowice, they had given way and agreed to both—thus running the unacceptable risk "of inflaming religious fanaticism among the working class."[113]

On the eve of the Pope's arrival on June 16, 1983, the underground Warsaw weekly *Tygodnik Mazowsze* expressed the hope that his visit would "enable people to break through the barrier of despair, just as his 1979 visit broke through the barrier of fear." In his first words after his emotional homecoming at Warsaw airport, John Paul II reached out to those imprisoned and persecuted by the regime:

> I ask those who suffer to be particularly close to me. I ask this in the words of Christ: "I was sick, and you visited me. I was in prison and you came to me." I myself cannot visit all those in prison [*gasps from the crowd*], all those who are suffering. But I ask them to be close to me in spirit to help me, just as they always do.[114]

At every stage during the next nine days, as during John Paul II's first visit four years earlier, the gulf between his immense moral authority and the discredited one-party state was plain for all to see. Even Jaruzelski sensed it during his first meeting with the Pope in the ornate surroundings of Belweder presidential palace. Though a non-believer, Jaruzelski later admitted that, "My legs were trembling and my knees were knocking together . . . The Pope, this figure in white, it all affected me emotionally. Beyond all reason . . ."[115]

For millions of Poles, the visit was equally unforgettable. Many walked across Poland to see John Paul II, often sleeping by the roadside during their journeys. Wherever the Pope stopped, there were rarely less than half a million people waiting for him.[116] "We have to deal with the most famous Pole in the world," grumbled Kiszczak, "and, unfortunately, we have to do it here in Poland!"[117] Though the Pope could not meet the leaders of the illegal Solidarity underground during his visit, he had sent an emissary, Father Adam Boniecki, to see them before he arrived and convey his gratitude and admiration to them.[118] At first the authorities refused to allow Wałęsa to meet the Pope; then, on the final day of his visit, they gave way and Wałęsa was flown to a meeting in the Tatra mountains. An underground cartoon of the time showed SB agents disguised as sheep and goats clutching boom microphones as they tried to listen in to the conversation.[119]

The formal ending of martial law a month after the Pope's visit did little to mend the regime's tattered reputation. Nor did Rakowski's visit to address Gdańsk shipyard workers on the third anniversary of the August 1980 accords. Having arrived to proclaim Solidarity dead and Wałęsa a has-been, he found himself upstaged by Solidarity hecklers. Wałęsa, in an admittedly stumbling statement, had the workers on his side when he accused Rakowski and his colleagues of using the 1980 strikes to lever

Gierek out of power and advance their own careers. It was probably this débâcle at Gdańsk which finally persuaded the regime to broadcast the libelous video of Wałęsa concocted by the SB at the end of the previous year. Film footage taken by a hidden SB camera of Wałęsa eating a birthday meal with his brother Stanisław was used as the basis of a bogus "documentary" entitled *Money,* which purported to expose Wałęsa's greed and corruption. The dialogue was constructed by splicing together some of Wałęsa's public statements, misleading extracts from the stolen tape-recording of his birthday celebrations and words spoken by a Warsaw actor imitating Wałęsa's voice.[120]

The Polish files seen by Mitrokhin end just too early to clarify who exactly was involved in the decision to go ahead with an active measure begun over a year earlier. Kiszczak later tried to put the blame on his SB subordinate, Adam Pietruszka, but he must certainly have been among those who authorized the use of the video. The film dialogue included a fabricated exchange about Wałęsa's supposed fortune in the West:

> LECH WAŁĘSA: You know all in all it is over a million dollars . . . Somebody has to draw it all and put it somewhere. It can't be brought into the country, though.
> STANISŁAW WAŁĘSA: No, no, no!
> LECH WAŁĘSA: So I thought about it and they came here and this priest had an idea that they would open an account in that bank, the papal one. They give 15 percent there . . . Somebody has to arrange it all, open accounts in the Vatican. I can't touch it though or I'd get smashed in the mug. So you could . . .

Part of the purpose of the SB active measure was to sabotage Wałęsa's prospect of winning the Nobel Peace Prize. The actor impersonating Wałęsa explains that the prize is worth a lot of money, then complains, "I'd get it if it weren't for the Church! But the Church is starting to interfere." "Yeah," says his brother, "because they've put up the Pope again."[121]

On October 5, however, came the news that Wałęsa had indeed been awarded the Nobel Peace Prize. To counter the SB's attempt to portray him as a corrupt fortune-hunter, Wałęsa announced that he was giving his prize money to a Church scheme to help private farmers modernize and mechanize the countryside.[122] Though now terminally ill, Andropov could barely contain his fury. From his sickbed he despatched a furious letter to Jaruzelski:

> The Church is reawakening the cult of Wałęsa, giving him inspiration and encouraging him in his actions. This means that the Church is creating a new kind of confrontation with the Party. In this situation, the most important thing is not to make concessions . . .

Jaruzelski appeared unmoved. A month later he wrote a remarkable letter to John Paul II saying that he still often thought of their conversations during his visit to

Poland because, "regardless of understandable differences in assessment, they were full of heartfelt concern for the fate of our motherland and the well-being of man."[123]

In April 1984, two months after Andropov's death, Jaruzelski was summoned to explain himself at another secret meeting in a railway coach at the border city of Brest-Litovsk, this time with foreign minister Gromyko and defense minister Ustinov. Gromyko gave a grim account of the meeting to the Politburo on April 26:

> Concerning the attitude of the Polish Church, [Jaruzelski] described the Church as an ally, without whom progress is impossible. He did not say a word about a determined struggle against the intrigues of the Church.

Andropov's successor, Konstantin Chernenko, declared that the Church was leading a counter-revolutionary offensive in Poland, "inspiring and uniting the enemies of Communism and those dissatisfied by the present system." The comments of Mikhail Gorbachev, who was to succeed Chernenko eleven months later, were curiously prophetic. "It seems to me," he said, "that we don't yet understand the true intentions of Jaruzelski. Perhaps he wishes to have a pluralistic system of government in Poland."[124]

As in Czechoslovakia during and after the Prague Spring, every stage of the Polish crisis was monitored by illegals on PROGRESS operations. In Poland, as in Czechoslovakia, there are indications that at least a few of the illegals became sympathetic to the reformers. The evidence is clearest in the case of Valentin Viktorovich Barannik (codenamed ORLOV) and his wife, Svetlana Mikhaylovna (codenamed ORLOVA), who, from 1978 onwards, were sent on a series of assignments in Poland using false West German passports. In the summer of 1982, ORLOV despatched to the center a devastating critique of the nature of the Polish one-party state:

> The absence of a legal opposition leads to the fact that only Yes men are successful. Views which are contrary to those of the leadership are not discussed, but suppressed and eliminated.
>
> The whole of the ruling stratum is engaged in a hidden struggle, individually and in groups, for an even higher post, a prestigious appointment and other advantages. Thus, the Party bureaucracy is not in a position to lead the country while taking a comprehensive account of all its problems and needs.
>
> Without creativity and free enterprise, a society is not viable, and it becomes the victim of bureaucracy.[125]

The files noted by Mitrokhin do not record the Centre's doubtless outraged response. There is little doubt, however, that there were other illegals who agreed privately with what ORLOV dared to say openly.

AS EARLY AS 1980 the Soviet Politburo had been forced into the reluctant recognition that the only effective defense against a Polish counter-revolution was the fear of

Soviet military intervention. That fear, however, was a dwindling asset based on memories of Budapest in 1956, Prague in 1968 and Kabul in 1979. Once the Politburo secretly turned against the idea of invading Warsaw in 1980, its policy was based on a bluff which could not be sustained indefinitely.

Gorbachev's rise to power in 1985 hastened the moment when the bluff would be called. In some of his first meetings as general secretary with east European leaders, he warned that they could no longer expect the Red Army to come to their rescue if they fell out with their fellow citizens. Gorbachev conveyed the same message more formally at a meeting of Comecon leaders in Moscow in November 1986.[126] Though the east European regimes were, predictably, unwilling to share the secret with their subjects, it was only a matter of time before they discovered it. It did not occur to Gorbachev, however, that he might be opening the way to the end of the Communist era in eastern Europe. He expected the hardliners, when they could hold out no longer, to be succeeded by a generation of little Gorbachevs anxious to emulate the reforms being introduced in Moscow. Few peacetime miscalculations have had such momentous consequences. Once a new crisis arose within the Soviet Bloc and it became clear that the Red Army would stay in its barracks, the "Socialist Commonwealth" was doomed.

The end game began in Poland. By the beginning of 1989, with the economy in dire straits and the return of labor unrest, the Polish Politburo was discussing new austerity measures which threatened to produce an explosion of discontent reminiscent of that in 1980. Jaruzelski refused to consider a return to martial law, convinced that it would lead to much greater loss of life than in 1981. The only option, he believed, was to hold discussions with the still-illegal Solidarity in return for its help in preserving the peace. Though Jaruzelski had the support of Czesław Kiszczak, interior minister in charge of the SB and one of the leading hardliners of 1981, he was able to push his proposal through the Politburo only by threatening to resign. Two months of tortuous negotiations led to Solidarity's relegalization and to general elections in June under rules which, though calculated to produce a large Communist majority, would give Solidarity a place in parliament. To the stupefaction of both itself and its opponents, however, Solidarity won a sweeping victory. A few months earlier the government spokesman, Jerzy Urban, had dismissed Solidarity as a "nonexistent organization" and Wałęsa as a "private citizen" of no political significance. After the Communist defeat he told the outgoing government, "This is not just a lost election, gentlemen. It's the end of an age."[127]

The end came more quickly than anyone thought possible. Any remaining doubts about Moscow's willingness to tolerate the removal of the Communist old guard disappeared during Gorbachev's visit to East Berlin in September to attend the fortieth birthday celebrations of the now-doomed "German Democratic Republic." He told Honecker in a phrase quickly made public by the Soviet delegation, "In politics life punishes severely those who fall behind." Honecker himself fell from power six weeks later. Even when it became clear that the whole Communist order, and not merely the old guard, was at risk in eastern Europe, Gorbachev did not draw back. He sent his close adviser Aleksandr Yakovlev to the capitals of the disintegrating Socialist

Commonwealth "to make the point over and over again: We are not going to interfere." Yakovlev said later:

> Please, we told them, make your own calculations, but make sure you understand that our troops will not be used, even though they are there. They will remain in their barracks and will not go anywhere, under any circumstances.[128]

After delirious East German crowds surged through the Berlin Wall on November 9 it took only the last seven weeks of the year for the remaining one-party states to topple like a house of cards.

The Centre accepted the collapse of the Soviet Bloc with far less equanimity than Gorbachev. Though the KGB devised active measures in a desperate attempt to stave off the downfall of the Communist regimes, it was refused permission to implement them. According to the head of the FCD, Leonid Shebarshin, the leaders of eastern Europe were told to fend for themselves. "But," he complains, "they were educated only to be friends of the Soviet Union; they were never prepared to stand on their own feet. They were just thrown to the wolves."[129]

CONCLUSION: FROM THE ONE-PARTY STATE TO THE YELTSIN PRESIDENCY

The Role of Russian Intelligence

Most academic historians have been slow to recognize the role of intelligence communities in the international relations and political history of the twentieth century. One striking example concerns the history of signals intelligence (SIGINT). From 1945 onwards, almost all histories of the Second World War mentioned the American success in breaking the main Japanese diplomatic cipher over a year before the attack on Pearl Harbor. British success in breaking German ciphers during the First World War was also common knowledge; indeed one well-publicized German decrypt produced by British codebreakers—the Zimmermann telegram—had hastened the US declaration of war on Germany in 1917. But, until the revelation of the ULTRA secret in 1973, it occurred to almost no historian (save for former intelligence officers who were forbidden to mention it) that there might have been major SIGINT successes against Germany as well as Japan. Even after the disclosure of ULTRA's important role in British and American wartime operations in the west, it took another fifteen years before any historian raised the rather obvious question of whether there was a Russian ULTRA on the eastern front.[1]

At the end of the twentieth century, many of the historians who now acknowledge the significance of SIGINT in the Second World War still ignore it completely in their studies of the Cold War. This sudden disappearance of SIGINT from the historical landscape immediately after VJ Day has produced a series of eccentric anomalies even in some of the leading studies of policymakers and international relations. Thus, for example, Sir Martin Gilbert's massive and mostly authoritative multivolume official biography of Churchill acknowledges his passion for SIGINT as war leader but includes not a single reference to his continuing interest in it as peacetime prime minister from 1951 to 1955.

There is even less about SIGINT in biographies of Stalin. While there are some excellent histories of the Soviet Union, it is difficult to think of any which devotes as much as a sentence to the enormous volume of SIGINT generated by the KGB and GRU. In many studies of Soviet foreign policy, the KGB is barely mentioned. The bibliography of the most recent academic history of Russian foreign relations from 1917 to 1991 (published in 1998), praised by a British authority on the subject as "easily the best general history of Soviet foreign policy," contains—apart from a biography of Beria—not a single work on Soviet intelligence among more than 120 titles.[2]

Though such aberrations by leading historians are due partly to the over-classification of intelligence archives (worst in the case of SIGINT), they derive at root from what psychologists call "cognitive dissonance"—the difficulty all of us have in grasping new concepts which disturb our existing view of the world.[3] For many twentieth-century historians, political scientists and international relations specialists, secret intelligence has been just such a concept. It is, of course, naive to assume, as some "spy writers" have done, that the most secret sources necessarily provide the most important information. But it is also naive to suppose that research on twentieth-century international relations and authoritarian regimes (to take only two examples) can afford to neglect the role of intelligence agencies. As a new century dawns the traditional academic disregard for intelligence is in serious, if not yet terminal, decline. A new generation of scholars has begun to emerge, less disoriented than most of their predecessors by the role of intelligence and its use (or abuse) by policymakers.[4] A vast research agenda awaits them.

Research on the Soviet era has already undermined the common assumption of a basic symmetry between the role of intelligence in East and West. The Cheka and its successors were central to the functioning of the Soviet system in ways that intelligence communities never were to the government of Western states. The great nineteenth-century dissident Aleksandr Herzen, perhaps the first real Russian socialist, said that what he feared for the twentieth century was "Genghis Khan with a telegraph"—a traditional despot with at his command all the power of the modern state. With Stalin's Russia, Herzen's nightmare became reality. But the power of the Stalinist state was, as George Orwell realized, in large part a secret power. The construction and survival of the world's first one-party state in Russia and its "near abroad" depended on the creation after the October Revolution of an unprecedented system of surveillance able to monitor and suppress all forms of dissent. In *Nineteen Eighty-Four* Orwell depicts a state built on almost total surveillance:

> There was . . . no way of knowing whether you were being watched at any given moment. How often, or on what system, the Thought Police plugged in on any individual wire was guesswork. It was even conceivable that they watched everybody all the time. But at any rate they could plug in your wire whenever they wanted to.[5]

Millions in Stalin's Russia felt almost as closely watched as Winston Smith in *Nineteen Eighty-Four*. "Because of the ubiquity of NKVD informers," writes historian Geoffrey Hosking, ". . . many people had no one whom they trusted completely."[6]

The foundations of Stalin's surveillance state were laid by Lenin, the Cheka's most ardent supporter within the Bolshevik leadership, who dismissed protests at its brutality as wimpish "wailing." With Lenin's personal encouragement, the Cheka gradually permeated every aspect of life under the Soviet regime.[7] When, for example, Lenin sought to stamp out celebration of the Russian Christmas, it was to the Cheka that he turned. "All Chekists," he instructed on December 25, 1919, "have to be on the alert to shoot anyone who doesn't turn up to work because of 'Nikola' [St.

Nicholas's Day]."[8] Stalin used the Cheka's successors, the OGPU and the NKVD, to carry through the greatest peacetime persecution in European history, whose victims included a majority of the Party leadership, of the high command and even of the commissars of state security responsible for implementing the Great Terror. Among Western observers of the Terror, unable to comprehend that such persecution was possible in an apparently civilized society, there were some textbook cases of cognitive dissonance. The American ambassador, Joseph Davies, informed Washington that the show trials had provided "proof beyond reasonable doubt to justify the verdict of guilty of treason." The historian Sir Bernard Pares, widely regarded as the leading British expert of his generation on all things Russian, wrote as late as 1962, "Nearly all [those condemned at the trials] admitted having conspired against the life of Stalin and others, and on this point it is not necessary to doubt them."[9]

After the Second World War the NKVD and its successor, the MGB, played a central role in the creation of the new Soviet empire in eastern and central Europe. Their role, according to a sanctimonious Soviet official history, was to "help the people of liberated countries in establishing and strengthening a free domestic form of government"[10]—in other words, to construct a series of obedient one-party states along the Soviet Union's western borders. Throughout the Soviet Bloc, security and intelligence services, newly created in the image of the MGB, played a crucial part in the establishment of Stalinist regimes. Informers in the German Democratic Republic were seven times more numerous even than in Nazi Germany. As in East Germany, many of the leaders of the new one-party states were not merely loyal Stalinists but also former Soviet agents.

Though post-Stalinist enemies of the people were downgraded by the KGB to the category of dissidents and subjected to less homicidal methods of repression, the campaign against them remained uncompromising. In order to understand the workings of the Soviet state, much more detailed research is needed on the KGB's methods of social control. Mitrokhin's notes on documents from internal KGB directorates which found their way into FCD files illustrate the enormous wealth of highly classified material on the functioning of the Soviet system which still remains hidden in the archives of today's Russian security service, the FSB.

Among the KGB's innovations during the Cold War was the punitive use of psychiatry against ideological subversion. The KGB recruited a series of psychiatrists at the Serbsky Institute for Forensic Psychiatry and other institutes who were instructed to diagnose political dissidents as cases of "paranoiac schizophrenia," thus condemning them to indefinite incarceration in mental hospitals where they could be drugged and tranquilized. One "plan of agent operational measures" implemented late in 1975 involved the use of four agents (KRAYEVSKY, PETROV, PROFESSOR and VAYKIN) and six co-optees (BEA, LDR, MGV, MZN, NRA and SAB) in the psychiatric profession.[11] There were, almost certainly, many more. Remarkably, most incarcerated dissidents retained their sanity, even after treatment by KGB psychiatrists. An examination of twenty-seven of them in 1977–8 by Aleksandr Aleksandrovich Voloshanovich, a doctor at the Dolgoprudnaya psychiatric hospital, concluded that none was suffering from any psychological disorder.[12] In 1983 Soviet psychiatrists resigned from the World Psychiatric Association, just in time to avoid expulsion for systematic abuse of their patients.

The KGB's most widely used methods of social control were the simpler, though immensely labor-intensive, techniques of ubiquitous surveillance and intimidation. Andropov's first-hand experience as ambassador in Budapest in 1956, reinforced by the Czechoslovak crisis during his first year as KGB chairman, convinced him that the KGB could not afford to overlook a single instance of ideological subversion. "Every such act," he insisted, "represents a danger."[13] None was too trivial to attract the attention of the KGB. The effort and resources employed to track down each and every author of an anonymous letter or seditious graffito criticizing the Soviet system frequently exceeded those devoted in the West to a major murder enquiry.

Among the many successful operations against such authors which were celebrated in the classified in-house journal *KGB Sbornik* was the hunt for a subversive codenamed KHUDOZHNIK ("Artist"), who in July 1971 began sending anonymous letters attacking Marxism-Leninism and various Party functionaries to CPSU and Komsomol committees. The letters were written in ballpoint pen and signed "Central Committee of the Freedom Party." Forensic examination revealed barely detectable traces on the back of some of the letters of pencil drawings—hence the codename KHUDOZHNIK and the hypothesis that he had studied at art school. Detailed study of the contents of the letters also revealed that he regularly read *Komsomolskaya Pravda* and listened to foreign radio stations. The fact that some of the letters were sent to military Komsomols led to an immense trawl through the records of people dismissed from military training establishments and the files of reserve officers. The search for KHUDOZHNIK was concentrated in Moscow, Yaroslavl, Rostov and Gavrilov-Yam, where his letters were posted. In all four places the postal censorship service (Sluzhba PK) searched for many months for handwriting similar to KHUDOZHNIK's; numerous KGB agents and co-optees were also shown samples of the writing and given KHUDOZHNIK's supposed psychological profile. An enormous research exercise was undertaken to identify and scrutinize official forms which KHUDOZHNIK might have filled in. Eventually, after a hunt lasting almost three years, his writing was found on an application to the Rostov City Housing Commission. In 1974 KHUDOZHNIK was unmasked as the chairman of a Rostov street committee named Korobov. After a brief period under surveillance, he was arrested, tried and imprisoned.[14] As in many similar cases, the triumphalist KGB report on the lengthy operation to track down KHUDOZHNIK showed no sense of the absurdity of devoting such huge resources to the hunt for an author of "libels against Soviet reality" none of which ever became public.

KGB officers were regularly reminded by articles in *KGB Sbornik* and other exhortations that even Western popular music was inherently subversive. Provincial KGBs went to enormous pains to discover the extent of local interest in such music, and were usually disturbed by what they discovered. The KGB in Dnepropetrovsk Oblast, where Brezhnev had begun his career as a party apparatchik, calculated after a presumably lengthy examination of young people's private correspondence in the mid-1970s, that almost 80 percent of the 15–20-year-old age group "systematically listened to broadcasts from Western radio stations," especially popular music, and showed other unhealthy signs of interest in Western pop stars such as trying to obtain their photographs. The almost surreal nature of the report on musical subversion in Dnepropetrovsk Oblast is a reminder of how the hunt for ideological dissidence frequently destroyed all sense of the absurd among those committed to the holy war against it:

> Even listening to musical programs gave young people a distorted idea of Soviet reality, and led to incidents of a treasonable nature. Infatuation with trendy Western popular music, musical groups and performers falling under their influence leads to the possibility of these young people embarking on a hostile path. Such infatuation has a negative influence on the interests of society, inflames vain ambitions and unjustified demands, and can encourage the emergence of informal [not officially approved] groups with a treasonable tendency.[15]

Michael Jackson and Pink Floyd, amongst others, were thus identified as potential threats to the Soviet system. The fact that the Communist one-party states felt so threatened by Western pop stars confirmed their status as symbols of youthful rebellion. Even in Albania, after the collapse in 1992 of the last and most isolated Communist regime in Europe (isolated even from Moscow), the elegant tree-lined Bulevard in the center of Tirana was full of young people wearing Michael Jackson (or "Miel Jaksen") T-shirts. The decapitated statue of Stalin was inscribed, in large red characters, with the words "Pink Floyd."[16]

All points of contact between Soviet citizens and Westerners were regarded by the Centre as potential causes of ideological contagion. Foreign residencies had Line SK officers whose chief duty was to prevent such contamination in the local Soviet colony, which invariably contained large numbers of KGB agents and co-optees. In the mid-1970s 15 percent of Soviet employees in New York were fully recruited agents.[17] It has long been known that Soviet groups traveling abroad were always carefully shepherded by KGB officers. What has not usually been appreciated, however, is the large proportion of agents and co-optees in each group (frequently over 15 percent) who monitored the behavior of their fellow travelers. When the Soviet State Academic Symphony Orchestra gave concerts in the FRG, Italy and Austria in October and November 1974, for example, two KGB officers, Pavel Vasilyevich Sobolev and Pyotr Trubagard, posed as members of the orchestra staff. The 122 members of the orchestra also included no less than eight agents and eleven co-optees. In the course of the tour "compromising materials" were obtained on thirty-five members of the orchestra, including evidence of "alcohol abuse," "speculation" (probably mostly involving attempts to purchase Western consumer goods), and—in the case of the Jewish musicians—"friendly" correspondence with individuals in Israel. Further "compromising" information was obtained on the musicians' families, such as the fact that the wife of one of the violinists (identified by name in Mitrokhin's notes) exchanged birthday greetings with acquaintances in France.[18] The

Moscow Chamber Orchestra also traveled to the West in October 1974 under the supervision of Mikhail Aleksandrovich Sizov of the KGB. Of the thirty members of the orchestra, three were agents and five co-optees. The "compromising information" gathered by the eight informers on the other twenty-two which most concerned the KGB was evidence that some of them corresponded with foreign acquaintances.[19]

It was chiefly because of the immense time and effort expended in the war on all fronts against ideological subversion that the KGB was many times larger than any Western intelligence or security service. One example of the overwhelming concentration by provincial KGBs on cases of ideological subversion is provided by the classified report for 1970 by the KGB directorate for Leningrad and Leningrad Oblast. Not a single case had been discovered of either espionage or terrorism. By contrast, 502 people were given "prophylactic briefings" (warnings) over their involvement in "politically harmful incidents"; forty-one were prosecuted for committing or attempting to commit state crimes (most almost certainly involving ideological subversion); thirty-four Soviet citizens were caught trying to cross the frontier. Extensive work was carried out in institutes of higher education "to prevent hostile incidents." The postal censorship service intercepted about 25,000 documents with "ideologically harmful contents"; a further 19,000 documents were confiscated at the frontier. One hundred and nine individuals (as compared with ninety-nine in 1969) were identified as distributing subversive leaflets and sending anonymous letters; twenty-seven of the culprits were tracked down. The KGB's huge agent network was reported to have grown by another 17.3 percent over the previous year. On the debit side the KGB surveillance service was reported to have crashed twenty-seven cars in the course of its operations.[20] Oleg Kalugin, who became deputy head of the Leningrad KGB in 1980, privately dismissed its work as "an elaborately choreographed farce," in which it tried desperately to discover enough ideological subversion to justify its existence.[21]

As head of the KGB from 1967 to 1982, Andropov sought to keep ideological subversion at the forefront of the leadership's preoccupations. Issues as trivial (by Western standards) as the activities of a small group of Jehovah's Witnesses in the depths of Siberia or the unauthorized publication in Paris of a short story by a Soviet author were liable to reach not merely Andropov's desk but also, on occasion, the Politburo. Though even the leading dissidents had little resonance with the rest of the Soviet population, at least until the Gorbachev era, they occupied many hours of Politburo discussions. Early in 1977 a total of thirty-two active measures operations against Andrei Sakharov, denounced by Andropov as "Public Enemy Number One," were either in progress or about to commence both within the Soviet Union and abroad.[22]

No group of Soviet dissidents during the Cold War could long avoid being penetrated by one or more of the KGB's several million agents and co-optees. Their capacity to make a public protest was limited to the ability to circulate secretly samizdat pamphlets or unfurl banners briefly in Red Square before they were torn down by plain clothes KGB men. Until the final years of the Soviet system, the dissidents were a tiny minority within the Soviet population with very little public support or sympathy. Therein lay much of their heroism, as they battled courageously against what must have seemed impossible odds.

The KGB helped to make the notion of serious political change appear an impossible dream. It simply did not occur to the vast majority of the Russian people that there was any alternative to the Soviet system. Despite grumbles about the standard of living, their almost unquestioning acceptance of the status quo had a profound effect on attitudes in the West, and thus on Western foreign policy. During the Cold War, most Western observers reluctantly assumed that the Soviet system would continue indefinitely. Hence the general sense of shock as well as of surprise when the Communist order in eastern Europe crumbled so swiftly in the final months of 1989, followed two years later by the almost equally rapid disintegration of the Soviet one-party state. Henry Kissinger claimed in 1992, "I knew no one . . . who had predicted the evolution in the Soviet Union."[23]

AS WELL AS underestimating the centrality of the KGB's system of social control to the functioning of the Soviet system, Western observers have often underestimated the power and influence of its security and intelligence chiefs.[24] Beria, who became head of the NKVD at the end of the Terror, emerged as the second most powerful man in the Soviet Union—"my Himmler," as Stalin once described him. In 1945 he was put in charge of the construction of the first Soviet atomic bomb. After Stalin's death in 1953, Beria became the first Soviet security chief to make a bid for supreme power. Fear of his ambitions, however, united the rest of the Soviet leadership against him and led to his execution at the end of the year.

It was frequently assumed thereafter that no KGB chief would ever again be given the opportunity by the rest of the Soviet leadership to make a successful bid for power. That assumption proved correct in the case of Aleksandr Shelepin, the dynamic and relatively youthful chairman of the KGB from 1958 to 1961, who made little secret of his desire to become general secretary, but was effectively sidelined after Khrushchev's overthrow by Brezhnev and the other leading plotters.

Yuri Andropov played a much subtler game than Beria or Shelepin in planning his own rise to power during the 1970s. As Brezhnev became progressively feebler, Andropov gradually established himself as heir apparent, succeeding him as general secretary in 1982. There is, however, not a single reference to Andropov either in the 2,000 pages of Henry Kissinger's memoirs of the period 1969–77, or in Cyrus Vance's memoirs on his term as secretary of state, in succession to Kissinger, from 1977 to 1980.[25] Vladimir Kryuchkov was similarly underrated as KGB chairman a decade later. Most Western observers were taken by surprise when he emerged as the ringleader of the abortive coup of August 1991 which sought to topple Gorbachev and install a hardline regime. Like Beria, however, Kryuchkov overreached himself. Though the KGB had hitherto been an indispensable bulwark of the Communist one-party state, Kryuchkov's mistimed attempt to shore it up merely hastened its collapse.[26]

Yevgeni Primakov, first head of the FCD's successor, the SVR, also attracted surprisingly little attention from most Western commentators. A much-praised American study of Yeltsin's Russia, published on the eve of Primakov's appointment as prime minister in September 1998, contained not a single reference to him.[27] By the spring of 1999, though disclaiming any ambition to succeed Yeltsin, Primakov topped opinion polls of potential candidates in the following year's presidential elections. Having apparently concluded that Primakov had become too powerful, Yeltsin sacked him in May 1999.

THE CHEKA AND its successors were central to the conduct of Soviet foreign policy as well as to the running of the one-party state. Kim Philby proudly told a KGB lecture audience in 1980, "Our service operating abroad is the Soviet Union's first line of defense."[28] The failure by many Western historians to identify the KGB as a major arm of Soviet foreign policy is due partly to the fact that many Soviet policy aims did not fit Western concepts of international relations. Surveys of Stalin's foreign policy invariably mention the negotiations on collective security against Nazi Germany, which were conducted by Litvinov and Soviet diplomats, but usually ignore entirely the less conventional operations against the White Guards in Paris, the plan to assassinate General Franco early in the Spanish Civil War, the liquidation of the leading Trotskyists in western Europe in the late 1930s and the plot to kill Tito in 1953—all of which were entrusted to the foreign intelligence service.[29] Even after Stalin's death, much of Soviet foreign policy was not cast in a Western mold.

INO, the interwar foreign intelligence agency, made its initial reputation by defeating a series of counter-revolutionary conspiracies involving anti-Bolshevik émigrés and imperialist intelligence agencies. Though the evidence now available indicates that none of these (in reality, rather trivial) conspiracies had the slightest prospect of success, they bulked large in the imagination of the Soviet leadership. Similarly, INO's liquidation of leading White Guards and Trotskyists outside the Soviet Union was, from Stalin's perspective, a major victory. At the outbreak of the Second World War, Stalin was more concerned by Trotsky than by Hitler.

During the 1930s Soviet foreign intelligence collection, thanks chiefly to the Great Illegals, led the world. The recruitment of the Magnificent Five and other high-flying ideological agents opened up the prospect of penetrating the very heard of imperialist power in Western capitals. The large number of British and other diplomatic documents obtained by INO had an important—though still little researched—influence on the making of Soviet foreign policy. Throughout the Stalin era, the Soviet intelligence contest with both Britain, the chief pre-war target, and the United States, the Main Adversary of the Cold War, was remarkably one-sided. SIS had no Moscow station between the wars; the United States possessed no espionage agency at all until 1941. INO's main pre-war defeats were self-inflicted: chief among them the massacre of many of its best officers who fell victim to the paranoia of the Great Terror.

Soviet intelligence penetration of the West reached its apogee during the Second World War. Never before had any state learned so many of its allies' secrets. At Tehran and Yalta Stalin was probably better informed on the cards in the hands of the other negotiators than any statesman at any previous conference. Stalin knew the contents of many highly classified British and American documents which Churchill and Roosevelt kept even from most of their cabinets. ULTRA, though revealed to only six British ministers, was known to Stalin. So was the MANHATTAN project, which was carefully concealed from Vice-President Harry Truman until he succeeded Roosevelt in April 1945. (Truman was then also informed of ULTRA for the first time.)[30] There is a peculiar irony about Truman's decision at the Potsdam conference in July 1945 to reveal to Stalin that "we had a new weapon of unusual destructive power."[31] Stalin seemed unimpressed by the news—as well he might, since he had known about plans to build the American atomic bomb for fifteen times as long as Truman.

Stalin was also much better informed than most American and British policy-makers about the first major American–British intelligence success against the Soviet Union during the Cold War, the VENONA decrypts, which revealed the codenames and clues to the identities of several hundred Soviet agents. Remarkably, Truman seems never to have been informed of VENONA at all. Nor, almost certainly, were more than a small minority of the Attlee cabinet in Britain. Because of internal rivalries within the US intelligence community, even the CIA was not told until late in 1952. The Centre, however, had learned of VENONA by early in 1947 from William Weisband, an agent in the US SIGINT agency, ASA. Thus, amazingly, Stalin discovered the greatest American intelligence secret of the early Cold War over five years before either the president or the CIA.[32]

The Centre's extraordinary successes in penetrating its allies during the Second World War, and the fact that some of its agents remained in place after victory, raised exaggerated expectations of what Soviet intelligence could achieve during the Cold War against the Main Adversary and its NATO allies. KGB post-war strategy was based on an attempt to recreate the pre-war era of Great Illegals, establish a large network of illegal residencies and recruit a new generation of high-flying ideological agents. Alongside the legal residencies in Washington, New York and San Francisco, the Centre planned as late as the early 1980s to set up six illegal residencies, each running agents at the heart of the Reagan administration. Its plans proved hopelessly optimistic.[33]

Despite some striking tactical successes, the KGB's post-war grand strategy for penetrating the corridors of power in its Main Adversary failed. At least until the early 1960s, its chief source of intelligence on American foreign policy was probably the penetration of the US embassy in Moscow. By the beginning of the Cold War the previously seductive myth–image of Stalin's Russia as the world's first truly socialist worker–peasant state, which had inspired the Magnificent Five and their American counterparts, was fading fast. Most of the idealistic student revolutionaries of the late 1960s, unlike their pre-war predecessors, turned for inspiration not to the old Communist parties but to a new left which seemed deeply suspect to the increasingly geriatric leadership of Brezhnev's Soviet Union.

The marginalization of the post-war Communist Parties in the United States and Great Britain deprived Soviet intelligence of what had previously been a major source of recruits and talent-spotters. Its most fertile Western recruiting grounds in the immediate aftermath of the Second World War were France and Italy, the two west European countries with the most powerful Communist Parties, both of which took part in post-war coalition governments. The longest-serving and probably most productive French and Italian agents identified in the files noted by Mitrokhin, JOUR and DARIO, both entered their respective foreign ministries during these years.[34]

By the 1950s the KGB was probably obtaining more high-grade diplomatic and political intelligence from the main NATO members in continental Europe than from the United States and Britain. As well as generating large numbers of diplomatic documents, the penetration of the French, Italian and other Western foreign ministries and Moscow embassies provided crucial assistance to KGB codebreakers. For most, if not all, of the Cold War the total number of diplomatic decrypts which the Centre considered sufficiently significant to forward to the Central Committee probably never dropped below 100,000 a year.[35] During the Cold War as a whole, as a result of the partition of Germany and the flow of refugees from East to West, the FRG was the major NATO member most vulnerable to agent penetration—though the KGB's successes were exceeded by those of its East German ally. The success of the HVA agent, Gånter Guillaume, in becoming aide to the Chancellor of West Germany at a crucial moment in East–West relations, just as Willy Brandt was beginning his *Ostpolitik,* was one of the greatest intelligence coups of the Cold War.

Though the Centre acquired a considerable volume of high-grade intelligence from NATO countries, it was never satisfied by what it achieved. In Europe, as in north America, it refused to abandon its early Cold War ambition to create a new generation of Great Illegals. During the 1970s it sought and obtained promises of assistance from Communist leaders around the world in finding further Richard Sorges. The files seen by Mitrokhin suggest, however, that few, if any Sorges were discovered. By the mid-1970s the brightest of the young Party members in the few west European countries where Communism remained a powerful force tended to be Eurocommunist heretics rather than blindly obedient pro-Soviet loyalists ready to sacrifice their lives in the service of the Fatherland of the Toilers. Even some Soviet illegals had difficulty in preserving their ideological commitment when confronted with the reality of life in the West. As the Cold War progressed, the KGB's best agents increasingly became mercenary (like Aldrich Ames) rather than ideological (like Kim Philby).

Residencies, however, remained under pressure from the Centre leadership, which had almost no first-hand experience of life in the West, to cultivate major political figures. Hence the hopelessly unrealistic KGB schemes, all doubtless approved by the political leadership, to recruit Harold Wilson, Willy Brandt, Oskar Lafontaine, Cyrus Vance, Zbigniew Brzezinski and other senior Western statesmen. Kryuchkov responded to these and other failures not with a more realistic recruitment policy but with greater bureaucracy, demanding ever longer reports and more form-filling. Residents must have groaned inwardly in April 1985 when they received from the Centre a newly devised questionnaire which Kryuchkov instructed them to use as the basis for reports on politicians and other "prominent figures in the West" being considered as possible "targets for cultivation." It contained fifty-six questions, many of them highly complex and minutely detailed. Question 14 in section 4 of the questionnaire, for example, demanded information on:

> Life style: hobbies, enjoyments, tastes; books—what writers does he prefer; theater, music, painting, and what he particularly likes; collecting; attitude to sport (riding, hunting, fishing, swimming, chess, football, games, motoring, sailing, etc.), prizes won; hiking; with what kind of environment and what kind of people does he prefer to associate; what kind of cuisine does he prefer, and so on.

The fifty-five other questions contained similarly detailed demands for reports on topics as diverse as "compromising information on subject" and "subject's attitude towards American foreign policy."[36] A full answer to the questionnaire on any "prominent figure in the West" would have required months of investigations by residency operations officers.

THE CENTRE'S MAIN weakness in the field of political intelligence was not, as it supposed, in intelligence collection but rather in its ability to interpret what it collected. Under both Stalin and Khrushchev, the Centre forwarded each day to the Kremlin a selection of foreign intelligence reports received from residencies and other sources, but usually shrank from offering more than perfunctory interpretation of the reports for fear of contradicting the views of the political leadership.[37] Both Stalin and Khrushchev acted as their own, ill-qualified chief intelligence analysts. Brezhnev, by contrast, spent little time interpreting intelligence or any other information, thus giving Andropov greater scope than any of his predecessors to submit intelligence assessments.

Intelligence assessment was worst in the Stalin era. Stalin himself bears a large measure of personal responsibility for the failure to heed repeated intelligence warnings of the 1941 German invasion. The institutionalized paranoia of the Stalinist system led to a series of other failures of assessment—among them the deluded belief in the middle of the war that the Magnificent Five, some of the Centre's most gifted and productive agents, were part of an elaborate British deception. Though intelligence analysis after Stalin's death never again descended to quite such paranoid depths, at moments of crisis in the Cold War the KGB tended to substitute conspiracy theory for balanced assessment. Within a year of becoming KGB chairman, Andropov was submitting distorted intelligence assessments to the Politburo designed to strengthen its resolve to crush the Prague Spring by armed force. His obsession with Western attempts to promote ideological sabotage in the Soviet Bloc made him unwilling to consider any evidence which suggested otherwise. In 1968 the Centre destroyed classified US documents obtained by the Washington residency which showed that neither the CIA nor any other American agency was manipulating the reformers of the Prague Spring.[38]

In both the early 1960s and the early 1980s the Centre believed that the United States was planning a nuclear first strike against the Soviet Union. Though some FCD officers in Western residencies, far better acquainted with the West than Soviet leaders and KGB chairmen, privately dismissed such fears as absurd alarmism, they did not dare dispute the Centre's judgment openly. The East German foreign intelligence chief, Markus Wolf, who resented the waste of time caused by KGB demands for HVA assistance in discovering non-existent plans for an American first strike, also knew better than to complain to Moscow. "These orders," he claims, "were no more open to discussion than other orders from above."[39]

The distortion of Soviet intelligence analysis derived, at root, from the nature of the one-party state and its inherent distrust of all opposing views. The Soviet Union thus found it more difficult than its Western rivals to understand, and therefore to use, the political intelligence it collected. Though the Soviet leadership never really understood the West until the closing years of the Cold War, it would have been outraged to have its misunderstandings challenged by intelligence reports. Heterodox opinions within the Soviet system always ran the risk of being condemned as subversive. Those intelligence officers who dared to express them openly during the late 1930s were likely to have their life expectancy dramatically reduced. Even during the post-Stalin era, when their survival was no longer threatened, their careers, like that of Mitrokhin, were almost certain to suffer. Closed or semi-closed societies have an inbuilt advantage over open societies in intelligence collection from human sources, because Western capitals invariably have much lower levels of security and surveillance than their counterparts in Communist and other authoritarian regimes. Equally, however, one-party states have an inherent disadvantage when it comes to intelligence analysis, since analysts usually fear to tell the Party hierarch what it does not want to hear.

Though careful to avoid offending the sensibilities of the political leadership, INO report-writers during the 1930s knew that they were on safe ground if they produced evidence of British anti-Soviet conspiracies. During the Cold War, their FCD successors similarly knew that they were taking no risks if they used the United States as a scapegoat. One Line PR officer, interviewed a few weeks after the abortive 1991 coup, told *Izvestia* that he and his colleagues had spent much of their careers acting on the principle "Blame everything on the Americans, and everything will be OK."[40] The intelligence reports received by the Soviet leadership thus tended to reinforce, rather than to correct, their misconceptions of the outside world.

There is no more convincing evidence of Gorbachev's "new thinking" towards the West during his first year as general secretary than his denunciation of the traditional bias of the FCD's political reporting. The fact that the Centre had to issue stern instructions at the end of 1985 "on the impermissibility of distortions of the factual state of affairs in messages and informational reports sent to the Central Committee of the CPSU and other ruling bodies" is a damning indictment of the KGB's subservience to the standards of political correctness expected by previous Soviet leaders.

For all their distortions, however, intelligence reports are sometimes crucial to an understanding of Soviet foreign policy. Khrushchev's policy towards the United

States, in particular the horrendously dangerous gamble of the Cuban missile bases, was heavily influenced by erroneous reports of American preparations for a nuclear first strike. The growing authority of Andropov in the 1970s and his policymaking *troika* with Gromyko and Ustinov is evidence of the influence of the Centre's intelligence assessments during the Brezhnev era. The increasingly apocalyptic language used by Andropov as Brezhnev's successor, culminating in denunciations of the "outrageous militarist psychosis" allegedly imposed on the American people by the Reagan administration, reflected, as in the early 1960s, alarmist Centre assessments of the (non-existent) threat of an American first strike.

Despite Gorbachev's early denunciation of KGB assessments, he came to rely on foreign intelligence in reorienting Soviet foreign policy to the United States. Hence his unprecedented decision to take the head of the FCD with him on his first visit to Washington in 1987 and his disastrous subsequent appointment of Kryuchkov as chairman of the KGB. Kryuchkov's successor as head of the FCD, Shebarshin, insists that foreign intelligence reports were by now free from past, politically correct distortions. As the Soviet system began to crumble in 1990–91, however, some of the old, anti-American conspiracy theories began to resurface. The United States and its allies were variously accused by Kryuchkov and other senior KGB officers of infecting Soviet grain imports, seeking to undermine the rouble, plotting the disintegration of the Soviet Union and training agents to sabotage the economy, administration and scientific research.[41]

THE SOVIET SYSTEM found it far easier to digest scientific and technological than political intelligence. While Western politics were inherently subversive of the one-party state, most Western science was not. "The achievements of foreign technology" had first been identified as a Soviet intelligence target by Dzerzhinsky in 1925.[42] By the Second World War S&T, particularly in the military sphere, was seen as crucially important. Nothing did more than intelligence on BritishAmerican plans to build the first atomic bomb to bring home to Stalin and the Centre the necessity of S&T in ensuring that Soviet military technology did not fall behind the West. As in the case of nuclear weapons, the early development of Soviet radar, rocketry and jet propulsion was heavily dependent on the imitation of Western technology. Stalin, indeed, had greater confidence in Western scientists than in his own. He did not trust Soviet technological innovation unless and until it was confirmed by Western experience.[43]

The enormous flow of Western (especially American) S&T throughout the Cold War helps to explain one of the central paradoxes of a Soviet state which was famously described as "Upper Volta with missiles": its ability to remain a military superpower while its infant mortality and other indices of social deprivation were at Third World levels. The fact that the gap between Soviet weapons systems and those of the West was far smaller than in any other area of economic production was due not merely to their enormous priority within the Soviet system but also to the remarkable success of S&T collection in the West. For most of the Cold War, American business proved much easier to penetrate than the federal government. Long before the KGB finally acquired a major spy in the CIA with the walk in of Aldrich

Ames in 1985, it was running a series of other mercenary agents in American defense contractors. Soviet agent penetration was accompanied by interception of the fax communications of some of the United States' largest companies.[44] During the early 1980s probably 70 percent of all current Warsaw Pact weapons systems were based on Western technology.[45] To an astonishing degree, both sides in the Cold War depended on American know-how.

Andropov and, at least initially, Gorbachev, saw greater use of S&T in non-military spheres as one of the keys to the rejuvenation of the Soviet economy as a whole. The real economic benefit of Western scientific and technological secrets, though put by Directorate T at billions of dollars, was, however, severely limited by the structural failings of the command economy. The ideological blinkers of the Soviet system were matched by its economic rigidity and resistance to innovation by comparison with the market economies of the West. Hence the great economic paradox of the 1980s: that despite possessing large numbers of well-qualified scientists and engineers and a huge volume of S&T, Soviet technology fell steadily further behind its Western rivals. Before Gorbachev's rise to power, the extent of that decline was concealed from the Soviet leadership. Politically correct FCD reports dwelt overwhelmingly on the economic problems of the capitalist West rather than on those of the "Socialist" East. In a biennial report on foreign intelligence operations completed in February 1984, Kryuchkov emphasized "the deepening economic and social crisis in the capitalist world," but made no mention of the far more serious crisis in the Soviet Bloc.[46] Even Gorbachev, in his speech to the Twenty-Seventh Party Congress in 1986 calling for "new thinking" in Soviet foreign policy, claimed that the crisis of capitalism was continuing to worsen.[47]

Until the closing years of the Cold War, there was an extraordinary contrast between the Kremlin's privileged access to the secrets of state-of-the-art Western technology and its failure to grasp the nature and extent of its own economic mismanagement. Gorbachev was the first post-war Soviet leader who gained access to moderately accurate statistics on the performance of the Soviet economy. Abel Aganbegyan, his most influential economic adviser in the early years of *perestroika*, calculated that between 1981 and 1985 there had been "a zero growth rate." The revelation of the extent of Soviet economic stagnation and long-term decline relative to the West had a much more profound effect on Gorbachev's policy than the successes of S&T collection against Western targets which had previously so impressed him. By the end of the decade, he had moved from trying to rejuvenate the command economy to accepting the market as the main economic regulator.[48]

The conclusion of the Cold War, so far from ending Russian S&T operations in the West, created new Line X opportunities through the expansion of East–West scientific exchanges and business joint ventures, which the SVR was eager to exploit. The reactivation in the early 1990s of the leading British Line X agent Michael Smith was one sign among many of the continued priority given to S&T collection in the Yeltsin era.[49] For the SVR, as for the FCD, the main Line X target remained the United States. The relaxation of US security checks, in an attempt to build bridges to Moscow and Beijing, led in 1994 to a dramatic increase in the number of

Russian and Chinese scientists allowed to visit the Los Alamos and Sandia nuclear laboratories, as well as other institutes conducting classified research. Line X, however, has found less enthusiasm for its product than during the Cold War. The collapse of the Russian command economy left the military–industrial complex—previously the chief customer for S&T—in disarray. During (and perhaps even before) the Yeltsin presidency, Russian S&T operations seem to have been upstaged by those of the Chinese. A congressional enquiry concluded in 1999 that, over the two previous decades, China had obtained detailed intelligence on every warhead in the US nuclear arsenal.[50] There is little doubt that the phenomenal achievements of Chinese S&T collection were inspired, at least in part, by the Soviet Union's earlier success in copying the first American atomic bomb and in basing the majority of its Cold War weapons systems on Western technology.

IT IS IMPORTANT not to judge the success of KGB foreign operations by purely Western standards. The Centre had, ultimately, an even higher priority than intelligence collection in the West. The Cheka had been founded six weeks after the Bolshevik seizure of power "for a revolutionary settlement of accounts with counter-revolutionaries." In that primary role—to defend the Bolshevik one-party state against dissent in all its forms—the Cheka and its successors were strikingly successful.

From the 1920s onwards the war against "counter-revolution" was waged abroad as well as at home. The FCD's role in combating ideological subversion has given rise, in Yeltsin's Russia, to a curious official amnesia. Like Kryuchkov and some other former senior FCD officers, the SVR maintains that the FCD was not involved in the persecution of dissidents and the abuse of human rights. In reality, it was centrally involved. Within the Soviet Bloc the war against ideological subversion was increasingly coordinated between the internal KGB and its foreign intelligence arm.

In the immediate aftermath of the suppression of the Hungarian Uprising by Soviet tanks in 1956, and again after the destruction of the Prague Spring in 1968, many Western observers doubted whether the genie of freedom could be quickly returned to its bottle. In fact, thanks largely to the KGB and its Hungarian and Czechoslovak allies, one-party states were restored in both Budapest and Prague with remarkable speed and success. From 1968 onwards the state of public opinion in the Soviet Bloc was carefully monitored by experienced illegals posing as Western tourists and business people, who sought out, and pretended to sympathize with, critics of the Communist regimes. In reporting on the results of these "PROGRESS operations," the FCD was franker than it would have dared to be in analyzing, for example, satirical comments by Soviet citizens on Brezhnev's increasing physical decrepitude.

Throughout the Cold War the KGB's war against ideological subversion was energetically waged in foreign capitals as well as on Soviet soil. Residencies in the West had standing instructions to collect as much material as possible to assist the persecution of dissidents, both at home and abroad:

In order to take active measures against the dissidents, it is important to know of disagreements among them, differences of views and conflicts within the dissident milieu, reasons why they have arisen, and possible ways of exacerbating them; and particulars discrediting the dissidents personally (alcoholism, immoral behavior, professional decline and so forth, as well as indications of links with the CIA, Western special [intelligence] services and ideological centers).[51]

Residencies were also required to target many of the dissidents' main supporters in the West. Among the KGB's targets in Britain was the London neurologist Harold Merskey, who had campaigned on behalf of the victims of Soviet psychiatric abuse. On September 20, 1976 the London residency posted a letter to Merskey, purporting to come from an anonymous wellwisher, warning him of an imminent attempt by unidentified assailants to cause him grievous bodily harm. Merskey, it was hoped, would become preoccupied with his own personal safety and spend less time supporting the incarcerated dissidents.[52]

So, far from being a mere adjunct to more conventional foreign intelligence operations, the FCD's war against the dissidents was one of its chief priorities. Among its most important operations in 1978, for example, was the attempt to ensure that the dissident Yuri Orlov did not receive the Nobel Peace Prize—as Sakharov had done three years earlier. The fact that the prize went instead to Anwar Sadat and Menachem Begin was claimed by the Centre as a major triumph—though, in reality, it probably owed little to KGB active measures. Suslov, the Politburo's leading guardian of ideological orthodoxy, was woken in the middle of the night by a phone call from the Oslo resident to be told the good news.[53] There are few better indications of the importance attached to a piece of information in any political system than the decision to wake a minister.

Residencies also followed with anxious attention the emergence in some leading Western Communist parties of the Eurocommunist heresy which challenged the traditional infallibility of the Moscow line, and thus qualified as a novel form of ideological subversion. Among the more unusual active measures devised in the later 1970s were those designed to discredit Eurocommunist party leaders.[54]

One of the FCD's chief priorities until the closing years of the Cold War was to seek to prevent *all* Soviet dissidents and defectors achieving foreign recognition—even in fields entirely divorced from politics (at least as understood in the West). Enormous time and effort was devoted by the Centre to devising ways to damage the careers of Rudolf Nureyev, Natalia Makarova and other defectors from Soviet ballet.[55] By the time the great cellist Mstislav Rostropovich (codenamed VOYAZHER, "Traveller") left for the West in 1974, the KGB had ceased to plan operations to cause physical injury to émigrés in the performing arts, but seems to have redoubled active measure campaigns intended to give them bad reviews in the Western media. In 1976, after Rostropovich and his wife, the singer Galina Vishnevskaya, were deprived of Soviet citizenship, the Centre appealed to all Soviet Bloc intelligence services for help in finding agents to penetrate their entourage. It was outraged by Rostropovich's appointment in 1977 as director of the National Symphony Orchestra in

Washington—a post he was to retain until his return to Russia seventeen years later—but encouraged by an untypically critical review of his work with the orchestra in the *Washington Post* in May 1978. The Centre circulated the review to Western residencies as an example of the kind of criticism they were to encourage, and demanded that they inspire articles attacking Rostropovich's alleged vanity, failure to live up to Western expectations, and—especially ironic in view of KGB active measures against him—his supposed attempts to manipulate the Western media.[56]

Dissident chess players were also the targets of major KGB operations designed to prevent them winning matches against the ideologically orthodox. During the 1978 world chess championship in the Philippines between the Soviet world champion, Anatoli Karpov, and the defector Viktor Korchnoi, the Centre assembled a team of eighteen FCD operations officers to try to ensure Korchnoi's defeat.[57] KGB active measures may well have determined the outcome of a close and controversial championship. After draws in the first seven matches, during which Korchnoi had the better of the play, Karpov refused to shake hands with his opponent at the start of the eighth. A furious Korchnoi, who was known to play poorly when angry, lost the game. After twelve games the scores were level, with Korchnoi once again appearing in better form. During the next five games, however, Korchnoi was thrown off his stride by the presence in the front of the audience of a Russian hypnotist, Dr. Vladimir Zukhar, who stared intently at him throughout the play. After seventeen games, Korchnoi was three points down. By the end of the match, he had pulled back two of his defeats but lost the championship by a single point.[58] A book remains to be written about the KGB's involvement in Soviet chess.[59]

POTENTIALLY THE MOST troublesome "ideological subversion" with which the KGB had to contend during the Cold War came from organized religion—especially Christianity, which failed to wither away as the Bolsheviks had hoped and expected. Though no other political party was allowed to exist within the Communist one-party state, Soviet rulers felt bound to proclaim a hypocritical respect for freedom of religion. By the end of the Second World War the attempt to eradicate religious practice had given way to subtler forms of persecution designed to ensure its steady decline and to discriminate against the faithful. Within the Russian Orthodox church the KGB was able to rely on an obedient hierarchy permeated by its agents. The Centre's main problems came from other Christian churches and a courageous minority of Orthodox priests who demanded an end to religious persecution. For freedom of religion to make progress within the Soviet Union, however, persecuted Christians required strong support from the worldwide church—in particular from the World Council of Churches. They did not receive it. KGB agents in the WCC were remarkably successful in persuading it to concentrate on the sins of the imperialist West rather than religious persecution in the Soviet Bloc. In 1975 agent ADAMANT (Metropolitan Nikodim) was elected as one of the WCC's six presidents.[60]

The importance attached by the KGB to controlling religious dissent and denying persecuted Soviet Christians support from the West was fully justified by events in Poland, where SB penetration never succeeded in bringing the Catholic Church under political control. By the early 1970s the KGB had already identified Karol Wojtyła, Archbishop of Kraków, as a potentially dangerous opponent, unwilling to compromise on either religious freedom or human rights. Though the SB wanted to arrest him, it dared not risk the outcry which would result in both Poland and the West. Wojtyła's election as Pope John Paul II in 1978 dealt the Polish Communist regime, and ultimately the cohesion of the Soviet Bloc, a blow from which they never recovered. During his triumphant tour of Poland in 1979, the contrast between the discredited Communist regime and the immense moral authority of the first Polish Pope was plain for all to see.[61]

The new freedoms of the Gorbachev era similarly went far to justifying the KGB's earlier fears of the potential damage to the Soviet regime if political dissidents were allowed to proceed with their "ideological subversion." In 1989, less than three years after Sakharov was freed from internal exile and allowed to return to Moscow, he established himself, as—in Gorbachev's words—"unquestionably the outstanding personality" in the Congress of People's Deputies. Almost all the main dissident demands of the early 1970s were now firmly placed on the political agenda.

Only when the vast apparatus of KGB social control began to be dismantled did the full extent of its importance to the survival of the Soviet Union become clear. The manifesto of the leaders of the August 1991 coup, led by Kryuchkov, which attempted to overthrow Gorbachev, implicitly acknowledged that the relaxation of the KGB campaign against ideological subversion had shaken the foundations of the one-party state:

> Authority at all levels has lost the confidence of the population . . . Malicious mockery of all the institutions of state is being implanted. The country has in effect become ungovernable.[62]

What the plotters failed to realize was that it was too late to turn back the clock. "If the *coup d'état* had happened a year and a half or two years earlier," wrote Gorbachev afterwards, "it might, presumably, have succeeded. But now society was completely changed."[63] Crucial to the change of mood was declining respect for the intimidatory power of the KGB, which had hitherto been able to strangle any Moscow demonstration at birth. Large crowds, which a few years earlier could never have assembled, gathered outside Yeltsin's headquarters in the Moscow White House to protect it from attack, and later circled the Lubyanka, cheering enthusiastically as the giant statue of Feliks Dzerzhinsky was toppled from its plinth.

At the time the speed of the collapse of the Soviet system took almost all observers by surprise. What now seems most remarkable, however, is less the sudden death of the Communist regime at the end of 1991 than its survival for almost seventy-five years. Without the system of surveillance and repression pioneered by Lenin and Dzerzhinsky, without the KGB's immense Cold War campaign against ideological subversion, the Communist era would have been much briefer. The KGB had indeed proved to be "the sword and the shield" of the Soviet system. Its most enduring achievement was to sustain the longest-lasting one-party state of the twentieth century.

WITH THE DISINTEGRATION of the one-party state went most of the KGB's vast system of social control. But though the power of the internal KGB directorates (reorganized successively as a security ministry, a counter-intelligence service and a security service) dramatically declined, the influence of the newly independent successor to the FCD, the Sluzhba Vneshnei Razvedki, quickly recovered. Indeed, the SVR soon became more publicly assertive than the FCD had ever been. In 1993, its head, Yevgeni Primakov, published a report attacking NATO expansion as a threat to Russian security—and he did so at a time when the Russian foreign ministry was taking a much softer and more conciliatory line. On the eve of President Yeltsin's visit to Washington in September 1994, Primakov once again upstaged the foreign ministry by publishing a warning to the West not to oppose the economic and political reintegration of Russia with other states which had formerly been part of the Soviet Union. Primakov's deputy, Vyacheslav Trubnikov, asserted the SVR's right to a public voice, even if it disagreed with the foreign ministry's: ". . . We want to be heard . . . We express our point of view as we deem necessary."[64]

The rivalry between SVR and foreign ministry during Yeltsin's first five years as president ended in decisive victory for the SVR with Primakov's appointment as foreign minister to replace the pro-Western Andrei Kozyrev in December 1996. Probably to the dismay of many Russian diplomats, Primakov took with him to the foreign ministry a number of SVR officers. Both as foreign minister and later as prime minister, Primakov remained in close touch with his former deputy, Trubnikov, who succeeded him as head of the SVR.[65]

The SVR is also more assertive behind the scenes than the FCD dared to be. The FCD regularly swore slavish obedience to the Party leadership—as, for example, in the typically ponderous preamble to its "work plan" for 1984:

The work of residencies abroad must be planned and organized in 1984 in strict accord with the decisions of the Twenty-sixth Party Congress, the November (1982) and June (1983) plenary sessions of the CPSU Central Committee, and the program directives and fundamental conclusions contained in the speeches of the Secretary General of the CPSU Central Committee, Comrade Yu. V. Andropov, as well as the requirements of the May (1981) All-Union Conference of the leadership of the [FCD].[66]

Today's SVR has abandoned such bureaucratic sycophancy. It reports direct to the president and sends Yeltsin daily digests of foreign intelligence somewhat akin to the *President's Daily Brief* produced by the CIA in the United States. Unlike the CIA, however, the SVR lists policy options and does not hesitate to recommend those which it prefers.[67]

How many SVR reports the ailing Yeltsin still bothers to read is uncertain. By the mid-1990s, when presented with his paperwork, he was already said to be frequently telling his long-suffering chief of staff, Viktor Ilyushin, not to bother him with "all that shit."[68] Like Primakov before him, however, Trubnikov has direct personal access to Yeltsin. In 1998 he helped to shape Russian policy during the dispute over UN weapons inspection in Iraq. Soon afterwards he was present at the Moscow talks on Kosovo between Yeltsin and Slobodan Milošević.[69] Unnoticed by the media, Trubnikov also accompanied Primakov on a visit to Belgrade in March 1999 for further discussions with Milošević. Trough the SVR is not a supporter of Saddam Hussein or Milošević, it does not wish either to be defeated by the West.

By the mid-1990s, the internal security service (then the FSK, now the FSB) had recovered some of its former influence, though only a fraction of its previous authority. Sergei Stepashin, who became its chief in 1994, was one of Yeltsin's closest advisers. A centrist politician with reformist credentials, he had declared in 1991, "The KGB must be liquidated." Once head of the FSK, however, he complained that his service had been "castrated" and was demanding greater powers. His influence was clearly evident in the crisis over Chechnya. In the late summer of 1994 Stepashin persuaded Yeltsin that an attack on Grozny, the Chechen capital, would overthrow its rebellious president, Dzhokhar Dudayev, almost overnight and bring Chechnya back under direct control from Moscow. The attack was to be mounted by Dudayev's Chechen opponents, armed and financed by the FSK. When most of the Chechen opposition pulled out of the operation at the last moment in November, however, the FSK went ahead using Russian troops instead—with (as Stepashin later acknowledged) disastrous consequences. Dudayev repulsed the initial attack and paraded captured Russian soldiers before the world's television cameras. Though Grozny later fell to Russian forces, the Chechens mounted a determined resistance from the countryside in a brutal war which, over the next two years, cost 25,000 lives. Yeltsin's reputation never recovered. Stepashin was sacked in June 1995 in an attempt to appease critics of the war in the Duma, but remained close to Yeltsin and was brought back into the government two years later, first as minister of justice, then in March 1998 as minister of the interior. In May 1999 Yeltsin chose him to succeed Primakov as prime minister.[70]

AS THIS VOLUME went to press in 1999, the Yeltsin decade which had begun triumphantly in 1991 with his election as the first democratically elected president of Russia and his defeat of the August coup, was tottering under his infirm and alcoholic leadership towards a tragically decrepit end. Both the SVR and FSB are already looking towards the post-Yeltsin era. Neither foresees a return to the Cold War. Both, indeed, now have well-established, though little-advertised, liaison arrangements with the main Western intelligence agencies. The SVR and FSB none the less expect a continuing conflict of interest with the West.

They have good reason to do so. The collapse of the Soviet system has revealed a much older East–West faultline which has more to do with events in the fourth century AD than in the twentieth century. It follows the line not of the Cold War Iron Curtain but of the division between Orthodox and Catholic Christianity which began with the establishment of Constantinople as the New Rome in 330 and was made permanent by the schism between the Orthodox and Catholic churches in

1054. Though the Orthodox East was invaded by Islam and the unity of the Catholic West fractured by the Protestant Reformation, the cultural divide between East and West persisted. "From the time of the Crusades," writes the historian Norman Davies, "the Orthodox looked on the West as a source of subjugation worse than the infidel."[71] It is precisely because the faultline is so deeply entrenched that it is so difficult to overcome.[72] Those east European states joining NATO at the end of the twentieth century, those likely to do so early in the twenty-first and the most probable future entrants into the European Union are all on the western side of the divide.[73] There is still no very promising candidate in Orthodox Europe.

To most Russians, the welcome given by Western statesmen in the late 1980s to Gorbachev's ambition of establishing Russia's place in the "common European home" now seems hollow, if not hypocritical. "A Russia shut out and disconnected," argued historian Jonathan Haslam, "will inevitably be troublesome."[74] Despite Russian membership of the Council of Europe, the Russia–NATO Joint Council and other Western attempts to bridge the East–West divide, the enlargement of NATO and the planned expansion of the European Union confirm Russia's relegation to the margins of Europe. The SVR, unsurprisingly, is resolutely opposed to both. Its opposition is strengthened by resentment at Russia's national decline. In the space of a few months in 1989 the revolutions in eastern Europe destroyed the Soviet Bloc. Two years later Russia lost, even more suddenly, almost half the territory previously ruled from Moscow and found itself smaller than in the reign of Catherine the Great. The signs are that some—perhaps many—SVR officers share the belief of the current leader of the Russian Communist Party, Gennadi Zyuganov, in a long-term Western plan first to destroy the Soviet state and then to prevent a revival of Russian power. Russia's historic mission, they believe, is to bar the way to American global hegemony and the triumph of Western values.[75]

The Yeltsin decade has been far too short a period for Russia to adjust to the disappearance of the Soviet Bloc and the break-up of the Soviet Union. Like post-war Britain, Yeltsin's Russia has, in Dean Acheson's famous phrase, "lost an empire and not yet found a role." But, whereas for Britain the loss of empire came at a time of political stability and economic recovery, in Russia it has been accompanied by economic collapse and political disintegration. Russia is in the unusual position at present of having a national anthem but little prospect of agreeing on words to go with it—one sign among many of its current crisis of national identity.[76]

In the search for its own identity, the SVR looks back to a heroic, reinvented version of its Soviet past. On December 20, 1995 it celebrated the seventy-fifth anniversary of the founding of the Cheka's foreign department as its own seventy-fifth birthday, and marked the occasion by publishing an uncritical eulogy of the "large number of glorious deeds" performed by Soviet foreign intelligence officers "who have made an outstanding contribution to guaranteeing the security of our Homeland." The SVR copes with the unfortunate fact that some of its past heroes perpetrated or collaborated in the atrocities of the Great Terror by denying, absurdly, that they played any part in them. In the SVR version of the Terror, the sole involvement of foreign intelligence was to produce martyrs who "perished in the torture chambers of Yezhov and Beria."[77] As head of the SVR, Primakov became "editor-in-chief" of a multi-volume history of Soviet foreign intelligence designed to demonstrate that Soviet foreign intelligence "honorably and unselfishly did its patriotic duty to Motherland and people."[78] Though Primakov's history has yet to reach the Cold War era, it is already clear that there will be no place in it for any account of FCD involvement in the persecution of dissidents and the abuse of human rights.

In 1996 the SVR issued a CD-ROM in both Russian and English, with the title *Russian Foreign Intelligence: VChK [Cheka]–KGB–SVR*, which claims to give "for the first time . . . a professional view on the history and development of one of the most powerful secret services in the world." The aim throughout its multimedia celebration of past successes, such as the recruitment of the Magnificent Five and atomic espionage, is to emphasize the direct links between Soviet foreign intelligence and today's SVR. The cover of the CD-ROM depicts the statue of Dzerzhinsky which the SVR and FSB now hope to see re-erected on its former pedestal outside the Lubyanka. Nothing better illustrates the continuity between the Soviet and Russian foreign intelligence services than the attempt by the SVR to reclaim its KGB past.

KGB CHAIRMEN, 1917–91

Feliks Edmundovich Dzerzhinsky (Cheka/GPU/OGPU)	1917–26
Vyacheslav Rudolfovich Menzhinsky (OGPU)	1926–34
Genrikh Grigoryevich Yagoda (NKVD)	1934–6
Nikolai Ivanovich Yezhov (NKVD)	1936–8
Lavrenti Pavlovich Beria (NKVD)	1938–41
Vsevelod Nikolayevich Merkulov (NKGB)	1941 (February–July)
Lavrenti Pavlovich Beria (NKVD)	1941–3
Vsevelod Nikolayevich Merkulov (NKGB/MGB)	1943–6
Viktor Semyonovich Abakumov (MGB)	1946–51
Semyon Denisovich Ignatyev (MGB)	1951–3
Lavrenti Pavlovich Beria (MGB)	1953 (March–June)
Sergei Nikiforovich Kruglov (MGB)	1953–4
Ivan Aleksandrovich Serov (KGB)	1954–8
Aleksandr Nikolayevich Shelepin (KGB)	1958–61
Vladimir Yefimovich Semichastny (KGB)	1961–7
Yuri Vladimirovich Andropov (KGB)	1967–82
Vitali Vasilyevich Fedorchuk (KGB)	1982 (May–December)
Viktor Mikhailovich Chebrikov (KGB)	1982–8
Vladimir Aleksandrovich Kryuchkov (KGB)	1988–91
Vadim Viktorovich Bakatin (KGB)	1991 (August–December)

HEADS OF FOREIGN INTELLIGENCE, 1920–99

Yakov Kristoforovich Davryan (Davydov) (Cheka)	1920–1
Solomon Grigoryevich Mogilevsky (Cheka)	1921
Mikhail Abramovich Trilisser (Cheka/GPU/OGPU)	1921–30
Artur Khristyanovich Artuzov (OGPU/NKVD)	1930–6
Abram Abramovich Slutsky (NKVD)	1936–8
Zelman I. Pasov (NKVD)	1938
Sergei Mikhailovich Shpigelglas (NKVD)	1938
Vladimir Georgiyevich Dekanozov (NKVD)	1938–9
Pavel Mikhailovich Fitin (NKVD/NKGB/NKVD/MGB)	1939–46
Pyotr Nikolayevich Kubatkin (MGB)	1946 (June–September)
Pyotr Vasilyevich Fedotov (Deputy Chairman, KI, 1947–9)	1946–9
Sergei Romanovich Savchenko (Deputy Chairman, KI, 1949–51)	1949–52
Yevgeni Petrovich Pitovranov (MGB)	1952–3
Vasili Stepanovich Ryasnoy (MGB)	1953 (March–June)
Aleksandr Semyonovich Panyushkin (MGB/KGB)	1953–5
Aleksandr Mikhailovich Sakharovsky (KGB)	1956–71
Fyodor Konstantinovich Mortin (KGB)	1971–4
Vladimir Aleksandrovich Kryuchkov (KGB)	1974–88
Leonid Vladimirovich Shebarshin (KGB)	1988–91
Yevgeni Maksimovich Primakov (SVR)	1991–6
Vyacheslav Ivanovich Trubnikov (SVR)	1996–

THE ORGANIZATION OF THE KGB

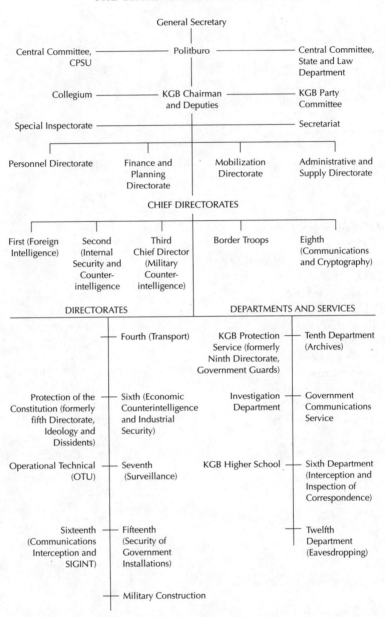

Source: Desmond Ball and Robert Windren, 'Soviet Signals Intelligence (Sigint): Organisation and Management,' *Intelligence and National Security*, vol. 4 (1989), no. 4; Christopher Andrew and Oleg Gordievsky, *KGB: The Inside Story of Its Foreign Operations from Lenin to Gorbachev*, paperback edition (London: Sceptre, 1991); and Mitrokhin.

THE ORGANIZATION OF THE KGB FIRST CHIEF DIRECTORATE
(FOREIGN INTELLIGENCE)

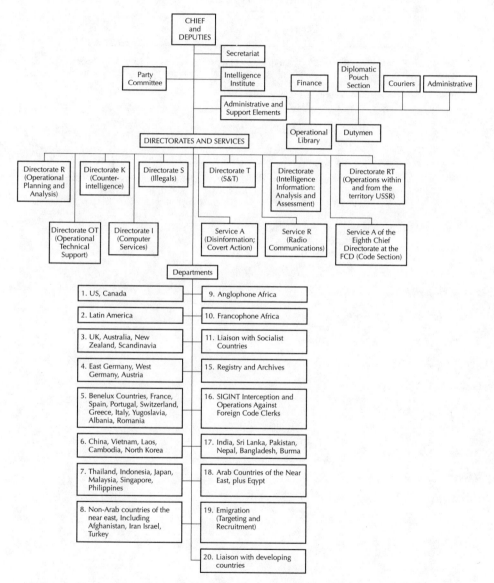

Source: Desmond Ball and Robert Windren, 'Soviet Signals Intelligence (Sigint): Organisation and Management,' *Intelligence and National Security*, vol. 4 (1989), no. 4; Christopher Andrew and Oleg Gordievsky, *KGB: The Inside Story of Its Foreign Operations from Lenin to Gorbachev*, paperback edition (London: Sceptre, 1991); and Mitrokhin.

THE ORGANIZATION OF A KGB RESIDENCY

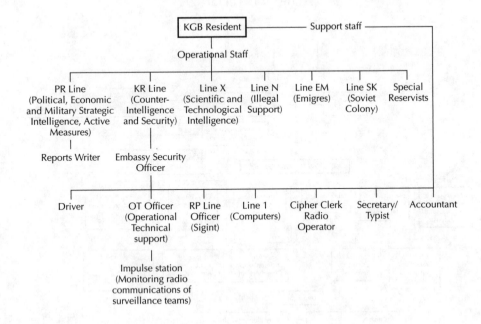

NOTES

Chapter One   The Mitrokhin Archive

1. *Nezavisimaya Gazeta,* December 10, 1996; Reuter reports, December 10, 1996.

2. Unless otherwise indicated, the account of Mitrokhin's career is based on his own recollections. Because of concern for his relatives in Russia, he is reluctant to reveal details of his family background. The SVR is still ferociously hostile to KGB defectors, whatever their motives. Most, even if—like Oleg Gordievsky—they betrayed not Russia but the now discredited Soviet one-party state through ideological conviction, remain under sentence of death. Though their relatives no longer face the overt persecution of the Soviet era, many understandably prefer not to have them identified.

3. For personal reasons, Mitrokhin does not wish to make public the location of this foreign posting, where he operated under an alias.

4. On the fall of Beria, see Moskalenko, "Beria's Arrest"; Volkogonov, *The Rise and Fall of the Soviet Empire,* pp. 185–93; Knight, *Beria,* ch. 9.

5. The FCD Archives, known in 1956 as the Operational Records Department (*Otdel Operativnogo Ucheta*), were subsequently renamed the Twelfth (later the Fifteenth) Department.

6. Volkogonov, *The Rise and Fall of the Soviet Empire,* p. 194.

7. Fleishman, *Boris Pasternak,* chs. 11,12; Levi, *Boris Pasternak,* chs. 8, 9.

8. Knight, *The KGB,* pp. 64–5.

9. k-9,183.

10. Medvedev, *Andropov,* p. 56.

11. Andrew and Gordievsky, *KGB,* pp. 434–5, 483–4; Arbatov, *The System,* p. 266; Dobbs, *Down With Big Brother,* p. 13.

12. k-25,1.

13. k-1,191. Because of the dissidents' contacts (both real and imagined) with the West and the expulsion of some of their leaders, FCD archives included material on them from both the Second (internal security) Chief Directorate and the Fifth Directorate, founded by Andropov to specialize in operations by domestic ideological subversion.

14. Mitrokhin later found evidence of similar plans to end the dancing career of another defector from the Kirov Ballet, Natalia Makarova.

15. The approximate size of the FCD archive *c.* 1970 is given in vol. 6, ch. 2, part 1.

16. When FCD Directorate S at the Lubyanka asked to consult one of the files transferred to Yasenevo, Mitrokhin was also responsible for supervising its return.

17. k-16,506.

18. Blake, *No Other Choice,* p. 265.

19. While working on the notes at the dacha, Mitrokhin kept them hidden at the bottom of a laundry basket, then buried them in the milk-churn before he left. He was not the first to bury a secret archive in a milk-churn. In the Warsaw Ghetto in 1942–3 Emanuel Ringelblum buried three churns, rediscovered after the Second World War, which contained a priceless collection of underground newspapers, reports on resistance networks, and the testimony of Jews who had escaped from the death camps. One of the milk-churns is among the exhibits at the United States Holocaust Memorial Museum in Washington.

20. Mitrokhin's archive is in four sections:

> (i) *k-series: handwritten material filed in large envelopes*
> (ii) *t-series: handwritten notebooks*
> (iii) *volumes: typed material, mostly arranged by country, sometimes with commentary by Mitrokhin*
> (iv) *frag.-series: miscellaneous handwritten notes*

Endnote references to Mitrokhin's archive follow this classification.

21. Solzhenitsyn's letter of complaint to Andropov and Andropov's mendacious report on it to the Council of Ministers are published in Scammell (ed.), *The Solzhenitsyn Files,* pp. 158–60. See also Solzhenitsyn, *The Oak and the Calf,* pp. 322–3, 497–8; Scammell, *Solzhenitsyn,* pp. 739–43.

22. Pipes (ed.), *The Unknown Lenin,* pp. 48–50.

23. Solzhenitsyn, *The Oak and the Calf,* p. 1.

24. Shentalinsky, *The KGB's Literary Archive,* pp. 80–1. In 1926 the OGPU had confiscated Bulgakov's allegedly subversive diary. Though Bulgakov succeeded in getting it back a few years later, he himself sub-

sequently burnt it for fear that it might provide evidence for his arrest. Happily, a copy survives in the KGB archives.

25. "Some aspects of the political and moral–psychological situation among members of the Moscow Theatre of Drama and Comedy on the Taganka." Report submitted to Andropov in July 1978 (k-25, appendix).

26. Solzhenitsyn, *The Oak and the Calf*, pp. 2–4.

27. See below, chapter 19.

28. The Afghan War will be covered in volume 2.

29. A characteristic example was a plan (document no. 150/S–9195) for agent infiltration into Russian émigré communities to monitor and destabilize dissidents abroad, signed jointly by Kryuchkov and Bobkov (head of the Fifth Directorate), submitted to Andropov on August 19, 1975, and approved by him a few days later; vol. 6, ch. 8, part 6. Kryuchkov now improbably maintains that he "had nothing to do with the struggle against dissent" (Remnick, *Resurrection,* p. 322).

30. vol. 10, ch. 3, para. 23.

31. vol. 6, app. 2, parts 3, 4; k-2,323; k-5,169.

32. Since he does not wish to reveal some details of his departure from the Soviet Union to the present Russian security service, Mitrokhin is unwilling to identify the Baltic republic in which he contacted SIS.

33. Kessler, *The FBI,* p. 433. Despite its limitations, the story confirms Kessler's well-deserved reputation for scoops.

34. Michael Isikoff, "FBI Probing Soviet Spy Effort, Book Says," *Washington Post* (August 18, 1993).

35. "Fun and Games with the KGB," *Time* (August 30, 1993).

36. The British media also assumed that the KGB defector had gone to the United States. See, for example, "Top US Officials 'Spied For KGB,' " *The Times* (August 19, 1993); "KGB Recruited 'Hundreds' of American Spies," *Independent* (August 19, 1993).

37. The first exposure of Hernu's alleged role as a Soviet Bloc agent was the article by Jérôme Dupuis and Jean-Marie Pontaut, "Charles Hernu était un agent de l'Est," *L'Express* (October 31, 1996).

38. "Le contre-espionnage français est convaincu que Charles Hernu a été un agent de l'Est," *Le Monde* (October 31, 1996). For British versions of the Hernu story, see, *inter alia*, the reports in the *Daily Telegraph, Guardian, Independent* and *The Times* on October 31, 1996, and in the *Sunday Times* and *Sunday Telegraph* on November 3, 1996.

39. Since Mitrokhin's notes, though voluminous, are not comprehensive, the absence of any identifiable reference to Hernu is not proof of his innocence, especially as his initial contacts were, allegedly, with Bulgarian and Romanian intelligence. Hernu's family insist that he is innocent of the charges against him.

40. *Focus* (December 1996, March 1997). *Focus*'s report in December 1996 provoked the vigorous SVR denunciation quoted at the beginning of this chapter.

41. Andreas Weber, "Die 'Grot' geschluckt: Die Lagepläne zu den KGB–Waffen- und Spreng-stoffdepots in Österreich sind überaus präzise," *Profil* (May 26, 1997).

42. t-7,65.

43. See below, chapter 22.

44. *Focus* (June 15, 1998). Other errors in the *Focus* story included the claim that the defector had "worked at KGB headquarters until the early 1990s."

45. *Focus* (June 15, 1998). Roger Boyes, "Defector Says Willy Brandt was KGB Agent," *The Times* (June 16, 1998).

46. ITAR/Tass interview with Yuri Kobaladze, June 19, 1998. Butkov's memoirs, so far available only in Norwegian, contain much of interest (including KGB documents) on his career in the FCD from 1984 to 1991, but include no reference to Brandt. In 1998, while living in Britain, Butkov was jailed for three years for his involvement in a confidence trick which persuaded companies in Russia and Ukraine to pay 1.5 pounds to enrol employees in a bogus business school in California. "Conman from Suburbia is KGB Defector," *Sunday Times* (April 26, 1998).

47. k-26,88.

48. See below, chapter 26.

49. vol. 6, ch. 11, parts 26, 28, 41.

50. Scott Shane and Sandy Banisky, "Lipka Was Wary of FBI's Spy Trap," *Baltimore Sun* (February 25, 1996); William C. Carley, "How the FBI Broke Spy Case that Baffled Agency for 30 Years," *Wall Street Journal* (November 21, 1996).

51. Julia C. Martinez, "Accused Spy Admits Guilt," *Philadelphia Inquirer* (May 24, 1997).

52. Joseph A. Slobodzian, "18-Year Sentence for Ex-Soviet Spy," *Philadelphia Inquirer* (September 25, 1997).

53. The first edition was published in New York by Reader's Digest Press.

54. vol. 6, ch. 8, part 54.

55. vol. 6, app. 1, part 28.

56. vol. 6, ch. 8, part 4.

57. Some of the KGB documents obtained by Gordievsky, all covering the period 1974 to 1985, were later published in Andrew and Gordievsky (eds.), *Instructions from the Centre* and *More Instructions from the Centre.*

58. Unattributable information. Since Mitrokhin had retired six years before the publication of the history by Andrew and Gordievsky, he had no access to KGB files on it.

59. Order of the Chairman of the KGB, no. 107/OV, September 5, 1990.

60. Costello later told Andrew and Gordievsky that he received the first order of KGB material shortly after the press conference to launch their book, at which he made an engagingly boisterous appearance to denounce their identification of John Cairncross as the Fifth Man as a plot by British intelligence. He subsequently changed his mind after seeing material from Cairncross's KGB file which confirmed that identification.

61. Costello, *Ten Days to Destiny.*

62. Costello and Tsarev, *Deadly Illusions*, pp. vi–vii. Costello's untimely death in 1996 has been variously attributed by conspiracy theorists to the machinations of British or Russian intelligence. While Costello was somewhat naive in his attitude to the SVR, there is no suggestion that either he or any of the other Western authors (some of them distinguished scholars) of the collaborative histories authorized by the SVR have been Russian agents.

63. The collaborative volumes so far published are, in order of publication: Costello and Tsarev, *Deadly Illusions;* Murphy, Kondrashev and Bailey, *Battleground Berlin;* Fursenko and Naftali, "*One Hell of a Gamble*"; West and Tsarev, *The Crown Jewels;* and Weinstein and Vassiliev, *The Haunted Wood.* Further publication details are given in the bibliography.

64. Extracts from the Philby file appear in Costello, *Ten Days to Destiny;* Costello and Tsarev, *Deadly Illusions;* Borovik, *The Philby Files;* West and Tsarev, *The Crown Jewels.*

65. See below, chapter 9.

66. Murphy, Kondrashev and Bailey, *Battleground Berlin,* p. 248. The authors rightly describe the SVR's claim that it has no file on Kopatzky/Orlov as "obviously disingenuous." The SVR's selection of documents for the most recent of the collaborative histories (on espionage in the USA in the Stalin era) shows some similar signs of archival amnesia on embarrassing episodes. It claims, for example, that "available records" do not indicate the fate of Vasili Mironov, a senior officer in the New York residency recalled to Moscow in 1944 (Weinstein and Vassiliev, *The Haunted Wood,* p. 275). In reality, his fate is precisely recorded in SVR files. After his recall, Mironov was first sent to labor camp, then shot after attempting to smuggle details of the NKVD massacre of Polish officers to the US embassy in Moscow.

67. See below, chapter 9.

68. Samolis (ed.), *Veterany Vneshnei Razvedki Rossii.* The editor, Tatyana Samolis, is spokeswoman for the SVR. One striking example of this volume's reverential attitude towards the pious myths created by the KGB is its highly sanitized account of the frequently unsavory career of Hero of the Soviet Union Stanislav Alekseyevich Vaupshashov.

69. Primakov *et al., Ocherki Istorii Rossiyskoi Vneshnei Razvedki.* Three volumes were published between 1995 and 1997. They are based, in part, on formerly classified articles in the KGB in-house journal *KGB Sbornik,* some of which were noted by Mitrokhin.

70. Though the former head of the SVR, Yevgeni Primakov (who in 1998 became Russian prime minister), was given the honorary title of "editor-in-chief" of *Ocherki Istorii Rossiyskoi Vneshnei Razvedki,* his role can scarcely have been much more than nominal. As "literary editor," Zamoysky is likely to have played a much more significant role. During the 1980s he regularly expounded his belief in a global Masonic–Zionist plot during briefing trips to foreign residencies. Oleg Gordievsky heard him deliver a lecture on this subject during his visit to the London residency in January 1985; Zamoysky was then deputy head of the FCD Directorate of Intelligence Information. Andrew and Gordievsky, *KGB,* p. 42.

71. "Freemasons," Zamoysky claimed, "have always controlled the upper echelons of government in Western countries . . . Masonry in fact runs, 'remotely controls' bourgeois society . . . The true center of the world Masonic movement is to be found in the most 'Masonic' country of all, the United States . . . Ronald Reagan has been characterized as an 'outstanding' Mason." Zamoysky's explanation of the Cold War was startling in its simplicity:

The first ever atomic attack on people, the use of atomic weapons for blackmail and the escalation of the arms race were sanctioned by the 33-degree Mason Harry Truman.

The first ever call for the Cold War was sounded by Mason Winston Churchill (with Truman's blessing).

The onslaught on the economic independence of Western Europe (disguised as the Marshall Plan) was directed by the 33-degree Mason George Marshall.

Truman and West European Freemasons orchestrated the formation of NATO.

Don't we owe to that cohort the instigation of hostility between the West and the Soviet Union . . . ?

(*Behind the Facade of the Masonic Temple*, pp. 6–7, 141.)

An important part of the explanation for the survival of some old KGB conspiracy theories into today's SVR is the continuity of personnel.

72. The third and latest volume of the SVR official history, which ends in 1941, concludes that Soviet foreign intelligence "honorably and unselfishly did its patriotic duty to Motherland and people." Primakov *et al.*, *Ocherki Istorii Rossiyskoi Vneshnei Razvedki*, vol. 3, conclusion.

73. That is why the SVR selected as the first subject for a collaborative history between one of its own consultants and a Western historian a biography of Aleksandr Orlov, a senior foreign intelligence officer who, despite being forced to flee to the West from Stalin's Terror, allegedly kept "faith with Lenin's revolution" and used his superior intelligence training to take in Western intelligence agencies for many years. Costello and Tsarev, *Deadly Illusions*.

74. See below, ch. 5.

75. See below, chs. 15, 16, 19, 20, 29, 30.

76. See below, ch. 18.

77. On the destruction of KGB files, see Knight, *Spies Without Cloaks*, p. 194.

Chapter Two   *From Lenin's Cheka to Stalin's OGPU*

1. Andrew and Gordievsky, *KGB*, pp. 56–63.

2. Andrew and Gordievsky, *KGB*, pp. 52–3.

3. vol. 6, ch. 3, part 3, *n.* 2; k-9,218.

4. Leggett, *The Cheka*, p. 17.

5. k-9,67.

6. Pipes, *Russia under the Bolshevik Regime*, 1919–1924, pp. 92–3.

7. k-9,67,204.

8. Tsvigun *et al.* (eds.), *V. I. Lenin i VChK*, no. 48.

9. Ostryakov, *Voyennye Chekisty*, ch. 1.

10. Andrew and Gordievsky, *KGB*, pp. 69–75. On the evidence for Lenin's involvement, see Brook-Shepherd, *Iron Maze*, p. 103.

11. Brook-Shepherd, *Iron Maze*, p. 107.

12. Andrew and Gordievsky, *KGB*, p. 79.

13. Before his execution, Kannegiser was twice interrogated personally by Dzerzhinsky. Though he had formerly been an active member of the Workers' Popular Socialist Party, he claimed—perhaps to protect other supporters of the Party—that, "as a matter of principle," he was not currently a member of any party. Kannegiser said that he had carried out the assassination entirely on his own to avenge those shot on Uritsky's orders as "enemies of Soviet power." According to his father, one of those shot had been a friend of Kannegiser. The family maid, Ilinaya, claimed that Kannegiser "was linked with some suspicious people who often came to see him, and that he himself would disappear from his house at night, returning only during the day." Rozenberg, another witness interrogated by the Cheka, claimed that Kannegiser had told him of his plan to overthrow the Bolshevik regime. Mitrokhin noted, after reading the Cheka interrogation records, that the conflicts in evidence had not been resolved. vol. 10, ch. 4.

14. The record of Kaplan's interrogation was published in 1923; Pipes, *The Russian Revolution*, p. 807.

15. Andrew and Gordievsky, *KGB*, pp. 75–81.

16. Pipes (ed.), *The Unknown Lenin*, pp. 48, 54.

17. Though the KGB files examined by Mitrokhin do not record Filippov's fate after his arrest by the Petrograd Cheka, he was never heard of again. k-9,67,204.

18. Andrew and Gordievsky, *KGB*, p. 237.

19. Leggett, *The Cheka*, p. 417 *n*. 21. Conquest, *The Great Terror*, pp. 325–7.

20. vol. 7, ch. 1, para. 5. Buikis subsequently wrote two brief memoirs of his early experiences in the Cheka in Rozvadovskaya *et al.* (eds.), *Rytsar Revoliutsii*, and Lyalin *et al.* (eds.), *Osoboie Zadanie*.

21. See, for example, Ostryakov, *Voyennye Chekisty*, ch. 1.

22. For the text of the official document certifying Ulyanov's "rights to hereditary nobility" (suppressed during the Soviet era), see Pipes (ed.), *The Unknown Lenin*, p. 19.

23. Pipes (ed.), *The Unknown Lenin*, pp. 3–5, 138–9.

24. Radzinsky, *Stalin*, pp. 11–12.

25. vol. 1, app. 3. Cf. Radzinsky, *Stalin*, pp. 12–14.

26. Radzinsky, *Stalin*, pp. 77–9. It is possible that Stalin's determination about changing the day of the month as well as the year of his birth in official records may have reflected the fear that Okhrana records contained some reference which had been overlooked to an agent, otherwise identified only by codename, who had his date of birth.

27. On June 11, 1919 the Central Committee of the Russian Communist Party stated: "[We] have noted Comrade Dzerzhinsky's announcement concerning the necessity of leaving illegal political workers in the areas occupied by the enemy . . . It is proposed that: (a) An Illegals Operations Department be created in the organizational office . . ." (vol. 6, ch. 5, part 1, *n*. 1).

28. vol. 6, ch. 5, part 1 and *n*. 1; vol. 7, ch. 1.

29. k-27,305.

30. Leggett, *The Cheka*, appendix C.

31. There is little doubt that *The State and Revolution* represented Lenin's innermost convictions. Had it been otherwise, he would scarcely have chosen to publish it in February 1918, at a time when the Cheka was already in existence and it was only too easy for Lenin's opponents to point to the contradictions between his words and his deeds. Its publication at such a difficult time was an act of faith that the regime's difficulties were only temporary and that he would live to see the fulfillment of his revolutionary dream.

32. Report from the Cheka of the town and district of Morshansk in the first issue of the Cheka weekly, dated September 22, 1918 (k-9,212).

33. Mitrokhin noted the following report (k-9,210) of an inspection by Cheka headquarters of Cheka operations in Dmitrov in 1918:

> Kurenkov, aged 18, operates as the chairman of the Dmitrov town Cheka of Moscow province. All his colleagues are young people, but young people who are competent, battle-tested and who work with energy.
>
> However, the work of the Cheka was carried out in a primitive manner. Searches were carried out without elected observers and without representatives of housing committees being present. Confiscated food stuffs were not handed over to the food department, and inventories were not drawn up.

34. Melgounov, *The Red Terror in Russia*. Figes, *A People's Tragedy*, pp. 646–9. The files for the period noted by Mitrokhin (mostly on foreign intelligence) make only indirect references to the atrocities of the civil war.

35. Speech by Lenin, December 23, 1921; text in Tsvigun *et al.*, *V. I. Lenin i VChK*, pp. 534f.

36. Brovkin, *Behind the Front Lines of the Civil War*, p. 424. The Dzerzhinsky Archive is Fond 76 in the All-Russian Center for the Preservation and Study of Documents of Modern History in Moscow.

37. Volkogonov, *Lenin*, p. 239.

38. Tsvigun *et al* (eds.), *V. I. Lenin i VChK*, no. 198. Andrew and Gordievsky, *KGB*, p. 69.

39. Pipes (ed.), *The Unknown Lenin*, pp. 127–9.

40. vol. 6, ch. 1, part 1, *n*. 1.

41. Pipes, *Russia under the Bolshevik Regime*, pp. 416–19.

42. Andrew and Gordievsky, *KGB*, pp. 99–100; Samolis (ed.), *Veterany Vneshnei Razvedki Rossii*, pp. 142–3; West and Tsarev, *The Crown Jewels*, p. 5.

43. Tsvigun *et al* (eds.), *Lenin i VChK*, no. 390. Andrew and Gordievsky, *KGB*, pp. 91–4.

44. West and Tsarev, *The Crown Jewels*, p. 5.

45. Tsvigun *et al.* (eds.), *V. I. Lenin i VChK*, no. 437.

46. Brovkin, *Behind the Front Lines of the Civil War*, pp. 334–56. Leggett, *The Cheka*, pp. 334–8, 464–6.

47. k-9,87.

48. The first of five foreign intelligence priorities set out in INO instructions of November 28, 1922 was "The exposure on the territory of each state of counter-revolutionary groups who are waging both active

and passive activity against the interests of the RSFSR and also against the international revolutionary movement." vol. 7, ch. 1.

49. Mitrokhin's handwritten note (k-9,87) makes it difficult to determine whether the date was June 16 or 26. Since Zavarny crossed into Romania on June 15 to negotiate details of Tutyunnik's return with him, it seems highly unlikely, particularly in view of earlier delays, that this could have taken place as early as June 16. Because CASE 39 was run by the internal departments of the OGPU, the file was kept in the special archival collections of the Second Chief Directorate, to which Mitrokhin did not have access. He was, however, able to note a classified history of the operation which was based on, and quoted, the CASE 39 file.

50. k-9,87. During the 1930s an illegal residency in Germany, headed by I. M. Kaminsky (codenamed MOREZ and MOND), specialized in operations against Ukrainian émigrés (vol. 7, ch. 9, paras. 1–2; vol. 6, ch. 5, part 1). The Administration for Special Tasks also carried out the assassination of several leading Ukrainian nationalists (Sudoplatovs, *Special Tasks,* chs. 1, 2).

51. vol. 6, ch. 8, part 6.

52. vol. 6, ch. 5, part 1, *n.* 1. Though Mitrokhin read a number of classified studies of the TREST and SINDIKAT operations, he did not have access to the files on them. Since the operations were run by the internal departments of the OGPU, their files—like that for CASE 39—were kept in the special archival collections (*spetsfondi*) of the Second Chief Directorate.

53. Andrew and Gordievsky, *KGB,* pp. 111–12. Costello and Tsarev, *Deadly Illusions,* pp. 33–4.

54. vol. 6, ch. 8, part 1. On the previous careers of Syroyezhkin and Fyodorov, see Samolis (ed.), *Veterany Vneshnei Razvedki Rossii,* pp. 138–40, 147–9.

55. Andrew and Gordievsky, *KGB,* pp. 112–13.

56. k-4,199.

57. Costello and Tsarev, *Deadly Illusions,* p. 35.

58. Andrew and Gordievsky, *KGB,* p. 114.

59. The complex use of multiple aliases for the same individual in the 37-volume TREST file, together with the baffling mixture of fact and invention recorded in it, confused a number of the KGB officers and historians who studied it over the years.

60. Andrew and Gordievsky, *KGB,* pp. 115–17.

61. Costello and Tsarev, *Deadly Illusions,* pp. 35–41 (based on partial access to the KGB TREST file); and photograph (following p. 258) of Reilly's corpse on display in the Lubyanka sickbay. Cf. Primakov *et al.,* *Ocherki Istorii Rossiyskoi Vneshnei Razvedki,* vol. 2, pp. 121ff. The brief SVR biography of Syroyezhkin identifies him as "especially prominent in the arrests of the subversive White Guard organization of B. Savinkov" and "an active participant in operation TREST during which the British agent S. Reilly was detained and arrested in September 1925." Samolis (ed.), *Veterany Vneshnei Razvedki Rossii,* p. 139.

62. Andrew and Gordievsky, *KGB,* pp. 118–21; Costello and Tsarev, *Deadly Illusions,* pp. 40–2.

63. vol. 7, ch. 14, item 1. Italian–Soviet diplomatic relations, broken after the Revolution, were not resumed until 1924, when the first legal residency was founded within the newly established Soviet diplomatic mission. The residency officer credited by KGB files with Constantini's recruitment was Sheftel, codenamed DOCTOR. Mitrokhin's notes give no further details on him. In 1997–8 the SVR gave privileged access to selected parts of Constantini's file to the authors of two histories of Soviet intelligence operations: Primakov *et al., Ocherki Istorii Rossiyskoi Vneshnei Razvedki,* vol. 3, ch. 13; and West and Tsarev, *The Crown Jewels,* ch. 5. Primakov *et al.* do not reveal Constantini's real name; West and Tsarev mistakenly refer to him as Costantini.

64. KGB files radically revise previous interpretations of leaks from the Rome embassy. A 1937 inquiry conducted by Valentine Vivian, head of SIS counter-intelligence, considered only leakage of classified documents to Italian intelligence. Though it was later discovered that some information had also gone to the OGPU/NKVD, the Foreign Office seems never to have realized that the original penetration was by the OGPU.

65. vol. 7, ch. 14, item 1.

66. Primakov *et al., Ocherki Istorii Rossiyskoi Vneshnei Razvedki,* vol. 3, ch. 13.

67. West and Tsarev, *The Crown Jewels,* pp. 94–9. Though Litvinov did not become Commissar for Foreign Affairs until 1930, *Izvestia* later noted that he had been *"de facto* head of our foreign policy from 1928." Haslam, *Soviet Foreign Policy, 1930–33,* p. 10.

68. Andrew and Gordievsky, *KGB,* p. 126. On the Crémet spyring, see Faligot and Kauffer, *As-tu vu Crémet?*

69. Andrew and Gordievsky, *KGB,* pp. 126–7.

70. Professor Matsokin was succeeded at a date not recorded in Mitrokhin's notes by another Japanese specialist, Kim Roman, an ethnic Korean from Nikolsk-Ussuriysk (k-9,73). Neither is mentioned in the

account of the Tanaka memorandum episode in Primakov *et al.*, *Ocherki Istorii Rossiyskoi Vneshnei Razvedki*, vol. 2, ch. 32.

71. k-9,73.

72. k-9,119. The official SVR history does not refer to ANO.

73. k-9,73. On the publication of the Tanaka memorandum, see Klehr, Haynes and Firsov, *The Secret World of American Communism*, pp. 52–3. The published version of the memorandum has been regarded by some scholars, unaware of the OGPU's success at this period in intercepting Japanese communications in Harbin and Seoul, as a forgery fabricated by the OGPU. The KGB record of its interception, however, describes it as genuine. It is possible, though Mitrokhin discovered no evidence of this, that the published version was doctored to improve its propaganda value.

74. Primakov *et al.*, *Ocherki Istorii Rossiyskoi Vneshnei Razvedki*, vol. 2, p. 257.

75. Article by Stalin of July 23, 1927, in Degras (ed.), *Documents on Soviet Foreign Policy*, vol. 2, pp. 233–5. The article also reflected alarm at the massacres of Chinese Communists by their former allies, the nationalist Kuomintang.

76. vol. 7, ch. 9, item 1. There is interesting detail on the Ilk-Weinstein residency in West and Tsarev, *The Crown Jewels*, ch. 3. The authors do not, however, appear to have had access to all the files seen by Mitrokhin, and conclude that the residency of Ilk and "Wanshtein" (*sic*—presumably a literal retransliteration from the Cyrillic) was "extremely effective" and pay tribute to "Ilk's great organizational skill." This judgment is somewhat at variance with the authors' acknowledgement that the quality of the residency's abundant British intelligence "left much to be desired"; the documents which they cite on Ilk's attempts to excuse the quality of the intelligence probably deserve a less charitable interpretation. Both Ilk and Weinstein are conspicuous by their absence from the biographies of seventy-five foreign intelligence heroes published by the SVR in 1995 on the seventy-fifth anniversary of the founding of the Cheka's foreign department. Since the "Great Illegals" of the inter-war period are included, the SVR evidently accepts that Ilk and Weinstein were not among them.

77. Trotsky, *My Life*, pp. 539ff; Deutscher, *Trotsky*, vol. 2, pp. 392–4; Volkogonov, *Trotsky*, pp. 305ff.

78. A "special courier," whom he refused to identify in his memoirs, delivered an additional eight or nine secret batches of correspondence from Moscow which, he claimed, kept him informed of "everything that was going on" in the capital. Trotsky replied to his Moscow informants by the same secret channel (Trotsky, *My Life*, p. 556). The KGB archives identify the "special courier" as a member of the carters' co-operative which transported freight between Alma-Ata and the nearest railway station in Frunze. OGPU surveillance teams reported that the carter would meet Trotsky's wife or elder son in the Alma-Ata market place, unobtrusively slip into their shopping baskets messages which had arrived at Frunze by the Trans-Siberian Express and collect the replies. vol. 6, ch. 3, part 1.

79. Volkogonov, *Trotsky*, p. 312. Menzhinsky became head of OGPU on Dzerzhinsky's death in 1927.

80. vol. 6, ch. 3, part 1.

81. Deutscher, *Trotsky*, vol. 3, pp. 1–3.

82. k-4,198.

83. Ostryakov, *Voyennye Chekisty*, ch. 2. Andrew and Gordievsky, *KGB*, p. 170. In this instance, the published KGB version of events (summarized by Ostryakov) agrees with its archival record (vol. 6, ch. 3, part 1). Volkogonov suggests that Blyumkin "was guilty of nothing more than having visited Trotsky" (*Trotsky*, p. 329), but overlooks the fact that Trotsky himself later acknowledged that Blyumkin was "trying to establish a connection between Trotsky and his co-thinkers in the USSR." Article signed "G. Gourov" [Trotsky] in *La Voix Communiste*, October 30, 1932; Vereeken, *The GPU in the Trotskyist Movement*, p. 13.

84. There is a sanitized version of Gorskaya's career in Samolis (ed.), *Veterany Vneshnei Razvedki Rossii*, pp. 53–5.

85. Agabekov, *OGPU*, pp. 202–3, 207–8, 219–21, 238–40. Poretsky, *Our Own People*, pp. 146–7. Orlov, *The Secret History of Stalin's Crimes*, pp. 200–3. There are minor discrepancies between these memoirs, based on the authors' varying personal knowledge of the affair. All agree, however, on Blyumkin's meeting with Trotsky, Gorskaya's involvement and Blyumkin's execution. The records noted by Mitrokhin contain no details of Blyumkin's recall to Moscow or of his interrogation; they mention only Blyumkin's attempt to set up "a line of communication for Trotsky with the Trotskyites in Moscow" and his subsequent execution. vol. 6, ch. 3, part 1.

86. Andrew and Gordievsky, *KGB*, pp. 165–6.

87. k-4,198,206.

88. Sudoplatovs, *Special Tasks*, pp. 32, 58. On its foundation in 1926, the Administration for Special Tasks had been intended chiefly to prepare for and execute sabotage operations behind enemy lines in time of war. On post-war "special tasks," see chapters 22–3.

89. Costello and Tsarev, *Deadly Illusions*, p. 439, *n*. 37.

90. k-4,198,206; the Kutepov operation is referred to in these files as "the liquidation of G."

91. k-4,199.

92. Andrew and Gordievsky, *KGB*, pp. 166–8.

Chapter Three   The Great Illegals

1. vol. 7, ch. 9.

2. vol. 6, ch. 12.

3. In 1930 there was no legal residency in the United States and only one illegal residency, staffed by four OGPU officers and four illegal agents. Much of the Centre's interest in the USA at this stage lay in the possibilities for operations against Germany and Japan offered by its large communities of expatriate Germans and Japanese. vol. 6, ch. 8, part 1.

4. vol. 7, ch. 9. The aim in 1930, never completely fulfilled, was to establish several illegal residencies in every major target country. By contrast, no country in the 1930s contained more than one legal residency.

5. vol. 7, ch. 9, para. 4.

6. vol. 7, ch. 9.

7. The most recent and best-documented biography of Sorge is Whymant, *Stalin's Spy*. Though a Fourth Department (later GRU) illegal, Sorge was still being cited by the KGB in talks with Western Communist leaders during the 1970s as representing the kind of illegal it wished to recruit.

8. Andrew and Gordievsky, *KGB*, pp. 46–50. See the forthcoming study of Tsarist diplomacy by Barbara Emerson, the first historian to gain full access to the *dossiers secrets* of decrypts in the archives of the Tsarist foreign ministry.

9. See above, chapter 2.

10. As with many other inter-war operations, the record of Bystroletov's foreign intelligence missions is incomplete. The main documents seen by Mitrokhin were a post-war memoir written by Bystroletov, some contemporary correspondence on his operations exchanged between the Center and residencies, and the 26-volume file on one of his leading agents, Ernest Holloway Oldham (ARNO). Though Bystroletov's memoir is colorfully written, some—but not all—of the main events recorded in it can be corroborated from other sources. The SVR has given partial access to its records on Bystroletov for the writing of two books co-authored by the former KGB officer Oleg Tsarev (now an SVR consultant) and Western historians: Costello and Tsarev, *Deadly Illusions;* and West and Tsarev, *The Crown Jewels*.

11. Samolis (ed.), *Veterany Vneshnei Razvedki Rossii*, pp. 19–21. The account of Bystroletov's career in the 1997 SVR official history also omits much that is of importance about it, including the identities of his main British agents. Primakov *et al.*, *Ocherki Istorii Rossiyskoi Vneshnei Razvedki*, ch. 22.

12. vol. 7, ch. 9, para. 16. The file noted by Mitrokhin identifies LAROCHE, in Cyrillic transliteration, as Eliana Aucouturier, born 1898. Samolis (ed.), *Veterany Vneshnei Razvedki Rossii*, says simply that Bystroletov "successfully cultivated a secretary at the French embassy who had access to secret correspondence and ciphers of the French foreign ministry" (p. 19), but does not give the secretary's name or codename, or refer to her seduction.

13. vol. 7, ch. 9.

14. The accounts of Bystroletov's career published by the SVR in 1995 and 1997, as well as the material supplied by the SVR for two books co-authored by the former KGB officer Oleg Tsarev and Western historians, do not mention that Bystroletov was not an OGPU/NKVD officer. Mitrokhin discovered, on examining Bystroletov's records, that he was simply an agent (vol. 7, ch. 9, para. 38). Even when fully rehabilitated in 1956, after spending sixteen years in prison from 1938 to 1954 as an innocent victim of the Stalinist terror, Bystroletov was denied a KGB pension on the grounds that he had never held officer rank. Since the SVR now portrays him as one of the main pre-war heroes of Soviet foreign intelligence, it is evidently embarrassed to admit his lowly status.

15. Though based in Berlin, Bazarov's residency operated against a number of countries, including—from 1929—Britain. Other illegals in the residency included Teodor Maly and D. A. Poslendy, vol. 7, ch. 1.

16. vol. 7, ch. 9, paras. 24–30. De Ry later also came to the attention of the French Deuxième Bureau as "*un trafiquant de codes*" with access to Italian ciphers (Paillole, *Notre espion chez Hitler*, p. 223).

17. vol. 7, ch. 9, para. 26. Though not present at this first encounter with ROSSI, Bystroletov was given details of it by the Paris residency in order to help track him down.

18. In Bystroletov's account (vol. 7, ch. 9, para. 26), the official who spoke to the walk-in at the Paris embassy is identified only as "a senior comrade." Other fragmentary accounts of the same episode indicate

that the comrade was Vladimir Voynovich, aka Yanovich and Volovich: Bessedovsky, *Revelations of a Soviet Diplomat*, pp. 247–8; Corson and Crowley, *The New KGB*, pp. 433–5; Costello and Tsarev, *Deadly Illusions*, p. 198.

19. vol. 7, ch. 9, para. 27. The photographer of the ciphers was identified as Voynovich's wife by the defector Grigori Besedovsky, then a senior diplomat in the Soviet embassy. Bessedovsky, *Revelations*, p. 247.

20. vol. 7, ch. 9. Corson and Crowley, *The New KGB*, pp. 140ff confuses the de Ry and Oldham cases, and claims that Oldham too was successfully defrauded. The authors, who had no access to KGB files, do not identify de Ry by name or codename and refer to Oldham as "Scott." Andrew and Gordievsky, (*KGB*, pp. 195–6) identify Oldham but follow Corson and Crowley in suggesting that he was defrauded by Voynovich. Surprisingly, Costello and Tsarev, despite their access to KGB documents, make no mention of de Ry and claim inaccurately in their paragraph on Oldham that he "was thrown out on his ear" by Voynovich, who "evidently suspected a British provocation plot" (*Deadly Illusions*, p. 198).

21. Besedovsky's memoirs, *Na Putiakh k Termidoru*, were published in Russian, French and German in 1930; an abridged English translation (in which the author's name is transliterated as "Bessedovslay") appeared in 1931. His insulting references to Stalin make the hypothesis that he was a bogus defector planted on the West untenable. There is, however, some indication that in the course of a sometimes bizarre life in exile, Besedovsky did co-operate to some degree with Soviet intelligence after the Second World War.

22. vol. 7, ch. 9.

23. The corrupt Italian diplomat was successively codenamed PATRON, CARTRIDGE and PATTERN by Soviet intelligence; vol. 7, ch. 9.

24. vol. 7, ch. 9.

25. vol. 7, ch. 9.

26. The only real post with which the non-existent position of head of intelligence at the Foreign Office might conceivably have been confused was that of head of political intelligence in SIS and liaison officer with the Foreign Office. The holder of that post from 1921 to early in the Second World War, however, was Major Malcolm Woollcombe.

27. vol. 7, ch. 9.

28. Mitrokhin found no note in the file querying the story.

29. vol. 7, ch. 9.

30. vol. 7, ch. 9, paras. 30–1. French intelligence records provide corroboration of both Lemoine's friendship with de Ry and their common interest in obtaining foreign diplomatic ciphers; Paillole, *Notre espion chez Hitler*, p. 223.

31. On Lemoine's career with the Deuxième Bureau and recruitment of Schmidt, see Paillole, *Notre espion chez Hitler*, p. 223.

32. French cryptanalysts were unable to exploit the intelligence on Enigma provided by Schmidt. The first steps in the breaking of Enigma were made by Polish military cryptanalysts with whom the Deuxième Bureau shared Schmidt's cipher material. The results achieved by the Poles were passed on to the British on the eve of the Second World War, Garlinski, *Intercept*, chs. 2, 3; Andrew, *Secret Service*, pp. 628–32.

33. vol. 7, ch. 9, para. 30. Neither Lemoine's name nor his codename, JOSEPH, appears in Bystroletov's 1995 SVR hagiography, which, however, confirms that "In the period between 1930 and 1936, whilst working with another agent, Bystroletov . . . established operational contact with a member of French military intelligence. He received from him Austrian cipher material and later Italian and Turkish cipher material and even secret documents from Hitler's Germany." (Samolis (ed.), *Veterany Vneshnei Razvedki Rossii*, p. 20.) It is clear from this censored account that Bystroletov's fellow illegal Ignace Reiss (alias Ignace Poretsky), with whom he shared the running of JOSEPH, remains an unperson in SVR historiography because of his later defection; he is referred to only as "another agent." There is no mention of JOSEPH in the account of Bystroletov's career in West and Tsarev, *The Crown Jewels*.

34. The file noted by Mitrokhin identifies OREL only as Lemoine's boss in the Deuxième Bureau; the Center may not have known his real identity (vol. 7, ch. 9, para. 30). Reiss was known to Lemoine and Bertrand as "Walter Scott." A Deuxième Bureau photograph, almost certainly taken without Reiss's knowledge, shows him at a meeting with Lemoine and Bertrand at Rotterdam in 1935 (Paillole, *Notre espion chez Hitler*, illustration facing p. 161).

35. vol. 7, ch. 9.

36. Paillole, *Notre espion chez Hitler*, p. 132. Which side provided what is generally unclear. Mitrokhin's notes, however, record that OREL (Bertrand) handed Reiss a new Italian cipher in November 1933.

37. vol. 7, ch. 9, para. 18. The decision to award Bystroletov his inscribed rifle is recorded in KGB files as order no. 1042 of September 17, 1932.

38. The date of Oldham's resignation is given in his "Statement of Services" in the 1933 *Foreign Office List*.

39. vol. 7, ch. 9.

40. vol. 7, ch. 11, para. 56.

41. vol. 7, ch. 9.

42. *Foreign Office List*, 1934. Andrew and Gordievsky, *KGB*, p. 196.

43. vol. 7, ch. 9.

44. See below, chapter 3.

45. vol. 7, ch. 9.

46. *Foreign Office List*, 1934. Oake's "Statement of Services" underlined his humble position. Whereas such statements for established staff gave full name, date of birth and a career summary, those for "temporary clerks" such as Oake gave only surname, initials and date of entry into the Foreign Office.

47. vol. 7, ch. 9, para. 20.

48. *Foreign Office List*, 1934.

49. Cornelissen, *De GPOe op de Overtoom*, pp. 156–7.

50. vol. 7, ch. 9, para. 22. King may or may not have believed Pieck's story that the money he received for his documents came from a Dutch banker anxious for inside information on international relations; Andrew and Gordievsky, *KGB*, p. 197.

51. West and Tsarev, *The Crown Jewels*, p. 94.

52. vol. 7, ch. 14, item 1; k-4,200.

53. Agabekov, *OGPU*, pp. 151–2, 204, 237–40.

54. vol. 7, ch. 14, item 1; k-4,200. Akselrod had previously used an Austrian passport in the name of "Friedrich Keil" (Agabekov, *OGPU*, pp. 240–2) and may well have used the same false identity in Italy. Significantly, the SVR version of Akselrod's early career omits all mention of his membership of Poale Zion. The KGB tradition that Soviet intelligence heroes were untainted by Zionism appears to be preserved by SVR historians. Primakov *et al.*, *Ocherki Istorii Rossiyskoi Vneshnei Razvedki*, vol. 3, pp. 158–9.

55. Primakov *et al.*, *Ocherki Istorii Rossiyskoi Vneshnei Razvedki*, vol. 3, ch. 13. The original text of the Foreign Office records of the talks with Hitler, Litvinov, Beck, Benes and Mussolini are published in Medlicott *et al.* (eds.), *Documents on British Foreign Policy 1919–1939*, 2nd series, vol. 12, pp. 703–46, 771–91, 803–10, 812–17; vol. 13, pp. 477–84; vol. 14, pp. 329–33. The version of the record of Simon's and Eden's talks with Hitler given to Stalin consisted of translated extracts rather than the full Foreign Office document. The same probably applies to the records given to Stalin of Eden's talks with Litvinov, Beck, Benes and Mussolini, which are not yet accessible.

56. Constantini may well not have been the only source for the document. The Foreign Office record of Simon's and Eden's talks with Hitler, also in March 1935, was provided by both King and Constantini.

57. Eden's meeting with Stalin took place in the Kremlin on March 30, 1935, following his talks with Litvinov during the previous two days. His telegram on the talks to the Foreign Office records that a copy was sent to the Rome embassy. Medlicott *et al.* (eds.), *Documents on British Foreign Policy, 1919–1939*, 2nd series, vol. 12, pp. 766–9.

58. Medlicott *et al.* (eds.), *Documents on British Foreign Policy, 1919–1939*, 2nd series, vol. 12, p. 820.

59. On Eden's policy on the Soviet Union and collective security, see Carlton, *Anthony Eden*, p. 63.

60. See below, chapter 3.

61. The report by a committee headed by Sir John Maffey concluded that British interests in and around Ethiopia were not sufficient to justify opposition to Italian conquest. Mussolini's decision to publish it in February 1936, at a time when the British government was considering oil sanctions against Italy, caused predictable embarrassment in the Foreign Office. Dilks, "Flashes of Intelligence," pp. 107–8. Andrew, *Secret Service*, pp. 567–8. There is no mention of the Italian publication of the Maffey report in the two accounts of Constantini's career based on authorized access to selected material from his file: West and Tsarev, *The Crown Jewels*, ch. 5; Primakov *et al.*, *Ocherki Istorii Rossiyskoi Vneshnei Razvedki*, vol. 3, ch. 13.

62. According to Mitrokhin's notes on KGB files, Francesco Constantini lost his job at the British embassy in 1936 (vol. 7, ch. 14, item 1). The current SVR version of his career claims that Constantini was sacked in 1931. (West and Tsarev, *The Crown Jewels*, ch. 5; Primakov *et al.*, *Ocherki Istorii Rossiyskoi Vneshnei Razvedki*, vol. 3, ch. 13.) In Mitrokhin's notes Constantini's codename appears as DUDLEN—probably an error of transcription for DUDLEY.

63. Andrew, *Secret Service*, pp. 568–9.

64. [Valentine Vivian], "Report on Measures to Enhance the Security of Documents, etc., in H. M. Embassy, Rome (February 20, 1937), PRO FO 850/2 Y775. This report, though not its authorship, was first revealed in Dilks, "Flashes of Intelligence," pp. 107ff. On Vivian's investigation in Rome and his authorship of this report, see Andrew, *Secret Service*, pp. 568–71, 771 *n.* 102.

65. Andrew, *Secret Service*, pp. 571–2.

66. Interview by Christopher Andrew with Lord Gladwyn (who, as Gladwyn Jebb, had served at the Rome embassy in the years up to the Ethiopian war), broadcast on *Timewatch*, BBC2 (July 10, 1984).

67. Andrew, *Secret Service*, p. 572.

68. The exact nature of the Centre's confused suspicions about Francesco Constantini at the height of the Great Terror in 1937 are unclear. Mitrokhin's one-sentence summary of the suspicions recorded in DUNCAN's file reads as follows: "He was in contact with the OVRA [Italian intelligence], was engaged in extortion, and the documents were probably supplied by the Special [intelligence] Services" (vol. 7, ch. 14, item 1. Cf. West and Tsarev, *The Crown Jewels*, ch. 5; Primakov *et al.*, *Ocherki Istorii Rossiyskoi Vneshnei Razvedki*, vol. 3, ch. 13).

69. "Mrs. Petrov's Statement Concerning Her Past Intelligence Work" (May 15, 1954), CRS A6283/XR1/14, Petrov papers, Australian Archives, Canberra.

70. As chairman of the Petrograd Cheka, Boky reported on October 15, 1918 that 800 individuals had been shot and 6,229 arrested. k-9,218.

71. Petrovs, *Empire of Fear*, pp. 129–31.

72. vol. 7, ch. 1, para. 13.

73. An official Soviet collection of intelligence documents for the period 1938 to 1941 includes a limited and far from comprehensive selection of (mainly German, Italian, Japanese and Turkish) intercepts; Stepashin *et al.* (eds.), *Organy Gosudarstvennoi Bezopastnosti SSSR v Velikoi Otechestvennoi Voine: Sbornik Dokumentov*, vols. 1 and 2.

74. Andrew and Gordievsky, *KGB*, pp. 237–42.

75. British interwar codebreakers were able to break all French diplomatic ciphers until 1935 (Andrew, *Secret Service*, p. 375). Given the classified French diplomatic cipher material supplied to Bystroletov by LAROCHE, it is barely conceivable that Boky's unit was entirely defeated by French diplomatic traffic.

76. Degras (ed.), *Documents on Soviet Foreign Policy*, vol. 3, p. 224. Andrew and Gordievsky, *KGB*, pp. 194–5. Though unusual, such public allusions to codebreaking were not unknown between the wars. In the 1920s, two British foreign secretaries and several other ministers had referred publicly to British success in breaking Soviet codes. Andrew, *Secret Service*, chs. 9, 10.

77. Andrew, *Secret Service*, pp. 471, 573.

78. Orlov, *A Handbook of Intelligence and Guerrilla Warfare*, p. 10. Costello and Tsarev, *Deadly Illusions*, p. 90. Fursenko and Naftali, "Soviet Intelligence and the Cuban Missile Crisis," p. 66.

79. Primakov *et al.*, *Ocherki Istorii Rossiyskoi Vneshnei Razvedki*, vol. 3, pp. 6, 161, 245.

80. The Foreign Office record of the meeting, held on March 25–6, 1935, is printed in Medlicott *et al.* (eds.), *Documents on British Foreign Policy 1919–1939*, 2nd series, vol. 12, pp. 703–45. In the course of the meeting Hitler suggested an Anglo-German naval agreement with a 100:35 ratio in favor of the Royal Navy. This formed the basis of an agreement concluded in London on June 18, 1935.

81. The abbreviated Russian translation of the Foreign Office record of the talks is published as an appendix to Primakov *et al.*, *Ocherki Istorii Rossiyskoi Vneshnei Razvedki*, vol. 3, pp. 461–7. An editorial note (appendix, *n.* 111) asserts that, by his statement on Austria, Simon "opened the path to the *Anschluss*."

82. Primakov *et al.*, *Ocherki Istorii Rossiyskoi Vneshnei Razvedki*, vol. 3, p. 6.

83. Primakov *et al.*, *Ocherki Istorii Rossiyskoi Vneshnei Razvedki*, vol. 3, p. 155.

Chapter Four   *The Magnificent Five*

1. Andrew and Gordievsky, *KGB*, p. 214. Primakov *et al.*, *Ocherki Istorii Rossiyskoi Vneshnei Razvedki*, vol. 3, p. 19.

2. "Nationale für ordentliche Hörer der philosophischen Fakultät": entries for Arnold Deutsch, 1923–7; "Rigorosenakt des Arnold Deutsch," 1928, no. 9929, with cv by Deutsch; records of Deutsch's 1928 PhD examination. Archives of University of Vienna.

3. vol. 7, chs. 9, 10.

4. Andrew and Gordievsky, *KGB*, pp. 214–15.

5. Sharaf, *Fury on Earth*.

6. Wilhelm Reich, *Sexualerregung und Sexualbefriedigung*, the first publication in the series *Schriften der Sozialistischen Gesellschaft für Sexualberatung und Sexualforschung in Wien*, carries the note "Copyright 1929

by Münster-Verlag (Dr. Arnold Deutsch), Wien II." When he later wrote a classified memoir for NKVD files, Deutsch seems to have considered it imprudent to mention his previous close association with the sex-pol movement and Reich, who by then was engaged in a somewhat bizarre program of research on human sexual behavior. There is no mention of Reich either in Mitrokhin's notes on the Deutsch file or in the two works by authors given some access to it by the SVR: Costello and Tsarev, *Deadly Illusions,* and West and Tsarev, *The Crown Jewels.* The 1997 SVR official history also makes no mention of Deutsch's involvement with Reich or the sex-pol movement in its hagiographic chapter on him; Primakov *et al.,* *Ocherki Istorii Rossiyskoi Vneshnei Razvedki,* vol. 3, ch. 1.

7. Viennese police reports on Deutsch of March 25 and April 27, 1934, ref. Z1.38.Z.g.p./34, Dokumentationsarchiv des Österreichischen Widerstandes, Vienna.

8. vol. 7, ch. 9, para. 10; ch. 10, para. 1. The illegal resident under whom Deutsch served in France was Fyodor Yakovlevich Karin, codenamed JACK.

9. Deutsch's address and profession as "university lecturer" are given on the birth certificate of his daughter, Ninette Elizabeth, born on May 21, 1936. Further information from residents of Lawn Road Flats.

10. vol. 7, ch. 9, para. 10. London University Archives contain no record of Deutsch as either research student or lecturer, probably because he was involved only on a part-time basis.

11. Andrew and Gordievsky, *KGB,* pp. 214–15. vol. 7, ch. 9.

12. vol. 7, ch. 10, para. 24.

13. vol. 7, ch. 10, para. 1. The files noted by Mitrokhin make clear that Deutsch was the first to devise this recruitment strategy.

14. A similar stroke of chance explains why Cambridge produced more British codebreakers than Oxford in both world wars. The Director of Naval Education in 1914, Sir Alfred Ewing, was a former professor of engineering at Cambridge. He recruited three Fellows of his former college, King's, who themselves became recruiters a quarter of a century later. In the Second World War, one third of the King's fellowship served in the wartime SIGINT agency at Bletchley Park—a far higher proportion than those recruited from any other Oxbridge college.

15. vol. 7, ch. 10, para. 2. Andrew and Gordievsky, *KGB,* pp. 209–13. Costello and Tsarev, *Deadly Illusions,* pp. 125–30.

16. Page, Leitch and Knightley, *Philby,* ch. 5; Knightley, *Philby,* ch. 3.

17. vol. 7, ch. 9, para. 11; ch. 10, para. 2. Costello and Tsarev, *Deadly Illusions,* fail to identify EDITH as an agent recruited by Deutsch.

18. vol. 7, ch. 9, para. 11. Cf. Costello and Tsarev, *Deadly Illusions,* pp. 133–7.

19. Costello and Tsarev, *Deadly Illusions,* p. 136.

20. vol. 7, ch. 10.

21. The text of the report on Deutsch's first meeting with Philby, sent to the Center by the London illegal resident, Ignati Reif, is published in Borovik, *The Philby Files,* pp. 38–40. Cf. Costello and Tsarev, *Deadly Illusions,* p. 137.

22. Borovik, *The Philby Files,* p. 29.

23. The exception was Philby, whose lack of attention to his studies earned him a third in part I of the Historical Tripos, followed by an upper second in part II Economics. Burgess gained a first in part I History but was ill during part II and awarded an aegrotat (the unclassed honors awarded to those unable to sit their examinations for medical reasons).

24. Cairncross, *When Polygamy was Made a Sin.*

25. Cairncross quotes Greene's letter to him in a postscript to his book *La Fontaine Fables and Other Poems.*

26. vol. 7, ch. 9 confirms the names of the illegal residents identified (with photographs) in Costello and Tsarev, *Deadly Illusions.*

27. Costello and Tsarev, *Deadly Illusions,* p. 132 and passim.

28. This claim appears in Orlov's file; vol. 5, ch. 7. In reality, Orlov did not meet Philby until Deutsch introduced him in Paris in 1937, a few months before Orlov's defection; West and Tsarev, *The Crown Jewels,* p. 110.

29. Costello and Tsarev, *Deadly Illusions,* ch. 15. Though containing valuable material from KGB archives on the recruitment of British agents in the 1930s, this SVR-sponsored volume not merely inflates Orlov's importance but is also misleading in some other respects. It omits James Klugmann (agent MER) from the list of early Cambridge recruits, and even implies that he was not recruited because of his open Party membership. It also wrongly identifies the agent who provided the first intelligence on the plan to build an atomic bomb in 1941 as Maclean rather than Cairncross. (Since Cairncross, alone of the Five, was still alive at the time of publication in 1993, the intention may have been to limit the material on him to aspects

of his career already admitted by him. The SVR now acknowledges that the atomic intelligence supplied by the London residency in 1941 came from Cairncross, not Maclean.) Among other examples of misleading mystification is the claim that agent ABO was a Cambridge contemporary of the "Magnificent Five," who had never been identified as a Soviet spy. In reality, ABO was Peter Smollett, who graduated from Vienna, not Cambridge, University; his career as a Soviet agent had already been discussed in Andrew and Gordievsky, *KGB*, pp. 334–9.

30. This is acknowledged, though somewhat lost sight of, in Costello and Tsarev, *Deadly Illusions*. In a number of respects the detailed evidence advanced by this volume is at odds with its overstatement of Orlov's importance by comparison with Deutsch. The 1997 SVR official history upgrades Deutsch's role to that of "the man who started the 'Cambridge Five' "; Primakov *et al., Ocherki Istorii Rossiyskoi Vneshnei Razvedki*, vol. 3, ch. 1. Cf. West and Tsarev, *The Crown Jewels*, pp. 103ff.

31. West and Tsarev (*The Crown Jewels*, pp. 103ff) give greater emphasis to Deutsch's role by companion with Orlov's than Costello and Tsarev, *Dangerous Illusions*. Their analysis, however, does not take account of the published material on Deutsch derived from the Vienna University Archives, the Dokumentationsarchiv des Österreichischen Widerstandes, the work of Wilhelm Reich published by Deutsch and the information obtained by Oleg Gordievsky during his career in the KGB (see Andrew and Gordievsky, *KGB*, ch. 5).

There is a considerable overlap between the KGB documents on Deutsch noted by Mitrokhin and those cited in West and Tsarev, *The Crown Jewels*. Each set of documents, however, contains material missing from the other. West and Tsarev do not, for example, appear to have seen Deutsch's important memorandum on the recruitment of student Communists. However, Mitrokhin did not note the interesting documents on Deutsch following his recall to Moscow late in 1937 which are cited by West and Tsarev.

32. vol. 7, ch. 10, para. 8.

33. Andrew and Gordievsky, *KGB*, pp. 223–6.

34. Costello and Tsarev, *Deadly Illusions*, pp. 186–8.

35. Andrew and Gordievsky, *KGB*, pp. 206–8.

36. Costello and Tsarev, *Deadly Illusions*, p. 224.

37. Costello and Tsarev, *Deadly Illusions*, p. 225.

38. Andrew and Gordievsky, *KGB*, pp. 216–19.

39. In this, as in other instances in this chapter, Mitrokhin's notes confirm the codename given by Costello and Tsarev, *Deadly Illusions*.

40. vol. 7, ch. 10.

41. Boyle, *The Climate of Treason*, p. 114.

42. Rees, *A Chapter of Accidents*, pp. 122–3; Straight, *After Long Silence*, pp. 94–5, 142.

43. Costello and Tsarev, *Deadly Illusions*, pp. 144–5, 159.

44. vol. 7, ch. 10, paras. 8, 9.

45. Andrew and Gordievsky, *KGB*, pp. 24–6. The only foreigners to achieve officer rank were some central European interwar illegals, such as Deutsch, who were used as agent controllers and recruiters.

46. Philby, *My Silent War*, p. 13. Emphasis added.

47. vol. 7, ch. 10, para. 24.

48. vol. 7, ch. 10, app., para. 2. On the misleading references to Klugmann in Costello and Tsarev, *Deadly Illusions*, see above, note 29.

49. Blunt, "From Bloomsbury to Marxism."

50. Boyle, *The Climate of Treason*, p. 72.

51. vol. 7, ch. 10, app., para. 2.

52. The first reference to Klugmann's recruitment based on material made available by the SVR is in West and Tsarev, *The Crown Jewels*, pp. 206, 294.

53. See below, chapter 17.

54. Deutsch, who was a decade younger than both Orlov and Maly and had joined the OGPU only in 1932, was evidently considered too junior for the post of resident.

55. Though some of his agents believed Maly had been a Catholic priest, his operational file shows that he had only deacon's orders when he volunteered for the army. West and Tsarev, *The Crown Jewels*, pp. 113–14.

56. Poretsky, *Our Own People*, pp. 214–15; Cornelissen, *De GPOe op de Overtoom*, ch. 11.

57. Andrew and Gordievsky, *KGB*, pp. 211–13, 229–30. Costello and Tsarev, *Deadly Illusions*, pp. 199ff.

58. vol. 7, ch. 10, app., item 3.

59. vol. 7, ch. 10, app., item 6.

60. Straight, *After Long Silence*, pp. 101–3, 120–1. The NKVD officer who met Straight did not identify himself, but Straight's description of him as stocky and dark-haired identifies him as Deutsch rather than the tall Maly, whose height earned him the nickname "*der Lange.*"

61. Details of Cairncross's academic career are in the archives of Glasgow University, Trinity College, Cambridge, and Cambridge University.

62. *Trinity Magazine*, Easter Term 1935 and Easter Term 1936.

63. Cairncross, *The Enigma Spy*, p. 42.

64. Colville, *The Fringes of Power*, p. 30 *n.*

65. vol. 7, ch. 10, item 1.

66. vol. 7, ch. 10, item 23.

67. Costello and Tsarev, *Deadly Illusions*, p. 214. West and Tsarev, *The Crown Jewels*, p. 207.

68. vol. 7, ch. 10, para. 23.

69. Cairncross, *The Enigma Spy*, pp. 61–2. Cairncross's account of the sequence of his initiation into the NKVD in successive meetings with Burgess, Klugmann and Deutsch agrees with KGB records both as noted by Mitrokhin and in the documents cited in West and Tsarev, *The Crown Jewels*. *The Enigma Spy* is, none the less, a textbook case of psychological denial. At almost every stage of his career as a Soviet agent (save for a heroic year at Bletchley Park in 1942–3, when he claims that the intelligence he provided on the eastern front was instrumental in "changing the course of World War Two"), Cairncross seeks to diminish or deny the significance of his role. His version of his career as a Soviet agent, save for the year at Bletchley Park, is comprehensively contradicted by the evidence of the KGB files.

70. West and Tsarev, *The Crown Jewels*, p. 208.

71. Minute by Cairncross, March 23, 1937, PRO FO371/21287 W7016. Andrew and Gordievsky, *KGB*, pp. 230–1.

72. There are very few references to such documents either in Mitrokhin's notes or in the material from KGB archives made available by the SVR for West and Tsarev, *The Crown Jewels*.

73. Though there is no positive evidence that this document was provided by Cairncross or Maclean, other sources can be excluded. The Center had recently broken contact with the two other agents who provided it with Foreign Office documents, Francesco Constantini and Captain John King. Since Halifax's record of his meeting with Hitler was not apparently sent as a telegram, the NKVD copy of it cannot have been obtained by SIGINT. The text of Halifax's record, together with details of its despatch to the Foreign Office, is published in Medlicott *et al.*, *Documents on British Foreign Policy, 1919–1939*, 2nd series, vol. 19, pp. 540–8.

74. Roberts, "*The Holy Fox,*" p. 70.

75. Primakov *et al.*, *Ocherki Istorii Rossiyskoi Vneshnei Razvedki*, vol. 3, pp. 6, 162.

76. Medlicott *et al.*, *Documents on British Foreign Policy, 1919–1939*, 2nd series, vol. 19, pp. 540–8; Roberts, "*The Holy Fox,*" pp. 70–5; Parker, *Chamberlain and Appeasement*, pp. 98–100.

77. Andrew and Gordievsky, *KGB*, pp. 216, 232–3.

78. Andrew and Gordievsky, *KGB*, p. 233. Borovik, *The Philby Files*, p. 80.

79. vol. 7, ch. 10, para. 4.

80. Borovik, *The Philby Files*, pp. 90–2.

81. Andrew and Gordievsky, *KGB*, p. 234.

Chapter Five   Terror

1. Serge, *Memoirs of a Revolutionary, 1901–1941*, p. 259.

2. For the text of the "Ryutin platform," see *Izvestia* (1989), no. 6; *Ogonek* (1989), no. 15.

3. Volkogonov, *Stalin*, p. 212.

4. k-4,198.

5. Volkogonov, *Trotsky*, p. 343.

6. Andrew and Gordievsky, *KGB*, ch. 4.

7. Andrew and Gordievsky, *KGB*, pp. 171–2; Volkogonov, *Trotsky*, pp. 334–6. Remarkably, a 1997 SVR official history makes a partial attempt to justify the anti-Trotskyist witch-hunt:

> [Trotskyist] criticism, though apparently aimed at Stalin personally, was essentially defamatory of everything Soviet. Largely thanks to the Trotskyists, a phenomenon developed abroad which became known as anti-Sovietism, which for many years hurt the USSR's domestic and foreign policy pursued at that time, as well as the international workers' and communists' movement . . . The Trotskyists were a fruitful agent base for the [Western] intelligence services.

Primakov *et al., Ocherki Istorii Rossiyskoi Vneshnei Razvedki,* vol. 3, p. 90.

8. k-4,198,206. Doriot's emotionally charged oratory caused him to perspire so profusely that after every major speech he was forced to change not merely his shirt but his suit as well. Brunet, *Jacques Doriot,* pp. 208–9.

9. k-4,198,206. A recent biography of Eugen Fried, the secret Comintern representative in the leadership of the French Communist Party, reveals that Comintern instructions were that the campaign against Doriot should go through three phases: "maneuverer, isoler, liquider." Without access to KGB files, the authors assume—reasonably but wrongly—that only "political," rather than "physical," assassination was intended. Kriegel and Courtois, *Eugen Fried,* p. 228.

10. On Doriot's break with the Communist Party and move to fascism, see Brunet, *Jacques Doriot,* chs. 9–12; Burrin, *La Dérive Fasciste,* chs. 5, 9.

11. k-4,198,206.

12. There are a number of examples in the VENONA decrypts of the use of the KHORKI ("Polecat") codename for the Trotskyists.

13. k-4,206. The codename of the task force appears in vol. 7, app. 3, *n.* 15.

14. k-4,206.

15. Deutscher, *Trotsky,* vol. 3, pp. 348–9.

16. vol. 7, appendix 3, *n.* 15.

17. Deutscher, *Trotsky,* vol. 3, p. 349.

18. Deutscher, *Trotsky,* vol. 3, pp. 125–6.

19. Minute by R. A. Sykes, October 23, 1952, PRO FO 371/100826 NS 1023/29/G.

20. vol. 6, ch. 12.

21. Among the growing number of studies of the Terror, the classic account remains that by Robert Conquest, *The Great Terror: A Reassessment.* There is, however, vigorous controversy over the numbers of the Terror's victims. In 1995 Colonel Grashoven, head of the Russian security ministry rehabilitation team, estimated that in the period 1935–45 18 million were arrested and 7 million shot. Olga Shatunovskaya, a member of Khrushchev's rehabilitation commission, gave the figure of those "repressed" (imprisoned or shot) from 1935 to 1941 as 19.8 million (a statistic also found in the papers of Anastas Mikoyan). Dmitri Volkogonov arrived at a total of 21.5 million (of whom a third were shot) for the period 1929–53. Conquest's own revised estimates are of a similar order of magnitude (Conquest, "Playing Down the Gulag," p. 8). Recent studies based on incomplete official records suggest considerably lower, but still large figures. Stephen Wheatcroft, one of the leading analysts of the official figures, believes it "unlikely that there were more than a million executions between 1921 and 1953. The labor camps and colonies never accounted for more than 2.5 million prisoners." What is striking even in the official records is the enormous rise in executions during the Great Terror: 353,074 in 1937 and 328,618 in 1938, as compared with a total of under 10,000 for the five year period 1932–6 (Wheatcroft, "The Scale and Nature of German and Soviet Repression and Mass Killings, 1930–45"). Controversy over the level of incompleteness in the official records (which do not, of course, include deaths in the camps or the millions who died from famine) will doubtless continue.

22. vol. 6, ch. 12.

23. Andrew and Gordievsky, *KGB,* pp. 149–61.

24. Radzinsky, *Stalin,* p. 371.

25. vol. 6, ch. 12.

26. Costello and Tsarev, *Deadly Illusions,* p. 281.

27. vol. 6, ch. 5, part 1, *n.* 1; vol. 7, app. 3, n. 15.

28. On Wollweber, see Flocken and Scholz, *Ernst Wollweber.*

29. k-4,206.

30. Costello and Tsarev, *Deadly Illusions,* p. 267.

31. See below, chapter 5.

32. Costello and Tsarev, *Deadly Illusions,* chs. 10, 11.

33. vol. 5, ch. 7. All these episodes are conspicuous by their absence from the official SVR hagiography: Samolis (ed.), *Veterany Vneshnei Razvedki Rossii,* pp. 21–4.

34. Castelo's personal file, archive no. 68312, registration no. 66160, once in the files of the FCD Fifteenth Department of the First Chief Directorate was transferred to the Eighth Department of FCD Directorate S. vol. 5, ch. 7.

35. After the defection of Orlov in July 1938, Eitingon succeeded him as resident.

36. vol. 5, ch. 7.

37. vol. 6, ch. 5, part 2.

38. Andrew and Gordievsky, *KGB*, pp. 177–8.

39. vol. 6, ch. 5, part 2.

40. k-4,198.

41. There is, however, one later reference to him being "killed"; vol. 6, ch. 12.

42. Andrew and Gordievsky, *KGB*, pp. 179–80. Volkogonov, *Trotsky*, pp. 359–60. Costello and Tsarev, *Dangerous Illusions*, pp. 282–4.

43. Deutscher, *Trotsky*, vol. 3, pp. 405–10. Costello and Tsarev, *Deadly Illusions*, pp. 319–21.

44. vol. 6, ch. 12.

45. Deutscher, *Trotsky*, vol. 3, pp. 407–8, 419–20. Sylvia Ageloff later described how, at an apparently "accidental meeting," the "handsome and dashing" Mercader, posing as a Belgian journalist, had "swept her off her feet with his charm, gallantry and generosity." Hook, *Out of Step*, p. 242.

46. k-4,198,206.

47. vol. 6, ch. 5, part 2, *n.* 4.

48. vol. 6, ch. 5, part 2, *n.* 4. Albam's file does not record his wife's arrest, so her denunciation of him may have saved her. Acquaintance with Albam was also among the evidence which led to the arrest of the military intelligence officers who had recruited him some years earlier: S. P. Uritsky and Aleksandr Karin. At the time of their arrest in 1937 they were, respectively, head and assistant head of military intelligence. Both were shot.

49. k-9,75.

50. k-9,76.

51. k-9,83. Bukharin was tried and sentenced to death in the last of the great show trials in February 1938.

52. vol. 6, ch. 8, part 1.

53. Orlov, *The Secret History of Stalin's Crime*, pp. 235–7. Though he had only deacon's orders when he gave up the monastic life, Maly was regarded within the NKVD as a former priest.

54. vol. 7, ch. 14, item 1. Cf. Primakov *et al.*, *Ocherki Istorii Rossiyskoi Vneshnei Razvedki*, vol. 3, p. 166.

55. Information from the son of the late Oscar Deutsch, David Deutsch, who recalls meeting Arnold Deutsch at sabbath dinners in Birmingham.

56. vol. 6, ch. 5, part 2.

57. The two most detailed accounts of the assassination of Poretsky, which disagree on some points of detail, are: Poretsky, *Our Own People*, pp. 1–3, chs. 9, 10; Krivitsky, *I was Stalin's Agent*, ch. 8.

58. vol. 7, ch. 9.

59. vol. 7, ch. 9, para. 22.

60. Andrew and Gordievsky, *KGB*, p. 233.

61. Rees, *A Chapter of Accidents*, pp. 110–11.

62. Rees, *Looking for Mr. Nobody*, pp. 87–90.

63. vol. 7, ch. 10, app., item 7.

64. Costello and Tsarev, *Deadly Illusions*, p. 245. Blunt had left Cambridge for the Warburg Institute in London, but returned for meetings of the Apostles and other occasions.

65. The files noted by Mitrokhin suggest that the intelligence supplied by Rees was of slender importance—items such as information on the correspondence of the Czech newspaper editor Hubert Ripka (later a member of the Czechoslovak government-in-exile in London) and the unsurprising news that the former British secret agent Sir Paul Dukes was still in touch with SIS. vol. 7, ch. 10, app., item 7.

66. Orlov, *The Secret History of Stalin's Crime*, pp. 237–8. An alternative version has it that Slutsky was smothered in his office; vol. 7, ch. 9, para. 37. The pretense was maintained that he had died from natural causes in order not to alarm other enemies of the people being recalled from foreign postings to retribution in Moscow.

67. Andrew and Gordievsky, *KGB*, p. 156.

68. vol. 7, ch. 9, para. 37.

69. Primakov *et al.*, *Ocherki Istorii Rossiyskoi Vneshnei Razvedki*, vol. 3, p. 17.

70. Radzinsky, *Stalin*, p. 417.

71. vol. 7, ch. 9, para. 36.

72. Dates of dismissal and arrest from KGB file cited by Costello and Tsarev, *Deadly Illusions*, p. 459, *n.* 63.

73. vol. 7, ch. 9, para. 36.

74. vol. 7, ch. 9, para. 37.

75. Costello and Tsarev, *Deadly Illusions*, p. 207. Mitrokhin's notes mention SAM but do not record the month of his arrival in London.

76. vol. 7, ch. 6, para. 2.

77. Costello and Tsarev, *Deadly Illusions*, pp. 208–10.

78. Foreign Office to Sir Eric Phipps (March 11, 1938), Phipps papers PHPP 2/21, Churchill College Archives Center, Cambridge.

79. West and Tsarev, *The Crown Jewels*, p. 209. Cairncross claimed in his memoirs (*The Enigma Spy*, p. 69) that, after Deutsch's recall to Moscow, he "provided no further data until after the Germans invaded Russia"—one of numerous falsehoods comprehensively demolished by his KGB file which Cairncross must have supposed would never be revealed.

80. Modin, *My Five Cambridge Friends*, pp. 79–80.

81. vol. 7, ch. 10, para. 23.

82. vol. 7, ch. 10, para. 23. West and Tsarev, *The Crown Jewels*, p. 210.

83. vol. 7, ch. 10, para. 15. ADA remained in Paris until Maclean departed with the rest of the British embassy in the summer of 1940, just before the arrival of the victorious German army.

84. vol. 7, ch. 10, paras. 15, 20. Cf. Costello and Tsarev, *Deadly Illusions*, pp. 216–17.

85. Andrew and Gordievsky, *KGB*, pp. 301–2. Costello and Tsarev, *Deadly Illusions*, pp. 239–40. Cf. vol. 7, ch. 10, para. 8.

86. vol. 7, ch. 1, para. 16.

87. Borovik, *The Philby Files*, p. 135.

88. vol. 7, ch. 1, para. 15.

89. Borovik, *The Philby Files*, p. 131.

90. Borovik, *The Philby Files*, pp. 132–3.

91. vol. 7, ch. 10, app., item 8. Cf. Costello and Tsarev, *Deadly Illusions*, pp. 241–2.

92. vol. 7, ch. 10, app., item 9. Cf. Costello and Tsarev, *Deadly Illusions*, p. 242.

93. vol. 7, ch. 10, app., item 4. On Smollett's wartime career, see Andrew and Gordievsky, *KGB*, pp. 334–7.

94. Rees, *Looking for Mr. Nobody*, pp. 273–7.

95. vol. 7, ch. 10, app., item 7.

96. Rees, *A Chapter of Accidents*, p. 191.

97. Borovik, *The Philby Files*, pp. 140–1.

98. vol. 7, ch. 1, para. 16.

99. Borovik, *The Philby Files*, p. 149.

100. Mitrokhin notes that "In 1940, when there was no contact with Burgess, he handed over material for the CPGB through MARY [Litzi Philby] and EDITH [Tudor Hart]"; vol. 7, ch. 10, app., item 4. He appears to have had little success. During a visit to the United States in the summer of 1940 he sought Straight's help in re-establishing contact, telling him, "I've been out of touch with our friends for several months" (Straight, *After Long Silence*, pp. 142–3).

101. Sudoplatos, *Special Tasks*, pp. 58–9. Though sentenced to death, Serebryanksy escaped execution. He was reinstated by the NKVD after the beginning of the Great Patriotic War and given the job of recruiting German POWs. He was re-arrested in 1953 as an alleged co-conspirator with Beria and died in prison in 1956.

102. Sudoplatos, *Special Tasks*, pp. 21–8, 68. Sudoplatov himself narrowly escaped arrest in the winter of 1938–9. His formal appointment as head of the Administration of Special Tasks occurred only in 1941. On the complicated administrative history of "special tasks" during the Second World War, see Sudoplatovs, *Special Tasks*, pp. 126–9.

103. Sudoplatovs, *Special Tasks*, pp. 65–9. Andrew and Gordievsky, *KGB*, pp. 181–3. The somewhat confused account of the assassination in Volkogonov, *Trotsky*, bizarrely suggests "the possibility that the American special services were following, and perhaps in some sense influencing, events" (p. 454). On the gaps in the KGB files on operation UTKA, see Primakov *et al.*, *Ocherki Istorii Rossiyskoi Vneshnei Razvedki*, vol. 3, ch. 8.

104. Levine, *The Mind of an Assassin*, p. 221. Though acknowledging Eitingon's "deserved reputation as a man of many affairs with women," Sudoplatov argues unconvincingly that his "close" relationship with Caridad Mercader did not involve sex, since this would have been a breach of regulations; *Special Tasks*, p. 70, *n.* 2.

105. On the codenames of Caridad and Ramón Mercader, see Primakov *et al.*, *Ocherki Istorii Rossiyskoi Vneshnei Razvedki*, ch. 8. After his arrest, Ramón's codename was changed to GNOM; there are a number of references to him under this codename in the VENONA decrypts.

106. Levine, *The Mind of an Assassin*, chs. 1–4. Sudoplatovs, *Special Tasks*, ch. 4.

107. k-2,369; k-16,518.

108. k-4,206; t-7,12; k-16,518. A sanitized account of Grigulevich's career in the Spanish Civil War appears in the 1997 SVR official history of pre-war intelligence operations. No reference, however, is made

to his role in the first major attempt to assassinate Trotsky, doubtless for fear of tarnishing his heroic image. Though the chapter on Trotsky's assassination refers to FELIPE, it gives no indication that FELIPE and Grigulevich were one and the same. Primakov *et al., Ocherki Istorii Rossiyskoi Vneshnei Razvedki,* chs. 8, 12.

109. t-7,12.

110. See below, chapter 10.

111. k-16,518.

112. k-2,354.

113. Primakov *et al., Ocherki Istorii Rossiyskoi Vneshnei Razvedki,* vol. 3, pp. 100–1.

114. k-2,369. The head of the Mexican secret police, General Leandro Sánchez Salazar, later reached the same conclusion. Though able to identify Grigulevich only as FELIPE (his codename within the assault group), Sánchez Salazar described him as "the real instigator of the attack." Sánchez Salazar believed the multilingual Grigulevich to be "a French Jew," partly as a result of discovering some of his underwear, which had been purchased in Paris on the Boulevard Saint Michel. Sánchez Salazar, *Murder in Mexico,* pp. 48–9.

115. Sánchez Salazar, *Murder in Mexico,* p. 45.

116. k-2,369.

117. Sudoplatovs, *Special Tasks,* p. 74. Cf. Deutscher, *Trotsky,* vol. 3, p. 488.

118. Deutscher, *Trotsky,* vol. 3, pp. 487–9.

119. Primakov *et al., Ocherki Istorii Rossiyskoi Vneshnei Razvedki,* vol. 3, p. 101.

120. Released on bail, Siqueiros escaped from Mexico with the help of the Chilean Communist poet Pablo Neruda. Sánchez Salazar, *Murder in Mexico,* pp. 211–14.

121. k-2,369,354; vol. 6, ch. 5, part 1.

122. Andrew and Gordievsky, *KGB,* pp. 183–5.

123. Levine, *The Mind of an Assassin,* chs. 5–9; Deutscher, *Trotsky,* vol. 3, ch. 5.

124. Note by Enrique Castro Delgado, the Spanish Communist Party representative at Comintern headquarters, on a conversation with Caridad Mercader, in Levine, *The Mind of an Assassin,* pp. 216–22.

125. See below, chs. 22, 23.

Chapter Six   War

1. k-27,app.

2. Primakov *et al., Ocherki Istorii Rossiyskoi Vneshnei Razvedki,* vol. 3, p. 247.

3. The visiting lecturers included Academicians I. M. Maisky, A. M. Deborin and A. A. Guber, and ambassadors A. A. Troyanovsky, B. Ye. Shteyn and Shenburg. k-27,appendix.

4. Primakov *et al., Ocherki Istorii Rossiyskoi Vneshnei Razvedki,* vol. 3, p. 248.

5. On June 5, 1943 SHON was reorganized as the Intelligence School (RASH) of the NKVD First (Foreign Intelligence) Directorate, and the training course extended to two years. By the end of the war about 200 foreign intelligence officers had graduated from it (k-27,appendix). During the Cold War it was known successively as the Higher Intelligence School (codenamed School no. 101), the Red Banner Institute and the Andropov Institute. In October 1994 it became the Foreign Intelligence Academy of the Russian Federation (Primakov *et al., Ocherki Istorii Rossiyskoi Vneshnei Razvedki,* vol. 3, ch. 23).

6. Slutsky, Pasov and Shpigelglas had been liquidated during 1938. Beria's acolyte, Vladimir Georgyevich Dekanozov, who briefly succeeded Shpigelglas, became Deputy Foreign Commissar in May 1939.

7. Fitin's career is summarized in Samolis (ed.), *Veterany Vneshnei Razvedki Rossii,* pp. 153–5, which acknowledges that he owed his promotion to "the acute shortage of intelligence personnel."

8. vol. 7, ch. 2, para. 1. A somewhat inaccurate hagiography of Gorsky's career (which, *inter alia,* attributes intelligence supplied by Cairncross to Maclean) appears in Samolis (ed.), *Veterany Vneshnei Razvedki Rossii,* pp. 31–2. There is no mention of Gorsky's disgrace in 1953 (Andrew and Gordievsky, *KGB,* p. 304). The SVR historians, however, indirectly give some indication of the extent of the disgrace when they acknowledge that they have been unable to establish the date of Gorsky's death.

9. Interview with Blunt cited in Cecil, *A Divided Life,* p. 66.

10. Bentley, *Out of Bondage,* pp. 173–7.

11. See above, chapter 5.

12. Borovik, *The Philby File,* pp. 153–4, 166–7. On SOE see Foot, *SOE.*

13. Andrew and Gordievsky, *KGB,* pp. 303–12. Though the identity of ELLI appears not to have been established by British intelligence for many years after the Second World War, it was in fact one of a num-

ber of somewhat transparent Soviet codenames of the period. In Russian ELLI means "Ls," an appropriate codename for Leo Long, whose initials were LL.

14. vol. 7, ch. 9, para. 22. The defector was Walter Krivitsky, codenamed GROLL. On King's arrest, see Andrew, *Secret Service*, pp. 606–7.

15. Andrew and Gordievsky, *KGB*, p. 272.

16. West and Tsarev, *The Crown Jewels*, pp. 214–17; Michael Smith, "The Humble Scot who Rose to the Top—But Then Chose Treachery," *Daily Telegraph* (January 12, 1992). Cairncross's KGB file corroborates the recollection of a former head of the Centre's British desk that he provided "tons of documents" (Andrew and Gordievsky, *KGB*, p. 272). Confident that his file would never see the light of day, Cairncross denied that he provided anything of significance to the London residency until after the Soviet Union entered the war. He admitted, however, that he had "no difficulty in having access to the secret papers in Hankey's office" (Cairncross, *The Enigma Spy*, pp. 90–1). When new War Cabinet regulations in June 1941 limited the circulation of diplomatic telegrams to Hankey, Cairncross as well as Hankey complained personally to the Foreign Office. The restrictions were quickly lifted. (G. L. Clutton (Foreign Office) to Cairncross (June 6, 1941); Sir Alexander Cadogan to Hankey (June 17, 1941). Hankey Papers, Churchill College Archives Center, Cambridge, HNKY 4/33.)

17. vol. 7, ch. 2, para. 7.

18. Samolis (ed.), *Veterany Vneshnei Razvedki Rossii*, pp. 63–5. Costello and Tsarev, *Deadly Illusions*, pp. 78–81. Andrew and Gordievsky, *KGB*, pp. 266. (Costello and Tsarev wrongly compute the period when the Center was out of touch with Harnack as fifteen rather than twenty-eight months.)

19. Samolis (ed.), *Veterany Vneshnei Razvedki Rossii*, p. 64; Costello and Tsarev, *Deadly Illusions*, pp. 82–5; Andrew and Gordievsky, *KGB*, pp. 266–7; Tarrant, *The Red Orchestra*, chs. 17–19.

20. Andrew and Gordievsky, *KGB*, p. 286.

21. Samolis (ed.), *Veterany Vneshnei Razvedki Rossii*, p. 64.

22. Samolis (ed.), *Veterany Vneshnei Razvedki Rossii*, p. 154. Some of the intelligence warnings of the preparations for BARBAROSSA are printed as appendices to Primakov *et al.*, *Ocherki Istorii Rossiyskoi Vneshnei Razvedki*, vol. 3.

23. The report and Stalin's comment on it were published in *Izvestia of the Central Committee of the CPSU* (April 1990). Cf. Costello and Tsarev, *Deadly Illusions*, p. 86.

24. Andrew and Gordievsky, *KGB*, pp. 275, 282. Prange *et al.*, *Target Tokyo*, chs. 42–7.

25. JIC(41)218(Final), CAB 81/102, PRO. On Churchill's warnings to Stalin, see Gorodetsky, *Stafford Cripps' Mission to Moscow 1940–42*, chs. 2–4. Exactly which JIC reports reached Stalin, and in what form, cannot be determined at present. But, given both the volume of highly classified intelligence from London and the numerous JIC assessments which contradicted Churchill's belief that Hitler was planning an invasion of Russia, Stalin must surely have been aware of the JIC view. The files noted by Mitrokhin show that Stalin had access to at least some of the telegrams exchanged between the Foreign Office and the British ambassador in Moscow, Sir Stafford Cripps. vol. 7, ch. 2, para. 10.

26. Andrew and Gordievsky, *KGB*, p. 274.

27. vol. 7, ch. 2, para. 11.

28. Whaley, *Codeword Barbarossa*, pp. 223–4, 241–3. An important new study by Gabriel Gorodetsky, *Grand Delusion: Stalin and the German Invasion of Russia*, was published just as this volume was going to press. It performs a valuable service by demolishing the main conspiracy theories (in particular those surrounding Hess's flight to Britain and Stalin's alleged preparations for an attack on Germany) which have confused some recent interpretations of the background of operation BARBAROSSA. Though there are some gaps in his analysis of Soviet intelligence, Professor Gorodetsky also adds much interesting detail from newly accessible Russian archives. His portrait of Stalin as "rational and level-headed" is, however, difficult to reconcile with, *inter alia*, Stalin's obsessive pursuit of Trotsky and his foreign supporters. *Grand Delusion* is, none the less, a major work.

29. Vaksberg, *The Prosecutor and the Prey*, p. 220.

30. One of the files noted by Mitrokhin records that Zarubin had been appointed deputy director of INO in 1937 (vol. 6, ch. 5, part 2). Over the next two years, three successive heads of INO were liquidated, and Zarubin only just escaped a similar fate. It is not clear precisely what position he held in the Center at the beginning of 1941.

31. vol. 6, ch. 5, part 2. On December 18, 1940 Hitler had ordered the completion of preparations for BARBAROSSA by May 15, 1941.

32. vol. 6, ch. 5, part 2.

33. Samolis (ed.), *Veterany Vneshnei Razvedki Rossii*, p. 154.

34. See below, chapter 7.

35. Interview with Shebarshin, *Daily Telegraph* (December 1, 1992). Even in the year before the abortive coup of August 1991, both the public rhetoric and inner convictions of the KGB leadership were influenced by crude anti-Western conspiracy theories. Andrew and Gordievsky (eds.), *Instructions from the Center*, pp. 218–22. Andrew and Gordievsky (eds.), *More Instructions from the Center*, pp. 125–8.

36. Andrew and Gordievsky, *KGB*, pp. 249–50, 281–3. Kahn, "Soviet Comint in the Cold War," pp. 11–13. PURPLE had been introduced in 1939. Soviet codebreakers had also broken the earlier and less complex Japanese RED cipher. On the breaking of PURPLE by US military cryptanalysts, see Kahn, "Pearl Harbor and the Inadequacy of Cryptanalysis." Mitrokhin did not have access to the archives of the KGB Sixteenth Directorate, which—together with those of the GRU—contain the main SIGINT files of the Great Patriotic War.

37. Erickson, *The Road to Stalingrad*, p. 329; Overy, *Russia's War*, p. 118.

38. Andrew and Gordievsky, *KGB*, p. 282.

39. On recruitment to Bletchley Park, see Hinsley and Stripp (eds.), *Codebreakers;* Andrew, "F. H. Hinsley and the Cambridge Moles"; Smith, *Station X.*

40. See below, pp. 156, 159. Andrew and Gordievsky, *KGB*, pp. 312–13.

41. Sudoplatovs, *Special Tasks*, p. 130. After the German invasion, Sudoplatov's Directorate for Special Tasks and Guerrilla Warfare (officially entitled Diversionary Intelligence), the successor of the pre-war Administration for Special Tasks, was officially removed from the NKVD First (Foreign Intelligence) Directorate as a new Fourth Directorate. Though the two directorates remained formally independent until April 1943, there was a constant interchange of personnel between them. Murphy, Kondrashev and Bailey, *Battleground Berlin*, pp. 28–9.

42. The official Soviet guide to the Museum of Partisan Glory is Balatsky, *Museum in the Catacombs.* At the time of writing, the Museum is still open daily with guided tours in Russian and Ukrainian catacombs.

43. Samolis (ed.), *Veterany Vneshnei Razvedki Rossii*, p. 101.

44. For details of the reconstruction, see Balatsky, *Museum in the Catacombs.*

45. vol. 5, sec. 13.

46. Samolis (ed.), *Veterany Vneshnei Razvedki Rossii*, p. 102–3. This account of Molodtsov's capture and execution is neither confirmed nor contradicted by Mitrokhin's notes on the Odessa file.

47. vol. 5, sec. 13.

48. vol. 5, sec. 13.

49. vol. 6, ch. 5, part 1.

50. Dear and Foot (eds.), *The Oxford Companion to the Second World War*, pp. 1240–1.

51. Dear and Foot (eds.), *The Oxford Companion to the Second World War*, p. 1240. Probably the best study of the eastern front, by Professor Richard Overy, concludes that, ". . . Where the NKVD did intervene the effect was to wound the war effort, not to invigorate it." One part of the complex explanation for increasing success of the Red Army was the demotion, under the pressure of war, of the political apparatchiks at the front in the autumn of 1942 and the new freedom given to officers to take decisions without being constantly checked for political correctness. Overy, *Russia's War*, pp. 329–30.

52. There was no legal residency in Argentina. At the outbreak of war no Latin American state had diplomatic relations with the Soviet Union. In October 1942 Cuba established diplomatic relations with the USSR. By the beginning of 1945 another eight Latin American republics had followed suit. Argentina did not establish diplomatic relations with the Soviet Union until 1946.

53. vol. 6, ch. 5, part 1. Mitrokhin's notes, which identify ARTUR as Grigulevich, provide the solution to a major unsolved problem in the VENONA decrypts. Though the decrypts contain frequent references to ARTUR, his identity was never discovered by NSA or the FBI (Benson, *VENONA Historical Monograph #5*, p. 5).

54. Humphreys, *Latin America and the Second World War*, vol. 1, pp. 154–6.

55. Macdonald, "The Politics of Intervention"; Newton, "Disorderly Succession."

56. Wartime Soviet agents with access to US policy documents on Argentina included Laurence Duggan, a Latin American expert in the State Department, and Maurice Halperin, chief of the Latin American division in the OSS R&A branch (Peake, "OSS and the Venona Decrypts," pp. 22, 25–6).

57. k-16,477.

58. k-13,370.

59. vol. 6, ch. 5, part 1; k-16,477.

60. Argentina did not declare war on Germany until March 1945.

61. Grigulevich's couriers to New York included the Chilean Communist Eduardo Pecchio and a member of the Latin American section of the Columbian Broadcasting Service, Ricardo Setaro (GONETS). VENONA decrypt, 2nd release, p. 26; 3rd release, part 2, p. 101.

62. VENONA decrypts, 5th release, pp. 11–12, 14–17, 20–1, 24–6, 31–2.

63. k-16,477.

64. See below, chapter 22.

65. The Center instructed the Montevideo residency on February 4, 1956:

> Do not re-establish contact [with Verzhbitksy]. Arrangements for his entry to the USSR must be made under MFA auspices in the usual way; do not get involved in the process and make no promises, including financial ones. Make a one-time payment of 1,500 pesos and we will then make no further monetary payments.
>
> (k-16,477)

66. k-16,477.

67. Andrew and Gordievsky, *KGB*, pp. 259–64.

68. Andrew and Gordievsky, *KGB*, pp. 259–64; Overy, *Russia's War*, pp. 232–3.

69. Volkogonov, *Stalin*, pp. 444–7.

70. k-4,204. The total number of sources was substantially greater than those accorded agent status by the Center. According to KGB files, the nationality of the agents was: 55 Germans; 14 French; 5 Belgians; 13 Austrians, Czechs and Hungarians; 6 Russians; and 16 others. The principal leaders, according to the same files, were: Belgian section: Leopold Trepper; German section: Harro Schulze-Boysen; French section (except Lyon): Henry Robinson; Lyon: Isidor Springer; Dutch section: Anton Winterinck; Swiss section: Sandor Rado.

71. Central Intelligence Agency, *The Rote Kapelle;* Milligan, "Spies, Ciphers and 'Zitadelle' "; Andrew and Gordievsky, *KGB*, pp. 285–9.

72. Glantz, *Soviet Military Intelligence in War;* Jukes, "The Soviets and 'Ultra' "; Andrew and Gordievsky, *KGB*, p. 289.

73. Beevor, *Stalingrad*, pp. 166–75, 201.

74. Under lend-lease agreements with Britain and the United States in 1941, the Soviet Union was supplied with 35,000 radio stations, 380,000 field telephones and 956,000 miles of telephone cable. Overy, *Russia's War*, pp. 193–4.

75. Andrew and Gordievsky, *KGB*, pp. 315–20; Milligan, "Spies, Ciphers and 'Zitadelle.' "

76. Kahn, "Soviet Comint in the Cold War," p. 14.

Chapter Seven   The Grand Alliance

1. Andrew and Gordievsky, *KGB*, pp. 241–2. At least in the early 1930s, the Fourth Department was probably primarily interested in the United States as a base from which to collect intelligence on Germany and Japan. Mitrokhin did not have access to Fourth Department files on its American agents and did not note references to these agents in KGB files. The case against Hiss, which has been strong but controversial ever since his conviction for perjury in 1951, is now overwhelming as a result of new evidence revealed during the 1990s from the VENONA decrypts, KGB files made available to Weinstein and Vassiliev which refer to his work for military intelligence, and Hungarian interrogation records of Hiss's fellow agent Noel Field. These sources also do much to vindicate the credibility of Hiss's principal public accuser, the former Fourth Department courier Whittaker Chambers. The best accounts of the Hiss case are the 1997 updated edition of Weinstein, *Perjury*, and Weinstein and Vassiliev, *The Haunted Wood*, chs. 2, 12.

2. Wadleigh, "Why I Spied for the Communists," part 7, *New York Post* (July 19, 1949).

3. vol. 6, ch. 5, part 2; vol. 6, ch. 8, part 1, *n.* 2.

4. Massing, *This Deception*, p. 155. The fact that Massing defected from the NKVD in 1938 makes her tribute to Bazarov all the more impressive.

5. vol. 6, ch. 5, part 2.

6. vol. 6, ch. 5, part 2.

7. The details in Mitrokhin's notes on "19" (date of birth, work in the Latin American division of the State Department, later transfer to the UN Relief and Rehabilitation Administration) clearly identify him as Duggan; vol. 6, ch. 5, part 2. By 1943, at the latest, however, Duggan's codename had been changed to FRENK (or FRANK); *VENONA*, 2nd release, pp. 278–9.

8. Weinstein, *Perjury*, pp. 182–3.

9. vol. 6, ch. 5, part 2.

10. See above, p. 84.

11. Straight, *After Long Silence*, pp. 110, 122–3, 129–36; Newton, *The Butcher's Embrace*, pp. 20–2.

12. Andrew and Gordievsky, *KGB*, pp. 240–3, 290. On Whittaker Chambers, see his memoir, *Witness*, and the biography by Sam Tanenhaus, *Whittaker Chambers*.

13. vol. 6, ch. 5, part 2.

14. Others recalled from the United States to be interrogated and liquidated in Moscow included the illegal CHARLIE, whose file was destroyed and whose identity is now unknown. Primakov *et al.*, *Ocherki Istorii Rossiyskoi Vneshnei Razvedki*, vol. 3, pp. 180–1.

15. vol. 6, ch. 5, part 2. Significantly, material on Morozov's denunciation of two successive residents was among that excluded from the documents selected by the SVR for the recent study of Soviet espionage in the United States in the Stalin era by Weinstein and Vassiliev, *The Haunted Wood*. While obliged to acknowledge the purge of many loyal foreign intelligence officers, the SVR is generally reluctant to reveal cases where they were denounced by their own comrades. Despite such examples of SVR censorship, for which Weinstein and Vassiliev are not, of course, responsible, *The Haunted Wood* is a very valuable contribution to the history of Soviet intelligence operations.

16. It is unclear from Mitrokhin's notes whether or not Akhmerov was given charge of an independent illegal residency *before* Bazarov's recall. However, Hede Massing's memoirs strongly suggest that both Bazarov and Akhmerov were members of the same illegal residency until at least 1937. Massing, *This Deception*, pp. 187–8, 191.

17. vol. 6, ch. 3, part 1. Significantly, the list of names noted by Mitrokhin did not include Samuel Dickstein, a Democratic congressman from Manhattan (codenamed CROOK), who had volunteered his services to the NKVD in 1937 but demanded a high price for his intelligence. Over the next two years, the NKVD oscillated between pride at having an agent in Congress and suspicion that Dickstein was recycling publicly available information. In June 1939 Ovakimyan denounced him in a message to the Center as "a complete racketeer and blackmailer." Weinstein and Vassiliev, *The Haunted Wood*, ch. 7.

18. On Duggan's codenames, see above, *n.* 7.

19. MORIS is described in Mitrokhin's note as an "archivist" at the Justice Department (vol. 6, ch. 3, part 1); this may, however, mean simply that he had access to department files and archives.

20. On the careers of Morros (who became an FBI double agent early in the Cold War), Martha Dodd Stern and William E. Dodd, Jr. (both of whom failed to live up to the Centre's high early expectations), see Weinstein and Vassiliev, *The Haunted Wood*, chs. 3, 6.

21. KHOSYAIN is identified as Buchman in vol. 6, ch. 5, part 2, but the spelling of his name ("Bukman" in Cyrillic transliteration) is uncertain.

22. vol. 6, ch. 5, part 2.

23. Straight, *After Long Silence*, pp. 143–4.

24. vol. 6, ch. 5, part 2; vol. 7, ch. 10, app. 6.

25. vol. 6, ch. 5, part 2. The claim in an SVR official history that Akhmerov was recalled in mid-1939 is difficult to reconcile with Straight's account of a meeting with him in late October. Primakov *et al.*, *Ocherki Istorii Rossiyskoi Vneshnei Razvedki*, vol. 3, ch. 15.

26. Primakov *et al.*, *Ocherki Istorii Rossiyskoi Vneshnei Razvedki*, vol. 3, ch. 15. On Ovakimyan's role in preparations for Trotsky's assassination, see Andrew and Gordievsky, *KGB*, pp. 183–4. The Centre's obsession with the pursuit of Trotskyists in the United States continued even after Trotsky's assassination.

27. Samolis (ed.), *Veterany Vneshnei Razvedki Rossii*, pp. 135–7. Primakov *et al.*, *Ocherki Istorii Rossiyskoi Vneshnei Razvedki*, vol. 3, pp. 177–8. There were two New York chemical institutes; the SVR histories do not make clear which is referred to.

28. vol. 6, ch. 6.

29. vol. 6, ch. 5, part 2. Samolis (ed.), *Veterany Vneshnei Razvedki Rossii*, pp. 169–71; Primakov *et al.*, *Ocherki Istorii Rossiyskoi Vneshnei Razvedki*, vol. 3, p. 177. Weinstein and Vassiliev, *The Haunted Wood*, p. 173.

30. vol. 6, ch. 3, part 1. The VENONA decrypts of NKVD wartime telegrams from the United States include the codenames of approximately 200 agents (about half of whom remain unidentified). Since these telegrams represent only a fraction of the wartime communications between the Center and its American residencies, the total NKVD network must have been substantially larger. Mitrokhin's notes give no statistics for the size of the network after 1941. The occupational breakdown for the network in April 1941 is highly incomplete. Apart from the forty-nine "engineers," Mitrokhin gives the occupations of only thirty-six others, of whom twenty-two were journalists. Many of the agents were immigrants and refugees. In 1940–1, sixty-six Baltic recruits emigrated to the United States (vol. 6, ch. 3, part 1).

31. Weinstein and Vassiliev, *The Haunted Wood*, p. 173.

32. Primakov *et al.*, *Ocherki Istorii Rossiyskoi Vneshnei Razvedki*, vol. 3, p. 178.

33. Andrew and Gordievsky, *KGB*, pp. 290–1. Weinstein, *Perjury*, pp. 292–3. KGB files cited by Weinstein and Vassiliev (*The Haunted Wood*, pp. 106, 159, 161–2) identify Lauchlin Currie as the agent PAGE referred to in a number of the VENONA decrypts. Mitrokhin's notes do not mention Currie.

34. vol. 6, ch. 5, part 2. Samolis (ed.), *Veterany Vneshnei Razvedki Rossii*, p. 53.

35. Samolis (ed.), *Veterany Vneshnei Razvedki Rossii*, pp. 50–3.

36. In 1929 Zarubina (then Gorskaya) had been used to seduce the pro-Trotskyist illegal Blyumkin and lure him back to execution in Moscow.

37. vol. 6, ch. 5, part 2.

38. vol. 6, ch. 12.

39. vol. 6, ch. 12. Klehr, Haynes and Firsov, *The Secret World of American Communism*, ch. 7.

40. A number of VENONA decrypts refer to Lee's work as a Soviet agent. Other important agents in OSS identified by VENONA include Maurice Halperin (HARE), J. Julius Joseph (CAUTIOUS) and Donald Niven Wheeler (IZRA). (For examples, see *VENONA*, 2nd release, pp. 118, 178–9; 3rd release, part 2, p. 196.) Soviet agents at OSS headquarters were probably well into double figures. Communists (not all of them agents) have been identified in the Russian, Spanish, Balkan, Hungarian and Latin American sections of OSS's R&A division, and in its operational German, Japanese, Korean, Italian, Spanish, Hungarian and Indonesian divisions. Peake, "OSS and the Venona Decrypts"; Andrew and Gordievsky, *KGB*, pp. 294–5; Klehr, Haynes and Firsov, *The Secret World of American Communism*, pp. 276–8.

41. Andrew and Gordievsky, *KGB*, pp. 450–1.

42. Klehr, Haynes and Firsov, *The Secret World of American Communism*, pp. 234–6.

43. vol. 6, ch. 12.

44. *VENONA*, 2nd release, part 2, p. 58.

45. Andrew and Gordievsky, *KGB*, p. 451.

46. vol. 6, ch. 5, part 2.

47. vol. 6, ch. 5, part 2.

48. Akhmerov told the Center in April 1944, "For your information: I have never met RULEVOY [Browder]." *VENONA*, 3rd release, part 1, pp. 26–8.

49. vol. 6, ch. 5, part 2.

50. Straight, *After Long Silence*, pp. 167–8.

51. vol. 6, ch. 5, part 2. Fearful that State Department security officers had discovered his earlier connection with Soviet intelligence, Duggan was less forthcoming during the war than he had been earlier. In June 1944 he left the State Department to join the newly founded United Nations Relief and Rehabilitation Administration as diplomatic adviser. Weinstein and Vassiliev, *The Haunted Wood*, pp. 16–19.

52. vol. 6, ch. 5, part 2.

53. We are indebted for information on Henry Wallace's plans for Duggan and White to Professor Harvey Klehr.

54. vol. 6, ch. 5, part 2.

55. Bentley, *Out of Bondage*, pp. 103–4, 115.

56. When Moscow changed control methods later in the War, the New York residency reported to the Center: "In ALBERT [Akhmerov]'s opinion our workers [Soviet intelligence officers] would hardly manage to work with the same success under the FELLOWCOUNTRYMAN [Communist Party] flag. We may possibly set up direct liaison with [members of the Silvermaster group], but it is doubtful whether we could secure from them the same results as ROBERT [Silvermaster], who, constantly dealing with them, has many advantages over us." The residency also reported that Silvermaster "did not believe in our orthodox methods." VENONA decrypts, 3rd release, part 3, p. 2.

57. Bentley, *Out of Bondage*, pp. 68–9, chs. 7, 8. Codenames from vol. 6, ch. 5, part 2 and VENONA decrypts. The sanitized SVR account of Golos's career makes no reference to his sexual indiscretion. "Russian [intelligence] operatives," it concludes, "will always honor and take pride in him." Primakov *et al.*, *Ocherki Istorii Rossiyskoy Vneshnei Razvedki*, vol. 3, ch. 16.

58. vol. 6, ch. 12. The VENONA decrypts indicate that Belfrage was also codenamed UCN/9.

59. On BSC, see Andrew, *For the President's Eyes Only*, pp. 96, 102–3, 127–30.

60. vol. 6, ch. 12. The KGB file noted by Mitrokhin confirms the main features of the account, contested by Belfrage during his lifetime, in Bentley, *Out of Bondage*, pp. 139–40—notably his espionage links with Golos and with V. J. Jerome, a close associate of Browder.

61. vol. 6, ch. 5, part 2.

62. On the woeful limitations of the intelligence on the Soviet Union available to Roosevelt early in the war, see Andrew, *For the President's Eyes Only*, pp. 132–3.

63. Andrew and Gordievsky, *KGB*, pp. 340–1; Zubok and Pleshakov, *Inside the Kremlin's Cold War*, p. 23.

64. vol. 6, ch. 12. Hopkins had been personally briefed by Hoover on Zarubin's visit to Nelson (Benson and Warner (eds.), *VENONA*, document 9). Hoover would doubtless have been outraged had he known that Hopkins had informed the Soviet embassy.

65. The source of the information on the talks between Roosevelt and Churchill was codenamed "19"— an example of the Centre's confusing habit of sometimes recycling the same codename for different people. Laurence Duggan had formerly been codenamed "19," but by now had the codename FRANK; he cannot, in any case, have provided this information. A detailed, meticulous and persuasive study by Eduard Mark concludes that it is "probable virtually to the point of certainty that Hopkins was *19*." Mark, "Venona's Source 19 and the 'Trident' Conference of 1943."

66. Andrew, "Anglo-American-Soviet Intelligence Relations," pp. 125–6. Crozier, *Free Agent*, pp. 1–2.

67. Hopkin's efforts to avoid US–Soviet friction also included securing the removal of officials he judged to be anti-Soviet: among them the US ambassador in Moscow, Laurence A. Steinhardt; the military attaché, Major Ivan D. Yeaton; and Loy W. Henderson, head of the Soviet desk in the State Department. When Soviet foreign minister Molotov visited Washington in May 1942, Hopkins took him aside and told him what to say to persuade Roosevelt of the need for an early second front in order to contradict contrary advice from the American military. Andrew and Gordievsky, *KGB*, pp. 297–300, 341; Mark, "Venona's Source 19 and the 'Trident' Conference of 1943," p. 20.

68. Bohlen, *Witness to History 1919–1969*, p. 148.

69. Dilks (ed.), *The Diaries of Sir Alexander Cadogan, OM, 1938–1945*, p. 582.

70. Cited by Kissinger, *Diplomacy*, p. 412. On relations between Churchill and Roosevelt at Tehran, see also Kimball, *Forged in War*, pp. 237–55.

71. Andrew and Gordievsky, *KGB*, p. 342.

72. The use made by Stalin of intelligence from Britain during the Tehran Conference remains more problematic, given the Centre's unwarranted suspicion at that time of its main British sources.

73. vol. 6, ch. 5, part 2.

74. vol. 7, ch. 2, para. 2; appendix 3, *n*. 21.

75. vol. 7, ch. 2, para. 5.

76. vol. 7, ch. 10, para. 15.

77. Philby, *My Silent War*, pp. 49–50, 67–8.

78. vol. 7, ch. 10, para. 5.

79. Borovik, *The Philby Files*, pp. 196–7. On SIS's lack of a Moscow station in the 1930s, see Andrew, *Secret Service*, p. 573.

80. The text of the report was first published, along with other KGB documents on atomic espionage, in *Voprossi Istorii Estestvoznania i Tekhniki* (1992), no. 3. This issue was withdrawn shortly after publication, but the documents are reprinted in Sudoplatovs, *Special Tasks*, appendix 2. Cf. Costello and Tsarev, *Deadly Illusions*, p. 218.

81. According to the minutes of the Scientific Advisory Committee, Cairncross briefly served as its joint secretary; SAC (DP)(41), CAB 90/8, PRO. In his memorably mendacious memoirs, Cairncross denied that he ever held this post. Even if he is correct in this instance (and Whitehall committee secretaries were, almost invariably, capable of ensuring that their names were correctly recorded), this would not have affected his access to SAC minutes since, by his own admission, he "had no difficulty in having access to the secret papers in Hankey's office." Cairncross, *The Enigma Spy*, pp. 9–10, 88–92.

82. The revelation that Cairncross, thanks to his access to Scientific Advisory Committee papers, was the first to warn the Center of the plan to construct the atomic bomb first appeared in 1990 in Andrew and Gordievsky, *KGB*, p. 321. Probably because Cairncross was then still alive, a series of KGB/SVR-sponsored publications suggested that the report of the Scientific Advisory Committee had come instead from Maclean. (See, e.g., Costello and Tsarev, *Deadly Illusions*, p. 218; Samolis (ed.), *Veterany Vneshnei Razvedki Rossii*, pp. 31, 60.) Following confirmation by Yuri Modin, who was given responsibility for Cairncross's file in 1944 and became his controller in 1947, that the Scientific Advisory Committee report came from Cairncross, the SVR changed its tune. In 1998 it released documents from Cairncross's file proving that he supplied the report and giving further details of his role as the first of the atom spies. West and Tsarev, *The Crown Jewels*, pp. 228–9, 234; Michael Smith,

"The Humble Scot Who Rose to the Top—But Then Chose Treachery," *Daily Telegraph* (January 12, 1998).

83. The text of Beria's report of March 1942, first published in *Voprossi Istorii Estestvoznania i Tekhniki,* 1992, no. 3, is reprinted in Sudoplatovs, *Special Tasks,* appendix 2, pp. 439–41. On the background see Holloway, *Stalin and the Bomb,* pp. 82–4.

84. Holloway, *Stalin and the Bomb,* pp. 84–9.

85. vol. 6, ch. 6. Roosevelt and Churchill agreed verbally on unrestricted exchange of information on the atomic project, but did not commit the agreement to writing. The Americans in charge of the MANHAT-TAN project afterwards claimed to be ignorant of the agreement. Not till the Quebec agreement of August 1943 was "full and effective collaboration" between Britain and the United States agreed in writing.

86. vol. 6, ch. 6.

87. Holloway, *Stalin and the Bomb,* p. 85.

88. Andrew and Gordievsky, *KGB,* pp. 321–2.

89. West and Tsarev, *Crown Jewels,* pp. 231–3.

90. Fuchs preferred meeting in London Underground stations. He later complained to Markus Wolf that Kremer's habit of constantly looking over his shoulder to see if he was being followed "seemed to attract more attention to us than simply getting on with it." Andrew and Gordievsky, *KGB,* pp. 322–4; Wolf, *Man without a Face,* p. 230. The best biography of Fuchs is Williams, *Klaus Fuchs, Atom Spy.*

91. The references to FIR in Mitrokhin's notes, including her involvement with Fuchs, identify her as SONIA (vol. 7, ch. 14, item 17). She is not to be confused with a British NKGB agent also codenamed FIR, an official of the Economic Commission for Asia and the Far East (ECAFE) recruited in China in 1943 (k-24,126).

92. Werner, *Sonya's Report,* pp. 250–3; Wolf, *Man without a Face,* p. 230.

93. Wolf, *Man without a Face,* p. 229.

94. vol. 7, ch. 14, item 17. It is just possible, though not probable, that an even stronger candidate for either of these titles is identified in files not seen by Mitrokhin. Like most, if not all, British agents recruited in the 1930s who were still active after the Second World War, Norwood had more than one codename in the course of her career. Though Mitrokhin's notes refer to her only as HOLA, her codename in 1945, shortly after she returned from GRU to NKGB control, was RITA. Extracts from KGB files made available by the SVR to Weinstein and Vassiliev, though not mentioning Norwood by name, identify RITA as an employee of the Non-Ferrous Metals [Research] Association (Weinstein and Vassiliev, *The Haunted Wood,* p. 194; cf. the reference to RITA in VENONA decrypts, 5th release, part 2, p. 247.)

95. vol. 7, ch. 14, item 17.

96. vol. 7, ch. 14, item 17.

97. Samolis (ed.), *Veterany Vneshnei Razvedki Rossii,* pp. 59–61. Cf. vol. 6, ch. 8, part 1.

98. vol. 6, ch. 6. In March 1943 Kurchatov sent similar reports to M. G. Pervukhin, Deputy Prime Minister and commissar of the chemical industry. The text, first published in *Voprossi Istorii Estestvoznania i Tekhniki* (1992), no. 3, is reprinted in translation in Sudoplatovs, *Special Tasks,* appendix 2, pp. 446–53.

99. vol. 6, ch. 6. Mitrokhin's notes do not reveal the identity of MAR.

100. VENONA decrypts, 1st release, pp. 1–4.

101. vol. 6, ch. 6. Mitrokhin's note does not identify the recipient of Kurchatov's top secret report. Given its importance, however, it was probably addressed, like his report of March 7 (also quoted in vol. 6, ch. 6), to Beria. Cf. Kurchatov's report to Pervukhin of July 3, 1943 in Sudoplatovs, *Special Tasks,* appendix 2, pp. 454–6.

102. Holloway, *Stalin and the Bomb,* p. 104.

103. vol. 6, ch. 6.

104. VENONA decrypts, 1st release, p. 5. Cf. Holloway, *Stalin and the Bomb,* p. 103.

105. Holloway, *Stalin and the Bomb,* p. 103.

106. There is some indication that later in 1944 FOGEL/PERS was providing intelligence from the Oak Ridge, Tennessee, laboratory of the MANHATTAN project. VENONA decrypts, 1st release, pp. 10, 29. Weinstein and Vassiliev, *The Haunted Wood,* pp. 190–1; Albright and Kunstel, *Bombshell,* p. 319.

107. Suggestions to the contrary derive chiefly from two sources: a fabricated version of the career of PERS (renamed PERSEUS), apparently devised by the SVR for purposes of mystification, perhaps to protect Theodore Hall (cf. Albright and Kunstel, *Bombshell,* p. 271; Weinstein and Vassiliev, *The Haunted Wood,* pp. 190–1*n*.); and the fallible memory of Pavel Sudoplatov, far less reliable on atomic espionage than on the "special actions" to which he devoted most of his career (cf. Holloway, "Sources for *Stalin and the*

Bomb"). The New York residency was dismayed to learn early in 1945 that FOGEL/PERS had declined an offer of employment as a construction engineer at Los Alamos, probably owing to a mixture of family pressures and fear of exposure. Weinstein and Vassiliev, *The Haunted Wood,* p. 192.

108. vol. 6, ch. 6.

109. vol. 8, ch. 12, para. 1.

110. vol. 6, ch. 6.

111. vol. 6, ch. 5, part 2.

112. vol. 7, ch. 2, para. 4

113. Andrew and Gordievsky, *KGB,* pp. 313–14. Pincher, *Too Secret Too Long,* p. 396. Early in the war, Philby had tried and failed to enter Bletchley Park.

114. vol. 7, ch. 2, para. 3.

115. Haslam, "Stalin's Fears of a Separate Peace 1942," pp. 97–9.

116. Andrew and Gordievsky, *KGB,* pp. 273–4, 305; Schmidt, "Der Hess-Flug und das Kabinet Churchill"; Schmidt, "The Marketing of Rudolf Hess."

117. Record of dinner conversation at the Kremlin, October 18, 1944, FO 800/414, PRO.

118. Some of the Hess conspiracy theories were examined in the BBC2 documentary, *Hess: An Edge of Conspiracy* (presenter: Christopher Andrew; producer: Roy Davies), first broadcast January 17, 1990.

119. Borovik, *The Philby Files,* pp. 216–18.

120. Andrew and Gordievsky, *KGB,* pp. 334–7.

121. Borovik, *The Philby Files,* p. 216.

122. Borovik, *The Philby Files,* p. 217*n.*

123. Samolis (ed.), *Veterany Vneshnei Razvedki Rossii,* p. 154. At a meeting with Christopher Andrew in August 1990, Cairncross admitted that he did supply intelligence from Bletchley Park to the NKGB before the battle of Kursk but declined to give details.

124. Andrew and Gordievsky, *KGB,* p. 314; Pincher, *Too Secret Too Long,* p. 396.

125. Borovik, *The Philby Files,* p. 218.

126. vol. 7, ch. 2, para. 1.

Chapter Eight   Victory

1. As late as 1990 Valentin Falin, head of the International Department of the Central Committee, which was largely responsible for determining foreign intelligence requirements, claimed that intelligence reports in 1943 showed that some in Washington as well as in London were considering "the possibility of terminating the coalition with the Soviet Union and reaching an accord with Nazi Germany, or with the Nazi Generals, on the question of waging a joint war against the Soviet Union":

> Therefore when we talk about Stalin's distrust with regard to Churchill, at a certain stage towards those surrounding Roosevelt, not so much towards Roosevelt himself, we should pay attention to the fact that he based this mistrust on a very precise knowledge of specific facts.

The "facts" produced by the Center were, in all probability, mere conspiracy theories of the kind which, in greater or lesser degree, distorted Soviet intelligence assessment throughout, and even beyond, the Stalinist era. (Interview by Christopher Andrew with Valentin Falin in Moscow for BBC2, December 12, 1990.)

2. On CPUSA operations against Trotskyists and heretics, see Klehr, Haynes and Firsov, *The Secret World of American Communism;* quotation from p. 89.

3. vol. 6, ch. 12. On the FBI bugging of Nelson, see also Klehr, Haynes and Firsov, *The Secret World of American Communism,* pp. 216–17. The disappointingly discreet account of Nelson's career, *Steve Nelson, American Radical,* by Nelson, Barrett and Ruck, makes a brief reference to his work on the secret Party control commission (p. 242).

4. vol. 6, ch. 12. On Hopkins, see above, chapter 7.

5. See above, chapter 7.

6. Benson and Warner (eds.), *VENONA,* p. xviii, *n.* 30 and document 10. The authors suggest the author of the letter to Hoover "might have been" Mironov. One of the files noted by Mitrokhin makes Mironov's authorship virtually certain. While imprisoned by the NKVD in 1945, Mironov tried to smuggle to the American embassy in Moscow information about the massacre of the Polish officer corps similar to that contained in the letter to Hoover in 1943 (vol. 5, section 11). A study of the letter by Ben Fischer, written without access to Mitrokhin's notes on KGB files, seeks to make sense of Mironov's bizarre claim that Zarubin and his wife were working for, respectively, Japanese and German intelligence, as a way "to grab

FBI attention" and ensure that Hoover acted against them. But Mr. Fischer also acknowledges evidence that Mironov "may have been mentally disturbed" (Fischer, " 'Mr. Guver,' " pp. 10–11.). KGB files suggest both an obsessional hostility to Zarubin from Mironov and a determination that the West should learn the truth about the massacre of the Polish officer corps. In the letter to Hoover, Mironov claimed that his real name was Markov; Mitrokhin's notes, however, refer to him as Mironov.

7. Zarubin to Center, June 3, 1943: VENONA decrypts, 2nd release, pp. 157–8. Zarubin moved to Washington during June.

8. Following the corrupt governorships of Huey and Earl Long, Sam Jones established a reputation for scrupulous honesty. On his term as governor, see Dawson, *The Louisiana Governors*, pp. 255–9.

9. vol. 6, ch. 5, part 2. The US "military intelligence officer" may have had knowledge of the information on Zarubin's involvement in the massacre of Polish officers contained in Mironov's letter to Hoover.

10. vol. 6, ch. 5, part 2.

11. Sudoplatovs, *Special Tasks*, pp. 196–7.

12. vol. 6, ch. 5, part 2.

13. Samolis (ed.) *Veterany Vneshnei Razvedki Rossii*, pp. 53–5. This SVR hagiography predictably makes no mention of Zarubin's various misadventures in the United States.

14. vol. 5, sec. 11. Sudoplatov wrongly claims that Mironov was simply "hospitalized and discharged from the service" on the grounds of schizophrenia; *Special Tasks*, p. 197.

15. VENONA decrypts, 4th release, part 4, pp. 115–16.

16. vol. 6, ch. 5, part 2; vol. 6, app. 2, part 7. Zarubin's immediate successor as resident in New York in the summer of 1943, probably on a temporary basis, had been Pavel Klarin (codenamed LUKA); VENONA decrypts, 2nd release, pp. 180ff. On Abbiate's previous career see above, chapter 4.

17. VENONA decrypts, 3rd release, part 2, pp. 205–6.

18. VENONA decrypts, 3rd release, part 3, p. 175. The telegram from the Center appointing Abbiate as resident refers to him by his codename SERGEI, identified in the NSA decrypt as Pravdin (Abbiate's alias in the USA). Apresyan's transfer to San Francisco was not necessarily a demotion in view of the forthcoming organizing conference of the United Nations, attended by NKGB agent Harry Dexter White and presided over by the GRU agent Alger Hiss.

19. vol. 7, ch. 2, 1; app. 3, *n.* 21.

20. Among the documents Philby passed to the NKGB were the German foreign ministry documents obtained by OSS in Switzerland and probably also supplied by NKGB agents in OSS. Philby, *My Silent War*, pp. 84–6; Andrew, *For the President's Eyes Only*, pp. 141–2.

21. Borovik, *The Philby Files*, pp. 232–3.

22. Philby, *My Silent War*, ch. 6; Cecil, "The Cambridge Comintern." On Krötenschield, see Modin, *My Five Cambridge Friends*, pp. 103–4, 124–5.

23. Modin, *My Five Cambridge Friends*, p. 114. From 1944 to 1947 Modin was responsible for the files of the Five at the Center, before being posted to London to act as their controller.

24. Andrew and Gordievsky, *KGB*, p. 314.

25. Pincher, *Too Secret Too Long*, p. 397.

26. Cecil, *A Divided Life*, pp. 74–5.

27. vol. 7, ch. 10, para. 9.

28. Andrew and Gordievsky, *KGB*, pp. 309–12; Cecil, "The Cambridge Comintern."

29. vol. 7, ch. 10, app., para. 2.

30. See above, chapter 7.

31. There are a number of references to Fuchs's codenames in the VENONA decrypts. Fuchs said later that he never knew which branch of Soviet intelligence he was working for. During his interrogation after his arrest in 1950 he claimed to have been previously unaware that more than one branch existed. Andrew and Gordievsky, *KGB*, p. 323.

32. vol. 6, ch. 6. The GRU did, however, keep control of its agents in the Anglo-Canadian atomic research center at Chalk River; Andrew and Gordievsky, *KGB*, pp. 325–6.

33. Norwood ceased contact with SONYA (referred to in KGB files as FIR) in 1944. However, the first contact between Norwood and her new (unidentified) controller recorded in Mitrokhin's notes took place in 1945. vol. 7, ch. 14, item 17.

34. vol. 7, ch. 14, item 17.

35. VENONA decrypts, 5th release, part 2, p. 249. Norwood's codename at this period was TINA.

36. West and Tsarev, *The Crown Jewels*, p. 234.

37. VENONA decrypts, 1st release, pp. 8–9.

38. FBI FOIA 65-58805, file 38, p. 7.

39. VENONA decrypts, 1st release, pp. 8–9.

40. FBI FOIA 65-58805, files 38, 40.

41. VENONA decrypts, 1st release, pp. 25, 27.

42. Gold's evidence to the FBI on renewing contact with Fuchs is reprinted in Williams, *Klaus Fuchs, Atom Spy*, pp. 206–12.

43. vol. 6, ch. 8, part 1.

44. The agents in Rosenberg's ring included the scientist William Perl (GNOME), who provided intelligence on jet engines, and the military electronics engineers Joel Barr (METRE) and Alfred Sarant (HUGHES), both of whom were radar experts; VENONA decrypts, 1st release, pp. 12, 18–19, 47, 51. On the origins of the Rosenberg spyring, run initially – according to Semenov – "on the principles of a Communist Party group," see Weinstein and Vassiliev, *The Haunted Wood*, pp. 177–9.

45. VENONA decrypts, 1st release, pp. 15, 36, 45–6.

46. Radosh and Milton, *The Rosenberg File*, ch. 3.

47. VENONA decrypts, 1st release, pp. 44–5; 3rd release, pp. 255–6, 261–6. Hall explained his belief that his atomic espionage had been a way "to help the world" in the BBC Radio 4 documentary *VENONA* (presenter: Christopher Andrew; producers: Mark Berman and Helen Weinstein), first broadcast March 18, 1998.

48. vol. 6, ch. 5, part 2.

49. VENONA decrypts, 2nd release, p. 424.

50. Bentley, *Out of Bondage,* pp. 160–1. The first VENONA decrypt in which Akhmerov reports intelligence from Bentley is dated December 11, 1943; VENONA decrypts, 2nd release, pp. 430–1.

51. Bentley, *Out of Bondage,* pp. 163–5. Bentley's story is, once again, largely corroborated by VENONA and other evidence. Cf. VENONA decrypts, 3rd release, part 1, pp. 26–8; and Klehr, Haynes and Firsov, *The Secret World of American Communism,* pp. 312–15.

52. vol. 6, ch. 5, part 2. Doubtless through a slip of the pen, Mitrokhin also refers to Perlo in this note as PEL. VENONA and other sources make clear that PEL (also codenamed PAL and ROBERT) was Greg Silvermaster. The other members of Perlo (RAIDER)'s group, all described as Communists, were Charles Kramer, Edward Fitzgerald, Harry Magdoff, John Abt, Charles Flato and Harold Glasser.

53. VENONA decrypts, 3rd release, part 1, pp. 26–8.

54. Bentley, *Out of Bondage,* pp. 166–7. Once again, VENONA confirms the substance of Bentley's version of events.

55. VENONA decrypts, 3rd release, part 1, p. 272.

56. Bentley, *Out of Bondage,* pp. 173–7.

57. VENONA decrypts, 1st release, part 1, p. 14; 3rd release, part 2, pp. 139, 152, 196.

58. Bentley, *Out of Bondage,* pp. 179–80.

59. VENONA decrypts, 3rd release, part 2, pp. 17–18. In January 1945 White was appointed Assistant Secretary of the Treasury.

60. Romerstein and Levchenko, *The KGB against the "Main Enemy,"* pp. 111–12. George Silverman, to whom (according to Bentley) Currie rushed to deliver his warning "sort of out of breath," is identified by the VENONA decrypts as a Soviet agent (codenamed ELERON [AILERON]). Currie himself may well be the agent codenamed PAGE to whom there are a number of references in the decrypts. Though denying that he had ever been a Soviet spy, Currie later acknowledged that he been entertained at Gorsky's home. Senior White House officials such as Currie were among the very small group privy to the highly classified information that OSS had obtained a charred NKGB codebook. There is no reference to Currie in Mitrokhin's notes.

61. The senior FBI agent who took part in the early analysis of the VENONA decrypts, Robert Lamphere, wrongly claims in his memoirs (*The FBI–KGB War,* p. 87ff) that the NKGB codebook was later used to assist the process of decrypting. National Security Agency, *Introductory History of VENONA and Guide to the Translations,* p. 8.

62. Andrew and Gordievsky, *KGB,* p. 295.

63. vol. 6, ch. 8, part 1. vol. 7, ch. 2, para. 22.

64. vol. 6, ch. 6.

65. Holloway, "Sources for *Stalin and the Bomb,*" p. 5.

66. vol. 7, ch. 2, para. 19.

67. Albright and Kunstel, *Bombshell,* pp. 121–7.

68. Albright and Kunstel, *Bombshell*, ch. 15. The career of Morris and "Lona" Cohen is summarized in vol. 6, ch. 5, part 2.

69. Albright and Kunstel, *Bombshell*, pp. 138–9.

70. NKGB report to Beria, July 10, 1945, first published in *Kurier Sovietski Razvedke* (1991); extract reprinted in Sudoplatovs, *Special Tasks*, appendix 4, pp. 474–5 (Sudoplatov misidentifies MLAD as Pontecorvo).

71. The story of Lona Cohen's trip to Albuquerque is briefly told in the short biography of her in Samolis (ed.), *Veterany Vneshnei Razvedki Rossii*, p. 71. See also Albright and Kunstel, *Bombshell*, ch. 17.

72. vol. 6, ch. 5, part 2. Unsurprisingly, this remarkable tale improved with the telling. In some recent Russian versions, Mrs. Cohen hid the documents in a box of Kleenex. The less elaborate account noted by Mitrokhin appears more reliable. He does not, however, identify the Los Alamos scientist who supplied the documents.

73. vol. 6, app. 2, part 5. The first VENONA reference to Yatskov's responsibility for ENORMOZ dates from January 23, 1945; VENONA decrypts, 1st release, p. 60.

74. Samolis (ed.), *Veterany Vneshnei Razvedki Rossii*, pp. 169–71.

75. VENONA decrypts, 3rd release, part 2, p. 268.

76. Though Mitrokhin's notes include references to most of the best-known, as well several hitherto-unknown, Soviet spies in the wartime United States, all refer to NKVD/NKGB agents. There is thus no reference to Hiss, who worked for Soviet military intelligence.

77. VENONA decrypts, 3rd release, part 3, p. 207.

78. k-27, appendix, para. 21.

79. Andrew and Gordievsky, *KGB*, pp. 343–8.

80. Kimball, *Forged in War*, p. 318.

81. VENONA decrypts, 3rd release, part 3, p. 207. A footnote to this decrypt, added by NSA in 1969, identifies ALES as "probably Alger Hiss." The corroborative evidence now available puts that identification beyond reasonable doubt. Of the four Americans (other than US embassy staff) who went on to Moscow after Yalta, only Hiss fits Gorsky's description of ALES (Moynihan, *Secrecy*, pp. 146–8). Gordievsky recalls a lecture in the Centre in which Akhmerov referred to his wartime contact with Hiss. Hungarian intelligence files on the Noel Field case show that Field also identified Hiss as a Soviet agent. Whittaker Chambers, the ex-GRU agent who exposed Hiss, testified that, as indicated by Gorsky's telegram, Hiss first began supplying intelligence to Moscow in 1935. Both Chambers and Bentley, like Gorsky, implicated some of Hiss's family, as well as Hiss himself, in Soviet espionage. Further evidence pointing to Hiss came from the Soviet defector Igor Guzenko in 1945. Though the statute of limitations prevented Hiss's prosecution for espionage in 1950, the evidence used to convict him of perjury in that year, for lying about providing government documents to a Communist spyring, remains compelling. See, *inter alia:* Breindel, "Hiss's Guilt," *New Republic* (April 15, 1996); Schmidt, "The Hiss Dossier," *New Republic* (November 8, 1993); Weinstein, *Perjury;* Andrew and Gordievsky, *KGB*. ALES, in the Cyrillic alphabet, looks like a contraction of "Alger Hiss"—one of a number of Soviet codenames at this period which contain clues to the identity of the agent concerned.

82. Andrew and Gordievsky, *KGB*, p. 347. On the basis of Akhmerov's contact with Hiss (very unusual in the case of a GRU agent), Andrew and Gordievsky wrongly deduced that Hiss was by now an NKGB agent, in common with other leading American GRU agents of the late 1930s.

83. vol. 5, sect. 4. Andrew and Gordievsky, *KGB*, pp. 350–1. In 1946 SMERSH was reorganized on a peacetime basis and returned to the control of the MGB, the post-war successor of the NKVD.

84. Bethell, *The Last Secret;* Tolstoy, *Victims of Yalta;* Tolstoy, *Stalin's Secret War*, ch. 17; Knight, "Harold Macmillan and the Cossacks"; Mitchell, *The Cost of a Reputation*, chs. 1, 3, 5. Tolstoy provides the most detailed and moving description of the forced repatriation of the Cossacks, but, as Knight demonstrates, exaggerates the personal responsibility of Harold Macmillan, minister-resident in Italy and political adviser to Supreme Allied Commander Field Marshal Alexander. Mitchell also concludes that Macmillan's "responsibility for what ultimately occurred must be adjudged as small." Tolstoy's charge that Lord Aldington (formerly Brigadier Toby Low) had committed war crimes in connection with the repatriation led to the award to Lord Aldington in 1989 of 1.5 million pounds damages for libel.

85. The fourth White general on Smersh's "most wanted" list, Timofei Domanov, was a former Soviet citizen whose fate, unlike that of the other three, had been sealed at Yalta.

86. vol. 5, sect. 4. A senior British officer reported, "All relations with Soviets most friendly with much interchange WHISKY and VODKA"; Knight, "Harold Macmillan and the Cossacks," p. 239.

87. vol. 5, sect. 4, paras. 2–4.

88. For legal reasons, six words have been omitted from the first sentence of Mitrokhin's note; they do not contain the name of the lieutenant-colonel. vol. 5, sect. 4, para. 5. The memoirs of the Deputy Chief of the Red Army, General Sergei Matveyevich Shtemenko, make no reference to bribery but confirm part of the sequence of events in the KGB files: "The Soviet government then made a firm representation to our allies over the matter of Krasnov, Shkuro, Sultan Ghirey, and other war criminals. The British stalled briefly; but since neither the old White guard generals nor their troops were worth much, they put all of them into trucks and delivered them into the hands of the Soviet authorities" (Tolstoy, *Stalin's Secret War*, p. 298).

89. Alexander instructed on May 22, 1945, "All who are Soviet citizens and who can be handed over to Russians without use of force should be returned by 8th Army. Any others should be evacuated to 12th Army Group." It has been argued that 5 Corps, the section of the Eighth Army which handed over the Cossacks, subsequently concluded that it had none the less been given "freedom of action" to use force if necessary. Controversy continues. Mitchell, *The Cost of a Reputation*, pp. 49–54. Brigadier Low left for Britain on May 22 or 23, some days before the "repatriation" began. There is no suggestion that, if bribery occurred, he was in any way cognizant of it.

90. Knight, "Harold Macmillan and the Cossacks," pp. 248–52.

91. Tolstoy, *Victims of Yalta*, pp. 182, 188, 193, 266–8. The execution of the generals was announced in a brief note in *Pravda* on January 17, 1947.

Chapter Nine   *From War to Cold War*

1. vol. 8, ch. 2.

2. The large literature on the Gouzenko case includes Bothwell and Granatstein (eds.), *The Gouzenko Transcripts;* Granatstein and Stafford, *Spy Wars*, ch. 3; Sawatsky, *Gouzenko;* Brook-Shepherd, *The Storm Birds*, ch. 21. Christopher Andrew interviewed Mrs. Gouzenko and her daughter (both of whom live under other names) in Canada in November 1992.

3. VENONA decrypts, 5th release, part 3, pp. 206–7.

4. vol. 8, ch. 2. Burdin served as resident from 1951 to 1953. In the records of the Canadian Ministry of External Affairs his name is transliterated as Bourdine. In 1952 Burdin recruited Hugh Hambleton, who later became one of the KGB's most important Canadian agents; see below, chapter 10.

5. vol. 8, ch. 10, paras. 7–8.

6. VENONA decrypts, 5th release, part 2, pp. 263–5, 272–3, 275.

7. The most reliable account of this episode is in Brook-Shepherd, *The Storm Birds*, ch. 4, which corrects a number of inventions in Philby's version of events.

8. Philby, *My Silent War*, pp. 114–15.

9. vol. 5, ch. 7.

10. Andrew and Gordievsky, *KGB*, p. 379.

11. Philby, *My Silent War*, p. 120.

12. vol. 5, ch. 7.

13. vol. 7, ch. 6, para. 6.

14. Modin, *My Five Cambridge Friends*, pp. 137, 155; Zubok and Pleshakov, *Inside the Kremlin's Cold War*, pp. 86–8.

15. Andrew and Gordievsky, *KGB*, pp. 375–6.

16. Andrew and Gordievsky, *KGB*, pp. 377, 396.

17. West and Tsarev, *The Crown Jewels*, p. 222.

18. Letters from Geoffrey A. Robinson to Christopher Andrew, October 19, 1997, September 14, 1998. Cairncross's memoirs are as unreliable about his post-war career as about his earlier work as a Soviet agent. He claims that he had virtually no access to secret material in the Treasury (*The Enigma Spy*, pp. 124–7). According to Robinson, though, "That is totally untrue. The TUBE ALLOYS [nuclear weapons] files themselves were many inches thick, let alone all the other Secret and Top Secret files."

19. Modin, *My Five Cambridge Friends*, p. 150. Cf. West and Tsarev, *The Crown Jewels*, pp. 222–6; Andrew and Gordievsky, *KGB*, p. 406.

20. vol. 7, ch. 6, para. 4.

21. vol. 7, ch. 6, para. 1.

22. Mitrokhin's notes do not give the exact dates of the surveillance team's presence at the London residency. It arrived late in the war and remained "for several years." vol. 7, ch. 2, para. 1; ch. 6, para. 5.

23. vol. 7, ch. 10, para. 11.

24. Andrew and Gordievsky, *KGB*, pp. 398–9; Boyle, *The Climate of Treason*, pp. 305, 341, 346–8. Mayhew, *Time to Explain*, p. 109.

25. Andrew and Gordievsky, *KGB*, p. 397. Modin, *My Five Cambridge Friends*, p. 201. Modin was unable to reveal Rodin's real name and refers to him by his alias "Korovin."

26. VENONA decrypts, 3rd release, part 3, pp. 150, 153.

27. Benson and Warner (eds.), *VENONA*, pp. 61–71. Hoover did not identify Bentley as his source. "At the present time," he wrote, "it is impossible to determine exactly how many of these people had actual knowledge of the disposition being made of the information they were transmitting."

28. Weinstein, *Perjury*, p. 357.

29. Bentley, *Out of Bondage*, pp. 204–7, 266–7.

30. If the Centre believed Gorsky to have been compromised by Gouzenko's defection, he would probably have been recalled earlier. By March 1946 the FBI was convinced that Bentley's defection was known to Silvermaster. Bentley, *Out of Bondage*, p. 267.

31. vol. 6, ch. 5, part 2. On Bentley's contact with Pravdin's wife, see Bentley, *Out of Bondage*, p. 329.

32. vol. 6, ch. 5, part 2.

33. Modin, *My Five Cambridge Friends*, p. 133.

34. See below, chapter 9.

35. Andrew and Gordievsky, *KGB*, p. 383.

36. See above, chapter 2.

37. Benson and Warner (eds.), *VENONA*, introduction. Two further studies of the decrypts were published just as this volume was going to press: Haynes and Klehr, *VENONA*; and West, VENONA.

38. Interview by Christopher Andrew with the late Dr. Cleveland Cram, October 2, 1996. Dr. Cram was one of the first CIA officers to be indoctrinated into VENONA in November 1952. Some of his recollections were included in the BBC Radio 4 documentary *VENONA* (written and presented by Christopher Andrew; producers: Mark Burman and Helen Weinstein), first broadcast on March 18, 1998.

39. Andrew, "The VENONA Secret."

40. Weisband had been recruited in 1934. From 1945 to 1947, however, contact was broken with him as part of the security measures which followed the defection of Elizabeth Bentley. Weinstein and Vassiliev, *The Haunted Wood*, p. 291.

41. Interviews with Cecil Phillips and Meredith Gardner broadcast in the BBC Radio 4 documentary *VENONA* (March 18, 1998).

42. Andrew and Gordievsky, *KGB*, pp. 388–9; Zubok and Pleshakov, *Inside the Kremlin's Cold War*, pp. 87–8.

43. vol. 6, ch. 5, part 1. Though initially made subordinate to the Council of Ministers, the Committee of Information was transferred to the Foreign Ministry in 1949; Murphy, Kondrashev and Bailey, *Battleground Berlin*, pp. 40–1.

44. vol. 7, ch. 6, para. 4.

45. The most detailed available account of the organization and development of the KI is a 24-page report based on information obtained during the debriefing of Vladimir and Yevdokia Petrov, following their defection in 1954: "The Committee of Information ('KI') 1947–1951" (November 17, 1954) CRS A6823/XR1/56, Australian Archives, Canberra.

46. vol. 6, ch. 5, part 2; vol. 6, appendix 2, part 7.

47. Dzhirkvelov, *Secret Servant*, p. 138.

48. Andrew and Gordievsky, *KGB*, p. 389. Panyushkin was ambassador in Washington from 1947 to 1951 and head of the FCD from 1953 to 1956.

49. Gromyko, *Memories*, pp. 318–19.

50. "The Committee of Information ('KI') 1947–1951" (November 17, 1954) CRS A6823/XR1/56, Australian Archives, Canberra.

51. "The Committee of Information ('KI') 1947–1951" (November 17, 1954) CRS A6823/XR1/56, Australian Archives, Canberra. According to vol. 7, ch. 11, para. 7, the GRU illegal section was not withdrawn from the KI until 1949.

52. t-7,187; vol. 6, ch. 5, part 4, *n.* 8; vol. 7, ch. 11, para. 5.

53. vol. 6, ch. 5, part 1; vol. 7, ch. 11, para. 7; vol. 7, app. 3, *n.* 62. On Korotkov's pre-war career, see Sudoplatovs, *Special Tasks*, p. 48. The official SVR version of Korotkov's career makes no mention of his post-war role as head of the Illegals Directorate; Samolis (ed., *Veterany Vneshnei Razvedki Rossii*, pp. 63–5.

54. Officers are not to be confused with agents, such as Philby.

55. His name appears on his birth certificate as Wilhelm August Fisher. His father, though Russian, came from a family with German origins. On the family background, see Saunders, "Tyneside and the Russian Revolution," pp. 280–4. Fisher's true identity was not revealed until after his death in 1971, when Western journalists noticed the name carved on his tombstone.

56. vol. 6, ch. 5, part 2 and *n*. 6. Cf. Samolis (ed.), *Veterany Vneshnei Razvedki Rossii*, pp. 156–9.

57. vol. 6, ch. 5, part 2 and *n*. 6. Fisher's entry in Samolis (ed.), *Veterany Vneshnei Razvedki Rossii* (pp. 156–9) refrains from mentioning any of the charges made against him.

58. vol. 6, ch. 5, part 2.

59. vol. 6, ch. 5, parts 1, 2.

60. vol. 6, ch. 5, part 2.

61. Recollections of MARK's New York friend and fellow artist, Burt Silverman; Bernikow, *Abel*, pp. 7–20.

62. vol. 6, ch. 5, part 2.

63. Samolis (ed.), *Veterany Vneshnei Razvedki Rossii*, pp. 68–70. Albright and Kunstel, *Bombshell*, pp. 179–85.

64. vol. 6, ch. 5, part 2. (Mitrokhin's note mistranscribes MLAD as MLADA.)

65. Albright and Kunstel, *Bombshell*, pp. 176–8.

66. Tchikov and Kern, *Comment Staline a volé la bombe atomique aux Américains*, p. 205.

67. vol. 6, ch. 5, part 2.

68. Samolis (ed.), *Veterany Vneshnei Razvedki Rossii*, pp. 158–9.

69. Samolis (ed.), *Veterany Vneshnei Razvedki Rossii*, p. 159.

70. OREL was Sixto Fernandes Donsel; FISH was Antonio Arjonilla Toriblo. vol. 6, app. 1, part 41.

71. vol. 6, ch. 5, part 2.

72. Interviews with Ted Hall and former FBI agent Robert McQueen, first broadcast in the BBC Radio 4 documentary VENONA (written and presented by Christopher Andrew; produced by Mark Burman and Helen Weinstein, March 18, 1998). Albright and Kunstel cite information from "confidential sources" that Hall had four or five meetings in New York with a Soviet agent whom he knew as "Jimmy Stevens" in 1952–3, before finally breaking contact with Soviet intelligence (*Bombshell*, ch. 25). Hall acknowledges that he had several meetings with a Soviet contact, but insists that he provided no information during this period (interview with Christopher Andrew, March 11, 1998).

73. vol. 6, ch. 5, part 2.

74. See below, chapter 17.

75. vol. 6, ch. 11, part 2. Kopatzky later claimed to have been born in Kiev on New Year's Day, 1922 (Wise, *Molehunt*, p. 183).

76. Wise, *Molehunt*, p. 184. Save for recording Kopatzky's date and place of birth, Mitrokhin's notes from his file contain nothing before 1946.

77. vol. 6, ch. 11, part 2.

78. Wise, *Molehunt*, pp. 182–3, 199.

79. Murphy, Kondrashev and Bailey, *Battleground Berlin*, p. 248. The SVR made available to the authors (David Murphy, head of the CIA Berlin station, 1959–61; Sergei Kondrashev, former deputy head of the FCD; George Bailey, former Director of Radio Liberty) a substantial number of files on KGB operations in Berlin before the building of the Wall. Its statement that no Kopatzky file exists—rightly dismissed by the authors as "obviously disingenuous"—is thus all the more extraordinary. The SVR claims that its only record of Kopatzky concerns his visit, under his new name Orlov, to the Soviet embassy in Washington in 1965 when he inquired about possible asylum in the USSR and complained that the FBI was "attempting to obtain an admission that he collaborated with Soviet intelligence while he was in Germany during the 1940s and 1950s."

80. vol. 6, ch. 11, part 2.

81. vol. 6, ch. 11, part 2. On Kopatzky's recruitment by the CIA, see also Murphy, Kondrashev and Bailey, *Battleground Berlin*, pp. 110–12.

82. vol. 6, ch. 11, part 2.

83. See below, chapter 11.

84. Kopatzky's case officers were Komarov, Galiguzov, Krasavin, V. V. Grankin, Krishchenko, Borisov, Komev, Fedorchenko, Melnikov, Chaikovsky, P. A. Shilov, Govorkov, Ye. P. Pitovranov, V. G. Likhachev, V. M. Biryukov, A. Ya. Zinchenko, Ya. F. Oleynik, M. I. Kuryshev, Yu. I. Arsenev, G. G. Fedorenko, Makarov, Myakotnykh, Sevastyanov, and the illegal DIMA. vol. 6, ch. 11, part 2.

85. Andrei Zhdanov told the founding meeting of Cominform (the post-war successor of Comintern) in September 1947 that "the principal driving force of the imperialist camp is the USA. Allied with it are Britain and France." Zhdanov, *The International Situation*.

86. k-11,112–13; k-7,84.

87. Buton, *Les lendemains qui déchantent;* Mortimer, *The Rise of the French Communist Party,* chs. 9, 10; Wolton, *La France sous influence,* chs. 1, 2.

88. vol. 9, ch. 1.

89. Zubok and Pleshakov, *Inside the Kremlin's Cold War,* p. 15.

90. vol. 9, ch. 1.

91. k-11,112–13; k-7,84.

92. vol. 9, ch. 1.

93. vol. 9, ch. 1, para. 86. Mitrokhin's notes contain very little information on the content of reports from the post-war Paris residency.

94. Dewavrin had resigned as head of SDECE in February 1946.

95. Vosjoli, *Lamia,* ch. 6; Porch, *The French Secret Services,* ch. 11.

96. vol. 9, ch. 1, para. 17.

97. k-6,91. WEST's other "contacts" in the DGER/SDECE, included members of the Italian and Spanish sections, and PASCAL who in 1946 was posted abroad.

98. k-6,92.

99. Recollection of the KGB defector Peter Deriabin: Schecter and Deriabin, *The Spy Who Saved the World,* p. 237*n.*

100. Wolton, *La France sous influence,* pp. 78–9; Buton, *Les lendemains qui déchantent,* p. 259.

101. t-1,24; t-2,25. Manac'h's other case officers were M. M. Baklanov, Tikhonov, Kiselev, Nagornov and S. I. Gavrilov.

102. k-4,32,176,179; t-1,42.

103. vol. 9, ch. 1, para. 6.

104. vol. 9, ch. 1, paras. 18–19.

105. vol. 9, ch. 1, para. 31.

106. vol. 9, ch. 1, para. 51. The Paris residency, however, complained of continuing staff shortages. In 1948 the Paris residency had a total of eighteen operational officers and technical support staff. Nine further intelligence officers whom the Centre had intended to send to Paris were refused visas. Attempts were made, with only limited success, to make good the shortfall both by setting up a new illegal residency and by coopting residency translators and typists as well as staff from the Soviet embassy, trade and other missions for operational intelligence work. vol. 9, ch. 1, para. 50.

107. See below, chapter 27.

108. Modin, *My Five Cambridge Friends,* pp. 159, 165.

109. Rees, *A Chapter of Accidents,* p. 7; Penrose and Freeman, *Conspiracy of Silence,* pp. 324–7.

110. vol. 7, ch. 10, para. 9.

111. vol. 7, ch. 10.

112. Cecil, *A Divided Life,* chs. 6, 7.

113. *The Times* (January 2, 1951).

114. Minute by Maclean (December 21, 1950), PRO FO 371/81613 AU 1013/52.

115. Philby, *My Silent War,* p. 134.

116. Though six telegrams in 1945 referred to Philby under the codename STANLEY, they appear not to have been decrypted until some years later; VENONA decrypts, 5th release, part 1, pp. 263–7, 272, 275–6. A total of thirty telegrams exchanged between the Centre and the London residency, mostly in 1945, were eventually decrypted in whole or in part by Anglo-American codebreakers.

117. Benson and Warner (eds.), *VENONA,* pp. xxvii–xxviii.

118. Fuchs told his interrogator that his last contact with Soviet intelligence had been in February or March 1949. That may have been his last meeting with his controller. Williams, *Klaus Fuchs, Atom Spy,* p. 186. See also Gorodetsky, *Grand Delusion,* ch. 12.

119. Benson and Warner (eds.), *VENONA,* pp. xxvii–xxviii. The US government lacked the evidence to prosecute Weisband for espionage, but he was sentenced to a year's imprisonment for contempt after failing to attend a federal grand jury hearing on Communist Party activity.

120. vol. 7, ch. 10, para. 7.

121. Philby, *My Silent War,* p. 146.

122. See above, chapter 9.

123. vol. 6, ch. 5, part 2. It is unclear from Mitrokhin's notes whether Philby refused contact with the legal residencies from the moment of his arrival in the United States in 1949 or in the following year. Unsurprisingly, Philby made no mention in his memoirs or published interviews of the failings of the American residencies.

124. vol. 6, ch. 5, part 2. Modin, *My Five Cambridge Friends*, pp. 186–7.

125. Philby, *My Silent War*, pp. 151–2. Burgess arrived at the Washington embassy as second secretary in August 1950. On Philby's house at 4100 Nebraska Avenue, NW, see Kessler, *Undercover Washington*, pp. 93–5.

126. Newton, *The Butcher's Embrace*, pp. 305–11; Knightley, *Philby*, pp. 167–8.

127. According to HARRY's KGB file, the out-of-date passport in the name of Kovalik was no. 214595, issued by the State Department in Washington on April 29, 1930. vol. 6, ch. 5, part 2.

128. vol. 6, ch. 5, part 2.

129. vol. 6, ch. 5, part 2. On the use of the *Batory* to transport Soviet agents to the United States, cf. Budenz, *Men Without Faces*, pp. 19, 64, 68.

130. vol. 6, ch. 5, part 2.

131. vol. 6, ch. 5, part 2. There is no suggestion that either Senator Flanders or his family were aware that HARRY was a Soviet illegal.

132. vol. 6, ch. 5, part 2.

133. Newton, *The Butcher's Embrace*, p. 281.

134. vol. 6, ch. 5, part 2.

135. Newton, *The Butcher's Embrace*, pp. 281–2.

136. Philby, *My Silent War*, pp. 152–4.

137. Cecil, *A Divided Life*, p. 118.

138. VENONA decrypts, 3rd release, part 1, pp. 240–1.

139. This is acknowledged by Yuri Modin (Modin, *My Five Cambridge Friends*, p. 199).

140. Philby, *My Silent War*, p. 156. The KGB claim that the escapades which led to Burgess's recall were pre-planned is not corroborated by Mitrokhin's notes; they were much in line with similar, unpremeditated "scrapes" over the previous few years.

141. vol. 6, ch. 5, part 2.

142. Modin, *My Five Cambridge Friends*, pp. 199–201.

143. Modin, *My Five Cambridge Friends*, pp. 202–3.

144. Modin, *My Five Cambridge Friends*, pp. 203–4; Costello and Tsarev, *Deadly Illusions*, pp. 338–9.

145. Andrew and Gordievsky, *KGB*, p. 404; Cecil, *A Divided Life*, pp. 135ff.

146. vol. 7, ch. 10, para. 16.

147. vol. 7, ch. 10, para. 17.

148. vol. 7, ch. 10, para. 19.

149. Modin, *My Five Cambridge Friends*, p. 251.

150. vol. 7, ch. 10, para. 19.

151. vol. 7, ch. 10, para. 18.

152. vol. 6, ch. 5, part 2.

153. Philby, *My Silent War*, pp. 157–9.

154. vol. 6, ch. 5, part 2.

155. vol. 6, ch. 5, part 2. In 1953 the illegal VIK also lost a hollow coin containing a microfilm message.

156. vol. 7, ch. 10, para. 19.

157. Andrew and Gordievsky, *KGB*, p. 406; Modin, *My Five Cambridge Friends*, pp. 213–18. Modin is apparently unaware that Colville had recorded his 1939 meetings with Cairncross in his diary, and is wrongly skeptical of his ability to identify Cairncross as the author of a note describing one of those meetings, found in Burgess's flat.

158. Modin, *My Five Cambridge Friends*, pp. 221–4, 229–32; Andrew and Gordievsky, *KGB*, pp. 406–7. Blunt finally confessed in 1964 in return for a guarantee of immunity from prosecution. He was not publicly identified as a former Soviet agent until 1979.

159. Philby, *My Silent War*, ch. 12; Andrew and Gordievsky, *KGB*, pp. 407–8; Knightley, *Philby*, pp. 147–8; Modin, *My Five Cambridge Friends*, pp. 224, 228–32.

160. Borovik, *The Philby Files*, p. 284.

161. Andrew and Gordievsky, *KGB*, pp. 24–6.

Chapter Ten The Main Adversary Part I

1. t-7,12; k-13,267; vol. 6, ch. 5, part 1. Mitrokhin's notes omit to record Grigulevich's alias as a Costa Rican diplomat, but the other details he provides (for example, the fact that on May 14, 1952 Grigulevich presented his letters of credence as Envoy Extraordinary and Minister Plenipotentiary of Costa Rica in Rome to the Italian president, Luigi Einaudi) clearly identify Grigulevich as "Teodoro B. Castro." The

members of the Costa Rican delegation to the Sixth Session of the UN General Assembly are listed in United Nations, *Official Records of the General Assembly Sixth Session, Plenary Meetings*, p. xiv.

2. See above, chapter 6.

3. k-13,370.

4. k-13,267; k-26,194. The two other leading members of the Costa Rican delegation to Rome were Francisco Orlich, Minister of Public Works, and Daniel Oduber, ambassador in Paris (later president of Costa Rica from 1974 to 1978, and in 1980 deputy chairman of the Socialist International). Grigulevich appears to have won their confidence, too; his wife was received by them when she visited Costa Rica in 1952. On Figueres's role in restoring constitutional government in Costa Rica, see Bird, *Costa Rica*, ch. 10.

5. k-13,267.

6. Acheson, *Present at the Creation*, pp. 580–1.

7. k-13,267; t-7,12; vol. 6, ch. 5, part 1. United Nations, *Official Records of the General Assembly Sixth Session, Ad Hoc Political Committee*, p. 20.

8. k-13,267.

9. See above, chapter 9.

10. The VENONA decrypts led to very few arrests of Soviet spies, largely because SIGINT was considered too secret to be used in court, even in closed session. Even had it been used, it would have been open to a variety of legal challenges.

11. See above, chapters 7–8.

12. Klehr and Haynes, *The American Communist Movement*, ch. 4.

13. See above, chapter 9.

14. The Illegals Directorate planned a network of 28 "documentation agents" in Austria, 24 in East Germany, 24 in West Germany, 15 in France, 13 in the United States, 12 in Britain, 12 in Italy, 10 in Canada, 10 in Belgium, 9 in Mexico, 8 in Iran, 6 in Lebanon and 6 in Turkey (vol. 6, ch. 5, part 4). The large number of agents in Germany and Austria reflected the high proportion of Soviet illegals posing as refugees from East Germany.

15. Operations officers specializing in illegal documentation were posted to the legal residencies in New York, Washington, Ottawa, Mexico City, Buenos Aires, London, Paris, Rome, Brussels, The Hague, Copenhagen, Oslo, Stockholm, Helsinki, Vienna, Athens, Istanbul, Tehran, Beirut, Calcutta, Karachi and Cairo. Those posted to New York were M. N. Korneyev, V. N. Danilin and A. M. Tikhomirov. vol. 6, ch. 5, part 4.

16. See above, chapter 9.

17. vol. 7, ch. 11, item 2.

18. vol. 8, ch. 8.

19. Sawatsky, *For Services Rendered*, p. 34.

20. vol. 8, ch. 8, paras. 5–6.

21. vol. 8, ch. 8, para. 7.

22. Sawatsky, *For Services Rendered*, p. 34.

23. Soboloff's father had left Canada to work at Magnitogorsk in 1931. David and his mother followed in 1935. vol. 8, ch. 8, para. 7.

24. Sawatsky, *For Services Rendered*, pp. 38–40.

25. Though the KGB file noted by Mitrokhin names HART's lover, it seems unfair to identify her.

26. vol. 8, ch. 8, paras. 14, 18.

27. Sawatsky, *For Services Rendered*, pp. 44–53, 66–7. Interviews by Christopher Andrew with Terry Guernsey in Toronto, October 1991.

28. vol. 8, ch. 2. On the Centre's criticisms of the Ottawa residency see above, pp. 180–1.

29. vol. 8, ch. 8, para. 9.

30. Sawatsky, *For Services Rendered*, pp. 53–4.

31. vol. 8, ch. 8, para. 9. On EMMA, see also k-8,82.

32. On Hambleton's career prior to his recruitment, see Heaps, *Hugh Hambleton, Spy*; Granatstein and Stafford, *Spy Wars*, ch. 8; Barron, *KGB Today*, ch. 9.

33. vol. 8, ch. 8; vol. 8, app. 1, item 87.

34. See below, chapter 12.

35. vol. 6, ch. 5, part 2.

36. vol. 8, ch. 8; vol. 6, ch. 5, part 2.

37. vol. 8, ch. 8, paras. 11, 20.

38. Sawatsky, *For Services Rendered*, pp. 64–71.

39. vol. 8, ch. 8, paras. 10, 20.

40. Sawatsky, *For Services Rendered*, p. 27.

41. vol. 8, ch. 8, para. 14.

42. vol. 8, ch. 8, paras. 10, 12.

43. vol. 8, ch. 8, para. 13.

44. vol. 8, ch. 8, paras. 15, 20.

45. vol. 8, ch. 8, para. 16. Remarkably, HART survived fifteen years' imprisonment (five in solitary confinement, three in a normal prison cell and seven in labor camp), and was later exfiltrated to the West by SIS. He now lives in Canada.

46. vol. 8, ch. 8, para. 20. In January 1964 a KGB officer traveling to Winnipeg with a scientific and cultural delegation and the Igor Moiseyev Folk Dance Group tried to reestablish contact with Morrison, but without success. An investigation by agent ANTHEA then established that he had moved house. The Centre later planned to involve Morrison in the hunt for two illegals, Yevgeni Runge (MAKS) and Valentina Rush (ZINA), who defected to the CIA in Berlin in 1967. But though attempts by the Ottawa residency to locate Morrison continued intermittently until 1974 they were unsuccessful (vol. 6, ch. 5, part 5; vol. 8, ch. 8, para. 21). In May 1986 Morrison was sentenced to eighteen months in jail for offenses against the Official Secrets Act (Granatstein and Stafford, *Spy Wars*, p. 149).

47. vol. 8, ch. 8, para. 19.

48. k-4,207; k-11,130. From 1961 to 1964 Grinchenko worked in Cuba as a consultant to the illegals directorate of the DGI; k-11,130.

49. On Fisher, see above, chapter 9.

50. Olavi Åhman (codenamed VIRTANEN) was a veteran of the International Brigades during the Spanish Civil War. vol. 6, ch. 5, part 2; k-27,451.

51. Bernikow, *Abel*, chs. 2–3.

52. The message was finally decrypted in 1957, with the assistance of cipher material given by VIK to the FBI and other material discovered by the Bureau in MARK's flat after his arrest. Lamphere, *The FBI–KGB War*, pp. 270–1, 274–5.

53. k-3,80; k-8,83. ORIZO's main motivation seems to have been financial. In Paris, he had been paid 40,000 francs a month; Mitrokhin's notes do not indicate how much he was paid in New York.

54. k-8,91.

55. k-3,80. ORIZO continued work as a Soviet agent until 1980.

56. Bernikow, *Abel*, pp. 171–2.

57. Bernikow, *Abel*, chs. 3–4. Even after his arrest, MARK failed to realize that VIK had never been under surveillance by the FBI. He told his lawyer that "he now believed that Hayhanen had been secretly apprehended in December [1956] by the FBI and had met [him] thereafter on orders from Federal agents" (Donovan, *Strangers on a Bridge*, p. 39).

58. vol. 6, ch. 5, part 2.

59. Bernikow, *Abel*, pp. 86–95.

60. vol. 6, ch. 5, part 2.

61. vol. 6, ch. 5, part 2.

62. vol. 6, ch. 5, part 2, *n.* 11.

63. Donovan, *Strangers on a Bridge*, pp. 179–80; Bernikow, *Abel*, pp. 242–4.

64. Donovan, *Strangers on a Bridge*, p. 257.

65. vol. 6, ch. 5, part 2.

66. Bernikow, *Abel*, pp. 223–4.

67. vol. 6, ch. 5, part 2.

68. Also on February 10, 1962 Frederic L. Pryor, a Yale student accused of espionage in East Berlin, was released at Checkpoint Charlie.

69. vol. 6, ch. 5, part 2.

70. vol. 6, ch. 5, part 2.

71. Donovan, *Strangers on a Bridge*, p. 418.

72. vol. 6, ch. 5, part 2.

73. vol. 6, ch. 5, part 2.

74. While in New York "Abel" had sent to Moscow, at the GRU's request, large-scale maps of American cities. Though this was not a very demanding assignment in the United States, similar maps were unobtainable for Soviet cities.

75. vol. 6, ch. 5, part 2.

76. Donovan, *Strangers on a Bridge*, pp. 275, 414.

77. vol. 6, ch. 5, part 2.

78. The SVR, which still propagates the heroic "Abel" myth, claimed in 1995 that, "Secrecy requirements do not yet allow the disclosure of many of the operations in which MARK participated." Samolis (ed.), *Veterany Vneshnei Razvedki Rossii,* pp. 156–9.

79. Gordievsky, *Next Stop Execution,* pp. 141–2.

Chapter Eleven   The Main Adversary Part 2

1. See above, chapter 9.

2. vol. 6, ch. 11, part 2.

3. vol. 6, ch. 11, part 2.

4. Wise, *Molehunt,* pp. 186–7.

5. Murphy, Kondrashev and Bailey, *Battleground Berlin,* pp. 245–6.

6. vol. 6, ch. 11, part 2.

7. Wise, *Molehunt,* pp. 188–9.

8. vol. 6, ch. 11, part 2. The Gallery Orlov, originally in South Pitt Street, Alexandria, later moved to King Street in the Old Town (Kessler, *Undercover Washington,* pp. 125–6).

9. Wise, *Molehunt,* pp. 191–4.

10. vol. 6, ch. 11, part 2.

11. vol. 6, ch. 11, part 2. Mrs. Orlov said later that her husband had told her the Soviet embassy had agreed to his request for asylum for them and their two young sons (Wise, *Molehunt,* p. 192).

12. Wise, *Molehunt,* ch. 13.

13. vol. 6, ch. 11, part 2; vol. 6, app. 1, parts 17, 41.

14. Kessler, *Undercover Washington,* p. 126.

15. k-4,136.

16. Barron, *KGB,* ch. 10. Andrew and Gordievsky, *KGB,* pp. 464–6.

17. k-4,136.

18. Andrew and Gordievsky, *KGB,* pp. 465–6.

19. Bamford, *The Puzzle Palace,* p. 144.

20. vol. 6, ch. 11, part 11.

21. Bamford, *The Puzzle Palace,* pp. 134–40.

22. vol. 6, ch. 11, part 11.

23. Bamford, *The Puzzle Palace,* p. 141.

24. vol. 6, ch. 11, part 11. From 1960 to 1963 the GRU had an important agent-in-place at NSA, Staff Sergeant Jack E. Dunlap (like Mitchell and Martin, a walk-in). In 1963 Victor Norris Hamilton, a former employee of NSA who had been forced to resign in 1959 because of mental illness, defected to the Soviet Union and gave a press conference much like Mitchell's and Martin's in 1960. Andrew and Gordievsky, *KGB,* pp. 462–4. Bamford, *The Puzzle Palace,* pp. 151–4.

25. Fursenko and Naftali, "Soviet Intelligence and the Cuban Missile Crisis," p. 77.

26. Bamford, *The Puzzle Palace,* pp. 142–3.

27. vol. 6, ch. 11, part 11. Mitrokhin's notes on the 500 rouble monthly allowance are taken from Mitchell's file and refer only to him. However, two years later, Martin told a reporter from *The New York Times,* whom he met in a chance encounter in a Leningrad café, that he been given the same allowance. Theodore Shabad, "Defector from US Resigned to Soviet Union," *The New York Times* (June 24, 1962). Bamford, *The Puzzle Palace,* p. 148. When Mitchell got a job, he was paid 100 roubles as a monthly salary and another 400 as a subsidy; vol. 6, ch. 11, part 11.

28. Information on Mitchell from vol. 6, ch. 11, part 11; on Martin from Shabad, "Defector from US Resigned to Soviet," *The New York Times* (June 24, 1962).

29. vol. 6, ch. 11, part 11.

30. Bamford, *The Puzzle Palace,* p. 149. Martin died in Moscow of acute leukemia in 1986.

31. The source of the alarmist KGB report of Pentagon plans for a nuclear attack was "a document sent by a[n unidentified] liaison officer with the CIA to his own government" (Fursenko and Naftali, "*One Hell of a Gamble,*" pp. 51–2). Though General Curtis LeMay, the belligerent head of Strategic Air Command, privately used the language of the pre-emptive strike, this never had any prospect of becoming the policy of the Eisenhower administration. Such language, however, caused some concern among the United States' NATO allies. The British JIC, though believing it "highly unlikely" that, with her democratic method of government and her close ties with other Western nations, [the USA] would ever provoke a war," concluded in 1954 that it was "just possible that given (a) a more extreme government in the US, (b)

increased US lack of confidence in some or all of her Western allies owing to political development in their countries, (c) some sudden advance in the USA in the sphere of weapons, etc., the counsels of impatience might get the upper hand." JIC(54) 37 (I owe this information to Alex Craig of Christ's College, Cambridge, currently completing a groundbreaking PhD on the JIC in the early Cold War).

Recently declassified US documents indicate that, under specified emergency conditions, senior American commanders had "predelegated" presidential authority to use nuclear weapons (Paul Lashmar, "Dr. Strangelove's Secrets," *Independent*, September 8, 1998). It is possible, but by no means certain, that a report of this from the KGB's source, together with LeMay's apocalyptic rhetoric, fueled the Centre's fear of an American first strike.

32. Feklisov, *Za okeanom i na ostrove*, pp. 199–201. Zubok and Pleshakov, *Inside the Kremlin's Cold War*, pp. 236–40.

33. Andrew, *For the President's Eyes Only*, pp. 257ff.

34. Zubok and Pleshakov, *Inside the Kremlin's Cold War*, p. 242.

35. Andrew, *For the President's Eyes Only*, pp. 267ff.

36. Shelepin to Khrushchev, memorandum no. 1861-Sh (July 29, 1961). Decree no. 191/75-GS. vol. 6, ch. 5, part 5. Cf. Zubok, "Spy vs. Spy," pp. 28–30; Zubok and Pleshakov, *Inside the Kremlin's Cold War*, pp. 253–5.

37. Andrew, *For the President's Eyes Only*, pp. 278–9; Dobrynin, *In Confidence*, pp. 52–4.

38. Fursenko and Naftali, "*One Hell of a Gamble*," pp. 155, 168. On American covert action against Castro, see Andrew, *For the President's Eyes Only*, pp. 271–2, 274–6, 280.

39. Fursenko and Naftali, "*One Hell of a Gamble*," ch. 9.

40. Andrew, *For the President's Eyes Only*, pp. 282–90.

41. Andrew, *For the President's Eyes Only*, pp. 285–95; Zubok and Pleshakov, *Inside the Kremlin's Cold War*, pp. 258–66; Dobrynin, *In Confidence*, pp. 52–4.

42. See above, chapters 7, 8.

43. Fursenko and Naftali, "Soviet Intelligence and the Cuban Missile Crisis." Mitrokhin's notes add nothing to this admirable analysis, based on privileged access to SVR files, of KGB sources of political intelligence in Washington during the missile crisis. There is no indication in files noted by Mitrokhin to which Fursenko and Naftali did not have access, notably those on illegals, of any significant source which they have overlooked.

44. Fursenko and Naftali, "Soviet Intelligence and the Cuban Missile Crisis," p. 65.

45. Kalugin, *Spymaster*, pp. 237–8. Sakharovsky's melancholy expression is clearly evident in the photograph which accompanies his official SVR hagiography (Samolis (ed.), *Veterany Vneshnei Razvedki Rossii*, pp. 133–5).

46. Fursenko and Naftali, "Soviet Intelligence and the Cuban Missile Crisis," pp. 66, 75, 85n.

47. Zubok and Pleshakov, *Inside the Kremlin's Cold War*, pp. 266–7. Fursenko and Naftali, "*One Hell of a Gamble*," ch. 14. On October 26, Feklisov, the Washington resident, had two, now celebrated, meetings with the ABC diplomatic correspondent, John Scali, whom he knew had good access to the White House, to discuss ways to end the crisis. Kennedy was convinced that Feklisov spoke for Khrushchev personally. The KGB archives, however, show that he did not. Feklisov played no role either in Khrushchev's proposal on October 26 to resolve the crisis by an American guarantee of Cuban territorial integrity, or in his attempt on October 27 to trade US bases in Turkey for Soviet missile sites in Cuba. It is possible that Shelepin, who—unlike Semichastny—was a member of the Presidium, had encouraged Semichastny to use a meeting between Feklisov and Scali to try to extract a US proposal to settle the crisis which would make the Soviet climbdown less humiliating. Because of the incomplete nature of KGB files on this episode, together with the conflict of oral evidence between Feklisov, Scali and Semichastny, it may never be possible to establish what led up to the meeting on the Soviet side. Fursenko and Naftali, "Using KGB Documents"; Fursenko and Naftali, "Soviet Intelligence and the Cuban Missile Crisis," pp. 80–3.

48. Zubok and Pleshakov, *Inside the Kremlin's Cold War*, p. 267. Fursenko and Naftali, "*One Hell of a Gamble*," pp. 284–6.

49. The fullest account of Penkovsky's career is Schecter and Deriabin, *The Spy Who Saved the World*.

50. vol. 6, ch. 1, part 1.

51. vol. 6, ch. 8, part 6.

52. vol. 6, ch. 8, part 6.

53. vol. 6, ch. 1, part 1.

54. vol. 2, app. 3.

55. On Golitsyn's impact on Angleton and the CIA, see Wise, *Molehunt*, and Mangold, *Cold Warrior*.

56. vol. 1, app. 3; vol. 6, ch. 1, part 1. On the US embassy's decision to return Cherepanov's documents, see Wise, *Molehunt*, pp. 121–3.

57. See below, chapter 22.

58. vol. 6, ch. 1, part 1; Nosenko's codename appears in vol. 6, ch. 5, part 5.

59. vol. 2, app. 3.

60. The VPK also tasked the GRU, the State Committee for Science and Technology (GKNT), a secret unit in the Soviet Academy of Sciences and the State Committee for External Economic Relations (GKES). Most of the S&T it received came from the KGB and GRU. Hanson, *Soviet Industrial Espionage;* Andrew and Gordievsky, *KGB,* pp. 622–3.

61. k-5,476.

62. k-5,473.

63. URBAN may be a post-war codename for the unidentified wartime agent PERS referred to in the VENONA decrypts. On KGB/SVR attempts to confuse identification of PERS, see Albright and Kunstel, *Bombshell,* pp. 156, 271.

64. Mitrokhin's note, in Russian, identifies BERG's employee as "Consolidated Vacuum." This is probably a reference to Sperry-Rand (UNIVAC); it is known that UNIVAC computers were high on the list of S&T targets (Tuck, *High-Tech Espionage,* ch. 11).

65. vol. 6, ch. 6.

66. Romerstein and Levchenko, *The KGB against the Main Enemy,* pp. 266–7; Richelson, *A Century of Spies,* pp. 279–82.

67. vol. 6, ch. 6.

68. Judy, "The Case of Computer Technology."

69. vol. 6, app. 1, part 27.

70. k-5,473.

71. k-5,369.

72. vol. 6, app. 1, part 39.

73. k-5,475.

74. On the time lag between US and Soviet computer technology, see Judy, "The Case of Computer Technology"; and Ammann, Cooper and Davies (eds.), *The Technological Level of Soviet Industry,* ch. 8.

75. Judy, "The Case of Computer Technology," p. 66.

76. k-5,476.

77. vol. 6, ch. 6.

78. vol. 6, ch. 3, part 1; vol. 10, ch. 2, para. 7.

Chapter Twelve   *The Main Adversary Part 3*

1. vol. 6, ch. 5, part 4. The KGB Collegium also proposed establishing networks of illegal residencies to take over the main burden of intelligence operations in Canada, Mexico, West Germany and China.

2. vol. 6, ch. 5, parts 2, 3. Unusually, Mitrokhin's notes from KONOV's file do not record the real name of either himself or his wife.

3. vol. 6, ch. 5, parts 2, 3. No details are available of KONOV's S&T.

4. vol. 8, app. 3a.

5. ALBERT's and GERA's KGB files record that they were issued with Belgian passports nos. 26862/37/41 and 26861/36/41 valid until April 8, 1961. vol. 8, app. 3a.

6. vol. 8, app. 3a.

7. vol. 6, ch. 5, part 3.

8. vol. 8, app. 3, item 7.

9. vol. 6, ch. 13, part 1.

10. Barron, *KGB Today,* pp. 294–320. vol. 6, ch. 13, part 1. During his interview with Barron, Valoushek used the cover name "Zemenek."

11. Barron, *KGB Today,* pp. 320–7; Granatstein and Stafford, *Spy Wars,* pp. 154–5.

12. vol. 6, ch. 13, part 1.

13. vol. 8, ch. 8, para. 3.

14. Barron, *KGB Today,* pp. 388–90; Granatstein and Stafford, *Spy Wars,* pp. 170–1.

15. vol. 6, ch. 11, part 5; vol. 8, ch. 8, paras. 3, 4. In 1975 alone Hambleton had meetings with Pyatin in Washington, with V. G. Matsenov in New York, with S. S. Sadauskas in Vienna and with A. Rusakov in Prague. His other foreign missions took in Haiti, Saudi Arabia, Egypt and Israel.

16. vol. 6, ch. 13, part 1. Mitrokhin's notes do not give IVANOVA's name.

17. Barron, *KGB Today*, pp. 330–1.

18. vol. 6, ch. 13, part 1; vol. 8, app. 8, item 87.

19. k-8,78; k-19,158; vol. 6, ch. 5, part 2. Mitrokhin's notes do not identify LENA.

20. k-8,78.

21. vol. 6, ch. 5, part 2.

22. vol. 6, app. 2, parts 3, 5.

23. vol. 6, ch. 5, part 2. It is not clear from Mitrokhin's notes whether Feder was a "live" or a "dead double."

24. vol. 6, ch. 5, part 2.

25. vol. 6, ch. 5, parts 2, 3. Like other Steinway customers, Governor Rockefeller can, of course, scarcely be blamed for failing to realize that his piano tuner was a KGB illegal. There is no evidence in Mitrokhin's notes that Rudenko had contact with him.

26. Dobrynin, Anatoly, *In Confidence*, p. 377.

27. Isaacson, *Kissinger*, pp. 90–3.

28. Kramer and Roberts, "*I Never Wanted to be Vice-President of Anything!*," pp. 8–9.

29. Schonberg, *Horowitz*, chs. 15–17. Mitrokhin's notes, probably like the KGB file on which they are based, do not make clear exactly how great a part RYBAKOV played in tuning Horowitz's pianos. The CD 186 was originally tuned by the Steinway chief technician, Franz Mohr.

30. vol. 6, ch. 5, part 2.

31. vol. 6, ch. 5, part 2; t-7,304.

32. vol. 6, ch. 5, part 2. RYBAKOV's file gives his Moscow address as 108 Mir Prospect, apartment 120.

33. Shevchenko, *Breaking with Moscow*, p. 375.

34. vol. 6, ch. 5, part 4. The main regional priorities for the establishment of illegal residencies in the period 1969–75, apart from North America, were the major states of western Europe, China and the Middle East. With the exception of the United States, where it was intended to establish ten residencies, no state was to have more than two.

35. vol. 6, ch. 5, parts 2, 3.

36. Barron, *KGB Today*, pp. 335–6.

37. vol. 6, ch. 5, part 3.

38. Barron, *KGB Today*, pp. 337–41, 349–51. vol. 6, ch. 13, part 1.

39. Barron, *KGB Today*, pp. 355–71.

40. Though not identified by Mitrokhin, LUTZEN was probably the defector Rupert Sigl, who had worked for the KGB in Karlshorst from 1957 to 1969.

41. vol. 6, ch. 13, part 1.

42. vol. 8, ch. 8, para. 3.

43. Granatstein and Stafford, *Spy Wars*, pp. 176, 179–83.

44. vol. 8, ch. 8, para. 4.

45. Granatstein and Stafford, *Spy Wars*, pp. 151–4, 184–5. In June 1986 Hambleton was moved to a Canadian jail and released under mandatory supervision in March 1989.

46. vol. 6, ch. 5, part 2; vol. 6, app. 2, part 1; k-16,89.

47. The fullest published account of the Koecher case is in Kessler, *Spy vs Spy* (based in part on interviews with the Koechers after their return to Czechoslovakia in 1986). There are some further details in Earley, *Confessions of a Spy*, ch. 6, and Kessler, "Moscow's Mole in the CIA," *Washington Post* (April 17, 1988). Karl Koecher's early career is summarized in k-8,110.

48. k-19,96.

49. Kessler, *Spy vs Spy*, pp. 52–63. Kessler, *Undercover Washington*, pp. 33–4.

50. k-19, 96. Hana Koecher was given the rather obvious KGB codename HANKA.

51. Kessler, *Spy vs Spy*, pp. 60, 245.

52. vol. 6, ch. 8, part 2; k-8,110.

53. t-7,306; vol. 6, app. 1 (misc.), part 2. Ogorodnik appears to have been recruited by the CIA while serving in Bogotá in 1974, and to have supplied microfilm copies of hundreds of secret Soviet documents, summaries of which were circulated by the CIA to the White House, the National Security Council and the State Department. Barron, *KGB Today*, pp. 428–9.

54. Kessler, *Spy vs Spy*, pp. 139–44, 152–8, 233–6; Kessler, "Moscow's Mole in the CIA," *Washington Post*, (April 17, 1988).

55. Hana Koecher sued the journalist, Egon Lansky, who had published the story about her and her husband. The case was dismissed and costs awarded against her. Tom Gross, "Spy's Wife Gets a Job with Our Man in Prague," *Sunday Telegraph* (March 5, 1995).

56. vol. 6, ch. 5, part 3.

57. vol. 6, app. 2, part 4.

Chapter Thirteen The Main Adversary Part 4

1. vol. 6, ch. 2, part 1*n.*

2. See below, chapter 15.

3. Dobrynin, *In Confidence,* pp. 209–10, 513. According to Dobrynin, "Andropov was cautious enough not to interfere in Gromyko's everyday management of foreign policy, and Gromyko for his part respected Andropov's growing influence in the Politburo."

4. Fursenko and Naftali, "Soviet Intelligence and the Cuban Missile Crisis," p. 85, *n.* 7. FCD intelligence analysis, however, seems to have remained comparatively undeveloped by the standards of the British JIC, the CIA's Directorate of Intelligence and other major Western assessment agencies.

5. See below, chapters 15 and 19.

6. Volkogonov, *The Rise and Fall of the Soviet Empire,* p. 322. The letter contained simply routine proposals for strengthening the role of the CPSU.

7. Kalugin, *Spymaster,* p. 257. During the final months of Brezhnev's life, however, Andropov began to circulate stories about the corruption of Brezhnev's family and entourage as part of his strategy to eliminate rivals to the succession. Service, *A History of Twentieth-Century Russia,* p. 426.

8. Dobrynin, *In Confidence,* p. 130.

9. Dobbs, *Down with Big Brother,* pp. 6–8; Chazov, *Zdorov'ye i Vlast,* pp. 115–44.

10. vol. 6, app. 2, part 6.

11. vol. 6, ch. 11, part 3; vol. 6, app. 1, parts 12, 41.

12. Kalugin, *Spymaster,* p. 83. Kalugin does not give Lipka's name or codename and refers to him only as "a 'walk-in' who came to us in the mid-1960s, explaining that he was involved in shredding and destroying NSA documents." A later analysis by the Centre singled out 200 documents from NSA, the CIA, State Department and other federal agencies as of particular value. Mitrokhin's notes, alas, give no details of their contents.

13. vol. 6, ch. 11, part 3; vol. 6, app. 1, parts 12, 26, 28, 41; k-8,78. Lipka's file includes his and his father's addresses during the 1970s, as well as details of his wife's work at St. Joseph's Hospital in Lancaster, Pennsylvania, together with her telephone number at the hospital.

14. Kalugin, *Spymaster,* pp. 84–9.

15. Studies of the Walker case include Barron, *Breaking the Ring;* Blum, *I Pledge Allegiance.*

16. Kalugin, *Spymaster,* p. 83.

17. Kalugin, *Spymaster,* p. 89. The fact that Walker's file was held by the Sixteenth Department, separately from most other FCD files, explains why Mitrokhin never saw it. There are probably other Sixteenth Department agents of whom he was also unaware.

18. Earley, *Confessions of a Spy,* pp. 7–8.

19. Kalugin, *Spymaster,* p. 89.

20. The KGB officers who took part in running MAREK were P. V. Yatskov, B. P. Kolymakov, Ye. N. Gorlitsyn, V. F. Perchik, Ye. V. Piskarev, G. N. Pustnyatsev, V. M. Bogachev, Ye. A. Belov, V. N. Gordeyev, A. V. Bolshakov, S. V. Sychev, V. N. Melnikov, A. A. Alekseyev, S. Ye. Muzhchinin, V. S. Miroshnikov, V. A. Revin, N. V. Medved, I. K. Baranov, V. I. Kucherov, V. S. Loginov, V. I. Shpakevich, I. S. Pakhmonov, V. V. Makarov, A. M. Gvosdev and L. K. Kostanyan. Even after Agee revealed that MAREK was a plant, some in the Centre did not regard the evidence as conclusive.

21. Earley, *Confessions of a Spy,* pp. 91–2.

22. Kalugin, *Spymaster,* pp. 111–12. Though Mitrokhin does not identify Sedov by name, he confirms the access to Kissinger by an "operations officer."

23. Schultz, *Turmoil and Triumph,* p. 117.

24. t-7,321.

25. Dobrynin, *In Confidence.*

26. Barron, *KGB,* pp. 25–7. Barron, *KGB Today,* pp. 240–3. vol. 6, ch. 10; vol. 6, app. 1, parts 19, 40.

27. vol. 6, ch. 10; vol. 6, app. 1, part 40. There is no evidence in Mitrokhin's notes that the cultivation of Waldheim was successful.

28. Shevchenko, *Breaking with Moscow,* pp. 331–2.

29. vol. 6, app. 1, parts 4, 19; t-3,69, k-24,228.

30. vol. 6, ch. 8, part 4, *n*. 1.

31. vol. 6, ch. 14, part 2, *n*. 2.

32. vol. 6, app. 1, parts 3, 41; t-2,258.

33. vol. 6, ch. 3, part 2; vol. 6, app. 1, part 41.

34. vol. 6, app. 1, part 16. The Turkish Cypriot newspaper *Malkin Sesi* reported on May 18, 1985 that, according to intelligence supplied by Washington to the Turkish government, Ozgur had worked as a Soviet spy from 1974 to 1977.

35. vol. 6, ch. 3, part 3.

36. vol. 6, ch. 4; k-8,103,447.

37. vol. 6, app. 1, part 38.

38. vol. 6, app. 1, part 4; t-3,56.

39. vol. 6, app. 1, parts 11, 39; k-22,71.

40. vol. 6, app. 1, part 33.

41. vol. 6, ch. 3, part 2. Mitrokhin does not give REM's identity. As was frequently the case, the same codename was given to several other agents. None of the others seems to fit the Washington REM.

42. k-22,207.

43. t-1,75.

44. vol. 6, ch. 4; vol. 6, app. 1, parts 16, 19.

45. vol. 6, ch. 14, part 2, *n*. 2.

46. vol. 6, ch. 3, part 3.

47. vol. 6, ch. 14, part 2, *n*. 2.

48. vol. 6, ch. 3, part 3.

49. Kalugin, *Spymaster*, pp. 72–5.

50. Kalugin, *Spymaster*, p. 103.

51. Dobrynin, *In Confidence*, p. 355.

52. vol. 6, ch. 3, part 3.

53. Kramer and Roberts, "*I Never Wanted to be* Vice-President *of Anything!*," p. 23.

54. vol. 6, ch. 3, part 3.

55. Dobrynin, *In Confidence*, pp. 377–8.

56. vol. 6, ch. 3, part 3.

57. In 1977 Lomov returned to New York with his deputy director, Yuri Mikhailovich Zabrodin, for a three-month visit. His main KGB mission on this occasion was to investigate research on interrogation techniques which, the Centre hoped, would cause those it interrogated to have no subsequent memory of their replies to questions. vol. 6, ch. 2, part 1; vol. 6, app. 2, parts 4, 5.

58. vol. 6, ch. 2, part 1; vol. 6, ch. 3, part 3.

59. vol. 6, ch. 2, part 1.

60. vol. 6, ch. 2, part 1.

61. See below, chapter 17.

62. vol. 6, ch. 7. Mitrokhin identifies VLADIMIROV as deputy director of the institute, but does not give his name. Cf. Barron, *KGB Today*, p. 265.

63. vol. 6, ch. 2, part 1; vol. 6, app. 2, parts 4, 6.

64. Kissinger, *White House Years*, p. 112.

65. vol. 6, app. 1, part 6.

66. Dobrynin, *In Confidence*, p. 485.

67. vol. 5, section 10.

68. vol. 6, ch. 3, parts 2, 3.

69. Andrew and Gordievsky (eds.), *Instructions from the Centre*, pp. 306–7.

70. vol. 6, ch. 2, part 1, *n*. 3.

71. Andrew and Gordievsky (eds.), *Instructions from the Centre*, ch. 4.

72. Kalugin, *Spymaster*, pp. 302–3. Kalugin considered the tone of Andropov's cable "paranoid."

73. Volkogonov, *The Rise and Fall of the Soviet Empire*, p. 351.

74. Dobrynin, *In Confidence*, p. 523.

75. Andrew and Gordievsky, *KGB*, pp. 582–603. Andrew and Gordievsky (eds.), *Instructions from the Centre*, ch. 4.

76. Shvets, *Washington Station*, pp. 29, 74–5. Shvets had access to Androsov's reports as a member of the

FCD First (North American) Department from 1982 to 1985, and was then posted to Washington as a Line PR officer in Androsov's residency.

77. Andrew and Gordievsky, *KGB*, pp. 591–605.

78. Andrew, *For the President's Eyes Only*, pp. 471–7.

79. *Izvestia* (September 24, 1991).

80. Garthoff, "The KGB Reports to Gorbachev," pp. 226–7.

81. vol. 6, ch. 6.

82. See, for example, Kryuchkov's 1984 analysis of "the deepening economic and social crisis in the capitalist world." Andrew and Gordievsky (eds.), *Instructions from the Centre*, pp. 33–4.

83. vol. 6, app. 1, part 41. Mitrokhin did not record the statistics for the San Francisco residency.

84. vol. 6, ch. 6.

85. Mitrokhin's notes give the recruitment dates of fifteen S&T agents who began work for the KGB in the 1970s: ANTON (1975), ARAM (1975), CHEKHOV/YAYKAL (1976), MAG (1974), MIKE (1973), OTPRYSK (1974), SARKIS (1974), SATURN (1978), SOFT (1971), TROP (1979), TURIST (1977), UGNYUS (1974), ZENIT (1978) and two others whose codenames cannot be published (recruited in 1975–6). VIL appears to have been recruited earlier. Other S&T agents active in the USA during the 1970s, whose recruitment dates do not appear in Mitrokhin's notes, were LONG, PATRIOT and RIDEL. Mitrokhin also identifies five trusted contacts recruited during the 1970s: KLARA (1972), KURT (1973), TSORN (1977), VELLO (1973) and VEYT (1973). In the case of a further eight members of the S&T network in 1970s (FOGEL, FREY, IZOLDA, OZON, ROZHEK, SPRINTER, TEPLOTEKNIK and VAYS), it is unclear from Mitrokhin's notes which were fully recruited agents and which were trusted contacts. The notes give no dates for the activities of another eight S&T agents and trusted contacts probably active in the 1970s: ALGORITMAS, AUTOMOBILIST, CHARLES, KLIM, LIR, ODISSEY, PAVEL and RUTH. Mitrokhin's notes on all those listed above are relatively brief, varying in length from a few lines to a paragraph. A majority of both agents and trusted contacts are identified by name. vol. 6, app. 1, parts 1, 2, 3, 5, 11, 14, 20, 27, 28, 29, 31, 32, 38, 39; k-14,171; k-18,380–2; t-1,138, 290,294–5,297–301; t-2,109,161–2; t-7,77.

86. FREY was an agent and PAVEL a trusted contact in IBM (vol. 6, app. 1, parts 5, 27). Agent SATURN occupied a senior scientific post in McDonnell Douglas (vol. 6, app. 1, parts 27, 32). Agent ZENIT was a scientist in TRW (vol. 6, app. 1, part 27).

87. vol. 6, app. 1, parts 2, 32.

88. vol. 6, app. 1, part 38. The case of another scientist at one of the best-known US universities cannot be referred to for legal reasons; vol. 6, app. 1, part 32.

89. vol. 6, app. 1, part 33.

90. vol. 6, app. 1, part 31. DARCOM has since become the Army Materiel Command (AMC).

91. The latest date for which Mitrokhin provides statistics on the total numbers of S&T agents run by the New York and Washington residencies is 1970; he provides no statistics on the agents run by the San Francisco residency.

92. Lindsey, *The Falcon and the Snowman*. Boyce escaped from prison in 1980, but was recaptured a year later and sentenced to an additional three years for escaping and twenty-five years for robbing seventeen banks while on the run (Lindsey, *The Flight of the Falcon*).

93. vol. 6, app. 1, part 27. Mitrokhin's brief note on ZENIT's recruitment gives no details of the intelligence he supplied. Other important intelligence on satellite surveillance included the operating manual for KH-11, the most advanced US SIGINT satellite. Early in 1978 William Kampiles, who had been briefly employed by the CIA Watch Center, presented a copy of it to the KGB residency in Athens. He was unaware, however, that the KGB officer who received it, Sergei Ivanovich Bokhan, had been recruited several years earlier by the CIA. Earley, *Confessions of a Spy*, p. 120.

94. This calculation appears to have been based on the estimated saving in imports paid for in hard currency. Brezhnev was informed that the economic benefit of S&T for the Soviet defense industry had not been calculated. vol. 6, ch. 6.

95. Similar reports on S&T successes were sent to Kosygin, the prime minister, and Ustinov, the Defence Minister.

96. vol. 6, ch. 6.

97. t-7,105.

98. vol. 6, ch. 6.

99. Andrew and Gordievsky, *KGB*, p. 622.

100. In 1965 the United States had accounted for over 90 percent of the VPK's requirements.

101. Documents supplied by the French agent in Directorate T, Vladimir Vetrov (codenamed FARE-WELL); cited by Brook-Shepherd, *The Storm Birds*, p. 260. On Vetrov, see Andrew and Gordievsky, *Le KGB dans le monde, 1917–1990*, pp. 619–23. For the text of some of Vetrov's documents, see Hanson, *Soviet Industrial Espionage.* Vetrov's documents and Mitrokhin's notes complement each other.

102. Hanson, *Soviet Industrial Espionage*, p. 31.

103. vol. 6, ch. 6. Mitrokhin's notes identify 106 of the KGB's agents within the Soviet scientific community; vol. 6, ch. 5, part 1, *n.* 6.

104. vol. 6, ch. 6.

105. vol. 6, app. 1, parts 2, 32.

106. vol. 6, app. 1, parts 27, 32.

107. vol. 6, ch. 6.

108. Kessler, *Spy vs Spy*, pp. 167–8.

109. Also targeted by western European residencies were the US Atomic Energy Commission, the Battelle Memorial Institute, Dow Chemicals, Dupont de Nemours, GTE, Arthur D. Little Inc., Litton Industries Inc., the Massachusetts Institute of Technology and RCA. Mitrokhin's notes do not indicate which—if any—residencies had particular responsibilities for these targets; k-5,424. The National Institute of Health was targeted because of its research on the effects of chemical and biological warfare; vol. 6, ch. 6.

110. vol. 6, app. 1, part 1; t-7,8,77.

111. vol. 2, app. 3.

112. Volkogonov, *The Rise and Fall of the Soviet Empire*, p. 338.

113. US government, *Soviet Acquisition of Militarily Significant Western Technology*

114. Brook-Shepherd, *The Storm Birds*, p. 260.

115. vol. 2, app. 3.

116. k-5,504.

117. Hanson, *Soviet Industrial Espionage*, pp. 10, 23.

118. Wolf, *Man without a Face*, p. 182.

119. Andrew and Gordievsky, *KGB*, pp. 641–2.

120. Andrew and Gordievsky (eds.), *Instructions from the Centre*, pp. 37, 49–50.

121. Recollections by Oleg Gordievsky of Gorbachev's address; Andrew and Gordievsky, *KGB*, p. 621.

122. Garthoff, "The KGB Reports to Gorbachev," pp. 228–9.

123. Brook-Shepherd, *The Storm Birds*, p. 260.

124. Andrew and Gordievsky (eds.), *Instructions from the Centre*, pp. 40–9, 115–17.

125. The fullest account of the Ames case, and the only one to benefit from interviews with Ames himself, is Earley, *Confessions of a Spy*. On the agents betrayed by Ames, see pp. 143–5. According to the SVR, several of the Western agents named by Ames had already been identified from other leads.

126. Interview with Shebarshin, *Daily Telegraph* (December 1, 1992).

127. Gates, *From the Shadows*, pp. 424–6.

128. Andrew and Gordievsky (eds.), *Instructions from the Centre*, pp. 212–17. Operation RYAN was not finally canceled until Primakov became head of foreign intelligence in October 1991; Richelson, *A Century of Spies*, p. 421.

129. Andrew and Gordievsky, *KGB*, pp. 627–8. Andrew and Gordievsky (eds.), *Instructions from the Centre*, pp. 217–18.

130. Shebarshin's foreign postings had included a term as main resident in India from 1975 to 1977.

131. Andrew and Gordievsky, *KGB*, pp. 620–1.

132. "Intelligence Service Divorces from the KGB," *Izvestia* (September 24, 1991).

133. Interview with Shebarshin, *Daily Telegraph* (December 1, 1992).

134. On the Soviet economy in the Gorbachev era, see Brown, *The Gorbachev Factor*, ch. 5.

135. BBC, *Summary of World Broadcasts*, SU/0955 (December 24, 1990), C4/3ff; SU/0946 (December 13, 1990), B/1.

136. Interview with Shebarshin, *Daily Telegraph* (December 1, 1992).

137. BBC, *Summary of World Broadcasts*, SU/0946 (December 13, 1990), B/1. Much the same conspiracy theory had been expounded in a secret circular to residencies almost six years earlier; Andrew and Gordievsky (eds.), *Instructions from the Centre*, pp. 152–9.

138. Andrew and Gordievsky (eds.), *Instructions from the Centre*, pp. 218–22; *More Instructions from the Centre*, pp. 125–8.

139. Kryuchkov continued to advance this preposterous conspiracy theory and to complain that, though he submitted a file on the case to Gorbachev, he repeatedly reneged on a promise to look into it. Remnick, *Resurrection*, p. 86.

Chapter Fourteen   Political Warfare

1. Marx, *Theses on Feuerbach*, no. 11.
2. "Chief Conclusions and Views Adopted at the Meeting of [FCD] Heads of Service," ref. 156/54 (February 1, 1984); Andrew and Gordievsky (eds.), *Instructions from the Centre*, pp. 30–44.
3. Andrew and Gordievsky, *KGB*, p. 629.
4. On Modin, see chapter 9.
5. See above, chapters 9 and 12.
6. An extract from the report appears in Yeltsin, *The View from the Kremlin*, appendix B, pp. 307–8.
7. Golson (ed.), *The Playboy Interview*, p. 135.
8. Posner, *Case Closed*, p. 371; Summers, *Conspiracy*, p. 36.
9. Hurt, *Reasonable Doubt*, p. 124.
10. Yeltsin, *The View from the Kremlin*, appendix B, p. 308.
11. Dobrynin, *In Confidence*, p. 111.
12. Yeltsin, *The View from the Kremlin*, appendix B, p. 308.
13. The best and fullest account of Oswald's period in the Soviet Union is in Mailer, *Oswald's Tale*. Mailer had access to many of the voluminous KGB files on Oswald, which include transcripts of conversations in his bugged flat in Minsk and surveillance reports from KGB personnel who followed him wherever he went, even spying on him and his wife through a peephole in the bedroom wall to record their "intimate moments."
14. Childs's warning about Oswald's letter was cited in a report by KGB chairman Semichastny to the Central Committee on December 10, 1963, of which an extract appears in Yeltsin, *The View from the Kremlin*, appendix B, p. 307. Yeltsin identifies the CPUSA informant as "Brooks," but does not reveal that this was the CPUSA alias of Jack Childs. For the text of Oswald's letter to the CPUSA of August 28, 1963, see Mailer, *Oswald's Tale*, pp. 594–5.
15. Posner, *Case Closed*, disposes of many of the conspiracy theories. Norman Mailer, the author of the best-documented study of Oswald, admits that he "began with a prejudice in favor of the conspiracy theorists" but finally concluded both that Oswald "had the character to kill Kennedy, and that he probably did it alone." The most difficult unsolved question is not *whether* Oswald shot the President but *why* he did so. Oswald was both a self-obsessed fantasist and a compulsive liar. There is general agreement, however, that he had no personal hostility to Kennedy himself. The best clue to Oswald's motives is probably that provided by the Intourist guide who first introduced him to Russia. "The most important thing for [Oswald]," she recalls, "was that he wanted to become famous. Idea Number One. He was fanatic about it" (Mailer, *Oswald's Tale*, p. 321). In Dallas on November 22, 1963 Oswald seized the opportunity to become one of the best-known Americans of the twentieth century.
16. Marzani was born in Rome in 1912 and emigrated with his parents to the United States in 1923. After graduating from Williams College, Mass., in 1935, he worked for a year in publishing, then studied at Exeter College, Oxford, from 1936 to 1938. According to his KGB file, while at Oxford University (perhaps during the 1937 long vacation) he served in an anarchist brigade in the Spanish Civil War, then joined the Communist Party. On his return to the United States (probably in 1938), he became a member of the CPUSA, using the Party alias "Tony Wells." In 1942 Marzani joined the Office of the Co-ordinator of Information (shortly to become OSS, which contained a number of other Communists and Soviet agents). When OSS was closed in September 1945, Marzani's section was transferred to the State Department. According to his KGB file, Marzani was first recommended to the New York residency by its agent, Cedric Belfrage (CHARLIE), who during the Second World War worked for British Security Co-ordination in New York (vol. 6, ch. 14, part 2). On his transfer to the State Department, Marzani signed a sworn statement that he did not belong to, or support, "any political party or organization that advocates the overthrow of the Government by force or violence." When later discovered to be a member of the CPUSA (officially considered to advocate that policy), he was sentenced in 1948 to two and a half years' imprisonment. Marzani gave some details of his pre-war and wartime career in testimony to the Senate Subcommittee to Investigate the Administration of the Internal Security Act and Other Internal Security Laws on June 18, 1953, but cited the Fifth Amendment and declined to answer the main questions put to him.
17. vol. 6, ch. 14, part 2.
18. Boffa, *Inside the Khrushchev Era*, p. 227.

19. The total advertising budget funded by the KGB during the seven-year period 1961–8 was 70,820 dollars. vol. 6, ch. 14, parts 1, 2.

20. Kalugin, *Spymaster,* p. 45. Marzani published over twenty books and pamphlets, written either by himself or by authors he had selected, on subjects chosen by the KGB. Several concerned the Vietnam War. Other active measures organized by Marzani included an attempt to discredit Stalin's daughter, Svetlana Alliluyeva (codenamed KUKUSHKA), after her flight to the United States in 1967. The KGB helped to refinance Marzani's publishing house after it was seriously damaged in a fire in 1969. During the early 1970s, however, the KGB became increasingly dissatisfied with Marzani. According to Mitrokhin's later notes on his file:

> The [New York] Residency began to notice signs of independent behavior on the part of NORD. He began to overestimate the extent to which the Residency depended upon him, and deluded himself in thinking that he was the only person in the country capable of carrying out Soviet intelligence tasks.
>
> Since 1974 NORD has been living in Puerto Rico; it has been difficult to communicate with him there, and he lost many intelligence opportunities.
>
> (vol. 6, ch. 14, part 2)

21. Joesten, *Oswald,* p. 4. (Page references are to the English edition.)

22. Joesten, *Oswald,* pp. 119, 149–50.

23. Joesten, *Oswald,* pp. 143, 145. In the second edition, Joesten acknowledged "substantial aid" from Marzani in the "research and writing" of an appendix criticizing the Warren report (Joesten, *Oswald,* p. 159*n.*).

24. Even the sympathetic Mark Lane later wrote somewhat critically of Joesten's book: "I had met with Carl Marzani, read proofs of the book at his request, and made some few suggestions. It was a very early work, written before the Warren Commission's evidence was released; therefore, while timely, it was of necessity somewhat flawed and incomplete" (Lane, *Plausible Denial,* p. 44*n*).

25. vol. 6, ch. 14, part 3.

26. Joersten, *Oswald,* p. 3.

27. Lane, *Plausible Denial,* p. 23.

28. vol. 6, ch. 14, part 3. There is no evidence that Lane did realize the source of the funding.

29. vol. 6, ch. 14, part 3; t-7,102. Borovik doubtless did not identify himself to Lane as a KGB agent.

30. Lane, *Plausible Denial,* pp. 4, 19. Posner, *Case Closed,* pp. 414–15.

31. Posner, *Case Closed,* p. 453.

32. vol. 6, ch. 14, part 3.

33. Posner, *Case Closed,* pp. 454–5.

34. vol. 6, ch. 14, part 3. Mitrokhin gives the text of the forged letter in Russian translation. For the original version, see Hurt, *Reasonable Doubt,* pp. 235–6. On Oswald's dyslexia, see Mailer, *Oswald's Tale,* appendix.

35. vol. 6, ch. 14, part 3.

36. Hurt, *Reasonable Doubt,* p. 236. Hurt refers to the letter as the most "singular and teasing" document to have emerged relating to the period immediately before the assassination.

37. vol. 6, ch. 14, part 3.

38. Lane, *Plausible Denial,* p. 187. KGB active measures probably encouraged, rather than accounted for, the Howard Hunt conspiracy theory.

39. Andrew, *For the President's Eyes Only,* pp. 311–12.

40. Also influential was the report of the House Select Committee on the JFK and King assassinations. Its draft report in December 1978 concluded that Oswald acted alone. Flawed acoustic evidence then persuaded the committee that, in addition to the three shots fired by Oswald, a fourth had been fired from a grassy knoll, thus leading it to conclude in its final report of July 1979 that there had been a conspiracy. It pointed to mobsters as the most likely conspirators. Posner, *Case Closed,* pp. 475–86, appendix A.

41. Andrew, *For the President's Eyes Only,* pp. 401–7, 410–11, 421. In private Church later admitted that his study of CIA assassination plots convinced him that the real rogue elephants had been in the White House: "The CIA operated as an arm of the presidency. This led presidents to conclude that they were 'super-godfathers' with enforcers. It made them feel above the law and unaccountable."

42. vol. 6, ch. 14, parts 1, 2, 3; vol. 6, app. 1, part 22.

43. On Agee's resignation from the CIA, see Barron, *KGB Today,* p. 228.

44. Kalugin, *Spymaster*, pp. 191–2. The KGB files noted by Mitrokhin describe Agee as an agent of the Cuban DGI and give details of his collaboration with the KGB, but do not formally list him as a KGB, as well as DGI, agent. vol. 6, ch. 14, parts 1, 2, 3; vol. 6, app. 1, part 22.

45. Agee, *Inside the Company*, p. viii. (Page references are to the Bantam edition.)

46. vol. 6, app. 1, part 22.

47. Agee, *Inside the Company*, p. 659.

48. The London residency eventually became dissatisfied with Cheporov, claiming that he "used his co-operation with the KGB for his own benefit" and "expressed improper criticism of the system in the USSR." k-14,115.

49. vol. 6, app. 1, part 22.

50. Agee, *On The Run*, pp. 111–12, 120–1.

51. Agee, *On The Run*, p. 123.

52. vol. 7, ch. 16, para. 46.

53. The defense committee also took up the case of an American journalist, Mark Hosenball, who had also been served with a deportation order. Unlike Agee, however, Hosenball had no contact with the committee and took no part in its campaign. In the KGB files noted by Mitrokhin there is no mention of Hosenball, save for a passing reference to the work of the defense committee.

54. Agee, *On The Run*, chs. 7, 8; Kelly, "The Deportations of Philip Agee"; vol. 7, ch. 16, para. 45.

55. On the residency's tendency to exaggerate in its influence on protest demonstrations, see Andrew and Gordievsky, *KGB*, p. 586.

56. At a private meeting of the Parliamentary Labour Party on February 17, 1977, however, the Home Secretary, Merlyn Rees, implied a KGB connection. Tony Benn's diary vaguely records that the gist of Rees's comments was that Agee and Hosenball "had been in contact or whatever with enemy agents or something." According to Benn, Rees "got quite a reasonable hearing from the Party." Benn, *Conflicts of Interest*, pp. 41–2.

57. vol. 6, ch. 14, parts 1, 2, 3; k-8,607.

58. Agee, "What Uncle Sam Wants to Know about You," p. 113. (Page references are to the 1978 reprint in Agee and Wolf, *Dirty Work*.)

59. vol. 6, ch. 14, part 1; vol. 7, ch. 16, para. 46.

60. Agee, "What Uncle Sam Wants to Know about You," p. 114.

61. Agee, *On The Run*, pp. 255, 280–1.

62. vol. 6, ch. 14, part 2.

63. Agee, *On The Run*, p. 255. Codenames of some of the RUPOR group in vol. 6, ch. 14, part 2. Mitrokhin's notes record that the group included "former CIA employees" apart from Agee, but do not identify Jim and Elsie Wilcott by name.

64. Agee, *On The Run*, pp. 276–82.

65. The document was also sent anonymously to the British journal *Leveller*, which published extracts from it in August 1979. vol. 6, ch. 14, part 2.

66. Agee, *On The Run*, p. 304.

67. vol. 6, ch. 14, part 2.

68. vol. 6, ch. 14, part 2.

69. Agee, *On The Run*, p. 306.

70. vol. 6, ch. 14, part 2.

71. Agee, *On The Run*, chs. 13–15.

72. vol. 6, ch. 14, part 1.

73. vol. 6, ch. 14, part 1.

74. "Miss Knight Pens Another Letter," *Washington Post* (August 4, 1966).

75. vol. 6, ch. 14, part 1. On Hoover's contacts with Knight, cf. Gentry, *J. Edgar Hoover*, p. 409.

76. vol. 6, ch. 14, part 1.

77. DeLoach, *Hoover's FBI*, ch. 4.

78. DeLoach, *Hoover's FBI*, p. 62.

79. vol. 6, ch. 14, part 1.

80. DeLoach, *Hoover's FBI*, ch. 9. The expurgated text of Sullivan's anonymous message to King, opened by his wife Coretta, is published in Theoharis, *From the Secret Files of J. Edgar Hoover*, pp. 102–3.

81. See below, chapter 17.

82. King, *Why We Can't Wait*; Colaiaco, *Martin Luther King, Jr.*, ch. 5.

83. vol. 6, ch. 14, part 2. The other civil rights leaders selected as targets for active measures were A. Philip Randolph, Whitney Young and Roy Wilkens.

84. vol. 6, ch. 14, part 2.

85. Colaiaco, *Martin Luther King, Jr.*, p. 183. Moscow disapproved, however, of the Black Panthers (whom Carmichael joined in 1968), the Black Muslims and other black separatist groups who lacked what it believed was a proper sense of solidarity with the worldwide struggle against American imperialism.

86. DeLoach, *Hoover's FBI*, p. 247.

87. vol. 6, ch. 14, part 2.

88. vol. 6, ch. 14, part 2. The file noted by Mitrokhin does not record the outcome of operation PANDORA. On present evidence, it is impossible to be certain which, if any, of the attacks on black organizations blamed on the Jewish Defense League were actually the work of the KGB.

89. vol. 6, ch. 10; vol. 6, ch. 14, part 1. The Soviet Union boycotted the Los Angeles Olympics in retaliation for the American boycott of the Moscow Olympics four years earlier.

90. US Department of State, *Active Measures*, p. 55.

91. Dobrynin, *In Confidence*, p. 176.

92. Andrew and Gordievsky, *KGB*, p. 539. Dobrynin, *In Confidence*, pp. 235–6.

93. Kissinger, *Years of Upheaval*, p. 256; Isaacson, *Kissinger*, p. 612. On the KGB targeting of Jackson and Perle, see vol. 6, ch. 14, part 1.

94. Isaacson, *Kissinger*, pp. 612–15.

95. Dobrynin, *In Confidence*, p. 269.

96. vol. 6, ch. 14, part 1.

97. On the Centre's short-lived hopes of using Brzezinski's Soviet contacts to exert influence on him, see above, chapter 8.

98. Andrew, *For the President's Eyes Only*, p. 433.

99. Dobrynin, *In Confidence*, p. 375.

100. vol. 6, ch. 14, part 1.

101. vol. 5, section 10.

102. vol. 5, section 10.

103. Andrew, *For the President's Eyes Only*, p. 455. Vance resigned as Secretary of State after opposing the unsuccessful mission to rescue the Teheran hostages in 1980.

104. vol. 6, ch. 14, part 1.

105. Reagan, *An American Life*, p. 33.

106. vol. 6, ch. 14, part 1.

107. Dobrynin, *In Confidence*, pp. 459, 470, 523. Cf. above, ch. 8. On RYAN, see Andrew and Gordievsky, *KGB*, pp. 583–605, and Andrew and Gordievsky (eds.), *Instructions from the Centre*, ch. 4.

108. Order of the KGB Chairman, no. 0066 (April 12, 1982). vol. 4, indapp. 3, item 47.

109. Andrew and Gordievsky, *KGB*, pp. 590–1.

110. Reagan, *An American Life*, pp. 329–30.

111. vol. 6, ch. 8, part 3. As well as deceiving Sekou Touré, Seliskov also made an unsuccessful attempt to recruit the CIA station chief during his visit to Conakry.

112. vol. 6, ch. 8, part 3.

113. Andrew and Gordievsky, *KGB*, p. 630. Active measures in the Third World will be covered in more detail in the next volume.

114. Andrew and Gordievsky, *KGB*, pp. 630–1.

115. Interview with Shebarshin after his retirement, *Daily Telegraph* (December 1, 1992).

116. Order of the Chairman of the KGB, no. 107/OV. (September 5, 1990).

117. Yeltsin, *The View from the Kremlin*, appendix B, pp. 306–9. Among those former KGB officers who continue to propagate the old JFK conspiracy theories is Oleg Nechiporenko, who twice met Oswald in Mexico City in October 1963 and was later concerned with active measures involving Philip Agee. After his official retirement from the KGB in 1991, Nechiporenko made a number of appearances on the American lecture circuit, published his memoirs in English and was interviewed by Dan Rather in a CBS special on the JFK assassination. Nechiporenko, however, has become confused by the distinction between the original version of the KGB conspiracy theory of the assassination involving oil magnate H. L. Hunt and a later version which targeted Watergate conspirator E. Howard Hunt. His book, *Passport to Assassination*, which argues that the "billionaire E. Howard Hunt played a special role" in the assassination, confuses the two Hunts. Nechiporenko also claims that the CIA was probably involved. *Passport to Assassination*, p. 135.

Chapter Fifteen   Progress Operations Part 1

1. Andrew and Gordievsky, *KGB*, ch. 9.
2. Leonhard, *Child of the Revolution*, p. 303. Leonhard accompanied Ulbricht back from Moscow.
3. Andrew and Gordievsky, *KGB*, ch. 9.
4. Szász, *Volunteers for the Gallows*, p. 105.
5. Flocken and Scholz, *Ernst Wollweber*.
6. After being expelled from the Party in 1958, Wollweiser lived in obscurity until his death in 1967. Childs and Popplewell, *The Stasi*, pp. 64–5.
7. Kopácsi, *Au nom de la classe ouvrière*, pp. 119–22. Mikoyan and Suslov, who also arrived secretly in Budapest at the beginning of the revolution, reported to Moscow on October 24, "One of the most serious mistakes of the Hungarian comrades was the fact that, before twelve midnight last night, they did not permit anyone to shoot at participants in the riots" ("Soviet Documents on the Hungarian Revolution," p. 29).
8. Kopácsi, *Au nom de la classe ouvrière*, pp. 122, 240–8.
9. The best account in English of the repression of the Hungarian Revolution, based on full access to Hungarian archives and limited access to Soviet sources, is contained in a volume edited by Professor György Litván, Director of the Institute for the History of the 1956 Hungarian Revolution, *The Hungarian Revolution of 1956*.
10. k-19,136.
11. t-7,299.
12. k-19,136.
13. t-7,299.
14. k-19,136.
15. Kalugin, *Spymaster*, p. 313.
16. Dawisha, *The Kremlin and the Prague Spring*, p. 16. In March 1968 Novotný was also forced to resign as president.
17. Andrew and Gordievsky, *KGB*, pp. 485–6.
18. Dubček, *Hope Dies Last*, p. 139.
19. Dobrynin, *In Confidence*, p. 179.
20. Pikhoya, "Chekhoslovakiya 1968 god," part 1, pp. 10–12.
21. See below, chapter 15.
22. Litván, *The Hungarian Revolution of 1956*, p. 58.
23. Shevchenko, *Breaking with Moscow*, p. 104.
24. Andrew and Gordievsky, *KGB*, pp. 434–5.
25. k-16,250. vol. 6, ch. 5, part 1. vol. 7, ch. 7, 68.
26. k-19,299.
27. t-7,280.
28. Their names are listed in k-20,93,94.
29. GROMOV was Vasili Antonovich Gordievsky, who at different times assumed the identities of Kurt Sandler, Kurt Molner and Emil Frank (t-7,279). SADKO was an Estonian, Ivan Karlovich Iozenson, who posed successively as a Canadian of Finnish origins, Valte Urho Kataja, and as the Germans Hans Graven and Pobbs Friedrich Schilling (vol. 8, ch. 8; k-8,23,167,574). SEVIDOV's real name is not recorded in Mitrokhin's notes. When traveling in the West, he usually carried a West German passport in the name of Heinrich Dremer or Kurt Ernst Tile; he also possessed an Austrian passport in the name of Dremer. At one stage a Swiss passport was also held in reserve for him at the KGB residency in Vienna. When traveling in Poland, he posed as the East German Willi Werner Neumann (k-16,455). VLADIMIR was a Soviet ethnic German, Ivan Dmitryevich Unrau, who obtained his first West German passport under an assumed identity in 1961; he used at least two different names, Hans Emil Redveyks and [first name unknown] Maykhert. His wife Irina Yevseyevna was the illegal BERTA (k-16,61). VLAS was a Soviet Moldavian (real name unrecorded) who posed as the West German Rolf Max Thiemichen. His wife LIRA was also an illegal (k-11,6; k-8,277). The aliases of all five illegals, like others, were noted by Mitrokhin in the Cyrillic alphabet; their retranslation into the Roman alphabet may in some instances produce spelling errors.
30. GURYEV was Valentin Aleksandrovich Gutin, who posed in Czechoslovakia as a businessman (alias not recorded), probably from West Germany; he accompanied GROMOV to Prague (k-19,655). YEV-DOKIMOV's real name is not recorded; he used the alias Heinz Bayer (k-20,94; t-2,65).

31. The first list of illegals selected for postings in Czechoslovakia contains the name of PYOTR, also known as ARTYOM. Later records reveal that his wife ARTYOMOVA, also an illegal, played an active role in Czechoslovakia, but Mitrokhin's notes contain no reference to operations by PYOTR/ARTYOM. ARTYOMOVA was a MGIMO graduate (real name unknown) who held a West German passport in the name of Edith Ingrid Eichendorf, but posed in Czechoslovakia as an Austrian businesswoman (alias unknown) (k-8,44; k-20,176). DIM (or DIMA) was V. I. Lyamin; he traveled to Prague on an Austrian passport (alias not recorded) (vol. 5, sec. 14; k-20,85). VIKTOR was a Latvian, Pavel Aleksandrovich Karalyun, who obtained a Brazilian passport in 1959 and later assumed Austrian nationality (vol. 6, ch. 5, parts 2, 4; k-16,483).

32. Mitrokhin notes that BELYAKOV used British identity documents but does not record either his real or his assumed name (vol. 6, ch. 5, part 4). USKOV was [first name not recorded] Nikolayevich Ustimenko, who used successively Irish and British passports (aliases not recorded). VALYA was USKOV's Norwegian-born wife, Victoria Martynova, who took Soviet citizenship on her marriage in 1961; like her husband, she used a British passport in Czechoslovakia (vol. 7, ch. 7; k-20,190).

33. ALLA was Galina Leonidovna Vinogradova (later Linitskaya and Kaminskaya), a Yugoslav woman whose first marriage was to a GRU illegal, Vladimir Ivanovich Vinogradov. In 1954 she obtained an Austrian passport in the name of Maria Machek. After her husband was dismissed from the GRU on charges of "political immaturity and ideological instability" in 1955, ALLA married the KGB illegal INDOR, then operating in Switzerland as Waldemar Weber, and acquired Swiss citizenship as Maria Weber. Her marriage to INDOR was dissolved "for operational reasons" in 1957 and she began a relationship with an Egyptian (codenamed PHARAOH) whom she met in Switzerland. Mitrokhin's notes on ALLA's bulky file record that she operated in Czechoslovakia in 1968 as Maria Werner. It is unclear whether ALLA had actually changed her alias from Weber or whether the apparent change is due to a clerical error related to the transliteration of her pseudonym to and from the Cyrillic alphabet. vol. 4, indapp. 3; vol. 4, pakapp. 3; k-20,187.

34. SEP was Mikhail Vladimirovich Fyodorov. From 1945 to 1951 he worked in Polish military intelligence under the alias Mikhail Lipsinski. In 1952 he and his wife ZHANNA (also an illegal) obtained Swiss passports. From 1953 to 1968 he was illegal resident in Switzerland; Mitrokhin's notes do not record his alias. k-20,94,201; vol. 7, ch. 7; vol. 7, app. 3.

35. YEFRAT was a Soviet Armenian, Ashot Abgarovich Akopyan, who assumed the identity of a living Lebanese double, Oganes Saradzhyan, who had migrated to the Soviet Union and obtained, successively, French and Lebanese passports. His wife, Kira Viktorovna Chertenko (TANYA), was also an illegal. k-7,9; k-16,338,419.

36. ROY (also known as KONEYEV) was Vladimir Igorevich Stetsenko, who assumed the identity of a Mexican citizen, Felipe Burns, allegedly the son of a Canadian father and Mexican mother. His wife PAT (also known as IRINA) was also an illegal. vol. 8, app. 3a.

37. The assumed nationality of the illegal JURGEN is not recorded in Mitrokhin's notes.

38. k-20,93.

39. k-19,331.

40. k-20,93.

41. k-20,86. On Bárak's imprisonment in 1962, see Renner, *A History of Czechoslovakia Since 1945*, p. 35.

42. k-20,87,189; vol. 3, pakapp. 3.

43. Gustav Husák, who was to succeed Dubček as First Secretary in April 1969, accused Bárak of personal responsibility for his brutal interrogation and trial on trumped-up charges in 1954. Skilling, *Czechoslovakia's Interrupted Revolution*, p. 380.

44. k-20,93.

45. k-20,96.

46. Dubček, *Hope Dies Last*, p. 150; Skilling, *Czechoslovakia's Interrupted Revolution*, pp. 231, 879.

47. k-20,79. Strougal lost his position in the CPCz secretariat during the April reshuffle. In January 1970 he succeeded ̌Cerník as prime minister.

48. August and Rees, *Red Star over Prague*, pp. 126–7; Dubček, *Hope Dies Last*, pp. 145–6; Dawisha, *The Kremlin and the Prague Spring*, p. 63.

49. Dubček, *Hope Dies Last*, p. 160.

50. k-19,655. k-20,95.

51. In April 1968 GROMOV was awarded the "Honoured KGB Officer" badge for his part in exfiltrating FAUST (Yevgeni Ivanovich Ushakov, who had assumed the identity of a "dead double," Olaf Carl Svenson). k-16,501; k-20,94. Cf. Gordievsky, *Next Stop Execution*, p. 188.

52. k-19,655.

53. k-19,655.

54. Skilling, *Czechoslovakia's Interrupted Revolution*, pp. 69, 568, 576, 696.

55. The KGB file noted by Mitrokhin records that the Service V thugs chosen to assist GUREYEV in kidnapping Černý were named Alekseyev and Ivanov; Petrov and Borisov, also from Service V, were to help GROMOV make off with Procházka (k-19,655).

56. k-19,655; k-20,95.

57. k-20,155,156,203.

58. k-20,89.

59. August and Rees, *Red Star over Prague*, p. 129; Valenta, *Soviet Intervention in Czechoslovakia, 1968*, pp. 63–4. k-20,203.

60. Pikhoya, "Chekhoslovakiya 1968 god," part 2, pp. 35ff; Gardner, "The Soviet Decision to Invade Czechoslovakia."

61. August and Rees, *Red Star over Prague*, p. 129; Valenta, *Soviet Intervention in Czechoslovakia, 1968*, pp. 63–4.

62. August and Rees, *Red Star over Prague*, pp. 140–1. Mitrokhin notes that KGB plans "to carry out special assignments on nine people" in Czechoslovakia in August 1968 were canceled by the Centre, but gives no further details (k-20,203).

63. k-19,644.

64. This is the interpretation of Frantisek August, an StB officer who later defected to the West. According to August, Frouz was "a Soviet agent" (August and Rees, *Red Star over Prague*, p. 128).

65. Interviews with Kalugin in *Komsomolskaya Pravda* (June 20, 1990) and *Moscow News*, 1990, no. 25; Andrew and Gordievsky, *KGB*, pp. 487–8; Kramer, "The Prague Spring and the Soviet Invasion of Czechoslovakia," part 2, p. 6.

66. The minutes of the Politburo meeting of August 15–17, 1968, which agreed the final details of the invasion, are not yet available.

67. Littell (ed.), *The Czech Black Book Prepared by the Czechoslovak Academy of Sciences*, pp. 64–70; August and Rees, *Red Star over Prague*, pp. 134–5.

68. Dubček, *Hope Dies Last*, p. 183.

69. Littell (ed.), *The Czech Black Book Prepared by the Czechoslovak Academy of Sciences*, p. 70.

70. Kramer, "The Prague Spring and the Soviet Invasion of Czechoslovakia," part 2, p. 3.

71. Dubček, *Hope Dies Last*, chs. 22–25.

72. *An Outline of the History of the CPCz*, p. 305.

73. k-19,644.

74. k-19,644. It is unclear from Mitrokhin's notes whether PATERA was an StB or KGB codename or an alias.

75. Kalugin, *Spymaster*, p. 107. Kalugin was "deeply moved by the resident's words."

76. Fourteen illegals were sent to Czechoslovakia in August 1968 (k-20,182); most had almost certainly been on previous short-term missions during the Prague Spring. The total sent, usually on more than one mission, to Czechoslovakia in 1968–9 was twenty-nine (k-20,203).

77. k-19,246.

78. k-20,181.

79. k-16,329; k-20,150,187.

80. k-16,329; k-20,176.

81. k-16,329; k-19,158.

82. k-16,329; k-19,158.

83. k-19,384.

84. vol. 8, ch. 8 and app. 1. ERNA, previously codenamed NORA, who had been born in France of Spanish parents in 1914, became a Communist militant and commanded a machine-gun company during the Spanish Civil War. In 1939 she moved to Russia, took Soviet citizenship and joined the NKGB in 1941. She worked as an illegal in France (1946–52) and Mexico (1954–57) before moving to Montreal in 1958. Despite her criticisms, ERNA told her shocked comrades in Budapest that she remained a committed Leninist. By the mid-1970s, however, she had become so disillusioned that she broke contact with the KGB.

85. Gordievsky, *Next Stop Execution*, pp. 81–2.

86. k-19,158.

87. vol. 3, pakapp. 3.

88. Gordievsky, *Next Stop Execution*, p. 187.

89. k-8,78; k-19,158,298,415,454; vol. 6, ch. 1, part 1; vol. 6, ch. 5, part 3.
90. Gordievsky, *Next Stop Execution*, pp. 172–3; Andrew and Gordievsky, *KGB*, pp. 491–2.

Chapter Sixteen   Progress' Operations Part 2

1. Dubček, *Hope Dies Last*, pp. 225–6.
2. The Ministry of the Interior existed at both federal and national levels. There were thus Czech and Slovak ministers in addition to the Czechoslovak minister.
3. Dubček, *Hope Dies Last*, pp. 236–9.
4. k-20,149.
5. k-20,189,177.
6. k-20,154. On Pachman, see Hruby, *Fools and Heroes*, ch. 4.
7. k-19,643.
8. Renner, *A History of Czechoslovakia Since 1945*, p. 98.
9. Jakeš's contact in the KGB liaison office was G. Slavin (first name and patronymic not recorded in Mitrokhin's notes; k-19,575).
10. k-19,552.
11. k-19,643.
12. k-19,615.
13. Mitrokhin's notes do not provide complete statistics for the purge of security and intelligence personnel. In 1970, however, 1,092 officials were dismissed from the central apparatus of the interior ministry and 3,202 individuals deprived of Party membership (k-19,551). During 1970 more than a hundred StB agents defected to the West (k-19,559).
14. k-19,566.
15. The KGB liaison office report cited as an example of the full and frank intelligence provided by Kaska the fact that he "told us all that he knew about Indra's behavior in connection with his visit to the GDR . . ." Mitrokhin's notes give no further information on this episode (k-19,645).
16. k-19,555.
17. k-19,576.
18. Sinitsyn reported that both Kaska and Husák had wanted to make further enquiries about KGB records on individuals "whose behavior in 1968–9 gave rise to doubts"; k-19,587.
19. Indra was seen by Husák as a potential rival, and his move in 1971 from his position as Party secretary to the prestigious but not very influential post of chairman of the National Assembly was probably intended to curtail his influence within the CPCz. Renner, *A History of Czechoslovakia Since 1945*, pp. 111–12.
20. k-19,554.
21. Kalugin, *Spymaster*, pp. 157–8.
22. k-19,554. On the problems of calculating the final total of the purge of the CPCz, see Kusin, *From Dubček to Charter 77*, pp. 85–9.
23. k-19,554.
24. k-19,541. The probable date of the meeting was April 1972.
25. k-16,329. k-19,158. Mitrokhin's notes do not give FYODOROV's real identity.
26. k-19,609.
27. k-19,600.
28. k-19,601.
29. Renner, *A History of Czechoslovakia since 1945*, pp. 100–1.
30. k-19,603.
31. k-19,606.
32. k-19,62.
33. k-19,68.
34. k-19,62,92,643.
35. Kusin, *From Dubček to Charter 77*, p. 194.
36. Dubček describes his surveillance and harassment by the StB in *Hope Dies Last*, ch. 29.
37. t-7,272,297. Dubček makes no mention of this episode in his memoirs.
38. k-19,330.
39. k-19,75.
40. k-19,77.
41. k-19,76.

42. The KGB team sent to Czechoslovakia "to help with the investigation of the Grohman case at a higher professional level" consisted of A. A. Fabrichnikov and V. A. Pakhomov of the Second Chief Directorate, and "others from the KGB Investigation Department." During the investigation, Bil'ak claimed that Grohman "was a close contact of Štrougal." k-19,67. On Grohman's subsequent trial, see: "Former Prague Minister on Spying Charge," *The Times* (January 5, 1977); "Viele Mitarbeiter des BND haben Angst vor Verrat," *Die Welt* (January 27, 1977).

43. k-19,77.

44. t-7,263,280,281. k-19,451.

45. Probably the KGB's main source on Moczar's active measures against Gierek and his bugging of much of the PUWP leadership was Szlachcic, later Polish Minister of the Interior. t-7,243.

46. For an analysis of the December 1970 protests, see Kurczewski, *The Resurrection of Rights in Poland*, ch. 5.

47. k-19,333.

48. k-19,322.

49. Crampton, *Eastern Europe in the Twentieth Century*, pp. 359–60.

50. t-7,243.

51. The other targets of cultivation assigned to BOGUN were W. Klimczak (not identified); the economist G. Nowakowski; the writer K. Busz, described as "leader of the Kraków intelligentsia"; and S. Kozinski, a photographer with "contacts in the Party and state apparatus" (k-19,415). The contact established by BOGUN with Bardecki was later continued by the illegal FILOSOV. Like others targeted by PROGRESS operations, Bardecki cannot be blamed for speaking to Western visitors whom he had no means of identifying as KGB illegals.

52. In addition to the seven illegals used for operations in East Germany, others were based there but operated elsewhere. k-19,399,415.

53. Mitrokhin's notes do not record the specific objectives of the illegals sent to Bulgaria.

54. Crampton, *Eastern Europe in the Twentieth Century*, pp. 354–5.

55. k-19,487.

56. k-19,455.

57. k-19,415,456.

58. Crampton, *Eastern Europe in the Twentieth Century*, pp. 350–2.

59. k-16,273; k-19,429. Mitrokhin's notes give no details on the content of the reports.

60. Andrew and Gordievsky, *KGB*, pp. 359–60.

61. k-19,287.

62. k-19,264.

63. Crampton, *Eastern Europe in the Twentieth Century*, pp. 357–8. Garton Ash, *In Europe's Name*, p. 77.

64. k-19,264.

65. k-19,270.

66. t-7,264.

67. Childs and Popplewell, *The Stasi*, p. 82. A KGB file, apparently for the period 1976–7, gives the total size of Stasi personnel as "over 60,000" (k-19,271). This is consistent with documents in the Gauck [Stasi] Archive, which record a rise from 59,500 in 1975 to 75,000 in 1980.

68. k-19,273.

69. t-7,184.

70. k-19,430.

71. k-19,458.

72. k-27,78.

73. k-19,627.

74. k-27,243.

75. t-7,94.

76. k-19,209.

77. k-26,162. The KGB file on the drug test incident identifies the Soviet player concerned, but, since he was never tested, it is unfair to mention his name.

78. k-26,162.

79. k-19,235.

80. Kusin, *From Dub'cek to Charter 77*, pp. 304–25; Renner, *A History of Czechoslovakia since 1945*, pp. 128–47; Crampton, *Eastern Europe in the Twentieth Century*, p. 384.

81. Cited in Renner, *A History of Czechoslovakia since 1945*, p. 102.

Chapter Seventeen   The KGB and Western Communist Parties

1. vol. 9, ch. 1, para. 17.

2. k-3,65,115. k-8,182. Though the earliest reference in Mitrokhin's notes to Plissonnier's collaboration with the KGB dates from 1952, it may well have begun earlier.

3. Robrieux, *Histoire intérieure du Parti communiste,* vol. 4, pp. 450–2. Bell and Criddle, *The French Communist Party in the Fifth Republic,* pp. 19, 21.

4. k-3,65,115. k-8,182.

5. k-3,65,115. k-8,182. Boumedienne was president of Algeria from December 1976 until his death in December 1978.

6. Ginsborg, *A History of Contemporary Italy,* pp. 84–7.

7. Andrew, *For the President's Eyes Only,* pp. 171–2.

8. Mitrokhin's notes do not include any examples of the intelligence obtained by DARIO and his female recruits from the foreign ministry.

9. At various stages in his career as a Soviet agent, DARIO was codenamed BASK, SPARTAK, GAU, CHESTNY and GAUDEMUS. He appears to have switched from GRU to MGB control immediately after the Second World War. k-10,109.

10. k-10,101–3,107,109. Mitrokhin's notes imply that in 1956 DARIO was also instrumental in the recruitment of MAGDA, a typist in the foreign ministry press department (k-10,100,103). Mitrokhin's notes also record the recruitment in 1970 of an agent in the Foreign Ministry, codenamed STRELOK, by Georgi Pavlovich Antonov. STRELOK subsequently became "reluctant to cooperate" (k-4,80,158; k-2,221,231,268).

11. k-10,109. See below chapter 18.

12. k-7,4,193; k-16,338,419; k-18,153; k-20,94.

13. Cronin, *Great Power Politics and the Struggle over Austria,* chs. 1–4; Barker, *Austria 1918–1972,* part 3.

14. Barker, *Austria 1918–1972,* p. 178.

15. k-18,52.

16. k-18,52.

17. k-16,214,216; vol. 5, sect. 6, paras. 5,6 and *n.*

18. k-14,722; k-2,175; t-7,1.

19. k-2,81,145,150.

20. k-13,55,61.

21. t-7,1.

22. The SKP fought elections as part of the *Suomen Kansan Demokraattinen Liitto* (SKDL), mainly composed of Communists and fellow travelers.

23. Zubok and Pleshakov, *Inside the Kremlin's Cold War,* pp. 118–19, 131–2.

24. Mitrokhin's notes unfortunately contain nothing on the Communist role in the post-war coalition governments and little on Finland before the Brezhnev era. Given the willing assistance given to the KGB by the SVK chairman (later honorary chairman), Ville Pessi, in the 1970s (k-26,191,211,228), it is scarcely conceivable that such assistance was not forthcoming earlier. Pessi was already a powerful figure as SVK secretary after the Second World War. The earliest post-war example of SVK assistance to Soviet intelligence operations noted by Mitrokhin was the help given in 1949–51 to the illegal VIK in adopting the identity of the Finn Eugene Maki. The first KGB agent in the Finnish police force referred to in Mitrokhin's notes is ZVEN, a CID officer recruited in 1959 (k-5,309).

25. Upton, *The Communist Parties of Scandinavia and Finland,* part 2, chs. 6, 7. Upton quotes from one of the few surviving copies of Leino's 1958 memoirs, *Kommunisti sisäministerinä,* withdrawn on the eve of publication.

26. Upton, *The Communist Parties of Scandinavia and Finland,* p. 405.

27. See above, chapter 7.

28. Klehr and Haynes, *The American Communist Movement,* ch. 4. This admirable volume omits the role of the undeclared Party members after 1958.

29. See above, chapter 10.

30. See below, chapter 24.

31. Mitrokhin's notes give the names of two Canadians who assisted in obtaining the passport in the name of "Robert Callan," no. 4-716255. The Centre also doctored a genuine Canadian passport, no. 4-428012, in the name of Vasili Dzogola (?Dzogol), inserting a photograph of "Abel" and changing the eye color and other particulars to match his. Because of "Abel's" arrest, this passport too was never used. vol. 6, ch. 5, part 2.

32. k-27,451.

33. k-3,122.

34. Since non-Soviet citizens could not normally qualify for officer status in the KGB, it was intended that the new recruits should become illegal agents rather than illegal officers.

35. k-26,331.

36. k-26,332.

37. k-26,333.

38. k-3,65,115; k-8,182.

39. k-26,327.

40. vol. 8, ch. 13. Mitrokhin's note on the meeting with Kashtan does not say explicitly that he was asked to talent-spot *illegal* agents. Given the previous role of the CPC in helping to fabricate illegals' legends, however, it is barely conceivable that Kashtan, unlike the other Western Communist leaders mentioned in the files noted by Mitrokhin, was asked to recommend only conventional agents.

41. k-26,217.

42. KGB Chairman's Decree no. 0099/OV of August 7, 1972, entitled "Measures for the Further Activation of Illegals Intelligence Activity and Increasing Its Role in the Foreign–Political Intelligence System of the KGB Under the USSR Council of Ministers," envisaged the recruitment of illegal agents recommended by the Communist Parties of the United States, Canada, Mexico, Brazil and Argentina for operations in North America; by the Communist Parties of Belgium, Britain, France, the FRG and Spain for operations in Europe; by the Communist Party of Japan for operations in Asia; and by the Communist Party of Israel for operations in the Middle East. vol. 6, ch. 5, part 4.

43. k-26,227.

44. k-26,94–5,308.

45. Soares, *Portugal's Struggle for Liberation*, p. 24.

46. k-26,108. In Angola, once the richest of Portugal's colonies, the end of Portuguese rule was followed in 1975 by full-scale civil war between the Marxist Popular Movement for the Liberation of Angola (MPLA) and the rival, non-Marxist FNLA and UNITA. Cunhal also promised "to do everything possible to give assistance to the MPLA, including using illegal channels to send people drawn from among experienced military cadres," though the PCP's assistance was dwarfed by that from the Soviet Union and Cuba. k-26,205,209.

47. Maxwell, *The Making of Portuguese Democracy*, pp. 69–70. According to Maxwell, the PIDE/DGS archives also revealed that "the PCP had some embarrassing skeletons of its own, not least the secret police informers within its own ranks."

48. k-26,4.

49. k-26,4. For examples of PIDE/DGS documents which appeared in the press, probably as a result of KGB active measures, see Maxwell, *The Making of Portuguese Democracy*, p. 70. Mitrokhin's notes give no details of these active measures. In 1994 the PIDE/DGS archive was opened to researchers, subject to a series of restrictions, at the Lisbon National Archive.

50. Maxwell, *The Making of Portuguese Democracy*, chs. 7–9.

51. Recruitment leads from the PCP leadership during the mid- and late 1970s included: the government lawyers BORETS and ZNATOK (k-16,180,182); the trade union lawyer ZHAK (k-16,179); MARAT, a registrar of births, deaths and marriages who was able to provide documentation for illegals (k-18,345); KAREKA, a newspaper editor used for active measures from 1977 to 1982 (k-14,272); and EMIL, a journalist with the ANOP agency (k-14,404). Some of the other Portuguese cultivations, agents and confidential contacts of which details are given in Mitrokhin's notes probably also stemmed from PCP leads.

52. k-18,345. Cf. k-26,210.

53. Pessi had further discussions on agent recruitment in both Moscow and Helsinki during 1978 and 1979; k-26,211,228,191.

54. k-8,79. Mitrokhin identifies the Dublin resident only by his codename KAVERIN; his real name (Shadrin) is given in Andrew and Gordievsky, *KGB*, appendix D3.

55. Andrew and Gordievsky (eds.), *Instructions from the Centre*, pp. 53–6. Kryuchkov's circular to residencies of April 6, 1978 referred to previous circulars of March 28, 1975 and June 17, 1976, apparently written in similar vein.

56. k-19,7. The main Asian Communist Parties mentioned in Mitrokhin's notes as taking part in the recruiting drive were those of the Indian subcontinent, Afghanistan and Japan. KGB relations with Third World Communist Parties will be covered in more detail in Volume 2.

57. It is possible, however, that a latter-day Sorge remains concealed in a file not seen by Mitrokhin. It is also possible that one or more of the recruits of the 1970s and early 1980s developed into an illegal of major importance after Mitrokhin ceased to have access to the files.

58. k-27,99. Mitrokhin's notes give Maria's full name, but it seems unfair to identify her.

59. k-14,519; k-18,409. Mitrokhin's notes reveal the identity of LIMB, DANA and MARCEL.

60. See below, chapter 18.

61. The FCD communication to Ponomarev of October 20, 1980 was numbered 2192-A/OV. The basic subsidy paid to Kashtan in the late 1970s was 150,000 US dollars, paid in two annual installments, with some supplements. By the 1980s the CPC had a membership of only about 4,000, and was thus receiving a subsidy of about $40 dollars per member. Subsidies were also paid to the Canada–USSR and Quebec–USSR Societies, and to the *Severny Sosed* ("Northern Neighbour") journal. In addition, subsidies were sometimes channeled through the CPC to the Haitian Communists, and perhaps other Parties. vol. 8, ch. 13.

62. Haynes and Klehr, " 'Moscow Gold,' Confirmed at Last?" pp. 281–4; L. Dobbs, *Down with Big Brother,* p. 414. Mitrokhin's notes provide numerous examples of "Moscow gold," especially during the 1970s, but no figures for the total subsidies received by any Communist Party.

63. Barron, *Operation Solo,* ch. 4; the aliases of Morris Childs (born Chilovsky) are given in vol. 6, ch. 12. (On Child's earlier career in the CPUSA, see Klehr, Haynes and Anderson, *The Soviet World of American Communism,* pp. 257–71.) Barron's account is based on interviews and other material from Childs, his wife Eva and FBI agents concerned with his case. *Operation Solo* somewhat exaggerates the importance of the intelligence he supplied to the FBI after his trips to Moscow (see Draper, "Our Man in Moscow," *New York Review of Books* (May 9, 1996)). Mitrokhin's notes from KGB files, however, largely corroborate, as well as making important additions to, Barron's account of Childs's role in channeling Soviet funds to the CPUSA. Mitrokhin, unlike Barron, rarely gives annual totals for the Soviet subsidies. But those he provides are compatible with, though not identical to, Barron's figures. According to the KGB files noted by Mitrokhin, the "allocations" to the CPUSA were 1.7 million dollars in both 1975 and 1976 (vol. 6, ch. 12). Barron gives figures of 1,792,676 dollars for 1975 and 1,997,651 dollars for 1976 (*Operation Solo,* appendix B); one possible explanation for the discrepancies is that, as sometimes happened, additional allocations were made in the course of the year.

64. vol. 6, ch. 12.

65. vol. 6, ch. 12.

66. The instructor's congratulations were reported by Friedman to the FBI. Barron, *Operation Solo,* pp. 144–5.

67. vol. 6, ch. 12.

68. Barron, *Operation Solo,* pp. 144–5. Mitrokhin's notes and Barron's book neatly complement each other. Mitrokhin summarizes the account of Friedman's career in KGB files (vol. 6, ch. 12); Barron describes his career as known to the FBI, though he omits his real name and identifies him only by his FBI codename, CLIP.

69. vol. 6, ch. 12.

70. Barron, *Operation Solo,* pp. 156–7.

71. vol. 6, ch. 12.

72. Barron, *Operation Solo,* ch. 3.

73. vol. 6, ch. 12.

74. Barron, *Operation Solo,* ch. 3; Draper, "Our Man in Moscow," *New York Review of Books* (May 9, 1996)

75. Barron, *Operation Solo,* p. 263.

76. vol. 6, ch. 12. Instead of Jackson, Dobrynin asked Hall to bring with him to meetings at the embassy Arnold Johnson, director of the CPUSA Information and Lecture Bureau, once improbably eulogized by Lee Harvey Oswald as "the Lenin of our country" (Posner, *Case Closed,* p. 149).

77. DeLoach, *Hoover's FBI,* pp. 213–14; Barron, *Operation Solo,* pp. 262–3. FBI reports to the White House said that Levison had been identified as a secret CPUSA member by "an informant who has furnished reliable information in the past as a secret member of the Communist Party," presumably Jack Childs. Friedly and Gallen, *Martin Luther King,* pp. 124, 136–7.

78. Garrow, *FBI and Martin Luther King Jr.,* ch. 1; Friedly and Gallen, *Martin Luther King,* pp. 23–8.

79. Barron, *Operation Solo,* p. 263; DeLoach, *Hoover's FBI,* p. 214; Friedly and Gallen, *Martin Luther King,* pp. 25–6, 133–5. Though he denied current membership of the CPUSA, O'Dell resigned from King's Southern Christian Leadership Conference in 1962. Mitrokhin's notes contain no specific reference to O'Dell but reveal that the magazine *Freedomways,* with which he became actively involved after leaving

the SCLC, had been founded with active Soviet support, continued to receive secret Soviet subsidies and was "close" to the CPUSA. vol. 6, ch. 12.

80. Barron, *Operation Solo*, pp. 265–6.

81. DeLoach, *Hoover's FBI*, p. 214–15; Friedly and Gallen, *Martin Luther King*, pp. 36–43.

82. vol. 6, ch. 12.

83. vol. 6, app. 1, part 34.

84. vol. 6, app. 1, part 4; t-3,76. Mitrokhin had access only to reports in FCD files based on intelligence provided by the agent, not to the agent's file itself—probably because he had been recruited by the Second (rather than the First) Chief Directorate during a visit to the Soviet Union. Within the United States he seems to have been run from the San Francisco residency.

85. The transliteration of these names into the Cyrillic alphabet in the KGB report of the meeting makes identification difficult. vol. 6, ch. 12.

86. vol. 6, ch. 12.

87. vol. 6, ch. 12.

88. Barron, *Operation Solo*, pp. xiii, 312–14, 329–31.

89. Klehr and Haynes, *The American Communist Movement*, pp. 173–4.

90. Haynes and Klehr, " 'Moscow Gold,' Confirmed at Last?"; Klehr, Haynes and Anderson, *The Soviet World of American Communism*, pp. 149–64.

91. Barron, *Operation Solo*, p. 300.

92. Healey and Isserman, *Dorothy Healey Remembers*, p. 273. Dorothy Ray Healey left the Party in 1973.

Chapter Eighteen   Eurocommunism

1. Urban, *Moscow and the Italian Communist Party*, pp. 254–6.

2. k-26,187,252,288,295,296.

3. k-26,258.

4. k-26,229.

5. k-26,59.

6. k-26,60.

7. The Centre concluded that the forgeries had probably been included in the money handed to the PCI in either April or July 1972. k-26,299.

8. k-26,306. From 1969 to 1976 the PCI emissary most frequently used to collect Soviet subsidies from the embassy was Barontini (codenamed CLAUDIO); other emissaries referred to in KGB files were Marmuggi (codenamed CARO) and Guido Cappelloni (codenamed ALBERTO). k-26,256,267,270,291,300,302, 303,305,306.

Smaller subsidies also went to the Italian Socialist Party of Proletarian Unity (PSIUP) and the San Marino Communist Party. In 1974 the San Marino general secretary sent Brezhnev a Capo di Monte marble clock, via the Rome residency, in gratitude for Soviet financial assistance. k-26,260,283,306.

9. k-26,246.

10. k-26,252,311. The supply of the SELENYA radio system to the PCI by the KGB had been approved in principle by Politburo decision no. P 91/3 of May 17, 1973, but it was agreed that, "The two-way radios must be handed over to our Italian friends [the PCI] only when there is a real need to organize radio communications, bearing in mind that if kept in store for a long period the radio stations require periodic checks, maintenance and repairs."

11. Berlinguer's articles, first published in the autumn of 1973, are reprinted in Valenza (ed.), *Il compromesso storico*, pp. 14–31.

12. k-26,229. Agostino Novella, a veteran member of the PCI Direzione, strengthened the case against Amendola, Pajetta and Ingrao by telling Ambassador Rhyzov that all three had tried to prevent Longo seeking medical treatment in the Soviet Union. k-26,230.

13. Urban, *Moscow and the Italian Communist Party*, ch. 8. Ginsborg, *A History of Contemporary Italy, 1943–1988*, ch. 10.

14. k-26,237.

15. Urban, *Moscow and the Italian Communist Party*, ch. 8.

16. Urban, *Moscow and the Italian Communist Party*, pp. 283–4, 290.

17. k-26,257. The KGB files noted by Mitrokhin do not record what use was made of its intelligence on Berlinguer's allegedly dubious building contracts.

18. k-26,264.

19. k-26,256. Mitrokhin gives no details of payments after 1976.

20. k-26,259,261. In 1998 a receipt by Cappelloni, dated June 27, 1976, for one million dollars from the CPSU for the 1976 election campaign was published in the Italian press. "Pci, ecco le ricevute dei miliardi di Mosca," *Il Giorno* (April 30, 1998).

21. The training was authorized by Politburo decision no. SG 143/8 GS of January 17, 1979. k-26,2.

22. Childs and Popplewell, *The Stasi*, p. 138.

23. k-26,158.

24. Ginsborg, *A History of Contemporary Italy, 1943–1988,* pp. 384–5.

25. k-26,158.

26. The PCI decision to dismantle the radio stations was reported by Kryuchkov to Ponomarev, head of the Central Committee International Department, in a communication of June 22, 1981, published in the Italian press in 1998. "Servizio segreto," *L'Avanti* (May 16, 1998).

27. Urban, *Moscow and the Italian Communist Party,* ch. 9; Cossutta, *Lo strappo;* "Cossutta Sempre Più Isolato," *La Repubblica* (January 2, 1982).

28. Hellman, "The Difficult Birth of the Democratic Party of the Left," p. 81.

29. Though details of the payments to Cossutta and other "healthy forces in the PCI" were passed by Moscow to the Rome Prosecutor's Office in 1992, they were not made public until 1998. "Pci, ecco le ricevute dei miliardi di Mosca," *Il Giorno* (April 30, 1998); "Ecco la Tangentopoli rossa," *Il Tempo* (April 30, 1998).

30. t-7,12.

31. Pike, *In the Service of Stalin,* p. 49; Thomas, *The Spanish Civil War,* p. 535.

32. Mujal-León, *Communism and Political Change in Spain,* pp. 107–9. After their expulsion, Gómez, García and Líster went on to found unsuccessful pro-Soviet splinter groups. Cf. k-3,12.

33. k-3,16.

34. Mujal-León, *Communism and Political Change in Spain,* ch. 6.

35. k-2,65; k-3,13,15,22; k-26,410.

36. k-3,18.

37. Mujal-León, *Communism and Political Change in Spain,* pp. 126–7.

38. k-3,17.

39. Thomas, *The Spanish Civil War,* p. 9.

40. Mujal-León, *Communism and Political Change in Spain,* pp. 127–31.

41. k-3,20.

42. k-5,879.

43. k-26,406.

44. In January, October and December 1980, Gallego was given payments of 10,000 dollars by the Madrid residency. k-26,405.

45. k-26,407.

46. The anti-Eurocommunist Catalan Communist Party, the PSUC (Partit Socialista Unificat de Catalunya), split away from the PCE.

47. Krasikov, *From Dictatorship to Democracy,* p. 188. Mitrokhin identifies Krasikov as a KGB officer; k-7,111. His book, originally published in Russian as *Ispanskii Reportazh,* was translated into a number of languages.

48. k-3,98.

49. Urban, *Moscow and the Italian Communist Party,* pp. 337–8.

50. Bell and Criddle, *The French Communist Party in the Fifth Republic,* pp. 19–20; Roy, *Somme tout,* pp. 156–7.

51. k-3,65,115; k-8,182.

52. Bell and Criddle, *The French Communist Party in the Fifth Republic,* p. 240.

53. k-3,140.

54. See below, chapter 27.

55. k-3,140.

56. k-3,140.

57. Adereth, *The French Communist Party,* pp. 208–13.

58. The text of the letters was later published in *Cahiers du Communisme* (October 1991).

59. k-8,148.

60. Bell and Criddle, *The French Communist Party in the Fifth Republic,* pp. 153–4, 164–5.

61. k-3,123.

62. k-3,140.

63. *L'Express* (July 27, 1970).

64. k-3,140.

65. Robrieux, *Histoire intérieure du Parti communiste,* vol. 2, pp. 657–65; vol. 3, pp. 344–5, 406–14.

66. Bell and Criddle, *The French Communist Party in the Fifth Republic,* pp. 154–6, 217–30. Though the Socialists won an overall majority at the 1981 legislative elections and did not depend on PCF support, four Communist ministers served in a Socialist-dominated coalition until 1984.

67. Urban (ed.), *Moscow and the Global Left in the Gorbachev Era,* pp. 5, 52–3.

68. Brown, *The Gorbachev Factor,* p. 75.

69. Urban (ed.), *Moscow and the Global Left in the Gorbachev Era,* ch. 2. While Gorbachev was publicly aligning himself with the PCI's reformist leadership, however, the International Department continued to subsidize the PCI old guard until 1987. In 1989 the PCI, led since 1988 by Achille Ochetto, changed its name to the PDS (Partito Democratico della Sinistra), the Democratic Party of the Left. A breakaway movement established itself in 1991 as the Partito della Rifondazione Comunista.

70. In 1987 the PCE, Gallego's PCPE, the Progressive Federation (founded by another former PCE member, Ramón Tamames), Pasoc (a breakaway Socialist group) and a number of independents combined to form the Izquierdo Unida; the PCE accounted for about two-thirds of the total membership.

71. Brown, *The Gorbachev Factor,* p. 116; Grachev, *Kremlevskaya Khronika,* p. 247.

72. Marchais's message was delivered by Gaston Plissonnier, who for the past twenty years had been the French conduit for the secret subsidies to the PCF. Dobrynin to Gorbachev (June 20, 1987); text in Stepankov and Lisov, *Kremlevsky Zagovor,* appendix.

73. Politburo decision of July 3, 1987, in Stepankov and Lisov, *Kremlevsky Zagovor,* appendix. Between 1981 and 1991 subsidies to the PCF totaled about 24 million dollars. Burke, "Recently Released Material on Soviet Intelligence Operations," p. 246; Albats, *The State within a State,* p. 222.

74. Haynes and Klehr, " 'Moscow Gold,' Confirmed at Last?", p. 283.

75. Hellman, "The Difficult Birth of the Democratic Party of the Left," p. 81.

Chapter Nineteen   Ideological Subversion Part 1

1. Scammell, *Solzhenitsyn,* p. 551.

2. vol. 10, ch. 3.

3. Labedz and Hayward (eds.), *On Trial,* p. 91.

4. vol. 10, ch. 3.

5. vol. 10, ch. 3. Cf. Zamoyska, "Sinyavsky, the Man and the Writer," p. 61.

6. vol. 10, ch. 3.

7. Aucouturier, "Andrey Sinyavsky on the Eve of His Arrest," p. 344.

8. Geli Fyoderovich Vasiliev, codenamed MIKHAILOV, had worked abroad as an illegal under the name Rudolf Steiner in Austria and Latin America. On returning to Moscow, apparently unable to stand the strain of life as an illegal, he began work in the Novosti Press Agency (k-16,446). Though the probability is that Vasilyev was the stoolpigeon placed in Sinyavsky's cell, it is just possible that the KGB used another agent with the same codename—though there is no identifiable record of such an agent in Mitrokhin's notes.

9. vol. 10, ch. 3.

10. vol. 10, ch. 3.

11. Mitrokhin's notes record simply that Remizov gave his interrogators "evidence against Sinyavsky." At the trial this evidence included an admission that he had delivered one of Sinyavsky's manuscripts to Hélène Zamoyska. Labedz and Hayward (eds.), *On Trial,* p. 153.

12. vol. 10, ch. 3.

13. Labedz and Hayward (eds.), *On Trial,* p. 306.

14. Labedz and Hayward (eds.), *On Trial,* pp. 196, 198, 209.

15. Asked if he had sent his manuscripts abroad "illegally," Sinyavsky replied, "No, unofficially." Sending manuscripts abroad was not illegal. But in his final address, the state prosecutor again claimed—inaccurately—that the defendants had sent their manuscripts to the West "illegally." Labedz and Hayward (eds.), *On Trial,* pp. 185, 308.

16. Labedz and Hayward (eds.), *On Trial,* pp. 253–4.

17. vol. 10, ch. 3; vol. 7, nzch. TANOV later took part in PROGRESS operations in Albania, Bulgaria, Czechoslovakia and Yugoslavia, using Austrian and forged Canadian passports, and carried out other intelligence assignments in Pakistan, India, France, the Lebanon, Syria, Kuwait and Spain. In 1982 he was recalled to Moscow on the grounds that he was producing little intelligence and had greatly overspent his budget (vol. 3, pakapp. 3).

18. Scammell, *Solzhenitsyn,* pp. 614–16.

19. vol. 10, ch. 3.

20. k-27,370

21. Scammell (ed.), *The Solzhenitsyn Files,* pp. xxv, 7, 41. This important collection of documents on "the Solzhenitsyn case," declassified by order of President Yeltsin in 1992, includes a number of KGB reports to the Central Committee and Politburo but not the KGB operational files to which Mitrokhin had access.

22. Andrew and Gordievsky, *KGB,* pp. 487–8.

23. Andrew and Gordievsky, *KGB,* p. 492.

24. Scammell (ed.), *The Solzhenitsyn Files,* pp. 138–41.

25. Scammell (ed.), *The Solzhenitsyn Files,* pp. xxix, 161–3.

26. Andropov instituted judicial proceedings against Shchelokov in December 1982, only a month after Brezhnev's death. Two years later, before his case had come to trial, Shchelokov committed suicide. Volkogonov, *The Rise and Fall of the Soviet Empire,* pp. 330, 348.

27. Scammell (ed.), *The Solzhenitsyn Files,* pp. 194–210.

28. Scammell, *Solzhenitsyn,* p. 615.

29. k-21,30.

30. k-21,17; vol. 6, ch. 5, part 4. The spelling of Boucaut in the Roman alphabet is uncertain; it appears in Cyrillic transliteration as "Buko." Mitrokhin's notes do not identify Nikashin's first name and patronymic.

31. k-21,114.

32. Sakharov, *Memoirs,* pp. 359, 369–70; Grigorenko, *Memoirs,* pp. 387–8.

33. Article by G. Kizlych and P. Aleksandrov on the Yakir and Krasin cases in the classified in-house quarterly, *KGB Sbornik,* no. 73; k-25,124.

34. vol. 10, ch. 5.

35. Protocols of Krasin's interrogation; vol. 10, ch. 5.

36. On Savinkov, see above, chapter 2.

37. Article by G. Kizlych and P. Aleksandrov on the Yakir and Krasin cases in the classified in-house quarterly, *KGB Sbornik,* no. 73; k-25,124.

38. vol. 10, ch. 5.

39. Scammell, *Solzhenitsyn,* p. 807; Solzhenitsyn, *The Oak and the Calf,* p. 522.

40. Grigorenko, *Memoirs,* p. 388.

41. Article by G. Kizlych and P. Aleksandrov on the Yakir and Krasin cases in the classified in-house quarterly, *KGB Sbornik,* no. 73; k-25,124.

42. Sakharov, *Sakharov Speaks,* pp. 212–15.

43. Scammell (ed.), *The Solzhenitsyn Files,* pp. 256–74, 340–6, 350–3.

44. Solzhenitsyn describes his forced departure from Russia in *The Oak and the Calf,* pp. 383–453.

45. k-21,123.

46. Scammell, *Solzhenitsyn,* p. 886. Though the woman who came to Solzhenitsyn's door on his first day in Zurich has never been identified, her Russian origins and the fact that within a few weeks, if not days, Valentina Holubová had established herself as his secretary and assistant make it probable that she was the caller. It is unlikely that a genuine native of Ryazan had tracked him down so rapidly. In reality, Holubová came not from Ryazan but from Vladivostok (k-21,123).

47. Scammell, *Solzhenitsyn,* p. 886. The fact that Dr. Frantiˇsek Holub was, like his wife, working for the StB, is implied rather than specifically stated in Mitrokhin's notes. For example, he records that the Holubs jointly recommended to Solzhenitsyn another StB officer posing as a Czech dissident, Tomáš Řezáč (k-21,123). It is inconceivable that the StB or the KGB would have allowed a husband and wife team to operate in this way unless both were working for them.

48. k-21,123,124. On Solzhenitsyn's first meeting with Krause, see Scammell, *Solzhenitsyn,* p. 886.

49. See above, chapters 2, 5.

50. k-21,124.

51. Scammell (ed.), *The Solzhenitsyn Files,* pp. 387–90.

52. k-21,25.

53. Scammell, *Solzhenitsyn,* pp. 887–8, 890–3, 987–90; Scammell (ed.), *The Solzhenitsyn Files,* pp. 431–2, 451–3. Rezác's scurrilous volume, *The Spiral of Solzhenitsyn's Betrayal,* described by the author as "an autopsy of the corpse of a traitor," appeared in Italian in 1977 and Russian in the following year, but failed to find a British or American publisher. While in Russia, Rezác also interviewed Sahkarov, who was unaware of his background (Sakharov, *Memoirs,* p. 591).

54. k-21,25.

55. Sakharov, *Memoirs*, p. 428.
56. Scammell, *Solzhenitsyn*, p. 890.
57. k-3(b),27. Mitrokhin copied or noted sections 1–5, 8, 9, 11, 16–19 of the 19-point "plan of agent operational measures."
58. k-3(b),27.
59. k-25,212.
60. Scammell, *Solzhenitsyn*, p. 955.
61. vol. 6, ch. 8, part 6.
62. k-25,29.
63. There is a vivid description of Solzhenitsyn's address and its reception in Thomas, *Alexander Solzhenitsyn*, pp. 460–3.
64. k-25,29. *The New York Times* and the *Washington Post* comments on the Harvard Address are quoted in Thomas, *Alexander Solzhenitsyn*, p. 462.

Chapter Twenty   Ideological Subversion Part 2

1. Dobrynin, *In Confidence*, pp. 346, 390.
2. k-21,16.
3. Sakharov, *Memoirs*, p. 429. The Nobel Peace Prize, presented in Oslo, is awarded by the Nobel Committee appointed by the Norwegian parliament. The other Nobel prizes, presented in Stockholm, are awarded by Swedish committees.
4. k-21,69. Before being passed for signature to Kryuchkov, head of the FCD, and Andropov, this document (reference no. 155/2422) was initialed by B. S. Ivanov, Kryuchkov's deputy, Oleg Kalugin, head of Counter-intelligence, and V.P. Ivanov of Section A. The alleged "criminals" who supported Sakharov were mostly, if not entirely, dissidents sentenced on trumped-up charges.
5. On the fabricated KGB claim that Sakharov supported the Pinochet regime, see Sakharov, *Memoirs*, pp. 389, 426.
6. k-21,64.
7. Scammell, *Solzhenitsyn*, p. 893.
8. vol. 6, ch. 8, part 6.
9. Kalugin, *Spymaster*, pp. 260–1.
10. k-21,104.
11. k-21,104.
12. Sakharov, *Memoirs*, pp. 585–92. On the KGB's use of Yakovlev to attack Solzhenitsyn, see Scammell (ed.), *The Solzhenitsyn Files*, pp. 394, 398, 409, 426–30.
13. k-21,1. Cf. Bonner, *Alone Together*, p. 46. YAK was used for a variety of active measures. One of the files noted by Mitrokhin records that in 1976 he was paid 500 dollars (probably per month). The same file records that *Russkiy Golos* had a circulation of only 1,500. k-21,106.
14. k-21,1. Bonner, *Alone Together*, pp. 37–8.
15. "CHI E" ELENA BONNER? Artifice di piu assassinii la moglie dell "accademico Sakharov," *Sette Giorni* (April 12, 1980). Cf. Bonner, *Alone Together*, pp. 31–2.
16. k-21,104. Cf. Bonner, *Alone Together*, pp. 37–8.
17. k-6,114; k-21,1,105.
18. "CHI E" ELENA BONNER? Artifice di piu assassinii la moglie dell "accademico Sakharov," *Sette Giorni* (April 12, 1980). k-21,1,82.
19. k-21,1,105; k-6,114. *Sette Giorni* also published an attack on Solzhenitsyn, based on an interview with his first wife (k-21,82).
20. k-21,82.
21. k-21,104.
22. k-21,104.
23. Bonner, *Alone Together*, p. 30.
24. Bethell, *Spies and Other Secrets*, p. 73.
25. Memorandum by Andropov and State Prosecutor Rudenko, no. 123-A (January 21, 1977); Albats, *The State within a State*, pp. 178–9.
26. k-21,153.
27. Bethell, *Spies and Other Secrets*, pp. 98–9.
28. The sentence was thirteen years. Shcharansky, *Fear No Evil*, pp. 205–6, 224–5.
29. k-21,157,159.

30. k-21,164.

31. k-21,156. Makarov was informed that the file recording the residency's success in preventing the award of the prize to Orlov had been passed to Andropov.

32. k-1,98.

33. vol. 6, ch. 1, part 1.

34. Sakharov, *Memoirs*, pp. 510–16.

35. k-21,80.

36. Gorbachev, *Memoirs*, p. 296.

37. Bethell, *Spies and Other Secrets*, pp. 315–16.

38. Brown, *The Gorbachev Factor*, p. 37. In public, in order not to alienate a majority on the Politburo, Gorbachev stuck to the official line. He declared in an interview with *L'Humanité* in February 1986: "Now about political prisoners, we don't have any . . . It is common knowledge that [Sakharov] committed actions punishable by law . . . Measures were taken with regard to him according to our legislation. The actual state of affairs is as follows. Sakharov resides in Gorky in normal conditions, is doing scientific work, and remains a member of the USSR Academy of Sciences. He is in normal health as far as I know. His wife has recently left the country for medical treatment abroad. As for Sakharov himself, he is still a bearer of secrets of special importance to the state and for this reason cannot go abroad." Sakharov, *Memoirs*, p. 607.

39. Grachev, *Kremlevskaya Karonika*, pp. 94–104; Brown, *The Gorbachev Factor*, p. 165.

40. Sakharov, *Memoirs*, p. 615.

41. Cited in Dobbs, *Down with Big Brother*, pp. 252–3.

42. Gorbachev, *Memoirs*, p. 295.

43. Dobbs, *Down with Big Brother*, pp. 253–64; Remnick, *Lenin's Tomb*, ch. 19.

44. Remnick, *Lenin's Tomb*, p. 282.

45. Brown, *The Gorbachev Factor*, pp. 7–10.

46. k-21,76.

47. k-21,153.

Chapter Twenty-one   SIGINT in the Cold War

1. Andrew, "Intelligence and International Relations in the Early Cold War."

2. Andrew, *For the President's Eyes Only*, seeks to assess the varying interest taken by US presidents in SIGINT.

3. Mitrokhin had no direct access to the files of either the Eighth Directorate or the Sixteenth (SIGINT) Directorate, founded in the late 1960s. He did, however, see some documents from both directorates in FCD files.

4. KGB to Khrushchev, "Report for 1960" (February 14, 1961), in the "special dossiers" of the CPSU Central Committee; cited by Zubok, "Spy vs. Spy," p. 23.

5. Garthoff, "The KGB Reports to Gorbachev," p. 228.

6. Kahn, "Soviet Comint in the Cold War."

7. Samouce, "I Do Understand the Russians," pp. 52–3, Samouce papers, US Army Military Institute, Carlisle Barracks, Pa.; Andrew and Gordievsky, *KGB*, pp. 237–40.

8. Kennan, *Memoirs 1950–1963*, pp. 154–7. Andrew and Gordievsky, *KGB*, pp. 454–6. Kennan was declared *persona non grata* in October 1952, though chiefly for reasons unconnected with the bugging incident.

9. Bohlen, *Witness to History 1919–1969*, pp. 345–6. Andrew and Gordievsky, *KGB*, pp. 456–7.

10. Dobrynin, *In Confidence*, p. 357.

11. Andrew and Gordievsky, *KGB*, p. 456. Remarkably, Nosenko's information was not sufficient to convince his CIA debriefers that he was a genuine defector.

12. vol. 6, ch. 9. For illustrations of some of the espionage equipment supplied by the FCD OT Directorate, see Melton, *The Ultimate Spy Book*.

13. k-18,342.

14. k-1,160. On KGB penetration of the Orthodox church, see below, chapter 28.

15. vol. 7, ch. 5, para. 44.

16. k-24,299; vol. 7, ch. 5.

17. Philby's career as an SIS officer had ended after his recall from Washington in 1951. Philby's later account to Borovik of his years in Beirut contains a number of inaccuracies, due partly to his attempt to discredit Lunn (transcribed by Borovik as "Lan"—an error derived, as in the KGB files noted by Mitrokhin, from the conversion of "Lunn" into Cyrillic). Philby attributes his successful escape in 1963 largely to Lunn's incompetence and adds that "amazingly, three or four years later [Lunn] received a high honour—the Cross of St. Michael

and St. George" (Borovik, *The Philby Files*, p. 354). In reality, as Philby had correctly informed the KGB after his defection, Lunn was awarded the CMG a decade earlier, in 1957 (vol. 7, ch. 5).

18. Lunn was the author of *High-Speed Skiing* (1935), *A Skiing Primer* (1948) and *The Guinness Book of Skiing* (1983). His father, Sir Arnold Lunn (1888–1974), was one of Europe's leading ski pioneers, as well as a leading Catholic apologist and a vocal opponent of both Nazism and Communism. His 63 books included 23 on skiing and 16 on Christian apologetics (*Dictionary of National Biography, 1971–1980*, pp. 522–3).

19. Lunn's recent *Who's Who* entries give the date of his entry into SIS. Earlier entries make no reference to his intelligence career.

20. Unless otherwise indicated, the account of operation RUBIN is based on k-24,299 and vol. 7, ch. 5.

21. k-26,223.

22. k-26,223.

23. The file noted by Mitrokhin does not reveal what the measures were.

24. On Philby's depression in the late 1960s and partial recovery during the 1970s, see Andrew and Gordievsky, *KGB*, pp. 24–6, 544–5, and Knightley, *Philby*, pp. 234–7.

25. One of the CIA officers on whom intelligence was gathered during operation RUBIN was selected by Andropov as the target of an attempted abduction.

26. k-18,342.

27. vol. 6, app. 1 (misc.), parts 1, 4; k-27,242. Mitrokhin's notes give no indication of what intelligence was obtained by bugging the CIA officer's flat. VERA's file records that the KGB lost contact with her in 1975 as a result of the Lebanese Civil War.

28. k-27,239.

29. KGB operations in Africa will be covered in volume 2.

30. Details of operation REBUS in k-17,49,59,185; vol. 6, ch. 10. On November 16, 1981 operation PHOENIX succeeded in bugging the residence of the US ambassador in Conakry. The agent responsible was a Guinean (probably a domestic servant) codenamed MURAT (k-17,145; k-8,519). The KGB also succeeded in intercepting the communications of US embassies in a number of other African capitals, among them Bamako and Brazzaville (vol. 6, ch. 10; k-17,168).

31. The last, reforming chairman of the KGB, Vadim Bakatin, appointed after the failed coup of August 1991, outraged his staff by giving the American ambassador blueprints of the highly sophisticated bugging system (Albats, *The State within a State*, pp. 311–13). There were several security alerts within the existing US embassy in Moscow during the 1980s. In 1984, however, bugs were discovered in electric typewriters in the US embassy in Moscow which had been in use for some years (Lardner, "Unbeatable Bugs"). In 1986 two marine guards admitted giving KGB agents access to the US embassy. Because of improved security procedures, however, the KGB do not seem to have gained access to the cipher room or other sensitive areas (Andrew and Gordievsky, *KGB*, p. 611).

32. k-22,135,232. The GRU already had posts in a number of its residencies designed to intercept US and NATO military communications.

33. vol. 6, ch. 9.

34. vol. 6, ch. 9.

35. Kalugin, *Spymaster*, p. 92. The POCHIN files noted by Mitrokhin confirm Kalugin's list of intercepted communications (vol. 6, ch. 9).

36. vol. 6, ch. 9.

37. See above, chapter 11.

38. See above, chapter 11.

39. vol. 6, ch. 2, part 2; vol. 6, ch. 9. There was a further operation to bug UN Secretariat offices in 1963 (k-8,138).

40. vol. 6, ch. 2, part 2.

41. After leaving GCHQ in 1977, Prime broke off contact with the KGB for the next three years. He had further meetings with his case officer in Vienna and Potsdam in 1980 and 1981. His work as a Soviet agent came to light after he was arrested for sexually molesting little girls in 1982. He was sentenced to thirty-five years' imprisonment for espionage and three for sexual assault (Andrew and Gordievsky, *KGB*, pp. 526–8, 530–1). A senior GCHQ officer was later quoted as saying, "On the political side, there was a time up to the mid-1970s when we used to get useful [Soviet] political and high-level military communications. But that dried up, partly as a result of Prime." (Urban, *UK Eyes Alpha*, p. 6.) Because Prime was a Third Directorate, not an FCD, agent, Mitrokhin did not have access to his file. The latest study of Prime, by the detective chief superintendent in charge of his case, is Cole, *Geoffrey Prime*.

42. Mitrokhin's notes do not give the date of foundation of the Sixteenth Directorate, but indicate that it

was in existence not later than 1968; k-22,232.

43. Andrew and Gordievsky, *KGB*, p. 529. vol. 6, ch. 9.

44. vol. 6, ch. 3, part 3.

45. vol. 6, ch. 9. Mitrokhin's notes do not record ANTON's real name.

46. Kissinger, *Years of Upheaval*, p. 1179.

47. vol. 6, ch. 9.

48. Kissinger, *Years of Upheaval*, p. 1192.

49. Kalugin, *Spymaster*, p. 92.

50. For illustrations of some of the complex antennae on the roofs of Soviet missions in the United States and elsewhere, see Ball, *Soviet Signals Intelligence (SIGINT)*, pp. 49–68.

51. vol. 6, ch. 9.

52. Andrew, *For the President's Eyes Only*, p. 359.

53. Dobrynin, *In Confidence*, pp. 357–8.

54. vol. 6, ch. 9.

55. vol. 6, ch. 3, part 2.

56. vol. 6, ch. 9.

57. vol. 6, ch. 2, part 1.

58. vol. 6, ch. 9. On the crisis over the Soviet "combat brigade" in Cuba, see Andrew, *For the President's Eyes Only*, pp. 444–7. Mitrokhin's notes on POCHIN files also record that "during the crisis in Lebanon the [Washington] residency was able to make a correct evaluation of the unfolding situation and inform the Centre on a timely basis that the United States had no plans for military intervention" (vol. 6, ch. 9). It is unclear which Lebanese crisis is referred to. Since the other material in this section of Mitrokhin's notes deals with the mid-1970s, however, the reference is probably to 1974, when Israel made a series of air attacks against villages in southern Lebanon, which it suspected of harboring terrorists.

59. vol. 6, ch. 9.

60. The FBI shortwave radio communications channels monitored continuously by the RAKETA post during the 1970s were:

- the radio link between surveillance vehicles and the six FBI posts responsible for observing the movements of Soviet personnel (167.4625 megahertz);
- the channel used by surveillance vehicles and observation posts monitoring the movements of members of Middle Eastern and some Western missions to the UN (167.2125 megahertz);
- the channel used for communications between the FBI department investigating bank robberies and surveillance vehicles (167.6887 megahertz);
- the channel used by those investigating other federal crimes (167.3756 megahertz);
- the channel used for communications between the FBI despatch centers in New York and New Jersey (frequency in the 167 megahertz band not recorded);
- the channel used for other communications between the New York dispatch center and FBI vehicles (167.7760 megahertz)

vol. 6, ch. 9).

61. vol. 6, ch. 9.

62. vol. 6, ch. 8, part 4, *n*. 1.

63. The running costs for the main intercept posts in KGB residencies around the world in 1979 were as follows (figures in thousands of hard currency roubles):

Washington (POCHIN): 26.0
New York (PROBA): 29.4
San Francisco (VESNA): 6.7
Ottawa (codename not recorded): figures unavailable (5.8 in 1977)
Montreal (VENERA): 3.3 (plus 3.5 for purchase of motorcar)
Cuba (TERMIT-S): 18.8
Brazil (KLEN): 4.8 (increased to 8.2 in 1980; 13.3 in 1981)
Mexico (RADAR): 3.5 (increased to 4.6 in 1980)
Reykjavik (OSTROV): 2.3
London (MERCURY): 7.1
Oslo (SEVER): 7.2
Paris (JUPITER): 10.1

Bonn (TSENTAVR-1): 11.3
Cologne (TSENTAVR-2): figures unavailable
Salzburg (TYROL-1): 1.3
Vienna (TYROL-2): 3.3
Berne (ELBRUS): 2.8
Geneva (KAVKAZ): 2.3
Rome (START): 15.0
Athens (RADUGA): 4.2
Ankara (RADUGA-T): 9.5 (plus supplementary 2.2)
Istanbul (SIRIUS): 5.3
Teheran (MARS): 5.0
Beijing (KRAB): 4.5
Tokyo (ZARYA): 10.4

vol. 6, ch. 9; 1977 figures for Ottawa from vol. 8, ch. 5)
   Because of the KGB's curious accounting methods, these figures doubtless do not represent the full running costs of the intercept posts. They do, however, give an approximate indication of the relative level of activity at each post. Other significant intercept posts, probably less important than those listed above, included Lisbon (ALTAY), Nairobi (KRYM), Cairo (ORION), The Hague (TULIP), Brussels (VEGA), Belgrade (PARUS), Hanoi (AMUR), Jakarta (DELFIN) and Damascus (SIGMA). Mitrokhin's notes do not give the budgets for these posts.
64. Ball, *Soviet Signals Intelligence (SIGINT)*, pp. 27–9; Rosenau, "A Deafening Silence," pp. 723–5.
65. vol. 6, ch. 9.
66. Ball, *Soviet Signals Intelligence (SIGINT)*, pp. 27–9.
67. vol. 2, app. 3.
68. k-22,136. Shorter reports were submitted by each intercept post at least once a month.
69. vol. 6, ch. 3, part 2.
70. vol. 6, ch. 6.
71. vol. 6, ch. 2, part 3; vol. 6, ch. 6; vol. 6, app. 2, parts 4, 5.
72. On the origins of the UKUSA agreement, see Andrew, "The Making of the Anglo-American SIGINT Alliance"; on its subsequent development, see Ball and Richelson, *The Ties That Bind* and Hager, *Secret Power*.
73. t-7,131.
74. t-7,130.
75. k-19,435.
76. vol. 6, ch. 8, part 5.
77. See above, chapter 6.
78. vol. 2, app. 3. The names of the head and deputy heads of the Sixteenth Department are given in k-22,134.
79. Interview by Christopher Andrew with Viktor Makarov, 1993. When Oleg Gordievsky became resident-designate at the London residency early in 1985, the Sixteenth Department officer told him that there was currently no British source providing high-grade cipher material (Andrew and Gordievsky, *KGB*, p. 610).
80. Interview by Christopher Andrew with Viktor Makarov, 1993; Kahn, "Soviet Comint in the Cold War," pp. 20–3.
81. Interview with Gurgenev (identified only by his first name and patronymic), *Izvestia* (September 24, 1991).
82. On March 25, 1985, for example, the London residency received an urgent telegram asking for British reactions to Gorbachev's meeting with the executive committee of the Socialist International. Sooner than report that the event had failed to excite great interest in Britain, the residency simply concocted a favorable reply without contacting any of its limited range of sources. (Recollection of Oleg Gordievsky, then resident-designate.)
83. See above, chapter 21.
84. Interview by Christopher Andrew with Viktor Makarov, 1993; Viktor Makarov, "The West Had No Aggressive Plans against the USSR," *Express Chronicle* (February 19, 1992), p. 5.
85. Urban, *UK Eyes Alpha*, ch. 19.
86. Ball, *Soviet Signals Intelligence (SIGINT)*. Ball and Windren, "Soviet Signals Intelligence (Sigint)."

87. Rosenau, "A Deafening Silence," p. 726.

88. Andrew, "The Nature of Military Intelligence," p. 5.

89. Rosenau, "A Deafening Silence," pp. 727, 732 *n.* 6.

Chapter Twenty-two   Tasks Part 1

1. Djilas, *Tito,* p. 29; Djilas, *Rise and Fall,* pp. 106–7; Radzinsky, *Stalin,* p. 399.

2. k-20,272; Ranković's codename is in k-20,287.

3. Djilas, *Rise and Fall,* pp. 82–3, 105–6.

4. k-20,281.

5. k-20,276.

6. k-20,290,292. Tishkov's cover name (Timofeyev) is given in Djilas, *Rise and Fall,* pp. 82–3, 105–6.

7. k-20,279.

8. k-20,289,290.

9. Djilas, *Rise and Fall,* pp. 84–5, 92, 95, 98–9, 105–6; Dedijer, *Tito Speaks,* p. 268.

10. k-20,292.

11. k-5,707.

12. Djilas, *Rise and Fall,* chs. 14, 15; Djilas, *Tito,* pp. 84–7; Andrew and Gordievsky, *KGB,* pp. 371–2. VAL is identified by Sudoplatovs, *Special Tasks,* p. 338.

13. Andrew and Gordievsky, *KGB,* pp. 415–17.

14. See above, chapters 5, 6, and 10.

15. MGB report to Stalin, first published by Dmitri Volkogonov in *Izvestia* (June 11, 1993); reprinted in Sudoplatovs, *Special Tasks,* pp. 336–7, and "Stalin's Plan to Assassinate Tito," p. 137.

16. MGB report to Stalin, first published by Dmitri Volkogonov in *Izvestia* (June 11, 1993).

17. "Stalin's Plan to Assassinate Tito," p. 137.

18. Wolff, "Leadership Transition in a Fractured Bloc," p. 1.

19. Sudoplatovs, *Special Tasks,* pp. 335–8.

20. k-13,267. Some examples of Grigulevich's works, published under his own name, the pseudonym I. R. Lavretsky and the hybrid Grigulevich-Lavretsky, are included in the bibliography.

21. Sudoplatovs, *Special Tasks,* pp. 249, 252–3.

22. Khokhlov, *In the Name of Conscience,* part 3; Andrew and Gordievsky, *KGB,* pp. 430–1.

23. vol. 3, pakapp. 3.

24. t-7,267.

25. t-7,267.

26. Each target file (*obektovoye delo*) had to give the following information:

1) The role of the target in peacetime and wartime, and its place in the enemy's military–industrial capabilities. Documents, photographs, films, maps and diagrams giving details on its location, work schedule, security system, personnel, neighbors, populated areas nearby and methods of approaching the target.

2) Detailed descriptions of the target's vulnerable points, methods of attacking each of them, estimates of the likely damage, and the type of personnel to be used in sabotage operations (agents, illegals, etc.).

3) Opportunities to reconnoitre and sabotage the target. This section of the file contains individual reports (*spravki*) on every information source available on the target, and on each combat agent (*agent-boyevik*) selected for operations against it.

4) Details of the special equipment needed for operations against the target, the precise use to be made of it, dead drops, storage arrangements and the role of each of those entrusted with its use.

5) Arrangements for giving instructions to those responsible for attacking the target, together with the codewords for the "special action" to begin. (This part of the file was placed in a sealed package.)

If information on any of the subjects listed above was missing, a note was added to the file on the action being taken to obtain it. vol. 6, ch. 5, part 5, *n.* 2.

27. k-16,255.

28. t-7,311.

29. vol. 6, ch. 5, part 5.

30. vol. 6, ch. 5, part 5.

31. Wolf, *Man without a Face*, pp. 211–12.

32. vol. 6, ch. 1, part 1.

33. Barron, *KGB*, pp. 421–6. Andrew and Gordievsky, *KGB*, p. 467.

34. The fullest account of Stashinsky's career is in Anders, *Murder to Order*.

35. Anders, *Murder to Order*, p. 107.

36. Andrew and Gordievsky, *KGB*, p. 468. See below, chapter 15.

37. Richard Beeston, "KGB Refused to Kill Khrushchev" [interview with Semichastny], *The Times* (December 23, 1997).

38. Andrew and Gordievsky, *KGB*, pp. 481–2.

39. The text of Khrushchev's secret speech of August 3, 1961 did not come to light until 1993. Zubok and Pleshakov, *Inside the Kremlin's Cold War*, p. 252.

40. vol. 6, ch. 5, part 5.

41. vol. 6, ch. 5, part 5. Fonseca was co-founder of the FSLN. Initially it was called the National Liberation Front. "Sandinista" was added, chiefly at Fonseca's insistence, in 1962 in honor of the "anti-imperialist" hero, General Augusto César Sandino. Volume 2 will give more detail on KGB links with the FSLN and on other operations in Latin America.

42. vol. 6, ch. 5, part 5.

43. vol. 6, ch. 5, part 5.

44. vol. 8, ch. 10.

45. t-7,173.

46. It was planned to put the Wilhemshaven-Wesseling oil pipeline out of action where it crosses the Lippe river and the Seitenkanal; t-7,277.

47. t-7,65; k-16,380.

48. k-2,186.

49. t-7,163,165,170–2. For examples of radio caches, see this chapter, appendices 2, 3.

50. k-5,483.

51. On the MOLNIYA device, see this chapter, appendix 1. Mitrokhin's notes do not always identify clearly which caches are booby-trapped.

52. See this chapter, appendix 2.

53. Reuter report (January 18, 1999).

54. k-5,382. The Belgian caches turned out not to be booby-trapped.

55. In 1968–9, the Thirteenth Department had one illegal, PAUL, assisted by his wife VIRGINIA, and two pairs of German illegal agents, on whom Mitrokhin's notes give no further details; vol. 3, pakapp. 3. There may have been others in files not noted by Mitrokhin.

56. The fullest account of PAUL's career is in vol. 7, ch. 7; there are a few further details in vol. 6, ch. 5, part 5. On RAG see also k-11,17. PAUL's file, on which Mitrokhin made detailed notes, gives little indication of the nature of the assistance provided by VIRGINIA.

57. vol. 7, ch. 7; vol. 8, ch. 9; vol. 6, ch. 5, part 5. Among other illegals seconded for shorter periods to Thirteenth Department operations was Vasili Gordievsky (GROMOV), who on a mission to Spain in the winter of 1964–5 selected seven landing sites and eight arms caches for DRG operations. Rodin, the head of the Thirteenth Department, requested the Illegals Directorate to give him an award to mark the success of his mission; t-7,279.

58. vol. 6, ch. 1, part 1.

59. See above, chapter 11.

60. Deryabin and Rastvorov defected in 1954 to the CIA in, respectively, Vienna and Tokyo. In the same year the Petrovs defected in Canberra.

61. vol. 5, sec. 7*n.*; vol. 2, app. 3.

62. vol. 6, ch. 8, part 6.

63. vol. 2, app. 3; vol. 6, ch. 5, part 5.

64. See above, chapter 11.

65. Wise, *Molehunt*, ch. 11; Mangold, *Cold Warrior*, ch. 12.

66. vol. 6, ch. 5, part 5.

67. vol. 6, ch. 5, part 5. The KGB also sought, unsuccessfully, to use its agent in the Canadian RCMP, Jim Morrison (FRIEND), to track down Runge.

68. vol. 2, app. 3.

69. Nureyev, *Nureyev*, pp. 96–7.

70. Percival, *Nureyev*, pp. 55–6.

71. vol. 2, app. 3.

72. Sheymov, *Tower of Secrets*, pp. 92–3. Probably because of the deep lingering hostility to Nureyev among the KGB old guard, he was not rehabilitated in Russia until September 1998, five years after his death in exile. See "Russia reinstates Nureyev," *The Times* (September 23, 1998).

73. vol. 6, ch. 5, part 5.

74. Percival, *Nureyev*, p. 99.

75. vol. 6, ch. 5, part 5.

76. vol. 2, app. 3. Both Nureyev and Makarova were also the targets of numerous KGB active measures designed to discredit them.

77. k-10,155.

78. k-10,154.

79. Ministère Public de la Confédération press release (January 18, 1999). The Swiss press release made no reference to the documents from Mitrokhin's archives used to locate the cache.

80. k-5,382.

81. k-10,156.

82. k-10,158.

83. k-10,157.

84. k-10,158.

Chapter Twenty-three   Special Tasks Part 2

1. vol. 3, pakapp. 3.

2. The earliest reference to Department V (the letter "V," not the Roman numeral) noted by Mitrokhin was contained in order no. 00197 of October 7, 1965 instructing other FCD departments with agents suitable for use in time of war or international crisis to hand them over to Department V. The Department had probably been founded not long before. vol. 2, app. 3.

3. vol. 3, pakapp. 3.

4. k-16,408.

5. k-26,317.

6. The earliest subsidies recorded by Mitrokhin were 135,000 dollars in February 1968, followed by 100,000 dollars in March. Mitrokhin's notes on Greek Communist Party files for 1967, however, are very thin and it is likely that the first subsidies to the underground Party were handed over in Budapest during the later months of 1967. k-26,319.

7. k-16,69.

8. See above, chapter 18.

9. k-27,61.

10. k-16,69.

11. k-27,61.

12. k-3,28.

13. k-3,23,24,29.

14. k-3,28; k-26,315,318,323,325,326,384,387,390,394.

15. k-26,322. The Iraqi Communist Party also deposited its archives in the Soviet Union for safekeeping; see volume 2.

16. k-14,531. The location for operation ZVENO was studied by the illegal YAKOV and the agent ROBBI of the Vienna residency. YAKOV was Gennadi Mikhailovich Alekseyev, based in Switzerland, who had assumed the identity of a Swiss man, Igor Mürner, who had died in the Soviet Union. In 1973 YAKOV was arrested by the Swiss authorities, who were unable to prove charges of espionage against him. He served two years in prison for using false identity documents (k-5,193; k-24,236). Mitrokhin is unable to identify ROBBI. Other KGB officers (at least three, and possibly all, from Department V) involved in preparations for operation ZVENO were Yu. V. Derzhavin, A. D. Grigoryev, B. N. Malinin, Ye. S. Shcherbanov, B. S. Olikheyko, A. S. Savin, Kovalik, and Ye. A. Sharov (k-14,531).

17. k-16,408.

18. vol. 7, ch. 15

19. vol. 3, pakapp. 3. Vol. 7, ch. 5, para. 35 gives the location of PEPEL as Istanbul, but neither reference identifies the type of special action employed in PEPEL. Mitrokhin did not see the PEPEL file. The 1969 report also noted that the 1955 requirement for the Thirteenth Department to steal Western military technology was out of date; this had become the primary responsibility of FCD Directorate T (Scientific and Technological Espionage).

20. O'Riordan's history of the Irish members of the International Brigades, *Connolly Column*, was printed in East Germany (though published in Dublin), and gratefully acknowledged the assistance of the Soviet agent and British defector to East Germany, John Peet.

21. The text of O'Riordan's appeal for weapons for the IRA is published in the appendix to Yeltsin, *The View from the Kremlin*, pp. 311–16. In December 1969, shortly before the split which led to the emergence of the Provisionals, a secret meeting of the IRA leadership approved a proposal by Goulding to establish a National Liberation Front including Sinn Fein, the Irish Communist Party and other left-wing groups. Coogan, *The Troubles*, p. 95.

22. Bishop and Mallie, *The Provisional IRA*, p. 88.

23. Eight memoranda on the subject by Andropov on the IRA appeal for arms are published, in whole or part, in the appendix to Yeltsin, *The View from the Kremlin*, pp. 311–16.

24. vol. 7, ch. 7; vol. 8, ch. 9; vol. 6, ch. 5, part 5.

25. On the FLQ, see Granatstein and Stafford, *Spy Wars*, pp. 206–10.

26. vol. 8, ch. 14.

27. Even Granatstein and Stafford, two of Canada's leading historians of intelligence, conclude that the CIA document, "if authentic . . . does suggest strongly that the CIA was operating in Quebec"; *Spy Wars*, p. 209.

28. vol. 8, ch. 14.

29. k-24,365.

30. "Soviets Protest to Argentina After Envoy Foils Kidnaping," *Washington Post* (March 31, 1970).

31. vol. 4, indapp. 3.

32. Rob Bull, "Defector Bares 'Secret' Past," *Vancouver Sun* (April 5, 1976).

33. vol. 4, indapp. 3.

34. Interview with Robert Gates by Christopher Andrew (March 14, 1994).

35. See above, chapter 22.

36. k-24,365.

37. k-24,365.

38. k-24,365.

39. See below, chapter 24.

40. Andrew and Gordievsky, *KGB*, pp. 524–5; Barron, *KGB*, pp. 110, 431ff; Brook-Shepherd, *The Storm Birds*, pp. 197–9.

41. Kalugin, *Spymaster*, pp. 131–2.

42. Bennett and Hamilton (eds.), *Documents on British Policy Overseas*, series 3, vol. 1, pp. 388–9.

43. Gordievsky, *Next Stop Execution*, p. 184.

44. Bennett and Hamilton (eds.), *Documents on British Policy Overseas*, series 3, vol. 1, pp. 337–43, 359.

45. Bennett and Hamilton (eds.), *Documents on British Policy Overseas*, series 3, vol. 1, p. 389*n*.

46. Barron, *KGB*, pp. 413–15. Kuzichkin, *Inside the KGB*, p. 81.

47. Kalugin, *Spymaster*, pp. 131–2.

48. Gordievsky, *Next Stop Execution*, p. 184.

49. vol. 6, ch. 1, part 1; vol. 6, ch. 5, part 5. It is, of course, impossible to exclude the possibility that plans to cripple Baryshnikov were contained in a file not seen by Mitrokhin.

50. Studies of the split between Officials and Provisionals include Bell, *The Secret Army*, ch. 18; Bishop and Mallie, *The Provisional IRA*, chs. 7–8; Coogan, *The IRA*, chs. 15–17; Coogan, *The Troubles*, ch. 3; Taylor, *The Provos*, ch. 5–6.

51. Smith, *Fighting for Ireland?*, pp. 88–90.

52. O'Riordan's letter to the Central Committee and Andropov's memorandum on operation SPLASH are printed in the appendix to Yeltsin, *The View from the Kremlin*, pp. 314–16. According to Yeltsin, the file on SPLASH in the archives of the General Secretary does not indicate whether it was implemented. The files noted by Mitrokhin, apparently withheld from Yeltsin, show that it was and identify the boat used in the operation. vol. 7, ch. 15, para. 2.

53. vol. 7, ch. 15, para. 2.

54. O'Riordan informed the Central Committee, "I will take no part in the transport operation, and my role will only involve transferring the technical information about this to Seamus Costello." Yeltsin, *The View from the Kremlin*, p. 314.

55. Bishop and Mallie, *The Provisional IRA*, pp. 221–2; Smith, *Fighting for Ireland?*, p. 90; Coogan, *The Troubles*, pp. 276–80. The Irish National Liberation Army (INLA), founded as the military wing of IRSP, became arguably the most violent of the republican paramilitary groups. Its victims included Airey Neave, MP, Conservative spokesman on Northern Ireland, killed in 1979 by a bomb, activated by a mercury tilt

switch, which was planted in his car in the Palace of Westminster car park.

56. k-27,393; vol. 6, ch. 5, part 5.

57. Hodges, *Intellectual Foundations of the Nicaraguan Revolution,* p. 228.

58. vol. 6, ch. 5, part 5. On Piñeiro, who in 1974 became head of a new Departamento Americano of the Cuban Communist Party's Central Committee, which took over responsibility for assistance to Latin American revolutionary movements, see Andrew and Gordievsky, *KGB,* p. 514.

59. vol. 6, ch. 5, part 5.

60. Pezzullos, *At the Fall of Somoza,* p. 58. Shelton's reports were widely regarded in diplomatic circles as reflecting only Somoza's views. On at least one occasion, his political officer, James R. Cheek, used the State Department's "dissent channel" to contradict his chief. Jeremiah O'Leary, "Shelton being Replaced as Ambassador to Nicaragua," *Washington Star* (April 19, 1975).

61. Pastor, *Condemned to Repetition,* p. 39.

62. vol. 6, ch. 5, part 5.

63. Booth, *The End and the Beginning,* p. 142, Pezzullos, *At the Fall of Somoza,* pp. 116–17. Shelton was replaced as ambassador in April 1975.

64. vol. 6, ch. 5, part 5.

65. On the three main factions within the FSLN which emerged in 1975, see Booth, *The End and the Beginning,* pp. 143–4; Hodges, *Intellectual Foundations of the Nicaraguan Revolution,* pp. 233–55.

66. On Fonseca's link with the USSR, see volume 2.

67. k-27,393.

68. The file seen by Mitrokhin records only Fonseca's request to visit Moscow. Though he saw no file on the trip itself, it is unlikely that the request was rejected.

69. Pezzullos, *At the Fall of Somoza,* pp. 117–19. On KGB relations with the Sandinistas, see volume 2.

70. t-7,135; vol. 2, appendix 3.

71. Kuzichkin, *Inside the KGB,* pp. 111–12.

72. Kalugin, *Spymaster,* pp. 238–9.

73. Kalugin, *Spymaster,* pp. 152–3.

74. vol. 2, app. 3.

75. Kalugin, *Spymaster,* pp. 152–9. Cf. Wise, *Molehunt,* pp. 195–7.

76. vol. 2, app. 3. The Line KR officer Vladimir Nikolayevich Yelchaninov (codenamed VELT), posted to the New York residency in 1978, also spent much of his time trying to track down defectors; vol. 6, app. 2, part 5.

77. Bereanu and Todorov, *The Umbrella Murder,* pp. 34–7, 70–3.

78. Kalugin, *Spymaster,* pp. 178–83; Andrew and Gordievsky, *KGB,* pp. 644–5. Bereanu and Todorov, *The Umbrella Murder,* adds usefully to previous accounts of Markov's murder but also introduces some implausible speculation. For an illustration of an earlier version of the weapon used to kill Markov, a KGB poison pellet cane of the 1950s, see Melton, *The Ultimate Spy Book,* p. 152.

79. Interviews with Alpha group veterans, broadcast in *Inside Russia's SAS* (BBC2, June 13, 1999).

80. vol. 1, ch. 4.

81. Westad, "Concerning the Situation in 'A,' " p. 130. Dobbs, *Down with Big Brother,* pp. 11–12.

82. See above, chapter 15.

83. vol. 1, ch. 4. Mitrokhin's account contains only a brief allusion to the attempts to poison Amin's food, which appears to have been the Eighth Department's preferred method of assassination. According to Vladimir Kuzichkin, who defected from Directorate S a few years later, the first choice of assassin was an Azerbaijani illegal, Mikhail Talybov, who was bilingual in Farsi and had spent several years in Kabul with Afghan identity papers forged by the KGB. Equipped with poisons from the OTU laboratory, Talybov succeeded in gaining a job as a chef in the presidential palace. But, according to Kuzichkin, "Amin was as careful as any of the Borgias. He kept switching his food and drink as if he expected to be poisoned." Kuzichkin, *Inside the KGB,* pp. 314–15; Kuzichkin, "Coups and Killings in Kabul," *Time* (November 22, 1982); Barron, *KGB Today,* pp. 15–16. A further, unsuccessful attempt to poison Amin took place at a lunch given by him for his ministers on December 27 (Dobbs, *Down with Big Brother,* p. 19).

84. Westad, "Concerning the Situation in 'A,' " p. 130.

85. "The Soviet Union and Afghanistan, 1978–1989," p. 159.

86. Westad, "Concerning the Situation in 'A,' " p. 131. The invasion plan was approved by the Politburo on December 12.

87. vol. 1, ch. 4.

88. Dobbs, *Down with Big Brother,* pp. 18–19.

89. vol. 1, ch. 4.

90. vol. 1, ch. 4.

91. vol. 1, ch. 4.

92. vol. 1, app. 2.

93. vol. 1, ch. 4.

94. On Kikot's previous career, see k-24,87,89; k-12,376; k-8,590.

95. vol. 1, app. 3.

96. Childs and Popplewell, *The Stasi*, pp. 138–40, 156–7; Gates, *From the Shadows*, pp. 206–7; Wolf, *Man Without a Face*, pp. 271–81. On Carlos's contacts with the KGB, see volume 2.

97. vol. 7, ch. 15.

98. Gates, *From the Shadows*, pp. 338–9.

99. Andrew and Gordievsky (eds.), *Instructions from the Centre*, pp. 82–5.

100. Accounts of the August coup include those in Stepankov and Lisov, *Kremlevsky Zagovor;* Albats, *The State within a State;* Remnick, *Lenin's Tomb;* and Gorbachev, *The August Coup.* Though Kryuchkov and other leading plotters were arrested after the coup, their trial was repeatedly postponed. By early 1993 all had been released. They were given formal amnesties by the Russian parliament elected in December 1993.

101. k-16,408.

Chapter Twenty-four   Cold War Operations against Britain Part 1

1. There is no support in any of the files seen by Mitrokhin that for the implausible theory that a major Soviet agent remained at work in MI5 after the demise of the Magnificent Five. Mitrokhin's notes contain no reference to Sir Roger Hollis, director-general of MI5, the most senior of the MI5 officers wrongly accused of being a Soviet agent. The Hollis story is now thoroughly discredited (Andrew and Gordievsky, *KGB*, p. 27).

2. On Norwood's early career, see above chapters 7 and 8.

3. vol. 7, ch. 14, item 17.

4. Hennessy, *Never Again*, p. 269.

5. vol. 7, ch. 14, item 17. Myakinkov's name was wrongly transcribed by Mitrokhin as Mekin'kov. (CBEN)

6. vol. 7, ch. 14, item 17.

7. For legal reasons neither HUNT's real identity nor the government departments for which he worked (included in Mitrokhin's notes) can be identified. HUNT's first controller was V. E. Tseyrov (then also Norwood's controller), followed by B. K. Stolenov and Yu. Kondratenko. After the mass expulsion of KGB and GRU personnel from London in 1971 HUNT was put on ice for several years as a security precaution. Contact was resumed in 1975 by MAIRE, an agent of the Paris residency. Following MAIRE's death in 1976, the London residency resumed control in 1977. HUNT's last two case officers were V. V. Yaroshenko and A. N. Chernayev. In 1979, following HUNT's establishment of a small business, his wife was recruited as a courier. By 1981, however, the Centre was dissatisfied with the quality of HUNT's intelligence and apparently fearful that he was under MI5 surveillance. Contact with him seems to have been broken at that point. vol. 7, ch. 14, item 16.

8. Blake, *No Other Choice*, chs. 2–5. Cf. Hyde, *George Blake*. Though acknowledging his affection and admiration for Curiel, Blake unconvincingly downplays his influence on him. According to Kalugin, Blake "already held far-leftist views at the outbreak of the Korean War" (Kalugin, *Spymaster*, p. 141.). For examples of other distortions in Blake's memoirs, see Andrew and Gordievsky, *KGB*, pp. 755–6, *n.* 117); Murphy, Kondrashev and Bailey, *Battleground Berlin*, pp. 217, 482–3, *n.* 36.

9. Murphy, Kondrashev and Bailey, *Battleground Berlin*, pp. 214–15 (an account based on partial access to KGB files and on the recollections of Kondrashev). Rodin was London resident from 1947 to 1952 and from 1956 to 1961; Andrew and Gordievsky, *KGB*, p. 663.

10. See below, chapter 26.

11. k-9, 65.

12. Blake, *No Other Choice*, pp. 207–8. Kalugin, *Spymaster*, p. 141. Andrew and Gordievsky, *KGB*, pp. 755–6, *n.* 117.

13. The best account of the Berlin tunnel operation, based both on material made available by the SVR and on newly declassified CIA files, is Murphy, Kondrashev and Bailey, *Battleground Berlin*, ch. 11 and appendix 5, which corrects numerous errors in earlier accounts. Mitrokhin's brief notes on the Berlin tunnel add nothing to *Battleground Berlin*.

14. Andrew and Gordievsky, *KGB*, p. 442. On Goleniewski see Murphy, Kondrashev and Bailey, *Battleground Berlin*, pp. 342–6.

15. Blake, *No Other Choice,* chs. 11, 12.

16. Kalugin, *Spymaster,* p. 142.

17. vol. 7, ch. 14, item 3. Driberg had joined the Communist Party while at public school but was expelled in 1941 when, according to his entry in the *Dictionary of National Biography,* the Party leadership "discovered that he was an agent of MI5, to which he had been recruited in the late 1930s" (*Dictionary of National Biography, 1971–1980,* p. 251). Though Driberg undoubtedly gave information to Maxwell Knight, a leading MI5 officer, much remains obscure about the relationship between them. According to Knight's personal assistant, Joan Miller, he was a bisexual who, for a time, was "crazy" about Driberg. In her view, Driberg was only "a casual agent" who would "turn in a bit of stuff" when Knight put pressure on him. (Interview with Joan Miller, *Sunday Times Magazine* (October 18, 1981); Miller, *One Girl's War;* Andrew, *Secret Service,* pp. 521–2.

18. Driberg, *Ruling Passions,* pp. 228–9.

19. Wheen, *Tom Driberg,* p. 309.

20. Vassall, *Vassall;* Andrew and Gordievsky, *KGB,* pp. 442–4. Andropov considered Vassall one of the KGB's most valuable agents.

21. Driberg, *Ruling Passions,* p. 235.

22. vol. 7, ch. 14, item 3. Mitrokhin's notes on Driberg's file record that he was "recruited in Moscow . . . chiefly on the basis of compromising material which recorded his homosexual relations with an agent," but give no further details of the "compromising material."

23. vol. 7, ch. 14, item 3.

24. Watkins's comments are quoted in Wheen, *Tom Driberg,* p. 328.

25. vol. 7, ch. 14, item 3.

26. Wheen, *Tom Driberg,* pp. 292–315. Francis Wheen's very readable and entertaining biography of Driberg dismisses all suggestion that his book on Burgess was influenced in any way by the KGB. Though shocked by the "stench" from the "acrid piss" of stories planted in the press by MI5 and MI6 (*Tom Driberg,* p. 317), Mr. Wheen failed to detect any unwholesome aroma emitting from the vast array of KGB active measures. Despite the SCD's addiction to compromise operations, it also does not occur to him that the KGB might have exploited Driberg's sexual adventures in Moscow lavatories.

27. Driberg, *Ruling Passions,* p. 229.

28. Driberg, *Guy Burgess.*

29. According to Mitrokhin's summary of Driberg's KGB file, he was used for "the publication of KGB themes in the British press," and "sent to the United States and other Western countries with a [KGB] brief"; vol. 7, ch. 14, item 3.

30. Wheen, *Tom Driberg,* p. 337.

31. Ziegler, *Wilson,* p. 313.

32. Wheen, *Tom Driberg,* pp. 353–4.

33. vol. 7, ch. 14, item 3.

34. Wheen, *Tom Driberg,* pp. 362–8, 400.

35. Ziegler, *Wilson,* p. 313.

36. Frolik also identified three other Labor MPs whom he claimed had been in the pay of the StB: Will Owen, John Stonehouse and agent GUSTAV (not so far reliably identified); Andrew and Gordievsky, *KGB,* pp. 523–4.

37. vol. 7, ch. 14, item 2.

38. Fletcher, *£60 a Second on Defence,* pp. 132–3.

39. vol. 7, ch. 14, item 2.

40. Fletcher claimed that MI5 had shown his wife intercepted letters in 1969 showing that he had had an affair during a visit to Hungary. Dorril and Ramsay, *Smear,* p. 197.

41. Dick Crossmann was less impressed, telling his diary that Wilson had done "a magnificent job of blowing out his information" in order to pose as a Soviet expert. Ziegler, *Wilson,* pp. 89–94.

42. vol. 7, ch. 14, item 18.

43. Ziegler, *Wilson,* p. 91.

44. vol. 7, ch. 14, item 18.

45. Ziegler, *Wilson,* p. 94.

46. vol. 7, ch. 14, item 18.

47. Wise, *Molehunt,* pp. 97–9. Mangold, *Cold Warrior,* pp. 95–7.

48. Wright, *Spycatcher.* Wright later disowned most of his own conspiracy theory and said in a *Panorama* interview that there had been only one serious plotter (BBC1, October 13, 1988).

49. vol. 7, ch. 16, item 15. In view of the connection of the future Labor leader, Michael Foot, with *Tribune* and the allegations made against him by the *Sunday Times* in 1995, for which he received libel damages, it seems appropriate to add that Mitrokhin's notes contain no reference to him.

50. Crankshaw, *Putting up with the Russians, 1947–1984,* p. xi.

51. Crankshaw, *Russia by Daylight,* p. 12.

52. *Dictionary of National Biography, 1981–1985,* p. 101.

53. vol. 7, ch. 14, item 42.

54. Crankshaw, *Putting up with the Russians,* p. 13.

55. vol. 7, ch. 14, item 42.

56. Crankshaw, *Putting up with the Russians,* p. 81.

57. vol. 7, ch. 14, item 42.

58. vol. 7, ch. 16, item 17.

59. Barron, *KGB,* pp. 343–5.

60. vol. 7, ch. 16, item 17. The KGB file on operation PROBA disproves suggestions that Courtney was the victim of a plot by MI5 rather than the KGB. Dorril and Ramsay, *Smear,* p. 107.

61. vol. 7, ch. 14, item 13. There is no record in Mitrokhin's notes of any major hemorrhage of information by any seduced member of the British embassy staff after Vassall.

62. See above, chapters 10 and 12.

63. Samolis (ed.), *Veterany Vneshnei Razvedki Rossii,* pp. 103–5. Though the main features of Molody's career as illegal resident in London, much of which came out at his trial in 1961, are already known, the files noted by Mitrokhin add some important details.

64. vol. 8, ch. 8. SVYASHCHENNIK had previously been used to "check" Hambleton before his recruitment by the KGB; vol. 8, app. 1.

65. vol. 8, ch. 8.

66. Granatstein and Stafford, *Spy Wars,* p. 119.

67. vol. 6, ch. 5, part 3.

68. k-11, 19.

69. Microdot letter found in BEN's possession after his arrest in 1961. Bulloch and Miller, *Spy Ring,* ch. 11; West, *The Illegals,* pp. 175–7.

70. vol. 6, ch. 5, part 3.

71. Agranovsky, "Profession: Foreigner."

72. vol. 6, ch. 5, part 2.

73. vol. 6, ch. 5, part 2. A KGB file for 1953 describes LONG as a "valuable agent" of the Paris residency; k-4, 99. According to their passports, "Peter Kroger" had been born in Gisborne, New Zealand, on July 10, 1910 and "Helen Kroger" had been born in Boyle, Alberta, on January 17, 1913; vol. 6, ch. 5, part 2. Their colleagues in the British book trade believed both to be Canadian.

74. Snelling, *Rare Books and Rarer People,* p. 208.

75. Blake, *No Other Choice,* p. 265.

76. Agranovsky, "Profession: Foreigner."

77. vol. 7, ch. 14, item 17.

78. vol. 7, ch. 12.

79. Houghton, *Operation Portland,* Andrew and Gordievsky, *KGB,* pp. 446–7.

80. Wright, *Spycatcher,* pp. 137–8; Rositzke, *The KGB,* pp. 76–7.

81. vol. 7, ch. 12.

82. vol. 6, ch. 5, part 2.

83. vol. 6, ch. 5, part 2.

84. Samolis (ed.), *Veterany Vneshnei Razvedki Rossii,* pp. 68–72.

85. Blake, *No Other Choice,* pp. 264–5.

86. vol. 7, ch. 12.

87. Andrew and Gordievsky, *KGB,* pp. 447–8.

88. vol. 7, ch. 12.

89. vol. 7, ch. 12.

90. RAG had been recruited in 1955; his work as a Soviet agent was known to at least one leader of the Belgian Communist Party. k-11, 17.

91. vol. 7, ch. 13. At the time of Koslov's recall, the Centre does not appear to have decided whether his final destination was to have been Britain or the United States.

92. Bagrichev later became head of the first department in Directorate S; a file noted by Mitrokhin records him as holding that post in 1975. vol. 7, ch. 8, para. 6.

93. Lopatin became acting resident, following Chizhov's sudden recall to Moscow in 1966 after he had apparently suffered a brain hemorrhage; Andrew and Gordievsky, *KGB*, p. 773, *n.* 121. Chizhov appears to have recovered. In the mid-1970s he was resident in Mogadishu. k-12, 452.

94. Andrew and Gordievsky, *KGB*, p. 517.

95. Frolik, *The Frolik Defection*, p. 82.

96. From 1964 to 1968 Savin was Lyalin's predecessor as the Thirteenth Department officer at the London residency; he later became head of Line N in Finland. vol. 7, app. 2, paras. 61, 84.

97. West, *A Matter of Trust*, p. 171. Brook-Shepherd, *The Storm Birds*, p. 198.

98. Andrew and Gordievsky, *KGB*, pp. 517–18. In 1971 sixteen Line X officers were operating under official cover in London: one (Sherstnev) as embassy first secretary; three as third secretaries; one as attaché; eight in the trade mission; one in Mashpriborintorg (International Machine Tool Trade Organization); and one as a trainee. Additional Line X officers were being selected for positions in the Moscow Narodnyy Bank and in an (unidentified) Anglo-Soviet organization. The number of Line X officers was seriously reduced as a result of the mass expulsion of September 1971. k-2, 124.

99. vol. 7, app. 1, item 65; k-2, 124. For legal reasons, it is not possible to include the names or other identifying details of the Line X agents contained in Mitrokhin's notes.

100. vol. 7, app. 1, item 51.

101. vol. 7, ch. 14, item 24; k-2, 120.

102. vol. 7, app. 1, item 70; k-2, 124.

103. vol. 7, ch. 14, item 4.

104. vol. 7, ch. 14, item 16.

105. vol. 7, app. 1, item 64; k-2, 124

106. vol. 7, ch. 14, item 36; k-2, 124.

107. vol. 7, app. 1, item 69; k-2, 124. The engineer DAN is not to be confused with the *Tribune* journalist with the same codename.

108. vol. 7, ch. 14, item 15; k-2, 124.

109. vol. 7, app. 1, item 96.

110. k-2, 124

111. vol. 7, ch. 14, item 31.

112. Andrew and Gordievsky, *KGB*, p. 518; West, *A Matter of Trust*, pp. 115–19.

113. Reports of the Security Commission in June 1965 (Cmnd. 2722) and November 1968 (Cmnd. 3856); Pincher, *Too Secret Too Long*, pp. 421–3, 463; West, *A Matter of Trust*, pp. 127–9, 161–2.

114. vol. 7, app. 2, item 64.

115. vol. 7, app. 2, item 31.

116. vol. 7, app. 2, item 14.

117. Andrew and Gordievsky, *KGB*, pp. 24–6.

118. Philby, *My Silent War*, p. 17.

119. vol. 6, app. 1, part 37

120. Philby's original codename had both Russian and German forms, respectively SYNOK and SÖHNCHEN, both meaning "Sonny."

121. vol. 6, app. 1, part 37

122. Andrew and Gordievsky, *KGB*, pp. 525–6.

123. See above, chapter 23.

124. Gordievsky, *Next Stop Execution*, p. 184.

125. Kalugin, *Spymaster*, p. 131.

Chapter Twenty-five   Cold War Operations against Britain Part 2

1. Andrew and Gordievsky, *KGB*, pp. 24–6. Knightley, *Philby;* pp. 234–7.

2. *Izvestia* (October 1, 1971).

3. See above, chapter 7.

4. SIS officers stationed in Beirut since Philby's defection in 1963 had been identified by the bugging of the British embassy and SIS station in operation RUBIN; vol. 7, ch. 5, para. 38.

5. *Izvestia* (October 1, 1971). Robert G. Kaiser, "Soviets Name 7 Britons as Mideast Spies," *Washington Post* (October 2, 1971).

6. vol. 7, ch. 5, para. 29. *Al Zaman* editorial (May 8, 1972).

7. BBC, *Summary of World Broadcasts*, ME/3823/i (October 27, 1971). *Al Zaman* editorial (May 8, 1972).

8. vol. 7, ch. 5, para. 36.

9. vol. 7, ch. 5, para. 29.

10. *L'Orient-Le Jour* (Beirut) (May 13, 1972); *The Times* (April 7, 1973). When later questioned by Knightley about the KGB's renewed contact with him in the early 1970s, Philby was "a little vague" (Knightley, *Philby*, p. 237). Philby could scarcely have forgotten the long interview in *Izvestia* on October 1, 1971, which marked his partial return to favor, but plainly preferred not to talk about it.

11. Kalugin, *Spymaster*, pp. 133–41. Andrew and Gordievsky, *KGB*, pp. 544–5.

12. vol. 7, app. 2, item 82.

13. Brook-Shepherd, *The Storm Birds*, p. 199; West, *A Matter of Trust*, pp. 171–2.

14. Andrew and Gordievsky, *KGB*, pp. 525–6.

15. vol. 7, ch. 6.

16. Andrew and Gordievsky, *KGB*, p. 526.

17. vol. 7, ch. 6, para. 9. Mitrokhin's notes do not record the date at which the bugging of the trade delegation was discovered. In 1989, however, the Soviets publicized their discovery of the bugs some years earlier. Christopher Andrew, Simon O'Dwyer Russell and Robert Porter, "Battle of the Bugs on the Wall," *Sunday Telegraph* (June 4, 1989).

18. Andrew and Gordievsky, *KGB*, p. 514.

19. vol. 7, app. 2, item 7. KGB agents in the London embassy on January 15, 1973 were Ivan I. Ippolitov (minister-counselor), Ralf Bernkhardovich Mikenberg (second secretary), V. I. Solovev (third secretary), Andreï Sergeyevich Parastayev (first secretary), Grigori Petrovich Dremlyuga (aide to naval attaché), Andrei Filippovich Pekhterev (senior assistant military attaché), Nikolai Nikolayevich Pleshakov (interpreter), I. A. Bardeyev, (assistant naval attaché), A. A. Abramov (attaché), I. M. Klimanov, Dmitri Alekhin (duty office keeper), Leonid A. Moskvin (third secretary), Vasili A. Tolstoy (duty office keeper), Viktor Mikhailovich Gribanov (trade attaché), Vladimir Petrovich Molotkov, Stanislav Pokrovsky, Lev. A. Konev, Viktor Mikhailovich Ivanov (trade representative) and Tamara Tikhonovna Nikulina.

20. vol. 7, ch. 3, para. 12; vol. 7, ch. 3, paras. 6–7.

21. vol. 7, app. 3; k-27, 453.

22. k-4, 154.

23. vol. 7, ch. 14, item 16.

24. vol. 7, ch. 14, item 17.

25. k-2, 124.

26. See above, chapter 24.

27. vol. 7, ch. 14, item 4.

28. vol. 7, ch. 3.

29. vol. 7, app. 3, *n.* 8. It does not follow that the KGB succeeded in sending agents or trusted contacts to all these colleges.

30. vol. 7, app. 2, item 77. Because of his difficulty in combining a career as a distinguished research scientist with work as an operational intelligence officer, Lednev was later allowed to leave the KGB, though he was no doubt expected to retain an association with it. According to KGB files, in 1981 he was deputy director of the Institute of Biological Physics in the city of Pushchino. vol. 6, app. 2, part 5.

31. vol. 7, app. 2, item 4. In 1979 Lopatin was succeeded as head of Directorate T by Leonid Sergeyevich Zaitsev, who had also begun specializing in S&T while at the London residency in the 1960s. vol. 3, pakapp. 3, items 294–5; Andrew and Gordievsky, *KGB*, p. 622.

32. k-2, 124. vol. 7, app. 1, item 66.

33. COOPER, who worked in the new products department of a pharmaceutical company; a virologist; a research scientist in a pharmaceutical company; and an engineer at a British nuclear reactor. vol. 7, ch. 14, item 31; k-2, 124; vol. 7, app. 1, item 96.

34. Meetings between STARIK and his controller took place in Paris, those with DAN in Western Europe. In 1975–6 contact with HUNT was maintained by an agent of the Paris residency. Other cases were run by the Copenhagen and Helsinki residencies (k-2, 124; vol. 6, app. 1, part 39; vol. 7, app. 1, items 65, 68).

35. vol. 7, ch. 14, item 12.

36. John Steele, "25 years for the Spy Who Stayed in the Cold," *Daily Telegraph* (November 18, 1993).

37. Report of the Security Commission (Cm 2930) (July 1995), chs. 2–4.

38. vol. 7, ch. 14, item 12.

39. On the information about Smith passed by MI5 to EMI in 1978, see "Phone Call that Trapped a Spy," *Independent* (November 19, 1993).

40. vol. 7, ch. 14, item 12.

41. The Security Commission later concluded that Smith had held on to some of the classified documents he had obtained at Thorn–EMI and given them to the KGB some time after he lost his security access in 1978. One or more of the payments recorded in his file may thus refer to a period after his loss of access. Since Mitrokhin's notes end in 1984, the details of KGB payments to Smith cannot refer to his later years as a Soviet agent.

42. " 'Boring' Idealist Who Spied for Russia Gets 25 Years," *The Times* (November 19, 1993).

43. Report of the Security Commission (Cm 2930) (July 1995), pp. 8–9. "Dear Maggie, Please Let Me Spy for the KGB!," *Daily Mirror* (September 21, 1993). Laurence Donegan and Richard Norton-Taylor, "Spy Who Slipped Through the Net," *Guardian* (November 19, 1993).

44. See below, chapter 25.

45. Britain ranked fourth in S&T collection.

46. Klöckner INA Industrial Plants Ltd was a British-based subsidiary of the West German firm Klöckner & Co., Kommanditgesellschaft auf Aktien.

47. The KGB officers who received commendations for their part in the operation were A. B. Maksimov, V. G. Goncharov, V. A. Andryevskaya, A. I. Baskakov, A. N. Belov, V. P. Varvanin, A. N. Kosarev, A. V. Smirnov, A. A. Shishkov, S. A. Agafonov, V. K. Gavrilov, S. Yu. Demidov, B. I. Danilin, O. I. Bukharev and V. A. Sedov. vol. 7, app. 3, *n*. 15.

48. See above, chapter 21.

49. vol. 7, ch. 14, item 14.

50. vol. 7, ch. 14, item 18. On Parastayev, see also vol. 7, app. 1, items 7, 42.

51. Ziegler, *Wilson*, p. 503.

52. vol. 7, ch. 14, item 18.

53. Ziegler, *Wilson*, pp. 508–9.

54. vol. 7, ch. 14, item 18.

55. Andrew and Gordievsky (eds.), *Instructions from the Centre*, p. 129.

56. vol. 7, ch. 16, items 54, 62.

57. vol. 7, ch. 16, item 62.

58. Andrew and Gordievsky (eds.), *Instructions from the Centre*, pp. 129–30.

59. See above, chapter 24.

60. Information from Oleg Gordievsky.

61. vol. 7, ch. 16, item 50.

62. *Morning Star* (October 31, 1975).

63. De-la-Noy, *Mervyn Stockwood*, pp. 214–15.

64. vol. 7, ch. 16, item 50. Tony Benn was also invited to dinner but declined because "Mervyn Stockwood is such an old gossip that he'd tell everybody that he's had a dinner party for the Secretary of the Communist Party and myself." Benn, *Against the Tide*, p. 482.

65. De-la-Noy, *Mervyn Stockwood*, p. 212.

66. vol. 7, ch. 16, item 51.

67. vol. 7, ch. 16, item 53.

68. Alasdair Palmer, "How the KGB Ran the *Guardian*'s Features Editor," *Spectator* (December 10, 1994). Interview with Richard Gott, *Guardian* (December 12, 1994).

69. Mitrokhin did not note either Gott's KGB file or references to other *Guardian* articles by him. His notes thus do not clarify the nature of Gott's relationship with the KGB. Gott acknowledges having met KGB officers in London, Moscow, Vienna, Athens and Nicosia, but claims that the only money he received from them was to pay travel expenses to and in the last three locations. Interview with Richard Gott, *Guardian* (December 12, 1994). Cf. Gordievsky, *Next Stop Execution*, pp. 281–2.

70. vol. 7, ch. 16, item 66. *Parliamentary Debates*, 5th series, *House of Commons Official Report*, Session 1977–78, vol. 944, col. 1200.

71. Andrew and Gordievsky, *KGB*, pp. 506–8.

72. Andrew and Gordievsky (eds.), *Instructions from the Centre*, pp. 101–2, 138–9.

73. *Observer* duly reported American claims that the document was forged but gave greater weight to evidence for its authenticity (*Observer*, January 22, 1984).

74. "A Girl's Best Friend," *New Statesman* (November 5, 1982).

75. Andrew and Gordievsky, *KGB,* p. 630.

76. vol. 6, app. 1 (misc.), part 1; k-12, 51.

77. Andrew and Gordievsky (eds.), *Instructions from the Centre,* pp. 130–7.

78. Andrew and Gordievsky (eds.), *Instructions from the Centre,* p. 118.

79. There is, for example, no reference in Mitrokhin's notes to Geoffrey Prime, the agent in GCHQ, who was—unusually—recruited and run outside the UK by the KGB Third Directorate, to whose files Mitrokhin did not have access.

80. vol. 7, app. 1, item 77. There is another tantalizing one-sentence reference to a SIGINT official (apparently British) codenamed ZHUR (JOUR), contacted in 1963 for the first time since 1938. Mitrokhin gives no indication whether or not the contact had any result. It is also possible that the reference was garbled, since the longest-serving agent providing intelligence on cipher systems, an employee of the French foreign ministry, was codenamed JOUR. vol. 7, app. 1, item 122.

81. vol. 5, ch. 14.

82. *The Times* (November 29, 1969, March 31, 1994).

83. vol. 5, ch. 14, para. 1; vol. 7, ch. 7, para. 74.

84. vol. 5, ch. 14, *n.* 4; vol. 7, ch. 7, para. 74.

85. vol. 5, ch. 14, para. 2 and *n.* 4.

86. vol. 7, ch. 7, paras. 73, 74; k-2, 171; vol. 5, ch. 14, paras. 2, 3, 7.

87. vol. 5, ch. 14, paras. 5, 6; vol. 7, ch. 7, para. 75. Since there is no indication that VERA behaved improperly, it would be unfair to reveal her identity or precise job in the Moscow embassy, both of which are recorded in Symonds's file.

88. vol. 5, ch. 14, paras. 7–9.

89. vol. 5, ch. 14, *n.* 6.

90. It was also considered too risky for Symonds to use his forged British passport to apply for an Australian visa; entry to New Zealand did not require a visa. From New Zealand he would need only Everett's birth certificate to gain entry to Australia. Symonds, however, was unable to book a direct flight from Tokyo to New Zealand and was forced to use his bogus British passport as a transit passenger in Sydney. When flying from New Zealand to Australia later in the year, he used the same passport with an Australian visa obtained in Wellington, fearing that if he used Everett's birth certificate an immigration service computer might detect that he had previously possessed a British passport containing the same name and date of birth. vol. 5, ch. 14, paras. 10–11.

91. vol. 5, ch. 14, paras. 12–44.

92. vol. 5, ch. 14, paras. 45–6.

93. vol. 7, ch. 7, para. 76.

94. vol. 5, ch. 14, paras. 51–2.

95. "The Fugitive Detective and His Secret Trips to Britain," *The Times* (April 15, 1981).

96. vol. 5, ch. 14, paras. 53–4.

97. "Bribes Trial Man Says He was Told to Flee," *The Times* (April 7, 1981). "Detective in 'Morass of Corruption' is Jailed," *The Times* (April 15, 1981). "Confessions of a Bent Copper," *The Times* (March 31, 1994).

98. Andrew and Gordievsky, *KGB,* p. 526. Lukasevics was unable to claim credit for Prime and Symonds, two of the KGB's most notable British agents of the 1970s; both had been recruited abroad.

99. Andrew and Gordievsky, *KGB,* pp. 585–7; Gordievsky, *Next Stop Execution,* pp. 249–52.

100. vol. 7, app. 2, item 69.

101. vol. 7, app. 2, 71. The file noted by Mitrokhin refers to Guk by his codename, YERMAKOV.

102. Zamuruyev was succeeded as head of Line N by Aleksandr Igorevich Timonov. vol. 7, ch. 7, para. 10; app. 2, para. 50.

103. Andrew and Gordievsky, *KGB,* p. 599. Gordievsky, *Next Stop Execution,* pp. 269–70.

104. Andrew and Gordievsky, *KGB,* pp. 582–605. Andrew and Gordievsky (eds.), *Instructions from the Centre,* ch. 4.

105. vol. 7, ch. 16, item 19.

106. Andrew and Gordievsky, *KGB,* p. 586.

107. vol. 7, app. 2, item 73.

108. vol. 7, app. 2, item 72.

109. Earley, *Confessions of a Spy,* pp. 139–45, 176–9.

110. Andrew and Gordievsky, *KGB,* pp. 28–35, 609; Gordievsky, *Next Stop Execution,* chs. 1, 14, 15.

111. vol. 7, ch. 14, item 12.

112. Report of the Security Commission (Cm 2930) (July 1995), p. 10.

113. Report of the Security Commission (Cm 2930) (July 1995), pp. 13–14, 32–3. "Phone Call Hoax that Trapped a Spy," *Independent* (November 19, 1993); "Vital Clues to a Traitor," *Daily Mail* (November 19, 1993).

114. Some indication of the intelligence provided by Kuzichkin and Butkov is provided in their memoirs. On Makarov, see Kahn, "Soviet Comint in the Cold War." Butkov's memoirs have so far appeared only in Norwegian.

115. Pasechnik, one of the scientific directors of Biopreparat, the world's largest and most advanced biological warfare research institute, made contact with SIS during a visit to France in 1989 and was exfiltrated to Britain. Interview with Pasechnik by Christopher Andrew in the 1995 Radio 4 series *New Spies for Old?* (presented by Christopher Andrew; produced by Dennis Sewell).

Chapter Twenty-six   *The Federal Republic of Germany*

1. See above, chapter 12.

2. In 1977 the KGB apparat at Karlshorst was training seven East German illegals and investigating another fifty-two potential recruits, most of whom would probably not make the grade; k-5, 774.

3. On its foundation in 1952, the Stasi's foreign intelligence arm was known as Hauptverwaltung XV (Main Department XV); it was renamed the HVA in 1956.

4. Childs and Popplewell, *The Stasi*, pp. 122–3.

5. Wolf, *Man without a Face*, p. xii.

6. k-16, 522. The residencies in Cologne and Hamburg were subordinate to that of Bonn, whose head had the title of Chief Resident.

7. k-19, 247.

8. The leader of the snatch squad was another German agent, WAGNER (later renamed FLORA). For this and other special actions, he was awarded the Order of the Red Star. While WAGNER was stationed in Belgium from 1964 to 1967, SERGEYEV acted as courier to him. k-5, 88; k-16, 212.

9. k-5, 88.

10. k-5, 283.

11. k-5, 284.

12. k-9, 65.

13. Höhne and Zolling, *The General was a Spy*, ch. 12. Rositzke, *The KGB*, pp. 189–94. Andrew and Gordievsky, *KGB*, pp. 412, 452–3; Murphy, Kondrashev and Bailey, *Battleground Berlin*, pp. 430–9. Mitrokhin's brief notes on Felfe contain no detailed examples of the intelligence he provided; they confirm, however, that Felfe's memoirs, *Im Dienst des Gegners*, contains disinformation fabricated by Service A (k-5, 284).

14. vol. 6, ch. 2, part 1, *n*.

15. Peet, *The Long Engagement*, pp. 3, 101–3, 184–5, 229–31.

16. Peet, *The Long Engagement*, ch. 30. Childs and Popplewell, *The Stasi*, pp. 145–6.

17. The best account of the Otto John case is Murphy, Kondrashev and Bailey, *Battleground Berlin*, ch. 10. Mitrokhin saw no file on the case.

18. Nationalrat der Nationalen Front des Demokratischen Deutschland, *Braunbuch* and *Graubuch*.

19. Schmeidel, "Shield and Sword of the Party," pp. 146–7.

20. k-26, 88. The fact that Brandt was given a codename is not, of course, evidence that he was an agent. Even Churchill and Roosevelt were referred to by codenames in wartime Soviet intelligence cables.

21. Brandt, *My Road to Berlin*, chs. 2–4.

22. k-26, 88. On Rein, see Brandt, *My Road to Berlin*, pp. 79–80.

23. The British also had ULTRA intelligence on the movements of the *Tirpitz*. After several unsuccessful British attacks, the battleship was finally sunk in November 1944 with the loss of 1,204 lives.

24. TERENTY was the Czech Communist journalist Walter Taube. Mitrokhin's note identifies VANYA as Vanek, a former Czech intelligence officer now working for the British. It is unclear whether "Vanek" is a forename or surname (k-26, 88).

25. k-26, 88.

26. k-26, 88.

27. k-26, 86.

28. Colitt, *Spy Master*, p. 97.

29. Brandt, *People and Politics*, pp. 47–8.

30. Operations against major foreign statesmen normally required the approval of the political leadership.

31. k-26, 88.

32. Mitrokhin's notes on Brandt's file go only to 1962. They do, however, include later references to Brandt from other files.

33. Brandt, *People and Politics*, pp. 102–3. Abrasimov, later accused of behaving like a Soviet pro-consul, was ambassador in East Berlin.

34. Wolf, *Man without a Face*, ch. 9; Colitt, *Spy Master*, ch. 4; Murphy, Kondrashev and Bailey, *Battleground Berlin*, p. 300.

35. Probably the best study of *Ostpolitik* is Garton Ash, *In Europe's Name*.

36. Wolf, *Man without a Face*, p. 156.

37. k-19, 248, 250.

38. Prittie, *Velvet Chancellors*, pp. 170–1.

39. Marshall, *Willy Brandt*, pp. 86–7.

40. k-2, 52.

41. Wolf, *Spionagechef im geheimen Krieg*, p. 261.

42. Marshall, *Willy Brandt*, pp. 88–90.

43. k-2, 52.

44. "Bank pay-in Slip Published in Bonn Bribes Scandal," *The Times* (June 20, 1973). "Steiner Tells of Work as an Agent," *Daily Telegraph* (August 8, 1973).

45. Wolf concludes that "it is impossible to establish whether [Steiner] was paid twice over for his services"—by Wienand as well as the HVA directly. Wolf, *Spionagechef im geheimen Krieg*, p. 261.

46. "Bonn Bribery Allegations 'Not Proven,' " *The Times* (March 28, 1974).

47. Genscher, *Erinnerungen*, pp. 197–201.

48. Wolf, *Man without a Face*, pp. 157–65. Wolf identifies a number of boastful inaccuracies in Guillaume's own account of his career.

49. Genscher, *Erinnerungen*, pp. 201–2.

50. Wolf, *Man without a Face*, pp. xi, 171–2.

51. Wolf, *Man without a Face*, p. 124.

52. Andrew and Gordievsky, *KGB*, pp. 238–40, 442–4, 456–7, 611.

53. The identity of Wolf's first "Romeo spy," codenamed FELIX, who began operations in the early 1950s, remains unknown. Wolf, *Man without a Face*, p. 124.

54. k-5, 30, 31.

55. k-5, 31.

56. Barron, *KGB*, pp. 198–9.

57. k-16, 139. The alias "Franz Becker" is not recorded by Mitrokhin, but was later revealed at Höke's trial.

58. k-10, 56; k-16, 139.

59. k-10, 56; k-16, 139.

60. k-16, 65.

61. k-16, 139; k-5, 19.

62. k-16, 65.

63. k-16, 139; k-5, 19.

64. k-10, 56; k-16, 139.

65. RENATA was married to RYBACHEK, a Czech illegal based in Switzerland, who was also working for the KGB. k-16, 94, 139; k-12, 5; k-8, 25-6; k-2, 46, 84.

66. "Russia May Have Learned War Secrets," *Observer* (September 1, 1985); "Bonn Spy Knew Army Secrets," *Observer* (September 8, 1985); "Glamour Spy's Love Ends in treachery," *Observer* (December 14, 1986); "Spionage: Wie ein Helmspiel," *Der Spiegel* (December 29, 1986); "KGB Lover Led Shy Secretary into Treason," *Daily Telegraph* (September 1, 1987).

67. Mitrokhin's notes on ROSIE do not give her real name. Press reports after her arrest in December 1976 identify her as Heidrun Hofer.

68. k-8, 7, 177; k-18, 385. According to k-8, 177, ROSIE was recruited in October 1971; according to k-16, 108, she was recruited in 1973. The two dates probably refer, respectively, to the point at which she began to supply information to ROLAND, and to her meeting with VLADIMIR in February 1973, after which the importance of her role as an agent appears to have increased.

69. k-16, 61. From 1970 to 1982 VLADIMIR was an illegal trainer based in Karlshorst, who performed various assignments in the GDR, FRG and Austria. His wife, Irina Yevseyevna (BERTA), was also an illegal.

70. "Bettgeflüster Nach Dienstschluss," *Quick* (January 13, 1977).

71. k-5, 20.

72. "Bettgeflüster Nach Dienstschluss," *Quick* (January 13, 1977). "Hat Spionin Hofer den BND auf Jahre gelähmt?," *Die Welt* (January 14, 1977).

73. k-16, 70; k-18, 5, 145. Details of the lonely hearts column and the alias used by GEORG (though not his real identity) were revealed at Falk's trial in 1989. Childs and Popplewell, *The Stasi*, p. 160.

74. Childs and Popplewell, *The Stasi*, p. 160.

75. k-16, 70; k-2, 374.

76. k-19, 357. Childs and Popplewell, *The Stasi*, p. 160.

77. k-18, 145.

78. Childs and Popplewell, *The Stasi*, pp. 160–1.

79. vol. 6, app. 1, part 5; k-14, 747, 748; k-11, 91; k-12, 435.

80. k-14, 747.

81. k-11, 91.

82. t-1, 45, 135; k-5, 193; k-24, 236; vol. 6, app. 2, part 3.

83. k-14, 237; k-8, 72.

84. Wolf, *Man without a Face*, pp. 142–8; Colitt, *Spy Master*, pp. 128–34. Gast was arrested on September 29, 1990, four days before the reunification of Germany, betrayed by a former senior official of the now defunct HVA.

85. Wolf, *Man without a Face*, pp. 188–94; Colitt, *Spy Master*, pp. 197–205, 235–7. In February 1992 Kuron was sentenced to twelve years' imprisonment and fined 692,000 marks—his total earnings from the HVA.

86. Wolf, *Man without a Face*, pp. 198–201; Colitt, *Spy Master*, pp. 203–4. Wolf ludicrously maintains that the prostitutes he employed to provide sexual services for Tiedge and other defectors "were not prostitutes but down-to-earth women, Party members and loyal to their country, who were prepared to do this in return for . . . a preferential flat or an advance up the waiting list for a car."

87. "Wienand zu zweieinhalb Jahren Freiheitsstrafe verurteilt," *Frankfurter Allgemeine Zeitung* (June 27, 1996); "Politik: Wegen langjähriger Spionage für die DDR: Karl Wienand zu zweieinhalb Jahren Haft verurteilt," *Süddeutsche Zeitung* (June 27, 1996); Imre Karacs, "Cold War Agent Jailed," *Independent* (June 27, 1996).

88. Genscher, *Erinnerungen*, p. 188.

89. Wolf, *Spionagechef im geheimen Krieg*, pp. 186–8. After a conversation with the former Soviet ambassador in Bonn, Valentin Falin, in 1992, Brandt wrote, "Since 1975, Karl W[ienand] committed himself to working for the services over there." Falin later denied having made a specific reference to Wienand. Roger Boyes, "Brandt Papers Revive Spy Claims," *The Times* (February 11, 1995). The files seen by Mitrokhin contain no reference to a KGB attempt to recruit Wienand.

90. *Observer* reported from Bonn on July 3, 1994 that Wehner was "now widely suspected of having been a Stasi spy."

91. k-3, 63.

92. Colitt, *Spy Master*, p. 250.

93. k-3, 63.

94. k-3, 63.

95. Wolf, *Man without a Face*, p. 169. Wolf's claims are not confirmed (or denied) by Mitrokhin. Mitrokhin's detailed notes on Wehner's file stop in 1941.

96. Wolf, *Spionagechef im geheimen Krieg*, pp. 185, 210–11. Most of the section of Wolf's memoirs on Wehner, like much else dealing with German politics, is omitted from the English translation.

97. Garton Ash, *In Europe's Name*, pp. 199, 321–2, 533–4.

98. Wolf, *Spionagechef im geheimen Krieg*, pp. 207, 209.

99. k-2, 53. Wolf then took his revenge on Van Nouhuys by leaking the story to *Quick*'s rival *Stern*, which published it on October 25, 1973. A long court battle followed, eventually decided in favor of *Stern*. Wolf, *Man without a Face*, pp. 237–8.

100. In 1994 Brandt's widow caused a political storm by referring publicly to his suspicions of Wehner.

101. Wolf, *Spionagechef im geheimen Krieg*, p. 218.

102. k-12, 505–6.

103. k-2, 162.

104. k-2, 165.

105. k-2, 179; k-10, 135–6.

106. k-5, 787.

107. Brezhnev's visit, however, led to enormous expenditure of KGB time and effort. Security procedures were overseen by a committee including the heads of no less than seven KGB directorates (Kryuchkov among them). Twenty-nine KGB and GRU operational groups were assigned to supervise Brezhnev's security during the visit. k-5, 788–9.

108. k-8, 104. Soviet–FRG negotiations on the natural gas pipeline from Siberia were successfully concluded in November 1981. According to Sir Percy Cradock, later Mrs. Thatcher's foreign policy adviser, the Reagan administration "found in the Polish crisis [of December 1981] a convenient pretext for sabotaging an agreement they did not like. Their action was at first confined to US companies, but in June 1982 it was extended, with little thought for the consequences, to US subsidiaries and foreign companies as well." After vigorous protests by Mrs. Thatcher as well as by Schmidt, the United States backed down in November 1982 in return for NATO acceptance of greater restrictions on trade with the Soviet Union. Cradock, *In Pursuit of British Interests*, p. 56.

109. k-8, 104.

110. Mitrokhin did not have access to the SCD files which reveal the agent's name.

111. k-13, 44. Mitrokhin's notes do not record any response by the Schmidt government.

112. k-19, 282. The active measures against Strauss give the lie to Wolf's suggestions since the publication of his memoirs that Strauss was an HVA informant.

113. k-5, 718, k-19, 282. Inge Goliath had been withdrawn to the GDR in 1979. Mitrokhin's notes summarize, but give few details about, a series of other KGB active measures designed to compromise the BND and BfV: operation JUNGLE, conducted jointly with the HVA from 1978 onwards to discredit the BND and disrupt its relations with other Western intelligence services (k-13, 61, 82, 102–3); operations ZHAK-RUZH, ROZA, BURGUNDER, OSMAN and PANTER (1978), designed, again in co-operation with the HVA, "to expose and impede the activity of the FRG special services in Europe and in the Near East" (k-13, 61); operation ONTARIO (1978), "to cause disagreements between the CIA, the SDECE and the BND" (k-13, 79); operation JAMES (1980), "to exacerbate disagreements between the BND and the CIA" (k-13, 102); operation KLOP (1981), to discredit the BfV (k-13, 85); operation ORKESTR (1981), to discredit West German journalists who were alleged to be BND officers or co-optees (k-13, 86); and operation DROTIK (1981), to compromise Western businesses allegedly used by the CIA and the BND as cover and for other operational purposes (k-13, 87).

114. k-5, 718, k-19, 282.

115. k-6, 102; k-19, 32.

116. Garton Ash, *In Europe's Name*, p. 320.

117. Wolf, *Man without a Face*, p. 222.

118. Andrew and Gordievsky (eds.), *More Instructions from the Centre*, pp. 38–9.

119. Hanson, *Soviet Industrial Espionage;* US Government, *Soviet Acquisition of Militarily Significant Western Technology;* Brook-Shepherd, *The Storm Birds*, p. 260.

120. RICHARD was first deployed in the FRG in 1964; k-16, 110, 129.

121. k-18, 441.

122. k-10, 39.

123. t-2, 34.

124. vol. 6, ch. 6.

125. Even when restrictions on the export of Western computers were relaxed during the Gorbachev era, fears that they were bugged or deliberately infected with viruses continued. Nikolai Brusnitsin, deputy chairman of the State Technical Commission, complained in 1990 that the software in a West German computer sold to a Soviet shoe-making factory had been deliberately pre-programmed to self-destruct. There had, he claimed, been a whole series of such incidents. Brusnitsin, *Openness and Espionage*, pp. 28–9.

126. Line X agents identified in the files seen by Mitrokhin include (in alphabetical order) BORIS, the manager of an electronics factory (k-18, 230); DAL, a laser technology and plasma specialist (k-10, 38); DYMOV, a computer programmer at a research center in West Berlin (k-12, 442); EBER, an employee of a major company (k-14, 570); EGON, an East German illegal working as an engineer (k-16, 112, 296); EMIL, an employee of Messerschmitt–Bölkow–Blohm (k-10, 37); ERICH, a chemical engineer (k-5, 232); FOTOGRAF, a scientist employed by the International Atomic Energy Agency (t-2, 54); FRIMAN, a rocket technology specialist (K-10, 32, 47); GUTSUL, the owner of a dye company (k-18, 318); HANS, an agent with access to two large engineering firms (k-14, 698); KARL, an expert in electro-magnetism

who for part of his career worked as an agent of the Paris residency against French targets; KERNER, a polymer chemist (k-10, 48; k-12, 414; k-16, 120-1); KEST, head of a research group at a medical institute (k-5, 341); KLEIN, a nuclear physicist (k-14, 429); LEONID, a computer scientist in a multinational chemical company (k-18, 277; k-27, 323); LETON, a trade official specializing in radio electronics (k-12, 129); LOTTS, who held a senior position in an aerospace research institute (k-10, 41, 44); MORZH, a Yugoslav who supplied embargoed chemical products (k-5, 9); MOST, founder of an electronics company (k-12, 87); PAUL, owner of an electronics company (t-2, 18); RASPORYATIDEL ("Organizer"), a company director who supplied equipment for assembling integrated circuits (k-14, 570); ROBERT, a rocket engineer (k-10, 35); SHMEL, head of a computer company (k-18, 283); TAL, a designer of chemical factories and polymer plants (t-2, 1); TART, who worked for the giant chemical company Bayer (k-14, 670); TSANDER, a polymer chemist (k-10, 48; k-12, 414; k-16, 120–1); VILON, a company director who supplied embargoed goods (k-5, 10); VIN, director of an electronics company (k-5, 216); YUNG, an aircraft computer systems engineer (k-2, 70, 120); WAGNER, an employee of a major petrochemical company (k-10, 33, 46).

127. *Die Welt* (July 17, 1986).

128. "Ex-KGB Agent to Return to West," *Guardian* (November 26, 1987).

129. k-10, 37.

130. "East Seen Escalating Drive for West's Industrial Secrets," *Washington Post* (October 24, 1986).

131. k-10, 37.

132. "Ex-KGB Agent to Return to West," *Guardian* (November 26, 1987). "Red Spy Returns for His Pension," *Today* (November 26, 1987).

133. Wolf, *Man without a Face*, ch. 1.

Chapter Twenty-seven   France and Italy During the Cold War

1. k-4, 91-9, 101. The 1953 list of "valuable agents" in Paris also includes the codename MES, but gives no indication of his or her occupation. The only codenames which can be identified on the basis of information in Mitrokhin's notes are PIZHO (Georges Pâques) and LONG (Paddy Costello). It is quite possible, however, that the other "valuable agents" include some of those recruited under other codenames during the few years after the Liberation. Pâques's most important period as a Soviet agent almost certainly came while he was working at the French general staff from 1958 to 1962.

2. vol. 9, ch. 1.

3. See above, chapter 9.

4. "Security Aspects of Possible Staff Talks with France." (February 24, 1948), JIC(48)5, CAB158/3, PRO. We are indebted for this reference to Alex Craig of Christ's College, Cambridge.

5. During the 1960s the FRG, as a result of penetration by both the HVA and KGB, became an even more important source of intelligence than France. See chapter 26.

6. "Miscellaneous Soviet Personalities Who Have Served Abroad," (September 29, 1954), CRS A6283/XR1/144, Australian Archives, Canberra.

7. vol. 9, ch. 1. For other examples of classified French documents on Berlin and the German question obtained by the Paris residency, see Murphy, Kondrashev and Bailey, *Battleground Berlin*, pp. 68–9, 75–7, 82–4, 95, 145. Though the authors were given access to some reports from the Paris residency, they were not allowed to see the files on agent penetration in France noted by Mitrokhin.

8. On JOUR, chapters 9 and 27.

9. Though given to no access to KGB files on JOUR, Fursenko and Naftali confirm KGB access during the Cuban Missile Crisis to diplomatic traffic between the Quai d'Orsay and French embassies in Moscow and Washington; "Soviet Intelligence and the Cuban Missile Crisis," pp. 70–1.

10. Wolton, *Le KGB en France*, pp. 204–6; Andrew and Gordievsky, *KGB*, p. 466.

11. vol. 9, ch. 6.

12. Wolton, *La France sous influence*, p. 70.

13. vol. 9, ch. 6, para. 47.

14. vol. 9, ch. 6, para. 43. Some doubt remains as to whether the FCD officer who calculated this total took fully into account the transition from "old" to "new" francs.

15. Wolton, *La France sous influence*, p. 70.

16. vol. 9, ch. 1.

17. k-4, 2-4. Mitrokhin's notes give no details of the intelligence supplied by GERMAIN, but the award of the Order of the Red Star is a reliable indication of its importance.

18. k-7, 178. After her false flag recruitment, ROZA was controlled by a female agent, JEANNETTE,

who doubtless posed as a member of the fictitious "progressive" group.

19. LARIONOV joined the foreign ministry from the army in 1960; k-4, 112.

20. k-4, 18.

21. FRENE became a *commissaire de police* in Paris in 1960; k-4, 114.

22. DACHNIK was recruited during a visit to the USSR in August 1962 by the Fourteenth Department of the FCD "for material reward"; k-14, 1.

23. ADAM was a chemist at the CNRS (Centre National de Recherches Scientifiques) recruited in 1959; k-4, 25.

24. SASHA was recruited in or before 1960. In that year he went to study electronics in Washington; k-4, 113.

25. k-4, 18.

26. Barron, *KGB*, pp. 169–82. Interview by Christopher Andrew with Yuri Nosenko (November 15, 1987); Wolton, *La France sous influence*, pp. 374–9. Because these were SCD operations, they do not appear in the FCD files seen by Mitrokhin.

27. k-4, 131. The LOUISA case, unlike those of Dejean and Guibaud, figured in the FCD files seen by Mitrokhin because of the unsuccessful attempt by the Paris residency to renew contact with her.

28. NN's name is not recorded in Mitrokhin's notes but can be identified from the biographical detail contained in them as Saar-Demichel; vol. 9, ch. 6, para. 5. Saar-Demichel later admitted his links with the KGB; Wolton, *La France sous influence*, p. 247. According to Wolton, his original KGB codename was ALEKSEI.

29. Wolton, *La France sous influence*, pp. 247–50.

30. Wolton, *La France sous influence*, pp. 374, 379, 411–12, 416–17, 426*n.*, 437.

31. vol. 9, ch. 6, para. 5.

32. vol. 9, ch. 4, para. 8.

33. vol. 9, ch. 6, paras. 43–5.

34. Mitrokhin's notes contain no reference to the radical (later socialist) politician Charles Hernu, who was to become defense minister from 1981 to 1985. It has been alleged that Hernu was recruited by the Bulgarian DS in 1953, later had contact with the Romanian Securitate and became a KGB agent in 1963. Dupuis and Pontaut, "Charles Hernu était un agent de l'Est."

35. k-6, 80, 128; t-1, 61. For legal reasons GILBERT's identity, though recorded in Mitrokhin's notes on KGB files, cannot be published. There is some indication that at one point GILBERT avoided contact with his case officer.

36. For legal reasons DROM's identity, though recorded in Mitrokhin's notes on KGB files, cannot be published. His file fills seven volumes. DROM's controllers were, successively, Spartak Ivanovich Leshchev (codenamed LARIN) from 1960 to 1964; Vladimir Filippovich Yashchechkin (YASNOV) from 1964 to 1967; Yuri Konstantinovich Semyonychev (TANEYEV) from 1967 to 1972; and Anatoli Nikolayevich Tsipalkin (VESNOV) in 1972–3. vol. 9, ch. 6, paras. 30–1; t-1, 58, 68; k-4, 27, 58.

37. vol. 9, ch. 6, para. 33.

38. vol. 9, chs. 2, 4

39. vol. 9, ch. 6, para. 5.

40. Myagkov, *Inside the KGB*, p. 24.

41. In the course of 1965 Saar-Demichel seems to have lost his influence at the Élysée. De Gaulle is reported to have said to a member of his entourage, "Saar-Demichel is a Soviet spy. He doesn't, of course, steal secrets to hand over to them, but he tells them everything he knows." Wolton, *La France sous influence*, pp. 382, 424–6.

42. Wolton, *La France sous influence*, p. 426.

43. vol. 9, ch. 6, paras. 33, 40.

44. vol. 9, ch. 2, para. 11.

45. During the period 1963–6 three unidentified French intelligence officers were members of the GRANIT group, and one of the BULAT group. BON, a former head of department at the Sûreté Générale, worked as an agent recruiter; k-27, 242. The latest reference in Mitrokhin's notes to penetration of SDECE is to the presence there of a KGB agent (not identified) in May 1969; k-4, 81.

46. k-4, 33, 34, 38.

47. vol. 9, ch. 6, para. 30.

48. vol. 9, ch. 6, para. 10. Mitrokhin's notes give few details of the regular (non-bonus) payments to these agents.

49. Mitrokhin's notes on his file do not specify what proportion of the large sums paid to him were in the

form of a regular salary or retainer, but they do make clear that he received very substantial bonuses for particularly important items of S&T (k-5, 460).

50. t-1, 47; k-4, 34.

51. k-4, 35, 65; k-14, 93; vol. 6, app. 1, part 33; t-1, 264-5.

52. k-5, 281; k-11, 87; t-1, 266.

53. t-1, 42.

54. Wolton, *Le KGB en France*, pp. 242-3; Favier and Martin-Roland, *La décennie Mitterrand*, vol. 1, pp. 271-2.

55. Kahn, "Soviet Comint in the Cold War," p. 20.

56. k-4, 176.

57. The six cipher personnel under cultivation were codenamed ALMAZOV, GROMOV, GUDKOV, KRASNOV, LAPIN and VESELOV. Mitrokhin gives details of only two. The cultivation of LAPIN began in 1980 and plans were made for it to continue after he was posted abroad in 1982. With the assistance of JOUR, an investigation was undertaken of KRASNOV's finances, home and leisure pursuits, and he was secretly photographed. At the end of 1981 an (unidentified) illegal began to cultivate him under false flag. Mitrokhin's notes do not record which, if any, of the cultivations ended in recruitment; k-4, 177.

58. t-1, 46; k-7, 145.

59. k-3, 81; t-1, 32.

60. t-1, 34; vol. 9, ch. 6, para. 7.

61. vol. 9, ch. 6, paras. 41-53; k-6, 3-5; t-1, 57.

62. vol. 9, ch. 6, para. 16; k-25, 120.

63. t-1, 27; vol. 3, pakapp. 1, 21.

64. t-1, 43; k-4, 180.

65. t-1, 44; k-14, 100.

66. t-1, 36; k-27, 292.

67. t-1, 46.

68. k-7, 145.

69. vol. 9, ch. 2, para. 17.

70. vol. 9, ch. 6, para. 7.

71. k-7, 145.

72. vol. 9, ch. 6, para. 7. Giscard d'Estaing's codename is given in k-3, 81.

73. For the two years 1976-7, BROK was paid a total of 217,000 francs: 72,000 francs basic salary, 83,000 bonuses, 62,000 expenses. From January to November 1978, the last period for which details of payments to BROK are available, he received a total of 182,000 francs: 55,000 francs salary, 83,000 bonuses, 62,000 expenses. k-3, 81.

74. Mitrokhin does not identify BROK's case officer(s) for the period 1946-51. Thereafter, his controllers were Ye. R. Radtsig (1951-7); V. K. Radchenko (1957-9); E. N. Yakovlev (1959-63); I. F. Gremyakin (1970-2); L. I. Vasenko (1972); R. F. Zhuravlev (1972-6); R. N. Lebedinsky (1974-5); Ye. L. Mokeyev (1976-8); and Ye. N. Malkov (1978-9). k-3, 81.

75. M. S. Tsimbal, A. I. Lazarev, A. V. Krasavin, V. P. Vlasov and N. N. Chetverikov; k-3, 81.

76. k-3, 81.

77. See above, chapter 12.

78. vol. 9, ch. 3, paras. 5, 6; t-7, 219.

79. vol. 9, ch. 6, paras. 15, 24.

80. Raymond Aron, "Il n'y a pas de quoi rire," *Le Figaro* (June 23, 1975). Aron, *Mémoires*, pp. 599-60. Other prominent critics of *Le Monde* included Pierre Nora and Jean-François Revel.

81. *Le Monde* (July 3, 1975).

82. *Le Monde* (September 12, 1975). This claim was subsequently withdrawn, but *Le Monde*'s critics complained that it continued, in its reporting on Solzhenitsyn, to "*prodiguer impunément quelques insultes sous le couvert de l'objectivité*." Legris, *Le Monde tel qu'il est*, p. 32.

83. A major operational plan for 1975, jointly signed by the heads of the First Chief, Second Chief and Fifth Directorates, aimed "to discredit PAUK [Solzhenitsyn] . . . through mass information media abroad." k-3b, 27.

84. Legris, *Le Monde tel qu'il est*.

85. Jacques Thibau's analysis of *Le Monde* in the 1970s concludes: " . . . *il repose à la fois sur ce que ses adver-*

saires 'de gauche' appellent l'ordre, et ses critiques 'de droite' la subversion. L'équilibre est difficile à tenir. Il requiert de la prudence et de la pratique de la casuistique, mais globalement il correspond à la fonction du journal." Thibau, *Le Monde, 1944–1996*, p. 433.

86. However, at least one regular Paris-based contributor to *Le Monde* in the 1970s, KRON, is identified as a KGB agent (k-24, 153). Mitrokhin's notes also identify MONGO, one of *Le Monde*'s African correspondents, as a KGB agent, but do not give his identity or the dates when he was posted in Africa (k-6, 116).

87. t-1, 46, 58; vol. 9, ch. 6, paras. 15, 24. Most of Mitrokhin's notes on influence operations directed against *Le Monde* are both brief and general. He identifies only two active measures articles by both author and exact date of publication. One is described as "entirely written on KGB themes" by a leading *Le Monde* journalist; the other was an article "using KGB arguments" by a leading socialist politician. Both were published in 1980. vol. 1, ch. 8; vol. 9, ch. 6, paras. 15, 24; k-8, 522; k-24, 153.

88. vol. 9, ch. 2, para. 23.

89. The same disproportion in the treatment of KGB and CIA active measures is evident, on a somewhat smaller scale, in the generally valuable history of *Le Monde* by Jacques Thibau. Thibau concludes, for example, that one notorious forgery published by *Le Monde*, the so-called "Fechteler report," which purported to reveal outrageously belligerent US designs in the Mediterranean, was almost certainly fabricated by the CIA and French intelligence. He does not consider the far more probable hypothesis that it was a KGB forgery (Thibau, *Le Monde, 1944–1996*, pp. 214–18). For an assessment of the revelations in the mid-1970s of malpractice by the US intelligence community, see Andrew, *For the President's Eyes Only*, ch. 10.

90. SIDOR was recruited in 1956 but later suspected of working for the DST (k-14, 3). JACQUES, an AFP correspondent in a number of Asian countries, was a KGB agent from 1964 to 1973; during that period he had seven different controllers (k-6, 53). MISHA was recruited during a visit to the Soviet Union in 1965; Mitrokhin's notes do not reveal how long his work as an agent continued (vol. 2, app. 1, para. 46; vol. 2, appendix 2, para. 68). LAN was an agent from 1969 to 1979, mostly—if not exclusively— in France (k-4, 85; k-27, 291). MARAT was an agent in Paris and abroad from *c.* 1973 to 1982 (k-6, 42). GRININ was recruited in 1980 (k-14, 379).

91. PIERRE, a confidential contact in the 1960s (k-14, 111, 134), and JOSEPH, a confidential contact from 1974 to 1977 (k-6, 84).

92. k-27, 291.

93. vol. 9, ch. 6, para. 33.

94. Shultz and Godson, *Dezinformatsia*, p. 134.

95. vol. 9, ch. 6, para. 40.

96. Shultz and Godson, *Dezinformatsia*, pp. 135–49.

97. k-5, 560.

98. vol. 9, ch. 6, paras. 37, 39–40. Sakharovsky was referred to at Pathé's trial by his alias, "Kuznetsov." The Paris residency believed that the DST had not succeeded in identifying him as the son of the former head of the FCD; k-5, 560.

99. Like DURANT, NANT, VERONIQUE, JACQUELINE and NANCY are identified in Mitrokhin's notes, but cannot be named for legal reasons; vol. 9, ch. 6, paras. 43–9; k-6, 3.

100. vol. 9, ch. 6, para. 11.

101. vol. 9, ch. 4, para. 33.

102. vol. 9, ch. 6, para. 28; vol. 9, ch. 2, paras. 25–30; vol. 9, ch. 6, paras. 13–15.

103. *L'élection présidentielle, 26 avril–10 mai 1981*, p. 34. Kahn, "Soviet Comint in the Cold War," p. 18.

104. vol. 9, ch. 3, para. 20. The "affair of the diamonds" had begun with the publication by one satirical weekly *Le Canard Enchaîné* on October 10, 1979 of an order placed by Bokassa six years earlier for the purchase of a diamond plaquette for Giscard d'Estaing. The Élysée tried to fend off this and similar stories over the next year and a half until it finally announced on March 23, 1981, just over a month before the first round of the presidential election, that diamonds given to Giscard in 1973, 1974 and 1975 had been valued at 115,000 francs and that this sum had been donated to the Red Cross and other good causes in the Central African Republic.

105. vol. 9, ch. 2, para. 31.

106. *Le Monde* reported during the campaign, *"C'est incontestablement le parti socialiste qui a la meilleure image de marque dans l'électorat juif."* *L'élection présidentielle, 26 avril–10 mai 1981*, p. 73.

107. vol. 9, ch. 2, para. 31.

108. Mitrokhin's notes give no details of the inside information provided by GILES; k-6, 128.

109. vol. 9, ch. 6, para. 3.

110. k-3, 81. BROK was not the only French journalist on whom the KGB radically revised its views. In 1979 the Centre concluded that LAN was providing "material not qualitatively different from material published in the press," and broke off contact with him. k-27, 291.

111. vol. 9, ch. 6, para. 3.

112. The statistics for Line X operations in European residencies in 1975 were as follows (figures for Line X officers certainly refer to 1975; those for agents are for approximately—probably exactly—1975):

Residency	Line X Officers [k-5, 420]	Line X Agents [k-5, 423]
Belgrade	3	?
Berne	3	?
Bonn	15	9
Brussels	7	4
Copenhagen	6	7
Geneva	3	2
The Hague	3	1
Helsinki	6	2
Lisbon	2	?
London	9	9
Oslo	3	0
Paris	22	22
Rome	9	10
Stockholm	7	1
Vienna	19	29

These statistics were compiled by the Second Department of FCD Directorate T, which was responsible for Line X operations in the residencies listed above. The figures for the Bonn residency account for only a part of Line X operations in the FRG; Line X operations were also run from Cologne. Line X in Karlshorst, which came under a different department of Directorate T, had fifty-nine agents in 1975 (k-5, 416). A probable majority of Line X operations in Vienna (which Mitrokhin's notes do not make it possible to quantify) were directed at non-Austrian targets.

113. k-5, 383, 386, 406. Though Mitrokhin's notes give no later statistics, it is possible that the 1977 record was subsequently surpassed.

114. Mitrokhin's notes give the following incomplete statistics of Line X officers stationed in European residencies for all or part of the period 1974–9:

Belgrade	4
Berne	6
Bonn	9
Brussels	10
Cologne	13
Copenhagen	13
Geneva	7
The Hague	6
Helsinki	10
Lisbon	?
London	?
Oslo	?
Paris	36
Rome	17
Stockholm	19
Vienna	38

(k-5, 459)

115. Line X in Paris also succeeded in penetrating an unquantifiable number of US companies and subsidiaries in France.

116. k-5, 460.

117. Though Mitrokhin's note merely records that Andropov recommended the award of the Order of the Red Star, it is barely conceivable that the recommendation was turned down. Kesarev's assistant, Yuri Ignatyevich Rakovsky, was recommended for accelerated promotion. k-5, 470.

118. Mitrokhin noted the following payments to ALAN which were recorded in his file: 409,000 francs for the period 1973 to 1976 (probably his basic salary with additional sums for particular items); 100,000 francs (undated) for information on the design of infra-red detectors; 40,000 francs (also undated) for samples of the detectors; 50,000 francs in September 1973 for two samples of missile-guidance systems; payments of 71,000 and 100,000 francs in 1974 for technical documentation; 40,000 francs in 1974 or 1975 for unidentified technical samples; 89,400 francs (purpose unspecified) in 1975; 110,000 francs in 1977 for documentation on missile guidance; 60,000 francs and approximately 200,000 francs (30,000 convertible roubles) in December 1977 (purpose unspecified); and 200,000 francs (purpose unspecified) in mid-1978. On the assumptions that these were all separate sums and that there were no other payments unrecorded by Mitrokhin, this would make a grand total of 1,429,400 francs. k-5, 460.

119. k-5, 460.

120. Favier and Martin-Roland, *La décennie Mitterrand*, vol. 1, p. 97.

121. Bourdiol was arrested in 1983 and later sentenced to five years' imprisonment, as a result of intelligence provided by the French agent FAREWELL. Wolton, *Le KGB en France*, p. 245; "Ariane: un ingénieur français incarcéré pour l'espionage," *Libération*, (December 2, 1983); *Early Warning* (March 2, 1984); Reuter reports (June 16, 1987). There is no identifiable reference to Bourdiol in Mitrokhin's notes.

122. Mitrokhin's incomplete notes on payments to KARL record that from January to November 1979 he was paid a monthly salary of 13,200 francs and an additional sum of 32,000 francs; and that from January to October he was paid 12,000 francs a month plus a single payment of 34,000 francs. KARL worked as a KGB agent from 1972 to 1982. k-5, 367–9.

123. k-5, 367.

124. On the FAREWELL case, see Wolton, *Le KGB en France*, part 5, and Brook-Shepherd, *The Storm Birds*, ch. 17. FAREWELL was first identified as Vetrov in Andrew and Gordievsky, *Le KGB dans le monde*, pp. 619–23.

125. Raymond Nart, head of the DST Soviet section, writing under the pseudonym Henri Regnard, gave the first public account of what had been learned from the FAREWELL operation in December 1983 in an article published in the journal *Défense Nationale*.

126. President Mitterrand, whose mind turned naturally to conspiracy, subsequently began to suspect bizarrely that the FAREWELL information might somehow have been planted on the DST by the CIA "as a way of testing socialist France and me personally," in order to see whether he would hold it back or pass it on to the Reagan administration. Favier and Martin-Roland, *La décennie Mitterrand*, vol. 1, pp. 94–8, 271–3.

127. Mitrokhin's notes contain the following comparative figures for the numbers of agents run by KGB residencies controlled by the FCD Fifth Department:

	1966	1971	1974
France	66	48	55 (+17 confidential contacts)
Italy	18	21	24 (+4 confidential contacts)
Belgium	24	19	19 (+7 confidential contacts)
Greece	18	6	18 (+3 confidential contacts)
Netherlands	2	2	?
Switzerland	2	8	8 (+2 confidential contacts)
Cyprus	2	5	?
Luxemburg	1	0	?
Yugoslavia	0	0	?

(k-8, 472; k-4, 33)

On January 1, 1975 the Rome residency had 23 agents (18 of them active) and 6 confidential contacts, as well as 4 agents in the Soviet community. A year later it had 21 non-Soviet agents (16 active), 7 confidential contacts and 9 Soviet agents (k-13, 135).

128. See above, chapter 17.

129. See above, chapter 17.

130. Mitrokhin's notes do not include any examples of the intelligence obtained by DARIO and his female recruits from the Foreign Ministry.

131. k-10, 101-3, 107, 109. Mitrokhin's notes imply in 1956 that DARIO was also instrumental in the recruitment of MAGDA, an employee of the foreign ministry press department; k-10,100,103. Mitrokhin's notes also record the recruitment in 1970 of an agent in the Foreign Ministry, codenamed STRELOK, by Georgi Pavlovich Antonov. STRELOK subsequently became "reluctant to co-operate" (k-4, 80, 158; k-2, 221, 231, 268).

132. k-16, 285. Mitrokhin notes that by 1965 LEDA "had lost her intelligence access."

133. k-10, 97, 109.

134. k-10, 109.

135. See above, chapter 17.

136. k-10, 63. Mitrokhin's notes do not give the date at which the various ciphers and surveillance lists were handed over by QUESTOR. In view of the Centre's dissatisfaction with the declining amount of intelligence obtained from QUESTOR by YEFRAT in the later 1950s, however, the bulk of the material was probably handed over in the mid-1950s.

137. Mitrokhin interpreted YEFRAT's file as placing the responsibility for the bankruptcy of the Italian firm on his mismanagement (k-7, 4, 193; k-16, 338, 419; k-18, 153; k-20, 94). In addition to being assisted by his wife TANYA, YEFRAT was given as deputy resident the illegal Aleksandr Vasilyevich Subotin (codenamed PIK), who had gained an Italian passport in the name of Adolfo Tolmer (k-16, 98, 285).

138. YEFRAT also cultivated CENSOR's wife, KAPA; Mitrokhin's notes do not record the outcome of the cultivation (k-16, 419; k-18, 153).

139. YEFRAT later took part in PROGRESS operations. In 1962 DEMID recruited his brother TIBER, who worked in the accounts department of the interior ministry, to act as radio operator for SAUL, a Lithuanian Catholic priest and KGB agent then studying at the Vatican. DEMID, CENSOR and QUESTOR continued to provide intelligence until at least 1963 (k-16, 419; k-10, 63; k-5, 688–91). After YEFRAT's departure, his former deputy, PIK, worked for the legal Rome residency until 1965, acting as LEDA's controller from February 1962 to September 1963 (k-16, 285).

140. k-2, 66. Mitrokhin's notes give no indication of whether IKAR continued to work as a KGB agent after his return to Italy.

141. k-5, 102.

142. k-9, 23; k-10, 126.

143. k-12, 516. IKAR, PLATON, ENERO and ARTUR were not the only SCD recruits in the Italian embassy in Moscow. Mitrokhin's notes also refer to the case of POLATOV (or POLETOV), an assistant service attaché, recruited by the SCD in the late 1970s, but give no details (k-10, 124). There may have been further embassy agents not mentioned in Mitrokhin's notes.

Other Italians recruited by the SCD in Moscow included an official in the legal department of the Italian interior ministry, recruited with the assistance of VERA, a swallow from the Polish SB (k-2, 273); and RITA, a female employee of the Fiat company recruited in 1976 (k-10, 132).

144. k-27, 240.

145. k-22, 72; k-26, 66; t-2, 158.

146. k-5, 256.

147. Cf. Andrew and Gordievsky, *KGB*, p. 459.

148. k-14, 262, 383. BUTIL broke contact in 1979 after his firm had failed to win Soviet contracts.

149. k-5, 420, 423.

150. The Italian businessmen identified in Mitrokhin's notes as Line X agents in the 1970s and/or early 1980s were CHIZ (k-14, 567), ERVIN (k-7, 37), KOZAK (k-14, 174), METIL (k-14, 383), PAN (k-12, 593) and TELINI (k-12, 389). It is unclear whether SAUST, a business consultant cultivated by the KGB, was actually recruited (k-14, 568).

151. Mitrokhin's notes identify a total of seventeen Line X officers stationed at the Rome residency for all or part of the period 1974–9 (k-5, 459).

152. k-5, 353, 425. The Soviet ambassador in Rome, N. S. Rhyzov, had opposed the establishment of a Soviet consulate in Milan in order to provide cover for a KGB residency in northern Italy, but the foreign ministry in Moscow gave way to pressure from the Centre (k-5, 422).

153. k-5, 353, 357.

154. k-5, 357.

155. Mitrokhin's notes give few details on MARIO save that he was recruited in 1972 and usually met his controller in the Soviet Union (k-6, 192).

156. k-14, 264; vol. 6, app. 1, part 40. As in other countries, Line X agents in Italy were also used to obtain S&T from US sources (k-5, 236).

157. vol. 6, app. 1, part 39. Mitrokhin's notes identify KULON and his research institute.

158. k-5, 425. Mitrokhin's notes do not indicate what happened to UCHITEL and Kuznetsov's other agents after his expulsion. It would have been normal practice for them to have been put on ice.

159. k-2, 415.

160. k-2, 217; k-3, 112.

161. k-2, 225, 243; k-20, 348.

162. k-2, 250, 275; k-4, 71; k-10, 52; vol. 6, app. 1, parts 39, 41.

163. k-2, 230, 242; k-13, 133; k-20, 347; k-21, 34; k-26, 68.

164. k-2, 274. Mitrokhin's notes transcribe his codename alternately as ACHERO and AGERO. The most likely codename is ACERO, pronounced "achero"—the Italian for "steel."

165. k-7, 126.

166. k-7, 48.

167. k-2, 212, 216, 220, 224, 229, 257–8; k-21, 32.

168. k-2, 211, 249.

169. k-2, 240, 271; k-25, 188. METSENAT's controllers in the Rome residency were, successively, Vladimir Yevgenyevich Strelkov, Anatoli Yegorovich Abalin, Valentin Mikhaolovich Yatsura and Konstantin Kazakov.

170. k-1, 1; k-2, 214, 222, 244; k-13, 143; k-14, 687.

171. k-13, 153, 148.

172. k-13, 148. The active measures statistics were much in line with those for the previous two years. In 1975 the Rome residency reported that "3 documentary [forged document] operations were carried out; 10 conversations of influence were held; 1 press conference, 1 conference [were arranged]; 4 oral reports were disseminated; 48 articles were published; 6 questions were asked in Parliament; 1 delegation was assembled and sent out; 4 appeals were drafted; 4 mailing operations were carried out; an Italy–Spain committee was set up; 2 leaflet operations were carried out and 2 anonymous letters were sent out" (k-13, 135). The active measures statistics for 1976 were as follows:

> articles placed [in the press]:   63
> conversations of influence: 6
> appeals made: 9
> working group organized: 1
> booklet distributed: 1
> leaflet operation carried out: 1
> anonymous letters distributed: 2
> demonstration held: 1
> parliamentary questions: 2
> question in the Senate: 1
> "Round Table" meeting held: 1

Of the total number of articles printed, 28 of the press articles were designed to discredit the Main Adversary; 21 alleged CIA interference in Italian affairs. The residency also claimed to have made "active use" of the "Italy–Spain" committee. Four active measures operations were intended "to discredit Maoism as an anti-socialist tendency." k-13, 151.

173. Mitrokhin's notes probably contain only an incomplete record of new agents recruited by the Rome residency during the period 1977–83. Among them, however, were ARO, who worked for the Ansaldo company in Genoa and was recruited at some point between 1978 and 1981 (k-14, 439); CLEMENT, a member of the international department of the Christian Association of Italian Workers (ACLI), recruited in 1978 but put on ice in 1981 after he had failed to supply intelligence of much significance (k-14, 395); KARS, an Italian physicist who worked as a Line X agent in both Italy and the United States in the early 1980s (k-14, 264; vol. 6, app. 1, part 40); KOK, a sinologist recruited in 1977 for operations against the PRC (k-13, 153); and KOZAK, the owner of an Italian engineering company, who was recruited not later than 1978 (k-14, 174).

174. k-14, 687.

175. k-7, 48.

176. k-10, 109; k-25, 188.

177. k-7, 126.

178. k-13, 112.

179. Andrew and Gordievsky (eds.), *Instructions from the Centre,* p. 10.

180. Andrew and Gordievsky (eds.), *Instructions from the Centre,* pp. 19–20.

181. Andrew and Gordievsky, *KGB,* pp. 629–31.

182. "Order of the Chairman of the KGB," no. 107/OV, September 5, 1990.

Chapter Twenty-eight   The Penetration and Persecution of the Soviet Churches

1. Lenin, *Works,* vol. 35, pp. 89–90; Shipler, *Russia,* pp. 270–1. KGB persecution of Islam and Judaism will be covered in volume 2.

2. Stalin may also have been influenced by the desire not to alienate his Anglo-American allies by continued religious persecution at a time when he was pressing them to open a second front. Pospielovsky, "The 'Best Years' of Stalin's Church Policy (1942–1948) in the Light of Archival Documents."

3. The work of Michael Bourdeaux and his colleagues at Keston College has impressively documented the vitality of religious life in the post-war Russian Orthodox Church, despite continued persecution and a mostly subservient hierarchy. See, *inter alia,* Bourdeaux, *Risen Indeed.*

4. Luchterhandt, "The Council for Religious Affairs."

5. vol. 5, sec. 9.

6. Meerson, "The Political Philosophy of the Russian Orthodox Episcopate in the Soviet Period," p. 221.

7. Revesz, *The Christian Peace Conference,* pp. 1–4.

8. k-1, 232.

9. k-1, 214.

10. Harriss, "The Gospel According to Marx," pp. 61–2.

11. Mitrokhin did not see the file on the 1961 WCC Central Committee meeting. Another file noted by him, however, identifies ADAMANT as Nikodim; vol. 7, ch. 5, para. 28.

12. "WCC Gives Eight-point Lead to Member Churches," *Church Times* (August 29, 1969).

13. "Elusive Goal" (leader), *Church Times* (August 29, 1969).

14. Harriss, "The Gospel According to Marx," pp. 61–2. On Buyevsky's role in the Moscow Patriarchate's foreign relations Department, see Ellis, *The Russian Orthodox Church,* p. 266.

15. Letter from the Bishop of Bristol to the *Church Times* (September 7, 1973); Smith, *Fraudulent Gospel,* pp. 2–3.

16. Babris, *Silent Churches,* p. 472.

17. Document cited by Harriss, "The Gospel According to Marx," p. 62.

18. KGB Church records temporarily accessible to journalists after the disintegration of the Soviet Union indicate that, at some stage after Nikodim's death in 1978, Yuvenali was given his former KGB codename ADAMANT. (It was not unusual for KGB codenames to be recycled.) Michael Dobbs, "Business as Usual for Ex-KGB Agents," *Washington Post* (February 11, 1992).

19. Pawley, *Donald Coggan,* pp. 244–8.

20. k-1, 24.

21. Polyakov, "Activities of the Moscow Patriarchate in 1991," p. 152.

22. Ellis, *The Russian Orthodox Church,* pp. 226–9.

23. *Daily American* (September 8, 1978). On September 29, 1978, less than a month after Nikodim's death in the Vatican, John Paul I also died suddenly, thus becoming the shortest-lived pope since Urban VII died of malaria twelve days after his election in 1590.

24. See above, chapter 28.

25. k-1, 30.

26. Ellis, *The Russian Orthodox Church,* pp. 215–16. On the authenticity of the report, see Oppenheim, "Are the Furov Reports Authentic?"

27. "His Holiness Patriarch Pimen's Address Before Panikhida in the Patriarchal Cathedral of the Epiphany in Moscow," *Journal of the Moscow Patriarchate* (1984), no. 3.

28. See, for example, Pimen's telegram to Brezhnev of December 17, 1976 in *Journal of the Moscow Patriarchate* (1977), no. 2, pp. 3–4.

29. "Soviet Peace Fund Awards," *Journal of the Moscow Patriarchate* (1976), no. 4.

30. "His Holiness Patriarch Pimen Awarded by the World Peace Council," *Journal of the Moscow Patriarchate* (1976), no. 6.

31. "World Conference: Religious Leaders for Lasting Peace, Disarmament and Just Relations among Nations," *Journal of the Moscow Patriarchate* (1977), no. 7, pp. 2–3 and no. 8, pp. 17–64.

32. k-1, 23; vol. 6, ch. 10. The Patriarchate was also involved in another KGB-sponsored production in 1982, the World Conference of Religious Workers for Saving the Sacred Gift of Life from Nuclear Catastrophe, which again attracted about 600 participants.

33. "Decree of the Presidium of the USSR Supreme Soviet on Conferring the Order of the Red Banner of Labor upon Patriarch Pimen of Moscow and All Russia," *Journal of the Moscow Patriarchate* (1977), no. 9, p. 3.

34. Ellis, *The Russian Orthodox Church*, p. 217.

35. The full text of the letter from Yakunin and Regelson was published in *Religion in Communist Lands*, vol. 41 (1976), no. 1.

36. Lefever, *Nairobi to Vancouver*, pp. 64–5; Ellis, *The Russian Orthodox Church*, pp. 355–68; Hudson, *The World Council of Churches in International Affairs*, pp. 286–7.

37. Norman, *Christianity and the World Order*, pp. 1–2, 90 *n*. 62.

38. Lefever, *Nairobi to Vancouver*, p. 65; Babris, *Silent Churches*, p. 475.

39. vol. 6, ch. 10.

40. Harriss, "The Gospel According to Marx," p. 63.

41. vol. 6, ch. 10.

42. "Interview Given by Metropolitan Filaret of Kiev and Gallich to a Novosti Press Agency Correspondent," *Journal of the Moscow Patriarchate* (1976), no. 5.

43. vol. 6, ch. 10.

44. Smith, *Fraudulent Gospel*, p. 68.

45. The text of the founding declaration of the Christian Committee was published in *Religion in Communist Lands*, vol. 6 (1978), no. 1. On the work of the committee, see Ellis, *The Russian Orthodox Church*, pp. 373–81.

46. k-21, 203.

47. *Documents of the Christian Committee for the Defense of Believers' Rights in the USSR*, 12 vols. (Vol. 3 consists of English translations; the remainder contain reproductions of the original Russian texts.) See also Scarfe (ed.), *The CCDBR Documents: Christian Committee for the Defense of Believers' Rights in the USSR*.

48. k-1, 65. On Varsonofy's resignation from the Christian Committee, cf. Ellis, *The Russian Orthodox Church*, p. 379.

49. k-27, 488.

50. Ellis, *The Russian Orthodox Church*, p. 379.

51. k-1, 50. On Fonchenkov's public career, cf. Ellis, *The Russian Orthodox Church*, pp. 380–1.

52. Ellis, *The Russian Orthodox Church*, p. 428.

53. Albats, *The State within a State*, p. 46.

54. Ellis, *The Russian Orthodox Church*, pp. 422ff.

55. Ellis, *The Russian Orthodox Church*, pp. 430–9.

56. It is impossible, however, to rule out the possibility, that Fonchenkov had become genuinely sympathetic towards Yakunin. Mitrokhin's notes on his career as agent DRUG are limited to the 1970s.

57. Ellis, *The Russian Orthodox Church*, pp. 439–41.

58. Lefever, *Nairobi to Vancouver*, pp. 3–5, 67–70, 73, 75, appendix A.

59. Andrew and Gordievsky (eds.), *Instructions from the Centre*, p. 20.

60. Kalugin, *Spymaster*, p. 197.

61. vol. 6, ch. 10, *n*. 1.

62. Mitrokhin's notes on the file of agent VORONOV, for example, record that during his period in New York in the late 1970s and early 1980s, he "was tasked to identify among his parishioners people who had a progressive and sympathetic view of the USSR—government workers, political party [members], union members, workers at scientific research institutes, diplomatic personnel, immigration officials, clergymen and church employees who were involved in the registration of births, marriages, and deaths [for assistance in the documentation of illegals] and agents of Zionist and anti-Soviet organizations" (vol. 6, app. 2, part 4).

63. Kalugin, *Spymaster*, p. 197.

64. vol. 6, app. 2, part 4

65. vol. 6, app. 2, part 4.

66. vol. 8, ch. 6, paras. 16–17.

67. vol. 8, app. 3, para. 20.

68. Albats, *The State within a State*, p. 46. Confirmation of DROZDOV's identity was provided by the release early in 1999 of a 1958 report on his recruitment, allegedly on "patriotic" grounds, by the Estonian

KGB. Though the report refers to the agent only by his codename, his year of birth and career details are identical with those of Aleksi. James Meek, "Russian Patriarch 'was KGB spy,' " *Guardian* (February 12, 1999).

69. "Metropolitan Aleksiy's Speech at the Founding Conference of the 'Rodina' Society," *Journal of the Moscow Patriarchate* (1976), no. 2.

70. Albats, *The State within a State,* p. 46.

71. Bociurkiw, "Suppression de l'Église gréco-catholique ukrainienne;" Pelikan, *Confessor between East and West,* ch. 8; Floridi, "The Church of the Martyrs and the Ukrainian Millennium," pp. 107–11; Tataryn, "The Re-emergence of the Ukrainian (Greek) Catholic Church in the USSR," pp. 292–4.

72. k-1, 246.

73. The intelligence agencies of the USSR, Bulgaria, the GDR, Hungary, Poland and Romania were represented by heads and deputy heads of directorates (k-1, 106).

74. k-1, 106. Mitrokhin's notes do not make clear which, if any, of the KGB representatives at the conference came from the FCD.

75. Though seeking confirmation of the report, the Centre took the alleged Vatican conspiracy seriously and drew up plans for a press exposé of it, if further details could be obtained (k-1, 2).

76. k-1, 71.

77. Babris, *Silent Churches,* pp. 149–50.

78. APOSTOL, RASS and SLUGA are not identified in Mitrokhin's notes (k-1, 2).

79. k-1, 3, 110. It is unclear whether the PETROV who studied at the Russicum was the cleric with the same codename later sent to North America.

80. k-1, 81-2, 109. ANTANAS arrived in Rome in January 1968; Mitrokhin does not record the date of arrival of VIDMANTAS.

81. k-1, 83-4. A KGB file also records that in October 1969 DAKTARAS visited Rome to attend "a gathering of bishops" (k-1, 2).

82. k-1, 2. Dudás appears in KGB files, in Cyrillic transliteration, as Dudast.

83. k-1, 2.

84. k-1, 133.

85. k-1, 133.

86. k-1, 36, k-5, 11, k-19, 82.

87. Unlike the similar 1967 conference, the 1975 conference was attended by the Cubans. On this occasion, however, there was no delegation from Romania. k-1, 13.

88. k-1, 13.

89. k-1, 246.

90. Borecky, Bishop Isidore, "The Church in Ukraine–1988;" Tataryn, "The Re-emergence of the Ukrainian (Greek) Catholic Church in the USSR;" Polyakov, "Activities of the Moscow Patriarchate in 1991," p. 152.

91. k-1, 146. The KGB estimate may have been too low. Published estimates for 1990, admittedly at a time when active persecution had almost ceased, were significantly higher; see Ramet (ed.), *Religious Policy in the Soviet Union,* pp. 355–6.

92. k-1, 73.

93. k-1, 146.

94. Ellis (ed.), *Three Generations of Suffering;* Bourdeaux, *Gorbachev, Glasnost & the Gospel,* p. 121.

95. k-1, 214.

96. Penton, *Apocalypse Delayed.*

97. k-1, 241.

98. Recollections of one of the deportees, Vasili Kalin, cited by James Meek, "Cult-busters Fight 'Sins of False Witness,' " *Guardian* (February 12, 1999).

99. k-1, 91.

100. Among the evidence ignored by the KGB conspiracy theorists who saw the Jehovah's Witnesses as vehicles for American ideological subversion was the fact that, from the First World War to the war in Vietnam, they consistently represented the largest group of Americans imprisoned for conscientious objection. In 1918 their leaders were imprisoned for contravening the American Espionage Act, though their sentences were overturned on appeal. Penton, *Apocalypse Delayed,* pp. 55–6, 142. Sadly, some of the conspiracy theories survived the collapse of the Soviet system.

101. k-1, 241. In reality, Jehovah's Witnesses behave in many ways as model citizens. Since 1962 they have been instructed to obey all human laws not directly in conflict with those of God. Penton, *Apocalypse Delayed,* p. 140.

102. Antic, "The Spread of Modern Cults in the USSR," pp. 257–8.

103. k-1, 92.

104. k-1, 91. There is no reference in the files noted by Mitrokhin to any successful KGB penetration either of the Jehovah's Witnesses" Brooklyn headquarters or of its west European offices.

105. k-1, 91.

106. k-1, 73.

107. Antic, "The Spread of Modern Cults in the USSR," p. 259.

108. Polyakov, "Activities of the Moscow Patriarchate in 1991; p. 147; Van den Bercken, "The Russian Orthodox Church, State and Society in 1991–1993," p. 164.

109. Walters, "The Defrocking of Fr. Gleb Yakunin," pp. 308–9.

110. Yakunin, "First Open Letter to Patriarch Aleksi II," pp. 313–14. Father Gleb was in dispute with the Patriarch over the decision by the Holy Synod in October 1993 that Orthodox clergy would no longer be allowed to stand as candidates for political office. He went ahead with his candidature in the elections two months later, was elected and then defrocked. Walters, "The Defrocking of Fr Gleb Yakunin," p. 310.

Chapter Twenty-nine   The Polish Pope and the Rise of Solidarity

1. k-19, 515.

2. See above, chapter 16.

3. k-19, 516.

4. On the arrests, see Karpiński, *Poland since 1944*, pp. 196–7.

5. Cywiński later read Wałęsa's acceptance speech for the 1983 Nobel Peace Prize at the ceremony in Oslo which Wałęsa was unable to attend.

6. k-19, 516.

7. Bernstein and Politi, *His Holiness*, p. 126.

8. See above, chapter 16.

9. k-19, 429. Bardecki cannot, of course, be blamed in any way for receiving, among his Western visitors, two men whom he had no possible means of identifying as KGB illegals.

10. k-19, 516.

11. Bernstein and Politi, *His Holiness*, p. 127.

12. Szulc, *Pope John Paul II*, p. 264.

13. k-19, 516.

14. Karpiński, *Poland since 1944*, pp. 200–1.

15. k-19, 473.

16. k-1, 45.

17. k-19, 515.

18. k-19, 506.

19. Szulc, *Pope John Paul II*, p. 289.

20. The KGB claimed in 1982 that there were 26,000 Catholic priests in Poland (k-19, 506).

21. Szulc, *Pope John Paul II*, p. 403.

22. Bernstein and Politi, *His Holiness*, p. 321.

23. k-1, 11.

24. Szulc, *Pope John Paul II*, p. 285.

25. k-1, 11.

26. Bernstein and Politi, *His Holiness*, p. 184.

27. vol. 8, ch. 8; vol. 8, app. 3. Tischner cannot, of course, be blamed in any way for receiving, among his Western visitors, an apparently well-recommended Canadian publisher seeking his help for a book on Polish missionaries, whom he had no possible means of identifying as a KGB illegal.

28. Bernstein and Politi, *His Holiness*, p. 373.

29. Szulc, *Pope John Paul II*, p. 299; Bernstein and Politi, *His Holiness*, p. 191.

30. k-20, 208.

31. k-20, 163.

32. k-20, 211.

33. Bernstein and Politi, *His Holiness*, pp. 217–18.

34. Szulc, *Pope John Paul II*, pp. 310–12; Bernstein and Politi, *His Holiness*, p. 308.

35. k-1, 19.

36. k-20, 245.

37. k-20, 245.

38. k-20, 220.
39. Kramer (ed.), "Declassified Soviet Documents on the Polish Crisis," p. 116.
40. Bernstein and Politi, *His Holiness,* p. 246.
41. k-20, 221.
42. Bernstein and Politi, *His Holiness,* p. 246.

Chapter Thirty   The Polish Crisis and the Crumbling of the Soviet Bloc

1. Kramer (ed.), "Declassified Soviet Documents on the Polish Crisis," pp. 117, 129–30.
2. k-20, 221.
3. Dobbs, *Down with Big Brother,* pp. 48–9.
4. k-20, 342.
5. k-20, 34.
6. k-20, 35.
7. Bernstein and Politi, *His Holiness,* pp. 247–8.
8. k-16, 409.
9. vol. 8, app. 3. Neither Bardecki nor Mazowiecki can be blamed in any way for receiving, among their Western visitors, someone whom they had no possible means of identifying as a KGB illegal.
10. t-7, 156.
11. Bernstein and Politi, *His Holiness,* p. 250.
12. k-20, 10, 26.
13. k-19, 29.
14. Bernstein and Politi, *His Holiness,* p. 254.
15. k-20, 28.
16. t-7, 154. On January 22 Mikhail Zimyanin returned to Moscow from a fact-finding mission in Poland and gave an equally gloomy report to the Politburo (Bernstein and Politi, *His Holiness,* pp. 255–6).
17. k-19, 511.
18. t-7, 155.
19. Bernstein and Politi, *His Holiness,* pp. 271–4.
20. k-20, 309.
21. Bernstein and Politi, *His Holiness,* pp. 276–84.
22. k-20, 110.
23. Kramer (ed.), "Declassified Soviet Documents on the Polish Crisis," pp. 130–1.
24. Szulc, *Pope John Paul II,* ch. 24. Bernstein and Politi, *His Holiness,* pp. 293–307.
25. At the time, opinions within the Centre were divided on whether the KGB had been involved in the assassination attempt. About half the FCD officers with whom Oleg Gordievsky discussed the attempt were convinced that the KGB would no longer contemplate such a risky special action, even if it were sub-contracted to the Bulgarian intelligence service. The other half, however, suspected that Department 8 of Directorate S, which was responsible for assassinations, had been involved; some told Gordievsky they only regretted that the attempt had failed. (Andrew and Gordievsky, *KGB,* p. 639.)
26. k-20, 101, 104.
27. k-20, 104.
28. k-20, 102. Olszowski was regarded as a KGB co-optee (k-19, 26).
29. k-20, 103. On June 7 Aristov, Kulikov and Pavlov telegraphed the Politburo to urge "the necessity of a direct dialogue with S. Kania about his departure from the post of the First Secretary" (k-20, 57).
30. k-20, 105.
31. k-20, 53.
32. k-20, 52.
33. k-20, 55.
34. k-20, 54.
35. k-19, 385.
36. k-20, 54, 102, 112.
37. Boyes, *The Naked President,* pp. 97–8.
38. k-19, 110.
39. k-19, 115.
40. Boyes, *The Naked President,* pp. 94–5.
41. k-19, 115.
42. k-19, 115.

43. k-19, 117.

44. k-19, 113.

45. k-19, 102.

46. k-19, 106.

47. k-19, 105.

48. k-19, 103.

49. k-19, 104.

50. Kramer (ed.) "Declassified Soviet Documents on the Polish Crisis," pp. 132–3.

51. CPSU Secretary K. V. Rusakov told Honecker after Kania's sacking, "We noticed that lately a difference began to appear between Kania and Jaruzelski in their approaches to basic questions. Jaruzelski began to show more and more readiness to accept violent measures in dealing with counter-revolution. We began to work with Jaruzelski. When doing this, we were influenced by the fact that Jaruzelski possessed greater authority in the army and also enjoyed the support of the ministers" (k-20, 338).

52. Bernstein and Politi, *His Holiness*, pp. 315–16.

53. k-20, 303.

54. Kramer (ed.), "Declassified Soviet Documents on the Polish Crisis," pp. 133–4.

55. k-20, 311.

56. k-20, 327.

57. k-20, 307.

58. k-20, 304.

59. k-20, 327.

60. k-20, 308.

61. Ustinov denied, not wholly convincingly, that Kulikov had actually referred to the possibility of Soviet military intervention; Kramer (ed.), "Declassified Soviet Documents on the Polish Crisis," pp. 134–7.

62. k-20, 315, 316.

63. k-20, 340.

64. k-20, 315.

65. k-20, 325.

66. k-20, 293.

67. k-20, 324.

68. Bernstein and Politi, *His Holiness*, pp. 334, 339.

69. Boyes, *The Naked President*, pp. 106–7.

70. k-20, 329.

71. k-20, 297.

72. Boyes, *The Naked President*, p. 107.

73. Bernstein and Politi, *His Holiness*, pp. 336–7.

74. k-20, 297.

75. k-20, 316.

76. Bernstein and Politi, *His Holiness*, pp. 337–9.

77. k-20, 323.

78. k-20, 296.

79. k-20, 298.

80. Bernstein and Politi, *His Holiness*, pp. 343–4.

81. k-19, 53.

82. k-19, 321.

83. k-19, 23.

84. Boyes, *The Naked President*, p. 108; Bernstein and Politi, *His Holiness*, p. 348.

85. k-20, 249.

86. k-19, 23.

87. Bernstein and Politi, *His Holiness*, p. 348.

88. Boyes, *The Naked President*, pp. 307–9.

89. k-20, 249.

90. k-19, 261.

91. Boyes, *The Naked President*, p. 117.

92. k-19, 381.

93. k-19, 380.

94. k-19, 411.

95. k-19, 312.

96. k-19, 252.

97. k-19, 253.

98. k-19, 257.

99. k-19, 258.

100. k-19, 261. Mitrokhin's notes do not record the content of Brezhnev's message to Jaruzelski. On prosecutions after the declaration of martial law, see Swidlicki, *Political Trials in Poland 1981–1986*.

101. k-19, 642.

102. k-19, 311.

103. k-19, 324.

104. k-19, 326.

105. k-19, 328.

106. k-19, 337.

107. k-19, 339.

108. k-19, 128.

109. k-19, 124.

110. k-19, 143. Kiszczak expressed his thanks for material and technical assistance already received; Mitrokhin's notes do not record the nature of this assistance.

111. k-19, 143.

112. k-1, 15.

113. k-19, 135.

114. Bernstein and Politi, *His Holiness*, pp. 376–7.

115. Szulc, *Pope John Paul II*, pp. 388–9.

116. Boyes, *The Naked President*, p. 131.

117. k-19, 143.

118. Bernstein and Politi, *His Holiness*, pp. 381–2.

119. Boyes, *The Naked President*, pp. 132–3.

120. Boyes, *The Naked President*, pp. 117, 134–6.

121. Boyes, *The Naked President*, pp. 117, 136–7.

122. Boyes, *The Naked President*, pp. 137–8.

123. Szulc, *Pope John Paul II*, pp. 395–6; Bernstein and Politi, *His Holiness*, pp. 387–8.

124. Bernstein and Politi, *His Holiness*, pp. 388–9; Szulc, *Pope John Paul II*, pp. 396–7.

125. k-16, 500.

126. Brown, *The Gorbachev Factor*, p. 249.

127. Dobbs, *Down with Big Brother*, pp. 265–9; Lévesque, *The Enigma of 1989*, ch. 6.

128. Dobbs, *Down with Big Brother*, p. 288.

129. Interview with Shebarshin, *Daily Telegraph* (December 1, 1992).

Conclusion. *From the One-Party State to the Yeltsin Presidency*

1. Jukes, "The Soviets and 'Ultra.' " Though Jukes's conclusions are debatable, his 1988 article remains a pathbreaking study.

2. Kennedy-Pipe, *Russia and the World, 1917–1991*. Dr. Kennedy-Pipe's otherwise valuable book is only one example of the continuing underestimation of the role of Soviet foreign intelligence even in some of the most recent work by leading Western scholars.

3. The significance of SIGINT was made clear by David Kahn's pioneering *The Codebreakers*, published in 1967. Though a bestseller, however, its contents appeared to stun, rather than to inspire, most historians of international relations.

4. A growing minority of international relations, history and other departments in British universities now offer courses on intelligence, though on a much smaller scale than in north America. There is a flourishing British Study Group on Intelligence, with a largely academic membership, and an increasing number of similar groups in north America and continental Europe.

5. Orwell, *Nineteen Eighty-Four*, p. 7.

6. Hosking, *A History of the Soviet Union*, p. 219.

7. Two of the leading historians of the Bolshevik Revolution, Orlando Figes and Richard Pipes, agree on describing the Cheka as "a state within a state."

8. Volkogonov, *The Rise and Fall of the Soviet Empire*, pp. 73–4.

9. Conquest, *The Great Terror*, pp. 468–70. It was a sign of the difficulty encountered by many Western historians in interpreting the Terror that Conquest's was the only full-scale history of it published during the life of the Soviet Union.

10. Ostryakov, *Voyennye Chekisty*, p. 258.

11. k-25, 78. On the punitive use of psychiatry in the Soviet Union, see Bloch and Reddaway, *Russia's Political Hospitals.*

12. k-25, 79. There is no suggestion in Mitrokhin's notes that Voloshanovich was working for the KGB.

13. See above, chapter 20.

14. frag. 1, 7. Mitrokhin's notes give no details of the precise charges leveled against Korobov or of the length of his sentence.

15. k-3b, 136.

16. I am grateful to Dr. Clarissa de Waal of Newnham College, Cambridge, for these recollections of Tirana in 1992.

17. A further 3 percent were KGB co-optees.

18. t-7, 284.

19. t-7, 286. The behavior of the informers should not, in most cases, be harshly judged. Those who refused invitations to inform were likely to incur the ill will of the KGB towards themselves and their families.

20. frag. 5, 3.

21. Kalugin, *Spymaster*, pp. 287–98.

22. See above, chapter 20.

23. Kissinger subsequently acknowledged that Senator Pat Moynihan had been an exception. "Your crystal ball," he told him, "was better than mine." Moynihan, *Secrecy*, p. 6.

24. For example, the Russian sections of Eric Hobsbawm's brilliant history of the twentieth century, *Age of Extremes*, include no mention of any of the heads of the Cheka and its successors, save for a passing reference to Andropov's career before becoming General Secretary as "chief of the security apparatus" (p. 476).

25. There is, however, a one-line reference to Andropov's subsequent emergence as Soviet leader in Vance's reflections on the period after his resignation (Vance, *Hard Choices*, p. 421).

26. Gorbachev, however, acknowledged that, eighteen months or two years earlier, the coup might have succeeded.

27. Remnick, *Resurrection*. The American edition of this generally admirable study appeared in 1997.

28. k-13, 268.

29. Kennedy-Pipe, *Russia and the World, 1917–1991*, is the most recent of the many studies of Soviet foreign policy which make no mention of these aspects of it.

30. Andrew, *For the President's Eyes Only*, pp. 149–52.

31. Truman, *Year of Decisions*, p. 346.

32. *VENONA*, BBC Radio 4 documentary written and presented by Christopher Andrew (producers: Mark Burman and Helen Weinstein), first broadcast March 18, 1998. Andrew, "The VENONA Secret." The Centre received progress reports on VENONA from Weisband until 1950 and from Philby from 1949 to 1951.

33. See above, chapter 9.

34. DARIO had already served in the Italian foreign ministry before the Second World War, and was reemployed there afterwards.

35. See above, chapter 21.

36. Andrew and Gordievsky (eds.), *Instructions from the Centre*, pp. 29–40.

37. Fursenko and Naftali, "Soviet Intelligence and the Cuban Missile Crisis," pp. 65–6.

38. See above, chapters 6, 7, and 15.

39. See above, chapter 26.

40. *Izvestia* (September 24, 1991).

41. The foreign intelligence reports submitted to Stalin and Khrushchev and the more elaborate assessments supplied to their successors will one day be a major source for the study of Soviet foreign policy. Thus far, however, very few are available for research.

42. k-9, 122; vol. 2, app. 3.

43. Holloway, *Stalin and the Bomb*, pp. 145–7.

44. See above, chapters 11, 13, and 21.

45. Pentagon estimate cited by Tuck, *High-Tech Espionage*, pp. 108–9.

46. Andrew and Gordievsky (eds.), *Instructions from the Centre*, p. 33.

47. Gorbachev's speech was reported in *Pravda* on March 26, 1986.

48. Brown, *The Gorbachev Factor*, pp. 134–5, 139.

49. See above, chapter 25.

50. Report of the House Committee, chaired by Representative Christopher Cox, of which a declassified version was published as this volume was going to press in May 1999.

51. k-3b, 137. Though this residency circular was sent out in 1977, it merely reiterated priorities formulated in previous instructions from the Centre.

52. k-25, 186.

53. See above, chapter 20.

54. See above, chapter 18.

55. See above, chapter 22.

56. vol. 6, ch. 1, part 1; k-25, 56; k-21, 74, 96, 99.

57. vol. 6, ch. 10. Mitrokhin's notes do not give the names of the operational officers assigned to the Karpov–Korchnoi match. Korchnoi's official "second," the British grandmaster Raymond Keene, believed that the head of the Soviet delegation at the championship, V. D. Baturinsky, was a KGB colonel (Keene, *Karpov–Korchnoi 1978*, p. 32). Korchnoi gives an account of his defection and career up to the 1978 world championship in his autobiography, *Chess is My Life.*

58. Keene, *Karpov–Korchnoi 1978*, pp. 56, 147–9, 153–4. During the rematch between Korchnoi and Karpov at Merano, Italy, in 1981, the KGB established a dedicated cipher communication circuit to report on the progress of matches and arranged a shuttle service between the Rome residency and the KGB operational group covering the World Chess Championship. No fewer than fourteen active measures were implemented in an attempt once again to ensure Korchnoi's defeat (k-5, 921). The undercover KGB advance party at Merano claimed to be monitoring the drinking water, the climate, noise levels, even levels of radioactivity (Kasparov, *Child of Change*, p. 76). Korchnoi, then past his best and, at fifty, a relatively elderly challenger for the world title, lost by eleven points to seven.

59. Karpov's eventual conqueror in the 1985 world championship, Gary Kasparov, has made much of the obstacles placed in his path by the Soviet establishment. He himself, however, owed much to the support of the head of the Azerbaijan KGB, Geidar Alyev. Lawson, *The Inner Game*, p. 17; Kasparov, *Child of Change*, p. 79.

60. See above, chapter 28.

61. See above, chapter 29.

62. The text of the appeal of the "State Committee for the State of Emergency," dated August 18, 1991, was published in *The Times* (August 19, 1991).

63. Gorbachev, *The August Coup*, p. 31.

64. Knight, *Spies Without Cloaks*, pp. 130–1. Trubnikov is a former senior FCD officer who made his reputation during operations in India, which will be covered in volume 2.

65. Unattributable information from Russian sources.

66. Andrew and Gordievsky (eds.), *Instructions from the Centre*, p. 17.

67. Unattributable information from Russian sources.

68. Remnick, *Resurrection*, p. 370.

69. Unattributable information from Russian sources.

70. Knight, *Spies Without Cloaks*, pp. 89–91, 106–8. Remnick, *Resurrection*, pp. 276–7. Anna Blundy, "Return to Grace of the Baby-faced Hawk," *The Times* (May 13, 1999). Stepashin is the only one of the original supporters of the war to admit his mistake.

71. Davies, *Europe*, pp. 328–32, 464–5.

72. The classic, though possibly overstated, analysis of the faultlines between cultures is Huntington, *The Clash of Civilizations and the Remaking of World Order.*

73. Pulled westward by a Western-educated élite often out of tune with its own population, Greece remains something of an anomaly as an Orthodox member of NATO and the EU. Stefan Wagstyl, Kerin Hope and John Thornhill, "Christendom's Ancient Split," *Financial Times* (May 4, 1999).

74. Haslam, "Russia's Seat at the Table," p. 129.

75. Vujacic, "Gennadiy Zyuganov and the 'Third Road.' "

76. Unusual but not unique. As a result of the divisive legacy of the Spanish Civil War, Spain also has no words to its national anthem. The Soviet Union found itself in a similar situation in 1956 after Krushchev suppressed the existing words to the Soviet national anthem as too Stalinist. New words were not devised until 1977.

77. Samolis (ed.), *Veterany Vneshnei Razvedki Rossii*, pp. 3–4.

78. Primakov *et al.*, *Ocherki Istorii Rossiyskoi Vneshnei Razvedki*, vol. 3, conclusion.

BIBLIOGRAPHY

1. Mitrokhin's Archive
Mitrokhin's notes and transcripts are arranged in four sections:

(i) k-series: handwritten notes on individual KGB files, stored in large envelopes;
(ii) t-series: handwritten notebooks containing notes on individual KGB files;
(iii) vol.-series: typed volumes containing material drawn from numerous KGB files, mostly arranged by country, sometimes with commentary by Mitrokhin;
(iv) frag-series: miscellaneous handwritten notes.

2. Published Collections of Soviet Documents Containing KGB Material
Andrew, Christopher, and Gordievsky, Oleg (eds.), *Instructions from the Centre: Top Secret Files on KGB Foreign Operations, 1975–1985* (London: Hodder & Stoughton, 1990); slightly revised US edition published as *Comrade Kryuchkov's Instructions: Top Secret Files on KGB Foreign Operations, 1975–1985* (Stanford, Calif.: Stanford University Press, 1993)

Andrew, Christopher, and Gordievsky, Oleg (eds.), *More Instructions from the Centre: Top Secret Files on KGB Global Operations, 1975–1985* (London: Frank Cass, 1991)

Cold War International History Project Bulletin: regularly publishes declassified Soviet official documents, including some KGB reports to the Politburo (see articles cited in section 3 of the bibliography)

Fond 89: documents assembled in late 1991 for the prosecution of the CPSU (including some KGB reports), available on Chadwyck-Healey microfilm

Hanson, Philip, *Soviet Industrial Espionage: Some New Information* (London: RIIA, 1987)

Koenker, Diane P., and Bachman, Ronald D. (eds.), *Revelations from the Russian Archives* (Washington, DC.: Library of Congress, 1997)

Russian Foreign Intelligence (VChk–KGB–SVR): 1996 CD-Rom produced by the SVR, containing brief extracts from declassified KGB documents

Scammell, Michael (ed.), *The Solzhenitsyn Files* (Chicago: Edition q, 1995): includes some KGB reports

Stepashin, Sergei, *et al* (eds.), *Organy Gosudarstvennoi Bezopastnosti SSSR v Velikoi Otechestvennoi Voine: Sbornik Dokumentov:* vol. 1 (November 1938–December 1940); vol. 2 (January–June 1941) (Moscow: Kniga i Biznes, 1995)

Tsvigun, S. K. *et al* (eds.), *V. I. Lenin i VChk: Sbornik Dokumentov (1917–1922gg)* (Moscow: Izdatelstvo Politicheskoi Literaturi, 1975)

VENONA: decrypted Soviet telegrams (many concerning intelligence operations), mostly for the period 1940–8, accessible on the NSA website: http://www.nsa.gov:8080/

3. Other Publications Cited in the Notes
Acheson, Dean, *Present at the Creation: My Years in the State Department* (New York: W. W. Norton & Co., 1969)

Adereth, M., *The French Communist Party: A Critical History (1920–84), From Comintern to "The Colors of France"* (Manchester: Manchester University Press, 1984)

Agabekov, Georgi, *OGPU* (New York: Brentano's, 1931)

Agee, Philip, *Inside the Company: CIA Diary* (London: Allen Lane, 1975; US paperback edition, New York: Bantam Books, 1976)

Agee, Philip, *On The Run* (London: Bloomsbury, 1987)

Agee, Philip, "What Uncle Sam Wants to Know about You: The KIQs," first published as a pamphlet in 1977; reprinted in Agee, Philip, and Wolf, Louis, *Dirty Work: The CIA in Western Europe* (London: Zed Press, 1978)

Agee, Philip, and Wolf, Louis, *Dirty Work: The CIA in Western Europe* (London: Zed Press, 1978)

Agranovsky, Valeri, "Profession: Foreigner," *Znamya* (September 1988)

Albats, Yevgenia, *The State within a State: The KGB and Its Hold on Russia—Past, Present, and Future* (New York: Farrar, Straus & Giroux, 1994)

Albright, Joseph, and Kunstel, Marcia, *Bombshell: The Secret Story of America's Unknown Atomic Spy Conspiracy* (New York: Times Books, 1997)

Ammann, Ronald; Cooper, Julian; and Davies, R. W. (eds.), *The Technological Level of Soviet Industry* (New Haven: Yale University Press, 1977)

Anders, Karl, *Murder to Order* (London: Ampersand, 1965)

Anderson, John, "The Archives of the Council for Religious Affairs," *Religion, State and Society*, vol. 20 (1992), nos. 3–4.

Andrew, Christopher, *Secret Service: The Making of the British Intelligence Community*, 3rd paperback edition (London: Scepter, 1991)

Andrew, Christopher, *For the President's Eyes Only: Secret Intelligence and the American Presidency from Washington to Bush* (London: HarperCollins, 1995)

Andrew, Christopher, "F. H. Hinsley and the Cambridge Moles: Two Patterns of Intelligence Recruitment," in Langhorne, Richard (ed.), *Diplomacy and Intelligence During the Second World War: Essays in Honor of F. H. Hinsley* (Cambridge: Cambridge University Press, 1985)

Andrew, Christopher, "The Nature of Military Intelligence," in Neilson, Keith, and McKercher, B. J. C. (eds.), *Go Spy the Land: Military Intelligence in History* (London: Praeger, 1992)

Andrew, Christopher, "The Making of the Anglo-American SIGINT Alliance," in Peake, Hayden B., and Halpern, Samuel (eds.), *In the Name of Intelligence: Essays in Honor of Walter Pforzheimer* (Washington: NIBC Press, 1994)

Andrew, Christopher, "Anglo-American–Soviet Intelligence Relations," in Lane, Ann, and Temperley, Howard (eds.), *The Rise and Fall of the Grand Alliance, 1941–45* (London: Macmillan, 1995)

Andrew, Christopher, "An Agenda for Future Research," in Andrew, Christopher, and Jeffreys-Jones, Rhodri (eds.), *Eternal Vigilance? Fifty Years of the CIA* (London: Frank Cass, 1997)

Andrew, Christopher, "Intelligence and International Relations in the Early Cold War," *Review of International Studies*, vol. 24 (1998)

Andrew, Christopher, "The VENONA Secret," in Robertson, K. G. (ed.), *War, Resistance and Intelligence: Essays in Honor of M. R. D. Foot* (Barnsley: Pen and Sword, 1999)

Andrew, Christopher, and Dilks, David, *The Missing Dimension: Governments and Intelligence Communities in the Twentieth Century* (London: Macmillan, 1984)

Andrew, Christopher, and Gordievsky, Oleg, *Le KGB dans le monde, 1917–1990* (Paris: Fayard, 1990)

Andrew, Christopher, and Gordievsky, Oleg, *KGB: The Inside Story of Its Foreign Operations from Lenin to Gorbachev*, paperback edition (London: Sceptre, 1991)

Andrew, Christopher, and Jeffreys-Jones, Rhodri (eds.), *Eternal Vigilance? Fifty Years of the CIA* (London: Frank Cass, 1997)

Antic, Oxana, "The Spread of Modern Cults in the USSR," in Ramet, Sabrina Petra (ed.), *Religious Policy in the Soviet Union* (Cambridge: Cambridge University Press, 1993)

Arbatov, Georgi, *The System* (New York: Times Books, 1992)

Aron, Raymond, *Mémoires: 50 ans de réflexions politiques* (Paris: Julliard, 1983)

Ash, Timothy Garton, *In Europe's Name: Germany and the Divided Continent*, paperback edition (London: Vintage, 1994)

Aucouturier, Alfreda, "Andrey Sinyavsky on the Eve of His Arrest," in Labedz, Leopold and Hayward, Max (eds.), *On Trial: The Case of Sinyavsky (Tertz) and Daniel (Arzhak)* (London: Collins and Harvill Press, 1967)

August, Frantisek, and Rees, David, *Red Star over Prague* (London: Sherwood Press, 1984)

Babris, Peter J., *Silent Churches: Persecution of Religion in the Soviet-dominated Areas* (Arlington Heights, Ill.: Research Publishers, 1978)

Balatsky, V., *Museum in the Catacombs: Guide* (Odessa: Mayak, 1986)

Ball, Desmond, *Soviet Signals Intelligence (SIGINT)*, Canberra Papers on Strategy and Defense, no. 47 (Canberra: Australian National University, 1989)

Ball, Desmond, and Richelson, Jeffrey, *The Ties That Bind* (London: Allen & Unwin, 1995)

Ball, Desmond, and Windren, Robert, "Soviet Signals Intelligence (Sigint): Organization and Management," *Intelligence and National Security*, vol. 4 (1989), no. 4

Bamford, James, *The Puzzle Palace* (Boston: Houghton Mifflin, 1982)

Barker, Elizabeth, *Austria 1918–1972* (London: Macmillan, 1973)

Barron, John, *KGB: The Secret Work of Soviet Secret Agents*, paperback edition (New York: Bantam Books, 1974)

Barron, John, *KGB Today: The Hidden Hand*, paperback edition (London: Coronet Books, 1985)

Barron, John, *Breaking the Ring* (New York: Avon Books, 1988)

Barron, John, Operation Solo: The FBI's Man in the Kremlin (Washington, DC: Regnery, 1996)

Beevor, Antony, *Stalingrad,* paperback edition (Harmondsworth: Penguin, 1999)

Bell, D. S. and Criddle, Byron, *The French Communist Party in the Fifth Republic* (Oxford: Clarendon Press, 1994)

Bell, J. Bowyer, *The Secret Army: The IRA 1916–1979* (Dublin: Poolberg Press, 1990)

Benn, Tony, *Against the Tide: Diaries 1973–6* (London: Hutchinson, 1989)

Benn, Tony, *Conflicts of Interest: Diaries 1977–80* (London: Hutchinson, 1990)

Bennett, G., and Hamilton, K. A. (eds.), *Documents on British Foreign Policy,* series 3, vol. 1: *Britain and the Soviet Union, 1968–1972* (London: The Stationery Office, 1998)

Benson, Roger Louis, *Introductory History of VENONA and Guide to the Translations* (Fort George G. Meade, MD: National Security Agency, 1995)

Benson, Roger Louis, *VENONA Historical Monograph #2: The 1942–43 New-York–Moscow KGB Messages* (Fort George G. Meade, MD: National Security Agency, 1995)

Benson, Roger Louis, *VENONA Historical Monograph #3: The 1944–45 New-York and Washington–Moscow KGB Messages* (Fort George G. Meade, Md.: National Security Agency, 1995)

Benson, Roger Louis, *VENONA Historical Monograph #4: The KGB in San Francisco and Mexico City. The GRU in New York and Washington* (Fort George G. Meade, MD: National Security Agency, 1996)

Benson, Roger Louis, *VENONA Historical Monograph #5: The KGB and GRU in Europe, South America and Australia* (Fort George G. Meade, MD: National Security Agency, 1996)

Benson, Roger Louis, and Warner, Michael (eds.), *VENONA: Soviet Espionage and the American Response, 1939–1957* (Washington, DC: National Security Agency/Central Intelligence Agency, 1996)

Bentley, Elizabeth, *Out of Bondage,* with afterword by Hayden Peake (New York: Ballantine Books, 1988)

Bereanu, Vladimir, and Todorov, Kalin, *The Umbrella Murder* (Bury St. Edmunds: TEL, 1994)

Bernikow, Louise, *Abel,* revised edition (New York: Ballantine, 1982)

Bernstein, Carl, and Politi, Marco, *His Holiness: John Paul II and the Hidden History of Our Time* (London: Doubleday, 1996)

Bessedovsky, Grigori, *Revelations of a Soviet Diplomat* (London: Williams & Norgate, 1931); abridged English translation of *Na Putiakh k Termidoru* (Paris, 1930)

Bethell, Nicholas, *The Last Secret* (London: André Deutsch, 1974)

Bethell, Nicholas, *Spies and Other Secrets* (London: Viking, 1994)

Bird, Leonard, *Costa Rica: The Unarmed Democracy* (London: Sheppard Press, 1984)

Bishop, Patrick, and Mallie, Eamonn, *The Provisional IRA* (London: Heinemann, 1987)

Blake, George, *No Other Choice: An Autobiography* (London: Jonathan Cape, 1990)

Bloch, Sidney, and Reddaway, Peter, *Russia's Political Hospitals: The Abuse of Psychiatry in the Soviet Union* (London: Victor Gonancz, 1977)

Blum, Howard, *I Pledge Allegiance* (New York: Simon & Schuster, 1987)

Blunt, Anthony, "From Bloomsbury to Marxism," *Studio International* (November 1973)

Bociurkiw, Bohdan, "Suppression de l'Église gréco-catholique ukrainienne après la deuxième guerre mondiale en l'URSS et en Pologne. Une comparaison," in *Millenium of Christianity in Ukraine: A Symposium* (Ottawa: Saint Paul University, 1987)

Boffa, Giuseppe, *Inside the Khrushchev Era,* Marzani, Carl (trans.) (London: George Allen & Unwin, 1960)

Bohlen, Charles E., *Witness to History 1919–1969* (London: Weidenfeld & Nicolson, 1973)

Bonner, Elena, *Alone Together* (London: Collins Harvill, 1986)

Booth, John A., *The End and the Beginning: The Nicaraguan Revolution,* 2nd edition (Boulder, Colorado: Westview Press, 1985)

Borecky, Bishop Isidore, "The Church in Ukraine–1988," *Religion in Communist Lands,* vol. 17 (1989), no. 2

Borovik, Genrikh, *The Philby Files* (London: Little, Brown, 1994)

Bothwell, Robert, and Granatstein, J. L. (eds.), *The Gouzenko Transcripts* (Ottawa: Deneau, n.d.)

Bourdeaux, Michael, *Risen Indeed: Lessons in Faith from the USSR* (London: Darton, Longman and Todd, 1983)

Bourdeaux, Michael, *Gorbachev, Glasnost & the Gospel* (London: Hodder & Stoughton, 1990)

Boyes, Roger, *The Naked President: A Political Life of Lech Walesa* (London: Secker & Warburg, 1994)

Boyle, Andrew, *The Climate of Treason* (London: Hutchinson, 1979)

Brandt, Willy, *My Road to Berlin* (London: Peter Davies, 1960)

Brandt, Willy, *People and Politics: The Years 1960–1975* (London: Collins, 1978)

Brandt, Willy, *Erinnerungen* (Frankfurt: Propyläen, 1989)

Brook-Shepherd, Gordon, *The Storm Birds* (London: Weidenfeld & Nicolson, 1988)

Brook-Shepherd, Gordon, *Iron Maze: The Western Secret Services and the Bolsheviks* (London: Macmillan, 1998)

Brovkin, Vladimir N., *Behind the Front Lines of the Civil War: Political Parties and Social Movements in Russia, 1918–1922* (Princeton: Princeton University Press, 1994)

Brown, Archie, *The Gorbachev Factor* (Oxford: Oxford University Press, 1996)

Brunet, Jean-Paul, *Jacques Doriot: du communisme au fascisme* (Paris: Éditions Balland, 1986)

Brusnitsin, Nikolai, *Openness and Espionage* (Moscow: Military Publishing House, 1990)

Budenz, Louis, *Men Without Faces: The Communist Conspiracy in the United States* (New York: Harper and Brothers, 1948)

Bulgakov, Mikhail, *The Master and Margarita*, Ginsburg, Mirra (trans.) (New York: Grove Weidenfeld, 1967)

Bulloch, John, and Miller, Henry, *Spy Ring* (London: Secker & Warburg, 1961)

Burke, James F., "Recently Released Material on Soviet Intelligence Operations," *Intelligence and National Security*, vol. 8 (1993), no. 2

Burrin, Philippe, *La Dérive Fasciste: Doriot, Déat, Bergery, 1933–1945* (Paris: Éditions du Seuil, 1986)

Buton, Philippe, *Les lendemains qui déchantent: Le Parti communiste français à la Libération* (Paris: Presses de la Fondation Nationale des Sciences Politiques, 1993)

Cairncross, John, *When Polygamy was Made a Sin* (London: Routledge, 1974)

Cairncross, John, *La Fontaine Fables and Other Poems* (Gerrards Cross: Colin Smythe, 1982)

Cairncross, John, *The Enigma Spy: The Story of the Man Who Changed the Course of World War Two* (London: Century, 1997)

Carlton, David, *Anthony Eden: A Biography* (London: Allen Lane, 1981)

Cecil, Robert, *A Divided Life* (London: Bodley Head, 1988)

Cecil, Robert, "The Cambridge Comintern," in Andrew, Christopher, and Dilks, David, *The Missing Dimension: Governments and Intelligence Communities in the Twentieth Century* (London: Macmillan, 1984)

Central Intelligence Agency, *The Rote Kapelle: The CIA's History of Soviet Intelligence and Espionage Networks in Western Europe 1936–1945* (Washington, DC: University Publications of America, 1984)

Chambers, Whittaker, *Witness* (New York: Random House, 1952)

Chazov, Yevgeni, *Zdorov'ye i Vlast'* (Moscow: Novosti, 1992)

Childs, David, and Popplewell, Richard, *The Stasi: The East German Intelligence and Security Service* (London: Macmillan, 1996)

Colaiaco, James A., *Martin Luther King, Jr: Apostle of Militant Nonviolence* (London: Macmillan, 1988)

Cole, D. J., *Geoffrey Prime: The Imperfect Spy* (London: Robert Hale, 1998)

Colitt, Leslie, *Spy Master: The Real-Life Karla, His Moles, and the East German Secret Police* (London: Robson, 1996)

Colville, John, *The Fringes of Power* (London: Hodder & Stoughton, 1985)

Conquest, Robert, *The Great Terror: A Reassessment*, revised edition (London: Hutchinson, 1990)

Conquest, Robert, "Playing Down the Gulag," *The Times Literary Supplement* (February 24, 1995)

Coogan, Tim Pat, *The IRA*, revised edition (London: HarperCollins, 1995)

Coogan, Tim Pat, *The Troubles: Ireland's Ordeal 1966–1995 and the Search for Peace* (London: Hutchinson, 1995)

Cornelissen, Igor, *De GPOe op de Overtoom* (Amsterdam: Van Gennep, 1989)

Corson, William R., and Crowley, Robert T., *The New KGB: Engine of Soviet Power*, revised edition (New York: Quill, 1986)

Cossutta, Armando, *Lo Strappo: USA, URSS movimento operaio di fronte alla crisi internazionale* (Milan: Arnaldo Mondadori, 1982)

Costello, John, *Ten Days to Destiny* (New York: William Morrow, 1991)

Costello, John, and Tsarev, Oleg, *Deadly Illusions* (London: Century, 1993)

Cradock, Percy, *In Pursuit of British Interests: Reflections on Foreign Policy under Margaret Thatcher and John Major* (London: John Murray, 1997)

Crampton, R. J., *Eastern Europe in the Twentieth Century* (London: Routledge, 1994)

Crankshaw, Edward, *Russia by Daylight* (London: Michael Joseph, 1951)

Crankshaw, Edward, *Putting up with the Russians, 1947–1984* (London: Macmillan, 1984)

Cronin, Audrey Kurth, *Great Power Politics and the Struggle over Austria, 1945–1955* (Ithaca: Cornell University Press, 1986)

Crozier, Brian, *Free Agent* (London: HarperCollins, 1993) Davies, Norman, *Europe: A History*, paperback edition (London, Pimlico, 1997)

Davies, Norman, *Europe: A History*, paperback edition (London: Pimlico, 1997)

Dawisha, Karen, *The Kremlin and the Prague Spring* (Berkeley, Ca.: University of California Press, 1984)

Dawson III, Joseph G. (ed.), *The Louisiana Governors: From Ibberville to Edwards* (Baton Rouge, La.: Louisiana State University Press, 1990)

Dear, I.C.B., and Foot, M.R.D. (eds.), *The Oxford Companion to the Second World War* (Oxford: Oxford University Press, 1995)

Dedijer, Vladimir, *Tito Speaks: His Self-Portrait and Struggle with Stalin* (London: Weidenfeld & Nicolson (1953))

Degras, Jane (ed.), *Documents on Soviet Foreign Policy*, 3 vols (London: Oxford University Press, 1951–3)

De-la-Noy, Michael, *Mervyn Stockwood: A Lonely Life* (London: Mowbray, 1996)

DeLoach, Cartha D. "Deke," *Hoover's FBI: The Inside Story of Hoover's Trusted Lieutenant* (Washington, DC: Regnery, 1995)

Deutscher, Isaac, *Trotsky*, vol. 2: *The Prophet Unarmed, 1921–1929;* vol. 3: *The Prophet Outcast, 1929–1940*, paperback edition (Oxford: Oxford University Press, 1970)

Dilks, David (ed.), *The Diaries of Sir Alexander Cadogan, OM, 1938–1945* (London: Cassell, 1971)

Dilks, David, ??? Andrew, Christopher, and Dilks, David (eds.), *The Missing Dimension: Governments and Intelligence Communities in the Twentieth Century* (London: Macmillan, 1984)

Djilas, Milovan, *Tito: The Story from the Inside* (London: Weidenfeld & Nicolson, 1981)

Djilas, Milovan, *Rise and Fall* (London: Macmillan, 1985)

Dobbs, Michael, *Down with Big Brother: The Fall of the Soviet Empire* (London: Bloomsbury, 1997)

Dobrynin, Anatoly, *In Confidence* (New York: Times Books, 1995)

Documents of the Christian Committee for the Defense of Believers' Rights in the USSR, 12 vols. (San Francisco: Washington Research Center, 1977–80)

Donovan, James, *Strangers on a Bridge: The Case of Colonel Abel* (London: Secker & Warburg, 1964)

Dorril, Stephen, and Ramsay, Robin, *Smear: Wilson and the Secret State* (London: Grafton, 1992)

Draper, Theodore, *The Roots of American Communism* (New York: Viking Press, 1957)

Driberg, Tom, *Guy Burgess: A Portrait with Background* (London: Weidenfeld & Nicolson, 1956)

Driberg, Tom, *Ruling Passions: The Autobiography of Tom Driberg* (London: Quartet, 1978)

Dubček, Alexander, *Hope Dies Last: The Autobiography of Alexander Dub'cek* (New York: Kodansha International, 1993)

Dupuis, Jérôme, and Pontaut, Jean-Marie, "Charles Hernu était un agent de l'Est," *L'Express* (October 31, 1996)

Dzhirkvelov, Ilya, *Secret Servant* (London: Collins, 1987)

Earley, Pete, *Confessions of a Spy: The Real Story of Aldrich Ames* (London: Hodder & Stoughton, 1997)

L'élection présidentielle, 26 avril–10 mai 1981 (Paris: Le Monde, 1981)

Ellis, Jane (ed.), *Three Generations of Suffering*, 2nd edition (London: Hodder & Stoughton, 1979)

Ellis, Jane, *The Russian Orthodox Church: A Contemporary History* (London: Routledge, 1988)

Erickson, John, *The Road to Stalingrad*, paperback edition (London: Panther Books, 1985)

Faligot, Roger, and Kauffer, Rémi, *As-tu vu Crémet?* (Paris: Fayard, 1991)

Favier, Pierre, and Martin-Roland, Michel, *La décennie Mitterrand*, vol. 1: *Les ruptures* (Paris: Seuil, 1990); vol. 2: *Les épreuves* (Paris: Seuil, 1991)

Feklisov, Aleksandr, *Za okeanom i na ostrove: Zapiski razvedchika* (Moscow: DEM, 1994)

Felfe, Heinz, *Im Dienst des Gegners: 10 Jahre Moskans Mann im BND* (Hamburg: Rasch und Roehring Verlag, 1986)

Figes, Orlando, *A People's Tragedy: The Russian Revolution 1891–1924* (London: Jonathan Cape, 1996)

Fischer, Ben, " 'Mr. Guver:' Anonymous Soviet Letter to the FBI," *[CIA] Center for the Study of Intelligence Newsletter* no. 7 (1997)

Fleishman, Lazar, *Boris Pasternak: The Poet and His Politics* (Cambridge, Mass.: Harvard University Press, 1990)

Fletcher, Raymond, *£60 a Second on Defence* (London: MacGibbon and Kee, 1963)

Flocken, Jan von, and Scholz, Michael F., *Ernst Wollweber: Saboteur–Minister–Unperson* (Berlin: Aufbau-Verlag, 1994)

Floridi, Alexis U., SJ, "The Church of the Martyrs and the Ukrainian Millennium," in *Millennium of Christianity in Ukraine: A Symposium* (Ottawa: Saint Paul University, 1987)

Foot, M.R.D., *SOE* (London: BBC, 1984)

Friedly, Michael, and Gallen, David, *Martin Luther King: The FBI File* (New York: Carroll & Graf, 1993)

Frolik, Josef, *The Frolik Defection* (London: Leo Cooper, 1975)

Fursenko, Alexander, and Naftali, Timothy, *"One Hell of a Gamble:" Khrushchev, Kennedy, Castro and the Cuban Missile Crisis, 1958–1964* (London: John Murray, 1997)

Fursenko, Alexander, and Naftali, Timothy, "Using KGB Documents: The Scali–Feklisov Channel in the Cuban Missile Crisis," *Cold War International History Project Bulletin*, no. 5 (1995), pp. 58–62.

Fursenko, Alexander, and Naftali, Timothy, "Soviet Intelligence and the Cuban Missile Crisis," *Intelligence and National Security*, vol. 13 (1998), no. 3

Gardner, A. R., "The Soviet Decision to Invade Czechoslovakia," Thesis for MPhil in International Relations, University of Cambridge (1996)

Garlinski, Jozef, *Intercept* (London: Dent, 1979)

Garrow, David, *The FBI and Martin Luther King, Jr.* (New York: Penguin, 1981)

Garthoff, Raymond L., "The KGB Reports to Gorbachev," *Intelligence and National Security*, vol. 11 (1996), no. 2

Garthoff, Raymond L., "Andropov's Report to Brezhnev on the KGB in 1967," *Cold War International History Project Bulletin*, no. 10 (1998)

Garthoff, Raymond L., "The Conference on Poland, 1980–1982: Internal Crisis, International Dimensions," *Cold War International History Project Bulletin*, no. 10 (1998)

Gates, Robert M., *From the Shadows: The Ultimate Insider's Story of Five Presidents and How They Won the Cold War* (New York: Simon & Schuster, 1996)

Genscher, Hans-Dietrich, *Erinnerungen* (Berlin: Siedler Verlag, 1995)

Gentry, Curt, *J. Edgar Hoover: The Man and His Secrets* (New York: W. W. Norton, 1991)

Ginsborg, Paul, *A History of Contemporary Italy: Society and Politics 1943–1988* (Harmondsworth: Penguin, 1990)

Glantz, David M., *Soviet Military Intelligence in War* (London: Frank Cass, 1990)

Golitsyn, Anatoli, *New Lies for Old* (New York: Dodd, Mead, 1984)

Golson, G. Barry (ed.), *The Playboy Interview* (New York: Wideview Books, 1981)

Gorbachev, Mikhail, *The August Coup: The Truth and the Lessons* (London: HarperCollins, 1991)

Gorbachev, Mikhail, *Memoirs* (London: Doubleday, 1996)

Gordievsky, Oleg, *Next Stop Execution* (London: Macmillan, 1995)

Gorodetsky, Gabriel, *Stafford Cripps' Mission to Moscow 1940–42* (Cambridge: Cambridge University Press, 1984)

Gorodetsky, Gabriel, *Grand Delusion: Stalin and the German Invasion of Russia* (New Haven, Conn.: Yale University Press, 1999)

Grachev, Andrei, *Kremlevskaya Khronika* (Moscow: EKSMO, 1994)

Granatstein, J. L., and Stafford, David, *Spy Wars: Espionage and Canada from Gouzenko to Glasnost* (Toronto: Key Porter, 1990)

Granville, Johanna, "Imre Nagy, Hesitant Revolutionary," *Cold War International History Project Bulletin*, no. 5 (1995)

Gribin, N. P., *Tragediya Olstera* (Moscow, 1980)

Grigorenko, Petro G., *Memoirs* (London: Harvill Press, 1983)

Grigulevich, I. R., *Myatezhnaya Tserkov v Latinskoi Amerike* (Moscow: Nauka, 1972)

Grigulevich, I. R., *Khristiantsvo i Rus* (Moscow: Nauka, 1988)

Grigulevich, I. R., and Koslov, S. Y. (eds.), *Contemporary Ethnic and Racial Problems* (Moscow: Progress Publishers, 1977)

Grigulevich-Lavretski, J. [Grigulevich, I. R.], *La Iglesia y la Sociedad en América Latina*, 2nd edition (Moscow: Academia de Ciencias de la URSS, 1983)

Gromyko, Andrei, *Memories* (London: Hutchinson, 1989)

Hager, Nicky, *Secret Power: New Zealand's Role in the International Spy Network* (Nelson, New Zealand: Craig Potton, 1996)

Hanson, Philip, *Soviet ??? Espionage: Some New Information* (London: Royal Institute of International Affairs, 1987)

Harriss, Joseph, "The Gospel According to Marx," *Reader's Digest* (February 1993)

Haslam, Jonathan, *Soviet Foreign Policy 1930–33: The Impact of the Depression* (London: Macmillan, 1983)

Haslam, Jonathan, "Stalin's Fears of a Separate Peace 1942," *Intelligence and National Security*, vol. 8 (1993)

Haslam, Jonathan, "Russia's Seat at the Table: A Place Denied or a Place Delayed?," *International Affairs*, vol. 74 (1998), no. 1

Hauner, Milan, "The Prague Spring–Twenty Years After" in Stone, Norman, and Strouhal, Eduard (eds.), *Czechoslovakia: Crossroads and Crises, 1918–88* (London: Macmillan, 1989)

Haynes, John Earl, and Klehr, Harvey, *VENONA: Decoding Soviet Espionage in America* (New Haven, Conn.: Yale University Press, 1999)

Haynes, John Earl, and Klehr, Harvey, " 'Moscow Gold,' Confirmed at Last?," *Labor History*, vol. 33 (1992), no. 2

Heaps, Leo, *Hugh Hambleton, Spy* (Toronto: Methuen, 1981)

Healey, Dorothy Ray, and Isserman, Maurice, *Dorothy Healey Remembers: A Life in the American Communist Party* (New York: Oxford University Press, 1990)

Hellman, Stephen, "The Difficult Birth of the Democratic Party of the Left," in Hellman, Stephen, and Pasqino, Gianfranco (eds.), *Italian Politics*, vol. 7 (London: Pinter, 1992)

Hennessy, Peter, *Never Again: Britain 1945–1951*, paperback edition (London: Vintage, 1993)

Hinsley, F. H., and Stripp, Alan (eds.), *Codebreakers: The Inside Story of Bletchley Park* (Oxford: Oxford University Press, 1993)

Hobsbawm, Eric, *Age of Extremes: The Short Twentieth Century, 1914–1991*, paperback edition (London: Abacus, 1995)

Hodges, Donald C., *Intellectual Origins of the Nicaraguan Revolution* (Austin, Texas: University of Texas Press, 1987)

Höhne, Heinz, and Zolling, Hermann, *The General was a Spy* (London: Pan, 1972))

Holloway, David, *Stalin and the Bomb* (New Haven: Yale University Press, 1994)

Holloway, David, "Sources for *Stalin and the Bomb*," *Cold War International History Project Bulletin*, no. 4 (1994)

Hook, Sidney, *Out of Step: An Unquiet Life in the 20th Century* (New York: Harper & Row, 1987)

Hosking, Geoffrey A., *A History of the Soviet Union* (London: Fontana, 1985)

Houghton, Harry, *Operation Portland: The Autobiography of a Spy* (London: Rupert Hart-Davis, 1972)

Hruby, Peter, *Fools and Heroes: The Changing Role of Communist Intellectuals in Czechoslovakia* (Oxford: Pergamon Press, 1980)

Hudson, Darrill, *The World Council of Churches in International Affairs* (London: Royal Institute of International Affairs, 1977)

Humphreys, *Latin America and the Second World War, vol. 1: 1939–1942* (London: Athlone, 1981)

Huntington, Samuel, P., *The Crash of Civilizations and the Remaking of World Order* (New York: Simon & Schuster, ???)

Hurt, Henry, *Reasonable Doubt: An Investigation into the Assassination of John F. Kennedy* (London: Sidgwick & Jackson, 1986)

Hyde, H. Montgomery, *George Blake, Superspy* (London: Constable, 1987)

The Intelligence War in 1941 (Washington, DC: CIA Center for the Study of Intelligence, 1991)

Isaacson, Walter, *Kissinger: A Biography* (New York: Simon & Schuster, 1992)

Joesten, Joachim, *Oswald: Assassin or Fall Guy?* (New York: Marzani & Munsell; London: Merlin Press, 1964)

Journal of the Moscow Patriarchate (Moscow: Moscow Patriarch 1971–93)

Judy, Richard W., "The Case of Computer Technology" in Wasowski, Stanislaw (ed.), *East–West Trade and the Technology Gap: A Political and Economic Appraisal* (New York: Praeger, 1970)

Jukes, Geoff, "The Soviets and 'Ultra,' " *Intelligence and National Security*, vol. 3 (1988), no. 2

Kahn, David, *The Codebreakers* (New York: Macmillan, 1967)

Kahn, David, "Pearl Harbor and the Inadequacy of Cryptanalysis," *Cryptologia*, vol. 15 (1991)

Kahn, David, "Soviet Comint in the Cold War," *Cryptologia*, vol. 22 (1998)

Kalugin, Oleg, *Spymaster: My 32 Years in Intelligence and Espionage against the West* (London: Smith Gryphon, 1994)

Karpínski, Jakub, *Poland Since 1944: A Portrait of Years* (Boulder, Colorado: Westview Press, 1995)

Kasparov, Gary, *Child of Change: The Autobiography of Gary Kasparov* (London: Hutchinson, 1987)

Keene, Raymond, *Karpov–Korchnoi 1978: The Inside Story of the Match* (London: Batsford, 1978)

Kelly, Phil, "The Deportations of Philip Agee" in Agee, Philip, and Wolf, Louis, *Dirty Work: The CIA in Western Europe* (London: Zed Press, 1978)

Kennan, George, *Memoirs 1950–1963* (New York: Pantheon Books, 1983)

Kennedy-Pipe, Caroline, *Russia and the World, 1917–1991* (London: Arnold, 1998)

Kessler, Pamela, *Undercover Washington* (McLean, Va.: EPM Publications, 1992)

Kessler, Ronald, *Spy vs. Spy* (New York: Scribner's, 1988)

Kessler, Ronald, *Inside the CIA* (New York: Simon & Schuster, 1991)

Kessler, Ronald, *The FBI: Inside the World's Most Powerful Law Enforcement Agency* (New York: Pocket Books, 1993)

Khokhlov, Nikolai, *In the Name of Conscience* (London: Frederick Muller, 1960)

Kimball, Warren, *Forged in War: Churchill, Roosevelt and the Second World War* (London: HarperCollins, 1997)

King Jr., Martin Luther, *Why We Can't Wait* (New York: Harper & Row, 1964)

Kissinger, Henry, *White House Years* (Boston: Little, Brown, 1979)

Kissinger, Henry, *Years of Upheaval* (Boston: Little, Brown, 1982)

Kissinger, Henry, *Diplomacy* (New York: Simon & Schuster, 1994)

Klehr, Harvey, and Haynes, John Earl, *The American Communist Movement: Storming Heaven Itself* (New York: Twayne, 1992)

Klehr, Harvey; Haynes, John Earl; and Firsov, Fridrikh Igorevich, *The Secret World of American Communism* (New Haven: Yale University Press, 1995)

Klehr, Harvey; Haynes, John Earl; and Firsov, Fridrikh Igorevich, *The Soviet World of American Communism* (New Haven: Yale University Press, 1998)

Knight, Amy W., *The KGB: Police and Politics in the Soviet Union* (London: Unwin Hyman, 1988)

Knight, Amy W., *Beria: Stalin's First Lieutenant* (Princeton: Princeton University Press, 1993)

Knight, Amy W., *Spies Without Cloaks: The KGB's Successors* (Princeton: Princeton University Press, 1996)

Knight, Robert, "Harold Macmillan and the Cossacks: Was There a Klagenfurt Conspiracy?," *Intelligence and National Security,* vol. 1 (1986), no. 2

Knightley, Phillip, *Philby: The Life and Views of the KGB Masterspy* (London: André Deutsch, 1988)

Kopácsi, Sándor, *Au nom de la classe ouvrière* (Paris: Editions Robert Laffont, 1979)

Korchnoi, Viktor, *Chess is My Life: Autobiography and Games* (London: Batsford, 1977)

Kramer, Mark, "The Prague Spring and the Soviet Invasion of Czechoslovakia: New Interpretations," *Cold War International History Project Bulletin,* part 1: no. 2 (1992); part 2: no. 3 (1993)

Kramer, Mark, "Poland, 1980–81: Soviet Policy During the Polish Crisis," *Cold War International History Project Bulletin,* no. 5 (1995)

Kramer, Mark (ed.), "Declassified Soviet Documents on the Polish Crisis," *Cold War International History Project Bulletin,* no. 5 (1995)

Kramer, Mark (ed.), "The Warsaw Pact and the Polish Crisis of 1980–81: Honecker's Call for Military Intervention," *Cold War International History Project Bulletin,* no. 5 (1995)

Kramer, Mark (ed.), "Ukraine and the Soviet–Czechoslovak Crisis of 1968 (Part I): New Evidence from the Diary of Petro Shelest," *Cold War International History Project Bulletin,* no. 10 (1998)

Kramer, Michael, and Roberts, Sam, *I Never Wanted to be Vice-President of Anything!: An Investigative Biography of Nelson Rockefeller* (New York: Basic Books, 1976)

Krasikov, Anatoly, *From Democracy to Dictatorship: Spanish Reportage* (Oxford: Pergamon Press, 1984)

Kriegel, Annie, and Courtois, Stéphane, *Eugen Fried: le grand secret du PCF* (Paris: Seuil, 1997)

Krivitsky, Walter, *I was Stalin's Agent* (London: Hamish Hamilton, 1939)

Kurczewski, Jurcek, *The Resurrection of Rights in Poland* (Oxford: Clarendon Press, 1993)

Kusin, Vladimir V., *From Dubcek to Charter 77: A Study of "Normalization" in Czechoslovakia 1968–1978* (Edinburgh: Q Press, 1978)

Kuzichkin, Vladimir, *Inside the KGB: Myth and Reality* (London: André Deutsch, 1990)

Labedz, Leopold and Hayward, Max (eds.), *On Trial: The Case of Sinyavsky (Tertz) and Daniel (Arzhak)* (London: Collins and Harvill Press, 1967)

Lamphere, Robert, *The FBI–KGB War: A Special Agent's Story* (London: W. H. Allen, 1987)

Lane, Mark, *Rush to Judgement* (New York: Holt, Rinehart & Winston, 1966)

Lane, Mark, *Plausible Denial: Was the CIA Involved in the Assassination of JFK?* (London: Plexus, 1992)

Lavretsky, I. R. [Grigulevich, I. R.], "Un análisis critico de la *Hispanic American Historical Review,* 1956–8" in Ortega y Medina, J. A. (ed.), *Historiografiá Soviética Iberoamericanista, 1945–60* (Mexico City: Universitad Nacional Autónoma de México, 1961)

Lawson, Dominic, *The Inner Game* (London: Macmillan, 1993)

Lefever, Ernest W., *Nairobi to Vancouver: The World Council of Churches and the World, 1975–87* (Washington, DC: Ethics and Public Policy Center, 1987)

Leggett, George, *The Cheka: Lenin's Political Police* (Oxford: Clarendon Press, 1981)

Legris, Michel, *Le Monde tel qu'il est* (Paris: Plon, 1976)

Lenin, Vladimir Ilich, *Collected Works,* 47 vols. (London: Lawrence and Wishart, 1960–80)

Leonhard, Wolfgang, *Child of the Revolution* (London: Collins, 1957)

Lévesque, Jacques, *The Enigma of 1989: The USSR and the Liberation of Eastern Europe* (Berkeley, Ca., 1997)

Levi, Peter, *Boris Pasternak* (London: Hutchinson, 1990)

Levine, Isaac Don, *The Mind of an Assassin* (London: Weidenfeld & Nicolson, 1959)

Lindsey, Robert, *The Falcon and the Snowman* (New York: Pocket, 1979)

Lindsey, Robert, *The Flight of the Falcon* (New York: Pocket, 1981)

Littell, Robert (ed.), *The Czech Black Book Prepared by the Czechoslovak Academy of Sciences* (London: Pall Mall Press, 1969)

Litván, György (ed.), *The Hungarian Revolution of 1956: Reform, Revolt and Repression 1953–1963* (London: Longman, 1996)

Luchterhandt, Otto, "The Council for Religious Affairs" in Ramet, Sabrina Petra (ed.), *Religious Policy in the Soviet Union* (Cambridge: Cambridge University Press, 1993)

Lyalin, S. N. *et al.* (eds.), *Osoboie Zadanie* (Moscow, 1968)

Macdonald, Callum A., "The Politics of Intervention: The United States and Argentina, 1941–1946," *Journal of Latin American Studies,* vol. 12 (1980), no. 2

Mailer, Norman, *Oswald's Tale: An American Mystery* (London: Little, Brown, 1995)

Mangold, Tom, *Cold Warrior; James Jesus Angleton: the CIA's Master Spy Hunter* (New York: Simon & Schuster, 1991)

Mark, Eduard, "Venona's Source 19 and the 'Trident' Conference of 1943: Diplomacy or Espionage?," *Intelligence and National Security,* vol. 13 (1998), no. 2

Marshall, Barbara, *Willy Brandt* (London: Cardinal, 1990)

Massing, Hede, *This Deception* (New York: Ivy Books, 1987)

Maxwell, Kenneth, *The Making of Portuguese Democracy* (Cambridge: Cambridge University Press, 1995)

Mayhew, Christopher, *Time to Explain* (London: Hutchinson, 1987)

Medlicott, W. N., *et al., Documents on British Foreign Policy* (London: HMSO, 1949 onwards)

Medvedev, Zhores, *Andropov: His Life and Death,* revised edition (Oxford: Basil Blackwell, 1984)

Meerson, Michael A., "The Political Philosophy of the Russian Orthodox Episcopate in the Soviet Period" in Hosking, Geoffrey A. (ed.), *Church, Nation and State in Russia and Ukraine* (London: Macmillan, 1991)

Melgounov, Sergei Petrovich, *The Red Terror in Russia* (London: J. M. Dent, 1925)

Melton, H. Keith, *The Ultimate Spy Book* (London: Dorling Kindersley, 1996)

Miller, Joan, *One Girl's War: Personal Experiences in MI5's Most Secret Station* (Dingle, Ireland: Brandon, 1986)

Milligan, Timothy P., "Spies, Ciphers and 'Zitadelle:' Intelligence and the Battle of Kursk, 1943," *Journal of Contemporary History,* vol. 22 (1987), no. 2

Mitchell, Ian, *The Cost of a Reputation; Aldington Versus Tolstoy: The Causes, Course and Consequences of the Notorious Libel Case* (Lagavulin, isle of Islay: Topical Books, 1997)

Modin, Yuri, *My Five Cambridge Friends* (London: Headline, 1994)

Mortimer, Edward, *The Rise of the French Communist Party, 1920–1947* (London: Faber & Faber, 1984)

Moskalenko, Kirill S., "Beria's Arrest," *Moscow News* (1990), no. 23

Moynihan, Daniel Patrick, *Secrecy: The American Experience* (New Haven: Yale University Press, 1998)

Mujal-León, Eusebio, *Communism and Political Change in Spain* (Bloomington: Indiana University Press, 1983)

Murphy, David E., Kondrashev, Sergei A., and Bailey, George, *Battleground Berlin: CIA vs. KGB in the Cold War* (New Haven: Yale University Press, 1997)

Myagkov, Aleksei, *Inside the KGB: An Exposé by an Officer of the Third Directorate* (Richmond, Surrey: Foreign Affairs, 1976)

National Security Agency, *Introductory History of VENONA and Guide to the Translations* (Fort Meade, MD: NSA, 1995)

Nationalrat der Nationalen Front des Demokratischen Deutschland, *Braunbuch: Kriegs-und-Nazi Verbrecher in der Bundesrepublik* (East Berlin: Dokumentationszentrum der Staatlichen Archivvervaltung der DDR, 1965)

Nationalrat der Nationalen Front des Demokratischen Deutschland, *Graubuch: Expansionspolitik und Neo-Nazismus in Westdeutschland–Eine Dokumentation* (East Berlin: Dokumentationszentrum der Staatlichen Archivvervaltung der DDR, 1967)

Nechiporenko, Oleg, *Passport to Assassination* (New York: Birch Lane Press, 1993)

Nelson, Steve, Barrett, James R., and Ruck, Rob, *Steve Nelson, American Radical* (Pittsburgh: University of Pittsburgh Press, 1981)

"New Evidence on Soviet Intelligence: The KGB's 1967 Annual Report," *Cold War International History Project Bulletin*, no. 10 (1998)

Newton, Ronald C., "Disorderly Succession: Great Britain, the United States and the 'Nazi Menace' in Argentina, 1938–1947," in Tella, Guido di, and Cameron Watt, D. (eds.), *Argentina Between the Great Powers, 1939–1946* (London: Macmillan, 1989)

Newton, Verne W., *The Butcher's Embrace: The Philby Conspirators in Washington* (London: Macdonald, 1991)

Norman, Edward, *Christianity and the World Order* (Oxford: Oxford University Press, 1979)

Nureyev, Rudolf, *Nureyev: An Autobiography with Pictures*, Bland, Alexander (ed.) (London: Hodder & Stoughton, 1962)

Oppenheim, Raymond, "Are the Furov Reports Authentic?" in Hosking, Geoffrey A. (ed.), *Church, Nation and State in Russia and Ukraine* (London: Macmillan, 1991)

O'Riordan, Michael, *Connolly Column: The Story of the Irishmen Who Fought in the Ranks of the International Brigades in the National-Revolutionary War of the Spanish People* (Dublin: New Books, 1979)

Orlov, Aleksandr, *The Secret History of Stalin's Crimes* (London: Jarrold's, 1954)

Orlov, Aleksandr, *A Handbook of Intelligence and Guerrilla Warfare* (Ann Arbor, Mich.: University of Michigan Press, 1963)

Orwell, George, *Nineteen Eighty-Four* (London: Secker & Warburg, 1949)

Ostryakov, Sergei Zakharovich, *Voyennye Chekisty* (Moscow: Voyenizdat, 1979)

An Outline of the History of the CPCz, 2nd updated edition (Prague: Orbis Press Agency, 1985)

Overy, Richard, *Russia's War* (London: Allen Lane, The Penguin Press, 1998)

Page, Bruce, Leitch, David and Knightley, Phillip, *Philby: The Spy Who Betrayed a Generation*, paperback edition (London: Sphere, 1977)

Paillole, Paul, *Notre espion chez Hitler* (Paris: Laffont, 1985)

Parker, R. A. C., *Chamberlain and Appeasement: British Policy and the Coming of the Second World War* (London: Macmillan, 1993)

Pastor, Robert A., *Condemned to Repetition* (Princeton, N.J.: Princeton University Press, 1988)

Pawley, Margaret, *Donald Coggan: Servant of Christ* (London: SPCK, 1987)

Peake, Hayden B., "OSS and the Venona Decrypts," *Intelligence and National Security*, vol. 12 (1997), no. 3

Peet, John, *The Long Engagement: Memoirs of a Cold War Legend* (London: Fourth Estate, 1989)

Pelikan, Jaroslav, *Confessor between East and West: A Portrait of Ukrainian Cardinal Josyf Slipyj* (Grand Rapids, Mich.: William B. Eerdmanns, 1990)

Penrose, Barrie, and Freeman, Simon, *Conspiracy of Silence* (London: Grafton Books, 1986)

Penton, M. James, *Apocalypse Delayed: The Story of Jehovah's Witnesses* (Toronto: University of Toronto Press, 1985)

Percival, John, *Nureyev: Aspects of the Dancer* (London: Faber and Faber, 1976)

Petrov, Vladimir and Evdokia, *Empire of Fear* (London: André Deutsch, 1956)

Pezzullo, Lawrence, and Pezzullo, Ralph, *At the Fall of Somoza* (Pittsburgh: University of Pittsburgh Press, 1993)

Philby, Kim, *My Silent War*, paperback edition (London: Granada, 1969)

Pike, David Wingeate, *In the Service of Stalin: The Spanish Communists in Exile, 1939–1945* (Oxford: Clarendon Press, 1993)

Pikhoya, R. G., "Chekhoslovakiya 1968 god," *Novaya a Noveishaya Istoriya*, part 1 (1994) no. 6, pp. 3–20; part 2 (1995), no. 1, pp. 24–8

Pincher, Chapman, *Too Secret Too Long* (London: New English Library, 1985)

Pipes, Richard, *The Russian Revolution, 1899–1919* (London: Collins Harvill, 1990)

Pipes, Richard, *Russia under the Bolshevik Regime, 1919–1924*, paperback edition (London: HarperCollins, 1995)

Pipes, Richard (ed.), *The Unknown Lenin: From the Secret Archive* (New Haven, Conn.: Yale University Press, 1996)

Polyakov, Yevgeni, "Activities of the Moscow Patriarchate in 1991," *Religion, State and Society*, vol. 22 (1994), no. 2

Porch, Douglas, *The French Secret Services* (New York: Farrar, Straus & Giroux, 1995)

Poretsky, Elizabeth, *Our Own People* (London: Oxford University Press, 1969)

Posner, Gerald, *Case Closed: Lee Harvey Oswald and the Assassination of JFK* (New York: Random House, 1993)

Pospielovsky, Dimitry, "The 'Best Years' of Stalin's Church Policy (1942–1948) in the Light of Archival Documents," *Religion, State and Society*, vol. 25 (1997), no. 2

Prange, Gordon W. *et al.*, *Target Tokyo: The Story of the Sorge Spy Ring* (New York: McGraw Hill, 1985)

Primakov, Yevgeni, *et al.*, *Ocherki Istorii Rossiyskoi Vneshnei Razvedki*, vol. 1: *Pre–1917; vol. 2: 1917–33; vol. 3: 1933–41* (Moscow: Mezhdunarodnye Otnosheniya, 1995–7)

Prittie, Terence, *The Velvet Chancellors: A History of Post-War Germany* (London: Frederick Muller, 1979)

Radosh, Ronald, and Milton, Joyce, *The Rosenberg File* (London: Weidenfeld & Nicolson, 1983)

Radzinsky, Edvard, *Stalin* (London: Hodder & Stoughton, 1996)

Ramet, Sabrina Petra (ed.), *Religious Policy in the Soviet Union* (Cambridge: Cambridge University Press, 1993)

Reagan, Ronald, *An American Life* (New York: Simon & Schuster, 1990)

Rees, Goronwy, *A Chapter of Accidents* (London: Chatto & Windus, 1971)

Rees, Jenny, *Looking for Mr. Nobody: The Secret Life of Goronwy Rees* (London: Weidenfeld & Nicolson, 1974)

Regnard, Henri [Nart, Raymond], "L'URSS et le renseignement scientifique, technique et technologique," *Défense Nationale* (December 1983)

Reich, Wilhelm, *Sexualerregung und Sexualbefriedigung* (Vienna: Münster–Verlag (Dr. Arnold Deutsch, 1929)

Religion in Communist Lands (Christehurst, Kent: Keston College, 1973–91); continued as *Religion, State and Society*

Religion, State and Society (Abingdon, Oxfordshire: Keston College, 1992–)

Remnick, David, *Lenin's Tomb: The Last Days of the Soviet Empire* (Harmondsworth: Penguin, 1994)

Remnick, David, *Resurrection: The Struggle for a New Russia* (London: Picador, 1998)

Renner, Hans, *A History of Czechoslovakia Since 1945* (London: Routledge, 1989)

Revesz, Laszło, *The Christian Peace Conference* (Conflict Study no. 91) (London: Institute for the Study of Conflict, 1978)

Richelson, Jeffrey T., *A Century of Spies: Intelligence in the Twentieth Century* (Oxford: Oxford University Press, 1995)

Roberts, Andrew, *"The Holy Fox:" A Biography of Lord Halifax* (London: Weidenfeld & Nicolson, 1991)

Robrieux, Philippe, *Histoire intérieure du Parti communiste*, 4 vols. (Paris: Fayard, 1980–4)

Romerstein, Herbert, and Levchenko, Stanislav, *The KGB against the 'Main Enemy'* (Lexington, Mass.: Lexington Books, 1989)

Rosenau, William, "A Deafening Silence: US Government Policy and the SIGINT Facility at Lourdes," *Intelligence and National Security*, vol. 9 (1994), no. 4

Rositzke, Harry, *The KGB: Eyes of Russia* (London: Sidgwick & Jackson, 1983)

[Rostovsky, Semyon,] "Letter from a Historical Optimist," *Druzhba Narodov* (March 1988)

Roy, Claude, *Somme tout* (Paris: Gallimard, 1976)

Rozvadovskaya, M. F., *et al.* (eds.), *Rytsar Revoliutsii: Vospominaniya Sovremennikov o Felikse Edmundoviche Dzerzhinskom* (Moscow, 1967)

Sakharov, Andrei, *Sakharov Speaks* (London: Collins & Harvill Press, 1974)

Sakharov, Andrei, *Memoirs* (London: Hutchinson, 1990)

Samolis, T. V. (ed.), *Veterany Vneshnei Razvedki Rossii: Kratkiy Biografichesky Spravochnik* (Moscow: SVR Press, 1995)

Sánchez Salazar, General Leandro A., *Murder in Mexico: The Assassination of Leon Trotsky* (London: Secker & Warburg, 1950)

Saunders, David, ??? *Northern History*, vol. 21 (1985)

Sawatsky, John, *For Services Rendered*, revised edition (Markham, Ont.: Penguin, 1986)

Sawatsky, John, *Gouzenko: The Untold Story* (Toronto: Macmillan, 1985)

Scammell, Michael, *Solzhenitsyn: A Biography* (London: Hutchinson, 1985)

Scarfe, Alan (ed.), *The CCDBR Documents: Christian Committee for the Defense of Believers' Rights in the USSR* (Glendale/Orange, Cal.: Door of Hope Press/Society for the Study of Religion under Communism, 1982)

Schecter, Jerrold L., and Deriabin, Peter S., *The Spy Who Saved the World* (New York: Scribner's, 1992)

Schmeidel, John, "Shield and Sword of the Party: Internal Repression, Exterior Espionage and Support for International Terrorism by the East German Ministry for State Security, 1970–1989," Ph.D. thesis, Cambridge University (1995)

Schmidt, Rainer F., "Der Hess-Flug und das Kabinet Churchill. Hitlers Stellvertreter im Kalkül der Britischen Kriegsdiplomatie," Vierteljahreshefte für Zeitgeschichte, vol. 42 (1993)

Schmidt, Rainer F., "The Marketing of Rudolf Hess: A Key to the 'Preventive War' Debate," *War in History* (forthcoming)

Schonberg, Harold C., *Horowitz: His Life and Music* (New York: Simon & Schuster, 1992)

Serge, Victor, *Memoirs of a Revolutionary, 1901–1941* (London: Oxford University Press, 1963)

Service, Robert, *A History of Twentieth-Century Russia,* paperback edition (Hammondsworth: Penguin, 1998)

Sharaf, Myron, *Fury on Earth: A Biography of Wilhelm Reich* (London: André Deutsch, 1983)

Shcharansky, Natan, *Fear No Evil* (London: Weidenfeld & Nicolson, 1988)

Shentalinsky, Vitaly, *KGB's Literary Archive* (London: Harvill Press, 1995)

Shevchenko, Arkadi N., *Breaking with Moscow,* paperback edition (New York: Ballantine, 1985)

Sheymov, Victor, *Tower of Secrets: A Real Life Spy Thriller* (Annapolis, Md.: Naval Institute Press, 1993)

Shipler, David K., *Russia: Broken Idols, Solemn Dreams* (London: Macdonald: 1984)

Shultz, George P., *Turmoil and Triumph: My Years as Secretary of State* (New York: Scribner's, 1993)

Shultz, Richard H., and Godson, Roy, *Dezinformatsia: Active Measures in Soviet Strategy* (Washington/Oxford: Pergamon-Brassey's, 1984)

Shvets Yuri B., *Washington Station: My Life as a KGB Spy in America* (New York: Simon & Schuster, 1994)

Skilling, H. Gordon, *Czechoslovakia's Interrupted Revolution* (Princeton, NJ: Princeton University Press, 1976)

Smith, Bernard, *The Fraudulent Gospel: Politics and the World Council of Churches* (London: Covenant Books, 1991)

Smith, M. L. R., *Fighting for Ireland? The Military Strategy of the Irish Republican Movement* (London: Routledge, 1995)

Smith, Michael, *Station X: The Codebreakers of Bletchley Park* (London: Channel 4 Books, 1998)

Snelling, O. F., *Rare Books and Rarer People: Some Personal Reminiscences of "The Trade"* (London: Werner Shaw, 1982)

Soares, Mário, *Portugal's Struggle for Liberation* (London: Allen & Unwin, 1975)

Solzhenitsyn, Aleksandr, *The Oak and the Calf: Sketches of Literary Life in the Soviet Union,* Willetts, Harry (trans.) (London: Collins and Harvill Press, 1980)

"Soviet Documents on the Hungarian Revolution, October 24–November 4, 1956," *Cold War International History Project Bulletin,* no. 5 (1995)

"The Soviet Union and Afghanistan, 1978–1989: New Documents from the Russian and East German Archives," *Cold War International History Project Bulletin,* nos. 8–9 (1996/97)

"Stalin's Plan to Assassinate Tito," *Cold War International History Project Bulletin,* no. 10 (1998)

Stepankov, Valentin, and Lisov, Yevgeni, *Kremlevsky Zagovor* (Moscow: Ogonek, 1992)

Straight, Michael, *After Long Silence* (London: Collins, 1983)

Sudoplatov, Pavel and Anatoli (with Schecter, Jerrold L. and Lorna P.), *Special Tasks* (London: Little, Brown, 1994)

Summers, Anthony, *Conspiracy: Who Killed President Kennedy?* (London: Fontana, 1980)

Swidlicki, Andrzej, *Political Trials in Poland 1981–1986* (London: Croom Helm, 1988)

Szász, Béla, *Volunteers for the Gallows* (London: Chatto & Windus, 1971)

Szulc, Tad, *Pope John Paul II: The Biography* (London: Scribner, 1995)

Tanenhaus, Sam, *Whittaker Chambers: A Biography* (New York: Random House, 1997)

Tarrant, V. E., *The Red Orchestra* (New York: John Wiley & Sons, 1995)

Tataryn, Miroslaw, "The Re-emergence of the Ukrainian (Greek) Catholic Church in the USSR" in Ramet, Sabrina Petra (ed.), *Religious Policy in the Soviet Union* (Cambridge: Cambridge University Press, 1993)

Taylor, Peter, ??? (London: Bloomsburg, 1997)

Tchikov, Vladimir, and Kern, Gary, *Comment Staline a volé le bombe atomique aux Américains: Dossier KGB no. 13676* (Paris: Robert Laffont, 1996)

Theoharis, Athan (ed.), *From the Secret Files of J. Edgar Hoover* (Chicago: Ivan R. Dee, 1991)

Thibau, Jacques, *Le Monde, 1944–1996: Histoire d'un journal, un journal dans l'histoire* (Paris: Plon, 1996)

Thomas, D. M., *Alexander Solzhenitsyn: A Century in His Life,* paperback edition (London: Abacus, 1999)

Thomas, Hugh, *The Spanish Civil War*, revised edition (London: Hamish Hamilton, 1977)

Tolstoy, Nikolai, *Victims of Yalta* (London: Hodder & Stoughton, 1977)

Tolstoy, Nikolai, *Stalin's Secret War* (London: Jonathan Cape, 1981)

Trotsky, Leon, *My Life* (Gloucester, Mass.: Peter Smith, 1970)

Truman, Harry S., Year of Decisions: 1945 (London: Hodder & Stoughton, 1955)

Tuck, Jay, *High-Tech Espionage: How the KGB Smuggles NATO's Strategic Secrets to Moscow* (London: Sidgwick & Jackson, 1986)

Upton, A. F., *The Communist Parties of Scandinavia and Finland* (London: Weidenfeld & Nicolson, 1973)

Urban, Joan Barth, *Moscow and the Italian Communist Party* (Ithaca, NJ: Cornell University Press, 1986)

Urban, Joan Barth (ed.), *Moscow and the Global Left in the Gorbachev Era* (Ithaca, NJ: Cornell University Press, 1992)

Urban, Mark, *UK Eyes Alpha: Inside British Intelligence* (London: Faber & Faber, 1996)

US Department of State, *Active Measures: A Report on the Substance and Process of Anti-US Disinformation and Propaganda Campaigns* (August 1986)

US Government, *Soviet Acquisition of Militarily Significant Western Technology: An Update* (September 1985)

Vaksberg, Arkady, *The Prosecutor and the Prey: Vyshinsky and the 1930s Moscow Show Trials* (London: Weidenfeld & Nicolson, 1990)

Valenta, Jiri, *Soviet Intervention in Czechoslovakia, 1968: Anatomy of a Decision* (Baltimore, Md.: Johns Hopkins University Press, 1979)

Valenza, Pietro (ed.), *Il compromesso storico* (Rome: Newton Compton Editori, 1975)

Vance, Cyrus, *Hard Choices: Critical Years in America's Foreign Policy* (New York: Simon & Schuster, 1983)

Van den Bercken, William, "The Russian Orthodox Church, State and Society in 1991–1993: The Rest of the Story," *Religion, State and Society*, vol. 22 (1994), no. 2

Vassall, John, *Vassall* (London; Sidgwick & Jackson, 1975)

Vereeken, Georges, *The GPU in the Trotskyist Movement* (London: New Park Publications, 1976)

Volkogonov, Dmitri, *Stalin: Triumph and Tragedy* (London: Weidenfeld & Nicolson, 1991)

Volkogonov, Dmitri, *Lenin: Life and Legacy* (London: HarperCollins, 1995)

Volkogonov, Dmitri, *Trotsky: The Eternal Revolutionary* (London: HarperCollins, 1996)

Volkogonov, Dmitri, *The Rise and Fall of the Soviet Empire: Political Leaders from Lenin to Gorbachev* (London: HarperCollins, 1998)

Vosjoli, P. L. Thyraud de, *Lamia* (Boston: Little, Brown, 1970)

Vujacic, Veljko, "Gennadiy Zyuganov and the 'Third Road,'" *Post-Soviet Affairs*, vol. 12 (1996), no. 2

Wadleigh, Henry Julian, "Why I Spied for the Communists," seven parts, *New York Post* (July 12–20, 1949)

Walters, Philip, "The Defrocking of Fr. Gleb Yakunin," *Religion, State and Society*, vol. 22 (1994), no. 3

Weinstein, Allen, *Perjury: The Hiss-Chambers Case*, revised edition (New York: Random House, 1997)

Weinstein, Allen, and Vassiliev, Alexander, *The Haunted Wood: Soviet Espionage in America—The Stalin Era* (New York: Random House, 1999)

Werner, Ruth, *Sonya's Report* (London: Chatto & Windus, 1991)

West, Nigel, *A Matter of Trust* (London: Weidenfeld & Nicolson, 1982)

West, Nigel, The Illegals: The Double Lives of the Cold War's Most Secret Agents (London: Hodder & Stoughton, 1993)

West, Nigel, *Venona: The Greatest Secret of the Cold War* (London, HarperCollins, 1999)

West, Nigel, and Tsarev, Oleg, *The Crown Jewels: The British Secrets at the Heart of the KGB's Archives* (London: HarperCollins, 1998)

Westad, Odd Arne, "Concerning the Situation in 'A:' New Russian Evidence on the Soviet Intervention in Afghanistan," *Cold War International History Project Bulletin*, nos. 8–9 (1996/97)

Whaley, Barton, *Codeword Barbarossa* (Cambridge, Mass.: MIT Press, 1974)

Wheatcroft, Stephen, "The Scale and Nature of German and Soviet Repression and Mass Killings, 1930–45," *Europe-Asia Studies*, vol. 48 (1996), no. 8

Wheen, Francis, *Tom Driberg: His Life and Indiscretions* (London: Chatto & Windus, 1990)

Whymant, Robert, *Stalin's Spy: Richard Sorge and the Tokyo Espionage Ring* (London: I. B. Tauris, 1966)

Williams, Robert Chadwell, *Klaus Fuchs, Atom Spy* (Cambridge, Mass.: Harvard University Press, 1987)

Wise, David, *Molehunt: The Secret Search For Traitors That Shattered The CIA* (New York: Random House, 1992)

Wolf, Markus (with McElvoy, Anne), *Man without a Face: The Autobiography of Communism's Greatest Spymaster* (London: Jonathan Cape, 1997)

Wolf, Markus, *Spionagechef im geheimen Krieg: Erinnerungen* (Munich: List Verlag, 1997)

Wolff, David, "Leadership Transition in a Fractured Bloc: Editor's Note," *Cold War International History Project Bulletin*, no. 10 (1988)

Wolton, Thierry, *Le KGB en France* (Paris: Bernard Grasset, 1986)

Wolton, Thierry, *La France sous influence. Paris–Moscou: 30 ans de relations secrètes* (Paris: Bernard Grasset, 1997)

Wright, Peter, *Spycatcher* (New York: Viking, 1987)

Yakunin, Father Gleb, "First Open Letter to Patriarch Aleksi II," *Religion, State and Society*, vol. 22 (1994), no. 3

Yeltsin, Boris, *The View from the Kremlin* (London: HarperCollins, 1994)

Zamoyska, Hélène, "Sinyavsky, the Man and the Writer" in Labedz, Leopold, and Hayward, Max (eds.), *On Trial: The Case of Sinyavsky (Tertz) and Daniel (Arzhak)* (London: Collins and Harvill Press, 1967)

Zamoysky, Lolly, *Behind the Facade of the Masonic Temple* (Moscow: Progress Publishers, 1989)

Zhdanov, Andrei, *The International Situation* (Moscow: Foreign Languages Publishing House, 1947)

Ziegler, Philip, *Wilson: The Authorized Life* (London: Weidenfeld & Nicolson, 1993)

Zubok, Vladislav, "Spy vs. Spy: The KGB vs. the CIA, 1960–1962," *Cold War International History Project Bulletin*, no. 4 (1994)

Zubok, Vladislav, "Soviet Intelligence and the Cold War: The 'Small' Committee of Information in 1952–1953," *Diplomatic History* (Winter 1995)

Zubok, Vladislav, and Pleshakov, Constantine, *Inside the Kremlin's Cold War: From Stalin to Khrushchev* (Cambridge, Mass.: Harvard University Press, 1996)

INDEX